C000262382

ANNUAL REVIEW OF IRISH LAW 2009

Annual Review of Irish Law 2009

Raymond Byrne
B.C.L., LL.M., Barrister-at-Law
Director of Research, Law Reform Commission

William Binchy
B.A., B.C.L., LL.M., F.T.C.D., Barrister-at-Law
Regius Professor of Laws, Trinity College Dublin

ROUND HALL

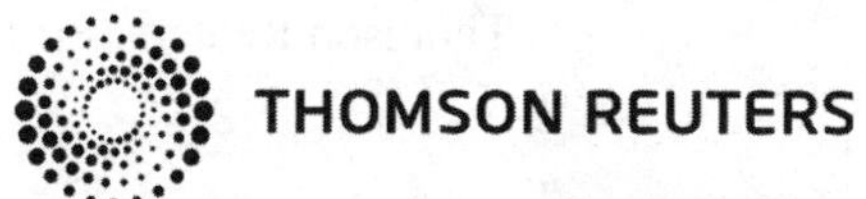

Published in 2010 by
Thomson Reuters (Professional) Ireland Limited
(Registered in Ireland, Company No. 80867.
Registered Office and address for service:
43 Fitzwilliam Place, Dublin 2)
trading as Round Hall

Typeset by
Gough Typesetting Services
Dublin

Printed by
MPG Books, Bodmin, Cornwall

ISBN 978-1-85800-562-1
ISSN 0791-1084

A catalogue record for this book
is available from the British Library

Table of Contents

Preface

This is the 23rd volume in the Annual Review series and, as with previous volumes, our purpose continues to be to provide a review of legal developments, judicial and statutory, that occurred in 2009. As with the previous volumes, we endeavour to discuss those Acts and statutory instruments enacted and made during the year. In terms of case law, this includes those judgments delivered in 2009 and which were available to us and our contributors by mid-2010 (whether in the law reports or through online sources).

Once again it is a pleasure to thank those who made the task of completing this volume less onerous. For this 23rd volume of the Annual Review series, we are delighted to have had the benefit of specialist contributions on Asylum and Immigration Law, Company and Insolvency Law, Constitutional Law, Contract Law, Criminal Law, Criminal Evidence, Employment, Equity, Information Law and the Ombudsman, Land Law, Landlord and Tenant Law and Conveyancing, Legislation, Planning and Development Law, Practice and Procedure, Probate and Succession Law, Social Welfare, and Whistleblower Protection included in this volume. We continue to take final responsibility for the overall text as in the past, but are especially grateful for the contributions of Nuala Egan and Patricia Brazil in Asylum and Immigration Law, Grainne Callanan in Company and Insolvency Law, Oran Doyle and Estelle Feldman in Constitutional Law, Fergus Ryan in Contract Law, John P. Byrne in Criminal Law, Yvonne Daly in Criminal Evidence, Desmond Ryan in Employment Law, Brian Tobin in Equity, Estelle Feldman in Information Law and the Ombudsman and Whistleblower Protection, Fiona de Londras in Land Law, Landlord and Tenant Law and Conveyancing, Brian Hunt in Legislation, Garrett Simons in Planning and Development Law, Martin Canny in Practice and Procedure, Albert Keating in Probate and Succession Law and Gerry Whyte in Social Welfare Law. Finally, we are very grateful to Round Hall, in particular Frieda Donoghue, Maura Smyth, Terri McDonnell and Nicola Barrett, and to Gough Typesetting Services, whose professionalism and patience ensures the continued production of this series.

Raymond Byrne and William Binchy,
Dublin
November 2010

Table of Cases

IRELAND

ENGLAND

NORTHERN IRELAND

EUROPEAN COURT OF JUSTICE

EUROPEAN COURT OF HUMAN RIGHTS

OTHER JURISDICTIONS

Table of Legislation

CONSTITUTIONAL PROVISIONS

TABLE OF STATUTES

IRELAND

Pre-1922 Statutes

Post-1922 Statutes

Broadcasting Act 2009—*contd.*

Statutory Instruments

Bills

EUROPEAN LEGISLATION

Directives

Regulations

Decisions

INTERNATIONAL TREATIES AND CONVENTIONS

ENGLAND AND WALES

UNITED STATES OF AMERICA

Administrative Law

APPROPRIATION

The Appropriation Act 2009 provided as follows. For the year ended December 31, 2009 the amount of supply grants in accordance with the Central Fund (Permanent Provisions) Act 1965 was €47,868,895,000. Reflecting the depth of the deteriorating fiscal difficulties for the State in 2009, for the first time in the 23 volumes of the *Annual Review of Irish Law*, this was significantly less in actual terms than the corresponding figure in the Appropriation Act 2008, which was €50,049,646,000. Under the Public Accounts and Charges Act 1891, the sum for appropriations-in-aid was €5,978,112,000 (higher than the 2008 figure of €4,472,799,000). The 2009 Act also provided, in accordance with s.91 of the Finance Act 2004, for carrying over into the year ending December 31, 2010 undischarged appropriations for capital supply services totalling €125,717,000 (less than the 2008 figure of €128,453,000). This, in effect, allowed this amount, which had not been spent on, for example, large infrastructure projects in 2009, to be carried over into 2010. The 2009 Act came into effect on its signature by the President on December 20, 2009. The 2009 Act also provided that the financial resolutions passed by Dáil Éireann on December 9, 2009 (after the 2009 budget) would have legal effect. This is subject to the proviso that, in accordance with s.4 of the Provisional Collection of Taxes Act 1927, legislation was enacted in 2010 to give full effect to the resolutions. These were included in the Finance Act 2010.

COMMISSION TO INQUIRE INTO CHILD ABUSE

The Commission to Inquire into Child Abuse Act 2000 (Section 5) (Specified Period) Order 2009 (S.I. No. 26 of 2009) extended to May 31, 2009 the specified period allowing for the completion of the work of the Commission established under the Commission to Inquire into Child Abuse Act 2000. This proved sufficient for the ultimate completion of the work of the Commission (which comprised Mr Justice Sean Ryan, Ms Marian Shanley, solicitor, and Dr Fred Lowe, clinical psychologist) and its enormous, and enormously significant, five-volume report was published in May 2009.

On its publication, the *Report of the Commission to Inquire into Child Abuse* (available at *www.childabusecommission.com*) received huge national and international media attention. The report confirmed the extensive testimony given to the Commission's investigative sub-committee from individual witnesses who had been detained in institutional facilities in the State between the 1940 and the 1970s that many of them had been subjected to systematic psychological, physical and sexual abuse. The following note of the main conclusions and recommendations in the report are based on the executive summary published by the Commission.

In Volume 4, Ch.6 of the report, the Commission arrived at 43 numbered conclusions. The general conclusions were:

1. Physical and emotional abuse and neglect were features of the institutions. Sexual abuse occurred in many of them, particularly boys' institutions. Schools were run in a severe, regimented manner that imposed unreasonable and oppressive discipline on children and even on staff.
2. The system of large-scale institutionalisation was a response to a 19th-century social problem, which was outdated and incapable of meeting the needs of individual children. The defects of the system were exacerbated by the way it was operated by the congregations that owned and managed the schools. This failure led to the institutional abuse of children where their developmental, emotional and educational needs were not met.
3. The deferential and submissive attitude of the Department of Education towards the congregations compromised its ability to carry out its statutory duty of inspection and monitoring of the schools. The Reformatory and Industrial Schools Section of the Department was accorded a low status within the Department and generally saw itself as facilitating the congregations and the resident managers.
4. The capital and financial commitment made by the religious congregations was a major factor in prolonging the system of institutional care of children in the State. From the mid-1920s in England, smaller more family-like settings were established and they were seen as providing a better standard of care for children in need. In Ireland, however, the industrial school system thrived.
5. The system of funding through capitation grants led to demands by managers for children to be committed to industrial schools for reasons of economic viability of the institutions.
6. The system of inspection by the Department of Education was fundamentally flawed and incapable of being effective.
7. Many witnesses who complained of abuse nevertheless expressed some positive memories: small gestures of kindness were vividly recalled. A word of consideration or encouragement, or an act of sympathy or understanding had a profound effect. Adults in their 60s and 70s recalled seemingly insignificant events that

had remained with them all their lives. Often the act of kindness recalled in such a positive light arose from the simple fact that the staff member had not given a beating when one was expected.

In Volume 4, Ch.7 of the report, the Commission made 20 recommendations, the first four under the general heading "to alleviate or otherwise address the effects of the abuse on those who suffered" and the remaining 16 under the heading "to prevent where possible and reduce the incidence of abuse of children in institutions and to protect children from such abuse."

1. A memorial should be erected, using the words of the special statement made by the Taoiseach in May 1999: "On behalf of the State and of all citizens of the State, the Government wishes to make a sincere and long overdue apology to the victims of childhood abuse for our collective failure to intervene, to detect their pain, to come to their rescue."
2. The lessons of the past should be learned.
3. Counselling and educational services should be available.
4. Family tracing services should be continued.
5. Childcare policy should be child-centred. The needs of the child should be paramount.
6. National childcare policy should be clearly articulated and reviewed on a regular basis.
7. A method of evaluating the extent to which services meet the aims and objectives of the national childcare policy should be devised.
8. The provision of childcare services should be reviewed on a regular basis.
9. It is important that rules and regulations be enforced, breaches be reported and sanctions applied.
10. A culture of respecting and implementing rules and regulations and of observing codes of conduct should be developed.
11. Independent inspections are essential.
12. Management at all levels should be accountable for the quality of services and care.
13. Children in care should be able to communicate concerns without fear.
14. Childcare services depend on good communication.
15. Children in care need a consistent care figure.
16. Children who have been in state care should have access to support services.
17. Children who have been in childcare facilities are in a good

position to identify failings and deficiencies in the system, and should be consulted.

18. Children in care should not, save in exceptional circumstances, be cut off from their families.
19. The full personal records of children in care must be maintained.
20. The 1999 report *Children First: The National Guidelines for the Protection and Welfare of Children* should be uniformly and consistently implemented throughout the State in dealing with allegations of abuse.

Separately, in November 2009, the *Dublin Archdiocese Commission of Investigation Report* was published (available at *www.dacoi.ie*). The commission (comprising Judge Yvonne Murphy, chairperson; Ita Mangan, barrister; and Hugh O'Neill, solicitor) had been appointed in 2006 under the Commissions of Investigation Act 2004 to investigate the full extent of complaints or allegations of child sexual abuse made to the Archdiocesan and other Catholic Church authorities and public and state authorities in the period January 1, 1975 to May 1, 2004 against Catholic clergy operating under the aegis of the Catholic Archdiocese of Dublin. The commission of investigation concluded that virtually all of the complaints could be substantiated and that there had been a substantial cover-up by church authorities, sometimes aided by state authorities. The concluding paragraph of Ch.1 of the report stated:

> "1.113 The Commission has no doubt that clerical child sexual abuse was covered up by the Archdiocese of Dublin and other Church authorities over much of the period covered by the Commission's remit. The structures and rules of the Catholic Church facilitated that cover-up. The State authorities facilitated the cover up by not fulfilling their responsibilities to ensure that the law was applied equally to all and allowing the Church institutions to be beyond the reach of the normal law enforcement processes. The welfare of children, which should have been the first priority, was not even a factor to be considered in the early stages. Instead the focus was on the avoidance of scandal and the preservation of the good name, status and assets of the institution and of what the institution regarded as its most important members – the priests. In the mid 1990s, a light began to be shone on the scandal and the cover up. Gradually, the story has unfolded. It is the responsibility of the State to ensure that no similar institutional immunity is ever allowed to occur again. This can be ensured only if all institutions are open to scrutiny and not accorded an exempted status by any organs of the State."

In the aftermath of the publication of the *Report of the Commission to Inquire into Child Abuse*, the Government committed to a phased implementation plan for the recommendations made in the report. By the end of 2009, and in the wake of the additional findings in the *Dublin Archdiocese Commission of Investigation Report*, a revised version of the *Children First: The National Guidelines for the Protection and Welfare of Children* had been published by the Office of the Minister of State for Children. Other recommendations of the Commission to Inquire into Child Abuse are likely to take some considerable time to implement, and some may be linked to the proposed amendment to Art.42 of the Constitution concerning the rights of the child.

ETHICS IN PUBLIC OFFICE

Anglo Irish Bank The Ethics In Public Office (Prescribed Public Bodies, Designated Directorships of Public Bodies and Designated Positions In Public Bodies) (Amendment) Regulations 2009 (S.I. No. 320 of 2009) prescribe directorships and positions of employment in Anglo Irish Bank Corporation Limited and in the subsidiaries of Anglo Irish Bank Corporation Limited specified in the Regulations as, respectively, "designated directorships" and "designated positions" for the purposes of the Ethics in Public Office Act 1995. This was required in the wake of the nationalisation of Anglo Irish Bank: see the Anglo Irish Bank Act 2009, discussed in the Commercial Law chapter, below. A person holding a "designated directorship" is required, inter alia, to furnish a statement of his or her registrable interests to the Standards in Public Office Commission and to such officer of the body, as determined by the Minister for Finance. Where no registrable interests exist, a nil statement is requested. A person occupying a "designated position" is required to furnish his or her statement to the relevant authority, as determined by the Minister for Finance. Where no registrable interests exist, a nil statement is requested. The Company Secretary and the Head of Human Resources in Anglo Irish Bank Corporation Limited are, respectively, the officer of the body and the relevant authority, as determined by the Minister for Finance.

FREEDOM OF INFORMATION

The Freedom of Information Act 1997 (Section 17(6)) Regulations 2009 (S.I. No. 385 of 2009) prescribe certain classes of individuals who may apply under s.17 of the Freedom of Information Act 1997 for amendment of records containing certain incorrect, incomplete or misleading information having regard to relevant circumstances and to guidelines published by the Minister for Finance. The Freedom of Information Act 1997 (Section 18(5a)) Regulations 2009 (S.I. No. 386 of 2009) prescribe certain classes of individuals who may apply under s.18 of the Freedom of Information Act 1997 for information regarding acts of public bodies having regard to relevant circumstances and to guidelines published by the Minister for Finance. The Freedom of Information Act 1997 (Section 28(6)) Regulations 2009 (S.I. No. 387 of 2009) prescribe the classes of individual whose records will be made available to parents and guardians, and the classes of requester to whom the records of deceased persons will be made available, having regard to relevant circumstances and to guidelines published by the Minister for Finance.

JUDICIAL REVIEW

The case law under Ord.84 of the Rules of the Superior Courts 1986 that arose in 2009 is discussed in the various chapters in this *Annual Review of Irish Law* where the substantive subjects arising are detailed, notably in the Immigration and Planning Law chapters. Further reference may also be obtained through the Table of Statutory Instruments under the entry for the Rules of the Superior Courts 1986.

OIREACHTAS

Houses of the Oireachtas Commission and Houses of the Oireachtas Service The Houses of the Oireachtas Commission (Amendment) Act 2009 (the "2009 Act") amended the Houses of the Oireachtas Commission Act 2003 (the "2003 Act") (*Annual Review of Irish Law 2003*, p.6). The primary purpose of the 2009 Act was to make available the funding for the Houses of the Oireachtas Commission for the three-year period 2010 to 2012. The 2009 Act provides the Commission a sum not exceeding €360 million to carry out its functions for the three-year period (which contrasted with the €393 million provided for 2007 to 2009).

The Commission came into being on January 1, 2004 under the 2003 Act. The Commission is composed of 11 members under the chairmanship of the Ceann Comhairle of Dáil Éireann. The Cathaoirleach of Seanad Éireann is an ex officio member, as is the Clerk of the Dáil, who also has the title of Secretary General of the Office of the Houses of the Oireachtas. There are also seven ordinary members, four from the Dáil and three from the Seanad, who are appointed by the Members of each House, and one representative of the Minister for Finance.

The responsibilities of the Commission include the payment of the salaries and allowances of deputies and senators, the payment of the salaries of staff, including Members' staff, the payment of certain pensions and the provision of other necessary facilities to enable the business of both Houses to be transacted.

During the Oireachtas debate on the 2009 Act, it was noted that since its inception, the Commission had instituted a number of significant improvements in the services provided to members. Among these was the creation of a research service for members. This involved increasing the library staff of about 12 by a further 20 to create a research service modelled on international standards. At the time of the Oireachtas debate on the 2009 Act, it was stated that this had been used by over 90 per cent of Members in the current Dáil and all feedback indicates that it was highly regarded by Members.

In addition to the financial provisions, the 2009 Act provided for renaming the Office of the Houses of the Oireachtas as the Houses of the Oireachtas Service. The purpose of this is to strengthen the identity of the Service. The distinct role of the civil service staff and senior management structures of the Oireachtas are specifically recognised in the staff of the Houses of the Oireachtas Act 1959. The renaming of the Office comprising the staff of the Houses as the Houses of the Oireachtas Service does not affect the operations of the Service or its relationship with the Commission under the 2003 Act. The Commission retains all the powers and functions conferred by the 2003 Act. However, the change in title may facilitate further development of the Service and closer integration of the Service with the Commission as its governing body.

Oireachtas allowances The Oireachtas (Allowances to Members) and Ministerial and Parliamentary Offices Act 2009 (the "2009 Act") amended the Oireachtas (Allowances to Members) Act 1938 and the Ministerial and Parliamentary Offices Acts 1938 to 2001 in order to alter the salaries payable to members of either House of the Oireachtas. The 2009 Act also altered the remuneration, allowances and pensions payable to former holders of ministerial and other offices who are members of either House or members of the European Parliament. The 2009 Act thus formed another component of the many Acts enacted in 2009 aimed at reducing public expenditure in the wake of the international and national financial and fiscal collapse. See also the various Emergency Financial Measure Acts discussed in the Commercial Law chapter, below.

Agriculture, Food and Forestry

ABATTOIRS

Emergency slaughter The Abattoirs Act 1988 (Veterinary Examination and Health Mark) (No.2) Regulations 2009 (S.I. No. 373 of 2009), made under the Abattoirs Act 1988 (*Annual Review of Irish Law 1988*, pp.37–38), provide for the possibility of meat, from an otherwise healthy animal, that is slaughtered due to, e.g. an injury that prevents transportation live to a slaughtering establishment (in accordance with Chapter VI of Section I of Annex III to Regulation 853/2004 laying down specific hygiene rules for food of animal origin intended for human consumption) being placed on the national market. The Regulations also require that this is subject to it being certified fit for human consumption and marked in a manner specified in the Schedule to the Regulations. They also revoked and replaced the Abattoirs Act 1988 (Veterinary Examination and Health Mark) Regulations 2009 (S.I. No. 154 of 2009) with effect from September 11, 2009.

ANIMAL HEALTH AND WELFARE

Bovine breeding and artificial reproduction The European Communities (Bovine Breeding) Regulations 2009 (S.I. No. 19 of 2009) (the "2009 Regulations") implemented Directive 77/504, which, as amended, governs trade in bovine breeding animals, including trade in their semen, ova and embryos. Over 40 EU instruments, set out in the preamble to the 2009 Regulations, have amended the original 1977 Directives, indicating the complexity of the regulatory regime involved in this area of agricultural trade, a far cry from the days of the "AI man". It should also be noted that the 2009 Regulations overlap with the requirements of the Live Stock (Artificial Insemination) Act 1947, although the 1947 Act is not referred to in the 2009 Regulations. The 2009 Regulations also revoked and replaced: the European Communities (Trade in Bovine Breeding Animals, their Semen, Ova and Embryos) Regulations 1996; the European Communities (Trade in Bovine Breeding Animals, their Semen, Ova and Embryos) (Amendment) Regulations 1996; the European Communities (Trade in Bovine Breeding Animals, their Semen, Ova and Embryos) (Amendment) Regulations 2004; and the European Communities (Trade in Bovine Breeding Animals, their Semen, Ova and Embryos)

(Amendment) Regulations 2007. The 2009 Regulations came into force on January 26, 2009.

Bovine identification The European Communities (Identification of Bovines) Regulations 2009 (S.I. No. 77 of 2009) (the "2009 Regulations") implemented Regulation 1760/2000 Title I in relation to the identification of bovine animals and laid down obligations and responsibilities in relation to the keeping of records and provision of information. The 2009 Regulations also revoked and replaced in full the following: the Bovine Tuberculosis (Attestation of State and General Provisions) Order 1996; the European Communities (Registration of Bovine Animals) Regulations 1996; the European Communities (Supply of Information on the Origin, Identification and Destination of Bovine Animals) Regulations 1999; the European Communities (Identification and Registration of Bovine Animals) Regulations 1999; the Bovine Tuberculosis (Attestation of State and General Provisions) Order 1999; the European Communities (Identification and Registration of Animals) (Amendment) Regulations 2000; the Brucellosis (General Provisions) (Amendment) Order 2001; the European Communities (Identification and Registration of Bovine Animals) (Amendment) Regulations 2002; the European Communities (Identification and Registration of Bovine Animals) (Amendment) Regulations 2004; the European Communities (Identification and Registration of Bovine Animals) (Amendment) Regulations 2006; and the Bovine Tuberculosis (Attestation of State and General Provisions) (Amendment) Order 2006. The 2009 Regulations also revoked and replaced: art.32(2) and art.39 of the Bovine Tuberculosis (Attestation of State and General Provisions) Order 1989 (inserted by the Bovine Tuberculosis (Attestation of State and General Provisions) (Amendment) Order 2006); and art.19(7) of the Brucellosis in Cattle (General Provisions) Order 1991 (inserted by the Brucellosis (General Provisions) (Amendment) Order 2001).

Calves The European Communities (Welfare of Farmed Animals) (Amendment) Regulations 2009 (S.I. No. 32 of 2009) provided that references in the European Communities (Welfare of Farmed Animals) Regulations 2008 (S.I. No. 14 of 2008), which implemented Directive 93/119 on the protection of animals at the time of slaughter, be adapted to conform to the codified provisions in Directive 2008/119, which lays down minimum standards for the protection of calves.

Chicken The European Communities (Control of Salmonella In Broilers) Regulations 2009 (S.I. No. 64 of 2009) implemented Regulation 646/2007 of June 12, 2007 as amended by Commission Regulation 584/2008 of June 20, 2008 on the control of salmonella in broilers, and require the testing of such flocks and provide for the approval of laboratories to conduct tests.

Notifiable diseases The Diseases of Animals Act 1966 (Notification and Control of Animal Diseases) (Amendment) Order 2009 (S.I. No. 292 of 2009) amended the Schedule to the Diseases of Animals Act 1966 (Notification and Control of Animal Diseases) Order 2008 in order to make Hendra virus, Piroplasmosis, Surra and West Nile Virus notifiable diseases under the Diseases of Animals Act 1966.

Pet passport The European Communities (Pet Passport) Regulations 2009 (S.I. No. 263 of 2009) implemented the administrative measures required by Regulation 998/2003 (the Pet Passport Regulation), as amended by Regulation 592/2004 and Regulation 454/2008, which deal with the movement of certain pet animals within the EU and from certain third countries.

Pig slaughtering The Slaughter of Animals Act 1935 (Approved Instruments) Order 2008 (S.I. No. 599 of 2008) provide that a chamber containing inert gas and certain electrodes are approved instruments for the slaughter of pigs under the Slaughter of Animals Act 1935. This was done pending the full implementation of the detailed humane arrangements in the European Communities (Welfare of Farmed Animals) Regulations 2008 (S.I. No. 14 of 2008), which implemented Directive 93/119 on the protection of animals at the time of slaughter.

Poultry vaccines The Diseases of Animals Act 1966 (Control on Animal and Poultry Vaccines) (Amendment) Order 2009 (SI No. 323 of 2009) provides for the removal of the disease "Salmonellosis (caused by or involving salmonella enteriditis or salmonella typhimurium) in poultry" from the First Schedule of the Diseases of Animals Act 1966 (Control on Animal and Poultry Vaccines) Order 2002 and its insertion in the Second Schedule, Pt 1, of the 2002 Order. The effect is to remove some restrictions on the use of vaccines for salmonella.

Rabies: import restrictions The Rabies (Importation, Landing and Movement of Animals) (Amendment) Order 2009 (S.I. No. 261 of 2009), made under the Diseases of Animals Act 1966, amended the Rabies (Importation, Landing and Movement of Animals) Order 1976 by removing the requirement for an import licence from Great Britain, in respect of imports of animals to which the 1976 Order, as amended by the 2009 Order, applies. The 1976 Order had already exempted imports from Northern Ireland.

Swill The Diseases of Animals Act 1966 (Prohibition on the Use Of Swill) (Amendment) Order 2009 (S.I. No. 12 of 2009) amended the Diseases of Animals Act 1966 (Prohibition on the Use Of Swill) Order 2001 by permitting the collection, assembly, processing and storage of swill at approved composting and biogas plants.

Transmissible spongiform encephalopathies (TSEs) The European Communities (Transmissible Spongiform Encephalopathies and Animal By-Products) (Amendment) Regulations 2009 (S.I. No. 291 of 2009) amended the European Communities (Transmissible Spongiform Encephalopathies and Animal By-products) Regulations 2008 and made it an offence to remove a spine, that is, vertebral column, in butchers' premises without an authorisation. They also provide for the issuing of such an authorisation and also provide for an appeal mechanism in the event of a refusal to issue such an authorisation and allow for the possibility of TSE sampling being carried out by someone other than a registered veterinary practitioner, in accordance with the instructions of an authorised officer. The 2009 Regulations also revoked the European Communities (Removal of Bovine Vertebral Column) Regulations 2004.

ANIMAL REMEDIES

Hormones The European Communities (Control of Animal Remedies and their Residues) Regulations 2009 (S.I. No. 183 of 2009) (the "2009 Regulations") implemented Directive 96/22 on the prohibition in stock farming of certain substances having hormonal or thyrostatic action and of beta agonists. They also implemented Directive 96/23 on measures to monitor certain substances and residues thereof in live animals and animal products. The 2009 Regulations overlap with the provisions of the Animal Remedies Act 1993 (*Annual Review of Irish Law 1993*, pp.34–37). The 2009 Regulations also revoked and replaced the European Communities (Control of Animal Remedies and their Residues) Regulations 2007.

Medicinal products and veterinary prescription The European Communities (Animal Remedies) (Amendment) Regulations 2009 (S.I. No. 182 of 2009) amended the European Communities (Animal Remedies) (No. 2) Regulations 2007 in order to implement Directive 2009/9, which amended Directive 2001/82 on the Community code relating to medicinal products for veterinary use. This included amending the specifics required in a veterinary prescription.

CROPS AND PLANTS

Harmful substances The European Communities (Control of Organisms Harmful to Plants and Plant Products) (Amendment) Regulations 2009 (S.I. No. 8 of 2009) amended the European Communities (Control of Organisms Harmful to Plants and Plant Products) Regulations 2004 in order to implement Directive 2008/109, which had amended Annex IV to Directive 2000/29 on protective measures against the introduction into the Community of organisms harmful to plants or plant products.

Pesticides The European Communities (Authorisation, Placing on the Market, Use and Control of Plant Protection Products) (Amendment) Regulations 2009 (S.I. No. 107 of 2009) amended the European Communities (Authorisation, Placing on the Market, Use and Control of Plant Protection Products) Regulations 2003 in order to implement the amendments to Annex I of Directive 91/414 made by a series of Directives adopted in 2008 and 2009. The effect of the amendments was to impose restrictions on the use of the following pesticides: bifenox, diflufenican, fenoxaprop-P, fenpropidin, quinoclamine, clofentezine, dicamba, difenoconazole, diflubenzuron, imazaquin, lenacil, oxadiazon, picloram, pyriproxyfen, tritosulfuron, diuron, abamectin, epoxiconazole, fenpropimorph, fenpyroximate, tralkoxydim, flutolanil, benfluralin, fluazinam, fuberidazole, mepiquat, aclonifen, imidacloprid, metazachlor, aluminium phosphide, calcium phosphide, magnesium phosphide, cymoxanil, dodemorph, 2,5-dichlorobenzoic acid methylester, metamitron, sulcotrione, tebuconazole, triadimenol, bensulfuron, sodium 5-nitroguaiacolate, sodium o-nitrophenolate, sodium p-nitrophenolate and tebufenpyrad.

FOOD

Food labelling The European Communities (Labelling, Presentation and Advertising of Foodstuffs) (Amendment) Regulations 2009 (S.I. No. 61 of 2009) amended the European Communities (Labelling, Presentation and Advertising of Foodstuffs) Regulations 2002 to 2008 in order to implement Directive 2008/5 on the compulsory indication on the labelling of certain foodstuffs of particulars other than those provided for in Directive 2000/13.

Organic produce labelling The European Communities (Organic Farming) (Amendment) Regulations 2009 (S.I. No. 30 of 2009) provided that the European Communities (Organic Farming) Regulations 2004 should be read as including references to Regulation 834/2007 and Regulation 889/2008 on controls on the production and labelling of organic products.

Dietary foods: baby food The European Communities (Dietary Foods for Special Medical Purposes) Regulations 2009 (S.I. No. 187 of 2009) (the "2009 Regulations") implemented Directive 1999/21 on dietary foods for special medical purposes, as amended by Directive 2006/82 and Directive 2006/141. The 2009 Regulations also revoke and replace the European Communities (Dietary Foods for Special Medical Purposes) Regulations 2001, the European

Communities (Dietary Foods for Special Medical Purposes) (Amendment) Regulations 2002, and the European Communities (Dietary Foods for Special Medical Purposes) (Amendment) Regulations 2007.

Infant formulae The European Communities (Infant Formulae and Follow-On Formulae) (Amendment) Regulations 2009 (S.I. No. 209 of 2009) (the "2009 Regulations") amended the European Communities (Infant Formulae and Follow-On Formulae) Regulations 2007 (the principal Regulations in this area) and the European Communities (Infant Formulae and Follow-On Formulae) Regulations 2004. The 2009 Regulations implemented Directive 2006/141, which had amended Directive 1999/21 on infant formulae and follow-on formulae. The 2009 Regulations also provided for the administrative implementation of Regulation 1243/2008, which had amended Directive 2006/141, Annexes III and VI, as regards compositional requirements for certain infant formulae.

Food hygiene and indictable offences The European Communities (Hygiene of Foodstuffs) (Amendment) Regulations 2009 (S.I. No. 380 of 2009) amended the European Communities (Hygiene of Foodstuffs) Regulations 2006 in order to provide for the administrative implementation of Regulation 1019/2008, which had amended Annex II to Regulation 852/2004 on the hygiene of foodstuffs. The 2009 Regulations also provided for the first time that breach of Regulation 852/2004 involved, potentially, the commission of an indictable offences and related penalties, implementing the power to do so conferred by the European Communities Act 2007 (see *Annual Review of Irish Law 2007*, pp.403–404). Thus, reg.18(4) of the 2006 Regulations originally provided that:

> A person who is guilty of an offence under these Regulations is liable on summary conviction to a fine not exceeding €5,000 or at the discretion of the Court to imprisonment for a term not exceeding 6 months or both.

The 2009 Regulations substituted the following new reg.18(4):

> A person who is guilty of an offence under these Regulations is liable:
> (a) on summary conviction to a fine not exceeding €5,000 or at the discretion of the Court to imprisonment for a term not exceeding 6 months or both, or
> (b) on conviction on indictment, to a fine not exceeding €500,000, or imprisonment for a term not exceeding 3 years, or both.

This indicates the extent of the power conferred by the 2007 Act to create offences carrying significant penalties that are comparable to very serious "traditional" crimes (of the *malum in se* variety). The notion that food hygiene offences are relatively trivial criminal matters (mere "regulatory" crimes or *mala prohibita*) is clearly no longer tenable.

FORESTRY

Coillte borrowing powers Coillte Teoranta, the Irish Forestry Board Ltd, the state authority with responsibility for forestry matters, was established under the Forestry Act 1988 (the "1988 Act") (*Annual Review of Irish Law 1988*, p.5). The Forestry (Amendment) Act 2009 (the "2009 Act") amended s.24(1)(b) of the Forestry Act 1988 by increasing Coillte's maximum borrowing power from £80 million (approximately €101.5 million) to €400 million. It was explained during the Oireachtas debate on the 2009 Act that it was necessary to increase the statutory borrowing limit, which had not changed since 1988, to make adequate provision for the borrowing requirements of Coillte for its capital expenditure programme. This includes reforestation, investment in forest infrastructure and plant and equipment.

It was noted during the Oireachtas debate on the 2009 Act that Coillte Teoranta had been established under the 1988 Act as a private commercial company. The 1988 Act provides that the principal objects of the company are to carry on the business of forestry and related activities on a commercial basis and in accordance with efficient silvicultural practices; to establish and carry on woodland industries; to participate with others in forestry and related activities consistent with its objects, designed to enhance the effectiveness and profitable operation of the company; and to utilise and manage the resources available to it in a manner consistent with these objects.

It was noted that, in the intervening 20 years since its establishment, Coillte had increased its forest estate by 37,000 hectares, developed its recreational facilities and extended its business base to include panel products. At the end of 2009, when the 2009 Act was being debated, it was noted that:

> "Coillte manages 445,000 hectares of forest land, of which 79% is forested with the remaining 21% encompassing open spaces, water, roads or land above the tree line. Such management induces maintenance of the forest estate, felling as appropriate and replanting. The company also supplies logs to the timber processing industry including sawmills, panel board mills and the emerging energy supply businesses. While the company provides direct employment, it also engages harvesting and haulage contractors thereby sustaining employment for a far greater number."

It was also noted that the company also owned two panel board businesses, manufacturing OSB and MDF boards, respectively, with more than 80 per cent of their output being exported. Coillte had also at that time entered into a joint venture arrangement with the Electricity Supply Board to develop a wind farm. Coillte's contribution to recreation by way of its forest parks and trails and its involvement in Lough Key Forest Park in Roscommon was also noted.

It is worth noting that the 2009 Bill that was enacted as the 2009 Act was published on December 2, 2009 and that all stages of the Bill were completed by both Houses of the Oireachtas in a single day, December 17, 2009. An early signature motion resulted in the President signing the Act on December 20, 2009, when the Act came into force.

Coillte bye-laws The Forestry Act 1988 (Section 37) (Coillte Teoranta) Bye-Laws 2009 (S.I. No. 151 of 2009) contain the detailed rules regulating public access to lands owned, managed or used by Coillte. In accordance with s.37(4) of the 1988 Act, under which the 2009 bye-laws were made, a person who contravenes a bye-law made under s.37 is guilty of an offence. Section 7 of the 1988 Act provides that a person guilty of an offence under s.37 is liable (a) on summary conviction to a fine not exceeding €1,270 and/or 12 months' imprisonment, or (b) on conviction on indictment to a fine not exceeding €12,700 and/or two years' imprisonment. The fines under the 1988 Act will be increased in accordance with the provisions of the Fines Act 2010 when that Act is brought into force.

Arts and Culture

BROADCASTING

Part-consolidation of Broadcasting Acts The Broadcasting Act 2009 (the "2009 Act") consolidated to a great extent, with significant amendments, much of the main Broadcasting Acts enacted in the State since the 1960s, and provided for significant changes to the regulation in the State of the broadcast media. In particular, the 2009 Act provided for the establishment of a single regulatory authority, the Broadcasting Authority of Ireland (BAI), which replaced the Broadcasting Commission of Ireland (BAI) and the Broadcasting Complaints Commission (BCC). While the BCI had previously regulated the "commercial" broadcasters, it had not been responsible for regulating the state-owned public service broadcasters, RTE and TG4. By contrast, the BAI is now, under the 2009 Act, the regulator for all broadcasters in the State. The BAI also takes responsibility for all individual complaints that the licensed broadcasters have breached the relevant statutory standards set out in the Broadcasting Acts. The Broadcasting Authority of Ireland (Establishment Day) Order 2009 (S.I. No. 389 of 2009) brought Pt 2, ss.49 and 157 and Pt 12 of the 2009 Act into operation on October 1, 2009. The key effect was to establish the BAI and dissolve the BCI.

The 2009 Act also significantly amended the legislative basis for: the RTE Authority and Teilifís na Gaeilge (TG4), the state-owned public service broadcasters; the award of broadcasting contracts; broadcasting duties, codes and rules; digital terrestrial broadcasting; the granting of monies for independent productions under the "Broadcasting Fund"; and the designation of major television events coverage. The 2009 Act also completely recast the basis for the collection of television licences.

In the context of EU law, the 2009 Act also implemented in large part the relevant provisions of the "Television Without Frontiers" Directives, that is, Directive 89/552 on television broadcasting activities, as amended by Directive 97/36, and Directive 2007/65, the 2007 Audiovisual Media Services Directive. In particular, while the "standard TV" elements of the 2007 Directive were implemented by the 2009 Act, the remaining elements of the Directive (concerning "on-demand" television services, whether provided by satellite or cable) were implemented by the European Communities (Audiovisual Media Services) Regulations 2010 (S.I. No. 258 of 2010).

When the 2009 Act comes fully into force, it will repeal in full: the Broadcasting Authority (Amendment) Act 1964; the Broadcasting Authority

(Amendment) Act 1966; the Broadcasting Authority (Amendment) Act 1971; the Broadcasting Authority (Amendment) Act 1973; the Broadcasting Authority (Amendment) Act 1974; the Broadcasting Authority (Amendment) Act 1979; the Broadcasting And Wireless Telegraphy Act 1988; the Broadcasting (Major Events Television Coverage) Act 1999; the Broadcasting Authority (Amendment) Act 1993; the Broadcasting (Major Events Television Coverage) (Amendment) Act 2003; the Broadcasting (Funding) Act 2003; and the Broadcasting (Amendment) Act 2007. In addition, the 2009 Act involves significant changes to the Broadcasting Act 1960, which established the RTE Authority.

Broadcasting Authority of Ireland Part 2 of the 2009 Act (ss.5 to 38) provides for the establishment of the Broadcasting Authority of Ireland (BAI) and its two statutory committees, the Contract Awards Committee and the Compliance Committee. Section 8 sets out the procedures for appointment of the membership of the BAI and its two statutory committees. The section provides that five members of the BAI shall be appointed by Government on the nomination of the Minister for Communications, Marine and Natural Resources and that four members of the BAI shall be appointed by Government on the nomination of the Minister, the Minister having regard to the advice of the Joint Oireachtas Committee with responsibility for broadcasting matters. It also provides that not less than four of the members of the Authority shall be men and not less than four of them shall be women. Section 8 also provides that half of the membership of each of the two statutory committees shall be appointed by Government on the nomination of the Minister and the remaining membership shall be appointed by the BAI from the membership of the BAI and its staff. Section 11 provides for the appointment by Government on the nomination of the Minister of the chairpersons of the BAI and its two statutory committees. Section 14 provides for the position of chief executive officer of the BAI. The chief executive shall be appointed, by means of a public competition, by the Authority with the consent of the Minister. Section 19 provides that the chief executive officer of the BAI is accountable to and must attend before the Committee of Public Accounts in respect of the expenditure of the BAI. Section 20 sets down the requirements for the chief executive officer and chairpersons of the BAI and its statutory committees to attend before committees of the Houses of the Oireachtas.

Section 25 sets out the objectives of the BAI. In general terms, s.25(1) of the 2009 Act provides that the BAI must:

> endeavour to ensure (a) that the number and categories of broadcasting services made available in the State by virtue of this Act best serve the needs of the people of the island of Ireland, bearing in mind their languages and traditions and their religious, ethical and cultural

> diversity, (b) that the democratic values enshrined in the Constitution, especially those relating to rightful liberty of expression, are upheld, and (c) the provision of open and pluralistic broadcasting services.

Section 25(2) sets out the detailed obligations in this respect.

Section 33 empowers the BAI to impose a levy on the broadcasting sector to meet the cost of regulation of the sector by the BAI and its statutory committees. Section 33 permits the BAI to distinguish between various categories of broadcaster when imposing a levy. Section 34 provides that Exchequer funding may be used to defray exceptional costs incurred by the BAI in the performance of its functions. In addition, s.34 provides that the BAI will be funded from the Exchequer for the first year of its operation. Section 36 provides that the Contract Awards Committee may impose a requirement for deposits in respect of an application for a broadcasting contract. The section also allows the BAI to charge fees in respect of services or facilities provided by it.

Duties, codes and rules for broadcasters Part 3 of the 2009 Act (ss.39 to 46) sets out a revised list of duties and regulatory codes for broadcasters. Section 39(1) sets out the following general duties:

> Every broadcaster shall ensure that—
> (a) all news broadcast by the broadcaster is reported and presented in an objective and impartial manner and without any expression of the broadcaster's own views,
> (b) the broadcast treatment of current affairs, including matters which are either of public controversy or the subject of current public debate, is fair to all interests concerned and that the broadcast matter is presented in an objective and impartial manner and without any expression of his or her own views, except that should it prove impracticable in relation to a single broadcast to apply this paragraph, two or more related broadcasts may be considered as a whole, if the broadcasts are transmitted within a reasonable period of each other,
> (c) in the case of sound broadcasters a minimum of—
> (i) not less than 20 per cent of the broadcasting time, and
> (ii) if the broadcasting service is provided for more than 12 hours in any one day, two hours of broadcasting time between 07.00 hours and 19.00 hours,
> is devoted to the broadcasting of news and current affairs programmes, unless a derogation from this requirement is authorised by the [BAI] under subsection (3),
> (d) anything which may reasonably be regarded as causing harm or offence, or as being likely to promote, or incite to, crime or as

tending to undermine the authority of the State, is not broadcast by the broadcaster, and

(e) in programmes broadcast by the broadcaster, and in the means employed to make such programmes, the privacy of any individual is not unreasonably encroached upon.

Section 40 requires broadcasters to record, and to hold for a specified period, every broadcast made by them for the purposes of the performance of the functions of the Compliance Committee. Section 41 imposes certain requirements in respect of the broadcast of advertisements.

Section 42 requires the BAI to prepare codes governing standards and practices to be observed by broadcasters. It also provides for the continuance of equivalent codes promulgated by the Broadcasting Commission of Ireland prior to the 2009 Act. When the 2009 Act was enacted, these were: (a) the Code of Programme Standards (April 10, 2007); (b) the Children's Advertising Code (January 1, 2005); and (c) the Advertising Code (April 10, 2007). Section 43 requires the BAI to prepare rules for broadcasters in respect of access to broadcasting services by persons with hearing or sight impairments and in respect of the maximum duration and frequency of broadcast advertisements. As with s.42, it also provides for the continuance of rules promulgated by the Broadcasting Commission of Ireland. When the 2009 Act was enacted, these were: a) Access Rules (January 1, 2005) prepared under s.19 of the Broadcasting Act 2001; and (b) rules with respect to the maximum daily and hourly limits on advertising and teleshopping continued under s.19 of the Broadcasting Act 2001. Section 44 requires that any draft broadcasting code or rule be subject to public consultation. Section 45 provides that any broadcasting code or rule prepared by the BAI may be annulled by a resolution of either House of the Oireachtas. Section 46 provides that the BAI may co-operate with other parties in the drawing up by such parties of self-regulating standards in respect of broadcasting content.

Redress Part 4 of the 2009 Act (ss.47 to 49) deals with redress for those making complaints in respect of broadcasts. Section 47 requires broadcasters to consider complaints made to them and to establish a mechanism for dealing with such complaints. Section 48 provides for the consideration of complaints made against broadcasters by the Compliance Committee of the BAI. Section 49 provides for a right of reply mechanism for persons whose honour and reputation has been impugned by an assertion of incorrect facts in a broadcast. Section 49 also deals with the effect of this in the context of a defamation action, which is now regulated in general terms under the Defamation Act 2009: see the Torts chapter, pp.740–742, below.

Enforcement of broadcasting standards Part 5 of the 2009 Act (ss.50 to 57) deals with the enforcement by the BAI of broadcasting standards. Section 50 empowers the Compliance Committee of the BAI to conduct an investigation into the affairs of a broadcasting contractor in respect of adherence by a commercial or community broadcaster with the terms of their contract with the BAI and with the terms of any associated wireless telegraphy licence. Section 51 provides that the BAI on the recommendation of the Compliance Committee may, in certain circumstances, suspend or terminate a broadcasting contract. Section 53 provides that the Compliance Committee may appoint investigating officers to investigate and report on apparent breaches by a broadcaster of certain requirements of Pt 3 of the 2009 Act. Section 54 sets out the procedures to be followed by the investigating officer and Compliance Committee in any investigation of an apparent breach by a broadcaster. It also provides that the BAI, on the recommendation of the Compliance Committee, may apply to the High Court for the imposition of a financial sanction in respect of a breach by a broadcaster. It also provides that a broadcaster may request that the matter be dealt with by the Compliance Committee rather than the High Court. Section 55 provides that the High Court or the Compliance Committee may make a determination in respect of a breach and may impose a financial sanction of up to €250,000. It also provides that a broadcaster may appeal a decision of the Compliance Committee to the High Court. Section 56 provides for the matters to be considered by the Compliance Committee and by the High Court in determining the amount of any financial sanctions imposed on a broadcaster under s.55.

Broadcasting contracts and content: commercial and community broadcasters Part 6 of the 2009 Act (ss.58 to 78) sets out detailed requirements concerning broadcasting contracts and the content provision contracts for commercial and community broadcasters. Section 59 provides that the BAI may not award a broadcasting contract without an associated wireless telegraphy licence issued by the Commission for Communications Regulation (ComReg). Section 60 provides that ComReg may, on certain specified grounds, vary the terms and conditions of any wireless telegraphy licence issued for the purposes of a broadcasting contract. Section 61 provides that the Minister may suspend certain wireless telegraphy licences issued to commercial and community radio and television broadcasters and multiplex operators in the event of a national emergency declared under the Wireless Telegraphy Act 1926. Section 62 provides that the BAI may not grant a sound (radio) broadcasting contract to a person who has been convicted in the last five years of certain offences relating to wireless telegraphy.

Section 63 provides that the BAI, on the recommendation of the Contract Awards Committee, may award sound broadcasting contracts. Section 64 provides that the BAI, on the recommendation of the Contract Awards

Committee, may award sound broadcasting contracts for the provision of community sound broadcasting services by persons representing local communities or communities of interest. Section 65 provides for the process by which the Contract Awards Committee seeks applications for the award of broadcasting contracts. Section 66 outlines the criteria against which the Contract Awards Committee must consider applications for the award of a broadcasting contract. It also requires the Contract Awards Committee to agree a common score for each applicant and to notify the applicant of the reasons for the decision, the score of the applicant and the score of the successful applicant. Section 67 provides for a "fast-track" procedure in respect of an incumbent broadcaster that the Contract Awards Committee may adopt in the event that there is a limited response to a call for expressions of interest for the award of a sound broadcasting contract. Section 68 provides that the BAI may award temporary or institutional sound broadcasting services. Section 69 sets out the terms and conditions that apply to broadcasting contracts including duration, change of ownership and conditions in relation to the preservation of certain categories of programming by sound broadcasting contractors.

Section 70 provides for the award of an analogue television broadcasting contract to a television service programme contractor and sets out certain terms and conditions that shall apply to the television service programme contractor. It also provides for the continuance of the existing contract held by TV3 Television Network Ltd.

Section 71 provides that the BAI may award content provision contracts to commercial and community radio and television broadcasters to make their services available on broadcasting platforms such as cable, IPTV, satellite, digital terrestrial television (DTT) and mobile television systems, for reception in Ireland or elsewhere. The holder of a contract under this section will be subject to the broadcasting duties, codes and rules imposed under Pt 3. Section 72 allows for the BAI to award community content provision contracts for the provision of community television services to persons representing local communities. Section 73 provides that the BAI may carry out an assessment of the needs of a community in respect of broadcasting.

Section 74 provides that the BAI shall enter into contracts for the provision of electronic programme guides (EPG) where such guides are made available and provide information in relation to the schedule of programme material on broadcasting services available in Ireland. The section provides for prioritisation of information regarding the broadcasting services provided by RTE, TG4 and the television programme service contractor. Section 75 provides that the BAI may, following consultation with ComReg, prepare rules in respect of EPGs.

Section 76 sets out rules in relation to the "must carry" of certain services on MMD systems. Section 77 sets out the rules for "must carry" of television services provided by RTE, TG4, and the television programme service contractor, of national radio services provided by RTE and broadcasting contractors, and of community content provision contractors on certain types of broadcasting transmission networks. Section 78 provides that a person who contravenes s.71(1) or s.74(2) commits an offence, and that the person is liable, on summary conviction, to a fine not exceeding €5,000, or, on conviction on indictment, to a fine not exceeding €100,000.

Public service broadcasting: RTE and TG4 Part 7 of the 2009 Act (ss.79 to 128) concerns public service broadcasting, including significant changes to the regulation of RTE and TG4.

Part 7, Ch.1 (ss.79 to 112) contains what are described as Common Provisions for all Public Service Broadcasting Corporations, in effect, RTE and TG4. Section 79 provides for the continuation of RTE and TG4 as corporate bodies. Section 81 provides for the appointment by Government of the members of the boards of RTE and TG4. It provides that each board will comprise 12 members; six to be nominated by the Minister, four to be nominated by the Minister, the Minister having regard to the advice of a Joint Oireachtas Committee with responsibility for broadcasting matters, one to be elected by staff interests and a director general who will hold his or her position on the board in an ex officio capacity. Section 81 also provides for gender balance in respect of board membership. Section 82 outlines the experience required of persons to be appointed as board members of RTE and TG4, the period of appointment and the necessary processes to effect a resignation from a board. Section 83 sets out the process for the election of staff members to be appointed to the board of RTE and TG4. Section 84 provides for the terms of office, and procedure for removal of the board members of RTE and TG4. Section 85 provides for appointment by Government, on the nomination of the Minister, of the chairpersons of the boards of RTE and TG4. Section 86 provides for the suspension or exclusion from membership of the boards of RTE and TG4 in certain specified circumstances.

Section 87 imposes certain duties on the board members of RTE and TG4, namely, to:

(*a*) represent the interests of viewers and listeners,
(*b*) ensure that the activities of the corporation in pursuance of its objectives as set out in *section 114(1)* or *118(1)* are performed efficiently and effectively,
(*c*) ensure that the gathering and presentation by the corporation of news and current affairs is accurate and impartial,
and
(*d*) safeguard the independence of the corporation, as regards, the conception, content and production of programmes, the editing and presentation of news and current affairs programmes and the definition of programme schedules from State, political and commercial influences.

Section 89 provides for the appointment of directors general of RTE and TG4. It provides that a director general shall:

(a) carry on and manage, and control generally, the administration of the corporation,
(b) act as editor-in-chief in respect of content published by the corporation in pursuance of its objects under this Act, and
(c) perform such other functions (if any) as may be determined by the board of the corporation.

Section 92 requires the directors general and chairpersons of RTE and TG4 to attend before committees of the Houses of the Oireachtas.

Section 101 requires RTE and TG4 to prepare public service broadcasting statements outlining the activities that they propose to undertake over a five-year period in order to fulfil their public service objects. Section 101 also provides that any such statement is subject to approval by the Minister, following consultation with the BAI.

Section 103 sets out the instances in which RTE and TG4 must seek the consent of the Minister to carry out certain new services, or to vary the number of television or radio channels provided by them. It also outlines the matters which the Minister must consider in deciding whether or not to grant such consent. Section 106 outlines the particular requirements placed on RTE and TG4 as regards advertising and sponsorship. Section 108 concerns the exploitation of commercial opportunities by RTE and TG4, and states that such exploitation shall be at arm's length basis and would be used to subsidise public service broadcasting objects. Section 112 requires RTE and TG4 to prepare, following guidance from the BAI, a code setting out the principles that they will apply when commissioning programming from independent producers. Any code prepared is subject to ministerial approval.

Section 113 of the 2009 Act provides for the formal continuance of RTE. It may be noted that s.113 also provided for a change in the full title of RTE from Radio Telefís Éireann to Raidió Teilifís Éireann. Section 114 outlines the objects and associated powers of RTE. These are:

(a) to establish, maintain and operate a national television and sound broadcasting service which shall have the character of a public service, be a free-to-air service and be made available, in so far as it is reasonably practicable, to the whole community on the island of Ireland,
(b) to establish and maintain a website and teletext services in connection with the services of RTE under paragraphs (a), (c), (d), (e), (f), (g), (h) and (i),
(c) to establish and maintain orchestras, choirs and other cultural

performing groups in connection with the services of RTE under paragraphs (a), (f), (g) and (h),

(d) to assist and co-operate with the relevant public bodies in preparation for, and execution of, the dissemination of relevant information to the public in the event of a major emergency,

(e) to establish and maintain archives and libraries containing materials relevant to the objects of RTE under this subsection,

(f) to establish, maintain and operate a television broadcasting service and a sound broadcasting service which shall have the character of a public service, which services shall be made available, in so far as RTE considers reasonably practicable, to Irish communities outside the island of Ireland,

(g) subject to the consent of the Minister, the Minister having consulted with the Authority, to establish, maintain and operate, in so far as it is reasonably practicable, community, local, or regional broadcasting services, which shall have the character of a public service, and be available free-to-air,

(h) subject to the consent of the Minister, the Minister having consulted with the Authority, to establish and maintain non-broadcast non-linear audio-visual media services, in so far as it is reasonably practicable, which shall have the character of a public broadcasting service (such consent not being required in respect of such services which are ancillary to a broadcasting service provided under paragraphs (a), (d), (f) and (g)),

(i) to establish, maintain, and operate one or more national multiplexes,

(j) so far as it is reasonably practicable, to exploit such commercial opportunities as may arise in pursuit of the objects outlined in paragraphs (a) to (i).

Section 115 provides that the Minister at the request of the BAI may direct RTE to require it to co-operate with the holder of a broadcasting contract in respect of access to, and use of, RTE's transmission infrastructure. Section 116 requires RTE to commission specified levels of television and radio programming from the independent production sector. Section 117 provides for the continuance of TG4, or Teilifís na Gaeilge. Section 118 outlines the objects and associated powers of TG4. These broadly mirror those for RTE, but with a specific statement that its range of programmes be "primarily in the Irish language". Section 120 requires RTE to supply the equivalent of one hour per day of television programme material to TG4, and for TG4 to supply programme material to RTE in respect of the provision by RTE of a television service to Irish communities abroad.

Section 121 provides that ComReg shall issue a wireless telegraphy licence to RTE and TG4 in respect of the provision of broadcasting services by them. Section 122 provides that in the event of a national emergency declared under the Wireless Telegraphy Act 1926 the Minister may suspend any wireless telegraphy licence issued to RTE or TG4.

Significantly, and in contrast to the commercial broadcasters, s.123 of the 2009 Act provides that the Minister for Communications, with the consent of the Minister for Finance, may pay to RTE, out of Exchequer funds, an amount equivalent to the total receipts from the television licence fee less the costs of collecting the television licence fee and amounts paid to BAI in respect of the "Broadcasting Fund". Section 123 also provides that the Minister, subject to consent of Minister for Finance, may make Exchequer funding available to RTE and TG4 for public service purposes. Section 124 provides that on an annual and five-year basis the BAI will conduct reviews and make recommendations to the Minister as to the requisite level of public funding for RTE and TG4 to fulfil their public service objects.

Section 125 provides that the Houses of the Oireachtas Commission and Houses of the Oireachtas Service may establish a free-to-air television service in respect of the proceedings of the Houses of the Oireachtas and certain other matters to be known as the Houses of the Oireachtas Channel. Section 126 amends the Schedule to the Houses of the Oireachtas Commission Act 2003 to permit the Commission to provide for the funding of the Houses of the Oireachtas Channel. See also the Administrative Law chapter, pp.6–7, above for the significant amendments made to the 2003 Act by the Houses of the Oireachtas Commission (Amendment) Act 2009. Section 127 allows the Irish Film Board to establish a free-to-air Irish film television channel to be known as the Irish Film Channel, exhibiting principally Irish cinematic works. Section 128 provides that the Commission of the Houses of the Oireachtas and the Irish Film Board must every five years prepare, in respect of the Houses of the Oireachtas Channel and the Irish Film Channel, a public service broadcasting charter. It also provides that every five years the BAI will review the adequacy of public funding to support the fulfilment of the functions of the Houses of the Oireachtas Channel and the Irish Film Channel.

Digital broadcasting and analogue switch-off Part 8 of the 2009 Act (ss.129 to 139) deals with the arrangements for the introduction of digital broadcasting, and the switching off of all analogue broadcasting services. Section 130 provides for the establishment and operation of digital broadcast systems by RTE. The 2009 Act describes these digital systems as "multiplexes" and s.129 defines "multiplex" as "an electronic system which combines programme material and related and other data in a digital form and the transmission of that material and data so combined by means of wireless telegraphy directly or indirectly for reception by the general public." Section 130 also requires that RTE and TG4 channels are carried on the first RTE television multiplex.

The RTÉ (National Television Multiplex) Order 2010 (S.I. No. 85 of 2010) specified that the date on which the national television multiplex is required to be operational and available free-to-air to approximately 90% of the population is October 31, 2010. Section 130 also provides for the carriage on the first RTE multiplex of the Houses of the Oireachtas Channel and the Irish Film Channel, if required by the Minister, and of other television services of a public service nature if designated by the Minister by order, and of the television programme service contractor, if requested by the Authority. Channels carried on the first RTE multiplex may make payments to RTE in respect of this provision and also in certain circumstances may request an increase in capacity for the carriage of their service.

Section 131 provides that the BAI shall make arrangements for the establishment and operation of multiplexes in addition to those provided by RTE. Section 132 provides that ComReg is required to make available licences for digital terrestrial television (DTT) services for both RTE and other multiplex service providers. These licences must allow for the possibility that multiplexes may, so far as it is reasonably practicable to do so, be made available to the whole community in the State. In addition, s.132 allows for the possibility that ComReg may allocate further licences for DTT and for other services. Section 133 provides that ComReg is required to make available licences, both to RTE and other providers, in a similar arrangement to that of s.132, but in respect of digital sound broadcasting.

Section 139 provides for consideration by the Minister for Communications of a date for analogue switch-off, having consulted with all relevant stakeholders. It provides that the Minister may issue a policy direction to ComReg under s.13 of the Communications Regulation Act 2002 to begin the process of analogue switch-off and it requires ComReg to revoke existing licences to facilitate analogue switch-off. It also provides for RTE and the BAI to provide information to the public with regard to analogue switch-off. At the time of writing (August 2010), it appears that 2013 is the anticipated date for the switch to digital broadcasting and the consequent analogue switch-off.

Television licences Part 9 of the 2009 Act (ss.140 to 152) involves a significant recasting of the systems for regulating television licences. Section 140 provides, for example, that the Minister may by order specify that individual rooms within a premises are to be regarded as separate premises for the purpose of television set licensing.

Section 142 reiterates the long-established requirement that possession of television set requires a licence and that the Minister may exempt certain classes of television set from the licensing requirement. The details of the exemptions are set out in the Television Licence (Exemption of Classes of Television Set) Order 2009 (S.I. No. 319 of 2009). The 2009 Order contains exemptions for: (a) portable devices with a display size of not more than 160 cm^2 capable of exhibiting television services, e.g. mobile phones or personal digital assistants; and (b) other devices, e.g. personal computers or laptops, capable of accessing the internet and television-like services streamed via websites. The 2009 Order does not exempt from the television licensing requirements devices (e.g. personal computers or laptops) with a display size of more than 160 cm^2, capable of displaying television channels (e.g. RTE 2, TV3, TG4, BBC 1, 3e) distributed by conventional broadcast networks (e.g. cable, satellite, IPTV, analogue terrestrial, digital terrestrial or MMDS) using a television tuner card or related device (whether or not such devices are also capable of accessing the internet or television-like services streamed via websites).

Section 143 provides that the Minister may grant a television licence to possess a television set in a premises. Section 144 provides that the Minister may make regulations in regard to television licences, including the making of regulations prescribing that television sets held within a particular class of premises require a particular class of television licence. Section 145 provides that An Post, or a person designated by the Minister, may act as the Minister's agent as regards the grant of television licences and the collection of licence fees. Section 146 provides that television licence inspectors shall be issued with evidence of identification, may enter onto a premises for the purposes of ascertaining whether or not a television set is on the premises and whether or not there is a television licence in force, and may request a person to produce evidence of having a television licence in respect of a television set. Section 147 provides that a special notice may be issued to a person requiring them to complete and return a form of declaration, including a statutory declaration as to whether or not the person has in their possession a television set and has or has not a current television licence. If a person fails to complete and return the declaration within 28 days, it is presumed that they have a television set and that there is no television licence in force. Section 147 also provides that a person commits an offence if they make any false or misleading statements in respect of the completion of a special notice under this section. Section 148 provides that it is an offence to not hold a television licence in respect of the possession of a television set and sets out the maximum fines applicable on summary conviction of such an offence: in the case of a first offence, a fine not exceeding €1,000, and, in the case of a second or subsequent offence, a fine not exceeding €2,000. Section 149 provides for the operation of a fixed penalty payment mechanism in respect of a failure to hold a television licence in respect of the possession of a television set. A fixed penalty payment notice may only be applied after the issue of two reminder notifications and a minimum period of 56 days. The extent of a fixed penalty payment notice is capped at one third of the value of the extant television licence fee. Section 151 provides for the prosecution of offences in respect of the failure to hold a television licence in respect of the possession of a television set.

Broadcasting fund Part 10 of the 2009 Act (ss.153 to 159) deals with the Broadcasting Fund. Section 154 provides for the preparation of a Broadcasting Fund Scheme, in effect, a grant scheme by the Authority, the terms of which are to be agreed with the Minister. Section 155 sets out the objectives of a broadcasting funding scheme. These are to:

(*a*) develop high quality programmes based on Irish culture, heritage and experience,
(*b*) develop these programmes in the Irish language,
(*c*) increase the availability of programmes referred to in *paragraphs (a)* and *(b)* to audiences in the State,
(*d*) represent the diversity of Irish culture and heritage,
(*e*) record oral Irish heritage and aspects of Irish heritage which are disappearing, under threat, or have not been previously recorded, and
(*f*) develop local and community broadcasting.

Section 156 provides for payments by the Minister equivalent to 5 per cent of the net revenue received from the sale of television set licence fees for the purposes of a broadcasting funding scheme. Section 157 provides that the BAI may establish current and investment accounts associated with broadcasting funding schemes under Pt 10.

Major events television coverage Part 11 of the 2009 Act (ss.160 to 173) involves a recasting of the existing arrangements on which events of major importance to society are to be available free to air. Section 162 provides that the Minister may by order determine and designate events of major importance to society to be available free to air. Section 163 sets out the consultation process required where it is intended to designate an event of major importance. Section 164 sets out the duties of the broadcaster whether they are qualified or not in respect of acquiring rights with respect to designated events. Section 165 sets out the duties of the broadcaster in respect of events designated as being of major importance by a Member State of the European Communities. Section 166 provides for civil remedies by an "aggrieved broadcaster" where it is alleged a broadcaster has not complied with ss.164 and 165. This includes injunctive relief and/or an award of damages.

Section 167 provides that the High Court may, on application by a broadcaster, make an order determining reasonable market rates for an event. Section 168 provides for circumstances where an event organiser has not, within 56 days of the event taking place, entered into a contract with a qualifying broadcaster for broadcasting rights to a designated event. Section 168 also provides that a qualifying broadcaster may apply to the High Court for an order directing the event organiser to provide access to the event subject to the payment of reasonable market rates and such other terms to be determined by the court, and that the High Court may, upon such terms as the court considers just and proper, direct an event organiser to give a qualifying broadcaster access to a designated event before the High Court has fixed all the terms for the acquisition of broadcasting rights including the fixing of reasonable market rates. It also provides that where an existing contract is in place between an event organiser and a non-qualifying broadcaster, the High Court shall, on receipt of an application from a qualifying broadcaster, decide to whom and in what proportion monies in respect of reasonable market rates should be paid. Section 168 also provides that the High Court may adjust, as it considers appropriate, the terms of an existing contract between an event organiser and a non-qualifying broadcaster. Section 169 provides for arbitration arrangements in respect of instances where an event organiser who is willing to sell broadcasting rights to a designated event has not been able to agree a price with a qualifying broadcaster for access to the event. Section 170 sets out the criteria which the High Court or arbitrator must have regard to when determining reasonable market rates or terms for the purposes of Pt 11. Section 171 provides that the Minister may, in the public interest, require an event organiser to provide the Minister with a copy of any agreement entered into by an event organiser with any broadcaster in respect of a designated event. Section 173 sets a three-year review timetable for the purposes of s.162.

Transitional provisions concerning BCI Part 12 of the 2009 Act (ss.174 to 179) deals with transitional arrangements concerning, in particular, the dissolution of the Broadcasting Commission of Ireland on the establishment of the BAI.

Wireless telegraphy Part 13 of the 2009 Act (ss.180 and 181) involve amendments to the Wireless Telegraphy Acts 1926 to 2009 to conform to the changes made by the 2009 Act. It also provides for increases in fines in respect of convictions for offences under the Wireless Telegraphy Acts.

Copyright and digital broadcasting Part 14 of the 2009 Act (ss.183 to 185) involves a number of miscellaneous changes. Notably, s.183 amended s.2 of the Copyright and Related Rights Act 2000 to ensure that the rules governing the acquisition of copyright by DTT providers are the same as those which apply to cable, MMDS, multichannel multipoint distribution service, and internet protocol television, IPTV. While there are changes to the definitions of the Copyright and Related Rights Act, the effective change is to the existing s.174 of the 2000 Act by including DTT retransmission along with MMDS and cable in the definition of cable programme services. DTT retransmission is put on the same footing as MMDS and cable. Section 174 reflects Directive 93/83, the

Cable and Satellite Directive, which requires Member States to have such rules for cable and MMDS. During the Oireachtas debate on this section, the Minister expressed satisfaction that it was consistent with the 1993 Directive.

Minister's powers generally concerning broadcasting Section 184 of the 2009 Act provides that, without prejudice to the Minister's functions under the 2009 Act or any other enactment, the Minister has the power and is deemed always to have had the power, by himself or herself, or in conjunction with any other person, to fund, install, own and operate electronic communications networks and to provide electronic communications services. This includes where such networks or services are for the purpose of providing broadcasting services.

Referendum Commission Section 185 of the 2009 Act amended s.5 of the Referendum Act 1998 to reflect the establishment of the BAI and the dissolution of the Broadcasting Commission of Ireland.

Asylum and Immigration Law

PATRICIA BRAZIL BL, Lecturer in Law, Trinity College Dublin and
NUALA EGAN BL

CASE LAW

Adoption of "fixed and rigid policy" in consideration of previous tribunal decisions In *LCL v Refugee Appeals Tribunal* [2009] IEHC 26; unreported, High Court, Clark J., January 21, 2009, the applicant sought leave to apply for judicial review of the decision of the Refugee Appeals Tribunal dated August 30, 2007, to affirm the earlier recommendation of the Refugee Applications Commissioner dated July 15, 2004, that the applicant should not be granted a declaration of refugee status. The applicant was an Angolan national who applied for asylum in the State on June 3, 2003, asserting a well-founded fear of persecution on the basis of political opinion by reason of his membership of the FLEC-FAC party in Angola. The Refugee Applications Commissioner issued a negative recommendation in respect of his application for refugee status on July 15, 2004. A notice of appeal to the Refugee Appeals Tribunal was filed on August 9, 2004. A medical report prepared by two doctors attached to the SPIRASI centre for the survivors of torture was attached. The applicant's legal representatives submitted country of origin information and six previous Refugee Appeals Tribunal decisions in support of the appeal.

On August 30, 2007, the Refugee Appeals Tribunal refused the applicant's refugee appeal. The applicant's credibility was rejected on the basis of a number of inconsistencies identified in his evidence. The tribunal member stated that he had considered the medical reports but found that evidence to be contingent upon whether he believed the applicant's story as to how he came to suffer the various injuries detailed therein. The tribunal member rejected the relevance of the six previous tribunal decisions which had been submitted in support of the appeal and stated that he had observed the applicant's overall demeanour and the way he gave his evidence, and found that they indicated that his account was not credible.

Among the grounds advanced by the applicant in his application for leave to apply for judicial review was a complaint that the tribunal member had failed to consider adequately the contents of the SPIRASI medical report when assessing his credibility and that the tribunal member failed to adequately assess the relevance of the six previous Tribunal decisions submitted by the applicant. In relation to the SPIRASI report, it was submitted that the tribunal member erred in making reference to the report only after assessing the applicant's credibility, and not as one of the factors considered in the context of that assessment. While it was accepted that it was ultimately a matter for the tribunal member to determine how much weight to be attributed to the medical report, "he was not entitled to relegate it to an afterthought of his credibility assessment".

In relation to the consideration of the six previous Tribunal decisions submitted in support of the appeal, the tribunal member in his decision stated:

> "The Applicant's legal advisers have submitted six previous decisions of the Tribunal relating to other appeals. The Tribunal has considered these Decisions in the context of the current appeal. The Irish Courts have made it clear on a number of occasions that the Tribunal is not bound in any way to follow previous decisions of the Tribunal concerning other Appeals (see *Fasakin* and *Atanasov*). Clearly this is a sound proposition in view of the ever changing facts and circumstances in the Countries of Origin concerned, and of the very individual nature of appeals in this context. As the Tribunal is frequently reminded by legal advisers, the refugee definition requires an analysis of the subjective, as well as the objective circumstances in each appeal. The Tribunal has taken into account the individual facts in the instant Appeal. Given the facts of this particular case the Tribunal finds that the previous decisions submitted are not of sufficient relevance to the instant appeal to warrant a conclusion that the current recommendation be overturned."

The applicant complained that this was a standard paragraph of a rote and formulaic nature routinely inserted into Tribunal decisions in cases where previous tribunal decisions have been submitted for consideration. It was argued that the use of this standard passage indicated a rejection of the decisions without considering their relevance in establishing relevant legal principles.

On behalf of the respondent it was submitted that it was clear from the decision of the tribunal member that it was clear as a matter of "forensic timing" that when the decision was read as a whole, the tribunal member did have regard to the SPIRASI report when considering the applicant's credibility. In relation to the consideration of the six previous Tribunal decisions, reliance was placed on the decision of O'Leary J. in *Fasakin v Refugee Appeals Tribunal* [2005] IEHC 423 where it was held:

> "Evidence from family members other than the applicant could be relevant in the event that a particular family was the subject of persecution. Similarly evidence of ethnic persecution can be persuasive though not yet personal to the applicant. However, the decision of a

> body in a particular case is neither evidence in an other case nor does it create a binding authority for future cases. Each case must be considered on its own merits."

It was further submitted that there was a finding that the applicant's evidence was consistent and credible in each of the six previous decisions submitted by the applicant, and it was contended that the facts of those cases constituted a very different situation to the present, where the applicant's credibility was impugned.

Clark J. was satisfied that the medical report from SPIRASI should have been "specifically referred to and was worthy of some analysis before its relevance was rejected". It was noted that while the findings made in that report may not have been highly placed on the hierarchy of probative value outlined in the Istanbul Protocol; nonetheless Clark J. was satisfied that:

> "[T]he report and its place in the credibility assessment and the consideration of explanations for errors in the applicant's questionnaire should have been stated in the decision."

In this regard, it was noted that the SPIRASI report referred to 12 small concentric scars on the applicant's arms which were consistent with the applicant's account of torture. Accordingly, Clark J. granted leave to seek judicial review of the Refugee Appeals Tribunal decision on this ground.

Clark J. was also satisfied that substantial grounds sufficient for leave had also been made out in relation to the tribunal member's treatment of the six previous decisions submitted in support of the appeal. This conclusion was arrived at following an examination by the court of the six decisions referred to. Clark J. noted that:

> "… there was no evidence in the decision impugned that the previous RAT decisions were considered, rejected or distinguished by the tribunal member. It was left to counsel for the respondents to seek to urge this court that credibility had been established in all those cases and that this was the distinguishing feature with this case. If that is correct, and it is unnecessary for me to make a finding on the point, then the differences between those decisions and the applicant's case should, at the very least, have been referred to in the decision. The quotation highlighted by the applicant from the decision has appeared verbatim in other decisions of the RAT and is suggestive of a blanket rejection of previous RAT decisions without further consideration or evaluation".

Concluding that the treatment of the medical report and the previous decisions of the tribunal was "suggestive of a want of fair process", leave was granted to seek judicial review.

Application to compel decision on naturalisation within reasonable period of time In *AN v Minister for Justice, Equality and Law Reform,* unreported, High Court, Clark J., July 29, 2009; [2009] IEHC 354, the applicant was a national of Pakistan who entered the State on a student visa in 2002 and was thereafter granted a work permit. He married an Irish national while in the State in April 2004 and was granted residency in the State on the basis of his marriage to an Irish national. The applicant lodged an application for a certificate of naturalisation in June 2007, pursuant to s.15A of the Irish Nationality and Citizenship Acts 1956–2004. He provided an amount of documentation in support of his application. Receipt was acknowledged and the application was deemed valid on September 4, 2007.

More than a year later, after the decision of Edwards J. in *KM and GD v Minister for Justice, Equality and Law Reform* [2007] IEHC 234,[1] two letters were sent to the Minister asking for an indication as to when the application would be decided. No response was received to the first letter. The Minister was then informed that proceedings would be commenced if a satisfactory response was not received and if the application was not determined within a reasonable time. On October 23, 2007, the applicant was informed in response to the second letter that there was a backlog and it would take 29 months to process an application for a certificate of naturalisation. This would mean that the applicant would have a decision in November 2009.

In October 2008 Edwards J. granted leave on an ex parte basis, stating that it was arguable that the Minister was obliged to deal with applications expeditiously and within a reasonable time. The relief sought was an order requiring the Minister to indicate to the applicant how long it would take for his application to be decided. The application was processed immediately thereafter and the Minister granted the applicant a certificate of naturalisation in February 2009. He was subsequently granted an Irish passport. The proceedings were therefore moot in respect of the substantive reliefs sought, and the only issue outstanding was that of costs. The applicant sought his costs against the respondent in respect of the proceedings, and the respondent sought his costs against the applicant.

Counsel for the applicant argued that it was reasonable for the applicant to commence proceedings in the context of the state of the law following the decision of Edwards J. in *KM and DG*. It was argued that a 29-month delay in processing the application was unreasonable and it was argued that the applicant was prejudiced because he would not be entitled to vote in elections in Ireland until he became a citizen. Counsel indicated that because there were differences between the rights enjoyed by citizens and non-citizens, this emphasised the importance of an application for a certificate of naturalisation being determined within a reasonable time. Counsel for the respondent accepted

---

1 See Brazil and Egan, "Asylum and Immigration Law" in Byrne and Binchy (eds), *Annual Review of Irish Law 2007* (Round Hall, 2008), pp.23–26.

that an application must be determined within a reasonable time, but argued that what is reasonable depends on a number of factors, the first of which is the nature of the application being made and the extent of the discretion of the decision-maker. It was pointed out that the Minister's discretion to grant a certificate of naturalisation was absolute, and that there was no constitutional entitlement to apply for naturalisation—this was a right conferred by statute (i.e. the Irish Nationality and Citizenship Acts 1956–2004). Counsel for the respondents argued that it was not reasonable for the applicant to seek from the court an order directing the Minister to act in a particular way or directing the Department of Finance to allocate more funds to a particular task. It was argued that if the court was minded to have regard to a "floodgates" argument, it should be borne in mind that 8,000 people made an application for a certificate of naturalisation in 2008 and not all of those applications had been determined; by the same token not all of the applications made in 2007 had been determined.

On June 26, 2009, Clark J. gave her decision ex tempore and refused the application; on July 29, 2009, a written decision was delivered setting out the reasons for the finding that the applicant was not entitled to the costs of bringing proceedings which the court considered inappropriate and unreasonable. At the outset, Clark J. noted that the applicant was a non-EU national who came to the State on a student visa and, after obtaining a work permit, married an Irish citizen. The applicant had a statutory right to apply for a certificate of naturalisation under s.15A of the Irish Nationality and Citizenship Acts 1956–2004 once he had lived in the State with his spouse for the requisite amount of time, being three years from the date of his marriage. It was noted that the 2004 Act states at s.15 that the Minister may, in his or her absolute discretion, grant a certificate of naturalisation provided that the applicant meets certain pre-conditions and criteria including being of good character, being married to a citizen in a subsisting and recognised marriage under the laws of the State for a period of at least three years and having the intention to reside in the State after naturalisation.

Having considered the legal principles identified in *KM*, Clark J. held that the facts of the present case could easily be distinguished from those recited in that decision. It was held that, unlike in *KM*, the circumstances of this case did not demonstrate any pressing social needs on the applicant's part as he was legally in employment, living with his spouse with no limitation as to the right to remain in the country. Clark J. was satisfied that there was no urgency such that would require an order of mandamus directed to the Minister to deal with this case within time limits identified by Edwards J. in *KM*, and that the facts of this case were therefore clearly distinguishable from the line of authority relied on, including *Phillips v Medical Council* [1992] I.L.R.M. 469, *Ó Murchú v Registrar of Companies and the Minister for Industry and Commerce* [1988] I.R. 112 and *Halowane v Minister for Justice, Equality and Law Reform* [2008] IEHC 130.

Clark J. noted that the applicant was informed from the first opportunity that there would be a delay in dealing with his application, and that no valid reason was advanced for the applicant to demand, require or insist on the consideration of his application before the identified period. Furthermore, the Minister was never informed of any special or pressing circumstance requiring a speedier determination. Clark J. concluded that:

> "[T]he act of the applicant in seeking to compel the Minister is evidence that he considered the granting of naturalisation as an absolute right rather than a privilege subject to policy considerations in the interest of the common good."

It was noted that a great number of applications for naturalisation are made to the Minister which must be individually considered and investigated, and that there was no question of accepting the contents of assertions made in an application form at face value:

> "[A] degree of investigation is required and then provided that the Minister does not act capriciously or arbitrarily, he determines in his discretion whether to grant a certificate of naturalisation."

Clark J. concluded by stating:

> "I do not believe that in the absence of cogent evidence of arbitrary or capricious behaviour in the consideration of applications of the nature in question it is appropriate for a court to direct a Minister to carry out his discretionary functions within any particular time limit. It would seem to me to encroach on the constitutionally recognised and protected doctrine of the separation of powers between executive and judicial functions. It does not seem appropriate in a case such as this that it is appropriate for the court to determine what constitutes a reasonable period within which the Minister should perform his functions. The Irish Nationality and Citizenship Acts 1956–2004 at s.15 uses the wording 'The Minister may, in his or her absolute discretion, grant a certificate of naturalisation'. These words have a meaning which would be reduced to an obligation to grant if the Minister were in ordinary circumstances to be directed by the Court to consider the application within a period determined by the Court."

Having determined that there was no evidence of unreasonable and unconscionable delay nor had the applicant established any prejudice, Clark J. concluded that it was not reasonable that the applicant should have instituted proceedings in the manner as occurred in this case or for the reliefs sought and thus refused the applicant's application for an order of costs.

Clark J. went on to consider whether the Minister was entitled to his costs against the applicant. It was held that while all persons in the State enjoy fundamental rights of access to the courts, that right is not unqualified and is subject to imposition of a penalty of costs incurred by the responding party if those proceedings have been inappropriately commenced. However, in the exercise of her discretion Clark J. made no order for costs in favour of the Minister as this was possibly the first time that the issue of costs in such a case has been tested. However, Clark J. warned that:

> "[I]t may be appropriate in subsequent cases arising from the same or similar facts that an order for costs against the applicant and in favour of the Minister should appropriately be made."

Assessment of credibility Many of the judicial reviews heard in the High Court in recent years have involved a challenge to the assessment of the applicant's credibility made by the decision-maker in the refugee process. In *IR v Minister for Justice, Equality and Law Reform* [2009] IEHC 353; unreported, Cooke J., July 24, 2009, Cooke J. sought to harmonise the various decisions of the High Court in relation to assessment of credibility to provide guidance for future challenges.

At the outset, Cooke J. noted that in most forms of adversarial dispute the assessment of the credibility of oral testimony is one of the most difficult challenges faced by the decision-maker. He accepted that the difficulty is particularly acute in asylum cases because:

> "[A]lmost by definition, a genuine refugee will be someone who has fled home in circumstances of stress, urgency and even terror and will have arrived in a place which is wholly strange to them; whose language they do not speak and whose culture may be incomprehensible."

It was noted that in such cases the decision-makers at first instance have:

> "… the unenviable task of deciding if an applicant can be believed by recourse to little more than an appraisal of the account given, the way in which it was given and the reaction of the applicant to sceptical questions, to the highlighting of possible discrepancies or to contradictory evidence from other sources".

Cooke J. noted that recourse will also be had in appropriate cases to country of origin information but accepted that:

> "[I]n most cases this will be of use only in ascertaining whether the social, political and other conditions in the country of origin are such

> that the events recounted or the mistreatment claimed to have been suffered, may or may not have taken place."

It was emphasised that in such cases, where the judgment of the primary decision-maker must frequently depend on the personal appraisal of an applicant, it is not the function of the High Court in judicial review to reassess credibility and to substitute its own view for that of the decision-maker:

> "[I]ts role is confined when a finding of lack of credibility is attacked, to ensuring that the process by which that conclusion has been reached is legally sound and not vitiated by any material error of law."

Cooke J. reviewed the statutory provisions and guidelines which govern decision-making in the asylum field, including s.11B of the Refugee Act 1996, reg.5 of the European Communities (Eligibility for Protection) Regulations 2006 and the UNHCR *Handbook on Procedures and Criteria for Determining Refugee Status*.

The applicant in the present proceedings sought to quash the decision of the Refugee Appeals Tribunal of April 17, 2007 which decision turned entirely upon the credibility of the applicant's account of his personal history and his claim of a well-founded fear of persecution in Belarus based on his political opinion and political activities as a member of an opposition party, the Belarus Popular Front (BPF). Cooke J. summarised the issues raised by the applicant as follows:

> "(i) how is this decision-maker to strike a correct balance when required to weigh evidence in different forms and of different quality:
> (ii) if the decision-maker doubts the plausibility of an account given in personal testimony what duty, if any, is there to consider and assess the probative value and effect of documentary evidence or other secondary information which appears to be supportive of the doubted testimony: and
> (iii) where the decision-maker rejects as incredible the personal testimony of an applicant what is the extent of the obligation, if any, to state the reasons for the rejection or discounting of other inconsistent documentary evidence or secondary information?"

Referring to previous judgments of the High Court in relation to the assessment of credibility,[2] Cooke J. set out 10 core principles governing the assessment of credibility which should be set out in full:

---

2 Including *Memishi v Refugee Appeals Tribunal*, unreported, Peart J., June 25, 2003; *Kramarenko v Refugee Appeals Tribunal* [2004] 2 I.L.R.M. 450; *Traore v Refugee*

"(1) The determination as to whether a claim to a well founded fear of persecution is credible falls to be made under the Refugee Act 1996 by the administrative decision-maker and not by the Court. The High Court on judicial review must not succumb to the temptation or fall into the trap of substituting its own view for that of the primary decision-makers.

(2) On judicial review the function and jurisdiction of the High Court is confined to ensuring that the process by which the determination is made is legally sound and is not vitiated by any material error of law, infringement of any applicable statutory provision or of any principle of natural or constitutional justice.

(3) There are two facets to the issue of credibility, one subjective and the other objective. An applicant must first show that he or she has a genuine fear of persecution for a Convention reason. The second element involves assessing whether that subjective fear is objectively justified or reasonable and thus well founded.

(4) The assessment of credibility must be made by reference to the full picture that emerges from the available evidence and information taken as a whole, when rationally analysed and fairly weighed. It must not be based on a perceived, correct instinct or gut feeling as to whether the truth is or is not being told.

(5) A finding of lack of credibility must be based on correct facts, untainted by conjecture or speculation and the reasons drawn from such facts must be cogent and bear a legitimate connection to the adverse finding.

(6) The reasons must relate to the substantive basis of the claim made and not to minor matters or to facts which are merely incidental in the account given.

(7) A mistake as to one or even more facts will not necessarily vitiate a conclusion as to lack of credibility provided the conclusion is tenably sustained by other correct facts. Nevertheless, an adverse finding based on a single fact will not necessarily justify a denial of credibility generally to the claim.

(8) When subjected to judicial review, a decision on credibility

---

Appeals Tribunal [2004] 4 I.R. 607; *Da Silviera v Refugee Appeals Tribunal*, unreported, Peart J., July 9, 2004; *Sango v Minister for Justice, Equality and Law Reform* [2005] IEHC 395; *Imafu v Minister for Justice, Equality and Law Reform* [2005] IEHC 182 (pre-leave Clarke J.); *Imafu v Minister for Justice, Equality and Law Reform* [2005] IEHC 416 (post-leave Peart J.); *Imoh v Refugee Appeals Tribunal* [2007] IEHC 220 (Clarke J.); *Banzuzi v Refugee Appeals Tribunal* [2007] IEHC 2 (Feeney J.); *Kikumbi v Minister for Justice, Equality and Law Reform* [2007] IEHC 11 (Herbert J.); *E v Refugee Appeals Tribunal* [2008] IEHC 339 (Hedigan J.); *VZ v Minister for Justice, Equality and Law Reform* [2002] 2 I.R.; *K v Minister for Justice, Equality and Law Reform*, unreported, Gilligan J., April 19, 2007 and *Simo v Refugee Appeals Tribunal*, unreported, Edwards J., July 4, 2007.

> must be read as a whole and the Court should be wary of attempts to deconstruct an overall conclusion by subjecting its individual parts to isolated examination in disregard of the cumulative impression made upon the decision-maker especially where the conclusion takes particular account of the demeanour and reaction of an applicant when testifying in person.
>
> (9) Where an adverse finding involves discounting or rejecting documentary evidence or information relied upon in support of a claim and which is prima facie relevant to a fact or event pertinent to a material aspect of the credibility issue, the reasons for that rejection should be stated.
>
> (10) Nevertheless, there is no general obligation in all cases to refer in a decision on credibility to every item of evidence and to every argument advanced, provided the reasons stated enable the applicant as addressee, and the Court in exercise of its judicial review function, to understand the substantive basis for the conclusion on credibility and the process of analysis or evaluation by which it has been reached."

It was noted that the case before the court was somewhat unusual in that the applicant's case did not rest solely upon his own personal testimony and its credibility; rather, the applicant submitted at the outset of his refugee application a number of documents which on their face appeared to be directly related to specific facts and events recounted by the applicant and which formed the basis of his claim to have suffered particular mistreatment on specific dates in given places. Among the documents submitted by the applicant were his military service book, birth certificate, an extract from his passport, a police report, a court decision, a court verdict, a police summons and a newspaper article. Cooke J. stated:

> "The Court considers that what is crucial about this material so far as concerns the legality of the process by which the conclusion on credibility in the Contested Decision was reached, is that none of it is referred to anywhere in that decision except insofar as it might be said to have been included in the phrase 'The Tribunal has considered all the relevant documentation…' which appears in the Conclusion at section 7."

The court accepted that, "the mere existence and submission of such documents does not necessarily render untenable a judgment as to the lack of credibility of the oral testimony of the applicant", but held that until such time as those documents and any issues arising therefrom had been properly considered by the tribunal member:

> "[T]he fundamental point is that this was, at least on its face, original, contemporaneous documentary evidence of potentially significant probative weight in corroborating key facts and events. If it is authentic, it may prove that the applicant has suffered persecution for his political activities. If that is so, then the judgmental assessment that is made of the quality of his answers to the questions about the BPF may possibly assume an entirely different weight when all of the evidence, both testimony and documentary, is objectively weighed in the balance."

It was further accepted that:

> "[T]here may well be cases in which an applicant relies partly on oral assertions, partly on documents, and partly on country of origin information and in which the decision-maker has sound reason to conclude that the oral testimony is so fundamentally incredible that it is unnecessary to consider whether the documents are authentic and whether the conditions in the country of origin are such that the claim could be plausible."

Cooke J. held that the present case was materially different:

> "… because the adverse finding of credibility is effectively based on the Tribunal member's premise as to the level of knowledge to be expected and the apparent lack of that knowledge, while the documents have the potential to establish that specific events did happen and happened to the applicant. It is this which gives rise to the need for the whole of the evidence to be evaluated and the analysis to be explained".

Cooke J. thus concluded that the process employed by the tribunal member in reaching the negative credibility conclusion was "fundamentally flawed" because the documentary evidence which had been expressly relied upon before the Commissioner and in the notice of appeal and which was on its face relevant to the events on which credibility depended, was ignored, not considered, and not mentioned in the decision to refuse the applicant's refugee appeal. In this regard, the court accepted:

> "… that a decision-maker is not obliged to mention every argument or deal with every piece of evidence in an appeal decision at least so long as the basis upon which the lack of credibility has been found can be ascertained from the reasons given".

However, it was held that this proposition is valid only when the other arguments and additional evidence are ancillary to the matters upon which the substantive finding is based and could not by themselves have rendered the conclusion unsound or untenable if shown to be correct or proven. In the present case, having regard to the fact that the documentary evidence submitted by the applicant in support of his refugee appeal were capable of objectively verifying key aspects of the applicant's claim, the court held that the failure to have regard to those documents rendered the decision-making process flawed and the tribunal member's analysis incomplete. Cooke J. accordingly quashed the decision of the tribunal member on the basis of an error of law in that the tribunal member failed to consider all of the relevant evidence on credibility and adequately and objectively to weigh it in the balance in reaching a conclusion on that issue, concluding:

> "Where, as here, documentary evidence of manifest relevance and of potential probative force is adduced and relied upon, the Tribunal member is under a duty in law to consider it and if it is discounted or rejected as unauthentic or unreliable or otherwise lacking probative value, there is a duty to state the reason for that finding."

This decision offers welcome clarification of the obligations on refugee decision-makers in the assessment of credibility. It is also notable that a subsequent application for a certificate of leave to appeal pursuant to s.5 of the Illegal Immigrants (Trafficking) Act 2000 was refused by Cooke J. on the basis that no novel proposition of law was contained in the judgment: "It merely applies to the special circumstances of this case the general principles derived from the settled case law" (*IR v Minister for Justice, Equality and Law Reform* [2009] IEHC 510; unreported, Cooke J., November 26, 2009).

Challenge to refusal of naturalisation In *AB v Minister for Justice, Equality and Law Reform* [2009] IEHC 449; unreported, High Court, Cooke J., June 18, 2009, the applicant sought to challenge a decision of the Minister dated July 21, 2008, in which the Minister refused to reconsider an earlier decision of March 13, 2008, to refuse the applicant's application for a certificate of naturalisation pursuant to s.14 of the Irish Nationality and Citizenship Act 1956 (as amended). Leave to seek judicial review was granted by Finlay Geoghegan J. on October 6, 2008, to seek an order of certiorari to quash the decision; the order also granted leave to seek additional reliefs including a declaration that the decision had been made in breach of the applicant's rights to constitutional and natural justice and an order of mandamus requiring the Minister to reconsider the original application.

The relevant provisions of the 1956 Act were ss.14, 15 and 16, which provide:

> 14. Irish citizenship may be conferred on a non-national by means of a certificate of naturalisation granted by the Minister.

15(1) Upon receipt of an application for a certificate of naturalisation, the Minister may, in his absolute discretion, grant the application, if satisfied that the applicant –

(a) (i) is of full age or

(ii) is a minor born in the State;

(b) is of good character

(c) has had a period of one year's continuous residence in the State immediately before the date of the application and, during the eight years immediately preceding that period has had a total residence in the State amounting to four years;

(d) intends in good faith to continue to reside in the State after naturalisation; and

(e) has made, either before a justice of the district court in open court or in such manner as the Minister, for special reasons, allows, a declaration in the prescribed manner, of fidelity to the nation and loyalty to the State.

(2) The conditions specified in paragraphs (a) to (e) of subsection (1) are referred to in this Act as conditions for naturalisation.

16. The Minister may in his absolute discretion grant an application for a certificate of naturalisation in the following cases, although the conditions for naturalisation (or any of them) are not complied with:

...

(g) where the applicant is a person who is a refugee within the meaning of the United Nations Convention relating to the status of refugees of 28th July, 1951, and the protocol relating to the status of refugees of 31st January, 1967, or is a stateless person within the meaning of the United Nations Convention relating to the status of stateless persons of 28th of September, 1954.

The grounds upon which leave was granted effectively related to the validity of the reason stated by the Minister for the original refusal of the certificate as contained in his letter of March 13, 2008, namely, that the Minister did not consider that the applicant fulfilled the naturalisation condition of being of "good character" as required by s.15(1)(b).

The factual background to the proceedings were that the applicant was born in Nigeria in 1973 but fled to the State in 2002 and successfully applied for refugee status which was granted on May 15, 2003. On July 7, 2005, he applied to the Minister for a certificate of naturalisation as an Irish citizen in accordance with s.14 of the Act. By letter of March 13, 2008, the Minister refused that application on the grounds that the applicant had come to the adverse attention of An Garda Síochána, having been charged before the District Court with the offence of having no driving licence and failing to produce a driving licence, in circumstances where the charges did not result in a conviction as the case was not called in court. The applicant averred that the reason for the refusal came as a surprise to him as he was not aware of having come to such "adverse attention". Upon making further enquiry he learned that it arose from an occasion when he had been stopped at a checkpoint on May 8, 2005, and requested to produce his driving licence; as he did not have it on him at the time, he was required to produce it within 10 days at a Garda station. It appeared that when he failed to do so an application was made to issue a summons in the District Court but this was never served or proceeded with and no conviction was recorded. The applicant obtained confirmation from the Dublin City Motor Tax Office that he had held a provisional driving licence since May 2003, and therefore held such a licence on May 8, 2005. The applicant conceded that he did not have the original driving licence on him on the occasion in question but claimed that he showed a photo-copy of it to the Garda and that he was not asked to produce the original within 10 days as a result.

Having assembled written confirmation of this background from the Gardaí and the Motor Tax Office the applicant had his solicitor write to the citizenship section of the Department on July 11, 2008, placing the information before it and pointing out that the applicant had been neither charged with nor convicted of any offence and was in those circumstances entitled to the benefit of the presumption of innocence and that a mere allegation could not constitute the basis for a finding by the Minister that he was not of "good character", especially when he had provided references attesting to his good character. Reference was also made to art.34 of the 1951 Convention relating to the status of refugees which obliges contracting states "as far as possible (to) facilitate the assimilation and naturalisation of refugees and in particular (to) make every effort to expedite naturalisation proceedings." It was submitted that the applicant was a recognised refugee since 2003 and had two Irish citizen children. The letter concluded:

> "[I]n the light of the above submissions, we now seek a review of the decision to refuse our client a certificate of naturalisation. We submit that a review of this decision should be taken in the interests of justice".

The Citizenship Section replied on behalf of the Minister by letter of July 22, 2008, and stated that, "applicants who have come to the adverse attention of An Garda Síochána are not considered of sufficient character to be granted Irish citizenship". The letter further noted that in refusing his application for naturalisation, the Minister had exercised his absolute discretion as provided by the Irish Nationality and Citizenship Act 1956 as amended. It was further stated that there was no appeals process under the Act but that it was open to the applicant to lodge a new application for a certificate of naturalisation at any time.

Cooke J. noted that while the relief for which leave was sought and granted is directed exclusively at the refusal of the Minister on July 22, 2008 to review the original decision of March 13, 2008, the arguments advanced were directed, in effect, at the legality of the original refusal of the certificate and, in particular, at the finding that the applicant was not of "good character" simply because he had come to the adverse attention of An Garda Síochána. It was submitted that to draw an inference adverse to the applicant's character on the basis of a District Court summons which had never been proceeded with and of which the applicant was wholly unaware was fundamentally unlawful in that it violated the applicant's presumption of innocence, was a patently unfair procedure in the decision-making process and a wholly irrational policy upon which to base the operation of s.15. Counsel for the applicant submitted that the Minister's refusal to reconsider reflected a policy in which "coming to the adverse attention of An Garda Síochána" was of itself adequate justification for the exercise of the Minister's absolute discretion to refuse the certificate, whether or not the adverse attention had any real bearing upon an applicant's character as such. It was submitted that there was, accordingly, no point in the applicant making a new application for a certificate so long as the Minister maintained such a policy. It was also submitted that even if the applicant had failed to fulfil the "good character" condition, the Minister had erred in law in failing to consider the exercise of his discretion under s.16 to waive compliance with that condition when the Minister knew that the applicant was a refugee.

Cooke J. noted that in the course of arguments on these issues considerable attention was paid to the role of the Minister's "absolute discretion" under both s.15 and s.16 and the extent to which it might render his decision immune from judicial review. However, on the facts of this case he stated that the refusal of the applicant's application for naturalisation did not appear to be an exercise of the Minister's absolute discretion, but rather was based on the applicant's failure to fulfil the statutory criteria for naturalisation. Cooke J. stated that the reality of the applicant's grievance in the present case was clearly the basis upon which the Minister considered him to fail to meet the "good character" condition. However, that was regarded as a matter which goes to the basis of the original decision refusing the certificate in the letter of March 13, 2008, which was not before the court as leave was granted to challenge the Minister's refusal to review that decision and not the decision itself. Cooke J. noted that where the Minister is not relying upon his absolute discretion to refuse an application under s.15 but is rejecting it upon the basis of non-compliance with one or more of the naturalisation conditions, his refusal is clearly amenable to judicial review and it would be one of the circumstances in which fair procedures would require the reason for refusal to be stated.

However, Cooke J. held that where the Minister gives a reason for refusal with which an applicant is dissatisfied, "the Minister cannot be compelled to reconsider his refusal or reopen the original application for fresh determination." Reference was made to the Minister's letters which clearly stated that there was no appeal against the Minister's decision as such but that every applicant is entitled to make a new application for the certificate at any time if he or she considers that the Minister has made a mistake or that some omission on the part of the applicant has since been rectified. Cooke J. also commented:

> "When a new application is lodged, however, the Minister is entitled, especially where there has been a lapse of time since the original application was made, to determine it on the basis of up to date information and new enquiries. The Minister cannot be compelled to confine himself to a reconsideration of the original application based on the state of the information available when the decision was made in disregard of any possible changes of circumstance (including the applicant's conduct and character) which have intervened subsequently."

The relief claimed in this application was accordingly refused because it was directed at the decision of July 21, 2008, to refuse to review the refusal of the applicant's application and, in the court's judgment, the Minister was not compellable to reconsider a decision taken under s.15 of the Act.

Challenge to refusal of visa In *RMR and BH v Minister for Justice, Equality and Law Reform* [2009] IEHC 279; unreported, Clark J., June 11, 2009, the applicants were a married couple who were Sri Lankan nationals. The husband resided in Ireland and the wife resided in Sri Lanka. The applicants sought judicial review of the refusal of the Minister to grant to the wife a visa to travel to Ireland to join her husband who had leave to remain temporarily in Ireland. The applicants sought an order of certiorari quashing that refusal and an order of mandamus ordering the Minister to determine the application for a visa. On December 15, 2008, Peart J. granted the applicants leave ex parte to seek judicial review.

The husband had arrived in the State in April 2002 and applied for refugee status. His application was refused by the Refugee Applications Commissioner and Refugee Appeals Tribunal, which found that although his credibility was accepted, he had failed to establish that he would face persecution in the event of his return to Sri Lanka. He was granted humanitarian leave to remain in the State on October 16, 2003. In 2007, he returned to Sri Lanka for a period of approximately three months to visit his mother who was dying; during this period, a marriage was arranged with the first-named applicant. On February 13, 2008, the wife made an application online for a long-stay "D" visa to join her non-EEA national spouse in Ireland. The application was made to her local embassy, which referred the application on March 10, 2008, to the visa office in New Delhi. The application was accompanied by a letter of reference from a Cork TD; a copy of her husband's Irish travel document and GNIB card; his wage slips, income tax information and bank statements; work references from their respective employers; their marriage certificate;

personal letters from herself, her mother and her husband; rent receipts and two ESB bills as evidence of the husband's residence in Cork; and a letter from his landlady. The applicant's work reference indicated that he had been working in a restaurant in Cork since April 2007. On April 2, 2008, the Irish Embassy in New Delhi refused the visa for a number of reasons, including the immigration history of the first-named applicant (namely that he had been refused refugee status and had married the second-named applicant less than four months after being granted leave to remain); inconsistencies in relation to marriage certificate; that the granting of a visa may result in a cost to public funds; that the granting of a visa may result in a cost to public resources and that the parties had not shown evidence of a relationship being in existence prior to the visa application/marriage and had failed to satisfy the visa officer that the relationship was bona fide. An appeal was lodged against the visa refusal, which appeal was refused in June 2008.

On August 19, 2008, a letter was written to the Minister on behalf of the wife asking the Minister to undertake a review of the visa refusal on the basis that the visa officer had failed to deal with the applicants' rights under art.8 of the European Convention on Human Rights and Art.41 of the Irish Constitution. The Dublin Visa Office agreed to undertake a full review of the case. The review was completed on October 7, 2008, and a fresh refusal to grant a visa issued. The reasons given were the immigration history of the first-named applicant; it was noted that he had temporary leave to remain under s.3(6) of the Immigration Act 1999 as amended, which Act made no provision for family reunification. It was also stated that the applicants had not shown evidence of a relationship prior to marriage, and that the visa officer was not satisfied that the relationship was bona fide. It was also stated that the granting of a visa may result in a cost to public funds. Detailed consideration was also given to art.8 of the Convention; it was accepted that family life arose between the applicants for the purpose of art.8 of the Convention and Art.41 of the Constitution. It was found, however, that in refusing a visa to the wife, there would be no lack of respect for family life under art.8(1) of the Convention and therefore no breach of art.8. This finding was made with reference to the decision of the Court of Appeal in *R. (Mahmood) v Secretary of State for the Home Department* [2001] 1 W.L.R. 840, where it was held that art.8 does not impose on a state any general obligation to respect the choice of residence of a married couple, and that a state has a right to control the entry of non-nationals into its territory, subject to its treaty obligations. It was also noted that there was no evidence that there were insurmountable obstacles to the applicants enjoying their family life in Sri Lanka.

The applicants complained that in refusing to grant a visa to the first-named applicant the Minister acted unreasonably and unlawfully by failing to consider the positive credibility findings made by the Refugee Appeals Tribunal in respect of the husband's asylum application, and that the Minister acted unlawfully by finding that because the applicants did not have a previous relationship their marriage was not bona fide. The respondent submitted that the grant of leave to remain does not create any entitlement to family reunification. It was submitted that in refusing a long stay visa to the wife the Minister was entitled to take into account the matters that he took into account and that it was entirely reasonable for him to reach the conclusions that he reached. It was noted that interference with the right to respect for private and family life in the interests of the economic wellbeing of the country is expressly envisaged under art.8(2) of the Convention.

Clark J. noted at the outset that there was no entitlement to family reunification for a person who has temporary leave to remain in the State. The court reiterated the well-established principle that it is for the Minister to determine the conditions under which foreign nationals enter, remain and leave the State. Clark J. was therefore satisfied that the Minister was under no legal obligation to grant a visa—"the grant or refusal of visas is entirely within his discretion and it is for the visa applicant to convince the Minister that he or she should be granted a visa."

It was noted:

> "Government policy determines which foreign nationals require visas to visit or transit the State and whether they can work in the State. The inherent executive power and responsibility of the Government to formulate immigration policy is supplemented by statutory provisions including the Aliens Act 1935 and the Immigration Acts 1999, 2003 and 2004. There is at present no statutory framework for issuing visas …
>
> It is a matter for the Minister to determine who is permitted to visit, work or live in the State in the exercise of an ordered immigration policy."

The court was satisfied that the Minister was entitled to consider the facts surrounding a request to come and live in the State in pursuance of an ordered immigration policy, and that the Minister was entitled to consider that the husband was a failed asylum-seeker with leave to remain for a temporary period and that the marriage was of very recent origin and duration. It was held that the Minister was also entitled to consider the possibility that the wife may become a charge to the State as she will not be permitted to work and the husband's available income might have been stretched were he to support and provide health insurance for a young wife. Clark J. therefore dismissed the application for judicial review.

Correct interpretation of reg.5(2) of the European Communities (Eligibility for Protection) Regulations 2006 The correct interpretation of reg.5(2) of the European Communities (Eligibility for Protection) Regulations was considered by the High Court in *MST v Minister for Justice, Equality and*

Law Reform [2009] IEHC 529; unreported, Cooke J., December 4, 2009. By order of Finlay Geoghegan J. of November 19, 2008, leave was granted to the applicants to seek an order of certiorari by way of judicial review to quash the decision of the Minister made on September 15, 2008, refusing their application for subsidiary protection under the European Communities (Eligibility for Protection) Regulations 2006 (the 2006 Regulations). The applicants were mother and daughter and were ethnic Serbs who came from Croatia. They arrived in the State in September 2004 and applied for asylum. They applied for asylum but were refused at first instance by the Refugee Applications Commissioner on April 11, 2005, and ultimately on appeal by the Refugee Appeals Tribunal on March 29, 2006.

By letter of April 25, 2006, the Minister advised the applicants of his proposal to make a deportation order and invited representations to be made as to why the applicants should not be deported. Deportation orders were made in respect of the applicants on June 28, 2006. An application was then made under s.3(11) of the 1999 Act to have those orders revoked. On November 23, 2006, the applicant's solicitors wrote applying for subsidiary protection for them under the 2006 Regulations and enclosed the relevant forms together with country of origin information documents and medical reports. By letter of March 14, 2008, the Minister agreed to consider an application for subsidiary protection on behalf of the applicants. By letter of September 15, 2008, the Minister refused the application for subsidiary protection, enclosing with that letter a copy of the analysis note on the application made.

Among the grounds advanced by the applicants in their judicial review was the claim that the decision to refuse the application for subsidiary protection was in breach of reg.5(2) of the 2006 Regulations by reason of the failure to consider whether the evidence of previous serious harm was alone sufficient to warrant the grant of subsidiary protection.

Regulation 5(2) of the 2006 Regulations provides:

> (2) The fact that a protection applicant has already been subject to persecution or serious harm, or to direct threats of such persecution or such harm, shall be regarded as a serious indication of the applicant's well-founded fear of persecution or real risk of suffering serious harm, unless there are good reasons to consider that such persecution or serious harm will not be repeated, but compelling reasons arising out of previous persecution or serious harm alone may nevertheless warrant a determination that the applicant is eligible for protection.

The applicants contended that medical evidence submitted in support of their subsidiary protection constituted evidence of "previous serious harm" which alone would have warranted the grant of protection and that the Minister had failed to consider it.

Cooke J. noted at the outset that the 2006 Regulations were made on October

6, 2006, for the express purpose of giving effect to Council Directive 2004/83 (the Qualifications Directive) which Directive was adopted for the purpose of laying down for the Member States:

> "... minimum standards for the qualification and status of third country nationals or stateless persons as refugees or as persons who otherwise need international protection and the content of the protection granted."

It was also noted that while the common standards required to be effected by the Member States are minimum standards, recital (8) and art.3 of the Qualifications Directive make it clear that the Member States are to remain free to introduce or maintain more favourable standards for determining who qualifies as a refugee or is eligible for subsidiary protection so long as those standards are compatible with the Directive.

The court compared the wording of reg.5(2) of the 2006 Regulations with art.4.4 of the Directive, which provides:

> The fact that an applicant has already been subject to ... serious harm or to direct threats of ... such harm, is a serious indication of the applicant's ... real risk of suffering serious harm, unless there are good reasons to consider that such ... serious harm will not be repeated.

Cooke J. noted that reg.5(2):

> "... has the object and effect of transposing article 4.4 of the Directive but does so with the addition of the words upon which the applicants now rely (hereafter referred to as 'the additional wording') and which are not used in the Directive namely ... but compelling reasons arising out of previous ... serious harm alone may nevertheless warrant a determination that the applicant is eligible for protection".

He continued:

> "29. The ordinary meaning of the additional wording appears to be that, what might be called a 'counter-exception' to para (ii) above is created to the effect that, even if there is no reason for considering that the previous serious harm will now be repeated, the historic serious harm may be such that the fact of its occurrence alone gives rise to compelling reasons for recognising eligibility."

Cooke J. concluded that notwithstanding the difficulties presented by the additional wording,

> "[T]here cannot be any doubt … that the additional wording can only be construed as intending to permit some limited extension to the conditions of eligibility prescribed in Art.4.4 designed to allow some latitude in according subsidiary protection based exclusively upon the fact of previous serious harm when it is accompanied by compelling reasons."

It was noted in this regard that "serious harm" is defined as including "inhuman or degrading treatment", and that it was possible to envisage a situation in which an applicant had escaped from an incident of mass murder, genocide or ethnic cleansing in a particular locality:

> "Even if the conditions in the country of origin had so changed that no real risk now existed of those events happening once again, the trauma already suffered might still be such as to give rise to compelling reasons for not requiring the applicant to return to the locality of the earlier suffering because the return itself could be so traumatic as to expose the applicant to inhuman or degrading treatment."

The court was accordingly satisfied that the additional wording had some limited effect in extending the possible scope of application of art.4.4. In particular, it was held that the wording appeared to be designed to grant some latitude to the Minister to recognise eligibility for subsidiary protection in a case of proven previous serious harm giving rise to compelling reasons for according international protection notwithstanding the fact that there may exist some doubt as to the likelihood of risk of repetition of that previous serious harm. In so concluding, Cooke J. agreed with the judgment of Charleton J. in *N v Minister for Justice, Equality and Law Reform*, unreported, High Court, April 24, 2008, where it was held that this additional wording did not operate so as to create a distinct new criterion for entitlement to subsidiary protection over and above that contained in art.4.4 of the Directive, but merely allowed the decision-maker the facility in a case where there were compelling reasons, to determine eligibility for protection as established without being obliged to be fully satisfied that the harm runs a risk of being repeated.

On the basis of the Minister's failure to have regard to the medical evidence and consider whether such evidence amounted to "previous serious harm" giving rise to "compelling reasons" such that subsidiary protection should be granted, Cooke J. quashed the decision to refuse the applicants' application for subsidiary protection.

Decision of Refugee Applications Commissioner quashed on grounds of breach of fair procedures In *JM v Refugee Applications Commissioner* [2009] IEHC 352; unreported, High Court, Clark J., July 29, 2009, the applicant sought an order of certiorari by way of judicial review of the recommendation of the Refugee Applications Commissioner dated February 5, 2008, that the applicant should not be granted a declaration of refugee status. Leave was granted on January 27, 2009, by Cooke J. The essence of the applicant's complaint was that the decision of the Refugee Applications Commissioner was fundamentally flawed and ought to be quashed by reason of the authorised officer's failure to explore with the applicant the potential for him to acquire nationality of Mozambique. The applicant argued that this flaw in the investigative process rendered this an appropriate case for judicial review rather than an appeal to the Refugee Appeals Tribunal.

The applicant applied for asylum in the State on December 1, 2006, claiming to be a citizen of Zimbabwe. The applicant had previously sought and been refused asylum in the United Kingdom on the grounds that the applicant had dual citizenship and that he could return to Mozambique. The applicant had entered the United Kingdom using a Mozambican passport and claiming to be a national of Mozambique although his claim for asylum centred on the ill-treatment he suffered in Zimbabwe as a result of his membership of the opposition Movement for Democratic Change (MDC) and his trade union activities. At the appeal stage in the United Kingdom asylum process, he claimed that the Mozambican passport was not genuine and that he was in fact a national of Zimbabwe. The applicant also furnished documentation in support of that assertion including copies of his Zimbabwean birth certificate, his passport, ID card and MDC membership card. It was not disputed in the United Kingdom that the applicant was tortured in Zimbabwe—a medical report submitted on behalf of the applicant confirmed that he had "a number of scars consistent with his account of torture" and that the examining physician "did not doubt that this man has been tortured as he describes". While accepting the torture claim, the Secretary of State and the special adjudicator found that the applicant was from Mozambique and not Zimbabwe. His appeal to the Immigration Appeal Tribunal (IAT) was refused in June 2006 on the basis that he had dual nationality. The applicant subsequently travelled to the State and applied for asylum. The applicant maintained that he was from Zimbabwe and not Mozambique and furnished country of origin information that dual nationality was not permissible in law in either Mozambique or Zimbabwe.

In a decision dated February 12, 2008, the Commissioner refused the applicant's application for refugee status. The decision was based on two alternative conclusions from the applicant's evidence: first that he was a national of Mozambique; and secondly, that even if he was not a national of Mozambique, his father was born there and the applicant would therefore be entitled to apply for citizenship through his parentage. The Commissioner accepted that the applicant had been a victim of torture in Zimbabwe but concluded that the applicant had:

> "… not presented a case that negates the protection of the country of

> his second available citizenship, Mozambique. Therefore the applicant would avail of the protection of Mozambique and is not in need of international protection".

The Commissioner also found that as the applicant had lodged a previous application for asylum in the United Kingdom, s.13(6) of the Refugee Act 1996 applied which meant that his appeal would be document-based only and without an oral hearing.

Leave was granted by Cooke J. on January 29, 2009, to argue that the s.13 report infringed the applicant's entitlement to fair procedures by reason of the failure of the Refugee Applications Commissioner: (1) to disclose and to afford the applicant an opportunity of rebutting or answering the Appendix 4 document extract on the laws of Mozambique citizenship; and (2) to adequately alert and permit the applicant to consider and answer the proposition that he could, either in his own right or through his father, obtain or reacquire Mozambique nationality and thereby have the protection of that country and not need international protection. Counsel for the applicant urged the court to bear in mind that it was accepted in the s.13 report that the applicant was tortured in Zimbabwe and that the reason for the negative recommendation was that the applicant could obtain citizenship of Mozambique and could seek protection there. It was argued that there was an almost total absence of any reference in the s.11 interview notes to the question of the applicant's potential to acquire citizenship and therefore the protection of Mozambique. It was submitted that while the mobility of the applicant between Zimbabwe and Mozambique was discussed, there was nothing further than a fleeting reference to his ability to acquire citizenship of Mozambique, which was described as a stark omission when, as it turned out, his citizenship of Mozambique became the core reason for the negative recommendation. The applicant also complained that the Refugee Applications Commissioner officer failed to disclose to the applicant the document relied on in the s.13 report and contained at Appendix 4 of that report, entitled *Citizenship Laws of the World* produced by the Office of Personnel Management of the US Government in 2000/2001, and that the applicant was therefore denied an opportunity of rebutting or answering this document. It was submitted that there was an obligation on the Refugee Applications Commissioner as a matter of fair procedures to put to an applicant all matters that are considered to be relevant, referring to *Idiakheua v Minister for Justice, Equality and Law Reform*, unreported, High Court, Clarke J., May 5, 2005 and *Moyosola v Refugee Applications Commissioner* [2005] IEHC 218.

The respondent argued that although the Refugee Applications Commissioner stage of the asylum process is inquisitorial or quasi-inquisitorial, the applicant is not merely a passive recipient of a decision. Pursuant to s.11C of the Refugee Act 1996, as amended, an applicant has a duty to co-operate in the investigation of his application and has a duty to furnish to the Commissioner as soon as reasonably practicable all relevant information in his or her possession, control or procurement. It was submitted that the issue of the applicant's nationality was a potentially significant matter at all stages of his application. The documentation furnished by the applicant to the Refugee Applications Commissioner made it clear that he was fully aware that his nationality was a live issue during his previous application in the UK and he must be taken to have known that it would be a live issue before the Commissioner. It was also argued that the requirements of fair procedures do not exist in a vacuum and while the Refugee Applications Commissioner officer might have further teased out the issue of nationality with the applicant this could not be said to be a fundamental breach of fair procedures in circumstances where the applicant was aware that dual nationality was a live issue.

In relation to the Commissioner's finding pursuant to s.13(6) of the 1996 Act, counsel for the applicant argued that judicial review should lie in this case because the applicant should not have to seek a remedy by way of a paper-based appeal. It was argued that the applicant should be entitled to fair procedures and natural and constitutional justice at the first instance before the Refugee Applications Commissioner and this was denied to him. It was emphasised that the applicant was not expressing a grievance with the quality of the s.13 report (as was the case for example in *AD (Diallo) v Refugee Applications Commissioner* [2009] IEHC 77, where Cooke J. found that judicial review did not lie), but rather he was complaining of "a fundamental and irremediable infringement of the entitlement to a fair procedure" which was recognised by Cooke J. in *Diallo* as the exceptional type case where judicial review rather than appeal might lie. Counsel for the respondents argued that even if it was accepted that there had been a breach of fair procedures (which it was not), the court must consider whether that breach was of such significance that the Refugee Applications Commissioner recommendation ought to be quashed and the matter remitted for reconsideration or whether, in the alternative, the breach could be remedied on appeal. It was submitted that this was a case that was capable of being directly cured by way of a paper-based appeal, as the question of whether the applicant was entitled to apply for Mozambican nationality by descent was a question of pure law which could be determined without an oral hearing.

Clark J. reviewed the jurisprudence on the circumstances where it is appropriate to seek judicial review of a decision of the Refugee Applications Commissioner rather than utilising the statutory appeal remedy before the Refugee Appeals Tribunal[3] and noted that the application of the principles

---

3 Including *Stefan v Minister for Justice, Equality and Law Reform* [2001] 4 I.R. 203, *AK (Kayode) v Refugee Applications Commissioner* (ex tempore judgment of Murray C.J., January 28, 2009) and the decisions of Hedigan J. in *BNN (Nganzunuj) v Minister for Justice, Equality and Law Reform* [2008] IEHC 308 and Cooke J. in *AD (Diallo) v Refugee Applications Commissioner* [2009] IEHC 77, January 27, 2009, the leave stage in the present case (*JM v Refugee Applications Commissioner* [2009] IEHC 64; *TTA*

set out in those cases to the facts and arguments in this case involved a basic two-step assessment:

> "First, the court must determine whether there has been a fundamental flaw or illegality such that a rehearing upon appeal before the Tribunal will be an inadequate remedy and that *certiorari* may lie. If it is found that *certiorari* may be granted, the court must then consider whether to exercise its discretion to grant the order."

In relation to the first question, Clark J. was satisfied that there was a breach of fair procedures by reason of the failure of the authorised officer to engage with the applicant on the question of his ability to acquire nationality of Mozambique. It was held that if the authorised officer had taken the view that the acquisition of Mozambican nationality derived from his father's origins would or could debar the applicant from protection, then it was incumbent on the authorised officer to tease out the issue a little further if only to establish the correctness of this view. Clark J. concluded:

> "As this issue formed the basis of the negative recommendation it seems to me that there has been a fundamental flaw in the investigation process which amounts to a breach of fair procedures."

Clark J. then proceeded to the second question, whether this was an appropriate case in which to grant certiorari, and concluded that having regard to the finding that there had been a fundamental flaw in the applicant's entitlement to a fair procedure, that flaw was not remediable at appeal. Having regard to the possibility that, "complex issues of nationality and general credibility will have to be addressed on paper, such an appeal would be an inadequate remedy for the error made in the first stage of the investigation." Accordingly, Clark J. made an order quashing the decision of the Refugee Applications Commissioner and directing that the case be remitted to the Commissioner for a fresh evaluation before a new authorised officer.

The decision in *JM* is significant as it would appear to be the only decision quashing a decision of the Refugee Applications Commissioner since the development of a new line of jurisprudence of the High Court on the circumstances in which judicial review lies against the Refugee Applications Commissioner.[4]

(Akintunde) v Refugee Applications Commissioner [2009] IEHC 215 and *RLA v Minister for Justice, Equality and Law Reform* [2009] IEHC 41.

4 See Brazil and Egan, "Asylum and Immigration Law" in Byrne and Binchy (eds), *Annual Review of Irish Law 2008* (Round Hall, 2009), pp.7–11.

EU nationals not eligible to seek leave to remain in the State pursuant to s.3 of the Immigration Act 1999 In *BB v Minister for Justice, Equality and Law Reform* [2009] IEHC 333; Cooke J., July 16, 2009, the High Court was asked to consider whether an EU national was entitled to maintain an application for leave to remain in the State pursuant to s.3 of the Immigration Act 1999. Leave to seek judicial review was granted by Edwards J. on February 16, 2009, to allow the applicant seek an order of mandamus directing the respondent to make a decision on an application made by the applicant for residence in the State. The applicant was a Romanian national who entered the State in October 1996 and claimed asylum. On March 17, 1998, his daughter was born to his then Irish citizen partner and he withdrew his application for refugee status and applied for residence as the father of an Irish citizen child. On November 10, 2003, the Minister notified the applicant of a proposal to make a deportation order in respect of him and representations were made to the Minister on his behalf, together with an application for leave to remain. These were considered and on May 23, 2006, the applicant was served with a deportation order dated May 12, 2006. Judicial review proceedings to quash that order were instituted, and on December 12, 2006, these were compromised on the basis that the Minister would revoke the deportation order in respect of the applicant and that the applicant could make fresh representations pursuant to s.3 of the Immigration Act 1999 within 15 working days, and that the Minister would then issue a decision on this application within 21 days of receipt of the submissions. On foot of that agreement, the deportation order was duly revoked and the applicant submitted fresh representations.

Nothing further was heard from the Minister until, on June 23, 2008, the Minister wrote to the applicant to inform him:

> "Since 1 January 2007, on the accession of Bulgaria and Romania to the EU, citizens in those countries are, in terms of immigration controls, covered by the provisions of the European Communities, (Free Movement of Persons), (No. 2), Regulations 2006. They have the same rights of access to the Republic of Ireland as a citizen of an existing European Union, (EU) Member State, with the exception of access to the labour market. There will, therefore, be no decision made on your client's application, for Humanitarian Leave to remain in the State, as such applications in respect of Romanian nationals are no longer valid."

On October 29, 2008, the applicant's solicitors wrote to the Minister requesting that a decision be made on his outstanding application for leave to remain in the State which would amount to an "unrestricted permission to remain in Ireland without the requirement of an employment permit". It was also pointed out that by refusing to consider the fresh representations under s.3 of the Immigration Act the Minister was in breach of the settlement agreement. It was claimed that the applicant was prejudiced by this failure on the Minister's part because, as an unskilled worker, he would be ineligible for an employment permit from the Department of Trade and Enterprise.

In his application for judicial review, the applicant submitted that his "application for humanitarian leave to remain" was still outstanding and that the Minister was compellable in law to make a decision on that application. Cooke J. noted that the use of the expression "humanitarian leave to remain" could give the impression that the relevant legislation provides for a specific category of non-national residence permission which can be applied for and granted as such, upon humanitarian grounds, much as a person might apply for a tourist visa, or for temporary residence to pursue a course of study. However, he stated that that did not appear to be the case.

It was noted that a non-national who is not an EU citizen and who enters the State and claims asylum is entitled to remain in the State until the application is refused or withdrawn as provided for in ss.8 and 9 of the Refugee Act 1996, and s.5 of the Immigration Act 2004. Cooke J. noted that such a person is illegally in the State from the date of withdrawal or rejection of the application and may be deported in accordance with s.3 of the Immigration Act 1999. Furthermore, where the Minister proposes to make a deportation order, s.3 requires him to notify the person of the proposal and invite him or her to make representations, that is, representations as to why the order ought not to be made. It was noted that in practice, the proposal letter sent by the Minister usually indicates that the addressee has three options, namely: 1) to leave voluntarily, before an order is made; 2) to consent to the making of the order; and 3) to make representations to remain temporarily in the State. Cooke J. noted that the expression "humanitarian leave" appears to derive from the fact that under s.3(3)(b) of the 1999 Act, one of the matters which the Minister must have regard to when deciding whether or not to make an order, in addition to any representations, is "humanitarian considerations"; "in effect therefore, what is described as 'humanitarian leave' is a decision by the Minister to postpone, or to temporarily refrain from making a deportation order on the basis of humanitarian considerations." Cooke J. noted that where a non-national is illegally in the State following the rejection or withdrawal of an asylum application, there is no entitlement to temporary leave or postponement of deportation; it is entirely a matter at the discretion of the Minister, albeit a discretion which must be exercised in accordance with the terms of the Act and in a reasonable and fair manner.

Cooke J. noted that the difficulty that arose for the applicant in these circumstances was attributable to the fact that on January 1, 2007 Romania, together with Bulgaria, acceded to the European Union and the applicant became a citizen of the EU with the benefit of the various rights and freedoms conferred by the Treaties but subject also to the exceptions and derogations agreed as transitional arrangements with those to new Member States. As a result, it was held that the regime of the asylum process in the 1996 and 1999

Acts ceased to apply to the applicant. Indeed, it was noted that the State cannot deport an EU citizen; rather, the arrangements governing the entry, residence and removal of nationals of other Member States are those contained primarily in the European Communities (Free Movement of Persons) (No. 2) Regulations 2006, which give effect to Directive 2004/38. By virtue of those regulations and Community law, an EU citizen in possession of a valid national identity card or passport may not be refused entry to the State (save for two reasons relating to health and personal conduct), and may reside in the State for three months.

Reference was also made to the Employment Permit Acts 2003 to 2006, which provide that a non-national seeking to enter the employment of an employer in the State must obtain a work permit from the Minister for Enterprise, Trade and Employment. However, Cooke J. noted that under the transitional arrangements for the accession of Romania to the European Union, it was agreed that the existing measures on freedom of movement of workers, in particular Regulation 1612/68 of the Council of October 15, 1968, would not apply to Romanian nationals during the transitional period of two years, which was extendable and was in fact extended to a full period of five years. Thus, Cooke J. noted that in practical terms, since January 1, 2007 nationals of Romania, while entitled to exercise the freedom of interstate movement within the EU, did not have access to the labour market in other Member States. Thus, the applicant did not have an entitlement to a work permit under the Employment Permits Acts 2003–2006 in the State. As a consequence, Cooke J. accepted the applicant's averment that he could be denied permission to continued residence in the State as an EU citizen beyond three months.

Cooke J. noted that the applicant's case was commenced on the basis that if the applicant was granted leave to remain pursuant to s.3 of the 1999 Act, instead of being deported, he could seek employment without needing an employment permit. However, as the Minister pointed out, that position was altered when s.2(10) of the Employment Permits Act 2003 was amended by s.3 of the 2006 Act, which had the effect of requiring any Romanian national in the State pursuant to a leave to remain under s.3 of the 1999 Act, to obtain a permit. Cooke J. commented:

> "An order of *mandamus* can only issue to compel a decision maker to take a decision which he or she has power to take and then only when the decision maker has either wrongfully refused to take the decision, or has delayed unreasonably long in so doing as to have failed unlawfully to discharge the statutory duty concerned."

Cooke J. was satisfied that the Minister had no power, since January 1, 2007, to grant leave to remain in the State pursuant to s.3 of the 1999 Act to a Romanian national. The provisions of the 1999 Act ceased to have any application to Romanian nationals as of that date, and such persons could only be required to leave the State pursuant to the procedure prescribed for removal of Union citizens in reg.20 of the 2006 Regulations. Cooke J. was satisfied that that position was not altered by the fact of the settlement agreement of December 2006, on the basis that the Minister's competence to perform that agreement, in so far as it involved making a decision for the purposes of s.3 of the 1999 Act, ceased on January 1, 2007.

Concluding that mandamus did not lie against the Minister to compel him to make the decision identified in the relief sought, the application was therefore refused.

Failure of Refugee Appeals Tribunal to reach clear finding of nationality In *ES v Refugee Appeals Tribunal* [2009] IEHC 335; unreported, High Court, Cooke J., July 15, 2009, the applicant sought leave by way of judicial review to challenge a negative decision of the Refugee Appeals Tribunal on the basis that it failed to reach a clear finding as to nationality. The applicant was a 30-year-old single woman who arrived in the State on February 6, 2005, having travelled from South Africa on a South African passport which she said was false and which she had bought from a man. She applied for asylum in the State on April 26, 2005. The applicant claimed that she had Zimbabwean nationality and that she had been forced to flee Zimbabwe to avoid a forced marriage.

In a report dated August 15, 2005, the applicant's claim to refugee status was recommended for rejection by the Refugee Applications Commissioner, essentially upon the ground that the story she told was not credible. In particular, the Commissioner's authorised officer had doubts as to whether the applicant was a national of Zimbabwe as she claimed. In addition to doubting her credibility, the report relied on a number of other factors as undermining her claim to a well-founded fear of persecution in Zimbabwe. The report made an express finding by reference to s.13(6)(c) of the 1996 Act—failure to apply for asylum as soon as practical on arrival thereby excluding an oral hearing on appeal.

On September 1, 2005, a notice of appeal was lodged against that report. Almost two years later, on August 9, 2007, the applicant's solicitors lodged with the tribunal a new schedule headed "further submissions", together with a large volume of documentary country of origin information relating to conditions in Zimbabwe and copies of a series of previous decisions of the tribunal. These submissions raised a number of new grounds, including a fear of persecution for political reasons and membership of a particular social group comprising people who are HIV positive. The court noted that in neither set of appeal grounds and submissions was any attempt made to address and to challenge the substantive content and findings of the appealed report. In particular, no challenge was raised to the factors identified as giving rise to the doubts as to whether the applicant was in fact from Zimbabwe and a national of that country. Following the lodging of the further submissions and before the determination of the appeal, an exchange of correspondence took place between the applicants and solicitors and the tribunal. Further representations and documentation were submitted on her behalf on December 14, 2007. By letter of February 8, 2008, the applicant was advised that the tribunal had requested that her South African passport be submitted to technical examination for verification of its authenticity. The results report from the Garda Technical Bureau stated that the document was listed on the Interpol database as a stolen document by the South African authorities.

The decision on the appeal was given on April 14, 2008. In its introduction it referred to the further submissions of August 2007 and recorded that her fear of persecution was claimed for the reasons of nationality, political opinion, membership of a particular social group, and the fact that she was HIV positive. In relation to the applicant's claim to be of Zimbabwean origin, the tribunal member referred to the negative credibility findings made by the Refugee Applications Commissioner on this issue. Negative credibility findings were made in respect of the claimed fear of persecution on the grounds of political opinion and membership of a particular social group on the basis of forced marriage. The tribunal member then noted that the applicant had been living in South Africa and had fled to France, and that the applicant had not sought asylum in France nor immediately upon arrival in the State. Finally, the tribunal member stated that she had also considered the claim to fear persecution as a failed asylum-seeker if returned and the applicant's medical status. In relation to the latter, the tribunal member stated:

> "The applicant's access to medical treatment in Zimbabwe and/or in South Africa is an issue which relates to an application for leave to remain. Such an application is a matter for another forum."

The applicant sought leave to apply for, inter alia, an order of certiorari to quash the decision of the tribunal on the basis that the tribunal member failed to consider the applicant's claim to fear persecution if returned to Zimbabwe as a failed asylum-seeker; and that the tribunal member erred in finding that her claim based on her medical status as a HIV-positive person was a matter of access to medical treatment in Zimbabwe and/or South Africa and therefore an issue which related to an application for leave to remain, and as such a matter for another forum.

Cooke J. noted at the outset that there was "an ambiguity and therefore an uncertainty as to the exact basis upon which the Tribunal member in this case finally decided to affirm the recommendation of the section 13 report." Like the Commissioner, the tribunal member expressed a serious doubt as to whether the applicant was in fact a national of Zimbabwe, but no distinct conclusion or finding was reached on that issue; instead it was merely one of the factors together with the failure to seek protection in South Africa and to apply for asylum in France, which form the basis cumulatively for the rejection of the appeal. The court also noted that it must be inferred that this rejection was on the basis that the tribunal member did not consider that the claim of a well-founded fear of persecution had been established because no explicit statement to that effect is made in the decision. Cooke J. went on to state:

> "It is axiomatic that the establishment of the country of origin of a claimant to refugee status is fundamental to the assessment of the claim because it is otherwise impossible to determine whether the claimant is outside that country owing to a Convention based fear of persecution. That is not infrequently an extremely difficult exercise and while the onus of establishing refugee status is on the claimant, the UNCHR handbook points out at paragraph 196:
>
> > 'While the burden of proof in principle rests with the applicant, the duty to ascertain and evaluate all relevant facts is shared between the applicant and the examiner. Indeed, in some cases it may be for the examiner to use all means at his disposal to produce the necessary evidence in support of the application.'"

Cooke J. stated that if the tribunal member was not satisfied that the applicant had established her Zimbabwean nationality and was possibly a national of South Africa, then the tribunal member had an obligation either to consider whether further enquiries were possible to resolve that issue or, alternatively, to find that she was not a national of Zimbabwe, in which case an examination of the various reasons for fear of persecution in Zimbabwe was irrelevant and unnecessary. It was noted in this regard that so far as the issue of credibility as to country of origin was concerned a significant development had occurred, namely that the South African passport on which the applicant had travelled had been found to be false. The court stated that it was remarkable that, while the report of the Garda Technical Bureau was one of the documents listed in the section 7 "Conclusion" of the decision, its actual effect and significance were not mentioned anywhere in the decision. The only reference to the passport was the somewhat ambivalent sentence in the section 6 analysis: "Apart from the South African passport on file, other matters arise which call into question the applicant's origins." Cooke J. commented:

> "The Tribunal Member does not appear to have averted to the possible implication of this for the reliability of the authorised officer's doubts about the applicant's nationality. If, as the applicant had claimed from the outset, she had travelled on a false South African passport, did that imply that she had no entitlement to a valid one as a South African national? If she was not a South African national, where else might she come from if not Zimbabwe?"

The court concluded that given the significance of this issue, in this case a substantial issue arose as to whether there had been an adequate determination by the tribunal of the country of origin or nationality of the applicant. Leave to seek judicial review was therefore granted on the ground, inter alia, that:

> "The Tribunal erred in failing to investigate and to determine to an adequate degree of likelihood the country of nationality or origin of the applicant and to state its reasons for its determination."

However, Cooke J. emphasised that the finding was one of a substantial ground only, and that no view was expressed as to whether upon full argument and examination the application was likely to succeed.

Failure to consider whether applicant had well-founded fear of persecution on grounds of return as failed asylum-seeker In *AO v Refugee Appeals Tribunal* [2009] IEHC 501; unreported, High Court, Cooke J., November 25, 2009, the High Court granted leave to challenge a decision of the Refugee Appeals Tribunal on the grounds of failure to assess whether the applicant had a well-founded fear of persecution on grounds of imputed political opinion in the event of her return to her country of origin as a failed asylum-seeker.

The first-named applicant was from the Democratic Republic of the Congo and was the mother of the second-named applicant. They both arrived in Ireland in June 2006 and claimed asylum. The mother was interviewed under s.11 of the Refugee Act 1996 on July 31, 2006 and the Refugee Applications Commissioner issued a negative section 13 report on September 7, 2006. The applicants appealed to the Refugee Appeals Tribunal and a hearing before a tribunal member took place on December 13, 2007. By decision dated January 27, 2008 the tribunal rejected the appeal. The applicants sought leave to seek judicial review of the tribunal's decision; one of the grounds advanced on behalf of the applicants was "the summary dismissal without examination of her fear of persecution as a returned asylum seeker because it was held to fall outside the jurisdiction of the Tribunal." The only finding made by the tribunal member in relation to this ground was the statement:

> "The Tribunal has considered the submission made in relation to failed asylum seekers and re-states the function of the Tribunal as outlined in the 1996 Act, as amended. It is the responsibility of the appropriate Minister of government to deal with the outcome of any decision from the Refugee Appeals Tribunal."

Cooke J. noted that this statement was a reference to the practice of the tribunal to treat alleged persecution of returning asylum-seekers as a matter to be dealt with by the Minister for Justice under the prohibition of refoulement in s.5 of the Refugee Act 1996 rather than as a matter coming within the definition of "refugee" in s.2. The court commented in this regard:

"It is, of course, undoubtedly the case that the prohibition on *refoulement* can apply to a situation in which a deportee faces persecution on return to a country of origin whether or not he or she has been unsuccessful in an asylum claim. That does not, however, appear to preclude persecution of returned asylum seekers also coming within the scope of the definition where the conditions of that definition are shown to be met."

The learned High Court judge accepted that:

"[C]ases can arise in which return as a failed asylum seeker is the occasion or pretext for the treatment of such persons as falling into some political or other category which attracts discrimination or persecution at the hands of a particular regime".

This referred to the decision of Clark J. in *G v Refugee Appeals Tribunal*, unreported, High Court, Clark J., February 26, 2008. Cooke J. concluded that:

"[I]f the statement in the present decision to the effect that it is the responsibility of the Minister to deal with the outcome of any decision is to be understood as meaning that a fear of persecution as a returned asylum seeker can never come within the definition of 'refugee' and thus within the jurisdiction of the Tribunal, the decision is clearly wrong in law."

The court then considered whether the documentation relied upon by the applicant was sufficient by way of cogent evidence of the systematic persecution of asylum-seekers on return to the DRC to put the tribunal member on inquiry as to whether this was a case in which the necessary Convention nexus was established. Cooke J. was satisfied that the possibility that the Convention nexus might arise from a fear of persecution for imputed political opinion could not be made in the present case as the applicant herself never claimed to have been persecuted for her political opinions. However, the court was satisfied that the documents relied on by the appellant before the tribunal in relation to the treatment of failed asylum-seekers on return to DRC were sufficient to put the tribunal member on inquiry as to whether the applicant's claimed fear of persecution as a returned asylum-seeker might come within the definition on the basis of imputed political opinion as the pretext for a systematic treatment of such persons in the DRC.

Cooke J. also went on to consider whether a Convention nexus could be made out in respect of the identification of returned asylum-seekers as a "particular social group" for the purpose of the definition. It was noted that the precise scope of the notion of "particular social group" in the Geneva Convention is an issue which has exercised the courts of many jurisdictions although its precise scope does not appear to have been considered in detail in any Irish judgment to date. Having cited key decisions from the United States, Canada and the United Kingdom[5] as well as the UNHCR "Guidelines on International Protection: Membership of a Particular Social Group", Cooke J. noted that it was arguable that in a particular society returning failed asylum-seekers were regarded as a distinct social group. The court was at pains to point out, however, that this was only an application for leave and that the issues raised in this regard required more extensive consideration on the hearing of the substantive application.

Accordingly, the court was satisfied that a substantial ground had been raised which was sufficient to require those issues to be examined on a substantive application, and leave to seek judicial review was granted on the ground that the decision of the tribunal was wrong in law in refusing to examine and consider as outside its jurisdiction the applicant's claim to be a refugee within the meaning of the definition of that term in s.2 of the Refugee Act 1996 (as amended) on the basis of her claim to fear persecution if returned to the Democratic Republic of Congo on the ground of imputed political opinion or, alternatively, as a member of a particular social group comprised of returning failed asylum-seekers.

Judicial review of decisions of the Refugee Applications Commissioner Reference was made in the *Annual Review of Irish Law 2008* to a recent body of jurisprudence from the High Court significantly limiting the extent to which judicial review is available in respect of decisions of the Refugee Applications Commissioner on the grounds that an alternative remedy of appeal to the Refugee Appeals Tribunal is more appropriate.[6] This trend was continued in a number of decisions in 2009, including *Diallo v Refugee Applications Commissioner*, unreported, High Court, January 27, 2009, where Cooke J. reviewed the existing jurisprudence on the issue of appropriateness of judicial review including the decision in *BNN*, and stated:

> "It follows accordingly from this case law, that leave to apply for judicial review to quash a report and recommendation of the Commissioner should only be granted in exceptional cases and that to bring an

5 Cooke J. referred to decisions of the American courts in *Re Toboso – Alfonso* (20 I & N Dec 819); *Re Acosta* (19 I & N Dec. 211); *Gatimi v AG* (7th Cir. August 20, 2009). The Canadian decision of *Attorney General of Canada v Ward* (1993) 103 D.L.R. 1 and the United Kingdom decisions in *R. v Immigration Appeal Tribunal Ex p. Shah* (1999) 2 A.C. 629 and *Fornah v Secretary of State for Home Department* (2007) 1 A.C. 412 were also cited.

6 See Brazil and Egan, "Asylum and Immigration Law" in Byrne and Binchy (eds), *Annual Review of Irish Law 2008* (Round Hall, 2009), pp.7–11 and in particular the discussion of the decision of *BNN v MJELR*, High Court, unreported, Hedigan J., October 9, 2008; [2008] IEHC 308.

> application within the category of such cases it is necessary to advance substantial grounds for the existence of some fundamental flaw or illegality in the Commissioner's report such that a rehearing upon appeal before the Tribunal will be inadequate to remedy it."

After referring to *Stefan* and Denham J.'s dictum to the effect that "a fair appeal cannot cure an unfair hearing", Cooke J. concluded at para.22:

> "While such a judicial aphorism has considerable attraction it does not offer an immediate solution for all these cases. It depends on what is meant by 'fairness'. An applicant may well consider it is unfair that part of his account has been judged incredible or that some contrary evidence is attributed more weight than his own. It is clear, however, from the case law already cited that unfairness in this sense means some fundamental error or irregularity at first instance amounting to a clear infringement of the right to fair procedures. The procedure at first instance must be shown to have been so flawed that, in the words of Lynch J. in *Gill v. Connellan* [1987] I.R. 381 describing the defectiveness of a District Court hearing, 'On appeal to the Circuit Court, therefore, the appeal could hardly be said to be by way of rehearing. The case would be more truly heard for the first time.'"

Two further decisions of Cooke J. in 2009 have reinforced the test of exceptionality which must now be met in order to justify the decision to institute judicial review proceedings in respect of a decision of the Refugee Applications Commissioner. In *TTA v Refugee Applications Commissioner*, unreported, High Court, April 29, 2009; [2009] IEHC 215 Cooke J. noted:

> "At the opening of the hearing of this application the Court invited counsel to make submissions on the issue as to whether this was a case in which, in the light of the grounds for which leave had been granted, the Court would or should exercise its discretion to issue an order of *certiorari* against the Commissioner when an appeal was available and had been commenced. It did so because this issue has now been considered by this Court in a number of judgments and on the 28th January, 2009, the issue was the subject of a judgment given in the Supreme Court in an appeal certified to it by the High Court under s. 5(3)(a) of the Illegal Immigrants (Trafficking) Act 2000 in the case of *A.K. v. The Commissioner*. In that judgment the Supreme Court reaffirmed its earlier view of the issue as given in *The State v. Dublin Corporation* [1984] I.R. 381 and more particularly, in the context of asylum cases, in its judgment in *Stefan v Minister for Justice* [2001] 4 I.R. 203. In his conclusion to an ex tempore judgment in the *A.K.* case Murray C.J. held that the appeal available was a more appropriate remedy

where the issue raised by the applicant principally (but not exclusively) related to the quality of the decision of the Commissioner."

Cooke J. thus concluded:

> "It follows from this case law in the Court's view, and it is accepted by both sides in the present case, that *certiorari* can, in principle, issue to quash the report and recommendation of the Refugee Applications Commissioner under the Act even where an appeal is available and has been initiated in good time. However, it is now equally clear that this Court should only intervene in exceptional and clear cases where it is necessary to do so".

He again endorsed the decision of Hedigan J. in *BNN*. Cooke J. was satisfied that both *BNN* and *Diallo* were consistent with the Supreme Court decision in *Kayode* (although neither was referred to in the decision of the Chief Justice), and held:

> "[I]t is in the light of those criteria that it is necessary to determine whether the appeal available to the applicant in the present case is adequate or whether the illegalities alleged in the Commissioner's decision are incapable of being remedied because they are such as must have continuing adverse effect upon the applicant in the course of the appeal".

Cooke J. then analysed the grounds on which leave had been granted, and held that none of the grounds met the threshold of exceptionality such as would entitle the applicant to relief by way of judicial review. He instead held that appeal was the more appropriate remedy, noting that the court:

> "…should confine itself to the necessary correction of significant illegalities in the first stage investigation by the Commissioner when it is indispensable to do so in order to preserve the effectiveness, fairness and integrity of the appeal that is otherwise available to the Tribunal".

In a decision the following day, *RLA v Refugee Applications Commissioner,* unreported, High Court, April 30, 2009; [2009] IEHC 216 Cooke J. adopted the same approach.

It is submitted that the grounds on which an applicant may seek judicial review of a decision of the Refugee Applications Commissioner are clearly more limited in light of these recent decisions of the High Court. It is unfortunate that certificates of leave to appeal pursuant to s.5(3)(a) of the Illegal Immigrants (Trafficking) Act 2000 were refused by both Hedigan and Cooke JJ. as a Supreme Court decision on the "exceptionality" test laid down by these decisions would have brought finality and certainty to this area. It would seem that judicial review of decisions of the Commissioner will remain available to applicants complaining of a fundamental procedural defect which will continue to cause prejudice in the context of the appeal, e.g. a finding pursuant to s.13(6) of the Refugee Act 1996 which has the effect of depriving the applicant of an oral hearing on appeal, with the appeal assessed on the papers only.

"Mixed motives" in respect of Convention nexus In *MSA v Refugee Appeals Tribunal* [2009] IEHC 435; unreported, High Court, Clark J., October 6, 2009 the High Court considered obiter the issue of "mixed motives" in determining whether an applicant had established a Convention nexus in respect of his claimed fear of persecution. The applicant was an Afghan national who sought refugee status in the State on October 16, 2006. The applicant's fear of persecution was based on his nationality and political opinion, including a fear of persecution at the hands of a local warlord because of the applicant's former connection with the Taliban. His application was refused at first instance by the Refugee Applications Commissioner and on appeal by the Refugee Appeals Tribunal by decision dated May 15, 2007. The decision of the Refugee Appeals Tribunal was based on negative credibility findings, including the fact that the applicant had failed to disclose that he had previously been in Greece for a period of over a year prior to his arrival in this State.

The applicant was granted leave to seek judicial review by Cooke J. on March 20, 2009. The grounds upon which the applicant sought to challenge the tribunal decision related to the assessment of the applicant's credibility, failure to have regard to country of origin information and error of law in determining whether there was a Convention nexus in respect of the applicant's fear of persecution.

Clark J. rejected the applicant's challenge to the negative credibility findings made against him on the basis that the tribunal "was entitled to view all the evidence furnished by the applicant … with a degree of scepticism" having regard to the applicant's failure to disclose that he had been in Greece prior to his arrival in the State, which was in breach of the applicant's obligation to co-operate with the investigation of his application pursuant to s.11C of the Refugee Act 1996. The court also rejected the applicant's complaint in respect of the alleged failure to have regard to country of origin information on the basis that this issue was subsidiary to the primary ground of refusal of the applicant's claim, namely that his credibility was found to be lacking. Clark J. held that "no convincing arguments were advanced to establish that this country of origin information could have affected a fair evaluation of the applicant's credibility."

The court then proceeded to address the third ground relating to the tribunal's assessment of whether there was a Convention nexus to the applicant's claimed fear of persecution. The court's comments in this regard were clearly obiter dictum because of the conclusion that the primary reason for the rejection of the applicant's appeal was his failure to satisfy the decision-maker as to his own credibility, and that the issue of the Convention nexus was subsidiary to the primary assessment in relation to credibility. Thus, Clark J. held that "any criticism on his approach to the subsidiary issues would not have made any significant difference to the overall decision."

Nonetheless, the court's comments on the issue of the Convention nexus are of interest as there remains little jurisprudence from the Irish courts in this area. The tribunal member, having rejected the applicant's credibility, went on to conclude that even if the applicant had established his general credibility, there was no Convention nexus because his claimed fear of persecution related to a local commander's desire to seek vengeance against the applicant because he had been implicated in the murder of the commander's brother. The tribunal member then concluded that:

> "[T]he reason for the perceived persecution (if the Applicant were credible) is linked to the unfortunate circumstance of his having been blamed for involvement with the killing of the commander's brother, and not 'because of' any imputed or active political involvement."

It was submitted on behalf of the applicant that the tribunal member erred in law in making this determination because the existence of mixed motives does not defeat a legitimate Convention nexus. Reliance was placed on the decision of the English Court of Appeal in *Noune v Secretary of State for the Home Department* [2000] EWCA Civ. 306, where Schiemann L.J. held that "[t]he motives of the persecutor may be mixed and they can include non-Convention reasons: it is not necessary to show that they are purely political." The court directed that further submissions be filed on the issue of mixed motives, whereupon the applicant filed additional authorities to support the argument that "mixed motives" do not negate a Convention nexus.[7] The applicant argued that the tribunal member applied an incorrect causative test by requiring the Convention reason (i.e. race, religion, nationality, political opinion or membership of a social group) to be the sole reason for the persecution. It was argued that it was well established that where a persecutor has more than one motive, as long as that motive has a connection to the Convention it is sufficient to satisfy the refugee definition set out in s.2 of the Refugee Act 1996.

The court rejected the contention that the tribunal member determined that as a matter of law the threat of persecution had to be solely by reason of the applicant's political opinion, noting that:

---

7 Reliance was placed on the decision of the American courts in *Singh v Ilchert* 63 F.3d 1501; Australia (*El Merhabi v Minister for Immigration and Multicultural Affairs* [2000] F.C.A. 42; *Chen Shi Hai v Minister for Immigration* [2000] I.N.L.R. 455); and the United Kingdom (*Sepet v Secretary of State for the Home Department* [2003] 1 W.L.R. 856; *R. (Sivakumaran) v Secretary of State for the Home Department* [2003] 1 W.L.R. 840.

> "[I]f he did, the Tribunal Member would have erred in law as the existence of personal motivation for persecution does not detract from a parallel political reason, provided that the political or other Convention connection is established. The need for acts of persecution to have a nexus with a Convention reason is outlined in Regulation 9(3) of the European Communities (Eligibility for Protection) Regulations 2006 (S.I. No. 518 of 2006) which clearly states that that there must be 'a connection' between the acts of persecution and the applicant's race, religion, nationality, membership of a particular social group or political opinion. It is well accepted that the existence of other motives does not necessarily mean that persecution for Convention reasons is not established."

Nonetheless, the court reiterated its view that the primary reason for the rejection of the applicant's appeal was his failure to satisfy the decision-maker as to his own credibility. The court was satisfied that the tribunal member's comments on state protection and the Convention nexus were subsidiary to the primary assessment in relation to credibility, and in circumstances where the court rejected the contention that the tribunal member erred in law or acted in breach of fair procedures in the assessment of credibility, the application for judicial review was refused.

No family life between adult woman and minor siblings and their mother on whom she was not dependant In *YO v Minister for Justice, Equality and Law Reform* [2009] IEHC 148; unreported, High Court, March 11, 2009 the applicant was a 22-year-old Nigerian woman who wished to remain in Ireland with her Nigerian mother, on whom she was not dependent, and with her two younger sisters who were Irish citizens. The respondent made a deportation order in respect of the applicant on September 18, 2008. The applicant sought leave by way of judicial review to challenge that decision. The basis of the challenge was that there had been an inadequate consideration of the applicant's family life in this State with her mother and sisters.

Charleton J. noted at the outset that the Supreme Court in *Oguekwe v Minister for Justice, Equality and Law Reform* [2008] 3 I.R. 795; [2008] 2 I.L.R.M. 481 set out a non-exhaustive list of factors to be considered by the Minister when making a decision to deport either foreign parent of an Irish citizen child, including the rights of the Irish child to reside in the State; to be reared and educated with due regard to his or her welfare; to have the society, care and company of his or her parents; and the general protection afforded to the family pursuant to Art.41. Charleton J. commented that:

> "While these rights are not absolute, it is clear on the case law opened to this Court that they are manifestly strongest as between an Irish child

> and his or her foreign parents who genuinely seek to stay in Ireland to nurture him or her."

However, Charleton J. went on to state:

> "I do not accept that the analysis conducted by the Supreme Court in *Oguekwe* is capable of being extended, save in the most exceptional circumstances, involving perhaps the death of a mother or genuinely nurturing father or very serious disability of an Irish child, circumstances where the family naturally looks to its own for nurture, to aunts, uncles, grandparents, siblings or cousins. Were I to hold otherwise, it would involve an extension of the law beyond the precise tests set down by the Supreme Court in *Oguekwe*. These are specifically geared to an analysis of a decision to deport either parent of an Irish child."

The court was further satisfied that none of the entitlements of an Irish child as enumerated by the Supreme Court in *Oguekwe* applied:

> "…to a newly-discovered sibling whose only connection with the State is that she followed her mother from a foreign land to Ireland after an absence of seven years with a view to establishing ties here on the basis of asserting a right to family life."

The learned High Court judge commented that he could:

> "…not see how, in ordinary circumstances, such family contacts cannot be nurtured from a distance, as has been the case throughout centuries of emigration from Ireland. I cannot see that having an Irish sister or brother gives a foreign citizen any constitutional or statutory right to come and live in Ireland."

In relation to the claim under art.8 of the European Convention on Human Rights, Charleton J. noted that particular objection was taken by the applicant to the analysis conducted on behalf of the Minister in so far as it stated that family life did not arise between her and her mother and two young sisters. Charleton J. accepted that that unlike Art.41 of the Constitution, art.8 of the European Convention was not solely confined to relationships based on marriage, but was capable of extending those rights to ties based on blood relationships. However, it was noted that an analysis of the relevant judgments made clear the qualified nature of entitlement to respect for family life under art.8 of the Convention. Particular reliance was placed in this regard on the judgment of Dunne J. in *S v Minister for Justice, Equality and Law Reform* [2007] IEHC

398,[8] as well as the judgment of Birmingham J. in *GO v Minister for Justice, Equality and Law Reform* [2008] IEHC 190. Charleton J. commented:

> "In the field of asylum law, consistency of approach is essential to the rational disposal of these difficult cases. Strong reasons would have to be shown to justify departure from carefully considered authorities".

He concluded that "the right to assert family life entitlements in favour of this applicant, as a grown and independent adult, do not arise under Article 8 of the Convention." Accordingly, leave to seek judicial review was refused.

Refusal of naturalisation quashed on ground that Minister took into account irrelevant considerations In *LGH v Minister for Justice, Equality and Law Reform* [2009] IEHC 78; unreported, High Court, Edwards J., January 30, 2009 the applicant was a Chinese national who arrived in the State on or about March 30, 2000 as a programme refugee. Some time in 2005 the applicant applied to the Minister for a certificate of naturalisation pursuant to s.15 of the Irish Nationality and Citizenship Act 1956 as amended. A decision on that application was communicated to her by letter dated May 18, 2007 which refused her application for naturalisation, essentially on the basis that while she herself had never come to the adverse attention of the Garda Síochána, two of her sons had convictions in respect of criminal offences committed in the State.

Edwards J. noted at the outset that while the applicant's sons had criminal convictions, "their convictions [were] not of a very serious nature"; one son had convictions for drunken driving and no insurance, while the other son had convictions for driving without reasonable consideration, failure to present an insurance certificate and using a vehicle without a licence. Edwards J. was satisfied that the offences in question were minor offences within the meaning of that term as used in the Constitution; they were prosecuted in the District Court, and their cases were disposed of in the District Court. In respect of the charge pending against one of the sons, the court noted that the prosecution had been initiated in the District Court and that was as much as could be said about that.

On November 12, 2007 the applicant was granted leave to apply for judicial review to seek an order of certiorari to quash the decision of the Minister to refuse her application for a certificate of naturalisation, and for an order of mandamus directing him to reconsider the application afresh. The principal grounds upon which the reliefs were sought were first that the Minister took into account irrelevant considerations, and secondly that the decision of the Minister was irrational.

[8] See Brazil and Egan "Asylum and Immigration Law" in Byrne and Binchy (eds), *Annual Review of Irish Law 2007* (Round Hall, 2008), p.131.

Referring to a number of authorities including *Tesco Stores v Secretary of State for the Environment* [1995] 1 W.L.R. 759, *Mishra v Minister for Justice* [1996] 1 I.L.R.M. 189, *State (Keegan) v O'Rourke* [1986] I.L.R.M. 95 and *Pok Sun Shum v Ireland* [1986] I.L.R.M. 3, Edwards J. stated that he would grant the applicant an order of certiorari quashing the decision of the Minister to refuse her application for a certificate of naturalisation and remit the matter to the Minister to be reconsidered. These orders were granted on the basis that "the Minister took into account irrelevant considerations in making his decision". At the outset, Edwards J. accepted that the Minister enjoyed an absolute discretion in relation to the grant of a certificate of naturalisation, and that an applicant for naturalisation had no right or entitlement to a particular outcome. Edwards J. accepted the submission on behalf of the applicant that it could be inferred that the reason why the applicant's application was refused was, inter alia, the fact that two of her sons had convictions for road traffic matters.

The court was satisfied that to the extent that her sons' convictions were taken into account, "those were irrelevant considerations and … they should not have been taken into account". Edwards J. stated:

> "This applicant is an applicant of good character. This applicant meets all of the statutory requirements for naturalisation. While the Minister has, at the end of the day, absolute discretion, he must act judicially in the exercise of that discretion. …
>
> [I]t is true that she lives with these two sons, but they are not in any sense persons under her control. They are in their late 20's, and are fully adult persons. The only conclusion that this court can come to is that the mere fact that the applicant is related through blood to these two men, who have unfortunately acquired convictions, or have gotten into trouble, is being held against her. I am satisfied that that is not something to which any consideration could be legitimately be given. The Minister was incorrect to have regard to the character of the applicants' sons when making his decision."

Edwards J. stated that it was:

> "… offensive to all notions of justice that a person can be prejudiced on account of his or her family associations, in circumstances where the person concerned is of acknowledged good character. We cannot help the families we are born into, anymore than a child can help it as to who his parents are."

Commenting that the applicant could not be held responsible in any way for the failures of her adult sons, directly or indirectly, Edwards J. held that these matters should not have been taken into account in consideration of the applicant's application for naturalisation.

Accordingly, the Minister's decision was quashed on the ground that irrelevant considerations were taken into account; no finding was made on the question of rationality.

Technical breach of s.16(8) of Refugee Act 1996 not sufficient to warrant quashing Refugee Appeals Tribunal decision In *MN v Refugee Appeals Tribunal* [2009] IEHC 301; unreported, Cooke J., July 1, 2009, substantive relief in respect of a decision of the Refugee Appeals Tribunal was refused because although a breach of s.16(8) was found, it was held to be a "technical" breach only. By order of July 2, 2008 Birmingham J. granted leave to the applicant to seek by way of judicial review an order of certiorari quashing the decision of the Refugee Appeals Tribunal dated July 19, 2006 to refuse the applicant's appeal against a report of the Refugee Applications Commissioner of November 30, 2005 recommending that the applicant's application for asylum be refused and that he should not be declared to be a refugee. Leave was granted to apply for judicial review of the tribunal decision on the ground, inter alia, that the tribunal had acted in breach of natural and constitutional justice by relying on country of origin information in the form of a lecture given by a named individual in circumstances where the tribunal had failed to make a copy of that lecture available to the applicant and his legal representative.

The applicant was from the Democratic Republic of the Congo and he claimed to have fled that country in 2005 in fear of persecution for his political activities as a member of the Union for Democracy and Social Progress (UDPS). He applied for asylum in the State on September 30, 2005. The report of the Refugee Applications Commissioner rejected the applicant's claim as lacking credibility based on discrepancies between the applicant's evidence and country of origin information. The tribunal also rejected the applicant's claim on grounds of credibility; Cooke J. noted that one factor which appeared to have influenced the conclusion of the tribunal member was information the tribunal member appeared to have gleaned from a lecture given in Dublin on June 14–16, 2004 by a UNHCR protection officer in Kinshasa. This information appeared to have been considered important by the tribunal member not only because it ran counter to the applicant's evidence but because the information, unlike much country of origin information downloaded from a variety of sources on the internet, was given personally in Dublin by a UNHCR official with personal first-hand experience of that country of origin.

The court noted at the outset that it was unclear as to what form the information may have taken. It appeared from the decision that the UNHCR officer had given a lecture in Dublin on June 14–16, 2004. However, it appeared that no text of that lecture was produced at the appeal hearing when the information was put to the applicant and it was not disputed that no such text was ever furnished by the tribunal in accordance with s.16(8) of the Refugee Act 1996 since the hearing. Section 16(8) provides:

> "(8) The Tribunal shall furnish the applicant concerned and his or her solicitor (if known) and the High Commissioner whenever so requested by him or her with copies of any reports, observations or representations in writing or any other document, furnished to the Tribunal by the Commissioner copies of which have not been previously furnished to the applicant or, as the case may be, the High Commissioner pursuant to section 11(6) and an indication in writing of the nature and source of any other information relating to the appeal which has come to the notice of the Tribunal in the course of an appeal under this section."

Counsel for the respondents emphasised that no request had been made on behalf of the applicant either at the appeal hearing or at any time since for the production of the lecture and it was submitted that there was no obligation on the tribunal under s.16(8) to furnish it in the absence of such a request. Cooke J. rejected this submission, holding that s.16(8) requires "that in compliance with the requirement for a fair procedure, documents and information not already given to the applicant at the earlier stage, are to be furnished by the Tribunal before the final decision is adopted."

In the present case, the court noted that it was unclear whether the material derived from the lecture upon which the tribunal member relied was from a written text or from something the UNHCR had stated in reply to a question during the course of the lecture. However, the court noted that if the material in question was derived from a lecture or newspaper report it came within the first part of s.16(8)—documents to be furnished—and if the tribunal member was simply relying on his recollection of what was said at the lecture, it came within the second part—information the nature and source of which should have been the subject of a written indication. Cooke J. concluded that "in that sense there may well have been a technical non-compliance with the requirement even in the absence of a request by the applicant."

Nevertheless, the court was satisfied that even if there had been non-compliance with the strict terms of the statutory requirement, it was "a technical defect which would not justify the quashing of the appeal decision on that ground alone." This conclusion was justified on the grounds that there was no substantive violation of the principle of natural or constitutional justice which s.16(8) reflects because the information was openly disclosed and put to the applicant at the hearing, and the applicant therefore had the possibility of disputing it or of demanding an opportunity of examining its source and context with a view to rebutting it after the hearing and before the decision was adopted. Secondly, Cooke J. noted that the item of information did not stand alone but rather was confirmed elsewhere in the country of origin information before the tribunal. Finally, Cooke J. held that the quashing of the decision on this ground would not be warranted by a procedural defect in respect of such an item of evidence when the decision turned upon a broader negative finding of credibility based upon a number of facets of the applicant's story unrelated to this information.

The court therefore concluded that the tribunal decision had neither been shown to have been vitiated by error of fact nor rendered sufficiently flawed by procedural defect in the form of non-compliance with s.16(8) of the 1996 Act as to require it to be quashed as unlawful. The application for relief was, therefore, to be refused.

Whether arrest pursuant to s.12 of the Immigration Act 2004 valid when made for ulterior purpose of refusing arrested person leave to land and arranging removal from the State In *Oladapo v Governor of Cloverhill* [2009] IESC 42; [2009] 2 I.L.R.M. 166, the Supreme Court considered the lawfulness of an arrest pursuant to s.13 of the Immigration Act 2004 (arising from the applicant's failure to produce a passport), which arrest was effected for the purpose of detaining the applicant in order to facilitate a decision to refuse the applicant leave to land in the State pursuant to s.4 of the 2004 Act and subsequently enable arrangements to be made to effect his removal from the State.

The applicant was a national of Nigeria and initially arrived in Ireland in 2002 and left the State on a number of occasions in the following years. He had been absent from the State from September 2007 to November 2008, when he returned. From that date he was unlawfully present in the State. On February 14, 2009 the applicant left the State to go across the border to shop. On his return on the same day he was stopped by the Gardaí who were aware of the applicant's background and departure on the day. The Gardaí requested the applicant to produce a valid passport pursuant to s.12 of the Immigration Act 2004 which he failed to do. The applicant was then arrested pursuant to s.13 of the Immigration Act 2004 and taken to Dundalk Garda station. Some time later he was denied permission to land pursuant to s.4(3)(e) and (g) of the 2004 Act.

Following upon that refusal the applicant was arrested pursuant to s.5(2) of the 2003 Act, which provides that a non-national refused a permission to land:

> … whom an immigration officer or a member of the Garda Síochána, with reasonable cause, suspects has been unlawfully in the State for a continuous period of less than 3 months … may be arrested by an immigration officer or a member of the Garda Síochána and detained under warrant of that officer or member in a prescribed place and in the custody of the officer of the Minister or member of the Garda Síochána for the time being in charge of that place …

The applicant was detained overnight in the Garda station and on the following day a warrant issued pursuant to s.5 for the detention of the applicant in Cloverhill prison pending the making of arrangements for his removal from the State. The arresting Garda stated in evidence in the High Court that at the time of the initial arrest he intended to refuse the applicant permission to land. It was apparent from the evidence available from the hearing in the High Court that at the time of the initial arrest the Gardaí had no intention of charging the applicant with the offence for which he had been initially arrested. The true intention was to take the applicant into custody so that he could be brought to the Garda station and then refused permission to land and be issued with a warrant pursuant to s.5 of the 2003 Act so that arrangements could be made for his removal from the state.

The applicant challenged the lawfulness of his detention by way of an inquiry pursuant to Art.40.4 of the Constitution on the grounds, inter alia, that the initial arrest pursuant to s.13 of the 2004 Act was unlawful because it was not made for the purpose of charging the applicant with the offence for which he had been arrested. In the High Court it was held that the applicant was lawfully detained pursuant to the warrant notwithstanding that the period of detention in the Garda station prior to his arrest pursuant to s.5 of the 2003 Act was unlawful. The applicant appealed to the Supreme Court, which held that the initial arrest pursuant to s.13 of the 2004 Act was itself unlawful as it was not made for the purpose of charging the applicant with the offence for which he was purportedly arrested. Murray C.J. stated that a person may only be lawfully arrested on a criminal charge where, apart from other criteria, there is a bona fide intention of charging that person with that offence. It was held that the powers of arrest for the purpose of investigation under s.4 of the Criminal Justice Act 1984 are an entirely separate matter. Thus, Murray C.J. stated:

> "The unlawful arrest and the consequential unlawful detention are the dominant circumstances in this case. Even though the later arrest and detention pursuant to s.5(2) of the Act of 2003 might otherwise have been lawful, that arrest and subsequent detention is dominated by the fact that it was deliberately facilitated and achieved by bringing the appellant into unlawful custody for that specific and ulterior purpose. This is not simply a question of an otherwise lawful arrest being potentially tainted by an unlawful period of detention because in this case the dominating factor which brought about the arrest under s.5(2) was the deliberate unlawful arrest and detention under s.13. What occurred in this case was a fundamental breach of the due process of law."

It was further held that if the Gardaí had legitimate grounds for arresting the applicant pursuant to s.5 of the 2003 Act he ought to have been freed from his unlawful custody before any such step was taken. The Supreme Court accepted that a person released from unlawful custody, including a person unconditionally released pursuant to an order under Art.40 of the Constitution, is not thereafter exempt from due process of law, referring to *People (DPP) v Pringle* [1981] 2 Frewen 57. However, Murray C.J. concluded:

> "The release of an unlawfully arrested person from unlawful custody in circumstances such as the present is not a mere formality even if such release were to be immediately followed by a lawful arrest or re-arrest. The release marks in a substantive manner the termination of what has been unlawful in a fundamental way from its inception. It is then for a Garda member effecting a subsequent arrest, if any, to justify that deprivation of liberty in accordance with law."

Whether court may refuse to accept plea of guilt in relation to charge of failure to produce evidence of identity or nationality on grounds of uncertainty as to identity of accused Section 12(1) of the Immigration Act 2004 requires every non-national to produce, on demand, evidence of identity or nationality unless he or she gives a satisfactory explanation of the circumstances which prevent him or her from doing so. Section 12(2) provides that any non-national who contravenes this section shall be guilty of an offence. Concern had been expressed by practitioners for some time that, on occasion, the District Court had refused to accept a plea of guilty in relation to a charge under s.12 of the 2004 Act on the basis that the accused had not proved his identity. This could have the consequence of an accused person being remanded in custody on successive occasions being unable to bring the criminal proceedings to a conclusion by reason of the court's refusal to accept the plea.

This issue was conclusively determined by O'Neill J. in *Olafusi v Governor of Cloverhill Prison* [2009] IEHC 558; [2010] 1 I.L.R.M. 534. On October 8, 2009 the applicant was arrested and charged with offences contrary to ss.12(1)(a) and (2) and s.13 of the Immigration Act 2004 for failure to produce on demand to a member of An Garda Síochána evidence of his identity and nationality and for failure to provide a satisfactory explanation of the circumstances that prevented him from doing so. He was remanded in custody to appear before Cloverhill District Court on October 15, 2009.

When the applicant appeared before the District Court judge on that date, a plea of guilty was entered by counsel on his behalf. The prosecuting Garda told the District Court judge that the Gardaí were not satisfied as to the true identity of the applicant and requested that he be remanded in custody. The District Court judge said that she could not accept a plea of guilty where there was an issue as to the identity of the accused. Counsel for the applicant told the District Court judge that other applicants had brought successful habeas corpus applications where guilty pleas had not been accepted. The District Court judge asked whether the applicant would give evidence regarding his lack of documents. Counsel for the applicant informed the District Court judge that he would not. The District Court judge remanded the applicant in custody to October 22, 2009.

On October 19, 2009 the applicant applied to the High Court for an inquiry into the legality of his detention pursuant to Art.40.4.2° of the Constitution. On October 20, 2009, the High Court found the applicant's detention to be unlawful and ordered that the applicant be released from custody. The judgment of the court was handed down on December 11, 2009. Referring to the decision of the Supreme Court in *People (DPP) v Redmond* [2006] 3 I.R. 188; [2006] 2 I.L.R.M. 182, O'Neill J. held:

> "[I]t is only in the most exceptional circumstances can there be a refusal to accept a plea. I am satisfied that this is all the more so in a case of a summary offence at the minor end of the criminal calendar. Without doubt, the refusal of a guilty plea for the purposes of enabling an adjournment to facilitate further enquiries concerning the identification of an accused is not a proper basis for refusing a plea. Therefore, the necessary conclusion of this court is that the detention of the applicant on foot of a decision to refuse a plea in the absence of appropriate exceptional circumstances was unquestionably illegal detention."

It was accepted that difficulties may arise in the identification of people who are found not to have normal proof of identification, but O'Neill J. concluded that:

> "[T]he criminal justice process cannot be used or adapted to facilitate the ascertainment of the identity of such a person. Where such a person offers a plea of guilty the court must, in the absence of appropriate exceptional circumstances, proceed to sentence."

It was held that in so far as there are difficulties encountered in establishing the identity of persons, this is a matter to be resolved by the immigration authorities and the Gardaí. In this regard, O'Neill J. noted that there are statutory provisions which provide for the detention of such persons apart from the criminal process, such as s.9(8) of the Refugee Act 1996, as amended.

The decision in *Olafusi* provides welcome and necessary clarification as to the entitlement of a person charged pursuant to s.12 of the Immigration Act 2004 to enter a plea of guilt and for that plea to be accepted notwithstanding that the Gardaí remain unsatisfied as to the identity of the accused person.

Whether Minister required to have regard to personal rights of unborn citizen child when considering application to revoke deportation order As noted in the *Annual Review of Irish Law 2008*, in *OE v Minister for Justice, Equality and Law Reform* [2008] 3 I.R. 760 it was held by the High Court (Irvine J.) that the Minister for Justice was required to have regard to the personal rights of an unborn citizen child when considering whether to deport a parent of that child. This issue was revisited in the case of *HU v Minister for Justice, Equality and Law Reform* [2009] IEHC 598; unreported, Cooke J., December 17, 2009.

By order of the High Court made by consent on May 28, 2009, the applicants were granted leave to seek by way of judicial review, inter alia, an order of certiorari to quash the decision of the Minister dated February 6, 2009, by which he refused to revoke the deportation order in respect of the first-named applicant.

The first-named applicant arrived in the State on June 17, 2008 and applied for asylum. His application was refused by both the Refugee Applications Commissioner and Refugee Appeals Tribunal, and by letter dated October 24, 2008, the Minister notified the first-named applicant that he was proposing to make a deportation order in respect of him, and invited representations as to why he should not be deported. Representations were furnished to the Minister by letter dated December 4, 2008, which representations referred to the fact of his marriage to the second-named applicant, an Irish citizen. On January 8, 2009, the first-named applicant was notified that a deportation order had been signed in respect of him on December 4, 2008. The Minister thus advised that the first-named applicant should submit an application for revocation of the deportation order pursuant to s.3(11) of the 1999 Act.

On January 15, 2009, the applicants submitted to the Minister an application for revocation of the deportation order in respect of the first-named applicant on the basis of his marriage and his wife's pregnancy. By letter dated February 6, 2009, the Minister refused the application for revocation. The applicants instituted judicial review proceedings seeking to challenge the refusal to revoke on the basis that the Minister had failed to consider the rights of the then unborn citizen child.

At the hearing of the action, it was not disputed that no consideration was given by the Minister in arriving at his decision to the rights of the then unborn child other than that implicit in the recognition of the fact that the child was expected and in the recognition of the first- and second-named applicants as constituting a family. The applicants claimed that in considering an application to revoke a deportation order, the Minister was obliged by law to give specific consideration to the effect that the deportation of a non-national father would have upon the personal constitutional rights of his unborn Irish citizen child and that the rights to be thus considered were the same as those which would fall to be taken into account if the application to revoke under s.3(11) of the 1999 Act were made after the birth of that child. The applicants relied in support of this submission on the judgment of Irvine J. in *OE v Minister for Justice, Equality and Law Reform* [2008] 3 I.R. 760.

The Minister submitted that he was under no obligation in law to consider the impact of the deportation order on any particular personal right of an unborn child. It was submitted on behalf of the Minister that the constitutional right of the unborn child was that of the right to life enshrined in the Constitution in

Art.40.3.3° by the Eighth Amendment to the Constitution and that alone. It was submitted that *OE* was not authority for the proposition that the unborn child has any other constitutional right capable of being invoked in aid of the first-named applicant. It was further submitted that if the *OE* case was considered by the court to be authority for such a proposition, the case was wrongly decided and that it ought not to be followed. As Cooke J. noted:

> "It is accordingly necessary to decide in this case which of these diametrically opposed contentions is correct. In other words, is the Minister constrained when proposing to deport the non-national parent of an unborn who may at birth be entitled to Irish citizenship, to give specific consideration to the personal constitutional rights of that unborn child as if the child was already born?"

In relation to the decision of Irvine J. in *OE*, Cooke J. concluded that this decision was not authority for the proposition advanced by the applicants or, at least, one which could be said to constitute a binding precedent for the purpose of the present case. This was held to be so having regard to the comment by Irvine J. at para.50 of her decision in *OE* that:

> "[T]he respondent did not ask the court to consider the constitutional rights of the unborn child in this case, having regard to its impending birth, as being any different from the rights which he would have enjoyed had he been born at the time the respondent was asked to exercise his power under section 3(11) of the Act of 1999."

Cooke J. thus concluded:

> "[T]he learned judge is expressly drawing attention to the fact that she was not asked to determine the issue to whether, as a matter of law, the unborn child had the same constitutional or Convention rights as the child born as an Irish citizen. That caveat by itself signals that the learned High Court judge did not intend her judgment to be read as a definitive determination of that issue."

Cooke J. noted that:

> "[A] previous judgment can only be said to be a precedent by reference to its *ratio decidendi* namely, the essential principle upon which the concrete decision in the case is based, abstracted from the specific peculiarities of the case. It is the *ratio* alone which has force of law."

Having regard to the comment of Irvine J. that the court had not been asked to consider whether the constitutional rights of the unborn child were different from the rights of the citizen child when born, Cooke J. was satisfied that "the subsequent expression of observations on that topic cannot be taken as statements of reasons or principle which were necessary to the legal basis upon which the decision in that case was made" and that the court was "not constrained by the judgment in the *OE* case and is thus obliged to examine on the merits the arguments on the substantive issue which have been put before it in the present case."

The learned High Court judge then proceeded to examine the proposition that it was already settled law prior to the *OE* judgment that by reference to Arts 40.3.1° and 2°, there existed in law no distinction in the protection afforded by the Constitution to the personal rights of a person depending upon whether the subject of the asserted right was a citizen child or an unborn within the jurisdiction of the State. It was noted that there had been some judicial references prior to the enactment of the Eighth Amendment in 1983 to the possibility that the right to life of the unborn child was one of the latent or unspecified personal rights that might fall to be protected by the State under Art.40.3. However, Cooke J. held that "contrary to the impression given by the *OE* judgment … it does not appear that any definitive judgment to that effect had been handed down."

Referring to a number of judgments concerning the interpretation of Art.40.3 including *G v An Bord Uchtála* [1980] I.R. 32, *McGee v Attorney General* [1974] I.R. 284 and *Finn v Attorney General* [1983] I.R. 154, Cooke J. concluded:

> "[N]otwithstanding the strong indications of judicial thinking to be found in observations made *obiter* by a number of learned members of the bench of great authority and experience in constitutional law, the legal fact remains that, at the date of adoption of the Eighth Amendment, no definitive ruling amounting to a binding precedent had yet been handed down to the effect that Article 40.3 as it then stood gave protection to the right to life of the unborn as one of the unspecified personal rights of the citizen. Much less was there any considered judicial pronouncement as to the possible scope or qualification of such protection."

Cooke J. thus held that:

> "[T]he right to life of the unborn and the scope and limitations with which it has been defined in the Constitution, must be taken as having been made explicit by the enactment of the Amendments so that they are now contained exclusively in the three subsections of subparagraph 3 alone."

The learned High Court judge concluded:

> "65. It is clear, therefore, that the purpose and effect of the Amendments was to deal specifically and separately with the acknowledged right peculiar to the unborn. As such, Article 40.3.3 explicitly guarantees 'the right to life' or, in other words, the right to be born. It is perhaps arguable that the 'right to life' encompasses more than the right not to have the natural course towards birth deliberately interrupted such that, for example, it includes the right of the unborn to bodily integrity. Given the acknowledgment of the right to be born, it is undoubtedly arguable that the unborn has a right not to have the natural course of gestation put at risk of deformity or handicap by some wilful misconduct on the part of the mother or of some third party. Thus, the right to be born includes the right to be born in the natural course and to be protected against any unnatural intervention short of termination which might harm or jeopardise the expectation of the unborn being born in normal good health and condition … Unlike the personal rights of the citizen in Article 40.3.1 therefore, the right to life of the unborn is not merely prospective but vested and justiciable and, as such, its effect in law is greater than the retroactive entitlement accorded to the child *en ventre sa mère* by the principle of common law. But if that proposition is valid, it is on the basis of the specific protection enshrined in the Constitution by the Amendments, as an integral facet of the right to be born rather than as a distinct personal right derived from paras 1 and 2 of Article 40.3."

The court thus considered that the objective and effect of the Eighth Amendment was to deal specifically in Art.40.3.3° by way of variation and addition with the full extent of the constitutional protection to be accorded to the unborn child and concluded that "Article 40.3 in its subsections 1 and 2 cannot be looked to as a source of further or different rights on the part of the unborn to be protected by the Constitution." On the basis that the Constitution "does not now accord to the unborn all of the unspecified personal rights enjoyed by the born citizen child", it was held that the Minister, when considering the possible deportation of an unborn child's non-national parent, was not required to consider "the personal rights of the child in relation to its own position in society, its progress in life and in education, its attachment to any community" as these rights remain purely prospective and inchoate until it is born. Cooke J. was satisfied that:

> "[T]hose rights do not attain any justiciable status such as would attract the obligation of respect and vindication by the State under the Constitution or that of respect under the Convention until the point at which that child acquires an existence in its own right independent of its mother."

Cooke J. concluded:

> "[T]he only right of the unborn child as the Constitution now stands which attracts the entitlement to protection and vindication is that enshrined by the Amendments in Article 40.3.3 namely, the right to life or, in other words, the right to be born and, possibly (and this is a matter for future decision) allied rights such as the right to bodily integrity which are inherent in and inseparable from the right to life itself. The deportation of a non-national parent cannot, in the court's judgment, be said to be in any sense an interference with that right."

The application for judicial review was therefore refused. The decision in *HU* is under appeal to the Supreme Court so a definitive decision is awaited as to the rights, if any, of the unborn citizen child to be considered in the immigration context.

Whether refusal of permanent residence application by Romanian national lawful In *IB v Minister for Justice, Equality and Law Reform* [2009] IEHC 447; unreported, High Court, Cooke J., October 15, 2009, the applicant sought to challenge the Minister's refusal of his application for permanent residence in the State pursuant to the European Communities (Freedom of Movement of Persons) No. 2 Regulations 2006 (the 2006 Regulations). Leave to seek judicial review was granted by Finlay Geoghegan J. on October 6, 2008.

The applicant was a national of Romania who came to the State in August 1999. He applied unsuccessfully for asylum but since October 2000 had permission to reside in the State and held a work permit which enabled him to obtain employment. In 2002 he was joined by his wife and children. On November 20, 2007, having resided in the State for over five years, he applied through his solicitor under the 2006 Regulations for a permanent residence certificate. The Department sought and was then sent further documentation in support of the application. In a letter of March 13, 2008, the Minister refused the application on the basis that the applicant had not resided in Ireland continuously for a five-year period. By letter of May 1, 2008, the applicant's solicitors queried the refusal and pointed out that since Romania had become a member state of the European Union on January 1, 2007, the applicant no longer required the permission of the Minister as he had in excess of five years' lawful residence in the State where he continued to be gainfully employed. The solicitor asked the Minister to reconsider his refusal but by letter of June 9, 2008, the refusal was confirmed. This letter stated that in order to make an application for permanent residence, an applicant must have resided in the State for more than five years as a European citizen. It was noted that Romania became a member of the EU on January 1, 2007 and that the applicant was therefore not eligible to make an application for permanent residence until January 1, 2012.

The applicant challenged this decision on a net ground which turned on the interpretation of reg.12(1) of the 2006 Regulations. Effectively, the issue arising for determination was whether the period of five years' continuous residence in the State required by the Regulations could be calculated so as to include the years of the applicant's residence in the State prior to January 1, 2007 or whether, as contended by the Minister, the full five years' continuous residence in the State must be subsequent to the accession of Romania to the EU on January 1, 2007.

Cooke J. noted that the 2006 Regulations were adopted by the respondent pursuant to s.3 of the European Communities Act 1972 for the purpose of giving effect to Directive 2004/38 of the European Parliament and of the Council of April 29, 2004, on the right of citizens of the Union and their family members to move and reside freely within the territory of the Member States. The regulations came into force on January 1, 2007 and it was on that basis that the applicant applied for the certificate of permanent residence in November 2007. Regulation 12, which sets out the entitlement to permanent residence, provides:

> "(1) Subject to paragraph (3) and Regulation 13, a person to whom these regulations apply who has resided in the State in conformity with these regulations for a continuous period of five years may remain permanently in the State.
>
> (2) For the purposes of paragraph (1) continuity of residence in the State shall not be affected by temporary absences not exceeding six months a year, or by absences of a longer duration for compulsory and military service or by one absence of a maximum of twelve consecutive months for important reasons such as pregnancy and childbirth, serious illness, study or vocational training, or a posting in another Member State of a third country.
>
> (3) The entitlement to remain permanently in the State pursuant to paragraph (1) shall cease to exist where the person concerned has been absent from the State for a period exceeding two consecutive years."

Cooke J. noted that reg.12 corresponds to and implements art.16(1) of the 2004 Directive which reads as follows:

> "Union citizens who have resided legally for a continuous period of five years in the host Member State shall have the right of permanent residence there. This right shall not be subject to the conditions provided for in chapter III."

It was noted that the "conditions provided for in Chapter III" were those attached to the rights of residence for up to and for more than three months such as, for example, being in employment or being self-employed, having sufficient resources not to become a burden on the social assistance system or being enrolled for a course of study. Thus, the court stated, the scheme of the Directive was that a Union citizen who has resided legally in a host Member State for upwards of five years acquires a right to a permanent residence there without having to comply further with such conditions.

The applicant contended that the Minister erred in considering that the applicant had not resided in the State "in conformity with" the 2006 Regulations for a continuous period of five years, having taken into account only the years of the applicant's residence since the accession of Romania on January 1, 2007. The court rejected this argument, holding that reg.12(1) of the 2006 Regulations correctly reflected and implemented art.16(1) of the 2004 Directive when read in conjunction with the explanatory motivation at recital 17 of the Directive which provides:

> "Enjoyment of permanent residence by Union citizens who have chosen to settle long-term in the host Member State would strengthen the feeling of Union citizenship and is a key element in promoting social cohesion, which is one of the fundamental objectives of the Union. A right of permanent residence should therefore be laid down for all Union citizens and their family members who have resided in the host Member State in compliance with the conditions laid down in this Directive during a continuous period of five years without becoming subject to an expulsion measure."

Cooke J. noted that prior to January 1, 2007, the applicant was not an EU citizen and his presence in the State, while lawful under national law, was not residence "in compliance with the conditions" of the Directive or of Community law as such. Rather, his presence was lawful by virtue of a purely domestic authorisation granted to a non-EU national. It was held that the recital was "a substantive statement of the motivation for laying down the right to permanent residence" and that the wording of the recital confirmed the coherent scheme of the Directive in giving effect to the Treaty rights of free movement and residence within the Member States. The court rejected the applicant's submission that the term "have resided legally" in a host Member State required only that the residence be lawful by reference to applicable national laws and conditions. It was held that this expression must be given a Community law meaning. Thus, Cooke J. concluded:

> "Prior to January 1, 2007 the applicant was not a Union citizen and his presence in the State was not 'residence in a host Member State'. Ireland was, of course, already a Member State when the applicant arrived here but it did not receive him as a 'host' Member State in the sense of the

> Directive provision. When read in the light of recital 17 to the Directive, it is clear that the continuous period of five years residence required is a period during which an applicant has resided in the host Member State pursuant to and on the basis of the Directive and in compliance with its conditions."

The court was satisfied that:

> "[T]o construe the provision in the sense contended for by the applicant would be inconsistent with ensuring the uniform application of the Directive by rendering its effect susceptible to the divergent conditions of national rules of 'legal residence' for non-nationals of Member States."

Accordingly, the court held that the ground of illegality asserted against the Minister's decision to refuse the certificate of permanent residence had not been made out and the application was therefore rejected.

Challenge to transfer of asylum applicants to Greece pursuant to Dublin II Regulation In *Mirza, Mamo and Abrahimi v Minister for Justice, Equality and Law Reform*, unreported, High Court, Clark J., October 21, 2009, the applicants sought judicial review of determinations of the Refugee Applications Commissioner in October 2008 that Greece was responsible for determining the applicants' asylum applications and that they should be transferred to Greece, pursuant to the terms of Council Regulation 343/2003/EC (the Dublin II Regulation).

Each of the applicants had applied for asylum in Ireland and in each case a Eurodac "hit" revealed that the applicant had previously entered Greece where his/her fingerprints were taken. The Commissioner determined that Greece was responsible for examining their asylum applications in all three cases pursuant to the Dublin II Regulation and that they should be transferred to Greece. A further common feature of the three cases was that the applicants were represented by the Refugee Legal Service (RLS) which made submissions to the Commissioner on behalf on each applicant, requesting that the Commissioner exercise his discretion under art.3(2) of the Dublin II Regulation to derogate from the normal application of that instrument and to accept responsibility for determining the applicants' asylum cases in Ireland.

The submissions made by the RLS to the Commissioner in each case concerned the asylum procedures in Greece, and included reliance on a report of the Committee on Civil Liberties, Justice and Home Affairs (LIBE) of the European Parliament (July 2007) which detailed the deplorable reception and detention conditions for asylum seekers and noted that refugee recognition rate in 2004 was 0.3% and in 2006 was 0.7% and total protection stood at

1.2%; the fact that in January 2008 the European Commission had commenced infringement proceedings against Greece before the European Court of Justice for non-compliance with the Dublin II Regulation; the fact that various other EU Member States including Norway, Germany, Sweden and Iceland had recently decided not to transfer asylum applicants to Greece; a UNHCR position paper of April 2008 which called on Member States to stop returning asylum-seekers to Greece and make use of art.3(2) of the Dublin II Regulation, pointing out "many obstacles faced by 'Dublin returnees' to having their asylum claim registered and examined, leading to exclusion from the procedures or to their refoulement"; the decision of the European Court of Human Rights to issue interim measures under rule 39 of the Rules of Court as an interim measure, restraining the transfer of an Iraqi applicant from Finland to Greece until further notice and seven subsequent rule 39 requests from the court to the Finnish authorities in respect of returns to Greece. It was submitted to the Commissioner that given the seriousness of the information widely available in relation to Greece, it was incumbent on the Irish authorities to investigate the status of the applicant's case in Greece and the likely conditions or risk of refoulement that he/she would face if returned there, in advance of taking a decision as to his/her return.

In the case of each applicant, a memo which formed the basis of the decision was prepared by an authorised officer from the Dublin Unit of the Commissioner's office. The memo in each case set out the details of the application, highlighting discrepancies in the evidence given by each applicant and noting that the applicants were less than forthcoming during the initial phase of their asylum applications in Ireland about their experiences in Greece. The memos then summarised the RLS submissions and concluded in relation to same that there was no risk of refoulement for asylum-seekers returned to Greece; that the UNHCR stated in 2007 that "there would appear to be substantial efforts to provide support to asylum applicants"; that applicants transferred from Ireland to Greece had been accepted into the asylum process; that there was no general application by other Member States of the sovereignty clause of the Dublin II Regulation and that any such derogations were in relation to specific and unique cases; that any Member State which suspended transfers to Greece did so on a temporary basis until they were satisfied that there was no risk to the applicant on transfer; and that each Member State has responsibility for the operation of its own asylum procedure and that any concerns about the operation of such procedures in relation to the requirements of EU law were a matter for complaint to the European Commission. The memo in each case concluded:

> "I am satisfied (on the basis of the evidence available both directly from the Greek authorities and from other Member States) that Greece meets its obligations to admit persons to its asylum procedure, to process their application and to avoid the risk of refoulement".

A recommendation was therefore made that a notice of determination issue to each applicant pursuant to the Refugee Act 1996 (Section 22) Order 2003 (S.I. No. 423 of 2003).

The applicants sought, inter alia, an order of certiorari quashing the Commissioner's determination that they should be transferred to Greece. Although a number of diverse grounds were advanced by the applicants in support of the reliefs claimed, Clark J. summarised the applicants' claim into two separate limbs: first that the Commissioner acted unfairly, irrationally and in breach of natural and constitutional justice in the manner in which it assessed the information and materials before it; and secondly that the Commissioner erred in law in refusing to exercise its discretion under art.3(2) of the Dublin II Regulation. Clark J. also noted that although reference was made in the applicants' grounds to the European Convention on Human Rights, that ground was abandoned at the hearing of the substantive application. The applicants also clarified that they were only challenging the Commissioner's determinations and not the subsequent decisions of the Minister to make transfer orders.

In relation to the first ground, Clark J. was satisfied that, "read as a whole", there was:

> "… little doubt that the issues raised by the RLS on behalf of the applicants were considered thoroughly and carefully. Each submission made was examined and attached country of origin information and other material furnished was considered. The applicant did not during the lengthy hearing point to any relevant matter which the Commissioner failed to consider."

Accordingly, the court was not satisfied that the Commissioner breached his obligations under reg.(4) of the Refugee Act 1996 (Section 22) Order (S.I. No. 423 of 2003) to take account of all relevant information known to him. Clark J. was satisfied that the Commissioner was entitled to seek information from Greece in relation to the criticisms made of its asylum application process, on the grounds that as a Member State of the European Union and a contracting state to the European Convention on Human Rights, there was "a presumption that it will comply with its international obligations". The court was satisfied that that the applicants' arguments relating to the undue deference by the Commissioner to Greece's position and response to the UNHCR paper and the criticism of humanitarian organisations and NGOs were not warranted. In relation to the applicants' reliance on statistics relating to the levels of successful asylum outcomes, Clark J. accepted that those statistics were "undoubtedly alarmingly low". Clark J. endorsed "[t]he approach taken by the Commissioner to those statistics" which was "to indicate that neither the RLS nor Ireland is a party to the determination process in Greece and that it would not be appropriate to draw conclusions on the figures". The court was satisfied that without information and explanations as to how those statistics were complied, "statistics can be meaningless" because "a low rate of recognition may be reflective of a state of affairs where the applicants are economic migrants fleeing poverty rather than persecution in its many forms and will not necessarily be indicative of an unfair or defective asylum determination system".

The court was satisfied that the Commissioner's summary of the LIBE delegation report of the European Parliament was neither selective nor unfair, and also rejected the applicants' complaint that the Commissioner did not disclose to them the information obtained regarding the position of other Member States vis-à-vis transfers to Greece nor did he afford them an opportunity to comment upon that information was in breach of natural justice. Clark J. commented that "[i]t is difficult to discern what exactly the applicants wished to do with such an opportunity", noting that the question of whether an asylum application should be determined in Ireland is a matter for the Commissioner pursuant to reg.4 of the Refugee Act 1996 (Section 22) Order 2003 and that:

> "[U]nless special circumstances exist this determination is intended to be a rapid process and not one which deals with the merits of the applicant's claim or a development of the applicant's arguments as to why Ireland should exercise its discretion to derogate from the Regulation."

Clark J. noted that the RLS made very extensive submissions and observations on behalf of each applicant and that those submissions and observations were considered and investigated and conclusions were reached, concluding:

> "In the absence of extraordinary changed circumstances relating either to Greece or to the applicants' personal circumstances, it is difficult to envisage that a right of rebuttal was anticipated by the obligation to consider 'all relevant matters' set out in section 4(2)."

Accordingly, the court was satisfied that the Commissioner acted rationally and in accordance with fair procedures and natural and constitutional justice once he had considered all relevant information known to him and the representations made on behalf of the applicants.

In relation to the second ground, Clark J. rejected the applicants' contention that Ireland was obliged to derogate from the general application of the Dublin II Regulation once cogent evidence established that Greece was not compliant with its obligations under EC law. It was held that the only identified situation where an obligation to derogate from the Regulation arose was "where the proposed transfer would give rise to a breach of a Member State's obligations under Article 3 of the European Convention for Human Rights (ECHR)." It was noted that:

> "[I]n the relatively recent past it was believed that persons being returned

> to Greece under the Dublin II Regulation might face being returned by Greece to their native countries where there existed a real risk that they would face torture or worse. Such return would constitute a breach of the prohibition of refoulement, contrary to Article 3 of the ECHR. It has since been clarified however that Greece has not in fact returned any persons to countries where such a risk exists and refoulement is no longer considered a risk."

Reference was made to the decisions of the Court of Appeal and House of Lords in *R. (Nasseri) v Secretary of State for the Home Department* [2008] 3 W.L.R. 1386; *AH (Iran), Zego (Eritrea) and Kadir (Iraq) v Secretary of State for the Home Department* [2008] E.W.C.A. Civ. 985 and *R. (Nasseri) v Secretary of State for the Home Department* [2009] 2 W.L.R. 1190 and the decision of the European Court for Human Rights in *KRS v United Kingdom* (Application No. 32733/08, December 2, 2008) which established that:

> "[W]here substantial grounds have been shown for believing that the person concerned would if deported or transferred face a real risk of being subjected to treatment contrary to Article 3, then that person should not be deported or transferred."

Clark J. concluded:

> "The Court is not aware of any other situation where there is an *obligation* to derogate from the Dublin II Regulation. In the circumstances, it follows that the Commissioner was correct when it was stated in the Memo accompanying the determination that each Member State is responsible for its own asylum process and that if a Member State has issues with another State's asylum process that is a matter for complaint to the European Commission. The European Commission is the 'guardian' of the EC Treaty as set out in Article 211 EC and one of its roles is to ensure the proper application of Community law.
>
> If a Member State is not complying with its obligations under Community law, it is the Commission that takes steps to put the situation right. As the Dublin II Regulation operates on the assumption that it is the Commission that should regulate standards, it cannot be appropriate for Member States to examine other countries' processes themselves."

Noting that the Common European Asylum System is based on mutual trust, confidence and solidarity between Member States with the object of pursuing co-ordinated, strong and effective working relations between Member States and the European institutions, Clark J. was satisfied that:

"... those objectives would be undermined if the application of the Dublin II Regulation in Ireland was subject to the oversight by domestic courts of the effectiveness of asylum system of Greece or if there were an obligation on the part of the Commissioner to consider whether the responsible Member State operated an asylum system which accorded with an applicant's concept of an effective asylum evaluation system".

It was held that "the authorities in this State are entitled to assume that other Member States act in compliance with their obligations under Community law and that any issues of non-compliance are for the Commission to investigate."

Clark J. noted that Ireland may derogate from the normal application of the Dublin II Regulation for a variety of reasons including humanitarian or compassionate grounds, and commented that there was "certainly an argument that burden sharing should be distributed more fairly throughout the EU by less exposed countries accepting prospective Dublin II returnees into the asylum system." However, it was held that there was no *obligation* on Ireland to derogate from the normal application of the Dublin II Regulation, absent substantial grounds for believing that there is a real and substantial risk of the transferee being subject to treatment contrary to art.3 of the ECHR as a result of the transfer. In so holding, Clark J. adopted the statement of Stanley Burnton L.J. in *Zego* where he stated:

"In my judgment it is right to distinguish between ill treatment in Greece and the risk of return to a country by Greece to another country in which an applicant will be mistreated. [...] a defective examination of an asylum claim, in my judgement, only becomes relevant if there is a real risk of return contrary to Article 3: that is to say a return of an applicant without examination complying with international standards of his asylum claim to a state in which he is liable to be mistreated. If there is no risk of return, the fact that there is no proper examination of the asylum claim cannot of itself either constitute a breach of Article 3 or supplement what otherwise would not amount to a breach of Article 3 within what is alleged to be a safe third country, here Greece."

Clark J. stated that it was important to distinguish between cases where there is a real risk of a breach of the European Convention on Human Rights and cases where there are concerns about the asylum determination process and reception conditions which fall short of breaches of art.3 of the Convention. While it was accepted that there may be an obligation to derogate in respect of the first category, there was no such obligation in respect of the second. Accordingly, it was held that the Commissioner's decision to issue notices of determination to the applicants pursuant to the Refugee Act 1996 (Section 22)

Order 2003 (S.I. No. 423 of 2003) was in accordance with law, fair procedures and natural and constitutional justice and the application was dismissed.

LEGISLATION

There was no primary legislation enacted in 2009 pertaining to asylum or immigration law. However, two statutory instruments were enacted relating to visa requirements.

Immigration Act 2004 (Visas) Order 2009 (S.I. No. 239 of 2009) On June 27, 2009, the Minister for Justice exercised his power pursuant to s.17 of the Immigration Act 2004 to make an order specifying the classes of non-nationals who are exempt from Irish visa requirements and those who are required to be in possession of a valid Irish transit visa when transiting within a port within the State. The principal change effected by the order is that Taiwan is, from July 1, 2009, no longer subject to an Irish visa requirement.

Immigration Act 2004 (Visas) (No. 2) Order 2009 (S.I. No. 453 of 2009) On November 16, 2009, the Minister for Justice exercised his power pursuant to s.17 of the Immigration Act 2004 to make an order specifying the classes of non-nationals who are exempt from Irish visa requirements and those who are required to be in possession of a valid Irish transit visa when transiting within a port within the State. The principal change effected by the order is that nationals of Mauritius are, from January 1, 2010, subject to an Irish visa requirement.

Business Occupations and Professions

LEGAL PROFESSION

Legal Services Ombudsman The Legal Services Ombudsman Act 2009 is discussed in the Legal Profession chapter, pp.559–603, below.

PRIVATE SECURITY SERVICES

Identity documents The Private Security (Identity Badge) Regulations 2009 (SI No. 332 of 2009) set out the detailed requirements concerning the wearing of identity badges by the holders of certain categories of licences granted under the Private Security Services Act 2004 (*Annual Review of Irish Law 2004*, pp.15–18). The form, content and size of the identity badge is also prescribed. The 2009 Regulations came into force on September 1, 2009.

Charities

Charities Act 2009 The Charities Act 2009 (the "2009 Act") constitutes the most significant legislative reform of the law on charities since the foundation of the State. The 2009 Act provides for the establishment of the first regulatory body for this important sector, the Charities Regulatory Authority, which will replace the non-regulatory Commissioners of Charitable Donations and Bequests for Ireland. The 2009 Act also contains the first statutory definition of "charitable purpose", replacing the so-called *Pemsel* classification, derived from the decision of the UK House of Lords in *Commissioners of Income Tax v Pemsel* [1891] A.C. 531. The 2009 Act provides for the registration of charitable organisations by the Charities Regulatory Authority, subject to appeals concerning registration and non-registration to the Charity Appeals Tribunal. The 2009 Act also includes detailed provisions concerning the financial regulation and protection of charitable organisations and also sets out some important duties of charitable trustees. It also modernises the statutory regulation of fund-raising by or on behalf of registered charitable organisations.

At the time of writing (August 2010), the central feature of the 2009 Act, the establishment of the Charities Regulatory Authority, has not yet been commenced. During the Oireachtas debate on the 2009 Act, the Minister of State in what is now the Department of Community, Equality and Gaeltacht Affairs stated that:

> "[I]n other common law jurisdictions, such as Scotland it has taken some time— approximately two years after enactment—for the regulatory framework to be put in place on a statutory basis and a similar scenario is likely here."

With the minor cavil that Scotland, although part of the United Kingdom has a shared common law and civil law heritage, this statement indicates the timeframe envisaged for completing commencement of the Act. The Charities Act 2009 (Commencement) Order 2009 (S.I. No. 284 of 2009) brought into force ss.2, 5, 10 and 99 of the 2009 Act. Section 99 deals with the offence of selling a mass card other than under an arrangement with a recognised person. The Charities Act 2009 (Commencement Order) 2010 (S.I. No. 315 of 2010) brought full commencement of the 2009 Act somewhat closer, firstly, by bringing s.4 of the 2009 Act into force. Section 4 empowers the Minister to make orders or regulations under the 2009 Act and would thus enable the

Minister to make regulations before the Charities Regulatory Authority is established, if considered appropriate. The 2010 Order also brought into force s.90 of the 2009 Act, which empowers the courts to grant relief to charity trustees from personal liability for breach of trust where, in the opinion of the court, while the trustee may be liable for the breach, he or she acted in good faith and ought to be excused.

Background to the 2009 Act The reform of the regulation of charities has been a matter of concern for many years. Recent estimates indicate that more than €2 billion passes through charities in Ireland. In recent years, calls for reform focused on the reality that, in the absence of a clear regulatory system, charities were being abused by some unscrupulous individuals for personal gain and, more worryingly, were also being used as a money-laundering facility connected to organised crime. At an international level, the OECD's Financial Action Task Force (FATF) on money laundering (see *www.fatf-gafi.org*), discussed below, has been influential in the development of national policies and, as with the 2009 Act, statutory regulation. At national level, major reform of the fundraising aspect was recommended by the 1990 *Report of the Committee on Fundraising Activities for Charitable and Other Purposes* (the Costello Report). No action was taken at that time on the Costello Report. In many other states, comprehensive reviews of charity law had been carried out and, by the late 1990s and the first decade of this century, significant reforms had been enacted, including in the United Kingdom.

Against this background, the Government commissioned a review of developments in this area, resulting in the publication in April 2002 of *Charity Law Review: a Report for the Department of Social, Community & Family Affairs*. In June 2002 the Programme for Government included a commitment to a "comprehensive reform of the law of charities... to ensure accountability and to protect against abuse of charitable status and fraud." In July 2002 the Law Reform Committee of the Law Society of Ireland published *Charity Law: the Case for Reform*, and this proved to be another influential catalyst for reform. The Government then began a major public consultation exercise on the reform of charity law. This resulted in the publication in December 2003 by the Department of Social, Community and Family Affairs of a Consultation Paper entitled *Establishing a Modern Statutory Framework for Charities*, followed in September 2004 by its *Response to Public Consultation.* The Department had, in tandem with this, also requested the Law Reform Commission to examine some aspects of the law, notably the role of charity trustees. This area, and trustee law generally, had already been included in the Commission's *Second Programme of Law Reform 2000–2007* and the Commission published two Consultation Papers on the law of trustees and on charitable trustees in 2005: *Consultation Paper on Trust Law: General Proposals* (LRC CP 35–2005) and *Consultation Paper on Charitable Trust Law: General Proposals* (LRC CP 36–2005) (see

Annual Review of Irish Law 2005, pp.507–509). This was followed by its 2006 *Report on Charitable Trusts and Legal Structures for Charities* (LRC 80–2006) (see *Annual Review of Irish Law 2006*, pp.432–433).

In the meanwhile, in February 2006, the Department had published a detailed *General Scheme for the Charities Regulation Bill 2006*, which largely implemented the Commission's 2005 provisional recommendations on charitable trustees. The 2006 scheme was, in turn, broadly the basis for the *Charities Bill 2007* and which, with significant changes (some of which "reinstated" provisions from the 2006 Bill Scheme that had been omitted from the 2007 Bill) was ultimately enacted as the 2009 Act. This indicative list of the various milestones in the enactment of the 2009 Act underline the extensive nature of the consultative elements involved in this reform process. For a detailed analysis by one of the major contributors to the reform of this area, see O'Halloran, "Charity Law Review in Ireland and the Challenges for the State/Third Sector Partnership" (2002) 5(1) *International Journal of Not-for-Profit Law* (available at *www.icnl.org/knowledge/ijnl/index.htm*) and O'Halloran, *Charity Law and Social Inclusion* (Routledge, 2006). We now turn to provide an overview of the specific contents of the 2009 Act.

Charitable purposes Section 3 of the 2009 Act contains the first statutory definition of "charitable purpose", replacing the so-called *Pemsel* classification, derived from the decision of the UK House of Lords in *Commissioners of Income Tax v Pemsel* [1891] A.C. 531. The *Pemsel* classification has been applied many times by the Irish courts in litigation on the charitable status of trusts, for example, by Keane J. in *Re the Worth Library* [1995] 2 I.R. 301 (*Annual Review of Irish Law 1993*, pp.294–297). It was pointed out during the Oireachtas debate that the *Pemsel* classification derived to some extent from the Preamble to the Statute of Charitable Uses 1601, which had not applied in Ireland but which contained a list of purposes or activities which the State believed were of general benefit to society and to which the State wanted to encourage private contributions. The list in the Preamble to the 1601 Statute, which has formed the foundation of the modern definition of "charitable purposes", had developed entirely through case law prior to the 2009 Act. Case law, notably *Commissioners of Income Tax v Pemsel* [1891] A.C. 531, had interpreted this as giving rise to four categories of purposes: (a) the prevention or relief of poverty or economic hardship; (b) the advancement of education; (c) the advancement of religion; and (d) any other purpose that is of benefit to the community. Section 3(1) and (2) of the 2009 broadly replicated these four headings, with some necessary updating of language. Thus s.3(1) and (2) state:

> (1) For the purposes of this Act each of the following shall, subject to subsection (2), be a charitable purpose:

(a) the prevention or relief of poverty or economic hardship;
(b) the advancement of education;
(c) the advancement of religion;
(d) any other purpose that is of benefit to the community.

(2) A purpose shall not be a charitable purpose unless it is of public benefit.

It was noted in the Oireachtas debate that the Revenue Commissioners have referred to these categories when deciding whether an organisation is eligible for charitable tax exemptions. In addition s.3(11) of the 2009 Act sets out in greater detail than had been the case prior to that what are to be considered "other purposes that are of benefit to the community", the fourth *Pemsel* category. Section 3(11) states:

> In this section "purpose that is of benefit to the community" includes—
> (a) the advancement of community welfare including the relief of those in need by reason of youth, age, ill-health, or disability,
> (b) the advancement of community development, including rural or urban regeneration,
> (c) the promotion of civic responsibility or voluntary work,
> (d) the promotion of health, including the prevention or relief of sickness, disease or human suffering,
> (e) the advancement of conflict resolution or reconciliation,
> (f) the promotion of religious or racial harmony and harmonious community relations,
> (g) the protection of the natural environment,
> (h) the advancement of environmental sustainability,
> (i) the advancement of the efficient and effective use of the property of charitable organisations,
> (j) the prevention or relief of suffering of animals,
> (k) the advancement of the arts, culture, heritage or sciences, and
> (l) the integration of those who are disadvantaged, and the promotion of their full participation, in society.

In enshrining these "charitable purposes" in primary legislation for the first time, the 2009 Act was described as "seeking neither to narrow nor to broaden the purposes that have emerged through case law over the years". As well as being required to be established for a charitable purpose only, s.3 provides that charities must show that there is a public benefit to their activities. This is a longstanding requirement of charities. This provision is to deter charities being set up to benefit only a limited number of persons who may have a personal connection with the founder of the organisation.

Although the 2009 Act does not allow charities to support either a political candidate or a party, charities will be permitted to promote a political cause but only one relating directly to their charitable purpose.

At common law, there had been a presumption of public benefit for religious charities, which if retained in the 2009 Act would have effectively required the Charities Regulatory Authority in dealing with applications, particularly from newer religious organisations that have emerged in recent years. To counteract this, at report stage in the Dáil debate on the 2009 Act, this automatic presumption was removed and replaced by a rebuttable presumption. As enacted, the relevant provisions on this point are contained in s.3(4), (5), (6) and (10):

> (4) It shall be presumed, unless the contrary is proved, that a gift for the advancement of religion is of public benefit.
>
> (5) The Authority shall not make a determination that a gift for the advancement of religion is not of public benefit without the consent of the Attorney General.
>
> (6) A charitable gift for the purpose of the advancement of religion shall have effect, and the terms upon which it is given shall be construed, in accordance with the laws, canons, ordinances and tenets of the religion concerned...
>
> (10) For the purposes of this section, a gift is not a gift for the advancement of religion if it is made to or for the benefit of an organisation or cult—
>
> (a) the principal object of which is the making of profit, or
>
> (b) that employs oppressive psychological manipulation—
>
> (i) of its followers, or
>
> (ii) for the purpose of gaining new followers.

Charitable registration separate from taxation matters Section 7 of the 2009 Act clearly separates the functions of the Charities Regulatory Authority, which will be to consider the charitable status of organisations, from that of the Revenue Commissioners, which will remain fully responsible for deciding whether an organisation is eligible for charitable tax exemptions.

Exclusion of securitisation Section 8 of the 2009 Act excludes organisations that are involved in securitisation activities from the provisions of the Act. The Minister of State stated during the Oireachtas debate that the 2009 Act:

> "... was never intended to comprehend such organisations which play an important role in the Irish financial services sector. It is considered that placing an additional layer of administration on such organisations might damage Ireland's position as a suitable base for such organisations

and threaten jobs in the sector. These organisations do not fundraise directly from the public, and are essentially dormant for the majority of their existence".

Offences and penalties Section 10 sets out the penalties for both summary and indictable convictions for an offence under the 2009 Act. It provides, on summary conviction, for a maximum fine of €5,000 and/or imprisonment for up to 12 months; and, on conviction on indictment, for a maximum fine of €300,000 and/or imprisonment for up to 10 years. This clearly marks out the seriousness of the offences involved, and that the offences also constitute arrestable offences.

Charities Regulatory Authority Part 2 of the 2009 Act (ss.12 to 38) provides for the establishment and functions of the Charities Regulatory Authority (in Irish, An tÚdarás Rialála Carthanas). As pointed out during the Oireachtas debate, the Authority is the centrepiece of the regulatory framework in the 2009 Act. Schedule 1 of the 2009 Act sets out the legal status of the Authority, the appointment of its members and the procedures to be followed by it. The Authority will have a minimum of nine and a maximum of 15 members. At least three members will have a legal background and provision is also made for persons with experience of charitable work to serve as members. Members will be appointed by the Minister with the approval of the Government. Schedule 1 also sets out how and why members of the Authority might be removed from office, how conflicts of interest involving members or members of staff should be handled and empowers the Authority to establish committees to assist and advise it or perform functions that might be delegated to it.

Section 14 of the 2009 Act sets out in detail the functions of the Authority. In addition to its regulatory powers, the Authority will also have a supportive role for charities themselves in recognition of the fact that most charities in Ireland are small volunteer-run entities. It will also have a role in disseminating information on charities, in particular by establishing and maintaining a register of charities. This was regarded during the Oireachtas debate as being of critical importance in increasing transparency and enabling donors to make more informed decisions as to which charities they choose to support and to verify the charitable bona fides of any organisation.

Section 19 relates to the appointment of the chief executive officer (CEO). The Minister may appoint a chief executive officer in advance of the Authority itself being set up. Subsequent CEOs will be appointed by the Authority with the consent of the Minister. Section 20 provides that the CEO will be responsible for the efficient and effective administration of the Authority. Sections 22 and 23 provide for the accountability of the CEO to, respectively, the Oireachtas Committee of Public Accounts and other Committees of the Oireachtas separate from the Committee of Public Accounts. Section 25 allows for the transfer of staff from the Office of the Commissioners of Charitable Donations and Bequests for Ireland, which will be dissolved, to the Authority. It specifies that the terms and conditions applicable to such employees shall not be affected by the transfer, unless any such change has been discussed and agreed with the relevant union or association. Previous service with the dissolved body will be also reckonable under the relevant employment legislation.

The Authority will work closely with other regulators and law enforcement bodies. Thus, s.27 allows for disclosure of information by specified regulators, law enforcement bodies, or other organisations as may be prescribed by the Minister, relating to possible offences under this legislation, to the authority. Conversely, s.28 empowers the Authority to share information with other regulators and law enforcement agencies, both within and outside the State, where it suspects an offence has been committed. Any such information may be used only for the purpose of detection, investigation or prosecution of an offence. Having regard to the money-laundering context to reform of the law on charities, discussed above, the 2009 Act applies to charities based in other jurisdictions that also operate in Ireland. EU or EEA charities will not be required to have a place of business in the State. Thus, s.34, which allows for information sharing and co-operation with regulators in other jurisdictions, will prove extremely useful. This will include co-operation at EU level and the wider international setting, including, in particular, in conjunction with the OECD's Financial Action Task Force (FATF) on money laundering (see *www.fatf-gafi.org*). Up to 2009, FATF had developed over 40 Recommendations on Money Laundering and nine Special Recommendations (SRs) on Terrorist Financing which are intended to influence national policy and legislation to combat money laundering and terrorist financing. The FATF Special Recommendation 8 deals with Non-Profit Organisations and is therefore of particular relevance to charities. Ministerial approval will be required for any such co-operation arrangements, and the Minister must also prescribe the foreign statutory bodies concerned.

Attorney General's previous role Prior to the enactment of the 2009 Act, the Attorney General had a longstanding role as the "protector of charities"; this formed part of the Attorney General's role, under s.6 of the Ministers and Secretaries Act 1924, "in the assertion of or protection of public rights": see *Byrne and McCutcheon on the Irish Legal System*, 5th edn (Bloomsbury Professional, 2009), para.3.95. This role involved initiating legal proceedings in defence of charities, participating in proceedings brought by others, or carrying out certain functions under the Charities Act 1961: see, for example, *Re the Worth Library* [1995] 2 I.R. 301 (*Annual Review of Irish Law 1993*, pp.294–297). In the context of the new statutory regulatory framework for charities in the 2009 Act, with a strong yet supportive authority as the centrepiece, it was agreed that it was no longer essential for the Attorney General to have such a role. Therefore, s.38 transfers any relevant functions that were previously vested in the Attorney General to the Authority on the establishment day.

Register of charities Part 3 of the 2009 Act (ss.39 to 63) sets out in greater detail how the Authority will regulate the charity sector in practice. A key measure is the establishment for the first time, under ss.39 and 40, of a register of charities. The register is to be available to the public, including by electronic means. Section 40 provides for any organisation that has qualified for charitable tax exemptions to be automatically deemed to be registered as a charity. This provision was inserted at report stage in the Dáil and was designed to ease the administrative burden for the charities themselves, and for the Authority, which would otherwise have had to deal with a huge volume of applications for registration within a very short period. Under s.40, organisations whose charitable bona fides have already been examined and accepted by the Office of the Revenue Commissioners—it was estimated that there are in excess of 7,000 such organisations in 2009—will not be required to submit to the Authority the full range of material normally required from new applicants. Any relevant information may be provided by the Revenue, or requested by the Authority from the charity, if necessary. Organisations that do not hold charitable tax exemptions will be required under s.39 to apply directly to the Authority for entry onto the register and to provide the information listed in subs.39(5).

Sections 39 and 40 refer to charities established in the State, charities established in another EEA state and charities established outside the EEA, in the context of their providing information on their principal place of business to the Authority. It was pointed out in the Oireachtas debate that the legal advice to Government (presumably given by the Attorney General) was that it is not appropriate to insist that charities established in the EEA, although operating in this jurisdiction, have a principal place of business in Ireland. By contrast, it was deemed possible to insist on charities from outside the EEA having a principal place of business in the State. Therefore, there is a differentiation in ss.39 and 40 in terms of information to be provided by Irish charities and their EEA-based counterparts.

In the case of new applicants under s.39, the Authority is required to make a decision as to whether the applicant is a charity before entering it onto the register, inform the applicant of its decision and state the reasons for its decision where an application is refused. It is an offence for an applicant knowingly to provide false or misleading information to the Authority. Any organisation on the register must inform the Authority when any of the particulars relating to it entered on the register cease to be correct. The Authority will be responsible for maintaining the accuracy and integrity of the register.

The Authority must inform the Registrar of Companies whenever a company applies for entry onto the register, as the 2009 Act makes special provision for co-operation between these two bodies to minimise dual filing and regulation.

Section 41 makes it an offence for anyone to promote, or collect moneys, property or gifts for, a charity that is not on the register. This also applies to companies that are charities but which are not registered. The exception to this is where a decision is awaited in respect of an existing charity that has applied for registration under s.39.

Section 42 allows the Authority to refuse to register an organisation where its name is the same or very similar to that of another charity on the register, where the name is considered misleading for the public, or where the name is considered offensive. The decision of the Authority is subject to appeal. Section 42 also provides that a registered charity cannot change its name without the consent of the Authority. The Authority may also remove an organisation from the register where, having consulted the Garda Síochána, it forms the view that the organisation is an excluded body. Similarly, an organisation can be removed from the register for changing its name without the consent of the Authority, or for failure to comply with the various accounts, audit and provision-of-information obligations contained in the 2009 Act. Where the Authority forms the view that an organisation is not a charitable organisation any longer, or that a charity trustee is no longer eligible to hold such a position, it can apply to the High Court for consent to remove the organisation in question from the register. Whenever an organisation is removed from the register under s.43, the Authority will enter onto the register a statement to this effect, and the reasons for its removal. Section 44 allows the Authority, in similar circumstances to those covered by s.43, to remove from the register organisations "deemed" to be registered under s.40.

Section 45 sets out the process of appeal for bodies whose application to register has been refused, or where a body is removed from the register. Appeals will be heard by the Charity Appeals Tribunal, and the decision of the tribunal will be binding on all parties to the appeal, including the Authority itself. The Minister is also given a reserve right of appeal against a decision by the tribunal.

Holding out unregistered body as a charity It was noted during the Oireachtas debate that a major difficulty facing the public is the problem of differentiating between genuine charities and other organisations that are not so altruistic. In this context, door-to-door collections of clothes that are presented as charitable, but whose charitable bona fides are questionable, were mentioned during the Oireachtas debate. Such collections, though not illegal prior to the 2009 Act, had, it was stated, impacted greatly on donations of clothes to genuine charity shops. Section 46 of the 2009 Act was inserted to address the practice of non-charities creating a perception that they are charities. While such bodies may be careful to avoid describing themselves as charities, s.46

makes it an offence for any non-charity to describe itself or its activities in a way that would cause members of the public to reasonably believe they are charitable, irrespective of whether they actually use the word "charity".

Section 46 also requires any registered charity, unless specifically exempted, to describe itself as a registered charitable organisation in all public documents or in any other documentation that the Minister may prescribe. Section 46 also makes it an offence for a person to mislead the public as to where an organisation was established.

Accounts Section 47 requires charities, apart from those incorporated as companies that already have such an obligation under company law, to have available, on an ongoing basis, proper books of account for inspection by a person so authorised by the Authority. It is an offence not to do so. Section 48 places an obligation on charities, apart from those incorporated as companies, to prepare an annual statement of accounts in such form as may be prescribed by the Minister. Similarly, it is an offence not to prepare this statement of accounts. Section 49 requires the Companies Registration Office to forward to the Authority the annual return, as required under company law, of any company that is a charity and any attached documents. Section 50 places an obligation on charities, again apart from those incorporated as companies, to have their accounts either audited, in the case of charities with income or expenditure in excess of a threshold, which the Minister may prescribe, or examined by an independent person, in the case of smaller charities below the threshold. An "independent person" may be so prescribed by the Minister, and the nature of the examination will be a matter for the Authority. This graduated approach was intended to alleviate the burden on smaller charities. However, the Authority is also empowered where it considers it necessary or where a charity has failed to meet its obligations under this section for the Authority to direct any charity to have a full audit or itself appoint an auditor. Where the Authority incurs any costs arising from such an audit, they may be recouped from the charity concerned. Section 51 allows the Minister to make regulations in respect of the duties and operations of auditors or independent persons under the previous section. It shall be an offence for any person not to co-operate with an auditor in respect of any such powers vested in him or her by the Minister.

Section 52 provides that all charities, including those incorporated as companies, will have to provide an annual report on their charitable activities to the Authority. The nature of the annual report will be prescribed in regulations by the Minister. In general, charities will be required to submit their annual report, annual statement of accounts and the auditor or independent person's reports together to the Authority. In the case of companies that are not required under company law to annex their accounts to their annual return to the Registrar of Companies, their annual report under this section should be submitted with their company law accounts directly to the Authority. As part of the increased transparency in the 2009 Act, s.54 requires the Authority to make available to the public a charity's annual report and any documents attached to it. Given that the majority of charities fundraise from the public, it was considered that this provision serves a public interest. However, it was not considered that the same public interest applies to private charitable trusts which do not fundraise from the public, such as those set up by philanthropists. Therefore, although the Authority will hold information in respect of such private trusts, it will not be available to the public.

Reporting of offences or suspected offences Section 59 requires relevant persons to report to the Authority in writing where he or she, in the course of carrying out their duties, forms the opinion that an offence under the Criminal Justice (Theft and Fraud Offences) Act 2001 has been, or is being, committed. A "relevant person" includes an auditor, a charity trustee, an investment business firm or a person involved in preparing the annual report. Section 60 provides for qualified privilege in respect of any report prepared under section 59. Sections 61 and 62, "whistleblower" provisions, protect persons who report a suspected offence under either this legislation or under the Criminal Justice (Theft and Fraud Offences) Act 2001 from civil liability once they have acted in good faith.

Protection of Charitable Organisations Part 4 of the 2009 Act (ss.64 to 74) sets out the investigative powers of the Authority and the rights of the Authority to seek documentation from charities. Under s.64, the Authority may appoint an inspector to carry out investigations and to report to the Authority on the investigation. Section 71 provides that any such report may be evidence in any proceedings arising. Under s.65, charitable organisations, including trustees, or other persons believed to be in possession of relevant information, are required to co-operate with any investigation in terms of appearing before an inspector and providing documentation or records to an inspector on request. Where reasonable grounds for concern exist, the inspector may also request records of bank accounts held by a charity or a trustee. Section 66 provides that any report, or interim report, submitted by an inspector to the Authority may be sent by the Authority to specified persons or organisations, or published in full or in part.

Outside the specific context of an investigation, the Authority may from time to time require books, documents or records from a charity or from a person believed to be holding such records and s.68 makes the necessary provision. It is an offence not to co-operate with such a request for information from the Authority, although s.72 provides that legal privilege will apply to the production of certain documents under this Part of the Act. The Authority may also, under s.69, apply to the District Court for permission to enter and search premises where a charity does not comply with a request for information under the previous section. It is an offence not to co-operate with such a search. Any documents taken by the Authority will be subject to certain restrictions in terms of their subsequent use and may only be passed on to the specific "competent authorities" listed in the section.

In order to avoid the necessity to issue proceedings for what may only be minor, or unintended, breaches of the 2009 Act, under s.73 the Authority may impose intermediate sanctions on an organisation rather than initiate full proceedings. Examples of this might include where an organisation has failed to comply with its reporting or accounting obligations under the legislation. Such intermediate sanctions might involve the removal of an organisation from the register until it complies fully with its obligations or entering a statement of the contravention on the register.

As already indicated, the Authority will take over the role previously carried out by the Attorney General as "protector of charities". In this context, s.74 allows the Authority, where it considers that a charity or its property is at risk and where it is considered to be in the best interests of the organisation, to apply to the High Court for either an interim, interlocutory or permanent order to, for example, suspend, remove or even appoint a trustee.

Charity Appeals Tribunal In the case of a dispute concerning a decision of the authority, Pt 5 of the 2009 Act (ss.75 to 80) provides for an extra-judicial appeals mechanism, to be known as the Charity Appeals Tribunal, to help to avoid the costs associated with going to the High Court. This dispute resolution mechanism is intended to be accessible by all charities, regardless of their size. The tribunal will have five members and membership will include persons with a legal background and persons with expertise relating to charities. Its proceedings will generally be in public, although a "non-disclosure" provision is available if required. Decisions of the tribunal may be appealed to the High Court on a point of law.

Dissolution of Commissioners of Charitable Donations and Bequests for Ireland The Authority is also required to carry out the functions under the Charities Acts 1961 and 1973 currently carried out by the Office of the Commissioners of Charitable Donations and Bequests for Ireland, which is to be dissolved when the Authority is established. Part 6 (ss.80 to 87), contains standard provisions which allow for the transfer of statutory functions from the Commissioners to the Authority. This includes, for example, the transfer of land or property and the transfer of any business in hand to the Authority from the Commissioners.

Charity trustees and personal liability It was noted during the Oireachtas debate on the 2009 Act that charity trustees play a key role in the operation of charities. The 2009 Act therefore contains a number of provisions relating to the role of charity trustees. It would have been preferable if these had been located together in the 2009 Act, as they had been in the Scheme of the Charities Bill 2006. Unfortunately, when the 2009 Act was initially published as the Charities Bill 2007, it contained only two limited provisions on trustees, which became ss.56 and 57 of the 2009 Act. At later stages in its passage through the Oireachtas, three other significant sections were reinstated from the Scheme of the 2006 Bill, and these were enacted as ss.89 to 91 of the 2009 Act.

Section 55 lays out the circumstances under which a person may become disqualified from acting as a charity trustee. These include where a person has been convicted on indictment of an offence, has been imprisoned or where serious specified financial difficulties, such as bankruptcy, have arisen. Any person so disqualified may apply to the High Court for an order allowing him or her to act as charity trustee again. In the public interest, the Authority is also required under this section to establish and maintain a register of disqualified persons. Section 56 makes it an offence for a disqualified person to act as a charity trustee, though any actions undertaken by such an individual whilst so serving will remain valid. Any costs occurring to the charity or any benefits accruing to the disqualified person as a consequence of their actions shall be repayable to the charity.

Section 57 deals with the situation where a person within a charity acts under the direction of a disqualified charity trustee. It is an offence for a person to so act unless he or she had reasonable grounds for not knowing that the person was so disqualified. On conviction under this section, the person will also cease to be qualified to serve as a charity trustee. Section 58 follows from ss.56 and 57 in that it provides that a disqualified charity trustee convicted under s.56 shall be personally liable for any debts accrued by the charity as a consequence of their actions while illegally serving as a disqualified trustee. The same applies to a person convicted under s.57 of knowingly acting for a disqualified charity trustee. However, this section allows for the court to grant relief from such personal liability where it is considered appropriate.

At report stage in the Dáil and in the Seanad Committee Stage debate, what became ss.89, 90 and 91 were also included in the 2009 Act. Section 89 allows trustees and persons personally connected with trustees to receive remuneration in respect of non-trustee services provided to a charity. Section 90 empowers the courts to relieve a charity trustee of liability in certain circumstances. Section 91 allows charities to take out indemnity insurance in order that charity trustees are not personally liable for any losses accruing to the charity as a consequence of the performance of their duties. As already mentioned, these had been included in the Scheme of the Bill published in 2006, and were based on recommendations made in the Law Reform Commission's review of this aspect the reform of charity law: see above.

Prior to the enactment of s.89, charity trustees were not permitted to receive any remuneration from their charity for non-trustee services provided. Under s.89, a trustee may provide professional or other services unrelated to their trustee role to the charity, perhaps for a fee less than the going rate. Certain controls are in place to prevent abuse of the privilege and remuneration may only be paid where it is in the best interests of the charity and it must not be for trustee services. Section 90 provides that, in any proceedings brought against a charity trustee for breach of trust, where it appears to the court that the charity trustee is or may be liable in respect of the breach of trust "but... he or she acted honestly and reasonably and... having regard to all of the circumstances of the case he or she ought fairly to be excused for the breach of trust, the court may relieve him or her in whole or in part from his or her liability on such terms as the court deems appropriate." Section 91 seeks to address the fact that charity trustees were, prior to the 2009 Act, potentially personally liable for any losses accruing to the charity as a consequence of the performance of their duties, which acted as a disincentive to potential charity trustees by leaving voluntary charity trustees exposed to an unreasonable personal risk. Section 91 thus encourages individuals to take on the role of charity trustee.

Street and house-to-house collections Sections 91 to 96 of the 2009 Act also update certain provisions of the Street and House to House Collections Act 1962. This included the need to include in the 1962 Act the concept of collecting "promises of money" through direct debits or standing orders, which did not arise in 1962, whereas it has in recent years become important to charities in providing a steady and secure income stream. The 2009 Act amends the 1962 Act to bring this method of fundraising within the collection permit regime administered by the Garda Síochána under the 1962 Act for the first time, as well as enhancing the security and transparency of collections generally. The definition of the word "money" in the 1962 Act was also broadened beyond notes and coins. Another development in the area of fundraising which the 2009 Act also deals with had been the practice of selling items or tokens for a specific price. The 2009 Act also significantly updated the penalties for offences under the 1962 Act, from £50 to €5,000.

Fundraising regulation generally Section 97 empowers the Minister to make statutory regulations on fundraising, although it was pointed out during the Oireachtas debate that, initially, it is intended that non-statutory codes will be developed.

Social finance lenders Section 95 of the 2009 Act exempts social finance lenders from supervision under the financial services regulatory elements of the Markets in Financial Instruments and Miscellaneous Provisions Act 2007. They will instead be regulated by the Authority, thus avoiding dual regulation.

Mass cards Section 99 of the 2009 Act was added at report stage in the Seanad debate on the 2009 Act, with a view to regulating the sale of mass cards within the Roman Catholic Church. Section 99 creates an offence of selling a mass card other than under an arrangement with a "recognised person". A recognised person for the purposes of s.99 means a bishop, or a provincial of an order of priests established under the authority of, and recognised by, the Holy Catholic Apostolic and Roman Church.

Further possible reforms While the 2009 Act involves a major modernisation of the law in this area, it is unfortunate that the opportunity was not taken to provide for a complete replacement of the existing Acts in this area, notably the Charities Act 1961, the Street and House to House Collections Act 1962 and the Charities Act 1973. Rather, these Acts have been retained, albeit in amended form, alongside the major reforms in the 2009 Act. Additional reforms recommended by the Law Society and the Law Reform Commission concerning a tailored corporate structure for charities, the Charitable Incorporated Organisation (CIO), and a comprehensive statement of the duties of charitable trustees will have to await further legislative action. The concept of a CIO has been legislated for in the United Kingdom, but the Government and Oireachtas took the decision not to include this in the 2009 Act, indicating that this might be reviewed in light of experience with CIOs in the UK and other States. Indeed, s.6 of the 2009 Act provides for a mandatory review of the operation of the Act after five years in operation. Separately, a comprehensive statement of the powers and duties of trustees, including charitable trustees, may be enacted in a Trustee Bill which the Government is committed to publish (Government Legislation Programme, Summer Session 2010, April 2010), taking into account the recommendations in the Law Reform Commission's *Report on Trust Law: General Proposals* (LRC 92–2008) (see *Annual Review of Irish Law 2008*, pp.418–421).

Commercial Law

ARBITRATION

Set aside of award of arbitrator: doing justice in remittal In *S & R Motors (Donegal) Ltd v Moohan and Bradley (trading as Bradley Construction)* [2008] IEHC 383, Clarke J. set aside part of an award that, on its face, had been made in excess of jurisdiction. Nonetheless, it remitting the matter Clarke J. also ensured that the elements of the award which were within jurisdiction were, in effect, retained in order to ensure justice between the parties. The applicant, S & R Motors, was in dispute with the respondent, Bradley Construction, arising from Bradley Construction's work in building car showrooms for S & R Motors. In earlier proceedings in which Bradley Construction were plaintiffs, *Moohan and Bradley (trading as Bradley Construction) v S & R Motors (Donegal) Ltd* [2007] IEHC 435, Clarke J. had given liberty for Bradley Construction to enter summary judgment against S & R Motors on the basis of sums certified in architects certificates arising out of the construction contract. In effect, therefore, it was clear that these sums were due. Clarke J. had, however, placed a stay on the execution of any sum in excess of €112,000 "until the determination of an arbitration in respect of the claims made by S & R Motors relating to defective construction". The arbitration contemplated by the order ultimately proceeded before the arbitrator, who ordered that S & R Motors pay €117,000 to Bradley Construction, together with the costs of the arbitration, and that Bradley Construction pay S & R Motors €9,600 in respect of its defective construction claim.

As already indicated, S & R Motors sought an order setting aside the arbitrator's award and, to some extent, Clarke J. made the order sought. Nonetheless, in setting aside and remitting part of the award, he also limited the effect of the setting aside. Clarke J. accepted that, in relation to the sums awarded to Bradley Construction by the arbitrator, his own previous decision in *Moohan and Bradley (trading as Bradley Construction) v S & R Motors (Donegal) Ltd* [2007] IEHC 435, had already determined the amount due to Bradley Construction on foot of the construction contract and the architect's certificates issued in accordance with it, and that final judgment had been entered for that sum. Therefore, the entitlement of the respondents to payment per se was *res judicata*; it was not a matter that could have properly been reopened before the arbitrator, and nor was it either necessary or appropriate for the arbitrator to deal with those sums in his award. That the arbitrator had exceeded his jurisdiction was, therefore, apparent on the face of the record and it followed that the award of the arbitrator should be remitted to him to correct that error, and so that he could make whatever award he considered appropriate on foot of the claim for defective construction. It followed from that finding that the award of costs by the arbitrator must also be remitted for further consideration. On this matter, Clarke J. commented:

> "It does not seem to me to be appropriate to determine that the arbitrator was bound to award full costs to S & R Motors. True it is that, for the reasons I have already sought to analyse, S & R Motors must now have an award in their favour for defective workmanship. However, it is clear from cases such as *Veolia Water UK plc and Ors v Fingal County Council* [2006] IEHC 240 that, in claims which are partly successful and partly unsuccessful, a court should attempt to do justice between the parties by crafting an order which reflects the extent, if any, to which unnecessary costs may have been incurred in litigating issues upon which the party who was generally successful, nonetheless failed. It is clear that S & R Motors maintained a significant claim in respect of delay which wholly failed. It seems to me that it is for the arbitrator to determine, in accordance with the principles identified in the relevant jurisprudence, what, in those circumstances, the appropriate order for costs should be. The arbitrator must, of course, start from the basis that S & R Motors have succeeded in establishing some entitlement on their claim for defective workmanship and, *prima facie*, therefore, the event which costs must be said to follow was, at least to that extent, resolved in favour of S & R Motors. Whether and to what extent there are other factors properly taken into account which should lead the arbitrator to depart from a full order for costs in favour of S & R Motors is, in my view, a matter for the arbitrator."

In relation to the claim of S & R Motors relating to defective workmanship, Clarke J. noted that there was little dispute as to the applicable legal principles, both at common law and under the Arbitration Act 1954, where a court is asked to set aside an award. He referred to his judgment in *Limerick County Council v Uniform Construction Ltd* [2005] IEHC 347 and of Laffoy J. in *Uniform Construction Ltd v Cappawhite Contractors Limited* [2007] IEHC 295 (*Annual Review of Irish Law 2007*, pp.146–149), in which they had both analysed the relevant law and had come to the same conclusions. On this basis, Clarke J. held that it was clear that "an award can only be set aside where there is an error of law on the face of the award which is so fundamental that the court cannot stand aside and allow it to remain unchallenged". In the present case, he noted that the arbitrator had not rejected, as such, the unchallenged evidence of any expert. He did not, for example, find that the valuation, engineering or accountancy evidence was incorrect. Rather, the arbitrator came to the view that the proper course of action which should have been adopted under the contract and in all the circumstances was to have permitted the contractor, Bradley Construction, to carry out remedial works while still on site. Clarke J. held that the arbitrator had been "well within the arbitrator's entitlement to reach such a conclusion". Therefore, no case had been made out for the court interfering with the substance of the determination by the arbitrator as to the two amounts to be allowed in respect of defects.

DEBT ENFORCEMENT

The Enforcement of Court Orders (Amendment) Act 2009 (the "2009 Act") constituted an immediate, though ultimately stop-gap, response to the decision in *McCann v Judge of Monaghan District Court* [2009] IEHC 276; [2010] 1 I.L.R.M. 17 (see also the discussion in the Constitutional Law chapter, at pp.200–201, below). In *McCann*, Laffoy J. had held that the relevant provisions of the Enforcement of Court Orders Acts 1926 and 1940, as amended, were unconstitutional and thus invalid. This was, in particular, because they empowered the District Court to order the imprisonment of a person, such as the plaintiff, for non-payment of a debt in circumstances where the debtor had not appeared in court and where the court had thus been unable to make a finding that there had been wilful refusal to pay the debt, as opposed to inability to pay the debt. Since the enactment of the Debtors (Ireland) Act 1872, imprisonment for non-payment of debt has, at least in principle, been limited to those who wilfully refuse to pay a debt, as opposed to those who are unable to pay. Since the enactment of the Enforcement of Court Orders Acts 1926 and 1940, however, the 1872 Act is rarely used as the basis on which non-payment of debts is enforced. Instead, the 1926 and 1940 Acts, as amended, provide for a process in which a debtor may challenge in the District Court the basis on which the enforcement of a debt is sought. For a variety of reasons, including because the debtor was unable to obtain legal advice or legal aid and/or was unwilling to have their debts discussed in open court in their local District Court with the attendant likelihood that the case would be reported in the local media, many debtors did not attend in the District Court at the hearing under the 1926 and 1940 Acts. The result was often that an order was made under those Acts holding the debtor in contempt and leading to their imprisonment for non-payment. In the *McCann* case, Laffoy J. held that this outcome rendered invalid these aspects of the 1926 and 1940 Acts.

The key elements of the 2009 Act were to provide that an order can only be made under the 1926 and 1940 Acts after the debtor has appeared in court, and to provide for an extension of the Civil Legal Aid Act 1995 to encompass proceedings under those Acts. To that extent, the 2009 Act constitutes a full response to the deficiencies identified in the *McCann* case. Nonetheless, the 2009 Act must be seen as a stop-gap response to wider problems surrounding the law on debt enforcement in Ireland. These wider problems had been identified by FLAC, the Free Legal Advice Centres Ltd, in its 2003 Report, *An End Based on Means?* (available at *www.flac.ie*), in which reform proposals were made to deal with this matter. In September 2009, as part of its *Third Programme of Law Reform 2008–2014*, the Law Reform Commission published a wide-ranging *Consultation Paper on Personal Debt Management and Debt Enforcement* (LRC CP 56-2009), which built on the work of FLAC and on comparative developments in this area. In the Law Reform Commission's *Interim Report on Personal Debt Management and Debt Enforcement* (LRC 96-2010), to which we will return in the *Annual Review of Irish Law 2010*, the Commission notes that, by the end of 2009, a clear consensus had developed that fundamental reform of this area was required. The 2010 *Interim Report* contains a 14 Point Action Plan containing specific initiatives in the short term, pending medium term legislative proposals to be made by the Commission in a final Report on this area, which the Commission expects will be published by the end of 2010. If so, we will also return to this in the *Annual Review of Irish Law 2010*.

FINANCIAL SERVICES: POTENTIAL COLLAPSE OF SOME RETAIL FINANCIAL INSTITUTIONS AND RESPONSE TO STATE FISCAL DEFICIT

As noted in the *Annual Review of Irish Law 2008*, pp.61–62, a series of Acts beginning in late 2008 and proceeding well into 2009 were enacted in response to the potential threat that some of the main retail banks operating in Ireland might collapse. This potential collapse of the retail financial services sector coincided with an unprecedented deterioration in the State's fiscal position—a major factor in which was the sudden collapse of the housing market which resulted in a huge reduction in State receipts from stamp duty on property transactions and a corresponding reduction in income tax receipts because of increased levels of unemployment, in which the level of employment fell from just over 2 million to 1.8 million in less than 2 years. These events placed huge strains on the State's international rating in terms of its sovereign debt liabilities, and the Acts enacted in 2009 arose against this background. While these two major occurrences—the retail bank collapse and the sudden emergence of a massive State fiscal deficit—were not directly connected, the legislative responses to both were debated and enacted in close proximity. The merits and demerits of the strategies surrounding the economic and fiscal solutions, which were legislated for in the Acts discussed below, are outside the scope of this *Annual Review*. It is sufficient to mention here that the outcomes arising from these Acts were widely debated and scrutinised at national and international level, and this analysis continued well into 2010. Indeed, the proponents of the solutions enacted in these series of Acts accepted that the ultimate cost to, or possible profit for, the State may not be known for a decade.

Anglo Irish Bank nationalisation The Anglo Irish Bank Corporation Act 2009, the first Act of the Oireachtas enacted in 2009, provided, in effect, for the nationalisation of Anglo Irish Bank. The 2009 Act was enacted for the purpose of "maintaining the stability of the financial system in the State". This element of the purpose of the 2009 Act was necessary in order to ensure that the effective nationalisation, accompanied by enormous financial transfers from the State running to billions of euro, did not breach EU law on State aid to industries. The specific elements involved in the effective nationalisation were: (a) the transfer to the Minister for Finance or the Minister's nominee of all the shares in Anglo Irish Bank Corp Public Ltd Co; (b) extinguishing certain rights in Anglo Irish Bank, notably those of existing shareholders; (c) the removal of persons from certain offices, positions or employment within Anglo Irish Bank, notably those with executive responsibility and those at board level, and the appointment of persons to those offices or positions or that employment; (d) to provide for the appointment of an assessor to assess whether compensation should be paid to persons whose shares were transferred to the Minister for Finance or whose rights were extinguished, and if so to determine the fair and reasonable amount payable as such compensation; and (e) to provide for the payment of any such compensation. At the time of writing (September 2010), it remains difficult, even for the Government, to state with accuracy the final amount of financial transfers required to recapitalise the nationalised bank, taking into account the enormous losses it had incurred by this time. At the time of writing (September 2010), it is estimated that over €25 billion, spread over a series of tranches promised over a 10 years period, may be involved.

State guarantee for financial institutions, including deposits In the *Annual Review of Irish Law 2008*, p.61, we noted that the Credit Institutions (Financial Support) Act 2008 provided a State guarantee in respect of the relevant liabilities of the "covered financial institutions", in effect, any Irish-based financial institution. The Financial Services (Deposit Guarantee Scheme) Act 2009 complemented the 2008 Act by confirming in primary legislation a State guarantee for all deposits held in the covered institutions up to a maximum of €100,000 per deposit-holder. The 2009 Act also provided for the maintenance of a deposit protection account by the Central Bank and Financial Services Authority of Ireland (renamed the Central Bank Commission: see the Central Bank Reform Act 2010, to which we will return in the *Annual Review of Irish Law 2010*).

The details of the upper limit of the deposit guarantee were set out in the European Communities (Deposit Guarantee Schemes) (Amendment) Regulations 2009 (S.I. No. 228 of 2009), which amended the European Communities (Deposit Guarantee Schemes) Regulations 1995 (S.I. No. 168 of 1995) (*Annual Review of Irish Law 1995*, p.40). The 2009 Regulations also implemented Directive 2009/14. The changes made to the 1995 Regulations included (as already mentioned) increasing the statutory limit for the scheme from €20,000 to €100,000 per eligible depositor per institution; discontinuing the 10 per cent co-insurance requirement; extending the cover of the scheme to credit union savers; reducing the minimum payout period under the scheme; increasing the minimum contribution requirement by credit institutions to €50,000 (but this does not apply to credit unions); and ending the set-off requirement when making payouts under the scheme.

The Credit Institutions (Financial Support) Act 2008 was also supplemented by the Financial Measures (Miscellaneous Provisions) Act 2009. This 2009 Act amended the 2008 Act to allow the extension of the period in which financial support under the 2008 Act could be provided.

The 2009 Act also provided for the transfer of the assets of certain pension funds held by publicly funded bodies, including universities, to the National Pensions Reserve Fund, and the continued payment of benefits formerly payable from those funds.

National Asset Management Agency The National Asset Management Agency Act 2009, enacted in November 2009, provided for the transfer to the body established by the Act, the National Asset Management Agency (NAMA), of the property-related loans of the main Irish retail financial services institutions, whether banks or building societies. In effect, NAMA was established specifically to acquire these property-related assets for two connected reasons. First, it had become clear that the value of these assets had been unsustainably inflated in the period up to about 2007 and that they had to be substantially written down in the accounts of the financial institutions concerned in 2008 and 2009 and beyond, thus requiring enormous recapitalisation of these institutions in order to meet legislative prudential capitalisation requirements. Second, because it became equally clear that some of the individuals and corporate entities to whom the loans were given, many of whom were involved almost exclusively in property development, would be unable to repay all these loans, it was necessary to provide financial support in the short term in the hope that, in the longer term (in the order of 10 years), the "impaired" loans would recover some value and involve, at the least, a fiscally neutral transaction for the State.

As with many of the other related Acts enacted in 2009, the National Asset Management Agency Act 2009 sought to conform to EU law by stating it was enacted "to address a serious threat to the economy and to the systemic stability of credit institutions in the State generally". The main functions of NAMA are: the acquisition by NAMA of certain assets from certain persons to be designated by the Minister for Finance; effecting the expeditious and efficient transfer of those assets to NAMA; the holding, managing and realising of those assets by NAMA (including the collection of interest and capital due, the taking or taking over of collateral where necessary and the provision of funds where appropriate); the taking by NAMA of all steps necessary or expedient to protect, enhance and better realise the value of assets transferred to it; the facilitation of restructuring of credit institutions of systemic importance to the economy; to provide for the valuation of the assets concerned and the review of any such valuation; to give NAMA certain powers over land, including powers relating to the development of land; and for the issuing of debt securities by the Minister for Finance and by NAMA.

Once the 2009 Act was enacted, a key matter that received considerable public debate and attention was the discount on the current market value of the assets which NAMA would impose in the transfer of the property assets from the financial institutions (colloquially referred to as the "NAMA haircut"). When the first tranches of loans were transferred in early 2010, the discount varied from about 40 per cent for some loans up to 70 per cent for the first tranche of loans from the by-then nationalised Anglo Irish Bank.

Use of National Pensions Reserve Fund The investment of the National Pensions Reserve Fund and Miscellaneous Provisions Act 2009 facilitated the use of a large amount of the funds invested in the National Pensions Reserve Fund to finance the nationalisation of Anglo Irish Bank and the acquisition by NAMA of the property-related assets/debts of the retail financial institutions discussed above. This was done by amending the National Pensions Reserve Fund Act 2000 to provide for this. The 2009 Act also amended the Markets in Financial Instruments and Miscellaneous Provisions Act 2007 (*Annual Review of Irish Law 2007*, p.84), to provide for greater transparency in relation to certain kinds of trading in financial instruments.

Emergency financial measures, including public sector pay cuts, to stabilise the State's fiscal position The Financial Emergency Measures in the Public Interest Act 2009 and the Financial Emergency Measures in the Public Interest (No. 2) Act 2009 were, respectively, enacted at the beginning and the end of 2009. Both Acts had as their main objective, the beginning of the process of bringing the State's diminishing income into line with its outgoings. As already indicated, the national and international financial collapse, allied to a global recession that began in 2008 resulted in a gap of almost €20 billion between the State's projected annual expenditure of over €50 billion and its projected annual income of just over €30 billion. In order to bring about a reduction in the projected borrowing requirement to sustainable levels, and meet the EU Treaty Growth and Stability Pact target of three per cent borrowing levels, the two Acts under discussion here provided for unprecedented impositions and pay reductions. The first of the Emergency Measures Acts provided for the imposition of a public sector pension/superannuation payment or levy. This was intended to reflect more fully the actual cost of meeting the ongoing costs of such pensions or superannuations, including those under the Superannuation

Acts 1834 to 1963. In effect, of course, they were a direct method of raising a levy from public servants. The second of the Emergency Measures Acts provided for unprecedented real cuts in pay for virtually all public servants, ranging, in gross pay terms, from 7 per cent at the lower end to 20 per cent at the higher levels of pay. While these pay cuts would have been unthinkable even two years previously, when pay increases under the most recent Partnership Agreements had been approved between the Government, employers and trade unions, they did not result in national strikes by public sector employees. These had seemed likely, particularly in the wake of failed discussions between the Social Partners which had attempted, unsuccessfully, to avoid the pay cuts ultimately legislated for. The absence of national strikes can be attributed directly to the intervention of the Labour Relations Commission, which led, in early 2010, to an agreement on public sector transformation, known as the Croke Park Agreement, and which (by a relatively small minority) was later ratified by the public sector trade unions. Under this Agreement, the Government committed itself to refraining, until 2014, from introducing further public sector pay cuts in return for a wide-ranging public sector transformation and modernisation programme.

Payment services The European Communities (Payment Services) Regulations 2009 (S.I. No. 383 of 2009) implemented Directive 2007/64, the Payment Services Directive, which repealed Directive 97/5 (on cross-border credit transfers), and amended Directives 97/7 (on distance contracts), 2002/65 (on distance marketing of consumer financial services), 2005/60 and 2006/48 (on the taking up and pursuit of the business of credit institutions). The 2007 Payment Services Directive establishes a harmonised legal framework for the provision of payment services in the European Union and European Economic Area. The Directive: establishes who may provide payments services; introduces an authorisation and supervision framework for a new category of payment services provider called a payment institution; establishes transparency and information requirements to ensure that payment service providers give requisite information to payment service users; and sets out the respective rights and obligations of payment service providers and payment service users. The 2009 Regulations designate the Financial Regulator as the competent authority for the general purposes of the 2007 Payment Services Directive. In respect of Pt 3 of the 2009 Regulations, which concerns access to payment systems, they designate the Central Bank Commission as the competent authority.

INDUSTRIAL DEVELOPMENT

Transfer of shares in start-up companies from Shannon Development to Enterprise Ireland The Industrial Development Act 2009 (the “2009

Act") amended the Industrial Development Act 1986 (as amended) for three main purposes. First, the 2009 Act provided for the transfer of shares held by Shannon Free Airport Development Co Ltd to Enterprise Ireland. Following a change in the Shannon Development mandate in 2007, Enterprise Ireland took over Shannon Development's responsibilities in relation to indigenous industry in the mid-west region. Shannon Development holds shares in 28 client companies (listed in the Schedule to the 2009 Act) and it was necessary to transfer ownership of this equity to Enterprise Ireland. Most of these companies were regarded by the agencies as high potential start-up companies (HPSUs). Enterprise Ireland were advised that legislation was the only practical means of effecting this transfer, and of substituting Enterprise Ireland for Shannon Development in the various Shareholder Agreements and other documents relating to those shares. The 2009 Act effected this.

Increased grant limits Secondly, the 2009 Act provided for increasing the statutory limit on aggregate payments by the Minister for Enterprise, Trade and Innovation to the enterprise development agencies, and to certain thresholds above which agency grant payments to individual companies require government approval. Section 3 provided for an increase in the previous thresholds under the Industrial Development Act 1986 (as amended) above which Government approval was required, from €5 million to €7.5 million in each of the following cases—employment grants to industry, training grants, power to purchase shares and total investment grants to one company. The total aggregate threshold in the 1986 Act was also increased from €10 million to €15 million.

Intellectual property rights The 2009 Act also provided for the transfer of all property of the Minister for Enterprise, Trade and Innovation under s.19 of the Industrial Research and Standards Act 1961 to Enterprise Ireland. Prior to the 2009 Act, s.19(1) of the Industrial Research and Standards Act 1961 provided that any discoveries or inventions resulting from research carried out by or on behalf of Eolas, Forbairt, Forfas and Enterprise Ireland and the Institute for Industrial Research Standards are the property of the Minister. It was explained in the Oireachtas debate on the 2009 Act that there were a small number of cases where patents arising from research covered by s.19 of the 1961 Act were applied for by the agencies and were granted in the names of the agencies rather than in the name of the Minister. A number of such patent applications were still pending at the time the 2009 Act was being enacted. Some of these applications for patents and associated intellectual property rights, also covered by s.19, had been licensed to Irish companies carrying out further research based on the applications for patents. It might have created a serious problem for these companies if their title to any new intellectual property rights subsequently developed was shown to be defective. In some cases, the

Irish companies had sub-licensed aspects of the intellectual property rights to other companies. In most of these cases the licensee would have relied on a warranty that the licensor had good title to the rights being licensed. The 2009 Act dealt with this issue.

INSURANCE

Solvency margins The European Communities (Non-Life Insurance) Framework (Amendment) Regulations 2009 (S.I. No. 25 of 2009) amended Annex II of the European Communities (Non-Life Insurance) Framework Regulations 1994 (S.I. No. 359 of 1994) with regard to the solvency margin requirements of non-life insurance undertakings.

INTELLECTUAL PROPERTY

Patents rules and Patent Law Treaty The Patents (Amendment) Act 2006 (Certain Provisions) (Commencement) Order 2009 (S.I. No. 196 of 2009) brought the relevant elements of the Patents Act 1992, as amended by the Patents (Amendment) Act 2006 (*Annual Review of Irish Law 2006*, pp.85–91), into force on 21 May 2009 in order to implement the 2000 WIPO Patent Law Treaty. The Patents (Amendment) Rules 2009 (S.I. No. 194 of 2009) amended the Patent Rules 1992 in order to conform to the detailed requirements of the Patent Law Treaty.

Patents and other intellectual property rights: transfer The effect of the Industrial Development Act 2009 in terms of the transfer of intellectual property rights of the Minister for Enterprise, Trade and Innovation under s.19 of the Industrial Research and Standards Act 1961 is discussed above.

INTERNATIONAL TRADE

Dual use goods and technology: detailed export licensing controls The Control of Exports (Goods and Technology) Order 2009 (S.I. No. 305 of 2009), made under the Control of Exports Act 2008 (*Annual Review of Irish Law 2008*, pp.65–66), provides that the 2008 Act applies to the lengthy list of specific goods and technology set out in the Schedule to the Order. The effect is that the export of any goods or technology, or both, specified in the Schedule is prohibited except under, and in accordance with, a licence issued by the Minister for Enterprise, Trade and Innovation (formerly, the Minister for Enterprise, Trade and Employment). The goods and technology listed in the Schedule are derived from the Common Military List of the European Union, which sets out a detailed list of goods and technology which EU Member States have agreed must be subject to export licensing controls. The Common Military List is updated from time to time, and is based on key principles agreed by the EU Member States, now contained in Council Common Position 2008/944/CFSP defining common rules governing the control of exports of military technology and equipment, OJ L335 13.12.2008, p.99. The 2008 Common Position was adopted under Title V of the EU Treaty, art.15. The 2009 Order also revoked the Control of Exports Order 2005.

The goods and technology in the Schedule to the 2009 Order are listed under the following headings: smooth-bore weapons; ammunition and fuse setting devices; bombs, torpedoes, rockets, missiles, other explosive devices and charges and related equipment and accessories; fire control, and related alerting and warning equipment, and related systems, test and alignment and countermeasure equipment specially designed for military use; ground vehicles and components, including tanks and other military armed vehicles and military vehicles fitted with mountings for arms or equipment for mine laying or the launching of munitions; chemical or biological toxic agents, riot control agents, radioactive materials, related equipment, components and materials; "energetic materials" and related substances, including precursors which, when combined, have an explosive effect; vessels of war (surface or underwater), special naval equipment, accessories, components and other surface vessels; aircraft, lighter-than-air vehicles, unmanned airborne vehicles, aero-engines and aircraft equipment, related equipment and components, specially designed or modified for military use; electronic equipment, not specified elsewhere on the EU Common Military List, including Global Navigation Satellite Systems (GNSS) jamming equipment; high velocity kinetic energy weapon systems and related equipment; armoured or protective equipment, constructions and components; specialised equipment for military training; imaging or countermeasure equipment specially designed for military use, including infrared or thermal imaging equipment; forgings, castings and other unfinished products; miscellaneous equipment, including self-contained diving and underwater swimming apparatus; production equipment and components, such as centrifugal testing apparatus or equipment; directed energy weapon systems (DEW), related or countermeasure equipment and test models, including laser systems specially designed for destruction or effecting mission-abort of a target; cryogenic and superconductive equipment; software specially designed for military use; and other technology required for the development, production or use of items specified in the EU Common Military List.

Company and Insolvency Law

GRÁINNE CALLANAN, Lecturer in Company and Insolvency Law,
Waterford Institute of Technology

EXAMINERSHIP

The onus on the petitioner Section 2 of the Companies (Amendment) Act 1990, as amended (the "Act") sets down the statutory tests which must be satisfied before the court may exercise its discretion to appoint an examiner. From an evidential point of view the most onerous of these tests is found in s.2(2) which provides:

> The Court shall not make an order under this section unless it is satisfied that there is a reasonable prospect of survival of the company and the whole or any part of its undertaking as a going concern.

The onus is on the petitioner to satisfy the court that the company has a reasonable prospect of survival and it is this evidential burden that proved insurmountable in a number of high profile cases during the year, which for the most part concerned companies involved in the construction industry. In *Re Gallium Ltd*, High Court (ex tempore), January 13, 2009, McGovern J. dismissed a petition by an investment company which specialised in sourcing and placing equity and mezzanine finance for property development projects. The information provided to the court by the petitioner was considered "vague and nebulous" and included notable discrepancies in financial information. Although the company succeeded on appeal in having an examiner appointed (*Re Gallium Ltd* [2009] 2 I.L.R.M. 11) it was only because the petitioner had submitted new evidence to the court to explain the existing discrepancies, and crucially the only two opposing creditors withdrew their opposition and supported the examinership. The failure to adduce accurate evidence to the court was central to the failure of one of the country's largest construction groups to secure court protection in *Re Vantive Holdings & Ors (No. 1)* [2009] IEHC 384. The group, which consisted of 51 interdependent companies, owed such enormous amounts to its banks it prompted Kelly J. to remark:

> "It is sometimes said that when small or modest borrowers from banks encounter difficulties in repaying their loans, then such borrowers have a problem. For those with large borrowings, it is the banks who have a

> problem. If ever a case demonstrated the accuracy of that proposition, it is this one."

The principal activity of the petitioner was to raise finance for onward lending to related companies. The principal activity of the related companies consisted of purchasing land, developing those lands, investments and sales. The group was insolvent. In the event of a winding up it appeared that there would be a shortfall of over €1 billion. If the group collapsed the consequences for the companies, their banks and indeed the property market itself would be disastrous. The lending banks took no action against the group because to do so would bring down a "house of cards". Indeed, some banks continued to advance money to the companies in suit to enable them pay off all the other creditors with the notable exception of the Revenue Commissioners. However, one bank, ACC Bank Plc, broke ranks and issued a statutory demand for the repayment of debt owing within the meaning of s.214 of the Companies Act 1963. Against this background a petition was presented for the appointment of an examiner.

The independent accountant's report, which recommended the formulation of a compromise and scheme of arrangement, was considered seriously flawed. It was based on a three-year business plan, prepared by the company—but not presented to the court—which projected that if the group's development sites were completed and there was an orderly disposal of assets over these three years there would be a remarkable turnaround in the company's fortunes from a deficit of circa €1 billion to having net assets of almost €300 million. These projections were based on valuations which, as the court observed, were seven months old. A turnaround in the fortunes of the property market was anticipated without any evidence to support same. No evidence was provided to the court in respect of future financing which would allow completion of the development sites. Commenting on the independent accountant's report, Kelly J. said:

> "Given current market conditions and with little or no prospect for improvement in the future, on the basis of all the current economic indicators, this degree of optimism on the part of the independent accountant borders, if it does not actually trespass, upon the fanciful."

Kelly J. found the independent accountant's report to be inadequate and unconvincing. Accordingly, he was not persuaded by either the submissions by the company or the report of the independent accountant, which in any case he did not consider to be independent and objective. He was not satisfied that the petitioners had discharged the onus of proof showing that there was a reasonable prospect of the survival of the companies as a going concern. Accordingly, he refused to appoint an examiner.

In a secondary conclusion, Kelly J. indicated that even if some basis had been shown for a reasonable prospect of survival of the companies concerned he would not have been inclined to exercise the court's discretion in favour of the appointment of an examiner. He considered the exercise as presented to be somewhat "artificial" in that it appeared to be designed to increase the value of the properties for realisation as opposed to facilitating the survival of the companies as going concerns. With respect to the saving of enterprises and jobs, it appeared to him that of the 650 jobs apparently at risk should the companies be wound up, only 100 were held by direct employees. He considered the appointment of the examiner was designed to help the shareholders and this was not an objective contemplated by the legislation.

The decision of Kelly J. was appealed (*Re Vantive Holdings & Ors (No.1)* [2009] IESC 68). Murray C.J. observed that the first step a court must take in examining an application for the appointment of an examiner is whether on "the material placed before the court" it is satisfied that the company has a reasonable prospect of survival. Unless so satisfied, the court does not have the jurisdiction to exercise its broader discretion to appoint an examiner (referring to *Re Tuskar Resources Plc* [2001] I I.R. 668). Murray C.J. made it clear that:

> "Mere assertions on behalf of a petitioner that a company has a reasonable prospect of survival as a going concern cannot be given significant weight unless it is supported by an objective appraisal of the circumstances of the company concerned and an objective rationale as to the manner in which the company can be reasonably expected to overcome the insolvency in which it finds itself and survive as a going concern."

Murray C.J. further stated that the petitioner cannot satisfy this evidential burden by demonstrating that the assets of the company could be disposed of in a more orderly fashion for the benefit of the creditors. Nor can it satisfy the burden by demonstrating that liquidation would be a far less attractive option from the point of view of the members or the creditors of the company.

In reviewing the independent accountant's report the court found that it was based on a number of assumptions which were not verified by evidence. Those assumptions were based on the company's own three-year plan which in turn was based on assumptions about the upturn in the market and the likely value of the assets during this upturn. That plan had not been submitted to the court and the valuation reports which underpinned this plan were not submitted either. The independent accountant's report had not expressed an objective opinion in relation to the plan or its underlying assumptions and could not, therefore, be regarded as having any evidential value. No evidence was provided by the petitioner or the independent accountant as to the manner in which this three-year turnaround plan would be funded. With regard to the statutory burden placed on the petitioner by virtue of s.2(2) of the Act, the court was satisfied that it had not been met. Murray C.J. observed:

> "In short there is a complete absence of any objective evidence or material in the affidavits filed by the petitioner ... which could lead the Court to conclude that there were some underlying objective rationale or material supporting the petitioner's contention that the market conditions would change in the short to medium term so as to permit the properties in question to be disposed of in an orderly manner so as to enable it to benefit from any enhanced value."

In conclusion, the court upheld the order of the High Court and dismissed the appeal. The court did not consider it necessary to address the secondary conclusion reached by Kelly J. in the High Court in which he had indicated that he would have been disinclined to exercise his discretion to appoint an examiner even if the statutory burden under s.2(2) of the Act had been satisfied.

Presentation of second petition In *Re Vantive Holdings & Ors (No. 2)* [2009] IEHC 408, Cooke J. was asked to consider whether the court would hear a second petition for the appointment of an examiner. The petitioners submitted that they had a number of supplemental materials and evidence which were regarded as deficient during the first application. In particular they now had the company's business plan and the underlying property valuations which had been absent during the first hearing. They accepted that some of this information had been available to them at the time of the first petition but it had been withheld on the instructions of one of the directors, who was a 50 per cent shareholder, and whose judgement was somewhat impaired due to ill health. Cooke J. was satisfied that the Companies (Amendment) Act 1990, as amended (the "Act") did not preclude the presentation of a second petition and there could be special circumstances whereby a court would be reluctant to refuse a second petition where there was a reasonable prospect of saving employment, paying creditors more than in a winding up and the company, or at least a part of it, surviving as a going concern. On this basis the question for the court was whether such special circumstances existed in the present application. The court was satisfied that the new information, which could be examined in detail at the hearing of the petition, was sufficiently cogent and detailed to warrant that the petition be heard and the material considered.

ACC Bank Plc, who opposed the second petition, submitted that the application was an abuse of process because the issue as to whether an examiner should be appointed had already been decided and the case now being made could and should have been made at the first hearing. They relied on a number of authorities to support their contention that the second petition was an attempt by the petitioners to circumvent the Supreme Court's determination of the issue (referring to *Henderson v Henderson* (1843) 3 Hare 100; *Johnson v Gore Wood & Co* [2002] 2 A.C. 1; *Carroll v Ryan* [2003] 1 I.R. 309 and *AA v Medical Council* [2003] 4 I.R. 302). The court distinguished these authorities as the application before the court did not concern inter partes litigation but a "plea for the intervention of the court to protect the undertaking in the interests of the companies, their creditors, employees and other interested parties". The court did not consider that the matter was res judicata in a strict sense as new evidence and information would be put before the court which had not been available in the first application. Although Cooke J. was critical of the manner in which the information was withheld at the first hearing, he did not consider the decision to be a "malevolent attempt to conceal matters from the court with a view to misleading it". In conclusion, the court was satisfied that the overriding consideration must be the legislative objective of securing, if possible, the interests of the creditors and employees, of those doing business with the companies and the economy in general, by investigating any reasonable prospect of survival of the enterprise in whole or in part. On this basis the court found that there were good grounds to give the petition a second hearing.

Clarke J. refused the second petition on its merits (*Re Vantive Holdings (No.3)* [2009] IEHC 409) but in any event ACC Bank Plc had appealed the decision of Cooke J. The Supreme Court (*Re Vantive Holdings & Ors (No. 2)* [2009] IESC 69) accepted that the Companies (Amendment) Act 1990, as amended, did not preclude the presentation of a second petition should special circumstances or explanations arise. However, it did not accept that such circumstances arose in the present applications. Information was available to the company at the time of the first petition. While the court accepted that there was no bad faith on the part of the petitioner, the deliberate decision to withhold this information, in the face of legal advice to the contrary, was done for strategic reasons and the petitioner must bear the responsibility of the consequences of this decision. The Supreme Court agreed with the High Court that the rule of estoppel in *Henderson v Henderson* [1843] 3 Hare 100 did not strictly apply to an application of the kind before the court. Nonetheless, the court had the jurisdiction "to protect the integrity of the due process of the administration of justice and the finality, in principle, of a judicial decision". Applying this principle to the present application Murray C.J. stated:

> "The appointment of an examiner on foot of a petition has laudable objectives which in general terms is designed to facilitate the survival of a company as a going concern notwithstanding its insolvency if it demonstrates that it has a reasonable prospect of survival. Once the petition is lodged the company is entitled to the protection of the Court which may be to the serious detriment of its creditors and that protection continues while the matter is pending before the Court ... The protection of the Court could be artificially obtained if it were possible for a petitioner, after its first petition had failed, to proceed (even though such a step was not envisaged at the time of the first petition) with one or more successive petitions on the basis of additional evidence, notwithstanding it had been available and deliberately withheld, at the first petition, and thus extend further the protection of the court from its creditors pending

> at least a hearing which resulted in its refusal. Again, to permit a party to make the same application on foot of withheld evidence by way of petition, without excusing exceptional circumstances, would undermine the principle of finality which the Courts have always considered essential to the integrity of the administration of justice. As Hamilton C.J. observed in Re Greendale Developments Limited (In liquidation) (No. 3) [2002] IR 514 '...the finality of proceedings both at the level of trial and possibly more particularly at the level of ultimate appeal is of fundamental importance to the certainty of the administration of law, and should not lightly be breached.'"

Murray C.J did not consider there to be any "excusing exceptional circumstances" in the present application. Concerns about the confidentiality of information and the health of the principal shareholder and director were not sufficient to justify the withholding of information from the court. Furthermore, there were no other overriding considerations which would require the court to permit the second petition to go ahead. The court accepted that at various stages of the examinership process there are other interests to be taken into account which include creditors, employees and others who might benefit from the survival of the company, but these considerations do not in themselves override the obligations placed by law on the petitioner whose responsibility it is for the conduct and prosecution of an application. In these circumstances the Supreme Court was satisfied that the second petition constituted an abuse of process and the appeal was allowed.

The nature of an "undertaking" In *Re Laragan Developments Ltd* [2009] IEHC 390 the company had successfully petitioned for the protection of the court and the examiner had prepared proposals for a scheme of arrangement, in accordance with s.18 of the Companies (Amendment) Act 1990, as amended (the "Act"). When the examiner presented the proposals for approval by the High Court there were a number of objections from creditors. The company is a subsidiary company of Laragan (Holdings) Ltd which is owned by Mr Alan Hanly to the extent of 74.33 per cent and one other shareholder. Mr Hanly effectively controlled the subsidiary, the holding company and a number of other companies in the group. In general terms the group was involved in the construction industry, the hotel sector and similar ventures. On the evidence before it, the court found that during its existence the company was not an independent trading company, but rather was employed as a construction company for the purposes of carrying out building works for Mr Hanly personally and for other companies in the group. The court further found that the relationship between Mr Hanly and the company was not at arm's length and the company was little more than a vehicle of convenience for them. On the basis of the manner in which the company was operated Clarke J. did not consider that "the company can properly be the subject of examinership on a standalone basis, divorced from the other companies in the group". There was no enterprise to be saved for the benefit of the community and it was clear that no additional jobs would be saved by approving the scheme of arrangement. Accordingly, he did not consider that it was proper to describe the company as being an "undertaking" within the meaning of the Act (referring to *Re Traffic Group Ltd* [2008] 3 I.R. 253). He refused to confirm the scheme of arrangement and further ordered that the company be wound up. In *Re Vantive Holdings (No.1)* [2009] IEHC referred to above, Kelly J. referred to the artificiality of the tentative proposals which appeared designed to protect the company's shareholders rather than the survival of an undertaking as a going concern (see above).

Post-scheme solvency requirement In *Re Sharmane Ltd & Ors*, High Court (ex tempore), February 17, 2009, Finlay Geoghegan J. declared that the Act required that a scheme of arrangement

> "... be such that it then renders the company to which it applies solvent on the date of entry into force of the scheme of arrangement in the sense of then being capable of paying its debts (as per the scheme of arrangement) as they fall due".

The requirement of solvency is not a statutory precondition to the confirmation of a scheme of arrangement but it is clear that if the company cannot pay its debts as they fall due then its prospects for survival are not "reasonable". In *Re Vantive Holdings & Ors (No. 3)* [2009] IEHC 409, Clarke J. had similar reservations about the solvency of the group once interest moratoriums agreed with certain banks came to an end. He noted that an important factor in any determination, albeit not the only one, was the ability of the company to pay its debts as they fall due once it comes out of court protection. In this regard he observed:

> "It is trite to say that any company will be able to survive as long as its creditors do not look to be paid. Any company will, therefore, have a prospect of survival for so long as a moratorium is placed on it having to make payments to its creditors (or at least make payments which go beyond its income). What would be achieved, however, by placing a moratorium on any payments which the company could not meet unless, at the end of the period of the moratorium concerned, the company was in a fit state to operate into the future with a reasonable prospect of survival. The answer is simple. All that would be achieved in such circumstances would be an orderly wind-down of the company's affairs followed by a final liquidation (or receivership) at the end of the

moratorium period. As pointed out by the Supreme Court in its judgment in relation to the first petition in this case, such is not the purpose of an examinership."

It would now appear from these decisions that the solvency of a company coming out of court protection is central to any "reasonable" prospects of its survival. Compromises and schemes of arrangements which provide a moratorium on debt or interest as opposed to a complete write-down will be scrutinised by the courts to ensure that the examinership process is not being used as an artificial "hold and wait" strategy rather than a mechanism for facilitating the survival of an enterprise as a real "going concern".

Vesting of powers in examiner In order to enable the examiner carry out his statutory functions the Companies (Amendment) Act 1990, as amended (the "Act"), confers a number of powers on the examiner. Some powers vest automatically by virtue of his appointment while others are exercisable only at the discretion of the court. Section 9 of the Act permits the court, on application by the examiner, to vest all or any of the functions and powers of the company's directors in the examiner. Until recently, such an application was often sought where the examiner was required to borrow money to allow the company to continue trading pending the formulation of a compromise or scheme of arrangement (*Re Atlantic Magnetics Ltd* [1993] 2 I.R. 561 and *Re Holidair Ltd* [1994] 1 I.R. 416). Section 9 of the Act provides as follows:

> (1) Where it appears to the court, on the application of the examiner, that, having regard to the matters referred to in subsection (2), it is just and equitable to do so, it may make an order that all or any of the functions or powers which are vested in or exercisable by the directors (whether by virtue of the memorandum or articles of association of the company or by law or otherwise) shall be performable or exercisable only by the examiner.
> (2) The matters to which the court is to have regard for the purpose of subsection (1) are—
> (a) that the affairs of the company are being conducted, or are likely to be conducted, in a manner which is calculated or likely to prejudice the interests of the company or of its employees or of its creditors as a whole, or
> (b) that it is expedient, for the purpose of preserving the assets of the company or of safeguarding the interests of the company or of its employees or of its creditors as a whole, that the carrying on of the business of the company by, or the exercise of the powers of, its directors or management should be curtailed or regulated in any particular respect, or

(c) that the company, or its directors, have resolved that such an order should be sought, or
(d) any other matter in relation to the company the court thinks relevant.

(3) Where the court makes an order under subsection (1), it may, for the purpose of giving full effect to the order, include such conditions in the order and make such ancillary or other orders as it sees fit.

(4) Without prejudice to the generality of subsections (1) and (3), an order under this section may provide that the examiner shall have all or any of the powers that he would have if he were a liquidator appointed by the court in respect of the company and, where such order so provides, the court shall have all the powers that it would have if it had made a winding-up order and appointed a liquidator in respect of the company concerned.

If the examiner does not seek an order under s.9 to have some or all of the functions and powers of the board vested in him, then the directors continue to manage the affairs of the company. While the examiner may be quite satisfied with leaving the board to continue with its functions and powers he may require that the court confer on him any or all of the powers of a liquidator pursuant to s.9(4) of the Act. Whether the examiner can apply for an order under s.9(4) independently of any application under s.9(1) was given judicial consideration in *Re Fate Park Ltd and Related Companies* [2009] IEHC 375. Here, the examiner of the company applied to the High Court under s.9(4) of the Act for certain powers that he would have as a liquidator of the company. In particular the examiner sought to disclaim an onerous contract between the company and a substantial shareholder—a power exercisable by a liquidator under s.290 of the Companies Act 1963. The examiner had formed the view that the contract in question was unprofitable and a termination could not be negotiated. The disclaimer was required by the proposed investor and was therefore necessary to ensure the success of the proposals for a compromise or scheme of arrangement. In seeking the order under s.9(4) the examiner had not sought an order under s.9(1) of the Act to have any of the functions or powers of the directors exercisable by the examiner.

The principal issue before the court related to whether s.9(4) of the Act conferred a distinct jurisdiction on the court to make an order that an examiner have any or all powers of a liquidator or whether an order under s.9(4) was dependent on an order being made under s.9(1) of the Act. Counsel for the examiner contended that the court had independent jurisdiction and to support this contention relied on the judgment of Finlay C.J. in *Re Holidair Ltd* [1994] 1 I.R. 41. In his judgment the former Chief Justice had suggested that subs.4 vested an "additional authority" in the court to give an examiner additional powers over and above those of the directors. Finlay Geoghegan J. distinguished *Holidair* on the grounds that the former Chief Justice's comments were made in the context of whether an examiner, in applying for the directors' power to borrow under s.9(1), was subject to the same contractual limitations on such borrowing as the directors of the company or whether an order could include powers not exercisable by the directors. The issue as to whether or not the court could make an order under s.9(4) independently of making an order under s.9(1) had not arisen.

In giving s.9 its ordinary meaning, Finlay Geoghegan J. was satisfied that an order could only be made under s.9(4) where an order had been made under s.9(1). Accordingly, s.9(4) could not be construed independently and the court did not have the jurisdiction to make an order under the subsection.

Counsel for the examiner then submitted that if the court did not construe s.9(4) as giving independent jurisdiction to the court then the court would now have jurisdiction to make an order under s.9(1) and then add a liquidator's power to disclaim. As the disclaimer was necessary to secure the proposed investment and to ensure the success of the compromise and scheme of arrangement then it should be considered a "matter in relation to the company" under s.9(2)(d) of the Act. The court rejected this submission. Finlay Geoghegan J. stated that the grounds upon which the court may transfer executive powers primarily related to the manner in which the directors were conducting the affairs of the company. Accordingly, the requirement by the proposed investor that the contracts be disclaimed was not a "matter in relation to the company" for the purposes of s.9(2)(d) in the absence of evidence as to what the directors did or did not do in the context of this request by the investor. She noted by way of example that there was no suggestion that the directors were requested by the examiner to procure that the company seek the approval of the court for a repudiation of the contract under s.20 of the Act and that they had refused to do so. On this basis Finlay Geoghegan J. was not satisfied that the examiner had made out any grounds under s.9(2) which would enable the court exercise a jurisdiction under s.9(1). In the absence of the court making an order under s.9(1) the court had no jurisdiction to make an order under s.9(4). The application was accordingly refused.

Repudiation of contracts during examinership An examiner's power to repudiate contracts entered into by the company prior to his appointment is very restricted by virtue of s.7(5A) of the Companies (Amendment) Act 1990, as amended, (the "Act"). However, where the examiner is formulating a compromise or scheme of arrangement, the company itself may apply to the court to have certain contracts repudiated pursuant to s.20(1) of the Act which provides:

> Where proposals for a compromise or scheme of arrangement are to be formulated in relation to a company, the company may, subject to the approval of the court, affirm or repudiate any contract under which

> some element of performance other than payment remains to be rendered both by the company and other contracting party of parties.

Where the court grants leave to repudiate, any person who suffers loss or damage as a result of such repudiation shall stand as an unsecured creditor for the amount of such loss or damage (s.20(2) of the Act). The court may hold a hearing to determine the loss of any affected party (s.20(3) of the Act). Section 20 does not specify the types of contracts which may be repudiated but it is clear from the section that an application will not be permitted if the only unperformed element of the contract is the payment of money. In *Re O'Brien's Irish Sandwich Bars Ltd* [2009] IEHC 465, Ryan J. questioned whether leasehold contracts could be repudiated pursuant to s.20(1). In this application the company ran a franchise business where the company licensed franchisees to operate under its name. One of the features of the business was that the company leased premises suitable for its business product and then sub-let those premises to the franchisees. When some of these franchisees experienced financial difficulties the company was left servicing the head-leases for premises which were unoccupied and for others where franchisees were continuing to operate but doing so in arrears on their rental payments. This was one of the main reasons why the company itself became insolvent.

An examiner had been appointed to the company and negotiations had taken place with an outside investor. The investor required that the company either surrender or repudiate all leases so that the business would become a strictly franchise operation with no leasing obligations. Essentially the scheme of arrangement envisaged, inter alia, the franchisees stepping up to become direct lessees in place of the company. Some landlords had agreed to the proposed arrangement but others had not done so and the deadline for the agreement with the proposed investor was looming. Accordingly, the company applied to the High Court for the approval of the repudiation of all the leases it held and in respect of which an agreement had not been reached.

Ryan J. contrasted the wording of s.20 with the disclaimer provisions of s.290 of the Companies Act 1963 which makes specific provision for the disclaimer of onerous leasehold contracts in liquidations (s.290(8)). He did not consider that this specifically excludes the application of s.20 to a lease but he did regard it as a significant omission. Turning then to the wording of s.20(1) he tentatively concluded that s.20 would not permit the repudiation of entire leasehold contracts. In this regard he observed:

> "There may well be circumstances where non-pecuniary obligations under a lease remain to be performed by an insolvent company, and the loss or damage resulting from repudiation can be determined by a court under sub-section (3) of section 20. However, I do not think that s.20 permits the repudiation of entire contracts with all elements of performance, including money payments, because that would, in my

view, be to ignore the restriction that is contained in sub-section (1) to residual performance elements other than payment."

In any case he was satisfied that even if his interpretation of s.20 of the Act was incorrect he did not consider that the court should exercise its discretion in this case. There were over 40 separate leasehold contracts to consider and the consequences of the repudiation had not been assessed in relation to the individuals affected. The time constraints required to ensure the scheme was implemented meant that the court could not hold a hearing to determine the amount of loss or damage consequent on repudiation. As s.20(3) envisaged such a hearing he was not prepared to put business exigencies "over fundamental requirements of justice and even constitutionally mandated protections".

In *Re Linen Supply of Ireland Ltd* [2009] IEHC 544 the release of a company from onerous leases was once again central to a proposed scheme of arrangement. The company was the leading vendor of washroom hygiene products, textile services and mats. It operated from a number of premises in which it held a leasehold interest. An examiner had been appointed to the company and in an attempt to formulate a scheme of arrangement two applications were made to the High Court. The first was on behalf of the company for an order pursuant to s.20(1) of the Act approving the repudiation of a number of leases, and the second was one made by the examiner for an order pursuant to s.9(1) of the Act transferring the functions and the powers exercisable by the directors to the examiner. The examiner had also sought an order under s.9(4) to have a liquidator's power to disclaim an onerous contract vested in him. This order was sought as an alternative to the application by the company and on the basis that the company would not succeed.

Counsel for the landlords of the premises opposed the application and submitted that s.20(1) did not apply to a repudiation of a lease. They argued that the only element of performance remaining to be rendered was the payment of rent and on that basis it did not come within the ambit of the s.20(1) of the Act. The company submitted that the leases involved duties and obligations on the parties to the lease which go beyond payment of rent and were therefore within the ambit of s.20(1). The court was invited to consider what was meant by the words "... any contract under which some element of performance other than payment remains to be rendered, both by the company and the other contracting party or parties". McGovern J. referred to the aforementioned judgment of Ryan J. in *Re O'Brien's Irish Sandwich Bars Ltd* and his commentary in relation to the application of s.20(1) to leasehold contracts. Counsel for the landlords referred the court to s.25B of the Act which states:

> 1. Subject to subsection (3), proposals for a compromise or scheme of arrangement shall not contain, nor shall any modification by the court under section 24 of such proposals, result in their containing a provision providing for either or both:

(a) a reduction in the amount of any rent or other periodical payment reserved under a lease of land that falls to be paid after the compromise or scheme of arrangement would take effect under section 24(9) or the complete extinguishment of the right of the lessor to any such payments,

(b) as regards a failure—

(i) to pay an amount of rent or make any periodical payment reserved under a lease of land, or

(ii) to comply with any other covenant or obligation of such a lease,

that falls to be paid or complied with after the date referred to in paragraph (a), a requirement that the lessor under such a lease shall not exercise, or shall only exercise in specified circumstances, any right, whether under the lease or otherwise, to recover possession of the land concerned, effect a forfeiture of the lease or otherwise enter on the land or recover the amount of such rent or other payment or to claim damages or other relief in respect of the failure to comply with such a covenant or obligation.

2. Subject to subsection (3), proposals for a compromise or scheme of arrangement in relation to a company shall not be held by the court to satisfy the conditions specified in paragraph (c)(ii) of section 24(4) if the proposals contain a provision relating to a lease of, or any hiring agreement in relation to property other than land and, in the opinion of the court—

(a) the value of that property is substantial, and

(b) the said provisions of like effect to a provision referred to in paragraph (a) or (b) of subsection (1).

3. Subsection (1) or (2) shall not apply if the lessor or owner of the property concerned has consented in writing to the inclusion of the provision referred to in subsection (1) or (2) in the proposals for the compromise or scheme of arrangement.

4. In deciding, for the purpose of subsection (2), whether the value of the property concerned is substantial, the matters to which the court shall have regard shall include the length of the unexpired form of the lease or hiring agreement concerned.

Counsel for the landlords submitted that s.25B is a self-contained provision dealing with the position of leaseholds where proposals or a compromise for a scheme of arrangement are being drawn up. If s.20 permitted a repudiation of a lease, s.25B would have no effect. The court accepted this submission. McGovern J. observed:

"It seems to me that the thrust of s. 25B of the Act is to the effect that

> a Scheme of Arrangement cannot provide for a reduction in rent or an extinguishment of the right of the lessor to the payment of rent that falls to be paid after the compromise or Scheme of Arrangement would take effect, unless the lessor or owner of the property concerned has consented in writing to the inclusion of such a provision in the proposals for the compromise or Scheme of Arrangement. If s. 20 of the Act was to permit the repudiation of a lease, it would be completely at variance with s. 25B. Since s. 25B specifically refers to leases, as does s. 290 of the Principal Act, I have come to the conclusion that s. 20 of the Act does not permit the court to make an order entitling the company to repudiate the leases in this case."

McGovern J. then turned to the examiner's application pursuant to s.9(1) of the Act. He observed that the examiner was seeking the order for the purpose of disclaiming the onerous leases. This, he stated, was problematic in the context of s.25B of the Act. This provision required that unless the landlord consents in writing, the examiner cannot curtail or extinguish any entitlement of the landlord to rental payments after the scheme of arrangement comes into effect. He concluded that while an examiner might be given all or any of the powers of a liquidator, those powers could not include the power to disclaim a lease for the purposes of preparing a scheme of arrangement. Accordingly he refused the application of the examiner.

The decision of McGovern J. caused some confusion for examiners. The de facto position, acknowledged by McGovern J., had been that the courts were permitting the disclaimer and repudiation of leases by companies or by the examiner up until this case. Unsurprisingly, the decision was appealed and given the time constraints involved in formulating schemes of arrangement the Supreme Court delivered an ex tempore judgment six days later (COS 467/2009).

In construing s.20 of the Act, Murray C.J. was satisfied that given its ordinary meaning, the term "contract" did include a lease, and had the legislature intended to exclude leases from the term "contract" it would have done so explicitly. With regard to the limitations of s.20(1) to contracts "under which some element of performance other than payment remains to be rendered" by the company and other contracting parties, he was satisfied that a lease involves the performance of obligations by both the lessor and the lessee other than payment of money. He gave by way of example, "the right to quiet enjoyment and to obligations to insure". He observed that it had not been shown that the obligations arising under the leases in this case were confined to the making of payments. He further rejected the finding that s.25B of the Act effectively removed leases from the repudiation provisions of s.20. He stated that s.25B is concerned only with the variation or even the complete extinguishment of the rights of the lessor to payment of any rent while the lessee continues to have the benefit of the property the subject of the lease.

Repudiation, involving the mutual release of both the lessor and the lessee from all rights and obligations, was an entirely different matter and not within the ambit of s.25B. Accordingly, he concluded that leases were repudiable under s.20 and he remitted the matter to the High Court to decide whether or not it should exercise its discretion under s.20(1) of the Act.

Costs and expenses of examiner In *Re Sharmane Ltd & Related Companies* [2009] IEHC 556 the High Court held that an examiner was not entitled to an order that all 13 companies in a group of companies to which he was appointed be jointly and severally liable for the costs and expenses of the examiner. The examiner had been appointed to Sharmane Ltd pursuant to s.2 of the Companies (Amendment) Act 1990 (the "Act"). He was also appointed pursuant to s.4 of the Act to a number of related companies. By order of the High Court, pursuant to s.26 of the Act, court protection eventually ceased for all companies. The examiner sought an order that all 13 companies to which he was appointed be jointly and severally liable for such amount as may be determined in respect of the aggregate remuneration, costs and expenses incurred by the examiner whilst appointed examiner of Sharmane Ltd and its related companies. Section 29 of the Act provides:

> (1) The court may from time to time make such orders as it thinks proper for payment of the remuneration and costs of, and reasonable expenses properly incurred by, an examiner.
> (2) Unless the court otherwise orders, the remuneration, costs and expenses of an examiner shall be paid and the examiner shall be entitled to be indemnified in respect thereof out of the revenue of the business of the company to which he has been appointed, or the proceeds of realisation of the assets (including investments).
> (3) The remuneration, costs and expenses of an examiner which have been sanctioned by order of the court (other than the expenses referred to in subsection (3A)) shall be paid in full and shall be paid before any other claim, secured or unsecured, under any compromise or scheme of arrangement or in any receivership or winding-up of the company to which he has been appointed.
> (3A) Liabilities incurred by the company to which an examiner has been appointed that, by virtue of section 10(1), are treated as expenses properly incurred by the examiner shall be paid in full and shall be paid before any other claim (including a claim secured by a floating charge), but after any claim secured by a mortgage, charge, lien or other encumbrance of a fixed nature or a pledge, under any compromise or scheme of arrangement or in any receivership or winding-up of the company to which he has been appointed.
> (3B) In subsections (3) and (3A) references to a claim shall be deemed

> to include references to any payment in a winding-up of the company in respect of costs, charges and expenses of that winding-up (including the remuneration of any liquidator).
> (4) The functions of an examiner may be performed by him with the assistance of persons appointed or employed by him for that purpose provided that an examiner shall, insofar as is reasonably possible, make use of the services of the staff and facilities of the company to which he has been appointed to assist him in the performance of his functions.
> (5) In considering any matter relating to the costs, expenses and remuneration of an examiner the court shall have particular regard to the proviso to subsection (4).

Finlay Geoghegan J. considered s.29 in the context of the overall statutory scheme which envisages the appointment of the same person as examiner to a company pursuant to s.2(1) of the Act, and also as examiner to each of one or more related companies pursuant to s.4 of the Act. She observed that s.4(4) emphasises that where an examiner is appointed to related companies he shall have the same powers and duties in relation to each company, taken separately, unless the court otherwise directs. The examiner submitted that much of the work done by him in the course of his appointment as examiner to Sharmane Ltd and to each of the related companies may have been simultaneously done for the purpose of formulating schemes of arrangement or otherwise performing his duties in relation to several of the companies. However, the court observed that the remuneration and costs now sought by the examiner were significantly higher than they would have been had he been appointed to only one company.

If the examiner obtained the order sought he could then look to any one of the companies to discharge the entire of his aggregate remuneration and expenses. The court considered that this was contrary to the provisions of s.29(2) having regard, in particular, to the priority given to remuneration, costs and expenses of an examiner under s.29(3) of the Act. As s.29(2) provides that the remuneration of an examiner is to be paid out of "the revenue of the business of the company to which he has been appointed, or the proceeds of realisation of the assets of that company", the court was satisfied that an examiner was only entitled to have his remuneration, costs and expenses incurred when acting as an examiner of a relevant company to be discharged from the revenue or assets of that company. There was no basis for construing s.29(2) as permitting an examiner who is appointed to a company and a related company to look to the revenue or assets of either company to discharge his aggregate remuneration, costs and expenses. This is the effect that an order for joint and several liability would have if granted. As the priority position given to the examiner's remuneration, costs and expenses by virtue of s.29(3) of the Act was a potentially significant interference with the property rights of secured creditors, the court considered that it should be construed strictly. In conclusion, the court refused the order sought and held that the examiner was entitled, pursuant to s.29 of the Act, to approval of such separate amounts as may be determined by the court for his reasonable remuneration, costs and expenses in respect of the work done as examiner for each of the companies from the separate revenue or assets of each of those relevant companies.

Examiners and NAMA By virtue of the National Asset Management Agency Act 2009 ("NAMA Act") s.2 of the Companies (Amendment) Act 1990 has been amended by the insertion of a new subs.(5) which provides:

> (5) The court shall not make an order under this section unless—
> (a) the court is satisfied that the company has no obligations in relation to a bank asset that has been transferred to the National Management Agency or a NAM group entity, or
> (b) if the company has any such obligation–
> (i) a copy of the petition has been served on that Agency, and
> (ii) the court has heard that Agency in relation to the making of the order.

Similar provisions apply in the case of a petition to appoint an examiner to related companies under s.4 of the Companies (Amendment) Act, 1990.

Under the NAMA Act, a statutory receiver may be appointed over acquired assets where a power of sale becomes exercisable or the power to appoint a receiver becomes exercisable. Where a statutory receiver is appointed in such circumstances he will have the same powers, rights and obligations that a receiver has under the Companies Acts 1963–2009. However, certain limitations normally applying to receivers by virtue of the Companies (Amendment) Act 1990 will not apply to statutory receivers. By virtue of s.150 of the NAMA Act, where an examiner is appointed to a company whose assets or any part of them are under the control of a statutory receiver, such an appointment will not displace the statutory receiver or affect his powers, authority or agency, prevent the statutory receiver from enforcing any security held by NAMA or cause the de-crystallisation of any charge created as a floating charge over assets that are under the control of the statutory receiver.

FRAUDULENT AND RECKLESS TRADING

Intentional under-declaration and under-payment of revenue liabilities In *Re PSK Construction Ltd (in voluntary liquidation)* [2009] IEHC 538 the liquidator sought various orders against the respondents including, inter alia, orders pursuant to s.297A of the Companies Act 1963 for fraudulent and reckless trading. The first-named respondent, Mr Killeen, the managing director of the company, had worked in the construction industry since his teens. In 2001 he incorporated his own construction company which obtained a number of contracts on substantial developments in Dublin. In its early years the company traded successfully. Despite the fact that the company had circa 200 employees during the year 2004/2005 and a turnover of circa €16 million, it did not employ a financial controller or an accountant. Basic accounting was done by under-qualified office employees. By 2004/2005 the company became involved in unprofitable contracts which ultimately led to its insolvency. The respondent had little education and had averred that he had no experience of employing professionals such as quantity surveyors.

By 2005 the company was in serious financial difficulty and the company's auditor had recommended the company cease trading. The respondent ignored this advice. As the company was still engaged in loss-making contracts the respondent took the decision to both under-declare and under-pay certain of the company's revenue liabilities for a number of months in 2005 with a view to trading out of the difficulties. The underpayment to the Revenue for this period was circa €1.6 million.

Section 297A(1) of the Companies Act 1963 provides:

> If in the course of winding up of a company or in the course of proceedings under the Companies (Amendment) Act, 1990, it appears that—
>
> (a) any person was, while an officer of the company, knowingly a party to the carrying on of any business of the company in a reckless manner; or
>
> (b) any person was knowingly a party to the carrying on of any business of the company with intent to defraud creditors of the company, or creditors of any other person or for any fraudulent purpose;
>
> the court, on the application of the receiver, examiner, liquidator or any creditor or contributory of the company, may, if it thinks it proper to do so, declare that such person shall be personally responsible, without any limitation of liability, for all or any part of the debts or other liabilities of the company as the court may direct.

With regard to the reckless trading provision of s.297A(1)(a) above, Finlay Geoghegan J. referred to the principal Irish authority of *Re Heffernon Kearns Ltd (No.2)* [1993] 3 I.R. 191. Here Lynch J. referred to the objective test of recklessness set out by the Supreme Court in its decision in *Donovan v Landys Ltd* [1963] I.R. 441 where Kingsmill Moore J. cited with approval a passage from the judgment of Megaw J. in the English High Court in *Shawninigan v Vokins* [1961] 1 W.L.R. 1206 as follows:

> "In my view, 'reckless' means grossly careless. Recklessness is gross carelessness - the doing of something which in fact involves a risk whether the doer realises it or not; and the risk being such, having regard to all the circumstances, that the taking of that risk would be described in ordinary parlance as 'reckless'. The likelihood or otherwise that damage will follow is one element to be considered, not whether the doer of the act actually realised the likelihood. The extent of the damage which is likely to follow is another element, not the extent which the doer of the act, in his wisdom or folly, happens to foresee. If the risk is slight and the damage which will follow if things go wrong is small it may not be reckless, however unjustified the doing of that act may be. If the risk is great, and the probable damage great, recklessness may readily be a fair description however much the doer may regard the action as justified and reasonable. Each case has to be viewed on its own particular facts and not by reference to any formula. The only test, in my view, is an objective one. Would a reasonable man, knowing all the facts and circumstances which the doer of the ace knew or ought to have known, describe the act as 'reckless' in the ordinary meaning of that word in ordinary speech? As I have said, my understanding of the ordinary meaning of that word is a high degree of carelessness."

As to the inclusion of the word "knowingly" Finlay Geoghegan J. referred with approval to the statement by Lynch J. where he observed at p.222:

> "The inclusion of the word 'knowingly' ... must have been intended by the Oireachtas to have some effect on the nature of the reckless conduct required to come within the sub-section. I think that its inclusion requires that the director is party to carrying on the business in a manner which the director knows very well involves an obvious and serious risk of loss or damage to others, and yet ignores that risk, because he does not really care whether such others suffer loss or damage or because his selfish desire to keep his own company alive overrides any concern which he ought to have for others."

Counsel for the respondents submitted that the court should pay attention to s.297A(2)(a), which provides:

> Without prejudice to the generality of subsection (1) (a), an officer of a company shall be deemed to have been knowingly a party to the carrying on of any business of the company in a reckless manner if—
>
> (a) he was a party to the carrying on of such business and, having regard to the general knowledge, skill and experience that may reasonably be expected of a person in his position, he ought to have known that his actions or those of the

> company would cause loss to the creditors of the company, or any of them, ...

In particular it was emphasised that the court should have regard "to the general knowledge, skill and experience that may reasonably be expected of a person in his position". Finlay Geoghegan J. rejected this submission. The provisions of s.297A(2), she stated, were directed at additional circumstances whereby the court could deem a person to have been knowingly a party to the carrying on of any of the business of the company in a reckless way. The reference to the knowledge, skill and experience of a person in those additional circumstances had no application to s.297A(1)(a) upon which the applicant had relied.

Turning then to s.297A(1)(a) and applying the test set out by Lynch J. in *Re Heffernon Kearns Ltd*, Finlay Geoghegan J. was satisfied that the respondent was a party to the carrying on of the business of the company in a reckless manner. He had knowingly decided to keep the company trading by under-declaring and under-paying revenue liabilities, the continuation of which posed an "obvious and serious" risk of loss or damage to the creditor. Such risk was ignored by the respondent in his desire to keep the company afloat. His intention that his behaviour in this regard would be of a temporary nature until the loss-making contracts were dealt with was not based on reasonable grounds.

The court then turned to the matter of whether the respondent had carried on the business of the company in a fraudulent manner under s.297A(1)(b) referred to above. The court was satisfied that the making of returns to the Revenue formed part of the "carrying on of the business of the company" within the meaning of s.297A(1)(b) of the Principal Act (citing *Re Hunting Lodges Ltd (In Liquidation)* [1985] I.L.R.M. 75). The under-declaration and under-payment of revenue liabilities was done for the fraudulent purpose of inducing the revenue commissioners to believe that the amount due by the company was the lesser amount declared and not the true amount. The respondent was by his own admission, knowingly a party to the company doing this and indeed he had taken the decision himself. On this basis the court was satisfied that the applicant liquidator had made out the claim against the respondent pursuant to s.297A(1)(b) of the Principal Act.

Having regard to the court's findings on the reckless and fraudulent trading provisions, the court considered whether it should make a declaration that the respondent be personally responsible, without any limitation of liability, for all or any part of the debts or other liabilities of the company. Finlay Geoghegan J. accepted the submission by counsel for the respondent that the principle of proportionality applied (*O'Keefe v Ferris* [1997] 3 I.R. 463). Although the respondent had not himself benefitted from the wrongdoing, the effect was nonetheless that the company had continued to trade during a period when it ought to have been wound up, liabilities had been incurred and the company continued to trade unprofitably. Applying the principle of proportionality the court assessed the liability of the respondent, based essentially on the entire deficit of the company at the time of the winding up, less an amount reflecting the reduction of asset values due to the liquidation and other miscellaneous deductions. The court was satisfied that the applicant was entitled to a declaration that the respondent is personally liable for the debts of the company in a sum not exceeding €1.6 million. The court also ordered that the first-named respondent be disqualified for a period of seven years.

The applicant had also sought an order under s.297A(1)(a) against the second-named respondent, who was the partner of the first-named respondent and the second director of the company. She was a non-executive director, had no executive or management role and merely took directions from the first-named respondent. She was essentially an office employee with responsibility for pricing materials and stock and general administration. She knew of the cash flow problems and the decision taken by the first-named respondent to under-declare and under-pay revenue liabilities. Nonetheless, the court was not satisfied that she had sufficient knowledge about the company's financial position to know that the continuation of trading and the actions of the first-named respondent would cause a serious risk of loss or damage to the revenue commissioners or other creditors. The court then turned to whether the second-named respondent could be "deemed" to have been knowingly a party to the carrying on of the business of the company in a reckless manner having regard to the provisions of s.297A(2)(a) referred to above. Finlay Geoghegan J. was satisfied that she was "a party to the carrying on of the business" in so far as she knew of the decision of the first-named respondent and had not made any objections. However, the court was not satisfied that, having regard to the "general knowledge, skill and experience" which might reasonably be expected of a person in her position, that she ought to have known that the decision taken by the first-named respondent would cause a loss to the revenue or other creditors. Accordingly, the application under s.297A(2)(a) was refused.

However, the court did agree that her complicity in the making of the under-declarations to the Revenue Commissioners over a period of five months rendered her unfit to be concerned in the management of the company. Accordingly, an order for disqualification was made against her for a period of five years.

PROVISIONAL LIQUIDATOR

Adjournment of winding-up petition to allow continuation of provisional liquidator In *Re Coolfadda Developers Ltd* [2009] IEHC 263, a petition was presented on April 22, 2009 for the winding up of the company on the grounds of insolvency. On application by the company, the court appointed a provisional liquidator on the same date. The company indicated that it intended to have the winding up petition adjourned from time to time to allow the continuation of the provisional liquidation. The company was involved in the construction business and its objectives in seeking the continuation of the provisional liquidation were two-fold. First, it wished to finish out existing building contracts which, it was represented, were at risk of termination by the employer if a winding up order were made. Second, the completion of the contracts would maximise funds for distribution to creditors. No creditors appeared to object to the proposed adjournments. Laffoy J. considered whether the adjournment of the company's petition to wind up and to continue the appointment of the provisional liquidator for an indefinite period was a proper exercise of the court's discretion. Section 216 of the Companies Act 1963 sets out the court's powers on hearing a petition for the winding up of a company. It provides:

> On hearing a winding-up petition, the court may dismiss it, or adjourn the hearing conditionally or unconditionally, or make any interim order, or any other order that it thinks fit, but the court shall not refuse to make a winding-up order on the ground only that the assets of the company have been mortgaged to an amount equal to or in excess of those assets, or that the company has no assets.

Laffoy J. noted the courts traditional reluctance to grant lengthy adjournments of winding up petitions. She cited with approval a passage from the *Companies Acts 1963 – 2006* (McCann & Courtney, 2008), p.436 where it was stated:

> "The Court is reluctant to grant lengthy adjournments of creditors' petitions. Adjournments are often undesirable because the winding up order (if made) dates back to the presentation of the petition. Furthermore if the matter is not dealt with quickly the books of the company tend to be out of date or lost (quite apart from any question of dishonest behaviour on the part of the Officers). Officers and employees who could provide valuable information sometimes leave and cannot be traced. Dispositions made between the presentation of the petition and the making of the winding up are void and any delay increases the number of these transactions and make their examination more difficult. In certain circumstances the Court has granted an adjournment pending litigation between the parties."

Various authorities were cited in relation to the court's discretion to refuse the winding up order or to postpone it. In *Re Genport Ltd* [1996] IEHC 34, McCracken J. stayed a winding up petition because of the alleged ulterior (though not necessarily improper) motives of the petitioner; the opinions of the ordinary trade creditor that their interests were best served by the company continuing to trade; and the impact that a winding up order would have on pending litigation involving the company. In *Re Demaglass Holdings Limited* [2001] 2 B.C.L.C. 633 the English High Court acceded to a request to have the hearing of a winding up petition adjourned. The receivers in this case sought the adjournment to allow them sell assets more advantageously than would occur in a winding up. The adjournment—for a 10-week period—was considered by Neuberger J. as a "temporary refusal" as distinct from an "outright denial" of the right of a petitioning creditor to a winding up order. He considered that the court should be less reluctant to adjourn the hearing of a winding up petition than it would be to dismiss the petition particularly where the adjournment was for a relatively short period. In the more recent case of *Re Minrealm Ltd* [2008] 2 B.C.L.C. 141 the English High Court stayed a winding up petition in circumstances where there was evidence to suggest that if monies owed by certain directors were repaid to the company it would return to solvency.

Laffoy J. observed that none of the authorities cited involved the adjournment of a winding up petition for the sole purpose of the continuation of a provisional liquidator. Reference was made to exceptional cases involving banking and insurance insolvency (*Re Rafidain Bank* (2000) L.T.L. 23/3/2000; *Re Novi Reinsurance Company Limited* (Record No. 2001 317 COS); *New Cap v HIH Casualty & General* [2002] 2 B.C.L.C. 228) where provisional liquidations were continued for a number of years. Laffoy J. distinguished these cases as they had no application to the present case.

Considering the unprecedented nature of the present application Laffoy J. then considered how the court's discretion should be exercised. She distinguished the procedure for appointing an examiner under the Companies (Amendment) Act 1990 from that involving the winding up of a company under the Companies Act 1963 (the "1963 Act"). The former involves the rehabilitation of a company which has reasonable prospects for survival, the latter is the gathering in and realising and distributing the assets of a company in an orderly manner. The former procedure was not pursued by the company presumably because it had no prospect of survival. Pending a decision by a court on a winding up petition, Laffoy J. was satisfied that the role of a provisional liquidator was to ensure the preservation of the company's assets. The application in this case—to adjourn for the purpose of enabling the continuation of the provisional liquidation—was not in keeping with the spirit and intendment of the 1963 Act.

While it was acknowledged that there may be exceptional cases where the court could countenance adjournment for the purpose of continuing a provisional liquidation, Laffoy J. did not consider the present application to be such a case. The company was "hopelessly insolvent" with no prospect of a return to solvency. The purpose of continuing the provisional liquidation was to complete a number of construction developments. It was conceivable that these developments could be completed by a receiver appointed by secured creditors or indeed an official liquidator if it was beneficial for the winding up. In conclusion, Laffoy J. did not consider that it was a proper exercise of the court's discretion to postpone the making of the winding up order to enable the provisional liquidator to continue to conduct most aspects of the business of the company with a view to maximising the company's assets.

The decision of Laffoy J. was appealed ([2009] IESC 54). Giving judgment for the Supreme Court, Denham J. agreed that in general a provisional liquidation is a "stop-gap" measure. However, she accepted that the court does have jurisdiction in an exceptional case to adjourn a winding up petition in favour of allowing the continuation of a provisional liquidation and that such jurisdiction is not contrary to the spirit of the winding up provisions in the Companies Acts (*Re MHMH Ltd* [2006] 1 B.C.L.C. 279 considered). However, there was no such exceptional circumstance in the present case. The appeal was dismissed accordingly.

LIQUIDATOR'S APPOINTMENT

Liquidator's appointment by creditors' meeting challenged In *Re Jim Murnane Ltd (in Liquidation)* [2009] IEHC 412 the company, by reason of its insolvency, had resolved in February 2009 to be wound up voluntarily and to appoint a liquidator. On the same day a creditors' meeting was held and, pursuant to s.266(3)(a) of the Companies Act 1963 (the "Principal Act"), a statement of affairs was laid before this meeting together with a list of the unsecured creditors and the estimated amount of their claims. In accordance with this list, the chairman of the creditor's meeting was the largest in value and the applicant was listed as the second largest in value of the creditors. The applicant's solicitor attended the meeting on its behalf and informed the chairman that the amount stated to be owed to the applicant was wrong. He suggested that the amount owing was almost three times that stated which would make him the largest creditor in value to the company. He also informed the chairman that where there was a dispute as to the debt owing, it was normal practice to allow the higher amount when it came to voting for the liquidator. The chairman stated that he would not allow the higher amount for voting purposes, but would only allow the figure in the estimated statement of affairs.

On the matter of the appointment of the liquidator, the chairman told the meeting that a Mr Mehigan was the nominee of the members of the company. When asked for any other nominations, the applicant nominated an alternate liquidator. The matter was put to a vote and the majority in value voted in favour of the company's nominee who was duly appointed liquidator. The applicant sought the following reliefs:

(i) An order pursuant to Ord.74 r.71 of the Rules of the Superior Courts 1986 (RSC) setting aside by way of appeal the decision of the chairman of the creditors' meeting, to reject the proof of the debt owed by the company to the applicant; and
(ii) an order pursuant to s.267(2) of the Principal Act, directing that

> the applicant's nominee be appointed as liquidator in place of the company's nominee.

Laffoy J. considered the statutory framework relevant to the application. Section 267 of the Principal Act provides:

> (1) Subject to subsection (2), the creditors and the company at their respective meetings mentioned in section 266 may nominate a person to be liquidator for the purpose of winding up the affairs of the company and distributing the assets of the company, and if the creditors and the company nominate different persons, the person nominated by the creditors shall be the liquidator, and if no person is nominated by the creditors, the person, if any, nominated by the company shall be the liquidator.
> (2) Where different persons are nominated as liquidator, any director, member or creditor of the company may, within 14 days after the date on which the nomination was made by the creditors, apply to the court for an order either directing that the person nominated as liquidator by the company shall be liquidator instead of or jointly with the person nominated by the creditors, or appointing some other person to be liquidator instead of the person nominated by the creditors.
> (3) If at a meeting of creditors mentioned in section 266(1) a resolution as to the creditors' nominee as liquidator is proposed, it shall be deemed to be passed when a majority, in value only, of the creditors present personally or by proxy and voting on the resolution have voted in favour of the resolution.

Order 74 r.71 of the RSC which regulates the admission and rejection of proofs for the purpose of voting at a creditors' meeting convened pursuant to s.266 provides as follows:

> The chairman shall have power to admit or reject a proof for the purpose of voting, but his decision shall be subject to appeal to Court. If he is in doubt whether a proof should be admitted or rejected, he shall mark it as objected to and allow the creditor to vote subject to the vote being declared invalid in the event of the objection being sustained.

Laffoy J. noted that Ord.74 r.71 of the RSC predated the insertion of subs.(3) of s.267 by the Company Law Enforcement Act 2001.

The respondents submitted that the decision taken by the chairman was in line with recommended practice and, in particular, in line with the recommendations of the Chartered Accountants Regulatory Body guidance document S8B – *Planning and Administration of Creditors Meetings*. Paragraph 31 of that document provides:

> "The amount for which the chairman admits the proof for voting purposes should normally be the lower of:
> (a) The amount stated in the proofs; and
> (b) The amount considered by the company to be due to the creditor.
>
> The amount for which the proof is admitted for voting purposes should be endorsed on it, and in most instances, it is expected that prior to the meeting, the chairman will do this."

No direct Irish authorities were cited on the function of the court on an appeal pursuant to Ord.74 r.71. Counsel for the respondents did refer to an ex tempore decision of McCracken J. in *A & M Construction Ltd (in liquidation),* unreported, High Court, February 22, 1995 where a dispute arose in relation to the conduct of a creditors' meeting where several creditors had been omitted or had their debts understated in the list of creditors provided by the company. The company had asserted that counter-claims by the company against these creditors had cancelled out or substantially reduced the debts due to them. In any case McCracken J. stated that he could not adjudicate definitely on the nature of the claims and appeared to accept that the company had acted bona fide in its assertions.

Laffoy J. considered helpful the decision of Blackburne J. in *Re A Company* [1995] 1 B.C.L.C. 459 where an appeal arose in respect of a similar provision in the United Kingdom, specifically, r. 4.70 of the Insolvency Rules 1986. Laffoy J. observed that the only difference in substance with this provision and r.71 was that the chairman's discretion to admit or reject is exercisable in respect of the whole or part of the proof. She further noted that the provision provided helpful guidance to the court as to the consequences of upholding an appeal. She referred to a passage by Blackburne J. where he outlined his understanding of the function of the court on an appeal under r.4.70 as follows:

> "In my view, the task of the court on an appeal under rule 4.70 (4) is simply to examine the evidence placed before it on the matter and come to a conclusion whether, on balance, the claim against the company is established and, if so, in what amount. I would only add that, in considering the matter, the court is not confined to the evidence that was before the chairman at the time that he made his decision but is entitled to consider whatever admissible evidence on the issue the parties to the appeal choose to place before the court."

Counsel for the respondents submitted that the court's role on an appeal under r.71 was not to determine the value of the debt, but rather to determine whether the correct procedure had been followed by the chairman at the creditors' meeting. Nonetheless, the court examined the nature of the disputed amounts and the complexities involved and concluded as follows:

> "Rule 71 is concerned with the admission or rejection of a proof of debt 'for the purpose of voting'. In other words, neither the decision of the chairman nor the determination of the Court on an appeal against that decision can be definitive as to the amount of the debt. Rule 71 as it exists seems to envisage admission or rejection of the proof of the debt in whole. Unlike the U.K. provision considered in *Re a Company*, it does not appear to address the difficulty which arose in this case – that the company's estimate of the debt represented only part of the amount claimed by the applicant creditor. It may be that there is a *casus omissus* in the legislative scheme constituted by s. 267 and the Rules since the insertion of subs. (3) in s. 267. As it exists, in my view, the rule requires the chairman to give the creditor the benefit of the doubt, subject to the possibility of his decision being set aside on appeal. In the situation which arose in this case, where the amount of the applicant's claimed debt exceeded the company's estimate of the debt, it must be assumed that there was a doubt. On the rule as it exists, the decision of the chairman should have been to allow the applicant to vote on the basis that the value of its claim was the value asserted by [the applicant]. As a matter of law, I see no basis for applying para. 31 of guidance document S8B in a situation to which r. 71 applies. In relation to an appeal to the Court under r. 71 against a decision of a chairman made under that rule, it seems to me that the Court is concerned with much more than whether the chairman acted properly procedurally. Rule 71 treats a doubt of the chairman as to the decision to be made, which, obviously involves a dispute between a creditor and the company as to the debt, as an objection and it envisages the Court making a determination as to whether the objection is sustainable. This means that the Court is required to make some sort of determination on the substance of the dispute."

The court was satisfied that in many cases on an appeal under r.71 a court would be unable to determine the amount of the debt so as to determine the substantive issue. Nevertheless it was necessary that there was some "rule of thumb" whereby the chairman of a creditors' meeting can resolve the type of dispute where quantum is at issue. While the court acknowledged that there may be better ways to deal with this matter, such policy decisions were not a matter for the court.

On this basis, Laffoy J. considered that on the facts of the case, the chairman should have allowed the proof in whole and treated the debt as the amount claimed by the applicant creditor. If this had been done, the applicant's liquidator would have been appointed. In consequence of this she made the following orders:

(a) a declaration that the vote in favour of the appointment of Mr Mehigan as liquidator of the company at the creditors' meeting on February 27, 2009 is invalid; and
(b) an order under s.267(2) appointing the creditors' liquidator.

(See also, *In Re Centrum Products Ltd (in voluntary liquidation)* [2009] IEHC 592 in respect of a similar but unsuccessful application).

WINDING UP PETITION

Substituting a petitioner for the purposes of winding up the company In *Re Lycatel Ltd* [2009] IEHC 264, Wavecrest (UK) Ltd ("Wavecrest") presented a petition to the High Court on April 6, 2009 to wind up Lycatel (Ireland) Ltd (the "company") under s.213(e) of the Companies Act 1963 (the "Principal Act") on the ground that the company, having been served a statutory demand under s.214 of the Principal Act, had not paid its debts and was therefore deemed to be insolvent. The petition was listed for April 27, 2009 on which date Wavecrest told the court that the petition had not been advertised and that it was being withdrawn. On that occasion another creditor of the company, Cronosell Telecom Ltd ("Cronosell") applied to the court to be substituted as petitioner on the same grounds invoked originally by Wavecrest. Cronosell sought to be substituted pursuant to Ord.74 r.18 of the Rules of the Superior Courts 1986 (RSC). Wavecrest opposed the application. The issue before the court was whether Cronosell had locus standi to be substituted and whether Wavecrest had locus standi to oppose the application to be substituted.

The court was satisfied that Cronosell was a creditor who could rely on s.213(e) of the Principal Act in the same manner as Wavecrest had relied. Laffoy J. inferred that Wavecrest's opposition to the substitution related to the combined effect of s.220(2) and s.218 of the Principal Act. The former provides that the winding up of a company is deemed to commence at the time of the presentation of the petition for the winding up, and the latter provides that post-commencement dispositions are void unless otherwise ordered by the court. If a compromise or settlement had been made between the company and Wavecrest after its petition was presented—the court was not formally advised of this—then such a compromise would be jeopardised if the substitution of the petitioner and the petition itself were ultimately successful. Order 74 r.18 of the RSC provides:

When a petitioner consents to withdraw his petition, or to allow it to

> be dismissed, or the hearing adjourned or fails to appear in support of his petition when it is called in Court on the day originally fixed for the hearing thereof, or on any day to which the hearing has been adjourned, or if appearing, does not apply for an order in the terms of the prayer of his petition, the court may, if, and upon such terms as it shall deem just, substitute as petitioner any person who would have a right to present a petition, and who desires to prosecute the petition.

Wavecrest opposed any order under r.18 on the basis that the rule is predicated on the petition having been advertised under Ord.74 r.10 of the RSC, which had not been done. The court did not agree (*Re United Stock Exchange Ltd, ex parte Philp & Kidd* (1884) 28 Ch D 183; *Re a Company* (1980) 35 A.C.T.R. 36 and *Re Creative Handbook Ltd* [1985] B.C.L.C. 1 distinguished). Laffoy J. referred to a passage from French on *Applications to Wind Up Companies*, 2nd edn (Oxford: OUP, 2008) where he observed:

> "Without provision for substitution, an insolvent company could delay being wound up by paying off petitioning creditors one by one, forcing other creditors to present and advertise new petitions, then waiting until the petition of each creditor was at or near hearing before paying that creditor off too. In order to counter these tactics, several creditors would have to present petitions simultaneously. As Needham J. said in D.M.K. Building Materials Pty Limited (1985) 10 ACLR 16 at p.19: 'The purpose of substitution, in my opinion, is to ensure that once a prima facie right to the winding up of a company has arisen, the company should not escape from that position except upon the basis of fair dealing with all its creditors, not merely by paying of the particular [applicant].'"

Laffoy J. rejected the submission by counsel for Wavecrest that r.18 is predicated on the petition having been advertised and made an order substituting Cronosell as petitioner. She further ordered that the amended petition be advertised in accordance with Ord.74 r.10 of the RSC.

NAMA AND LIQUIDATIONS

By virtue of the National Asset Management Agency Act 2009 ("NAMA Act"), s.216 of the Companies Act 1963 has been amended by the insertion of a new subs.(2) which provides:

> (2) The court shall not make an order for the winding up of the company unless—
>
> (a) the court is satisfied that the company has no obligations

in relation to a bank asset that has been transferred to the National Management Agency or a NAMA group entity, or

(b) if the company has any such obligation—

(iii) a copy of the petition has been served on that Agency, and

(iv) the court has heard that Agency in relation to the making of the order.

The fraudulent preference provisions of s.286 of the Companies Act 1963 will not apply where a company makes a payment to NAMA or to another person at NAMA's direction. By virtue of s.150 of the NAMA Act where a liquidator is appointed to a company whose assets or any part of them are under the control of a statutory receiver, such an appointment will not displace the statutory receiver or affect his powers, authority or agency.

RECEIVERS' DUTIES

Receivers' duties when managing company assets Both common law and statute (s.316A of the Companies Act 1963) impose a specific duty of care on receivers when selling company assets. The duty of a receiver when his conduct does not involve the sale of an asset but the management of an asset remains a more contentious matter. In such circumstances, his duty to the debenture holder to service and ultimately repay the company's debt is without doubt. However, the thorny question of whether the receiver has a remaining duty to the company when managing the company's assets remains to some extent unanswered. Keane J. (*Company Law*, 4th edn (Dublin: Tottel Publishing, 2007)) has observed that where a receiver acts as a manager, he will not be liable to the company provided he acts in good faith. This view follows a line of authorities in the United Kingdom (*Downsview Nominees Ltd v First City Corp* [1993] 1 A.C. 295 and *Re B. Johnson & Co. (Builders) Ltd* [1955] 1 Ch. 634) which were cited with approval in this jurisdiction in *Kinsella v Somers*, unreported, High Court, Budd J., November 23, 1999. Notwithstanding this line of authorities, in the English case of *Medforth v Blake* [2000] Ch. 86, Sir Richard Scott V.C. went beyond the good faith test and set out the following propositions in relation to the functions of receivers:

> "(1) A Receiver managing mortgaged property owes duties to the mortgagor and any one else with an interest in the equity of redemption.
>
> (2) The duties include, but are not necessarily confined to, a duty of good faith.

> (3) The extent and scope of any duty additional to that of good faith will depend on the facts and circumstances of a particular case.
> (4) In exercising his powers of management the primary duty of the Receiver is to try and bring about a situation in which the interest on the security can be paid and the debt itself repaid.
> (5) Subject to the primary duty, the Receiver owes a duty to manage the property with due diligence.
> (6) Due diligence does not oblige the Receiver to continue to carry on a business on the alleged premises previously carried out by the mortgagor.
> (7) If the Receiver does carry on a business on the mortgaged premises, due diligence requires reasonable steps to be taken in order to do so profitably."

The application of this expanded view of a receiver's potential liability in this jurisdiction arose in *Moorview Developments Ltd & Ors v First Active Plc & Ors* [2009] IEHC 367. Following the collapse of a number of companies associated with the Cunningham Construction Group a receiver was appointed to some of these companies by First Active Plc. A number of connected proceedings had already been adjudicated upon but some issues remained outstanding including, inter alia, a claim by the plaintiffs that the receiver was negligent in the management of a building development site in Malahide, Co. Dublin. Prior to the appointment of the receiver a number of problems had arisen between Mr Cunningham and First Active Plc and the relationship between them had deteriorated. In order to recommence funding of the development site, Mr Cunningham agreed to step down from any involvement in the day-to-day running of the site and the management of the site would be handed over to Construction Site Services (CSS). Despite this, delays continued and issues arose as to the quality of the management by CSS of the site. When the receiver was ultimately appointed in April 2003, Mr Cunningham warned him of possible fraud on the site by CSS. The site continued to experience delays and cost overruns and part of the cost overruns was an admitted fraud committed by CSS staff. Following the admission of fraud, CSS were dismissed in January 2004 and the site was not completed until 2006.

The Cunningham Group alleged, inter alia, that the receiver failed in his duty with respect to the management of the Malahide site. They contended that he was vicariously liable for the acts of the professional team under whose management the site was conducted. They further submitted that the receiver could have avoided cost overruns had he taken the advice of an insolvency quantity surveyor. They argued that the receiver was under a duty to the company to manage the business with due diligence and he had failed to do so. Reliance was placed on the propositions laid down in *Medforth v Blake* referred to above.

Counsel for the receiver argued that *Medforth v Blake* did not represent the law in Ireland and a receiver/manager should not be subject to liability where he decides to manage and does so in good faith with the object of preserving and realising the assets for the benefit of the debenture holder. Reliance was placed on the *Downsview Nominees Ltd v First City Corp Ltd* [1993] 1 A.C. 295 line of authorities referred to above.

In considering the application of *Medforth v Blake* in Ireland, Clarke J. observed that all the authorities, including *Medforth v Blake*, accepted that the underlying obligation of a receiver is to the debenture holder who had appointed that receiver. On this basis he summarised the approach of the *Downsview* line of authorities as follows:

> "[I]t is impossible to impose any obligation on the receiver in respect of the management of the property when his primary obligation is to the debenture holder. In a sense it is said that the receiver cannot serve two masters. As the position of the debenture holder is superior (because the company has allowed itself to get into default) then the receiver must serve the interests of the debenture holder, and not the company. On that basis it is suggested that to attempt to impose some residual obligation on the receiver would be a recipe for difficulty, with the court being constantly faced with an attempt to strip out from the primary obligation of the receiver towards the debenture holder, some residual obligation in respect of the company."

With regard to the apparent conflict between this approach and the *Medforth v Blake* approach he observed:

> "Medforth v Blake seeks to get around that difficulty by recognising that the primary duty of the receiver is to procure that the debt be paid, but suggests that, subject to that primary duty, there remains a duty on the receiver to manage the property with due diligence in order that the business of the company be carried out profitably."

Without addressing whether this residual obligation, identified in *Medforth v Blake*, represents the law in Ireland, Clarke J. concluded that even if it did, it would not avail to the Cunningham Group as no sufficient case had been made out for negligence against the receiver and more importantly, there was no causal link between the alleged negligence and any consequences for the Cunningham Group. Accordingly, he did not consider it appropriate to make a definitive ruling on the application of *Medforth v Blake* as such a view would necessarily be obiter. However, he did consider that there are at least arguable grounds for the proposition that *Medforth v Blake* does represent the law in Ireland and in this regard he stated:

> "While understanding the practical difficulties which have led courts in the common law world to shy away from imposing a liability on receivers in such circumstances, (and in particular the difficulty in identifying the responsibility of a receiver to a company where the primary responsibility of that receiver is to the debenture holder), I am not convinced that a blanket immunity from liability on the part of receivers for the management of businesses placed in their hands is an appropriate response to the undoubted difficulties which arise. On the other hand, it is also necessary to take into account the fact that the legislature has decided to enact a specific provision providing for the liability of receivers in cases of sale at an undervalue without specifying any similar liability in cases of mismanagement. It is at least open to the view that in so doing the legislature impliedly declined to extend the potential liability of receivers beyond the category of sale at an undervalue traditionally established at common law."

The comments by Clarke J., albeit obiter, leave open the question of whether a receiver could be liable in circumstances even where he acts in good faith in managing a company's assets rather than selling them. This is particularly relevant in the current economic climate where receivers who have been appointed over large complex building developments are managing these developments rather than selling them in a continually depreciating property market. As Irish banks' lending practices almost invariably require personal guarantees in addition to asset securities, there is no doubt that guarantors will eagerly monitor the management of these projects by receivers and it may not be long before a definitive judicial statement on the application of *Medforth v Blake* will be made.

SHADOW DIRECTORS

Is a financial institution a shadow director? In *Moorview Developments Ltd & Ors v First Active Plc & Ors* [2009] IEHC 367, referred to above, the Cunningham Group also asserted that First Active Plc was a shadow director of the Group and as such it owed certain duties which it had breached. Counsel for the Cunningham Group submitted that First Active Plc had gone beyond merely being the group's banker and had become a shadow director by virtue of certain incidences. In particular, it was contended that First Active Plc had appointed the board of the Cunningham Group, had insisted that Mr Cunningham be excluded from any part in the management of the company, had chosen and appointed quantity surveyors and project managers to run sites, and had insisted on the sale of one of the company's substantial assets. First Active Plc vigorously rejected this contention or that it was in breach of any alleged duty.

Section 27 of the Companies Act 1990 (the "1990 Act") defines a shadow director as a person:

> … in accordance with whose directions or instructions the directors of a company are accustomed to act … unless the directors are accustomed so to act by reason only that they do so on advice given by him in a professional capacity.

Clarke J. observed that courts in Ireland had never made a finding of shadow directorship against a financial institution. Counsel for the Cunningham Group relied upon the decision of the English Court of Appeal in *Re Tasbian Ltd (No. 2)* [1993] B.C.L.C. 297 to support their claim. In that case the company's bankers had appointed an expert to report on the company's financial position and to advise on measures which the company should take to trade its way out of its difficulties. The expert was paid by the company, had negotiated a moratorium with creditors, had monitored the company's trading, assisted the board, negotiated with the Revenue and other regulatory authorities and was a signatory to the company's bank account. The English Court of Appeal held that there was an arguable case that he was a de facto or a shadow director for the purposes of disqualification proceedings.

First Active Plc submitted that it had acted only in the protection of its commercial interests, attaching reasonable conditions to the continuation of its financial support to the company and it had not played a hands-on role in the affairs of the Cunningham Group thus distinguishing it from the role played by the "company doctor" in *Re Tasbian Ltd.* To support its submissions it relied on the decision in *Re PFTZM Ltd (In Liquidation)* [1995] B.C.C. 280. Here the English High Court considered the question of whether officers of the company's lending institution were shadow directors. The company had incurred serious financial difficulties and it was agreed that officers of the company lending institution would attend weekly meetings of the company. The court considered the institution was merely acting to protect their commercial interests by imposing terms on which it was prepared to continue to advance lending facilities. The board still retained the power to accept or reject these terms and accordingly, the officers were not shadow directors of the company.

Clarke J. considered the facts of *Re PFTZM Ltd* to be more analogous to the current proceedings than those of *Re Tasbian Ltd.* The court then turned to the circumstances which the Cunningham Group claimed gave rise to their submission that First Active was a shadow director. The court noted that the Cunningham Group's own advisors had recommended strengthening the board with independent members given the expanded business of the Group. In relation to First Active Plc's role in vetting these additional members of the board, Clarke J. was satisfied that a lending institution was entitled to satisfy itself as to the strength of the board and its role in this regard was "nothing more than the exercise of legitimate concern in respect of the management strength of the borrower".

With regard to the exclusion of Mr Cunningham from an active role in the management of sites, the court was satisfied that this development was not initiated by the board of directors or by First Active, but rather was a requirement of a key customer who had expressed serious concern about his involvement. First Active plc had supported this view. Furthermore, as the company's financial situation had deteriorated it became clear that relations between Mr Cunningham and the independent members of the board had broken down and in such circumstances, "it was more than reasonable for a lender to express, even in trenchant terms, its view that its continuing support is dependent on those management difficulties being sorted out".

With regard to the remaining circumstances, the court concluded that given the highly leveraged financial position of the company it was acceptable for a lending institution to insist on certain conditions being satisfied before it would advance facilities to a troubled company. He observed that:

> "[T]he actions which a lender may take must be viewed in the context of the circumstances pertaining at the relevant time. Actions which might be unusual in one set of circumstances might be regarded as entirely expected in another set of circumstances."

In conclusion, Clarke J. was satisfied that neither individually nor cumulatively did any of the circumstances provide a basis for the suggestion that the Cunningham Group was accustomed to act on the instructions of First Active Plc and accordingly a finding of shadow directorship could not be sustained.

SECTION 201 SCHEME OF ARRANGEMENTS

Jurisdiction of court to categorise meetings at stage one of section 201 procedure In *Re Millstream Recyling Ltd* [2009] IEHC 571 the company was engaged in the collection of food by-products which were processed by it and sold as pig and cattle feed ingredients. In December 2008, the Department of Agriculture, Fisheries and Food found that certain of the company's feeds were contaminated with dioxins and polychlorinated biphenyls and restricted the movement of cattle and pigs on all farms which used food products supplied by the company. Equivalent orders were made in Northern Ireland. In both jurisdictions it was ordered that certain livestock be slaughtered. Various Government compensation schemes were put in place for those affected by these orders. However, additional claims were also made against the company for material loss, consequential loss and third party claims arising from the use of the contaminated feed, estimated at over €40 million. If these claims proved successful they would render the company insolvent. Arising from this development the company proposed a compromise with its creditors under s.201 of the Companies Act 1963 (the "Principal Act").

This proposed scheme is designed to make provision for those parties entitled to compensation as a result of the contamination (the "contamination creditors"). It does not apply to ordinary trade creditors. The company applied for various orders pursuant to s.201(1) including, inter alia, an order directing the summoning of a meeting of the contamination creditors to consider the proposed scheme on July 10, 2010. The company also sought a stay in the further prosecution of all claims to which the scheme relates against the company and/or the issuing of any further proceedings against the company. The proposals for the scheme envisage two sources of funding to meet the claims of the contamination creditors: the proceeds of an insurance policy; and the proceeds of a pending action by the company against the supplier of the oil used by the company which allegedly caused the contamination. The creditors' meeting could not take place until matters relating to the insurance policy had been clarified and the proceedings against the supplier had been concluded. Although the resolution of these matters is not within the control of the company, it appeared to be satisfied that the funds would be identified by that date. The company submitted that the contamination creditors would be better served by the proposed scheme compared to their position in the event the company was wound up. A winding up would cause difficulties in the context of payments under the insurance policy by virtue of s.62 of the Civil Liability Act 1961 and it could jeopardise the pending action against the aforementioned oil supplier.

The court considered the various reliefs sought. In particular, it observed that a crucial element of the reliefs sought was the stay on existing proceedings against the company by the contamination creditors. Those contamination creditors who had already initiated these proceedings were strongly opposed to the relief sought. The court considered its jurisdiction under s.201 of the Principal Act. It referred to the decision of the Court of Appeal of England and Wales in *Re Hawk Insurance Company Ltd* [2002] B.C.C. 300 where Chadwick L.J. identified the three-stage process involved. First, an application is made to court for an order that a meeting(s) be summoned. The second stage involves the putting of the scheme proposals to the meeting(s), and finally if the meeting accepts the proposals an application is made to court to sanction the compromise or scheme. At this latter stage the court must ensure that the proper meetings have been summoned, the proposals have been approved by the requisite majorities and the views of those who have not approved the proposals receive consideration.

Some of the contamination creditors had actions pending against the company; others did not. The question which then arose was whether the court had any role to play under s.201(1) to pronounce on the categorisation in classes of the creditors proposed to be subject to the scheme. The court observed that if the correct decision as to the summoning of the meetings at stage one is not made correctly, then the court may find that it is without jurisdiction at the third stage. While the court acknowledged that it has no statutory obligation to give directions as to the different class meetings which must be held—this being a matter for the company itself—it noted that the existing three-stage statutory process is not without difficulties. Referring to *Re Hawk Insurance Ltd, Re Pye (Ireland) Ltd*, unreported, High Court, Costello J., March 11, 1985; *Re T & N (No.3)* [2007] 1 All E.R. 851 and the *UK Practice Direction* [2002] 3 All E.R. 96 where certain difficulties were identified Laffoy J. observed:

> "... as a matter of common sense, the first stage of the exercise of the useful and beneficial discretion which the entirety of s.201 confers on this Court to sanction a scheme of arrangement may be rendered useless and a waste of money if the Court postpones consideration of whether separate classes of meetings are required until the third stage. Sub-section (1) of s.201 gives a very broad discretion to the Court in directing the creditors' meeting or meetings. Obviously, the discretion can only be exercised if the parties who are likely to be affected by the Court's determination have an opportunity to be heard on the issue, which necessitates the Court being satisfied that they are on notice of the application under s.201 either having been served or by advertisement. In this case, compliance with the notice and advertising requirements of the order of 16th November, 2009 has been proven. Therefore, in my view, the Court has jurisdiction to determine whether separate class meetings are required and, having regard to the procedure adopted on this application can properly exercise the jurisdiction."

In determining these different classes, Laffoy J. relied on the test formulated by Bowen L.J. in *Sovereign Life Assurance Co. v Dodd* [1892] 2 Q.B. 573 where on the construction of the word "class" he stated:

> "The word 'class' is vague, and to find out what is meant by it we must look at the scope of the section, which is a section enabling the Court to order a meeting of a class of creditors to be called. It seems plain that we must give such a meaning to the term 'class' as will prevent the section being worked as to result in confiscation and injustice, and that it might be confined to those persons whose rights are not so dissimilar as to make it impossible for them to consult together with a view to their common interest."

Applying this test to the contamination creditors who would be affected by the scheme the court was satisfied that their rights were not so dissimilar as to make it impossible for them to consult together with a view to their common interest. The advanced stage of litigation by some of the contamination creditors or their rights in the event of a liquidation of the company vis-à-vis the application of s.62 of the Civil Liability Act 1961 did not give them any additional rights or distinguish them in any respect from the other contamination creditors affected by the scheme. The court found that an exception did apply to certain contamination creditor companies that are related to the company, and that these connected creditors should constitute a separate class of creditor for the purposes of the meetings to be summoned (*Re Pye Ireland Ltd* followed).

On this basis the court made an order under s.201(1) of the Principal Act that two meetings be held; one of the contamination creditors unconnected to the company and one of the contaminated creditors connected to the company, The court also ordered, pursuant to s.201(2) of the Principal Act, a stay on all proceedings and restraining all further proceedings against the company for damages in relation to claims arising out of the contamination event until further order of the court.

MINORITY OPPRESSION

Corporate restructuring squeezes out minority shareholder from share in profits In *Re Emerald Group Holdings Ltd* [2009] IEHC 440, the petitioner Banfi Ltd (Banfi) was a minority shareholder in Emerald Group Holdings Ltd (EGHL). Banfi claims, as a member of EGHL, pursuant to s.205 of the Companies Act 1963 (the "Act"), the affairs of EGHL are being conducted, or the powers of the directors are being exercised, in a manner oppressive to it or in disregard of its interests as a member. EGHL was a holding company in a corporate structure which had developed following the incorporation of a company to carry on the business of growing, marketing and selling Christmas trees. The petitioner's interest in EGHL was held through a nominee company, ICT Nominees Ltd. When that nominee company transferred the shares to the petitioner in order that it could pursue section 205 proceedings, the directors refused to register the transfer. Following successful litigation the court ordered that the shares be registered in the petitioner's name (see *Annual Review of Irish Law 2006*).

EGHL experienced a number of financial difficulties which resulted in the respondents arranging a corporate restructuring, debt compromises and refinancing of the group. As a result of this restructuring a further corporate entity, Best Christmas Trees Limited (BCTL), was created which was fully owned by the respondents and in which the petitioner had no legal or beneficial interest. BCTL effectively became the new holding company and EGHL was effectively sidelined in terms of development. When the fortunes of the Christmas tree business eventually turned around due to the restructuring, the petitioner did not benefit as EGHL remained the only company in the group with a deficit on its balance sheet while BCTL was the profitable company. The petitioner alleges that the manner in which the group's affairs were developed and conducted resulted in him being excluded from participating in the benefits of the now successful business. It submits that such conduct was and continues to be oppressive to it or in disregard of its interest as a member of EGHL within the meaning of s.205 of the Act.

The primary dispute arose in relation to the timing of the conduct which formed the basis of the complaint. Section 205(1) of the Act provides that any member of a company who complains that the affairs of the company "are" being conducted in an oppressive manner may petition the court. The respondents submitted that the conduct complained of had commenced at a time when Banfi was not a member of the company, and as such, cannot form the basis of a claim by Banfi pursuant to s.205(1) of the Act. The court referred to the decision of *Re Greenore Trading Company Ltd* [1980] I.L.R.M. 94 where Keane J. stated:

> "It is true that the wording of the section envisages that the oppression complained of is operative at the time when the petition is launched. (See *Re Jermyn Street Turkish Baths Ltd.*). In this case, the transfer of shares took place in March 1978. The accounts for the year were certified by the company's auditors on 9 June 1978. The petition was presented just over a year later on 15 June 1979, after protests had been made in correspondence on behalf of the petitioner at the manner in which the company's affairs were being conducted. The company had not merely failed to take any steps to deal with these gross irregularities in its affairs prior to the issuing of the petition; it had also wholly ignored letters written on behalf of the petitioner which clearly called for an answer. It seems to me that in these circumstances the oppressive conduct can properly be regarded as having continued up to the date of the issuing of the petition."

On the basis of the wording of s.205 of the Act and the judgment of Keane J., Finlay Geoghegan J. was satisfied that the effect on the petitioner of the conduct complained of must be continuing up until the date of the presentation of the petition. However, she was also satisfied that where the conduct complained of relates to a transaction which has already taken place, provided the transaction has continuing effects which are oppressive to the member or in disregard of its interests as a member and the effects have not been remedied, then the alleged conduct can be considered operative at the date of the presentation of the petition. The conduct complained of had commenced in 2002 when the petitioner's beneficial interest in the company was held by ICT Nominees Ltd. The respondents knew of this beneficial ownership and the court was satisfied that there was nothing in the legislation to preclude Banfi complaining of conduct—even though the conduct commenced at a time when it was the beneficial owner and not a member—provided the effects of such conduct was continuing at the date of the petition.

The court referred to the converse situation which arose in *Re Via Net Works*

(Ireland) Ltd [2002] 2 I.R. 47 where the petitioner had entered into a binding contract to transfer the shares prior to the presentation of the petition, but had not done so. When the issue of locus standi arose Keane J. observed:

> "Persons, such as the petitioners, who have voluntarily disposed of their entire shareholding in a company, could not conceivably have been contemplated by the legislature as persons who would be entitled to relief under s. 205. Nor is it any answer to say that, because the petitioners have not transferred their shares, as they are contractually bound to do, they remain registered as members of the company. It is undoubtedly the case that a person who has become entitled to be registered as a shareholder may be unable to exercise any of his rights as a shareholder until his name has been entered on the register. But if does not follow that a person who, conversely, has voluntarily divested himself of all his shares in the company, but remains on the register must be treated as a member of the company for all the purposes. I have no doubt that, when the legislature enacted s. 205(1), it was not envisaged that persons without any interest in the company but who, for whatever reason, remained on the register as members would be entitled to present a petition grounded on alleged oppression of them as members."

In regard to the present petition Finlay Geoghegan J. observed:

> "Similarly, it appears to me, that when the legislature enacted s. 205(1), whilst it required a person to be a member to bring proceedings pursuant to the section, it did not envisage that a person who was the beneficial owner of shares, but not yet a member of the company, would, once he became a member and entitled to exercise his rights pursuant to s. 205(1), be precluded from relying upon conduct which commenced whilst he was the beneficial owner of the shares which he now held as a member."

Turning then to the question of whether the complaint complained of was conduct which has the continuing effect of being oppressive to or in disregard of its interests as a member of EGHL, the court was satisfied that it was. The decision taken to restructure the group by the respondents had the effect of excluding the petitioner from the benefit of a turnaround in the business of the group and that position had continued up to the date of the presentation of the petition. The court ordered that the respondents should purchase the shares of Banfi at a fair value which takes into account an estimated fair value of BCTL.

DISQUALIFICATION OF DIRECTORS

In *Director of Corporate Enforcement v Byrne* [2009] IESC 57 the appellant was disqualified by order of the High Court on July 31, 2008 following an application by the Director pursuant to a report of the inspectors appointed to investigate certain matters at National Irish Bank and National Irish Bank Financial Services Ltd. The inspectors made two criticisms of the appellant in the report. The first was that the appellant, after a DIRT Theme Audit Report and a subsequent related meeting in February 1995, failed in his responsibility to raise the issue of potential retrospective liability for DIRT due in respect of interest on accounts wrongly classified as DIRT exempt. The second criticism related to the drafting of circulars to branch staff in relation to the operation of non-resident accounts subsequent to that meeting. Murphy J. had concluded that the appellant should be disqualified under s.160(2)(e) of the Companies Act 1990, because in consequence of the inspectors' report, his conduct made him "unfit to be concerned in the management of a company" (See *Annual Review of Irish Law 2008*).

On appeal to the Supreme Court, the court found that the High Court had no jurisdiction, on the basis of its own findings, to have made a disqualification order. Denham J. reviewed the general authorities and legal propositions relating to disqualification (referring to *Business Communications Ltd v Baxter and Parsons*, unreported, High Court, July 21, 1995; *Re Newcastle Timber Ltd (In Liquidation)* [2001] 4 I.R. 586; *Cahill v Grimes, Re Readymix Ltd* [2002] 1 I.R. 372; *Re Lo-line Motors Ltd* (1988) B.C.L.C. 698; *Director of Corporate Enforcement v D'Arcy* [2006] 2 I.R. 163) and applied them to the criticisms of the appellant found by the inspectors. She observed that the High Court had found that in relation to the appellant there was no evidence of gross negligence or total incompetence or of him being a danger to the public. She affirmed these findings. Nonetheless, the High Court found that despite the fact that the inspectors had not made a finding of tax evasion against the appellant he had a responsibility to raise the issue of retrospective tax liability and he had failed to do so. On this basis the High Court found that the appellant displayed a lack of commercial probity. Denham J. concluded that the High Court had "fell into error in this analysis". In this regard Denham J. was satisfied that the key ingredient of "probity" is honesty and the Director had not alleged dishonesty on behalf of the appellant. She observed:

> "At its height the Inspectors' Report criticised the appellant for not exercising a responsibility, which he did not have, and which he did not realise arose. Commercial misjudgement is not sufficient. However, this did not arise as an issue in this case. The conduct complained of must display a lack of 'commercial probity', although in an extreme case of gross negligence or total incompetence disqualification could be appropriate. The High Court held that there was no evidence of gross

> negligence or total incompetence. There was no issue of dishonest behaviour by the appellant. Thus these aspects of the legal test are not met."

In conclusion, Denham J. was satisfied that the burden of establishing that a disqualification order should be made was not discharged. Fennelly J. considered that the primary dispute centred on the meaning of the term "unfit" in s.160(2)(e). He referred to the often cited passage of Browne-Wilkinson V.C. in *Re Lo-Line Motors Ltd* (1988) B.C.L.C. 698 where he had stated:

> "What is the proper approach to deciding whether someone is unfit to be a director? The approach adopted in all the cases to which I have been referred is broadly the same. The primary purpose of the section is not to punish the individual but to protect the public against the future conduct of companies by persons whose past records as directors of insolvent companies have shown them to be a danger to creditors and others. Therefore, the power is not fundamentally penal. Ordinary commercial misjudgment is in itself not sufficient to justify disqualification. In the normal case, the conduct complained of must display a lack of commercial probity, although I have no doubt that in an extreme case of gross negligence or total incompetence disqualification could be appropriate."

Fennelly J. accepted that whilst this passage was not definitive in relation to the concept of unfitness (referring to *Re Sevenoaks Stationers Ltd* [1991] Ch. 164) it did provide "useful pointers" as to how the court should assess the concept of "unfitness". The issue to be considered is whether the findings of the inspectors were such to warrant the conclusion that the appellant displayed a lack of commercial probity to the extent which warranted the disqualification order. Fennelly J. was satisfied that they did not and, accordingly, the High Court's findings could not be permitted to stand. The appeal was allowed.

COMPANIES (AMENDMENT) ACT 2009

The Companies (Amendment) Act 2009 was signed into law and commenced on July 12, 2009 and introduces a significant number of changes to Irish company law. The principal objective of the Act is to strengthen the compliance and enforcement related provisions of existing legislation by eliminating certain disclosure exemptions which applied to licensed banks in respect of director loans. The powers of the Director of Corporate Enforcement (the "Director") have been substantially amended, in particular in the area of search and seizure of relevant company documents and electronic information where that company is under investigation. Furthermore, the evidential burden on the Director when taking action against companies who breach provisions regarding directors' loans has been reduced. The key sections of the Act are as follows:

1. Section 2 amends the provisions of s.194 of the Companies Act 1963 which impose a duty on directors to declare their interests in contracts made by the company and a corresponding obligation on the company to maintain a book containing a copy of those declarations. Section 194 has been amended by the insertion of a new subs.5A. This subsection requires companies, if required by the Director, to produce the book containing a copy of those declarations to the Director and to make facilities available to the Director for inspecting or copying the book. Failure to comply with this provision renders the company and every officer of the company who is in default guilty of an offence and liable to a fine. If any inspection or production is refused the court may by order compel an immediate inspection or production.
2. Section 4 substitutes s.19(3) of the Companies Act 1990 and inserts a new s.19(3A). Essentially these amendments clarify the Director's power to require the production of books or documents from a third party where those books or documents relate to a company under investigation under s.19(2) of the Companies Act 1990. Where the Director exercises his power to direct a third party to produce such books or documents, it is now a criminal offence for that third party to destroy, mutilate, falsify or conceal any book or document which is the subject of the Director's directions.
3. Section 5 amends s.20 of the Companies Act 1990 by expanding the Director's powers in relation to entering and searching a premises including allowing a court to extend the period of validity of a warrant and allowing the Director to seize and remove papers and electronic information for examination elsewhere. Furthermore, an officer of the Director may seize anything at the premises named on the search warrant (or in the custody or possession of any person found on the premises) if he has reasonable grounds for believing that it may contain material information and it is not reasonably practicable for him to make a determination at the premises as to whether that item falls within the scope of the search warrant. The officer may also take information and documents outside the scope of the search warrant provided it is not reasonably practicable for him to separate that information and documents from material information which are within the scope of the search warrant. These powers must be exercised judiciously as they are subject to judicial review. Furthermore, the powers can only be exercised where the officer has made arrangements for the safe and confidential storage of those documents and ensures

that the lawful owner has access to them. The officer must make a determination within a specific timeframe and following this determination must return the non-material information within a prescribed period.

4. Section 6 is one of the more controversial aspects of the legislation. It amends s.23 of the Companies Act 1990 by permitting the Director to seize information that is claimed to be legally privileged. The confidentiality of this information must be maintained and it must be stored securely by the Director pending determination by the High Court as to whether any privilege attaches.
5. Section 7 substitutes s.40 of the Companies Act 1990 which relates to the criminal penalties for breach of the provisions relating to the general prohibition imposed on companies on the giving of loans and related credit transactions for its directors under s.31 of the Companies Act 1990. The new provision simplifies the offence and the proofs required as the offence is now directed at any "officer of the company who is in default" compared with the more cumbersome requirement in the former provision whereby the offence was directed at "an officer of a company who authorises or permits the company to enter into a transaction or arrangement knowing or having reasonable cause to believe that the company was thereby contravening section 31".
6. Section 8 amends ss.41 and 43 of the Companies Act 1990 which relate to the disclosure by companies of loan transactions and related arrangements and any other substantial transactions involving directors and connected persons in the company's financial statements. Prior to this amendment licensed banks or their holding companies were exempt from such disclosure requirements. Rather, the financial statements would set out the aggregate amount of relevant transactions to all directors and connected persons. Under the new provisions licensed banks are no longer exempt and must disclose the same details of all transactions (including those entered into in the ordinary course of business) with directors as other companies. Transactions with connected persons, which are entered into in the ordinary course of business, need only be disclosed on an aggregate basis as before. However, transactions entered into with connected persons and which are not entered into in the ordinary course of business and on non-commercial terms must be fully disclosed.
7. Section 9 amends s.44 of the Companies Act 1990 in relation to clarifying the additional disclosure rules imposed on licensed banks in respect of loan and related transactions and certain contracts involving directors and connected persons. Under s.44

licensed banks must maintain registers of certain transactions with directors and connected persons. Under the amended section these registers must include the additional disclosure requirements mentioned in the previous paragraph. Furthermore, the Director may now have access to these registers.

8. Section 10 amends the residency requirements of directors as set out in ss.43 and 44 of the Companies (Amendment) (No. 2) Act 1999. The requirement that at least one director of Irish companies had to be resident in the State (subject to certain exemptions) has now been replaced by the requirement that such a director be resident in any Member State of the European Economic Area (the European Union States and Iceland, Norway and Liechtenstein). This amendment was required to address the concerns that the previous provision was contrary to the EU's freedom of establishment principles.

COMPANIES (MISCELLANEOUS PROVISIONS) ACT 2009

The Companies (Miscellaneous Provisions) Act 2009 was enacted on December 23, 2009. The principal objective of the Act is to provide in limited circumstances, for a transitional period only, for the use by certain parent undertakings of internationally recognised accounting standards other than those recognised and required by existing legislation. In many cases these companies have moved or are moving to Ireland but as they are listed on the US Stock Exchange they are obliged to produce US GAAP accounts. The existing regime in Ireland is principally the International Financial Reporting Standards (IFRS) and Irish GAAP, but under these new measures these companies may continue to prepare their financial statements using US GAAP for such of its first four financial years (up until December 31, 2015) after it is incorporated in Ireland subject to specific criteria. These criteria are as follows:

(1) The relevant parent undertaking does not have securities admitted to trading on a regulated market in the EU or the EEA;
(2) The relevant parent undertaking has its securities registered with the Securities Exchange Commission of the United States of America (SEC) or which is otherwise subject to reporting to the SEC under the laws of the USA; and
(3) The relevant parent undertaking has not made and was not required to make, prior to the commencement of this Act, an annual return to the registrar of companies to which accounts were required to have been annexed.

The Act limits the extent of the use of US GAAP where it contravenes any provision of the Companies Acts or of any regulations made thereunder that: (a) a true and fair view of the state of affairs and profit or loss of a relevant parent undertaking may be given by the use by that undertaking of those principles in the preparation of its Companies Act individual accounts; and (b) a true and fair view of the state of affairs and profit or loss of a relevant parent undertaking and its subsidiary undertakings as a whole may be given by the use by that relevant parent undertaking of those principles in the preparation of its Companies Act group accounts. The Act provides that where such accounts are prepared in accordance with these provisions, the notes of those accounts must contain a statement to that effect.

The Act also empowers the Minister to make regulations that may prescribe other specified internationally recognised accounting standards subject to specified criteria.

The Act also amends the provisions of s.7(3) of the Companies Act 1990 whereby the court may, where it appoints an inspector to investigate the affairs of the company, require the applicant to give security for the costs of the investigation up to a certain amount. This limit has now been removed giving the court absolute discretion in this regard. Minor changes have also been made in relation to the market purchase of own shares under the Companies Act 1990 whereby, by order of the Minister, certain overseas Stock Exchanges outside the State may be recognised for the purposes of the market purchase rules. This provision is designed to facilitate international companies that are relocating their parent undertaking to Ireland, that are not listed on the Irish Stock Exchange and that wish to make market purchases of their own shares.

The UCITS Regulations have also been amended to provide a mechanism whereby collective investment funds can move their registered offices into Ireland without having to wind up in their current jurisdiction. These funds will be regulated by the Irish Financial Regulator.

SECONDARY LEGISLATION

Shareholders' Rights (Directive 2007/36/EC) Regulations 2009 (S.I. No. 316 of 2009) These regulations give effect to Directive 2007/36/EC of the European Parliament and of the Council relating to shareholders' rights where the company is trading on a regulated market (which includes the ISEQ). The key amendments introduced by these regulations relate to the rights of shareholders at meetings of these companies and are as follows.

Section 133 of the Companies Act 1963 (the "1963 Act") sets out the notice requirements for the different types of companies depending on the nature of the general meeting. The notice requirements of s.133 of the 1963 Act have been amended by these regulations by restricting the circumstances in which companies trading on a regulated market (including the ISEQ) can rely on the

14-day notice period for general meetings (other than annual general meetings or general meetings for the passing of a special resolution). These companies may only have a 14-day notice period where the company offers electronic voting to all holders of shares with voting rights and a special resolution authorising the 14-day notice period has been passed at the immediately preceding general meeting.

The regulations insert s.133A into the 1963 Act which provides for additional notice requirements for companies traded on a regulated market and to make available specified information on its internet site for a continuous period beginning not later than 21 days before a general meeting. The additional information includes, inter alia, the place and time of the meeting, the proposed agenda, a clear and precise statement of any procedures a member must comply with in order to participate and vote in the meeting, the record date for eligibility for voting, where and how the full unabridged text of the documents and draft resolutions, and the internet site at which, the information shall be made available.

The regulations insert s.133B into the 1963 Act which gives shareholders of companies traded on a regulated market the right to put items on the agenda of the general meeting and to table draft resolutions subject to the members concerned holding 3 per cent of the issued share capital, representing at least 3 per cent of the total voting rights of all the members who have a right to vote at the meeting to which the request for inclusion of the item relates and other notice criteria.

The regulations insert s.134A into the 1963 Act which provides new requirements for participation and voting in general meetings of companies traded on a regulated market. Essentially in order to participate and vote, a person must be entered in the relevant register of securities by the "record date" which is a date not more than 48 hours before the general meeting to which it relates. Members are entitled to sells their shares after the record date if the right to sell is not otherwise restricted.

The regulations insert s.134B into the 1963 Act which allows companies trading on a regulated market to conduct their general meetings by electronic means including voting mechanisms, real time electronic transmission of the meeting including two-way communication enabling member to address the meeting externally. Where companies elect to provide for such participation they are subject to certain requirements and restrictions.

The regulations insert s.134C into the 1963 Act which provides for the first time a statutory right of a member of a company traded on a regulated market to ask questions relating to items on the agenda of a general meeting and to have those questions answered.

Section 136 of the Companies Act 1963 is amended by the insertion of s.136(1A) and (1B) which clarifies the rules in relation to proxies for companies trading on a regulated market including their appointment electronically. Furthermore, in the case of those companies no limitation may be placed on the right to appoint more than one proxy to attend and vote at a general meeting in respect of shares held in different securities accounts (s.136(2A)(a) of the 1963 Act) provided that a member shall not be entitled to appoint more than one proxy to attend and vote on the same occasion unless the member is an intermediary acting on behalf of clients.

Section 138 of the Companies Act 1963 has been substituted by new provisions which permit companies traded on a regulated market to provide for voting by correspondence subject to minimal identification requirements. The company is only required to count those votes where they are received before the date and time specified by the company, which cannot be more than 24 hours before the time at which the vote is to be concluded.

Section 145 of the Companies Act 1963 has been amended by the insertion of a new s.145A which provides that any member of a company trading on a regulated market has the right to request a full account of a vote before or on the declaration of the result of a vote at a general meeting. Where no such request is made the company may proceed by way of a show of hands.

Companies (Auditing and Accounting) Act 2003 (Procedures Governing the Conduct of Section 24 Investigations) Regulations 2009 (S.I. No. 355 of 2009) These Regulations set out the procedures governing the conduct of investigations by the Irish Auditing and Accounting Supervisory Authority pursuant to s.24 of the Companies (Auditing and Accounting) Act 2003 (the "2003 Act"). The Irish Auditing and Accounting Supervisory Authority (the "Authority") was established pursuant to the provisions of the 2003 Act and one of its functions is to undertake, under s.24 of the Act, investigations into possible breaches of the prescribed accountancy bodies' standards by a member/member firm. Pursuant to s.28 of the 2003 Act, in September 2008 the Authority adopted and issued interim regulations governing the conduct of investigations under s.24. At that time the Authority also published a Consultation Paper for the purpose of seeking interested parties' views on the interim regulations and indicated that, upon completion of the consultation exercise, the interim regulations would be superseded by final regulations. These regulations are the culmination of that process.

European Communities (Directive 2006/46) Regulations 2009 (S.I. No. 450 of 2009) The European Communities (Directive 2006/46) Regulations 2009 (S.I. No. 450 of 2009) give effect to Directive 2006/46 of the European Parliament and of the Council, of 14 June 2006 amending Council Directives 78/660 on the annual accounts of certain types of companies, 83/349 on consolidated accounts, 86/635 on the annual accounts and consolidated accounts of banks and financial institutions and 91/674 on the annual accounts and consolidated accounts of insurance undertakings.

Companies (Auditing And Accounting) Act 2003 (Commencement) Order 2009 (S.I. No. 113 of 2009) This order sets January 27, 2009 as the day upon which s.36 of the Companies (Auditing and Accounting) Act 2003 comes into effect. Section 36 inserts a new s.192A into the Companies Act 1990 which provides statutory backing for the disciplinary procedures of prescribed accountancy bodies.

Companies Act 1963 (Alteration Of Eight Schedule) Order 2009 (S.I. No. 302 of 2009) This order alters the Eight Schedule to the Companies Act, 1963 by replacing Pt 1 of the existing schedule relating to the fees to be paid to the Registrar of Companies. It further revokes the Companies (Fees) (No.4) Order 2005 (S.I. No. 737 of 2005) and the Companies (Fees) Order 2006 (S.I. No. 502 of 2006).

Conflicts of Law

INTERNATIONAL CHILD ABDUCTION

Habitual residence The concept of habitual residence is relatively straightforward where adults are concerned but considerably less so in relation to children, as the jurisprudence on the Hague Child Abduction Convention reveals. The reason is clear enough: children, especially when very young, do not determine where they live. Decisions about their country of residence are made by adults, usually their parents; sometimes one parent, in making this decision, will be acting contrary to the wishes, or legal entitlements, of the other parent. If might were right and courts had to look only to the objective facts of the child's residence, ascriptions of habitual residence would be easier but would also yield results that some courts are not willing to countenance from the standpoint of justice or practicality of implementation of the Convention's policy goals. In seeking fair solutions, courts have allowed themselves to become enmeshed in analysis of the intentions of the spouses, with the consequent danger of creating an elaborate conceptual edifice, contradicting the original primary rationale of habitual residence, which was its simple factual character, and yielding unpredictable outcomes.

In *S v S* [2009] IESC 77, affirming [2009] IEHC 345, the Supreme Court grappled with these confusions. In one sense the case is straightforward. An Irish mother and Australian father met in Australia, quickly produced a child and married in December 2007, the child being born the following April. They all came to Ireland in mid-December 2008. The father left Ireland before the end of January and returned to Australia at the beginning of February 2009. The mother refused the father's request that their daughter also return to Australia. The crucial question in the case concerned the habitual residence of the child: had it changed from Australian to Irish in that very short period? If it had not, then of course the Hague Convention was engaged; if it had, the Convention would have no application.

MacMenamin J. examined the evidence as to the spouses' relationship, their stated intentions and conduct. He concluded that the infant's habitual residence had remained Australian. There had been "no long term continuity to the residence in Ireland". MacMenamin J. observed:

> "The time in question here is certainly not 'appreciable'. [The infant] is not in her mother's sole lawful custody. Looked at another way, the

> issue which this Court must determine is whether there existed a *joint settled intention* that the child should not return to Australia, at least in the foreseeable future, and instead should take up residence in Ireland. I am not convinced that the evidence establishes even this. The unilateral intent of one parent does not establish a joint settled intention. There is evidence that the hope and aspiration of the respondent was that she would return to Ireland. She may well have hoped that the applicant would join her in this intention. But looked at objectively, I think the evidence only establishes that the applicant was simply prepared, in the colloquial sense, to 'give it a go' in Ireland, but that at no time did he abandon his long term intention to reside in Australia. He did not break his ties with that country. He did not give up his job completely or resign from it. Both parties retained some at least of their household goods in Australia, although they bought others here. Insofar as there was a joint common intention, the parties may have agreed that they would not live in Australia for a significant period, but this does not establish that they intended to set up a joint residence in Ireland on a continuous basis. Certainly the material does not establish that they resided here in such a manner as to be 'settled'."

The mother appealed unsuccessfully to the Supreme Court. Macken J. (Kearns P. and Fennelly J. concurring) observed that:

> "[the] Convention itself does not define 'habitual residence'. That of a small child, being utterly reliant on parents in relation to its place of residence, is, *ipso facto*, dependent in turn on assessing the parents' movements, actions and intentions, so as to ascertain therefrom their habitual residence and therefore, except in what must be very rare cases indeed, where the child's habitual residence also is. This is well established in the *jurisprudence*, and in any event, is clearly a matter of common sense."

Macken J. concentrated her analysis on the notion of "a settled purpose" (or, by way of variant, "settled purposes") which emerged in Lord Scarman's speech in *R. v Barnet London Borough Council, Ex p Shah* [1983] 2 A.C. 309 and had since assumed canonical status. Lord Scarman was seeking to define "ordinary residence" but in later decisions the courts had accepted that there was no difference in the core meaning of the term from that of "habitual residence". Lord Scarman had stated:

> "Unless … it can be shown that the statutory framework or the legal context in which the words are used requires a different interpretation, I unhesitatingly subscribe the view that 'ordinarily resident' refers to man's abode in a particular place or country, *which he has adopted*

> *voluntarily and for settled purposes as part of the regular order of his life for the time being, whether of short or of long duration*" (emphasis added by Macken J.).

He had gone on to observe: "All that is necessary is that the purpose of living where one does has a sufficient degree of continuity to be properly described as settled."

He had also stated:

> "For if there be proved a regular habitual mode of life in a particular place, the continuity of which was persisted despite temporary absences, ordinary residence is established provided only it is adopted *voluntarily and for a settled purpose*" (emphasis added by Macken J.).

This conceptual apparatus found its way into Waite J.'s judgment in *Re B: (Minors: Abduction) (No. 2)* [1993] 1 F.L.R. 993 which was in turn incorporated with approval into Fennelly J.'s judgment in the Supreme Court decision of *PAS v AFS* [2005] 1 I.L.R.M. 306, analysed in the *Annual Review of Irish Law 2004*, pp.134–139.

Macken J. discerned a difference between a "settled purpose" and a "settled intention", to which she attached some significance:

> "The nub of the difficulty is that the extracts from cases in which habitual residence is determined by assessing whether there was a 'settled purpose' to the move do not fall to be easily applied to facts in other cases where no similar or analogous settled purpose can necessarily be established, including the present case. In such cases, the formula mentioned by Waite, J. in *Re B (Minors: Abduction*) [(No.2) [1993] 1 FLR 993], that the assumption of habitual residence requires 'an appreciable period of time and a settled intention' may be more apt to be applied. I do not see in the case law any suggestion that a move for a 'settled purpose voluntarily undertaken' is always the same as having a 'settled intention' to acquire a new habitual residence. This also flows from the judgment of Scarman L. in the *Shah* case, and also from the judgment of Thorpe L.J. in *Al Habtoor* [*v Fotheringham* [2001] 1 FLR 951].
>
> The reason I consider it necessary to draw some distinction between the presence and absence of a 'settled purpose' which may permit a court, on the facts, to find with ease that habitual residence, even for a very short period of time, has been established and the latter test, is because the absence of a settled purpose, if that phrase is to apply in all cases, may lead to a child being left with no clear habitual residence. This is especially so in the case of parents leading, as is no longer a rarity, peripatetic, nomadic or transient lifestyles. I would, in the case of

> a doubt, lean against leaving a young child in such a position. That this possibility is real is evident from the large numbers of persons travelling between Member States of the European Union, even travelling without a clear settled purpose to two or more member States, over quite short periods of time. The requirement to establish a settled intention on the part of the parents to acquire an habitual residence is, in my view, essential, to guard against such uncertainty."

In the instant case, on the question whether Ireland had been "adopted voluntarily and for settled purposes" as the country where the parties would live as part of the regular order of their life for the time being, whether of short or long duration, MacMenamin J. had before him:

> "... sufficient evidence upon which he could properly conclude that, while the parties intended to come to Ireland, it was only to 'give it a go' even for up to one year if matters developed, [and] that [the] evidence did not go so far as to suggest that they had a joint settled purpose in doing so".

Applying the joint settled intention test, Macken J. considered that MacMenamin J. had reached the correct conclusions based on the findings of fact which he made following upon cross-examination and his assessment of the evidence and demeanour of the witnesses.

Macken J.'s distinction between a "settled purpose" and a "settled intention" has not been recognised in England. Cheshire, North & Fawcett, *Private International Law,* 14th edn, by James Fawcett & Janeen Carruthers (Oxford: OUP, 2008), p.189, fn.339 observe that "[t]here does not appear to be any difference between the two". Nevertheless, it may be useful to point to the complexities and ambiguities of the word "settled" and the notion of settlement as well as the subtleties and uncertainties of the distinction between "purpose" and "intention".

It is most unfortunate that Lord Scarman should have chosen the word "settled" in this context because of its strong association with long-term residence, which is not actually required for establishing either ordinary or habitual residence. Settlers are people who move to a country with an intention to stay there for the very long haul. More modestly, a person becomes settled in a new environment only after having put down some roots. What Lord Scarman was seeking to deal with was to provide the extra ingredient which would transform mere physical presence into ordinary residence. He chose "settled purpose" because it distinguishes presence of a completely uncommitted and tentative character from one that involves some mental commitment on the part of the propositus. What is important to note here is that the existence of a "settled purpose" makes it easier for a court to find ordinary (or habitual) residence even where the period is short. This is in contrast to the position of a drifter, disconnected from his or her environment, with no clear life plan. A month's residence in a country based on a clear purpose, even one of a temporary character, is more likely to be characterised as constituting ordinary (or habitual) residence than the same period where the propositus lacks focus or is entirely tentative as to whether to go or stay throughout that period. Yet it is clear that the establishment of a habitual residence does not *depend* on any settled purpose: provided the residence is long enough, then, even without such purpose, it will—eventually—become habitual. This distinguishes habitual residence from domicile because, without the necessary intent to reside permanently or indefinitely in a particular country, the person's domicile will not be changed, no matter how many years pass.

The word "intention" in this context is also unfortunate as its precise contours are hard to discern. We have only to think of the morass into which criminal law has sunk when trying to give an exact meaning to the term, which is a key element of mens rea. Intention is here contrasted with motive; yet what is the relationship between "intention" and "purpose"? A purpose might, in some contexts at least, be regarded as more specific and potentially less immediate than an intention. A person enters a shop intending to buy a hammer for the purpose of using it to put a nail in the wall to hang a picture. Of course, one could also say that the person has the intention of using the nail in that way and that the person, when entering the shop, has the purpose of buying a hammer; yet, in ordinary discourse, there can be nuanced contextual preferences for one or other word.

In the context of the habitual residence of parents, it seems entirely reasonable to use "settled purpose" and "settled intention" interchangeably; yet the word "intention" could be regarded as involving a somewhat less clearly focused commitment to one's place of residence. If I go to another country with no clear plans (as the parents did, when coming to Ireland in the instant case), it is very hard to identify a "purpose" but somewhat less difficult to identify an "intention". The parents in the instant case definitely intended to spend some time in Ireland, though their purpose was more opaque.

Complicating matters further is the fact that, in cases such as this, courts seek to identify a common purpose or intention between two individuals. The word "settled" here assumes further ambiguity since it may connote an *agreement between the parents* rather than the individual settlement of purpose or intention. Such an agreement could of course be arrived at expressly but in most cases courts will be searching for an implied agreement, a far more elusive, and frankly contentious concept.

Macken J.'s analysis has therefore served to highlight the difficulty of the notion of "settled purpose" in this context. It is interesting to note that courts in the United States of America are divided on its utility or precise meaning. Some have embraced it enthusiastically, focusing on parental intentions. *Mozes v Mozes*, 239 F. 3d 1067 (9th Cir. 2001) is perhaps the clearest example. Others have placed less emphasis on the intentions of the parents. In *Feder v*

Evans-Feder, 63 F. 3d 217 (3rd Cir. 1995) it was stated that the child's habitual residence "is a place where he or she has been physically present for an amount of time for acclimatization and which has a 'degree of settled purpose' from the child's perspective". For analysis of the competing approaches, see Gadic Zohar, "Habitual Residence: An Alternative to the Common Law Concept of Domicile?" 9 Whittier J. of Child and Fam. Advocacy 169 (2009).

In *EB v AG* [2009] IEHC 104, Finlay Geoghegan J. threw some light on the extent to which courts should expand their consideration beyond the facts to take account of parental entitlements when determining a child's habitual residence. The applicant and the mother had a relationship in 1995, resulting in the birth of child in 1996. All parties were nationals of Latvia. The child lived with his mother and maternal grandparents in Latvia from birth until 2003, and thereafter with his maternal grandmother in Latvia until August 2007. The applicant acknowledged that he was the father of the child some years after his birth.

The mother came to Ireland in 2003. The child remained in Latvia and visited his mother in Ireland during school holidays. He had access visits with the applicant whilst in Latvia. In 2006 the child's mother married the respondent, a national of Romania who had resided in Ireland since 2000. The mother was diagnosed with cancer in 2006 and returned to Latvia with the respondent for a number of months to receive medical treatment. The mother and the respondent brought the child to Ireland in August 2007 and he commenced school the following month. The mother died in May 2008.

The child travelled with the respondent to Latvia on May 14, 2008 for the mother's funeral. On May 15 the applicant determined that the child should return to live in Latvia, though not necessarily when this should happen. He consented to his son's returning to Ireland with the respondent until the end of the school year in June. (There was some confusion as to whether this was on June 15 or 27 but nothing turned on the difference.) The child and respondent came back to Ireland on May 28. The respondent subsequently declined to permit the child to go back to Latvia.

When the applicant sought the child's return, the crucial question related to his habitual residence on June 15. There was no dispute that on his mother's death the child's habitual residence was Irish. Counsel for the applicant argued that the applicant's unilateral determination on May 15 that the child should return to Latvia had the effect of changing his habitual residence to Latvian. Finlay Geoghegan J. did not agree. It appeared to her that the argument ran counter to the "well established view" of the courts in Ireland and in England that the terms "habitual residence", or "habitually resident", as used in art.3 of the Convention, were not to be treated as terms of art with some special meaning, but rather to be understood according to the ordinary and natural meaning of the two words they contained. In her view:

> "[T]he child during June 2008 continued to reside in Ireland and attend

> school in Dublin as he had done prior to May 2008. This residence in Ireland was without objection from the applicant either until 15th June, 2008, or more probably the end of the Irish school year which is stated to have been 27th June, 2008. During this period, the child continued as a matter of fact to be resident in Ireland and by reason of his prior habitual residence also I have concluded to continue to be habitually resident in Ireland. There was no decision that his place of residence should change prior to the end of the Irish school year. There was no change in this period in his place of habitual residence. Without a change in his habitual residence, he cannot have acquired a habitual residence in Latvia."

This conclusion was sufficient to determine the issue but Finlay Geoghegan J. did not wish to be understood as accepting the submission of counsel for the applicant that a decision taken by the applicant, as the sole person entitled to determine where the child should live, that the child return to live in Latvia, had the effect of changing the child's habitual residence from Ireland to Latvia after the date upon which the decision was intended to come into effect without any change in where the child lived:

> "Where as on the facts herein the child is 12 and has an acquired habitual residence in Ireland it does not appear to me that such decision alone changes the habitual residence of the child. Whilst there may be a settled intention by the applicant as sole guardian that the child return to reside in Latvia at a specified date, if the child does not comply with the decision and continues to reside in Ireland after that date, then for so long as he does so it does not appear to me on an assessment of all the facts and giving the words 'habitual residence' their natural or ordinary meaning I should conclude that there has been a change in the habitual residence of the child from Ireland to Latvia. There has been no change in the country of residence of the child. He has not ceased to reside in Ireland albeit this factual position may be contrary to the decision by the applicant as his sole guardian. Nevertheless, it is the factual position and as such essential to the determination of habitual residence."

Consent In *S v S* [2009] IESC 77, affirming [2009] IEHC 345, where spouses who had been living in Australia came to Ireland in mid-December 2008 and had split up within a month, the husband leaving Ireland to return to Australia without his child at the end of January 2009, the defence of consent failed hopelessly. MacMenamin J. held that there had been no clear evidence of consent. At best it showed that the spouses had agreed in January that the marriage was not going to survive; that "was not ... tantamount to the [husband's] consenting to [the child's] being retained" in Ireland. There had been "no real positive or unequivocal consent"; nor had there been any words or conduct from which consent could be informed. On appeal, the Supreme Court considered the defence to be so "wholly unsustainable" that it did not require to hear counsel for the husband on this ground.

Acquiescence In *N v N* [2009] IEHC 213, Sheehan J. had little hesitation in rejecting the defence of acquiescence where a recently divorced mother had wrongfully removed her six-year-old child from Lithuania to Ireland on June 18, 2008 to stay with her parents. The father made several attempts to contact her on her Lithuanian mobile phone before getting in touch with the Child Protection Services in Lithuania on July 17. In his initial contact with the Child Protection Services, the father had indicated an intention to seek a communication order from the courts rather than an order for the return of his son. He gave them her email address. He had not communicated with the mother by email during the period since she had gone to Ireland but, when the Child Protection Services did so, the following day, she responded immediately. Thereafter the applicant had intermittent contact with his son and former wife.

In Sheehan J.'s view, while there was "a degree of ambivalence" in the father's approach to his son's living in Ireland, it did not amount to acquiescence. Although there had been some delay on his part in approaching the Lithuanian authorities, it was also the case that he had indicated to them an intention "to approach the court about the child's abduction".

Grave risk of harm In *A v A (aka McC)* [2009] IEHC 460, Finlay Geoghegan J. held that the defence of grave risk of harm under art.13(b) of the Child Abduction Convention had not been made out where the mother of three children alleged that the father had been violent towards her and had caused her in the past to live with the children in women's refuges in England, being forced to move from one to another between 2004 and the beginning of 2008. Even if this evidence were to be accepted, it did not appear to Finlay Geoghegan J. that there was any evidence that the English courts and other relevant authorities were not in a position at the time of judgment to protect the children and their mother from any potential threat of violence by the father. During the period since the mother had sought and obtained a non-molestation order in early 2008, there had been no evidence that the father had acted in breach of it.

In *Li v La* [2009] IEHC 585, a boy aged 10 and a half years, who had been taken to Ireland by his mother from Poland, said to a consultant clinical psychologist appointed by the High Court that his father had hit him in the face following a football match, giving him a black eye. The father in evidence strongly contradicted this claim. Edwards J. ordered the return of the boy and his younger brother, rejecting the defence of grave risk of harm. While he took into account the psychologist's concern about physical abuse, he did not regard the allegation as having been "next or near proven". Nothing in the paperwork from the proceedings in the Polish courts supported it, nor had it been supported by medical evidence. While the mother had made a "bald assertion" in a letter to the Polish court that the children were in fear of their father, there had been "no evidence to put flesh on the bones of that very skeletal assertion".

The mother's failure to turn up to court to participate in the hearing must undoubtedly have made the court's assessment of this issue a more difficult one. Edwards J. had regard to "the absence of evidence from the mother who I believe would have attended Court, or at least have put in an affidavit, if there was substance to this".

The child's objection to being returned Under art.13 of the Abduction Convention, the judicial authority may refuse to order the return of a child if it finds that the child objects to being returned and has attained an age and degree of maturity at which it is appropriate to take account of the child's views. In *A v A (aka McC)* [2009] IEHC 460, the mother of three children, aged nine, six and five, took them to Ireland in January 2009, in breach of an order of an English court. She alleged that in the past she had been the victim of violence from the father; she had obtained a non-molestation order against him in early 2008. Her argument that the children should not be returned on account of grave risk of harm failed as Finlay Geoghegan J. considered that the evidence had not established that the English courts and other relevant authorities would be unable to provide the necessary protection: see above, p.176. The argument that the children's wish not to be returned should be heeded was treated as being of greater significance.

A child psychologist interviewed the two elder children. In her report she concluded that, notwithstanding evidence of coaching, each of the children objected to being returned to England. Finlay Geoghegan J. was satisfied that the nine-year-old child was of an age and degree of maturity that the court should take her views into account. The six-year-old child appeared to be "marginally of an age and degree of maturity where the court should take his views into account". On balance, Finlay Geoghegan J. concluded that she should do so, while observing that "of course the child's young age and relative immaturity is a significant factor in determining the weight which should be given to the child's objections".

On the question whether, in light of the children's objections, the court should exercise its discretion against an order for return, Finlay Geoghegan J. drew inspiration from passages of the speech of Baroness Hale of Richmond in *Re M (Abduction: Child's objections)* [2008] 1 A.C. 1288, in one of which Baroness Hale had observed:

> "In child's objections cases, the range of considerations may be even wider than those in the other exceptions. The exception itself is brought into play when only two conditions are met: first, that the child herself objects to being returned and second, that she has attained an age and

degree of maturity at which it is appropriate to take account of her views. These days, and especially in the light of Article 12 of the United Nations Convention on the Rights of the Child, courts increasingly consider it appropriate to take account of a child's views. Taking account does not mean that those views are always determinative or even presumptively so. Once the discretion comes into play, the court may have to consider the nature and strength of the child's objections, the extent to which they are 'authentically her own' or the product of the influence of the abducting parent, the extent to which they coincide or are at odds with other considerations which are relevant to her welfare, as well as the general Convention considerations referred to earlier. The older the child, the greater the weight that her objections are likely to carry. But that is far from saying that the child's objections should only prevail in the most exceptional circumstances."

Finlay Geoghegan J. expressed agreement with:

"... the nuanced approach suggested to considering the balance to be achieved on the particular facts of each case, and having regard to a number of factors including the nature and strength of the child's objections, the extent to which they are 'authentically her own' or may have been influenced by others and the age and maturity of the child".

In this context it is worth noting that the overall tenor of Baroness Hale's treatment of art.12 of the Convention on the Rights of the Child is less than effusive: her comments surround this important provision with references to other factors that tend, cumulatively, to weaken its force.

Counsel for the mother made the novel argument that the policy of the Convention must be considered in the context of art.11(6) to (8) of the Brussels II *bis* Regulation. Whereas, in Convention cases where the Regulation did not apply, if a requested court determined not to make an order for return of a child then, subject to appeal in that jurisdiction, it was a final order, that was no longer the case where the Regulation applied. Article 11(6) to (8) of the Regulation gave to the court of prior habitual residence the entitlement, in effect, to override an order for non-return. Finlay Geoghegan J. observed that:

"[i]t does not appear that the potential for the Court of habitual residence to make an enforceable order for return pursuant to Article 11(8) takes away from the requirement that this Court take into account the policy of the Convention, not only to secure the prompt return of abducted children, but also to deter abduction in the first place, and to respect the judicial process of other contracting states. Nevertheless, it is a factor to be taken into account and the weight to be attached would depend

> upon the facts of the particular application. Care must be taken that the policy of the Convention to deter abduction is not undermined by giving an advantage in any subsequent hearing to a parent who wrongfully removed children. If the Court of the jurisdiction of habitual residence is required to consider custody issues, including an issue of return in the context of the Court of another member state having made an order for non-return, there may be such an advantage or a perceived advantage."

With regard to the children's objections, Finlay Geoghegan J. considered that they were in part based on their preference for their life in Ireland. On balance, she concluded that, having regard to the nature of the children's objections and their ages and degrees of maturity:

> "[t]he court should not depart from the policy of the Convention, even when combined with a consideration of the provisions of Article 11(6) to (8) of the Regulation, having regard, in particular, to the existence of the English order … prohibiting the mother from doing what she did."

Accordingly, Finlay Geoghegan J. exercised her discretion so as to make an order for the return of the three children. Finlay Geoghegan J. placed a stay on the order for return for about two months in order to permit the mother to pursue her application for permission to relocate to Ireland, on her undertaking that she would do so promptly and attend, with the children if required, any court hearings or meetings that the English courts might direct.

In *N v N* [2009] IEHC 213, the child whose views were in issue was six years old. The consultant clinical psychologist appointed by the court reported that he did not wish to return to Lithuania since this would mean that he would no longer live with his natural grandparents in Ireland. In the psychologist's opinion, the boy was capable of forming a view of whom he wanted to live with and was able to give clear reasons for his choice, not unduly influenced by his concern that a return to Lithuania would upset his mother. In earlier proceedings, Finlay Geoghegan J. had consented to the mother's application for an order that the boy be interviewed and assessed: [2008] IEHC 176. Finlay Geoghegan J. provided a comprehensive analysis of the circumstances in which such an order should be made: see the *Annual Review of Irish Law 2008*, pp.109–114. Sheehan J., in the light of this judgment and the evidence before him, concluded that the child had attained an age and a degree of maturity at which it was appropriate to take into account his views.

Turning to the question of the weight to be attached to the child's objection to being returned, Sheehan J. made the following important observation:

> "While it is clearly important to take the objections of the child into account, one has to be careful when considering the views of

> a young male child who has expressed a preference for his mother. The importance of a father's role in a child's upbringing may not be sufficiently appreciated by a young person, and is something that this Court is obliged to acknowledge. Indeed, this seems to be implicit in Article 24(3) of the Charter of Fundamental Rights of the European Union which states:
>
> > 'Every child shall have the right to maintain on a regular basis a personal relationship and direct contact with both his or her parents, unless that is contrary to his or her interests'.
>
> In light of the above I hold that the child's views in this case cannot be determinative, particularly when one takes into account his young age."

This passage is interesting because it identifies a reason for overruling the objection of the child. In most cases the applicant will be the father. If the principle underlying art.24(3) of the Charter is to be used as an a priori ballast for fathers' claims for the return of their children, this is a factor of some general importance. It is to be noted that Sheehan J. merely holds that, in light of this consideration, the child's views "cannot be determinative", but that is clear from the text of art.13 of the Hague Convention, which does not make the child's objection *decisive* but rather a matter to which regard may be given once the requirements it specifies have been met. The thrust of Sheehan J.'s analysis is that the principle underlying art.24(3) should be ascribed a certain weight, to be placed on the scales opposite the child's objection.

Sheehan J. went on, as Finlay Geoghegan J. did in *A v A (aka McC)* [2009] IEHC 460, to invoke the observations of Baroness Hale in *R v M (Abduction: Child's Objections*) [2008] 1 A.C. 1288 as further ballast against the child's objections to being returned. He considered that they "echoed" the eight factors that Denham J. had outlined in *B v B (Child Abduction)* [1998] 1 I.R. 299 in regard to the court's exercise of discretion. He observed that the Lithuanian court had already considered the issue of the father's access; it seemed to him that that court was the appropriate one to decide further access arrangements. He exercised his discretion in favour of an order for return, subject to a stay to enable the mother to make an application in Lithuania to have the matter of the child's access to his father reviewed by the Lithuanian court in light of the mother's existing circumstances.

It is worth noting that in both *A v A (aka McC)* and *N v N*, the court counterbalanced the child's objection with overwhelmingly a priori considerations. Presumably it is open to a court, while applying these considerations uniformly, to come to varying conclusions from case to case as to whether to order the return of the child, based on the particular facts of each case. In that regard, a court will be likely to tend to give greater weight to the views of older and more mature children.

In *Li v La* [2009] IEHC 585, Edwards J. endorsed the approach that Sheehan

J. had adopted in *N v N* [2009] IEHC 213 in relation to the principle underlying art.24(3) of the European Charter of Fundamental Rights, in overriding the objection of a 10-and-a-half-year-old boy to being returned to Poland on the application of his father. Edwards J. was not satisfied on the evidence that it was contrary to the interest of either the boy or his younger brother, that they "should have the society of their father".

JURISDICTION

Prorogation of jurisdiction Article 23 of Brussels 1 provides as follows:

> 1. If the parties, one or more of whom is domiciled in a Member State, have agreed that a court or the courts of a Member State are to have jurisdiction to settle any disputes which have arisen or which may arise in connection with a particular legal relationship, that court or those courts shall have jurisdiction. Such jurisdiction shall be exclusive unless the parties have agreed otherwise. Such an agreement conferring jurisdiction shall be either:
>   a. in writing or evidenced in writing; or
>   b. in a form which accords with the practices which the parties have established between themselves; or
>   c. in international trade or commerce, in a form which accords with a usage of which the parties are or ought to have been aware and which in such trade or commerce is widely known to, and regularly observed by, parties to contracts of the type involved in the particular trade or commerce concerned …

In *O'Connor v Masterwood (UK) Ltd* [2009] IESC 49, the Supreme Court had no hesitation in holding that the parties had agreed to confer exclusive jurisdiction on the Italian courts where the plaintiffs, who had a joinery business in Kerry and who sought a specialised woodcutting machine from an Italian company, had signed and returned an order form and document headed "General Conditions of Sale" faxed to it by the Italian company. The document included a clause which stated: "For any controversy arising from the present contract or connected to the same, the Court of Rimini shall have sole jurisdiction."

When the plaintiffs sued the defendants in Ireland alleging defects in the machine, the second defendant challenged the jurisdiction of the Irish courts, invoking art.23.

In the view of Fennelly J. (Denham and Geoghegan JJ. concurring), subpara.(a) applied:

> "The clause is in a written document which was signed. Nothing more is required … The jurisdiction clause is both in writing and evidenced in writing. Article 23 does not appear expressly to require the signature of the party to be bound. In any event, the contract and the clause are signed."

While it was strictly unnecessary to consider whether subpara.(c) applied, Fennelly J. considered it equally clear that it did. He thought it unnecessary to repeat the analysis set out in his judgment in *Bio-Medical Research Ltd v Delatex SA* [2000] 4 I.R. 307, which we discussed in the *Annual Review of Irish Law 2000*, pp.64–65. He noted that, in *MSG v Gravères Rhénanes* [1997] ECR 1-911, the European Court of Justice had recalled that the original form of art.17 of the Convention had been amended so as to provide that:

> "[i]n international trade or commerce, any jurisdiction clause may be validly concluded in a form which accords with practices in that trade or commerce of which the parties are or ought to have been aware."

While laying emphasis on the need to establish consensus on the application of the clause, the court had nonetheless continued:

> "To take the view, however, that the relaxation thus introduced relates solely to the requirements as to form laid down by Article 17 by merely eliminating the need for a written form of consent would be tantamount to disregarding the requirements of non-formalism, simplicity and speed in international trade or commerce and to depriving that provision of a major part of its effectiveness.
>
> Thus, in the light of the amendment made to Article 17 … consensus on the part of the contracting parties as to a jurisdiction clause is presumed to exist where commercial practices in the relevant branch of international trade or commerce exist in this regard of which the parties are or ought to have been aware."

Fennelly J. considered that it "would be to overlook the obvious" if the court were to ignore the admitted signature of the first-named plaintiff on a set of printed conditions containing a clear and express jurisdiction clause:

> "It may well be that the first-named plaintiff paid little attention to the terms of printed conditions. That is commonplace. However, people engaged in trade, certainly in international trade, must be taken to be aware that printed conditions contain clauses which can affect their rights. They choose to ignore them at their peril. That is why Article 23, section 1, subparagraph (c) refers to practices of which parties '*ought to have been aware.*'

> In my view, it is inescapable that the jurisdiction clause was part of any agreement between the plaintiffs and the second-named defendant."

Accordingly the Supreme Court dismissed the appeal.

In *Ryanair Ltd v Bravofly Ltd* [2009] IEHC 41, Ryanair took proceedings in Ireland in relation to the use of automated systems and software to extract real time flight information from its website for the purposes of presenting it on websites facilitating flight search and booking services. This practice, known as "screen scraping", was alleged to constitute an infringement of Ryanair's intellectual property rights as well as the torts of conversion and trespass to goods. The second-named defendant, Travelfusion, an English company, invoked art.23 on the basis of a clause in the Terms of Use of the Ryanair website which provided as follows:

> "Disputes arising from the use of this website and the interpretation of these Terms of Use of the Ryanair website are governed by English Law. All disputes relating to these Terms of Use and the use of the Ryanair Website are subject to the exclusive jurisdiction of the English court, save that Ryanair may, at its sole discretion, institute proceedings in the country of your domicile."

Clarke J. noted that the parties had accepted that the circumstances giving rise to the issue in the case were highly unusual. The party who had produced the standard form containing a choice of jurisdiction clause was the one saying it did not apply. Equally the party denying that there was any contract at all was the one who was placing reliance on a clause which arose out of a contract alleged by its opponent but denied by it.

Clarke J. identified two important principles regarding the construction of the Brussels I Regulation. The first involved an autonomous Community law rule for the determination of whether the requirements for the application of a choice of jurisdiction clause had been met. The second was that decisions as to whether a choice of jurisdiction clause applied should be made in a relatively straightforward way. The issue between the parties so far as the choice of jurisdiction clause was concerned was whether there was a consensus as to that clause. It appeared to Clarke J. that:

> "[I]t would be most unsatisfactory if a court were required to enter into a detailed inquiry in relation to the underlying facts giving rise to the proceedings, similar to that which would need to be conducted to determine the central issues in the substantive proceedings, in order for the court to determine jurisdiction. In such a circumstance the court could hardly be said to be able to 'readily decide' the jurisdiction issue…

> While Travelfusion does deny the applicability of the Terms [of Use], it seems to me that it would do significantly less damage to the jurisdiction regime specified in the Brussels Regulation to permit, for the purposes of an action, a party to accept, for jurisdictional purposes only, the applicability of a jurisdiction clause sought to be imposed by the other side (while denying in the substantive proceedings the existence of any agreement) rather than creating a situation where it would be necessary to embark on a level of inquiry into the facts which would very closely parallel the inquiry that would be necessitated by a hearing of the substantive proceedings themselves."

It may be suggested that another view is possible. Article 23 becomes operative only when its preconditions have been fulfilled. It is not enough for a party to assert that the article applies to the case. Unless the preconditions specified by the article have been fulfilled to the satisfaction of the Irish court, the article has no effect in overriding the application of the other jurisdictional ground or grounds that the Regulation prescribes.

Lis pendens In *Goshawk Dedicated Ltd v Life Receivables Irl Ltd* [2009] IESC 7, the Supreme Court referred to the European Court of Justice the question whether, when a defendant is sued in its country of domicile, it is inconsistent with Regulation 44/2001 (Brussels 1) for the court of a Member State to decline jurisdiction or to stay proceedings on the basis that proceedings between the same parties and involving the same cause of action are already pending in the courts of a non-Member State and therefore first in time.

This question had been left unanswered in *Owusu v Jackson* [2005] ECR 1-1383, where the ECJ had made it clear that the *forum non conveniens* doctrine had no application even where the issue related to a state other than a Contracting State under the Brussels Convention. It had held that:

> "[t]he Brussels Convention precludes a court of a Contracting State from declining the jurisdiction conferred on it by Article 2 of that convention on the ground that a court of a non-Contracting State would be a more appropriate forum for the trial of the action even if the jurisdiction of no other Contracting State is in issue or the proceedings have no connecting factors to any other Contracting State."

See further Edwin Pecl, "*Forum non conveniens* and European Ideals", [1995] Lloyd's Maritime & Comm. L.Q. 363 and Adrian Briggs. "*Forum non conveniens* and Ideal Europeans", [1995] Lloyd's Maritime & Comm. L.Q. 378.

In the instant case, an Irish company had sued English companies in a United States federal court seeking a range of reliefs for alleged securities fraud. The European companies had later taken proceedings in Ireland against the Irish company claiming, in effect, that they had no such liability. Under traditional Irish rules of private international law, the *lis pendens* principle might be invoked against the Irish proceedings: see W. Binchy, *Irish Conflicts of Law* (Butterworths, 1988), pp.162–171. Brussels I contains rules for *lis pendens* where the claims are litigated in Member States. These rules do not deal with cases where a third state is involved. Article 34(4), however, does make reference to judgments in third states. It provides that a judgment should not be recognised:

> "... if it is irreconcilable with an earlier judgment given in another Member State or in a third State involving the same cause of action and between the same parties, provided that the earlier judgment fulfils the conditions necessary for its recognition in the Member State addressed".

In the instant proceedings in the High Court ([2008] IEHC 90; [2008] 2 I.L.R.M. 460), Clarke J. had held that an Irish court was required to exercise the mandatory jurisdiction conferred on it by art.2, notwithstanding the fact that there might be proceedings in a non-Member State which were first in time, involving the same subject matter, where a judgment from the court of the non-Member State would be recognised in Ireland.

Clarke J. acknowledged the unsatisfactory consequences of this rule but he considered that the difficulties had arisen because those who framed the Brussels Convention and Brussels I had not resolved the position in the texts.

JUDICIAL SEPARATION

In *S v S* [2009] IEHC 579, Abbott J. provided an important interpretation of the meaning of "habitual residence" as a ground, or an element of a ground, founding jurisdiction in proceedings for judicial separation under the Brussels II *bis* Regulation. He contrasted the interpretation of that term under the Hague Child Abduction Convention, which allows for the possibility that a person may have more than one place of habitual at one time, stating:

> "While I accept that if the court were dealing with a case involving child abduction I would be bound by these decisions, I do not consider them relevant to the issue as to whether there can be only one habitual residence at a time to be taken into consideration by a court in deciding whether it should accept jurisdiction under Brussels II *bis* of a case of which it is seized. *Marinos v. Marinos* [2007] EWHC 2047 (Fam.) and another English case *Monroe v. Monroe* [2007] EWHC 3315 (Fam.) are both authorities which I find to be of convincing persuasive effect

> for the reasons advanced in these judgments for the above proposition and particularly, by reason of the fact that the dynamic jurisdiction of Brussels II *bis*, arising from the intervention of the operation of the principle *lis alibi pendens*, absolutely compels the court to engage in a disciplined process to ascertain with certainty where the jurisdiction lies in the event of two courts of Member States being seised at the one time. It also arises from the requirement that the jurisdiction conferred on the courts of Members States by Brussels II *bis* is exclusive, that is to say there is no jurisdiction arising other than that which arises under the criteria set out in the Regulation. If the interpretation of habitual residence does not include a requirement that, it too, must be exclusive, then the whole working of the process ascertainment of jurisdiction under Brussels II *bis* would fall into chaos and the parties moving from one Member State to another would be denied the predictability and certainty in relation to jurisdiction and consequently enforceability of court decisions which Brussels II *bis* is primarily designed to provide."

In the instant case, Abbott J. considered that the centre of interest of the family:

> "… should be adjudicated upon the basis, *inter alia*, of the welfare of the children as defined by s. 3(1), para. (b) of the [Judicial Separation and Law Reform] Act [1989], not as an absolute guide, but as an appropriate model of analysis under the categories mentioned therein, where the definition is as follows:
>
> > '"welfare" comprises the religious and moral, intellectual, physical and social welfare of the children concerned'."

The family in the instant case was very rich; the spouses had established residences in both Ireland and the Cayman Islands, intending to reside for nine months each year in Ireland and the remaining three months in the Cayman Islands. Abbott J. considered that the "centre of interest" of the family was "predominantly and mainly Ireland" for four reasons. The spouses had placed importance on bringing up their six children in a Catholic culture; the husband's business was "in effect" administered from Ireland; the children's welfare interests were more effectively advanced in Ireland, which offered better educational and sporting facilities and a more integrated community life than the Cayman Islands; and greater protection was afforded by Irish law—the Family Home Protection Act 1976—to the wife and children.

There are some curious aspects to Abbott J.'s analysis. He placed considerable emphasis on assessing the children's welfare as defined by s.3(2)(b) of the Judicial Separation and Family Law Reform Act 1989 when determining the habitual residence of the spouses. Yet the test for determining habitual residence is one of factual connection rather than one of comparative benefit of application of competing legal systems. Moreover, the welfare of children is an entirely different question from the habitual residence of either of their parents. Abbott J. appears to be applying a normative rather than empirical test for determining a spouse's "centre of interests" in the context of habitual residence.

A further curiosity about Abbott J.'s approach is his apparent application of an "ordinary residence" test in conjunction with that of habitual residence. Under s.31(4) of the Judicial Separation and Family Law Reform Act 1989, the Irish courts have jurisdiction where either spouse is domiciled in the State or "is ordinarily resident in the State throughout the period of one year ending on th[e] date" of the application commencing proceedings. This jurisdictional ground is trumped by the grounds specified in the Brussels II *bis* Regulation. Only if a spouse is unable to establish a ground under the Regulation will s.31(4) come into play. In the instant case, Abbott J. concluded that jurisdiction was established under indents 1 and 3 of art.3(1)(a) of the Regulation—that the spouses were habitually resident in the State and that the respondent was habitually resident in the State. Once such Regulation-based grounds of jurisdiction were established, s.31(4) had no relevance.

Constitutional Law

ORAN DOYLE, Trinity College Dublin, and
ESTELLE FELDMAN, Trinity College Dublin

ACCESS TO JUSTICE

Isolated, vulnerable and impecunious It was noted without comment in *VTS v HSE* [2009] IEHC 106 that, citing *State (O) v Daly* [1977] I.R. 312, as discussed elsewhere in this chapter, the State had argued that a person compulsorily detained in isolation under s.38 of the Health Act 1947 had no entitlement to have their legal representation funded by the State. The judgment described the circumstances of the detainee in question as follows:

> "The patient in this case is particularly weak and vulnerable. She is believed to have not just one, but two, life- threatening medical conditions, namely full blown AIDS and MDR-TB. She is a foreign national in a foreign land with no family network here and no significant social network here. She faces a deportation order. Her children are in care. Although of normal intelligence she is almost certainly of limited education. While she understands and speaks some English it is not her first language. Her literacy skills, if any, are uncertain. She is detained in a highly controlled environment with limited opportunities for interaction with other persons. Those she does have contact with, with the exception of her children, and her mother who has only recently had an opportunity to visit her, are culturally alien to her. All of her visitors must wear masks, gowns and gloves. Some also wear goggles. There is a security man at her door around the clock. She is sometimes depressed. She continues to refuse treatment and in this respect, and in some other respects from time to time, is not behaving rationally. There is, though it can be put no higher than this at the present time, a question mark over her capacity to take decisions in her own interest. She is presumed to be compos mentis but only on the basis of a limited, and less than wholly satisfactory, psychiatric evaluation. That presumption, like all presumptions, may be capable of being rebutted. There are huge cultural issues at play as well as issues of trust and confidence. The patient unquestionably faces numerous adversities, though some of these are of her own making."

In the reported sworn evidence in the same case, the assigned social worker had stated that "a lot of us were putting in our own money to buy her things".

This generosity, in fact as well as spirit, of the much-maligned employees in the health service serves to highlight the unsympathetic attitude of the State to any grant of civil legal aid, no matter how exceptionally vulnerable the impecunious potential litigant may be. This is not to suggest that there should be an open-ended facility available. However, if a person's constitutional rights are in issue and vindication of those rights requires access to the courts, even in these financially straitened times, it behoves the agents of the State to demonstrate some compliance with constitutional requirements by facilitating legal representation to such impecunious and vulnerable potential litigants. Whilst Art.45 is not cognisable by the courts it is intended for the guidance of the Oireachtas, and Art.45(1) provides:

> "The State shall strive to promote the welfare of the whole people by securing and protecting as effectively as it may a social order in which justice and charity shall inform all the institutions of the national life."

Means to litigate In last year's *Annual Review* we considered *Grant v Roche Products (Ireland)* [2008] 4 I.R. 679; [2008] IESC 35, in which a unanimous Supreme Court (Hardiman J., Murray C.J. and Geoghegan J. concurring) affirmed that the right to litigate to achieve an appropriate remedy is an unenumerated right under Art.40.3.1°. *Grant* was also considered in the chapters on Practice and Procedure and Tort Law, *Annual Review of Irish Law 2008* (see index for entries). In this ongoing case, a bereaved father, inter alia, is seeking an inquiry into the accountability for the death of his son who took his own life allegedly as a consequence of taking a prescribed medication. Hardiman J. stated at para.68:

> "It is quite contrary to any holistic view of human nature to fail to acknowledge that each and every one of these people [the father and extended family circle] will benefit from a resolution of the suspicions which they clearly hold, that the deceased was led to take his own life by the ingestion of a prescription drug known or believed to be associated with grave adverse psychiatric consequences. Moreover, where a very young man has died by his own hand, there is a manifest benefit to his father and other relatives in establishing, if it be the case, that his death had an exogenous cause and was not the result of a free decision on his part. The overwhelming majority of humanity, including the 'reasonable man' beloved of the law, would recognise this instinctively and, in my view, correctly."

However, if we look to 2009 and the case we now consider, we must question whether this judgment of the Supreme Court represents merely high-flown and elegant expressions of constitutional law without any application to the circumstances of a considerable section of the population, namely those without the means to litigate. In *Magee v Farrell* [2009] 2 I.L.R.M. 453; [2009] IESC 60, another unanimous Supreme Court (Finnegan P., Murray C.J., Fennelly J. concurring) overturned the High Court decision and held that the plaintiff has no entitlement to legal aid so that she may be represented at the inquest into the death of her 19-year-old son who had died in Garda custody, apparently from a cocaine-related collapse. The appeal was on the sole issue as to whether the State is in law required to provide the plaintiff with publicly funded legal aid or assistance so that she could attend at, and participate in, the inquest held into her son's death. The Supreme Court held:

> "There is a constitutional right to State funded legal aid when facing a criminal charge with serious consequences and certainly where there is the possibility of loss of liberty. The right has not been extended to proceedings other than in the Criminal Courts. Merely because a constitutional right is in issue and there is a right to be heard and to be legally represented it does not follow that there is an obligation on the State to fund legal representation."

Finnegan J. was at pains to interpret the jurisprudence of the Supreme Court as clearly limiting a constitutional entitlement to legal aid for criminal proceedings. Such an interpretation appears at odds with two explicit statements in *Grant*, in which the Supreme Court was at pains to deny that there can be a distinction between criminal and civil law in the vindication of personal rights. Hardiman J. said ([2008] 4 I.R. 679 at para.77):

> "I wish specifically to reject a central proposition upon which the ... defendants relied, that the vindication of personal rights is a matter only for the 'criminal or regulatory' law and not civil law. *This highly artificial distinction has no basis in the Constitution or in the law itself. Above all, it does not conduce to justice which, by Article 34.1 of the Constitution, is what the courts are to administer"* (emphasis added).

Not satisfied with one statement in this respect, four paragraphs later, at para.81, he said:

> "I have already indicated that I would reject the view that civil, as opposed to 'criminal or regulatory' law has nothing to do with the implementation of the State's duty to vindicate personal rights. *I believe it to be absolutely contrary to established authority and to the opinion of the legal academic exponent of the Constitution, the late Professor Kelly*" (emphasis added).

Two distinctions between *Grant* and *Magee* may be noted: the first relates to the nature of the proceedings and the second to the circumstances of the young men's tragic deaths. The bereaved parent in *Grant* was seeking to take an action in tort and, in order to proceed, inter alia sought and was granted a declaration from the court that he had an unenumerated right to seek an inquiry into the accountability for the death of his son. Secondly, the deceased had taken his own life allegedly as a consequence of taking prescribed medication. By contrast, the bereaved parent in *Magee* sought to be facilitated to be independently represented at the inquest into the death of her son. Her son had died whilst in the custody of the State.

However, the key distinction between the two grieving parents is that the parent in *Magee* was impecunious and without access to the resources necessary to mount any litigation, whereas the parent in *Grant* had access to those resources. The unanimous Supreme Court in *Magee* made no reference whatsoever to the right the court had declared in *Grant*, finding that the State's civil aid scheme does not extend to such matters, and denied the bereaved parent the opportunity of being independently represented at the inquest into her son's death. To paraphrase Hardiman J. in *Grant*: the overwhelming majority of humanity, including the "reasonable man" beloved of the law, would recognise this right of this mother instinctively and, in our view, correctly. The sad conclusion is that the impecunious litigant is a contradiction in terms.

Vexatious litigant The dilemma for the courts when confronted with a vexatious litigant is how to ensure that the litigant is afforded his constitutional right of access to justice whilst ensuring that any potential abuse of process is kept to a minimum. This was summarised as follows by Murray C.J. (Denham, Hardiman, Geoghegan, Fennelly JJ. concurring), in *Riordan v Government of Ireland* [2009] IESC 44:

> "All citizens have a right of access to the Courts which, in other cases, the Courts have been sedulous in protecting. But this right of access is for the purpose of resolving justiciable issues and not for the purpose of constituting the Courts as a sort of debating society or deliberative assembly for the discussion of abstract issues. In the words of Henchy J. in Cahill v. Sutton:
>
> > 'It would be contrary to precedent, to constitutional propriety and the common good for the High Court and this Court to proclaim itself an open house for the reception of such claims'.
>
> The Court agrees with the learned trial judge [Smyth J.] that:
>
> > 'In vindicating the constitutional rights of any person it is of importance that the rights of the community as a whole or identifiable persons or officers or offices in it are not disregarded (e.g. by being open to harassment oppression or scandalous or vexatious litigation). The common good and the respect of society as a community for a justice system is not served or ensured by a disproportionate concern for the rights of the individual at the almost inevitable expense of a disregard for the rights of society by an over indulgence of every or any complaint of an individual.

> The Courts in respecting the rights of all of those who seek access to the Courts must also have some self respect. Otherwise there is the real possibility, nay probability, that the justice system will be abused and/or manipulated for unworthy purposes'.
>
> It must also be borne in mind that all litigation, even groundless litigation, causes expense to the individuals or entities impleaded in it and that this expense will often fall on the taxpayer."

The Supreme Court dismissed the appeal, upholding the order of Smyth J. in the High Court, [2006] IEHC 312, *Annual Review of Irish Law 2006*, p.165 et seq., that:

> "[A]ny further applications by the appellant for leave to commence or continue proceedings should be made by application in writing on notice to the intended defendants or respondents supported by an affidavit referring in full and complete detail to all earlier applications, motions, actions or proceedings of any nature whatever in which the matters intended to be raised in the proposed proceedings were previously raised by him in such earlier matters or proceedings."

ADMINISTRATION OF JUSTICE AND OF THE COURTS

The substantive issue in *Riordan v Government of Ireland* [2009] IESC 44 might be of interest to law students, if not legal scholars. The Supreme Court engaged in a patient textbook exposition on the appointment and jurisdiction of judges and the composition of the courts arising from a constitutional challenge by the appellant, see above ACCESS TO JUSTICE. Smyth J.'s resounding denial of the claim ([2006] IEHC 312, *Annual Review of Irish Law 2006*, p.165 et seq.), was upheld with consideration of Arts 12.3.1°,26, 34, 35 and 36 and various statutory provisions regulating the courts.

AGE DISCRIMINATION

In *D v Residential Institutions Redress Review Committee* [2009] IESC 59, the Supreme Court allowed the State's appeal against the High Court's conclusion that the definition of "child" in s.1 of the Residential Institutions Redress Act 2002 was unconstitutional. (See *Annual Review 2008*, pp.135–137 for an analysis of the High Court judgment.) The Act, which applied retrospectively to institutions operative mainly between the 1930s and the 1980s, provided a scheme of redress for those abused as children in certain residential institutions. The said definition of "child", combined with s.7 of the Act, effectively limited the scheme of redress to those who were under the age of 18 while resident in one of the prescribed institutions. The applicant had entered a prescribed institution shortly after her 18th birthday for the purposes of having a baby. Her application for redress was refused and she sought judicial review of the decision of the Residential Institutions Redress Review Committee. The case essentially turned on the constitutionality of the definition of "child", however. The applicant was a minor at the time at which she was sent to the home by her parents in 1968. She argued that all persons between the ages of 0 and 21 were in the same class, similarly situated. The age discrimination introduced by the 2002 Act differentiated within this class: it was arbitrary and irrational, as it related to no age relevant to those who resided in the institutions covered by the Act. Instead, it appeared to be based on an assessment of the age of majority at the time the Act was enacted.

Murray C.J., delivering the judgment of the Supreme Court, emphasised the presumption of constitutionality that attached to the legislation. He noted that the applicant's challenge was directed to the choice of the age of 18 rather than the decision to limit redress to those who were children at the time they resided in residential institutions. He considered the general principles applicable to such legislative classifications:

> "[A]lmost all legislation addressed to the regulation of society resorts to some form of classification. Age is frequently used as a classification of inclusion or exclusion for multitudes of legislative purposes. There is nothing in such classification, taken on its own, to suggest that it is invidious, unfair or, in the legal sense, discriminatory."

Except in cases involving "invidious discrimination", such as those listed in *Re Article 26 and the Employment Equality Bill 1996* [1997] 2 I.R. 321 (sex, race, language, religious or political opinion), the onus was on the applicant to establish a prima facie basis for the claim that the classification was discriminatory. The court implicitly rejected the applicant's contention that it was for the State to identify a possible justification.

The court also rejected the premise of the applicant's claim, noting that counsel for the State had pointed to many definitions of "child" prevalent in the law at the time the applicant was sent to the residential institution. The age of majority was not the converse of childhood. Having come to this view, the court relatively quickly concluded:

> "In deciding as a matter of policy to establish a special scheme of redress for abused children the Oireachtas necessarily had to define the scope and limits of its application. The court is satisfied that the choice of an age limit of 18 constituted a legitimate legislative designation of the persons who naturally and normally have been described as children. The definition of 'child' as a person under the age of eighteen years represents an objective classification, containing no element of discrimination. It is neither arbitrary nor irrational."

The court also unanimously rejected the applicant's cross-appeal under the European Convention on Human Rights Act 2003.

Several interesting points emerge from the Supreme Court's judgment applying Art.40.1 of the Constitution. First, the court has identified a new category of legislation that is "in the legal sense" discriminatory. This terminology has never been used before by the courts but appears to overlap with the old, generally considered unhelpful, terminology of "invidious discrimination". However, "invidious discrimination" is now understood to refer to those grounds of discrimination identified by the court in the Employment Equality Bill case as being presumptively proscribed: namely, sex, race, language, religious or political opinion. The court does not consider that age falls within the list and may—although this is less clear—consider that the list is closed. As the categorisation of discrimination as invidious or as discrimination "in the legal sense" carries important consequences, it would be regrettable if the court were to consider the list of invidious discrimination to be closed. One might imagine that other grounds of discrimination, such as ethnicity, nationality, disability and sexual orientation, could raise concerns similar to those that exercised the Supreme Court in the Employment Equality Bill case.

Secondly, the characterisation of a discrimination as invidious carries with it important consequences. In such circumstances, the Supreme Court appears to accept that the onus of justification shifts onto the State. What happens in other circumstances is less clear. The applicant had argued that the State was required to identify a possible justification for the age discrimination, then leaving it to the applicant to demonstrate that the proffered justification could not withstand scrutiny. The court rejected this proposition, leaving the applicant in the impossible position of having positively to establish a negative, i.e. that there was no conceivable justification for the legislation. This was of significant importance in the case, given the inability of the State to identify any reason, no matter how tenuous, as to why the age of 18—as distinct from any other age—was chosen. As noted by the court, the State instanced many situations in which the word "child" was not taken as being synonymous with a person who had not attained majority. However, the State could instance no situation in which the word "child" was—at the material time—taken as being synonymous with a person under the age of 18. The legislative examples proffered involved ages of 12 and 16, but not 18.

The court suggested that it was for the applicant to establish a prima facie basis for the claim that the classification was discriminatory. However, it is entirely unclear how the court considered this could be achieved in respect of discriminations other than those listed by the court in the Employment Equality Bill case. It may be that the court considered that only invidious discriminations of that type were amenable to judicial scrutiny at all, and not just amenable to scrutiny with a reversed onus of proof. This position, although stark, is consistent with the actual result of the case: outside the domain of "invidious discriminations", the Oireachtas is entitled to establish legislative classifications without any reason.

Thirdly, to a certain extent, the court's judgment is a further reflection of the impact of *Somjee v Minister for Justice* [1981] I.L.R.M. 324. In that case, Keane J. held that a discriminatory provision which conferred a benefit on one class of persons could not be challenged under Art.40.1 by a member of the class that did not receive the benefit: a declaration that the benefit was unconstitutional would provide no advantage to the litigant. There is a logic to this position but its net effect is to leave significantly discriminatory measures beyond the review of the courts (see discussion below in connection with *D v Ireland* [2009] IEHC 206.) In order to ensure that a declaration of constitutionality would assist her—and thereby avoid the problem stemming from *Somjee*—the applicant was required to argue that she would fall within the understanding of "child" if the statutory definition were declared unconstitutional. This may have distracted from the core of her argument as to why there was unconstitutional discrimination. At the material time, those aged between 0 and 21 in residential institutions were fundamentally the same in an important respect and fundamentally different from those over the age of 21. Under s.1 of the Guardianship of Infants Act, the applicant was an infant. Under s.6 of this Act, her parents were her guardians. Under s.10 of this Act, her guardians were entitled to her custody and entitled to take proceedings for the restoration of custody against any person who wrongfully took her away. Also under s.10, her guardians were entitled to the possession and control of all her property. It was against this legal background that the applicant was sent to the home. Like all other persons under the age of 21, she was there because she was—in law—an infant deemed incompetent of deciding where she should live or how she should manage her resources. Her parents, notwithstanding that they had allowed a situation whereby she was raped by her brothers and made pregnant by one of them, were legally entitled to make all decisions as to her custody and as to the management of any property that might otherwise have facilitated an independent existence outside the home. If the applicant had been over the age of 21, she would have been legally competent to decide to leave the residential institution concerned. In that context, the distinction drawn by the Oireachtas between persons aged under and over 18—in respect of events that occurred prior to 1985—appears of questionable relevance to anything.

CONSTITUTIONALITY OF LEGISLATION

Breach of the principles and policies test The Freedom of Information Act 1997 (section 28(6)) Regulations 2009 (S.I. No. 387 of 2009) were issued to replace regulations issued in 1999. The comments below also apply to the replacement regulations issued under s.17, right to amend personal information, and under s.18, right to reasons for decisions. The impetus for replacement is considered in detail in the Information Law and the Ombudsman chapter of this *Annual Review* and previously in the *Annual Review of Irish Law 2005*, pp.452 et seq. These Regulations deal with access to the personal information of minors, and access to records of deceased persons. As noted, the Information Commissioner, in calling for urgent review of the 1999 Regulations, had commented in 2006:

> "While I appreciate the difficulties of drafting amending primary legislation in this area, I am convinced that it is necessary. I do not believe that it is appropriate that key decisions as to the rules for access to records of deceased persons (particularly health records) should be left to the effective discretion of the Minister for Finance. I would hope that the Minister will undertake a comprehensive review of the whole issue of access to deceased persons' records (and medical records in particular) and, following that review, bring forward detailed amendments to the FOI Act for consideration by the Oireachtas. In the short term, I would hope that the Minister will amend article (1)(b)(iii) of the 1999 Regulations to overcome the difficulties [initially] highlighted." ("Access to Records of Deceased Persons under Freedom of Information" published in Feldman (ed.), Freedom of Information: Law and Practice (Dublin: FirstLaw, 2006) also available at *www.oic.gov.ie/en/MediaandSpeeches/PublishedArticlesExtracts/2006*)

Section 28(6) Freedom of Information Act 1997 provides:

> Notwithstanding subsection (1), the Minister may provide by regulations for the grant of a request under section 7 where—
> (a) the individual to whom the record concerned relates belongs to a class specified in the regulations and the requester concerned is the parent or guardian of the individual, or
> (b) the individual to whom the record concerned relates is dead and the requester concerned is a member of a class specified in the regulations.

As the Commissioner has pointed out, a major difficulty in devising any regulations is to discern the principles and policies set down by the Oireachtas in the primary legislation. With regard to 28(6)(b) three classes of requester are specified in the Regulations:

> "i) a personal representative of the individual acting in due course of administration of his or her estate or any person acting with the consent of a personal representative so acting,
> ii) a person on whom a function is conferred by law in relation to the individual or his or her estate acting in the course of the performance of the function, and

iii) the spouse or the next of kin of the individual where in the opinion of the head, having regard to all the circumstances and to any relevant guidelines published by the Minister, the public interest, including the public interest in the confidentiality of personal information, would on balance be better served by granting than by refusing to grant the request."

In relation to requests by parents or guardians the Regulations refer to a head of a public body "having regard to all the circumstances and to any guidelines drawn up and published by the Minister".

It is not unreasonable to question whether authority for the categories of requester who may access records of the deceased lies within the policies and principles of the Act. Moreover, introducing a requirement to have regard to guidelines may well be a good idea but it appears to have no basis in the primary legislation. As noted in the Information Law and the Ombudsman chapter the guidelines published by the Minister Guidance Notes on Access to records by parents/guardians Access to records relating to deceased persons under section 28(6) of the Freedom of Information Act 1997 ("Guidance Notes") appear most thorough and laudable in attitude. However, some of the advice, which is of course NOT a part of the law, if followed might well result in the public body being in breach of Arts 41 and 42. A clear example is section 2.1 Factors to be considered (B) Minors (persons who have not reached the age of majority - persons under 18 years who are not or have never been married):

"(iii) Are the records held in the minor's own right? If so, the general position is that such records would not be released to a parent or guardian unless such release was in the minor's best interest. Examples of records in this area would be:

- Lone Parent's Allowance in the Department of Social, Community and Family Affairs (which are not age related),
- Motorcycle licenses in the Department of the Environment which can be issued to 16 year old applicants in their own right.
- Certain medical records which may not be appropriate for automatic release to parents/guardians, such as records a GP might have on prescribing contraceptives to a minor." (emphasis as in Guidance Notes p.5)

The question of confidentiality of a GP's records when contraceptives are prescribed to a minor has not been tested in this jurisdiction and the advice would appear to be written without due regard to the courts' interpretation of parental autonomy and family rights, see below FAMILY RIGHTS **Consent to medical treatment**.

Trespass on High Court's jurisdiction In *Minister for Justice, Equality and Law Reform v Director of the Equality Tribunal* [2009] IEHC 72, Charleton J. held that the Equality Tribunal, as a body whose powers are defined by statute, was not entitled to commence a hearing that had the result that it assumed a legal entitlement to overrule a statutory instrument. He stated at para.8:

> "There is no principle of European law which allows an administrative body or a court of limited jurisdiction to exceed its own authority in order to achieve a result, whereby it is of the view that European legislation has not been properly implemented at national level and that this situation is to be remedied by the re-ordering in ideal form of national legislation. The limit of jurisdiction is of primary importance to the exercise of authority, whether the court be one established as an administrative body, or is one of the courts under the Constitution. In the event that a view emerges that national legislation has not properly implemented European legislation, this is no more than an opinion. The respondent does not have the authority to make a binding legal declaration of inconsistency or insufficiency on a comparison of European and national legislation. The High Court has that power as this has been expressly reserved to it by Article 34 of the Constitution".

CONTEMPT OF COURT

Criminal contempt The preliminary issues involved in *DPP v Independent Newspapers* [2008] IESC 8 were considered in *Annual Review of Irish Law 2008*, pp.129 and 144 et seq. This case related to the criminal jurisdiction of the High Court and, at the time, we noted that on the substantive issue in 2009 the Supreme Court did allow the Director of Public Prosecution's appeal against the High Court's refusal to grant the order for criminal contempt. In that appeal ([2009] IESC 20) Geoghegan J. (Murray C.J., Hardiman, Fennelly, Finnegan JJ. concurring) concluded:

> "A long time has elapsed however in the appeal process in this case having regard to the unusual and complex problems which arose. By any standard the case is now somewhat stale. It was important from the point of the view of the Director of Public Prosecutions to establish the correct legal position both in relation to procedures and the substance. That has been achieved and in all the circumstances, I would be of the view that the court should exercise its discretion against ordering a new trial".

With regard to criminal contempt, relying on the judgment of Henchy J. in *State (DPP) v Walsh* [1981] I.R. 412, the Supreme Court held that a trial with a jury of a motion for attachment and committal in respect of a non-minor criminal contempt has to be conducted differently from an ordinary trial for indictable crime:

> "Certain issues which would in the ordinary way be regarded as issues of fact and, therefore to be determined by a jury must, in the overall interests of the due administration of justice, be deemed to be issues of law and left to the determination of the judge."

Hardiman J. (Fennelly J. concurring), in a very short judgment, whilst agreeing with the nature of the jury trial, maintained his opinion from his earlier dissenting judgment, that trial for criminal contempt was not sui generis. He made the following general observation about media commentary on criminal trials:

> "Many Irish people will remember how strange and how utterly unfair it seemed, thirty years ago, when the media in another jurisdiction appeared, with impunity, to assume the guilt of certain Irish people facing criminal charges. It is no less inappropriate in this jurisdiction. In relation to almost every sort of criminal charge there are some persons who will be gratified or advantaged if the alleged criminals are 'led out in handcuffs'. But such persons, especially if they are newspaper editors or others who are powerful or influential in the shaping of public opinion, must take care not to pollute the fountain of justice by expressing, or seeming to express, a view as to the guilt or innocence of accused persons, especially in lurid or vivid terms. Apart from anything else, such views are rarely based on an examination of the evidence which will eventually come before the trial court".

COURT OF FINAL APPEAL

Exceptional jurisdiction to vary finality The lay litigant in *Talbot v McCann Fitzgerald* [2009] IESC 25 was denied his motion to vacate a final judgment of the Supreme Court. Denham J. (Kearns and Clarke JJ. concurring) at paras 31.6 and 31.7 found that whereas the fundamental principle is that the order of the Supreme Court is final, in rare and exceptional cases a jurisdiction to vary a final order may arise: (a) where there has been an accidental slip in the judgment; (b) where the judgment as drawn up does not correctly state what the court intended and decided; (c) in separate proceedings for fraud; and/or (d) in rare and exceptional cases to protect constitutional rights and/or justice.

EXECUTIVE PRIVILEGE

Privileged documents In *O'Neill v An Taoiseach* [2009] IEHC 119, Murphy J. upheld a claim of statutory privilege over the archive of the MacEntee

Commission, a private statutory inquiry into the explosions collectively known as the Dublin–Monaghan bombings of 1974. Mr Patrick MacEntee SC, QC, had been appointed in May 2005, as the sole member of the Commission of Inquiry. Murphy J. reiterated the principles stated in *Murphy v Dublin Corporation* [1972] I.R. 215 and *Ambiorix v Minister for the Environment (No. 1)* [1992] 1 I.R. 277, which established that it is for the courts to determine which public interest shall prevail in the event of a conflict between the public interest in the administration of justice and the public interest involved in the confidentiality, or exemption from disclosure, of documents pertaining to the executive powers of the State. In the event he had not deemed it necessary for the court to examine the documents. The claim was upheld "on the basis of a description of the nature and contents of the documents, namely that they comprise the archive of the MacEntee Commission and having regard to that Commission's terms of reference."

FAIR PROCEDURES

In *McCann v Judges of Monaghan District Court* [2009] IEHC 276, the plaintiff challenged the validity of an order for her arrest and imprisonment (the 2005 order) under the Enforcement of Court Orders Acts 1926 and 1940. She also challenged the constitutionality of the legislation. Laffoy J. held that the legislation breached both Art.40.3 (fair procedures) and Art.40.4 of the Constitution. Laffoy J. explained the conclusion in relation to fair procedures in the following terms:

> "There are fundamental deficiencies in s. 6 which render it invalid having regard to the provisions of the Constitution because it violates the debtor's constitutional guarantee of fair procedure.
>
> First, on its proper construction, it confers jurisdiction on the District Court to make an order for the arrest and imprisonment of a defaulting debtor even if the debtor is not present before the Court and even if the Judge is not in a position to determine whether the absence of the debtor is due to a conscious decision.
>
> Secondly, it confers jurisdiction to order the arrest and imprisonment of an impecunious debtor without there being in place some legislative or administrative scheme under which the District Court is empowered to make provision for the legal representation of the debtor at the expense of the State.
>
> Thirdly, s.6 is also invalid in that, while it recognises that an order for arrest and imprisonment should only issue if the default on the part of the debtor is attributable to wilful refusal or culpable neglect, it expressly puts the onus on the debtor to disprove such conduct on his part. If, instead of leaving it to the creditor to pursue the committal of a defaulting debtor for non-compliance with an instalment order,

> the Oireachtas had made it an offence punishable on three months' imprisonment to wilfully or culpably negligently fail to comply with the instalment order, the hypothetical provision would be invalid having regard to the provisions of the Constitution if it purported to put the onus of disproving the offence on the debtor."

Laffoy J. held that the legislation could not be interpreted in such a way as to remove the constitutional difficulty and therefore granted a declaration of unconstitutionality.

FAMILY LIFE

In *McD v L* [2009] IESC 81, the Supreme Court restated the traditional constitutional approach to family rights and expressed strong views about the circumstances in which the European Convention on Human Rights might be applied by the Irish courts. The respondents were two lesbian partners who decided that they wished to have a child. They agreed with a friend, the applicant, that he would act as sperm donor. They signed an agreement under which the father would not be anonymous; the child would have knowledge of the father, but would remain with the respondents, the father adopting a role as a "favourite uncle". The child was born in May 2006. After the birth of the child, the relationship between the applicant and the respondents deteriorated. The respondents felt that the applicant was seeking to be more intrusive into their relationship than had been agreed. For various reasons, they wished to travel to Australia and stay there for a year. The applicant obtained an interim injunction from the High Court preventing the respondents from taking the child out of the jurisdiction. At the full hearing in the High Court, Hedigan J. relied on the European Convention on Human Rights Act 2003 and referred to cases decided by the European Court of Human Rights interpreting art.8 of the Convention. He concluded that the respondents and the child constituted a de facto family. He considered it highly possible that the integrity of this family would be seriously—and perhaps fatally—undermined by any order granting guardianship or access to the applicant. He refused the applicant both an Order appointing him guardian and an Order allowing him access to the child. The applicant appealed.

The Supreme Court unanimously reversed the High Court judgment in relation to access, although not in relation to guardianship. Denham J., in a judgment similar to those of other members of the court, endorsed the constitutional position laid down by Hamilton C.J. in *WO'R v EH* [1996] 2 I.R. 248: the unmarried father had rights of interest or concern in the context of guardianship and access applications, but the primary consideration was the welfare of the child. She considered that the High Court had given too little weight to these rights of interest or concern on the part of the father. Although the agreement between the parties was unenforceable, it was a helpful indication of a previously agreed scheme that might serve the best interests of the child. Most importantly, from the constitutional perspective, Denham J. rejected Hedigan J.'s conclusion that it was open to the court to recognise the existence of a de facto family. Reviewing the case law on this issue, she concluded:

> "63. There is no institution in Ireland of a de facto family. Reference has been made in cases previously, as set out earlier in this judgment, to a de facto family, but it is a shorthand method of referring to the circumstances of a settled relationship in which a child lives. In cases where the issue of guardianship, custody and access arise the kernel issue is the welfare of a child. In assessing the welfare of a child all the circumstances require to be analysed. These include the biological parents, the age of the child, the relationships which the child has formed, the situation in which he or she lives. If a couple have lived together in a settled relationship for years and have a child in that relationship then these are critical factors. A child will know and have a relationship with the people with whom he lives—it will be an important aspect of his life, and therefore weigh heavily in determining his welfare. On the other hand, if a couple have a child and do not live together, there may be little or no relationship between the child and the father and thus the relationship with the father will not weigh so heavily. These will be factors in the balance to be considered by the court in determining the welfare of the child. It is a question of considering the welfare of the child in all the circumstances of the case. If the circumstances include a long standing relationship with a parent that is an important factor for the court.
>
> 64. The same analysis will apply to circumstances where same sex couples live together. Circumstances, in which a child is living a settled life, and has a relationship with those with whom he lives, are critical factors.
>
> 65. On the issue of a de facto family, the learned High Court judge fell into error. However, that has little significant effect on the analysis in the circumstances of this case of what is in the best interests of the child. The respondents are a loving couple, taking care of the child, in a settled environment. These are key factors in considering the welfare of the child."

The Supreme Court also expressed reservations about the manner in which Hedigan J. had relied on the European Convention on Human Rights. The Chief Justice reiterated the constitutional position that Ireland had a dualist system and that international conventions could only become part of the law of the State if adopted by the Oireachtas. The European Convention on Human Rights 2003 did not give general effect to the Convention but rather imposed certain obligations related to the Convention, in certain circumstances. Section 2 of the European Convention on Human Rights Act 2003 allows for interpretative claims that can apply to existing rules of law. However, it does not allow for autonomous claims based purely on the Convention. There was no existing rule of law at issue in respect of which s.2 could apply to create recognition in Irish law for a de facto family.

FAMILY RIGHTS

Breach of parental rights *FP v Information Commissioner* [2009] IEHC 574 is analysed in detail in the Information Law and the Ombudsman chapter and referred to in the Whistleblower Protection chapter of this Annual Review. In para.2 Clark J. referred to a series of disturbing events which eventually gave rise to the case. One of these which merits mention in this chapter is that, unknown to the appellant, his wife applied for a birth certificate to be amended so that the biological father's name was substituted for the appellant's name. The appellant had believed the child to be his biological daughter and he had formed a strong parental bond with her. They had lived together as a family unit. This birth occurred in 1993. Under s.19 of the more recent Civil Registration Act 2004 it is the duty of the parents, plural, to register a birth. It is not unreasonable to suggest that facilitating the amendment of a birth certificate by one parent without the knowledge of their legal spouse is a breach of parental rights.

Consent to medical treatment Section 38 of the Health Act 1947, which provides for compulsory detention for public health reasons, was declared constitutional in *VTS v HSE* [2009] IEHC. In s.2 of the Act, an "adult person" is defined "as a person who is sixteen years of age or older" and a child is defined "as a person who is less than sixteen years of age". Where a s.38 order has been made s.38(h) states that "the patient (or the parent of the patient, where the patient is a child) may at any time appeal to the Minister in writing to direct the release of the patient". It is clear that the terms of the statute create an anomalous situation which purports to confer adult status on persons between the ages of 16 and 18. It is arguable that such contention is unconstitutional with respect to Arts 41 and 42 of the Constitution. This view is supported by the Law Reform Commission in its *Consultation Paper on Children and the Law: Medical Treatment* (LRC CP59–2009), para.4.03, where it considers a parallel provision, s.23(1) of the Non-Fatal Offences Against the Person Act 1997:

> "The consent of a minor who has attained the age of 16 years to any surgical, medical or dental treatment which, in the absence of consent, would constitute a trespass to his or her person, shall be as effective as it would be if he or she were of full age; and where a minor has by virtue of this section given an effective consent to any treatment it shall not be necessary to obtain any consent for it from his or her parent or guardian."

The LRC holds that "section 23 does not serve as an explicit acknowledgement of the right of a child to participate in decisions regarding his or her medical treatment".

FREEDOM OF EXPRESSION

Gag clauses Are statutory provisions that require a person to be, in effect, mealy-mouthed, a breach of that individual's constitutional right to express freely convictions and opinion? Article 40.6.1° states: "The State guarantees liberty for the exercise of the following rights, subject to public order and morality: i.e. the right of the citizens to express freely their convictions and opinions." According to the *Oxford Dictionary of English* (2nd edn, 2005), "mealy-mouthed" is an adjective meaning "afraid to speak frankly or straightforwardly". This does not appear to be an unfair description of the gag clauses which are becoming a common feature of statutorily appointed regulators as highlighted in the chapter "Information Law and the Ombudsman" in this *Annual Review*. Section 16(2) of the Legal Services Ombudsman Act 2009 states:

> The Legal Services Ombudsman when giving evidence under this section shall not question or express an opinion on the merits of any policy of the Government or on the merits of the objectives of such policy.

Similar draconian strictures are included, for example, in the Charities Act 2009 (ss.22 and 23), Broadcasting Act 2009 (s.19), National Management Agency Act 2009 (ss.58 and 59) and Labour Services (Amendment) Act 2009 (s.4). This is not a matter of upholding confidentiality in relation to matters that should remain confidential. This is a specific injunction statutorily imposed on certain office-holders when called before Oireachtas committees, most particularly the Public Accounts Committee, to prevent the expression by that person of an opinion. The case law referred to later in this section considered European Convention of Human Rights jurisprudence concerning art.10, and freedom of expression, in the context of journalistic sources. However, certain principles of universal application are contained in those European Court of Human Rights judgments, e.g. *Sunday Times v The United Kingdom* (1979) 2 E.H.R.R. 245 (limitation on restrictions as not justified by "pressing social need" thus not "necessary"); *Lingens v Austria* (1986) 87 E.H.R.R. 329 (criminal defamation of Austrian Chancellor violated art.10); *Castells v Spain* (1992) 14 E.H.R.R. 445 (insults to government); *Goodwin v United Kingdom* (1996) 22 E.H.R.R. 123 (overturned House of Lords fine and requirement to disclose source). The European Court in *Lingens* stated at paras 40 and 41, as cited by Fennelly J. on behalf of the Supreme Court in *Mahon v Keena* [2009] IESC 64, at para.47:

"'The Court must determine whether the interference at issue was "proportionate to the legitimate aim pursued" and whether the reasons adduced by the Austrian courts to justify it are "relevant and sufficient".

41. In this connection, the Court has to recall that freedom of expression, as secured in paragraph 1 of Article 10, constitutes one of the essential foundations of a democratic society and one of the basic conditions for its progress and for each individual's self-fulfilment. Subject to paragraph 2, it is applicable not only to "information" or "ideas'" that are favourably received or regarded as inoffensive or as a matter of indifference, but also to those that offend, shock or disturb. Such are the demands of that pluralism, tolerance and broadmindedness without which there is no "democratic society".'"

Were the constitutionality of these gag provisions challenged and a proportionality test applied as is now a matter of course, is there any "legitimate aim" that is in the public interest that could be pleaded in defence? Could one reasonably argue that the Oireachtas is entitled to gag, by prior restraint, those that are called before its own subcommittees to prevent any potential embarrassment to the Executive? That would probably be to rely too much on the legal fiction that we enjoy a tripartite separation of powers. The Oireachtas is largely powerless in the face of an overly dominant Executive. Moreover, the chilling effect of such a gag clause is more likely than not to restrict those in the affected functions from questioning government policies and from expressing any incisive opinions on those policies in any forum. This could hardly be considered either in the public interest or a justifiable interference with those who are appointed to regulate and to control bodies performing public functions and/or which are in receipt of public funds.

Right to dignity In the course of his judgment in *VTS v HSE* [2009] IEHC 106, Edwards J. criticised the failure of the health authorities to explain properly to the patient the consequences of resisting her detention in the context of her right to human dignity and to freedom of expression:

"While the patient is aware that she is being forcibly denied her liberty, she is seemingly unaware that her right to freedom of expression within the hospital is restricted by law. Despite the desperateness of her situation, she cannot even shout out in frustration. If she does so, she potentially commits the criminal offence of failing to submit to her isolation 'in a peaceful and orderly manner'. Does her right to human dignity not entitle her to be appraised of the full implications of her situation?"

Subverting rule of law In *Mahon v Keena* [2009] IESC 64, the Supreme Court granted an appeal against the order of a Divisional High Court (Johnson

P., Kelly, O'Neill JJ.) [2007] IEHC 348, compelling *The Irish Times* editor, Geraldine Kennedy, and journalist, Colm Keena, to disclose their sources to the Mahon Tribunal of Inquiry into Certain Planning Matters which had led to the publication of leaked confidential documentation. An additional aspect of the case had been the fact that *The Irish Times* admitted destroying the initiating document (*Annual Review of Irish Law 2007*, p.312). In the Supreme Court, Fennelly J. (Murray C.J., Geoghegan, Macken and Finnegan JJ. assenting), overturned the High Court which held that an order compelling the appellants to answer questions for the purpose of identifying their source could only be "justified by an overriding requirement in the public interest." In this case, as the source seemed to be anonymous, the High Court had erred by issuing the order to appear for questioning at the Tribunal. Fennelly J. observed at para.60:

> "The courts cannot and should not abdicate their responsibility to decide when a journalist is obliged to disclose his or her source. The unilateral decision of a journalist to destroy evidence with intent to deprive the courts of jurisdiction is, as the High Court has held, designed to subvert the rule of law. The Courts cannot shirk their duty to penalise journalists who refuse to answer questions legitimately and lawfully put to them."

He queried whether it was:

> "… in accord with the interests of a democratic society based on the rule of law that journalists, as a unique class, have the right to decide for themselves to withhold information from any and every public institution or court regardless of the existence of a compelling need, for example, for the production of evidence of the commission of a serious crime. While the present case does not concern information about the commission of serious criminal offences, it cannot be doubted that such a case could arise. Who would decide whether the journalist's source had to be protected? There can be only one answer. In the event of conflict, whether in a civil or criminal context, the courts must adjudicate and decide, while allowing all due respect to the principle of journalistic privilege. No citizen has the right to claim immunity from the processes of the law" (at para.61).

Fennelly J. did not disagree with the language used by the High Court in reference to the deliberate destruction by the appellants of the very documents that were at the core of the inquiry. The High Court, for example, considered the conduct of the respondents as "anathema to the rule of law and an affront to democratic order". However, the Supreme Court judgment accepted that:

> "[T]he issue is not whether that act was a wrongful one and deserving of the opprobrium applied to it by the High Court, but the narrower question of whether, in circumstances where the documents no longer

exist, there is a logical or causal link between that act and the order made. It does not appear to me that there is."

Penalising journalists With regard to costs which normally follow the event in *Mahon v Keena* [2009] IESC 78, Murray C.J., for a unanimous Supreme Court, (Geoghegan, Fennelly, Macken and Finnegan JJ. all concurring) awarded all costs against the appellants stating that:

> "[I]t was the very act of destroying the document that decisively shifted the balance and deprived the Tribunal of any effective power to conduct an inquiry and, by extension, deprived the courts of any power to give effect to any order of the Tribunal. This act was calculated and deliberate and was performed with that clear purpose in mind. That 'reprehensible conduct' determined the course which these proceedings took and was at the root of balancing the issue which the Court had to determine. In the view of the court the deliberate behaviour of the appellants was directly related to and was intended to achieve the outcome of the case, which has in fact occurred."

LANGUAGE RIGHTS

In *Ó Gríofáin v Éire* [2009] IEHC 188, Charleton J. rejected an application from an accused person to prohibit his trial for driving while under the influence of alcohol on the basis that the machine which produced an automatic read-out of the alcohol level in his body did not print that form, which he was required to sign by way of acknowledgement, in Irish. Relying on *Ó Beoláin v Fahey* [2001] 2 I.R. 279, Charleton J. rejected the contention that there was a real risk of unfairness to the accused such as would warrant an order of prohibition. He also expressed views on the circumstances in which personal rights should be allowed to interfere with the processes of the criminal law. He rejected the view expressed by the Canadian Supreme Court in *Beaulac v The Queen and the Attorney General of Canada* [1999] 1 S.C.R. 76, to the effect that language rights must be preserved, even at a cost to the administration of justice, as a way of preserving language communities:

> "10. I do not accept that. Justice is the aim of every legal proceeding. Truth is the object of every judicial exercise. The principle of true social order attendant on the purpose of our Constitution, and as declared in the Preamble, must place the disposal of criminal business as being a value of particular importance in the maintenance of a cohesive society. Were the argument of the applicant to succeed, then any person stopped in his and her vehicle and suspected of drunken driving would only have to greet the Garda in Irish for the entire process to be made to grind to a halt, unless the Garda happened to be highly competent in Irish.

> Rights are a vital component of the Constitution. The exercise of a right is not an academic exercise that occurs divorced from a factual matrix. There is a right to privacy, to be let alone. It is not enough, as a matter of law, simply to assert that right. A court must look at the circumstances in which it is argued to operate and the rights, legal entitlements and obligations such exercise is claimed to be superior to. For instance, no one can reveal the contents of a telephone conversation without the permission of at least one party to the call; see the analysis of the Court of Criminal Appeal in The People (DPP) v Geasley [2009] I.E.C.C.A. 22. In telephoning someone, in addition to statutory rights, one is normally asserting a constitutional right to privacy; an exception might be phoning a radio programme for public broadcast. If a journalist were to take the phone of a citizen in order to pretend an identity and record a call with a public figure with a view to a public report, as has happened in other countries, the right to privacy could clearly be asserted. A police officer in possession of a suspected drug dealer's phone who might engage in an exercise of deception in order to make an arrest would be in a different category. Could it be asserted the constitutional right to privacy extends to organizing a crime in private? I would doubt that. Finally, in some circumstances the motive for exercising a right may be part of the required legal analysis. A citizen has the right to sell his property. But if his purpose is to make himself judgment-proof and so cheat his creditors, the constitutional rights attendant on private property may conflict and be resolved in favour of what is fair according to the standards of decent people."

LEGAL REPRESENTATION

Criminal legal aid payment Counsel representing indigent defendants need to ensure that they are properly listed on the barristers' panel or they may well find themselves seriously out of pocket, as was the situation in *Walsh v Minister for Justice, Equality and Law Reform* [2009] IEHC 102. The plaintiff, a practising senior counsel, had been removed from the panel for failure to produce a tax clearance certificate as required by the Criminal Justice (Legal Aid) (Tax Clearance Certificate) Regulations 1999 (S.I. No. 135 of 1999). Laffoy J., whilst sympathising with the plaintiff's plight, dismissed his claim for payment based, inter alia, on an accused's constitutional right to legal representation. She observed:

> "The obligations of the State to which a practical effect was given in The State (Healy) v. Donoghue were owed to the accused person whose personal rights under the Constitution were at issue. Those obligations extended to the accused person who was represented by the plaintiff in Wexford, who had corresponding rights which were protected by

> the Constitution. If his rights had been violated, the accused would have had locus standi to seek a remedy. However, the proposition that a lawyer who represents an accused person, who has the benefit of a legal aid certificate, can 'piggy-back' on the constitutional rights of the accused person and assert a constitutional right to be paid for the legal services provided, although not in compliance with the statutory scheme for funding the provision of such legal services, in my view, is wholly untenable."

Right to apply for counsel In a significant development in *Carmody v Minister for Justice, Equality and Law Reform* [2009] IESC 71, the Supreme Court upheld the High Court that "a defendant in criminal proceedings before the District Court has a constitutional right to apply for legal aid to include counsel". It may be noted that at the time of writing, July 2010, no mechanism exists whereby a defendant can vindicate that constitutional right.

When we considered *Carmody v Minister for Justice, Equality and Law Reform* [2005] IEHC 10 (*Annual Review of Irish Law 2005*, p.188 et seq.) we noted that whereas the case falls into the criminal justice classification it did, nonetheless, "air important considerations in relation to the nature of the legal representation that should be provided by the statutory legal aid scheme". The appeal was heard in November 2009 and Murray C.J., on behalf of the court (Denham, Hardiman, Geoghegan, Fennelly JJ.), engaged in a wide-ranging judgment on the right to legal representation in the context of the right to a fair trial. He held that "a defendant in criminal proceedings before the District Court has a constitutional right to apply for legal aid to include counsel". Nevertheless, he upheld the High Court finding of constitutionality of s.2 of the Criminal Justice (Legal Aid) Act 1962 which, only in the case of murder, permits legal aid for counsel. The judgment also established that when there is a challenge to both the constitutionality of a statutory provision and the compatibility of that provision with the European Convention of Human Rights (ECHR), the constitutionality of the impugned provision should be considered first. This aspect is considered elsewhere in this chapter.

Since the details of the case have been outlined in the *Annual Review 2005*, these will not be repeated. What we will review is the apparent contradiction in the judgment expressed in the final paragraph of the reasoning:

> "Accordingly, the absence of a right to apply for legal aid to include counsel in appropriate cases must properly be considered as stemming from a failure of the State to make by one means or another, specific provision for such legal aid rather than from any provision, in particular any prohibition, in the Act of 1962."

Consequent on this finding, in the final paragraph of the judgment the court ordered:

> "Accordingly, for the reasons set out in this judgment the Court will allow the appeal and make a declaration that the appellant, as a defendant in a criminal prosecution before the District Court has a constitutional right, prior to being tried, to apply to and have determined by a court or other appropriate body whether he should be granted legal aid to include representation by counsel as well as by a solicitor. The Court will make an order prohibiting the State from proceeding with the prosecution unless and until he is afforded that right."

Upholding constitutionality The onus is on the person challenging the constitutionality of legislation to establish that the legislation is unconstitutional. In this instance, the court, finding for the applicant that there is a constitutional right to apply for criminal legal aid for counsel in circumstances not envisaged during the passage of the 1962 Act, held that the exclusion in s.2 of the 1962 Act does not in any way render that provision invalid.

Section 2 of the Criminal Justice (Legal Aid) Act 1962 states:

> (1) If it appears to the District Court—
> (a) that the means of a person charged before it with an offence are insufficient to enable him to obtain legal aid, and
> (b) that by reason of the gravity of the charge or of exceptional circumstances it is essential in the interests of justice that he should have legal aid in the preparation and conduct of his defence before it,
>
> the Court shall, on application being made to it in that behalf, grant in respect of him a certificate for free legal aid (in this Act referred to as a legal aid (District Court) certificate) and thereupon he shall be entitled to such aid and *to have a solicitor and (where he is charged with murder and the Court thinks fit) counsel assigned to him for that purpose* in such manner as may be prescribed by regulations under section 10 of this Act (emphasis added, see below **Severability**.)
>
> (2) A decision of the District Court in relation to an application under this section shall be final and shall not be appealable (emphasis added).

The first basis on which the constitutionality of s.2 was challenged was that it breaches the constitutional right to a trial according to the due process of law, because it arbitrarily excludes the District Court from even considering the possibility of providing, by means of legal aid, the assistance of counsel in cases being tried by the District Court, even if it could be established that the interests of justice require that the defendant be provided with such counsel because of the gravity, complexity or exceptional circumstances of the case. The Supreme Court described the background to the Act and the provision of criminal legal aid, plus the curiosity of Ireland including a derogation restricting legal aid when it ratified the ECHR, a derogation still in existence but not relied upon by the respondents in the instant case:

> "It may seem extraordinary now but prior to the adoption of the Criminal Justice (Legal Aid) Act 1962 no legal aid was available for poor persons except when they were charged with the crime of murder (then a capital offence) or in certain circumstances where a retrial was ordered by the Court of Criminal Appeal or the Supreme Court. That situation had for a long time been considered by many to be inconsistent with the notion of a fair trial although no issue concerning it had been raised before the Courts. When Ireland ratified the European Convention on Human Rights in February 1953 the State must have foreseen that the absence of legal aid for poor persons in nearly all cases might place it in breach of Article 6 of the Convention on the right to a fair trial because, as regards that Article, it inserted in its instrument of ratification a reservation pursuant to Article 15 of the Convention that Ireland did not 'interpret Article 6.3.c of the Convention as requiring the provision of free legal assistance to any wider extent than is now provided in Ireland.'"

Article 6.3.c of the ECHR states:

> "Everyone charged with a criminal offence has the following minimum rights: … (c) to defend himself in person or through legal assistance of his own choosing or, if he has not sufficient means to pay for legal assistance, to be given it free when the interests of justice so require."

Thus, the court observed, the framework for criminal legal aid in the District Court:

> "… fashioned in the mindset and circumstances of now nearly half a century ago as a first and valuable step in this area, remains applicable today notwithstanding the substantially changed legal environment in which the District Court functions in the area of criminal justice".

The judgment then referred to the seminal case, *State (Healy) v Donoghue* [1976] I.R. 325, the first case in which the right to criminal legal aid arose as a substantive issue some 14 years after the adoption of the 1962 Act.

Principles governing right to criminal legal aid According to the Supreme Court, "the principles expressed in the judgments of the court [in *Healy*] are directly relevant to any consideration of the constitutional right of poor persons to legal aid in criminal cases." In *Healy*, the court made it quite clear that:

> "… the right to legal aid does not stem from a statute. It is a constitutional

> right. The Act of 1962, to the extent that it does make provision for legal aid, is merely a means of vindicating that right".

The judgment then cited O'Higgins C.J. [1976] I.R. 325 at 350:

> "If the right to be represented is now an acknowledged right of an accused person, justice requires something more when, because of a lack of means, a person facing a serious criminal charge cannot provide a lawyer for his own defence. In my view the concept of justice under the Constitution, or constitutional justice … requires that in such circumstances the person charged must be afforded the opportunity of being represented.
>
> This opportunity must be provided by the State. Only in this way can justice be done, and only by recognising and discharging this duty can the State be said to vindicate the personal rights of the person charged. To hold otherwise would be to tolerate a situation which the nature and extent of a man's ability to defend himself, when accused, would depend on the nature and extent of his means. That would be to tolerate injustice."

Henchy J. was then cited: [1976] I.R. 325 at 354:

> "A person who has been convicted and deprived of his liberty as a result of a prosecution which, because of his poverty he has had to bear without legal aid has reason to complain that he has been meted out less than his constitutional due. This is particularly true if the absence of legal aid is compounded by the factors such as a grave or complex charge."

Henchy J. was further cited as expressing the view that, once the interests of justice required that a person be afforded legal aid, a trial without it "could not be said to be a trial 'in due course of law'" within the meaning of that phrase in Art.38.1.

The affirmation of *Healy* principles concluded by citing Griffin J. [1976] I.R. 325 at 354:

> "The principles enshrined in these principles of the Constitution require fundamental fairness in criminal trials—principles which encompass the right to legal aid in summary cases no less than in cases tried on indictment—whenever the assistance of a solicitor or counsel is necessary to ensure a fair trial. Ours is an adversary system of criminal justice. On the one side is the State with all its resources, which it properly and justifiably uses in the prosecution of crime. It has available to it a trained and skilled police force, and lawyers who prosecute in the interest of the public. On the other side is the person charged with a crime; if he has the resources, he will retain the best solicitor and counsel obtainable for the preparation and conduct of his defence. If he is too

> poor to engage a solicitor or counsel, can he be assured of a fair trial unless legal aid is provided for him? It seems to me beyond argument that if lawyers are necessary to represent persons with means to pay for them, they are no less necessary for poor persons who are unable to provide for them out of their own resources"(emphasis added).

The Supreme Court then added its own view of the principle:

> "The right is a constitutional right. Everyone has a right to be represented in a criminal trial but justice requires something more than the mere right to be represented when a person, who cannot afford legal representation, is facing a serious criminal charge. Such a person has a constitutional right to be granted legal aid by the State to enable him or her to have legal representation at the trial. The nature and extent of that right may be affected by the gravity and complexity of the charge. In addition, although the Act does not require it, every unrepresented defendant must be informed of his or her right to legal aid if they cannot afford it themselves."

The Supreme Court noted that the *Healy* judgments were clearly based on the assumption that, as the 1962 Act and consequent regulations provided, in all trials before the Circuit Court or the Central Criminal Court an accused had a right to be represented by solicitor and counsel and in some instances two counsel:

> "The unquestionable right of a poor accused to be provided with legal aid for solicitor and counsel in such cases undoubtedly arises from a range of factors inherent in the trial of indictable offences before such Courts. It is sufficient to mention two of them. There is the particular seriousness attached to offences tried in such Courts because of their nature or the range of severe sentences which the Court of trial has power to impose. There is the process of trial before a Judge and jury, which for many self evident reasons is more complex than a summary trial in the District Court and which necessarily requires representation by an advocate skilled in the conduct of such trials. Again the Oireachtas itself has recognised that necessity and so provided in the case of trials before a judge and jury."

Solicitor and counsel There followed comments on the two legal professions which, presumably of interest to all engaged with law, are quoted in extenso:

> "In the second of two articles entitled "Competition in the cab rank and the challenge to the independent bar", Judge John Cooke, as he then was as a member of the Court of First Instance of the European Communities, in referring to the underlining rationale of the two professions stated, inter alia:

> '...From a practical point of view, the common law system of litigation with its emphasis upon direct proof by witnesses of all essential facts and the oral exposition of legal argument, effectively requires that the presentation of cases in court be a specialised activity. That is why even in those common law jurisdictions where two branches of the profession have been amalgamated as a distinct advocacy bar continues to emerge. An effective trial bar has evolved in the United States and a similar trend can be seen in Australia. Where, as in Western Australia, there is a unified profession, some law firms give over an entire floor to 'litigation counsel'. These are partners and associates in the firm who effectively operate as barristers. They have no direct dealings with clients. They are brought into cases by other partners or associates in the same firm whenever advocacy is required. It is a separate bar in all but name. But it is considered necessary if the firm was to maintain the same level of litigation expertise as they would face at federal level when opposing leading silks from New South Wales.'

The bar is a referral profession. That is to say it does not deal directly with clients but has clients referred to it when necessary by solicitors whose practice brings them in direct contact with the public. One of the many functions of a solicitor is to advise a client when the engagement of counsel is either desirable or necessary and as to who that counsel should be. Of course there are solicitors who are or have been skilled advocates in criminal trials before a judge and jury, having devoted much of their professional practice developing those skills just as there are or have been barristers who do not profess to have full professional skills in advocacy having specialised exclusively in non court work such as conveyancing but these are very much in a minority in both professions and an exception to the general rule. In general the nature of a solicitor's professional practice is such that he or she is committed to working on behalf of clients principally in their offices, a professional practice which they could not maintain if they were to prepare for and appear in jury trial courts with regularity. Most of the legal services required by most clients can be fully provided by a solicitor. When a client needs, exceptionally, for the purpose of legal representation or advice, the professional advice or representation of a barrister, the solicitor has at his disposal an ad hoc 'partner' so to speak who can be briefed according to that barrister's general or specialised skills that best serves the particular needs of the client on a particular matter.

Solicitors, as well as barristers, are of course professionally skilled to deal with cases in the District Court, particularly those who are on legal aid panels, because that is where they have professionally exercised and developed their skills in the course of their career. The fact is that District Court cases are heard in a local court and are in the main short

> cases (as opposed to criminal trials which can last many weeks). Again they are in general less complex and there is less at stake. That is not in any way to suggest that they are not important or serious cases which at times will give rise to complex legal issues.
>
> There are many criminal cases which come before the District Court which are serious and complex. Solicitors are professionally well qualified to represent and conduct defences on behalf of defendants in such cases so as to meet the requirements of constitutional justice. But the question, as properly raised by the appellant, is whether that can be said of all cases where there is a confluence of the gravity of the charges and particular complexity or other factors."

The court reiterated the view that constitutional justice requires that a person charged with an offence before the District Court and without the means to pay for legal representation be provided by the State with the legal representation necessary to enable preparation and the conduct of the defence to the charge:

> "The legal representation provided must be that which is essential in the interests of justice having regard to the gravity of the charge, the complexity of the case including the applicable law and any exceptional circumstances."

The Supreme Court then considered the factual situation of this statement of law in the context of the District Court and within the context of Kenny J.'s observation in Healy: "It would be foolish to lay down what constitutes a fair trial because its requisites change from generation to generation".

The judgment recognised the seriousness of offences which may be tried in the District Court and stated further, that "even where no detention or imprisonment is imposed, conviction for an offence before the District Court may, because of its nature, result in serious reputational damage to a citizen in the eyes of the community." Nevertheless, District Courts deal with thousands of relatively trivial cases and, as a general rule, "the more serious or complex criminal cases requiring legal aid could not, in the Court's view, require more than the services of a professional solicitor to meet the essential requirements of justice".

The judgment continued by noting that the legal environment to which the District Court exercised its criminal jurisdiction has changed significantly since 1962. At that time, under s.5 of the Criminal Justice Act 1951, the District Court could not impose any consecutive term of imprisonment exceeding 12 months. The Criminal Justice Act 1984 had amended this section, substituting two years for the earlier stated period of 12 months:

> "Thus, since 1984 where the District Court imposes two or more sentences to run consecutively the aggregate term of imprisonment

may be twice the amount which it was in 1962. No change was made as regards the provision of legal aid."

The Supreme Court observed:

> "Perhaps of even more pertinence is the fact that there is a wide range of potentially complex offences created in recent decades for which the District Court now has jurisdiction and which have serious import from both the perspective of the public interest and defendants. Many of these offences arise from the introduction of modern regulatory regimes often accompanied by regulatory bodies with powers of prosecution.
>
> Such offences arise in areas such as competition law, (enforced by the Competition Authority), consumer protection (enforced by the Consumer Protection Agency), environmental law including illegal dumping, handling of hazardous waste, environmental pollution, and planning (enforced by the Environment Protection Agency, local authorities, planning authorities and other agencies), food safety (enforced by the Food Safety Authority), company law including corporate governance (Director of Corporate Enforcement) to name at least some.
>
> In addition of course the nature and volume of crime has changed dramatically over the decades. For example dealing in and supplying illicit drugs was virtually unknown in the 1960s. Successive statutes, apart from amending legislation governing long standing criminal offences, have created new ones. The offence of possession of child pornography, which may in certain circumstances be tried summarily, is an example. Another obvious example is the regulation of the farming or agriculture industry which has seen a host of regulatory measures often, as in this case, designed to protect a vital industry from the hazards of animal disease and also public health. Such regulatory measures may be introduced in the implementation of national policies or be required to be introduced as a result of obligations arising from EU legislation."

The Supreme Court concluded that over recent decades the enforcement and application of criminal law in the District Court has become more complex. It then considered the right to seek legal aid in the "contemporary" circumstances. With regard to the decision of an agency or authority which has the responsibility for enforcing the regulatory regime in the courts throughout the country to engage counsel, this may be for reasons that are not germane to the gravity or complexity of a particular case. However, the court did not exclude the possibility that the very reason for engaging counsel may be due to particularly contentious issues of fact or the particular complexity of the law governing an offence. It acknowledged that the State:

> "…with all the resources which it has at its disposal, is at liberty to

> engage counsel to act for the prosecution before the District Court irrespective of whether the services of counsel in addition to that of a solicitor are strictly required by the circumstances of the case. More relevantly it may do so because the State considers representation by counsel is necessary due to the complexity or gravity of the case".

Equality of arms The judgment briefly adverted to the concept of "equality of arms" relying on the submission of the amicus curiae of the Human Rights Commission and adopting the European Court of Human Rights observation in *Steel & Morris v United Kingdom* (2005) 41 E.H.R.R. 22:

> "'The adversarial system … is based on the idea that justice can be achieved if the parties to a legal dispute are able to adduce their evidence and test their opponent's evidence in circumstances of reasonable equality.'"

It was also noted that the court had not found that simple parity of representation is required by the principle of "equality of arms". Referring again to Henchy J. in *Healy*, the court held that:

> "… a defendant is entitled to have his or her trial conducted in the manner which would not 'shut him out from a reasonable opportunity of establishing his innocence; or, … of receiving a sentence appropriate to his degree of guilt and his relevant circumstances".

Essentially, the judgment viewed equality of arms as meaning that "neither party in criminal trials should be procedurally disadvantaged as compared to the other party."

Right to just or fair trial The key issue in the case fell to be decided within the broader notion of right to a just or fair trial which is a right of both the prosecution and a defendant:

> "Within that broader concept the fact that the State prosecutor is represented by solicitor and counsel may be a relevant factor should a court or other body have to determine whether the defendant should also be represented by counsel as well as a solicitor. If such a question fell to be determined by the District Court, which of course it has no power to do at present, and it was satisfied that granting legal aid for a solicitor only, notwithstanding the appearance of counsel for the State, was sufficient to meet the essential requirements of justice in providing effective legal representation then the constitutional obligation to the defendant would be met. On the other hand, in deciding whether legal aid should be granted to include counsel as well as solicitor such a court would in such instance, be entitled to take into account the fact that the State were represented by counsel in determining whether there

were particular aspects of the case as regards the gravity, complexity or other exceptional circumstances which required the grant of legal aid for counsel in all the circumstances of that case."

Rights of the accused The Supreme Court directed some critical comments at the popular and uninformed view of criminal justice:

> "Sometimes simplistic and unthinking comments surface in the public arena suggesting that fairness and fair procedures at a criminal trial only exist for the benefit of criminals. So far as a defendant is concerned these are protections in place for every citizen charged with a criminal offence, who enjoys the presumption of innocence unless proven guilty. Furthermore the constitutional guarantee to a fair trial minimises as far as reasonably possible the risk of an innocent person being convicted of an offence. The fact that an accused's defence can be effectively and fairly advanced at a trial is essential for the purpose of public confidence in the system of trial. It also gives confidence to the victims that the true perpetrator of the crime has been convicted. It is of no benefit, to say the least, to a victim or society in general if a conviction is later set aside on the grounds of a miscarriage of justice at a time when the trail to the true culprit may have become obliterated or difficult to pick up again with the passage of time."

District Court's limitations The Supreme Court then commented on the limitations of the District Court's jurisdiction to grant criminal legal aid:

> "[W]hatever 'the gravity of the charge', whatever 'exceptional circumstances' may exist and whatever 'the interests of justice' might require, a defendant in a trial before the District Court has no right to apply for legal aid to include counsel.
>
> Unless it could be assumed that no criminal case which comes before the District Court could ever require representation by counsel, in order to ensure that the trial was in accordance with the requirements of constitutional justice, this limitation on a poor defendant's right to apply for legal aid must be considered arbitrary.
>
> Having regard to the extremely wide scope and range of offences which come within the jurisdiction of the District Court in the field of criminal law and the increased complexity of modern legislation and regulatory measures, with which the Court is by no means unfamiliar, the Court is satisfied not only that the necessity in the interests of justice for a defendant to be represented by counsel as well as solicitor cannot be excluded but that cases, however infrequently that may be, will inevitably arise where it would be essential that an indigent defendant be afforded such legal aid.
>
> In order to vindicate the constitutional right of an indigent defendant

> in the District Court to a fair trial he or she must be entitled to legal aid with representation by counsel as well as solicitor where it is established that because of the particular gravity and complexity of the case or other exceptional circumstances such representation is essential in the interests of justice. It follows that any such defendant must have a right to apply for such legal aid and have the application determined on its merits."

This part of the judgment, in some sense repetitious, is reproduced verbatim, since despite this determination the Supreme Court, somewhat mystifyingly, proceeded to hold constitutional the restrictive provision which limits the District Court from vindicating that constitutional right. The reasoning of the court is, of course, laudable, but at the end of the day, the Supreme Court, in upholding the constitutionality of the impugned provision, has denied the ultimate remedy to the appellant in this case and, indeed, to the State and potential defendants in future cases until such time as the State remedies the situation. The Supreme Court acknowledged that the State fulfilled the constitutional obligation to vindicate the rights of an indigent defendant to legal representation by providing legal aid to obtain such representation for the preparation and conduct of a defence which is essential to the interests of justice, but no more: "The State is not bound to provide what might be perceived by an individual defendant to be the optimum form of representation or that which he or she desires." The court took the reasonable view that when the District Court grants legal aid in criminal cases, the defendant's right to legal aid will normally continue to be met by aid for a solicitor only. This includes cases which may be considered to be grave, complex or involve other exceptional circumstances. As District Court trials are less formal than jury trials there are also procedural options available which may facilitate the defence in certain circumstances. The court found that:

> "[I]t would be a question of judgment in each case for the Judge (assuming that a Court was conferred with such jurisdiction) concerned based on the degree of gravity and complexity in conjunction with any other exceptional circumstances of the case which may be taken into account, and which taken together necessitate a conclusion that the legal aid granted should include counsel. The object is to enable a defendant to be legally represented so that his or her defence can be properly prepared and fairly put.
>
> In considering the legal aid to be granted a court would be bound to take into account any procedural measures which may assist the defendant in the preparation and presentation of his case."

Constitutionality issue The Supreme Court was at pains to point out the positive rather than prohibitive or restrictive effect of the impugned provision which in 1982, for the first time, conferred on the District Court jurisdiction to grant legal aid in specified circumstances in the furtherance of a constitutional right. In the majority of cases, the provision must be considered sufficient to vindicate that right:

> "The absence of a right to apply for such legal aid in the District Court, prior to 1962 and since, stems not from the specific provisions of the Act of 1962 and in particular from any prohibition in that Act, but from the failure of the Oireachtas to confer at any time on the District Court or any other body, jurisdiction to consider an application for legal aid to include solicitor and counsel in the exceptional circumstances to which the Court has referred above."

The judgment held that "the mischief complained of by the appellant stems not from the effect of its provisions but from the failure of the State to make provision at any time for such legal aid."

The Supreme Court then observed that in order to apply Art.15.4.2 there must be a determination that the provision of an Act is in some respect repugnant to the Constitution. The appellant had claimed that a failure to include the right to apply for, and obtain, legal aid for counsel as well as a solicitor in appropriate circumstances is a constitutional deficiency in the Act. The court did not accept this argument:

> "However, as previously pointed out, and as emphasised in the Healy case, the duty of providing adequate legal representation in criminal cases to persons who cannot afford it themselves rests with the State. It is a matter in the first instance for the State to provide the mechanism or procedures by which this right may be vindicated. It may do so by statutory or administrative means provided the provision of such legal aid is secured in a sufficiently clear and certain manner. There is nothing in the provisions of the Act of 1962, and in particular in s. 2(1), which could be said to prohibit or create an obstacle to the introduction by the State of procedures or means which would enable a defendant in a criminal prosecution before the District Court to apply for legal aid which could, in particular circumstances, include representation by counsel. This is so even if the State chose to provide such legal aid by supplemental or other provisions amending the Act of 1962.
>
> So far as the right to be represented by a solicitor in such cases is concerned the Court is satisfied that s.2(1) insofar as it goes secures that constitutional right, although to a limited extent, and cannot be considered repugnant to the Constitution in any respect. There may be circumstances where the provisions of an Act facilitate the exercise of a constitutional right to a limited extent only but nonetheless limit the exercise of the constitutional right in a manner which has other consequences which are incompatible with the Constitution such as invidious discrimination. As regards the Act of 1962 the Court does

not consider that any other consequences of that nature arise in this case."

What is the State? As noted above, on a number of occasions the Supreme Court made reference to the "State" and its failure and/or obligation to provide the appropriate mechanisms of legal aid so that the constitutional right to a fair trial may be vindicated. The court referred to the failure of the Oireachtas to confer the necessary jurisdiction on the District Court or on any other body. Referring to itself as one of the organs of government it observed that in exercising its judicial functions it must seek to vindicate personal rights in accordance with Art.40.3. It noted that Barrington J. pointed out in *McDonnell v Ireland* [1998] 1 I.R. 134 at 148 that "… when the Legislature has failed in its constitutional duty to defend or vindicate a particular constitutional right pursuant to the provisions of Article 40.3 of the Constitution … this Court, as the Court of last resort, will feel obliged to fashion its own remedies."

The remedy which the Supreme Court fashioned was to prohibit the trial of the defendant while he is denied the right to apply for legal aid to include solicitor and counsel and have that application determined on its merits. This, the court declared, would be unjust and contrary to the appellant's right to a trial "in due course of law" as required by Art.38.1:

> "To allow a trial to proceed without any possibility of determining whether it was essential to a fair hearing that the defendant be represented by solicitor and counsel would be, in the words of O'Higgins J., in the Healy case, 'to tolerate injustice'."

Severability Upholding the constitutionality of s.2(1) leaves a situation whereby the District Court may only grant aid for a solicitor other than in the case of murder and there is no alternative mechanism available that may grant legal aid for counsel in the District Court. At a minimum, therefore, based on the Supreme Court judgment, it would seem that an amending statute is required to enable a decision awarding aid for counsel in accordance with the Supreme Court's decision. The likelihood that the State would act in accordance with the judgment and actually vindicate a constitutional right to legal aid might have been enhanced if there had been a declaration of unconstitutionality. The doctrine of severability is expressed in the words "to the extent only of such repugnancy". We submit that to have severed as unconstitutional the words "to have a solicitor and (where he is charged with murder and the Court thinks fit) counsel assigned to him for that purpose" would not have impacted negatively on the continuing exercise of the free criminal legal aid scheme by the District Court yet, would have left the way open for the District Court to consider applications for legal aid for counsel; furthermore, in *Carmody*, the Supreme Court has set out in some detail the type of case where counsel would be appropriate and, perhaps more significantly, where awarding aid for counsel might not be appropriate. Thus, such a severing would not have left a "gap in the law" so rightly deplored in *State (P Woods) v Attorney General* [1969] I.R. 385. Of course, the Supreme Court might have been leery of such action following its judgment in *C v Ireland (No. 2)* [2006] IESC 33; [2006] 2 I.L.R.M. 161 (*Annual Review of Irish Law 2006,* see index). However, since *A v Governor of Arbour Hill Prison* [2006] IESC 45; [2006] 2 I.L.R.M. 481 (*Annual Review of Irish Law 2006,* see index), the striking down of a law no longer means that floodgates would be opened for disaffected litigants who did not have the opportunity to apply for counsel. Of course, one might argue that this would be a usurpation by the courts of the legislative function as per *Maher v Attorney General* [1973] I.R. 140, but to uphold the section has the consequence of continuing the ill that is contained therein. As it stands, the particular applicant awaits trial until such time as the Government may introduce a new scheme or an amended scheme which would then vindicate a constitutional right which ranks very high in the hierarchy of rights, namely the right to legal representation where liberty is at stake. But what of the right to a speedy trial where liberty is at stake? If the applicant may not be tried for want of a scheme to enable him to apply for legal aid for counsel, will his prosecution fall for delay?

LIBERTY

Voluntary without consent The question of unlawful detention under the Mental Health Act 2001 also featured in 2009 and, once again, we raise concerns that the fundamental right to liberty as guaranteed under Art.40.4 may not be treated by the courts with the strict scrutiny it deserves, see *Annual Review of Irish Law 2007*, p.133 et seq. and *Annual Review of Irish Law 2008*, p.151 et seq. This year we consider just one case in which it was decided that persons may be deemed as voluntary patients in a locked psychiatric unit, despite the undisputed fact that the persons in question are non compos mentis, i.e. do not possess the mental capacity to make a full and informed decision with regard to medical treatment and are incapable of giving consent. Each of the two applicants in *McN v HSE* [2009] IEHC 236 had been originally detained involuntarily suffering from a mental disorder within the meaning of s.3 of the Mental Health Act 2001. Subsequently, and immediately prior to any review of that detention by a Mental Health Tribunal, the appropriate consultant psychiatrist had concluded that each was no longer suffering from a mental disorder as defined in the Act and the admission orders had been revoked. Nevertheless, each applicant had remained in the same locked psychiatric unit as a voluntary patient. On their behalf it was submitted that each was in de facto detention and since the admission orders had been revoked, they had ceased "to enjoy the panoply of rights and safeguards which the Act provides for patients being detained involuntarily". Peart J. refused the applications that each was being unlawfully detained, stating as follows:

> "It does not seem to me that there is any statutory requirement under the Act that a person must be capable of expressing, and express, a consent to being in an approved centre on a voluntary basis before that person can be categorised as being a 'voluntary patient'. The term 'voluntary patient' has a specific definition as appearing in s. 2 of the Act. As provided therein, and as referred to already a voluntary patient is defined as being '[save where the context otherwise requires] ...a person receiving care and treatment in an approved centre who is not the subject of an admission order or a renewal order'. There is not in my view any context in relation to these applicants which mandates that this definition is not appropriate to be applied. Having been lawfully admitted on an involuntary basis, these applicants' state of mental health improved as a result of medication and care provided, yet not to the point where they were capable of being discharged in the sense of released home."

Further in his decision he stated:

> "The order must be revoked if the patient no longer suffers from a mental disorder as defined. It seems to me to make complete sense that following the revocation order, a consultant psychiatrist must retain the capacity to ensure that a patient is not thereupon discharged from the hospital into a situation of, say, danger, to himself or others. As I have said, this follows from the ongoing duty of care owed to a particularly vulnerable person."

The question of procedural safeguards available to such patients does not appear to have been addressed.

Compulsory detention orders Section 38 of the Health Act 1947 as amended by s.35 of the Health Act 1953 provides for the detention and isolation of a person suffering from an infectious disease who is a probable source of infection. According to the Director of Public Health for HSE South in her testimony in *S* or *VTS v HSE* [2009] IEHC, s.38 orders are "very, very rare" and "the invoking of s.38 was considered to be a measure of last resort". Consequently, we might satisfactorily treat this judgment as a case in which the detention of the patient was deemed lawful, and the impugned statutory provisions were held constitutional. However, while the judgment is confined to an inquiry under Art.40.4, the variety of issues raised, as detailed by Edwards J., are highly significant:

> "... matters of public policy; the risk of epidemic; the public interest both local and national; the adequacy of existing legislation; the need to balance the public's right to protection with the patient's rights to liberty, to bodily integrity, to self determination, and to privacy;

> the patient's mental capacity and ability to take decisions; cultural difficulties; the legal requirement of consent to medical treatment, possible limits on the right to refuse medical treatment; whether the patient might be medicated against her will in any circumstances and, if that were possible, the theoretical means by which she could be treated involuntarily; possible invocation of the wardship jurisdiction; and so on, this Court is constrained in that it can only have regard to those issues to the extent that they have a bearing on the legality of the patient's detention. Save to that limited extent, they are not matters to be appropriately considered within the bounds of an inquiry under Article 40.4, and, although they might be legitimately canvassed in other proceedings on another day, there are not, in so far as the Court is aware, any such proceedings presently in being."

The applicant in *S v HSE* [2009] IEHC 106, also referred to as *VTS v HSE*, had challenged the legality of the detention of her daughter, a 33-year old South African national (the patient) at the Mercy University Hospital in Cork. At the time of the hearing the patient had been compulsorily detained in isolation for almost a year under s.38 of the Health Act 1947. The s.38 order was issued on December 11, 2007:

> "… on the basis that the patient is a probable source of infection with an infectious disease, to wit tuberculosis (TB), and that her isolation is necessary as a safeguard against the spread of infection and that she cannot be effectively isolated in her home. The order specified that the patient be detained and isolated in a specialised negatively pressurized room within the Mercy University Hospital until certified by the said Medical Officer of Health that she is no longer a probable source of infection."

Wardship jurisdiction Edwards J. delivered his decision ex tempore on November 26, 2008, "mindful of the need for expedition in a matter involving the right to personal liberty". The introduction to the judgment concluded:

> "Moreover, it should be stated that I have, of my own motion, decided that it is appropriate to bring the very particular and unusual circumstances of the patient's case to the attention of the President of the High Court so that he might consider it the context of the wardship jurisdiction that is reserved to him. Accordingly, my judgment incorporates a much more detailed review of the evidence heard in the course of the inquiry than would otherwise be necessary."

This is, indeed, a lengthy judgment and the review of evidence is not merely very detailed but highly illuminating and instructive for anyone who may be interested in the actions and decision-making processes of health professionals in the Health Service Executive and in a busy city hospital.

The law Section 38 of the Health Act 1947 states:

(1) Where a chief medical officer is of opinion, either consequent on his own inspection of a person in the area for which such medical officer acts or consequent upon information furnished to him by a registered medical practitioner who has inspected such person, that such person is a probable source of infection with an infectious disease and that his isolation is necessary as a safeguard against the spread of infection, and that such person cannot be effectively isolated in his home, such medical officer may order in writing the detention and isolation of such person in a specified hospital or other place until such medical officer gives a certificate (for which no charge shall be made) that such person is no longer a probable source of infection.

(2) Where an order is made under this section in relation to a person (in this subsection referred to as the patient), the following provisions shall have effect:-

(a) the medical officer who made the order in this subsection referred to as the committing officer) shall forthwith send a copy of the order to the Minister and to the Health Authority for which he acts,

(b) the committing officer, and also any other person, to whom the duty of acting under this section has been assigned by or with the consent of the Minister and who has been authorised in writing by the committing officer to act in the particular case, may detain the patient,

(c) the person detaining the patient shall, on or before doing so –

(i) produce for inspection by the appropriate person his written authorisation from the committing officer, if he is not himself the committing officer, and

(ii) give to the appropriate person a copy of the order and a statement in writing of the right of appeal under paragraph (h) of this subsection,

(d) if the patient, when detained, is outside the area for which the committing officer acts, the committing officer, may, with the consent of the chief medical officer of the area in which the person is detained, amend the order to allow for the patient's isolation in a hospital or other place convenient to the place where he is detained, and the order as so amended shall have effect accordingly,

(e) where the committing officer amends the order, he shall forthwith send a copy of the order as amended to the Minister and to the health authority for which he acts and to the health authority of the area in which the patient is detained and to the appropriate person,

(f) after the patient is detained, he shall be taken to the hospital or other place specified in the order and shall, subject to the provisions of this subsection, be there detained and isolated until the committing officer certifies that he is no longer a probable source of infection,

(g) the person in charge of such hospital or other place shall afford to the committing officer all reasonable facilities for visiting such hospital or other place and examining the patient therein,

(h) the patient (of the parent of the patient, where the patient is a child) may at any time appeal to the Minister in writing to direct the release of the patient.

(i) the person in charge of such hospital or other place shall afford all reasonable facilities for the purposes of any appeal under paragraph (h) of this subsection, including where appropriate facilities for the inspection of any reports and records relating to the patient and available in such hospital or other place and the provision of copies of any such reports or records,

(j) on receipt of an appeal under paragraph (h) of this subsection, the Minister shall give notice in writing of the date on which such appeal was received by him to the person making the appeal and to the person in charge of such hospital or other place,

(k) if no determination of an appeal under paragraph (h) is made by the Minister and communicated to the person in charge of such hospital or other place within twenty one clear days from the receipt by the Minister of such appeal, such person shall release the patient and notify the committing officer of such release and if necessary arrange for conveyance of the patient to his usual place of residence,

(l) if at any time the Minister directs the release of the patient, he shall be released by the person in charge of such hospital or other place in accordance with the direction and such person shall, if necessary, arrange for his conveyance to his usual place of residence

(m) where an appeal is made under paragraph (h) of this subsection the Minister shall cause one of his medical officers to examine the patient and report the result of such examination,

(i) as soon as practicable after the appeal is received by the Minister, and

(ii) at intervals thereafter not exceeding six weeks during the detention,

(n) the person in charge of such hospital or other place shall provide all reasonable facilities for an examination under paragraph (m) of this subsection,

(o) force may, if necessary, be used for the purpose of carrying out any provision of this subsection.

(3) In this section the expression 'the appropriate person' means in relation to a patient –

(a) where the patient appears to be under sixteen years of age and his parent can be ascertained and reached within a time which is reasonable having regard to all the circumstances of the case – his parent,

(b) where the patient appears to be under sixteen years of age and his parent cannot be ascertained and reached within a time which is reasonable having regard to all the circumstances of the case – the person for the time being in charge of the patient,

(c) where the patient, being an adult person, is for any reason unable to act for himself – the person for the time being in charge of the patient,

(d) in any other case – the patient himself.

(4) A person to whom an order under this section relates who –

(a) resists being detained under this section or resists being brought under this section to the hospital or other place specified in the order, or

(b) wilfully misbehaves while detained in such hospital or other place,

(c) escapes or attempts to escape from detention under this section, or

(d) does not submit himself in a peaceful and orderly manner to the exercise of any power conferred by this section, shall be guilty of an offence under this section.

(5) A person who –

(a) prevents or attempts to prevent the detention under section of any person or the bringing under this section of any person to a hospital or other place for detention and isolation, or

(b) assists in an escape or an attempted escape of any person from detention and isolation under this section, or

(c) obstructs or interferes with the exercise of any power conferred by this section, shall be guilty of an offence under this section.

(6) A person who is guilty of an offence under this section, shall, on summary conviction thereof, be liable to a fine not exceeding fifty pounds or, at the discretion of the court, to imprisonment for a term not exceeding three months or to both such fine and such imprisonment.

(7) The cost of the maintenance and treatment of a person to whom an order under this section relates in the hospital or other place mentioned in the order (including the cost of anything done under paragraph (f), (k) or (l) of subsection (2) of this section) shall be paid by the health authority for which the medical officer who made the order acts."

Section 35 of the Health Act 1953 amended s.38 as follows:

> An order made after the commencement of this section under subs.(1) of s.38 of the Principal Act shall have no effect unless, in addition to being signed by the chief medical officer, it is also signed by another registered medical practitioner.

Edwards J. referred to the appropriate statutory provisions which, "in so far as possible", effected "a seamless transfer of statutory functions and powers" allowing for the administrative changes in the health services since 1947 to date. He concluded with the statutory definitions and list of infectious diseases for the purposes of a section 38 order. These are contained in the Infectious Diseases Regulations 1981 (S.I. No. 390 of 1981), as amended, made under s.29 of the Health Act 1947. All diseases currently specified as infectious diseases are listed in the Schedule thereto. Regulation 8 of those regulations, as amended by reg.4(4) of the Infectious Diseases (Amendment) (No 3) Regulations 2003 (S.I. No. 707 of 2003) provides:

> "Infectious diseases 'All the infectious diseases listed in the Schedule to these Regulations, except acute anterior poliomyelitis, cholera, diphtheria, paratyphoid, plague, severe acute respiratory syndrome (SARS), smallpox, tuberculosis, typhoid, typhus and viral haemorrhagic fevers (Lassa, Marburg, Ebola, Crimean-Congo) shall be excluded from the application of Section 38 of the Health Act 1947 as amended by Section 35 of the Health Act 1953.'"

The patient was deemed a probable source of infection of Multi (or Multiple) Drug Resistant Tuberculosis (MDR-TB). Expert evidence was that ordinary drug-resistant TB represents a significant public health risk in itself. Moderately contagious and, although not difficult to treat, it nevertheless requires a lengthy period of treatment. The mortality incidence is significant. Treatment of MDR-TB, which the patient in the present case was suspected to have, is much more difficult, much more protracted, and it has a much higher mortality incidence. Edwards J. continued:

> "Further, and much more sinisterly, incomplete or inconsistent treatment with antibiotics of MDR-TB patients creates a risk of the emergence of XDR-TB which is virtually untreatable. The patient in this case, who is believed to suffer from MDR-TB, has had incomplete or inconsistent treatment of her condition with antibiotics. [The expert witness in microbiology] characterises the potential spread of a virulent airborne disease such as MDR-TB, and in particular XDR-TB, as being 'one of the worst nightmare scenarios for epidemiologists, conjuring up images of numerous TB sanatoria that were common in Europe and the United States prior to the development of antibiotic treatment'. He says that the potential risk to the public from MDR-TB or XDR-TB is

> very serious, and is significantly more serious than the risk to the public from diseases such as MRSA."

In consideration of the evidence Edwards J. was satisfied that the patient, for so long as she remains infectious, "represents a grave danger to the general public unless she effectively isolated."

Lack of safeguards of rights Edwards J. acknowledged that the power of detention provided by s.38 represents a significant impingement upon the constitutional rights of the person against whom it is invoked. He held that there must be due recognition of this at all stages, stating that "it is incumbent on the person invoking s.38 to take positive steps to ensure respect for, and the vindication of, the subject patient's rights to the greatest extent possible consistent with the need to protect the public against the spread of disease". He had regrettably been forced to the conclusion based on the evidence that Dr Keane, the relevant medical officer who had issued the section 38 order, had focused primarily on the public health risk and had given:

> "… little or no thought to how the unfortunate patient's constitutional rights might be respected or vindicated. The patient had been in detention for almost eleven months when the matter came before this Court, and there was no care plan in place for this patient to ensure the vindication of her rights".

He found that Dr Keane was required to be, and remains, centrally involved. He continued:

> "The patient will remain in isolation until she, Dr. Keane, is in a position to certify that the patient is no longer a probable source of infection. Accordingly, she is obliged to stay in close touch with the primary care team and to maintain the case under constant review. Moreover, Dr. Keane is the person who is ultimately responsible for not just for the physical care of the patient but for all aspects of the patient's welfare. Her responsibility in this regard is an onerous one. She must ensure that the patient's rights are impinged upon to the very minimum extent necessary. She is required to vigilant and pro-active to ensure that the patient's rights are respected and vindicated in so far as is possible. Her duty in that regard is all the greater in circumstances where the patient is particularly weak and vulnerable and the statutory provision containing the power of detention is an old one that provides little or nothing in the way of built in safeguards for the protection of the patient's rights. It is unfortunately the case that s. 38 does not incorporate many of the safeguards that one might reasonably expect to see in a more modern piece of legislation e.g., it does not provide for regular periodic reviews

> of the patient's case, or for the provision of an independent advocate for the patient."

HSE and hospital share responsibility Edwards J. was nevertheless satisfied that at all times Dr Keane had acted in good faith, and that she did so within the scope of her job as Director of Public Health for HSE South and Medical Officer of Health for the Counties of Cork and Kerry. Thus, the HSE shared, and continue to share, her responsibilities towards the patient and are obliged to support the doctor in her role:

> "… not least by providing her with comprehensive and reliable legal advice concerning what to do in the very unusual situation of the s.38 power needing to be invoked and, where necessary, by providing her with material and administrative assistance".

He was of the view that the second-named respondent, as the physical custodian of the patient, has parallel responsibilities with those of the first-named respondent in respect of the patient's non-medical welfare: "It goes without saying that it has primary responsibility for her medical welfare".

Absence of rights-based care plan Edwards J. continued with strong criticism of a failure to apprise fully the patient of her situation:

> "The Court has already criticised the absence of a rights based care plan for the patient in this case. Although the various professionals concerned with her welfare are all well disposed towards her, are caring, and are doing their best in a very difficult situation, their approach to her non-medical welfare has been ad hoc and largely unplanned. There have been failures on account of this. To give just one example, the evidence establishes that the patient has from time to time resisted detention, has attempted to escape, has wilfully misbehaved and has not submitted to the exercise of s.38 powers 'in a peaceful and orderly manner'. Yet it has never occurred to anybody, either before or since, to advise the patient of the implications of these behaviours, that each one of them constitutes a criminal offence under s.38 (4), attracting a potential custodial sentence of up to three months in jail. The Court would ask how, in the absence of this information, it could be contended that the patient's right to self determination is being respected? To make a proper decision a person has to have all necessary information".

He further observed that s.38(2)(o) provides that "force may, if necessary, be used for the purpose of carrying out any provision of this subsection":

> "There is no evidence that the patient has been advised of this feature of the circumstances in which she is detained. It is possible that if, out

> of frustration or otherwise she becomes unruly, she could be forcibly restrained. Does she realise this? Has anybody told her?
>
> Now while the Court accepts that it is inherently unlikely that this patient would ever be prosecuted for a s.38(4) offence, that is not the point. The point is that no one has sat down to work out, or to plan, exactly what information the patient needs to have, how it is to be communicated, how issues of trust and confidence tending to undermine effective communication are to be addressed, what special skills may be necessary to ensure effective advocacy both with and on behalf of the patient, and who is to have responsibility for it."

Despite his criticisms of the historical circumstances, Edwards J. declared himself on balance satisfied that, notwithstanding past failure:

> "[T]he patient's constitutional rights are now being sufficiently respected and vindicated to enable the Court to express the view that her detention is, at this time, lawful. There is, however, room for considerable improvement in terms of the formulation of a specific rights based care plan, and the implementation of a system of regular periodic reviews not just of the patient's medical situation but of all aspects of her welfare."

Presumption of constitutionality With regard to the constitutionality of s.38, it enjoys a presumption of constitutionality. Moreover, in accordance with *East Donegal Co-op v Attorney General* [1970] I.R. 317, there is a further presumption that decisions taken under s.38 will be made in accordance with the principles of natural and constitutional justice and that the relevant decision-makers will have regard to the constitutional right to liberty. Edwards J. concluded that the power created by s.38:

> "… supports an important public interest objective, namely, it assists in safeguarding against the spread of particular infectious diseases amongst the general population by facilitating, where necessary, the compulsory effective isolation of a person who is suffering from such a disease".

Therefore, he was satisfied that "the provision is therefore benign, and that it is of an essentially paternal character".

Misunderstandings and misapprehensions As noted above, this is a lengthy judgment and it has given rise to some errors by some commentators. Whilst HIV infection is a complicating factor in the medical diagnosis and prognosis, it was incidental to the section 38 order. This related to infectious TB and was a last resort required, it would seem, solely because of the patient's refusal to accept and maintain treatment. It is recommended that anyone who wishes to understand the reasons for the patient's confinement in isolation as described elsewhere in this chapter should read the judgment in full, including the sworn evidence. It is made clear in the judgment that the patient will stay in this situation until she dies unless she starts and maintains treatment. Taking the required medication intermittently will only result in the infection becoming more drug-resistant and the patient will remain a probable source of infection. The reason there is a security guard continuously outside her door is not because of the detention order, but because she had attempted to escape the detention. Not all visitors to her room wear goggles; some do for fear that she will spit into their eyes, as she has done on occasion. One psychiatrist is of the opinion that the patient's refusal to co-operate and her outbursts are a reasonable reaction based on anger and frustration; another psychiatrist contends that it is mental disorder. The difference of opinion between psychiatrists as to her mental state is perhaps the most informative aspect of the evidence, especially as the court concluded that the order was essentially paternal in character. It might be recommended as required reading to all involved in decision-making situations where liberty is at stake under health, especially mental health legislation.

MASS CARDS

Background Section 99 of the Charities Act 2009 provides as follows:

> 99—(1) A person who sells a Mass card other than pursuant to an arrangement with a recognised person shall be guilty of an offence.
>
> (2) In proceedings for an offence under this section it shall be presumed, until the contrary is proved on the balance of probabilities, that the sale of the Mass card to which the alleged offence relates was not done pursuant to an arrangement with a recognised person.
>
> (3) In this section-
>
> 'Church' means the Holy Catholic Apostolic and Roman Church;
>
> 'Mass card' means a card or other printed material that indicates, or purports to indicate, that the Holy Sacrifice of the Mass (howsoever described) will be offered for –
>
> (a) the intention specified therein, or
>
> (b) such intentions as will include the intentions specified therein;
>
> 'priest' means a priest ordained according to the rites of the Church;
>
> 'recognised person' means –
>
> (a) a bishop of the Church, or
>
> (b) a provincial of an order of priests established under the authority of, and recognised by, the Church;
>
> 'sell' includes, in relation to a Mass card, offer or expose the card for sale or invite the making by a person of an offer to purchase the card.

This provision was added to the Charities Bill at a relatively late stage in the drafting process, responding to concerns about the practice of selling Mass cards. The Catholic Church has long held a practice of allowing Masses to be offered for particular intentions. In Ireland (almost uniquely), a practice has developed of having a card, signed by the priest, to note the offering of the Mass for the particular intention. This allows the person requesting the Mass to provide evidence, in a tasteful format, to the person on whose behalf the Mass was offered or—more usually—a relative of the deceased person on whose behalf the Mass was offered. Over time, the expression of sorrow contained in the card may have become as important—for some people—as the offering of the Mass itself. To facilitate people who might not know their priest or who, due to working commitments, might find it difficult to meet a priest to arrange for the offering of a Mass, a practice developed of providing pre-signed Mass cards. Under this system, pre-signed Mass cards could be purchased with the names of those for whom Masses were to be offered retained for transmission to the priest who had pre-signed the card. As well as providing solace for the bereaved faithful, this whole system also provided a method of people supporting their priests. It is customary to make an offering to the priest who says the Mass although—of fundamental importance from a theological perspective—the offering in no way represents a payment for the Mass. As well as supporting local priests, Irish people have a tradition of arranging for Masses to be said by priests on the missions. The transfer of offerings to those priests provides one of their few sources of income. This entire scheme has the potential to become extremely murky and is heavily regulated by Canon law. In Ireland, there developed a substantial industry of Mass card sales operated by private persons on a for-profit basis. Concerns arose as to whether these private operators were compliant with Canon law and whether consumers of Mass cards were receiving what they thought they were buying, namely a Mass card and a Mass offering compliant with all requirements of the Catholic Church.

Section 99 of the Charities Act 2009 was enacted to address these concerns. It operates by effectively setting up a licensing system for the sale of Mass cards—the sale of Mass cards, other than pursuant to an arrangement with a recognised person, is an offence. Recognised persons are bishops or provincials of the Catholic Church. This legislation was challenged by Mr McNally, a producer and seller of Mass cards. MacMenamin J. took some time to characterise the nature of Mr McNally's business. He noted that, "[b]y way of notices, signs and advertisements MCC makes every effort to convey the impression that their pre-signed Mass cards are 'authentic', that is, in accordance with Roman Catholic Church teaching". However, it was questionable whether this was in fact the case. Mr McNally sold his cards through commissioned agents, each of whom would provide retail outlets with a form on which would be written the names of the purchasers of cards. These forms were sent back to Mr McNally's business, where they were routinely destroyed after two or three weeks. Mr McNally had an arrangement with a Fr Latus in Bermuda, whereby he paid Fr Latus a stipend of €300 a month. Each month, Fr Latus offered three Masses, collectively for the dead, the sick and the living. Mr McNally's annual turnover was in the region of €250,000, whereas Fr Latus received just €3,600. Moreover, Fr Latus was saying Masses without ever knowing the names of those for whom the Mass had been requested. Each Mass must have applied in respect of hundreds or possibly thousands of persons, even though Mr McNally's cards created an impression (somewhat qualified by small type) that a Mass was said for each person for whom a card was bought. There had previously been an issue with a priest who signed Mr McNally's Mass cards, as he had been suspended from his ministry by his bishop in Tanzania. Around this time, the Gardaí in Longford sent a file to the Director of Public Prosecutions. The Director's office responded that a prosecution for any offence would present significant evidential difficulties, particularly in establishing that Masses had or had not been said by the named priest, and also with regard to the status of that priest.

For the purposes of applying the proportionality test, MacMenamin J. reasoned that it was sufficient that the following had been established:

> "There was ample material to show that certain of the activities of MCC and other businesses could mislead ordinary Roman Catholic consumers or purchasers as to the 'authenticity' of their Mass cards and their compliance with canon law and other Roman Catholic teaching (at [63])".

The challenge under Art.44 of the Constitution The plaintiff argued that s.99 infringed the right to the free profession and practice of religion under Art.44.2.1, discriminated on the basis of religious profession, belief or status contrary to Art.44.2.3, and amounted to a quasi-establishment of the Roman Catholic Church contrary to Art.44.2.5. Mr McNally's argument placed heavy reliance on the jurisprudence of the United States Supreme Court, interpreting the First Amendment to the US Constitution. MacMenamin J., while reviewing the US case law in detail, was sceptical of this line of argument:

> "[A] court considering foreign authority is entitled to enquire whether the decision is in fact 'authoritative' in representing well settled law. In law context is all important. A United States authority, even if representing well settled law on a fundamental issue such as the constitutional separation of church and state may be of persuasive force and assistance only where the relevant provisions of the constitutions of the two states are akin textually and in their application in established jurisprudence. If the tests applied in the application of the First Amendment actually run counter to the provisions of the Constitution of Ireland, then clearly such decisions cannot assist an Irish Court. One must start from the fundamental premise that it is the task of judges in Ireland who make the declaration of office under the Constitution to uphold and apply the provisions of that Constitution of 1937 and no other one. This case cannot concern an 'issue' of whether s.99 of the Act of 2009 runs

> counter to the terms of the First Amendment clause. The task which the plaintiff takes on therefore, must be to establish that any jurisprudence sought to be 'transplanted' is not to be 'rejected' at the outset because it is in its terms inimical to what was enacted by the people of Ireland and the manner in which these have been interpreted."

MacMenamin J. considered that the two Constitutions, while sharing some common objectives such as the value of freedom of religious practice, differed in significant ways as to the mode of achievement of those objectives. He endorsed Keane J.'s comments in *Campaign to Separate Church and State Ltd v Minister for Education* [1998] 2 I.L.R.M. 81 to the effect that Art.44.2 was markedly different from the First Amendment to the US Constitution. While the terms of the US Establishment clause are neutral or blind towards religion, Art.44.2 specifically recognises religious establishments and protects certain rights. Article 44.1 contains an acknowledgement of a monotheistic, Christian and pluralist State. Having quoted the famous extracts from *McGrath v Trustees of Maynooth College* [1979] I.L.R.M. 166 and *Re Article 26 and the Employment Equality Bill 1996* [1997] 2 I.R. 321, in which the Supreme Court recognised that the State may give effect to religious discrimination in order to secure the free practice of religion, MacMenamin J. continued:

> "[T]he two emphasised quotations demonstrate that in our jurisprudence there may arise circumstances which are by no means analogous, but may run entirely counter to the idea of State avoidance of any 'entanglement'. The expression of priorities in Article 44.2.5 finds no reflection in the ideas of Paine, Jefferson or Madison. Subject to the proviso identified by Hamilton C.J., the State may lend its weight to disability or discriminations which derive from within a denomination but only insofar as it is necessary to give life and reality to the constitutional guarantee of freedom of religion."

MacMenamin J. summarised the differences between the US and Irish approaches in the following way:

> "In summary therefore it is true that Article 44.2.1 guarantees freedom of conscience, profession and practice of religion but subject to public order and morality. Article 44.2.3 prohibits any disabilities or discrimination on the grounds of religious belief or status. But these provisions must be seen as being embedded within the overall constitutional framework of Article 44, informed by its pluralistic Christian values, but to be interpreted harmoniously inter alia by reference to the Article 44.2.5 guarantee of religious autonomy, which, far from eschewing internal disabilities and discriminations which flow from the tenets of a particular religion, may on occasion actually allow for support subject to other constitutional rights guarantees. In this way the State may on occasion

> justifiably 'lend its weight' to the support of one denomination in autonomous affairs. This is entirely at variance with United States authority and the terms of that constitution. Here engagement may be permitted in the United States it is to be entirely avoided actually or symbolically. At its height what is in question here is, as pointed out below not a support or "buttress" but a mere identification for statutory purposes involving a matter of where public order and morality is concerned."

MacMenamin J. then held that Mr McNally did not have locus standi under Art.44.2.1 to invoke the free profession and practice of religion, as he had given no evidence that his freedom to practise religion was affected in any way. The plaintiff's sister was a party to the proceedings and, based on an affidavit filed in relation to an interlocutory application, might have claimed that Mr McNally's cards provided her with solace even if they were not in accordance with the tenets of the Catholic Church. However, she did not give evidence at the trial.

There was a similar problem in relation to the plaintiff's claim under Art.44.2.3 (discrimination on the grounds of religious status) as there was no evidence as to who was suffering from that discrimination. In any event, MacMenamin J. rejected this claim on its merits. He accepted the proposition that Art.44.2.3 applied to both positive and negative discriminations. In so far as there might be said to be a positive discrimination here, it had to be seen in light of Art.44.2.5 which provides that every religious denomination shall have the right to manage its own affairs. In giving effect to this provision, the legislature was entitled to identify bishops and provincials of the Catholic Church as the persons who would, in effect, establish the authenticity of cards. This identification did not amount to discrimination on the grounds of religious status.

Claims other than those based on Art.44.2 Section 99(2) contains a reverse-onus provision, whereby it is assumed that Mass cards are not sold in accordance with a valid arrangement until the contrary is proved. Mr McNally challenged this as a breach of the presumption of innocence, protected by Art.38. MacMenamin J. accepted that a proportionality analysis could be applied to the rights protected by Art.38. He noted the difficulty of positively proving that there was no arrangement with any one of thousands of recognised persons while, on the other hand, if there were such an arrangement it would be peculiarly within the knowledge of the accused person. For these reasons, all limbs of the proportionality test were satisfied.

Finally, MacMenamin J. also rejected a challenge by Mr McNally to the potential severity of the penalties under the Act (10 years' imprisonment or €100,000). These were maximum penalties that applied to all the offences under the Act. There was no guarantee that such a sentence would be imposed for an offence under s.99, if committed. Accordingly, Mr McNally's challenge was premature.

PROCEDURES OF CONSTITUTIONAL LITIGATION

In the related cases of *Equality Authority v Portmarnock Golf Club and Portmarnock Golf Club v Ireland* [2005] IEHC 235, the High Court had held that Portmarnock Golf Club was not a discriminating club within the meaning of ss.8 and 9 of the Equal Status Act 2000. However, O'Higgins J. proceeded to consider the club's challenge to the constitutionality of the Act in the alternative. The Equality Authority appealed against the High Court's conclusion in relation to the interpretation of the Act and the Club cross-appealed in relation to the High Court's decision on the constitutional issue, specifically objecting to the Court's decision to embark on the constitutional question. The Supreme Court (Hardiman and Geoghegan JJ., Macken J. concurring, Denham and Fennelly JJ. dissenting) upheld the judgment of the High Court on the issue of statutory interpretation; see [2009] IESC 73. As such, the court did not need to consider the constitutionality of the sections. Nevertheless, several members of the court reiterated the principle of constitutional litigation, that it was inappropriate for the trial judge to embark on a consideration of the constitutionality of the legislation when it was not necessary to do so. Hardiman J. expressed the point in the following way:

> "As the learned trial judge pointed out, there is ample authority for the proposition that a court should not embark upon a constitutional issue if the dispute between the parties can be resolved otherwise. I may say that I fully understand why, nevertheless, he addressed the Constitution issue: he considered that it would be economical of time to do so in case his decision were taken further. But I cannot consider that an adequate reason for embarking, without necessity, on a constitutional 'comment'.
>
> The club's proceedings make it quite clear that it is only in the event of their losing on the issue of the construction of the statute that they wish to agitate the constitutional questions. This is a perfectly proper attitude: they would have been open to legitimate criticism had they asked the court to decide on the constitutionality of the statute without first seeking to establish whether if, on its true meaning, they could claim the benefit of s.9.
>
> It is further to be noted that the learned trial judge did not make an order on the constitutional issues, presumably because they are hypothetical only, and described his own statements on the constitutional topics merely as 'comments'. But he made an order for the costs of the issue. It is not desirable that comments from an authoritative source on the constitutional issues should exist, as it were, in a vacuum. I

> would therefore set aside so much of the judgment of the learned trial judge that consists of commentary on the constitutional issues raised, and affirm the balance of the judgment, that set out up to p.22 of the approved text. I would also discharge the order for the costs of the constitutional issue."

Regular readers of the *Annual Review of Irish Law* might wish to refer to pp.199–201 of the 2005 volume.

Constitutional issue first, Convention incompatibility last As noted elsewhere in this chapter, *Carmody v Minister for Justice, Equality and Law Reform* [2009] IESC 71 ([2005] IEHC 10 considered in *Annual Review of Irish Law 2005*, p.188 et seq.) established that when there is a challenge to both the constitutionality of a statutory provision and the compatibility of that provision with the European Convention of Human Rights, the constitutionality of the impugned provision should be considered first. The essence of the issue raised by the appellant was that the State, by virtue of the terms of s.2 Criminal Justice (Legal Aid) Act 1962, wrongfully denied him the possibility of applying to the District Court for the grant of legal aid to include counsel and, or alternatively, the refusal to actually grant such legal aid in the circumstances of his particular case to the appellant. He had also sought a declaration of incompatibility with the Convention. The decision to defer the issue of compatibility until such time that the constitutionality issue is determined at first glance appears to overturn one of the canons of judicial review of legislation that arises from the presumption of constitutionality, namely, "that a court should not enter upon the question of constitutionality unless it is necessary for the determination of the case before it", per Henchy J., in *State (Woods) v Attorney General* [1969] I.R. 385. The court noted that this principle has been reiterated in a number of cases including *Murphy v Roche* [1987] I.R. 106, where Finlay C.J. stated at 110:

> "Where the issues between the parties can be determined and finally disposed of by resolution of an issue of law other than constitutional law, the Court should proceed to determine that other issue first, and, if it determines the case, should refrain from expressing any view on the constitutional issue that may have been raised."

It was this latter case that had informed Laffoy J.'s decision in the High Court to consider the claim for a declaration of incompatibility under s.5 of the European Convention of Human Rights Act 2003, prior to the constitutional issue. Section 5 states:

> (1) In any proceedings, the High Court, or the Supreme Court when exercising its appellate jurisdiction, may, having regard to the provisions of section 2 , on application to it in that behalf by a party, or of its own

motion, and where no other legal remedy is adequate and available, make a declaration (referred to in this Act as 'a declaration of incompatibility') that a statutory provision or rule of law is incompatible with the State's obligations under the Convention provisions.

(2) A declaration of incompatibility—

(a) shall not affect the validity, continuing operation or enforcement of the statutory provision or rule of law in respect of which it is made, and

(b) shall not prevent a party to the proceedings concerned from making submissions or representations in relation to matters to which the declaration relates in any proceedings before the European Court of Human Rights.

(3) The Taoiseach shall cause a copy of any order containing a declaration of incompatibility to be laid before each House of the Oireachtas within the next 21 days on which that House has sat after the making of the order.

(4) Where—

(a) a declaration of incompatibility is made,

(b) a party to the proceedings concerned makes an application in writing to the Attorney General for compensation in respect of an injury or loss or damage suffered by him or her as a result of the incompatibility concerned, and

(c) the Government, in their discretion, consider that it may be appropriate to make an ex gratia payment of compensation to that party ('a payment'),

the Government may request an adviser appointed by them to advise them as to the amount of such compensation (if any) and may, in their discretion, make a payment of the amount aforesaid or of such other amount as they consider appropriate in the circumstances.

(5) In advising the Government on the amount of compensation for the purposes of subsection (4), an adviser shall take appropriate account of the principles and practice applied by the European Court of Human Rights in relation to affording just satisfaction to an injured party under Article 41 of the Convention.

She had noted that in accordance with s.5(2) of that Act "if a declaration of incompatibility is made, it will not affect the validity, continuing in operation or enforcement of s.2 of the Act of 1962". However, she had observed that there had been no debate as to whether "obtaining such a declaration would resolve the issues between the parties to the extent that the court should refrain from expressing any view on the constitutionality of s.2 in accordance with the self-restraint principle as formulated in Murphy v. Roche". The Supreme Court, noting that a declaration of incompatibility did not "accord to a plaintiff any direct or enforceable judicial remedy", observed that it would have been more desirable for the parties to have debated in the High Court whether the obtaining of such a declaration would resolve the issue between them:

> "This would have more readily enabled the learned trial Judge to examine this question in the context of the case as a whole which could have led to a different order of priority being accorded to the issue of constitutionality on the one hand and that arising from the claim for a declaration of incompatibility on the other.
>
> In any event, the order in which issues in proceedings should be determined, where one of them involves the constitutionality of an Act, is ultimately and finally a matter for the Court rather than the parties while taking into account any views or submissions tendered on their behalf."

The court reaffirmed the principle as enunciated in the High Court that the question involving any validity of a statute or a section thereof should be postponed until consideration has been given to any other question of law, the resolution of which could determine the issues between the parties. Nonetheless, in the circumstances, the court was satisfied that a declaration of incompatibility was not a remedy which would resolve the issue between the parties. Even with such a declaration, the appellant would be in the same position with regard to his claimed constitutional right to legal representation in the prosecution pending against him in the District Court as he was prior to the commencement of proceedings. While of itself that was sufficient for the court to address the constitutional issue first, additionally the Supreme Court noted that s.5(1) of the 2003 Act conferred jurisdiction to make a declaration concerning a statutory provision or rule of law only "where no other legal remedy is adequate and available". The judgment continued:

> "Where a citizen's constitutional rights are violated, statute law or some other rule of law may provide a remedy which vindicates such rights. Where a statute or a rule of law does not provide a remedy for the violation of such a right the citizen is entitled to rely on the provisions of the Constitution for a remedy in vindication of the right. That is what the appellant has done in this case in relying on the provisions of the Constitution, and the principles which flow from it, as affording him a remedy for the alleged breach of his rights. It hardly needs to be said that the provisions of the Act of 2003 cannot compromise in any way the interpretation or application of the Constitution, a principle which is acknowledged in the long title to the Act which states that the effect of the Act is 'subject to the Constitution'."

Accordingly, the Supreme Court held that when a party challenges the constitutional validity of an Act or any of its provisions and at the same time applies for a declaration of incompatibility of such Act or some of its provisions with the State's obligations under the Convention, the issue of constitutionality must first be decided. This part of the judgment concluded as follows:

> "If a Court concludes that the statutory provisions in issue are incompatible with the Constitution and such a finding will resolve the issues between the parties as regards all the statutory provisions impugned, then that is the remedy which the Constitution envisages the party should have. Any such declaration means that the provisions in question are invalid and do not have the force of law. The question of a declaration pursuant to s.5 concerning such provisions cannot then arise. If, in such a case, a Court decides that the statutory provisions impugned are not inconsistent with the Constitution then it is open to the Court to consider the application for a declaration pursuant to s.5 if the provisions of the section including the absence of any other legal remedy, are otherwise met."

As de Londras and Kelly write in *European Convention on Human Rights Act: Operation, Impact and Analysis* (Round Hall, 2010), para.2-37:

> "The Supreme Court decision in Carmody therefore appears to finally resolve the matter of sequencing in favour of primary constitutional analysis with Convention matters being considered secondarily, and while a finding that a provision is constitutional will not prohibit the court from issuing a declaration of incompatibility, in cases where a finding of unconstitutionality has been arrived at the Convention matters may not be considered at all. Arguably this position as to sequencing removes any incentive for an applicant to make a stand-alone section 5 argument unless the matter under consideration has been determined from a constitutional perspective in previous jurisprudence."

With respect to *Carmody*, the Supreme Court found the impugned section constitutional and refused a declaration of incompatibility, as it was satisfied "that the remedies which are being afforded to the appellant in these proceedings are adequate to remedy the complaints which he has made with regard to his constitutional rights to legal aid". The so-called remedy is an order that he may not be tried before the District Court until he has exercised his constitutional right "to apply to and have determined by a court or other appropriate body whether he should be granted legal aid to include representation by counsel as well as by a solicitor". Since the District Court has no such jurisdiction, and no other appropriate body has made an appearance, it is difficult to view the decision as either a "determination" or a "resolution" of the issue between the appellant and the State. It is merely an amber light holding the appellant in a limbo awaiting trial.

RESTRICTION OF CONSTITUTIONAL RIGHTS IN LIGHT OF THE FINANCIAL SITUATION OF THE STATE

In *J & J Haire & Company Ltd v Minister for Health and Children* [2009] IEHC 562, McMahon J. assessed a challenge by pharmacists to the Financial Emergency Measures in the Public Interest Act 2009, as well as certain regulations made under that Act. The pharmacists had entered into a standard form contract with the Minister to provide medicines as ordered under a prescription to GMS and other eligible persons. In consideration of this service, the HSE paid funds to the pharmacists. Of crucial importance was clause 12(1) of the contract:

> "12(1) The Board shall in consideration of the service provided by the pharmacy contractor in accordance with these terms and conditions and on foot of claims made in the form and at the times directed by the Minister, make payments or arrange for payments to be made to the pharmacy contractor for prescriptions dispensed at his/her contracted community pharmacy *in accordance with such rates as may be approved or directed by the Minister from time to time after consultation with the Pharmaceutical Contractors Committee*" (emphasis added [by McMahon J])."

The 2009 Act commenced with a number of recitals recording the financial situation in which the State found itself and the need to reduce State expenditure. Section 9 of the Act authorised the Minister for Health and Children, notwithstanding any other enactment, contract, arrangement, understanding, expectation, circular or instrument or other document, by regulation to reduce, whether by formula or otherwise, the amount or the rate of payment to be made to health professionals, or classes of health professionals, in respect of any services that they render to, or on behalf of, a health body from the date of the regulation. The section applied to services rendered from the date of the regulation, even if the health professional concerned had commenced the provision of the service prior to the date of the regulation. Section 9(4) imposed an obligation on the Minister to engage in such consultations as she considered appropriate prior to making a regulation. Section 9(5) required the Minister to fix an amount or rate that she considered to be fair and reasonable in the light of the purposes of the Act, having regard to a number of matters, including any submissions made and views expressed during the consultation process. Pursuant to this section, the Minister made the Health Professionals (Reduction of Payments to Community Pharmacy Contractors) Regulations 2009 (S.I. No. 246 of 2009). For the purposes of the case, it was accepted that the reduction in fees effected by the Regulations was in the order of 24 per cent. The pharmacists contended that the reduction was in the order of 30 per cent but were prepared to argue the case on the basis of the lower figure. Part of the pharmacists' case turned on the fact that the reduction of 24 per cent was considerably greater than the reduction of 8 per cent required of other professionals providing services to the public sector. The State maintained that the differential was justified based on the greater state involvement in this sector of the economy and the rebate that wholesalers granted to pharmacists as a result—on the State's evidence—of the State's existence as a bulk-buyer in the market.

The main focus of the pharmacists' case was that the Regulation constituted an unjust attack on their property rights. The State did not dispute that a contractual right was a property right and that such rights are protected by the Constitution. In this regard, McMahon J. endorsed the comments of McWilliam J. in *Condon v Minister for Labour (No. 2)*, High Court, June 11, 1980 to the effect that a right under contract is a right protected by Arts 40.3 and 43 of the Constitution. However, the crucial question concerned what rights were granted by the contract: the Constitution could not protect anything greater than the contract provided. In this regard, McMahon J. reasoned as follows:

> "In the Contract between the pharmacist and the HSE, the pharmacist agrees to supply goods and provide a service on behalf of the HSE for certain rates of payment. The 2009 Regulations purport to reduce these rates from a certain date forward. It is important to appreciate that the Regulations do not purport to introduce the changes retrospectively. Neither is there any attempt to confiscate property in the sense of seizing goods or land. If such were attempted, of course, it could only be done under certain conditions and could not normally be done without reasonable compensation.
>
> The plaintiffs' property rights in this instance are no more and no less than those rights which are accorded to him in the Contract. Either the Minister is entitled to make the changes under the Contract or she is not. If she is entitled to do so, then she is not in breach of the Contract; if she is not entitled to do so, she is first and foremost in breach of the Contract and the plaintiff's primary remedies are in contract. Bearing in mind the terms of the Contract in this case, and particularly clause 12(1) which allows the Minister to change unilaterally the rate of remuneration, admittedly after consultation, there is little doubt that had the Minister chosen to effect the rate changes by following the procedure provided for in clause 12(1) of the Contract, the plaintiffs could not complain. There would have been no breach of the Contract and there would have been no infringement of a constitutional right which, by definition, is no greater than the plaintiffs' contractual right. A close look at the Contract between the pharmacists and the HSE, does not disclose that the pharmacists have any right or entitlement for the rates of remuneration to continue indefinitely into the future.
>
> The so called right claimed by the pharmacists under the Contract

> is not in fact a right at all. At most it is merely a spes, a hope that the present rates will continue. Whether they do, however, is not a matter which is to be determined by the pharmacists. It is a matter exclusively for the Minister. From this analysis it can be seen that this is the height of the pharmacists' entitlement under the Contract."

For that reason, McMahon J. rejected the pharmacists' arguments that their constitutional rights had been interfered with. Furthermore, he also considered that—even if there were a property right in being that was affected by the legislation—the legislation did not constitute an unjust attack on the property right. In comments that may give some indication of how the courts will assess constitutional challenges to other measures adopted by the State in response to the financial crisis, McMahon J. reasoned that the Act and the Regulations were a proportionate and well-tailored response to an exceptional situation:

> "Given the exceptional threat to the economic well being of the State and to the people, I have no difficulty in accepting that the 2009 Act is exceptional. Clearly it is capable of affecting persons adversely and that was one of the objectives of the legislation. I am not satisfied, however, that it could properly be described as draconian in the circumstances where it is clearly a measured, proportionate and carefully drawn piece of legislation with a number of significant safeguards inbuilt. I have already referred to these, but it may be well in the present context to refer briefly to them again. Regulations may be made under s.9 only after a process of consultation (s.9(4)); s.9(5) of the Act stipulates a list of matters which have to be considered when Regulations are being made; the Regulations must be laid before both Houses of the Oireachtas and are subject to annulment by resolution by either House (s.9(16)); the Minister for Health and Children must annually review the operation, effectiveness and impact of the amounts and rates fixed by the Regulations and she is obliged to consider the appropriateness of the amounts and rates having regard to any change of circumstances and, in particular, any alteration of relevant matters (s.9(13)); similarly the Minister for Finance has an obligation to annually review the Regulations (s.13); a health professional is also entitled to terminate his/her contractual obligations by giving 30 days notice (s.9(8))."

McMahon J. also rejected an argument that the Regulations abrogated the pharmacists' property rights. He considered that the Regulations only altered one term of the contract—albeit an important one relating to rates—and that this could not be characterised as an abrogation. If it were an abrogation, it was justified by the extreme financial crisis or fundamental disequilibrium in the public finances, as anticipated by the Supreme Court in *Re Article 26 and the Health (Amendment) (No 2) Bill 2004* [2005] IESC 7. In any event, as the contract itself allowed for the Minister unilaterally to alter the charges, no property right was being affected by the legislation, let alone abrogated thereby.

In a separate part of his judgment, McMahon J. considered the proportionality of the Regulations, although this analysis must be taken also to concern the legitimacy of the restriction on the pharmacists' property rights. Adopting the proportionality test as applied by the Supreme Court in *Re Article 26 and Part V of the Planning and Development Bill 1999* [2000] 2 I.R. 321, he reasoned as follows:

> "As to the size of the cuts made to the rates of remuneration for pharmacists under the regulations, it is not appropriate for the court to assess their appropriateness. That is not the court's function. Suffice to say, as I have already done, that the determination of the level of the cuts was arrived at after serious, detailed and prolonged study of the pharmacy sector and after many studies and various calculations were considered in great detail."

The pharmacists also argued that the difference in treatment between them and other professionals providing services to the State and state bodies breached Art.40.1. In this regard, McMahon J. held that as no evidence of disparate treatment had been adduced by the pharmacists, this argument could not succeed. The presumption of constitutionality meant that the onus of proof lay on the pharmacists to show that any discrimination was unconstitutional. Following the judgment of the Supreme Court in *D v Residential Institutions Redress Review Committee HSE* [2009] IESC 59 (discussed above), McMahon J. considered that there was no element of invidious discrimination here such as would reverse the onus of proof.

J & J Haire is an important case for a number of reasons. First, it appears to reflect a new collective wisdom that contractual entitlements amount to constitutionally protected property rights. As this point was not contested by the State, it cannot be taken to have been definitively settled by the courts. Nevertheless, it appears unlikely that the State will contest this position in future. Secondly, McMahon J.'s judgment importantly emphasises that the extent of the constitutionally protected property right can be no greater than the right actually provided under contract. This conclusion was largely determinative of the case. However, it may not be so important in other cases where the State seeks to alter contractual terms between private parties or public contracts in which the State does not have a unilateral power—under the contract—to alter the terms of the contract. Thirdly, McMahon J.'s judgment illustrates that the courts accept that the State is facing a severe financial crisis and will, therefore, be exceptionally slow to second-guess the State's assessment of the measures necessary to resolve that crisis.

STATUS OF THE EMBRYO

In *Roche v Roche* [2009] IESC 82, the Supreme Court was required to address the question of whether the unborn outside the womb (in vitro) was protected by Art.40.3 of the Constitution. The plaintiff was married to the first defendant. In 2002 the plaintiff underwent IVF treatment. In preparation for this, the plaintiff agreed to the removal of eggs from her ovaries and a mixing of the eggs with the sperm of her husband. Both signed a document in which they consented to the cryo preservation (freezing) of their embryos and undertook full responsibility on an ongoing basis for those embryos. The first defendant also signed documents in which he consented to the fertilisation of his wife's eggs and the implantation of three embryos. He acknowledged that he would become the father of any resulting child. As a result of the IVF treatment, six viable embryos were created and three were implanted in the plaintiff's womb, the other three being frozen. As a result of this process, the plaintiff gave birth to a daughter. Towards the end of the pregnancy, marital difficulties arose and the plaintiff and her husband separated. The issue came before the court because the plaintiff wished to have the three frozen embryos implanted in her uterus. Her husband did not want this to happen and did not wish to become the father of any child that might be born as a result of the implantation of the frozen embryos.

In the High Court, McGovern J. had directed a trial of a preliminary issue. This established that there was no agreement between the husband and wife as to what should happen to the frozen embryos and that the husband had given neither express nor implied consent to the implantation of the frozen embryos. If there had been agreement or consent to implantation on the part of the husband, there would have been no possible conflict between the wishes of the parties and constitutional requirements. However, as there was no consent to implantation on the part of the husband, the court was required to assess whether there was any constitutional reason as to why the embryos should be implanted. Addressing this substantive issue, McGovern J. concluded that the word "unborn" used in the Eighth Amendment was not intended to include the unborn child in vitro. The Eight Amendment was intended solely to deal with the issue of abortion and, as such, was not relevant to the status of the embryo outside the womb. On appeal, the Supreme Court unanimously held that Mr Roche was not party to any contract relating to the implantation of the embryos; nor was he estopped by conduct from objecting to the implantation of the embryos. Accordingly, the members of the court all addressed the substantive issue of constitutional interpretation.

Murray C.J. took a different approach from that adopted by McGovern J. in the High Court. He noted that Art.40.3.3 had not been framed in such a way as to address a specific mischief (such as "no law shall be enacted permitting an abortion to be performed"). Rather, he identified the ethos of the provision as a whole:

> "In my view the subsection 3 of Article 40.3. is clear in its intent. It is intended to protect human life before birth. The key words in the English version are 'life of the unborn' and in particular, in my view the much more apt expression, 'mbeo gan breith' (beo in its genitive case). I think 'ceart na mbeo gan breith chun a mbeatha' can be fairly interpreted as meaning the right of life not yet born to live or to its life. The life referred to, in a provision on personal rights is, obviously, human life…
>
> If the objective at the time had been to just address some perceived statutory frailties that could have been achieved more readily and easily by the adoption of legislation. But the public debate transcended that and the object obviously was, as the result demonstrates, to place in the Constitution a protection for human life before birth."

Murray C.J. also rejected an argument based on the reference in Art.40.3.3 to the "equal right to life of the mother." It was argued on appeal that this implied that Art.40.3.3 was concerned with gestation, where the presence of an unborn child might pose a threat to the mother. Murray C.J. rejected this limitation on two grounds. First, he commented that in vitro fertilisation and the maintenance of frozen embryos outside the womb was probably not contemplated at the time of the 1983 amendment. However, given that the first test tube baby was born in 1978, with considerable public attention, this assumption about the enacter's state of mind in 1983 is questionable. Secondly, he commented that the need for such a provision would apply in respect of babies conceived through IVF as they, too, would need to gestate in a mother. This is a fair observation although, of course, one of the features of IVF is that there is no physical requirement for the genetic mother to be the birth mother. In any event, Murray C.J. proceeded to focus on the core question of when human life begins. This question was avoided by the High Court but is central to the legal and moral issues raised by the case. Accordingly, it is welcome that the Chief Justice addressed the point directly.

Addressing the question of when human life begins, Murray C.J. noted that there were two predominant views: life begins at conception or life begins at implantation in the womb. He observed that there was no consensus on these issues, either at the present time or at the time when the Eighth Amendment was adopted by the People. All were agreed that the embryo—even pre-implantation—held a special status connected with human dignity. Nevertheless, the issue was whether the court should consider a frozen embryo to be human life for the purposes of Art.40.3.3:

> "In the course of the appeal counsel for the appellant acknowledged that the issue is polycentric. That is to say it is an issue which must be viewed from many standpoints, moral, ethical, philosophical, theological and scientific. It is an issue on which engenders passionate views on one side or the other in virtually all disciplines.

I do not consider that it is for a Court of law, faced with the most divergent if most learned views in the discourses available to it from the disciplines referred to, to pronounce on the truth of when human life begins.

Absent a broad consensus on that truth, it is for legislatures in the exercise of their dispositive powers to resolve such issues on the basis of policy choices.

The learned trial Judge quoted from the report of the Constitution Review Group of the Oireachtas published in July 1996 to the following effect:

> 'Definition is needed as to when the "unborn" acquires the protection of the law. Philosophers and scientists may continue to debate when human life begins but the law must define what it intends to protect.'

In my view that sums up the role of the Oireachtas in relation to this matter as the organ of State with at least initial responsibility for the protection and regulation of constitutional rights.

Therefore in the context of this case, there is uncertainty or no consensus as to when human life begins. The choice as to how life before birth can be best protected, and therefore the point which in law that protection should be deemed to commence, is a policy choice for the Oireachtas. It is one which falls to be made having taken into account all the factors and strands of thought which it considers material and relevant.

The Courts do not have at its disposal objective criteria to decide this as a justiciable issue. Issues are not justiciable before the Courts where there is, as Brennan J., put it in his opinion in Baker v. Carr 9US 1962), 'a lack of judicially discoverable and manageable standards for resolving it; or the impossibility of deciding without an initial policy determination of a kind clearly for non judicial discretion; …' That is the position of this Court in this case. The onus rests in the Oireachtas, to make the initial policy determination so as to define by law when 'the life of the unborn' acquires protection. The other alternative is an amendment to the Constitution."

Holding that the issue was non-justiciable, the Chief Justice rejected the appeal.

Denham J. differed from the Chief Justice's approach, identifying several reasons why the unborn in Art.40.3.3 encompassed only unborn life in the womb. First, she analysed the statutory law that applied prior to the enactment of the Constitution and held that it concerned the human life in vitro. She reasoned that Art.40.3.3 was an attempt to copper-fasten that statutory position, precluding the sort of expansive interpretation of the word "unlawful" taken by the courts of England and Wales in *R v Bourne* [1939] I K.B. 687. Secondly, she differed from the Chief Justice in her identification of the mischief addressed by the Amendment as the termination of pregnancy, the procurement of a miscarriage, and abortion. Thirdly, she again differed from the Chief Justice in reading the words of Art.40.3.3 as limiting the scope of the provision to the gestational context:

> "62. This analysis may be put in a slightly different form. The right to life of the unborn is not stated as an absolute right in Article 40.3.3°. Rather, it is subject to the due regard to the right to life of the mother. The right to life of the mother is not stated as an absolute right either. Article 40.3.3° refers to a situation where these two lives are connected and a balance may have to be sought between the two lives. Thus the physical situation must exist to require such a balancing act. No such connection exists between the plaintiff and the three surplus embryos now frozen and stored at the Clinic. There is no such connection between the lives of the mother and the embryos at the moment. The relationship which might require the consideration of the right to life of the unborn and the equal right of the mother does not arise in the circumstances.
>
> 63. This connection, relationship, between the embryos and the mother does not arise until after implantation has occurred. After the implantation of an embryo the relationship between the embryo and the mother changes. The mother has carriage of the embryos, becomes pregnant, and the embryo enters a state of 'unborn'. At that time an attachment begins between the two lives. It is that attachment which gives rise to the relationship addressed in Article 40.3.3°.
>
> 64. The words of Article 40.3.3° refers to a situation where the rights of the mother and the unborn are engaged. This occurs after implantation. Thus Article 40.3.3° does not apply to pre-implantation embryos."

Fourthly, attempting to harmonise the meaning of "unborn" with other constitutional values and provisions, Denham J. reasoned that family autonomy, protected by Art.41, would be breached if the State were to intervene to facilitate implantation against parents' wishes. However, it is questionable whether this reasoning properly applies to a situation where the parents are divided as to whether the embryos should be implanted. Furthermore, a duty on the State to allow the implantation of the embryos does not necessarily imply that those embryos must be implanted in the genetic mother. It might be possible for the State to arrange for a scheme of embryo adoption. It is therefore not necessarily the case that an expansive reading of "unborn" would infringe family autonomy.

Hardiman J. undertook a detailed analysis of the Irish text to reach a similar conclusion to that of Denham J. in relation to the gestational context of Art.40.3.3:

> "Accordingly, in a strictly linguistic sense and perhaps more generally,

> the right of the 'living without birth' to their lives is placed in apposition, perhaps in juxtaposition to the right of the mother to her life. But that linkage makes no sense, either as a matter of law, logic, language or ordinary human experience unless the life of the 'living without birth' is so connected with the right of the mother to her life that the former is capable of impinging negatively on the latter. If this were not so it would be quite pointless to condition or qualify the undertaking of the State in relation to the life of the unborn with a need to consider the mother's right to her life."

Accordingly, Hardiman J. considered that Art.40.3.3 was limited to the temporal scope of pregnancy. He also reviewed the mischief addressed by the Eighth Amendment and came to a similar conclusion as Denham J. in that regard.

Geoghegan and Fennelly JJ. also dismissed the appeal, on similar grounds as Hardiman J.

Although all five judges agreed that the appeal ought to be dismissed, there is a marked difference between the approaches taken by Murray C.J. and the other members of the Court. Murray C.J. disagreed with the four other members of the court over whether the mischief addressed by Art.40.3.3 was limited to the prohibition of abortion. In this regard, Murray C.J.'s approach seems preferable. One cannot overlook the fact that the People did not amend the Constitution just to prohibit abortion (despite the presence of other constitutional provisions in similar form) but rather chose to articulate the philosophical basis for such a prohibition: namely, the right to life of the unborn. As such, it is unwarranted to limit the intent of the People in this way. Murray C.J. also disagreed with the other four members of the court as regards the significance to be attached to the phrase "with due regard to the equal right to life of the mother". The analysis of Denham and Hardiman JJ. as to why this implicates a gestational context is compelling: the equal right to life of the mother only comes into play once there is a pregnancy. However, it does not necessarily follow that this limits Art.40.3.3 to the gestational context. As Murray C.J. pointed out, the implanted embryo will also be brought to term through pregnancy. Approaching the provision in this way, it could be argued that the phrase "with due regard to the equal right to life of the mother" is intended to qualify the ways in which the State may defend and vindicate the right to life of the unborn but is not meant to limit the right to life of the unborn to situations in which there is a potential conflict with the mother's right to life.

It is thus questionable whether the linguistic and purposive approaches adopted by Denham, Hardiman, Geoghegan and Fennelly JJ. actually dispose of the issue. If those approaches do not dispose of the issue, however, are we forced—with Murray C.J.—to conclude that the issue is non-justiciable? In this regard, Murray C.J. elided the propositions that there was neither certainty nor consensus on the issue of when human life begins. However, there is a significant difference between uncertainty and lack of consensus. Although *some* people *may* be uncertain as to which is the correct approach, many people—on both sides of the debate—are certain that theirs is the correct approach. The import of the Chief Justice's comments is that where people disagree on fundamental moral and philosophical questions, the courts are not entitled to determine the issue, even where that issue arises from the document that judges are sworn to uphold. In Murray C.J.'s view, the decision is a "policy choice" for the Oireachtas which the Oireachtas must make "taking into account all the factors and strands of thought which it considers material and relevant". However, it does not seem right to characterise this question as one of "policy", nor to suggest that the answer is to be reached having taken into account different factors. Moreover, if the status of the embryo is a contested question of philosophy and politics, so too must be the meaning of equality, all personal rights and the separation of powers. Once the Constitution explicitly or implicitly adopts a position on these issues—however indeterminate—it surely falls to the courts to articulate their best interpretation of the contested concept.

The judgments in *Roche v Roche* leave the Oireachtas with considerable latitude in devising a new regulatory scheme to deal with the issues raised by the existence of non-implanted embryos, in the context of both parenthood and scientific research. Many members of the court specifically emphasised the need for the Oireachtas to address these issues as a matter of urgency. Murray C.J.'s approach would have left the Oireachtas with the broadest discretion as, under his approach, the Oireachtas may determine whether the unborn has constitutional protection (under Art.40.3.3) from conception or from implantation. In contrast, under the approach adopted by the other members of the court, the Oireachtas must take as its starting point that the embryo receives constitutional protection only once implanted in the womb. Although the Oireachtas might choose to provide additional protection (even to the extent of recognising a right to life) to a pre-implantation embryo, it would not be entitled to rely on constitutional protection for doing so in the face of any other constitutional rights that such an approach might infringe. As such, it would be required to defend such legislation on the grounds of proportionality, rather than the balancing of rights exercise permitted by the Supreme Court in *Tuohy v Courtney* [1994] 3 I.R. 1.

STAY ON CRIMINAL PROCEEDINGS PENDING CONSTITUTIONAL CHALLENGE

In *D v Ireland* [2009] IEHC 206, Clarke J. considered an application to stay a criminal prosecution pending a challenge to the constitutionality of the Sexual Offences Act 2006. Mr D, a minor, was prosecuted under s.3 of the Act for having sexual intercourse with another minor. As the other minor was a female, s.5 of the Act precluded any prosecution of her. Mr D argued that this legislative position infringed Art.40.1 of the Constitution. He sought to postpone his trial until after the resolution of the constitutional challenge. Clarke J. referred to the Supreme Court decisions of *Pesca Valentia Ltd v Minister for Fisheries Ltd* [1985] I.R. 193 and *CC v Ireland* [2006] IESC 33. These established both that the courts had a jurisdiction to prevent the operation of a statute pending the determination of its constitutionality (although the jurisdiction ought to be exercised sparingly) and that the courts had a jurisdiction to stay criminal proceedings while considering the constitutionality of a statute, although the normal course would be for a person to challenge the constitutionality of the statute post conviction. In relation to the *Pesca Valentia* issue, it is noteworthy that the relief sought by Mr D was limited in character. He did not seek to prevent the statute coming into force pending the determination of its constitutionality. Rather he sought to prevent certain official steps being taken on foot of the statute, while accepting that those steps could later be taken in respect of events that occurred before the constitutionality of the legislation was determined.

From these cases, Clarke J. identified the following factors that a court must consider when deciding whether to stay criminal proceedings pending a constitutional challenge:

(a) Whether a fair case to be tried has been made out as to the validity of the statute concerned including a consideration of whether any successful challenge would materially affect the pending criminal proceedings;
(b) If so (given that it is difficult to see that damages could be an adequate remedy) where the balance of convenience lies affording a very significant weight indeed to the need to ensure that laws enjoying he presumption of constitutionality are enforced; but
(c) Also considering any special or unusual countervailing factors which might render it disproportionate to require the criminal trial concerned to go ahead immediately, including having due regard to the possibility of minimising any effect on the proper progress of criminal litigation.

The State contended that Mr D had not shown that there was a fair question to be tried as it was not possible for him to surmount the procedural impasse implicit in his challenge to the Act. The only discrimination appeared in s.5 of the Act, providing an exception for females. However, striking down the exception would provide no benefit for Mr D, as the offence itself, contained in s.5, would remain in place. Although noting the difficulty for Mr D, Clarke J. still considered that there was a fair issue to be tried. If s.5 were struck down, it might be possible for Mr D to argue that it was impermissible for the DPP to elect to prosecute one of the parties to the criminal act but not the other. Such an approach would not be far removed from the remedy fashioned by the

Supreme Court in *Carmody v Minister for Justice* (discussed above)—namely, a refusal to declare the legislation unconstitutional but a prohibition on the authorities from taking steps on foot of legislation until other legislation was enacted to remedy the constitutional defect.

Clarke J.'s approach to this issue is a welcome indication that the courts might not be entirely happy with the rationale of *Somjee v Minister for Justice* [1981] I.L.R.M. 324. In that case, Keane J. held that a discriminatory provision which conferred a benefit on one class of persons could not be challenged under Art.40.1 by a member of the class that did not receive the benefit: a declaration that the benefit was unconstitutional would provide no advantage to the litigant. There is a logic to this position, but its net effect is to leave significantly discriminatory measures beyond the review of the courts. As I have argued previously, one could construct an entire apartheid regime in a manner that, on the basis of *Somjee*, makes it immune from judicial review. (See Oran Doyle, *Constitutional Equality Law* (Thomson Round Hall, 2004), p.86.) First, the legislator must enact a comprehensive ban on access to a particular location or resource and then enact a number of exceptions that provide the privilege of accessing the location or resource to one group. Striking down any such exceptional privilege would provide no benefit to the other group (as the situation would revert to the comprehensive ban). Accordingly, following *Somjee*, the courts cannot intervene and must leave the apartheid system in place. Of course, the Oireachtas has never enacted such odious legislation. Nevertheless, once *Somjee* is established as part of the constitutional architecture, it provides a positive incentive to the Oireachtas to enact unconstitutional legislation in the knowledge that it can never be challenged. Indeed, in *D* itself, Clarke J. suggested that the legislation may well have been drafted specifically to take advantage of the *Somjee* position:

> "It seems likely that the way in which the relevant legislation was crafted was designed precisely to deal with a situation where it might be determined that it was impermissible to discriminate between underage males and underage females in the way in which this legislation does."

Furthermore, the *Somjee* rule does not just deprive standing to some plaintiffs but rather ensures that there can be no plaintiff in respect of certain discriminatory laws, provided they are framed in the correct way. Nevertheless, it is only a rule of procedure and does not cure the unconstitutionality that affects the law in question. As such, the law remains unconstitutional but immune from judicial review. It is difficult, if not impossible, to reconcile the *Somjee* rule with the courts' jurisdiction to assess the constitutional validity of any law and the prohibition, contained in Art.15.4, on the Oireachtas from enacting unconstitutional laws.

As far as these authors are aware, Ireland is the only country in the world with a written Constitution to operate a rule along the lines of *Somjee*. Many other jurisdictions, such as Canada and South Africa, operate a system of suspended declarations. Under this approach, a declaration is granted that the impugned legislation is invalid, but this is suspended for a period of time to give the legislature an opportunity to bring the legislation into line with constitutional requirements. This allows the legislature to choose whether the legislation should be "levelled up" or "levelled down" but ensures that, either way, the unconstitutional discrimination is removed. This is a far preferable approach to that adopted by Keane J. in *Somjee* and argued for by the State in D. Moreover, in *A v Governor of Arbour Hill Prison* [2006] IESC 45, both Murray C.J. and Denham J. cited the Canadian practice of granting suspended declarations. In particular, Denham J. commended the practice as one which supported both democracy and the ordered running of the State, suggesting that its adoption in Ireland was open for argument in an appropriate case. Although the *Somjee* point was not at issue in *A*, the comments of Murray C.J. and Denham J. do suggest that there is sufficient leeway in Irish constitutional law for the point to be argued, thereby supporting Clarke J.'s conclusion that Mr D had an arguable case.

Addressing the other factors, Clarke J. held that it was appropriate to stay the criminal proceedings. He had particular regard to the fact that Mr D had commenced his proceedings in a timely fashion, that there had been a (not extreme) delay by the State in filing its defence, and that it should be possible to arrange for the proceedings to be advanced in a manner that caused only minimal delay to the trial.

This constitutional challenge came on for hearing in December 2009. Dunne J. held against Mr D in a judgment delivered on March 26, 2010 ([2010] IEHC 101). This judgment will be considered in next year's *Annual Review of Irish Law*. It is currently under appeal to the Supreme Court.

TRIBUNALS OF INQUIRY

Supreme Court affirmation In *Lawlor v Planning Tribunal* [2009] IESC 50, Murray C.J., on behalf of the Court (Denham, Geoghegan, Fennelly, Kearns JJ.) upheld the High Court in denying claims of Hazel Lawlor, widow of the late Liam Lawlor, that a standard of proof of beyond a reasonable doubt would be required to make a finding of serious misconduct against her late husband and with regard to provision of costs for legal representation, *Annual Review of Irish Law 2008*, p.177. Whilst the Supreme Court judgment is an affirmation of existing law, it is nevertheless interesting for the succinct manner in which the Chief Justice re-stated issues that have been rehearsed on many occasions. It is also of interest that Murray C.J. did not express the now frequent frustration of some of his judicial colleagues regarding the duration of the tribunal as evidenced by the concluding sentence of the following quotation:

> "Tribunals of Inquiry perform a unique role in Irish public life. A tribunal

> is an inquisitorial body which derives its authority and existence and its terms of reference from resolutions passed by the Oireachtas. In this instance, the Oireachtas determined that this Tribunal should be constituted to inquire urgently into allegations that corrupt acts had occurred in relation to the process of granting planning permissions in the Dublin area. The Tribunal was charged with the task of conducting that inquiry and reporting to the Clerk of the Dáil having made such findings and recommendations as it saw fit. This exercise was required to be undertaken in the context that the Oireachtas considered that the subject matter of the investigation was one of 'urgent public importance'. Given the nature and wide ambit of the terms of reference given to the Tribunal this could not be taken to imply that its inquiries would be of modest duration."

Moreover, Murray C.J. observed that the court had been informed that:

> "[I]n excess of 20 judicial review applications have been brought during the course of this Planning Inquiry, some successful, some not, and some of which, intentionally or otherwise, have slowed and delayed the work of this Tribunal."

The court acknowledged that a feature of a public inquisitorial tribunal process which is difficult to avoid is the reputational damage which may attach to any individual against whom allegations are aired before a tribunal, notably in its public sittings, not least because of the length of time which may elapse before the person concerned can rebut such allegations. This could only be justified by reference to "the critical requirement that matters of such public importance and concern be properly investigated when the Oireachtas so determines".

Fair procedures With regard to the rights of individuals attending a Tribunal of Inquiry, Murray C.J. continued:

> "The legislation which provides for tribunals has survived constitutional scrutiny and the courts in this jurisdiction have repeatedly upheld the right of tribunals to purposively inquire into matters the subject of their terms of reference. Nonetheless, the courts have stressed repeatedly the obligation of tribunals to apply fair procedures and to trench upon the rights of the individual as little as possible, consistent with the aims and objectives of the inquiry itself. In this regard the invocation by persons under investigation of the panoply of rights identified by this Court in In Re Haughey [1971] I.R. 217 is an entitlement repeatedly upheld and supported by the Courts. That said, the Courts have been quick to acknowledge that considerable adverse reputational consequences can flow both from allegations aired at tribunals and from supposedly 'legally sterile' tribunal findings. The term 'legally sterile' has been

used as an allusion to the fact that the findings of a tribunal are the conclusions only of the Chairperson, and its members where there is more than one member, and in no sense, as pointed out above, has the status of a judicial finding, civil or criminal, notwithstanding that in order to ensure the independence of a tribunal, its chairman and members are judges. Persons the subject of inquiry by such a tribunal are never charged with any offence nor are they on trial. A tribunal can never be seen as a substitute for or an alternative mode of criminal trial. That does not of course take away from the fact that the adverse findings of grave wrongdoing can have devastating consequences for the standing and reputation of a person in the community."

Standard of proof With regard to standard of proof Murray C.J. observed:

> "It would, nonetheless be wrong to infer from these comments that a tribunal of inquiry is at large in terms of the requirements of proof or that the standard of proof is simply a matter of procedure which it may regulate as it sees fit. Such an approach could lead to a situation where, for example, on the bare balance of probabilities, a finding of the utmost gravity could be made against a particular individual. In principle evidential requirements must vary depending upon the gravity of the particular allegation. This is not to adopt the 'sliding scale' of proof advocated by counsel for the applicant, but rather to simply recognise, as an integral part of fair procedures, that a finding in respect of a serious matter which may involve reputational damage must be proportionate to the evidence upon which it is based. For example, a finding that a particular meeting occurred on one day rather than another may be of such little significance that a tribunal could make a finding in that respect on the bare balance of probabilities. A finding of criminal behaviour on the other hand would require a greater degree of authority and weight derived from the evidence itself."

VINDICATION OF RIGHTS

Orwellian horizons *VTS v HSE* [2009] IEHC 106 is considered in detail elsewhere in this chapter. In his probing analysis of the execution of a detention order under s.38 of the Health Act 1947, Edwards J. appears to have held that health officials may remove a person unlawfully from place A to place B providing a) that the initiating order is lawful and intra vires, b) despite the fact that the subject of the order has not been identified by any address or other personal identification other than name, and c) providing that the lawful order specifies the ultimate destination correctly, namely place B. With regard to point b), this breach was excused on the basis that there was only one person in the patient's circumstances and that this person was known to those involved in the process and thus easily identifiable. This is understandable in the context of the circumstances of the case, and one might infer that Edwards J. was concerned only with the specifics of the case. However, what if there were an epidemic of some infectious nature involving not easily identifiable African asylum seekers who had a record of ongoing healthcare in the place of detention but Irish citizens with first names such as Mary and Patrick, and common surnames such as Murphy or Ryan, who might easily be confused with each other in records as a consequence? Would the process of removal from point A to point B of subjects of section 38 orders be as easily discounted as lawful but irrelevant to the vindication of personal rights? Would the public interest in controlling an epidemic or pandemic be the deciding factor in suppressing individual rights in a constitutional challenge? It is not entirely improbable, since in those circumstances a care plan for the vindication of personal rights of those detained, whilst recommended, is not mandated in either the Constitution or statute, and is unlikely to be high on a list of healthcare priorities to control and contain a serious public health risk. Moreover, unless a writ of habeas corpus were sought under Art.40.4 whereby the State might exercise its discretion to provide legal aid to impecunious litigants, the State has already indicated its intention to refuse legal aid to challenge such detention, as evidenced from the reported submission of the third and fourth respondents in this case, Ireland and the Attorney General.

It was noted without comment in the judgment that the State parties had argued that a person detained under s.38 has no entitlement to have their legal representation funded by the State, citing *State (O) v Daly* [1977] I.R. 312 as authority for this. In that case which concerned detention under s.207 of the Mental Treatment Act 1945 in the Central Mental Hospital of an offender unfit to plead, O'Higgins C.J. ([1997] I.R. 312) observed at 316 that whilst the District Justice was exercising his criminal jurisdiction in such circumstances:

> "…it is very much ancillary and preparatory. No trial can take place and no punishment can be imposed. What is involved is an enquiry as to the mental health of the person charged, there being prima facie evidence that he has committed the offence."

It is, at the very least, interesting that the State should seek to rely on *State (O) v Daly*, since the statutory provision in question was declared unconstitutional in 1995 by Costello P. in *RT v Director of Central Mental Hospital* [1995] 2 I.R. 65 for, inter alia, the very reason that Edwards J. had such concerns about the detention of the patient in the instant case; namely inadequate safeguards for the patient and no requirement for regular reviews of the patient's situation. It was subsequently repealed by s.6 of the Mental Health Act 2001, which eventually came into force on November 1, 2006. Readers are referred to Whelan, *Mental Health Law and Practice* (Round Hall, 2009) for details.

Of course, as the judgment in *VTS* noted, refusal to cooperate with a section

38 order is a criminal offence. It may be genuinely difficult for the health authorities in an epidemic or pandemic situation to differentiate between a potential detainee who is refusing to co-operate with the isolation order because they have been wrongly identified and a correctly identified person who is fearful, for whatever reason, of being so detained. In such circumstances the wrongly identified subject becomes caught in an authoritarian Orwellian world, giving real meaning to Edwards J.'s eloquent comment that "while the Court accepts that it is inherently unlikely that this patient would ever be prosecuted for a s.38(4) offence, that is not the point."

For all of these reasons it is imperative that the Oireachtas act with dispatch to amend the provisions of s.38 of the Health Act 1947 so that the statute mandates protection of individual rights in all actions taken in the interests of public health. As Connell commented in "Detaining Swine Flu Sufferers post S. v Health Service Executive" (2009) 27 I.L.T. 204 (footnotes excluded):

> "However, the criticisms of s.38's safeguards offered by Edwards J. are a stark reminder of the necessity for legislative reform in this controversial but critical area of State power: the power to detain a person for the purposes of preventing the spread of a prescribed infectious disease. Arguably, the necessity for the statutory enshrinement of a proper care plan and periodic review mechanism coupled with this necessary power of detention would afford persons subject to such an order a modicum of respect for their own welfare and dignity. Such statutory reform would further preempt any possible challenge to s.38 by way of an Article 234 preliminary reference to the European Court of Justice on the grounds of the incompatibility of the provision with the Treaty principle of the free movement of workers.
>
> In the criminal law sphere, the superior courts have regularly overturned the imposition of sentences that incorporate an element of preventative detention, i.e. the imprisonment of individuals solely on the basis of their risk of re-offending. It is somewhat disconcerting that the Health Act 1947 provides for a form of preventative detention, not as regards the risk of re-offending, rather, as regards the risk of spreading a prescribed disease but does so without the necessity for specific court authorisation.
>
> While such detention is of course required in extreme cases where a patient cannot be effectively isolated in his or her home, it is nevertheless regrettable that the procedure pursuant to s.38 is an anachronistic mechanism for this form of detention and, as such, represents an inadequate statutory vehicle ... In a modern democratic European Union Member State, patients in the unenviable position of Ms S. deserve greater express protection of their rights and welfare than that contained in s.38."

Contract Law

FERGUS RYAN, Lecturer in Law, Dublin Institute of Technology

ARBITRATION

See also, *Kastrup Trae-Aluvinduet A/S v Aluwood Concepts Ltd,* High Court, MacMenamin J., November 13, 2009; [2009] IEHC 577 discussed below under INCORPORATION OF TERMS

Introduction The general reluctance on the part of the courts to set aside an arbitrator's award, discussed in the contract law chapters in previous years of the *Annual Review*, is highlighted again this year by a number of decisions.

As noted by Kelly J. in *Clancy v Nevin* [2008] IEHC 121, a party seeking to set aside an arbitral award faces "an uphill struggle". In *SJW Facades Ltd v Bowen Construction* [2009] IEHC 49, MacMenamin J. declined a request to set aside an arbitrator's verdict on the basis of alleged misconduct, concluding that the arbitrator had in fact appropriately conducted the arbitration. In the course of his decision, the judge noted the desirability of finality in relation to arbitration awards. He also highlighted the reluctance of the courts to interfere with an arbitral award unless there is a serious irregularity in the process resulting in real injustice or unfairness. Mere error on the part of the arbitrator, for instance, in the interpretation of the law or in coming to conclusions on the facts would not be sufficient to amount to misconduct.

Likewise, in *Moohan v S & R Motors (Donegal) Ltd* [2009] IEHC 391, Clarke J., while agreeing to an extension of time for challenging an arbitral decision, declined to set aside the award. Citing *Uniform Construction Ltd v Cappawhite* [2007] IEHC 295 (discussed in the *Annual Review 2007*, pp.146–149), the judge noted that an award would only be set aside:

> "... on the grounds of an error on the face of the award where that error is so fundamental that the court cannot stand aside and allow it to remain unchallenged".

On the facts, he was not satisfied that such an error had transpired in this case.

Two other rather novel issues are dealt with in the following cases. *Clarke Quarries* addresses the interaction between adjudication and arbitration clauses in a building contract, while *Kelly v Lennon* considers the effect on court proceedings of a "partial arbitration" addressing some but not all disputed matters in a case.

***Clarke Quarries Ltd v PT McWilliams Ltd*, High Court, Laffoy J., August 24, 2009; [2009] IEHC 403** The net question in this case was whether it was possible for a party to invoke an adjudication clause, provided for in a building contract, while matters in dispute between the parties were simultaneously the subject of a pending arbitration. Laffoy J. determined that, under the contract, the adjudication could proceed in parallel with the arbitral process, even though the adjudication concerned matters that would also be considered at arbitration.

Adjudication is a process that differs from arbitration in certain important respects. It is generally intended to provide the option of a speedy interim resolution of certain disputed matters. In a construction contract, the main purpose of such a clause is to facilitate cash flow. It is generally envisaged as interim in its effects, and is not considered as a replacement for litigation or arbitration as a means of final dispute resolution. It is primarily intended as a quick, provisional means of addressing specific disputed matters, often pending the final resolution of a dispute.

The defendant builder had agreed to build a multi-storey car park at a development in Monaghan. In late 2008 the parties fell out, the defendant serving a notice of suspension of building on the basis that there had been, it alleged, a "contractor termination event". The plaintiff counterclaimed that this step constituted a breach of contract on the defendant's part entitling the plaintiff to terminate the contract. The defendant in turn asserted that the plaintiff's purported termination was wrongful, a view later confirmed by the adjudicator.

The defendant claimed, in particular, that it was still owed €4.45 million in compensation in respect of the works. In March 2009, the defendant sought to initiate an arbitration relating, inter alia, to the plaintiff's alleged wrongful termination of the contract and the alleged failure on the part of the plaintiff to pay monies due to the defendant. The plaintiff had also, separately, referred certain matters in dispute for arbitration.

Nonetheless, in tandem with this process the defendant sought to refer the issue of outstanding compensation to a separate adjudicator, as envisaged by the building contract. The plaintiff objected to the simultaneous referral of substantially the same issue to both arbitration and an adjudicator. It claimed that the attempt to have the same issue considered simultaneously by two separate bodies constituted an abuse of process, in short, that "a litigant cannot vent the same issue in two different forums".

The parties' contract provided mechanisms for the resolution of disputes. While it made provision for either party to refer a dispute to arbitration, it also envisaged an adjudication process. This adjudication process was intended to yield quicker verdicts than either arbitration or litigation. In particular, an adjudicator was required to deliver his or her decision within 20 days of referral. A fast-track procedure applying in certain cases (including in relation to matters of compensation) required a response within 10 days of referral. The decision of the adjudicator was deemed to be final, though this was subject to the right of the parties to refer the matter to arbitration or to agree an alternative settlement.

Laffoy J. concluded, on the basis of the specific contract's terms, that the referral to arbitration did not preclude a separate reference of similar issues to adjudication. Although not ruling definitively on the point, she "incline[d] to the view" that the contract, as written, stipulated for adjudication as a preliminary to arbitration, the normal sequence envisaged by the dispute resolution clause being informal attempts at resolution, followed by adjudication and then arbitration. She concluded that the contract did not, in any event, contain any provision preventing a party who had invoked the arbitration procedure in the contract from simultaneously referring the same matter to adjudication pending the completion of the arbitration. The purpose of the adjudication process was, she noted, to "give a party to a contract a speedy mechanism for settling disputes on a provisional interim basis". In other words, adjudication was designed to facilitate speedy interim redress "pending finality through determination by arbitration, legal proceedings or the agreement of the parties". In this regard, she distinguished adjudication from arbitration, arbitration having the effect of staying litigation in the same matter; adjudication does not have this consequence.

In support, she cited the decision of Dyson J. in *Herschel Engineering Ltd v Breen Property Ltd* [2000] B.L.R. 272, to the effect that a party was entitled to refer a matter to adjudication (under a UK statute) even while the same matter was the subject of litigation. Dyson J. observed that the purpose of adjudication in this context was to allow a fast-track mechanism for dispute resolution pending the final resolution of the matter in arbitration or litigation, or by agreement between the parties. The decision of the adjudicator was different from that of the arbitrator, an adjudication decision being of "temporary effect" and being, in particular, subject to a different verdict at arbitration or following litigation. The apparent purpose of such clauses (and the clear purpose of the Act considered in *Herschel*) was to ensure continuity of cash flow while disputes were proceeding; in other words, that an arbitration or litigation would not have the effect of stalling payment to the parties pending the final resolution of a dispute.

***Kelly and O'Sullivan v Lennon*, High Court, Clarke J., July 2, 2009; [2009] IEHC 320** This case concerned a contract for the sale of lands for €46.7 million, and in particular the status and effect of an arbitration clause therein. The arbitration clause in this case required some, but not all, matters in dispute to be referred to an arbitrator. The net question that arose was whether this "partial arbitration clause" required the court to place a stay on proceedings in which other matters in dispute, which were not subject to the arbitration clause, had been raised for consideration by the court. In his decision, Clarke J. considered the effect of such a "partial arbitration" requirement on the proceedings before the court, setting out the sequence that the arbitration and court proceedings should follow.

The plaintiffs in this case, being the intended purchasers, claimed that the contract for the sale of lands had been terminated, entitling them to rescind the contract. They claimed also that they were entitled to have their deposit of just over €9 million returned to them. The vendor, Mr Lennon, by contrast, argued that the agreement was still in force. He claimed, moreover, that certain aspects of the dispute were governed by an arbitration clause in the contract (which incorporated the Law Society's General Conditions of Sale). On foot of this arbitration clause, he sought to have the court proceedings stayed pending the determination of the disputed matters at arbitration.

A number of disputes had arisen between the parties. In particular, differences arose in the course of investigating title as to the consistency of the boundaries set out in the folios in the registry of title with the physical boundaries of the lands. There was some disagreement also as to the matter of tenancies subject to which the land was to be sold (some of the tenants having vacated the land prior to completion), as well as disagreement in relation to the sequence in which the completion notices had been issued.

The defendant contended that the specific dispute over the boundaries had to be considered, under the contract, by an arbitrator. Condition 51 of the General Conditions required that any dispute as to, inter alia, "(c) any issues on foot of Condition 33, including the applicability of said Condition, and the amount of compensation payable thereunder…shall be submitted to arbitration by a sole Arbitrator".

Condition 33 relates to errors in the memorandum or particulars of the contract, which included, the judge ruled, "an alleged discrepancy between the physical boundaries and the folios concerned". It stipulates that an error will not validly terminate the contract unless the error was the result of fraud or recklessness, was so substantial as to cause material prejudice, or had occurred in circumstances where it would prove impossible to calculate damages. Otherwise, condition 33 contemplated that the contract would still be binding subject to compensation being payable in respect of the error (unless the error was trivial in its consequences). The question that thus arose was whether the error as to boundaries was sufficiently material to cause prejudice and thus to allow the parties to "walk away from the contract". It was clear to the judge that general condition 51 required that the issue as to whether the error was sufficiently serious was one that the contract stipulated should be determined by the arbitrator.

The plaintiffs, however, claimed that the effect of a valid rescission of a contract is to terminate any arbitration clause therein such that disputes could no longer be referred to an arbitrator. Citing *Doyle v Irish National Insurance Company* [1998] 1 I.L.R.M. 502, the judge roundly dismissed this contention, the law being clear that an arbitration clause "survives any contended termination of the contract" (see also *McCormack Fuels v Maxol Ltd* [2008] IEHC 197, discussed in the *Annual Review of Irish Law 2008*, pp.185–188).

The plaintiffs further asserted that the defendant's unconditional appearance in the court proceedings prevented him from invoking the arbitration clause. The judge also dismissed this second contention as being "manifestly ill-founded", s.12(1) of the Arbitration Act 1954 having expressly clarified "that an appearance is not to be treated as taking a step in the proceedings" that would preclude a stay pending arbitration; "indeed, the application for a stay is to take place after appearance".

It was clear, nonetheless, that the scope of the specific arbitration clause in this case was unusually limited. In particular, it applied only to the dispute relating to the boundaries, and not in relation to the other disputed matters which were, the judge concluded, "matters purely for the court". Thus "some, but not all of the issues" in dispute were subject to arbitration.

In these circumstances, where some but not all disputed issues in a single cause of action were required to be referred to arbitration, the remaining issues being properly the subject of court proceedings, the question that arose was whether the court should place a stay on court proceedings pending the conclusion of the arbitration. In such unusual circumstances, where there was a "single cause of action", Clarke J. determined that he had a discretion as to whether to grant a stay in respect of the court proceedings.

In determining how that discretion should be exercised, the judge had to have regard to the need to ensure "a speedy resolution of all the issues which arise". This did not entitle the court to usurp the role of the arbitrator in relation to the matters reserved for determination by arbitration. The issue instead was:

> "... how the various elements of the case (being those properly within the jurisdiction of the court and those validly referred to arbitration) *should be sequenced* so as to maximise the likelihood of a speedy and just resolution of all issues between the parties" (my emphasis).

On the facts of this specific case, the judge concluded that a full stay on proceedings pending arbitration would not be appropriate. Even if the defendant were to succeed at arbitration, Clarke J. observed, the remaining matters in dispute would still have to be determined by the court. On the other hand, if the plaintiffs were to win in relation to those matters in dispute that were not subject to arbitration, the issue before the arbitrator "would almost certainly become irrelevant". Given this background:

> "… it seems to me that it would be inappropriate to fully stay these proceedings pending arbitration, for it is clear that the other issues, which are substantive stand alone issues, will need to be determined in any event. On the other hand, it seems to me that any question of the issues arising under General Condition 33 must be stayed for to do otherwise would be to usurp the function which the parties have, by agreement, referred to arbitration".

The judge thus placed a stay on court proceedings relating to those matters that were to be the subject of arbitration only. He went on to suggest that it would be preferable for the arbitration of those limited matters to be concluded before the court considered the other issues at trial. Notice of trial would thus not be served until the arbitrator had issued its verdict, as this would "allow the court, when embarking on the trial, to have a full picture of all of the legal issues available to it and to reach a single concluded determination".

Nonetheless, this did not preclude the matters not subject to arbitration from being progressed up to the service of the notice of trial. The judge thus allowed pleadings to be completed and matters such as discovery to be addressed pending trial. While the parties would be able in the interim to raise issues relating to matters properly before the arbitrator, this would be subject to the caveat that:

> "… what is being relied on is the possible determination in their favour on that issue by an arbitrator. No pleading should be filed which might be construed as attempting to invite the court to determine those issues because, for the reasons which I have set out, any consideration by the court of those issues is being stayed pending arbitration".

Clarke J. thus ordered a stay on that part of the proceedings that related to the issues before arbitration, but allowed the remaining matters to "proceed in an orderly fashion", though notice of trial would not be served until the arbitrator's decision was made.

BREACH OF CONTRACT

***Lynch v Duffy*, High Court, Murphy J., February 12, 2009; [2009] IEHC 59** In contract law, time is usually not of the essence, particularly in contracts for the sale of land. That said, where a contract *expressly* stipulates that time is of the essence, the importance of prompt action in meeting deadlines becomes imperative, as illustrated by this cautionary tale.

This case relates to a contract for the sale of land, subject to a condition as to planning permission. It related to the sale of lands in Co. Cavan for €4 million, the plaintiff in this case being the vendor, while the defendants were the purchasers. Although the details were essentially agreed in January 2007, the contract for sale was formally executed on April 4, 2007. A deposit of €400,000 was paid in respect of the lands. The agreement in question stipulated that it represented the entire agreement between the parties on the matter and thus superseded all preceding "agreements, arrangements and understandings" in relation to the subject matter of the contract.

The agreement contained a special condition as to the acquisition of planning permission for the building of private homes on the land. Effectively, the contractual terms required that the purchasers apply for planning permission as soon as possible after the contract was entered into. The purchasers were, moreover, required to make all reasonable endeavours to ensure that the application was successful and permission obtained. Should planning permission be refused, the parties agreed that the contract would come to an end. Additionally, should the necessary planning permission not issue by June 30, 2007, interest of 5 per cent per annum would be payable to the vendor on the balance of the purchase price until such time as the contract closed. Finally, the contract stipulated that should planning permission not be successfully obtained by October 31, 2007 (time being of the essence for this purpose), either party would be entitled to terminate the contract by notice in writing, the deposit being repayable in such circumstances.

There were, however, considerable delays in the application process for planning permission. In particular, while the defendants lodged an application for planning permission in July 2007, the council rejected the application owing to non-payment of the required application fee. (A cheque drawn in respect of the fee was not honoured.) A fresh, valid planning application was made on October 24, 2007, only a week before the October 31 deadline stipulated in the contract. Two days later, on October 26, the defendants wrote to the plaintiff, stating that as planning permission would not issue prior to the October 31 deadline, they did not wish to proceed with the purchase. They also requested a refund of their deposit. This request was repeated by letter of November 15, 2007.

The net question that arose was whether the defendants in this case had used all reasonable endeavours promptly to obtain planning permission, as required by the contract. Murphy J. concluded that they had not.

Although the contract was not formally executed until April 2007, the defendants had already made substantial preparations for the purpose of seeking planning permission, with plans being at an advanced stage by June 2007. Indeed, by that date, the defendants had already incurred costs of €190,000 in respect of work preliminary to the application.

Nonetheless, the defendants did not submit an application for planning permission until July 2007; indeed, this was only received on August 1, 2007. While the defendants included a cheque for the application fee, this was not honoured. Despite reminders from the council, the fee was never paid and the application was thus rejected for non-payment of the application fee. A proper application (including the fee) was not submitted until late October 2007.

The court noted that the contract itself (drafted in late 2006) stipulated that the planning permission be sought before February 26, 2007. As this date preceded the date on which the contract was executed, Murphy J. ruled that compliance with this term was impossible and ordered that the February deadline be deleted from the contract. What was left, in the judge's view, was a requirement that the defendants used all reasonable endeavours to ensure that planning permission was obtained as soon as possible after the contract was formally executed in April 2007. Nonetheless, there were significant delays, with a proper application only being submitted one week before the end of October deadline.

In the circumstances, Murphy J. ruled that the defendants had not complied with their obligation to seek planning permission as soon as possible after the contract was entered into, and thus were in breach of the special condition. The defendants had delayed some five months in making a proper application. Given that they had already made substantial and costly preparations for the application by June 2007, it was unclear why the defendants had delayed so long in submitting a proper application. The application of October 24, 2007 was, in particular, "lodged too late to comply with the obligation to use reasonable endeavours to obtain planning permission", the defendants thus being in breach of contract in relation to this clause.

The contract allowed either party to terminate the contract should planning permission not issue by October 31, 2007, time being of the essence for this purpose. However, this last condition, Murphy J. noted, necessarily had to be read alongside the requirement that the defendants make all reasonable endeavours to obtain planning permission in as timely a manner as possible. In other words, the right to terminate was conditional upon having made reasonable efforts to obtain planning permission. The judge concluded that because they had failed to comply with the requirement to use all reasonable endeavours to obtain planning permission, the defendants had lost the right of termination provided for under the contract. Additionally, the judge concluded that the defendants' letter of October 26, 2007 seeking the return of their deposit was not operative as a termination of the contract, as the deadline of October 31 had not passed. Even ignoring the long delay in applying for permission, the defendants had no right under the contract to terminate before that deadline. Nor had a subsequent letter from the defendants dated November 15, 2007 served to terminate the contract.

The final question related to the return of the deposit, a matter not specifically provided for in the special conditions but nonetheless governed by clause 41 of the Law Society's General Conditions of Sale (2001). Clause 41 stipulates that should the purchaser fail in a material respect to fulfil the conditions of sale, the vendor would be entitled to forfeit the deposit and re-sell the property. Given the breach of the condition as to prompt endeavours to seek planning permission, Murphy J. concluded that the vendor was entitled to keep the deposit and resell the property.

CONTRACTS FOR THE SALE OF LAND

See also FORMALITIES

Land and Conveyancing Law Reform Act 2009 Section 52 of the Land and Conveyancing Law Reform Act stipulates that an enforceable contract for the sale or other disposition of land has the effect of passing the entire beneficial interest in the land to the purchaser on the making of that enforceable contract. Notably, this provision extends only to contracts that are enforceable either on the basis of s.51 of the Act (requiring that contracts for the sale of land be in writing or be enforced in writing) or on foot of part-performance of an oral contract. (See further, the discussion below under FORMALITIES).

This rule is also subject to any provision to the contrary contained in the relevant contract. In other words, the parties may expressly provide in their contract that the vendor will in fact retain the beneficial interest pending completion. Section 52, moreover, does not absolve the vendor from the obligation to maintain the land for so long as the vendor retains possession thereof, nor does it remove the vendor's liability for loss or damage to the land under any contractual provision dealing with such a risk. The transfer of the beneficial interest is, furthermore, without prejudice to the vendor's right to rescind the contract for failure to complete or for breach of contract.

DAMAGES

See also, *James Keating v Catherine and Patrick Keating,* High Court, Laffoy J., August 24, 2009; [2009] IEHC 405 discussed below under IMPROVIDENT TRANSACTIONS

Land and Conveyancing Law Reform Act 2009 Section 53 of the Land and Conveyancing Law Reform Act 2009 abolishes with prospective effect the much-criticised rule in *Bain v Fothergill* (1874) LR 7 HL 158 (see also *Flureau v Thornhill* (1776) 2 Wm. Bl. 1078 and *Buckley v Dawson* (1854) 6 Ir. Jur. Rep. 374). The rule in question limited the ability to recover damages for failure to transfer good title, where there is an irremovable defect in the title. Unless the purchaser could show that the vendor had acted fraudulently or in bad faith, the purchaser would be restricted to recovering expenses only, namely his or her deposit, any interest payable thereon, and any reasonable monies spent investigating the title or preparing the conveyance. Damages for loss of bargain would not be awarded. The rule was confirmed in Ireland in *Kelly v Duffy* [1922] 1 I.R. 82 and *McQuaid v Lynam* [1965] I.R. 564.

The rationale behind the original rule lay in the complexities involved in showing good title. The limitations placed on those seeking damages reflected a concern that because of the complexity of establishing good title in former times, vendors might easily fall foul of the requirement to show good title, through no fault of their own. With the adoption of land registration legislation, this rationale bears less weight today than at the time of its formulation and thus, the rule is arguably no longer either necessary or justifiable. Nonetheless, the removal of this limitation on damages arguably enhances the need for vigilance by practitioners in ensuring that there are no defects in title.

It is important to note that the abolition of this rule will only apply to contracts made after the commencement date for Ch.1 of Pt 9 of the Act and not otherwise. The commencement date for this purpose is designated as December 1, 2009 by the Land and Conveyancing Law Reform Act 2009 (Commencement) Order 2009 (S.I. No. 356 of 2009).

The rule in *Bain v Fothergill* has been the result of relatively consistent criticism. Indeed, several commentators have espoused its outright abolition. In particular, as far back as 1989, the Law Reform Commission commended its removal in its *Report on Land Law and Conveyancing* LRC–30–1989, a stance reiterated more recently in its *Report on the Reform and Modernisation of Land Law and Conveyancing Law* LRC–34–2004. Notably, the rule has already been abolished in England and Wales by s.3 of the Law of Property (Miscellaneous Provisions) Act 1989 (c. 34).

***Joyce v O'Shea*, High Court, Laffoy J., July 31, 2009; [2009] IEHC 415** This case relates to the calculation of damages for breach of contract for the sale of land, and specifically the appropriate date for the valuation of the property for the purpose of calculating damages. It concerned approximately 16 acres of land (hereinafter termed "Plot B") located near Tullow, Co. Carlow, with planning permission for the building of residential homes. The contract in question was entered into in May 2007, the plaintiffs being the vendors, while the defendant was the intended purchaser. The purchase price was €10.7 million, with a nominal deposit of €100 being paid on execution of the contract. In January 2009, in default of appearance by the defendant, the plaintiffs sought and obtained an order for specific performance of the contract. The court also ordered the payment of interest for delayed completion, amounting to approximately €585,000. The defendant, however, failed to comply, with the result that in June 2009 the plaintiffs sought and obtained an order for damages in lieu of specific performance, Charleton J. setting aside his earlier order for specific performance. (The order in respect of interest payable, however, stood.)

Unfortunately, between May 2007 and June 2009, the market value of the land had dropped considerably. This meant that the vendors' chances of mitigating their losses owing to the breach of contract were slim. In particular, the price of residential homes had dropped sharply in Tullow, with the result that the land in question would more than likely not have been sold for anywhere near the original €10.7 million contract price.

The land in question that was the subject of the contract (termed "Plot B" in the proceedings) was adjacent to a 15-acre plot ("Plot A"). The defendant had previously bought Plot A from the plaintiffs. The terms of the relevant planning permission for both plots required the construction of additional roads to cater for the anticipated development. As it happened, Carlow County Council had been planning to build a relief road around the town of Tullow, which would have provided access to Plot B. Nonetheless, because of the position of Plot A, Plot B was effectively land-locked, with access to Plot B being blocked. The council had sought but failed to obtain agreement with the defendant to facilitate the building of the relief road adjacent to Plot A. As a result, government funding for the relief road had been lost, and was unlikely to be forthcoming again.

Consequently, it was unlikely that the relief road would be built by the time the planning permission for the development expired in October 2011. In particular, the evidence of the plaintiff was to the effect that it would be difficult, if not impossible, to acquire a new buyer for the land without the access provided by the relief road. While there was a possibility of selling Plot B for agricultural purposes, the price for this purpose was unlikely to exceed €10,000 per acre or €160,000 in total. Given the lack of relief road access, coupled with the stark decline in house prices in the area, a local estate agent gave evidence to the effect that the probable market value of Plot B as of July 2009 was €40,000 per acre or €639,000 (as compared with an intended purchase price of €10.7 million).

Clearly then, the land had suffered a significant drop in value since the contract had been concluded. The plaintiffs thus were unlikely, in a subsequent sale, to receive anything like the €10.7 million agreed for Plot B under the 2007 agreement. The plaintiffs were clearly entitled to damages in respect of this loss. The question that arose, however, was the relevant date by reference to which the loss was to be assessed.

The plaintiffs had alleged that the appropriate date for the purpose of calculating the loss in value of the land was the date of assessment of such losses by the court. In her judgment, Laffoy J. referred to a passage from Wylie and Woods, *Conveyancing Law*, 3rd edn (Dublin: Tottle Publishing, 2005), which sets out the relevant principles for the calculation of damages for the breach of a contract for the sale of land. There the authors note that:

> "... the general rule is that the damages are to be assessed as the difference in value between the contract price and the value of the land *at the date of the breach of contract*".

In other words, losses are *generally* assessed as of the date on which the contract was first deemed to have been broken. If followed, this of course would significantly limit the liability of the defendant. The authors noted, however, that the general rule as stated above may lead to hardship, particularly in inflationary circumstances (though also, presumably in a case such as this where the land has sharply diminished in value). The authors thus conclude that:

> "It is now accepted that the common law rule is not inflexible and that the court has a discretion to choose the most appropriate date at which to value the land for the purposes of calculating the damages to be awarded" (see, in particular, *Johnson v Agnew* [1980] A.C. 367).

For instance, a party may not immediately seek damages but may instead initially take some other action that it is entitled to take to compel performance of the contract, such as by pursuing an action for specific performance. In such cases, the party will not be prejudiced by any such action on its part. In support, the decision of McWilliam J. in *Vandaleur v Dargan* [1981] I.L.R.M. 75 was cited. This decision suggests that where a vendor pursues an order for specific performance which, through no fault of the vendor, is either unsuccessful or is aborted, the appropriate date for assessment of damages in lieu of specific performance is the date on which the order for specific performance was dissolved. Applied to this specific case, this would mean that the date on which the court vacated the order for specific performance (due to the defendant's failure to comply with that order), namely June 22, 2009, is the appropriate date for calculation of the loss sustained by the plaintiffs.

Applied to the facts of this case, Laffoy J. determined that the defendant was liable for damages in respect of the loss in value of the land up to June 22, 2009, the date on which the order for specific performance was vacated. For this purpose, she accepted the valuation offered in court by the local estate agent, namely that the land was worth €639,000 as of July 2009. This resulted in a total loss of €10.1 million, representing the contract price of €10.7 million less the market value as of July 2009. From this amount the deposit of €100 was also subtracted, with the result that the defendant was ordered to pay damages of just under €10.1 million. The judge also affirmed an order of January 2009 awarding €585,000 in interest arising from the defendant's delay in completing the contract.

DURESS

See *James Keating v Catherine and Patrick Keating,* High Court, Laffoy J., August 24, 2009; [2009] IEHC 405 discussed below under IMPROVIDENT TRANSACTIONS

ESTOPPEL

See also, *Liberty Asset Management Ltd v Gannon*, High Court, Laffoy J., October 14, 2009; [2009] IEHC 468 discussed below under FORMALITIES and *Mary Roche v Thomas Roche,* Supreme Court, December 15, 2009; [2009] IESC 82 discussed below under INTERPRETATION OF CONTRACTS

***Healy v Ulster Bank Ireland Ltd,* High Court, McGovern J., July 17, 2009; [2009] IEHC 360** This case concerned a claim of estoppel. The plaintiff was a medical doctor. In 2005 he had entered into a partnership with another doctor, Dr Cullen, their plan being to build and run a medical centre in Coole, Co. Westmeath. In order to fund the development, the partners obtained a loan from Ulster Bank, the defendant. Both of the doctors also entered into personal guarantees in respect of the loan.

The business partners' relationship having deteriorated markedly, they decided to dissolve the partnership in 2007. Dr Cullen agreed that he would assume sole responsibility for the liabilities and assets of the partnership. In consequence of the dissolution, Dr Cullen paid the plaintiff €2.2 million. In August 2007 the plaintiff lodged this money to the defendant bank. He claimed that he did so on foot of assurances by Mr Leech, an assistant manager at the bank, that the plaintiff was no longer subject to the guarantee that he had made in favour of the bank in respect of the partnership loan. Had he not been given such an assurance, the plaintiff claimed, he would not have lodged the monies to the bank.

A year later, in August 2008, the bank sought to set off the money on credit in his account against debts owed by the partnership, representing a set-off of just under US$994,000 or approximately €680,000 (one of Dr Healy's accounts having been in dollars). The plaintiff claimed that the bank was not entitled to do this.

The main question that arose for determination was whether Mr Leech had assured Dr Healy that the guarantee was no longer enforceable, and if so whether Dr Healy had relied to his detriment on this statement. In the Supreme Court decision in *Doran v Thompson Limited* [1978] I.R. 223, Griffin J. set out the relevant principles that apply in this context:

> "Where one party has, by his words or conduct, made to the other, a clear and unambiguous promise or assurance which was intended to affect the legal relations between them and to be acted on accordingly, and the other party has acted on it by altering his position to his detriment, it is well settled that the one who gave the promise or assurance cannot afterwards be allowed to revert to their previous legal relations as if no such promise or assurance had been made by him, and that he may

> be restrained in equity from acting inconsistently with such promise or assurance. The representation, promise or assurance must be clear and unambiguous to found such an estoppel" (see also, *Ryan v Connolly* [2001] 1 I.R. 627).

On the evidence, the judge concluded that the bank officials had not in fact offered any assurance as regards the liability of the plaintiff under the guarantee. In particular, McGovern J. accepted the evidence of the assistant manager that he would not have given such an assurance, nor would he have had the authority to do so. While acknowledging that he could not recall precisely what he had said at the meeting, Mr Leech unequivocally insisted that he had not given the plaintiff any such assurance, adding that he would not have been entitled to do so without the permission of the bank's credit control department.

The guarantee in question was formal in nature, written and made under seal. To be released from liability thereunder, a formal release was required. Indeed, the partnership dissolution agreement expressly anticipated the need for a formal letter of release from Ulster Bank. In the judge's view, the evidence suggested "that the plaintiff himself appears to have understood that a letter of release would be required to free him of his liability under the guarantee".

Dr Healy further claimed that, in conversation with his solicitor before visiting the bank, the latter had reassured him that Dr Healy's liability under the guarantee had ended and that he could safely deposit his money with Ulster Bank. The solicitor, however, "quite trenchantly" denied offering any such assurance, evidence that the court accepted as preferable to that of the plaintiff. The solicitor insisted that he did not and could not have told him this as the guarantee was still in force, a point that the plaintiff appeared later to have conceded.

Mr Leech, for his part, insisted that he "had absolutely no discretion to restructure existing facilities or release existing security in relation to customers". Such matters had to be dealt with by the credit department. The plaintiff alleged that he had told Mr Leech that his solicitor had assured him that the guarantee was no longer in force. Given that the court accepted the solicitor's evidence denying such an assertion, it logically followed that if such a statement was made to Mr Leech, it was misleading.

After the set-off had taken place, the plaintiff had secretly taped two conversations with bank officials in which he had attempted to press bank staff to admit that he had been given the assurances that he claimed were offered by Mr Leech. Though nothing in the tapes supported the plaintiff's contention, the judge declined to consider the secretly taped evidence, regarding the manner of recording as "quite improper".

The plaintiff had also claimed that as a result of the set-off, he was prevented from purchasing a property in Florida for US$900,000, claiming that he had thus sustained lost profits of up to US$3 million. In fact, the building was unlikely to have earned the plaintiff considerable profit and would have proved difficult to resell. The property, indeed, sold in 2008 for only US$750,000, effectively negating the plaintiff's claim that he had sustained a loss of potential profits. The plaintiff ultimately admitted on cross-examination that he had not in fact paid a deposit of US$90,000, which he had falsely claimed had been lost.

Nor did bank documents produced in evidence support the plaintiff's claim that he had been released from the guarantee. At most, a proposal had been made to clear the plaintiff's liability, which proposal was rejected. These documents, far from assisting the plaintiff, supported Mr Leech's contention that he could not have given the alleged assurance that Dr Healy claimed had been offered by the bank.

The judge considered that Mr Leech was a candid and credible witness. He noted that, during the August 2007 meeting, Mr Leech had left the room to enquire on the plaintiff's behalf about available interest rates. He would hardly have done so in order to check interest rates, and yet have given a blanket assurance regarding the guarantee without also checking this first. By contrast, the judge observed that the plaintiff was "lacking in candour and credibility", had proved untruthful in relation to several matters, and had secretly recorded conversations during which he made statements that he had known to be false. Noting that the burden of proof lay on the plaintiff, the judge added that "the credibility of the plaintiff is essential to enable him to establish these facts as they depend on the plaintiff's account of what occurred at the meeting on 1st August, 2007". In the circumstances, the plaintiff had failed to establish that the assurance had in fact been given.

The claim of estoppel was thus rejected, the guarantee being enforceable. Although it is not of great consequence given the ultimate verdict, it is notable that the decision does not expressly reference the species of estoppel sought, whether it was the equitable remedy of promissory estoppel, or estoppel by representation or by convention at common law. The decision of Geoghegan J. in *Courtney v McCarthy* [2008] 2 I.R. 376 suggests some blurring in the distinction between the various categories of estoppel, such that it may no longer be as important to identify the precise type of estoppel being invoked. The notable lack of clarity in *Healy* on the precise type of estoppel sought arguably lends some support to this trend.

EXCLUSION CLAUSES

***Smith v Meade, Meade, FBD Insurance, Ireland and the Attorney General,* High Court, Peart J., February 5, 2000; [2009] IEHC 99** While this case turns primarily on a point of EU law, it has some relevance in the context of motor insurance contracts, and in relation to the validity of exclusion clauses therein.

In 1999, the plaintiff was injured while travelling as a passenger in the back of a van driven by the first defendant. The rear of the vehicle was not, however, equipped to accommodate passengers.

The second defendant had taken out compulsory insurance in respect of the vehicle with FBD Insurance. The policy covered third parties in cases of loss or injury caused as a result, inter alia, of the negligence of either the second defendant or of a person driving the van with his consent. The insurance cover, however, expressly excluded liability in respect of injuries caused to a passenger seated in any part of the vehicle that had not been "designed and constructed with seating accommodation for passengers".

FBD claimed that this exclusion was permitted by s.65 of the Road Traffic Act 1961, as amended (on foot of s.3 of the European Communities Act 1972) by S.I. No. 347 of 1992. The Road Traffic Act 1961 mandates the compulsory insurance of motor vehicles. Section 65, as amended, however, exempted from the requirement of compulsory insurance persons injured while seated in a part of a vehicle not designed for carrying seated passengers. FBD thus claimed that it was not required by law to indemnify the first and second defendants in respect of the plaintiff's injuries. Such injuries were, it claimed, exempt from the requirement of compulsory insurance, as the passenger was in a part of the vehicle that did not contain proper fixed seating.

The question arose as to whether this clause was void because it was in breach of a series of EU Directives stipulating that Member States take steps to require compulsory coverage for *all* passengers in a vehicle. In particular, Council Directive 90/232 of 1990 (the "Third Directive") required that motor insurance cover should "cover liability for personal injuries to all passengers, other than the driver, arising out of the use of a vehicle" (art.1). Notwithstanding this Directive, the domestic legislation that applied in Ireland at the date of the accident expressly excluded from the requirement for compulsory insurance liability in respect of passengers travelling in any part of a vehicle where that part did not contain seating to accommodate passengers (S.I. Nos 346 and 347 of 1992).

This exclusion was, the plaintiff alleged, contrary to the requirements set out in the 1990 Directive. In particular, the European Court of Justice in *Farrell v Whitty* [2007] E.C.R. I-3067 had ruled that art.1 of the 1990 Directive precluded statutory exemptions in respect of personal injuries to a person travelling in a part of a vehicle not equipped with seating for passengers. This requirement, moreover, had direct effect, it being sufficiently precise and unconditional.

In its defence, FBD claimed that its policy complied with the law in force in Ireland at the time the contract was issued. While the 1990 Directive required Member State implementation by the end of 1995, Ireland had missed that deadline for proper transposition. S.I. No. 347 had purported to implement that Directive by making changes to the 1965 Act, but had in fact included the exemption relating to persons not seated in a part of a vehicle designed to accommodate seated passengers. As a result, the 1990 Directive had not been properly implemented as of the date of the accident.

The insurer thus submitted that it had complied with Irish law as it stood at the date of the accident. In respect of the failure to transpose the Directive correctly, the appropriate claim, FBD asserted, was against the State, not the insurer. In so far as the Directive had direct effect, this placed an obligation only on the State and any emanation of the State, which did not include a private insurer such as FBD. Thus, the insurer maintained, the implications of the failure to transpose the Directive correctly could not be "visited upon" the insurer. The direct effect of an improperly transposed or untransposed directive may only be pleaded; FBD argued against the State or an emanation of the State and does not cast any new obligation or liability upon a private individual or corporation.

Against this, the plaintiff invoked the decision in C-106/89 *Marleasing SA v La Comercial Internacionale de Alimentacion SA* [1990] E.C.R. I-4135. While affirming that an unimplemented directive does not directly impose obligations on private persons, the European Court of Justice confirmed that a national court is required to interpret its own national legislation in the light of the directive, with a view to achieving the purpose set out therein. In particular, the primacy of EU law imposed an obligation on the courts to seek to give effect, where possible, to the terms of directives. Thus:

> "… in applying national law, whether the provisions in question were adopted before or after the directive, the national court called upon to interpret it is required to do so, as far as possible, in the light of the wording and the purpose of the directive in order to achieve the result pursued by [the directive]".

Given the primacy of EU law, the plaintiff thus claimed that he was entitled to the benefit of the Directive, and that the court was obliged to declare the exclusion clause void on the basis that it infringed the 1990 Directive.

Peart J. agreed. Noting the primacy of community law and the need for harmonious interpretation of Irish and EU legal provisions, the judge concluded that Irish law as it stood at the time of the accident was "out of line" with what was required by the relevant EU Directives. The relevant Directives stipulated that all passengers in vehicles were to be insured, whether or not they were accommodated in designated, fixed passenger seating. The objective to be achieved by these directives was clear, namely that all passengers throughout the community, without exception, should be covered by compulsory motor vehicle insurance regardless of the condition of the part of the vehicle in which they were accommodated.

On the basis of the decision in *Marleasing,* Peart J. thus concluded that the national court is obliged:

> "… when applying national law to do so as far as possible in the light of the wording and purpose of the directive in order to pursue the result sought to be pursued by the directive. It seems inescapable that in the

> present case this court is required to read s.65 of the Act as amended by S.I. 346 and 347 of 1992 by overlooking or ignoring the exclusion permitted therein in respect of liability for injuries caused to persons such as the plaintiff in this case".

As a result, it "inevitably" followed that the exclusion clause in FBD's contract was void, such that FBD could not rely thereon.

From the insurer's point of view, this is quite a remarkable decision. While it is clear that Irish law was, at that time, out of line with EU law, the relevant Irish legislation was nonetheless clear in permitting such an exemption. The relevant provision of the Directive had direct effect, but this does not of itself impose obligations on private persons who are not an emanation of the State. The decision suggests that, notwithstanding clear compliance with the terms of Irish law, a term in a contract between private parties may be deemed void and thus unenforceable on the basis that it infringes an EU Directive which has not yet been properly implemented into Irish law.

Notably, the law has since been changed by S.I. No. 248 of 2008, the European Communities (Motor Insurance) Regulations 2008. These regulations extend the requirement for coverage by compulsory motor insurance to *all* passengers, thus giving full effect to the relevant provision in the Third Directive.

A similar issue concerning exclusion clauses in motor insurance contracts, albeit with a different result, arose in *James Power v Guardian PMPA Insurance Ltd,* High Court, Laffoy J., February 2, 2007; [2007] IEHC 105, discussed in the Contract Law chapter in the *Annual Review of Irish Law 2007,* pp.177–181. The accident in that case took place in 1991 and thus preceded the deadline for implementation of the 1995 Directive, such that the enforcement of the latter was not at issue.

FORMALITIES

See also, *Sheridan Quinn v Gayner* [2009] IEHC 421, discussed below under FORMATION OF A CONTRACT

Land and Conveyancing Law Reform Act 2009 Part 9, Chapter 1 of the Land and Conveyancing Law Reform Act 2009 updates and consolidates the law as it relates to contracts for the sale of land. For a full discussion of the implications of this important Act see Neil Maddox, *Land and Conveyancing Law Reform Act 2009: A Commentary* (Dublin: Round Hall, 2010) and J.C.W. Wylie, *The Land and Conveyancing Law Reform Act 2009: Annotations and Commentary* (Dublin: Bloomsbury, 2010).

Notably, s.51 of the Act restates and updates the well-worn requirements of the Statute of Frauds (Ireland) 1695, in so far as it relates to the sale of land. Under the 2009 Act, a contract for the sale or other disposition of land will not be enforceable unless the contract, or a note or memorandum thereof, is in writing. Additionally, in order for the contract to be enforced against a particular person, the contract, or a note or memorandum thereof, must have been signed by that person, or by an authorised agent of that person.

In the Act, "disposition" is defined as including "a conveyance and a devise, bequest or appointment of property by will". "Land" includes any estate or interest in or over land (whether corporeal or incorporeal), any buildings or structures thereon, the airspace above the surface of land as well as land which is underwater, mines, minerals and other substances below the surface, and any part of land (see s.3 of the 2009 Act). The creation of interests in land such as easements, freehold covenants, rent charges and profits à prendre will be covered by the new requirements as they were by the old, as the definition of land for the purposes of the Act includes "any interest or estate in land, whether corporeal or incorporeal". This view is supported by s.11(4) of the 2009 Act, which sets out a number of "legal interests" in land, expressly including the interests specified above.

Section 51 substantially restates and replaces the relevant provisions of s.2 of the Statute of Frauds (Ireland) 1695 to the extent that that section related to the sale or disposition of land. The relevant provisions of s.2 of the Statute of Frauds, however, are repealed only to the extent that they relate to the "sale of lands, tenements, or hereditaments" or of any interest therein *but not otherwise*. Schedule 2 to the 2009 Act removes the words "or upon any contract or *(sic)* sale of lands, tenements, or hereditaments, or any interest in or concerning them" from s.2 of the 1695 Act, but otherwise leaves the latter section untouched. Thus, the other formalities contained in the Statute of Frauds that relate to other contracts not for the sale of land—such as contracts providing guarantees—still stand.

Section 51 also expressly preserves the equitable doctrine of part-performance that qualifies the rigours of the Statute of Frauds. This allows the part-performance of a contract to continue to facilitate the enforcement of an oral contract for the sale of land, notwithstanding the lack of written evidence concerning the contract. By the same token, s.51(3) of the Act clarifies that it is not necessary for a deposit to be paid in order for a contract for the sale of land to be enforceable, although it remains possible for the parties to expressly provide to the contrary in their contract.

***Liberty Asset Management Ltd v Gannon*, High Court, Laffoy J., October 14, 2009; [2009] IEHC 468** The net issue in this case was whether there was a concluded and enforceable contract for the sale of a leasehold interest in an office building in Dublin. The case turns, in particular, on the application of the Statute of Frauds (Ireland) 1695 and the equitable doctrine of part-performance.

The plaintiff and defendant in this case had their offices in two adjoining premises, the defendant occupying No. 52 and the plaintiff No. 54, Northumberland Road. The plaintiff had acquired a leasehold interest in respect of No. 54, entered into in 2003 for a term of nine years and eleven months. Both parties needed further space for their respective businesses. The defendant owned an office building at "Richview" in Clonskeagh, Dublin 14, to which the plaintiff had expressed an interest in moving, provided it could find a new tenant for its existing office. (This latter caveat was insisted upon by the plaintiff's parent company, Friends First, as a condition of taking a lease on new offices.)

In May 2006, the plaintiff wrote to the defendant proposing that it would lease the Clonskeagh premises from the defendant, Gannon, on the understanding that Gannon would reciprocate by taking over the plaintiff's lease at No. 54. Following detailed discussions and correspondence, the lease for the Clonskeagh office was agreed in July 2007, with the plaintiff moving into the premises and vacating No. 54. A purported contract for the transfer of the lease in respect of No. 54 was signed by the defendant in September 2006 but was never executed by the plaintiff.

In August 2007, however, the defendant wrote to the plaintiff stating that he no longer wished to proceed with the transfer of the lease in respect of No. 54. The defendant's ostensible reason for so doing was that the plaintiff had failed to exercise a break clause in the plaintiff's lease of No. 54. This clause allowed the plaintiff to break the lease five years into the duration of the lease, provided 12 months' notice was given. The defendant argued that if the plaintiff had done so, this would have placed the defendant in a better position to pursue the landlord for the full freehold interest in No. 54.

On the facts, Laffoy J. concluded first that prior to May 2006 there was an agreement in principle to transfer the Clonskeagh office to the plaintiff, in consideration for which the defendant would take over the lease on No. 54. This agreement was, she added, not in any way contingent on the plaintiff exercising the break clause in the lease in respect of No. 54. In particular, the plaintiff was not, on the facts, ever contractually required to exercise the break clause, such a requirement not having formed part of the contract. Indeed, the judge seemed to intimate that the argument in relation to the break clause was in fact a "red herring" not germane to the defendant's complaint.

The plaintiff had fulfilled its end of the bargain by moving into the Clonskeagh premises. When this occurred, the judge observed, the agreement in principle to take over the lease in respect of No. 54 "crystallised into a completed contractual arrangement which concluded a contractual obligation on the part of the defendant to take No. 54". The only condition that remained precedent to the transfer of No. 54 was the agreement to the transfer by the plaintiff's landlord, which had since been forthcoming. Once obtained, the landlord's consent to the transfer rendered the obligation to take over the No. 54, Northumberland Road lease unconditional.

The plaintiff thus sought specific performance of the agreement to transfer No. 54, as well as damages for losses sustained as a result of the defendant's refusal to take over the envisaged lease. The defendant counter-argued that there was in fact no concluded agreement for the sale of No. 54. Even if there was such agreement, the defendant claimed that it was not enforceable as there was no sufficient written memorandum or note of that agreement to satisfy the requirements of the Statute of Frauds (Ireland) 1695.

The first question was whether there was a concluded contract in this case for the transfer of No. 54. Laffoy J. ruled that there was in fact such an agreement, though, notably, she observed that it did not come into existence until the entry into force of the lease for the Clonskeagh premises in July 2007. In relation to this agreement, however, there was no note or memorandum sufficient to satisfy the terms of the Statute of Frauds. Notably, a great deal of the correspondence that passed between the parties was expressly stated to be "subject to contract", "subject to lease" or was headed "lease and agreement denied". These were phrases that negated the existence of a concluded contract and could not thus satisfy the terms of the Statute, as confirmed in *Boyle v Lee* [1992] 1 I.R. 555. While the defendant had signed a letter of May 2006 and a contract dated September 2006 (neither of which documents were expressed to be subject to contract), neither document constituted a sufficient note of the agreement as, according to the judge:

> "… there was no concluded agreement in existence at the time either document came into being. There was no concluded agreement between the parties until 6th July, 2007".

In other words, neither of these documents could be taken as having evidenced a concluded agreement, as the concluded agreement in relation to No. 54 did not come into being until July 2007 when the plaintiff moved to Clonskeagh, *after* those documents had been signed. They could not thus have provided written evidence of an agreement that post-dated their creation.

In particular, Laffoy J. noted that the reference in the defendant's letter of May 2006 to No. 54 did not create a freestanding obligation to take over the lease. Instead, the letter recognised that the consideration for the completion of the lease for the Clonskeagh premises would be the transfer of No. 54 to the defendant. The reference to No. 54 in that letter was thus "merely an aspect of the defendant's contractual liability in return for the plaintiff taking the [Clonskeagh lease]…". Nor could the September 2006 contract satisfy the Statute, given that both parties' correspondence in the days just following the signing of that contract expressly used the terms "subject to contract/contract denied" in reference to that deal. This clearly indicated the parties' stance that the contract in respect of No. 54 would not be executed until the Clonskeagh lease was finalised.

This was not, however, the end of the matter. Laffoy J. determined that the plaintiff's conduct in entering into the Clonskeagh lease, and vacating No. 54, constituted part-performance of the concluded oral agreement regarding the vacated premises. Following *Steadman v Steadman* [1976] A.C. 536 and *Mackey v Wilde* [1998] 2 I.R. 578, Laffoy J. noted that equity would not permit the Statute of Frauds to be used as "an engine of fraud" allowing the defendant to "break faith" with the plaintiff in circumstances where the plaintiff had acted to its detriment by performing its end of the bargain. According to Barron J. in *Mackey v Wilde*, the test for part-performance required, first, that there was a concluded oral contract in respect of which one of the parties had indicated, by its actions, an intention to perform. Secondly, the other party must have "induced such acts or stood by while they were being performed", such that "… it would be unconscionable and a breach of good faith to allow the defendant to rely upon the terms of the Statute of Frauds to prevent performance of the contract".

On all counts, the plaintiff had satisfied these criteria. First, there was a concluded contract that came into being on the making of the agreement relating to the lease of the Clonskeagh premises. On foot of that agreement, the plaintiff had moved into Richview, vacating its Northumberland Road premises. The defendant had "not merely induced or acquiesced" in this conduct, but had "actively participated" therein, having itself agreed to lease out the Clonskeagh office premises. Given the circumstances, Laffoy J. concluded that it would "undoubtedly be unconscionable and a breach of good faith" to permit reliance on the Statute of Frauds to avoid the transfer of the lease over No. 54. The judge also dismissed the contention that there had been delay in this case sufficient to deny the plaintiff relief.

Although ruling that it was not relevant to the resolution of the case (part-performance having been established), Laffoy J. also observed that the plaintiff, if it had no other remedy, would have been entitled to plead estoppel in this case. As a result, the defendant would have been prevented from avoiding its commitment to acquire the lease in respect of No. 54. Citing *Courtney v McCarthy* [2008] 2 I.R. 376, Laffoy J. noted that the defendant could not "reneg[e] on his assurance" regarding No. 54, as the plaintiff had relied on that assurance to its detriment by leaving No. 54 and entering into the Clonskeagh lease. The plaintiff had relied upon this commitment to its clear detriment, and thus the defendant could be estopped from backtracking on its word. The precise species of estoppel upon which the judge relied is unclear—it may well be proprietary estoppel, given that an interest in land is involved, but this is not clear from the judgment. It is arguable, however, that the precise category may no longer be of great consequence given the blurring of those categories evidenced in the decision of Geoghegan J. in *Courtney v McCarthy* [2008] 2 I.R. 376. In any case, given that the contract already contained such a commitment, and that part-performance had occurred, the issue of estoppel did not require a definitive ruling.

The judge thus awarded specific performance of the contract for the lease in respect of No. 54. The judge also awarded the plaintiff damages for rent in respect of No. 54 from January 2008 onwards, as well as insurance, rates and water rates paid on the premises. Additionally, compensation was ordered in respect of the maintenance of No. 54 as well as for professional fees paid in respect of a rent review. Notably, by the time this case was decided, there were only two and a half years left to run on that lease, the plaintiff also having waived any statutory right to renew this lease for No.54 when it ran out.

FORMATION OF A CONTRACT

***Sheridan and Quinn t/a Sheridan Quinn v John Gaynor; Cecilia Gaynor v Sheridan and Quinn t/a Sheridan Quinn*, High Court, Feeney J., September 14, 2009; [2009] IEHC 421** The net question in this case was whether the plaintiff, Ms Cecilia Gaynor, held an interest in land that was the subject of a judgment mortgage that had been registered against her brother, John Gaynor. The key principle arising is the requirement for certainty in a contract for the sale of land. Absent a specific identification of the property to be transferred, an arrangement in relation to the transfer of land is unlikely to be enforceable.

The facts of the case are unusual. John and Cecilia Gaynor were nephew and niece respectively of a Mr Edward Rogers, who owned approximately 16 hectares in Co. Westmeath. At the relevant time this land was valued at £40,000 (€50,800). In 1996, Edward and his nephew John entered into an agreement to sell the land to John for £25,000 (€31,750). A deposit of £2,500 was paid upfront, while the remaining sums were to be paid in instalments of £2,000 each year commencing December 1996. The arrangement between the parties was that Edward would continue to enjoy a right of residence for the rest of his life in a bungalow situated on the land. It appeared, however, that parallel to this legal agreement, a secret arrangement had been made whereby John's sister, Cecilia, would pay an additional £20,000 in respect of the land. The purpose of this parallel—and clandestine—arrangement was to avoid certain implications for Edward, who was worried that payment of full market value for the land would potentially affect a small pension to which he was entitled.

Edward and John signed a deed of transfer in respect of the land in early 2007. The transaction was effected against the strong advice of Mr Rogers' solicitor, who correctly observed that the stated contract price amounted to a "gross undervalue" of the land. While Mr Rogers obtained independent legal advice, he was not for turning and the transaction proceeded.

While the evidence supported the existence of the parallel agreement, the contract and deed made no mention of Cecilia's claimed interest in the property. A judgment mortgage having been registered against the land, the question arose as to whether Cecilia had any legal or equitable interest in the property, and if so what legal implications this might have for the judgment mortgage.

Feeney J. accepted that the true arrangement envisaged by the parties was that the full price to be paid to the uncle was £40,000 with £20,000 emanating from each of the siblings. While the transaction would name only John and his uncle, the true intent was that on Edward's death, the land would be divided equally between John and Cecilia. In particular, it was the understanding of all the parties (including the uncle) that Cecilia would take that portion of the land that included Edward's home, which portion would be registered separately in a new folio. Two separate written documents attested to this understanding. First, a letter signed by Edward in November 1996 acknowledged receipt of £20,000 from Cecilia in respect of the "dwelling house and surrounding area after my death". A hand-written document signed by the siblings and their uncle shortly before Edward's death in 2000 confirmed also that Cecilia Gaynor was intended to have a "50% claim on the property" to be registered in a new folio after the uncle's death.

While the judge accepted, on the evidence, that such was the true intent of all the parties, he nonetheless concluded that Cecilia did not have any interest, either equitable or legal, in the land. A key factor in this conclusion was that the portion of the land to which Cecilia claimed entitlement had not been identified with sufficient precision. Although it was understood that she would occupy that portion of the land on which Edward's house was located, the exact boundaries of this portion had not been identified. The true intention of the parties was that this precise portion would be identified after the uncle's demise, whereupon the relevant portion of land would be transferred to Cecilia.

In other words, the agreement of 1996 did not operate to transfer any land to Cecilia. The agreement by its express terms transferred the property into the sole name of John. The parallel secret arrangement was that John would transfer an as yet unidentified portion of land to Cecilia after the uncle's death. The lands otherwise had been purchased "in their entirety" by John, subject to a separate understanding that after Edward's death, John would transfer half of the property to his sister. The court thus concluded that:

> "… Cecilia Gaynor does not have an interest in the lands and property… The lands were transferred by contract to John Gaynor and under that contract Cecilia Gaynor has no interest in the lands".

Certainly there was an agreement that once Edward passed away, the lands would be sub-divided by a future agreement between the siblings. Nonetheless, there had never been any agreement to transfer a specifically identified portion of the lands to Cecilia.

It was this lack of certainty as to the exact parameters of the portion of land to be transferred to Cecilia that was crucial. As Feeney J. remarked:

> "It is clear that any property which is the subject matter of a contract

> or agreement for sale must be described with sufficient certainty to be capable of being clearly identified."

The agreement in this case did not adequately specify the lands to be transferred. Instead there was effectively an "agreement to agree" the boundaries at some later stage. In short:

> "There is not and never was a sufficient identification of the property sufficient to establish a legal or equitable interest therein on the part of Cecilia Gaynor."

In this regard the requirements of s.2 of the Statute of Frauds 1695 (see the discussion above under FORMALITIES) had not been met, as the exact property to be transferred had not been sufficiently identified.

It was this lack of certainty that was fatal to Cecilia's case. Quoting Wylie, the judge adverted to the general principle that a contract "must be sufficiently certain" so that "if necessary, a court will be able to see precisely what it is they have agreed" (Wylie, *Conveyancing Law*, 2nd edn (Dublin: Butterworths, 1996), p.141). As noted by Geoghegan J. in *Supermacs Ireland v Katesan (Naas)* [2000] 4 I.R. 273:

> "There cannot be a concluded agreement unless everything intended to be covered by the agreement has been either expressly or impliedly agreed."

At most here there was "no more than an agreement to agree".

The court did note that Cecilia had paid £20,000 towards the purchase price. There is an exception to the requirement that a contract be in writing or evidenced in writing under the Statute of Frauds where there is part performance of an oral contract. Traditionally, the payment of money was not deemed sufficient in itself to constitute part-performance thereof (*Clinan v Cooke* (1802) 1 Sch. & Lef. 22), although this blanket rule has been qualified by *Steadman v Steadman* [1976] A.C. 536 which allows exceptions in specified cases. While Feeney J. acknowledged the possibility that one might thus feasibly argue against a "general rule that payment of money can never be part performance", he was satisfied that this was not a case where such an argument would succeed. Again, the lack of agreement as to the precise portion of land to which Cecilia would allegedly be entitled was crucial in this regard, the court reiterating that there was no specific agreement as to the precise portion of the property to be assigned to her.

Arguably, the clandestine nature of the parties' arrangements more or less sealed their fate. Indeed, the judge himself concluded that even if there had been an enforceable contract in Cecilia's favour, considerations of public policy would have militated against its enforcement. The purpose of the particular arrangement being to conceal the amount of money available to Edward Rogers, it would be "a breach of public policy" to enforce a contract the purpose of which was "to conceal from the Revenue Authorities the true nature of the transactions".

McCabe Builders (Dublin) Limited v Sagamu Developments Ltd, Laragan Developments Ltd and Hanly Group Ltd, **Supreme Court, April 1, 2009; [2009] IESC 31** This is an appeal from a decision of the High Court, delivered by Charleton J. on November 23, 2007; [2007] IEHC 391, and discussed in the *Annual Review of Irish Law 2007*, pp.192–196. This intricate case essentially concerns the issue of contract formation, specifically whether the parties in this case had entered into a concluded building contract. The case also raises the complex issue as to the correct construction of that contract, and in particular whether the contract as agreed required the completion of the works as described in a tender document known as a "Bill of Approximate Quantities".

The crux of the High Court decision was that the parties had in fact reached no conclusion at all on the central terms of their contract. Charleton J. ruled that there had been no meeting of minds on matters fundamental to any concluded agreement. In particular, there had been no agreement as to whether the plaintiff had agreed to carry out the works by reference to a description of those works contained in a bill of approximate quantities included with the tender documents or whether, in the alternative, the bill simply constituted a schedule of rates for the work actually completed. On appeal this verdict was reversed, the Supreme Court ruling that, on a correct interpretation of the parties' dealings, there had in fact been a binding agreement, though the Supreme Court split 2:1 on the correct construction of this agreement.

The defendants in this case were related development companies, the first and second defendants being subsidiaries of the third. They wished to build 32 houses and 14 apartments at a site in Kilmacanogue, Co. Wicklow. In July 2005 the plaintiff building company successfully tendered for the project, the parties ultimately setting a price of €15.3 million for the work (though they subsequently disputed what this price included). The parties differed, however, in relation to the scope of the works that the plaintiff was contractually bound to carry out.

The plaintiff contended that it was entitled to extra payment in respect of extra costs flowing from unforeseen difficulties with the works, the project having been complicated by a number of unforeseen factors. In particular, the amount of rock to be excavated exceeded considerably the amount originally estimated by the defendants. The defendants counter-argued that it was their understanding that the contract was (except for certain specified matters) essentially a fixed-price contract. In particular, they contended that the plaintiff had agreed to carry out the work as described in a bill of approximate quantities (BAQ), which was one of the tender documents, the terms of which had placed the risk of any unforeseen extra costs in relation to the works squarely on the plaintiff.

The defendants relied on the BAQ which stated, as a general condition, that:

> "[T]he Contractor shall carefully examine the drawings and other Contract documents and satisfy himself as to their accuracy and ensure that they cover and embody the proposed works. *The Contractor shall properly execute the Works whether or not shown on the drawings or described in the Bill of Approximate Quantities, provided that same may be reasonably inferred therefrom*" (emphasis added).

The conditions in the BAQ also stipulated that the plaintiff should visit the site:

> "… and is to be taken to have made himself acquainted with the nature of the works, the character, dimensions, levels and other features of the site…and all other things in so far as they may have any connection with, or effect, the works…".

Thus, if this particular BAQ formed part of the agreement, the parties would be taken to have agreed to carry out the full works described therein for the fixed price of €15.3 million. The plaintiff would therefore assume the risk of any extra costs associated with the development.

The plaintiff, for its part, contended that the description of the works in the BAQ did not form part of the concluded contract. It asserted that under the express terms of the written contract signed by both parties, the BAQ, in so far as it was relevant, constituted only a schedule of rates for work actually carried out on the site. The plaintiff claimed, in particular, that under the express terms of the written contract it was bound only to complete the works as described in the drawings and in a specification which were included with the tender documents. The plaintiff thus claimed that it was entitled to be paid extra for any work carried out beyond what was set out and described in those drawings and specification (despite the clear inadequacy of both these documents).

If the BAQ had not formed part of the contract, but instead constituted a schedule of rates, as contended by the plaintiff, the latter would have been able to claim for the full costs of the work actually completed at the rates set out in the BAQ. It would, moreover, only have been bound to carry out the works as described in the admittedly incomplete drawings and specification, allowing it to claim extra payment for work not described therein.

In the High Court, Charleton J. concluded that the description of the works contained in the BAQ had not formed part of the contract. The defendants, in particular, had chosen to rely on the "blue form" of the RIAI standard form of building contract, which it had issued to the plaintiff following the conclusion of the tender process. Both parties had signed this form. The RIAI form expressly *excluded* the BAQ from forming part of the contract, the BAQ thus "dropping away" and becoming merely a schedule of rates for the materials and work. In sum, far from providing clearly that the terms of the BAQ should be included as part of the contract, the articles of agreement, as set out in the RIAI form, expressly negated such inclusion. It thus, the High Court concluded, "becomes impossible to conclude that the parties have agreed that descriptions in the Bill of Quantities should be part of the contract obligation."

The defendants nonetheless contended that the course of dealings between the parties, comprising a number of letters, documents and discussions, evidenced an agreement to displace this express provision, thus incorporating into the contract the descriptions as set out in the BAQ. In particular, they claimed that a letter of August 2005, which had been signed and countersigned by each party, required that the plaintiff complete the works as described in the BAQ for the fixed sum of €15.3 million. This letter was accompanied by the BAQ itself, and thus was alleged to constitute acceptance, by reference to the BAQ, of the description of works contained therein.

The High Court judge, however, concluded that, on the facts, there had been no concluded contract. Fundamentally "the minds of the parties never met as to central issues that are crucial to their different understandings of what would otherwise be their mutual obligations." The parties had never agreed the crucial matter of pricing and responsibility for unforeseen extra costs in completing the works. They effectively held two completely opposing views of their obligations. The defendants believed that the contract was an all-in, fixed-price affair for the works as described in the BAQ. By contrast, the plaintiff assumed that it would be recompensed for what it claimed were extra costs for works above and beyond what were set out in the drawings and specification. The mutual obligations of the parties, in short, had not been finalised. Charleton J. thus ruled that, in the absence of a concluded contract, the plaintiff was to be remunerated on a quantum meruit basis, the precise amount of compensation to be fixed at arbitration.

On appeal, all three judges in the Supreme Court agreed that there had in fact been a concluded contract, though the court split 2:1 in relation to the correct construction of that contract. Fennelly J., with whom Hardiman J. concurred, issued the majority verdict. Fennelly J. ruled that a contract had been concluded which had incorporated the description of the works as set out in the BAQ. Murphy J. agreed that there had been an agreement between the parties, although he believed based on the evidence that the entire agreement was as comprised in the RIAI form, which expressly *excluded* the description contained in the BAQ.

In his judgment, Fennelly J. leaned heavily in favour of the existence of a concluded contract. He placed particular emphasis on the fact that both parties had come to court claiming that they had a concluded contract, although they differed as to the content of that contract. It was thus "striking", in Fennelly

J.'s view, that Charleton J. had ruled that there was no contract *at all*.

There were, the Supreme Court judge noted, three distinct phases of contractual negotiations in this case. At each stage it was "indisputable" that the parties "wished their agreement for the carrying out of a very substantial development to be contained in a formal written agreement". Fennelly J. noted, in particular, that the task of ascertaining the intentions of the parties was to be carried out by reference to the objective standard, in other words by reference to the parties' outward conduct and the documents that they had exchanged, as opposed to the subjective intentions or understandings as expressed by the parties when giving evidence. The implication is that Charleton J. had perhaps relied excessively on the subjective perspectives of the parties as to what they had agreed, rather than by looking to the objective intention as evidenced by the documents exchanged between the parties.

The potential outcome of the High Court decision was also of significance to Fennelly J. Charleton J.'s finding, the Supreme Court judge felt, was one that had fostered considerable uncertainty. It meant, in particular, that there were no limits on the amount owed to McCabe, as the amount was to be determined on a quantum meruit basis rather than by reference to agreed contractual terms. In particular, the decision that no contract had been concluded "between parties who have negotiated a hard-won deal" was "liable to produce injustice". If there was no contract there would, in particular, be no reason to restrict payment to the agreed sum on the basis of which McCabe had been awarded the tender.

The High Court had observed that its verdict may have facilitated the plaintiff claiming twice for the same work, though Charleton J. had suggested that such a conclusion was excluded "by implication". In the Supreme Court, Fennelly J. noted that the possibility that the plaintiff might claim twice was probably inconsistent with the High Court ruling that there was no contract for the tendered sum. Clearly, the plaintiff could not have claimed payment by reference to that contract sum, if there was in fact no contract, *and* simultaneously claim on a quantum meruit basis for the completed work. Fennelly J. was also not satisfied that the purported right to claim on the double would have been "excluded by implication", as Charleton J. had contended, the Supreme Court observing that "it is not clear how such a term could be implied in the absence of a contract". Nor would the plaintiff's agreement not to claim twice have been contractually binding. (That said, of course, had the contract been upheld without incorporating the description contained in the BAQ, the potential for claiming twice for the same work would have arisen, a point discussed further below.)

The parties had, Fennelly J. noted, clearly intended to enter into a formal legally binding contract. The court should, he added, seek to give effect to such apparent intentions, particularly in commercial arrangements, where there is a strong presumption (according to McDermott, *Contract Law* (Dublin: Butterworth's, 2001) "that the parties intended to create legally binding contracts". The parties in this case had manifestly "intended that their relationship would be governed by a formal legal contract" and the court should seek, where possible, to give effect to this intention.

Turning to the terms of such a contract, the judge noted that there was no doubt but that, at tender stage, the description of the works as set out in the BAQ "was central". Thus, as Fennelly J. remarked:

> "Looking at the object of the contract as a whole, therefore, there is no doubt that the intention of the parties was that the contract specified in the RIAI form would represent the consideration *for the carrying out of the works for which McCabes had submitted their tender*" (my emphasis).

As against this, the plaintiff contended that the references in the RIAI standard form expressly excluded the descriptions as set out in the BAQ from the concluded contract. In particular, it claimed that the RIAI contract (and the documents stated to be incorporated thereby) comprised the entire contract between the parties. The RIAI form, by its express words, had excluded the BAQ from the contract except to the extent that it constituted a schedule of rates. In short, the plaintiff argued that once the RIAI form was signed, the BAQ "dropped away" from the contract, except in so far as the BAQ governed the rates of compensation for the actual work completed.

While Fennelly J. saw "very great merit" in this approach, he nonetheless looked to "the apparent intention of the parties as shown by [the] course of dealing between them, thus including the August correspondence and the Bill of Approximate Quantities." Fennelly J. was, in particular, not convinced that the specific terms of the RIAI form constituted the parties' full agreement. He believed, instead, that the true terms of the contract necessarily included the BAQ and the description of the works contained therein. The judge determined that this was so by reference to the full course of dealings between the parties. In particular, he had regard to the original tender process on foot of which McCabe won the tender as well as the later exchange of correspondence between the parties. Notably, the August 2005 letter, signed by both parties, clearly indicated an intention that the works would be completed as described in the BAQ. It was clear then from both the original tender and the subsequent correspondence between the parties that the true objective intention was that the works would be completed as described in the BAQ.

The judge then turned to consider the effect of the RIAI form, which had purported to exclude from the contract the description of the works as set out in the BAQ. Condition 1 of the RIAI form notably required by its express terms that the plaintiff would carry out the works "shown upon the Contract Drawings and/or described in the Specification and Conditions". These works as described in those drawings and specification were not, however, the entirety of the works as contemplated by the original tender. Indeed, the RIAI form itself had referred to those works as those works that were "the subject of the tender documents". The judge thus felt that condition 1 was "not exhaustive" of the works to be completed. It was instead to be read in the light of the earlier tender documents which had included the description in the BAQ.

Nonetheless, a clause in the RIAI form clearly purported to exclude the BAQ except to the extent that it constituted a schedule of rates. If this were to prevail, Fennelly J. noted, the effect would be that the works would be defined "only by reference to the drawings and specification, the latter being, by common consent, utterly inadequate".

Fennelly J. remarked that this clause had to be considered in the light of the entire dealings between the parties. Notably, McCabe had tendered on the basis of the description of the works contained in the tender documents, which included the BAQ and the general conditions contained therein. Those conditions defined, in part at least, the plaintiff's obligations under the contract. To rule otherwise would potentially have allowed the plaintiff to claim twice for the same work—once as part of the agreed contract price on the basis of which the tender was won by the plaintiff, and again as "extra costs"—a "potentially unjust interpretation" which the court should, the judge concluded, strive to avoid.

Fennelly J. had particular regard to the August 2005 letter that had been signed and countersigned by both parties. This letter had indicated an agreement for the fixed price of €15.3 million to carry out the works as described in the letter and the documents included with the letter, which included the BAQ. The judge believed that this letter reflected the true agreement of the parties, to which they had intended the RIAI form would give effect. To the extent that the RIAI form did not give effect to that agreement "it is in conflict with the intentions of the parties." Given such conflict, Fennelly J. preferred to enforce "the clear intention of the parties", which was to prevail in case of conflict. While conceding that the RIAI form normally would take precedence in cases of discrepancy, the whole course of dealings between the parties in this case, he believed, clearly indicated that the parties had intended, objectively speaking, that the works were to be as described in the BAQ. In this regard the letter of August 2005 was particularly significant, indicating as it did an objective intention to be bound by the description of the works set out in the BAQ. Fennelly J. thus concluded that the contract was intended to include that description of the works, notwithstanding the purported exclusion in the RIAI form.

Notably, Fennelly J. did not feel it was necessary to order rectification of the contract, indicating that the above interpretation of the relevant documents would yield the correct result. While agreeing that there had been a concluded contract, Murphy J. dissented from the majority verdict that that contract required completion of the works as described in the BAQ. For his part, Murphy J. concluded that the express terms of the RIAI form were to prevail, and that this standard form contract, together with the contract documents to which it referred, constituted the entire contract of the parties. That standard form, by its terms, expressly excluded the terms contained in the BAQ except to the extent that they constituted a schedule of rates for the work completed. Unless a special condition to the contrary was expressly included in the contract as contained in the RIAI form, the form used by the parties meant that "only the drawings and specification, inadequate though they appear, can form the definition of works." The "contract documents", therefore, in his opinion included only those drawings and that specification. He thus concluded that:

> "… the RIAI contract without quantities binds the parties…However, I am unable to accept the appellant's contention that the RIAI contract can incorporate the description in the Approximate Bill of Quantities as being a definition of the works or as being part of the contract documentation".

Although Murphy J. made reference to the August 2005 correspondence, he does not appear to have accepted that this correspondence altered the terms of the contract as contained in the RIAI form.

The decision in this case undoubtedly raises complex issues of construction. The nub of the majority decision is that one should consider the true construction of the contract by reference to the entire dealings of the parties, including the initial tender process and the subsequent correspondence. The majority verdict thus prevents the plaintiff from claiming extra for works that it had essentially offered, in its initial tender, to complete for the fixed price of €15.3 million. The decision also effectively confers on the plaintiff the risk of any extra costs ensuing from unforeseen difficulties and delays encountered with those works.

The difficulty with this conclusion is that the express terms of the RIAI standard-form building contract clearly excluded the description and conditions contained in the BAQ. That Fennelly J. was able to gloss over this undoubted obstacle is testimony to the holistic method of interpretation favoured by the majority in this case. The decision of Murphy J., by contrast, appears to rely solely on the terms of the RIAI contract, as signed by the parties. This arguably yielded a more orthodox verdict, focussing as it does on the express terms of the RIAI document. The decision of both of the judges, however, clearly indicates a shared inclination to identify agreement between the parties, and a desire to avoid the uncertainty engendered by the High Court finding that there was no concluded contract at all.

FRUSTRATION

***Ringsend Property Limited v Donatex Ltd and Bernard McNamara,* High Court, Kelly J., December 18, 2009; [2009] IEHC 568** A number of issues of contract law arise in this case, which concerned the ill-fated purchase of the former Irish Glass Bottle site in Ringsend, Dublin. Although the proceedings were for summary judgment, some interesting points of contract law are explored, most notably the doctrine of frustration and the use of implied terms.

The site in question formerly belonged to a company called South Wharf Ltd. A company called Becbay subsequently acquired the site by purchasing the entire share capital in South Wharf for the princely sum of €410 million. (At the time of the judgment the site was estimated to have declined in value to a mere €60 million.)

A consortium behind Becbay included the second defendant Bernard McNamara (who held a 41 per cent stake), and the Dublin Docklands Development Authority (DDDA) which held a 26 per cent interest therein. The purpose of the purchase was an ambitious development of the former Glass Bottle site. For this purpose it was proposed that Becbay would seek an exemption from the normal requirement for planning permission by obtaining a certificate under s.25 of the Dublin Docklands Development Act 1997, if it was in line with an approved planning scheme for the Docks area. This would effectively allow for fast-tracked approval for the development of the site, exempting the development from the normal requirements of the Planning Acts.

With a view to financing Mr McNamara's end of the purchase, the first defendant (a company owned by Mr McNamara) issued loan stock to the value of €62.5 million. It did so on generous terms (notably with annual interest of 14 per cent and a 3 per cent redemption premium). The loan stock was ultimately transferred to the plaintiff company, which was to hold the stock on trust and as agent for the various stockholders. For his part, Mr McNamara issued a personal guarantee making him liable in case of default in respect of the loan principal issued to the first defendant (but not for the interest thereon).

While the loan stock was intended to be repayable after seven years, the loan stock instrument entered into with the plaintiff provided for accelerated repayment in certain stipulated circumstances. Notably, clause 5 of the instrument stipulated that if, within 30 months of the date of the execution of the loan stock instrument, Becbay had not either applied for the required s.25 certificate in respect of the site or in the alternative had not received planning permission from Dublin City Council, the loan stock would be repayable *with immediate effect*, with interest due up to the date of repayment.

The loan stock agreement was entered into in January 2007. More than 30 months later, Becbay had neither applied for a section 25 certificate nor had it obtained any planning permission in respect of the site, with the result that the anticipated site development had not commenced. In these circumstances the plaintiff sought summary judgment to redeem the €62.5 million loan stock, with interest, bringing the total sum claimed to in excess of €98 million. It also sought to enforce Mr McNamara's personal guarantee for the principal advanced.

Where summary judgment is sought, the question that arises is whether there existed a "fair or reasonable probability of the defendants having a real or bona fide defence" (see *First National Commercial Bank v Anglin* [1996] 1 I.R. 75 and *Aer Rianta Cpt v Ryanair Ltd* [2001] 4 I.R. 607). If the defendant could establish that there was a credible defence or a fair and reasonably possibility of mounting a real or bona fide defence, summary judgment would not be granted. Notably, it was not necessary, for this purpose, to demonstrate that the defence put forward is likely to succeed, or that success is "not improbable". In *Aer Rianta v Ryanair,* Hardiman J. summarised the criteria for the granting of a summary judgment, noting that:

> "[T]he fundamental questions to be posed…remain: is it 'very clear' that the defendant has no case? Is there either no issue to be tried or only issues which are simple and easily determined? Do the defendant's affidavits fail to disclose even an arguable defence?"

In response to the request for summary judgment, the defendants raised five possible defences, the first of which was abandoned in the course of argument. The remaining defences will be dealt with in turn:

Failure to comply with the terms of the agreement The defendants made a rather pedantic assertion that the plaintiffs, in seeking repayment, had not complied with the terms of the loan stock agreement. In particular, they submitted that the plaintiff was required by clause 4 of the agreement to surrender loan stock certificates when seeking to redeem its stock. The defendants asserted that the plaintiff had merely demanded repayment and had not surrendered the relevant certificates. In dismissing this contention as lacking "any arguable defence", Kelly J. noted that the plaintiff had in its letter of demand committed to releasing the stock certificates once it was paid the amount due, an approach that the judge felt was "perfectly in order". The judge, moreover, questioned the business efficacy of a term that would have required the plaintiff to surrender the loan stock certificates *before* repayment was made.

Frustration/partial frustration The defendants claimed that because of a prior verdict of the High Court in relation to the powers of the DDDA to grant s.25 certificates, the contract had been frustrated. They claimed that the effect of the decision of Finlay Geoghegan J. in *North Wall Property Holding Company Limited v Dublin Docklands Development Authority* [2009] IEHC 11 was to frustrate the loan stock agreement in this case. The defendants asserted that the judgment in the earlier case prevented the DDDA from granting s.25 certificates in cases where the DDDA was itself an interested party. This therefore meant that the contract could not be performed, and thus had been frustrated and could be regarded as discharged.

The doctrine of frustration operates so as to allow the contract to be discharged where, through no fault of either party, an unanticipated event takes place that prevents the performance of the core element of the agreement. Because of the event, the contract as anticipated cannot be performed—that which was contracted for cannot be delivered. As noted in *Davis Contractors Ltd v Fareham UDC* [1956] A.C. 696:

> "[F]rustration occurs whenever the law recognises that without default of either party a contractual obligation has become incapable of being performed because the circumstances in which performance is called for would render it a thing radically different from that which was undertaken by the contract."

It is not enough that the event causes hardship, inconvenience or loss in the performance of the contractual obligation, or renders its performance more costly or onerous. Nor is it sufficient that the agreement is simply a bad bargain. The circumstances must be such that the performance of the contract would result in "a different thing from that contracted for".

Kelly J. did not at this stage have to determine whether the contract had in fact been frustrated. He simply had to determine whether the defendants had a credible defence on this ground. In this regard, there were two specific difficulties. First, the loan stock agreement itself provided expressly for the possibility that a s.25 certificate would not issue, or that the council would not grant planning permission within the 30-month window. In other words, it had expressly anticipated what would happen in the event that permission was not granted. The doctrine of frustration, however, only applies in respect of an event that the contract has not itself anticipated or for which it has not provided. It is always open to the parties to make their own provisions for a contingency, thus apportioning the risk of such events. Where the parties have anticipated the risk of an event occurring, and have allocated the risk in relation to such an event, frustration on the basis of such an event is thus foreclosed. The parties therefore cannot claim frustration of a contract occurring as a result of an event which is itself anticipated by the contract.

Thus, although Kelly J. acknowledged that the defence might be "arguable", there were "formidable hurdles" to its success. The contract, after all, had anticipated the prospect of a s.25 certificate and/or planning permission not issuing on time. In the event of such a contingency, the agreement very clearly placed the risk on the defendants. As the judge noted, the money had been invested on the basis that it would be repayable immediately if a certain specific state of affairs came to pass, which plainly did.

Another more fundamental objection to the defence lay in the fact that were the defence of frustration to succeed, the contract would thus be at an end, rendering the loan stock repayable with immediate effect. The defendants thus argued that it was possible for the court to accept a defence of 'partial frustration', discharging only that part of the contract that required immediate repayment should the certificate or planning permission not issue within 30 months. Effectively, the defendants argued that there could be frustration of a specific section of a contract only, leaving the remaining obligations in situ. Part of this argument comprised the contention that the immediate repayment clause could be suspended for the time being, but revived at some future point absent the 30-month deadline, through what an obviously sceptical Kelly J. termed "some unexplained and, I suspect, inexplicable alchemy".

The concept of partial frustration is known in civil law jurisdictions, such that destruction of a part of subject matter may lead to discharge in respect of that part only. Kelly J. concluded, nonetheless, that this was not a concept that operated at common law. According to Treitel, *The Law of Contract*, 11th edn (London: Sweet & Maxwell, 2003) "there is no such concept as partial or temporary frustration on account of partial or temporary impossibility". Partial discharge may be available where obligations are severable, if the relevant part could be severed from the remainder of the contract. In this case, however, the repayment clause was "an integral part of the contract" and could not be severed from the remainder of the contract in the same way as an arbitration clause would be severable from a contract that had otherwise been ended or discharged.

Mistake of law The defendants raised a defence of mistake as to the law. The contract was entered into, they claimed, on the basis of an understanding that the DDDA had the power to grant s.25 certificates. They contended, on the basis of the decision in *North Wall Property*, that they had entered into the contract under a mistake as to the law.

While traditionally a mistake as to the law did not afford relief to a litigant, the decision in *Kleinwort Benson Ltd v Lincoln City Council* [1999] A.C. 349 qualified this traditional bar, ruling that a party could seek restitution on the basis of a mistake as to the law. Kelly J. did not believe, however, that on the facts there was an arguable defence on the basis of a mistake as to the law. The defendants had specifically claimed that were it not for representations made by the DDDA to the defendants that the latter had the power to grant s.25 certificates and to guarantee a specified minimum plot density, the defendants would not have entered into the loan stock agreement. This seems to suggest (though the judgment is quite opaque on the point) that the issue being raised was not mistake, but misrepresentation. While noting that Mr McNamara might have some action on the basis of this claim against the DDDA, the testimony as presented did "not provide a defence on this claim on the basis of the contract having been entered into under a mistake of law."

The basis for this finding is somewhat unclear, there being relatively little detail on the reasoning for excluding this defence. Kelly J. did note that the case was "nowhere near the situation which obtained in *Kleinwort Benson*" or in other cited precedents. He suggested that the circumstances in which a mistake as to law would be actionable were "extremely limited". This suggests (though it is unclear) that the departure from the old exclusionary rule in relation to mistake in law is—in the judge's view—a limited one, with application only in exceptional cases. Based on the pleadings of the defendants, one might also surmise that the defence raised was in fact properly a claim for misrepresentation on the part of the DDDA rather than a claim for relief for mistake, though in the absence of a more detailed discussion, this point remains speculative.

Implied terms Finally, the defendants had contended that a term should be implied into the contract stipulating that the DDDA had the necessary legal power to grant the s.25 certificate. The judge rejected this proposition. There are two alternative tests for the implication in fact of terms into a contract on the basis of the presumed intention of the parties. The first is that the term in question is necessary to give business efficacy to the contract (*The Moorcock* (1889) 14 PD 64, *Butler v McAlpine* [1904] 2 I.R. 445). Kelly J. ruled, however, that no such implication was required, the loan stock instrument being "…perfectly workable and efficacious from a business point of view". There was thus no basis for its implication.

Nor did such an implied term satisfy the requirements of the alternative test set out in *Shirlaw v Southern Foundries* [1939] 2 K.B. 206. This test requires that if an ordinary reasonable person had asked the parties if they had intended to include this term, the parties would readily have responded "yes, of course, that is so obvious that it goes without saying." The investors had signed up to the loan stock on the basis that they would be repaid if the development did not receive a s.25 certificate or, alternatively, regular planning permission. The reasons for such failure would have been irrelevant to them. All that concerned the investors was that they would be repaid should that contingency arise. It could not therefore be said that the investors, as reasonable persons, would have regarded the caveat contended for by the defendants as so obvious as to go without saying. Noting that the relevant clause clearly cast the risk of the contingency upon the defendants, the judge remarked that "no sensible businessman investing monies of the type involved here would, in my view, have even contemplated the implication of a clause such as is contended for."

Closing remarks Kelly J. had proceeded in this case on the assumption that the defendants' interpretation of *North Wall Property* was correct. The defendants had contended that the latter decision entirely precluded the DDDA from issuing a s.25 certificate in relation to the Irish Glass Bottle site, because of its involvement in the development. On a closer examination of that decision, Kelly J. observed that its true impact was more limited than that contended for by the defendants. In *North Wall Property*, Finlay Geoghegan J. quashed a decision of the authority to grant a s.25 certificate in respect of a site, on the basis of objective bias. The authority in that case had, after the applicant had applied for a s.25 certificate but before it was granted, entered into an agreement with the applicant. Under this agreement, it was envisaged that the applicant would, if a s.25 certificate was granted, transfer land to the DDDA for public use. On the grounds that this deal created a reasonable apprehension of bias, the decision to grant the certificate was quashed.

On a close reading of the decision, the judge doubted the defendants' interpretation of this decision as entirely precluding the Authority from issuing a certificate in this case. What the judge had in fact decided was that the Authority should take practical steps "to free itself in taking a decision…not merely from actual bias, but the apprehension of bias in the minds of reasonable people." Absolute neutrality was not required; the Authority after all had a development function, and thus understandably may be inclined to favour granting a certificate. Nonetheless, while pre-application discussions may take place and may be appropriate, the Authority and its executives should refrain from committing itself to a particular course of action prior to its decision; nor should it seek any benefit in exchange for the grant of a certificate.

The judge thus suggests that the implications of the judgment were much narrower than suggested by the defendants—that what the earlier decision precluded was the Authority or its staff members supporting or committing themselves to a particular result before the Board ruled on the section 25 certificate. The implications of the earlier decision were, Kelly J. felt, thus much narrower than claimed, a view that "copper-fastened the lack of any arguable defence in this case." Whether this meant that the s.25 certificate could in fact have been issued in this case remains, however, somewhat unclear. While the Authority admittedly has a development function, the implication of bias may be hard to avoid in a case where the Authority itself has a direct financial interest in the development for which a section 25 certificate is being sought.

This was, Kelly J. added, a formal commercial contract, entered into on a speculative basis, planning permission not yet having been obtained in respect of the site. The document, the judge noted, "[spoke] for itself": it imposed a clear obligation on the defendants to repay the loan in circumstances that had in fact transpired. The defendants had unequivocally assumed the entire risk that planning permission would not be obtained. Noting the seminal importance of certainty in commercial contracts, Kelly J. dismissed attempts by the defendants to rely on pre-contractual representations made to the defendants before the loan stock instrument was issued. This was not, he noted, a case where rectification of the contract was sought. Secondly, the representations had not been made by the plaintiff or any of the stockholders, and thus could not be held against them. Thirdly, the accelerated repayment clause was clear and unambiguous and "no aid to the matrix of surrounding fact is required".

In relation to this last point, Kelly J. cited the decision in *Charterbrook Limited v Persimmon Homes* [2009] 3 W.L.R. 267 to the effect that "resort to any form of background in aid of interpretation" should be kept to a minimum. To the greatest extent possible the express words of a contractual document should speak for themselves. This contract was clear in its terms, and should be enforced. There being no arguable defence available to the defendant, summary judgment was issued in the sum of €98 million against Donatex and €62.5 million against Mr McNamara based on his personal guarantee.

IMPLIED TERMS

See *Mary Roche v Thomas Roche,* Supreme Court, December 15, 2009; [2009] IESC 82 discussed below under INTERPRETATION OF CONTRACTS and *Ringsend Property Limited v Donatex Ltd and Bernard McNamara,* High Court, Kelly J., December 18, 2009; [2009] IEHC 568 (discussed above under FRUSTRATION)

IMPROVIDENT TRANSACTIONS

See also, *Kevin Prendergast and Monica Joyce v Dermot Joyce, Bank of Ireland and Allied Irish Banks,* High Court, Gilligan J., February 13, 2009; [2009] IEHC 199 discussed below under UNDUE INFLUENCE

***James Keating v Catherine and Patrick Keating,* High Court, Laffoy J., August 24, 2009; [2009] IEHC 405** This case relates to a transfer of land belonging to the plaintiff, James Keating, made in favour of his first cousin's wife and son, the first and second defendants respectively. It concerns an allegation that the land was transferred as a result of duress and undue influence, or in the alternative that the bargain was an improvident one.

The plaintiff was, at the time of the relevant transfer, a bachelor aged 61. He was in considerable financial straits and in poor health. He owned a farm of modest proportions in West Clare, close to Loop Head. The defendants in this case were Catherine and Patrick Keating, the widow and son respectively of the plaintiff's first cousin. They lived on an adjoining farm. In July 1999 the plaintiff transferred his lands to Catherine Keating for total consideration of £45,000. He subsequently sought to set aside this transaction, alleging that it was the result of duress and/or undue influence, or in the alternative that it constituted an improvident or unconscionable transaction. He also alleged that a purported transfer to the first defendant of a suckler cow premium quota was not the product of his agreement, and that his signature had been forged on the relevant document of transfer. The plaintiff, furthermore, claimed damages for detinue and conversion in respect of what he claimed was the unauthorised removal from his farm of cattle, as well as the destruction and/or removal of farm machinery. He also asserted that the second defendant, Patrick, had cut the plaintiff's water supply and "closed in" his septic tank. Finally, the plaintiff claimed for damages for trespass and assault in respect of an incident that took place in 2002, the defendant Patrick Keating having (it was established) attacked and damaged the plaintiff's home following the service of summons in these proceedings.

The defendants for their part denied the allegations of duress and undue influence. They claimed, furthermore, that the plaintiff had received full value for the land. In relation to the cattle, they asserted that 12 of the cattle were included in the land transfer, 18 were transferred along with the quota transfer and that the remainder had been sold for full market value, the proceeds having been paid to the plaintiff.

At the time of the transfer, it was clear that the plaintiff's financial and personal fortunes were in serious decline. He owed at least £17,878 to ACC bank, while from around the end of 1998 his personal health had deteriorated as a result of a severe bout of ulcerated shingles. His doctor described the plaintiff's condition in February 1999 as "shocking". He ate little and had lost weight. The plaintiff's farm also suffered, with evidence of his cattle being underfed, of the farm being poorly managed and of machinery being in a poor state of repair.

Around this time, James Keating consulted with his solicitor as regards his financial options. One of the options discussed was the possibility of availing of an EU Early Retirement from Farming scheme. This would have afforded the plaintiff a small pension on condition that he withdraw from farming, selling his land and stock, as well as any associated quotas, to a younger, qualified person.

In relation to the land transfer the plaintiff alleged that he had, on a continuing basis, been bullied, intimidated and assaulted by his first cousin, the first defendant's husband, and then by the second defendant with a view to selling the farm. The judge concluded that the allegation of assault by his first cousin had not been substantiated—that James's cousin had not assaulted him.

For his part the second defendant, Patrick Keating, alleged that the plaintiff had in fact taken the initiative in offering to sell Patrick the land, together with his quota and the cattle associated with the quota, in early 1999. The second defendant discussed this offer with his mother, who subsequently agreed to buy the land on the understanding that the plaintiff would continue to reside in his home on the land for the remainder of his life. In March 1999 the plaintiff approached his solicitor, indicating that he intended to sell the farm to Catherine for £45,000 in total. £40,000 was to be paid upfront on the conclusion of the transfer with the remaining £5,000 being payable in yearly instalments of

£1,000 per annum. In March 1999 the plaintiff personally received and cashed a deposit of £3,000 in respect of the proposed agreement. (On the evidence, the judge discounted an allegation that the second defendant had, by means of threats, forced the plaintiff to pay over the deposit to him once received.) The contract was subject, James added, to Catherine being approved as a qualifying transferee for the purpose of the "early retirement from farming" scheme, and her securing adequate finance.

Unusually, two months prior to the formal transfer, and prior to the signing of a formal contract, Catherine Keating had given the plaintiff's solicitor a draft for £17,000, endorsed in favour of James, for the purpose of discharging his indebtedness to ACC bank. These monies were paid over to ACC bank in April 1999 in full and final settlement of the plaintiff's debts. This all happened notwithstanding the fact that the sale had yet to be completed. This was apparently done with a view to securing the release of the land certificate in respect of James's farm.

In April 1999 both parties signed a formal contract, James promising to transfer the land to Catherine subject to a condition as to James's right of residence for life in his home on the land. Under the terms of the agreement, James was to retire from farming. While there was some delay in closing, due mainly to the plaintiff's procrastination, the sale was closed on July 12, 1999.

At the end of May 1999, Catherine Keating completed a transfer form in respect of James's suckler cow quota, which purported to transfer the benefit of the quota to her. While the form suggested that £10,000 would be paid to James in respect of the transfer of the quota, he in fact never received any money therefor. Although the plaintiff's signature had ostensibly appeared on the transfer form, the plaintiff claimed that his signature had been forged. Evidence from a forgery expert suggested that the signature was not in fact that of James, but rather that it had more than likely been replicated using a tracing of James's signature as it appeared on the contract for the sale of the farm. Applying as the correct evidential criterion for this purpose the civil standard of proof, the judge concluded (though "not lightly") that either Catherine or Patrick had inserted James's signature on the quota transfer form, without his knowledge or consent.

Despite signing up to the early retirement scheme, James was in fact a reluctant retired farmer. In particular, he did not want his neighbours to know that he had left farming. Notwithstanding the requirement (as a condition for receiving the pension under the early retirement scheme) that he dispose of his herd, he continued to keep his cattle on the land for some time after the transfer. While the first defendant had acquired his herd number, the plaintiff proved reluctant to allow the sale of the cattle. The defendants sold some of the cattle, forwarding the proceeds to James, though in respect of at least some of the cattle, the cheques for the proceeds of sale were returned uncashed to the defendants. Further tensions arose when the second defendant removed machinery from the land, while disposing of other items of machinery on the land. When the plaintiff issued a plenary summons in this case, Patrick Keating reacted by going to the plaintiff's home, throwing a battery through the window in his door and a spare wheel through another window. While Patrick was charged in respect of the event, he received the benefit of the Probation Act, subsequently admitting his regret in respect of the incident.

The judge first considered the issue of alleged undervalue in respect of the land. Evidence was offered on behalf of the plaintiff, suggesting that in 1999 the land (even with the plaintiff's right of residence being preserved) was worth as much as £240,000 on the open market. This valuation included a "hope value" that planning permission might be obtained for residential development on the land.

This valuation (of what was, after all, agricultural land) was, the judge asserted, "grossly exaggerated" and "totally divorced from the reality which prevailed in 1999". In particular, she rejected the contention that "any prospective purchaser would factor any development value into the price of the land". While she found it impossible to determine what the land with vacant possession would have earned on the open market, she concluded that the plaintiff could possibly have secured more than £45,000 for the land. In this regard, however, she noted that the 1999 transaction secured certain benefits to the plaintiff, not least the right to remain in his home. It also guaranteed him access to the early retirement scheme. Both of these benefits would not have been guaranteed had he sold the land on the open market.

The judge also dismissed the plaintiff's allegations of duress and undue influence as unfounded. Notably, the plaintiff was seeking to establish actual as opposed to presumed undue influence in this case. On the facts, Laffoy J. ruled that up until March 1999, the point where the plaintiff had sought to instigate the sale, there had been no undue influence or duress brought to bear by either Mr Keating Senior, the plaintiff's cousin, or by his son Patrick, the second defendant, with a view to forcing the sale. In particular, based on the evidence, she discounted allegations that Messrs Keating Snr and Jnr prior to March 1999 had bullied, intimidated and beaten James with a view to securing the transfer.

In fact the "true position", in the judge's estimation, was that *it was the plaintiff himself* who had sought to persuade his relatives to buy the land. Laffoy J. based this conclusion on "an overview of the evidence", noting James's concern to clear his debts with ACC as well as his interest in acquiring the early retirement pension. In short, he had in fact instigated the agreement for sale (cf. *Grealish v Murphy* [1946] I.R. 35 where the transferor's initiative in relation to the transfer of land precluded a finding of undue influence (though not a finding of improvidence)).

The failure of these claims did not, however, preclude the plaintiff from pursuing an alternative equitable remedy. The plaintiff had further alleged that the land transfer constituted an improvident transaction or unconscionable bargain on his part, such that it should be set aside. The test for improvidence is set out in Delany, *Equity and the Law of Trusts in Ireland*, 4th edn (Dublin: Thomson Round Hall, 2007), p.701:

> "A transaction may be set aside in equity where one party is at a serious disadvantage by reason of poverty, ignorance or some other factor such as old age, so that unfair advantage may be taken of that party. Equity will intervene particularly where a transfer of property is made for no consideration at all or at an undervalue and where the transferee acts without the benefit of independent legal advice."

As noted in *Grealish v Murphy* [1946] I.R. 35, "equity comes to the rescue whenever the parties to a contract have not met on equal terms." In such circumstances, the transferee must establish that the transferor has received adequate protection to defend his interests. Laffoy J. noted that the fact that the plaintiff had in fact been the prime mover in relation to the sale of the land did not preclude him from having the transaction set aside for improvidence. In *Grealish*, for instance, it was the plaintiff who had instigated the plan for the sale of his land, a fact that did not prevent the court from concluding that the resulting transaction was nonetheless improvident (though this factor did mean that he could not claim that he had entered into the contract as a result of undue influence).

Laffoy J. cites *Alec Lobb (Garages) v Total Oil (GB) Ltd* [1983] 1 W.L.R. 87 as establishing as a requirement for improvidence that, inter alia, "this weakness of the one party has been exploited by the other in some morally culpable manner". There must be some impropriety, the court observed, not only "in the terms of the transaction itself" but also "in the conduct of the stronger party". Notably, this proposition is at odds with the conclusion of Gilligan J. in *Prendergast v Joyce* [2009] IEHC 199 (discussed below under UNDUE INFLUENCE) in which he expressly discounted the requirement that the plaintiff must demonstrate wrongdoing on the part of the stronger party. This point is considered further in the context of that case.

The contract for the sale of land undeniably offered some benefits to the plaintiff. It allowed him to clear his debts to ACC and to avail of the early retirement scheme. The plaintiff had, prior to the conclusion of the contract, some understanding that this was the best option for him. He also had sufficient capacity to understand the requirements of the early retirement scheme, and to renegotiate downwards his liability to ACC. Nonetheless, Laffoy J. considered that the plaintiff did not entirely understand or appreciate that by selling his land and signing up to the early retirement scheme he would have to give up farming. In particular, he seemed conflicted and reluctant to abandon farming, as evidenced by his resistance to the defendants' moves to remove his cattle from the land. He was reluctant, once the contract was signed, to close the deal, and in particular to give up his livestock. In this regard, Laffoy J. considered it probable that he was "pressurised by the defendants to close after the 30th April, 1999 and his resistance to the pressure was weak because of his physical and psychological condition."

In looking to the issue of transactional undervalue, Laffoy J. observed that one could not look to the land transfer alone. That transaction had to be viewed in the context of the associated dealings with the cattle and with the quota. While the quota was valuable in its own right, the plaintiff had not received any consideration therefor. Certainly, the plaintiff had secured a right of residence and a regular pension on foot of the transfer. Laffoy J. was unable to determine definitively what would have been a reasonable price for the land, taking into account these benefits. Nonetheless, taking into account in the round the *entire benefit* gained by the defendants—including the land, the farm buildings, the quota, the cattle, and the plaintiff's house, subject to his right of residence for life—the judge was satisfied that the overall transaction was "improvident…oppressive and unfair".

Laffoy J. refused to accept that either the contract and land transfer included a transfer of the quota and the cattle attached to the quota. It was not normally the case, she observed, that the transfer of the quota rights would also serve to transfer the cattle attached to that quota. The quota was, in other words, separate from the cattle to which the quota related. The quota transfer, at any rate, had been forged. The judge doubted that 12 of the animals taken in March 1999 were the subject of any agreement or had been paid for, but even if there had been an agreement as to their sale, the second defendant "rode roughshod over the plaintiff in selecting and removing animals without the consent of the plaintiff."

In short, the entire dealings between the parties indicated that, from March 1999 onwards, the defendants had taken unfair advantage of the plaintiff in relation specifically to the quota and most notably the cattle. Laffoy J. had previously concluded that there was no evidence of bullying and pressure prior to March 1999, in particular in advance of the plaintiff's first instructions to his solicitor regarding the proposed sale. Nonetheless, the judge ruled that in the two months preceding the deed of transfer, it was probable that Patrick Keating had indeed bullied and intimidated the plaintiff.

Once he had contracted to sell the land, the plaintiff was, the judge ruled, at a serious disadvantage because of his impaired understanding of the full implications of these transactions. His poor physical condition contributed to this state of disadvantage. Once the contract was in place, the defendants exploited this situation of weakness to their advantage. The necessary protection from such exploitation was not, she added, available to him. In particular, the plaintiff's solicitor had not acted to secure the plaintiff's best interests, in that he had allowed the plaintiff to receive and spend almost half of the proceeds of sale before the transfer was completed (in particular, in discharging his debt to ACC). Once the contract was signed, the judge suggested, the solicitor's priority appeared to be to complete the sale, and to obtain vacant possession for the first defendant. In such circumstances, the focus of the solicitor was on completing the sale as quickly as possible, and not on offering protection to his client. As a result, the court felt that the plaintiff had not received independent legal advice. Citing Barron J. in *Carroll v Carroll* [1999] 4 I.R. 241 at 265, the judge concluded that the plaintiff had not received the benefit of independent legal advice in the matter.

Accordingly, the judge set aside the land transfer. There was, she added, no *laches* or affirmation in this case. James had not been aware of his right to have the contract set aside, or had not been in a position to set it aside, until he had consulted with his solicitors in December 2001. As such, he could not be said to have delayed unduly in seeking relief on foot of the alleged improvidence.

The judge ordered that the land transfer was to be set aside. As a result, the first defendant was entitled to the return of £40,000 or €50,790 paid in respect of the property (four of the remaining instalments for £1,000 each had been rejected and the final instalment had not been paid). With a view to achieving *restitutio in integrum* (i.e. restoring the parties to their pre-contractual position) the judge ordered that the plaintiff be registered as the full owner of the land. This was subject to the discharge of the charge for the £5,000 of the property price that had remained unpaid. An award of €39,527 was also conferred in respect of the benefits accrued to the defendant on foot of the transfer of the quota.

The plaintiff's claim for €190,000 for lost profits in respect of the running of the farm (with interest) was, however, dismissed as "wholly unrealistic and exaggerated". Given the plaintiff's age, his financial position prior to the contract, and his difficulties in managing the farm prior to 1999, the judge was satisfied that there was no basis for the claim that he had lost any profits as a result of the sale of his farm. Notably, no evidence had been offered as to the profitability of the farm pre-1999, more than likely because the farm was not in fact profitable. The plaintiff certainly would not have made profits in excess of what he had received under the early retirement scheme and old age pension combined. Thus, no damages were awarded for loss of profit.

The judge also dismissed as inflated a claim for €10,000 (plus interest of €7,000) in respect of four items of machinery which were destroyed or appropriated by the second defendant, ruling that a sum of €2,000 was more realistic. €12,000 was awarded in respect of 30 misappropriated cattle, taking into account the fact that, in the wake of the land transfer, the plaintiff had neglected the animals and that the second defendant had had to care for them. The judge declined, however, to award the €40,000 which the plaintiff had claimed for the restocking of his land.

Damages of €12,500 were also awarded in respect of the 2002 assault and trespass by Patrick Keating. Laffoy J. did not, however, accept that the plaintiff had established that he was suffering from post-traumatic stress disorder as a result of this incident or as a result of his treatment by the defendants. A report from a doctor suggesting the existence of PTSD post-dated the incident by seven years. It could not therefore be accepted as having been caused by the incident or by the defendants' earlier treatment of the plaintiff.

The judge did not consider, moreover, that it was appropriate to award aggravated or punitive damages against the second defendant, Patrick Keating. While the latter had not apologised directly to the plaintiff, he had acknowledged his wrong both in the course of this case and in criminal proceedings. The judge also pointed out, in support of her conclusion, that the plaintiff had, in the course of the proceedings, made unfounded allegations against Patrick relating to his behaviour pre-March 1999.

Whether this verdict will be to the plaintiff's ultimate benefit was, the judge concluded, questionable. He was now 72, and unlikely to be in a position to work the farm himself. The landscape of EU grants and supports had changed considerably in the intervening years, with the result that he may not be entitled to the single farm payment. The awards in the case may also affect his non-contributory old-age pension, while his return to farming may well affect his entitlement to early retirement payments. The judge added that, given the value of the land, and the costs involved therein, it may have been wiser to take the case at Circuit Court level, rather than escalating it to the High Court.

The decision is notable in several respects. It again illustrates, should further illustration be required, the need for vigilance and care in relation to transactions involving elderly and infirm transferors of land. Notably, in determining the improvidence of the transaction, the judge took a holistic view of the entire dealings between the parties. In particular, while the land transfer in itself may not have been at considerable undervalue per se, the transfer of the quota (by means of forgery and for no value) and the appropriation of 30 of the cattle brought the entire dealings between the parties within the realm of improvidence. The decision is also notable in that the plaintiff had initiated the sale himself, apparently free from any pressure from the defendants. It was instead the actions of the defendants after the sale had been proposed that amounted to exploitation of the plaintiff, most notably their actions in respect of the cattle and the quota. Whether the requirement of moral turpitude of the transferee as a prerequisite to improvidence will stand is an open question, given the opposing views of Gilligan J. in *Prendergast v Joyce* discussed below. Arguably this is not a requirement, although the removal of this requirement would hardly have changed the verdict against the defendants.

INCORPORATION OF TERMS

***Kastrup Trae-Aluvinduet A/S v Aluwood Concepts Ltd,* High Court, MacMenamin J., November 13, 2009; [2009] IEHC 577** This case relates to the enforcement of a Danish arbitration award made in April 2009. In particular, it examines the criteria for the incorporation by notice of an arbitration clause in a contract between businesses contracting at arm's length. The net point that arises is that an arbitration clause may be incorporated by sufficient notice of terms not themselves reproduced in full in the body of contractual correspondence, but contained elsewhere. In other words, terms and conditions may be incorporated "by reference" provided that sufficient notice is given that these terms form part of the contract. There is no requirement that the party to be bound by them must have read these terms and conditions, provided that the party has been given sufficient notice of their inclusion in the contract.

The applicant in this case, Kastrup, is a Danish company that manufactures and supplies doors and windows. For some years, the respondent purchased these products from the applicant on foot of individual contracts. In 2008 a dispute arose regarding unpaid invoices, the respondent citing defects in some of the products supplied as the reason for non-payment. When matters remained unresolved, the applicant notified the respondent of its intention to refer the matter to the Danish Court of Arbitration for the Building and Construction Industry. Despite repeated extensions to the time allowed for making an appearance before the Danish arbitrator, the respondent consistently dragged its heels, claiming that it could not afford representation before the arbitrator. While a last-minute defence was emailed to the Danish arbitrator the night before arbitration, the respondent chose not to be represented before the arbitrator.

The net question was whether the parties had in fact agreed that, if a dispute arose, the Danish Court of Arbitration would have jurisdiction to resolve the matter. While the applicant claimed that this was a term of the contract, Aluwood denied that it had agreed to such a term. Notably, at the very commencement of the parties' business dealings, the applicant had written to the respondent, expressly indicating that the basis for their relationship would be the Common Sales and Delivery Conditions of the Danish window producers' organisation. This statement was repeated when the first order was confirmed in writing some days later. These Common Sales and Delivery Conditions contained an arbitration clause requiring that, in cases of dispute, the Danish Court of Arbitration for the Building and Construction Industry would have jurisdiction to hear the dispute.

Aluwood claimed, in short, that the arbitrator did not have jurisdiction, as Aluwood had never agreed to the relevant arbitration clause. It asserted, in particular, that the contents of the Common Sales and Delivery Conditions containing the arbitration clause were never specifically drawn to its attention, and that therefore these conditions were not binding. The bedrock of its defence was that although the terms were referred to in the correspondence, the specific and detailed content of those terms and conditions was not specifically brought to Aluwood's attention. It claimed in particular that it had never received or read a copy of those conditions.

MacMenamin J. roundly rejected the respondent's claim that it was not bound by the arbitration clause. The judge first noted that Aluwood was not a "simple consumer" but rather a company engaged in business. Both parties were in a business where arbitration agreements were "prevalent if not universal". The incorporation of arbitration terms in contracts in the relevant trade was a "near universal practice", something that could hardly be regarded as a "bolt from the blue" by Aluwood.

The New York Convention on the Recognition and Enforcement of Foreign Arbitral Awards 1958 governs the recognition of foreign arbitration awards. The proceedings in this case were governed by the Arbitration Acts 1954–1998, since repealed by the Arbitration Act 2010. Under s.7 of the Arbitration Act 1980 an award made in pursuance of an arbitration agreement in a convention state was generally enforceable and binding in Ireland. It could, in particular, be enforced under s.41 of the Arbitration Act 1954. Section 9 of the Act of 1980 set out an exhaustive range of grounds upon which a person might resist enforcement of the foreign award, one of which grounds was that the "composition of the arbitral authority or the procedure adopted therein *[is not] in accordance with the agreement of the parties* or the law of the country where the arbitration took place…" (emphasis added).

Aluwood's key defence in this case was that it had never agreed to the arbitration clause by reference to which the arbitration had proceeded; in other words that the applicant's terms and conditions had not been incorporated into the parties' contract. Its basis for so claiming was that although the correspondence may have referred to these terms, it did not directly replicate or supply the terms. It instead referred to extraneous documents in which those terms were contained. As such Aluwood claimed that the content of the terms had not been sufficiently notified.

MacMenamin J. rejected this contention. He first noted that the decision as to whether the arbitrator had jurisdiction was a matter for the court rather than the arbitrator. In particular, the decision of the arbitrator that it did have authority under an agreement did not preclude the court from reaching an opposite conclusion.

The judge noted that in the initial correspondence from the applicant, the latter had referred to the Common Sales and Delivery Conditions of the Danish window producers' organisation (which in turn contained the arbitration clause) as governing the dealings between the parties. This reference appeared in the initial quotation and in the correspondence confirming the first order. Thus, "on the plain face of the correspondence, the common terms were incorporated into the contract". The relevant letters referred to the contract as being subject to the aforementioned Common Sales and Delivery Conditions, which included the arbitration clause. The respondent thus had been put on notice of the relevant conditions. The judge also placed particular emphasis on the fact that the respondent's objection to the arbitration clause came very late in the day, at the "eleventh minute of the eleventh hour".

In support, MacMenamin J. cited the decision of O'Hanlon J. in *Sweeney v Mulcahy* [1993] I.L.R.M. 289. In that case, the defendant had stated in correspondence that the conditions of engagement and scale of charges set out by the Royal Institute of Architects of Ireland (RIAI) would apply to a contract for the renovation of the plaintiff's home. Although the defendant had not sent the plaintiff a copy of the RIAI conditions, the latter was nonetheless bound by those terms. The defendant had expressly referred to these conditions as the terms upon which she was willing to contract, the plaintiff not having objected to such conditions. Had the plaintiff wished to review a copy of the terms it was open to him to ask for them, but he had not done so.

The fact that in the instant case, both companies were commercial entities was of particular note. In *Holfeld Plastics v ISAP Omv Group Spa* [1999] IEHC 24, Geoghegan J. noted that commercial companies should anticipate that, in the normal course of business, suppliers will attach terms to their sales. In *Holfeld* the defendant had referred, in its initial quotation, to the terms upon which it was willing to contract. In the circumstances, Geoghegan J. concluded that the plaintiff had been put on notice of the relevant clauses, whether or not he had in fact read them.

The test for determining whether there was actual agreement as to the terms was on the balance of probabilities. As noted by O'Neill J. in *Stryker Corporation v Sulzer Metco AG* [2006] IEHC 60, even where there is no proof of actual agreement, it is open to a court to infer agreement:

> "… where the circumstances are such as to demonstrate that in the commercial context in which the agreement exists, the existence of that consensus or agreement is in those circumstances a probability rather than otherwise".

(Though in *Stryker*, on the facts, there was not sufficient evidence of consensus regarding the relevant term.)

Where general conditions are expressly referred to on the face of a contract, even if their content lies elsewhere, a court is entitled to infer, on the balance of probabilities, that those conditions form part of the contract. Citing *Credit Suisse v Société Génerale d'Enterprises* [1997] ILPT 165, MacMenamin J. observed that "where the text of the contract contains an express reference to the relevant conditions, the fact that the other party does not have a copy of these is irrelevant." The question, according to the Court of Appeal in *Credit Suisse* (per Saville L.J.), was:

> "… whether the express reference in the written contract…amounts to a clear and precise demonstration that the clause conferring jurisdiction was the subject of consensus between the parties".

There was no requirement, the Court of Appeal added, that such terms would not be incorporated until a copy of the terms referred to in the contract were supplied to a defendant, still less read by him. Thus, a reference in the contract to a 1992 Master Agreement was sufficient to incorporate the terms of the Master Agreement into the contract.

Thus MacMenamin J. concluded, on the balance of probabilities, that the arbitration clause did form part of the contract between the parties, and had been appropriately incorporated by notice. MacMenamin J. also rejected the respondent's claim of unfair procedures on the part of the Court of Arbitration. The nub of the respondent's complaint was that the proceedings and the associated documentation were issued in Danish rather than English. The respondent had been given all necessary documentation to facilitate its defence. It could, if it wished, have translated the documentation but made no effort to do so. It had chosen not to defend itself in Denmark owing to the costs, though the judge considered that the expense would not have been inordinate. In short, the Court of Arbitration had done all that it could to safeguard the respondent's interests. The respondent's woes were entirely of its own making, having chosen "to bury its corporate head in the sand". Only "minimal steps" were required to protect its interests, steps that the respondent had failed to take.

The judge also rejected the contention that the Danish arbitrator had failed to take note of Aluwood's last minute objections and counterclaims, noting that in fact it had done so, but that they were—in the main—not proven. The fact that the applicant accepted two points of the counterclaim, lowering its own claim in response, shows that the respondent's counterclaims were in fact considered.

The central lesson in this case is simple: contractual terms may be incorporated if sufficient notice is given that the terms contained in a named document are to form part of the contract. This is the case even if the terms themselves are not directly replicated in the body of contractual correspondence provided that sufficient notice is given of their existence and of the fact that they form part of the contract. Thus, where a party to a contract gives sufficient notice of terms which it wishes to incorporate by reference, those terms are binding provided the other party has been given notice of this fact and has not objected to their incorporation. Once put on notice of these terms, a contractor is bound by them, even if it has not read them or received a copy thereof. The situation may possibly be different in the case of standard-form consumer contracts, where a more stringent interpretation may apply, but in business relations contracting parties would be well advised to familiarise themselves with the specific terms of documents "incorporated by reference".

INSURANCE CONTRACTS

See *Smith v Meade, Meade, FBD Insurance, Ireland and the Attorney General,* High Court, Peart J., February 5, 2000; [2009] IEHC 99 discussed above under EXCLUSION CLAUSES

INTENTION TO CREATE LEGAL RELATIONS

See the decision of Geoghegan J. in *Mary Roche v Thomas Roche,* Supreme Court, December 15, 2009; [2009] IESC 82 discussed below under INTERPRETATION OF CONTRACTS and in *McCabe Builders (Dublin) Limited v Sagamu Developments Ltd, Laragan Developments Ltd and Hanly Group Ltd,* Supreme Court, April 1, 2009; [2009] IESC 31 discussed above under FORMATION OF A CONTRACT

INTERPRETATION OF CONTRACTS

See also, *Ringsend Property Limited v Donatex Ltd and Bernard McNamara,* High Court, Kelly J., December 18, 2009; [2009] IEHC 568 discussed above under FRUSTRATION

Introduction The principles relating to the interpretation of contracts containing a rent review clause are considered in *Anthony Kidney & Ronan McNamee v Julian Charlton & Edward Charlton* [2009] M.R. 1, discussed below in Dr de Londras' chapter on Land Law, Landlord and Tenant Law and Conveyancing.

***Emo Oil Limited v Sun Alliance and London Insurance Company,* Supreme Court, Kearns J. (Denham and De Valera JJ. concurring), January 22, 2009; [2009] IESC 2** The plaintiff in this case, inter alia, imports and supplies oil products to businesses, including petrol stations. This case concerned the interpretation of an insurance contract entered into by the plaintiff and defendant. The contract specifically comprised a policy for credit insurance in respect of losses incurred owing to the "insolvency" (as defined by the contract) of one of the plaintiff's customers. The insurance policy indemnified the plaintiff against losses incurred should one of its buyers became insolvent (as defined by the policy) during the lifetime of the policy. Insolvency for the purpose of this contract was defined as meaning that one of a number of events had occurred in respect of one of the plaintiff's buyers, including where "[a] resolution has been passed for the voluntary winding up or an order for winding up has been made by the Court…[under the relevant legislation]". Notably, the policy in question commenced in May 1997 and was renewed on various occasions, the term expiring on August 31, 2002.

On August 29, 2002 Emo Oil submitted a petition to wind up one of its buyers, Dev Oil & Gas Ltd. While the petition was presented to the court just two days before the credit insurance policy was due to expire, the court order to wind up the company was not made until September 11, 2002, 11 days after the policy had expired. As a result of Dev Oil's insolvency, Emo Oil claimed it had lost approximately €648,000, which it sought to claim back from the defendant insurer.

The net question in this case was whether the insolvency of Dev Oil (as defined by the terms of the contract) "occurred" during the period of insurance ending August 31, 2002. The plaintiff argued that the effect of a winding up order was retrospective. It claimed that, under Irish law, once a court order for winding up was made, the company was deemed to have been wound up with effect from the date on which the petition for winding up had first been presented. This interpretation is supported by company law legislation, and in particular s.220(2) of the Companies Act 1963. The latter provision specifically deems that, except in certain cases, "the winding up of a company by the court shall be deemed to commence at the time of the presentation of the petition for the winding up". In other words, the Act endorses a principle of "relation back" whereby the order for the winding up of a company is statutorily deemed to take effect from the date on which the petition was first presented, notwithstanding the later court order. This had important implications for the plaintiff as, while the order for the winding up of Dev Oil had been made after the policy ended, the petition for winding up had been presented *before* the date of expiry.

In the High Court, Gilligan J. accepted this argument, ruling that the winding up of the company was deemed to have taken place, for the purpose of the contract of insurance, as of the date on which the petition for winding up was first made. The judge placed particular emphasis on the "relation back" principle contained in s.220(2), noting that under Irish law once a winding up order was made by a court, it was deemed to have commenced as of the date of presentation of the petition, which fell within the period of insurance.

On appeal to the Supreme Court, this verdict was reversed. The appeal court ruled that, as a matter of contractual interpretation, the policy of insurance clearly required that the actual court order for winding up had to have been made within the time period stipulated in the contract. On the proper construction of the contract, the principle of relation back did not apply in this specific context, the contract having expressly required that a court order for winding up be issued before the company would be deemed "insolvent" for the purpose of the contract.

Kearns J. (Denham and De Valera JJ. concurring) stressed first that this case turned on a matter of contractual rather than statutory interpretation. While accepting the application of the relation back principle in company law, Kearns J. noted that the issue at stake in this case was not the position in company law but rather the specific interpretation of the relevant insurance contract. The issue was whether *for the purposes of the contract* the insolvency was deemed to have taken place at the time a petition for winding up is presented or, in the alternative, when an order for winding up is actually made by the court.

In the course of delivering the Supreme Court verdict, Kearns J. reiterated some important general principles on the interpretation of contracts. In particular, he cited the decision in *UPM Kymmene Corp v BWG Limited,* unreported, High Court, Laffoy J., June 11, 1999 where Laffoy J. neatly summarises the correct approach as follows:

> "The court's task is to ascertain the intention of the parties, and the intention must be ascertained from the language they have used, considered in the light of the surrounding circumstances and the object of the contract. Moreover, in attempting to ascertain the presumed intention of the parties the court should adopt an objective, rather than subjective approach and should consider what would have been the intention of reasonable persons in the position of the parties."

Elaborating on these principles, Kearns J. cited the decision of Lord Hoffman in *ICS v West Bromwich BS* [1998] 1 W.L.R. 896 at 912–913 (adopted with approval in Ireland in *Analog Devices BV v Zurich Insurance Company* [2005] 1 I.R. 274). Lord Hoffman, in *ICS,* rehearsed the well-established principle that a court, in interpreting a contract, must look to the objective meaning of the contract, in other words what the "document would convey to a reasonable person having all the background knowledge which would reasonably have been available to the parties in the situation in which they were at the time of the contract". In short, a contract should be interpreted by reference to what a reasonable person would take it to mean, rather than what the contracting parties subjectively thought it meant. The private understandings of the parties as to the meaning of their contract are effectively irrelevant in this context.

Nonetheless the court, Lord Hoffman continued, must also have regard to the background or the "matrix of fact" against which the contract was made. The contract should be interpreted not in a vacuum but in the light of the context and business scenario in which it was made. This may mean that words that, in their ordinary and natural sense, convey a particular meaning, may bear a different interpretation when viewed against the background to the contract. (See also the comments of Lord Wilberforce in *Reardon Smith Line Limited v Hansen-Tangen* [1976] 3 All E.R. 570 at 574–575.) In seeking to construe the contract, the court should have full regard to the situation of the parties, investing in the hypothetical reasonable person full knowledge and understanding of the background and surrounding context in which the contract is forged.

Turning to the case before the Supreme Court, the plaintiff had claimed that should there be any ambiguity in the meaning of the relevant clause, the clause should be read *contra proferentem*, giving the benefit of any doubt to the plaintiff. Counsel for the plaintiff, in particular, suggested that the existence of the relation back principle in company law had fostered an ambiguity in the interpretation of the contract that should, he submitted, be resolved in his client's favour.

In his response, Kearns J. observed that the *contra proferentem* rule may only be deployed where an ambiguity already exists. It should be used, he asserted, only to resolve a genuine ambiguity, and not to foster such ambiguity where the meaning of a contract was perfectly clear. In support of this proposition, Kearns J. cited Clarke's *Law of Insurance Contracts*, 5th edn (London: Informa Publishing, 2006). Clarke asserts that the *contra proferentem* rule should only be employed "for the purpose of removing a doubt, not for the purpose of creating a doubt or magnifying an ambiguity, where the circumstances of the case raise no real difficulty." Clarke suggests that the *contra proferentem* rule is often abused so as to sow doubt where contracts are in fact perfectly clear in their meaning.

Kearns J. had no doubt that there was, in this case, "no ambiguity in the relevant clause of the insurance contract". The terms of the agreement clearly indicated as alternative prerequisites that either "a resolution has been passed for the voluntary winding up" or that court has *made* an order for the winding up of the company. Here, there was "no ambiguity of language". The terms of the contract require that "an order for winding up has been made by the court". Had the parties wished to do so, they could have stipulated that the term "insolvency" would include a situation where "a winding up has commenced". This formula would have allowed the insolvency to date from the submission of the petition, the deemed statutory beginning of the winding up. Instead, the parties had expressly agreed as one of the alternative prerequisites the making of a court order for winding up, a formula that clearly necessitated the making of a court order and not simply the presentation of a petition.

It is important to note that the judge readily accepted, as a matter of company law, the application of the relation back principle in the context of company law. As a matter of company law it was well established, he accepted, that once an order for winding up is made in respect of a company, it is deemed to take legal effect from the date on which the petition for winding up was first presented. The purpose of this rule was to protect creditors and to ensure the validity of any actions of a provisional creditor taken pending the court order, considerations that did not arise in relation to the specific insurance contract being considered in this case.

The issue in the instant case, however, was not the correct interpretation of the Companies Acts but, rather, the proper construction of a contract. The contract having expressly referred to an order being made by the court for winding up, the contract could not be interpreted as having incorporated the "relation back" principle. In support of this conclusion, Kearns J. relied on two analogous UK cases, *Mettoy Pension Trustees v Evans* [1990] 1 W.L.R. 1587 and *Re Walter Jacob and Co Ltd* [1993] BCC 512, in each of which cases the courts concluded that, on a specific interpretation of the relevant provisions, the relation back principle did not apply.

In support of this conclusion, Kearns J. noted the "significant problems" that would arise in practice should the date on which the insolvency commenced be deemed to be the date on which the petition was submitted rather than the date on which the court order was granted. In particular, such a conclusion would, he asserted, "flout business common sense, notably in circumstances where the presentation of a winding up petition might not result in any winding up order being made." He noted, in particular, that the interpretation favoured by the plaintiff would potentially lead to "open-ended exposure" being placed on the insurance company where, for instance, there was a delay in making the order, or where the order was appealed to a higher court. The insurer would thus potentially be exposed to liability for a period far beyond the date on which the policy expired.

The decision of Kearns J. raises a number of important points. First, the Supreme Court decision underlines the distinction between statutory interpretation and contractual interpretation. In particular, a term used in a generally applicable statute may not necessarily bear the same meaning when employed by the specific parties to a contract. Secondly, the judgment highlights the limitations of the *contra proferentem* rule, and its inapplicability in cases where the terms of a contract are unambiguous. The judgment also illustrates implicitly the fact that a court, in interpreting a contract, may have regard to the business efficacy of the particular interpretation that is adopted, Kearns J. having noted the difficulties that would arise had the interpretation favoured by the High Court been upheld. It is important finally to note that the decision does not qualify the application of the relation back principle in the context of company law. It simply confirms that, on the specific interpretation of this particular contract, the date of insolvency must be taken to be the date on which the court order for winding up was granted, a verdict that is confined to the particular construction of the relevant contract. The decision nonetheless highlights the importance of drafting with particular care the provisions of insurance contracts relating to insolvency so as to ensure that there is clarity as to whether the relation back principle does or does not apply.

***Mary Roche v Thomas Roche,* Supreme Court, December 15, 2009; [2009] IESC 82** The Supreme Court verdict in *Roche,* while primarily turning on the definition of the term "unborn" in Art.40.3.3 of the Constitution of Ireland, addresses in part some important points in relation to contractual interpretation and the implication of implied terms. The case arises on appeal from the decision in *MR v TR*, High Court, McGovern J., July 18, 2006; [2006] IEHC 221, discussed in *Annual Review of Irish Law 2006,* pp.270–272.

The plaintiff and first defendant in this case were respectively a wife and her husband. The couple already had a son, but as a result of an ovarian cyst it subsequently proved difficult for the wife to conceive again by natural means. Wishing to have another child, the couple undertook a course of IVF treatment. For this purpose, six eggs were extracted from the wife's ovaries and fertilised outside the womb. Three of the resulting embryos were then placed in the plaintiff's womb, while the remaining three were frozen with the apparent intention that they would be used if the first implantation did not succeed. As egg extraction is painful, and the prospect of impregnation on the first implantation is not assured, the clinic involved generally preferred to keep some embryos in reserve should the first implantation not succeed.

Prior to implantation, the husband signed a consent form, acknowledging that he was the husband of the plaintiff, that the sperm used for fertilisation of her eggs was his, and that he consented to the "course of treatment" proposed for his wife, namely the fertilisation of the eggs with his sperm to create the required embryos. Separately, the wife signed forms consenting to the extraction of her eggs, the mixing thereof with her husband's sperm and the implantation of three of the resulting embryos in her womb. Following the implantation, the wife became pregnant and had a daughter, the couple's second child.

Unfortunately, the couple subsequently separated. Some time after the separation, the wife sought to have the three remaining frozen embryos implanted in her womb with a view to having a third child. She claimed that, at the time when the original three embryos were implanted, her husband had consented, either expressly or implicitly, to such a further course of action. The husband objected, claiming that he had never agreed to the implantation of the additional embryos in such circumstances as these, where the parties were now separated and where the first implantation had been successful. He further asserted that, if the implantation were permitted, it would force him to become a parent against his will. Absent the husband's consent, the clinic involved refused to facilitate the implantation. This gave rise to two distinct questions:

- By signing the original consent form, had the husband agreed to the implantation of the remaining embryos for the purpose of allowing his estranged wife to have another child?
- If not, and having regard to the terms of the Constitution guaranteeing the right to life of the unborn, what was to happen to the embryos? The plaintiff claimed, in particular, that the embryos had a right to life and a right to a family life and, thus, that the destruction of the embryos would be unlawful.

On the extent and nature of the husband's consent, McGovern J. in the High Court concluded that the husband had not consented to a second implantation. There was essentially no agreement on his part as to the fate of the remaining embryos. In particular, there was no agreement between the parties as to what would occur should the parties separate or divorce. Nor was it possible, McGovern J. added, either as a matter of fact or of law, to imply a term as to the implantation of the remaining embryos. There was nothing in the parties' conduct or in the relevant consents to support the implication of terms relating to the implantation of the remaining embryos. At most the parties had agreed to freeze the remaining embryos and had accepted that they would remain responsible for them on an ongoing basis. The parties could not, the High Court concluded, be taken implicitly to have agreed that the frozen embryos could be used in circumstances where a child had already been born as a result of the first implantation, and where the couple had subsequently separated. Nor was there any aspect in the nature of the contracts agreed to suggest that such a conclusion was legally necessitated. In subsequent proceedings McGovern J. also concluded that the frozen embryos did not fall within the definition of "the unborn" in Art.40.3.3 of the Constitution of Ireland, and were thus not entitled to constitutional protection by virtue of that provision.

The Supreme Court agreed on both counts. While the preponderance of the judgments are dedicated to the meaning of the term "the unborn" in Art.40.3.3, the court also unanimously affirmed McGovern J.'s conclusions on the issue of contractual interpretation. Murray C.J. made only brief reference to the contractual issue, agreeing that the wife had:

> "... not established that there was any contractual arrangement between these parties obliging the husband to consent to the implantation of the frozen embryos nor was there otherwise an implied consent to do so".

Fennelly J. also agreed that the husband was not bound either in contract or "by the application of equitable principles" to allow the implantation.

Murray C.J. further agreed that in the specific circumstances of the case, the husband could not be estopped from opposing further implantation. Nonetheless, he added that the situation might possibly be different where a woman who had no children ("though not necessarily just in such cases") wished to have previously frozen embryos implanted, if this offered her the only prospect of pregnancy. In such cases, he suggests (though the point is clearly speculative and thus obiter) that the implantation might possibly take place notwithstanding the absence of consent of the man involved, if he had consented to the creation and freezing of the embryos. (In doing so, Murray C.J. indicated agreement with a similar point made by Denham J., though the latter made a somewhat narrower point relating to the *withdrawal* of the man's previous consent to implantation rather than its initial absence.)

Hardiman J. also made a relatively succinct contribution in relation to the contractual issue, agreeing again with the decision of the High Court. He noted, in particular, that the parties had "simply never discussed" the fate of the frozen embryos should the parties subsequently separate or should either of them die. There was no express agreement in relation to the matter, nor could such agreement be implied either as a matter of presumed intention or as a clause required by law.

By contrast with the other contributions, the verdicts of Denham and Geoghegan JJ. deal at some length with the matter of contractual obligation. Denham J. first noted that the wife had signed a form consenting to the extraction of her eggs, and the mixing of those eggs with her husband's sperm.

This was, she concluded, a consent form that addressed the relationship between the wife and the doctors only. It did not, in particular, establish any agreement between the spouses:

> "It is not a contract between the plaintiff and the husband. There is no question of an offer or acceptance or consideration, or an intention to create a legal contract, leading to an agreement between the plaintiff and her husband."

On the reverse of this form was another consent form, by virtue of which the husband had agreed to the course of treatment envisaged for his wife, acknowledging that he would become the legal father of any resulting child. Again, Denham J. observed that this consent addressed only the relationship between the doctors and the husband, and did not have the effect of creating a contract between the spouses.

The third consent form, by which the couple agreed to the freezing of the remaining embryos, was again, Denham J. observed, not a contract between the spouses but rather a consent form permitting a particular course of action by the clinic, namely the freezing of the embryos. It did not, she added, give rise to any agreement between the spouses. In fact, as Denham J. observed:

> "None of the documents are contracts creating or evidencing an agreement between the plaintiff and her husband expressing consent to the implantation of these three surplus embryos in the plaintiff's uterus … [T]he fact that the husband consented to the treatment and to the freezing does not establish a consent so as to enable the plaintiff to avail of the surplus frozen embryos for implantation."

The husband's consent to the IVF treatment and to the freezing of embryos, she concluded, was not an agreement permitting the subsequent implantation of the surplus embryos.

Nor had there been implied agreement. In support, Denham J. refers to two conversations between the parties, post-separation, where the wife raised the question as to what would happen to the frozen embryos. The evidence of the wife was to the effect that the husband had first suggested that they be destroyed, and subsequently that they be donated. This supported, in the judge's view, the conclusion that the husband's agreement could not be implied from the facts, as he had clearly set his mind against their implantation. (With respect, it might be counter-argued that these conversations took place after the couple had separated. They may not thus have afforded good evidence as to the parties' state of mind at the time of the original IVF treatment.)

Counsel for the plaintiff had further alleged that, even if the husband had not expressly consented or impliedly agreed to the further implantation, the whole chain of events leading to the creation of the surplus embryos (to which the husband had knowingly consented) precluded him by means of estoppel from objecting to their implantation. This was not, however, Denham J. noted, a case in which the husband had agreed to the implantation of the reserve embryos and then changed his mind. There had never been any agreement as to their fate, other than the consent to freezing the three additional embryos. This was not, therefore, a case where the husband could be prevented from reneging on a representation made, as he never made any representation or promise as to the possibility of implantation of the remaining embryos. Thus, no estoppel arose in this case.

While reiterating that the husband had not agreed to the use of the surplus embryos, Denham J. observed that even if he had previously agreed to their implantation, this did not mean that he could not subsequently and validly change his mind and withdraw his consent. In such a case, the court would have to consider all the facts carefully. One relevant factor in considering the effect of the withdrawal of consent would be if the wife had no children and no alternative means of becoming pregnant. In this case, however, the wife already had two children. The parties, moreover, were separated and the husband did not want any more children with the plaintiff. He would be forced, if her contentions were accepted, to become a father against his will. Just as the Constitution guarantees the right to procreate (see *Murray v Ireland* [1991] 1 I.L.R.M. 465), there is also "an equal and opposite right not to procreate". While the plaintiff did have a right to procreate, her estranged husband's objections constituted a proportional interference in this right.

Geoghegan J. also concluded that there was no enforceable contract permitting the wife to use the embryos against her estranged husband's wishes. As such, the judge did not have to consider whether such an agreement would have been enforceable, though the preponderance of US case law, he added, suggests that the matter of what should happen to spare embryos is generally left to the parties to determine by agreement (subject, in some jurisdictions, to a right to change one's mind).

Geoghegan J. noted in particular (though for information only and not with a view to propounding "any value judgment" on the matter) that if the wife succeeded in requiring implantation she would have considered any resulting child as the child of her estranged husband. The potential consequences for the husband were profound. Against his will, he would be compelled to become a parent again, "with all the financial and other responsibilities that fatherhood involves". Given that three embryos would have been implanted, the prospect of multiple births was also possible. While there was no statutory framework regulating IVF treatment and the treatment of frozen embryos, the judge had regard to the Guidelines of the Medical Council and the Report of the Commission on Assisted Human Reproduction. While noting the respect shown in these documents for the surplus embryos, nowhere in these guidelines, he observed, was there any intimation that a person could be forced to become a parent without their consent.

Turning to the contractual position of the parties, Geoghegan J. agreed that there was no evidence of express or implied agreement on the part of the husband to a further implantation. Indeed, the judge considered that McGovern J. could not have concluded otherwise, given the evidence before him. The husband had consented, if at all, only to the implantation of the first three embryos. (One might argue that the husband technically had only consented to the creation of those embryos. He had not expressly agreed in any of the documents to the implantation of the first set of embryos, though he had agreed to the "course of treatment" for his wife, and that he would become the legal father of any resulting child, all of which may necessarily be said to have presupposed the implantation of the first three embryos. At any rate, the husband did not object to the implantation of the first three embryos.)

While there may have been an understanding that the surplus embryos were frozen in case the first implantation did not succeed, there was certainly "no prior agreement" as to their fate:

> "At most, there would have been an understanding that the question of using the frozen embryos in the event of a failure following the first implantation would be considered or indeed that it might be considered for the purpose of producing a second child. Even that is doubtful."

Yet even if there was such an understanding, Geoghegan J. concluded that it would never "have been intended to give rise to a legally binding contract". In so concluding Geoghegan J. considered the enforceability of agreements between husbands and wives, invoking the presumption that arrangements made between spouses ordinarily do not presuppose an intention to create legal relations. For a contract to be enforceable, there must, inter alia, be an intention to create legal relations. In business transactions, this intention ordinarily is easily inferred, though it may be displaced by express evidence of the parties' agreement to be bound only as a matter of honour and not as a matter of law (*Rose and Frank Co v JR Crompton and Bros* [1925] A.C. 445). By contrast, it is generally presumed that agreements made between close family members are not intended to give rise to legal relations (*Balfour v Balfour* [1919] 2 K.B. 571, *Jones v Padvatton* [1969] 1 W.L.R. 328). While this presumption may be displaced (most notably where the parties are separated or at loggerheads), the general assumption is a fair one.

Given this stance, in Geoghegan J.'s view, "in a domestic agreement between husband and wife … it would be rare that even express terms would be held to constitute a legally binding agreement". The prospect that implied terms would give rise to such a legally binding contract was, the judge continued, even less plausible.

In this case, there was, the judge concluded, no evidence that the parties intended to create legal relations inter se. There was, moreover, no evidence to the effect that they had intended, between themselves, to agree the fate of the surplus embryos. In particular, the consent forms that they signed indicated their consent to the actions of the clinic and could not "be construed as contracts". (One might say that these formed, at best, a contract with the clinic and did not constitute a spousal agreement.)

This last point begs the question whether any spousal agreement would be enforceable, though the presumption against an intention to create legal relations in domestic situations may of course be rebutted on the facts by clear evidence that the spouses intended their agreement to be legally enforceable.

The case in its entirety emphasises above all the importance of legislating to regulate the complex and sensitive area of assisted human reproduction. Although the judgments offer some very valuable insights, the need for legislative clarification of the law relating to assisted human reproduction remains pressing.

PRIVITY OF CONTRACT

***Bowen Construction Ltd v Kelcar Developments Ltd,* High Court, Ryan J., October 16, 2009; [2009] IEHC 467** The net question in this case concerns the operation of the doctrine of privity of contract and the exceptions thereto. Essentially, the issue is whether the defendant could seek to invoke the rights of third parties to sue for defects allegedly arising as a result of the plaintiff's work.

The case concerned the development of a Co. Cork golf resort which boasted a golf course, a hotel and clubhouse and 56 cottages. While the course was owned and operated by the defendant, Kelcar Developments Ltd, the various buildings thereon had been transferred to a variety of other companies and individuals, some though not all of which were associated with Kelcar. The resort as a whole was operated by BGR Ltd (a subsidiary of Kelcar), while the hotel and clubhouse belonged to private investors. Approximately two-thirds of the cottages belong to the shareholders of Kelcar, the remainder having been sold. Thus, while Kelcar owned and operated the golf course, most of the buildings on the resort had been transferred to third parties, albeit in many cases to companies and individuals that were closely associated with the defendant company.

Bowen Construction had constructed the buildings in question, under a contract entered into with Kelcar Ltd. The agreement between the parties required Bowen to execute collateral warranties conferring on those to whom the buildings were transferred the right to sue for any defects in the work performed by Bowen. In the case of the owners of the clubhouse and hotel, this had occurred. While the warranties in favour of the cottage owners had not been executed, it was accepted that Bowen was willing to issue such warranties, if called upon to do so.

Kelcar alleged that the building work was defective, resulting in losses being sustained by the owners of the various buildings on the resort. In particular, it was alleged that as a result of the defects, the resort would have to be closed for some time to rectify the resulting problems. For its part, Bowen disputed this claim and asserted further that, under the terms of the contract, it was owed money by Kelcar. An arbitrator was appointed to adjudicate between the parties.

In the course of the arbitration, Kelcar argued that it was entitled to set off against monies allegedly owed by it to Bowen, damages in respect of the alleged defects and consequential losses. Against this, Bowen argued that Kelcar was not entitled to claim for losses that had been sustained by parties other than the defendant itself. The crux of Bowen's defence was that Kelcar was not the owner of the properties and therefore had no standing to seek damages in respect of the alleged defects, as it was the third parties, and not Kelcar, that had suffered the losses. While Kelcar may have been closely associated with many of the affected parties, as a separate legal person it did not own any of the relevant buildings, nor did it run the resort.

Pursuant to s.35 of the Arbitration Act 1954 (since repealed and replaced by the Arbitration Act 2010), the arbitrator referred a question of law to the court. The net question was whether Kelcar was precluded from relying on the alleged losses of third parties with a view to setting these losses off against it alleged liability towards Bowen.

By virtue of the doctrine of privity of contract, only a party to a contract may sue or be sued under the relevant contract. Third parties may not generally rely on a contract to which they were not privy. A related point is that a person cannot seek a remedy in respect of losses sustained by a third party (in other words, one cannot invoke a *jus tertii*, claiming relief for a loss that is incurred not by the litigant but by another person). By rights, Kelcar was seeking compensation not for its own losses but for those sustained by other parties—associated companies, certainly, but nonetheless entities that in law were separate and distinct from the defendant.

The judge first dismissed the contention that the contract itself allowed for a claim in respect of the specific losses sustained by third parties. Clause 21A of the contract allowed Kelcar to claim from Bowen "in respect of any loss, damage or injury to personal property that arises out of or in the course of or by reason of the works" owing to Bowen's negligence or fault. Ryan J. concluded, however, that this entitlement applied only while the works were ongoing and expired once there was "practical completion" of the buildings. In particular, the clause itself excluded liability in respect of damage caused to the buildings that were the subject of the works. In other words, this clause applied only for the duration of the building works, and then only in respect of property other than the buildings which Bowen was constructing.

While accepting as a general proposition that "a claimant cannot recover more than the amount required to compensate him for *his own and not another's* loss" (emphasis added), Ryan J. nonetheless acknowledged that this rule may

in specific cases give rise to injustice. In particular, it may create a "legal black hole" in cases where there is a clear breach of contract if a third party to a contract has no remedy in respect of a loss sustained following a breach of that contract.

Ryan J. referred to UK jurisprudence establishing an exception to the normal privity rules where such a "legal black hole" would otherwise arise. This exception allows a contractor to sue in respect of losses sustained by third parties, provided there is no alternative remedy available to those third parties. This exception was first established in *Dunlop v Lambert* (1839) 6 Cl & F 600, in the specific context of the carriage of goods, and extended to building contracts in *Linden Gardens Trust v Lenesta Sludge Disposal Ltd* [1994] 1 A.C. 85.

In *Linden Gardens Trust*, the House of Lords accepted the proposition that a party to a building contract, A, could sue a building contractor, B, for losses that were sustained on a building site which was subsequently transferred to a third party to the contract, C. The law lords so ruled on two alternative grounds. Lord Griffiths propounded the broader of the two grounds. He suggested that in a building contract for work, labour and materials, A was entitled in its own right to the performance of the contract. It thus could sue for substantial damages with a view to claiming "the benefit of the bargain which the defendant [B] had promised but failed to deliver". In other words, A was entitled in its own right to have the contract performed as agreed. This was subject to a requirement that A use the damages to remedy the defect (though this requirement has been doubted in subsequent cases), but otherwise A was entitled to performance of the contract as anticipated by the parties' agreement.

A narrower proposition emanated from the majority of the law lords, who based their verdict on the decision in *"The Albazero": Albacruz (Cargo Owners) v Albazero (Owners)* [1977] A.C. 774. They ruled that A could seek a remedy where it was known that third parties were likely to acquire and occupy the property, such that the contractors foresaw or anticipated that those third parties were likely to suffer loss as a result of any defects in the works. (Later case law suggests that this principle also applies where the land on which construction is carried out already belongs to the third party.) In such a case, the contract would be regarded as having been entered into for the benefit of those third parties who acquired or had an interest in the property and would thus be prejudiced by any damage to the property. As Lord Browne-Wilkinson observed in *Linden Gardens Trust*, A would be afforded a remedy "where no other would be available to a person sustaining loss which under a rational legal system ought to be compensated by the person who has caused it". The promisee would thus be able to "enforce the contractual rights for the benefit of those who suffered from defective performance" (although, as *Dunlop v Lambert* establishes, the promisee may (depending on the basis for the award of damages) be "accountable to the true owner for the proceeds of his judgment").

To this principle one must add an important caveat, namely that the third party itself had, in Chitty's words "not acquired any rights under the building contract and it was foreseeable…that he would not do so." In *Alfred McAlpine Construction Ltd v Panatown Limited* [2001] A.C. 518, the House of Lords confirmed that the exception adopted in *Linden Gardens Trust* only applied where it was necessary to avoid a "legal black hole", that is, to prevent the builder, B, from getting off "scot-free" in respect of defects arising from its negligence or fault. In *Panatown*, a building contract was entered into between A and a builder, B, in respect of a site which, for tax avoidance purposes, was owned by C. Notably, a separate contract was concluded between B and C whereby B accepted a duty of care towards C in respect of the building works. Because C, the owner of the site, had thereby acquired "an independent contractual right against the contractor", the exception applied in *Linden Gardens Trust* was not required here. In short, as a result of the separate legal commitment to C, there was no risk of the legal black hole that the House of Lords had so proficiently shored up in the earlier case.

Thus, Ryan J. concluded that a party to a contract could not seek to claim substantial damages for losses sustained by third parties "where those other parties *enjoy their own legal rights* to claim in respect of losses that they may have sustained" (my emphasis). In short, there was no legal black hole in the instant case. Under the terms of the parties' agreement, Bowen had entered into separate warranties with the owners of the clubhouse and hotel. It was required, moreover, separately to indemnify the owners of the cottages, a commitment that Bowen did not dispute. Under such warranties, the third parties would be entitled to a remedy in respect of any losses sustained. In other words, the third parties in this case had separate rights that they could themselves enforce, such that it was not necessary to cede to Kelcar's claim in order to do justice in the matter.

The judge also rejected Kelcar's attempt to rely on the broader ground proposed by Lord Griffiths in *Linden Gardens Trust,* namely that Kelcar had "…a right to have the contract performed according to its terms… despite not being the owner of the building at the time of the claim, provided it is clear that [it] actually intends to carry out the repairs." While Ryan J. was content to follow English law as it had developed, the authorities established that the exception to the privity rule propounded in *Linden Gardens Trust* did not apply if the third party had available to it an independent remedy in respect of the wrong. In short, "where the party suffering the loss has a right of action against the person in breach, the exception does not apply." If this caveat were not to be employed, that is, if the exception was not necessary in the case "in order to avoid injustice", the wrongdoer could potentially be found liable on the double, to both the original contractor and to the third party or parties. If Kelcar were to succeed in its own right, there would nonetheless be nothing to stop the third parties from also suing Bowen.

As such, the judge concluded that the exception to the privity rule did not

apply, and Kelcar would thus not be entitled to set off damages for loss against what it owed to Bowen. In so ruling, Ryan J. added that "a party is best left to make its own case for loss or damage and can be disadvantaged by having another make that case on its behalf."

The decision of Ryan J. is arguably authority for the proposition that in an appropriate case the Irish courts would be entitled to follow *Linden Gardens Trusts* so as to offer a remedy to a contracting party in a case where third parties would not have a remedy, thus avoiding a legal black hole that would effectively free the offending party from liability. This remedy would be of particular benefit in cases where work is done on foot of a contract with A, but where the work is carried out by B on property belonging to or subsequently transferred to a third party, C, in a case where B has no contractual obligation towards C. The narrower ground requires that both parties knew that the land was owned by a third party, or foresaw that a third party was likely to acquire the land, such that it was foreseeable that any defects in the building work were likely to result in the third party suffering losses. If accepted, this would represent a very significant exception to the rigours of the privity doctrine, though one that will only apply where the third party itself does not have a separate remedy available to it.

RESCISSION

***Marlan Homes Ltd v Walsh and Wedick,* High Court, Clarke J., December 21, 2009; [2009] IEHC 576** This case concerned a proposed development of lands in Dublin and two inter-related agreements concerning such developments. The defendants, Mr Walsh and Mr Wedick, owned two parcels of the relevant land. The third parcel of land belonged to Dublin City Council. The case turns on the proper construction of a contract, and whether it required the defendants to procure the consent of the city council to a charge over the defendants' interest in the council's land made for the purpose of securing lending to the plaintiff. It also deals with the operation of the equitable remedy of rescission, some interesting and topical points being made on the impact of an intervening diminution in the value of assets.

Under a November 2006 agreement with the defendants, Marlan Homes agreed to build a residential development on two parcels of land belonging to the defendants and a third parcel that was owned by the council. The agreement granted Marlan an exclusive building licence, permitting it to enter upon the lands with a view to carrying out construction thereon. The agreement also required that the lands be transferred either to Marlan or to the purchasers of the homes built on the land once they had been constructed. Under this agreement, Marlan paid the defendants €4.9 million. In substance, the agreement was to transfer the lands to Marlan (or to its nominees) once the development had been completed.

Under a separate agreement with Dublin City Council, made in December 2006, the defendants obtained permission from the council to develop, together with the defendants' own land, an adjoining property belonging to the council. This was to occur in line with planning permission already obtained by the defendants in respect of the lands. Subject to conditions precedent that the development would be completed "to wall-plate level" and to a satisfactory standard, the council agreed to confer on the defendants a 999-year lease in respect of the council lands. The agreement stipulated, however, that the benefit of the agreement could not be transferred to a third party except by way of a mortgage/charge in favour of a financial institution for the purpose of securing a loan made to the defendants (and to them alone) to fund the development. The agreement stipulated a strict 18-month time limit for completion of the development.

Under the November agreement, the defendants had agreed that they would allow their interest in the lands to be charged for the purpose of securing any loan sought by Marlan in order to fund Marlan's development of the lands. This included a commitment in respect of the defendants' interest in the Dublin City Council lands. In an earlier decision in the same dispute, *Marlan v Walsh and Wedick* [2009] IEHC 135, Clarke J. ruled the defendants were therefore "obliged to enable their interest in the Dublin City Council lands…to be the subject of security in favour of Marlan's lenders". In other words the defendants would be obliged to execute a mortgage/charge not only in relation to their own lands but also in respect of their interest in the council's property.

In November 2007, Marlan approached Bank of Scotland (Ireland) with a view to obtaining funding for the development. The bank offered a loan on the condition that the defendants execute a third party charge over the lands—including that portion owned by the council—in favour of the bank. The loan would be limited in recourse to the subject lands. The bank further stipulated that it would require the consent of the city council to the charge and to the assignment of the benefit of the December agreement to the plaintiff. Despite efforts to secure this consent, it proved impossible to obtain the agreement of the council.

The question first arose as to whether the defendants were required, under the November agreement, to deliver or procure the consent of Dublin City Council to the creation of a security over the council's lands in favour of Marlan's lender. While the court ruled that the agreement did not require the defendants to offer any guarantee or indemnity in respect of Marlan's liabilities, it nonetheless concluded that the defendants had committed themselves in substance to delivering the council's consent to any mortgage or charge over the council's lands made with a view to securing a loan issued to Marlan.

It is worth noting the interest that the defendants themselves had over the council's land. Effectively, the December agreement with the council constituted an agreement to grant a lease, subject to certain conditions. The defendants had a right thereunder to enter upon and develop the council lands, and a conditional right to have the lands transferred to them, provided development had reached a particular stage. The December agreement had expressly stated that the agreement was not transferable except with a view to securing a loan made in favour of the defendants themselves. It was thus clear that the agreement could not be transferred for the purpose of securing a loan made to the plaintiff without the further consent of the council.

The fundamental question was what interest a lender would have in respect of the council's lands should Marlan default on its loan. Had it secured the consent of the council, the lender would have been in a position to require the council to transfer Marlan's entitlements under the December agreement to a third party purchaser, thus recovering the monies loaned to the plaintiff should the latter default. The third party purchaser could more than likely then enter on the lands, complete the development and obtain a lease over the entire lands. Without such consent, however, the lender would have been placed in a difficult position in relation to its security. The planning permission granted to the defendants clearly anticipated development of the council lands as being integral to the permission granted. Thus, an effective charge over the development necessarily required that the charge apply to all the lands contemplated in the planning permission. It would not have been sufficient, thus, to confer a mortgage only in respect of the defendants' lands. A charge would also be required in respect of the defendants' interests in the council's land, under the December agreement.

The December agreement, however, was by its express terms not transferable to any third party other than a financial institution granting a charge in exchange for a loan to the defendants in respect of development on the relevant lands. The agreement thus clearly required that for a valid charge to be created in favour of Marlan's lender, the benefit of the December agreement would have to be transferred to Bank of Scotland (Ireland):

> "If it were considered possible for [the defendants] to provide security to a lender without transferring, in some way, the benefit of the agreement to that lender, then [the clause expressly permitting a mortgage/charge in favour of a bank lending to the defendants] would have been unnecessary. Put another way, it seems clear from the clause in question that both [the council and the defendants] contemplated that the conferring of an interest by way of security on a lending institution would amount to a transfer of the benefit of the agreement and could, therefore, only be done within the parameters set out in that clause."

The December agreement only contemplated a transfer in favour of a financial institution loaning money to the defendants and not in respect of a loan to a third party. Clarke J. thus concluded that the agreement to charge the defendants' interest in the council's lands (i.e. a charge over the agreement for a lease) so as to allow money to be lent to the plaintiff, necessarily required the consent of the council.

Thus, in practical terms the consent of the council was required in order to ensure that the bank would receive an appropriate and effective security over *all* the lands so that, in a case of default, it could sell on Marlan's entitlements under the December agreement to a third party. The consent of the council was necessary in order to allow an "an effectual charge" to be made in favour of Marlan's lender. It would not have been possible to offer such an effective charge over all the lands without the consent of the council. The November agreement therefore necessarily required that the defendants obtain the consent of the council to the charge in favour of the bank. As the defendants had not succeeded in doing so, as agreed, they were in breach of contract.

While the council's consent was being sought, Mr Seán Quinn, the father of the directors of Marlan, had made contact with the council with a view to assisting in the delivery of the required consent. The defendants alleged that these contacts had potentially undermined efforts to secure the council's consent. The judge discounted this contention, ruling that there was nothing untoward or improper in these contacts, and that the contacts had not in fact had such an effect. Even if they had, he added, the plaintiff was entitled to assume that the council knew of its involvement in the scheme. It appeared that the defendants had been "coy" with the council regarding their agreement with Marlan Homes, choosing to conceal from the council the interest conferred by the November agreement. Thus, if there was any fallout from the discovery by the council of the true state of affairs, "those difficulties can only be placed at the door of Mr. Walsh and Mr. Wedick".

Notably, nearly a year passed between the date upon which construction was set to commence and the date on which the council's consent was requested as a condition for funding the plaintiff. The judge, however, did not believe that this delay had prejudiced the defendants' interests. While the contract with the council stipulated strict time limits, the council had not in fact sought to terminate the agreement when they first became aware of the delay in commencement. The council's failure at this earlier stage to terminate estopped them from doing so now. The most the council could have required was immediate commencement of the works, with their completion over a reasonable period of time. As such, the judge concluded that the agreements could still have been commenced in early 2008 provided the necessary finance was forthcoming. It followed that the defendants had not been prejudiced by any delay on the part of the plaintiff in raising the requirement of the council's consent. The only remaining obstacle to the commencement of the works was the defendants' failure to procure the council's consent.

Given this breach of contract, Clarke J. ordered that the November agreement be rescinded. Rescission is available where "one party has been in breach of a fundamental term of a contract, having thereby failed substantially to perform its obligations." Where just and equitable to do so, a court will seek to restore the parties to the positions that they would have been in prior to the breach. Rescission requires that it be possible to restore the parties substantially ("as nearly as may be") to their respective original positions, without suffering injustice.

In this case, the judge concluded, there had been a fundamental breach. The agreement required, as a fundamental term thereof, that Marlan would be assisted in getting effective security over all of the subject lands so as to facilitate funding of the development. Any breach that had the effect of preventing such security from being granted went "to the very heart and root of the contractual arrangements between the parties". After all, without effective security, Marlan would be deprived of the necessary funding. As a result Marlan was, prima facie, "entitled to rescission".

The fact that the assets involved had since depreciated in value (owing to the intervening recession) did not prevent such rescission. As the judge noted:

> "[D]eterioration of the subject-matter does not destroy the right to rescind nor prevent true restoration to the original position. Being an equitable remedy, a court has full power to make all just allowances although it may not be able to restore the parties precisely to the state in which they were before they entered into the contract."

Thus, the fact that the asset involved is a "wasting asset"—that is, that it has lost value since the contract was entered into—does not mean that the court cannot grant rescission (see *Armstrong v Jackson* [1917] 2 K.B. 822, and *Northern Bank Finance Corporation Limited v Charlton* [1979] I.R. 149). In this case, Clarke J. was satisfied that the parties could be put back in the position that they had been in prior to the contract, with the defendants recovering their property and the plaintiff recouping the money paid for that property. The fact that the property was now less valuable than in 2006 was, the judge concluded, of no consequence.

As regards alleged delays, the judge was not satisfied that there had been any delay on the plaintiff's part in seeking rescission, once the breach of contract had been established. That said, the delay in seeking the consent of the council had stalled the development, a delay that was primarily due to the plaintiff's conduct. The defendants alleged that this would prevent them from being restored to their original position under the December agreement, as their right to complete the development was now in doubt due to long delays in commencement. Clarke J. observed, however, that the council had not sought to terminate the December agreement when it first became aware of delays in commencement. This factor more than likely meant that the council would have difficulty subsequently terminating the agreement without first offering the defendants a reasonable opportunity to commence and complete the work. As such, the judge was not satisfied that there would be any difficulty returning the defendants to their original position under the December agreement.

The November agreement was thus rescinded, the defendants being ordered to repay the €4.9 million paid by the plaintiff.

RESTRAINT OF TRADE

***Tejo Ventures International Ltd v O'Callaghan*, High Court, Laffoy J., July 31, 2009; [2009] IEHC 410** This case concerned a restraint of trade clause in a contract between the plaintiff, a franchisor and the defendant franchisee. The franchise in question related to the business of floor sanding and wood floor maintenance in general. As a result of a 2007 agreement, the parties had pledged (in clause 19.2 of the agreement) that should the franchise agreement be terminated for reasons other than the default of the plaintiff, the defendant would be restricted from engaging in business (whether as a rival trader or employee) in competition with the franchise business. The period of restriction varied depending on the geographical territory to which it related. A restriction applied in respect of the entire area of the Republic of Ireland for six months after termination, while a 12-month restriction applied specifically to West Cork and Kerry (the territory to which the specific franchise agreement applied). The agreement further prevented the franchisee from competing with another of the plaintiff's franchisees (or in their franchise territory) for a period of nine months after the end of the agreement. The defendant had also agreed, for a period of one year after the agreement was terminated, not to solicit business from those who had been former customers of the defendant at any time within the year immediately preceding the end of the agreement. Likewise a 12-month restriction applied preventing the defendant from soliciting the employees of the plaintiff or of the latter's franchisees as well as those persons who, at any time during the period of six months before the end of the agreement, had been the defendant's employees. Under clause 19.3 of the agreement, both parties expressly confirmed that the restraint of trade terms were "reasonable".

In February 2009 the parties agreed to bring the agreement to an end. The plaintiff, however, complained that the defendant had subsequently established a rival floor-sanding business. The plaintiff thus sought an interlocutory injunction seeking compliance with the no-compete clauses.

In its defence, the defendant alleged that as a result of the agreed manner of termination, he was not bound by the non-compete clause. He further asserted that clause 19.2 amounted to an unlawful restraint on trade and/or was in breach of s.4 of the Competition Act 2002. In the alternative he claimed that the non-compete clause specifically (and not the solicitation clause) was unlawful. He noted also that he had, by letter, already agreed to abide by the non-solicitation provisions and that, in any event, he had not sought to poach any former customers. Given that, at most, previously sanded floors would not require re-sanding for at least two years, the defendant further alleged that the likelihood of poaching was slim, and therefore that the restriction on soliciting former customers was superfluous and unreasonable. Finally, the defendant alleged that damages would provide an adequate remedy should the plaintiff ultimately win at trial, while the balance of convenience lay, he claimed, against granting the injunction.

Laffoy J. first noted that the purpose of an interlocutory injunction was to maintain the status quo pending full trial. It was not, she added, for the court to determine at this stage the true facts of the case or to seek to resolve the legal dispute between the parties. While acknowledging that the issues of law were "undoubtedly difficult" the judge noted that the main issue was whether there is a "fair issue to be tried that the defendant's activity is in contravention of clause 19.2".

Laffoy J. concluded that there was, in the circumstances, a fair issue to be tried that the restraint of trade clause was valid at common law and that the defendant was in breach thereof. In support she cited the seminal decision of Costello J. in *John Orr Ltd and Vescom BV v John Orr* [1987] I.L.R.M. 702, setting out the principles to be applied in such cases. The judge in *Orr* noted that, absent special justifying circumstances, all restraints of trade were contrary to public policy and thus prima facie void. Nonetheless, a restraint "may be justified if it is reasonable in the interests of the contracting parties and in the interests of the public", the onus of proving such reasonability lying on the party seeking to enforce the restraint. Costello J. had added that where the agreement was between a seller and a buyer of a business, the courts recognised a "greater freedom of contract" than might be the case in relation to a contract between employer and employee. In particular, "a covenant against competition entered into by the seller of a business which is reasonably necessary to protect the business sold is valid and enforceable". Even where a covenant went beyond what was reasonable, he added, it could nonetheless be enforced in part "by severance of the void parts from the valid parts".

Laffoy J. cited *Vendo Plc v Adams*, Chancery Division, High Court, Northern Ireland, January 14, 2002, but intimated that it may ultimately be deemed distinguishable on the facts. In that case, a request for an injunction was declined on the basis that the duration of the restraint was 18 months, a period that was deemed to be unreasonably restrictive.

Returning to the current case, Laffoy J. added that there was an arguable case that the clause would not be considered anti-competitive under the terms of the Competition Act 2002. Section 4 of the Act bans and invalidates any agreement between undertakings that has the object or effect of preventing, restricting or distorting competition in the provision of goods or services. That Act, however, allows for exceptions, and it was at least open to the plaintiff to argue that the agreement did not distort the market or, in the alternative,that the restraint clause was permitted by virtue of the statutory exceptions to s.4.

The judge was most persuaded by the plaintiff's arguments that it would be a "worthless exercise" for the plaintiff to grant a franchise if the franchisee could, without penalty, subsequently end the franchise and proceed to compete in the same field of business. In other words, without the clause in question, the business efficacy of the franchise contract would be greatly undermined. This did not in itself, she noted, mean that the restraint would necessarily be found reasonable as to time and geographical scope, but the judge did appear to indicate that at least prima facie there was an arguable case that the clause was necessary and reasonable in all the circumstances.

The plaintiff having established that there was a fair issue to be tried, Laffoy J. proceeded to conclude that, given the potential harm to "its business, goodwill and reputation", damages would not afford an adequate remedy should the plaintiff succeed at trial in the absence of the interlocutory injunction. In short, the balance of convenience lay in favour of granting the injunction.

SPECIFIC PERFORMANCE

See also, *Liberty Asset Management Ltd v Gannon*, High Court, Laffoy J., October 14, 2009; [2009] IEHC 468 discussed above under FORMALITIES

Introduction The issue of the specific performance of an options agreement was considered in *Devereux v Goff* [2009] IEHC 398. On the facts, specific performance of the contract for the sale of land was not granted, the court having concluded that the defendant had the right under the express terms of the agreement not to proceed with the purchase in circumstances where planning permission was granted on conditions that were not satisfactory to the defendant. As the defendant purchaser had not been satisfied with the conditions in respect of which planning permission had been granted, the court ruled that a condition precedent to the enforcement of the contract had not been satisfied.

Land and Conveyancing Law Reform Act 2009 Section 54 of the Land and Conveyancing Law Reform Act 2009 allows a court to make certain orders in lieu of an order for specific performance in respect of land. In particular, where a court refuses to order specific performance of a contract for the sale or other disposition of land, it may, where it considers it just and equitable to do so, "order the repayment of the whole or part of any deposit paid in respect of the land, with or without interest". This provision is enabling rather than mandatory.

STATUTE OF FRAUDS (IRELAND) 1695

See the discussion of s.51 of the Land and Conveyancing Law Reform Act 2009 and *Liberty Asset Management Ltd v Gannon*, High Court, Laffoy J., October 14, 2009; [2009] IEHC 468, both of which are discussed above under FORMALITIES, and *Sheridan Quinn v Gaynor* [2009] IEHC 421, discussed above under FORMATION OF CONTRACT

UNCONSCIONABLE BARGAINS

See *James Keating v Catherine and Patrick Keating*, High Court, Laffoy J., August 24, 2009; [2009] IEHC 405 discussed above under IMPROVIDENT TRANSACTIONS and *Kevin Prendergast and Monica Joyce v Dermot Joyce, Bank of Ireland and Allied Irish Banks*, High Court, Gilligan J., February 13, 2009; [2009] IEHC 199 discussed below under UNDUE INFLUENCE

UNDUE INFLUENCE

See also, *James Keating v Catherine and Patrick Keating*, High Court, Laffoy J., August 24, 2009; [2009] IEHC 405 discussed above under IMPROVIDENT TRANSACTIONS

***Kevin Prendergast and Monica Joyce v Dermot Joyce, Bank of Ireland and Allied Irish Banks*, High Court, Gilligan J., February 13, 2009; [2009] IEHC 199** This case concerns the setting aside of a transaction owing to undue influence and improvidence. The case offers some useful discussion of the principles applicable in relation to the presumption of undue influence as well as the operation of the doctrine of improvidence.

The case centres on the transfer of sums in various bank accounts into the joint names of Monica Joyce, an elderly woman, and her late husband's nephew, Dermot Joyce. The sums in question were substantial, amounting to €143,342 (not including interest accrued of approximately €14,000.) The transactions were effected by Mrs Joyce at the Bank of Ireland and Allied Irish Bank offices in Claremorris, Co. Mayo on January 21, 1998, very shortly after the death of Monica's husband Jack.

In the words of the judge, Monica and Jack had been a "very close couple", Monica being "effectively totally dependent on Jack". It was clear from the evidence that Monica placed great trust in her husband and tended to defer to his wishes, particularly in matters of business. Prior to his death, Jack had been the owner and manager of a small petrol station. The couple had no children, but had a number of nieces and nephews, including the first defendant, Dermot Joyce. Although the latter claimed that he had often assisted in the running of Jack's petrol station, the judge doubted, on the evidence, that Dermot's contribution was as significant as he claimed. The evidence did establish, however, that Jack regarded Dermot as "better than a son to them". On a number of occasions Jack had indicated his desire to transfer the contents of bank accounts that were held in Monica and Jack's joint names into Dermot's name, though Jack never took firm steps to give effect to this stated intention.

From around 1993 onwards, Monica's mental condition deteriorated significantly. She became forgetful and disorientated, and was becoming increasingly incapable of taking care of herself or of her affairs. As the years progressed her mental condition deteriorated. By early 1998, her doctor was satisfied that her state of mental impairment was such that "she was incapable of living alone or of making her own decisions". The doctor, in particular, considered that she was incapable of understanding legal documentation such as a will.

On January 14, 1998 Jack died of a heart attack. Exactly one week later, at the respective offices of the Bank of Ireland and Allied Irish Banks, Monica transferred the contents of three accounts held jointly in her and Jack's names into the joint names of Dermot Joyce and Monica Joyce. Monica's relatives challenged this transaction, seeking to set it aside.

Gilligan J. first considered whether the presumption of undue influence applied to the transactions. Where the presumption of undue influence arises in respect of a transaction, the onus is conferred on the person seeking to defend the validity of the transaction by showing that it was the product of a free exercise of the donor's independent will. Unless it can be shown that the transaction was the spontaneous and free act of the donor, it will be set aside. For this purpose it is not necessary to establish that the donee has in fact committed a wrongful act. The presumption, according to Cotton L.J. in *Allcard v Skinner* (1887) 36 Ch D 145 at 171, is grounded in public policy, the purpose of the presumption being "to prevent the relations which existed between the parties and the influence arising therefrom being abused".

The list of relationships to which the presumption may apply is neither fixed nor closed. While the presumption is deemed to apply automatically in respect of certain classes of relationship (e.g. in respect of parents and their minor children, solicitors and clients) outside the context of these specific relationships the question of whether the particular relationship between two parties gives rise to the presumption depends on the particular facts of each case. The question ultimately is whether the particular relationship between the parties is one where one party has reposed trust and confidence in the other such that the opportunity for exercising influence exists. Notably the presumption was deemed to arise in the particular context of a relationship between a nephew and his illiterate elderly aunt in *Inche Noriah v Shaik Allie Bin Omar* [1929] A.C. 127. As Budd J. observed in *Gregg v Kidd* [1956] I.R. 183, disparity of age and mental infirmity may give rise more easily to a relationship of dependence. "Mere blood relationship", however, is not sufficient:

> "To bring the principle into play it must be shown that the opportunity for the exercise of the influence or ascendancy on the donor existed, as where the parties reside together or meet frequently…it must be shown that the actual relations between the parties give rise to the presumption of influence" (*Gregg v Kidd* [1956] I.R. 183 at 195).

The question that thus arose was whether the actual relationship between Dermot Joyce and Monica Joyce was such as to give rise to the presumption. On the particular facts, the court concluded that the presumption did arise in this case. Gilligan J. placed particular emphasis on the very vulnerable position of Mrs Joyce. Her age, combined with her confused and deteriorating state of mind, put her in an especially vulnerable position, exacerbated by the grief and confusion caused by her husband's very recent death. She was, in the judge's view, "undoubtedly vulnerable to exploitation".

While the judge was satisfied that the defendant had overstated his contribution to Jack's business, the evidence showed that "he occupied a position of trust in relation to his uncle". Given that Monica was inclined to defer to her husband in respect of matters of business and money, Gilligan J. concluded that "it seems reasonable to infer…that she would tend to repose trust in those in whom her husband trusted, provided that she herself was familiar with them." The widow's deteriorating state of health placed her in a particularly vulnerable position, heightening the risk of exploitation by trusted persons. The defendant, moreover, had received a substantial benefit from the transactions.

As such, the court concluded that the presumption arose on the facts. In so ruling, Gilligan J. expressly rejected the contention that the presumption would only arise where it could be shown that the transaction was itself wrongful in the sense that the donee had actually taken advantage of the donor. The judge was satisfied that this proposition, made by Lord Scarman in *National Westminster Bank v Morgan* [1985] A.C. 686, did not form part of Irish law. In particular, this proposition appeared to confuse the criteria for actual undue influence with the criteria prerequisite to the presumption arising. For the presumption to arise, it was not necessary to show that the donee had acted improperly or had in fact taken advantage of the relationship of trust. According to Denham J. in *Carroll v Carroll*, the presence of the relationship of trust, coupled with the conferring of a substantial benefit, is sufficient to raise the presumption. Indeed, in *Carroll* itself the court accepted that the son in that case had not acted improperly or sought to take advantage of his father, though the presumption nonetheless arose. The onus is then cast on the recipient to adduce evidence to establish that the transaction was not the product of undue influence but rather the free act of the donor's independent will. Another way of putting this is that the presumption, as a matter of public policy, places on the recipient the onus of establishing the "propriety of the transaction" (Clark, *Contract Law in Ireland*, 6th edn (Dublin: Thomson Round Hall, 2008), p.376. This occurs because of the risks of abuse inherent in such relationships, the recipient being required to prove that no such abuse arose.

Turning to whether the presumption had been displaced, the court concluded that, on the facts, the defendant had failed to establish that the transfer was the result of the free and spontaneous act of the donor. While accepting that Jack Joyce had stated his intention to give money to his nephew, the deceased had never followed through on this plan. (Indeed, the judge doubted whether Jack ever seriously intended to do so.) The deceased's will did make some provision for his nephew, but only in the event that Monica predeceased Jack. The will otherwise left everything to Monica. The court, moreover, thought it highly unlikely that Jack would have intended to leave his wife without significant resources in the case of his death. Other than the bank accounts, Monica had very modest resources, namely a small pension and approximately €34,000 in death benefits.

The evidence, moreover, indicated that Monica's independence of mind was, even ignoring her weakened mental condition, not to the fore. In financial and business matters at least, she tended, according to the judge, to "agree with everything Jack said".

The court also concluded that Monica had not received independent advice prior to concluding the transaction in question. "The advice", the judge observed, "must be such as a competent adviser would give if acting solely in the interests of the donor". Although the local Bank of Ireland bank manager had been present at the transaction in that bank, and had advised Monica as to the effect of the transaction, Gilligan J. concluded that the advice given was not independent. The bank manager, he observed, had a vested financial interest in the transaction, namely that it would contribute towards his target in terms of the number of business transactions effected by his branch. This meant that he could not be considered independent in his role. Gilligan J. noted that Jack and the bank manager had previously discussed Jack's intention to transfer the funds to Dermot, though the transfer was never made during Jack's lifetime. According to the judge, these previous discussions had fostered a view in the bank manager's mind that his role was to give effect to Jack's intentions. As such, the court concluded that the bank manager had never adequately considered whether the transaction was in Monica's interests.

Particular care is required, Gilligan J. added, where a donor is susceptible to exploitation, to ensure that the donor understands fully the nature and impact of the transaction. It was clear in this case that an independent adviser would have warned Mrs Joyce as to the very substantial transfer she was making, something that had not in this case occurred. Gilligan J. further refuted the contention that Mrs Joyce was mentally capable of conducting the transaction on the day in question, an assertion which was clearly negated by the professional view of her doctor that she was not capable of understanding her actions.

The judge finally turned to the matter of motivation. The defendant had claimed that the transfer was made in recognition of the assistance and help offered to Jack and Monica by the defendant, particularly in respect of his work at Jack's garage. The judge again doubted the extent of Dermot's contribution thereto. He added that Monica had other relatives to whom she was closer than Dermot, some of whom had taken care of her during her last years. It was thus:

> "…difficult to understand why she would have made greater provision for the defendant, a nephew by marriage, than she would for those who were closer to her both in family ties and in the care they showed for her."

There was no suggestion, moreover, that the defendant was in need of money. In sum, it was implausible that such a large transfer would have been made solely out of natural love and affection. As such the defendant had failed to rebut the presumption of undue influence and thus the judge ordered that the transaction be set aside.

Gilligan J. additionally concluded that the transaction was improvident. The criteria for improvidence (sometimes termed 'unconscionability') are threefold:

1. that, owing to a factor such as age, poverty or ignorance, the donor is at a serious disadvantage relative to the donee/recipient, such that the potential arose that a person would take unfair advantage of the donor;
2. the transaction in question was made at an undervalue; and
3. the donor lacked independent advice.

Gilligan J. first noted that the court's jurisdiction in relation to improvidence was not confined to transactions supported by consideration (where value was exchanged) but applied also to gifts made by the donor. Nor was it necessary, the judge added, to establish moral turpitude or wrongdoing on the part of the recipient. Although the proposition has been put forward in a number of cases that wrongful behaviour is required on the part of the transferee, the decision of Shanley J. in *Carroll v Carroll* [1998] 2 I.L.R.M. 218 indicated that no such evidence of wrongdoing is required. Older cases bear this out, as in *Evans v Peacock,* 16 Ves. Jun. 512 at 518 where a bargain was set aside despite there having been "nothing dishonourable or immoral in the stronger party's conduct". Likewise, in *Longmate v Ledger*, 2 Giff. 157, a bargain was struck between an aged man and his creditor, the former being so weak and eccentric as not to be "competent to exercise a prudent care for his own interests". Although the defendant in that case was acknowledged not to have "used any of the arts to induce the vendor to enter into this contract" the bargain was set aside. In *Rooney v Conway,* unreported, Northern Ireland High Court, March 8, 1986 an elderly man had transferred his farm to a young man not of his family for less than a quarter of its true price. The bargain was deemed improvident despite a lack of evidence of unconscionable behaviour on the part of the young man.

It was clear in this specific case that Monica was seriously disadvantaged by her mental state. As a result, she was "unequal to protecting herself". The transaction, moreover, was made not simply at an undervalue but without any consideration, and without independent advice. Indeed the transfer was particularly disadvantageous and improvident given that the contents of the bank accounts "represented the great majority of her liquid assets". In Gilligan J.'s words:

> "At a stroke, she deprived herself of those monies in exchange for no benefit immediately following the loss of a husband on whom she had become almost totally dependent. The evidence in this regard discloses a clear case of improvidence."

The transfer of monies into the joint accounts was thus set aside.

***Danske Bank t/a National Irish Bank Plc v John Madden,* High Court, McGovern J., July 3, 2009; [2009] IEHC 319** This case explores the circumstances in which a bank is taken to have notice of wrongdoing on the part of a third party. It suggests that where a bank has sought and received undertakings from the borrower and his solicitor, the bank may thus be relieved from any obligation to look behind these assurances and to check the averred statements of the parties.

The defendant in this case, a businessman involved in car sales, had borrowed just under €1.36 million from the bank. The purpose of this loan, according to the loan agreement, was to invest in property. As security, a house in Saggart, Co. Dublin was offered, the defendant having falsely represented to the bank that he was the owner of this property.

The defendant later claimed that the purpose of the loan was in fact to *buy* this property in Saggart from the owner, who was the defendant's solicitor, Mr Thomas Byrne. This purchase followed a previously aborted purchase in which the defendant and the solicitor had been involved, the purpose of the new arrangement being to compensate the defendant for losses sustained as a result of the earlier aborted transaction. Previously, the defendant sought to buy a site for his car dealership, agreeing to pay €1.3 million for the site and a 10 per cent deposit up front. Mr Byrne had agreed to participate in the purchase as a partner. It transpired, however, that Mr Byrne had failed to pay the deposit and to return the contracts. The property was subsequently sold on to another purchaser for €3.75 million. When the defendant threatened to sue and to report Mr Byrne to the Law Society, the solicitor offered to sell him the house in Saggart for €1.3 million although it was probably worth twice that amount.

The plaintiff for its part claimed that it had been led to believe that Mr Madden already owned this property in Saggart and that it was being offered as security for a loan to purchase *other* property. The defendant, indeed, had admitted that he had not told the bank that he was in fact using the loan money to buy the house in Saggart from his solicitor. The evidence clearly established, the judge ruled, that the bank had been led to believe that the defendant owned the Saggart property when this was not in fact the case, and that this property was being used as security for the loan. The bank had been led to believe, moreover, that the purpose of this loan was to purchase property other than the house offered as security. For his part, Thomas Byrne offered a solicitor's undertaking in respect of the property. The defendant also signed a family home declaration to the effect that the Saggart property was not a family home, further evidence that the defendant was being falsely represented as the true owner of the property.

The loan in question was paid to the defendant's solicitor, but never passed on to the defendant. In mid-2006 the defendant wished to sell the Saggart house, but was dissuaded from doing so by Mr Byrne, who encouraged him instead to mortgage the house to the Irish Nationwide Building Society. The defendant did so, borrowing a sum of €1.4 million. The defendant believed that this money had been used to discharge his liability to the plaintiff. In fact, Mr Byrne had retained the money, and (unbeknownst to the defendant) had mortgaged the property to another lender.

In the meantime the plaintiff bank kept drawing down money from the defendant's bank account to meet the loan repayments, and had written to the defendant to warn him about falling into arrears. While the defendant did ask his solicitor to check this, he admitted that he had not personally contacted the bank to clarify the matter (a fact that the judge found surprising).

The defendant claimed that the loan agreement was the product of the undue influence of his solicitor. He also asserted that he had been the victim of fraud and deception on the part of Mr Byrne. He suggested, moreover, that the plaintiff bank had constructive notice of this as it was aware, or ought to have been aware, that the defendant did not originally own the house in Saggart.

First, in relation to undue influence, it is well established that the relationship between solicitor and client gives rise automatically to the presumption of undue influence. Here, however, the judge was satisfied that, on the facts, the presumption had been rebutted. The judge first noted that the defendant was "an established businessman", there being no evidence that he was either "vulnerable or dependent". While the defendant and his solicitor had previous dealings in relation to the aborted property deal, the judge was nonetheless satisfied that Mr Byrne had been in a position to offer independent legal advice to his client:

> "The usual meaning of such advice is that it is advice obtained by the party himself from a lawyer retained by him and not advice coming from the legal advisor of a third party with whom he is entering into a legal relationship. If there was an issue on the question of Mr. Byrne acting for the defendant in what was, in effect, the transfer of his interest in the property to the defendant, that was a matter between the defendant and his solicitor and did not concern the bank."

In other words, in so far as the bank and its loan agreement was concerned, the advice was independent in that it did not emanate from the bank itself or from its own legal adviser. In this regard, the judge appears to have confined his examination of the independence of the advice to the specific advice offered in respect of the loan. The wider involvement of Mr Byrne in the transaction was not deemed relevant. In other words, the fact that the loan was for the purpose of buying Mr Byrne's house was not germane to the issue as to whether what was offered was independent advice. With respect, this seems an unduly narrow, technical approach to the issue of independent advice. Arguably the solicitor did have a vested interest in the transaction with the bank, though admittedly not one of which the bank was itself aware.

Nonetheless, the judge was satisfied that the evidence clearly negated the contention that the defendant's solicitor had exercised undue influence in relation to the loan. Certainly, the defendant more than likely was the victim of fraud "but this is quite a separate matter from undue influence". In accepting the loan he was receiving "what he wanted", namely finance for the purchase of a house at a significant discount. Given the circumstances, the judge rejected the contention that the loan had been sought under the solicitor's influence.

Turning to the issue of fraud, the judge considered the circumstances in which a bank will be affected by the fraud perpetrated by a third party on a person taking out a loan. In such a case, "it is necessary that the party seeking to enforce the contract had actual or constructive notice of the fraud or undue influence". The burden of proving such knowledge rests with the defendant.

The defendant contended that the plaintiff either knew or ought to have known that he was not the original owner of the Saggart property. He claimed that the plaintiff would have discovered this had it made reasonable inquiries and searches (e.g. in the registry of deeds). In the circumstances, however, the judge felt that the plaintiff had made such inquiries as could reasonably be expected. He relied in particular on a statement of affairs setting out the assets of the defendant (which had indicated that the defendant had originally owned the house in Saggart). The defendant's solicitor had furnished this document to the bank at a meeting with bank officials prior to the issuing of the loan. The defendant had also attended this meeting and did not correct the statement to the effect that he already owned the Saggart property. Given these signed assurances, McGovern J. did not consider that it would have been reasonable to require the bank to verify this statement of affairs. The defendant's contemporaneous completion of a family home declaration, in particular, clearly was consistent only with the contention that he already owned the Saggart property.

The judge effectively accepted that the bank was entitled, in line with normal banking practice, to rely on the statement of affairs and the solicitor's undertaking. The fact that the defendant himself had represented himself as the owner of the house was crucial in this regard.

The judge noted the purpose of the doctrine of constructive notice, which is to determine which of two or more innocent parties should bear the loss when there is undue influence or fraud. Although the judge did not flesh this out, the implication was that the defendant himself had not been entirely frank with the bank, and thus could not have claimed to be entirely innocent in the matter. Certainly, one might argue that it was doubtful that the maxim "she who seeks equity must come with clean hands" had been satisfied, such that equity should come to the defendant's rescue.

Citing *Bank of Ireland v Rockfield* [1979] 1 I.R. 21, the judge doubted whether the doctrine of constructive notice was, at any rate, applicable in the context of commercial transactions. The judge also distinguished *Northern Bank Limited v Henry* [1981] I.R. 1, where a bank was deemed to have had constructive notice of a wife's equitable interest in the family home. The bank in that case had made no inquiries, apart from a search in the registry of deeds, into the ownership of the home and thus was fixed with notice of the wife's interest. In the instant case, by contrast, the defendant had himself sought the loan (which he subsequently drew down), signed documents in order to do so, and allowed his solicitor to enter into an undertaking in order to support the loan. Given these circumstances, the judge "[did] not accept that the bank had any obligation to go further than they did before granting the loan and taking steps to secure it." The defendant had signed a number of documents, and was bound by his signature thereof. The fact that he had not read these documents was irrelevant—to rule otherwise would lead to "chaos in the day-to-day workings of commercial life". A person who signs documents is ordinarily regarded as bound by their contents.

Thus, while accepting that the defendant had been the victim of fraud and deception, the court held that in so far as the liability to the bank was concerned, the defendant was still bound to pay back the loan. While the facts of the case—and the defendant's own responsibility for the misrepresentation of ownership—may have been instrumental in determining this case, the judgment appears to set a very low threshold for a bank seeking to establish that it has made all reasonable inquiries. Given recent events, it is certainly questionable to say the least that banks should be considered to have acted with due diligence simply by accepting the assurances of interested parties.

Criminal Evidence

DR YVONNE DALY, Lecturer in Law, Socio-Legal Research Centre, School of Law and Government, Dublin City University

LEGISLATIVE DEVELOPMENTS

Criminal Justice (Surveillance) Act 2009 While surveillance activity has for many years been a part of policing in Ireland, in July 2009 the Oireachtas introduced specific statutory provision for varying forms of surveillance under the Criminal Justice (Surveillance) Act 2009. This Act allows for covert surveillance to be carried out by the Gardaí (or members of the defence forces or the revenue commissioners in certain circumstances) and for the evidence obtained in that manner to be admitted at trial. "Surveillance", according to s.1 of the Act, includes monitoring, observing, listening to or making a recording of a particular person or group of persons or their movements, activities and communications; or monitoring or making a recording of places or things, by or with the assistance of surveillance devices.

A judge of the District Court may grant an authorisation for surveillance on the application of a superior officer (a Garda, member of the defence forces or officer of the revenue commissioners of appropriate rank). Section 4(1) provides that, in the context of the criminal justice system, an applicant Garda, not below the rank of superintendent, must have reasonable grounds to believe that:

(a) as part of an operation or investigation being conducted by Gardaí concerning an arrestable offence, the requested surveillance is necessary for the purposes of obtaining information as to whether the offence has been committed or as to the circumstances relating to the commission of the offence, or obtaining evidence for the purposes of proceedings in relation to the offence,

(b) the requested surveillance is necessary for the purpose of preventing the commission of arrestable offences, or

(c) the requested surveillance is necessary for the purpose of maintaining the security of the State.

Under s.4(5) the applicant must also have reasonable grounds for believing that the surveillance for which authorisation is sought is:

(a) the least intrusive means available, having regard to its objectives and other relevant considerations,
(b) proportionate to its objectives, having regard to all the circumstances including its likely impact on the rights of any person, and
(c) of a duration that is reasonably required to achieve its objectives.

Once in possession of an authorisation, the applicant Garda named therein or other Gardaí designated by him may enter any place for the purposes of initiating or carrying out the authorised surveillance, and withdrawing the authorised surveillance device, without the consent of a person who owns or is in charge of that place (s.5(7)). Reasonable force may be used if necessary (s.5(7)). The authorisation is to last no longer than three months (s.5(8)).

In cases of urgency, s.7 makes provision for a Garda to carry out surveillance under the approval of a superior officer (i.e. a Garda not below the rank of superintendent), in the absence of judicial authorisation. Such approval is only to be given by a superior officer on application from a Garda where: (i) the conditions for the grant of a judicial authorisation are in place; and (ii) before judicial authorisation could be obtained one or more of a number of specifically listed occurrences are likely to take place, i.e. a person would abscond for the purpose of avoiding justice, would obstruct the course of justice or commit an arrestable offence, the security of the State would be compromised, or, information or evidence relating to the commission of an arrestable offence would be destroyed, lost or otherwise become unavailable (s.7(2)). Section 7(8) provides that an urgent approval will last for 72 hours at most.

Under s.8 tracking devices may be utilised by Gardaí with the approval of a superior officer without any need to have recourse to the courts.

Section 14 of the Act provides that evidence obtained as a result of authorised or approved surveillance may be admitted as evidence in criminal proceedings. Notably, the Act provides that information or documents obtained as a result of an authorised or approved surveillance may be admitted as evidence notwithstanding any error or omission on the face of the relevant authorisation or written record of approval if the court decides that (a) the error or omission concerned was inadvertent, and (b) the information or document ought to be admitted in the interests of justice (s.14(3)(a)). In making this decision the court should take the following into account (s.14(3)(b)):

(i) whether the error or omission concerned was serious or merely technical in nature;
(ii) the nature of any right infringed by obtaining the information or document concerned;
(iii) whether there were circumstances of urgency;

(iv) the possible prejudicial effect of the information or document concerned; and,

(v) the probative value of the information or document concerned.

Furthermore, s.14(4) provides that information or documents obtained as a result of authorised or approved surveillance may be admitted as evidence in criminal proceedings notwithstanding any failure by a Garda to comply with a requirement of the relevant authorisation or approval if the court decides that (a) the Garda or officer concerned acted in good faith and the failure was inadvertent, and (b) the information or document ought to be admitted in the interests of justice, taking the s.14(3)(b) list into consideration.

It is noteworthy that the legislature made specific provision within this Act for the carrying out of a balancing test in relation to the admissibility of relevant evidence. Given that important constitutional rights including privacy and the inviolability of the dwelling are likely to be affected by the covert surveillance powers provided under the terms of this Act, the suggestion that evidence obtained in breach of the requirements of the Act which is obtained nonetheless in "good faith" should be admissible seems to undermine the strict exclusionary rule set out in *People (DPP) v Kenny* [1990] 2 I.R. 110 and applied in Ireland for the past 20 years. Under that rule evidence obtained in violation of constitutional rights must automatically be excluded (in the absence of extraordinary excusing circumstances) regardless of the knowledge of the violator that his actions were interfering with such rights, and regardless of his motivation. It remains to be seen whether any constitutional challenge to this or other elements of the Criminal Justice (Surveillance) Act 2009 might arise in the future.

Criminal Justice (Amendment) Act 2009 On April 9, 2009 a man named Roy Collins was shot dead in Limerick. A family member of his had given evidence in a "gangland crime" trial five years previously and it was generally believed that his murder was related to this. The Oireachtas enacted the Criminal Justice (Amendment) Act 2009, aimed at tackling "organised crime" in the wake of this murder, despite some controversy. 133 lawyers objected to its introduction by way of a letter to the *Irish Times* and the President considered referring the Bill to the Supreme Court under Art.26 of the Constitution. However, following consultation with the Council of State, she signed the Bill into law on July 23, 2009.

A new definition of a "criminal organisation" is provided under s.3 of the Criminal Justice (Amendment) Act 2009, which amends s.70 of the Criminal Justice Act 2006. It defines a "criminal organisation" as "a structured group, however organised, that has as its main purpose or activity the commission or facilitation of a serious offence".

A "structured group" is defined by the section as:

> … a group of 3 or more persons, which is not randomly formed for the immediate commission of a single offence, and the involvement in which by 2 or more of those persons is with a view to their acting in concert; for the avoidance of doubt, a structured group may exist notwithstanding the absence of all or any of the following: (a) formal rules or formal membership, or any formal roles for those involved in the group; (b) any hierarchical or leadership structure; (c) continuity of involvement by persons in the group.

One of the most notable features of the Act is the "block booking" of the non-jury Special Criminal Court for the trial of specific "organised crime" offences. Section 8 of the Act declares that, "the ordinary courts are inadequate to secure the effective administration of justice and the preservation of public peace and order" in relation to specific offences, of an "organised crime" nature. The relevant offences are set out in Pt 7 of the Criminal Justice Act 2006, as amended by the Criminal Justice (Amendment) Act 2009, and include:

- s.71(A) – directing a criminal organisation;
- s.72 – participating in or contributing to activities intending to, or being reckless as to whether that could, enhance the ability of a criminal organisation to commit a serious offence or facilitating a criminal organisation in committing a serious offence;
- s.73 – committing a serious offence for a criminal organisation; and
- s.76 – those same offences when committed by a body corporate.

These offences are scheduled by s.8(2) of the 2009 Act and therefore are directly sent forward for trial in the non-jury Special Criminal Court, unless the Director of Public Prosecutions (DPP) specifically provides otherwise.

For many years the DPP has had the power to send any case to the Special Criminal Court where he has certified that the ordinary courts are inadequate to secure the effective administration of justice and the preservation of public peace and order (under s.46 of the Offences Against the State Act 1939), and indeed many "organised crime" cases have previously been heard in that court. However, s.8 of the Criminal Justice (Amendment) Act 2009 is the first provision to specifically designate a group of offences of a particular nature for hearing in the Special Criminal Court, other than the subversive offences provided for in the Offences Against the State Acts. Section 8 must be renewed by the Oireachtas every 12 months.

In terms of the law of criminal evidence, another particularly notable aspect of this Act is that Garda opinion evidence can be admitted by the courts as expert evidence in relation to the existence of a particular criminal organisation. Section 7 of the 2009 Act inserts s.71B into the Criminal Justice Act 2006 and provides that a court may hear the opinion evidence of a Garda or former Garda of any rank in relation to the existence of a criminal organisation where it appears to the court that he possesses "the appropriate expertise". Such expertise is to be based on experience, specialised knowledge or qualifications and the relevant Garda may have formed his opinion in relation to the existence of the organisation on the basis of any previous convictions for arrestable offences of persons believed by him to be part of that organisation, amongst other things (s.71B(3)). Of course, Garda opinion evidence is admissible in relation to the offence of membership of an unlawful organisation by virtue of s.3(2) of the Offences Against the State (Amendment) Act 1972. This provision was unsuccessfully challenged as being unconstitutional and contrary to the European Convention on Human Rights in the 2009 case of *Redmond v Ireland and the Attorney General* [2009] IEHC 201; [2009] 2 I.L.R.M. 419 (discussed below).

Other evidence which the court may admit in considering whether a particular group is in fact a criminal organisation includes any document or other record emanating from the relevant group from which it can be inferred (i) that the group is a criminal organisation or (ii) that the group committed or facilitated a serious offence or engaged in related activity, or, in which a name, word, symbol or other representation is used which identifies the group as a criminal organisation or from which it can be inferred that the group is a criminal organisation. Documents or records, the legislation provides, may include a photograph, a disc, tape or other sound-storage device, a film, tape or other visual image-storage device (s.71B(5)).

Section 71B(4)(b) also refers, albeit a little confusingly, to admissible evidence potentially taking the form of:

> … the provision by a group of 3 or more persons of a material benefit to the defendant (or a promise by such a group to provide a material benefit to the defendant), which provision or promise is not made in return for a lawful act performed or to be performed by the defendant.

A procedural matter provided for in the Criminal Justice (Amendment) Act 2009 is the potential for detention extension hearings to be heard otherwise than in public. Sections 21, 22 and 23 of the 2009 Act make this provision for suspects detained under s.30 of the Offences Against the State Act 1939, s.2 of the Criminal Justice (Drug Trafficking) Act 2006 or s.50 of the Criminal Justice Act 2007. The respective sections provide that where application is made to the District Court for an extension of the detention period of a detained suspect and the judge is satisfied that it is desirable to do so in order to "avoid a risk of prejudice to the investigation concerned" he may:

(i) direct that the application be heard otherwise than in public, or
(ii) exclude from the Court during the hearing all persons except officers of the Court, persons directly concerned in the proceedings, *bona fide* representatives of the Press and such other persons as the Court may permit to remain.

More specifically, the legislation (ss.30(4BA)(b) of the 1939 Act, 2(3A)(b) of the 1996 Act and 50(4A)(b) of the 2007 Act, as inserted by ss.21, 22 and 23 of the 2009 Act) provides that a judge at a detention extension hearing under the relevant provisions may direct that, in the public interest, particular evidence at the hearing be given in the absence of every person, except the Garda giving the evidence and a clerk or registrar of the court. The exclusion from the court even includes the relevant detained suspect and his legal representative. The type of evidence deemed by the legislation to potentially warrant such an exclusion direction is evidence which:

> "… concerns steps that have been, or may be, taken in the course of any inquiry or investigation being conducted by the Garda Síochána with respect to the suspected involvement of the person to whom the application relates, or any other person, in the commission of the offence to which the detention relates or any other offence…[and] the nature of those steps is such that the giving of that evidence concerning them could prejudice, in a material respect, the proper conducting of any foregoing inquiry or investigation".

While the rationale for these provisions may be clear, the lack of transparency in the criminal process and the inequality of arms provided for thereunder may raise challenges in the future.

Another important provision of the Criminal Justice (Amendment) Act 2009 is s.9, which inserts s.72A into the Criminal Justice Act 2006 and relates to the drawing of inferences at trial from the pre-trial silence of the accused in the context of an investigation into an "organised crime" offence. Section 72A operates only in the context of "organised crime" and provides that an inference may be drawn at trial from the pre-trial failure of a suspect to "answer a question material to the investigation of the offence". This is similar to s.2 of the Offences Against the State (Amendment) Act 1998; however, the only offence covered by that provision is membership of an unlawful organisation. Section 72A applies to any offence under Pt 7 of the Criminal Justice Act 2006 and is therefore much broader in application, and those offences carry potential penalties which are much higher than the two-year maximum term which attaches to membership of an unlawful organisation.

Under s.72A, a person is not to be convicted solely or mainly on an inference drawn from the relevant pre-trial failure to answer; the suspect must have been told in ordinary language when being questioned what the effect of such a failure might be; he must have been afforded a reasonable opportunity to consult a solicitor before such a failure occurred; and the relevant interview must have been recorded by electronic or similar means unless the suspect consented in writing to it not being recorded.

"Any question material to the investigation of the offence" is defined within s.72A(7) as including, inter alia:

- a request that the suspect give a full account of his or her movements, actions, activities or associations during any specified period relevant to the offence being investigated;
- questions related to statements or conduct of the suspect implying or leading to a reasonable inference that he was at a material time directing the activities of a criminal organisation; and
- questions relating to any benefit which the suspect may have obtained from directing a criminal organisation or committing a serious offence within a criminal organisation.

A question is not to be regarded as being material to the investigation of the offence unless the Garda concerned reasonably believed that the question related to the participation of the defendant in the commission of the offence (s.72A(7)).

Section 72A seems to differ from the main inference-drawing provisions that are already on the Irish statute books. Section 19A of the Criminal Justice Act 1984, as inserted by the Criminal Justice Act 2007, is the broadest inference-drawing provision in this jurisdiction. It applies to all arrestable offences and operates where the accused failed to mention a particular fact in the pre-trial period which at that time "clearly called for an explanation" and which he then sought to rely on at trial as part of his defence. Sections 18 and 19 of the 1984 Act, as substituted by the 2007 Act, allow for inferences to be drawn from the accused's failure to account for very particular matters (objects, substances, marks on one's person or clothing, or one's presence in a particular place) in the pre-trial investigatory stage, where such an account was again "clearly called for". Section 72A involves a different concept which raises issues in relation to the presumption of innocence and the burden of proof in a criminal trial. The court may draw an inference against the accused, basically on the grounds that he refused to co-operate with the Garda investigation into his guilt. An inference, it seems, may be drawn whether or not an answer to the particular question was "clearly called for" or the failure to provide such an answer is a specifically relevant matter in the context of the later trial. Failure alone gives rise to the inference: there is no threshold of trial reliance or pre-trial objective necessity in place.

In relation to legal advice, s.72A requires that the suspect must have been afforded a reasonable opportunity to consult a solicitor prior to the relevant failure to answer a question. This entitlement may be waived, however, and the restrictive interpretation of a "reasonable opportunity" to consult a solicitor in Irish pre-trial law gives some cause for concern (see *People (DPP) v Healy* [1990] 2 I.R. 73; *Barry v Waldron,* unreported, High Court, ex tempore, May 23, 1996; and *Lavery v Member-in-Charge, Carrickmacross Garda Station* [1999] 2 I.R. 390). Furthermore, there is no prohibition on questioning the suspect prior to this consultation (see *People (DPP) v Cullen,* unreported, Court of Criminal Appeal, March 30, 1993; *People (DPP) v Buck* [2002] 2 I.R. 268; and *People (DPP) v O'Brien* [2005] 2 I.R. 206). It is foreseeable that pre-consultation interrogation could cloud the mind of a suspect and even though he may have received legal advice in the intervening period, subsequent interrogation may be influenced by his earlier interaction with the Gardaí. A stronger level of protection would be to allow no interrogation prior to consultation.

Beyond all of this, it seems likely that a new caution taking account of s.72A will be required to facilitate clarity for Gardaí and suspects alike in this area. In *People (DPP) v Campbell,* unreported, Court of Criminal Appeal, December 19, 2003 it was argued that the appellant had been confused by the contradiction between the traditional caution administered, which states that there is no obligation to say anything, and the explanation of s.2 of the Offences Against the State (Amendment) Act 1998. On the facts, the Court of Criminal Appeal rejected such submissions, but a future case may have different results. The operation of s.2 of the 1998 Act was also considered in 2009 in *DPP v Mark Doran* [2009] IECCA 113 (discussed below).

Section 72A seems to move the focus of the criminal case from the courtroom and the legal defence of the charge to the Garda station and the initial investigation of the offence, and it places a heavy onus on the suspect within the pre-trial process to provide the Gardaí with information on which to base their further investigations. This is symptomatic of the ongoing movement backwards from the public courtroom to the Garda interrogation room. Other examples of this shift in focus include the provision of extended pre-trial detention periods (e.g. under s.50 of the Criminal Justice Act 2007) and courtroom reliance on Garda testimony (e.g. under s.71B of the Criminal Justice Act 2006 as inserted by s.7 of the Criminal Justice (Amendment) Act 2009).

CASE LAW DEVELOPMENTS

Duty to seek out and preserve evidence In the course of their investigations into alleged criminal activity, Gardaí are obliged to seek out and preserve all relevant evidence, both that which might implicate and that which might exonerate a suspect. This has previously been emphasised by the superior courts in cases such as *Murphy v DPP* [1989] I.L.R.M. 71; *Braddish v DPP*

[2001] 3 I.R. 127; *Dunne v DPP* [2002] 2 I.R. 25; *Scully v DPP* [2005] 1 I.R. 242; *Savage v DPP* [2009] 1 I.R. 185; and *Ludlow v DPP* [2009] 1 I.R. 640. A number of principles relating to this issue have been set down by the courts in these and other related cases (for further analysis see Heffernan, "The Duty to Preserve Evidence" in Bacik and Heffernan (eds), *Criminal Law and Procedures: Current Issues and Emerging Trends* (Dublin: FirstLaw, 2009), pp.53–71).

One of the central principles emanating from the courts is that to obtain an order prohibiting the progression of a trial due to the absence of evidence which ought to have been preserved, the accused must show that there is a real risk that his trial would be unfair and that directions or rulings by the trial judge would be insufficient to avoid such unfairness. Generally, the courts are slow to prohibit a trial on the grounds of "missing evidence", particularly where alternative, relevant evidence is available to the defence.

A number of cases seeking prohibition of trial on the basis of "missing evidence" came before the courts in 2009. While the High Court held in *English v DPP* [2009] IEHC 27 that no unfairness would result in the applicant's trial for arson as a result of the loss of a CCTV recording, a number of interesting statements were made by O'Neill J. in relation to the absence of appropriate facilities in Garda Síochána stations for the storage of evidence of this nature:

> "[I]t is incomprehensible that every Garda station does not have a facility for the secure storage of this kind of evidence. It is wholly unacceptable that evidence of this kind invariably ends up in the personal locker of investigating Gardaí. I appreciate that Gardaí do they best they can to safeguard evidence in this way, where there is no dedicated storage facility for that purpose.
>
> What is required is neither elaborate or expensive. A locked cupboard or filing cabinet would suffice into which the evidence, properly labelled, namely, with the name of the accused, the investigating Gardaí and the numbers of the charge sheets or summonses attached."

He went on to state that the consequence of the absence of such a simple and basic facility was that:

> "… dozens of criminal trials have been delayed for lengthy periods and a great deal of money has had to be needlessly expended on judicial review proceedings. In addition, a small number of trials have been prohibited with the consequent defeat of the right of the public to have these matters prosecuted to a lawful conclusion".

O'Neill J. expressed a wish that, "after almost a decade of these cases", the root cause of the loss of evidence such as this could be addressed.

Approaching the matter from a slightly different angle, Fennelly J. in the Supreme Court in *CD v DPP* [2009] IESC 70 noted that in less than two years the Supreme Court had heard eight appeals in "missing evidence" cases. He then said:

> "It is not easy to avoid the suspicion that a practice has developed of trawling through the book of evidence in search of the silver bullet—rather the absent missing bullet—which can put a stop to any trial."

In *CD*, the High Court had refused an order prohibiting the trial of the appellant in relation to the sexual assault of a female Garda outside Leinster House. The Supreme Court held that there was no basis to disturb the High Court decision of O'Neill J. on the facts. For the Supreme Court to overturn the High Court decision it would need to be shown some error in approach, not merely called upon to take a different view. Furthermore, Fennelly J. held that the appellant's claim that still images at half-second intervals ought to have been obtained by the Gardaí, rather than those obtained which were at one second intervals, was "far-fetched" and did not impart a fair or reasonable standard in terms of the Garda duty to seek out and preserve evidence. The appeal was dismissed as there was no evidence of a real risk of unfairness in the trial due to the absence of half-second interval still images.

In *McG v DPP* [2009] IEHC 294, it was held that there was no risk of an unfair trial for the offence of rape where, inter alia, the Gardaí had decided not to re-interview the complainant and another witness and not to forensically examine certain items. Herbert J. noted, as had Hardiman J. in *Dunne v DPP* [2002] 2 I.R. 25, that the Garda duty to seek out and preserve evidence extends only to evidence which might realistically afford an applicant a real opportunity of rebutting the prosecution case, not that which could "remotely, theoretically or fancifully" do so.

Bermingham J. in *Keogh v DPP* [2009] IEHC observed that the legal principles applicable to "missing evidence" cases are now well settled, but he also noted that, "the situation is often less straightforward when it comes to applying those principles to the facts of a particular case". In applying the law to the facts in this case, the learned judge deemed it one of the rare cases where prohibition of trial was appropriate. The accused in this case was charged with possession of a firearm and claimed that CCTV footage from a local pub ought to have been sought by the Gardaí. The Gardaí had been called to a laneway behind a pub to investigate suspicious activity and two other persons had been present there with the applicant directly prior to his arrest. The claim was that although the CCTV footage would have been unlikely to show clearly the exact place where the applicant was arrested, and where the firearm was found in a bag, it may well have been able to show occurrences leading up to the arrival of the Gardaí and may have shown the relevant bag and firearm to have in fact been in the possession of someone other than the applicant. Bermingham J.

held that if the CCTV footage could have shown the applicant and those with him at the time which aroused suspicion prior to the arrival of the Gardaí, it may have been of "enormous significance" and that it was reasonable to have expected therefore that the Gardaí would seek to obtain the CCTV footage. It was noted by the court also that the applicant's solicitor had requested that the Gardaí seek the relevant footage within eight days of the applicant's arrest. Due to the unsatisfactory state of affairs presented by the facts of this case, the applicant succeeded in obtaining an order prohibiting trial.

An application for an order to prohibit a criminal trial on drugs charges due to several items of evidence going missing was rejected by Hedigan J. in *Kelly v DPP* [2009] IEHC 525. The missing evidence included, amongst other things, receipts, carbon paper, garden forks, gloves, plastic bags, a carpet mat from the boot of the applicant's car, car keys, and original statements. Hedigan J. held that the fact that some of these items of evidence were missing was in fact to the advantage of the applicant and that any conceivable injustice could be adequately addressed by the trial judge.

In the Supreme Court in *Dunne v DPP* [2009] IESC 14, a High Court order prohibiting trial was overturned. This case involved missing CCTV footage of a robbery. There was other evidence in existence linking the respondent to the offence, most notably the fact that he had been apprehended not long after the robbery with a bag in his possession containing much of the material which had been stolen and that he had given a full statement of admission to the Gardaí. While Quirke J. in the High Court had held that there was "a risk, however, remote, of a miscarriage of justice", Fennelly J. in the Supreme Court reiterated the requirement that there be a "real risk" in order for prohibition of trial to be warranted.

An order of prohibition handed down by Quirke J. in the High Court was upheld by the Supreme Court on the specific facts of *McHugh v DPP* [2009] IESC 15. The respondent in that case was charged with the theft of a leather jacket at a supermarket. On the date of the incident, CCTV footage of the supermarket had been viewed by a Garda, the manager of the supermarket and a private security guard, thus identifying the respondent. The Garda requested that a copy of the CCTV footage be created for him but what he in fact received were five still images from the CCTV footage, rather than the moving video which he had previously viewed. The Supreme Court found that the still images from the CCTV did not clearly indicate that the respondent had stolen a jacket. The main difficulty arose in the case due to the fact that the central prosecution evidence was based on the accounts of the Garda, supermarket manager and security guard who viewed the CCTV footage, but that footage had never been available to the defence. Accordingly, the Supreme Court held that there was, in the specific circumstances of this case, a real risk to the fairness of the trial where the original footage was not made available on an equal footing to both the prosecution and the defence. The court clearly confined this case to its own facts, however, and overtly stated that it was not holding that still images taken from a missing video were generally inadmissible.

Interestingly, however, in the later case of *CD v DPP* (outlined above), Fennelly J., who seemed concerned about the high number of "missing evidence" cases coming before the courts, said in relation to *McHugh*:

> "At this point, on reflection, I wonder whether even that case could not properly have been left on the basis that it would be unfair to admit evidence of identification from unavailable CCTV footage, which would be a matter for the trial judge."

In the Supreme Court case of *O'Driscoll v DPP* [2009] IESC 23, Macken J. drew a distinction between a criminal damage charge and a burglary charge which were pending in relation to the appellant. The court held that the failure of the Gardaí to inform the appellant and/or his legal representative that a car involved in the ramming and burglary of a video store was to be returned to its owner from whom it had been stolen, denied the appellant the opportunity to have the car forensically examined. This interfered with his ability to construct his defence and engage with the prosecution case, but only in relation to the criminal damage charge. There was separate evidence, including identification and arrest at the scene, in relation to the burglary charge. Therefore, the Supreme Court granted an order prohibiting trial on the criminal damage charge, but not on the burglary charge.

In *RC v DPP* [2009] IESC 32, the appellant had been charged with sexual assault of a minor and a central element of the investigation and the prosecution case related to telephone communications between the appellant and the complainant. The Gardaí, in their investigations, had accessed the mobile phone records of the appellant, showing only the outgoing calls from his phone. The appellant claimed that calls incoming to his phone from the complainant's phone were of central importance as proof that he had only responded to communication she initiated, supporting his denial of all allegations against him.

Denham J., in the Supreme Court, noted that an order to prohibit prosecution should only be given in exceptional circumstances. She further noted that while, in general, the absence of phone records is not a reason to prohibit a trial, in the specific circumstances of this case the absence of the relevant records created circumstances where there was a real risk of an unfair trial, and an order for prohibition was appropriate.

Delay The central principle which applies to prohibiting a trial on the basis of missing evidence is the same as that which applies to prohibiting a trial on grounds of delay: an order of prohibition will only be granted where there is a real risk that an unfair trial will occur, which can not be remedied by appropriate directions or rulings by the trial judge.

In *C v DPP* [2009] IEHC 400, the applicant sought an order prohibiting further steps in his prosecution on charges relating to a series of sexual offences against his niece which were alleged to have occurred between April 1, 1973 and December 31, 1978, when she was aged between 12 and 17 years, on the basis of delay. In January 1999 the complainant had, for the first time, told a counsellor that she had been abused by the applicant as a child. She did not make any formal complaint to the Garda Síochána until February 2005 and a criminal investigation was then commenced. The applicant was not formally charged until May 2007.

The main submissions of the applicant were that the lapse of time between the dates of the alleged offences and the date on which the complainant first contacted the authorities resulted in unavoidable and incurable prejudice; there was a real and substantial risk of an unfair trial by virtue of the death of a number of key witnesses, the applicant's age and his present physical condition; and that the delay on the part of the prosecution in advancing the proceedings was oppressive and amounted to a violation of his right to a trial with due expedition and in due course of law.

Hedigan J. noted the jurisprudence of the Irish courts in cases such as this in recent years, observing that there is a balance to be achieved between "an applicant's right to a trial in due course of law and the community's right to see that serious crimes do not go unpunished". This balance is achieved by only granting an order of prohibition where there is a real risk that the accused would not receive a fair trial, and any unfairness which might arise could not be avoided by appropriate rulings and directions on the part of the trial judge.

Hedigan J. noted that there are different strands to the issue of delay: prosecutorial delay and complainant delay, and he further noted that the court is entitled to consider the cumulative effects of all factors in a case—what is sometimes referred to as the "omnibus test".

On the facts of the instant case, the learned High Court judge considered that while the prosecutorial delay was not ideal, it was not sufficient of itself to presume irreparable prejudice and direct the prohibition of the trial. The more pressing issue in this case was the delay on the part of the complainant, which the High Court deemed to have significantly prejudiced the applicant's ability to raise a defence to the charges. This was mainly based on the fact that important witnesses had died in the intervening years and that the applicant could not prove his case by alternative means. Furthermore, Hedigan J. considered that the demonstrable prejudice which arose against the applicant could not be avoided or ameliorated by appropriate warnings and directions of the trial judge if the case were to proceed. Taking this finding into account, along with the prosecutorial delay, Hedigan J. granted the order for prohibition which was sought in this case.

In more general terms, Hedigan J. made the following statements:

> "The courts do not lightly interfere with the decision of the Director of

> Public Prosecutions to bring a prosecution. However, it is ultimately the courts that must decide where lies the balance between society's undoubted interest in the prosecution of serious offences and an accused's right to a fair trial which itself is something in which society also has an undoubted interest."

Search The Court of Criminal Appeal in *DPP v Lynch* [2009] IECCA 31 considered whether a squatter/trespasser in a flat could claim a breach of constitutional rights when that flat was searched under the purported authority of what was in fact an invalid search warrant. Here, a search warrant had been issued in the District Court under s.48 of the Criminal Justice (Theft and Fraud Offences) Act 2001 for the search of the relevant premises based on the suspicion that stolen property would be found there. While that provision requires that a specific Garda be named on the warrant, this did not occur. Therefore, the warrant was deemed invalid at trial. However, the trial judge considered that where the occupant of the flat was a squatter, or trespasser, it could not be right or just that he would be afforded the same constitutional protections as the owner or lawful occupier of a dwelling. He held accordingly that the evidence of stolen property had been obtained unlawfully, not unconstitutionally, and he exercised his discretion to admit the evidence.

Considering whether or not the applicant in this case could claim the protection of the constitutional right to the inviolability of the dwelling under Art.40.5, the Court of Criminal Appeal looked at the Irish version of the text, which refers to the English term "dwelling" as "ionad cónaithe" (living place). The court held that the Irish version reinforced the view that it was a question of fact in each individual case as to whether a particular premises was someone's dwelling. Further, Fennelly J. stated that:

> "… the constitutional protection would extend to a wide variety of people with dubious legal titles, such as an overholding tenant, the widow of a deceased legal owner, or a person in *bona fide* possession on foot of an invalid title".

On the facts of the instant case, the court noted that the Gardaí had this premises on a list of a number of addresses for the applicant, and indeed the search warrant was sought because the Gardaí believed that the applicant lived there and that stolen property would be found there for that reason. The Court of Criminal Appeal thus held that the flat was the "dwelling" of the applicant and, accordingly, the search under the invalid warrant was contrary to Art.40.5 of the Constitution. Therefore, the learned trial judge had no discretion to admit it and the strict exclusionary rule from *People (DPP) v Kenny* [1990] 2 I.R. 110 ought to have been applied. The conviction was quashed as a result.

Although the specific point raised in this case had not come before the courts before, in the past it seemed that only the lawful owner/occupier of a dwelling could lay claim to the constitutional protection under Art.40.5. In *DPP v Forbes* [1994] 2 I.R. 542, for example, the accused was arrested on the forecourt of the private property of a third party. He sought to argue that the arrest was unlawful as a result, but this was rejected by the Supreme Court. It was held that there was no breach of constitutional rights when a Garda goes on to the forecourt of a householder's dwelling with their permission, and that every householder is presumed to give an implied authority to the Garda Síochána to come onto such forecourt "in order to see the enforcement of the law or prevent a breach thereof". This implied authority could be rebutted on the evidence.

The facts of *Forbes* obviously differ from those presented in *Lynch*, both in terms of the appellant in *Lynch* actually residing in the premises and the Gardaí in *Lynch* entering that premises rather than remaining on any forecourt or driveway. Indeed, in *Forbes* the Supreme Court expressly noted that it was not called upon in that case to consider any entry of a dwelling. The Court of Criminal Appeal was not obliged in any way to follow *Forbes* given the distinction in the facts, although it is interesting that there was no discussion of that case at all in the judgment of Fennelly J. in *Lynch*.

The power of the Gardaí to stop and search a vehicle was the subject of *DPP (Higgins) v Farrell* [2009] IEHC 368, an appeal by way of case stated from the conviction of the appellant in the District Court in relation to possession of a knife. The Garda who had stopped and searched the appellant's vehicle stated in evidence at trial that he had stopped the car in order to conduct a search under the Misuse of Drugs Act 1977 as there was a drugs problem in the area.

Looking at *DPP (Stratford) v Fagan* [1994] 3 I.R. 265, which related to stopping cars to investigate drink-driving, Clark J. stated:

> "I see little reason why, if a Garda can randomly stop a driver and speak to him/her in an attempt to detect drunk driving, the same Garda cannot also set up road blocks in areas known for the distribution of drugs to randomly stop and seek to search a vehicle in order to determine whether that vehicle is being used to transport drugs."

However, the learned High Court judge went on to state that while the Garda in this case was empowered to stop without any specific suspicion any car in pursuit of the detection and prevention of crime, and to have the driver provide his name and address, he did not hold the right, either at common law or under statute, to search the car without permission in those circumstances. In order to invoke the statutory power to search the vehicle under s.23 of the Misuse of Drugs Act 1977, the Garda would have to have reasonable suspicion that the appellant specifically was in possession of a controlled substance. Interestingly, the judge also suggested that if the Garda had requested to search the vehicle and had been refused permission, this may have led to reasonable cause to suspect that the appellant was in possession of drugs and to invoke the statutory search powers. Furthermore, it was held that the Gardaí are obliged to inform a person in general terms as to why their car is being searched.

In *People (DPP) v Valiukas,* unreported, ex tempore, Court of Criminal Appeal, Kearns, Budd, McMahon JJ., April 27 2009, it was held, amongst other things, that the Garda protocol for conducting searches of a house was not unlawful, at least not on the facts of this case. Here, when executing a search warrant the Gardaí had asked the four occupants of the house at that time to wait in the kitchen while the search was conducted. An argument was made that they were effectively detained from that time onwards, but this was rejected and the court held that the applicant, and the other occupants of the house, were not restrained or prohibited from leaving the house. Kearns J. did state that the situation may have been different if the applicant had endeavoured to leave the house and had been told that he could not do so. However, that did not arise and, at least on the basis of the facts in the instant case, the Gardaí were entitled to act as they had done in searching the house.

Arrest and detention In *Oladapo v Governor of Cloverhill Prison* [2009] IESC 42; [2009] 2 I.L.R.M. 166, the Supreme Court held that the appellant had been unlawfully arrested and detained by the Gardaí. The arrest was deemed unlawful as it was not made for the purpose of charging the appellant with the offence for which he was purportedly arrested. The appellant was a non-national who was arrested on re-entering the State following a shopping trip to Northern Ireland. He was purportedly arrested under s.13 of the Immigration Act 2004 for failure to produce documents, contrary to s.12 of that Act, but, in fact, the arresting Garda admitted at trial that his intention at the time of arrest was to refuse the appellant leave to land and to seek a warrant under s.5(2) of the Immigration Act 2003 which would allow for arrangements to be made for his removal from the State.

While he was later arrested and detained under s.5(2) of the 2003 Act, the appellant had been held in unlawful detention directly prior to that, consequent to the initial unlawful arrest. Murray C.J. held that the subsequent arrest and detention under s.5(2) was "dominated by the fact that it was deliberately facilitated and achieved by bringing the appellant into unlawful custody for that specific and ulterior purpose". This was found to entail a fundamental breach in the due process of law, even though the arresting Garda may not have realised this. The appeal was therefore allowed and an order for release under Art.40.4 was made.

DPP v Bullman [2009] IECCA 84 involved an appeal against a conviction of membership of an unlawful organisation which had been handed down by the Special Criminal Court, the salient part of which related to the detention of the appellant prior to arrest. The appellant, along with two others, was in a jeep at the rear of Heuston Station when Gardaí, who had been involved in surveillance in the area, approached the jeep and spoke with them. The Gardaí sought to identify the men and to check certain details relating to the ownership of the jeep. Ten minutes elapsed while the Gardaí carried out these checks. At some point during that time the appellant asked a Garda if he could get out of the jeep to have a cigarette. The Garda replied: "No, I would prefer if you stayed seated in the back."

The suggestion that this discouragement in terms of exiting the vehicle amounted to unlawful detention was dismissed on the facts in the Special Criminal Court, and the Court of Criminal Appeal saw no reason to disturb that decision. Although the Gardaí had some information relating to the appellant and his colleagues, they were entitled to seek to verify this before being satisfied as to the identity of the occupants of the jeep. The suggestion seemed to be that without this satisfaction in terms of identity the Gardaí had not reached the point of holding a suspicion sufficient to warrant an arrest and therefore no arrest needed to be made at that point. Furthermore, on the facts there was no true detention, merely a discouragement, and the appellant made no real effort to challenge that discouragement.

The applicant for judicial review in *Broe v DPP* [2009] IEHC 549 had been originally arrested and detained by the Gardaí under s.4 of the Criminal Justice Act 1984 in connection with an assault. Shortly before he was to be released, the DPP gave instructions that he should be charged with specified offences. He was released and immediately re-arrested. Section 10(2) of the Criminal Justice Act 1984 provides that where a person is released from section 4 detention he can only be re-arrested by order of the District Court or for the purpose of charging him "forthwith". In this case, there was a delay of three hours and 45 minutes between the time of re-arrest and charging. During this time the Gardaí were trying to arrange for a special sitting of the District Court to which they could bring the applicant and they needed to know the venue of the court in order to complete the charge sheet. The applicant argued that the delay in charging him meant that s.10(2) was not complied with as charging did not happen "forthwith". His consequent argument was that all that followed the delay was invalid and void.

Applying *O'Brien v Special Criminal Court* [2008] 4 I.R. 514, which dealt with an analogous, though not identical, situation under s.30A(3) of the Offences Against the State Act 1939, Ryan J. held that s.10(2) of the 1984 Act involves a statutory obligation to charge the relevant person "forthwith" and that the word "forthwith" should be given its ordinary meaning of "at once" or "immediate". Although Ryan J. was unsure whether the Supreme Court meant to set down an absolute rule that would apply in all conditions and circumstances in *O'Brien*, he held that if that judgment did mean "immediate and nothing else" then the applicant in this case was not charged "forthwith".

Even if the correct approach in a case such as this was to examine the individual circumstances of each case, it was clear to the court that the delay in the instant case was longer than delays in other cases and the justification for the delay was not comparable to other cases. In any event, Ryan J. held that *O'Brien* was binding on him and accordingly held that the delay in this case meant that the applicant had not been charged forthwith.

The learned High Court judge then moved on to consider the implications of this finding. He noted the general rule that the fact that a person is unlawfully brought before the court for charge does not invalidate the subsequent court proceedings. While certain exceptions to this rule exist, specifically, for example, in relation to the Special Criminal Court (s.43 of the Offences Against the State Act 1939) or where the process by which the individual is brought before the court involves a breach of constitutional rights (such as in *State (Trimbole) v The Governor of Mountjoy Prison* [1985] I.R. 550), no such exceptions were in existence in this case. Ryan J. considered that the delay in charging the applicant did not amount to a breach of his constitutional rights. Despite the fact that the applicant was not charged forthwith, the application was dismissed on the grounds that this did not invalidate the subsequent court proceedings.

European Arrest Warrant (EAW) *Minister for Justice, Equality and Law Reform v Gotszlik* [2009] IESC 13; [2009] 3 I.R. 390 was a most interesting case in relation to the execution of EAWs, centering on the interpretation of s.22 of the European Arrest Warrant Act 2003 as substituted by s.80 of the Criminal Justice (Terrorist Offences) Act 2005. This case is particularly interesting as the Supreme Court therein exercised its discretion to hear and determine an issue of law, despite the fact that the factual basis for the original case had altered, rendering the legal decision moot in this case but important for the future. That factual basis, which for the purposes of deciding the legal issue the Supreme Court was presumed to still persist, was that two separate EAWs had been issued by the Polish authorities for the surrender of the respondent in relation to two separate offences.

The wording of s.22(1), in pertinent part, is as follows:

> In this section, except where the context otherwise requires, "offence" means, in relation to a person to whom a European arrest warrant applies, an offence (other than an offence specified in the European arrest warrant in respect of which the person's surrender is ordered under this Act) under the law of the issuing state committed before the person's surrender, but shall not include an offence consisting, in whole, of acts or omissions of which the offence specified in the European arrest warrant consists in whole or in part.

Section 22 gives effect to the "speciality rule" in the context of the EAW. This rule, applied for many years in extradition cases, exists to protect the subject of an EAW from prosecution or sentence in the requesting State for offences committed prior to the execution of the EAW (which were not included in the requesting EAW), unless he is given reasonable opportunity to leave the requesting state. Giving a literal interpretation to s.22, the High Court refused to execute the EAW; however, this was deemed "absurd" by Denham J. in the Supreme Court as it meant that two valid EAWs were not executed. The learned Supreme Court judge preferred a purposive approach to the interpretation of s.22. She noted that:

> "... while the European Arrest Warrant Act, 2003, as amended, may not be drafted in optimum terms, it is clearly intended to give effect to the Council Framework Decision of 13 June 2002 on the European arrest warrant and the surrender procedures between Member States. The Framework Decision sought to establish a simplified system of surrender between Member States. By this system it was sought to reduce issues such as delay and complexity. Section 22, and the Act as a whole, may be construed as implementing in the Statute the specialty rule as addressed in Article 27 of the Framework Decision".

Applying a purposive approach, Denham J. (Fennelly and Macken JJ. concurring) held that a court may order the surrender of a person on more than one EAW. This approach preserved the protection of the speciality rule and was consistent with the terms of s.22 and the purpose of the Framework Decision. Although there were no longer two EAWs in place in relation to the respondent in this case, the legal principle set out by the Supreme Court provides important clarity for the future.

Drink-driving cases A number of cases arose in 2009 which addressed procedure and evidence in the context of drink-driving investigations and trials. The question of errors in procedure being merely "technical" or otherwise is central to much of the judicial discussion in these cases. Generally, if only non-essential evidence is affected by a breach in procedure, the accused will have to show some specific prejudice in order to have evidence excluded or charges dismissed. If an essential item of evidence in the case is affected, this may be enough in itself for exclusion or dismissal of charges.

DPP v Freeman [2009] IEHC 179 concerned s.17 of the Road Traffic Act 1994, which relates to the taking of specimens of breath from an individual suspected of driving while above the legal alcohol limit. Section 17(2) provides that when such specimens are taken and the apparatus used determines the level of alcohol in the relevant specimen to be potentially in contravention of the law, the suspected person shall be supplied by a member of the Garda Síochána with two identical statements automatically produced by the apparatus and "duly completed by the member in the prescribed form". These statements will state the concentration of alcohol in the specimen given by the suspect, as determined by the apparatus.

Section 17(3) states that on receipt of those statements, the suspected person shall "forthwith acknowledge such receipt by placing his signature on each statement" and return one of the statements to the member. It is an offence not to comply with s.17(3).

Section 21 of the Road Traffic Act 1994 states that a statement:

> … purporting to have been supplied under section 17 shall, until the contrary is shown, be sufficient evidence in any proceedings under the Road Traffic Acts, 1961–1994, of the facts stated therein, without proof of any signature on it or that the signatory was the proper person to sign it, and shall, until the contrary is shown, be sufficient evidence of compliance by the member of the Garda Síochána concerned with the requirements imposed on him …

The Road Traffic Act 1994 (Section 17) Regulations 1999 also outline the manner in which s.17 is to operate and state, amongst other things, that, "following the automatic production of the statements by the apparatus", the relevant member of the Garda Síóchána should sign the statements (reg.5).

This High Court appeal in this case arose by way of case stated from the District Court and the relevant facts are as follows. The accused was arrested on October 20, 2006 on suspicion of drink-driving, having been stopped at a Garda check-point. At Pearse Street Garda station, following arrest, an intoxilyser test was carried out, which required the appellant to provide two specimens of breath. The main issue which arose was the order in which the statements printed by the intoxilyser machine were signed: the accused first signed the statements and they were *then* signed by the relevant Garda. Thereafter the accused took one copy of the statement and the Garda kept the other. In the District Court it was held that the requirements of s.17 were not properly complied with and the charges against the accused were dismissed.

The High Court embarked on a review of precedent and determined that an essential element of earlier decisions has been the nature and effect of the error or omission, and whether or not it was such as to necessarily give rise to a "direction" of no case to answer. Looking at the earlier highly relevant authority of *DPP v Keogh,* unreported, High Court, ex tempore, Murphy J., February 9, 2004, MacMenamin J. observed that, in cases such as this, "while the error may indeed be 'technical', it involves a breach of a penal provision which must be interpreted and applied strictly". He held that the instant case could not be distinguished from *Keogh* and accordingly deemed himself bound to follow it. On the facts of the instant case, MacMenamin J. stated that:

> "[T]he phrase in the section '*duly completed*' can only be read as meaning full compliance other than by the signature of the person providing a sample. A form not signed by the Garda first is 'not duly completed'; and therefore the statutory presumption cannot apply to

> it. Once signed by the Garda first, it is only then 'duly completed' and must be signed by the recipient."

Accordingly the High Court held that the District Court judge had been correct to dismiss the charges against the accused.

Issues of procedure in the context of drink-driving investigations also arose for consideration by way of case stated from the District Court to the High Court in *DPP (O'Brien) v Hopkins* [2009] IEHC 337. The accused here was charged with drink-driving on May 6, 2007, having been initially stopped at a Garda check-point on that date. Following arrest, a blood sample was taken from the accused by a doctor at Store Street Garda station. A mistake was made on the labelling of one container of the blood sample, which was kept by the accused. Instead of recording the date of the sampling on the label, the doctor accidentally recorded the (incorrect) date of birth of the accused. The District Court judge held that the error on the label was in breach of s.18 of the Road Traffic Act 1994 and, in the absence of any explanation for this error, she dismissed the charges against the accused.

On appeal, the prosecutor argued that the error in this case was trivial in nature and that it did nothing to undermine the admissibility of a certificate prepared by the Medical Bureau of Road Safety pursuant to s.19 of the 1994 Act, relating to the specimen retained by the Gardaí, which was the central item of proof in the case. Hedigan J. in the High Court distinguished this case from the above-outlined case of *Freeman*, as in *Freeman* the statement from the intoxilyser was itself the essential piece of evidence in the case, which was not true of *Hopkins*. In light of this difference between the two cases, and basing his decision on other earlier precedents, Hedigan J. held that to succeed in having the case dismissed, the accused in *Hopkins* would have to show that the technical flaw which existed in some way prejudiced him or appreciably hampered his defence. In this regard, the learned judge stated that:

> "In considering the issue of prejudice, the court is obliged to examine any tangible and credible impediment which might arise as against the accused, in the conduct of his case, as a result of the error made by the relevant authorities."

On the facts, it was held that the breach was a purely technical one and accordingly it did not require a specific explanation from the prosecution at trial as it was clear that it was merely a slip. The District Court ought to have sought some real prejudice to the accused before deciding to dismiss the charge against him. In the absence of evidence of such prejudice the District judge erred in law in dismissing the charge.

Related issues arose by way of a consultative case stated from the District Court in *DPP v Kennedy* [2009] IEHC 361. A sample of blood was obtained from the accused by a doctor in Westport Garda station, following his arrest on suspicion of drink-driving. The blood sample was divided into two containers and the accused was informed by a member of the Garda Síochána that he could retain one of those, which he chose to do. The doctor handed one of the containers to the accused. The question for the High Court was whether s.18(2) of the 1994 Act requires that in "offering" the sample to the accused a member of the Garda Síochána must physically proffer or tender it to the accused. The relevant text of the section provides that:

> Where a specimen of blood or urine of a person has been divided into 2 parts pursuant to subsection (1), a member of the Garda Síochána shall offer to the person one of the sealed containers …

McMahon J., in the High Court, considered that it would be "wholly artificial" to follow the arguments made on behalf of the respondent in this case, having regard to both the language and the purpose of s.18(2). He held that the true meaning of the salient part of the provision is that, "the Garda must tell the accused that he may have one container to retain for himself". For clarity, the learned High Court judge stated that it is not necessary for the Garda to have the containers in his hand in order to make the relevant offer—even if they were on a table in another part of the room, the statutory requirements would be fulfilled so long as the Garda tells the accused that he may retain one of the containers. The court also dismissed any reliance on a mistake made by the doctor in filling out a particular form detailing what occurred on the occasion of his taking the blood sample. The doctor stated on this form that he had handed both containers to a Garda, whereas in fact he had handed one of the containers to the accused. The High Court held this to be merely a mistaken statement in respect of a non-essential requirement.

As in *Hopkins*, the High Court in *Kennedy* distinguished the instant case from that of *Freeman*. McMahon J. also set down a number of principles emanating from the case law of the courts in this area of criminal evidence and procedure. The three main principles which he identified are as follows:

> "(i) If there is a mandatory provision in the relevant statute or in the Regulations, the prosecution must in normal situations comply with it.
>
> (ii) Failure to complete a form accurately, where the Regulation only obliges the doctor 'to complete the relevant form', will not be fatal to the prosecution if it does no injustice to the party being prosecuted and if it is a minor or technical error.
>
> (iii) Where the Regulation itself provides that the statements averred to in the form are to be taken as proof of the facts averred to, then failure to complete the form in a non-essential matter only means that the evidentiary presumption is lost and may be proved

> independently by the prosecution if it has alternative ways of doing so."

The final case of this nature to come before the courts in 2009 was *DPP (Murphy) v Davenport* [2009] IEHC 506. This was a consultative case stated from Letterkenny District Court. Following a traffic accident, the accused was detained at the scene for approximately 15 minutes by Sergeant Michael Murphy, while Garda John Healy went to get an alcometer from Letterkenny Garda station in order to test the accused's breath for the presence of alcohol. When Garda Healy returned with the alcometer he administered it to the accused and a positive response was returned. Garda Healy then cautioned the accused and arrested him. Sergeant Murphy was standing beside Garda Healy throughout this time.

The defence sought a direction from the District Court on the grounds that s.12 of the Road Traffic Act 2003 had not been properly complied with. The main argument in this regard was that, under the legislation, it ought to be the same member of the Garda Síochána who both detains the suspect under s.12 and administers the alcometer test thereunder.

Section 12(2) provides that:

> A member of the Garda Síochána may require a person to whom this section applies—
>
> (a) to provide, by exhaling into an apparatus for indicating the presence of alcohol in the breath, a specimen of his or her breath,
>
> (b) to accompany him or her to a place (including a vehicle) at or in the vicinity of the public place concerned and there require the person to provide, by exhaling into such an apparatus, a specimen of his or her breath, or
>
> (c) where the member does not have such an apparatus with him or her, to remain at that place in his or her presence or in the presence of another member of the Garda Síochána until such an apparatus becomes available to him or her (but the member shall not require the person to so remain for more than one hour) and the member may then require the person to provide, by exhaling into such an apparatus, a specimen of his or her breath, and the member may indicate the manner in which the person is to comply with the requirement.

Hedigan J. extrapolated two relevant principles from previous case law in this area and stated that:

> "(1) Courts should not readily interpret legislation in a way that would lead to an artificial or absurd result.
>
> (2) A minor flaw of no significance in complying with a statutory provision is not fatal to the prosecution of an accused where it cannot cause prejudice of itself or work an injustice to the accused."

Accordingly, the learned High Court judge held that it would be:

> "… an absurd and artificial interpretation of the relevant section if it meant that the Sergeant in charge at the scene of an accident could not detain under s.12(2)(c) and then require another member to conduct the alcometer test".

He further held that as long as the accused is aware that he is being detained pending an alcometer test and he is made aware he will be required to give a sample when the apparatus is available, the legislative purpose and intent is met. In any event, Hedigan J. stated that no prejudice to the accused arose from this minor flaw and no direction could therefore be forthcoming.

Pre-trial right to legal advice Several issues relating to the constitutional right of reasonable access to legal advice in the pre-trial period arose before the courts in 2009. The first case in fact links back to the previous section as it arose in the context of a drink-driving investigation.

DPP (Lavelle) v McCrea [2009] IEHC 39 was an appeal by way of case stated to the High Court from the District Court relating to procedures surrounding the refusal of an arrested person to provide a specimen of breath pursuant to s.13 of the Road Traffic Act 1994 as amended. The accused had provided a specimen of breath when his car was stopped by the Gardaí on June 9, 2007 due to his erratic driving. Having failed that roadside breath test, the accused was arrested and brought to Blanchardstown Garda station. He was requested to provide two further specimens of breath at the Garda station, pursuant to s.13, and the consequences of failure to provide such specimens were explained to him, i.e. it is an offence not to provide the specimens. The accused refused and stated that he wished to consult a solicitor. The Garda operating the intoxilyser machine, Garda Synott, then told the accused that he could speak with a solicitor after he had provided the required breath samples. Garda Synnott explained to the accused in ordinary language that he was required to provide a breath sample under the law and that his solicitor would tell him the same thing. The accused continued to refuse, somewhat verbally aggressively, to provide a breath sample.

The accused was charged with failure to provide a specimen of breath under s.13(2) of the Road Traffic Act 1994 as amended. On questioning by the trial judge, Garda Synnott stated that the reason for her failure to allow the accused to consult a solicitor was that she believed she could only make one request pursuant to s.13(1)(a) and that if she aborted the process midway through, in order to provide the accused with an opportunity to speak to his solicitor, she would be precluded from making any further such request at a later stage.

The defence argued that the accused had been denied his right of reasonable access to a solicitor and that this had led to the evidence put forward by the prosecution against him. Finding that there was a breach of the constitutional right to legal advice, the District judge dismissed all charges against the accused.

The High Court, on appeal, held that the accused had indeed been denied his constitutional right of reasonable access to legal advice and that such denial had led to his being held in unlawful detention. Although the court accepted that Garda Synott was acting bona fide, it nonetheless recognised that the breach of constitutional rights in this case was deliberate and conscious in the sense in which that phrase was employed in *People (DPP) v Kenny* [1990] 2 I.R. 110. From the moment that the request to consult a solicitor was denied the accused was in unlawful detention and the exclusionary rule had to be applied by the court to evidence obtained during that period. The High Court rejected any assertion that the lack of culpability of Garda Synott, the subjective reasonableness of her actions, or the asserted prudence underlying her actions could be viewed as extraordinary excusing circumstances.

While Edwards J. then did apply the exclusionary rule from *Kenny* in this case, he did not seem overly enamoured with the rule and he noted that an appeal from the High Court decision in *DPP (Walsh) v Cash* [2007] IEHC 108 was pending before the Supreme Court. Edwards J. stated that he agreed with the view expressed by Charleton J. in that case, that:

> "[T]he automatic exclusion of evidence due to a mistake made in good faith arguably represents an unjustifiable anomaly in the law and something which is inimical to the public's interest in the prosecution of crime."

He supported Charleton J.'s call for a re-examination of the exclusionary rule. He further stated that he believed the rule was in need of re-examination, 18 years after *Kenny*:

> "… particularly in the light of the changed circumstances in which the Criminal Courts now find themselves, where the previously ubiquitous trial within trial seeking the exclusion of evidence on the grounds of alleged Garda misconduct has become … not quite a thing of the past, that would be to overstate it, but … very much the exception rather than the rule."

In relation to the requirement for a causative link to exist between the breach of rights and the obtaining of the impugned evidence, Edwards J. held that it is no longer the position that a causative link is necessarily required in order for the impugned evidence to be excluded, rather an individual's detention will be rendered unlawful if he is denied his right of reasonable access to a solicitor, and it will remain unlawful for so long as he remains deprived of a solicitor. He based this view on *People (DPP) v Buck* [2002] 2 I.R. 268 and *People (DPP) v O'Brien* [2005] 2 I.R. 206.

On the facts of the instant case, Edwards J. held that from the point of denial of the right to legal advice the accused was in unlawful detention and as such he was entitled from there on to be released and was not obliged to remain in the Garda station to fulfil the demand which had been made of him, to provide a specimen of breath. In this regard, the learned judge held that there was not a requirement for a causative link in order for the evidence of failure to comply to be excluded. Although the denial of the right to legal advice was not necessarily the reason for non-compliance, the accused was in unlawful detention at the time and Garda Synott therefore had no lawful authority to request that he comply with her demand for a breath sample.

In relation to the prosecution argument that as the evidence of non-compliance was obtained passively the exclusionary rule should not apply, Edwards J. held that, in the circumstances:

> "It matters not whether the evidence was acquired by means of some positive action taken by the Gardaí, or whether it was gathered incidentally, serendipitously or by mere passive observation."

In *DPP v Gormley* [2009] IECCA 86, the applicant had been convicted of attempted rape contrary to s.4 of the Criminal Law (Rape) (Amendment) Act 1990. Following a complaint from the complainant, who knew the applicant quite well, the Gardaí went to the apartment complex in which the applicant lived. They met the owner of the apartment complex there and he admitted them to the apartment block. They went up to the applicant's apartment and found that the door was open. They called out, entered the apartment and went up an internal staircase. The applicant was upstairs reading a newspaper and invited them to come in. The Gardaí cautioned the applicant and then put a number of questions to him. He identified the clothing he had been wearing the night before and admitted climbing a drainpipe at the back of the complainant's house and entering through an upstairs window. The applicant was arrested and conveyed to the Garda station where two interviews later took place.

Having been informed of his rights on arrival at the Garda station, the applicant requested to consult with his solicitor, either Mr Cathal Quinn or Mr Kieran Dillon. Neither of these were in their respective offices and no mobile phone numbers for them could be obtained. A Garda car was sent to search for Mr Dillon and it called at both his parents' house and his own home. At his home Gardaí spoke with his wife who agreed to try to contact Mr Dillon.

Around 20 minutes after this Mr Dillon rang the Garda station and indicated that he would call to the station in about one hour. In fact, Mr Dillon did not make it to the station until approximately one hour and 45 minutes later. At that time he met with the applicant for 45 minutes. The applicant was interviewed both prior to and following his consultation with Mr Dillon.

The central issues in this appeal related to an alleged denial of the constitutional right of reasonable access to legal advice and the alleged unlawful entry of the Gardaí into the applicant's dwelling.

In relation to the latter ground of appeal, Finnegan J., giving the judgment of the court, held that on entering without permission the Gardaí were trespassers, but the situation altered once the applicant invited them in. The presence of the Gardaí in the apartment became authorised at that point. At the time that statements in relation to the applicant's clothing and other matters were made and the applicant was arrested there was no illegality in the Garda presence.

The claim in relation to the right to legal advice was based on an assertion that, although the Gardaí were genuinely attempting to contact a solicitor, they did not allow sufficient time for his arrival prior to conducting the first interview. Basing its decision on *People (DPP) v Buck* [2002] 2 I.R. 268, the Court of Criminal Appeal held that so long as Gardaí are making genuine, bona fide attempts to contact a requested solicitor there is no prohibition on the questioning of a suspect. On the facts of this case, Finnegan J. suggested that, "having regard to the circumstance that it was a Sunday afternoon, the Gardaí used diligence and resourcefulness in locating the solicitor nominated by the applicant." Accordingly, the applicant was refused leave to appeal on both grounds.

DPP v Creed [2009] IECCA 95 also dealt with the question of pre-trial legal advice. The applicant had been convicted of robbery and unauthorised use of a mechanically propelled vehicle. The relevant facts are as follows: the applicant was arrested on the night of Saturday, October 21, 2006 and was brought to Naas Garda station. He requested the services of a particular solicitor, Ms Gráinne Malone. The member-in-charge telephoned the landline of Ms Malone's office (late on a Saturday night) a couple of times and got no answer. The member-in-charge did not try to obtain a different number on which to contact the solicitor and, in fact, never informed the applicant that he had been unable to contact Ms Malone, which might have given the applicant the opportunity to suggest a different solicitor.

The trial judge held that these failures on the part of the member-in-charge were not conscious and deliberate. The Court of Criminal Appeal supported the judge's right to make such a finding and distinguished the case from both *People (DPP) v Kenny* [1990] 2 I.R. 110 and *DPP (Lavelle) v McCrea* (discussed above) on the basis that *Kenny* entailed deliberate entry into the dwelling house of the accused without authorisation and *McCrea* entailed a deliberate refusal to provide the accused with access to legal advice. On the facts of the instant case, the court held that the member-in-charge did not deliberately deprive the applicant of his right of access to legal advice.

Geoghegan J., delivering the court's judgment, suggested that:

> "Where … there has been no deliberate and conscious violation of the constitutional right to access to a solicitor but where reasonable efforts have not been made to obtain a solicitor … it must then be a matter of discretion for the trial judge to rule as to whether any particular evidence obtained in that context should be admitted or not. It does not at all follow that because there was no deliberate and conscious violation of the right, that it would be a fair procedure towards the accused to admit evidence obtained in the absence of a solicitor when reasonable efforts have not been made to obtain one."

Despite his findings that there had been no deliberate and conscious breach of the applicant's right to pre-trial legal advice, the trial judge had agreed to exercise his discretion to exclude from evidence certain statements made by the applicant under questioning by the Gardaí on that occasion. This was arguably a good decision as the efforts of the member-in-charge in this case to secure legal advice for the detained suspect were in no way as extensive as those in the above-outlined case of *DPP v Gormley* [2009] IECCA 86, for example.

In any event, the broader question of admissibility in circumstances such as this case was still relevant as a hair sample from the applicant's head was taken during his detention for the purposes of DNA analysis and had been admitted at trial. It was held that the trial judge had not erred in admitting the hair sample as that was taken the following morning when an entirely different Garda was dealing with the applicant. That Garda was not requested to obtain a solicitor for the applicant—he considered that any such matters had been for the member-in-charge on the night before, and the applicant had made no enquiry as to the absence of his requested solicitor. Although this lack of continuity in the applicant's detention is somewhat concerning, and it could be contended that the obligation to fulfil a request for legal advice should not lapse merely because the member-in-charge has gone off duty, the Court of Criminal Appeal did not focus on this aspect of the case.

Geoghegan J. instead held that:

> "Given that under the Criminal Justice (Forensic Evidence) Act, 1990, the hair sample could be procured without consent, it would have been reasonable to assume that the applicant did not require a solicitor in connection with it. His request for a solicitor the previous evening was clearly related to the questioning which he was about to undergo."

As a result, the Court of Criminal Appeal refused leave to appeal and supported the manner in which the trial judge conducted the case.

Silence and admissions Two cases arose in 2009 in which the argument was made that the manner in which evidence was presented at trial made it clear that the appellant had exercised his right to silence when interviewed by Gardaí, and that this amounted to a breach of the right to a fair trial. These cases were based on events which occurred prior to the enactment of s.19A of the Criminal Justice Act 1984, as inserted by the Criminal Justice Act 2007, which allows for inferences to be drawn at trial from the pre-trial failure of the accused to mention any fact which he later relies upon, which "clearly called for an explanation" in the relevant pre-trial period. While s.19A may thus be invoked in future cases, the view of the Court of Criminal Appeal in the 2009 cases is nonetheless significant and relevant for future cases where no specific fact is relied upon which ought to have been mentioned in the pre-trial process, in accordance with s.19A, but reference is still made at trial to pre-trial interviews giving rise to nothing of evidential value.

The relevant cases were *DPP v O'Reilly* [2009] IECCA 18 and *DPP v Kearney* [2009] IECCA 112, both appeals against murder convictions. The Court of Criminal Appeal dismissed both appeals on the right to silence grounds, holding, in both cases, that it has never been held that any evidence from which it might be inferred that an accused exercised his right to silence should be excluded from the jury for that reason alone. While it could be excluded on the grounds of irrelevance in appropriate circumstances, it need not be excluded merely because it allowed the jury to know that the accused did not answer Garda questions. In *Kearney*, Kearns J. stated that there is "nothing procedurally wrong in telling a jury that an extensive interviewing process took place where nothing of evidential value arose from those interviews."

In both cases, the jury had not been invited to draw inferences from the fact that nothing of evidential value arose from the Garda interviews with the accused and the trial judge had directed the jury that they were not to draw such inferences.

Another issue which arose on appeal in *O'Reilly* was the admissibility of a statement taken from the appellant early on in the Garda investigation, which was taken without caution. At that stage in the investigation the appellant was not a suspect. The Court of Criminal Appeal noted that, "[t]he notion or term 'suspect' has a rather elastic meaning" and observed that in the context of a Garda investigation:

> "A person who comes under Garda suspicion so as to be regarded as a 'suspect' or 'potential suspect' (and it would be at least sometimes difficult to draw a line of distinction between those two terms) may be eliminated and replaced by another 'suspect' or 'suspects' as an investigation progresses. The degree to which a person might be considered a 'suspect' may vary greatly. A person on the one hand, may be the subject of an investigation in order to either eliminate that person as a suspect or confirm the need for further investigation. On

the other hand a person in respect of whom the investigating Gardaí have formed a firm opinion that he or she is the culprit, requires proof to charge such a person. This will depend on the gathering of sufficient evidence by further investigation."

It was held on the facts of this case that the Judges' Rules and the obligation to issue a caution did not apply when the statement was made as, even though he was a suspect, the Garda taking the statement had not made up his mind to charge him at that time and he was not in custody. In relation to the argument that there was a breach of fundamental fairness, the Court of Criminal Appeal distinguished the case of *People (DPP) v Breen*, unreported, Court of Criminal Appeal, March 13, 1995 in which the failure to administer a caution in the particular circumstances had been said to breach the requirements of basic fairness. In that case, the failure to administer a caution was coupled with a Garda encouraging an admission while the accused was in some distress. This was not the case in *O'Reilly* and the court held that there is no rule stating that a mere failure to caution a person being interviewed, even if they are a suspect, would constitute unfairness; there must be something more specific in the circumstances of the case which would render it necessary for a caution to be administered in order to ensure fairness.

In *DPP v Mark Doran* [2009] IECCA 113, the Court of Criminal Appeal made a number of notable statements in relation to the operation of s.2 of the Offences Against the State (Amendment) Act 1998. This provision, which allows for inferences to be drawn at trial for membership of an unlawful organisation from the accused's pre-trial failure to answer any question material to the investigation of that offence, is similar in its terms to the newly introduced s.72A of the Criminal Justice Act 2006, inserted by s.9 of the Criminal Justice (Amendment) Act 2009 (discussed above). The court in *Doran*, referring also to the admissibility of Garda belief evidence under s.3(2) of the Offences Against the State (Amendment) Act 1972, stated that:

> "The exception to the normal rules of proof provided for in s.2 must be construed appropriately, which may mean fairly strictly, given that the inferences permitted to be drawn are themselves to be used to corroborate belief evidence which, in turn, is not capable of being challenged against a claim to confidentiality invoked, as here, by all Chief Superintendents, and which this court fully accepts and affirms."

The court also stated that:

> "The Act of 1998 provides that inferences may be drawn from responses made to questions posed. The trial court can draw inferences…from questions posed, but those inferences must have regard for and be judged on the basis of the questions actually posed and the responses

> actually given. This is evident from the actual wording of the Act of 1998, (as amended). Those responses to the questions posed can then be considered against factual material presented … by which the responses can be assessed for evasiveness or for failure to respond."

The Court of Criminal Appeal was wary of the fact that, in this case, the trial court failed to acknowledge the limitations of questions asked of the appellant in relation to telephone contact between him and another person, Patrick Dermody, on a series of relevant dates. It felt that the Special Criminal Court had been swayed by evidence relating to the fact that telephone contact had been had *in itself*, rather than by any failure or refusal to answer questions relating to that. While the appellant had been asked only about telephone contact on certain days and had replied in somewhat vague terms, he had not been asked about all of the dates on which evidence showed that contact occurred. The Special Criminal Court judgment contended that the appellant "could not have forgotten the many telephone calls with Patrick Dermody which took place within days prior to the interviews". There was no evidential basis for this statement as the appellant had not been asked about all of those days and the Court of Criminal Appeal held that the Special Criminal Court had inappropriately invoked s.2 on this matter.

Bail Confirmation that hearsay evidence can be admitted in certain circumstances at bail hearings was given by the Supreme Court in *DPP v McLoughlin* [2009] IESC 65; [2010] 1 I.L.R.M. 1. Citing *People (DPP) v McGinley* [1998] 2 I.R. 408, the court held that the right to liberty must yield to the public interest in the administration of justice and, to this end, hearsay evidence may become admissible at a bail hearing where the court hearing the application is satisfied that there are sufficient grounds for not requiring relevant witnesses to give viva voce evidence. It would then be up to the court to consider what weight to attach to the hearsay evidence admitted.

Although expressly stating that his view on the issue of hearsay evidence in bail applications was obiter in the context of his judgment in this case, Hardiman J. addressed the matter in some detail and stated that, "there is a *prima facie* right in an applicant for bail to have the evidence deployed against his application given orally, by its author and not simply by a person who heard it said". This right, he suggested, was necessary in order not to "deny to an applicant the essential and vital tool of cross-examination of the persons giving evidence against him". However, Hardiman J. said:

> "[T]he exigencies of the practice of criminal law, particularly in interlocutory applications, make it absolutely necessary that hearsay be admissible *in some such interlocutory applications*, but on a very restricted basis."

He continued:

> "[H]earsay evidence may be admissible in a bail application, but quite exceptionally, and when a specific, recognised, ground for its admission has been properly established by ordinary evidence."

He emphasised that the admission of hearsay evidence in bail applications was a rare exception and it is for the courts to monitor the extent of the attempted use of hearsay in such applications and to keep it within proper bounds. He further outlined that:

> "Where it is proposed to adduce hearsay evidence, and where that proposal is objected to, there must be a full and proper hearing of the objection and of the evidence relied on in support of the admission of hearsay, and a proper ruling on this question."

On the facts of the instant case, where Gardaí testified that witnesses had been intimidated and therefore would not attend at the hearing, the Supreme Court found that it had been reasonable for the judge to admit the hearsay evidence. However, the appellant in this case succeeded in his appeal on other grounds, namely that the judge hearing the bail application had failed to expressly set out his reasons for being satisfied of the probability of the risk that the applicant would interfere with or intimidate witnesses.

In *Devoy v Governor of the Dóchas Centre* [2009] IEHC 380; [2009] 3 I.R. 673 it was held that a District Court judge had incorrectly revoked the bail of the applicant. The applicant had been on bail for a period of time and had come before the District Court in relation to a number of offences including drink driving, dangerous driving, driving without insurance and driving without a licence. The District judge had before her a pre-sentence probation report but certain information was not included therein. The judge ordered another probation report, put the case back until that report was provided and remanded the applicant in custody until that time. There was no application before the District Court for the revocation of the applicant's bail and, although the judge is entitled to revoke bail on her own motion, the High Court held that fair procedures in such an instance would require that the grounds for revocation would be notified in some reasonable way to the accused person or her representative in order to provide a reasonable opportunity to address them either by way of evidence or by way of submissions. Peart J., in the High Court, held that the revocation of bail on the facts of this case, in the absence of lawful grounds for such revocation such as a risk of interference with witnesses, absconding or committing other offences, amounted to a de facto sentence which "offends against constitutional justice".

Trial right to legal advice In *Carmody v Minister for Justice* [2009] IESC 71; [2010] 1 I.L.R.M. 157, it was argued that s.2 of the Criminal Justice (Legal Aid) Act 1962 was both repugnant to the Constitution and incompatible with the European Convention on Human Rights as it did not allow for the District Court to grant legal aid to an accused person in a criminal trial in that court such as to include the retention of a barrister, only the retention of a solicitor. In terms of the Constitution, one of the arguments was that this was contrary to the right to a fair trial as counsel could not be provided for, by means of legal aid, even if the District Court considered that the assistance of counsel would be in the interests of justice given the gravity, complexity or exceptional circumstances of the case.

The Supreme Court in this case restated that the right to criminal legal aid is a constitutional right, and further stated that:

> "Everyone has a right to be represented in a criminal trial but justice requires something more than the mere right to be represented when a person, who cannot afford legal representation, is facing a serious criminal charge. Such a person has a constitutional right to be granted legal aid by the State to enable him or her to have legal representation at the trial. The nature and extent of that right may be affected by the gravity and complexity of the charge. In addition, although the Act does not require it, every unrepresented defendant must be informed of his or her right to legal aid if they cannot afford it themselves."

Murray C.J., giving the judgment of the court, observed that the District Court deals annually with thousands of "relatively trivial cases" and that, as a general rule, the more serious or complex criminal cases requiring legal aid in the District Court would not be beyond the capabilities of a professional solicitor. However, the learned Chief Justice also noted that the legal environment of the District Court has changed significantly in the intervening years since the promulgation of the Criminal Justice (Legal Aid) Act 1962. One example given of this change was that where consecutive terms of imprisonment were imposed in the District Court in the past the total term of imprisonment could not exceed 12 months. This was altered under the Criminal Justice Act 1984 to allow for an aggregate term of two years in such circumstances. Furthermore, many modern regulatory offences (e.g. in competition law, environmental law, company law, etc.) have been introduced into the criminal jurisdiction of the District Court in recent years, some of which are potentially complex in nature. The court also recognised that the volume and nature of criminal law have altered since the 1960s, a time at which offences such as dealing in and supplying illicit drugs, or possession of child pornography would have been almost unheard of. In summation on this matter, Murray C.J. observed that, "[t]here can be no doubt that over recent decades the enforcement and application of the criminal law in the District Court has become more complex".

In relation to the offences at hand in the instant case, related to illegalities around the moving of cattle, it was submitted to the court that the State, in prosecuting such offences, routinely engaged counsel. While the court noted that the concept of "equality of arms" did not necessitate parity of representation, it did observe that "equality of arms" is part of the broader notion of the right to a fair trial. Murray C.J. said that:

> "Having regard to the extremely wide scope and range of offences which come within the jurisdiction of the District Court in the field of criminal law and the increased complexity of modern legislation and regulatory measures… the Court is satisfied not only that the necessity in the interests of justice for a defendant to be represented by counsel as well as solicitor cannot be excluded but that cases, however infrequently that may be, will inevitably arise where it would be essential that an indigent defendant be afforded such legal aid.
>
> In order to vindicate the constitutional right of an indigent defendant in the District Court to a fair trial he or she must be entitled to legal aid with representation by counsel as well as solicitor where it is established that because of the particular gravity and complexity of the case or other exceptional circumstances such representation is essential in the interests of justice. It follows that any such defendant must have a right to apply for such legal aid and have the application determined on its merits."

Having said that, the court noted that the State is not obliged to provide what might be seen as the "optimum" form of representation for an indigent defendant in a criminal trial, or the form which he or she desires; rather the State should provide the defendant with legal aid so as to enable him to be legally represented so that his defence can be properly prepared and fairly put.

On the central issue in the case, the Supreme Court held that s.2 of the 1962 Act could not be declared repugnant to the Constitution as it in fact contained positive provision for legal aid in the District Court in so far as access to a solicitor was provided. The mischief which occasioned the claims of the appellant in this case was in fact the lack of provision by the Oireachtas for a mechanism through which he could apply for criminal legal aid which would include access to counsel in an appropriate case. This failure to provide in fact amounted to a denial of a constitutional right, the right to a fair trial, and the Supreme Court held that the appellant in this case could not be tried unless and until he was afforded an opportunity to apply for legal aid, to include solicitor and counsel, and to have that application determined on its merits. The court further granted a declaration that, "the appellant has a constitutional right to apply, prior to being tried, for legal aid in the criminal proceedings brought against him in the District Court and to have that application heard and determined on its merits" and an order prohibiting the prosecution from proceeding in this case unless and until the appellant was afforded that right.

Having made the above determinations, the court considered it unnecessary to explore the ECHR issues.

DNA evidence In *DPP v Horgan* [2009] IECCA 85, DNA evidence taken from the appellant in the pre-trial period in relation to the offences with which he was charged and later convicted, had been unlawfully retained beyond the statutorily allowed period. As a result, at trial the DPP relied on DNA evidence which had been taken from the appellant in relation to an entirely different matter some years previously and had, the court was told, been lawfully retained. Amongst other things, the appellant argued that it was an error of law on the part of the trial judge to allow the prosecution to rely on that retained DNA evidence. However, this argument was rejected and the Court of Criminal Appeal considered that reliance on that evidence did not lead to any breach of basic fairness.

Evidence by video link In *O'D v DPP* [2009] IEHC 559 the applicant was accused of committing offences contrary to s.5 of the Criminal Justice (Sexual Offences) Act 1993 in regard to two complainants, who were his cousins and were both now in their 40s. Section 5 provides for the offence of having sexual intercourse with mentally impaired persons. The phrase "mentally impaired" is defined in s.5(5) as:

> … suffering from a disorder of the mind, whether through mental handicap or mental illness, which is of such a nature or degree as to render a person incapable of living an independent life or of guarding against serious exploitation.

Application had been made and granted in the Dublin Circuit Criminal Court for the complainants to give their evidence to the court by way of live video link. This application was made pursuant to s.13(1)(b) of the Criminal Evidence Act 1992. Section 13(1) of the 1992 Act provides that:

> In any proceedings for an offence to which this Part applies [including sexual offences] a person other than the accused may give evidence, whether from within or outside the State, through a live television link—
>
> (a) if the person is under 17 years of age, unless the court sees good reason to the contrary,
> (b) in any other case, with the leave of the court.

By virtue of s.19 of the 1992 Act, s.13(1)(a) also applies in the context of a person of any age who has a "mental handicap". As the question of the complainants having a "mental handicap" was an essential ingredient of the offence under s.5, the application for the giving of evidence by video link was made and granted under s.13(1)(b) in order to avoid pre-judging that issue. Nonetheless, the argument before the High Court in the instant case was that allowing the complainants to give evidence in this manner could or would convey to a jury that they were persons with a mental impairment. The applicant, as part of his defence to the charges against him, disputed the suggestion that the complainants had a mental impairment and therefore sought to have the order allowing for the complainants to give evidence by video link overturned.

Handing down the decision of the High Court, O'Neill J. held that the danger of the jury perceiving that the complainants were persons with mental impairment if they gave evidence by way of video link could not be avoided by directions from the trial judge and he stated that in his view:

> "… it is clear that evidence by video link in the circumstances of this case does carry with it a real risk of unfairness to the accused person which probably cannot be remedied by directions from the trial judge or statements from the prosecution".

He considered that there is a difficult balance to be achieved in cases such as this between the applicant's right to a fair trial and the prosecution's right to have evidence given by video link. O'Neill J. went on to state that where the court concludes that there is a serious risk of unfairness to the accused in allowing evidence to be given by video link, which could not be remedied by an appropriate statement from the prosecution or direction from the trial judge:

> "… it should only permit the giving of evidence by video link where it was satisfied by evidence that a serious injustice would be done, in the sense of a significant impairment to the prosecution's case if evidence had to be given in the normal way, viva voce, thus necessitating evidence by video link in order to vindicate the right of the public to prosecute offences of this kind. The fact that the giving of evidence viva voce would be very unpleasant for the witness or coming to court to give evidence very inconvenient, would not be relevant factors. In all cases of this nature the giving of evidence by the alleged victim will be very unpleasant and having to come to Court is invariably difficult and inconvenient for most persons. Most witnesses have vital commitments which have to be adjusted to allow them to come to Court. The real question is whether the circumstances of the witness are such that the requirement to give evidence viva voce is an insuperable obstacle to giving evidence in a manner that does justice to the prosecution case. The evidence must establish to the satisfaction of the Court hearing

> the application under s.13 of the Act of 1992 that the probability is that the witness in question will be deterred from giving evidence at all or will, in all probability, be unable to do justice to their evidence if required to give it viva voce in the ordinary way, This is necessarily a high threshold, but I am satisfied that in order to strike a fair balance between the right of the accused person to a fair trial and the right of the public to prosecute offences of this kind, it must be so".

O'Neill J. considered that the correct test had not been applied by the Circuit Court judge in this case. While she had considered that the order to allow evidence to be given by video link was appropriate due to the relationship between the applicant and the complainants, certain reports received on the mental assessment of the complainants, the awkwardness and inconvenience which would be caused to them, and the unpleasantness of the experience of giving evidence for them, she did not appear to have considered whether these factors amounted to or supported evidence which established that the complainants would not be capable of giving their evidence viva voce or would not be capable of doing justice to their evidence in that setting. Accordingly, the High Court quashed the order and remitted the case to the Circuit Court for a rehearing of the application under s.13.

Opinion evidence *Redmond v Ireland and the Attorney General* [2009] IEHC 201; [2009] 2 I.L.R.M. 419 addressed s.3(2) of the Offences Against the State (Amendment) Act 1972 which allows for the opinion evidence of a Garda not below the rank of Chief Superintendent to be admitted at trial in relation to the offence of membership of an unlawful organisation contrary to s.21 of the Offences Against the State Act 1939 as amended. The plaintiff in this case, who had been convicted of the section 21 offence in a trial in which evidence was received from a Chief Superintendent in accordance with the impugned section, sought a declaration that s.3(2) was contrary to both the Constitution and the European Convention on Human Rights and that his conviction was therefore unsafe and unsatisfactory and should be set aside. No such declaration was given in the High Court.

McMahon J. noted the Irish jurisprudence which has upheld the constitutionality of s.3(2) in the past (including *O'Leary v Attorney General* [1993] 1 I.R. 102, *DPP v Martin Kelly* [2006] 3 I.R. 115 and *People (DPP) v Binéad and Donohue* [2007] 1 I.R. 374) and found no reason to depart from that position. In terms of the European Convention on Human Rights, McMahon J. was of the opinion that this could not be relied upon by the plaintiff as the relevant trial occurred before the coming into force of the European Convention on Human Rights Act 2003. Nonetheless, he adverted to examinations of relevant European Court of Human Rights case law in *DPP v Martin Kelly* [2006] 3 I.R. 115 and *People (DPP) v Binéad* [2007] 1 I.R. 374 and held that there was no interference with convention rights, even if the argument made thereunder could be heard by the court.

Considering the right to a fair trial, under Art.38.1 of the Constitution, McMahon J. made the following general observations which are of interest:

> "[T]he concept of a fair trial must be seen in the wider context of the administration of justice where other interests must also be accommodated. There is the public interest, for example, in the security of the State. The right to life is another. Many States in recent years have had to introduce anti-terrorist measures which inevitably modified to some degree the traditional indicia of the ordinary criminal trial. Our legislation, reflecting our own political history of social disturbance, predates these recent enactments in other jurisdictions and has been challenged and considered by our courts on many occasions. The arguments advanced by the plaintiff here are not unfamiliar and have surfaced in the case law in one guise or another over the years.
>
> Fairness is not an absolute term. It is limited by the social and political circumstances in which it is being considered. Accepting that there are minimum standards below which the courts will not go in defending the citizen's right to a fair trial, it must be acknowledged that in times of crisis, where the security of the State is threatened, for example, the State may have to take measures which it would not wish to take in normal peaceful social conditions. It may have to depart, for example, from the norm of a jury trial. This is what has been done in this State by the establishment of the Special Criminal Court, a legal development which has been challenge-proofed by our Supreme Court on more than one occasion.
>
> It must be clear, however, that such erosion of the citizen's right to a fair trial does not, in difficult social circumstances, fall below the minimum guarantee to which the citizen is entitled. There are basic protections, core principles, which the individual is entitled to insist on even in times of crisis and social upheaval; a floor level below which any civilised State must not descend. It is for the courts in this State to ensure that this does not happen."

Looking more specifically at s.3(2), McMahon J. observed that it does not require the court to act on the opinion evidence of the Chief Superintendent, only to admit it. Furthermore, even though the Chief Superintendent may be able to claim privilege over his sources and the defendant in a given case may thereby be disadvantaged, the weight of the evidence must be considered by the trial court, and in considering the weight to attach thereto, the trial court would "no doubt, bear in mind the unusual nature of this evidence and all the weaknesses it has, as evidence being unavailable to, and untested and unchallenged by, the defence." Also, the Chief Superintendent is required to give his opinion evidence in court such that the court can consider the honesty of his belief and the belief can be subjected to cross-examination. Moreover, if it considers it necessary to do so, the trial court can examine the material on which the belief is based, in the absence of the accused where privilege has been claimed, and can accordingly determine for itself whether it is sufficient evidence to support the belief expressed. Finally, an appeal lies from the decision of the trial court, and McMahon J. (as he had in *Kemmy v Ireland and Attorney General* [2009] IEHC 178) noted that the presence of an appeal system is an important aspect of the right to a fair legal system, which he distinguished from the right to a fair trial.

For all of the above-outlined reasons and because of the "ongoing threat that the named organisations still present to the security of the State", McMahon J. held that s.3(2) was not repugnant to either the Constitution or the ECHR.

In *DPP v Mark Doran* [2009] IECCA 113, the Court of Criminal Appeal considered that the Special Criminal Court had fallen into error by relying on evidence presented by a Garda other than a Chief Superintendent in relation to the appellant's membership of an unlawful organisation. While the belief evidence of a Chief Superintendent has specific status in a trial on that charge, conferred upon it by virtue of the Offences Against the State Acts 1939 and 1998, the evidence of any other Garda has no such special status. The Court of Criminal Appeal could not be sure that the erroneous reliance on the evidence of a Detective Superintendent was not of significant influence in the decision made by the Special Criminal Court.

As noted above, s.7 of the Criminal Justice (Amendment) Act 2009 Act inserts s.71B into the Criminal Justice Act 2006 and provides that a court may hear the opinion evidence of a Garda or former Garda of any rank in relation to the existence of a criminal organisation where it appears to the court that he possesses "the appropriate expertise". Clearly then the difficulty encountered in *Doran* will not arise in this context. While s.71B relates only to the existence of a particular criminal organisation, not, for example, a given accused's membership of such an organisation, it is nonetheless broader in its operation than s.3(2) of the Offences Against the State (Amendment) Act 1972 as it allows for a Garda or a *former* Garda of *any* rank to provide the relevant opinion evidence to the court. This may reflect the reality that Gardaí working at the coal face of the criminal justice system have more knowledge of the existence of specific criminal organisations than chief superintendents or others of superior rank. Nonetheless, it is a step beyond what the Irish criminal justice system has previously accepted and, even though the protections which apply to the operation of s.3(2) and were outlined in *Redmond* should apply to the operation of s.71B also, there may be scope to challenge the constitutionality or ECHR compliance of s.71B given the greater breadth of its operation, in terms of those who it permits to give opinion evidence to the court.

Hearsay In *DPP v Albie Lonergan* [2009] IECCA 52, much of the evidence at trial was hearsay, admitted under the spontaneous declarations element of the res gestae exception to the general rule against hearsay. The accused was convicted by a jury of the murder of his brother. The relevant statements were from various persons who had spoken with the deceased moments after the fatal stabbing occurred. The deceased had variously stated "the bastard stabbed me", "the bastard stabbed me, my own brother stabbed me", "he is after stabbing me, Albie is after stabbing me" and similar phrases. The prosecution at trial had sought to have these statements admitted as forming part of the res gestae, not as being "dying declarations". In that sense, the statements were said to be spontaneous declarations forming part of the criminal act for which the accused was being tried. The trial judge admitted all such statements, including those made some 10 or 15 minutes after the relevant stabbing.

One of the arguments put forward for the applicant in this case was that the trial judge had admitted the hearsay evidence on the basis of an assessment of the exception to the rule against hearsay which strayed beyond the rationale adopted for the rule in Irish law, and involved a "composite approach" including elements of English law based on a different rationale. In the leading Irish authority on the spontaneous declarations aspect of res gestae, *People (Attorney General) v Crosbie* [1966] I.R. 490, Kenny J. stated that the impugned statements made in that case were:

> "… spoken within one minute of the stabbing. They related directly to the incident which was being investigated (the stabbing), and they were spoken immediately after it … the words were so clearly associated with the stabbing in time, place and circumstances that they were part of the thing being done and so an item or part of real evidence and not merely a reported statement" (making reference to the dicta of Normand L. in *Teper v R* [1952] A.C. 480).

The approach of the trial judge in the instant case, according to Kearns J., gave due weight to both the requirement of contemporaneity and the possibility of concoction or fabrication. Counsel for the applicant argued that contemporaneity was the only rationale for the admission of statements of this nature under Irish law and that the concept of concoction or fabrication had not been applied in this jurisdiction. However, the Court of Criminal Appeal held that the trial judge was correct in his "composite approach" and Kearns J. stated that:

> "It would be quite wrong to hold that admissibility should be determined by reference solely to a given time period as to do so would lead to arbitrary and unfair results. Time in this context is an important factor but not a determinant. The true importance of the requirement of contemporaneity is to eliminate the possibility of concoction. Where

> it is clear that no such opportunity existed on the facts of a given case it would be quite wrong to exclude statements on some arbitrary time basis. It is more a matter of factoring in both components when deciding whether or not to admit such statements as part of the *res gestae*. In every case the trial judge will have to exercise his discretion having regard to the particular circumstances of the case."

Looking at the facts of the instant case, the court noted that no suggestion existed that the relevant statements had not been made, there was no alternative version of events or other perpetrator possible on the evidence, and there was no motive for concoction or fabrication. Accordingly, the appeal failed on this ground.

Jury A second ground of appeal in *DPP v Albie Lonergan* [2009] IECCA 52 related to the failure of the trial judge to discharge the jury because of a possible interference with one of its members. One juror was approached in a pub and told by an unidentified person to "make the correct decision". The trial judge was informed of this matter and questioned the juror as to whether or not he felt intimidated by this occurrence. The juror said that he did not and when asked if he thought he could try the case only on the evidence before him in court, he replied that he could. Counsel for the applicant contended that the form of the question put by the trial judge invited only a positive response and that the judge effectively left no real alternative to the relevant juror other than to affirm the position as presented by the learned trial judge, that he was in a position to continue on the evidence in court alone.

The Court of Criminal Appeal held, however, that the trial judge had applied the correct test in this issue, namely that set out in *People (DPP) v Mulder* [2007] 4 I.R. 796, considering from an objective perspective whether a reasonable person would have a reasonable apprehension that the accused would not in the circumstances receive a fair and impartial trial. The appeal was accordingly dismissed on this ground also.

Another case relating, amongst other things, to the ability of a juror, or the jury as a whole, to fulfil their obligations to the court was *People (DPP) v MR* [2009] IECCA 87. This case involved an appeal against conviction on sexual offence charges and a number of grounds for appeal were pursued, most pertinently, that the judge erred in not particularising the elements of one of the offences in his charge to the jury, that there was pressure of time on the jury which rendered their verdict unsafe, and that counsel for the prosecution had inappropriately commented on the truthfulness of evidence given by the complainant.

On the first of these grounds, the Court of Criminal Appeal held that there is merit to the approach which requires that each and every member of the jury (or a majority thereof, following a direction) should agree on the fundamental facts of a case, i.e. the factual basis for the charge. In certain cases, which may be rare, a direction in this regard would be required from the trial judge. On the facts of the instant case it was held that a more particularised charge should have been given to the jury, and where this was not done, the verdict on the first count of sexual assault was unsafe.

The second issue related to a specific problem which arose with one member of the jury in this case. The juror had not been aware that she might be expected to deliberate beyond 6pm and there was no one to collect her six-year-old son from his crèche. As a result, she was visibly upset and informed the court Garda of her difficulties. The trial judge, with the help of counsel and the Gardaí, arranged for her son to be collected by uniformed Gardaí, even though the juror intimated that the child would be upset by this. While these arrangements were being made, the juror was absent from the rest of the jury for some time, although they had been directed by the trial judge not to deliberate during this time. When the juror rejoined the rest of the jury, it took just 22 minutes for them to reach a majority verdict on the second count.

The Court of Criminal Appeal held that the separation of the juror from the rest of the jury on the facts of the instant case was not detrimental to the verdict later reached. Neither was the short length of time which it took to obtain the majority verdict to be viewed as a ground to grant leave to appeal per se. However, the short length of time indicated that there may have been pressure on the juror or the jury. In this regard, Denham J., giving the judgment of the court said "[a] jury should not reach a verdict in circumstances where it is under pressure to reach a decision quickly, or under time constraints in any way". On the facts, the court considered that the pressure placed on the relevant juror due to her concerns about collecting her son could have spilt over into the rest of the jury and while the Court of Criminal Appeal could only engage in speculation about all of this, it considered that there was a real likelihood of pressure on the juror in question to reach a decision, and upon the jury which was aware, or some of whom were aware, of her anxiety to leave. Denham J. said:

> "A jury should be free to deliberate free from any form of time pressure. A jury should not be made to feel that a juror is under pressure to remain in the jury room in circumstances where he or she is under a degree of stress."

In relation to counsel for the prosecution expressing a view in his closing statement as to the truthfulness of the complainant, Denham J. stated that:

> "[I]t is not appropriate for counsel to personalise his role or to give a personal opinion on evidence and or on the credibility of witnesses. There is a danger that a jury might regard him as giving expert evidence."

However, on the facts of the instant case the statements made by counsel were not thought to lead to an unfair trial. Nonetheless, based on the failure to particularise the facts of the offence and the pressure of time on the jury, the Court of Criminal Appeal allowed the appeal and quashed the convictions of the applicant.

Evidence at sentencing hearings The case of *DPP v McDonnell* [2009] IECCA 16 raised issues before the Court of Criminal Appeal as to the strictness or otherwise of the rules of evidence at a sentencing hearing. It was claimed on behalf of the appellant that his sentence on drugs charges had been based on, amongst other things, hearsay and opinion evidence presented to the court by a member of the Garda Síochána. Kearns J., delivering the judgment of the court, stated that:

> "It is an undeniable fact that a wider range of evidence has historically been regarded as being admissible for the purpose of sentencing than would be admissible at the pre-conviction stage of a trial."

The court examined a number of cases, including the ex tempore judgment in *Director of Public Prosecutions v Philip Delaney*, unreported, Court of Criminal Appeal, February 28, 2000, along with the law in America, Canada and Australia, and the Irish Law Reform Commission, *Consultation Paper on Sentencing* (Dublin, 1993). Kearns J. then summarised the position as follows:

> "[I]t seems quite clear to this Court that the admission at a sentencing hearing of hearsay evidence to suggest the commission of prior criminal offences on the part of a convicted person for which he has not been tried and found guilty or even if charged, he does not require to be taken into account, would infringe Article 38 and Article 40.4.1 of the Constitution which former provides for a trial in due course of law for any such alleged offence and, which latter provides that no citizen should be punished on any matter on which he has not been convicted … Hearsay evidence of character, antecedents, and as to the background to the particular offence being dealt with, including the extent of the role played therein by an accused may, at the discretion of the sentencing judge, be received, subject to the requirement that if a particular fact assumes specific significance or is disputed the court's findings should require strict proof. It is a matter for the sentencing judge to decide what weight should be attached to such hearsay evidence as is received, noting any objection taken thereto and any arguments or evidence offered in rebuttal."

On the facts of the instant case it was held that the majority of the evidence presented to the court in the sentencing hearing was properly admitted and received. Although it did involve hearsay and opinion evidence, it was relevant to the specific offence then being addressed by the court and the Court of Criminal Appeal held that it was correct to receive the evidence:

> "… not to aggravate or increase the sentence, but to assist the judge in determining what mitigating factors (if any) should properly influence the sentence he was about to impose on the various co-accused".

Certain questions posed by the trial judge had strayed beyond what was permissible, however, by enquiring into the length of time for which the applicant had been involved in the drugs trade. The Court of Criminal Appeal considered this to be both irrelevant and improper due to the suggestion of other uncharged criminality in it. Despite this error in principle, the Court of Criminal Appeal upheld the sentence imposed by the trial judge as there was other evidence before the sentencing court on which to rely when handing down this sentence.

Criminal Law

DR JOHN P BYRNE, BCL, LLM, Barrister-at-Law, PhD

In 2009 the Criminal Justice (Amendment) Act 2009 was enacted, an Act which introduces additional measures targeted at combating organised crime. The Act targets those who direct the activities of criminal organisations and those who participate in the activities of such organisations. The Act also addresses the increasing levels of violence and intimidation directed at witnesses and other members of the public. In addition to increased penalties, it makes provision for the use of the Special Criminal Court for the hearing of particular organised crime offences unless the Director of Public Prosecutions directs otherwise. The Act also amends Garda detention, re-arrest and search powers. Because of the importance of the legislation the provisions of the legislation will be considered in some detail in this chapter.

BAIL

Higher threshold for bail pending appeal In *DPP v Harry Dunne*, Court of Criminal Appeal (ex tempore), Fennelly J. (Fennelly, Budd, McMahon JJ.), January 16, 2009, an application for bail was made pending an appeal on the basis of a point of law arising from the judge's charge. Applying the decision of the CCA in *DPP v Corbally* [2001] I.R. 180 the court ruled that bail can only be granted in a case of this sort where "some definite or discrete ground of appeal can be identified and isolated and is of such a nature that there is a strong chance of success on the appeal". Thus cases of this sort are treated differently to a case where an applicant is still awaiting trial, as in that case the presumption of innocence continues to apply, whereas in the present, as the CCA stated, the applicant had already been convicted by a judge and jury. The court was not satisfied that any such ground existed and the application for bail was rejected.

In *DPP v John Forrester*, Court of Criminal Appeal (ex tempore), Kearns J. (Kearns, Murphy, Clarke JJ.), March 26, 2009, the CCA also applied the *Corbally* decision in ruling that the threshold for bail had not been satisfied. The applicant had pleaded guilty to taking a car in Portmarnock, using it for rallying purposes and damaging the vehicle. The applicant had a string of previous convictions for that type of offence. The CCA indicated that if the applicant proceeded with the appeal he was at risk of having the sentence increased rather than decreased. The application for bail was refused.

Offence committed while on bail In *DPP v Adewale Idowu*, Court of Criminal Appeal (ex tempore), Finnegan J. (Finnegan, Herbert, McKechnie JJ.), March 30, 2009, a consecutive sentence imposed by the sentencing court at trial was upheld in circumstances where the applicant had committed the offences while on bail (and not while under temporary release). The applicant had applied for leave to appeal after he had pleaded guilty to five counts, three in relation to possession of false passports, contrary to s.29 of the Theft and Fraud Offences Act 2001, and two in relation to inducing another to accept a false instrument—a credit card—contrary to s.26 of the Theft and Fraud Offences Act 2001. The court noted that the offences were committed while the applicant was on bail, and so required consecutive sentences under s.11 of the Criminal Justice Act 1984, and it was noted that under s.10 of the Bail Act 1997 the fact that the offence was committed on bail is an aggravating circumstance. The sentences therefore must be consecutive to the sentence which he was serving, the CCA stating that:

> "[T]his court does not see that any lesser sentence than that of three years would be appropriate for the offences which he committed having regard to the fact that they were committed while on bail and the statutory provisions that affect that."

DURESS AND NECESSITY

Law reform In 2009 the Law Reform Commission published its *Report on Defences in Criminal Law* which made 46 specific recommendations for reform of the law, and included a draft Criminal Law (Defences) Bill 2009 to implement those recommendations. The report dealt with: legitimate defence (self-defence); defence of the home; use of force in law enforcement; the defence of provocation; and the defences of duress and necessity.

The Commission recommended that the defence of duress, which applies where threats of death or serious injury are made ("do this, or else …"), should continue to apply as a defence to most crimes (with the exception of treason, murder and attempted murder), and should also include threatening situations (duress of circumstances).

The defence of necessity, which applies in very limited situations (such as where damage to property is committed to save a life, or in cases of medical necessity such as the case of operating on conjoined twins), should continue to develop on a case-by-case basis.

EVIDENCE

Inference following failure to answer Section 9 of the Criminal Justice (Amendment) Act 2009 provides a new s.72A in the Criminal Justice Act 2006. Subsection (1) of this new provision permits inferences to be drawn as a result of the failure, in particular circumstances, of an accused to answer questions. It applies to the organised crime offences under Pt 7 of the Criminal Justice Act 2006, including the additional offence of directing the activities of a criminal organisation introduced in this Act. The remaining provisions of the section contain safeguards common to other similar existing provisions in Irish law such as, that the accused must be informed of the effect of a failure to answer a question; that a reasonable opportunity must be given to the accused to consult a solicitor; and that the questioning is recorded unless the accused consents otherwise. Subsection (8) confirms that the section shall not apply in relation to a failure to answer a question if the failure occurred before the passing of the section.

Exclusion of evidence Section 13 confirms that a court may exclude evidence if, in the opinion of the court, the prejudicial effect of evidence outweighs its probative value.

New evidence must have been unknown at time of trial In *DPP v Griffin*, unreported, Court of Criminal Appeal, Macken, deValera, Gilligan JJ. (Macken J.), July 24, 2008, the applicant sought leave to appeal against conviction. Counsel for the applicant sought to introduce a bundle of documents consisting of extracts from certain newspapers and television or radio reports published during or after the trial of the applicant which took place in December 2006 and January 2007. The documents sought to be introduced were of two types:

(a) those which had already unsuccessfully been the subject of applications for the jury to be discharged made on behalf of the applicant by his then senior counsel in the course of the trial; and
(b) others, published variously during the same period as the above publications, or in the course of the Christmas break in 2006 when the trial court was not in session, and the last one published in May 2007 after the applicant had been convicted and sentenced.

As regards those which fell into category (a), the CCA ruled that where a ground has not been raised in the course of a trial, either by way of requisitions on a charge, or by seeking a ruling, such as on an application to discharge the jury by virtue of media exposure considered by an applicant to be adverse to his interests, two criteria must be met. Those are: first, that the failure to have raised the matter must have occurred as a result of some inadvertence on the part of the applicant's legal advisers; and secondly, that there must be a reason tendered to this court as to why a point was not taken.

Considering the transcript from the trial and submissions made by counsel for the applicant, the CCA concluded that there was no evidence that those criteria were satisfied. The court concluded by stating:

> "There is no suggestion made on behalf of the applicant that counsel did not follow instructions fully, nor that counsel did not make all appropriate applications concerning media coverage when he did."

As regards those documents that fell into category (b)—those which were not the subject of a ruling at trial—the CCA considered various judgments which the court had delivered in the past on the rules concerning the introduction of new evidence, including the detailed judgment of Kearns J. in *DPP v Willoughby*, unreported, Court of Criminal Appeal, February 18, 2005, in which, having considered the entire range of jurisprudence on the issue, he stated, inter alia:

> "(a) Given that the public interest requires that a defendant bring forward his entire case at trial, exceptional circumstances must be established before the court should allow further evidence to be called. …
>
> (b) The evidence must not have been known at the time of the trial and must be such that it could not reasonably have been known or acquired at the time of the trial …"

After its examination of the authorities, the CCA noted that the evidence sought to be admitted in the instant case was clearly in existence during the course of the trial, with the exception of one document which was published after the trial had concluded. The evidence, in the view of the court, was "wholly procurable, even without having to exercise any due diligence". The CCA stated:

> "The transcript of the evidence makes it clear that the counsel for the applicant and his legal advisers were extremely alert to the existence of possible media coverage, and the jury had given an undertaking to the court that they would not be influenced in any way by any such media coverage."

The court concluded that in the circumstances, the various applications for leave to appeal should be refused.

Griffin reinforces the strict approach adopted by the CCA on the question of the introduction of new evidence at the appeal stage. As a general rule, it appears the court is quite disinclined to admit evidence which was available to the defendant at the time of the trial. Even new evidence satisfying that burden will not be admitted absent "exceptional circumstances".

Fresh interpretation of the *res gestae* In *DPP v Albie Lonergan* [2009] IECCA 52; Court of Criminal Appeal, Kearns J. (Kearns, Murphy, Clarke JJ.), May 8, 2009, the CCA applies a fresh approach to the interpretation of the *res gestae*. Briefly, the facts of the case were that on the date in question an altercation broke out between the two brothers outside the porch of a dwelling house in the course of which Michael Lonergan sustained two stab wounds to the chest and one stab wound to the right thigh, as a result of which he died later on the same day. The prosecution sought successfully to lead evidence from a number of people in whose presence the wounded victim made statements in the aftermath of the stabbing. Louise O'Brien, the partner of Emmet Coffey, a brother of the deceased's wife, told the court that Michael Lonergan turned to her and said he had been stabbed. His exact words were, "the bastard stabbed me". She also gave evidence that in the immediate aftermath of the incident, her partner Emmet Coffey chased the applicant down the road before returning some 10 or 15 minutes later, at which point, according to Louise O'Brien, Michael Lonergan said to Emmet Coffey, "the bastard stabbed me, my own brother stabbed me". Louise O'Brien clarified that no other person was involved in the fight with the applicant other than Michael Lonergan.

Emmet Coffey stated in evidence that on returning to the house having chased the applicant, Michael Lonergan said to him, "he is after stabbing me, Albie is after stabbing me". Yvonne Lonergan, the wife of the deceased, also testified that when she went out to the hallway of the house the deceased told her it was the applicant who had stabbed him. Another witness, Jonathan Bentley, was also present in the house when the argument took place. He left the room in which he was sitting to go to the toilet and encountered Michael Lonergan in the hallway. He had his hand on his stomach and he was "all blood". He caught Michael Lonergan as he was going to fall to the ground. Asked if the deceased had said anything, Mr Bentley stated that the deceased replied "the cunt stabbed me".

At the outset of the trial, an objection was raised by counsel for the applicant that only those statements immediately contemporaneous with the stabbing should be admitted in evidence and that statements made some 10 or 15 minutes later, notably that of Mr Emmet Coffey, should not be regarded as admissible because they did not form part of the *res gestae*.

Before ruling on this objection, the learned trial judge conducted a voir dire examination of each of the afore mentioned witnesses. As a result of a measure of agreement between the prosecution and the defence, the proposed evidence to be given by the various witnesses was edited and limited to that outlined above. The prosecution argued that all of the statements made by the deceased, which clearly identified the applicant as his assailant, were admissible as forming part of the *res gestae*, including statements made by the deceased some 10 or 15 minutes after the stabbing incident.

Following lengthy submissions involving much citation of relevant case law on the topic, the learned trial judge ruled that all of the statements of the deceased were admissible.

Giving judgment, the CCA, citing a number of authorities, including McGrath, *Evidence* (Dublin: Thomson Round Hall, 2005), para.5.53, stated that it is well established in Irish law that spontaneous declarations constitute an exception to the hearsay rule:

> "Statements concerning an event in issue, made in circumstances of such spontaneity or involvement in an event that the possibility of concoction, distortion or error can be disregarded, are admissible as evidence of the truth of their contents. The rationale for the admission of this category of out of court statements is evident from the formulation of the exception—they are made in circumstances where the declarant's mind is so dominated by a startling or overwhelming event that the statement is a spontaneous and instinctive reaction, made without any opportunity for the declarant to devise a false statement."

In the instant case it was never put or suggested to any of the witnesses that the statements as having been made by the deceased were not in fact so made. There was no other possible perpetrator or alternative version of events on the prosecution evidence other than that the applicant had killed his brother. No motive for concocting or fabricating evidence was suggested to any of the witnesses, nor was any evidence led by the defence to supply any such motive. Furthermore, counsel for the applicant had not really challenged the admissibility of the statements made by the deceased in the immediate aftermath of the stabbing. The challenge is effectively confined to the statements made by Michael Lonergan following the return of Emmet Coffey to the dwelling house following his chase of the applicant down the street. The CCA stated it was:

> "… entirely satisfied that the statements made some ten minutes after the stabbing were correctly admitted. They formed part of the same transaction, were sufficiently contemporaneous, and furthermore the Court is satisfied that there was no opportunity on the part of Michael Lonergan to concoct or fabricate an explanation, and indeed no motive for his having done so was ever identified".

The appeal was dismissed.

Interestingly, when reaching its decision, the court in *Lonergan* has indicated that the correct approach to cases of this type should not be confined to a question of contemporaneity, but should apply a composite approach, by also considering the possibility of concoction or fabrication of evidence. By adhering to this approach, which follows the approach of the House of Lords in *R. v Andrews* [1987] A.C. 281, the CCA has ruled that statements of this type should not be assessed solely on the basis of the time lapse between the statement and the incident at issue—which was the thrust of the CCA decision in *People (at the suit of the Attorney General) v Crosbie* [1966] I.R. 490—but should apply "the more evolved formulation of principle" from *Andrews*, and should consider all of the various circumstances. These would include, as in the instant case, the question of whether there was an alternative perpetrator, or whether the fact that the statement was made was in issue. *Lonergan* is now the leading Irish authority on the *res gestae*.

JURISDICTION OF COURTS

Jurisdiction Section 8 of the Criminal Justice (Amendment) Act 2009 provides, at s.8(1), a declaration that the ordinary courts are inadequate for the purpose of the effective administration of justice and the preservation of public peace in relation to the offences contained in Pt 7 of the Criminal Justice Act 2006 (excluding the conspiracy offence under s.71). This provision is not permanent and, depending on the threat posed by organised crime gangs, will have to be renewed on a regular basis. Section 8(2) has the effect of scheduling the offences specified in subs.(1) for the purpose of the provisions under the Offences against the State Act 1939 relating to the use of the Special Criminal Court. It allows the Special Criminal Court to hear prosecutions for the offence in question without prejudice, inter alia, to the power of the DPP to direct that a person not be sent forward for trial by that court (s.8(3)). Subsections (4) to (6) are the renewal provisions providing for the duration of this section. Section 8(4) sets down the expiry of operation of the section after one year unless a resolution continuing the section has been passed by both Houses of the Oireachtas. Section 8(5) allows further resolutions permitting, as needed, the continuation in force of the section. Under s.8(6), the Minister for Justice, Equality and Law Reform shall, before a resolution is passed by either House of the Oireachtas, place a report before each House concerning the operation of the provision to date.

Section 18 provides for jurisdiction over obstruction of justice offences relating to interference with the actions of the judiciary or law enforcement authorities and where committed on board an Irish ship, aircraft, or such offences committed by an Irish citizen/resident while in another jurisdiction. This is an important new provision to ensure that persons involved in organised crime can be pursued in respect of transnational offences. These provisions also meet our obligations under the UN Convention against Transnational Organised Crime.

Section 19 provides for jurisdiction over the offence of inducement of witnesses to give false testimony where committed on board an Irish ship, aircraft, or such an offence committed by an Irish citizen/resident while in another jurisdiction. This provision ensures that persons involved in organised crime can be pursued in respect of transnational offences. These provisions also meet our obligations under the UN Convention against Transnational Organised Crime.

LEGITIMATE DEFENCE (SELF DEFENCE)

Law reform In its 2009 *Report on Defences in Criminal Law* the Law Reform Commission made recommendations for the law on legitimate defence (self-defence). The Commission recommended that self-defence should be renamed legitimate defence to underline that: (1) a person is justified in using force against an unlawful attack in certain situations; and (2) the defence applies not just to protect the person themselves but also other people, such as their family, and to protect their home.

The defence of legitimate defence should be divided into four key elements: (1) a threshold requirement (only certain types of unlawful attack can justify use of defensive force, especially lethal defensive force); (2) the attack must be immediate; (3) the use of defensive force must be necessary (a person should usually retreat if possible); (4) the defensive force must be proportionate to the unlawful attack.

The test of whether the use of force is necessary and proportionate is based on an objective standard of a reasonable person (if the person attacked used lethal force, and subjectively believed it was necessary and proportionate but objectively it was not, the person should be found guilty of manslaughter, not murder: this is usually referred to as excessive or disproportionate force).

Defence of the dwelling The Law Reform Commission also made recommendations for the law on defence of the dwelling. The commission recommended that the general requirements for legitimate defence (self-defence) should apply to defence of the dwelling and its vicinity. The commission recommended that the general rule that a person should retreat where possible does not apply where the attack is in the home, and that, if all the requirements of the defence are met, use of lethal force would be a complete defence to murder and would lead to an acquittal.

Law enforcement The Commission also considered the issue of the use of force in law enforcement. It recommended that the use of such force (to assist in arresting a person, to deal with serious public disorder such as a riot, or to prevent prison escapes) should be limited to members of An Garda Síochána and prison officers. The use of force, including lethal force, is permitted only when it is necessary and proportionate in the circumstances.

MENS REA

Evidence of mental state at time of trial "entirely irrelevant" In *DPP v Anton Mulder*, Court of Criminal Appeal, Kearns J. (Kearns, Irvine, Edwards JJ.), April 27, 2009, the applicant had pleaded not guilty to the murder by strangulation of his wife at their family home in Dunshaughlin, County Meath in 2004. Following a trial in the Central Criminal Court, the applicant was convicted of murder and received a sentence of life imprisonment.

This was the second occasion upon which the applicant had been tried for this offence. In a previous trial in May 2006, the applicant was also convicted of the same offence, but that conviction was set aside by the CCA because a brother of the deceased had spoken to a member of the jury outside the courtroom (*DPP v Mulder* [2007] 4 I.R. 796). At the time of the second trial, there had been a change in the law by virtue of the enactment of the Criminal Law (Insanity) Act 2006, which introduced into Irish law the concept of diminished responsibility. On arraignment, however, the applicant simply pleaded "not guilty" to the offence of murder.

Section 6 of the Criminal Law (Insanity) Act 2006 states that:

> (1) Where a person is tried for murder and the jury or, as the case may be, the Special Criminal Court finds that the person—
> (a) did the act alleged,
> (b) was at the time suffering from a mental disorder, and
> (c) the mental disorder was not such as to justify finding him or her not guilty by reason of insanity, but was such as to diminish substantially his or her responsibility for the act,
> the jury or court, as the case may be, shall find the person not guilty of that offence but guilty of manslaughter on the ground of diminished responsibility.
> (2) Subject to section 5(4), where a person is tried for the offence specified in subsection (1), it shall be for the defence to establish that the person is, by virtue of this section, not liable to be convicted of that offence …

As the onus of proof in respect of this issue fell on the applicant, the defence led evidence as to the mental state of the applicant from Dr Harry Kennedy, who first examined the applicant on December 20, 2004, some three days after the offence. The main defence psychiatrist, however, was Dr Conor O'Neill who interviewed the applicant at Wheatfield Prison in a series of interviews commencing in May 2006. The defence also sought to call another psychiatrist, Dr Sally Lenihan, who first assessed the applicant in August 2007 with the stated aim of assessing the mental condition of the applicant at the time of trial. The prosecution objected to the admission of the evidence of Dr Lenihan on the basis that it was irrelevant and could say nothing to the mental state of the applicant at the time of the offence. In ruling on the application, the trial judge indicated that he would not admit the evidence *de bene esse* but would defer any final decision until a proper basis for the introduction of such evidence had been laid by the other psychiatrists intended to be called by the applicant. Having adduced the evidence of Dr Kennedy and Dr O'Neill, the defence made no further application thereafter to call Dr Lenihan as a witness in the case.

The main ground of appeal was that the trial judge had erred in not allowing Dr Lenihan to give evidence as to the current mental condition of the applicant. He submitted that such evidence would give weight and support to the opinion given by Dr O'Neill as to the mental condition of the applicant at the time of the offence.

Giving judgment, the CCA ruled that the trial judge had not ruled out altogether the possibility that the evidence of Dr Lenihan might be given at some stage. His ruling simply was to the effect that he would not accept such evidence *de bene esse* until a proper foundation for the leading of such evidence had been laid. As stated the defence made no further application to call Dr Lenihan as a witness in the case and the court was strongly of the view that such evidence "would have been entirely irrelevant".

OFFENCES

Participation Section 5 of the Criminal Justice (Amendment) Act 2009 inserts a new s.71A into Pt 7 of the Criminal Justice Act 2006. Section 71A(1) defines "directs" and provides that "activities" includes activities that do not constitute criminal offences, or that take place outside the State. Subsection (2) of the new s.71A makes it an offence for any person to direct, at any level of a criminal organisation, the activities of such an organisation. The maximum penalty following conviction on indictment is imprisonment for life. The section seeks to target those in a criminal organisation who give the orders. Some of these people may not themselves directly participate in the commission of criminal offences. By including the words "at any level of the organisation's structure" in s.71A(2), it is ensured that persons directing the activities need not necessarily be one of those at the top of the organisation or that they be shown to be such. Section 71A(3) of the new offence permits any statement or conduct of the accused causing a reasonable inference that the person was directing the activities of a criminal organisation, to be admissible as evidence. Section 71A(4) provides guidance for a court or jury, as the case may be, in determining whether or not an offence has been committed. Section

71A(5) makes provision for inferences that may be drawn from documentary evidence. Section 71A(6) provides that the definition of document or record is as defined in s.71B.

Section 6 amends the Criminal Justice Act 2006 by substituting a new section for the existing s.72 which relates to participation in organised crime. The new section will simplify the existing offence of participation in a criminal organisation. Subsection (1) of the new section makes it an offence to participate in any activity in the knowledge that doing so could reasonably, or reckless as to whether such participation would, enhance or facilitate the commission of an offence by a criminal organisation. Section 72(2) provides a penalty where convicted of this offence of a fine and/or up to 15 years' imprisonment. Section 72(3) confirms that the commission of a serious offence includes an act done outside the State. Section 72(4) provides that it is not necessary to prove that an offence has actually been carried out or that the defendant actually enhanced or facilitated an offence, or that the defendant knew the specific nature of any offence. Section 72(5) provides that the court may consider evidence whether or not the person uses a name, word or symbol which is associated with the organisation, or receives any benefit from the organisation. Section 72(6) provides that certain incriminating articles can be used as evidence that the defendant's state of mind was such that he/she had a deliberate intention to commit the offence.

Section 7 inserts a new section s.71B of the Criminal Justice Act 2006 to provide for proof of the evidence of the existence of a criminal organisation. This will enhance the ability to bring prosecutions for offences of directing or participating in organised crime. Sections 71B(1) and (2) allow for the admissibility of expert opinion evidence of a member of the Garda Síochána in determining the existence of a criminal organisation. Section 71B(3) further details the types of evidence which may be put forward by a member of the Garda Síochána, including evidence of previous convictions of gang members for arrestable offences. Sections 71B(4) and (5) provide that documents and records relevant to the criminal organisation are admissible as evidence.

Section 10 amends s.73 (Commission of offence for a criminal organisation) of the Criminal Justice Act 2006, to increase the penalty for that offence from 10 to 15 years.

Section 11 amends s.74 of the Criminal Justice Act 2006 to apply the jurisdiction provisions of s.74 (Proceedings relating to offences committed outside the State) to the offences of directing and participating in organised crime. Section 12 creates a new s.74A of the Criminal Justice Act 2006 establishing as an aggravating factor, for the purpose of sentencing, the fact that a serious offence was committed within the framework of a criminal organisation. This provision, in addition to providing an additional tool for the punishment of offences involving organised crime, fulfils an obligation arising under art.3.2 of the European Union Council Framework Decision of October 24, 2008 on the fight against organised crime.

Section 15 amends the Schedule to the Bail Act 1997. The Schedule lists the offences that are defined as "serious offences" and s.2 of the Bail Act provides for the circumstances in which bail may be refused for such offences. As a result of this amendment, the new directing offence under s.5 will also be added to the Bail Schedule.

POSSESSION

Possession of an article The Criminal Justice (Miscellaneous Provisions) Act 2009 s.44 amends s.15 of the Theft and Fraud Offences Act 2001 by inserting an additional offence—a person commits an offence if he or she is in possession, without lawful authority or reasonable excuse, of any article made or adapted for use, in the course of or in connection with, the commission of a number of the offences under the 2001 Act including theft and burglary. The amendment also inserts a defence for a person charged with the offence concerned.

PROCEDURE

Detention Section 20 of the Criminal Justice (Amendment) Act 2009 amends ss.30 and 30A of the Offences against the State Act 1939, as amended. Section 20(1) amends s.30. Section 30 provides that a person suspected of committing any offence under the 1939 Act or any offence that is scheduled for the purposes of Pt V of the Act (i.e. may be tried before the Special Criminal Court) may be detained for up to 72 hours where that is necessary for the proper investigation of the offence in question. The first 48 hours are subject to Garda authorisation and the remaining 24 hours are subject to judicial authorisation. Section 20(1)(a) inserts a new s.30(3A) in order to provide that a person detained under s.30 may continue to be detained for an offence other than the offence to which the detention relates. In order for this provision to apply: the "other offence" must come within the category of offences to which s.30 applies; a member of the Garda Síochána must have reasonable cause to suspect the detained person's involvement in the other offence; and the member in charge of the Garda station or, in the event that the person is detained in a place other than a Garda station as permitted by the section, a member of the Garda Síochána not below the rank of inspector, must have reasonable grounds for believing that the continued detention of the person is necessary for the proper investigation of the other offence concerned. The person may not be detained in excess of the maximum allowed, i.e. 72 hours. The other statutory detention powers already include a provision along these lines.

Section 20(1)(b) makes a number of changes to the procedures applying to the extension of time application under s.30(4). A new s.30(4BA) is inserted in order to minimise the risk of prejudice to the criminal investigation concerned arising from the disclosure of information during the hearing of the extension of time application. The judge is given discretion to direct that the application be heard otherwise than in public; to limit attendance at the hearing to the persons directly concerned with the application, officers of the court and bona fide representatives of the press; and to direct that certain information be disclosed in the absence of the suspect and legal representatives. The new subsection also prohibits the publication or broadcasting of any information about an application under s.30(4), other than the fact that the application has been made by the Gardaí in relation to a particular investigation and the decision on the application. Breach of this prohibition is a criminal offence.

A new s.30(4BB) is inserted in order to make it clear that the lawfulness of the arrest or detention of the suspect is not a matter to be raised during the hearing of an application for an extension of time. Such matters are properly the subject of a habeas corpus application to the High Court. A new s.30(4BC) is inserted in order to provide that the officer of the Garda Síochána making the application for an extension of time (who must be a superintendent or above) may give evidence of matters related to the application not within his/her personal knowledge but within the personal knowledge of another member, i.e. hearsay evidence may be given by the applicant officer. The judge hearing the application may, in the interests of justice, direct another member to attend to give direct oral evidence. The hearing may be adjourned to allow time for the member to attend.

Section 20(1)(c) substitutes s.30(4D) (inserted by s.187 of the Criminal Justice Act 2006) in order to provide that where the detention period expires during the time that the suspect is at the venue for the hearing of the extension of time application, it shall be deemed not to expire until such time as the application is determined by the judge. This provision is subject to the safeguard that the time of arrival must be certified by a court clerk in attendance at the venue. As the law stands at present it only addresses the situation where the detention period would expire during the hearing. Section 20(2) amends s.30A (inserted by s.11 of the Offences against the State (Amendment) Act 1998) in order to add to the grounds on which a court may authorise the re-arrest of a person previously detained under s.30 of the 1939 Act but released without charge. Section 30A provides that a warrant issued by a District Court judge is required to arrest a person again for the offence to which his or her detention related or for an offence which at the time of the first arrest the arresting member suspected or ought reasonably to have suspected the person of having committed. Under the existing law, in order for the judge to issue the warrant, information concerning the person's suspected participation in the offence for which his or her arrest is sought that has come to the knowledge of the Gardaí since the person's release must be supplied on oath. This amendment adds an alternative ground, viz. that notwithstanding that the Gardaí had knowledge of the person's suspected participation in the commission of the offence for which his or her arrest is sought, prior to his or her release, the questioning of the person in relation to that offence prior to release would not have been in the interests of the proper investigation of the offence. An application for an arrest warrant under this section is to be heard otherwise than in public. Section 20(3) makes a consequential amendment to s.30A(2) arising from the amendment to s.30.

Section 21 amends ss.2, 4, 5 and 11 of the Criminal Justice (Drug Trafficking) Act 1996. Section 21(1) amends s.2 of the Act. Section 2 provides that a person suspected of committing a drug trafficking offence (as defined in s.3(1) of the Criminal Justice Act 1994) may be detained for up to seven days for the proper investigation of the offence—48 hours under Garda authority and a further 120 hours under judicial authority.

Section 21(1)(a) makes a number of changes to the procedures applying to the extension of time application under s.2(2). A new s.2(3A) is inserted in order to minimise the risk of prejudice to the criminal investigation concerned arising from the disclosure of information during the hearing of the extension of time application. The judge is given discretion to direct that the application be heard otherwise than in public; to limit attendance at the hearing to the persons directly concerned with the application, officers of the court and bona fide representatives of the press; and to direct that certain information be disclosed in the absence of the suspect and legal representatives. The new s.2(3A) also prohibits the publication or broadcasting of any information about an application under s.2(2) other than the fact that the application has been made by the Gardaí in relation to a particular investigation and the decision on the application. Breach of this prohibition is a criminal offence.

A new s.2(3B) is inserted in order to make it clear that the lawfulness of the arrest or detention of the suspect is not a matter to be raised during the hearing of an application for an extension of time. Such matters are properly the subject of a habeas corpus application to the High Court. A new s.2(3C) is inserted in order to provide that the officer of the Garda Síochána making the application for an extension of time (who must be a chief superintendent or above) may give evidence of matters related to the application not within his/her personal knowledge but within the personal knowledge of another member, i.e. hearsay evidence may be given by the applicant officer. The judge hearing the application may in the interests of justice direct another member to attend to give direct oral evidence. The hearing may be adjourned to allow time for the member to attend. Section 21(1)(b) substitutes s.2(7A) (inserted by s.10 of the Criminal Justice Act 2006) in order to provide that where the detention period expires during the time that the suspect is at the venue for the hearing of the extension of time application, it shall be deemed not to expire until such time as the application is determined by the judge. This provision is subject to the safeguard that the time of arrival must be certified by a court clerk in attendance at the venue. As the law stands at present it only addresses the situation where the detention period would expire during the hearing.

Section 21(2) amends s.4 of the Act in order to add to the grounds on which a court may authorise the re-arrest of a person previously detained under s.2 of the Act but released without charge. Section 4 provides that a warrant issued by a judge of the District Court or a judge of the Circuit Court is required before such a person may be arrested again for the offence to which his or her detention related, or for an offence, which at the time of the first arrest, the arresting member suspected or ought reasonably to have suspected the person of having committed. Under the existing law, in order for the judge to issue the warrant, information concerning the person's suspected participation in the offence for which his or her arrest is sought that has come to the knowledge of the Gardaí since the person's release must be supplied on oath. This amendment adds an alternative ground, viz. that notwithstanding that the Gardaí had knowledge of the person's suspected participation in the commission of the offence for which his or her arrest is sought, prior to his or her release, the questioning of the person in relation to that offence prior to release would not have been in the interests of the proper investigation of the offence. An application for an arrest warrant under this section is to be held otherwise than in public. Subsection (3) amends s.5 of the Act. It applies an amendment to s.4 of the Criminal Justice Act 1984 (see s.23 of the Act) to persons detained under s.2 of the 1996 Act.

Section 21(4) repeals s.11 of the Act. The effect of this is to make ss.2, 3, 4, 5 and 6 of the Act permanent, thereby eliminating the need for these sections to be renewed every two years by a resolution of the Houses of the Oireachtas.

Section 22 amends ss.50, 51 and 52 of the Criminal Justice Act 2007. Section 50 provides that a person suspected of committing murder involving the use of a firearm or explosive; murder to which s.3 of the Criminal Justice Act 1990 applies (capital murder); an offence under s.15 of the Firearms Act 1925 (possession of firearms with intent to endanger life); or an offence under s.15 of the Non-Fatal Offences Against the Person Act 1997 involving the use of a firearm (the offence of false imprisonment); may be detained for up to seven days for the proper investigation of the offence—48 hours under Garda authority and a further 120 hours under judicial authority.

Section 22(1) amends s.50(1) of the Act in order to extend the list of offences to which the section applies. The offences under Pt 7 of the Criminal Justice Act 2007 (organised crime offences) are added. Section 22(2) amends s.50 in order to make a number of changes to the procedures applying to the extension of time application under s.50(3).

A new s.50(4A) is inserted in order to minimise the risk of prejudice to the criminal investigation concerned arising from the disclosure of information during the hearing of the extension of time application. The judge is given discretion to direct that the application be heard otherwise than in public; to limit attendance at the hearing to the persons directly concerned with the application, officers of the court and bona fide representatives of the press; and to direct that certain information be disclosed in the absence of the suspect and legal representatives. The new subsection also prohibits the publication or broadcasting of any information about an application under s.50(3), other than the fact that the application has been made by the Gardaí in relation to a particular investigation and the decision on the application. Breach of this prohibition is a criminal offence.

A new s.50(4B) is inserted in order to make it clear that the lawfulness of the arrest or detention of the suspect is not a matter to be raised at the hearing of an application for an extension of time. Such matters are properly the subject of a habeas corpus application to the High Court. A new s.50(4C) is inserted in order to provide that the officer of the Garda Síochána making the application for an extension of time (who must be a chief superintendent or above) may give evidence of matters related to the application not within his/her personal knowledge but within the personal knowledge of another member, i.e. hearsay evidence may be given by the applicant officer. The judge hearing the application may in the interests of justice direct another member to attend to give direct oral evidence. The hearing may be adjourned to allow time for the member to attend.

Section 22(1)(b) substitutes s.50(9) in order to provide that where the detention period expires during the time that the suspect is at the venue for the hearing of the extension of time application, it shall be deemed not to expire until such time as the application is determined by the judge. This provision is subject to the safeguard that the time of arrival must be certified by a court clerk in attendance at the venue. As the law stands at present it only addresses the situation where the detention period would expire during the hearing.

Section 22(3) amends s.51 in order to add to the grounds on which a court may authorise the re-arrest of a person previously detained under s.50 of the Act but released without charge.

Section 51 provides that a warrant issued by a District Court judge or a Circuit Court judge is required to arrest such a person again for the offence to which his or her detention related or for an offence which at the time of the first arrest the arresting member suspected or ought reasonably to have suspected the person of having committed. Under the existing law, in order for the judge to issue the warrant, information concerning the person's suspected participation in the offence for which his or her arrest is sought that has come to the knowledge of the Gardaí since the person's release must be supplied on oath. This amendment adds an alternative ground, viz. that notwithstanding that the Gardaí had knowledge of the person's suspected participation in the commission of the offence for which his or her arrest is sought, prior to his or her release, the questioning of the person in relation to that offence prior to release would not have been in the interests of the proper investigation of the offence. An application for an arrest warrant under this section shall be heard otherwise than in public. Section 22(4) amends s.52 of the Act. It applies an amendment to s.4 of the Criminal Justice Act 1984 (see s.23 of the Act) to persons detained under s.50 of the 2007 Act.

Section 23 amends ss.4, 9 and 10 of the Criminal Justice Act 1984. Section

4 of the Act provides that a person may be detained for up to 24 hours subject to Garda authorisation where this is necessary for the proper investigation of an arrestable offence (an offence punishable by five years or more). The 24-hour maximum does not include any periods not to be reckoned in its calculation, e.g. absences from the Garda station connected with the making of a habeas corpus application (s.4(8A)) and to attend hospital (s.4(8)). Section 23(1) amends s.4 of the Act by inserting a new s.4(8B). Section 4(8) already provides that any time that a person detained under s.4 is absent from the station for the purpose of hospitalisation is to be excluded in the reckoning of the detention period. A new subs.(8B) seeks to address the situation where a detainee is assessed as unfit for questioning but does not require hospitalisation, for example, where the detainee is intoxicated. It is proposed that where a medical practitioner certifies that the detainee is unfit for questioning, no questioning shall take place during the period certified and that period shall not be included in the reckoning of the detention period. The period cannot exceed six hours and a certificate can be provided on one occasion only.

Section 23(1)(b) makes a consequential amendment to s.4(9). Section 23(2) amends s.9 of the Act. The effect of this is to apply s.4(8B) to persons detained under s.30 of the Offences against the State Act 1939. Section 23(3) amends s.10 of the Act in order to add to the grounds on which a court may authorise the re-arrest of a person previously detained under s.4 of the Act but released without charge. Section 10 provides that a warrant issued by a District Court judge is required before such a person may be arrested again for the offence to which his or her detention related, or for an offence which at the time of the first arrest the arresting member suspected or ought reasonably to have suspected the person of having committed. Under the existing law, in order for the judge to issue the warrant, information concerning the person's suspected participation in the offence for which his or her arrest is sought that has come to the knowledge of the Gardaí since the person's release must be supplied on oath. This amendment adds an alternative ground, viz. that notwithstanding that the Gardaí had knowledge of the person's suspected participation in the commission of the offence for which his or her arrest is sought, prior to his or her release, the questioning of the person in relation to that offence prior to release would not have been in the interests of the proper investigation of the offence. An application for an arrest warrant under this section shall be heard otherwise than in public.

Interference with witnesses/jurors Section 16 of the Criminal Justice (Amendment) Act 2009 increases the penalty for the offence of intimidation of witnesses, jurors or others from 10 years to 15 years. Section 17 provides that the procedure available under s.13 of the Criminal Procedure Act 1967 whereby the District Court may, in circumstances where an accused person pleads guilty to an indictable offence, deal with that offence summarily or send the accused forward for sentencing, shall not apply to the directing the activities of a criminal organisation offence introduced by this Act. Section 29 of the Criminal Procedure Act 1967 is also amended to provide that a person charged with the directing offence may be admitted to bail only by the High Court. This is consistent with the treatment of the other offences under Pt 7 of the Criminal Justice Act 2006.

In *DPP v Albie Lonergan* [2009] IECCA 52; Court of Criminal Appeal, Kearns J. (Kearns, Murphy, Clarke JJ.), May 8, 2009, the CCA considered an interference with a juror during the course of the trial. On the fourth day of the trial it transpired that one of the members of the jury had been approached by an unidentified party in a public house and was told by this party to "make the correct decision". On being advised of this matter, the learned trial judge conducted a discussion initially with counsel in the absence of the jury. The jury was then recalled and the juror recounted the circumstances whereby he was in his local pub, was going to the bathroom and got tapped on the shoulder by a gentleman who was unknown to him and who said, "I hope you make the proper decision next week". The juror protested saying that the individual had got "the wrong guy". Asked if he was intimidated by this approach, the juror responded "no".

There then followed a series of questions as follows:

> JUDGE: It is very good of you to bring it to our attention. It is, dare I say it, one has heard of more serious approaches, if you like. And if I may say so you seem to be, you weren't put in fear or anything?
>
> JUROR: No.
>
> JUDGE: I must ask you this. You have taken an oath to try this case on the evidence and not on any other basis. It is a perfectly human reaction for you, and for all of you, that this might, might perhaps subconsciously even, taint your view of the case one way or another. And it is to be presumed, of course, that you will act in accordance with your oaths. But I wonder do you feel, some people would feel that they might have been tainted by it and are prepared to say they would be. Do you feel you can continue this case purely on the evidence and excluding from your mind any, how should we put it, sinister implications?
>
> JUROR: Yes, your honour.

At the appeal hearing the defence submitted that the form of the question put by the trial judge to the juror invited only a positive response. Senior counsel for the respondent argued that the learned trial judge had applied the correct test as set out in the decision of *DPP v Mulder* [2007] 4 I.R. 796, in that he applied the objective test as to whether a reasonable person would have a reasonable apprehension that the accused would not in the circumstances receive a fair and impartial trial.

The CCA considered that the trial judge applied the correct test as set out in the decision of *Mulder*. In that case there had been a series of incidents:

(a) At the arraignment in front of the jury panel the deceased's brother shouted from the public gallery.
(b) At that stage the judge questioned the deceased's brother in relation to the shouting and he stated that it was just his reaction at seeing his sister's husband who had allegedly strangled her.
(c) On the third day of the trial, prosecution counsel applied for an order excluding the deceased's brother and his wife from court while the evidence continued, due to concerns by the Gardaí as to the behaviour of the deceased's brother and his wife in court.
(d) The note from the foreman of the jury stated that the deceased's brother was making himself "familiar" with some members of the jury.
(e) After the trial judge's request to the foreman to ascertain the correct facts, the foreman addressed the court and referred to the outburst at the arraignment by the deceased's brother, and stated that while the jury were waiting in the corridor outside the court, the deceased's brother borrowed a newspaper from one of the jurors and read out an article referring to the outburst indicating that this was him.
(f) The foreman stated that the juror felt that the deceased's brother was familiarising himself with him and at the end of that day he greeted the juror with a smile and a nod.
(g) He further stated that the juror in question felt somewhat intimidated and uncomfortable.
(h) When the juror was questioned by the judge there was a conflict between his answers and that which the foreman had reported.

Geoghegan J., observing how cases of this nature should be dealt with, stated:

> "While courts should be reluctant to discharge a jury because of individual incidents involving communication with a juror, the nature of this intervention and the cumulative effect of the incidents and the conflict to some extent in the reports given to the judge would have all led an observer to be concerned that there would be a risk of an unfair trial."

The CCA ruled that no such problems arise in the instant case. The incident consisted of a simple remark or approach made in a public house which had no effect on the juror in question. The court was satisfied that the trial judge dealt with the matter in an entirely appropriate manner.

Thus, the *Mulder* and *Lonergan* decisions read together set out an objective test to be applied in cases of this type and show that a trial judge when dealing with an alleged interference should conduct a brief enquiry to ascertain the facts, should determine whether the juror in question (or the entire jury) is no longer capable of fulfilling their oath to try the case only on the basis of the evidence, and thus whether in all the circumstances a reasonable observer would have a reasonable apprehension that a risk of an unfair trial arises. In the result, the series of interferences in *Mulder* were sufficient to have the conviction in that case set aside, while the interference in *Lonergan* was not enough to taint the jury verdict. Thus the matter, in a given future case, will depend both on the nature of the interference, and the manner in which the trial judge deals with the matter.

Adverse comment by trial judge could be remedied at trial In *DPP v Kim Kavanagh*, unreported, Court of Criminal Appeal, Finnegan, Budd and Hanna JJ. (Finnegan J.), July 24, 2008, the applicant applied to the CCA for leave to appeal against both conviction and sentence for a robbery at a pharmacy on Manor Street, Dublin 7.

Several grounds of appeal were argued, including that the learned trial judge erred in making an adverse and prejudicial comment about the accused during her evidence, and in front of the jury, and erred in refusing a defence application for a discharge of the jury following those comments. The matter in question occurred on the fifth day of the hearing, the fourth day of evidence, while the applicant gave evidence. During the luncheon adjournment the applicant's car was stolen and counsel drew this and the fact that the applicant was upset as a result to the attention of the trial judge. That this was indeed the case appears from the transcript. The learned trial judge inquired of the applicant if she needed time to compose herself and offered her a glass of water. She accepted the judge's invitation to tell the jury why she was upset. Her initial answers were not audible and she was exhorted by counsel to speak up. Notwithstanding this, counsel had difficulty hearing her answers which had to be repeated on a number of occasions.

The applicant was subjected to a lengthy cross-examination which continued throughout the afternoon; on three occasions she was required to repeat her answers. On the fifth day of evidence she returned to the stand for cross-examination to continue. The learned trial judge wished her good morning and again exhorted her to keep her voice up. Within a relatively short space of time she was required to repeat her answers on three occasions. On the fourth occasion the learned trial judge addressed her as follows:

> "Ms Kavanagh, before the jury came out this morning and you were sitting in the courtroom, you were entirely composed as I saw you and you have only resorted to this demeanour when you have come to the witness box. You would help yourself greatly, frankly, if you spoke up to the jury. If you want to take a few moments to compose yourself again you are welcome to do so."

Counsel for the applicant, in the absence of the jury, immediately objected in the strongest of terms to the learned trial judge's intervention and applied to have the jury discharged. The learned trial judge responded to the application by stating:

> "Right. I am quite satisfied that what I have said to Ms Kavanagh is not anything of the moment that Mr Fitzgerald suggests or anything approaching requiring the jury to be discharged. I am concerned that the accused is not doing herself any service. I have—I did notice her on coming to court, into the courtroom this morning, and she seemed to be entirely composed. And her persistence in looking away from the microphone and whimpering, for want of a better description, is not helping her in getting across to the jury what it is she wants to tell them, because often times she is simply not audible and not making sense. So for that reason I have my suspicion that a great deal of what is going on is contrived but I would not for a moment suggest that in the presence of the jury …"

In the trial judge's charge to the jury it was stated:

> "To the extent that I am the person in charge of the law equally you are the people in charge of the facts, and you decide the case based upon your assessment of the facts that come to you from the evidence. No one can take that from you, and it is important for me to emphasise that in the course of my remarks if I make reference or comment on the facts, I stand, as has been said to you, like the other two barristers in the case who have spoken to you, that if what I say makes some sense to you, helps you reach your conclusion, by all means take it on board and apply it to your view of the case. If on the other hand you disagree with me on anything I say on the facts then simply say so. 'I don't agree with the judge. He's wrong. I have my view and that is what holds.'"

Giving judgment, the CCA relied on the decision of the Court of Appeal in *R. v Iroegbu*, *The Times*, August 2, 1988, where objection was taken to a considerable number of interventions by the trial judge. Of one such intervention, the Court of Appeal stated:

> "It must be said at once, in the view of this court, no such comment should ever be made by a judge in the course of summing up even in a case in which, as prosecuting counsel told us was the position here, the manner or content of a witness's evidence appear to warrant incredulity. It is axiomatic that it is the function of the judge to remain, and to appear to remain, objective, leaving the jury, in accordance with customary forms of direction, to decide the facts for themselves. While the judge should, as he did elsewhere in his summing up, instruct the jury to ignore, if they disagree with it, any view of the evidence which the judge may appear to express, it can never be appropriate for a judge to give an express indication of his own disbelief in relation to the evidence of a witness let alone that of the defendant.
>
> That said, however a single remark of that kind will not *ipso facto* render a verdict which accords with the judge's indication of view unsafe or unsatisfactory, and indeed this court does not consider that it did so in this case. Not only did the judge give a customary form of direction at the outset, but throughout his judgment, in the passages above mentioned and elsewhere, he repeatedly made clear to the jury not only that the issue was one of credibility, but the decision was entirely one for them. While the court considers that, taken alone the indication complained of was one which should never have been given, when the summing up is read as a whole we do not consider that the jury would have been misled or improperly influenced by it."

The CCA considered that the instant matter should be decided in the same manner. The court ruled that while the comment of the trial judge ought not to have been made, taken in the context of the trial as a whole and in the context of the learned trial judge's charge and his conduct throughout the trial, the comment objected to did not render the verdict unsafe or unsatisfactory.

Kavanagh is a sensible decision. It points to the importance of the trial judge's charge to the jury and in particular on the important matter of the role of the jury as the arbiter of the facts. It appears that once this is clearly put to the jury in a manner satisfactory to counsel on both sides, then a mere "once-off" comment by the judge during the trial, can be effectively remedied at trial stage. Such an approach is welcomed.

Garda protocol for conducting searches lawful In *DPP v Valdas Valiukas*, Court of Criminal Appeal (ex tempore), Kearns J. (Kearns, Budd, McMahon JJ.), April 27, 2009, the applicant was convicted in Naas Circuit Court of possession of certain items facilitating credit card theft contrary to s.15 of the Criminal Justice Act 2001. In what the court described as "a very able submission" by defence counsel, it was argued, inter alia, that the arrest of the applicant had effectively taken place one hour and 40 minutes before the official arrest on the basis that while a search was conducted of the applicant's house, the applicant had been detained there against his will and was not free to move anywhere nor was he told he was free to leave. Counsel for the DPP responded that the Gardaí had a protocol for conducting searches and that they had asked the various occupants of the house to wait in the kitchen while the search was conducted and they did this to ensure an orderly search and to ensure there would be no interference with the search, citing the Criminal Justice Theft and Fraud Offences Act 2001 s.48(3)(d), which provides, in relation to searches, that:

> [A] member of the Garda Síochána alone or accompanied by such other persons as may be necessary may take any other steps which may appear to the member to be necessary for preserving any such thing and preventing interference with it.

The CCA considered the matter and concluded that the submission advanced on behalf of the DPP was correct—there was no evidence of the Gardaí restraining or prohibiting the applicant from leaving the house. The appeal was dismissed.

Surveillance The Criminal Justice (Surveillance) Act 2009 came into effect on July 12, 2009. A key section in the Act deals with the admissibility of evidence gained by surveillance. Section 1 provides the definitions of the key words and phrases that are used throughout the Act, including the meaning of arrestable offence, surveillance, surveillance device and tracking device. Section 2 provides for the application of the Act. Section 3 provides that they shall carry out surveillance only in accordance with the provisions of the Act. Section 4 makes it clear that only members/officers of a sufficiently high level in each of the agencies concerned may apply to the District Court for authorisations, on the basis of strict criteria. In each case, reasonable grounds must exist also for believing that the surveillance sought to be approved is the least intrusive means available, is proportionate from a rights perspective, and is for a period which is limited to its objectives.

Section 5 provides that an authorisation may be applied for to a District Court judge on oath on an ex parte basis in private. The authorisation will be in writing and contain the relevant details as set out in s.5(7). It will be valid for a period of up to three months, which is renewable or variable in accordance with the provisions of s.6. It may allow the authorised member/officer, accompanied if necessary by any other person, to gain entry to property for the purposes of surveillance. This may involve the use of such reasonable force as is necessary in the particular circumstances.

Section 7 deals with a situation where time is of the essence and the matter is urgent to prevent a person absconding to avoid justice, the possible destruction of evidence, or where the security of the State would likely be compromised. In such a case a superior officer, as defined, in the relevant agency may give approval for surveillance on grounds connected with the issuing of an authorisation for a limited operational period of up to 72 hours. If continued surveillance is required, an authorisation will have to be obtained from a judge of the District Court. The section requires the keeping of written records and the making of reports by the parties involved.

Section 8 is concerned with internal approvals for the use of tracking devices for a maximum period of four months. Judicial authorisations are not required for their use, but the approval of a superior officer is necessary based on the strict qualifying criteria set out in the Act. The Act requires that written records and reports have to be maintained in these cases.

Section 9 provides for the retention for specified periods of all official documents relating to authorisations for surveillance, reports, written records of approval sanctioning surveillance in urgent cases, the use of tracking devices and surveillance. Section 10 deals with the secure storage of, and authorised access to, information and documents generated as a result of the carrying out of surveillance, to protect privacy and other rights. The Minister for Justice, Equality and Law Reform in the case of the Garda Síochána, the Minister for Defence in the case of the defence forces and the Minister for Finance in the case of the Revenue Commissioners, may make regulations in this regard in so far as their respective functional areas are concerned. The Minister for Justice, Equality and Law Reform may, in the interests of privacy and other rights, make regulations prescribing a period of less than four months for the use of tracking devices, or for different periods for different purposes.

Section 11 provides for a procedure for dealing with complaints where a person believes that they may be the subject of surveillance. In such cases, the matter will be dealt with by a complaints referee who is the judge of the Circuit Court who handles similar issues arising from the operation of the telephone interception legislation, i.e. the Interception of Postal Packets and Telecommunications Messages (Regulation) Act 1993. In a case where there has been a contravention of a provision of ss.4 to 8 of the Act, the referee has the power to recommend payment of compensation up to €5,000. The matter may also be referred to the Garda Síochána Ombudsman Commission, the Minister for Defence or the Minister for Finance depending on the particular state agency concerned.

Section 12 also follows the 1993 Act in relation to the appointment of a judge of the High Court to oversee the operation of the main provisions of the Act and to make regular reports to the Taoiseach in the matter. Such reports will be laid before both Houses of the Oireachtas.

Section 13 is a confidentiality provision. It prohibits the disclosure of any information about the operation of the Act, unless it is made to an authorised person, as defined, and it is connected with specified criteria. The section applies both to members/officers of the agencies concerned, as well as to persons engaged on contract work. It also applies to persons generally.

Section 14 is a core provision of the Act. It deals with the issue of admissibility of evidence in the narrow and very specific context of evidence obtained by means of surveillance. It provides that such evidence, notwithstanding any error or omission on the face of an authorisation or a written record of approval, or notwithstanding any failure by any member/officer to comply with a requirement of an authorisation or written record, is admissible in certain clearly defined circumstances as set out in the section. In effect, this means that a breach of statute-based procedures or a failure to fulfil particular statutory requirements will not, of themselves, mean that the material in question must be excluded.

Section 15 deals with the issue of disclosure of information about surveillance in proceedings. It provides that disclosure by means of discovery or otherwise shall not be made unless a court authorises otherwise.

Section 16 provides that, as already noted, the Minister for Justice, Equality and Law Reform, the Minister for Defence and the Minister for Finance may make regulations in so far as their areas of functional responsibility are concerned. Any such regulations have to be laid before each House of the Oireachtas.

Section 17 amends the Garda Síochána Act 2005 to provide, in line with existing policy, for the non-application of the provisions of the Act to the Garda Síochána Ombudsman Commission. Section 18 amends the Courts (Supplemental Provisions) Act 1961 to take account of the provisions of the Act in relation to the issuing, renewal and variation of authorisations for surveillance by a judge of the District Court.

Section 19 provides for the short title of the Act.

PROVOCATION

Law reform In its 2009 *Report on Defences in Criminal Law* the Law Reform Commission made recommendations for the law on provocation. The Commission recommended that the defence of provocation should continue to operate as a partial defence, reducing what would otherwise be murder to manslaughter. The defence should be based primarily on whether the provocation (words or acts, such as assault) was such that it was reasonable for the accused, based on the standard of an ordinary person, to have lost self-control.

The fact that the killing did not immediately follow the provocation does not, in itself, mean that the defence cannot be raised. Instead, the presence or absence of an immediate response to provocation should be a matter which a jury is to take into account, along with all the other evidence, in deciding whether the accused lost self-control. This could be especially relevant in the context of cumulative violence.

SENTENCING

Failure to impose Probation Act In *DPP v Christina Buckley*, Court of Criminal Appeal (ex tempore), Fennelly J. (Fennelly, Budd, McMahon JJ.), January 16, 2009, the DPP applied pursuant to s.2 of the Criminal Procedure Act for the court to review a sentence imposed in the Circuit Court on the grounds of undue leniency. The case was described as unusual by the court: "an unfortunate case in which one woman assaults another". While the judge at trial had indicated his intention to follow the "entirely laudable" course of applying the Probation Act, in doing so he did not follow through by imposing the procedure required. The CCA ordered that the offender be discharged conditionally pending her entering into a recognisance without sureties to be of good behaviour for six months.

Offender cannot buy his way out of trouble In *DPP v Lawrence Connors*, Court of Criminal Appeal (ex tempore), Kearns J. (Kearns, Budd, McMahon JJ.), April 27, 2009, the CCA heard an appeal against a sentence of five years (with the last two years suspended) imposed in the Circuit Court in respect of an offence of burglary at a house in Nenagh. There was evidence at trial of damage to the value of €2,000 at the house in question and that all the rooms in the house were badly ransacked. The occupier was in poor health and had been traumatised by the offence. The offender made an offer of compensation which the CCA indicated was "to his credit", though the court continued that "as the jurisprudence of this court shows, you can not simply buy your way out of trouble having committed an offence of such gravity". The CCA was satisfied that the sentencing judge considered the case in the round and had regard to all the factors before passing sentence correctly. The appeal was dismissed.

"Lethargic" application for review of sentence In *DPP v Gerard Murphy*, Court of Criminal Appeal (ex tempore), Kearns J. (Kearns, Budd, McMahon JJ.), April 27, 2009, the DPP brought an application under s.2 of the Criminal Justice Act 1993, for a review of the sentence imposed on the respondent—a three-year suspended sentence—in respect of a single count of possession of cocaine having a value in excess of €15,000. The CCA noted that the application for review of sentence had been put forward "on a somewhat lethargic basis", referring presumably to the fact that the DPP appeared to acknowledge that this was a marginal case.

The respondent was described as "a roadie going around the country with pop groups" and pursuant to such a lifestyle became introduced to cocaine. The trial judge had identified the case as particularly unusual and put the case "right on the margin as to whether a custodial prison sentence should be imposed". It was acknowledged that the respondent had subsequently received support from relevant services and that he had passed a random test for drugs—which indicated that he had made a good rehabilitation. The CCA concluded as follows:

> "All in all, while this Court in dealing with this case *ab initio* might have approached the question of sentencing in a quite different way and might have come down on the other side of the marginal line in favour of a custodial sentence, overall this strikes the Court as being a marginal case. Given that the Court must afford to the sentencing judge a proper margin of appreciation, and given that it had been accepted on behalf of the applicant [the DPP] that this is a marginal case, the Court has decided it will refuse the application."

Applicant had "turned his life around" In *DPP v James Regan*, Court of Criminal Appeal (ex tempore), Kearns J. (Kearns, Budd, McMahon JJ.) April 27, 2009, an appeal was brought against severity of sentence imposed in the Wicklow Circuit Court for conviction for possession of cocaine with a street value of €329, 301, under s.15A. The sentence imposed was seven years' imprisonment. The CCA noted that when the applicant was arrested he made a full admission and pleaded guilty. The applicant was 39 years of age, was in a relationship, and following the death of his father he had "gone off the rails". The court referred to the exceptional circumstances in terms of how the applicant had "turned his life around". In those circumstances the court varied the sentence by suspending the last two years.

Concurrent sentence for blackmail was preferred over consecutive sentence In *DPP v Keith Doheny*, Court of Criminal Appeal (ex tempore), Finnegan J. (Finnegan, Herbert, McKechnie JJ.), March 30, 2009, the applicant pleaded guilty to two offences of demanding with menaces, otherwise blackmail, contrary to the Criminal Justice (Public Order) Act 1994. The menaces concerned allegations of immorality against a woman. He was sentenced to a term of imprisonment for 18 months on each count to run consecutively. It appears the applicant wrote two letters demanding money. The court looked at the circumstances of the case and described it as "a despicable crime". The court said that "one can well imagine the anguish caused to the victim in the case". The applicant had been co-operative, had made a full admission, expressed remorse, and had no previous convictions. The CCA noted that the sentencing court was entitled to impose consecutive sentences as there had been two separate demands for different amounts in two separate letters. However, the CCA stated that it would prefer to treat the offences as a single transaction and a single event. The court imposed a concurrent sentence of three years on each count with the last 12 months of each suspended.

CCA re-enters consecutive sentences to take account of seriousness of offences In *DPP v Zach Moloney*, Court of Criminal Appeal (ex tempore), Finnegan J. (Finnegan, Herbert, McKechnie JJ.), March 30, 2009, the applicant was convicted of possession of an article, namely a broken glass bottle, with intent to cause injury to another contrary to s.9 of the Firearms and Offensive Weapons Act 1990, in circumstances where he had waited outside a convenience store wearing cling film across his face in order to disguise his appearance, and was on temporary release from prison. The court considered that he was intercepted when he intended to commit another offence which was to cause injury to another. He received a sentence of two years for that offence and a further two sentences of two years, to run concurrently, on other counts, as well as a three-month sentence for possession of cannabis. All sentences were to run consecutively with a five-year sentence he was then serving.

It appears the trial judge was misinformed by the DPP on the issue of whether the four counts in the instant case should be consecutive to the sentence he was already serving, pursuant to s.13 of the Criminal Law Act 1976. The DPP conceded on appeal that there was no such obligation. Thus, the CCA had to impose an appropriate sentence in respect of those offences. It was noted that the applicant had 64 previous convictions and there was nothing to suggest he had reached a turning point in his life. Thus the court struck out the original sentences and re-entered the same consecutive sentences, while not obliged to do so by statute, in order to take into account the seriousness of the offences, the circumstances of the applicant, and the totality principle.

Court should not allow tactical use to be made of the plea of guilty In *DPP v Glen Geasley*, unreported, Court of Criminal Appeal, Fennelly J., March 24, 2009, an important matter was considered within the context of the principle of stare decisis. In the case, the applicant applied for leave to appeal in circumstances where he argued he pleaded guilty at his trial after the trial judge abandoned the principle of stare decisis and ruled admissible evidence of certain telephone conversations, thus denying the applicant the protection of the law. He argued that his trial lacked the fundamental attributes of a fair trial so that he was left with no option but to plead guilty.

The applicant was tried at Cork Circuit Criminal Court before Judge Patrick Moran and a jury on three counts of conspiracy to possess firearms or ammunition and one of an attempt to possess firearms. On the ninth day of the trial, the applicant pleaded guilty to count 2 on the indictment which was as follows:

> "Glen Geasley and other persons did on a date between the 22nd February 2007 and 20th April 2007, both dates inclusive and within the State, conspire together to commit crime(s) punishable by law, namely:-Possession of firearms to wit two RPG7 rocket launchers, five

> AKM assault rifles 7.62 × 39mm calibre, 5 AKR 15 semiautomatic assault rifles .223 inch calibre, two Uzi submachine guns 9mm calibre, three Smith & Wesson 9 mm calibre semi automatic pistols, two Browning semiautomatic pistols 9 mm calibre, five Sig Saur 9mm calibre semiautomatic pistols in such circumstances as to give rise to a reasonable inference that such possession was not for a lawful purpose."

The DPP accepted that plea and entered a *nolle prosequi* in respect of the other counts. The learned trial judge sentenced the applicant to a term of imprisonment of 12 years with five years suspended.

The case against the applicant was that, with others, one of them a co-accused, he conspired to obtain a large cache of weapons and ammunition for the unlawful purposes of a group of people engaged in organised crime in Limerick. Virtually all of the evidence resulted from an undercover operation organised by An Garda Síochána in cooperation with an English law enforcement body called the Serious Organised Crime Agency (SOCA). Two enforcement officers employed by SOCA, using the cover names John and Raj, were the State's central witnesses. John and Raj met the applicant at a warehouse in London on February 22, 2007. They posed as arms dealers. They showed him photographs of weapons on a laptop and quoted prices. They each had a clean mobile phone, which was used solely for contact with the applicant. They supplied the applicant with the numbers for these mobiles. A significant part of the incriminating evidence against the applicant consisted of telephone conversations between the applicant and SOCA agents via these mobiles.

The applicant put forward several grounds of appeal. The first and principal matter to be considered was whether, notwithstanding his plea of guilty, the applicant could be permitted to pursue his appeal. That question depended, in turn, on his contention that he was left with no choice but to plead guilty by reason of an incorrect and unlawful ruling admitting the evidence of the mobile phone conversations, a ruling made in defiance of the binding decision of the Court of Criminal Appeal (CCA) in *DPP v Dillon* ([2002] 4 I.R. 501).

The applicant's basic point was that the telephone conversations between the applicant and the SOCA agents were unlawfully intercepted for the purpose of the relevant legislation and should have been ruled inadmissible pursuant to the ruling of the CCA in *Dillon*. The applicant had conversations with "John" and "Raj", believing them to be arms dealers, whereas they were in fact law enforcement officers.

The learned trial judge conducted a voir dire. He heard the evidence of "John" and submissions from counsel in the absence of the jury. He ruled that the evidence that had been obtained by means of the mobile phones, notwithstanding the decision in *Dillon*, was lawfully obtained. On the day following that ruling the applicant indicated his intention to plead guilty.

The CCA, considering whether the applicant could be permitted to pursue his appeal, ruled that in such circumstances the applicant must show that his decision to plead guilty followed on an erroneous ruling or material irregularity of a fundamental kind, such that proceeding with the trial would have been pointless. The CCA emphasised that the court should not allow tactical use to be made of the plea of guilty to obtain a new trial in more favourable circumstances.

Circuit Court not bound to follow decision of CCA decided per incuriam The CCA then considered whether the trial judge had committed a fundamental error of law. In effect the trial judge had ruled that the *Dillon* case was decided per incuriam and refused to follow it. The applicant contended that the trial judge had erred in not following *Dillon*. In *Dillon*, the basic facts were that a Garda inspector came into possession of a mobile phone which he had reason to believe was likely to be used for the purpose of arranging unlawful drug dealing. He answered a number of calls which were made to this phone. One of these was from a man with a Limerick accent who asked for Nicky. The inspector said that Nicky was not available and asked who the caller was. The caller said he was Joe. The caller asked who the inspector was and the latter said that he was Mick, which was of course an invented name. This led to a conversation about drug dealing, incriminating to the caller. Thus, the inspector assumed a false name for the purpose of the conversation and did not, of course, identify himself as a member of the Garda Síochána. He assumed the persona of someone who was privy to a previous arrangement with "Nicky".

The judgment of the CCA, delivered by Hardiman J., identified the issues as being: whether the action of the Garda inspector in listening to the conversation on the mobile phone amounted to an "interception" for the purposes of s.98 of the Postal and Telecommunications Services Act 1983 (the "1983 Act"); if so, whether the interception was unlawful or constituted an unconstitutional invasion of a right to privacy; and finally the consequences of such a finding for the admissibility of the evidence. The court went on to examine the provisions of the 1983 Act and in particular s.98(5) which no longer existed in the form in which it had been originally enacted. It had been replaced by s.13(3) of the Interception of Postal Packets and Telecommunications Messages (Regulations) Act 1993 (the "1993 Act").

However, the applicant in the instant case did not engage in any argument on the effect of the provision at s.98 of the 1983 Act but rather argued that the Circuit Court was bound to follow and apply the decision of the CCA in *Dillon*, being a superior court.

Giving judgment on this important matter the CCA indicated that the notion of a decision reached per incuriam is an essential part of the doctrine of stare decisis. On that issue it stated as follows:

> "Where a court has reached a decision without taking account of a

> relevant argument, an important judicial precedent or a relevant statutory provision, its decision may be disapproved in a later case, by a court of concurrent jurisdiction. Its authority, to borrow the language of Kingsmill Moore J, may be reduced 'to vanishing point'. Normally, it will remain binding, however, on courts of inferior jurisdiction."

However, the CCA noted that the instant case presented "an unusual, even an extreme example of a court deciding a matter without making any reference to the legal provision which was actually in force". The CCA remarked that the *Dillon* decision was entirely founded upon the interpretation of a statutory provision which was no longer in force and that, "faced with this unusual, even unprecedented, situation, the learned trial judge decided, at the urging of counsel for the prosecution, that he was not bound by *Dillon*".

This CCA ruled that the learned judge was correct in his ruling. In so far as *Dillon* stood as a precedent, it conveyed at most a binding interpretation of s.98(5) in its original form. It was not an authority on the interpretation of the new provision introduced by the 1993 Act. In that sense it was entirely academic, except for its effect on the application it decided. Once it was clear that the subsection was no longer in force, *Dillon* ceased to be relevant. The CCA stated as follows:

> "A trial judge is not only bound by decisions of this court and of the Supreme Court. The doctrine of precedent is not the sole source of law in the State. A judge is equally bound to give effect to legislation passed by the Oireachtas which is declared by the Constitution to be the sole and exclusive maker of our laws. The learned trial judge was faced with a direct and explicit conflict …"

Considering the report of the decision in *Dillon* the CCA felt that the amending provision had not been drawn to the court's attention in that case. The court continued that the learned trial judge was not only entitled but bound to apply the statutory provision and to give effect to the law as passed by the Oireachtas. Application for leave to appeal was dismissed.

This is a significant decision which impacts on our understanding of the scope of the doctrine of stare decisis. The argument raised by the applicant was novel in that he argued that while *Dillon* may have been decided per incuriam the principle of stare decisis meant an inferior court was still bound to follow it. The CCA ruled against that argument on the basis that the Circuit Court had an obligation to consider all the laws of the State, both decisions of the CCA and the Supreme Court, as well as the Oireachtas. The applicant could not, in other words, argue that the Circuit Court was bound to follow a decision of the CCA in circumstances where that would allow the applicant to circumnavigate a law enacted by the legislature. This is an entirely justifiable position to take for several reasons, not least because the CCA upheld the laws of the Oireachtas as well as those of the courts.

This matter withstanding, the case does set a potentially troublesome precedent in a future case, that an inferior court is not always bound to follow a decision of a superior court—where a decision of a superior court has been decided per incuriam it appears that the inferior court may disregard it. It is envisaged that a dispute may arise in a future case where an inferior court must decide whether a superior court had, or had not, actually had regard to a legislative provision. Nor, it appears, can the decision in *Geasley* be confined to its own facts, for while the CCA indicated that the case presented an "extreme example" the court clearly went on to state that the Circuit Court judge had been correct to rule that he was not bound to follow the CCA decision in *Dillon*.

Reactivation of part of suspended sentence In *DPP v Ryan*, unreported, CCA, Finnegan J., March 20, 2009, the applicant was charged and convicted on one count of wounding with intent to do grievous bodily harm contrary to s.18 of the Offences Against the Person Act 1861, the particulars of the offence being that on September 12, 1995 at O'Connell Street, Limerick he unlawfully and maliciously wounded Anthony O'Mahony with intent to do him grievous bodily harm. On March 23, 2000 he was sentenced to a term of imprisonment of 12 years with the last six years of that term suspended on terms that he keep the peace and be of good behaviour. He was released from prison having served that sentence on April 26, 2003.

On April 19, 2005 the respondent applied to have the suspended portion of the sentence reactivated. The evidence was that the applicant had committed a number of offences including obstructing a Garda contrary to s.29(5) of the Offences against the State Act 1939; two charges under s.13 of the Criminal Justice Act 1984 of failing to answer to bail; and two offences under the Criminal Justice (Public Order) Act 1994.

The issue for the court was whether s.99 of the Criminal Justice Act 2006 could be relied on in circumstances where that section had been enacted subsequent to the imposition of the suspended sentence at issue; in other words, whether that section had retrospective effect. Section 99 was enacted to apply to situations involving the reactivation of a suspended sentence. The provision enables a court to respond appropriately and proportionately by reactivating a sentence in part—in circumstances where commission of offences at issue could not be considered as de minimis breaches (thus allowing reactivation of a suspended sentence) but yet were such that the reactivation of an entire suspended sentence would be disproportionate. The section states:

> 99(1) Where a person is sentenced to a term of imprisonment (other than a mandatory term of imprisonment) by a court in respect of an offence that court may make an order suspending the execution of the sentence

in whole or in part, subject to the person entering into a recognizance to comply with the conditions of, or imposed in relation to, the order.

…

(9) Where a person to whom an order under subsection (1) applies is, during the period of suspension of the sentence concerned, convicted of an offence, the court before which proceedings for the offence were brought shall, after imposing sentence for that offence, remand the person in custody or on bail to the next setting of the court that made the said order and

…

(17) A court shall, where it is satisfied that a person to whom an order under subsection (1) applies has contravened a condition of the order, revoke the order unless it considers that in all the circumstances of the case it would be unjust to do so and where the court revokes the order the person shall be required to serve the entire of the sentence originally imposed by the court, or such part of the sentence as the court considers just having regard to all the circumstances of the case, less any period of that sentence already served in prison and any period spent in custody pending the revocation of the said order.

…

As against the applicability of s.99, the DPP argued that as the offences had been committed prior to the commencement of that section, the matter at issue was still governed by common law. The decision of *DPP v Alan Murray*, unreported, CCA, March 18, 2003 was cited where McCracken J. indicated that the option of reinstating part of a suspended sentence was not open to a judge in this jurisdiction. He said:

> "She (the learned trial judge) clearly took the view that this was a material and serious breach of the conditions in respect of residing where he is supposed to reside and visiting Mrs Kennedy. It is suggested in some way that reactivating the entire sentence is unjust, but no authority has been quoted to this court, and none of us are aware of any authority, whereby in a situation like this, where there has been a breach of a condition on which a sentence was suspended, that there is any discretion in the trial judge to do anything other than treat it as *de minimis* and simply almost ignore it and allow the suspension to continue, or else reactivate the entire sentence."

Again in *DPP v Stewart*, unreported, CCA, January 12, 2004, Hardiman J. said:

> "There is power to activate the sentence but it is not mandatory to do

> so in that a judge may decline to do so if the court considers that the breach might be described as trivial or *de minimis*. In the view of this court this breach in the circumstances in which it occurred could not possibly be so described. The second issue was whether the sentences could be partially, not totally, activated. The terms in which the sentences were suspended clearly indicate that the applicant must 'come up if called upon to do to serve the sentence of the court this day imposed but suspended on your entering into this bond.' Mr Maguire has referred us to English statutory authority for the proposition that the sentence may be re-imposed, if it is to be re-imposed, in whole or in part. There is no Irish equivalent. It therefore seems to us that Judge Dunne was constrained to act as she did."

Thus, the instant case turned on the applicability of s.99. Giving judgment, the CCA stated that central to the interpretation of s.99 was the provision at s.99(17). The wording of s.99(17) confers a benefit on those who have been sentenced with the entire or a portion of the sentence suspended and where another subsection, s.99(9), has not operated or has no application. Section 99(1) was considered "merely a statutory restatement of the common law". The court said:

> "[T]he object of the section as a whole is to deal with a perceived injustice where reactivation of a suspended sentence or a suspended portion of a sentence could be perceived as disproportionate in the absence of a power in the court to reactivate the sentence in part."

Further, the court stated:

> "[T]here was nothing in the wording of subsection (17) to impose a temporal restriction on the jurisdiction thereby conferred so that only those whose sentences are imposed after the commencement of section 99 should benefit."

Thus, the court had power to reactivate the suspended portion of a sentence in part, notwithstanding that the sentence was imposed prior to the commencement of s.99 of the Criminal Justice Act 2006. The court indicated it would hear submissions as to whether the matter should proceed as an application for leave to appeal against sentence or as an appeal pursuant to Criminal Justice Act 2006 s.99(12) to the Circuit Court.

While the result in *Ryan* is justifiable, there are two points of contention over the manner in which the court arrived at its conclusion. First, it is submitted, retrospective effect of legislative provisions should only apply where there is a clear intention from the Oireachtas that the provision should apply in that manner. In this particular case, the court has used a combination of the various subsections of s.99, in particular s.99(17), to read the section as having retrospective effect. That type of legislative interpretation is not without its difficulties.

The second point of contention is the reference by the court to s.99(1) being "merely a statutory restatement of the common law". Restatement of the law, in an Irish context, as set out in the Statute Law Restatement Act 2002, is a process of administrative consolidation of legislation—a task currently performed by the Law Reform Commission. The reference by the CCA to the restatement of the common law is, however, entirely understandable when ascribed the meaning given to restatement in another jurisdiction by the American Law Institute.

Value and quantity of drugs a "critical factor" in sentencing In *DPP v Derek Long*, unreported, Court of Criminal Appeal, Kearns, Budd, Clark JJ. (Kearns J.), October 31, 2008, a case concerning a review of sentence on grounds of undue leniency, the Court of Criminal Appeal ruled on "a point of considerable importance" in the area of sentencing under s.15A of the Misuse of Drugs Act 1977 (as inserted by ss.4 and 5 of the Criminal Justice Act 1999), namely, to what extent should the court take into account the quantity, value and type of drugs seized when determining the appropriate sentence?

The instant case concerned an application brought on behalf of the applicant under s.2 of the Criminal Justice Act 1993 for a review of a sentence of two years imposed on the respondent in Dublin Circuit Court following his guilty plea to possession of 1,591 grams of cocaine having an uncontested street value of €111,370, following a search of the respondent's family home in Blackrock. The respondent was not in the home at the time of the search.

On his return, the respondent was brought to the local Garda station by his father where he made various admissions. He claimed to be holding the cocaine on behalf of another person to whom he owed €500 which was due for payment of debts in relation to cocaine he, himself, had consumed. While not accepting that he was addicted to drugs, the respondent did admit to consuming cocaine at weekends, consuming approximately two €100 bags of cocaine per week.

The respondent, who was aged 21 at the time of commission of the offence, and who was 23 when the matter was decided by the Court of Criminal Appeal (CCA), was the youngest of a family of three children and resided with his parents. He left school at 16 years of age and held a variety of different jobs. There was evidence at the hearing of significant family difficulties in his background. The respondent's mother had a history of severe depression with a number of attempted suicides. Following one such episode, in March 2005, the respondent himself became depressed and was put on medication. He was unable to find work in 2006 and began drinking heavily and using cocaine. During this period, he ran up a series of debts which he could not repay.

At the sentencing hearing, a psychological report and a report from the respondent's GP were made available to the court. Those reports were used to impress upon the sentencing judge that the respondent was an immature and vulnerable person with low self-esteem who would be prone to abusing alcohol and drugs for those reasons. The managing director of a development company also gave evidence to state that the respondent had worked with his company between January and June 2007 and had shown himself to be a helpful and co-operative worker who applied himself in assisting main contractors with painting and decorating.

There was also evidence that the respondent had weaned himself off drugs from the time of the offence and had demonstrated signs of genuine remorse and a determination to put his life in order. The respondent had no previous drug-related convictions. His only prior convictions related to minor road traffic offences.

In the course of his plea for leniency on behalf of the respondent in the Circuit Court, counsel compared the facts of the instant case with those of *People (DPP) v David Spratt* [2007] IECCA 123, a case in which the CCA substituted a two-year term of imprisonment for a five-year suspended term. In pointing out contended similarities between the two cases, counsel was careful to point out that the street value of the drugs in that case was significantly less—about €35,000. On being given this information in the instant case the sentencing judge stated, "that is not a material factor".

Shortly afterwards, the sentencing judge gave judgment which the CCA cited in full, owing in part to "its exceptional brevity". The court had stated:

> "The accused man in this case has pleaded guilty to a very serious offence, that of s.15(A) of the Drugs Act. The minimum sentence as stipulated by the Act is ten years. Obviously, in special circumstances, I can go below that. It seems to me that those special circumstances (exist): his plea of guilty, his assistance in the investigation of the crime in question, and, in particular, as pointed out to me, his personal circumstances. What I think is very relevant in this case is the relative youth of the accused man on the date of the commission of the crime; he was twenty-one years of age. It seems to me from reading the medical evidence and psychological reports that he was particularly immature for his age. It also seems to me that he was suffering from a condition that would certainly impair his judgement and certainly weaken his defence against committing acts that would get him into trouble. So in all the circumstances, particularly bearing in mind his youth, psychological condition on the date in question and the special circumstances outlined, the plea of guilty and the assistance (given by the respondent), and taking into account the case of *DPP v. Spratt*, I will impose the same sentence as indicated in that case. I think that the appropriate sentence is one or two years' imprisonment."

The application for review of sentence in the instant case was primarily grounded on the assertion that, when imposing sentence, the Circuit Court erred in failing to take into account the gravity of the offence—in particular the substantial value of the drugs which formed the subject-matter of the charge. Further, it was submitted that the sentencing court erred in attaching undue weight to both the personal circumstances of the respondent and the manner in which the respondent had met the case. Giving decision, the CCA indicated that due regard should be given in all cases concerning s.15A to factors which may disapply the provisional minimum sentence, such as an early plea of guilty, the rendering of material assistance, or the fact that the offender is a foreign national.

The CCA continued by stating that:

> "[O]ther considerations might include the fact that the respondent was a vulnerable person, that it was a *'one off'* offence where the offender was unlikely to re-offend, that the offender was an addict himself or owed debts to the gang for whom he was holding drugs or that he was under duress or in fear of his own safety."

The court continued that it was concerned with the role which the quantity, value and type of drugs seized should play when sentencing. The quantity and value of drugs seized were considered "critical factors" to be taken into account in evaluating the overall seriousness of the offence. The court rejected as "mistaken" the views of the Circuit Court judge in the instant case which were unambiguously to the effect that the value of a particular haul or the difference in value of a particular haul between €35,000 and €111,370 was "not a material factor" when it came to sentencing. The court considered that while the *Spratt* case and the instant case were similar, the critical difference between them was the value of the drugs haul which placed the offence in the instant case "on a completely different level of seriousness and gravity".

As regards the type of drugs, and whether that was a relevant factor when sentencing, the CCA stated that:

> "[T]he extent that a particular drug may be shown to be actually or potentially more harmful than another is a factor of some value to which a sentencing judge may have regard in an appropriate case. The critical factor, however, in determining sentence is clearly the value of the drugs in question."

The CCA was also satisfied that the learned sentencing judge in the instant case attached "excessive importance to the respondent's age, immaturity and psychological vulnerability". The court was satisfied that none of those factors, either individually or collectively, were such as to warrant or justify the course adopted by the sentencing judge.

The court was satisfied that those errors "led to a substantial departure in the instant case from the appropriate sentence which should have been imposed". In a separate ex tempore decision, the CCA considered reports from the educational service and from a psychologist which both indicated that the respondent was "making significant progress". In the end, the court quashed the sentence of two years and substituted a sentence of six years' imprisonment, with the last three years suspended—owing to the unique circumstances which arose.

In *Long*, the CCA acknowledged that hitherto it had not made a statement to the effect that the quantity and value of the drugs is a critical factor when sentencing. The court considered that the matter was "self-evident" from the legislative provision. However, whilst iterating that position, the court threw light on the manner in which those factors should be taken into account.

Aside from indicating that both quantity and value of the drugs—and to a lesser extent, the type of drug—are significant factors in the sentencing process, the CCA ruled that there may well be cases where the person found in possession of the drugs is unaware and could not have known of the quantity or value of the drugs, such as in the case of a "drugs mule" who is handed a suitcase at a foreign airport and asked to import it into Ireland for reward. In those cases, it appears a different approach should be taken. The court indicated that each case will necessarily turn upon its own particular facts.

Another notable point which arises is the manner in which the CCA felt compelled to address "the terseness of the judgment" delivered in the Circuit Court, which, it said, gave rise to "a measure of concern". The CCA stated that it was important, particularly in cases of this nature, that the sentencing judge delivers a "reasoned judgment". While the court accepted the argument that the sentencing transcript was a "living transcript", it made clear its dissatisfaction with the judgment as delivered.

Error of principle Finally in *DPP v Paul Kelly*, Court of Criminal Appeal (ex tempore), Kearns J. (Kearns, Irvine, Edwards JJ.), March 31, 2009, the applicant had pleaded guilty to possession of a sizeable quantity of ecstasy tablets having a value of €86,000 which were stored in a car on Ormond Quay, for which he received a sentence of eight years with the final two years suspended. Following his arrest he made what the court described as "straight up admissions"—he indicated that he had run up significant drug debts amounting to €6,000, he was acting as a courier, and he was drug dependent. The court noted that there were "quite exceptional testimonials" which had been submitted on his behalf and he had provided 52 drug-free samples since the arrest, which was "quite an unusual but very encouraging development". The court said it would take into account the "material assistance in this instance" and that failure to take this into account amounted to an error of principle in the imposition of the original sentence such as would allow the CCA to substitute its own sentence. The CCA substituted a sentence of five years with the last two years suspended.

Electricity and Energy

EXPLORATION OUTSIDE TERRITORIAL SEAS

The Continental Shelf (Designated Areas) Order 2009 (S.I. No. 163 of 2009), made by the Government under s.2(3) of the Continental Shelf Act 1968, set out the designated area within which the rights of the State are exercisable outside the territorial seas over the sea bed and subsoil for the purpose of exploring such sea bed and subsoil and exploiting their natural resources. The "territorial seas" are defined under Pt 3, Ch.5 of the Sea-Fisheries and Maritime Jurisdiction Act 2006 (*Annual Review of Irish Law 2006*, p.394), which repealed and replaced the Maritime Jurisdiction Act 1959. The 2009 Order came into force on March 31, 2009.

ELECTRICITY

EU Internal Market in Electricity The European Communities (Internal Market in Electricity) Regulations 2009 (S.I. No. 226 of 2009) (the "2009 Regulations") inserted s.34(1B) into the Electricity Regulation Act 1999 (the "1999 Act") in order to give further legal effect to Directive 2003/54 concerning common rules for the EU Internal Market in Electricity. The 2003 Directive, which also repealed Directive 96/92, had largely been implemented by the European Communities (Internal Market in Electricity) Regulations 2000 (S.I. No. 445 of 2000), the European Communities (Internal Market in Electricity) Regulations 2005 (S.I. No. 60 of 2005) and the European Communities (Internal Market in Electricity) Regulations 2006 (S.I. No. 524 of 2006), each of which had also previously amended the 1999 Act. Section 34(1B) of the 1999 Act, as inserted by the 2009 Regulations, provides that an offer under s.34(1) of the 1999 Act, made for the purpose of connecting a generating station to the distribution system, may, on request of the applicant, be on the basis that the applicant constructs, or that either or both the applicant and the distribution system operator arranges to have constructed, the connection to the distribution system, and any such connection constructed or arranged to be constructed by the applicant shall be the property of the person with whom the agreement is made, and shall, for the purposes of s.37(4) of the 1999 Act, be deemed to be a direct line. This amendment to the 1999 Act provides for the construction of what are referred to as "contestable connections" between electricity generating plants and the distribution system. The 2009 Regulations came into force on June 15, 2009.

Licensing of combined heat and power (CHP) sources The Energy (Miscellaneous Provisions) Act 2006 (Commencement of Section 6) Order 2009 (S.I. No. 298 of 2009) brought s.6 of the 2006 Act (*Annual Review of Irish Law 2006*, p.358) into operation on July 29, 2009. Section 6 of the 2006 Act, which amended ss.2 and 7 of the Electricity Regulation Act 1999, deals with the licensing of combined heat and power (CHP) sources, in accordance with Directive 2004/8 on the promotion of cogeneration. The Electricity Regulation Act 1999 (Appointment of Person to Calculate Power to Heat Ratios of Combined Heat and Power Units) Order 2009 (S.I. No. 299 of 2009) appointed the Commission for Energy Regulation to calculate and certify, from July 30, 2009, the actual power to heat ratios of the cogeneration technologies specified in Annex 1 to Directive 2004/8.

GAS AND OIL

Bord Gáis Éireann: borrowing powers The Gas (Amendment) Act 2009 amended s.23(2) of the Gas Act 1976 (as last amended by s.31 of the Sustainable Energy Act 2002) in order to increase the statutory borrowing limit of Bord Gáis Éireann from €1.7 billion to €3 billion. It was explained during the Oireachtas debate on the 2009 Act that this change would give Bord Gáis Éireann the ability to access funds to develop the strategic direction set out in its five-year corporate plan up to 2012 and beyond.

Gas installers regulation Sections 9F to 9J of the Electricity Regulation Act 1999 (the "1999 Act"), inserted by s.13 of the Energy (Miscellaneous Provisions) Act 2006 (the "2006 Act") (*Annual Review of Irish Law 2006*, pp.359–360), provided for the regulation of registered gas installers. The details of the regulatory regime were set out in 2009. The Electricity Regulation Act 1999 (Gas Works) Regulations 2009 (S.I. No. 225 of 2009) designated certain classes of works to be gas works for the purposes of s.9G(3) of the 1999 Act, as inserted by the 2006 Act. For the purposes of s.9G(3) of the 1999 Act, "works which are gas works" cover the installation, removal, repair, servicing, maintenance or replacement of a natural gas fitting covered by the NSAI standard I.S. 813:2002 which is used or designed to be used by a domestic gas customer, or which is designed to be used by a domestic gas customer but which is installed in a commercial or an industrial premises. Complementing this, the Energy (Miscellaneous Provisions) Act 2006 (Section 13) (Commencement of Remaining Provisions) Order 2009 (S.I. No. 238 of 2009) brought into operation on June 29, 2009 the amendments made to the 1999 Act by s.13(3) and (4) of the 2006 Act. Thus, with effect from June 29, 2009, the Commission for Energy Regulation (CER) may prosecute any person who is not a registered gas installer but who carries out the gas works designated by the Electricity Regulation Act 1999 (Gas Works) Regulations 2009.

National Oil Reserves Agency Borrowing Powers The European Communities (Repeal of Section 26(4) of the National Oil Reserves Agency Act 2007) Regulations 2009 (S.I. No. 247 of 2009) provided for the repeal of s.26(4) of the National Oil Reserves Agency Act 2007 (the "2007 Act"), which dealt with aspects of the basis on which the National Oil Reserves Agency may raise or borrow money. The stated purpose of the repeal of s.26(4) of the 2007 Act by the 2009 Regulations was to make the 2007 Act compatible with art.3(1) of Directive 2006/67 imposing an obligation on Member States to maintain minimum stocks of crude oil and/or petroleum products.

National Oil Reserves Agency Levy The National Oil Reserves Agency Act 2007 (Returns and Levy) (Amendment) (No.2) Regulations 2009 (S.I. No. 220 of 2009) amended the National Oil Reserves Agency Act 2007 (Returns and Levy) Regulations 2007 (S.I. No. 567 of 2007) and revoked the National Oil Reserves Agency Act 2007 (Returns and Levy) (Amendment) Regulations 2009 (S.I. No. 214 of 2009) in order to provide for the variation in the amount of the National Oil Reserves Agency (NORA) levy to be paid with effect from October 1, 2009.

Offshore installations: hazardous substances discharge European Communities (Control Of Dangerous Substances From Offshore Installations) Regulations 2009 (S.I. No. 358 of 2009) (the "2009 Regulations") implemented Directive 2006/11 on pollution caused by certain dangerous substances discharged into the aquatic environment (the "2006 Directive"), insofar as it relates to the discharge of certain dangerous substances from offshore installations into the Irish territorial sea. The 2009 Regulations provide that a person shall not discharge or cause or permit the discharge of a dangerous substance from an offshore installation into the territorial seas except under and in accordance with a discharge permit given by the Minister for Communications, Energy and Natural Resources under the 2009 Regulations. Regulation 6 provides that a discharge permit shall be subject to conditions: (a) limiting the discharge of a dangerous substance; (b) establishing, in relation to the discharge of a dangerous substance, emission standards, set in accordance with art.6 of the 2006 Directive; (c) identifying, by means of a map or otherwise, the boundaries or limits of the place or waters in relation to which discharge of a dangerous substance may take place; (d) relating to monitoring and inspection of discharges and emission standards;

(e) specifying operational practices; (f) relating to the use and storage of any dangerous substance on offshore installations; and (g) requiring the keeping of records relating to a condition to which reg.6 relates. Regulation 17 of the 2009 Regulations provides that the Minister shall, after consultation with the Irish Marine Institute, publish or cause to be published a programme, in accordance with art.6 of the 2006 Directive, containing measures aimed at reducing pollution from dangerous substances used on offshore installations, within 12 months of the commencement of the Regulations. The Minister's programme must take account of other programmes established to achieve the objectives of Directive 2000/60 or other acts of the institutions of the European Communities that are, in the opinion of the Minister, necessary, ancillary or supplementary to achieving the objectives of the 2000 Directive. Regulation 22 of the 2009 Regulations provides that a person who commits an offence under reg.6 is liable: (a) on summary conviction, to a fine not exceeding €5,000, or (b) on conviction on indictment, to a fine not exceeding €500,000. The 2009 Regulations came into force on September 7, 2009.

Employment Law

DR DES RYAN, Lecturer in Law, Trinity College Dublin

INTRODUCTION

The focus of this chapter is on developments in Irish employment law in 2009. As ever, employment law continues to develop at a remarkable pace. Following the approach adopted in this chapter of the *Annual Review* in previous years, a number of key areas are selected for detailed analysis here. The areas considered this year are those concerning: (i) part-time and fixed-term workers; (ii) employment equality; (iii) claims of penalisation under the Safety, Health and Welfare at Work Act 2005; (iv) stress and harassment at work; (v) vicarious liability; and (vi) injunctions restraining dismissal. This range of topics enables an assessment of key developments to have taken place in 2009 not only in both the distinctive statutory and common law contexts but also across a broad selection of the multiplicity of different fora in Irish employment litigation.

PART-TIME AND FIXED-TERM WORKERS

Identification of comparator In the context of developments in 2009 concerning the Protection of Employees (Part-Time Work) Act 2001, two significant cases in the Labour Court this year were *Blackrock College v Browne* (PTD091, February 2, 2009) and *Catholic University School v Dooley* (PTD092, April 22, 2009), both Labour Court appeals under the Protection of Employees (Part-Time Work) Act 2001 (and, in *Dooley*, also under the Protection of Employees (Fixed-Term Work) Act 2003) in which the Labour Court afforded detailed consideration to the question of identifying a legitimate comparator for the purposes of a claim of discrimination on grounds of part-time status. Given the striking similarity of the two cases, it will be helpful to consider them both together so as to explore their significance.

***Browne v Blackrock College*: The background** The claimant in *Browne*, a part-time teacher employed by the respondent college, taught 14 hours per week, compared to full-time teachers who taught 22 hours. As a private school, the respondent paid some teachers out of its own funds and other teachers were remunerated by the Department of Education and Science. Those paid by the department were on a scale agreed with the relevant trade union. Those paid directly by the college, including the claimant, were paid at a lower rate and their conditions of employment were generally less favourable. Thus, the claimant was not entitled to sick pay and did not have access to the occupational health scheme.

The claimant brought a claim before a rights commissioner alleging less favourable treatment in terms of her pay and conditions of employment compared to full-time colleagues paid by the department. She succeeded before the rights commissioner. On appeal to the Labour Court, the respondent sought a ruling on the preliminary issue of whether the claimant in fact had a cause of action under the 2001 Act; accordingly, this was the sole question addressed by the Labour Court.

The approach of the Labour Court in *Browne* The court began by finding that the claimant and the comparator were employed by the same employer, even though the funds to pay the comparator came from the Department of Education and Science and the claimant's wages came from the college. The college argued that as it also employed full-time teachers whom it paid out of its own resources, that was the appropriate comparison for the part-time claimant to make rather than the nominated comparator paid for by the department who had a different status. As a result, given that full-time teachers paid directly by the college were employed on the same terms and conditions pro rata as the part-time claimant, there was no less favourable treatment involved. In rejecting this argument, the court examined its decision in the case of *McArdle v State Laboratory* (Determination No. FTD063 (the appeal to the High Court in *McArdle* on a point of law, reported at [2007] 2 I.L.R.M. 438, is not relevant for this point)). It will be recalled that in *McArdle* an unestablished civil servant working on a fixed-term contract successfully compared her treatment with an established permanent civil servant with whom she was engaged in like work. In that case the Labour Court, following the decision of the High Court (O'Sullivan J.) in *Wilton v Steel Company of Ireland* [1999] E.L.R. 1, concluded that it was for the claimant to choose his or her comparator provided the statutory criteria were met. The only test was whether the claimant and the comparator were engaged in like work.

The Labour Court in *Browne* then addressed the question of like work. The college argued that there were a number of differences in the conditions applicable to privately paid teachers and those paid directly by the department. Amongst these were requirements relating to registration, qualifications, negotiation arrangements, probation, access to posts of responsibility, career breaks and job sharing. The court observed that while these differences might be relevant to the contractual terms under which both categories were employed, they were not relevant to assessing whether like work was being performed. As the claimant and comparator were both secondary school teachers (although teaching different subjects) their work was "undoubtedly of the same or a similar nature within the meaning of s.7(2)(b) or 7(2)(c) of the [2001] Act".

Arguments as to transposition of Framework Directive on Part-Time Work Another point of significance about *Browne* was that a number of complex arguments were advanced on behalf of the college concerning the extent to which the Irish legislation correctly transposed the Framework Agreement on Part-Time Work ([1998] OJ L14/9). It was contended, for example, that a part-time teacher who was paid by the college would be entitled to claim equal pay and conditions with a full-time teacher paid by the department but a full-time teacher paid by the college could not claim such equal treatment. This, it was argued, would inevitably result in a reduction in opportunities for part-time teaching work which would run counter to the purpose of the legislation and the EU Framework Agreement, one of the aims of which is to facilitate the development of part-time work and to contribute to the flexible organisation of working time in a manner that takes into account the needs of both employers and workers (Clause 1 of the Framework Agreement). The Labour Court's determination in *Browne* focused more closely on the second (but related) submission put forward on behalf of the college, namely that Clause 4 of the Framework Agreement—which provides that in respect of employment conditions part-time workers shall not be treated in a less favourable manner than comparable full-time workers solely because they work part-time, unless the different treatment is justified on objective grounds—should influence the interpretation of the transposing domestic legislation (the 2001 Act). In essence, it was argued (in both *Browne* and the later 2009 case of *Dooley*, analysed below) that if the less favourable treatment was not related to the claimant's part-time status but to the status of the comparator, discrimination had not taken place. The court did not accept this interpretation of Clause 4 in either of the two cases, on the basis that to do so would mean that any consideration unrelated to an employee's part-time status which influenced the decision to treat him or her less favourably would provide a full defence. Even if this interpretation were correct, the court held that Clause 6 of the Framework Agreement specifically permitted Member States to provide better protection for part-time workers in its domestic legislation.

Ultimately, the Labour Court in *Browne* concluded that the claimant's complaint was legitimately made and that she was entitled to succeed in her claim unless the impugned treatment could be shown to be justified on objective grounds.

The approach of the Labour Court in *Dooley* In its later determination in *Dooley*, the Labour Court considered the employer's similar argument to the effect that the claimant was treated differently because he was paid out of private rather than public funds, and not because of his status as a part-time or fixed-term worker. It was argued that this was evidenced by the fact that other teachers, who were similarly privately funded and who were full-time and permanent, were treated in exactly the same manner as the claimant. Again, the Labour Court rejected this argument. In the course of its analysis the court set out in strong language its interpretation of the word "solely" in Clause 4 of the Framework Agreement:

> "If the word were to be interpreted literally, it would mean that any factor, no matter how trivial, which influenced an employer in not applying the principle of equal treatment could operate as a full defence to a claim made under the [2001 and 2003] Acts or the Directives. In that event the protection afforded by both Acts would be rendered nugatory and the objects pursued by the Directives would be subverted. This arises because there would rarely be a case in which an employer could not point to some status-neutral consideration, which influenced an impugned decision, to avoid liability for what would otherwise be unlawful discrimination. Such a result could not have been intended."

The Labour Court in *Dooley* went on to reject the argument of objective justification advanced by the school since it related solely to cost which is in and of itself not capable of amounting to objective justification (the court invoking in this regard the decision of the European Court of Justice in Case C-243/95 *Hill and Stapleton v Revenue Commissioners* ([1998] E.L.R. 225; [1999] I.C.R. 48)).

Subsequent appeal to High Court on point of law An appeal on a point of law was heard before the High Court in the case of *Catholic University School v Scannell*, heard before Dunne J. in March 2010. That judgment is currently awaited with interest and once delivered will be the subject of detailed analysis in this chapter of the *Annual Review*. For the time being, however, it is clear that these 2009 determinations of the Labour Court analysed above underline very significant questions about the scope of the 2001 and 2003 Acts concerning part-time and fixed-term workers respectively: this is evidently a very important aspect of Irish employment law that will be clarified by the outcome of this High Court appeal in *Dooley*.

EMPLOYMENT EQUALITY

In last year's chapter of the *Annual Review*, in assessing the most significant developments to emerge from the jurisprudence of the Equality Tribunal in 2008, the race ground was amongst those selected for special focus. This year, attention must again be given to the many developments concerning race discrimination to have occurred in 2009. In particular, case law of the Labour Court and the Equality Tribunal in 2009 concerning the race ground raises a number of interesting points demonstrating the relationship of this aspect of equality legislation with other significant employment law statutes, most notably the Safety, Health and Welfare at Work Act 2005. In addition, the effects of Irish language requirements in particular employment contexts have been the subject of focus this year, in a determination analysed below.

Race discrimination in the context of Irish language requirements The case of *NUI Galway v McBrierty* (ADE/08/1, Determination No. EDA091, January 26, 2009) concerned an appeal by the complainant employee against a decision of an equality officer rejecting her claims of discrimination on grounds of race and gender and a complaint that she had been victimised in response to her complaints of discrimination. For present purposes, the most significant aspect to note about this case is the race discrimination aspect of the claim, which concerned discrimination in terms of access to employment.

The complainant, a United Kingdom national, applied for work with the respondent University, which had a practice of filling secretarial and clerical posts from two panels: the first for full-time, long-term jobs carrying the potential for permanency, the second for short-term and casual work. The key difference between the eligibility requirements for the two panels was a necessity, pursuant to the University's statutory obligations, for proficiency in the Irish language in order to qualify for the former panel. The complainant applied for the second panel and worked in a number of different roles for a continuous period of almost seven months, when she applied to transfer to the first panel. She was subsequently informed that such a transfer was not possible and that she required Leaving Certificate Irish. She argued that this treatment was discriminatory on the nationality aspect of the race ground and that the requirement was not reasonable in all the circumstances.

The Labour Court accepted that such a requirement was discriminatory in principle in that non-Irish nationals do not, in general, have qualifications in the Irish language. However, it also pointed out that national languages have been accorded special protection by the European Court of Justice, citing the well-known ruling of that court in *Groener v Minister for Education and City of Dublin* (Case C-379/87, [1990] I.L.R.M. 335), where the ECJ held that a linguistic requirement may be valid where it is part of a policy to promote the first official language. Given the location of the respondent University and its special relationship with surrounding Gaeltacht areas, the Labour Court held that the requirement was reasonable in this case.

It is instructive to consider the Labour Court's analysis of *Groener* in the following passage:

> "Although [*Groener*] relates to the free movement of persons rather than equal treatment, the Court accepts that the European Court of Justice has always regarded the promotion of indigenous languages as a worthy policy aim and provided that such a policy is reasonable and proportionate it has accepted that a requirement for a candidate to be proficient in the language of the country in which they are applying for employment (where such a proficiency requirement obtains) is not discriminatory. In these circumstances, the Court finds that the requirement of the Respondent, given its statutory obligations deriving from both the Irish language and its special relationship with local Gaeltacht areas, that its employees have proficiency in the Irish language is not unreasonable. This would not necessarily apply in all other cases."

Accordingly, the Labour Court held that the employer could avail of the defence within s.31(d) of the Employment Equality Act 1998. On the facts of *McBrierty*, the Labour Court found that there had been some confusion caused, due to the use of misleading language in an advertisement, as to whether Leaving Certificate Irish or merely proficiency in Irish generally was a requirement for placement on the first panel. Ultimately, however, the Labour Court found that the situation had been clarified by a letter the complainant received that clearly explained that she could apply in the future for posts on the first panel provided that she was in a position to sit and pass an Irish proficiency examination. As such, the Labour Court concluded that it "could not be said to be discriminatory vis-à-vis the complainant as she had been informed of the true situation and indeed had previously applied for a position in which proficiency in Irish was a requirement".

Race discrimination in the context of health and safety requirements The determination of the Equality Tribunal in *Valpeters v Melbury Developments Ltd* [2010] 21 E.L.R. 64 highlights important issues surrounding the obligation to provide translations of documentation such as health and safety information. This case provides an interesting example from 2009 of how employment equality law can be developed by reference to other distinctive regimes in the framework of employment law, in this case, the Safety, Health and Welfare at Work Act 2005.

This case concerned a claim by an employee, whose command of the English language was described in the equality officer's determination as "fairly limited", that his employer had discriminated against him on the ground of race contrary to s.6(2)(h) of the Employment Equality Acts 1998 to 2004, in, inter alia, not making available to him health and safety information translated into the appropriate language. The equality officer stated (at para.4.11):

> "I now turn to the complainant's case that he was not given health and safety information in a language he could understand. The complainant gave his evidence at the hearing through an interpreter, and I am satisfied that his English is fairly limited. The complainant stated he was not given safety information. The respondent stated that it satisfied itself that the complainant held a valid FÁS SafePass, which largely covered the hazards the complainant would encounter in his general operative duties. Training for the SafePass scheme is provided in a number of languages. The respondent further stated that safety information was given to all workers, although they did admit that they did not furnish translation or interpretation for this site-specific safety information."

The equality officer cited the well-known determination of the Labour Court in *Campbell Catering v Rasaq* [2004] E.L.R. 310, in which the Labour Court had observed that:

> "It is clear that many non-national workers encounter special difficulties in employment arising from a lack of knowledge concerning statutory and contractual employment rights together with differences of language and culture. In the case of disciplinary proceedings, employers have a positive duty to ensure that all workers fully understand what is alleged against them, the gravity of the alleged misconduct and their right to mount a full defence, including the right to representation. Special measures may be necessary in the case of non-national workers to ensure that this obligation is fulfilled and that the accused worker fully appreciates the gravity of the situation and is given appropriate facilitates and guidance in making a defence. In such cases, applying the same procedural standards to a non-national workers as would be applied to an Irish national could amount to the application of the same rules to different situations and could in itself amount to discrimination."

It is significant that the above passage in *Rasaq* was articulated in the context of disciplinary proceedings, but applied by the equality officer here in the broader context of an employer's obligations pursuant to the health and safety legislation. The equality officer added:

> "I find that the complainant's right to safety information is one such statutory right arising from the relevant health and safety legislation. The complainant would therefore have had a right to have specific safety information given to other workers translated or interpreted into a language he could understand. I therefore find that the complainant has established a prima facie case with regard to less favourable treatment on the ground of race in this matter that the respondent has not rebutted."

The equality officer concluded that the employer had discriminated against the complainant regarding his conditions of employment in relation to the provision of health and safety information, contrary to s.8(1)(b) of the Acts (at para.4.13).

This case thus comprises an interesting example of the interface between employment equality law and other distinct employment law regimes: here, the Safety, Health and Welfare at Work Act 2005. Although the 2005 legislation is not specifically referred to in the determination of the equality officer, it is clear that the latter had in contemplation s.9 of the 2005 Act. This section imposes a duty on an employer regarding the provision of information to his or her employees. Section 9(1) of the 2005 Act includes a requirement that the employer, when furnishing information to employees regarding health and safety matters, do so in a manner, form and as appropriate, language that is reasonably likely to be understood by his or her employees.

Section 9(1) states:

> Without prejudice to the generality of *section 8*, every employer shall, when providing information to his or her employees under that section on matters relating to their safety, health and welfare at work ensure that the information—
>
> (*a*) is given in a form, manner and, as appropriate, language that is reasonably likely to be understood by the employees concerned …

The use of the words "as appropriate" in this section indicates that each case will turn on its own facts; thus the above example of the Equality Tribunal's approach provides an illustration of a case in which such translation will be appropriate.

PENALISATION CLAIMS UNDER THE SAFETY, HEALTH AND WELFARE AT WORK ACT 2005

The ambit of s.27 of the Safety, Health and Welfare at Work Act 2005 Just as the prohibition on penalisation marks an important feature of the part-time and fixed-term workers' protective legislation, so is the equivalent provision in the Safety, Health and Welfare at Work Act 2005 increasingly generating litigation. 2009 saw a number of interesting developments in this regard.

Section 27 of the 2005 Act provides, in so far as is relevant:

> (1) In this section "penalisation" includes any act or omission by an employer or a person acting on behalf of an employer that affects, to

his or her detriment, an employee with respect to any term or condition of his or her employment.

(2) Without prejudice to the generality of *subsection (1)*, penalisation includes—

(*a*) suspension, lay-off or dismissal (including a dismissal within the meaning of the Unfair Dismissals Acts 1977 to 2001), or the threat of suspension, lay-off or dismissal,

(*b*) demotion or loss of opportunity for promotion,

(*c*) transfer of duties, change of location of place of work, reduction in wages or change in working hours,

(*d*) imposition of any discipline, reprimand or other penalty (including a financial penalty), and

(*e*) coercion or intimidation.

(3) An employer shall not penalise or threaten penalisation against an employee for—

(*a*) acting in compliance with the relevant statutory provisions,

(*b*) performing any duty or exercising any right under the relevant statutory provisions,

(*c*) making a complaint or representation to his or her safety representative or employer or the Authority, as regards any matter relating to safety, health or welfare at work,

(*d*) giving evidence in proceedings in respect of the enforcement of the relevant statutory provisions,

(*e*) being a safety representative or an employee designated under *section 11* or appointed under *section 18* to perform functions under this Act, or

(*f*) subject to *subsection (6)*, in circumstances of danger which the employee reasonably believed to be serious and imminent and which he or she could not reasonably have been expected to avert, leaving (or proposing to leave) or, while the danger persisted, refusing to return to his or her place of work or any dangerous part of his or her place of work, or taking (or proposing to take) appropriate steps to protect himself or herself or other persons from the danger.

(4) The dismissal of an employee shall be deemed, for the purposes of the Unfair Dismissals Acts 1977 to 2001, to be an unfair dismissal if it results wholly or mainly from penalisation as referred to in *subsection (2)(a)*.

The causation inquiry that will attend consideration of this section was well captured by the Labour Court in its 2009 determination in *Toni & Guy Blackrock v Paul O'Neill* [2010] E.L.R. 1 when it observed:

> "It is clear from the language of this section that in order to make out a complaint of penalisation it is necessary for a claimant to establish that the determent of which he or she complains was imposed '*for*' having committed one of the acts protected by subsection 3. Thus the detriment giving rise to the complaint must have been incurred because of, or in retaliation for, the Claimant having committed a protected act. This suggested that where there is more than one causal factor in the chain of events leading to the detriment complained of the commission of a protected act must be an operative cause in the sense that '*but for*' the Claimant having committed the protected act he or she would not have suffered the detriment. This involves a consideration of the motive or reasons which influenced the decision maker in imposing the impugned determent."

Key 2009 Labour Court determinations involving penalisation In a series of 2009 decisions that includes the above-quoted determination, the Labour Court has illustrated the seriousness with which this penalisation provision will be treated. In *Allied Foods Ltd v Sterio* (HSD097, July 29, 2009), for example, the complainant was employed as a general operative. In May 2008 he discovered that his forklift licence was out of date and he alerted the company to this. Following clarification from the Health and Safety Authority, the complainant was moved to alternative duties. The company set up a refresher training course for workers with expired licences; the complainant claimed that he was initially overlooked for this training and that he was impeded in returning to the contract on which he was working. He referred his case to the rights commissioner under s.27 of the 2005 Act. The rights commissioner held that the complaint was well-founded, and directed that the employer relocate the claimant back to the duties he had been performing immediately before he had reported the licence issue. In addition, the rights commissioner directed that compensation in the amount of €5,000 be paid to the complainant. The employer appealed the rights commissioner's decision to the Labour Court.

Disallowing the appeal, the Labour Court was satisfied that what occurred subsequent to the complaint being made—not placing the claimant on the refresher course, and his subsequent loss of earnings—constituted penalisation within the meaning of s.27.

Significantly, the Labour Court relied on the decision of the European Court of Justice in *Von Colson and Kamann v Land Nordrhein-Westfalen* (C14/83) [1984] E.C.R. 1891, and the principles emphasised therein to the effect that where an individual right is infringed, the judicial redress provided should not only compensate for the claimant's economic loss but must also provide a real deterrent against future infractions. Accordingly, the Labour Court varied the rights commissioner's determination to provide for total compensation of €6,000.

Another instructive 2009 authority on the nature of a claim for penalisation under s.27 of the 2005 Act is *Flynn Concrete Products Ltd v Timma Gundars* (HSD096, July 20, 2009). The claimant contended that his dismissal was a direct result of his making a complaint under the 2005 Act which, he alleged, constituted penalisation within the terms of s.27(3)(c).

The employer rejected this contention and claimed that the dismissal flowed from the claimant's failure to co-operate fully with, and in other respects to act properly concerning, an internal investigation of a complaint made by the claimant against his supervisor; and the claimant's attitude towards the company and his work prior to the termination of his employment. The company insisted that there was no connection between the complaint and the dismissal. There was no evidence that the letter had arrived in the company before the complainant was dismissed.

The Labour Court emphasised that, given the fact that there was a complaint, followed by a dismissal, the onus was on the company to demonstrate that there was no causal connection. In the view of the court, the company had not succeeded in so demonstrating, and the court, on the balance of probabilities, preferred the evidence put on behalf of the claimant, concluding that penalisation under s.27 of the 2005 Act had been made out. The court took the view that an award of compensation was appropriate and measured the level of this compensation at €10,000.

In a further 2009 case already referred to above, *Toni & Guy Blackrock v Paul O'Neill* [2010] E.L.R. 1, the Labour Court noted that the 2005 Act was "silent on the question of how the burden of proof should be allocated as between the parties". Referring to its earlier 2008 determinations in *Department of Justice, Equality and Law Reform v Philip Kirwan* (HSD082, January 16, 2008) and *Fergal Brodigan T/A FB Groundworks v Juris Dubina* (HSD0810, December 10, 2008) which had acknowledged that the normal rule of he who asserts must prove is subject to the exception of the "peculiar knowledge principle", the court in *O'Neill* continued:

> "In the instant case what is at issue is the motive or reason for the Claimant's dismissal. That is to be found in the thought process of the decision makers at the time the decision to dismiss the Complainant was taken. That is something which is peculiarly within the knowledge of the Respondent. It would be palpably unfair to expect the Claimant to adduce direct evidence to show that the Respondent was influenced by his earlier complaints in deciding to dismiss him. Conversely, it is perfectly reasonable to require the Respondent to establish that the reasons for the dismissal were unrelated to his complaints under the Act.
>
> Having regard to these considerations, it seems to the Court that a form of shifting burden of proof, similar to that in employment equality law should be applied in the instant case. Thus the Claimant must establish, on the balance of probabilities, that he made complaints

concerning health and safety. It is then necessary for him to show that, having regard to the circumstances of the case, it is apt to infer from subsequent events that his complaints were an operative consideration leading to his dismissal. If those two limbs of the test are satisfied it is for the Respondent to satisfy the Court, on credible evidence and to the normal civil standard, that the complaints relied upon did not influence the Claimant's dismissal."

Applying this test to the facts of *O'Neill*, the Labour Court concluded that the claimant had been penalised in that his dismissal had flowed from his having made the relevant complaints, and awarded the substantial sum of €20,000 in compensation.

HARASSMENT AND STRESS IN THE WORKPLACE

In last year's edition of the *Annual Review*, it was noted that the most significant development in 2008 concerning bullying and harassment at work was undoubtedly the Supreme Court decision in *Quigley v Complex Tooling and Moulding* [2008] IESC 44; [2008] E.L.R. 297; [2009] 1 I.R. 349. In 2009, the Supreme Court delivered another extremely important judgment in this general area in the case of *Berber v Dunnes Stores* [2009] IESC 10; [2009] E.L.R. 61. *Berber* represents the first occasion on which the Supreme Court has had to deal with the issue of whether and when an employee can recover damages from an employer for psychological injury caused by stress in the workplace, as distinct from a situation such as that in *Quigley* where the stress in question was alleged to be the result of bullying.

***Berber*: The background** The plaintiff in *Berber* had been an employee of the defendant since he was 19 years of age in 1980, and had worked successfully in the company for some years. At a particular point in his employment relationship he felt that his superiors' view of him changed. He was, for example, given far less opportunity to travel abroad for work purposes. He also felt that there was an increased interest in the state of his health. This revolved largely around the fact that he had Crohn's disease. He felt that various events over the course of a year involved him being demoted and ignored by management within the company. Moreover, he felt that such actions represented a clear threat to his mental health, despite the fact that his solicitors had, from an early stage, put the company on written notice that he was suffering from stress. Eventually his employment relationship with the defendant company was terminated.

For present purposes, the relevant part of the High Court proceedings was the stress claim which itself was composed of two strands, namely:

(a) that the stress to which he had been exposed had exacerbated his ongoing problems with Crohn's disease; and
(b) that this stress had also led to him suffering a recognisable psychological injury.

The approach of the High Court In the High Court judgment (reported at [2007] E.L.R. 1), Laffoy J. took as her starting point the "three questions" approach to the issue of workplace stress first posited by Clarke J. in *Maher v Jabil Global Services Limited* [2008] 1 I.R. 25. It will be recalled that those three questions are as follows:

(a) has the plaintiff suffered an injury to his or her health as opposed to what might be described as ordinary occupational stress?;
(b) if so is that injury attributable to the workplace; and
(c) if so was the harm suffered by the particular employee concerned reasonably foreseeable in all the circumstances? ([2008] 1 I.R. 25, per Clarke J. at 39).

In *Berber*, the High Court answered these questions as follows:

(a) Laffoy J. accepted that the plaintiff *had* suffered a genuine injury to his health (a psychiatric condition known as adjustment disorder) as distinct from mere ordinary occupational stress. Moreover, she concluded that this disorder had exacerbated the plaintiff's Crohn's disease symptoms and hampered the treatment thereof.
(b) Laffoy J. also accepted that these conditions were caused by workplace stress—in other words that it was not the symptoms and treatment of his Crohn's disease that were the stressors affecting his mental health. The court was not, however, prepared to find that a particular flare-up in his Crohn's disease in March 2000 or a deterioration in his symptoms in 2005 could be attributed to the manner in which he was dealt with by the defendant.
(c) Finally, Laffoy J. held that the possibility of the plaintiff suffering from psychological injury as a result of the manner in which he was treated was reasonably foreseeable, especially in light of the fact that the defendants had been informed about the fact that the plaintiff was suffering from stress.

It was still necessary, therefore, for Laffoy J. to address the question of what the nature and scope of an employer's duty of care should be, once it was found that one existed. In this respect Laffoy J. accepted that the obligation on the employer was not to act as an insurer of the employee's safety but merely to do "what a reasonable and prudent employer would have done in the circumstances". Because she had already concluded that the defendants had actually breached the implied term of trust and confidence, Laffoy J. had no difficulty in concluding that their conduct fell short of what a reasonable and prudent employer would have done in the circumstances. Accordingly damages (both for the psychological symptoms suffered by the plaintiff *and* for the exacerbation of his physical symptoms) were assessed at €40,000.

The Supreme Court judgment Amongst the principal discussion points about the Supreme Court's 2009 decision in *Berber* [2009] IESC 10; [2009] E.L.R. 61 is arguably the fact that whereas it appeared to endorse the approach taken by the High Court to the law on workplace stress, it nonetheless overturned many of the conclusions of fact reached by the High Court on the question of the respective roles of employee and employer in the breakdown of the employment relationship.

In dealing with the stress claim itself, Finnegan J. for the Supreme Court accepted that the correct legal position in Irish law was that stated in the decisions of the High Court in *Maher v Jabil Global Services Ltd* [2008] 1 I.R. 25 and of the Court of Appeal in *Sutherland v Hatton* [2002] 2 All E.R. 1, although significantly it was the "three questions" posed by Clarke J. in *Maher* that Finnegan J. used as the template for his approach to the matter.

Notwithstanding this explicit recourse to the *Maher* three-step test, Finnegan J. in *Berber* cited the 16 practical propositions laid down in *Sutherland v Hatton*, and the inference would appear to be that these principles are of considerable authority in Irish law and possibly that they *are* now the Irish law in this area. Such a conclusion seems fortified by a consideration of what was said in *Maher* itself in relation to the approach of the High Court in *McGrath*, as for example, in the following passage of the judgment of Clarke J.:

> "In *McGrath v Trintech Technologies Ltd*, Laffoy J reviewed the authorities in relation to an employer's liability for psychiatric illness induced by stress and pressures at work. In the course of her judgment Laffoy J cited with approval 16 'practical propositions' set out in the judgment of Hale LJ in *Hatton v Sunderland* which are designed to assist in the assessment of such cases. While not all of those practical propositions will be relevant in each case, it was accepted by both sides that the principles identified by Laffoy J represent the law in this jurisdiction" (*Maher v Jabil Global Services Ltd* [2008] 1 I.R. 25, per Clarke J. at 38 (internal citations omitted)).

In *Berber*, as far as the question of the duty of care was concerned, Finnegan J. accepted that because the plaintiff had put the employer on written notice of his vulnerability to mental injury, therefore it was reasonably foreseeable on the part of the employer that "if it should fail to take reasonable care, it would cause stress". In addition, unlike the position adopted by the Supreme Court in *Quigley* analysed in last year's *Annual Review*, Finnegan J. in *Berber* did not regard causation as an issue in the case. Moreover, it was clear that the plaintiff had suffered psychological harm. Hence three of the four elements of the tort of negligence (those captured in Clarke J.'s three questions in *Maher* set out above) were made out and the key remaining issue was whether the employer had breached the standard of care by acting unreasonably in the circumstances. On the facts, Finnegan J. found that the defendant employer *had* acted reasonably in dealing with the plaintiff's known vulnerabilities and consequently that the claim must fail.

Berber comprises the only occasion to date on which the Supreme Court has afforded consideration to a stress at work claim. As noted above, it can now be added to the court's 2008 decision in *Quigley v Complex Tooling and Moulding* [2008] IESC 44; [2008] E.L.R. 297; [2009] 1 I.R. 349. In relation to these two decisions, a number of points emerge. First, whilst each such case is clearly highly fact-specific, it is significant that in both instances, the findings of fact in the High Court were overturned on appeal. It is, perhaps, unusual for the Supreme Court to reverse a decision of the High Court exclusively on a factual and not a legal basis. Whilst the result in both cases amounted to the reversal of successful plaintiff wins in the High Court, it must be emphasised that because the Supreme Court found no fault in the statements of law propounded by Lavan J. and Laffoy J. in the High Court judgments in *Quigley* and *Berber* respectively, the legal principles set out in those judgments remain authoritative propositions of law in this area.

The judgment in *Berber* may well support the argument that workplace stress claims—certainly in the manner in which they are treated by the Irish courts—are "in essence quite different to other negligence claims, and it would be appropriate for this reality to be accepted" (Neville Cox, "Recent Developments in the Rules Relating to Workplace Stress: The Supreme Court Decision in *Berber v Dunnes Stores*" (2008/9) 3(3) Q.R.T.L. 17, 27). Whether the effect of *Berber* and *Quigley* will be to make it more difficult for plaintiffs to recover in such cases remains to be seen; but an analysis of subsequent reports later in 2009 reveals several instances of cases for bullying, harassment and stress at work coming before the High Court that year (see for example, "Case against HSE settled", *The Irish Times*, November 6, 2009; "Women's refuge manager sues HSE over bullying claim", *The Irish Times*, November 26, 2009).

VICARIOUS LIABILITY

In last year's chapter in the *Annual Review*, the Supreme Court decision in

O'Keeffe v Hickey [2008] IESC 72; [2009] 2 I.R. 302; [2009] 1 I.L.R.M. 490 was analysed, and the ambiguous state of vicarious liability in Irish law noted. This ambiguity as to the status in Irish law of decisions such as that of the Supreme Court of Canada in *Bazley v Curry* [1999] 2 S.C.R. 534 and that of the House of Lords in *Lister v Hesley Hall Ltd* [2001] UKHL 22; [2002] 1 A.C. 215; [2001] 2 W.L.R. 1311 has, if anything, arguably been compounded by the subsequent decision of the Supreme Court in March 2009 in *Reilly v Devereux* [2009] IESC 22; [2009] 3 I.R. 660. This was an appeal from the High Court judgment in 2007 ([2007] IEHC 252) in which Johnson P. proceeded on the basis that *Lister* represented the law in Ireland. Having referred to *Bazley* and *Jacobi* and then to the key passages from the judgments of both Lord Steyn and Lord Clyde in *Lister*, Johnson P. continued:

> "In the Irish case of *Delahunty v South Eastern Health Board* the [*Lister*] principles were adopted with approval by Mr. Justice O'Higgins. In that case it was decided on the facts that the young man assaulted had not been in the care of the defendants but had merely been a visitor to their establishment. However, the remainder of the principles were adopted and it is quite clear that law is now as stated in [the High Court judgment in *O'Keeffe*]. It would appear that the principles as stated by Mr. Justice Costello in *Health Board v BC* have now been moved such that, if the tort and/or indecent assault was conducted in the course of and within the scope of the employment, then there can be vicarious liability" (internal citations omitted).

A difficulty with the above analysis is, with respect, that neither the approach of the High Court in *Delahunty* nor its approach in *O'Keeffe* was as clear on this point as suggested by Johnson P. For, in *Delahunty*, O'Higgins J. had expressly referred to the opposing approaches between *BC* and *Lister* and refrained from commenting as to which approach represented the law in this jurisdiction; nor did the High Court in *O'Keeffe* decide the status of *Lister*. In this regard it is significant that in delivering the judgment of the Supreme Court on appeal in *Reilly*, Kearns J. (Denham and Finnegan JJ. concurring) commenced his analysis of the vicarious liability point with the following statement:

> "The learned trial judge conducted a thorough review of the relevant case law on this topic and it has not been suggested that he stated the legal position incorrectly but only that he applied the legal principles incorrectly to the facts of the case. *The legal review may thus be brief*" (at 668, emphasis added).

Two points arise from this statement. First, given how unsettled the position was (and is) in relation to the status of *Lister*, it is not at all obvious why the defendant would not have taken issue with the approach to the law taken by Johnson P.—particularly in light of the fact that more than a year after the judgment of the High Court in *Reilly* the Supreme Court had, of course, delivered its judgment in *O'Keeffe*. Further, it may be that this acceptance of the correctness of the legal position as identified by the High Court led the Supreme Court in *Reilly* to take the view that it should not explore at length the status of *Bazley* or *Lister* in this jurisdiction (as perhaps seen, for example, in the italicised last sentence of the statement of Kearns J. in the passage quoted immediately above).

Kearns J. emphasised how the plaintiff in the appeal in *Reilly v Devereux* relied "almost exclusively on the principles laid down in the *Bazley* case" (at 670). In so doing, three parallels were sought to be drawn between the factual backgrounds in *Bazley* and *Reilly*. First, the environment of the defence forces was such that the normal rules of adult interaction did not apply, since the disparity in rank between the plaintiff, who was a gunner, and the perpetrator, a sergeant major, led to a situation where the latter "exercised great power over the plaintiff and could command unquestioning obedience from him". Secondly, it was argued that "an element of intimacy and camaraderie was encouraged in the Army in circumstances where employees worked in close quarters together". Finally, it was suggested that within a culture where complaining was both discouraged and "largely fruitless", a person in the plaintiff's position was particularly vulnerable to the wrongful exercise of power by a superior officer.

Rejecting the attempt to draw these parallels between the facts of *Bazley* and *Reilly*, Kearns J. did not accept that the nature of the employment relationship in *Reilly* supported the imposition of vicarious liability. The relationship between the plaintiff and defendant "could hardly be more different" from that between a school teacher and a child at a residential school; nor was there intimacy or a quasi-parental role implicit in the relationship as had been the case in *Bazley*.

What is significant about the approach of Kearns J. in *Reilly* in distinguishing *Bazley* is the strong suggestion in the judgment that, were the parallels with the latter case more strongly resounded on the facts of *Reilly*, then *Bazley* would govern the court's vicarious liability inquiry. With respect, this analysis is entirely question-begging since, as we have seen, not only did the Supreme Court in *O'Keeffe* three months earlier not resolve the status of *Bazley*, but it indicated a sharp division of approach even amongst the members of the majority as to this fundamental question.

A further source of confusion arising from *Reilly* is a degree of inconsistency arguably apparent within the judgment of Kearns J. It is, for example, confusing that Kearns J. in declining to impose vicarious liability in *Reilly* invoked the following passage from the judgment of Hardiman J. in *O'Keeffe*:

> "In my view, both justice and the basic requirements of an ordered society require that the imposition of strict liability on a no fault basis

> be done (if at all) only on the clearest and most readily understandable basis. I do not regard the Canadian cases cited as providing such a basis: quite the opposite, as the two conflicting decisions cited demonstrate, in my view. I do not believe that the expanded basis of vicarious liability represents the law in this jurisdiction, or can be made to do so except by legislation. The consequences of doing this, social as well economic, would be immense… (*O'Keeffe*, 526–527)."

Given Kearns J.'s emphasis on how *Bazley* could be distinguished in *Reilly*, it is difficult to see why support would then be drawn from that passage of Hardiman J.'s judgment in *O'Keeffe* which explicitly rejects the very notion that *Bazley* could represent the law in this jurisdiction.

This confusion is deepened in the following passage of Kearns J.'s analysis (at 671) of the position of Hardiman J. in *O'Keeffe*:

> "Hardiman J. went on to note the 'chilling effect' of any extension of the doctrine of vicarious liability whereby the State would become liable for criminal activities of those in their employment in circumstances where there was no fault attaching to the State. To do so would be not only to make the taxpayer liable for the criminal acts of employees of State bodies, but it would also affect that body's actions in ways which would require to be considered as a matter of policy before such an extension of the law could be allowed."

On the basis of the above passage, it appears that Kearns J. is signalling a strong note of caution about the acceptance of the *Bazley* and *Lister* approaches in Irish law. Once again, however, this is rendered less than clear by the passage immediately following this statement, in which Kearns J. observes (at 671–672):

> "While the able submissions advanced on behalf of the plaintiff make reference to the *Bazley* principles, they do so in a necessarily limited way and counsel was obliged to frankly concede that not all of the criteria elaborated by the Canadian Supreme Court were met in the instant case. I believe this case falls short by a considerable margin of establishing the prerequisites for a finding that the defendants should be held vicariously responsible for the criminal activities of the first named defendant in this case."

With respect, the references in this passage to the *Bazley* "criteria" being "met" and to the "prerequisites" for vicarious liability could be interpreted as suggesting that the *Bazley* approach applies in Ireland. This view is, however, extremely difficult to reconcile either with the passages from Kearns J.'s judgment, quoted above, in which reliance is placed on the Hardiman approach in *O'Keeffe*, or indeed with the complicated picture emerging from the various judgments in the latter case already analysed in last year's edition of the *Annual Review*.

INJUNCTIONS RESTRAINING DISMISSAL

Another important development this year was the Supreme Court judgment in *Cahill v DCU* [2009] IESC 80, a long-running case in which the plaintiff/respondent (who formerly held the post of Associate Professor in the School of Biotechnology in Dublin City University) sought an injunction restraining his dismissal from that post. (The High Court judgment is analysed in detail in the Employment Law chapter of the *Annual Review of Irish Law 2007* (pp.258–260)).

The salient facts may be briefly rehearsed. The plaintiff, while employed in DCU, had attended a meeting with the President of the University at which he informed the President that there was an offer on foot from NUI Galway for him (and his two researchers) to move to Galway and take up the Chair of Molecular Medicine with NUIG. He claimed that he had informed the President that this offer had been made both as a matter of courtesy and with a view to ascertaining whether there might be an improved offer to him from DCU in light of his proposed move, but he emphatically denied that he had informed or indicated to the President that he would definitely be relinquishing his post in DCU. The President, on the other hand, claimed that he had been left with the clear impression at the meeting that there was no doubt whatsoever about the respondent leaving DCU and moving to Galway even though it was accepted that he never tendered a formal resignation. This latter concession on the part of the University meant, significantly, that if the respondent's employment had terminated it was common case that this was by virtue of a dismissal.

In the months following on from that discussion, Professor Cahill never indicated the date of his proposed departure despite constant requests to him to do so by the University's Director of Human Resources. Naturally this created difficulties from the perspective of the University, in that it made it virtually impossible for it to plan effectively for its future. Therefore (and after a very long period of vacillation on the part of the plaintiff), the University decided that the only course open to it was to dismiss Professor Cahill. The latter therefore sought both injunctive and declaratory relief, claiming both that his purported dismissal was invalid and also that the University should be precluded from treating him as if he was dismissed.

It will be recalled that the High Court ([2007] IEHC 20; [2007] E.L.R. 113) had concluded that the dismissal of the employee was invalid and thus granted the relief sought (which, at the full hearing of the matter, amounted to a declaration that the dismissal was invalid and an order requiring Professor Cahill to be retained in office and paid his salary which in turn would lead to an obligation on the part of DCU to ensure that suitable academic duties were found for him) on three separate grounds, viz.:

- because the dismissal was other than in conformity with the terms of the Universities Act 1997;
- because it violated the concept of "tenure";
- because of the absence of fair procedures shown to the employee, and specifically because "… of a failure [on the part of the University] to at least give him some opportunity to make representations as to why his contract of employment should not have been determined".

On appeal, the Supreme Court (while accepting that the plaintiff's position was "less than fully meritorious") upheld the finding of the High Court (namely that the dismissal was invalid), but confined itself to analysis of the third of the points referred to by the High Court (the absence of fair procedures). Thus Geoghegan J. concluded that:

> "I think it only fair to say that a decision by the University to bring matters finally to a head in such a way that it knew exactly where it stood as to what (if any) new arrangements had to be put in place, was more than reasonable. Nevertheless whatever course the appellant took towards that end had to be lawful. I find myself in agreement with the learned High Court judge that the respondent was an officer of the University and under the terms of the Universities Act, 1997 and the appellant's own statutes, the respondent was entitled to fair procedures before he could lawfully be dismissed. In the context of this particular case, that meant, quite simply, that the respondent had to be given a final warning, that in accordance with the terms of the contract which he had entered into with the University (and to which I will be referring), it was proposed to serve notice of termination of his employment and then had to be given an opportunity to make submissions to the appellant as to why that should not be done. No such opportunity was afforded to him and … I am satisfied that in the absence of such fair procedures the termination was not valid."

It is significant to note, however, that the Supreme Court was not prepared to grant any specific form of order to the plaintiff. It may be remembered that, in the High Court, Clarke J. had originally—that is, at the interlocutory stage—been willing to make an order of reinstatement in favour of the plaintiff, on the basis that no compelling arguments had been advanced as to why the plaintiff could not continue with his employment, but by the time the matter came to full hearing the court concluded that "much water ha[d] passed under the bridge" and hence that it would no longer be possible for this to happen, and as such, the only appropriate order would be one declaring that he remained in office and was entitled to his salary but not reinstating him in any practical way. When the matter came to the Supreme Court, it was clear that such a measure of reinstatement was even more unrealistic than it had been when the High Court gave its judgment in the case. As such, Geoghegan J. concluded:

> "Not only did time elapse between the purported termination and the hearing in the High Court but almost three further years have elapsed since the High Court hearing. In accordance with well established principles neither the High Court nor this court can permit an injunction to be made against the appellant which is wholly impracticable or cannot properly be supervised by the court. In my view, the appeal should be dismissed but no final decision should be made as to the form of order without a further hearing preceded by written submissions from both parties as to the form of order and any relief to be granted."

Equity

BRIAN TOBIN, School of Law, Trinity College Dublin

CHARITABLE TRUSTS

Charities Act 2009 Under the Charities Act 2009 (Commencement) Order 2009 (S.I. No. 84 of 2009), only ss.1, 2, 5, 10 (other than subss.(3) and (4)) and 99 of the Charities Act 2009 came into effect on September 1, 2009.

Section 13 of the Charities Act 2009 (hereafter "the 2009 Act") provides for the establishment of a Charities Regulatory Authority which will take over the functions that were exercised by both the Attorney General and the Commissioners for Charitable Donations and Bequests. Section 14 outlines the general functions of the Charities Regulatory Authority and these include increasing public trust and confidence in the management and administration of charitable trusts and organisations as well as promoting the effective use of the property of such trusts or such organisations and ensuring and monitoring the compliance of charitable organisations with the 2009 Act. The Authority must also establish and maintain a register of charitable organisations, encourage and facilitate their better administration and management, ensure their accountability to donors and beneficiaries and the public, and carry out investigations in accordance with the Act. The Authority must also promote compliance by charity trustees with their duties in the management of charitable trusts/organisations. The trustees must keep proper books of account, have the accounts audited, and prepare and submit an annual report to the authority or provide it with information if so requested. Section 90 provides that where a charity trustee is responsible for a breach of trust the High Court can relieve him/her from personal liability if it considers that he/she has acted honestly and reasonably and ought fairly to be excused. Section 91 enables a charitable organisation to enter into an agreement with a charity trustee for the purchase of indemnity insurance against personal liability out of the charity's funds in respect of any act done or omitted to be done by him/her in good faith and in the performance of his/her functions as a charity trustee. Section 75 provides for the establishment of a Charity Appeals Tribunal that will hear appeals from decisions of the Authority while s.80 allows a party to appeal a decision of this tribunal to the High Court on a point of law.

Section 3 of the 2009 Act includes a statutory definition of "charitable purpose" for the first time in the Republic of Ireland which is almost identical to the four *Pemsel* categories. The four stated charitable purposes are "the prevention or relief of poverty or economic hardship", "the advancement of education", "the advancement of religion" and "any other purpose that is of benefit to the community". This last category includes the following:

a) the advancement of community welfare, including the relief of those in need by reason of youth, age, ill-health or disability;
b) the advancement of community development, including rural or urban regeneration;
c) the promotion of civic responsibility or voluntary work;
d) the promotion of health, including the prevention or relief of sickness, disease or human suffering;
e) the advancement of conflict resolution or reconciliation;
f) the promotion of religious or racial harmony and harmonious community relations;
g) the protection of the natural environment;
h) the advancement of environmental sustainability;
i) the advancement of the efficient and effective use of the property of charitable organisations;
j) the prevention or relief of suffering of animals;
k) the advancement of the arts, culture, heritage or sciences; and
l) the integration of those who are disadvantaged, and the promotion of their full participation, in society.

As we can see, "other purposes" that have previously been recognised in case law as being "of benefit to the community" are now expressly outlined in s.3(11) of the 2009 Act. Gifts for the aged, the disabled and the sick are referred to in subss.(a) and (d). Gifts to advance community development and related purposes are referred to in subss.(a), (b), (c) and (l), and gifts for the benefit of animals are referred to in subs.(j). However, gifts for sporting and recreational purposes are not recognised under s.3(11), and neither are gifts for political purposes because an "excluded body" under s.2 includes a political party, or a body that promotes a political party or candidate, or a body that promotes a political cause, *unless* the promotion of that cause relates directly to the advancement of the charitable purposes of that body. Thus, it would appear that a body that is primarily charitable may use political means to achieve its charitable goals under s.2, as recognised by Oonagh Breen in (2008) 59 *Northern Ireland Legal Quarterly* 223 at 227.

Public benefit Section 3(2) provides that a purpose shall not be regarded as charitable for the purposes of the 2009 Act unless it occasions public benefit. Section 3(3) stipulates that a gift shall not be regarded as being of public benefit unless it is intended to benefit the public or a section thereof, and in a case where it confers a benefit on a person other than in his capacity as a member of the public or a section thereof, any such benefit is reasonable in all the circumstances and is ancillary to and necessary for the furtherance of public benefit. Section 3(4) states that it shall be presumed, unless the contrary is proved, that a gift for the advancement of religion is of public benefit, and thus the presumption of public benefit that was originally provided for by s.45(1) of the Charities Act 1961 remains valid today. Section 3(7) provides that in determining whether a gift is of public benefit under the remaining three categories outlined in *Pemsel,* account shall be taken of any limitation imposed by the donor of the gift on the class of persons who may benefit and whether this limitation is justified and reasonable having regard to the nature and purpose of the gift; and, the amount of any charge payable for any service provided in furtherance of the purpose for which the gift is given and whether it is likely to limit the number of persons/classes of person who will benefit from the gift. Section 3(8) provides that a limitation on the class of persons who may benefit from the gift shall not be justified and reasonable if all of the intended beneficiaries of the gift or a significant number of them have a personal connection with the donor of the gift. Section 2(2)(a) states that for the purposes of the Act a person is connected with an individual, inter alia, if they are a parent, brother, sister, spouse, grandparent or grandchild of the individual or a child of the spouse of the individual or if they are in partnership with the individual or even employed by the individual under a contract of service.

Section 3(7) and (8) and s.2(2)(a) of the 2009 Act are significant provisions in that they effectively make it impossible for trusts for poor relations/employees to attain charitable status in this jurisdiction from now on given the personal connection between the donor and beneficiaries of the gift. These sections will also enable the Irish courts to continue to disqualify trusts for the advancement of education from charitable status where there is a personal connection between the donor and the intended beneficiaries.

Trusts for sporting and recreational purposes It was recently reiterated in *National Tourism Development Authority v Coughlan* [2009] IEHC 53 that trusts for sporting and recreational purposes are not charitable in law. Charleton J. had to consider if a trust that promoted tourism could be charitable when its subject-matter was a set of three scenic golf courses and a club house in Killarney. The High Court judge examined whether the trust could arguably come under the fourth category in the *Pemsel* case of trusts for "other purposes beneficial to the community". It had been argued that the trust was charitable because it allowed the golf courses to be used by their members and those who travel to play golf as a major attraction in circumstances where any profits must be ploughed back into the golf courses and the club house. Furthermore, it was argued that the trust was of major benefit to the town of Killarney, not only as a tourist facility which brings high-spending visitors into an area which otherwise lacks substantial alternative employment, but because it had resulted in the preservation of the land on which the golf courses are situated, which would otherwise have been subject to unsightly rural building development in recent years.

Charleton J. observed that for a member of the public to join the golf club costs around €7,000 but thereafter annual membership is much less. For travelling golfers the official website indicates green fees of around €100 but by booking in advance or playing at less busy times a considerable saving on this may be incurred. Charleton J. noted that clause 1 of the trust document refers to use of the trust property by "visiting golfers" and felt that this should be read in the context of clause 2 which refers to "tourism objects" and includes tourists who wish to play golf but also excludes others who are sightseers, hill walkers or picnickers. The judge held that tourism has never been recognised as charitable in law and that if it was:

> "[t]hen any recreation, activity or attraction that would bring tourists into an area, or keep them there for a longer stay, would thereby assume charitable status. On an extreme level, therefore, if tourism were to be recognised as a category that is charitable because it benefits the community, every trust setting up a casino or a fun park would enjoy the benefits in law of charitable status. Moreover, a tourist enterprise is an economic enterprise."

Charleton J. recognised that almost any economic enterprise can be of benefit to the community by providing gainful employment and hence enabling people to pay their taxes. Such enterprises have direct and indirect economic benefits for neighbourhoods and for the nation as a whole, but the judge held that the object of a trust has to be exclusively for charitable purposes so as to attain charitable status.

Charleton J. also believed that it was very hard on the case law to see that a golf course as a place for sport can properly be the object of a charitable trust. The learned judge held that:

> "Sport has never been recognised to be an object of sufficiently wide benefit to the community as to enjoy charitable status. The law has traditionally regarded sport as a form of recreation and, in consequence, trusts for sporting purposes are not recognised as charitable."

He then noted that incidentally a very small piece of countryside had been preserved in this case when so much else had been submerged by field destruction and suburban dwelling. Charleton J. held that among the indicia of a charity are that it is disinterested in commercial return for investors, is of genuine benefit to the community at large and, finally, that whatever benefit it dispenses is widely available to the community in the sense that it does not need to be bought into at exclusive levels of finance. He observed that while the profits had been used for the purpose of enhancing the facilities, it was clear from the wording of the trust document that the land was to be used as a golf course as opposed to a public area because those who wished to wander the land or take refreshments on it were to be denied entry. He further held that the case law makes it clear that exclusivity is an indication against charitable status because the wider public is less likely to be benefiting from the facility. Therefore, in conclusion Charleton J. held as follows:

> "The subject-matter of this trust is a golf course. That cannot be the subject of a charitable trust under ordinary circumstances; an exception that might arise could be the setting up of a trust for the use of a golf course by members of the army or by people with disabilities. Membership is, on the standards that are not defined but are clearly indicated by the case law, exclusive. The golf club certainly benefits the community and attracts tourist traffic but, no matter how it is analysed, it is still an ordinary golf club which you may join in order to avoid green fees and which, if you are visiting, whether from America or another part of Kerry, you may use in the ordinary way through paying a substantial sum in green fees by way of joining as a daily member. For these reasons, therefore, this trust cannot be a charitable one."

INTERLOCUTORY INJUNCTIONS

In an employment context In *Nolan v EMO Oil Services Ltd* [2009] IEHC 15, the plaintiff was a permanent employee of the defendant company as its credit manager pursuant to a written contract of employment which had commenced on November 1, 2001. The contract contained a provision enabling the defendant to terminate the plaintiff's employment on the giving of four weeks' notice. Due to the difficult economic downturn in 2008, upon his return from annual leave the plaintiff was informed by the defendant's managing director that he was being made redundant from his position as credit manager and he was given three months' notice which was more than sufficient to terminate his employment in accordance with his contract. Nonetheless the plaintiff contended that genuine bona fide redundancy did not exist in relation to the position of credit manager or alternatively that if a redundancy situation did exist he had been unfairly selected for redundancy. These of course were issues that would be dealt with at the trial of the action but pending the hearing the plaintiff was seeking relief in the form of a mandatory interlocutory injunction restraining the defendant from giving effect to his purported dismissal by reason of redundancy from the post of credit manager.

In deciding the case in the High Court Laffoy J. stated that:

> "[A]s, in effect, the plaintiff is seeking a mandatory interlocutory

> injunction, the first hurdle he has to overcome is that he must 'show at least that he has a strong case that he is likely to succeed at the hearing of the action' (per Fennelly J. in *Maha Lingham v Health Service Executive* [2006] 17 E.L.R. 137)."

The plaintiff contended that he could meet that test but the learned judge felt that he could not because both of his contentions, that the redundancy was not a valid one or that he should not have been selected for redundancy, could not be litigated in the proceedings currently before the court and could only be pursued via a claim under the Unfair Dismissal Acts 1977–2008. Laffoy J. then outlined an employee's two potential avenues to secure redress for dismissal from employment which he contends is unlawful:

> "One is to bring an action at common law for wrongful dismissal where he contends that the dismissal was in breach of contract or in violation of his constitutional rights. The other is to pursue a claim for unfair dismissal under the Unfair Dismissal Acts 1977–2008. That the two avenues are mutually exclusive has been consistently recognised."

Laffoy J. observed that in this case the plaintiff's contract of employment had been lawfully terminated as he had effectively been given three months' notice by the managing director. Thus, no common law action for wrongful dismissal arising from a breach of contract arose nor was there any question of violation of the plaintiff's constitutional rights by the company. Counsel for the plaintiff sought to rely on the implied term of mutual trust and confidence in contracts of employment, but this argument was rejected by the High Court because Laffoy J. held that such an implied term does not operate so as to prevent an employer from terminating a contract of employment by giving proper notice as emphasised by Fennelly J. in the above-mentioned *Maha Lingham* case. Laffoy J. noted that what the plaintiff was trying to achieve by these proceedings was to get his job back with the defendant company. The judge stated that, "if, as he contends, his dismissal is unfair, then the remedy available to him is the remedy provided by statute" and "that is the only remedy he could pursue because, in my view … [i]n the circumstances, there is no remedy which he can pursue in this court". Laffoy J. quoted from Lord Nicholls' speech in the case of *Johnson v Unisys Ltd* [2003] 1 A.C. 58 where His Lordship stated that:

> "Parliament has occupied the field relating to unfair dismissal … The statutory code provides remedies for infringement of the statutory right not to be dismissed unfairly. An employee's remedy for unfair dismissal, whether actual or constructive, is the remedy provided by statute."

Thus, Laffoy J. dismissed the plaintiff's application for a mandatory interlocutory injunction.

The outcome was again unfavourable from the plaintiff's viewpoint in *Buckley v National University of Ireland Maynooth* [2009] IEHC 58. The plaintiff had been employed under two fixed-term contracts at the defendant university. The first three-year fixed-term contract ran from October 1, 2003 to September 30, 2006 and the second two-year fixed-term contract ran from October 1, 2006 to September 30, 2008. In November 2007 the plaintiff, Dr Buckley, wrote to the personnel officer at NUI, Maynooth stating that she believed herself to be a permanent employee of the institution pursuant to s.9 of the Protection of Employees (Fixed-Term Work) Act 2003. The university did not agree with the plaintiff's interpretation of this provision of the 2003 Act and it refused to confirm that she was a permanent employee of the institution. In August 2008 the plaintiff brought her case to a rights commissioner pursuant to the mechanism provided for by the 2003 Act. The rights commissioner upheld the plaintiff's claim that she was entitled to a contract of indefinite duration with the university. Later that month the Director of Human Resources at NUI, Maynooth informed the plaintiff that she was being made redundant when her fixed-term contract expired on September 30, and she was provided with a statutory form of redundancy together with a copy of the university's appeal against the decision of the rights commissioner to the Labour Court. At the Labour Court hearing on October 16, the defendant made a new case that the plaintiff was never an employee of the university, so the Labour Court granted an adjournment for the plaintiff to consider this new case. It was alleged in evidence that the defendant gave an undertaking at the Labour Court hearing to maintain the status quo in relation to the plaintiff. Following the hearing the plaintiff was asked to vacate her office at the university and she was informed that the institution would cease to pay her with effect from January 12, 2009. Subsequent to the date of cessation of pay the plaintiff was unable to obtain access to her office as the door locks had been changed.

On February 13, 2009 the plaintiff sought an interlocutory injunction from the High Court restraining the defendants from terminating her contract of employment and restraining them from interfering with her remuneration and directing payment to her of this remuneration. She sought an interlocutory injunction restraining the defendant from breaching the terms and conditions of her employment and from interfering with the discharge by her of her role as Senior Research Fellow at NUI, Maynooth. The defendant argued that there was currently no continuing contract between it and the plaintiff and that even if she was successful before the Labour Court the redundancy notification given to her in August 2008 by its Director of Human Resources would effectively determine any indefinite contract. The defendant argued that its undertaking to maintain the status quo communicated to the Labour Court related only to salary and was offered as a goodwill gesture on an ex gratia basis in circumstances where the Labour Court does not have the power to require a party to give a legally binding undertaking to another.

Murphy J. held that the plaintiff's claim for a mandatory interlocutory injunction against the defendant must be assessed by reference to the common law remedy of wrongful dismissal. In considering whether there was a subsisting contract of employment between the parties, the learned judge held that the defendant would not be bound by the rights commissioner's decision regarding the plaintiff unless its appeal to the Labour Court was unsuccessful. He felt that this could reasonably be inferred from s.15(8) of the Act of 2003. As for the undertaking given by the defendant, Murphy J. held that the statutory scheme provided for in the 2003 Act makes no provision for the Labour Court to request an undertaking from either of the parties. Therefore, it was held that the defendant was entitled to resile from its alleged undertaking of October 16, 2008 to make an ex gratia payment of salary to the plaintiff because this promise was unenforceable by the Labour Court or the High Court as a matter of law.

Murphy J. then considered whether the plaintiff satisfied the first limb of the test for a mandatory interlocutory injunction by establishing a strong and clear case likely to succeed at the trial of the action. He observed that counsel for the plaintiff sought to rely on the implied term of mutual trust and confidence in contracts of employment, but he held that this implied term may avail an employee in the context of a dismissal in very limited circumstances such as where the employer undermined the contract of employment to such an extent as to deprive him/her of the right to terminate the contract on reasonable notice. Murphy J. did not feel that the implied term could benefit the plaintiff in this case because, quoting from the judgment of Fennelly J. in the Supreme Court case of *Maha Lingham v Health Service Executive* [2006] E.L.R. 137:

> "[T]he principle that there is an implied term of mutual trust and good faith in contracts of employment does not extend so as to prevent the employer terminating a contract of employment by giving proper notice..."

Murphy J. noted that the defendant claimed that even if the plaintiff was successful before the Labour Court, the statutory notice of redundancy given would operate so as to terminate any contract of employment of indefinite duration. He stated that there was no allegation that the period of notice given to terminate the plaintiff's contract of employment was inadequate and thus the plaintiff could not avail of the common law remedy of wrongful dismissal. Finally, the learned judge observed that it was not his place to adjudicate on the validity or otherwise of the purported redundancy and that the plaintiff would be best to have recourse to the statutory law of unfair dismissals. Accordingly, Murphy J. refused the plaintiff's application for mandatory interlocutory relief because she had failed to establish a strong case that she was likely to succeed at trial.

Both of the above-mentioned decisions make it clear that if an employee is to succeed in obtaining a mandatory interlocutory injunction against an employer s/he must have a strong case that is likely to succeed at a trial of the action. In general, both cases would appear to affirm that where there has been no violation of a plaintiff's constitutional rights, and his/her employment has simply been lawfully terminated in accordance with the terms of his/her contract of employment and on the grounds of redundancy, the courts are unlikely to allow him/her to avail of the common law remedy of wrongful dismissal and afford him/her relief via a mandatory interlocutory injunction. It seems that an argument based on the implied term of mutual trust and confidence in employment contracts will be given short shrift unless an employer has radically undermined the employee's employment contract. If a plaintiff nonetheless contends that s/he was indeed unfairly dismissed then s/he should avail of the remedies provided by statute, specifically the Unfair Dismissal Acts 1977–2008. Perhaps in this recessionary climate the Irish courts are attempting to deter hordes of disgruntled employees from inappropriately seeking mandatory interlocutory relief as a means of getting their jobs back when it might be far more prudent for such people to instead have recourse to unfair dismissals law where they have genuine grounds for believing that their redundancy was indeed an invalid one?

In a defamation context The jurisdiction to grant interlocutory injunctions in defamation cases has been described by Sullivan C.J. in the Supreme Court case of *Sinclair v Gogarty* [1937] 1 I.R. 377 at 384 as one "of a delicate nature" which should only be exercised "in the clearest cases". This cautious approach is undoubtedly due to the constitutional protection of the right to freedom of expression contained in Art.40.6.1.i. In *Quinlivan v O'Dea* [2009] IEHC 187 the plaintiff election candidate sought two interlocutory injunctions against the defendant TD. One was an injunction restraining the repetition of an alleged slander and the other was an injunction pursuant to s.11(5) of the Prevention of Electoral Abuses Act 1923 restraining a repetition of the making or publication of false statements in relation to the personal character or conduct of the plaintiff as a candidate in local government elections. The plaintiff claimed that he was slandered by the defendant in the course of an interview which the latter party gave to a journalist and which was reported in the *Limerick Chronicle*. The plaintiff claimed that the defendant made false and defamatory statements to the effect that he was involved as a co-owner or otherwise in the operation of a brothel at an apartment located at Clancy Strand in Limerick.

The plaintiff sought to rely on the title to the article, on its opening paragraph and on a direct quotation from the defendant in the article. The title to the article read "Quinlivan says he may sue O'Dea over brothel". The opening paragraph said:

> "Sinn Féin's Maurice Quinlivan says he's considering legal action against Willie O'Dea after the Minister for Defence claimed he part-

> owned a Clancy Strand apartment where a brothel was discovered in Garda raids."

The relevant quotation read, "I suppose I am going a bit too far when I say this but I'd like to ask Mr Quinlivan is the brothel still closed?"

The defendant admitted making the direct quotation but he categorically denied saying to the journalist that the plaintiff was a co-owner of the Clancy Strand apartment in Limerick. The court observed that s.11 of the 1923 Act creates a criminal offence of making or publishing a false statement of fact in relation to a candidate and it felt that the section should therefore be strictly construed and applied. Cooke J. held that a specific statement of fact must have been made or published by a defendant, that it must relate to the personal character or conduct of a candidate, and that it must be false. He observed that the crucial falsehood upon which the plaintiff relied in seeking the statutory injunction was the proposition that he was stated to be a co-owner of the Limerick apartment in which the brothel was discovered. The plaintiff relied in effect upon the article's opening paragraph to challenge the defendant's denial of having made such a false statement. However, the court held that the opening paragraph suggested that the journalist was not quoting the defendant but rather the reason given to him by the plaintiff as to why he was considering legal action against Mr O'Dea. In the court's judgment the injunction provided for in s.11 of the 1923 Act was against clearly identifiable statements of fact and not against possible interpretations of statements capable of two or more meanings, and it was held that the opening paragraph of the article did not constitute clear evidence of the making or publication of a false statement of fact. Cooke J. refused to grant the statutory injunction.

Cooke J. held that different considerations arose in relation to the other injunction sought:

> "The well-known criteria for the grant of interlocutory relief apply namely, whether the plaintiff has raised a fair issue to be tried; whether damages will be an adequate remedy and, if not, whether the balance of convenience lies in granting or refusing the injunction. Those criteria fall to be applied in cases where an injunction is sought to restrain publication or repetition of a defamation with the additional requirement that there is not only a fair issue to be tried but that there is no doubt that the words complained of are defamatory."

Regarding the crucial substantive complaint that the defendant claimed to the journalist that the plaintiff was a co-owner of the apartment, Cooke J. observed that there was a full dispute as to whether the slanderous words were ever uttered as the defendant not only denied it but the article itself was ambiguous on the point. Moreover, the article as a whole did not support the proposition that any reader of the *Limerick Chronicle* understood that the plaintiff was a co-owner of the apartment because it accurately recorded the true ownership of the apartment and the fact that the brothel was run by the tenants. Thus the court found that the plaintiff had not established a fair issue to be tried as to the uttering by the defendant to the journalist of the slanderous words to the effect that the plaintiff was a co-owner of the apartment. The court felt that damages would in any event be an adequate remedy because the defendant's communication, if proved to have taken place, had no irreparable effect in itself upon the political prospects of the plaintiff because it was accompanied by the full explanation of the context to the brothel incident and by the plaintiff's robust denial.

The court held that the plaintiff had established a fair issue to be tried as to whether the question posed by the defendant could possibly be defamatory by virtue of innuendo. The question takes on its possibly defamatory innuendo when the reader knows that the apartment is owned by the plaintiff's brother and the question implies that the addressee is in a position to give it an authoritative answer. The court held that here damages may not be an adequate remedy because if an election candidate is unsuccessful it may be impossible to know if the damage to his reputation had a material influence upon the election result. However, the court felt that because the plaintiff had raised a fair issue in respect of an admitted statement already made, the damage had been done and his remedy was in damages.

Cooke J. held that a repetition of the alleged defamatory statement was unlikely on the evidence and he refused an interlocutory injunction. The defendant had emphatically denied ever making the substantive statement as to the plaintiff's co-ownership of the apartment and the true position as to that ownership and the absence of any involvement on the part of the plaintiff had already been made clear in the article. In conclusion, Cooke J. emphasised that:

> "Accordingly, even if it were necessary to have regard to the balance of convenience, the undesirability of fettering the freedom of speech of an elected representative must clearly outweigh the slim possibility, if such there be at this point, of any repetition of a clearly defamatory statement relating to the Clancy Street apartment between now and the trial."

European Union and International Law

EUROPEAN PARLIAMENT ELECTIONS

The European Parliament (Irish Constituency Members) Act 2009 provided for the arrangements concerning the 2009 European Parliament election. The 2009 Act also repealed and replaced the European Assembly (Irish Representatives) Act 1979, as amended.

LISBON TREATY RATIFICATION

The Twenty-Eighth Amendment of the Constitution (Treaty of Lisbon) Act 2009 amended Art.29.4 of the Constitution in order to provide for the ratification and implementation in Irish law of the changes effected by the 2007 Lisbon Treaty, formally entitled the Treaty of Lisbon amending the Treaty on European Union and the Treaty establishing the European Community. The European Union Act 2009 amended the European Communities Act 1972 to provide that the Lisbon Treaty, and the amendments it made to the EU Treaties, forms part of Irish law. We discuss briefly here the effect of the ratification of the Treaty.

Rejection of Lisbon Treaty in 2008 and Council Decision of June 2009 In June 2008, the people of Ireland rejected in a referendum the proposal to ratify the Lisbon Treaty. In the wake of this, the Government engaged in extensive discussion and consultation nationally and with other EU Member States to address the perceived reasons for its rejection. These discussions culminated in a Statement and Annexed Decision of the European Council of Ministers on June 19, 2009 (formally entitled: Decision of the Heads of State or Government of the 27 Member States of the EU, Meeting Within The European Council, on the Concerns of The Irish People on the Treaty of Lisbon) in which a number of specific matters were addressed. The Statement and Decision provided that, assuming ratification of the Lisbon Treaty, each EU Member State would retain a Commissioner and that Ireland was given a number of "guarantees and assurances" in the areas of concern to Irish voters which emerged in the June 2008 referendum. The Decision provided that:

- nothing in the Treaty of Lisbon makes any change of any kind, for any Member State, to the extent or operation of the Union's competences in relation to taxation;

- the Treaty of Lisbon does not prejudice the security and defence policy of Member States, including Ireland's traditional policy of neutrality; and
- the provisions of the Constitution of Ireland in relation to the right to life, education and the family are not in any way affected by the fact that the Treaty of Lisbon attributes legal status to the EU Charter of Fundamental Rights or by the justice and home affairs provisions of the Treaty.

The Decision also included a Solemn Declaration on workers' rights which confirms the high importance that the Union attaches to:

- social progress and the protection of workers' rights;
- public services;
- the responsibility of Member States for the delivery of education and health services;
- the essential role and wide discretion of national, regional and local authorities in providing, commissioning and organising services of general economic interest.

The June 2009 Decision also provided that if the Lisbon Treaty entered into force, the Decision would be annexed to the Treaties as a Protocol at the time of the conclusion of the next Accession Treaty for a new Member State.

Constitutional amendment to implement Lisbon Treaty In the wake of the June 2009 decision, the second referendum on the Twenty-Eighth Amendment to the Constitution (Lisbon Treaty) took place on October 2, 2009 when the Treaty was approved. The Twenty-Eighth Amendment had the effect of amending Art.29.4 of the Constitution by inserting the following after Art.29.4.3°:

> 4° Ireland affirms its commitment to the European Union within which the member states of that Union work together to promote peace, shared values and the well-being of their peoples.
>
> 5° The State may ratify the Treaty of Lisbon amending the Treaty on European Union and the Treaty establishing the European Community, signed at Lisbon on the 13th day of December 2007 ("Treaty of Lisbon"), and may be a member of the European Union established by virtue of that Treaty.
>
> 6° No provision of this Constitution invalidates laws enacted, acts done or measures adopted by the State, before, on or after the entry into force of the Treaty of Lisbon, that are necessitated by the obligations

of membership of the European Union referred to in subsection 5° of this section or of the European Atomic Energy Community, or prevents laws enacted, acts done or measures adopted by—

- i the said European Union or the European Atomic Energy Community, or institutions thereof,
- ii the European Communities or European Union existing immediately before the entry into force of the Treaty of Lisbon, or institutions thereof, or
- iii bodies competent under the treaties referred to in this section,

from having the force of law in the State.

7° The State may exercise the options or discretions—

- i to which Article 20 of the Treaty on European Union relating to enhanced cooperation applies,
- ii under Protocol No. 19 on the Schengen acquis integrated into the framework of the European Union annexed to that treaty and to the Treaty on the Functioning of the European Union (formerly known as the Treaty establishing the European Community), and
- iii under Protocol No. 21 on the position of the United Kingdom and Ireland in respect of the area of freedom, security and justice, so annexed, including the option that the said Protocol No. 21 shall, in whole or in part, cease to apply to the State,

but any such exercise shall be subject to the prior approval of both Houses of the Oireachtas.

8° The State may agree to the decisions, regulations or other acts—

- i under the Treaty on European Union and the Treaty on the Functioning of the European Union authorising the Council of the European Union to act other than by unanimity,
- ii under those treaties authorising the adoption of the ordinary legislative procedure, and
- iii under subparagraph (d) of Article 82.2, the third subparagraph of Article 83.1 and paragraphs 1 and 4 of Article 86 of the Treaty on the Functioning of the European Union, relating to the area of freedom, security and justice,

but the agreement to any such decision, regulation or act shall be subject to the prior approval of both Houses of the Oireachtas.

9° The State shall not adopt a decision taken by the European Council to establish a common defence pursuant to Article 42 of the Treaty on European Union where that common defence would include the State.

Main elements of Lisbon Treaty It is not possible in this *Annual Review of Irish Law* to provide a summary of the many changes effected by the Lisbon Treaty. In very broad terms, the Lisbon Treaty has accurately been described as having incorporated a very large percentage of the changes proposed in the rejected 2004 EU Constitutional Treaty but did not involve the creation of a unified Treaty to replace the existing EU Treaties. The Lisbon Treaty provides for significant changes to the Treaty on European Union and also to the EC Treaty, now renamed the Treaty on the Functioning of the European Union (TFEU). The following discussion is based on *A Summary Guide to the Treaty of Lisbon (EU Reform Treaty)* published in January 2008 by the National Forum on Europe (chair: Maurice Hayes).

The Lisbon Treaty changed the format of the EU Treaty and what is now the TFEU as follows. The Treaty on European Union (TEU) now has 6 Titles:

Title I Common Provisions
Title II Democratic Principles
Title III Institutions
Title IV Enhanced Cooperation
Title V External Actions and Common Foreign and Security Policy
Title VI Final Provisions

Title II (Democratic Principles) and Title III (Institutions) are new, although many of their provisions reflect existing rules, and the provisions on Freedom, Security and Justice have been moved to the Treaty on the Functioning of the European Union (TFEU). The TFEU now contains all the detailed rules on the workings of the EU and contains 7 Parts:

Part One Principles
Part Two Non-discrimination and citizenship of the Union
Part Three Union Policies and Internal Actions
Parts Four Overseas Countries and Territories
Part Five External Action by the Union
Part Six Institutional and Budgetary Provisions
Part Seven General and Final Provisions

The bulk of the TFEU is contained in Parts 2 and 3. A notable change in the TFEU's structure, by comparison with the EU Treaty, is the addition of Pt Five dealing with the EU's external action, which is linked to Title V of the Treaty on European Union (TEU).

The Lisbon Treaty also contains a series of Protocols and a number of Declarations have been made regarding the Treaty. A number of these protocols and declarations are directly relevant to Ireland, particularly the Protocol and Declaration relating to the ability of the Irish and UK to opt-out of proposals concerning judicial co-operation in criminal matters and police co-operation.

Integration of the "Three Pillars" An important effect of the Lisbon Treaty is to replace the EU's previous structure of "Three Pillars". The First Pillar was based on the EC Treaty, which included what was originally the concept of the Common Market, which later became the Single Market and, later, the Internal Market. First Pillar decision-making normally involved a proposal from the Commission with a qualified majority vote in the Council. The role of the European Parliament depended on the nature of the proposal. The Second Pillar dealt with the Common Foreign and Security Policy while the Third Pillar dealt with Police and Judicial Co-operation in criminal matters. The Second and Third Pillars involved inter-governmental procedures, with national vetoes for most decisions and a limited role for the European Parliament. The Lisbon Treaty abolished this inter-governmental pillar system while retaining special voting procedures for Common Foreign and Security Policy. The nature of the European Union's Second and Third Pillars had given rise to questions about its legal status. After the ratification of the Lisbon Treaty, the European Union replaces the European Community and the existing European Union with a single legal personality which has treaty-making powers.

Specific changes made by the Lisbon Treaty Among the specific changes made by the Lisbon Treaty are the following:

1. Qualified majority voting (QMV) becomes the normal rule for the Council of Ministers. National vetoes are removed in many areas, although some vetoes remain, such as in the area of rates of income tax and corporation tax.
2. Decisions by qualified majority (QMV) now require a "double majority" in the Council (55 per cent of Member States representing 65 per cent of the EU's population).
3. The European Parliament has gained co-decision powers in many policy areas, and this is now referred to in the TFEU as the "ordinary legislative process".
4. A European Council President now chairs the European Council for up to five years, replacing the six-monthly rotating Presidency.
5. A High Representative of the Union for Foreign Affairs and Security Policy combines two previous posts (Vice-President of the Commission and High Representative for Foreign and Security Policy.
6. While the Lisbon Treaty states that the number of Commissioners would be reduced, the June 2009 European Council Decision already mentioned agreed that this would not occur.

7. The number of MEPs is set at a maximum of 750, plus the Parliament's President (with a minimum of 6 and a maximum of 96 MEPs per country; Ireland currently has 12 MEPs).
8. National parliaments have the right to raise objections against draft EU legislation where national or local action would be more effective, thus giving clear effect to the principle of subsidiarity.
9. The EU is given a single legal personality.
10. An "exit clause" provides for the first time a procedure for a Member State to leave the EU.
11. Asylum, immigration, police and judicial co-operation no longer have a separate "pillar" but Ireland, with the UK, have an opt-out/opt-in concerning any proposals in this area.
12. Foreign and Security Policy is integrated with other areas of the EU but special procedures still apply, including unanimity for policy decisions.
13. The Treaty maintains full respect for Ireland's policy of military neutrality. It mandates Member States to increase their own military capabilities with a view to increasing the capabilities available for the EU's Common Security and Defence Policy.
14. New areas, such as climate change and energy solidarity, are included in the TFEU.
15. A Protocol is added on services of general interest, including economic services of general interest.
16. The EU is given greater controls in the area of macro-economic policy and additional tools to curb Member States with excessive budget deficits.
17. New procedures provide for simplified Treaty revisions in certain specified areas.
18. The 2000 EU Charter of Fundamental Rights is given Treaty status.

The Lisbon Treaty came into effect on December 1, 2009, after the Czech Republic and Poland completed their ratification processes.

INTERNATIONAL LAW

Diplomatic relations and immunities: European Centre for Medium-Range Weather Forecasts The European Centre for Medium-Range Weather Forecasts (Privileges and Immunities) Order 2009 (S.I. No. 328 of 2009), made under s.42A of the Diplomatic Relations and Immunities Act 1967 (the "1967 Act"), provides that the privileges, immunities and facilities provided for in the 1967 Act are afforded to the European Centre for Medium-Range Weather Forecasts. This was done to implement the 1973 Protocol on the Privileges and Immunities of the European Centre for Medium-Range Weather Forecasts, as amended by the 2005 Amending Protocol. The text of the 2005 Amending Protocol was annexed to the 2009 Order. The State had previously, in the European Centre for Medium-Range Weather Forecasts (Designation) Order 1974 (S.I. No. 381 of 1974), designated that Centre as an organisation to which Pt VIII of the 1967 Act applied.

Family Law

ADOPTION

In *S v The Adoption Board* [2009] IEHC 429, O'Neill J. was called on to interpret the scope of s.7F(2) of the Adoption Act 1952, as inserted by s.4 of the Adoption Act 1998. It provides as follows:

> Where on an application by an adoption agency that proposes to place a child for adoption, the Board is satisfied that, having regard to the nature of the relationship between the father and the mother or the circumstances of the conception of the child, it would be inappropriate for the agency to contact the father in respect of the placement of the child, the Board may authorise the agency to, and the agency at any time thereafter may, place the child for adoption.

The case concerned the adoption in 2007 of a girl born in 2001 to young unmarried parents. The father was named on the birth certificate. The relationship between the parents had not been a stable one. It began in 1999, when the father was 19 and the mother was 15. They had not initially lived together. In February 2003, the mother alleged that the father had attempted to strangle her in the course of an argument. He was charged with assault. The mother withdrew her statement the day before the prosecution was scheduled to go ahead. (She later explained this by saying that the father had threatened to take his own life if she ended the relationship.) In spite of this, they jointly applied to the local authority for housing and they went to live together in a local authority house in July 2003. In September 2003 a violent incident occurred which prompted the mother to return to her mother's home with the child. After consulting a solicitor, she received undertakings from the father that he would vacate their home, undergo counselling and desist from behaving in a threatening and abusive manner. The parties' relationship improved for a short period, but in December 2003, after an incident which involved the Gardaí being called, the father set their house on fire in an attempt to kill himself. He was charged with arson and granted bail on condition that he would not contact the mother or his child. He was imprisoned for a week for breach of that condition.

In May 2004 the mother obtained an interlocutory injunction against the father restraining him from any further assault and prohibiting him from entering her home. The father absconded to Britain. The only contact he had with his daughter during his period there was through birthday cards and Christmas cards. In July 2006 the father returned to Ireland and made contact with the Gardaí. He pleaded guilty to the arson charge and received a three-year suspended sentence.

In August 2007 the father applied to the District Court for access to his daughter. It transpired that the mother had married another man in 2005 and the two had adopted the daughter in June 2007, without any notice having been given to the father.

The father sought an order of certiorari quashing the adoption order on the basis that the Adoption Board had acted ultra vires and in breach of his natural and constitutional rights in failing to consult him before the adoption order was made.

O'Neill J. provided a comprehensive analysis of the law in Ireland and under the European Convention on Human Rights. Interpreting s.19A(3) in a manner compliant with the Convention required that "its effect be ring-fenced", so as to ensure that its application was confined to the kind of extreme or exceptional cases discussed in the jurisprudence of the European Court of Human Rights. The subsection mentioned only two circumstances which could be considered as a basis for not notifying the natural father: conception and the nature of the relationship between the natural father and the mother. Whilst the section made it clear that these could be considered separately, in a great many cases it was likely there would be a considerable overlap. When considering the circumstances of conception, clearly what the Oireachtas had in mind was:

> "... a distinction between conception as a result of rape, or an isolated casual encounter or some other incident of sexual contact which right-thinking people would readily recognise as failing to confer on the natural father any of the normal rights of paternity".

In clear contradistinction was the conception of a child "out of a normal relationship between the father and the mother".

A wider variety of considerations arose when dealing with the nature of the relationship between the natural father and the mother. A literal interpretation of the language used in the subsection did not include the relationship between the father and the child. Such an exclusion could hardly have been contemplated by the Oireachtas as it would lead to patently absurd results:

> "It could not seriously be suggested that an abusive relationship between the natural father and the child would have to be ignored where the relationship between the father and mother did not justify withholding notification. Conversely, where the relationship between the father and the child was good, it could not be the case that the abusive nature of the relationship between the father and the mother would, alone, be decisive on the question of notification."

A purposive approach was required. O'Neill J. observed:

> "In my judgment, a child centred approach is appropriate to the interpretation of s.19A(3) not only for consistency with the cases decided in the European Court of Human Rights but, more immediately, to comply with s.2 of the Act of 1974 which, in its clear terms, obliges the respondent and this Court and all other courts when dealing with arrangements for or the making of an adoption, in deciding 'that' question to have regard to the welfare of the child as the first and paramount consideration … With this in mind and also the obligation under s.2 of the [European Convention on Human Rights] Act … 2003, where possible to construe in compliance with the State's obligations under the Convention, I have come to the conclusion that the 'nature of the relationship between the father and the mother' must be construed as including the relationship between the father and the child."

O'Neill J. stressed that what was at stake in s.19A(3) was simply the decision whether to notify the father rather than whether … to make the adoption order itself. Different considerations would apply to the decision to make the adoption order. The welfare of the child had to be viewed in that context. Consideration of factors properly relating to the final decision might be premature and impermissible in making the decision whether to notify the father. Into this latter category would fall those considerations relating to the effect of the adoption order sought, as against its refusal, on the ultimate welfare of the child. In so far as the welfare of the child was concerned, the range of considerations of a decision to notify the natural father should be confined to the effect on the child's welfare of consulting the father in the adoption application "and no more".

Under the umbrella of the "nature of the relationship" a critically important factor in deciding to notify would be the duration of any relationship between the father and the child and hence the degree of any engagement between the father and the child or the depth (or lack of it) of any commitment by the father to the child. If the relationship was one of some longevity such that the normal parental bond was formed between father and child, unless there was present in that relationship an abusive element of some sort such as to lead to a conclusion that the relationship should be terminated in the interest of the welfare of the child, the Adoption Board "should be swayed towards notification".

O'Neill J. emphasised that, in a child-centred approach to discerning the meaning of s.19A(3), the factors relating specifically to the relationship between the father and the child should be paramount. Turning to the relationship between the father and the mother, O'Neill J. commented:

> "Where a relationship of significant duration between the mother and the father comes to an end, in my judgment, the [Adoption Board] must

> be careful not to be drawn into a punishment of the father for what may have been ill treatment by him of the mother. This may arise in the context of allegations by the mother of violence and other forms of abuse perpetrated by the father. Of particular concern in this regard is where it is alleged that there is a continuing threat of violence or harm from the father either directed at the mother or perhaps members of her family. Whilst this may be alarming to the Adoption Board, it must be realised that the safety or security of the applicant for an adoption order, or other persons connected to the applicant, is not primarily the concern of the [Adoption Board]. Where there is a material threat of violence or other harm or indeed an apprehension in that regard, this is a matter which is the responsibility of An Garda Síochána, who are in a position to deal with such matters and for that reason recourse should be to them in such situations. As far as the [Adoption Board] is concerned, while it is natural that there would be alarm when matters of this kind are raised, as they were in this case, great care must be taken to ensure that the [Adoption Board] is not impelled by the threat or apprehension of violence into a decision driven solely by that concern. Indeed the futility of a decision prompted in this way is apparent when one considers that the eventual adoption order will inevitably become known to the natural father and indeed the making of an adoption order without consulting a natural father would, in all probability, be more likely to exacerbate a potentially violent situation (if it existed) rather than easing it or avoiding it, in circumstances where the identity of all the parties are known to the natural father and vice-versa."

O'Neill J. went on to emphasise the "grave risk of a very serious breach of the natural father's constitutional right to fair procedures and natural justice and his rights under art.6 of the Convention, resulting in a very serious injustice being done to the natural father and, by extension, the child", if he was excluded from the process on the basis of reliance solely on information supplied by the mother. This risk placed on the Adoption Board a very heavy onus of ensuring that the procedures it adopted in order to reach a determination on whether to withhold notification in reliance on s.19A(3) were adequate to ensure that the injustice mentioned is avoided. It was not sufficient simply to accept the uncorroborated or unsupported word of the applicants for the adoption order. Their version of events, in so far as the core allegations against the father were concerned, had to be corroborated or supported by reliable independent evidence.

O'Neill J. went on to review in detail the process whereby the Adoption Board had decided not to consult the father and the evidence on which that decision was based.

He concluded that the information given to the Adoption Board which had persuaded it to withhold notification "was not only wholly inadequate, when compared to the fuller picture which has emerged in these proceedings, but also unjustly damnified the applicant". The father's relationship with his daughter had been a "relatively normal" one which was of considerable duration, for the first three years of her life. His relationship with the mother had also been of lengthy duration. The threat of violence had been remote in view of the long period that the father had lived separately from the mother after 2003.

O'Neill J.'s judgment is to be welcomed. It preserves the statutory provision from attack under the European Convention of Human Rights, albeit by, in effect, replacing the word "mother" by "child". Its child-centred approach yields a far more satisfactory outcome than one that would concentrate on the relationship between the parents, as the provision appears to require.

One might reflect further on what is envisaged by the phrase "circumstances of the conception of the child". O'Neill J. identifies rape as the quintessential example. One might perhaps also consider artificial insemination by donor or even certain surrogacy arrangements as also falling within the scope of the phrase. Again that shadow of the European Convention falls over the section, requiring further judicial inventiveness in statutory interpretation.

ASSISTED HUMAN REPRODUCTION

The past three decades have witnessed a transformation in the ways in which children are conceived, gestated, born and reared. The traditionally close association between sexual intercourse, pregnancy and birth and the cultural emphasis on marriage as the preferred context for having children have been broken down by a complex process of technological, medical, social and cultural changes.

In *Roche v Roche* [2009] IESC 82, the Supreme Court grappled with the new world of children conceived in a test tube. Its effort to produce a coherent interpretation of the relevant constitutional provisions was, unfortunately, less than successful. For comprehensive analysis of the decision, see Andrea Mulligan, "*Roche v Roche*: Some Guidance for Frozen Embryo Disputes" 13 *Trinity College Law Review* 168 (2010). The analysis that follows is based on the unapproved version of the Supreme Court determination.

The case involved a married couple, now separated, who had already parented a son and who had in 2002 engaged in assisted human reproduction. The husband signed a document consenting to the fertilisation of his wife's eggs and the implantation of three embryos and acknowledging that he would become the legal father of any resulting child. Both spouses signed a document in which they consented expressly to the freezing of the embryos they would create and to their taking "full responsibility on an ongoing basis for those cryo preserved embryos". As a result of the IVF treatment six viable embryos were created. Three were inserted in the wife's uterus and the other three were frozen. The wife became pregnant and gave birth to a daughter. Marital difficulties arose around this time. The spouses eventually entered into a judicial separation. The wife wished to have the remaining embryos implanted in her uterus; the husband opposed this.

In the High Court proceedings McGovern J. rejected the wife's contention that a term requiring the embryos to be implanted could be derived from the nature of the agreement between the spouses; he held that the husband was not estopped from denying that he had consented to the implantation. As regards the constitutional status and rights of the frozen embryos he held that Art.40.3.3° of the Constitution afforded them no protection.

The Supreme Court affirmed. The evidence, in the view of the members of the court, simply did not support a finding of implied agreement to implant the embryos. No estoppel arose as, in contrast to the American decision of *Re the Marriage of Witten III*, 672 NW 2d 768 (Iowa, 2003), there had been no initial agreement as to what would happen to the embryos other than that they be frozen.

The constitutional issue dominated the analysis of the five judges. It may be useful to set out the terms of Art.40.3.3° as originally promulgated, without reference to the later amendments effected in 1992, since they had apparently no influence on the case:

> "The State acknowledges the right to life of the unborn and, with due regard to the equal right to life of the mother, guarantees in its laws to respect, and, as far as practicable, by its laws to defend and vindicate that right."

The analysis that found favour with most of the members of the court can be summarised as follows. The Amendment in 1983 should be interpreted as restricting its remit to intra-uterine entities. Embryos before implantation, accordingly, can claim no protection under Art.40.3.3°. This is for two principal reasons: the People intended the Amendment to address the question of abortion rather than life at pre-implantation stage and the language of Art.40.3.3°, in referring to the mother, necessarily restricted the scope of the Amendment to a context in which the mother's life could be balanced with that of the unborn; no such balancing process arose before implantation.

The interpretation of the Amendment as being one intended to address abortion cannot easily be reconciled with the actual debate at the time the Amendment was before the People. Of course concern about the danger of possible judicial developments that would facilitate or require the legalisation of abortion was very real, but this was on account of what had actually happened in courts in other countries in the context of abortion. Unquestionably, abortion served as the focus of these concerns but equally unquestionably the concerns were not limited to abortion. They were about values and human rights—the value of unborn human life, of the lives of human beings at all stages. So far as abortion had been legally permitted in other countries, this process had involved the devaluation of the lives of human beings before birth, either on the basis of a comparison with the "yet more precious life of the mother" (*R. v Bourne* [1939] 1 K.B. 687) or on the basis of the lack of value attributed to unborn life by a particular constitution or on account of a perceived irreconcilability of philosophical perspectives on the value of the unborn human life. This process occurred during a period where societies were gradually coming to terms with the serious injustice and discrimination that had been imposed on women by law and culture. So far as the debate affected life before birth, the focus of public, legislative and judicial discussion was abortion, but this was not because that sad subject represents the totality of philosophical concern for the value and rights of unborn human beings. Abortion involves the intentional termination of the life of these human beings but there are other circumstances in which the life of an unborn human being can be terminated intentionally. A person may, for example, kill a child in the womb for reasons of hatred of the mother or of the child or to avoid legal obligations to the child in relation to maintenance. In 1983, the process of assisted human reproduction did not involve the creation of "spare" embryos and embryos were not destroyed as serving no utility, but clearly the intentional destruction of embryos requires courts to consider the value of their lives from philosophical and legal standpoints.

The point at issue here is that those who argued for, and supported, the Amendment did so, not on account of some fixation with abortion, but rather on account of a broader philosophical and normative concern: that human life before birth should not be devalued. Neither the fact that the process of devaluation, internationally, occurred in the context of abortion (though the effect of that devaluation extended beyond that context) nor the fact that a well-founded fear that abortion might be the context in which that devaluation might occur in Ireland in the absence of specific constitutional protection for the unborn warrants the conclusion reached by the court that the Amendment was designed, and should be interpreted as seeking only, to address the issue of abortion. Clearly this was not so. The text, on any fair reading, reveals its philosophical character. Nowhere does it refer expressly to abortion. Its language is rights-based. Naturally, it has to be capable of addressing the issue of abortion, which it does in philosophical terms, with its emphasis on the equality of the right to life of the mother and her unborn child (a norm which, incidentally, was rejected, implicitly by the majority and explicitly in McCarthy J.'s judgment in the Supreme Court decision of *Attorney General v X* [1992] 1 I.R. 1).

That the Amendment was not merely about abortion but rather addressed the wider philosophical and normative perspectives is plain from the heated debates that took place between proponents and opponents on the issue of the implications of the Amendment for the 'morning after' pill. The opponents of the Amendment certainly did not interpret it as being limited only to the context of abortion. Equally, no proponent of the Amendment sought to protect it from the attacks of its opponents on the basis that the Amendment was simply an anti-abortion measure. The well-recorded history of these debates refutes the interpretation of the Amendment adopted by the court.

Let us now consider whether the court was right to interpret Art.40.3.3° as excluding protection from unborn human beings before implantation because its language envisaged the necessity to balance the right to life of the unborn with the equal right to life of the mother. Denham J. expressed this view as follows:

> "The right to life of the unborn is not stated as an absolute right in Article 40.3.3°. Rather, it is subject to the due regard to the right to life of the mother. The right to life of the mother is not stated as an absolute right either. Article 40.3.3° refers to a situation where these two lives are connected and a balance may have to be sought between the two lives. Thus the physical situation must exist to require such a balancing act. No such connection exists between the [wife] and the three surplus embryos now frozen and stored at the Clinic…
>
> This connection, relationship, between the embryos and the mother does not arise until after implantation has occurred. After the implantation of an embryo the relationship between the embryo and the mother changes. The mother has carriage of the embryos, becomes pregnant, and the embryo enters a state of 'unborn'. At that time an attachment begins between the two lives. It is that attachment which gives rise to the relationship addressed in Article 40.3.3°."

One may reasonably doubt whether the inclusion in Art.40.3.3° of reference to the mother's right to life justifies the conclusion that the Amendment should be interpreted as excluding protection to unborn human beings outside the womb. Indeed the logic of the court's position is that Art.40.3.3° should be limited even further to the context where the lives of mother and child are being addressed in conjunction. Surely this is an unwarranted restriction? It was essential for any consitutional provision dealing with the protection of the right to life of the unborn to address the obvious context of pregnancy and the mother's right to life. Not to have done so would be unthinkable. Yet the fact that the Amendment did what was essential is no reason to interpret its broad language so narrowly as to deal exclusively with that particular context. Article 40.3.3° protects the life of the unborn against being killed by a hostile third party. (At least this proposition seemed clear before *Roche v Roche*.) To restrict its perspective to the context of pregnancy seems unwarranted by its language and contrary to any theory that retains philosophical or normative coherence.

Murray C.J. adopted a strikingly different approach to that favoured by his colleagues. As Attorney General in 1982, he was acknowledged as the author of the terms of the amendment. He did not consider that Art.40.3.3° was simply an anti-abortion measure:

> "If the objective … had been to just address some perceived statutory frailties that could have been achieved more readily and early by the adoption of legislation. But the public debate transcended that and the object obviously was, as the result demonstrates, to place in the Constitution a protection for human life before birth … Instead of addressing abortion as such by a prohibitive amendment such as 'no law shall be enacted permitting an abortion to be performed' or the like, reference to the specific mischief, so to speak, was omitted and the provision turned to focus on the positive protection of human life before birth.
>
> In my view the provision of the Constitution was intended to embrace human life before birth and to extend to it, in express positive terms, the constitutional protection available to life after birth already provided for in Article 40.3.3°."

Again in contrast to his colleagues, Murray C.J. did not conclude from the reference to the mother that Art.40.3.3° necessarily restricted the remit of its protection to unborn lives within the womb:

> "In short, th[e] statute or proviso concerning the equal right to life of the mother is there to ensure respect and protection for her rights in certain circumstances and cannot logically, in my view, be interpreted as devaluing the equal right to life of the unborn. Therefore, I cannot accept the argument that simply because the embryo exists outside the womb that it is incapable of falling under the protection of Article 40.3.
>
> *If*, and I accept it is a very important if, the frozen embryos fall to be considered as having the qualities of human life then, inevitably in my view, they would fall under the rubric of the constitutional provision. Outside the womb, they have the same qualities as they would have in the womb."

Murray C.J. then went on to provide an analysis which must rank as addressing one of the most important issues that have arisen in a generation of constitutional jurisprudence since it goes to the very core of the philosophical and normative character of the Constitution. There is no way in which that analysis can fairly be discussed without quoting it *in extenso*:

> "We know that human life begins in the womb. That is not in issue. I speak in the context of what is referred to as the act of procreation, of sexual intercourse between a man and a woman. The question is: at what point does human life begin. Again I suppose it could be said that there was a broad consensus among all disciplines that human life begins at implantation of the embryo in the womb or at least not long thereafter.

Of course Courts take judicial notice, without having to expressly say so, of obvious and accepted truths concerning the nature of the world we live in. Thus a party, in appropriate proceedings, would not have to prove that a foetus of three months constituted human life no more than a party would be required to prove the existence of the law of gravity. The issue here has an altogether different dimension.

Debate and discourse as to when human life begins has for very many decades, and indeed long before that, focused, though not always exclusively, on whether human life begins at conception or at implantation. Inevitably, this featured as part of the public debate on the proposed Amendment but the provision is resoundingly silent as to when human life should be deemed to begin for the purposes of enjoying its protection.

I think it is safe to assume that at the time when the proposed Amendment to the Constitution was being debated and its form being decided by the Oireachtas that there was no clear view or consensus on the question of when human life begins or perhaps more important when it can be deemed or treated as having begun.

The status of the embryo, that is to say its moral status, and the issue as to when human life begins, continues to be debated and discussed as part of a virtually world wide discourse in diverse fora including the most prestigious universities and halls of learning. The many facets of the various sides to that debate, and there are cogent arguments from every perspective, is evident from the evidence given by the expert witnesses in the High Court. The range of views expressed or referred to in that evidence underscore the absence of any broad multi disciplinary consensus as to when life begins and in particular as to whether it should be considered as beginning at conception or implantation, which are the two reference points with which we are concerned for present purposes.

However, I think it can be said that the human embryo is generally accepted as having moral qualities and a moral status. However else it may be characterised the fertilisation of the ovum is the first step in procreation and contains within it the potential, at least, for life. Its enactment and use cannot be divorced from our concepts of human dignity. The Council of Europe Convention on Human Rights and Bio Medicine with a view to, inter alia, preventing the misuse of biology in medicine which may lead to acts endangering human dignity prohibits, in Article 18, the creation of human embryos for research purposes. Article 3 of the Charter of Fundamental Rights of the European Union prohibits the use of embryos for the cloning of human beings as does a declaration of the United Nations. Such provisions and the fact that many countries regulate and protect the manner and circumstances in which in vitro embryos may be created and dealt with, reflect the ethical and moral status of embryos as being extricably associated with human dignity. There is inevitably within the ambit of that moral appreciation of the embryo much debate particularly concerning the parameters of regulatory measures and what should be permitted and what should be prohibited.

The moral status of embryos and the respect or protection which society may feel they are owed is a different issue to the question under consideration and I do not propose to consider it any further.

One comes back to the fundamental issue in this case namely whether this Court should consider that the frozen embryo is human life within the meaning of Article 40.3.3.

In the course of the appeal counsel for the appellant acknowledged that the issue is polycentric. That is to say it is an issue which must be viewed from many standpoints, moral, ethical, philosophical, theological and scientific. It is an issue … which engenders passionate views on one side or the other in virtually all disciplines.

I do not consider that it is for a Court of law, faced with the most divergent if most learned views in the discourses available to it from the disciplines referred to, to pronounce on the truth of when human life begins.

Absent a broad consensus on that truth, it is for legislatures in the exercise of their dispositive powers to resolve such issues on the basis of policy choices.

The learned trial Judge quoted from the report of the Constitution Review Group of the Oireachtas published in July 1996 to the following effect:

> 'Definition is needed as to when the "unborn" acquires the protection of the law. Philosophers and scientists may continue to debate when human life begins but the law must define what it intends to protect.'

In my view that sums up the role of the Oireachtas in relation to this matter as the organ of State with at least initial responsibility for the protection and regulation of constitutional rights.

Therefore in the context of this case, there is uncertainty or no consensus as to when human life begins. The choice as to how life before birth can be best protected, and therefore the point which in law that protection should be deemed to commence, is a policy choice for the Oireachtas. It is one which falls to be made having taken into account all the factors and strands of thought which it considers material and relevant.

The Courts do not have at [their] disposal objective criteria to decide this as a justiciable issue. Issues are not justiciable before the Courts where there is, as Brennan J., put it in his opinion in *Baker v. Carr* [369 US 186 at 217 (1962)], 'a lack of judicially discoverable and

> manageable standards for resolving it; or the impossibility of deciding without an initial policy determination of a kind clearly for non judicial discretion; …' That is the position of this Court in this case. The onus rests in the Oireachtas, to make the initial policy determination so as to define by law when 'the life of the unborn' acquires protection. The other alternative is an amendment to the Constitution.
>
> Accordingly in my view it has not been established by the appellant, and it is not a justiciable issue for this Court to decide, that the frozen embryos, constitute 'life of the unborn' within the meaning of Article 40.3.3."

What is one to make of this analysis? The first difficulty concerns Murray C.J.'s assertion that the determination of when human life begins is not a justiciable question. The passage quoted above contains unqualified statements to this effect; but it also contains statements that suggest that the courts do retain a determinative role, after the legislature has exercised an initial policy choice. If the courts retain that role, the further question arises as to the criteria by which they should be guided. If these criteria are not effective in enabling them to exercise any role initially, how can they become effective once the legislature has acted?

The idea that the existence of a lack of consensus, globally or nationally, on the question of when human life begins should render its determination beyond the judicial pale is, it may respectfully be suggested, entirely wrong. There is no scientific controversy about the fact that the human embryo is alive and that it is an entity completely distinct from the parental elements that generated it. The controversy is not of the empirical order, but rather of the philosophical and normative orders. What does it mean to be human? And, prior that question, how should the notion of being human relate to the framework of rights? Murray C.J. is therefore mistaken in using empirical language. In this regard one should reflect, with some concern, on his statement that:

> "[o]f course Courts take judicial notice, without having to expressly say so, of obvious and accepted truths concerning the nature of the world we live in. Thus a party, in appropriate proceedings, would not have to prove that a foetus of three months constituted human life no more than a party would be required to prove the existence of the law of gravity."

Judicial notice is a concept of the law of evidence that relates to empirically provable facts, not to normative propositions. It is no more or less an empirically provable fact that a foetus of three months constitutes human life than that an embryo does, or a person in a permanent vegetative state or a person with severe dementia, or, indeed, a person with impressive intellectual powers.

In the world of philosophy as opposed to empirical fact, there is not, contrary to Murray C.J.'s confident assertion, universal acceptance that a foetus of three months is human life. Charles Hartshorne ("Concerning Abortion: An Attempt at a Rational View", *The Christian Century*, January 21, 1981, p.42) observed:

> "Of course an infant is not fully human. No one thinks it can, while an infant, be taught to speak, reason or judge right and wrong. But it is much closer to that stage than is a three-month foetus."

Somewhat more moderately, but noteworthy nonetheless, another professor in one of those "prestigious universities and halls of learning", Peter Singer of Princeton, has argued that:

> "[i]f we compare a severely defective human infant with a nonhuman animal, a dog or a pig, for example, we will often find the nonhuman to have superior capacities, both actual and potential, for rationality, self-consciousness, communication and anything else that can plausibly be considered morally significant."

He and Helga Kuhse (*Should the Baby Live?: The Problem of Handicapped Infants* (OUP, 1985)) suggest that a period of 28 days after birth might be allowed before an infant is accepted as having the same right to life as others.

In the context of the right to life of people with severe restrictions on brain capacity or with other significant disabilities, yet again there is no global or national consensus on the value to be ascribed to the lives in question. Some have gone so far as to argue that people in a deep coma, in a permanent vegetative state, are not alive; others have argued that, though alive, they lack sufficient interests to protect them from having their lives terminated. Professor Julian Savulescu, of yet another prestigious hall of learning, Oxford, has commented ("Death us and Our Bodies: Personal Reflections", (2003) 29 *Journal of Medical Ethics* 127, 130) that "[s]ince I believe we die when our meaningful mental life ceases, organs should be available from that point, which may signficantly predate brain death."

Article 40.3.1, which protects the right to life of citizens, makes no attempt to address this lack of consensus. The logic of Murray C.J.'s analysis is that the courts should retreat from this area of normative controversy in the absence of prior legislation. Of course, these cases differ from those relating to the earlier stages of life, since the constitutional protection for the lives in question has already started, in contrast to the early stages of life, where the Chief Justice proposes that the legislature should have the power to delay the commencement of that protection. But if the existence of a lack of consensus as to whether a particular human being is entitled to be characterised as "human life" is sufficient to repel the courts from an adjudicative competence in the early stages of life's journey, why should a similar lack of consensus not result in the same compulsory retreat of the courts in the later stages, enabling the legislature to deny constitutional protection to older human beings on the same basis as human beings at the earliest stage of their life?

Murray C.J.'s invocation of the "political question doctrine" from the jurisprudence of the United States Supreme Court seems hard to explain. That doctrine does not extend to the kind of normative issue that arose in *Roche v Roche*. Most, if not all, normative issues involve debate in society. If the lack of consensus on crucial normative issues were to place them beyond the adjudicative competence of courts, the heart of constitutional jurisprudence would be destroyed.

Let us now consider the extent to which Murray C.J. seeks to qualify this proposition that the issue of when human life begins is not justiciable and that it should be determined by the legislature. Although he makes an unqualified claim to non-justiciability twice in the passage quoted above, he qualifies this twice by indicating that it is the Oireachtas which has "at least initial responsibility" for the matter and that "[t]he onus rests in the Oireachtas, to make the initial policy determination so as to define by law when 'the life of the unborn' acquires protection". The Chief Justice makes no attempt to explain how these qualified statements are capable of reconciliation with his unqualified assertions of non-justiciability; nor does he indicate how the courts are to engage with what apparently is to become a justiciable issue once the legislature has acted. Must they concede to the Oireachtas the entitlement to delay the commencement of constitutional protection to human beings after conception for such period as the Oireachtas may choose? Is the Oireachtas entitled to delay affording constitutional protection up to the point where a consensus, global or national, exists that human life exists? If the latter is the position, then it is noteworthy that the Chief Justice's careful use of language does not commit him to the proposition that implantation represents that point in life's journey at which such a consensus exists. He noted that conception and implantation were the two reference points with which the court was concerned "for present purposes". He observed that he supposed "it could be said that there was a broad consensus among all disciplines that human life begins at implantation of the embryo in the womb or at least not long thereafter". Yet the only point which the Chief Justice definitively identifies as being that where human life exists beyond argument is that of three months' gestational age. This is not of course to interpret the Chief Justice's remarks as suggesting that legislation delaying legal protection to close to that age would be constitutional; it is, however, noteworthy that he specifically disdained identifying implantation as the latest point at which the Oireachtas was entitled to delay protection and that his use of the absence of consensus as a justification for affording legislative entitlement to delay protection opens the possibility of further delay in light of increasing international divergence on the value of unborn life.

The primary weakness of Murray C.J.'s approach is its failure to interpret the Constitution in a coherent philosophical and normative way. Some constitutions limit themselves to normatively neutral provisions relating to such matters as the separation of powers and the respective roles of executive, legislature and judiciary. Other constitutions—of which the Irish Constitution is a striking example—contain a discernable philosophical and normative perspective. They may be based on the theory of human rights that is premised on an understanding of certain rights—including the right to life—as being inherent in human beings, not the mere product of legislation, but prior to positive law. The notion of dignity—the inherent equal worth of every human being—underlies these constitutions. (The Chief Justice indeed refers to human dignity in the international context but fails to develop any substantial analysis of the concept and its implications for human beings and the protection of their rights.)

The Supreme Court was called on to interpret Art.40.3.3° in light of the philosophical and normative framework of the Constitution. The court's task was greatly eased by the fact that the clear intent of the Amendment had been to clarify what was implicit in the Constitution rather than to insert a set of values inconsistent with those underlying that framework (as the divorce amendment of 1995 did: see the *Annual Review of Irish Law 1995*, pp.138–144). The lack of consensus which Murray C.J. identified as a reason for the court's disentitlement to engage in this process was in fact the inspiration of the Amendment: to ensure that, in times of normative controversy and debate, the unborn would be protected in accordance with the identifiable human rights philosophy of the Constitution as originally promulgated, until the People at some future date might choose to remove that protection by way of a further constitutional amendment. While concerns were concentrated on the dangers of judicial developments which might have these negative effects, the intent was not to surrender to the Oireachtas the power to restrict or remove constitutional protection from unborn human beings.

It may be interesting in this context to consider what Walsh J. intended to convey in *McGee v Attorney General* [1974] I.R. 284 at 312 in a passage in his judgment, quoted by Murray C.J., to the effect that:

> "[a]ny action on the part of either the husband or the wife or the State to limit family sizes by endangering or destroying human life must necessarily not only be an offence against the common good but also against the guaranteed personal rights of the citizen."

As Murray C.J. notes, "that passage was at the time referred to by some as a reason for considering that the then constitutional amendment was unnecessary." Walsh J. was speaking in a context where contraception was the issue requiring constitutional analysis and it seems reasonable to interpret his observation as casting doubt on the lawfulness of abortifacients. That Walsh J. had abortifacients in mind receives some support from Griffin J.'s observation in *McGee* that his judgment was confined "to contraception as such" and was "not intended to apply to abortifacients, though called contraceptives, as in the case of abortifacients entirely different considerations may arise". (The Health (Family Planning) Act 1979, enacted six years after *McGee*, specifically provided in s.10(c) that nothing in that Act should be construed as authorising the sale, importation, manufacture, advertising or display of abortifacients.) The issue relating to abortifacients is significant as it raised the question of the protection of life at pre-implantation stage.

The point worth noting here is that, in *McGee*, neither Walsh J. nor Griffin J. took the view that courts were required to refrain from considering who fell within the constitutional protection of the right to life under Art.40.3.1 on account of the absence of a consensus on the question. It would be curious if the implications of Murray C.J.'s analysis should be that the Constitution as promulgated in 1937 provided protection to the right to life of embryonic human life while an amendment specifically designed to copperfasten that protection actually dismantled it, on the basis of a rationale—the absence of consensus—which, if sound, should have applied also to the Constitution as promulgated.

NULLITY OF MARRIAGE

In the *Annual Review of Irish Law 2004*, pp.280–285, we analysed the High Court decision of *LB v T MacC* [2004] IEHC 409, in which O'Higgins J. dismissed an uncontested petition for nullity of marriage based on fraud and the respondent's lack of capacity to maintain a normal marriage relationship with the petitioner. The parties had married in 1993. The gravamen of the petition, supported by the evidence of the psychiatrist appointed by the court to carry out a psychiatric evaluation of the parties, was that the respondent had a personality disorder to such an extent as to make it impossible for him to consent to, and sustain, marriage to the petitioner.

Unquestionably the respondent, a Scottish chartered surveyor, had not prospered in a succession of business enterprises and was financially irresponsible. The psychiatrist, who interviewed each party for four hours, came to his conclusion that the respondent had a narcissistic personality disorder based on a "triad for diagnosis" of "self-importance or grandiosity, the need for admiration and the inability to empathise with others".

O'Higgins J. critically analysed some of the facts that grounded the psychiatrist's conclusion. These included a letter seeking employment in which the respondent said that he had been "head-hunted" by a particular company and correspondence with Scottish art dealers in which the respondent had sought to have three pictures sent to his Dublin address at a time when he was in debt to the dealers. O'Higgins J. considered that the claim in the letter was "nothing but a minor puff to cover up a gap in his curriculum vitae and to account for a period of unsuccessful business activity". As regards the correspondence with the art dealers, O'Higgins J. found nothing strange in the request; the respondent's letter indicated that the cheque enclosed with it reduced the respondent's indebtedness to £12.88.

In the appeal heard five years later, the Supreme Court affirmed O'Higgins J.'s judgment. Kearns J. (Macken and Finnegan JJ. concurring) considered that O'Higgins J. had been perfectly entitled to assess the respondent's assertion as to having been "head-hunted" as a "minor puff". Kearns J. considered that this was "a far from unusual or untoward experience in human affairs". It was a "given" that a person would try to exaggerate his talents in such a situation. Similarly, O'Higgins J. had been entitled to take the view that it was in no way unusual for a person to deal with a company to whom one owed money as the respondent had done. The amount due to the art dealers was hardly a matter of any significance. Kearns J. had:

> "... no difficulty in accepting the proposition that, from the petitioner's point of view, the respondent transpired to be something other than the man she thought she was marrying, but indeed one may regretfully observe that the same could be said of many marriages. The petitioner's complaints are almost entirely addressed to the conduct of the respondent, conduct which was undoubtedly feckless, irresponsible and immature. Nearly all of the behaviour relied upon occurred subsequent to the marriage and does not relate to the respondent's capacity at the time of the marriage. Further, the evidence does not support a view of the respondent as a confidence trickster cut from the same cloth as the eponymous anti-hero of Thomas Mann's novel 'Confessions of Felix Krull, Confidence Man' (Penguin, 1958). Even if it did, the evidence comes nowhere close to establishing that the respondent lacked capacity to contract to a valid marriage."

Kearns J. was particularly mindful in this context of the passages from the judgment of McGuinness J. in *PF v G O'M (otherwise GF)* [2001] 3 I.R. 1 where she had drawn a clear distinction between conduct on the one hand and incapacity and disability on the other. It seems clear enough that the Supreme Court no longer adheres to the curiously broad approach to grounds for annulment based on lack of consent which it had favoured in *M O'M (otherwise OC) v B O'C* [1996] 1 I.R. 208. The more restrained test elaborated in *PF v G O'M otherwise GF* is now the established limit. As Kearns J. acknowledged in the instant case, the Constitution "imposes a clear obligation on the court to uphold the marriage contract..."

FINANCIAL PROVISION

Protection of a spouse's self-esteem In the *Annual Review of Irish Law 2006*, pp.377–378, we critically analysed Abbott J.'s decision in *SN v P O'D*, High Court, November 29, 2006, awarding the husband of a very rich and successful wife €1,648,800 to compensate him for his comparative lack of success in business and his consequent lack of esteem. He observed:

> "[W]ith the children and their day to day care on the husband's side giving rise to an equality of self-esteem issue I consider that the husband requires further assets if they cannot be justified under any other criterion."

Abbott J. emphasised:

> "... the need to ensure by way of ancillary relief provisions that the husband in this case when dealing with the children when in his care or while on holidays, is not shown up by an embarrassing gap in wealth when compared with the children's mother. Such a gap in wealth in my view could easily result in the husband suffering such loss of self esteem, grieving or obsession with the litigation that he would easily lose the capacity to celebrate, enjoy, and be bubbly with his children as a father should".

On appeal to the Supreme Court, Abbott J.'s approach received no support. Fennelly J. (Denham and Finnegan JJ. concurring) could find no basis in s.20 of the Family Law Act 1995 or in any notion of "proper provision" for an award designed to compensate one party for loss of self-esteem. Fennelly J. noted that the wife had claimed that, in effect, Abbott J.'s order of this sum had amounted to discrimination in favour of her husband on the grounds of gender. She had not pressed this argument at the hearing of the appeal, however, Fennelly J. commenting, "in my view correctly so. The ground upon which the learned judge awarded th[is] su[m] could equally apply to either husband or wife."

While of course Abbott J. did not expressly base his award on the husband's gender and used language that was capable of applying to either spouse regardless of gender, it remains a remarkable phenomenon that there is no record of an Irish court's ever having awarded a wife compensation for the loss of self-esteem she would suffer when rearing her children in financial circumstances that did not match those of her husband. To interpret Abbot J.'s remarks as gender-neutral seems frankly implausible.

Order for sale In *DH v GH* [2009] IEHC 517, in judicial separation proceedings, Sheehan J. considered that the interests of justice were best met by ordering the sale of all of the seven properties, including the family home, in which the spouses had beneficial interests. They had married in 1980 and had two adult children. The wife was 53 years old, her husband 61. Neither was still working. The properties (including one in France) were valued at over €9 million, with charges on them coming to around €6 million. Sheehan J. observed in this context that:

> "[n]otwithstanding the significant equity placed on this property portfolio by the [wife]'s valuer, the valuations must nevertheless be seen in light of the [husband]'s failure to raise a further €200,000 in or about July 2009."

The husband was "primarily responsible" for the property portfolio, much of which he had acquired before the marriage; the wife had worked for two years following the marriage in employment outside the home; thereafter, she had been "primarily involved in looking after the home and family", though she had been involved for a few years after 1999 in the family business on a part-time basis. At the time of judgment, the spouses were residing, though not together, in what had been their family home. Neither seriously envisaged being able to retain it.

Sheehan J., when crafting his order, laid emphasis on the need to avoid any risk to the husband's ability to discharge all debt. He considered it preferable to order that all the properties be sold than to follow the suggestion of counsel for the wife to order the immediate sale of the family home in order to realise interim funds for providing her with accommodation.

Judge's role in ruling settlement In *P v Judge McDonagh* [2009] IEHC 316, in judicial separation proceedings which were being converted into divorce proceedings, the question of allocation of the spouses' substantial assets came into focus. The Circuit Court judge, when perusing the terms of a settlement agreement reached by the spouses during the course of the proceedings, expressed the view that a 49 per cent/51 per cent split in favour of the wife was not proper provision and that he wanted to see a 55 per cent/45 per cent split in her favour. In relation to a proposed lump sum payment of €120,000 to her, the judge said he "wanted to see the figure of €240,000" before he would rule the settlement. When the husband indicated that he was not prepared to vary from the agreed settlement terms, the judge stated that the husband "could give a further one acre" to the wife. The husband's counsel pointed out that the value of the field was around €175,000. The husband refused to renegotiate the settlement terms. The judge then said words which the husband's solicitor and counsel understood to be on the lines that, if the husband was not prepared to give the sum, there was an easy solution: the judge would "just make an order in those terms". The solicitor for the wife understood the words to have been that the judge would "hear the case and then make an appropriate order". Counsel for the husband requested the judge to discharge himself from the remainder of the case. The judge declined. Judicial proceedings against the judge were successful.

In an insightful analysis, Clarke J. discreetly qualified Barron J.'s unwise insistence in *Orange Ltd v Director of Telecoms (No. 2)* [2000] 4 I.R. 159 that bias would "always predate the actual decision or contemplated decision. Bias does not come into existence in the course of a hearing." Clarke J. considered that there was a form of pre-judgment:

> "... which arises where the adjudicator indicates that the adjudicator has reached a conclusion on a question in controversy between the parties, at a time prior to it being proper for such adjudicator to reach such a decision (indeed it might well be more accurate to describe such a situation as premature judgment rather than pre-judgment). It can hardly be said that a reasonable and objective and well informed person would be any the less concerned that a party to proceedings was not going to get a fair adjudication if, at an early stage of the hearing, comments were made by the adjudicator which made it clear that the adjudicator had reached a decision on some important point in the case at a time when no reasonable adjudicator could have, while complying with the principles of natural justice, reached such a conclusion".

In the instant case it was accepted that the judge had a jurisdiction, and indeed a statutory and constitutional duty, to consider whether the settlement concerned provided adequate provision for the wife. He had been "more than entitled" to come to the view, on the basis of the information then currently before him, that the settlement had not made such adequate provision. It was also accepted that where, on the basis of the information then currently available, a particular level of settlement in matrimonial proceedings appeared insufficient to amount to proper provision, a judge was entitled to give an indication as to the sort of provision that would so satisfy the judge. However, when so doing it was important that a judge make clear that the exercise engaged in was a determination by the judge as to whether, on the basis of the information *then* available, the settlement proposed appeared to make proper provision. It was also important that it be clear to the parties that, in the event that the case continued, the judge had not closed his or her mind to any further evidence or argument that might be made thereafter that might legitimately alter the judge's view as to what might be the minimum amount of provision that might be regarded as proper:

> "It is one thing for a judge to say, before a case has ended, that he is not satisfied that proper provision is being offered on the basis of the information then currently available. It is another thing entirely for a

judge to say, at the same stage, that the final order is going to be of a particular type and, by inference, that that would be so irrespective of what other evidence or argument might be addressed."

MAINTENANCE ENTITLEMENTS

Lump sum order where parents are not married In *E McE v J O'S* [2009] IEHC 52, the Circuit Court judge had made an order under s.11(1) of the Guardianship of Infants Act 1964 (the "1964 Act") requiring the father of a child born outside marriage in 2000 to pay €500,000 to the child's mother for the purchase of appropriate accommodation for her and the child. The father was a married man with three children of his marriage as well as two children born outside marriage. On appeal, Sheehan J. reversed this order. In his view, Budd J.'s decision in *MY v A Y*, High Court, December 11, 1995 was not a supporting precedent since in that case the parties had been married. In Sheehan J.'s view, the court was required to consider the constitutional provision of the family when approaching the interpretation of the 1964 Act. He noted that, in *Murphy v Attorney General* [1982] I.R. 241, the Supreme Court stated that:

> "[t]he pledge … to guard with special care the institution of marriage is a guarantee that this institution in all its constitutional connotations, including the pledge given in Article 41, s.2, sub-s.2, as to the position of the mother in the home, will be given special protection so that it can continue to fulfil its function as the basis of the family and as a permanent, indissoluble union of man and woman."

In *Ennis v Butterly* [1996] I.R. 426, Kelly J. had stated:

> "[N]otwithstanding the extensive reform of family law which has taken place in this country over the last 20 years, nowhere does one find any attempt on the part of the legislature to substantially enhance the legal position of, or to confer rights akin to those of married persons upon, the parties to non-marital unions, e.g. a right to maintenance."

In reaching this conclusion Kelly J. had found support in what Henchy J. had said in *State (Nicolaou) v An Bord Uchtála* [1966] I.R. 567:

> "For the State to award equal constitutional protection to the family founded on marriage and the 'family' founded on an extramarital union would in effect be a disregard of the pledge which the State gives in Article 41, s.3, sub-s.1 to guard with special care the institution of marriage."

Taking all the above matters into consideration Sheehan J. considered himself "obliged to conclude" that the Circuit Court had no jurisdiction under s.11 of the 1964 Act to make the order directing payment of a lump sum of €500,000.

Sheehan J.'s conclusion is of some considerable importance, raising a number of questions. Must legislation that does not on its face distinguish between the rights of children nonetheless be interpreted as having this effect in light of the constitutional provision of the family based on marriage? It will be recalled that in *O'B v S* [1984] I.R. 316, the Supreme Court held that Art.41 authorised the Oireachtas to make such distinctions but it did not hold that the Oireachtas was required to do so. No one has seriously suggested that the Status of Children Act 1987, removing many of these distinctions, is unconstitutional in light of Art.41.

Of course, what must have been on Sheehan J.'s mind was the fact that, in the instant case, the father was married. An order requiring him to pay €500,000 to a woman who was not his wife would substantially deplete the resources available for the support and financial welfare of his wife and his children born within marriage. At the heart of the issue is the nature of a lump sum payment made under s.11. Is it for the benefit of the child or the child's mother? If it is for the benefit of the child, then, it may be suggested, there is no difficulty whatsoever in making a lump sum order under s.11 in respect of a child born outside marriage, regardless of whether the father is married. (The same applies in relation to a lump sum order made against a mother of a child born outside marriage where she is a married woman with children born within marriage.) Indeed, it may be argued that any distinction in this context based on the marital status of the child's parents would be unconstitutional. Whatever merit there may be in interpreting the Constitution as permitting, though not requiring, discrimination in relation to succession entitlements of children—and one suspects that *O'B v S* could well be reconsidered by the Supreme Court were the issue to arise again—it surely is not the case that discrimination in relation to children's maintenance is permissible. The idea that a child should be denied proper maintenance so as to protect the institution of marriage seems highly controversial, since it targets an innocent, dependent person. Whether a distinction can justly be made between maintenance and succession is not clear. Of course in many cases children will not succeed to their parents' estate until they have grown up and are no longer in need of maintenance, but in some cases children lose their parents when they still depend on them for support.

At all events, questions of characterisation arise in regard to an order for a lump sum payment of €500,000 to the mother of a child born outside marriage for appropriate accommodation for her and her child. Is this truly and exclusively an order for maintenance of the child, or more broadly, an order for the child's welfare? Is there no independent element of benefit for the mother? Should any benefit that she may derive from living in the house be regarded as no more than collateral to the benefit that will inure to the child?

Clarification of prior order In *DO v Her Honour Judge Olive Buttimer* [2009] IEHC 162, Hedigan J. dismissed judicial review proceedings alleging, inter alia, lack of fair procedure, where the respondent judge, when clarifying the terms of an order for maintenance which she had made in earlier proceedings, had not asked the applicant for his financial documentation. The applicant had, however, submitted to the judge that he objected to the amount being claimed and also indicated his inability to pay. Allowing for "a certain measure of informality in the manner in which such hearings are conducted", it appeared to Hedigan J. that the applicant's claim had not been sustained on the evidence. The earlier order for maintenance, which was being clarified, had been made following a hearing in which both sides had been heard. The clarification had not involved a change of mind on the part of the judge.

GUARDIANSHIP OF CHILDREN

Guardianship agreements In *ER O'B (a minor) v Minister for Justice, Equality and Law Reform* [2009] IEHC 423, O'Neill J. rejected a claim that, under the Constitution and the European Convention on Human Rights, the State was required to maintain a register of guardianship agreements. The claimant was a child born outside marriage in 2006, whose parents had elected to exercise a joint statutory declaration that they would be her joint guardians. The essence of the claim made on her behalf was that, if the guardianship agreement were lost or destroyed, she would risk losing her rights associated with having her father as a guardian unless his guardianship could be proved by other evidence. This contrasted with the position of children whose parents were married since the law required the registration of the marriage.

O'Neill J. considered that the decision of the Supreme Court in *North Western Health Board v HW and CW* [2001] 3 I.R. 622, analysed in detail in the *Annual Review of Irish Law 2001*, pp.316–338, was a barrier to the claim. This had held that parents had primary responsibility for their children's upbringing and welfare. The State was, in O'Neill J.'s view, entitled to expect parents to take "reasonable precautions in the interests of their children", which would include looking after a guardianship agreement. All that needed to be done was to create a number of copies, to have them certified if desired and to place them in safekeeping. Even if a guardianship agreement were lost or destroyed, secondary evidence as to its existence could be given, though O'Neill J. acknowledged that this would not deal with emergency cases where it was immediately necessary to establish who the guardians were. At all events, he was satisfied that the absence of a register did not constitute a violation of the child's rights under Art.40.3.

Neither did the present position constitute invidious discrimination under Art.40.1. The primary purpose of the register of marriages was "for relevant reasons of social policy in that regard", to record all marriages solemnised in the State rather than to disclose the guardianship of marital children. Whilst from birth the guardians of a marital child could be gleaned from the register, changes that might occur later in the life of a child in relation to guardianship, as when a testamentary guardian or court-appointed guardian came into being on the death of a parent, were not recorded on the register.

O'Neill J. also rejected a claim based on art.8 of the European Convention. While States had a positive duty to vindicate article 8 rights where there was "a direct and immediate link between the measures sought by the applicant and the latter's private and/or family life" (*Botta v Italy* (1998) 26 E.H.R.R. 241, para.34), O'Neill J. was satisfied that no such link existed in the instant case between the risk of loss or destruction of the guardianship agreement and the introduction of a public register of guardianship agreements. Such a risk could "easily be eliminated entirely" by the exercise of care by the parents. The legislatively ordained entitlements of parents to enter guardianship agreements, exercisable through the mechanism provided in the Guardianship of Children (Statutory Declaration) Regulations 1998 (S.I. No. 5 of 1998), in O'Neill J.'s view exceeded any obligation that might rest on the State in this context.

Counsel for the State had argued that decisions on the allocation of public funds were exclusively a matter for the executive and that, even if the costs involved in establishing a public register were minimal, this could not permit an infringement of the principle of the separation of powers. O'Neill J. accepted this argument though it is notable that he laid emphasis on the policy choices that the executive and legislature might have to make rather than forming an objection to justiciability in terms of the need for courts to avoid implicating the State in how specifically to allocate some of its resources.

PRACTICE AND PROCEDURE

Delay In *M v Judge Ó Donnabháinn* [2009] IEHC 167 the applicant, in family law proceedings initiated by his wife in 2001, had counterclaimed for nullity of marriage in 2002. Until 2004 he had legal representation; from then on he represented himself. Matters proceeded very slowly thereafter. A date for trial was eventually settled, in 2007. On the morning of the hearing the report of a psychologist, appointed by the court to act as medical inspector, was made available to the parties and to the court. The applicant applied unsuccessfully for an adjournment to enable him to consider the report. The case went ahead, with neither party electing to call the psychologist as a witness. The applicant's nullity proceedings were dismissed.

Judicial review proceedings, alleging breach of the applicant's right to fair proceedings, were unsuccessful. O'Neill J. emphasised the failure of the applicant to have assembled the proofs necessary to support his case. In this respect, the refusal to grant an adjournment had not affected the applicant's claim:

> "The appointment of the Medical Examiner is not for the purpose of providing an applicant with the proofs necessary to make out the nullity case. The role of the Medical Examiner is to assist the court with independent expert evidence on the issues which arise in the nullity application which would in the ordinary course, in the context of the grounds alleged by the applicant, involve expertise, generally in the areas of psychiatry or psychology.
>
> Notwithstanding this, the applicant proceeded into this nullity case without any attempt, apparently, on his part, to obtain evidence to support his case."

In O'Neill J.'s view, the respondent judge has been:

> "... entitled to be conscious of the fact that these family law proceedings were at that time in being for six years, and regardless of what determination was made on the nullity application, further proceedings would be necessary in order to bring the original application to a conclusion. Thus, in my opinion, having regard to the court's independent obligation to ensure and promote the expeditious determination of proceedings, the respondent was manifestly entitled to have regard to the extraordinary delay that had already occurred in the case, in dealing with any application for an adjournment".

A further reason for dismissing the judicial review proceedings was that the applicant's ex parte application was about eight days outside the time limit prescribed by Ord.84 r.1 of the Rules of the Superior Courts. The applicant had mistakenly believed that he could commence the application in the Central Office rather than to the court. O'Neill J. thought there was "considerable merit" in the contention of the notice party, the applicant's wife, that the delay had exacerbated the prejudice she had suffered in putting off the day when she could finally have the break-up of her marriage and her status thereafter regulated.

In *Mannion v Bergin practising as O'Connor and Bergin Solicitors* [2009] IEHC 165, the defendants had acted for the plaintiff in family law proceedings culminating in a hearing in judicial separation proceedings in 1997. In 1999, the plaintiff had issued a plenary summons alleging negligence on their part. In July 2008 the defendants sought dismissal of the claim on the basis of inordinate and inexcusable delay and for want of prosecution. The plaintiff sought to explain the delay in claiming that his attention had been focused on the family law proceedings until their conclusion in 2004; since then, he said, he had been trying to ascertain how to obtain evidence from a solicitor as to the extent of the duty of a solicitor conducting family law proceedings. Hedigan J. rejected these excuses as the plaintiff had:

"... solicitors on record in these proceedings to progress them whilst his family law proceedings came to conclusion. His claim of difficulty in obtaining a professional witness to prove the standards required of a solicitor in conducting family law proceedings seems to me to be quite hollow".

Payment from proceeds of sale In *Keogh v Brian P Doyle trading as Heritage Solicitors* [2009] IEHC 313, Murphy J. declined to order a mandatory injunction requiring the solicitor of the mother of the plaintiff's child to deliver up the plaintiff's share of the proceeds of sale of property held jointly by her and the plaintiff. The property had been purchased in 1998 with a loan of £67,000 and a contribution by the mother of £20,000. An agreement between her and the plaintiff provided that she should have the option to have the house sold at a price to be agreed between her and the plaintiff (or a reputable valuer, in default of agreement); out of the proceeds, the sum of £20,000 should be paid to her and the balance equally divided between her and the plaintiff; each would contribute equally to the repayment of the mortgage and the plaintiff's payment in this respect should be deemed to discharge his legal responsibility for the financial maintenance of his child. The mother had obtained an interim maintenance order against the plaintiff in 2004. This order had not been enforced. When the property was sold in 2008, for €300,000, the mother objected to the release of proceeds unless the plaintiff made a compensatory payment in respect of maintenance for his child. Murphy J. noted that the 1998 agreement had been drafted by the plaintiff's solicitors and that the mother had not been separately advised. He referred to s.27 of the Family Law (Maintenance of Spouses and Children) Act 1976, which provides that an agreement is to be void in so far as it would have the effect of excluding or limiting the operation of any provision of that Act (other than s.21, relating to household allowances, which was not of relevance in the instant case). He considered that the payments made by the plaintiff in respect of the property were either maintenance or a contribution to the mortgage; they could not be both. The position relating to the plaintiff's possible liability under the interim maintenance order was not entirely clear. In the circumstances, Murphy J. considered it "clear" that the solicitor could not pay out any balance until the issues were resolved between the plaintiff and the mother, who, Murphy J. noted, was not a party to the instant application.

Discoverability of judges' notes In *O'Q v Judge Buttimer* [2009] IEHC 25, where a dispute had arisen between spouses as to the exact terms of an order relating to maintenance made by a Circuit Court judge and the judge later clarified what she had originally ordered, the husband took judicial review proceedings seeking an order for certiorari to quash the maintenance order. Before the Master of the High Court he obtained an order for discovery of the judge's notes in regard to the original hearing but an appeal to the High Court was successful.

Edwards J. emphasised the principle of judicial independence. In his view, "a strong argument" could be made in favour of the existence of a constitutional immunity or privilege rendering a judge's notes non-compellable in any proceedings:

> "A judge's notes are a personal *aide memoire* taken by the judge in the course of a case. They are intended for the judge's use and the judge's use alone. They are not intended to be referred to or used by any other person. A judge's notes are unlike, for example, hospital or medical notes in that there is no requirement that they should be generated and kept according to any established protocol. Nor is a judge required to use any standard form of notation. Some judges may write everything down in every case. Other judges may do that in some cases but in other cases may prefer to listen carefully to the evidence or to the arguments, or to observe the demeanour of a witness, taking only essential notes … The extent of the note taken in any case and the system of note taking employed is entirely up to the individual judge. The judge may use his or her own shorthand or none at all. He or she may have their own system of memory prompts. He or she may cross reference different pieces of evidence according to their own system. The notes may also record a judge's impression of a witness's credibility and reliability. There may be case citations or references to published material. Simply put the notes may be more or less comprehensive as the judge sees fit, and they may take any form that the judge sees fit."

The difficulty with making such notes available to a third party was that they would frequently require deciphering or explanation by the note-taker. This raised the spectre of a judge's having to explain, and possibly being cross-examined upon, his or her notes, which would be "inimical to the notion of judicial independence and contrary to the public interest".

Edwards J. did not consider it necessary in the circumstances of the instant case to express a definite view of whether judges' notes were non-compellable on grounds of constitutional immunity, since oral or affidavit evidence was a viable option, rendering the need for discovery nugatory. He expressed the strong view, however, that if discovery of judges' notes were theoretically possible, this could only happen in the most exceptional circumstances where the necessity for it was clearly demonstrable.

Fisheries and Harbours

FISHERIES

Designated European Union law offences Section 14 of the Sea-Fisheries and Maritime Jurisdiction Act 2006 (the "2006 Act") (*Annual Review of Irish Law 2006*, pp.390–394) provides that, without prejudice to the generality of s.3(1) of the European Communities Act 1972, the Minister for Agriculture, Fisheries and Food may, by Regulations, prescribe measures to give effect to any provision either of the EU Treaties or Community law. Section 14(3) of the 2006 Act provides that a contravention of such a Regulation is a criminal offence. The Sea-Fisheries (Recording of Catches) Regulations 2009 (S.I. No. 253 of 2009), which were made under s.14 of the 2006 Act and relate to fisheries control systems and rules for the recording of fish catches, thus provide that a contravention of any provision of Regulation 2807/83, as amended, Regulation 2847/93, as amended, and Regulation 1006/2008 is an offence under the 2006 Act. The 2009 Regulations came into force on July 2, 2009.

Prosecution of offences by Director of Public Prosecutions The Sea-Fisheries (Prosecution of Offences) Order 2009 (S.I. No. 314 of 2009) appointed August 1, 2009 as the day from which the Director of Public Prosecutions became the prosecutor, in lieu of the Attorney General, of sea-fisheries offences as specified in s.39(1) of the Sea-Fisheries and Maritime Jurisdiction Act 2006 (*Annual Review of Irish Law 2006*, p.393).

HARBOURS

The Harbours (Amendment) Act 2009 (the "2009 Act") amended the Harbours Act 1996 (the "2006 Act") (*Annual Review of Irish Law 1996*, pp.390–396) in a number of significant respects in order to implement certain aspects of the Government's 2005 *Ports Policy Statement*, which followed a 2003 High Level Review of the State's commercial ports and the 2001–2002 statutory performance audit of the port companies (the Packer audit).

Limits of a port company's harbour Section 3 of the 2009 Act inserted a completely new text of s.9 of the 1996 Act, which deals with the limits of a port company's harbour. Section 9 of the 1996 Act, as amended, now contains a list of principles and policies a Minister must have regard to when considering an application to alter a company's harbour limits. It was specifically noted in the Oireachtas debate that the insertion of such principles and policies arose from advice received from the Attorney General to ensure that s.9 would be consistent with the decision of the Supreme Court in *Cityview Press Ltd v An Chomhairle Oiliúna* [1980] I.R. 381. The principles in the amended s.9 of the 1996 Act include: planning applications or planning permissions under the Planning and Development Acts 2000 to 2006, various regulatory processes under the Foreshore Act 1933, and navigational safety as well as the current and expected capacity of the harbour. It was also noted that the changes made to s.9 of the 1996 Act had specific implications for the proposed development of a new deep water facility at Bremore by Drogheda Port Company and its partners.

Investing outside the State The 2009 Act also sought to enhance the ability of port companies to invest outside the limits of their harbours. Section 11(4)(d) of the 1996 Act restricted port companies from investing outside the State unless such investment would "promote the interest of trade or tourism in the State". Section 4 of the 2009 Act deleted this restrictive provision in s.11(4)(d) of the 1996 Act, and s.5 inserted a new s.12A into the 1996 Act, which provides for port companies to invest outside their harbour limits, including outside the State, provided consent from both the Minister for Transport and the Minister for Finance has been granted. The removal of this restrictive limitation is in line with the strategic objective of enhancing and underpinning the commercial ethos of the commercial ports sector, and it was pointed out in the Oireachtas debate that this brought the sector into line with other State commercial bodies such as the Electricity Supply Board and the Dublin Airport Authority.

Role of An Bord Pleanála Section 7 of the 2009 Act amended a number of sections of the Planning and Development Act 2000 in order to transfer certain functions of the Minister for Transport regarding the compulsory purchase of land by port companies to An Bord Pleanála. Prior to the 2009 Act, port companies seeking to make a compulsory purchase order needed to apply for a ministerial acquisition order under the Fourth Schedule to the Harbours Act 1996. It was stated during the Oireachtas debate that, while this function had been exercised only once since 1996, it was felt more appropriate that this power be transferred to An Bord Pleanála given its role, pursuant to the Planning and Development (Strategic Infrastructure) Act 2006, as the determining body in respect of planning consent for strategic infrastructure developments at commercial ports. It was thus anticipated that An Bord Pleanála would, over time, acquire and build up a body of expertise and experience in the planning aspects of major infrastructural development generally, and particularly, in this case, on port projects. It was also pointed out that similar functions with regard to the compulsory acquisition of land by Aer Rianta (now the Dublin Airport Authority) were transferred to An Bord Pleanála under the Air Navigation and Transport (Amendment) Act 1998 and that similar transfers of ministerial functions had taken place in respect of compulsory acquisition of land by local authorities under the Roads Acts and Housing Act 1966.

Borrowing capabilities of port companies Section 9 of the 2009 Act amended s.23 of the 1996 Act in order to enhance the capabilities of port companies by introducing a greater degree of flexibility into a port company's borrowing capabilities. The 1996 Act had restricted the port companies to borrowing a sum up to 50 per cent of the value of their fixed assets, subject to the consent of the Minister for Transport and the Minister for Finance. The changes made to s.23 of the 1996 Act by s.9 of the 2009 Act empowers a port company, or a subsidiary, to borrow up to €200 million or 50 per cent of the value of its fixed assets, whichever is higher. This remains subject to the consent of the Minister for Transport and the Minister for Finance. In addition, s.23 of the 1996 Act, as amended, inserted the principles and policies a Minister must have regard to when making an order to vary the 50 per cent limit, as required by the *Cityview Press* decision: see also the discussion of s.3 of the 2009 Act above.

Reform of port company board structure It was pointed out during the Oireachtas debate on the 2009 Act that the *Ports Policy Statement* had referred to the need to enhance the commercial mandate of the port companies by facilitating improved port company board performance through the reform of board structure. The Harbours Act 1996 had provided for port company boards to consist of 12 members, comprising three directors appointed on the nomination of the relevant local authority, one or two employee directors—depending on the size of the company—either directly elected by the employees or appointed by the Minister for Transport to represent employee interests, and a chief executive officer. The remaining directors were to be appointed at the discretion of the Minister. It was noted that, in the case of some of the smaller port companies, the number of directors exceeded the total number of employees and had the potential to create an additional financial burden on those companies. Section 8 of the 2009 Act, therefore, amended the articles of association of each port company to provide for a total of eight directors on each board. To achieve this reduction, s.11 of the 2009 Act amended the 1996 Act by removing the statutory representation of local authority directors on boards and by standardising the number of employee directors at one per port company. The removal of the statutory representation of local authority directors implemented, belatedly, a recommendation to that effect made in the *Report of the Commercial Harbours Review Group*, which had broadly shaped the contents of the Harbours Act 1996.

Regional harbours Section 18 of the 2009 Act inserted a new s.87A into the 1996 Act to deal specifically with two regional harbours, Bantry Bay Harbour and Tralee and Fenit Pier and Harbour. This was intended to implement recommendations in the 1999 *Review of Regional Harbours*, and reiterated in the 2003 High Level Review of the State commercial ports and the 2005 *Ports Policy Statement*. Section 87A of the 1996 Act, as inserted by the 2009 Act, introduced an enabling provision allowing for a ministerial order to be made transferring Tralee and Fenit Harbour to the control of Shannon Foynes Port Company and Bantry Bay to Port of Cork Company. This added a third option in addition to the two options that already existed under the 1996 Act, that is, establishment of a private company or transfer to local authority control. During the Oireachtas debate on the 2009 Act, a requirement was included for a consultation period prior to any order being made to transfer these particular harbours to port company control.

Consistent with this approach to regional harbours, s.17 of the 2009 Act amended s.87 of the 1996 Act by providing for the future transfer to local authority control of Arklow Harbour. It was stated during the Oireachtas debate that, at the time of drafting the 1996 Act, consideration had been given to establishing a commercial port company in respect of Arklow Harbour. Therefore, the harbour was not included in the list of regional harbours listed in s.87(2) of the 1996 Act that may, subject to a ministerial order, be transferred to a relevant local authority. Since, by 2009, Arklow Harbour no longer had any significant level of commercial traffic, it was considered appropriate that the harbour should appear in this list, which will permit its transfer to local authority control along with other similar harbours. While the changes made removed Arklow Harbour from the list of harbours to be established as commercial port companies, inclusion in the list to be transferred will also mean that a company could be established in respect of the harbour subject, once again, to ministerial order. It was noted, however, that that provision had never been invoked since the enactment of the Harbours Act 1996.

Pilotage Sections 12 to 16 of the 2009 Act also contain a number of amendments to ss.57, 64, 70, 72 and 79 of the Harbours Act 1996 regarding pilotage and pilotage services. These addressed a number of issues identified since the 1996 Act was enacted as well as changes that were required on foot of the separate provision to alter harbour limits. Towards the end of the Oireachtas debate on the 2009 Act, s.15 of the 2009 Act amended s.72 of the 1996 Act to raise the upper age limit for retirement of marine pilots from 60 to 65 years of age. This had been the subject of extensive consultation between the Department of Transport and the Association of Marine Pilots of Ireland, as well as the Irish Ports Association.

Garda Síochána

RANKS AND NUMBERS OF GARDAÍ

The Garda Síochána (Ranks) (No.2) Regulations 2009 (S.I. No. 390 of 2009) (which revoked and replaced the Garda Síochána (Ranks) Regulations 2009 (S.I. No. 53 of 2009)), made under s.122 of the Garda Síochána Act 2005 (*Annual Review of Irish Law 2005*, p.417–423), provide for the dividing of the Garda Síochána into nine specified ranks as well as the maximum number of members in each rank. The effect is that the Order sets out the maximum number of members of the Garda Síochána, as follows:

Rank of Garda Síochána (1)	*Maximum Number of Members of Garda Síochána in each rank (2)*
1. Commissioner	1
2. Deputy Commissioner	3
3. Assistant Commissioner	12
4. Surgeon	1
5. Chief Superintendent	53
6. Superintendent	191
7. Inspector	390
8. Sergeant	2,460
9. Garda	12,500

The effect of the 2009 Order was to provide for an increase of one Superintendent and 700 Gardaí compared to 2008: see *Annual Review of Irish Law 2008*, p.343.

Health Services

HEALTH INSURANCE

Prudential requirements: VHI The Voluntary Health Insurance (Amendment) Act 2008 (Appointment of Date Pursuant to subsection (5)(b) of Section 2 of the Voluntary Health Insurance (Amendment) Act 1996) Order 2009 (S.I. No. 124 of 2009) and the Voluntary Health Insurance (Amendment) Act 2008 (Appointment of Date Pursuant to subsection (5)(b) of Section 2 of the Voluntary Health Insurance (Amendment) Act 1996) (No.2) Order 2009 (S.I. No. 342 of 2009) both amended the date by which the Voluntary Health Insurance Board is obliged to accrue the capital reserve required for authorisation as a health insurance provider, as provided for in the Voluntary Health Insurance (Amendment) Act 2008 (*Annual Review of Irish Law 2008*, p.344).

HEALTH SERVICE BODIES

Dissolution of various health bodies The Health (Miscellaneous Provisions) Act 2009 provided for the dissolution of a number of health bodies and the integration of their functions as units within the Department of Health and Children. The bodies were: the National Council on Ageing and Older People, the Women's Health Council, the National Cancer Screening Service Board, the Drug Treatment Centre Board and the Crisis Pregnancy Agency. It also provided for amendments to the National Cancer Registry Board (Establishment) Order 1991 to provide for the appointment by the Minister for Health and Children of a seven-person Board with knowledge or experience of the collection, recording and analysis of information, or the use of such information in research projects and the management and planning of services, or have other relevant competencies to assist the Board in the performance of its functions.

Protected disclosures/"whistleblowing" Section 103 of the Health Act 2007 (the "2007 Act") inserted a new Pt 9A into the Health Act 2004, comprising 20 sections (ss.55A to 5T), which concerned protected disclosures or "whistleblowing" in the health care setting. On whistleblowing generally, and criticism of the scope of the changes made to the 2004 Act by the 2007 Act, see the detailed discussion in *Annual Review of Irish Law 2007*, pp.586–598. The Health Act 2007 (Section 103) (Commencement) Order 2009 (S.I. No.

27 of 2009) appointed March 1, 2009 as the date on which the majority of the changes made to the 2004 Act by s.103 of the 2007 Act came into operation (except in so far as the changes in the 2007 Act relate to s.55C and 55G(b) of the Health Act 2004 (inserted by s.103(1) of the 2007 Act) and in so far as they relate to the Chief Inspector in Sch.2A of the Health Act 2004 (inserted by s.103(2)(b) of the 2007 Act).

MEDICINAL PRODUCTS

Advanced therapy medicinal products The Medicinal Products (Control of Placing on the Market) Regulations 2007 (Amendment) Regulations 2009 (S.I. No. 3 of 2009) facilitate the operation of Regulation 1394/2007 relating to advanced therapy medicinal products. The 2009 Regulations also provide for controls in respect of advanced therapy medicinal products which are prepared on a non-routine basis according to specific quality standards, and used within the State in a hospital under the exclusive professional responsibility of a medical practitioner, to comply with an individual medical prescription for a custom-made product for an individual patient. Provisions are also included in respect of the traceability of all advanced therapy medicinal products.

MEDICAL PRACTITIONERS

Medical Practitioners Act 2007 fully in force The Medical Practitioners Act 2007 (Commencement) Order 2009 (S.I. No. 40 of 2009) brought into effect the remaining provisions of the Medical Practitioners Act 2007. These related to the registration of medical practitioners, the role of the Medical Council and the Health Service Executive in relation to medical education and training, provisions transposing Directive 2005/36 on the recognition of professional qualifications, as amended by Directive 2006/100 (insofar as the 2005 Directive relates to medical practitioners). The 2009 Order also provided for the repeal of all remaining operational provisions of the Medical Practitioners Acts 1978 to 2002 and the revocation of related statutory instruments.

NURSING HOMES/DESIGNATED CARE CENTRES FOR OLDER PERSONS

Nursing home care standards The Health Act 2007 (Commencement) (No.2) Order 2009 (S.I. No. 237 of 2009) brought into effect s.101 of the Health Act 2007, which concerns the regulation of certain designated care centres for older persons, namely, public and private nursing homes and their inspection and registration by the Chief Inspector of Social Services. The 2007

Act established the Health Information and Quality Authority (HIQA) as the main regulator in this area, and brought public residential care centres (what were previously called the "county homes", some of which had previously been workhouses built under the 19th Century Poor Law (Relief) Acts) under an independent regulatory system for the first time (private nursing homes having been regulated for many decades).

The Health Act 2007 (Care and Welfare of Residents in Designated Centres for Older People) Regulations 2009 (S.I. No. 236 of 2009) (the "2009 Regulations") contain the detailed provisions for designated centres for older people. The 2009 Regulations contain requirements organised in 12 Parts that deal with: the maintenance, care, welfare and well-being of persons resident in designated centres; the numbers, qualifications and availability of persons employed in a designated centre; the design, repair, cleaning and cleanliness, ventilation, heating and lighting of and the accommodation provided; the food provided for residents; the records to be kept; the insurance contracts to be effected; the management and control of the operation of; notification of incidents occurring; notification of periods when the person in charge is absent and the procedures and arrangements put in place for these periods; and the arrangements for dealing with complaints in a designated centre. The 2009 Regulations also revoked (and replaced) the Nursing Homes (Care and Welfare) Regulations 1993, as amended (*Annual Review of Irish Law 1993*, pp.346–347). The 2009 Regulations are complemented by the 2009 *National Quality Standards for Residential Care Settings for Older People in Ireland,* which were published by HIQA. These contain 32 standards under seven groupings: Rights, Protection, Health and Social Needs, Quality of Life, Staffing, the Care Environment and Governance and Management.

The Health Act 2007 (Registration of Designated Centres for Older People) Regulations 2009 (S.I. No. 245 of 2009) set out the detailed requirements for designated centres for older people to register with the Chief Inspector of Social Services in accordance with the 2007 Act. They also deal with the issuing of certificates of registration; changes to information supplied for registration purposes; applications for the variation or removal of conditions of registration; the payment of certain fees; and notice to be given of intention to cease to carry on the business of a designated centre.

Nursing Homes Support Scheme: "Fair Deal" Scheme The Nursing Homes Support Scheme Act 2009 (the "2009 Act") provided for the establishment of the Nursing Homes Support Scheme, commonly referred to as the "Fair Deal" Scheme, under which financial support may be made available to persons in respect of long-term residential care services out of resources allocated to the Health Service Executive (HSE). For these purposes, the 2009 Act amended the Health Act 1970 and the Health (Nursing Homes) Act 1990.

The Nursing Homes Support Scheme Act 2009 (Commencement) (Specified

Forms) Order 2009 (S.I. No. 394 of 2009) brought into force s.44 of the Nursing Homes Support Scheme Act 2009 to enable the HSE to specify the general forms required under the Nursing Homes Support/Fair Deal Scheme.

The Nursing Homes Support Scheme Act 2009 (Commencement) (Care Representatives and Regulations) Order 2009 (S.I. No. 381 of 2009) brought into force ss.21 and 22 of the 2009 Act to enable the appointment, through a court application, of a care representative. A care representative is required where an applicant to the Nursing Homes Support/Fair Deal Scheme lacks the mental capacity to apply for ancillary State support under the 2009 Act and to consent to the creation of any charge on any relevant property, including the person's home. The 2009 Order prescribed the format of reports submitted to the court under the 2009 Act where a care representative is being appointed. In effect, such a care representative is akin to an attorney appointed under an enduring power of attorney and this process is required in the absence of a generally applicable modern statutory framework on mental capacity. Such a statutory framework was recommended by the Law Reform Commission in its 2006 *Report on Vulnerable Adults and the Law* (*Annual Review of Irish Law 2006*, pp.364–366) and proposed in the *Scheme of a Mental Capacity Bill* published by the Department of Justice, Equality and Law Reform in 2008. At the time of writing, a Mental Capacity Bill is expected to be published by the end of 2010. In the absence of such a statutory framework, and to avoid the need to place those who lack mental capacity into wardship (currently regulated by the Lunacy Regulation (Ireland) Act 1871, which would be repealed and replaced by a Mental Capacity Bill), the care representative arrangement under the 2009 Act represents a suitable mixture of a rights-based approach which also recognises the need to protect against potential exploitation. The protection against exploitation is made clear because any funds in the control of the care representative must be applied solely to the care of the person involved.

PHARMACY

Pharmacy Act 2007 fully in force The Pharmacy Act 2007 (Commencement) Order 2009 (S.I. No. 281 of 2009) brought into effect the remaining provisions of the Pharmacy Act 2007 (other than s.64(9)) on August 1, 2009. The Pharmacy Act 2007 (Section 64(9)) Order 2009 (S.I. No. 282 of 2009) provided that s.64(9) of the Pharmacy Act 2007 came into force on May 1, 2010. Section 64(9) applies in relation to a registered retail pharmacy business or medical practice which was lawfully carried out immediately before the passing of the Pharmacy Act 2007.

Information Law and the Ombudsman

ESTELLE FELDMAN, Research Associate, Trinity College, Dublin

This chapter of the *Annual Review* considers, in separate sections, significant issues relating to the Information Commissioner, the Commissioner for Environmental Information, the Ombudsman, and the statutory sectoral ombudsmen. There is also a section noting statutes and statutory instruments affecting information disclosure in general and the statutory ombudsmen.

DO NOT QUESTION OR EXPRESS AN OPINION

The officials considered in this chapter are all creatures of statute of greater or lesser independence established to regulate public bodies. The failure of the financial regulatory regime to exercise effective control over banks and banking systems remains a major topic of discussion nationally and internationally. Regrettably, that discussion has not extended to any significant extent to rigorous review of the restricted independence of other regulatory regimes and the manner in which there appears to be increasing disregard for their roles. This is particularly the case in relation to the independent officers who do not report to, and are not as a consequence under the control of, a Government Minister, namely the Information Commissioner, the Commissioner for Environmental Information and the Ombudsman. In this *Annual Review* once again we highlight failures of the Oireachtas to ensure that major public bodies are required to answer to regulatory regimes the function of which is to facilitate openness, transparency and, above all, accountability. Moreover, a failure to insist that every public body or every organisation in receipt of public funds must come within the remit of the Ombudsman exposes a frame of mind that is content to permit maladministration to go unchecked. One would hope that the nadir has been reached with the controversy surrounding the refusal of the former Minister for the Marine and Natural Resources to accept the Ombudsman's recommendations in the Lost at Sea Scheme inquiry.

Ombudsman spurned In an address entitled "Challenge and Change in the Irish Public Service in 2010" delivered at the Public Affairs Ireland Conference, March 24, 2010, the Ombudsman referred to the recent debacle in relation to the Lost At Sea Scheme Report—the treatment of which directly threatened the future effectiveness of her Office and "the ability of thousands of ordinary people to achieve fair and proper outcomes for their complaints against public bodies". She called for an enhancement of the strength of the Office "to guard against future acts such as that we have witnessed". The Constitution Review Group 1996 had recommended a constitutional amendment to ensure the independence of the Office of the Ombudsman, see *Annual Review of Irish Law 2000*, p.276. The Lost At Sea Report was published in 2009 and is considered below. However, it is salutary at this point to quote from the Ombudsman's statement on that matter to the Joint Oireachtas Committee on Agriculture, Fisheries and Food, April 21, 2010. The speeches are available at *www.ombudsman.gov.ie/en/SpeechesandArticles/Ombudsmansspeeches*.

> "In speaking to you here today I am mindful that my Office has been working since 1984 on behalf of members of the public who felt they had been unfairly treated by public bodies. By the end of 2009 my Office had handled almost 73,800 valid complaints. In doing its work my Office has established a hard fought reputation for impartiality, objectivity and independence. My officials, some of whom have been with the Office since its establishment, have a vast knowledge of public administration and wide experience in evaluating the merits of individual complaints and in deciding which complaints stand up and which don't. My Office is scrupulous in ensuring that it treats public bodies as fairly and impartially as it treats complainants. As you know, this is only the second time ever that my Office has deemed it necessary to lay a Special Report before the House of the Oireachtas. I don't need to remind the Committee that there is a huge political and public debate raging in Ireland at the moment about financial regulation and there is a near unanimous view that to be properly effective it needs to be thorough, it needs to ensure accountability, it needs to impose sanctions where necessary without fear or favour and it needs to be free from outside interference in fulfilling its role on behalf of the public and in the public interest. My Office concerns itself with administrative accountability and to my mind members of the public need to be assured that my Office is also being properly effective."

Later in that address the Ombudsman continued:

> "The whole point in having an Ombudsman is that complaints are investigated by an independent, experienced, professional and authoritative office; logically, except an investigation of equivalent weight is conducted elsewhere, or unless the investigation is shown to have somehow erred in law, then the investigation findings and recommendations should be accepted. In my view, it should only be in very exceptional circumstances that an Ombudsman recommendation is not accepted and implemented. As my colleague Ann Abraham, the UK Parliamentary Ombudsman, said last year, speaking to a House of

> Commons Select Committee: 'Unless the Ombudsman has gone off her trolley, let us leave the findings undisturbed'."

Party whip imposed to stifle support for independent regulators *Lost At Sea Report* In her concluding remarks to the Joint Oireachtas Committee on Agriculture, Fisheries and Food, April 21, 2010, on the *Lost At Sea Report*, the Ombudsman referred to the imposition of the party whip to the potential detriment of a family's rights.

> "I am not blind to the fact that the divisions of opinion on this case have broken down on party political lines due to the fact that a former Minister was one of the parties involved in the Lost at Sea Scheme. I think that in the heat of the debate that people have lost sight of the fact that my findings relate to both the officials and the former Minister. I should also make the point that I had no difficulty with the decision to introduce the Scheme or indeed many elements of the criteria which the Minister introduced himself and how all the applications of which I am aware, apart from that of the Byrne family, were processed and I have said this in my report.
>
> I will tell you candidly that I always recognised that this matter might break down on party political lines but I felt duty bound to try and get a fair hearing for the Byrne family and I would ask everybody to try and approach the matter in a calm, reasonable and objective manner and consider the case on its merits. As Committee members and public representatives, I know that you deal with complaints from constituents on a regular basis and I would ask you to ask yourself the question I ask myself when I get a new complaint. Has this family been treated fairly?"

Non-disclosure enactments Similarly, the Joint Committee on Finance and the Public Service divided on party lines in relation to the Information Commissioner's recommendations to change certain statutory non-disclosure provisions. This matter is considered below, but again, it is salutary at this point to quote from the *Annual Report of the Information Commissioner 2009* at p.21:

> "In appearing before the Joint Committee, I felt that my detailed arguments that certain non-disclosure provisions should be changed were understood and, broadly speaking, accepted. However, when the Joint Committee presented its Report to the Oireachtas, its recommendation, in the case of those non-disclosure provisions on which I disagreed with the relevant Minister, was to support the Minister in each case. Subsequently, it became clear that the whip was applied so that the Committee's vote divided along party political lines. I have commented several times that I found this outcome deeply depressing."

Failure to comply with own regulations Unfortunately, a number of examples in the following pages show that disregard for the statutory regulations and the statutory regulator seems to have become ingrained in Irish public life. Two examples are evident in 2009 decisions of the Commissioner for Environmental Information (CEI). In *Cullen v Department of Environment, Heritage & Local Government* CEI/08/0012, the Department appears comprehensively to have misapplied its own regulations and is subjected to major criticism in her decision by the CEI who "calls into question the efforts made by the Department to fully identify all relevant [requested] information at the outset"; further, she expressed concern that the original decision and the internal review decision "failed to comply with the Regulations and with the Department's own published Guidelines on the Regulations through its inexplicable omission of the mandatory consideration of the public interest when refusing access to information". In the second case, *Geoghegan and the Environmental Protection Agency (EPA)* Case CEI/09/0004, the EPA seems not to have understood elements of its own licensing regulations concerning publication of records and the incomplete manner in which the EPA makes files publicly available also came in for criticism. Both cases are considered below.

Gag clauses Furthermore, the appointment of so-called "independent" regulators by statute now appears automatically to preclude any criticism of any nature of Government policy. This is evidenced by the strictures placed when appearing before Oireachtas committees. Section 16(2) of the Legal Services Ombudsman Act 2009 (considered later in this chapter) states:

> The Legal Services Ombudsman when giving evidence under this section shall not question or express an opinion on the merits of any policy of the Government or on the merits of the objectives of such policy.

Similar draconian strictures are included, for example, in the Charities Act 2009 (ss.22 and 23), Broadcasting Act 2009 (s.19), National Management Agency Act 2009 (ss.58 and 59) and Labour Services (Amendment) Act 2009 (s.4). The constitutionality of these gag clauses is considered in this *Annual Review* in the Constitutional Law chapter.

INFORMATION COMMISSIONER

All statutory references in this section are to the Freedom of Information Acts 1997 to 2003 unless otherwise stated. The Act has been previously considered in *Annual Review of Irish Law 1997*, p.2 et seq.; *Annual Review of Irish Law*

1999, p.1 et seq.; p.350 et seq.; *Annual Review of Irish Law 2000*, p.273 et seq.; *Annual Review of Irish Law 2001*, p.391 et seq.; *Annual Review of Irish Law 2002*, p.306 et seq.; *Annual Review of Irish Law 2003*, p.373 et seq.; *Annual Review of Irish Law 2004*, p.319 et seq.; *Annual Review of Irish Law 2005*, p.430 et seq.; *Annual Review of Irish Law 2006*, p.430 et seq.; *Annual Review of Irish Law 2007*, p.347 et seq.; and *Annual Review of Irish Law 2008*, p.342 et seq. In addition to hard copy, documents referred to may be found at the Information Commissioner's website *http://www.oic.gov.ie*. Since the Freedom of Information Act 1997 came into force there have been two Information Commissioners, Mr Kevin Murphy 1997–2003, and the present incumbent, Ms Emily O'Reilly, since mid–2003; hence references to publications may refer to "he" or "she" depending on the date of publication. It may be noted that in 2007 the separate role of Commissioner for Environmental Information was assigned to the office-holder.

CHANGES IN ANNUAL REPORTS

Under the heading "Saving money and trees" the Ombudsman records a move to "a primarily web-based report to cut costs in printing and posting and to deploy our staff resources more effectively. Not only will this be cheaper, more efficient and accessible, it is, of course, more environmentally friendly and sustainable." This is a commendable action particularly as the report itself is so informative and easy to access and to read. The Office of the Ombudsman, conscious that there are people who do not have access to the internet or downloading facilities, will make copies of the report available free of charge, on request. The Information Commissioner's report is also web based as is that of the Commissioner for Environmental Information.

SUPREME AND HIGH COURT APPEALS

Section 42 of the Act governs the right to take an appeal from a decision of the Information Commissioner on a point of law to the High Court. Such decisions issue consequent on a section 34 review (*Annual Review of Irish Law 1999*, p.351 et seq.). The statutory barrier preventing appeals from the High Court to the Supreme Court was withdrawn by the Freedom of Information (Amendment) Act 2003 (*Annual Review of Irish Law 2003*, p.391). In 2009, the High Court issued judgments in three cases, one of which has been appealed to the Supreme Court. It is noted in the Annual Report of the Information Commissioner 2009 (p.20) that another case was rejected for consideration by the court for procedural reasons.

Liberal access in non-restrictive manner There are now well in excess of 20 reported High Court judgments and one Supreme Court judgment with a second awaited. The body of law that this establishes has resulted in the High Court consistently referring to Fennelly J.'s judgment, albeit dissenting, in *Sheedy v Information Commissioner* [2005] 2 I.R. 272 (*Annual Review of Irish Law 2005*, p.431 et seq.) and the finding of McKechnie J. in the High Court in *Deely v Information Commissioner* [2001] 3 I.R. 439 (*Annual Review of Irish Law 2001*, p.405 et seq.) regarding the nature of the appeal to the High Court. It is no longer remarkable to refer to judgments as upholding the principles of the widest possible access to publicly held information. It would now be remarkable if the courts did not interpret the Act in light of Fennelly J.'s description of the Act:

> "The passing of the Freedom of Information Act 1997 constituted a legislative development of major importance. By it, the Oireachtas took a considered and deliberate step which dramatically alters the administrative assumptions and culture of centuries. It replaces the presumption of secrecy with one of openness. It is designed to open up the workings of government and administration to scrutiny. It is not designed simply to satisfy the appetite of the media for stories. It is for the benefit of every citizen. It lets light in to the offices and filing cabinets of our rulers. The principle of free access to publicly held information is part of a world-wide trend."

Malicious allegations of child abuse In order to understand the basis for the decision in *FP v Information Commissioner* [2009] IEHC 574, it is necessary to present details of the complicated background which gave rise to the initial request for records and to the appeal to the Information Commissioner. Clark J. set aside the Commissioner's decision to uphold the refusal to release requested records by the two public bodies concerned and remitted the matter for fresh consideration. The main issue in the case centred around the Commissioner's finding that a report to the appropriate authority regarding child abuse was not (i) an allegation, and further (ii) was not a false or malicious allegation. There were two parts to the judgment order: the first set aside the Commissioner's application of the public interest test set out in s.28(5) and the second part was a declaration that the Commissioner had misdirected herself as to the application of the public interest test in s.25(5A), namely she had not considered it necessary to apply it.

Whilst this case is about access to information, Clark J. made some significant comments about the manner in which allegations of child abuse are handled. She concluded at para.47:

> "The Court cannot review the legality of a decision which was not made but I nevertheless voice my belief that for many of the reasons which I

> have expressed in relation to personal information, the public interest is not served when a request for access to records is refused because the records contain information that was provided in circumstances where the motive for the complaint was highly suspect in the context of recently commenced access proceedings on almost unique facts. The laudable protection to providers of information of child abuse was never intended to guarantee a blanket embargo on the release of that information in appropriate circumstances."

Access requests The appellant had sought access to records pertaining to allegations of child sexual abuse made against him; two requests were made to the former Eastern Health Board ("the board") and a further request to Our Lady's Hospital for Sick Children ("the hospital"). Both bodies released some records to him and withheld the remainder, largely on the grounds that they contained information given in confidence (s.26), and personal information of third parties (s.28). The Commissioner's decisions, Cases 000478 & 000549 (which concerned the requests made to the board) and Case 0000479 (which concerned the request to the hospital) may be viewed at *www.oic.ie*.

Background By way of introduction (at para.2) Clark J. referred to "a series of disturbing events". In 1993, the appellant's wife had given birth to a daughter, a child he believed to be his biological daughter and with whom he formed a strong parental bond. However, the child was the result of his wife's extra-marital relationship with another man. Unknown to the appellant, his wife applied for the child's birth certificate to be amended so that the biological father's name was substituted for the appellant's name. She also secretly obtained DNA tests confirming the other man's paternity of the child and obtained court orders providing for birth expenses and support for the child from the biological father which were expenses already provided for by the appellant. In 1997, "not surprisingly" the couple split acrimoniously. "It is fair to say that the appellant had great difficulty in accepting that the child who he had raised as his daughter and who he deeply loved was not his" (at para.3). In January 1998, within seven days of the commencement by the appellant of proceedings for access under the Guardian of Infants Act 1964, his estranged wife reported to the Eastern Health Board that the child had told her that she had been touched inappropriately by the appellant. The child was referred to St Louise's Unit of Our Lady's Hospital, Crumlin, for assessment and the Gardaí were notified.

Having been invited to take part in the unit's assessment the appellant declined to do so. He had sought assurances that fair procedures would be accorded to him:

> "The Unit could not ensure that any interviews with the appellant would

> be recorded or that he would be furnished in advance with guidelines under which the Unit operated. It subsequently appeared that no such written guidelines were in existence" (at para.5).

Clark J. continued:

> "This Court cannot help but feel that the events which occurred thereafter could have been avoided if the social workers had agreed to meet the appellant's concerns by furnishing him with a full account of the allegations which were reported to have been made by the child to her mother concerning him. If, in addition, he had been permitted to have a transcript or a record of his interviews with the social workers to protect his interests, much expense and grief could have been avoided. I also use the word 'allegation' to describe what the notice parties in this case have been careful to refer to as 'concerns' expressed by the mother of what the child is alleged to have told her concerning the appellant's behaviour which if established would have profound effects on both the appellant and the child" (at para.6).

Towards the end of 1999 the appellant and the Gardaí were notified that the "concerns or allegations are unconfirmed". Clark J. noted that the Board explained to the appellant that there are three categories of outcome—confirmed, unconfirmed and unfounded and that the "unfounded" category was used only where there was proof that the concern raised was factually incorrect (at para.8). With regard to the access proceedings she went on to note that whilst a report compiled for those proceedings was sympathetic to the appellant it noted that he had not seen the child in two years:

> "The child had been told who her biological father was but she had not met him and she was aware that her mother was in a new relationship with a further man, with whom she went on to have five more children. The report concluded that, given her confusion as to the roles of the various men in her life, it would not be in her interests to add further confusion."

Thus the appellant's application for access rights failed (at para.9).

It was at this time that the appellant had requested records under FOI. In his appeal to the Commissioner he clarified that he was not pursuing any records as related exclusively to the child but was seeking all records that referred to himself and to the child and also each and every record that was considered by the hospital in its assessment of the alleged abuse (at para.13). During the course of the Commissioner's review he was invited to demonstrate that, on balance, the public interest in granting access to the records outweighed the child's right to privacy within the meaning of s.28(5).

The judgment noted as follows at para.15:

> "[The appellant] was at pains to present the allegations made against him as malicious and untrue and as having been made in the context of a matrimonial break-up. He submitted that it was in the public interest that false allegations should be investigated and that his constitutional right to a reputation should be vindicated. He pointed out that because he had no access to the records he was unable to assess whether to pursue a civil action in the event of the allegations having been made maliciously. He also argued that there was a public interest in individuals having access to their personal records in order to be in a position to ensure that such records are not incorrect or misleading."

The law Section 28.1 refers to the personal information exemption (*Annual Review of Irish Law 2008*, p.352). It is a complicated provision, certainly not written with any standard of plain English in mind. With regard to deceased individuals, this was at issue in another of the 2009 High Court cases, the Rotunda Hospital birth certificate case, discussed below. This matter is also considered with regard to the new Regulations on access to records of the deceased.

Section 28(1) states:

> Subject to the provisions of this section, a head shall refuse to grant a request under section 7 [request for records] if, in the opinion of the head, access to the record concerned would involve the disclosure of personal information (including personal information relating to a deceased individual).

The rest of the provision is quoted directly from the case (paras 28–31), as it includes comment from Clark J. at paras 29, 30 and 31 which might facilitate understanding:

> "28. The exemption provided for by s.28(1) is subject to sub-sections 2 to 5B of section 28. Sub-sections 2 (b) to (e) of section 28 are of no relevance to this case nor are sub-sections (3), (4) or 5A . Of particular relevance however are sub-sections 2(a), 5 and 5B . Section 28(2) (a) provides that section 28(1) does not apply if the information concerned relates to the requester concerned. This is in turn subject to section 28(5B) , as inserted by section 23 of the Freedom of Information (Amendment) Act 2003 , which provides:-
>
> > 'Notwithstanding paragraph (a) of subsection (2), a head shall, subject to paragraphs (b) to (e) of that subsection and subsections (5) and (6), refuse to grant a request under section 7 if, in the opinion of the head, access to the record concerned would, in addition to

> involving the disclosure of personal information relating to the requester, also involve the disclosure of personal information relating to an individual or individuals other than the requester.'
>
> 29. It is clear that this provision is applicable in the case of the appellant, as the grant of access to the records will result in the disclosure of information relating not only to the appellant (i.e. the requester) but also to the child. Thus, the Health Board, the Unit and the Commissioner were, on the face of it, justified in refusing the application made by the appellant seeking access to the records, pursuant to s.28(1) of the Act of 1997, as amended.
>
> 30. That is not the end of the matter however. The operation of s. 28(1) and s. 28(5B) are subject to an overriding public interest test imposed by s. 28(5) which provides:
>
> 'Where, as respects a request under section 7 the grant of which would, but for this subsection, fall to be refused under subsection (1), in the opinion of the head concerned, on balance -
>
> (a) the public interest that the request should be granted outweighs the public interest that the right to privacy of the individual to whom the information relates should be upheld, or
>
> (b) the grant of the request would benefit the individual aforesaid,
>
> the head may, subject to section 29 , grant the request.'
>
> 31. Section 29 sets out consultation requirements which are not at issue in this case."

The Commissioner had found that all of the withheld records disclosed personal information relating not just to the appellant but also to the child. Examining the appellant's submissions with respect to the public interest, she noted that "the complaints or allegations were unconfirmed".

She stated that the hospital had taken the position that this was a category covering a wide spectrum ranging from "almost sufficient evidence to confirm" to "nearly no evidence" and where it is not possible to form a clear opinion in that the allegations have neither been confirmed nor completely ruled out. In those circumstances she took it to be the position of the Hospital that "it does not regard the allegations as having been made maliciously". She stated that she understood the position of the Board to be in line with the Hospital's position and she stated that this was not a case where she would feel entitled to take a view as to whether a particular allegation had been made falsely. She concluded:

> "It is clear from the records in question that the information provided to the Board, and which formed the basis for the Board's decision to refer [the child] to the Hospital, was provided on the basis of possible

grounds for concern; the person conveying the information did not make any allegation. In the absence of any evidence that the matter was raised with the Board for malicious purposes, and in the light of the positions adopted by the Board and the Hospital, I have no basis for concluding that the approach to the Board was malicious" (at para.19, emphasis added by Clark J.).

Acknowledging that the appellant's submissions contained elements which supported the public interest in granting his request, her overall finding was that:

> "'[T]he cumulative impact of these public interest arguments is not such as to displace the very strong public interest served by the protection of the privacy rights of [the child] in relation to an aspect of [the child]'s life which is particularly sensitive. On this basis, I find that the public interest in granting your request does not outweigh the public interest in upholding [the child]'s right to privacy'" (at para.21).

Allegations and malice Since the question of malice in allegations of sexual abuse was at the heart of the court's decision, and in view of the multiplicity of proceedings concluded and in contemplation, it seems proper to quote directly from Clark J.'s judgment and her finding that the Commissioner had made an error of law in this matter:

> "33. The appellant argues that the Commissioner's determination that the report made by his wife to the Health Board was not a malicious allegation constitutes an error of law. He argued strenuously that the timing of the allegations, immediately after his application for access to the child, demonstrates that the allegations were made for malicious purposes and in the context of their marital animosity. He reminded the Court that while he was engaged in establishing fair procedures which he believed would protect him in his proposed interview with the Board he was informed that his wife has withdrawn the allegations. Then they were revived and enhanced following the birth of a new child in October. He argued that in the circumstances there was a clear public interest in granting a request for access to the documents, particularly as he was contemplating the commencement of proceedings pursuant to s.5 of the Protections for Persons Reporting Child Abuse Act 1998.
>
> 34. The Court with the consent of all parties has examined the video recordings and the documents in dispute and is satisfied that the inferences that the Commissioner drew that the complaints did not constitute allegations and that they were not made maliciously were incorrect. It is the view of the Court that in assessing the allegations, the Commissioner placed undue emphasis on the position of the Board

and the Hospital, in protecting the processes of the receiving and investigating of possible child sexual abuse. It seems to the Court that in ensuring the protection of their sources and the very valuable work in investigating those allegations, the Commissioner failed to give adequate consideration to the circumstances in which the allegations were reported in this case. The circumstances were that the mother's marriage to the appellant had broken down and the appellant had commenced access proceedings in respect of the child who he loved and had treated since birth as his biological daughter. The records reveal that the appellant's wife had refused to engage in the Hospital's assessment for a period of time (this is said to be because she was pregnant with a different partner) and it seems that she pursued the allegations at a time when it became apparent that the appellant might possibly be granted access.

35. The Commissioner gave no consideration to the unusual role of the complainant as the mother of the child and the estranged wife of the applicant. The appellant was not a stranger to the child and had been considered by the learned Judge of the Circuit Court as being a person entitled to seek access to the child subject to a Consultant Psychiatrist's report on the child's best interests. The documents which the Commissioner had available to her and which the Court has seen indicate that from the earliest stage that caution was advised regarding the allegations. The documents indicate evidence of a woman who was prepared to go to great lengths to prevent disclosure of the documents to the appellant. She had refused to proceed with the investigation of the allegations at the Unit unless her child was referred to by the surname of her biological father, who the child had never met. As previously noted, she had the child's birth certificate altered so that the appellant's name was removed without his knowledge and she pursued the biological father through the courts for expenses already paid by the appellant."

No reasonable decision-making body could make finding Clark J. then set aside the Commissioner's finding, citing *Deely v Information Commissioner* [2001] 3 I.R. 439 (*Annual Review of Irish Law 2001*, p.405 et seq.) as authority for such action:

"In the circumstances, I do not believe it was correct for the Commissioner to draw the inference from material before her that there was an absence of any evidence that the matter was raised with the Health Board for malicious purposes and that there was no basis for concluding that the approach made by the appellant's wife to the Board was malicious. The Court is struck by the conspicuous temporal connection between the court proceedings for access and the making of the report to the Health Board. Having seen the documents this court would go so far as to find that no reasonable decision-making body could draw the inference that the appellant's submissions as to the malicious nature of the allegations were of no significance to the application of s.28(5)(a). The Court is of the view that any reasonable decision-maker would find those submissions to be of particular significance to the weighing of the public interest in disclosure of the documents against the right to privacy of the child" (at para.36).

Child's right to privacy The court expressed discomfort with the very heavy emphasis placed in this case on the right to privacy of the child and noted the irony that if the allegations were deemed well-founded and the appellant had been charged, he would have been entitled to all the files, reports and video recordings:

> "The information deemed extremely sensitive personal information concerning the child is in fact information relating to the applicant alleged to have come from the child" (at para.39).

Clark J. was of the view:

> "... that the Commissioner placed an undue emphasis on the right to privacy of the very young child who it was asserted had made allegations against a person who until recently she had known as her father and whose allegations had been determined as unconfirmed" (at para.40).

In an interesting, and itself ironic, development, Clark J. then as good as lectured the Commissioner on the purpose of the Freedom of Information Acts 1997 to 2003, quoting McGovern J. in *Minister for Information and Science v The Information Commissioner* [2008] IEHC 279 at para.14 (*Annual Review of Irish Law 2008*, p.350) who held that the 1997 Act provides that:

> "... it was the intention of the Oireachtas that it is only in exceptional cases that members of the public should be deprived of access to information in the possession of public bodies".

She continued by reaffirming Fennelly J.'s judgment in *Sheedy*, quoting his description of the Act given above and then quoted from McKechnie J.'s judgment in *Deely*, mistakenly attributing it to Fennelly J., who quoted it in *Sheedy* and prefaced it by stating that he agreed with McKechnie J. who had made a "number of statements of general importance":

> "As can thus be seen the clear intention is that, subject to certain specific and defined exceptions, the rights so conferred on members of the public and their exercise should be as extensive as possible, this viewed, in the

> context of and in a way to positively further the aims, principles and policies underpinning this statute, subject only to necessary restrictions. It is on any view, a piece of legislation independent in existence, forceful in its aim and liberal in outlook and philosophy" (*Deely v Information Commissioner* [2001] 3 I.R. 439 at 442).

Clark J. in turn contributed her own statement of general importance:

> "In the light of those decisions it is clear that the intention of the Oireachtas was that the exemptions allowed by Part III of the Act of 1997 are to be interpreted restrictively and applied sparingly. If the exemptions are afforded too wide an interpretation, the refusal of access could become the rule instead of the exception and this would clearly frustrate the primary objectives of the Act of 1997" (at para.43).

Right to record of mother's age *The Governors and the Guardians of the Hospital for the Relief of Poor Lying-In Women, Dublin [Known as the Rotunda] v Information Commissioner* [2009] IEHC 315. The request in this case was, on the face of it, very straightforward and considered the right to personal information (s.28) and the confidentiality exemption (s.26). A woman sought access on behalf of her father, to a record of her grandmother's age when she gave birth to him in 1922. The hospital's refusal to grant access to the records was overturned by the Commissioner (Case No. 050148, December 14, 2007). McCarthy J. in the High Court upheld the Commissioner's decision. The hospital has appealed to the Supreme Court and the reserved judgment is awaited at the time of writing.

The High Court's lengthy judgment reflects a case that, far from being simple, is multi-layered and complex, considering issues that include: whether or not an appellant may raise matters that were not raised before the Commissioner; whether or not a hospital may successfully claim the confidentiality of records that contain information in the public domain; the standard of proof for presuming a person to be deceased; whether the deceased have rights; whether a child and/or a grandchild has a right to access to the records of their presumed deceased grandmother; whether corporate bodies may claim constitutional rights; what the correct balance is between a child's right to know the identity of its mother and the birth mother's right to privacy. Assuming that the Supreme Court will deal with these issues in its judgment which will be the subject of analysis in next year's *Annual Review*, it is deemed sufficient for the time being to recite McCarthy J.'s concluding summary of his findings in dismissing the appeal. It may be noted that with regard to the access of records of the deceased this case dealt with the Freedom of Information Act 1997 (s.28(6)) Regulations 1999 (S.I. No. 47 of 1999) which have been replaced by the 2009 Regulations considered elsewhere in this chapter:

"(a) I am entitled, and do, address a fresh or new issue of law even when not canvassed or dealt with by or before the Commissioner. I am not entitled to receive additional evidence since the appeal is on a point of law only.

(b) The new issue raised by the hospital is that of whether or not the record in question, created, as it was, before the commencement of the Act, falls within the Act's ambit. This is dependent on whether or not the information contained in the record is personal information which relates to Mr. Walsh.

(c) In as much as such information is personal information which relates to him, the Act is applicable.

(d) The question arises as to whether or not the record contains information of the same kind as that contained in the record in respect of individuals generally, or a class of individuals that is, having regard to all the circumstances, of significance size and is available to the general public: it is.

(e) Whether or not it was, in strictness, part of the Commissioner's decision I consider that Mr. Walsh as next of kin of the late Bridget Walsh has an entitlement to access by virtue of the provisions of s.28(6)(b)accordingly falls within the class of persons entitled to disclosure by virtue of the regulations made by SI No. 47/1999:

(f) That the record does not enjoy the necessary quality of confidentiality for the purpose of prima facie prohibiting disclosure, under the provisions of s.26 of the Act.

(g) No necessity arises to consider the discretionary disclosure of either personal information or confidential information but in as much as the latter was addressed by the Commissioner and at the hearing, I have sought to address certain principles which must be applied by the Commissioner when exercising the latter discretion" (at para.111).

Potential prejudice to examinations *Kruse v Information Commissioner* [2009] IEHC 286 concerned a medical student in UCD who had sought access to records relating to multiple choice examinations which he had sat in 2006. Sheehan J. upheld the Commissioner's decision affirming UCD's refusal of access to the requested records. The appeal related to the interpretation of s.21(1) and (2) of the FOI Act 1997 which granted an exemption on the basis that release of the records would prejudice the effectiveness of examinations. He noted the University policy to refuse requests from candidates to retain copies of the questions set and answered as part of a multiple choice question assessment:

"This was because the questions were drawn from a pool of validated questions, the question pool is finite and the questions used in one assessment would be used again in future assessments. A gradual accumulation of questions in the pool by students over a period of time would render it possible to circulate likely questions and correct answers among the student body in advance of future assessments, which would threaten the integrity and future viability of this method of assessment" (at para.9).

Section 21(1) and (2) have been previously considered in *Annual Review of Irish Law 2005*, p.431 and *Annual Review of Irish Law 2007*, p.347.

STATUTORY CERTIFICATES AND NOTICES

Certificates of exemption *Section 20* Section 20 of the Freedom of Information (Amendment) Act 2003 gives discretionary power to Secretaries General of Government departments to certify that a record of whatever nature relates to a deliberative process of Government and is thus exempt from release. Such a certificate is not amenable to internal review and cannot be appealed to the Information Commissioner. Section 20(1)(c) states, inter alia, that such a certificate shall be final. Effectively this means that the decision is entirely in the hands of the senior civil servant and that all Ministers, not just the departmental Minister, are bound by this unreviewable decision. In 2006, the first such certificate was issued by the Secretary General of the Department of Justice, Equality and Law Reform. The constitutional implications of issuing a section 20 certificate were discussed in *Annual Review of Irish Law 2006*, Constitutional Law chapter, pp.236–237. One new certificate was issued under this section in 2009 by the Secretary General of the Department of Defence further to a request from the *Irish Examiner* for a copy of the Department's risk register.

Under s.21A(b), if the Secretary General of the Department of State concerned is satisfied that the deliberative processes that led to the issue of the section 20 certificate of exemption have ended, "he or she shall, by certificate in writing, revoke the certificate" and the exemption regarding the record(s) at issue shall cease. The first certificate, issued by the Secretary General of the Department of Justice, Equality and Law Reform in August 2006, was not revoked in 2009. Copies of the statutory notifications to the Information Commissioner are reproduced in Appendix I of the Annual Report of the Information Commissioner 2009.

Section 25 Under s.25(1) a Government Minister may exempt a record from the application of the Freedom of Information Act (*Annual Review of Irish Law 2000*, p.275). Two certificates were issued with expiry dates of February 2, 2002 and March 29, 2002; *Annual Review of Irish Law 2001*, p.409, one certificate issued; *Annual Review of Irish Law 2002*, p.308, two certificates issued; *Annual Review of Irish Law 2003*, pp.391–392, one previously issued certificate renewed for further two years; *Annual Review of Irish Law 2004*, p.326, two previously issued certificates renewed; *Annual Review of Irish Law 2005*, pp.467–468, one previously issued certificate renewed; *Annual Review of Irish Law 2006*, pp.410–427, two previously issued certificates renewed; *Annual Review of Irish Law 2007*, pp.352–353, one previously issued certificate renewed; *Annual Review of Irish Law 2008*, pp.361–362, two previously issued certificates renewed). In 2009 three new certificates were issued, two by the Minister for Justice, Equality and Law Reform and one by the Minister for Foreign Affairs. Hitherto only the Minister for Justice, Equality and Law Reform had issued s.25 certificates; he also renewed a previously issued certificate related to phone tapping. A copy of the notification in respect of these certificates is reproduced in Appendix I of the Annual Report of the Information Commissioner 2009.

Section 25 review: notice from Department of the Taoiseach Section 25(7)(a) requires that the Taoiseach shall review the operation of s.25(1) at regular prescribed intervals, first described in *Annual Review of Irish Law 2005*, p.468. The Information Commissioner was informed by the Department of the Taoiseach on September 16, 2009, that the Taoiseach, the Tánaiste and Minister for Enterprise, Trade and Employment, and the Minister for Finance reviewed five existing certificates (all issued by the Minister for Justice, Equality and Law Reform, two during 2008 and three during 2009) that were in operation for the period ended August 2008, and decided that it was not necessary to request their revocation. A copy of the notification is reproduced in Appendix II of Annual Report of the Information Commissioner 2008.

Statutory notices of non-compliance with Information Commissioner requests *Section 37 notice* The Act provides for the issue of a notification under s.37 to the head of the public body requiring the production of information and/or records.

Section 35 notice Section 35 of the Act provides that, where a statement of reasons for refusing a request is inadequate the Commissioner may require the head concerned to furnish a further statement (*Annual Review of Irish Law 2002*, p.275; *Annual Review of Irish Law 2003*, p.393; *Annual Review of Irish Law 2004*, p.326; *Annual Review of Irish Law 2005*, p.468; *Annual Review of Irish Law 2006*, p.421; *Annual Review of Irish Law 2007*, p.353; *Annual Review of Irish Law 2008*, p.362).

No section 35 notices were issued by the Commissioner in 2009, and three section 37 notices were issued, one each to the Department of Justice, Equality and Law Reform, RTÉ and Cavan County Council. A certain level of frustration might be discerned from comments in the Annual Report. The Department of Justice, Equality and Law Reform did not act to provide requested records after two reminders were sent and the Commissioner noted that it was "difficult to understand why it took over five weeks to forward these records, and why they could not have been provided initially when first requested by my Office" (Annual Report of the Information Commissioner 2009, p.17). In the case of RTÉ the Commissioner stated:

> "I do not accept that RTÉ was not aware that the records fell to be released under FOI, and in taking the stance that it did, RTÉ caused many hours of unnecessary work to be undertaken, both by my officials and its own administrative staff, and also unnecessarily delayed receipt by the applicants of records they were fully entitled to get. Following many hours of work on this case by my officials, RTÉ released the records administratively which means it accepted that it was not necessary for me to make a binding decision requiring such release" (Annual Report of the Information Commissioner 2009, p.17).

With regard to Cavan County Council the Commissioner recorded that a "straightforward decision could have been taken 4 weeks earlier if the Council had not delayed provision of the necessary records to my Office" (Annual Report of the Information Commissioner 2009, p.18).

NON-DISCLOSURE ENACTMENTS

Section 32 of the FOI Act refers to non-disclosure enactments that are not included under any other section of the Act. Access shall be refused to any record whose disclosure is prohibited, or whose non-disclosure is authorised in certain circumstances, by statute (including statutory instrument). In circumstances where such a statute is listed in the Third Schedule to the Act, the disclosure of records is assessed solely by reference to the other provisions of the FOI Act. Section 32 has been previously considered in *Annual Review of Irish Law 1999*, p.354 et seq.; p.350 et seq.; *Annual Review of Irish Law 2001*, p.398 (as part of School League Tables case analysis); *Annual Review of Irish Law 2003*, p.394; *Annual Review of Irish Law 2004*, p.320 (as part of School League Tables case analysis) p.328 et seq.; *Annual Review of Irish Law 2005*, p.460 et seq.; *Annual Review of Irish Law 2006*, pp.415 et seq.

In *Annual Review 2006*, the Commissioner's Report to the Joint Oireachtas Committee on Finance and the Public Service for the Purpose of Review of Non-Disclosure Provisions in accordance with the Freedom of Information Act 1997 [s.32] was considered. In her Annual Report 2006, the Commissioner dealt at some length with the Oireachtas Committee members' response to her submission. In 2009, the Commissioner revisited the issue. She described the statutory procedure and her response to the outcome as follows:

> "Section 32 requires that a Joint Committee of both Houses of the Oireachtas, in this case, the Joint Committee on Finance and the Public Service, must review the non-disclosure provisions in all statutes to ascertain if any of them should be amended or repealed or included in the Third Schedule to the FOI Act. As part of this review, Ministers must report to the Joint Committee on all non-disclosure provisions in the legislation within their areas of authority. The Ministers must state their view on whether the non-disclosure provisions should be amended, repealed or allowed to continue in force and, additionally, whether a reference to any of those provisions should be included in the Third Schedule to the FOI Act. Each Minister must lay a copy of his or her report before each House of the Oireachtas and also forward it to the Information Commissioner. The Joint Committee is obliged to prepare and furnish to each House, a report of the operational review.
>
> Such reports fall due every five years since April 1999 (the date of the first report) and in accordance with section 32(5) of the FOI Act, I presented my opinions and conclusions relating to the 2004 reports to the Joint Committee in December 2005. In appearing before the Joint Committee, I felt that my detailed arguments that certain non-disclosure provisions should be changed were understood and, broadly speaking, accepted. However, when the Joint Committee presented its Report to the Oireachtas, its recommendation, in the case of those non-disclosure provisions on which I disagreed with the relevant Minister, was to support the Minister in each case. Subsequently, it became clear that the whip was applied so that the Committee's vote divided along party political lines. I have commented several times that I found this outcome deeply depressing."

The Commissioner continued by noting that a further round of reports fell due in 2009. She expressed concern lest there be any further delay in completing this further round of reports and concluded: "In the light of previous experience, I also hope that this time round, the Joint Committee will find the means to take a more considered view of my submissions" (*Annual Report of the Information Commissioner 2009*, pp.21–22).

ACCESS TO RECORDS OF MINORS* AND OF DECEASED PERSONS

(* We use the term "minor" as shorthand for those for whom parents and legal guardians remain responsible in law.)

Section 28(6) Regulations and Guidelines Section 28 of the Freedom of Information Act refers to requests for personal information. Section 28(6) provides:

> Notwithstanding *subsection* (1), the Minister may provide by regulations for the grant of a request under *section 7* where—
> (a) the individual to whom the record concerned relates belongs to a class specified in the regulations and the requester concerned is the parent or guardian of the individual, or
> (b) the individual to whom the record concerned relates is dead and the requester concerned is a member of a class specified in the regulations.

Pursuant to this section regulations were issued in 1999, Freedom of Information Act 1997 (section 28 (6)) Regulations 1999 (S.I. No. 47 of 1999) (the "Regulations"). In the *Annual Review of Irish Law 2005*, pp.452 et seq. it was recorded that the Information Commissioner had called for a total review of these Regulations as a matter of real urgency (*Annual Report of the Information Commissioner 2005*, pp.23–27). This was with particular reference to the issue of access to the personal records of deceased persons and arose from an initiative at the Fourth Annual Freedom of Information Conference held at Trinity College in October 2005 (Feldman, *Personal Information, Minors and Deceased Persons: Some Policy Issues*, available from School of Law, TCD). The Commissioner's comments on the Regulations were further developed as "Access to Records of Deceased Persons under Freedom of Information" published in Feldman (ed.), *Freedom of Information: Law and Practice* (Dublin: FirstLaw, 2006) also available at *www.oic.gov.ie/en/MediaandSpeeches/PublishedArticlesExtracts/2006*. In her 2006 and 2007 reports the Commissioner renewed her call for immediate review of this highly unsatisfactory situation. In 2008 the Commissioner recorded that the Department of Finance had consulted with FOI practitioners in the health sector on draft amended regulations and guidelines covering this area. She further noted, that in early 2009 the Department sought her comments on its proposals. Thus, after a long gestation period the Department of Finance finally issued new Regulations on the access to records of deceased persons, Freedom of Information Act 1997 (section 28 (6)) Regulations 2009 (S.I. No. 387 of 2009). Based on the foregoing and in the absence of any further publication on the official website, it is not unreasonable to assume that the Commissioner's views as expressed in the 2006 publication remain her opinion. The 2009 Regulations are consequently analysed through that focus. At that time she concluded:

> "While I appreciate the difficulties of drafting amending primary

legislation in this area, I am convinced that it is necessary. I do not believe that it is appropriate that key decisions as to the rules for access to records of deceased persons (particularly health records) should be left to the effective discretion of the Minister for Finance. I would hope that the Minister will undertake a comprehensive review of the whole issue of access to deceased persons' records (and medical records in particular) and, following that review, bring forward detailed amendments to the FOI Act for consideration by the Oireachtas. In the short term, I would hope that the Minister will amend article 3(1)(b)(iii) of the 1999 Regulations to overcome the difficulties [initially] highlighted."

Information Commissioner's analysis of Regulations The Commissioner introduced her analysis with five case studies all based on actual reviews that had been dealt with by her Office. These raised fairly complex issues and required that competing interests be balanced. Amongst the issues raised were:

"whether deceased people have any right to privacy;
whether the express wishes of a person, concerning who may access his or her personal information, should be given any recognition after that person's death;
whether medical confidences must be protected after death;
whether there should be a hierarchy of access rights as between the various parties with a family or other connection to the deceased;
whether, in such cases, one party should be recognised as being the "guardian" of the deceased's privacy and access by others would require that "guardian's" consent;
whether, in the case of individuals raised apart from their natural families, their need for information on their "origins" should be given priority over other considerations."

Legislative amendment required The first and most important point to note is that the Commissioner considered secondary legislation to be an inadequate and inappropriate mechanism to deal with such a serious matter as the records of deceased persons, most particularly health records. In finding that the current Irish arrangements were far from being satisfactory the Commissioner observed as follows:

"There are two particular difficulties, as I see it. The first has to do with the mechanism, provided for in section 28(6), whereby the Minister for Finance is delegated to deal with the matter by way of regulations.

> The second difficulty has to do with the content of the Minister's 1999 Regulations" (emphasis added).

As noted in the Constitutional Law chapter in this *Annual Review* the Commissioner found that a major difficulty in devising any regulations was discerning what are the principles and policies set down by the Oireachtas in the primary legislation. Absent those principles and policies any regulations may be constitutionally suspect.

> "Within the body of the FOI Act, it may be argued that the Oireachtas has established relevant principles and policies insofar as it seeks to protect information obtained in confidence (section 26) and personal information, including that of deceased persons (section 28). Furthermore, section 29 establishes the principle of consultation with the third party concerned where confidential, personal or commercially sensitive information is proposed to be released in the public interest.
>
> In the case of deceased persons, and as argued by Ms. Feldman, it would appear that there is no right to privacy. If so, then the principle of respecting privacy is not relevant to the Minister's regulations. In the case of confidentiality, there is also a problem in that it is unlikely that a duty of confidence could be owed to a deceased person. If a duty of confidence may be owed to the dead, how can the Minister frame regulations which will circumvent such a duty?
>
> It does seem to me that, in setting about the task of specifying classes of requester to whom a deceased person's records may be released, the Minister for Finance has very little to go on in terms of principles and policies contained in the FOI Act itself. It is arguable that of the principles and policies within the FOI Act, as identified above, the two of immediate relevance are (a) the use of a public interest test and (b) the desirability of consultation with whoever may be regarded as the "guardian" of the records of the deceased person ...
>
> A further matter of some concern is that the delegation given to the Minister, under section 28(6)(b), is to specify classes of persons to whom records of deceased persons may be released. What the Minister has actually done in article 3(1)(b)(iii) of the 1999 Regulations is to prescribe classes of persons by reference to a test of being *'appropriate having regard to all the circumstances ...'* and to guidelines which do not form part of the statutory instrument itself. Whether this is a valid prescription of classes, as envisaged in the primary law, may be open to question."

Content of Regulations Since the Minister for Finance chose to issue new Regulations rather than accept the considered advice of the Commissioner, the Commissioner's comments on the content of those Regulations becomes even more significant. These comments are reproduced in full, followed by an examination of the new Regulations to see whether or not the short-term solution has resolved the highlighted difficulties.

> "*Content of 1999 Regulations*
> It will be clear from my comments above that I do not regard the content and approach of the 1999 Regulations as amounting to anything like the kind of comprehensive and clear-cut provision which this very sensitive area demands. While I appreciate that any comprehensive arrangements in this area are likely to continue to involve some level of assessment and exercise of judgement by the decision-maker (and by my own Office), the current Regulations are too general by far. I would like to make it clear that I am not making any specific recommendations as to what might be contained in any amended set of provisions. Rather, my intention is to draw attention to matters which should be given serious consideration in the context of drafting amendments to the FOI Act.
>
> Article 3(1)(b)(iii) of the 1999 Regulations identifies 'a next of kin' as a class with a potential right of access to the records of a deceased person. There is a difficulty with this in as much as the reference is to 'a' next of kin rather than 'the' next of kin. Indeed, even were the reference to be to 'the' next of kin, this might not improve matters given that the term is not defined in the FOI Act, nor in the 1999 Regulations, nor is there any single agreed definition, generally. While the dictionary definition will define 'next of kin' as the nearest blood relative, general usage is frequently at odds with this definition. Many married people regard their spouse as their next of kin. Furthermore, hospitals generally have a practice, when recording patient details on admission, of asking a patient to nominate next of kin. As I understand it, this is not intended to identify that person who is the closest blood relative; rather, it is intended to identify that person whom the hospital should contact in case of an emergency; this might be a spouse, a sibling, a more distant relative or simply a friend. The main criterion, it appears, is that the nominated person is someone whom the patient is happy to have contacted and who is authorised by the patient to take decisions on his or her behalf, should this be necessary.
>
> It seems to me that if next of kin is to be used as an identifier for a class of person to whom a deceased person's records are to be released, much greater clarity and definition is needed in the use of that term. Even more so is it true that the reference to such 'other person or persons', in article 3(1)(b)(iii) of the 1999 Regulations, is problematic.
>
> As already cited above, the 1999 Regulations adopt a very broad definition of what constitutes a 'spouse' for the purpose of the Regulations. While the principle of recognising the rights of non-marital spouses and of former spouses may be laudable, it seems to me to be

essential that the rights of such spouses should be set within a statutory framework. Furthermore, the principles upon which access will be granted to such spouses should be contained in the primary legislation. In particular, there is a need for a hierarchy of rights as between the various sub-classes which constitute the current class of 'spouse'; and this hierarchy should be set down in primary legislation. There is also the difficulty, referred to earlier, that purporting to afford a right to a non-marital spouse may in some cases be at odds with the protection of the 'institution of Marriage', as provided for at Article 41.3 of the Constitution."

The 2009 Regulations The earlier 1999 Regulations are revoked in s.3 of the 2009 Regulations. Thus, s.4 is the relevant section when considering the content of the 2009 Regulations. This is reproduced in full below:

4 (1) Notwithstanding section 28(1), a request under section 7 in relation to a record access to which involves the disclosure of personal information (including personal information relating to a deceased individual) shall, subject to the other provisions of the Freedom of Information Act, 1997, be granted where:

(a) the requester is a parent or guardian of the individual to whom the record concerned relates and that individual belongs to one of the following classes of individual:
   (i) individuals who, on the date of the request, have not attained full age (within the meaning of the Age of Majority Act, 1985 (No. 2 of 1985)), or
   (ii) individuals who have attained full age (within the meaning aforesaid), who at the time of the request have a mental condition or mental incapacity or severe physical disability, the incidence and nature of which is certified by a registered medical practitioner and who, by reason thereof, are incapable of exercising their rights under the Act,

being individuals specified in clauses (i) and (ii) access to whose records would, in the opinion of the head having regard to all the circumstances and to any guidelines drawn up and published by the Minister, be in their best interests, or

(b) the individual to whom the record concerned relates is dead ("the individual") and the requester concerned belongs to one of the following classes of requester:
   (i) a personal representative of the individual acting in due course of administration of his or her estate or any person acting with the consent of a personal representative so acting,
   (ii) a person on whom a function is conferred by law in relation

to the individual or his or her estate acting in the course of the performance of the function, and

(iii) the spouse or the next of kin of the individual where in the opinion of the head, having regard to all the circumstances and to any relevant guidelines published by the Minister, the public interest, including the public interest in the confidentiality of personal information, would on balance be better served by granting than by refusing to grant the request.

(2) In this Regulation, "spouse" includes:

(a) a party to a marriage that has been dissolved, being a dissolution that is recognised as valid in the State, or who is living apart from his or her wife or husband pursuant to a deed of separation, and

(b) a man or woman who was not married to but cohabited as husband or wife, as the case may be, with the deceased individual,

and,

"next of kin" is the person or persons standing nearest in blood relationship to the individual in accordance with section 71(2) of the Succession Act, 1965.

By comparison to the 1999 Regulations, with regard to s.4(1)(a)(i) and (ii), the wording and punctuation is identical but there is a formatting difference whereby in the 1999 Regulations, s.3(1) (a)(ii) was a single paragraph from the word "individuals" to "in their best interests, or".

Sections 4(1)(b)(i) and (ii) are identical to the earlier ss.3(1)(b)(i) and (ii) which were effectively non-contentious. There are some differences in s.3(1)(b)(iii) and 3(2) from the 1999 Regulations and these are indicated in those earlier provisions which are reproduced below:

(1)(b)(iii) the spouse or <u>a</u> (replaced by "the") next of kin of the individual <u>or such other person or persons</u> (deleted) <u>as the head considers appropriate having regard to all the circumstances and to any relevant guidelines drawn up and published by the Minister.</u>(varied)

(2) In this Regulation, 'spouse' includes:

(a) a party to a marriage that has been dissolved, being a dissolution that is recognised as valid in the <u>State or,</u> (replaced by "State, or") (additional category of separated spouse inserted) ("and" inserted)

(b) a man or woman who was not married to but cohabited as husband or wife, as the case may be, with the deceased <u>individual.</u>" (replaced by individual,) (definition of "next of kin" inserted)

It may be noted that whereas some of the Commissioner's concerns appear to have been addressed the overall effect of the new Regulations is that lack of clarity continues in relation to a definition of "the" next of kin and no hierarchy of spousal/cohabiting partner rights has been included. The Department of Finance may contend that these issues are clarified in the newly issued Guidance Notes but we cannot over emphasise that guidelines are NOT the law.

Guidance Notes *Issued in accordance with Regulations* New Guidance Notes have been issued entitled *Guidance Notes on Access to records by parents/guardians Access to records relating to deceased persons under section 28(6) of the Freedom of Information Act 1997* ("Guidance Notes"). It had been identified in the 2005 critique that whereas the 1999 Regulations provided for decision-makers having regard to "any relevant guidelines drawn up and published by the Minister [for Finance]", no such guidelines had been drawn up and published by the Minister. The Department of Finance's website had published Guidance Notes in this area but they were described as "approved by the FOI Interdepartmental Working Group - March 1999" rather than as guidance drawn up and published by the Minister. The newly issued set of Guidance Notes are clearly marked as "Drawn up and published by the Minister for Finance pursuant to S.I. 387 of 2009 – *Freedom of Information Act 1997 (Section 28(6) Regulations) 2009*".

NOT the law As has been pointed out on many previous occasions, Guidance Notes and Guidelines are NOT a part of the law and must not be used in preference to the provisions of a statute, e.g. *Annual Review of Irish Law 2007*. For instance, the Guidelines issued by the Minister for the Environment, Heritage and Local Government under art.14 of the European Communities (Access to Information on the Environment) Regulations 2007 (S.I. No. 133 of 2007) note that under art.14, "public authorities are obliged to take account of these Guidelines in performing their functions under the Regulations. Nonetheless, the Guidelines do not purport to be a legal interpretation of the Regulations" (emphasis added). No such warning appears on the Department of Finance section 28(6) Guidance Notes. Of greater concern is that the final sentence states as follows: "Decision makers should, therefore, be aware that decisions on release of records under these Guidance Notes cannot be taken in isolation from the other provisions of the FOI or other Acts." Since, as we point out below and in the Constitutional Law chapter in this *Annual Review*, aspects of these Guidance Notes go far beyond anything specified in the primary legislation, or, indeed, the Regulations, we are concerned that these Guidance Notes might lead practitioners into grave legal error not excluding constitutional irregularities.

Content of Guidance Notes So far in this section we have been concentrating on issues relating to the records of deceased persons. However, the first section of s.28(6) deals with the personal information of minors, i.e. those still legally subject to parents or guardians and the Regulations include in that category individuals who are 18 and older, who at the time of the request have been certified by a registered medical practitioner as being incapable of exercising their rights under the Act. The guidance appears most thorough and is laudable in its attitude. It advises that in general, "decision makers are advised to put themselves in the place of the person to whom the records relate as far as practicable when examining requests. In this way, they would be better able to assess the impact of release of material on the person", Guidance Notes p.3. One cannot question that in general terms this may be good advice but it establishes what might be considered a subjective legal test which has no basis in the statute nor, we submit, in the Regulations. Moreover, even were such a test to be established in the Regulations, as the Commissioner pointed out with great clarity in 2006, this is in breach of the requirements of the principles and policies test relating to secondary legislation. These comments apply to the Guidance Notes in their entirety as, even though the section on access to records of deceased persons presents sound and clear advice to decision-makers based on the 2009 Regulations, the inclusion of a public interest test in the Regulations not present in s.28(6) in the primary statute, renders the whole suspect in law.

Law as wished not as is As the Guidance Notes do not fall to be classified as legislation in any sense it seems as if the authors of the Guidance Notes are rewriting law as they wish it to be rather than as it is. One is left wondering why the Minister did not follow the Commissioner's strong recommendation and seek an amendment of the primary statute to incorporate all the substantive issues.

Medical records We conclude with the Commissioner's comments on the issue that perhaps most concerned her, the confidentiality of medical records.

> "I think it is important to recognise the very genuine concerns of hospitals and medical practitioners arising from the release of the medical records of deceased patients. Unfortunately, neither section 28(6) of the FOI Act nor the 1999 Regulations address these concerns in any adequate way. By definition, where a public body holds the personal information of a deceased person, it is invariably information obtained or created in confidence. However, section 28(6) envisages that such confidential material will be released and, to this extent, appears to be at odds with the protections provided for at section 26 (information

> obtained in confidence). I take the view that, where release of records is found to be warranted under section 28(6) and the 1999 Regulations, then this amounts to an authorised release. In this situation, where disclosure is not unauthorised, one of the key requirements necessary to establish a breach of a duty of confidence - and the activation of section 26 - is missing."

The 2009 Regulations too are silent on this matter.

Section 17(6) and 18(5A) Regulations As noted at the end of this chapter, new regulations have also been issued in relation to s.17, right to amend personal information, and s.18, right to reasons for decisions. These regulations similarly relate to the classes of individuals who may apply on behalf of minors or regarding records of deceased persons.

COMMISSIONER FOR ENVIRONMENTAL INFORMATION

The role of the Commissioner for Environmental Information is to decide on appeals taken by members of the public who are not satisfied with the outcome of their requests to public authorities for environmental information. The Access to Information on the Environment Regulations (S.I. No. 133 of 2007) ("AIE Regs") assigned this legally distinct role of Commissioner for Environmental Information to the holder of the Office of Information Commissioner. The Regulations give effect to Directive 2003/4 of the European Parliament and of the Council of January 28, 2003. The activities of the Commissioner for Environmental Information were previously considered in *Annual Review of Irish Law 2007*, pp.355 et seq; *Annual Review of Irish Law 2008*, pp.368 et seq. In addition to hard copy, documents referred to may be found at the Environmental Information Commissioner's website *http://www.ocei.gov.ie/en/*. Part II of the Information Commissioner's Annual Report 2008 (pp.56–68) is devoted to the Annual Report of the Commissioner for Environmental Information.

Guidelines Article 14 of the AIE Regs allows the Minister to publish guidelines which, under art.14(2), a public authority "shall ... have regard to", in the performance of its functions under the AIE Regs (*Annual Review of Irish Law 2007*, p.355). It is worth repeating that these Guidance Notes are not, nor do they purport to be, a legal interpretation of the AIE Regs. It should also be noted that in appeals to the Commissioner for Environmental Information, to the extent relevant, she has regard to the guidelines. The Regulations and the

Guidance Notes can be found on the Department of the Environment, Heritage and Local Government website *www.environ.ie/en*.

Two distinct access to information regimes There have been statutory obligations to release environmental information since 1990 under European law and 1993 under domestic law. Since the enactment of the Freedom of Information Act in 1997, both legislative codes have operated in parallel but as fully distinct and separate systems. It is important to note that there are significant differences between the two regimes: see *Annual Review of Irish Law 2007*, pp.355–359; *Annual Review of Irish Law 2008*, pp.366–386. However, there are strong similarities in the processes for making requests and appealing refusals.

Making a request for environmental information All articles summarised below are contained in the AIE Regs unless otherwise stated. It is recommended that requesters refer to the comprehensive detail of the AIE Regs and to the Guidance Notes.

Article 6(1) governs requests which must be in writing or electronic form and state that the request is made under the AIE Regs. Article 6(2) specifies that the interest of the applicant is not required in making the request. Article 7 governs the public body's response to the request including time limitations for reply. Article 7(4) requires, inter alia, that in case of refusal reasons must be specified and rights of appeal must be provided. Article 8 details mandatory grounds for refusal. Article 9 outlines discretionary grounds for refusal. Article 10 refers to requests for information regarding emissions into the environment. Internal review of a refusal is governed by art.11.

Public interest test In her Annual Report 2008 the CEI made the following very important comment:

> "While some of these grounds are described as 'mandatory', this is misleading in that all of the exemption grounds are subject to certain restrictions, as set out in article 10 of the Regulations. For instance, requests for environmental information relating to emissions into the environment cannot, in general, be refused. In all cases, a potential exemption must be subjected to a public interest test."

Moreover, art.10(4) states: "The grounds for refusal of a request for environmental information shall be interpreted on a restrictive basis having regard to the public interest served by disclosure."

Appealing a refusal to grant information Article 12 establishes the Office of Commissioner for Environmental Information (CEI) and the right of appeal to the CEI. The CEI's decision is binding on the public authority, which must comply within three weeks (art.12(7)). The strength of the CEI's powers can be seen from art.12(6), which states:

The Commissioner may, for the purposes of this article, do any of the following:

(a) require a public authority to make available environmental information to the Commissioner and, where appropriate—
  (i) require the public authority concerned to attend before the Commissioner for that purpose, and
  (ii) where the public authority is a body corporate, require its chief officer to attend,

(b) examine and take copies of any environmental information held by a public authority and retain it in his or her possession for a reasonable period,

(c) enter any premises occupied by a public authority and there require to be furnished with such environmental information as he or she may reasonably require, or take such copies of, or extracts from, any environmental information found or made available on the premises.

Article 12(8) further empowers the CEI to apply to the High Court for an order directing the public authority to comply. Article 12(9) states:

(a) The Commissioner may refer any question of law arising in an appeal under this article to the High Court for determination and shall postpone the making of a decision until after the determination of the court proceedings.

(b) The High Court or, on appeal from that Court, the Supreme Court, may order that some or all of the costs of an applicant or other person affected in relation to a reference under this sub-article be paid by the public authority concerned.

Appeal to the High Court Article 13 governs an appeal to the High Court on a point of law by any interested party arising from a decision of the CEI. Article 13(3) empowers the High Court, and in case of appeal, the Supreme Court, to award costs against the public authority concerned if the court considers that the point of law is of exceptional public importance.

Fees Article 15 concerns fees. There are no up-front fees for a request for environmental information, nor for an internal review. However, a fee of €150 is required for an appeal to the CEI. The public authority may, nonetheless, charge a fee for providing environmental information (art.15(1)), but must publicise details of those fees (art.15(2)). This section was subject to a decision of the CEI in 2008, see *Annual Review of Irish Law 2008,* pp.368–369.

DECISIONS OF THE COMMISSIONER FOR ENVIRONMENTAL INFORMATION

All of the decisions may be found on the Office of the Commissioner for Environmental Information's website. These are the first decisions of the CEI and are of significant precedental value. Hence, they are dealt with in some detail including extensive quotes.

In her annual report the Commissioner notes that during 2009 18 appeals were received in contrast to 12 in 2008. The two formal decisions are considered below. Of the remainder, two cases were deemed to have been withdrawn as settled once the records were released following the CEI's intervention, one case was withdrawn and six appeals were deemed invalid on the grounds that internal review had not been requested or the statutory appeal fee was not paid. Thirteen cases were on hand at the end of 2009:

> "While most of the appeals arose from requests to local authorities and Government Departments, An Bord Pleanála, the Environmental Protection Agency, the Attorney General's Office and RTÉ were among the public authorities whose decisions were appealed. It is fair to say that most of the appeals arose from disputes as to whether any or further environmental information within the scope of a request was held, the format in which it was available or whether the body was a public authority for the purposes of the Regulations as opposed to cases where my Office had to decide whether or not the exceptions provided for in the Regulations had been properly applied."

Failures to manage environmental information However, the two decisions of the CEI in 2009 are perhaps more significant as a commentary on the overall health of the body politic. In both cases the public body charged with protecting the environment on behalf of the people not only acted improperly based on their own guiding regulations but misrepresented the information it held and did not hold. In the case of the Department of Environment, Heritage and Local Government the CEI noted in *Cullen*:

> "Overall, based on what occurred in this case, I am very disappointed in the Department's level of awareness of and compliance with the

> Regulations which give effect to Ireland's obligations under the Directive."

With regard to information not held by the Department and in *Geoghegan*, not held by the Environmental Protection Agency, the CEI said the following in both cases:

> "I note that the Directive has its origins in the UNECE Convention on Access to Information, Public Participation in Decision-Making and Access to Justice in Environmental Matters (the Aarhus Convention). 'The Aarhus Convention: an Implementation Guide' [ECE/CEP/72] says that if the public authority does not hold the information requested, it is under no obligation to secure it. It goes on to suggest that failure to possess environmental information relevant to a public authority's responsibilities might be a violation of Article 5, paragraph 1(a) of the Convention which relates to the requirement that public authorities collect, possess and disseminate environmental information."

Both cases are considered below in some detail. Nevertheless, in order to appreciate the full extent of the failures of both the Department and the EPA, readers are recommended to read the cases in full. The issue of information not held, common to both cases, is dealt with in *Geoghegan*.

Department wrongly refuses files on illegal dumping in Co. Wicklow *Cullen & Department of Environment, Heritage & Local Government (the Department)* CEI/08/0012, October 27, 2009, considered the following articles of the AIE Regs: art.3(1) definition of environmental information and the definition of an "applicant"; art.7(5) information which is not held; art.8(a)(ii) exception for confidentiality of third party information; art.8(a)(iv) confidentiality exemptions in the Freedom of Information Acts 1997 to 2003; art.9(1)(b) discretionary exception adversely affecting the course of justice; art.9(2)(c) discretionary exception in relation to incomplete or draft material; art.10(3) mandatory public interest test; art.10(4) grounds for refusal restrictive; art.11(5)(b) request inadequately answered. The CEI found that the Department's decision to refuse parts of the request was not justified except in relation to those parts of the information which she found qualified for legal professional privilege. She found that certain records and parts of records came within the exception in art.8(a)(iv) of the AIE Regs and that, in accordance with art.10, the public interest in granting that part of the request did not outweigh the interest served by refusing it. In her decision the CEI was critical of the Department's handling of the request. Since this is the Department responsible for the Regulations and Guidance Notes, which it appears to have comprehensively misapplied, direct comments from the CEI's decision are extensively quoted:

The articles quoted below are as they appear in the decision as the CEI included the headings which are not legally binding:

"Article 8(a)(ii) and 8(a)(iv)

Article 8 of the Regulations carries the side heading: 'Grounds that, subject to article 10, mandate a refusal'. Article 8 includes among the grounds that, subject to article 10, 'mandate a refusal' the following provisions:

'8. A public authority shall not make available environmental information in accordance with article 7 where disclosure of the information -

(a) would adversely affect -

... (ii) the interests of any person who, voluntarily and without being under, or capable of being put under, a legal obligation to do so, supplied the information requested, unless that person has consented to the release of that information,

... (iv) without prejudice to paragraph (b), the confidentiality of the proceedings of public authorities, where such confidentiality is otherwise protected by law (including the Freedom of Information Acts 1997 and 2003 with respect to exempt records within the meaning of those Acts);

Article 9(1)(b) and Article 9(2)(c)

Article 9 of the Regulations is headed 'Discretionary grounds for refusal of information'. Article 9(1) provides that a public authority may refuse to make available environmental information where disclosure would adversely affect:

(b) the course of justice (including criminal inquiries and disciplinary inquiries)

Article 9(2)(c) of the Regulations provides that:

(2) A public authority may refuse to make environmental information available where the request -

(c) concerns material in the course of completion, or unfinished documents or data

Articles 8 and 9 are subject to Article 10 which provides:

'10. (1) Notwithstanding articles 8 and 9(1)(c), a request for environmental information shall not be refused where the request relates to information on emissions into the environment.

(2) The reference in sub-article (1) to information on emissions into

the environment does not include a reference to any discussions on the matter of such emissions at any meeting of the Government.

(3) The public authority shall consider each request on an individual basis and weigh the public interest served by disclosure against the interest served by refusal.

(4) The grounds for refusal of a request for environmental information shall be interpreted on a restrictive basis having regard to the public interest served by disclosure

(5) Nothing in article 8 or 9 shall authorise a public authority not to make available environmental information which, although held with information to which article 8 or 9 relates, may be separated from such information.'"

The appellant, a Wicklow County Councillor, sought access to:

> "(a) and (b) all correspondence, reports, minutes of meetings and memos and internal communications between the Department and Wicklow County Council, the Environmental Protection Agency (EPA) and all other parties on the issue of illegal dumping in Wicklow in the period January 2001 to July 2008;
>
> (c) all records including those of the Local Government Audit Office on the issue of a waste licence at Ballybeg, Rathnew, Co. Wicklow and
>
> (d) all communications between the Department and the Council and internal records concerning the making of the Baltinglass Town Plan."

Status of the appellant The CEI pointed out that the Regulations and the Directive which give her jurisdiction "do not make any distinction between the rights of ordinary members of the public and the rights of elected representatives to have access to environmental information held by public authorities."

Thirty four additional records identified as result of CEI's review Following the initial request the Department had granted access to several files with the exception of some documents withheld on the grounds of exceptions provided for in the AIE Regs. It had mentioned that some of the documents related to European Court of Justice (ECJ) proceedings against Ireland, some contained legal advice or were connected with separate legal proceedings, some were internal communications of public authorities and one was being withheld by the Local Government Audit Service by reference to a provision of the Freedom of Information (FOI) Acts. The CEI noted that the Department had said that it would be "a better use of resources" if the appellant were to inspect the files and mark those pages he wished to have copied. This he apparently did, then requested internal review which released four additional records. In relating this background the CEI noted that the scope of her review was limited to that of the original request dated July 18, 2008. The four additional records had been released on October 3, 2008 and the appeal had been received by the CEI on November 4, 2008.

During the review by the CEI's Office the Department identified further relevant records, 16 of which were released to the appellant in December 2008. The appellant identified further records which he believed were relevant to his request and which had not been made available to him or included in the schedule. Following further enquiries from her office, the Department identified six additional records of which all except one page were released. Subsequently, in April 2009, the Department identified a further 12 records of which nine were released.

The CEI had this to say about the identification of records by the Department:

> "A particular difficulty which has arisen in dealing with this appeal is the identification of records relevant to the request. Considerable resources have been put into determining whether all records within the scope of the request and of this appeal have been identified. While I acknowledge that the original request was quite broad and that the Department has cooperated with all requests from my Office, it is disappointing to have to note that further relevant records were being identified as late as April 2009, despite the fact that the relevant information was first sought from the Department by my Office in November 2008. I am glad to note that the Department is currently reviewing its Records Management Strategy with a view to informing staff of best practice in this area. However, it seems to me that, irrespective of whether a request to the Department fell to be processed under FOI legislation or under the Regulations on Access to Environmental Information, the systems in place in the Department to identify information held in various sections failed in this case. I find the situation all the more worrying in view of the fact that the provisions of the FOI Act have been in place for over 11 years so that any claim that this is a new regime in which the Department has had little experience of or requirement to identify and retrieve similar records is simply not tenable."

She continued by noting that art.11(5)(b) of the AIE Regs provides that a reference to a request refused includes a request which has been inadequately answered:

> "In this case, while the Department adhered to the relevant deadlines in dealing with the original and internal review requests, and facilitated the applicant in viewing of files, it has since emerged as outlined above

> that additional records relevant to the request were identified following requests from this Office. Three further sets of relevant records came to light. This calls into question the efforts made by the Department to fully identify all relevant information at the outset."

Failure to consider the public interest A further concern of the CEI related to the level of consideration given by the Department's decision makers to the request under the AIE Regs:

> "In particular, I consider that the original decision and the internal review decision failed to comply with the Regulations and with the Department's own published Guidelines on the Regulations through its inexplicable omission of the mandatory consideration of the public interest when refusing access to information. Article 10 of the Regulations ... provides for this.
>
> While the matter of the public interest is addressed ... in my decision, I must emphasise that at no point does the Department appear to have addressed these crucial provisions, either in general terms or in relation to specific records in spite of the fact that the necessity to address the public interest was specifically raised by this Office in correspondence with the Department as far back as November 2008. Indeed, the Department's handling of the audit information [see below] was seriously deficient because, even if its assumption that the material came within one of or more of the provisions of the Regulations allowing refusal of such information was held to be correct, the public interest in releasing the information would have had to be considered. Overall, based on what occurred in this case, I am very disappointed in the Department's level of awareness of and compliance with the Regulations which give effect to Ireland's obligations under the Directive."

With reference to the Department's grounds for refusal the CEI continued:

> "While the Regulations do not explicitly provide that the burden of proof rests with the public authority in relation to justifying the use of the exceptions when refusing to make information available, I take it that the scheme of the Directive and the Regulations makes it clear that there is a presumption in favour of release of environmental information. This is reinforced by the provision at Article 10(4) which provides that the grounds for refusal shall be interpreted on a restrictive basis having regard to the public interest served by disclosure. One of the difficulties my Office has had in this case in analysing whether the grounds for refusal have been properly applied in relation to the withheld records. The Department has, in its decisions and in its submissions, put forward very little detailed argument as to what adverse effect it expects would

> result from the granting of the request in respect of specific records by reference to the detailed provisions of sections 8, 9 and 10 of the Regulations. This means that while I will, of course, consider the applicability of the Articles cited by reference to the content of the records remaining at issue in the light of the Department's views, I do not consider that there is an onus on me in this appeal to make the Department's case for it or to import into my analysis a consideration of any potential adverse affects that the Department has not put before me. I am satisfied that the Department has had adequate opportunity to make arguments in support of its position and to have them considered in the course of this review."

With regard to information which is not held by the public body (art.7(5)), this is dealt with in a similar fashion to the *Geoghegan* case below. Returning to *Cullen*, the CEI noted that:

> "... despite the fact that additional records were identified following enquiries made by this Office, I think it reasonable to now conclude on the balance of probabilities that adequate searches have been carried out across the various sections of the Department in the course of my review and that the officials with which my Office has been dealing have not given misleading information about the existence of additional records".

The CEI concluded further that it was no longer feasible to pursue the possibility that additional records might exist and, having regard to the appellant's requirements and the reasonable use of her Office's resources, it was necessary "to bring this protracted case to a conclusion".

A missing audit file The CEI then noted that the Department has advised that one particular file did exist but is now "missing". That file related to the Local Government Audit Service's (LGAS) examination of the circumstances surrounding the issue of a waste permit for lands at Ballybeg, Co. Wicklow. Following intervention by her staff, a draft version of the LGAS report was located and a copy provided to her office:

> "The remainder of the missing file is not available to me. I understand from the Department's Director of Audit that its staff carried out unsuccessful searches to locate the file. It appears that the file was held in Dublin as a draft report was prepared after the LGAS had, as part of its investigation, assembled relevant papers made available to it by Wicklow County Council and that, on reviewing the file, it was decided

> within the Department that it was not appropriate for the LGAS to issue a report on the matter."

Legal professional privilege The CEI considered that legal professional privilege is the type of claim for confidentiality that could be protected by law as envisaged in art.8(a)(iv). If certain records met the test for legal professional privilege under the common law rule (incorporated into the s.22(1)(a) exemption in the Freedom of Information Acts 1997–2003), the Department would be entitled to rely on art.8(a)(iv) in relation to those records subject to consideration of whether there is a public interest in releasing them. The CEI defined legal professional privilege as enabling the client to maintain the confidentiality of two types of communication: confidential communications made between the client and his/her professional legal adviser for the purpose of obtaining and/or giving legal advice, and communications made between the client and a legal adviser or the legal adviser and a third party or between the client and a third party, the dominant purpose of which is the preparation for contemplated or pending litigation.

Course of justice The CEI found that under art.9(1)(b) the Department has not made the case that release of these records would adversely affect the course of justice nor, in the case of the "legal advice"-type records, did she find in favour of the Department.

The CEI noted that both arts 8(a)(iv) and 9(1)(b) are subject to the public interest test at art.10(3) of the AIE Regs. Commenting that there would have to be exceptional public interest factors at play before legal professional privilege could be set aside, she nonetheless noted that "the Directive and the Regulations clearly envisage that circumstances will arise where information qualifying for legal professional privilege would be released in the public interest." In upholding legal professional privilege in this case she reasoned as follows:

> "The Appellant agues that the importance of the water pollution risk and the alleged corruption in relation to the illegal dumping situation is sufficient to set aside the privilege and confidentiality claimed. I have considered whether the factors in favour of disclosing the Department's legal advice are of sufficient weight to set aside the normal principles designed to protect the confidentiality of legal exchanges between the client (the Department) and its lawyers. I recognise that there is a public interest in government being open and transparent in relation to environmental matters. There is also a public interest in individual members of the public being able to understand the basis for decision making involving matters that affect the environment and involve alleged breaches of environmental law. However, against this I must weigh the strong and long established public interest in upholding legal

professional privilege as interpreted by the Courts. While it would be open to the Department to waive the privilege claimed over the information containing its legal advice, it has chosen not to do so as is its right under the law. Public authorities need to be reasonably certain that they can seek and obtain full and frank legal advice in confidence. In this case, while I cannot, of course, describe in any detail the advice sought or given, I can say that it is concerned primarily with the legal powers of the Minister in relation to investigation of the issues in Wicklow. I do not consider that the public interest factors here, though considerable, are of sufficient strength to justify the setting aside of legal professional privilege and therefore my findings in relation to [identified records] are that the information in them is properly exempt from disclosure."

With regard to other records the claim of legal professional privilege was rejected by the CEI. A very detailed account of her review is included in the case record. As succintly recorded in her annual report, no indication was found that these were prepared with the dominant purpose of preparing for litigation:

> "Further, the Department claimed privilege for correspondence with the EC Commission and, after a detailed examination of the circumstances of the creation of these and the [European Court of Justice] cases cited by the Department, I was not satisfied that preparation for litigation was the dominant purpose in their creation" (Annual Report of the Commissioner for Environmental Information, p.65).

Confidentiality of proceedings of public bodies Similarly, the case gives a detailed account for the rejection of this exemption. The annual report more succinctly states that some of the withheld material contained information which the Department said had been given in confidence:

> "I considered that the identities of the persons named in the records and the nature of their allegations were already in the public domain. The Department did not provide sufficient justification for its position to enable me to find that the providers of the information did so in the expectation of confidence or in circumstances imposing an obligation of confidence. Furthermore, Article 10(3) provides for a restrictive interpretation of the grounds for refusal to be applied. I concluded that making available the information would not adversely affect the confidentiality of the proceedings of public authorities where such confidentiality is otherwise protected by law nor would it adversely affect the interests of any persons who supplied the information"

(Annual Report of the Commissioner for Environmental Information, p.65).

Department's "bizarre" claim Referring to the missing Local Government Audit Service file, the CEI noted again that this file was missing and the only part of it available to her was a draft report prepared by the LGAS which was held in electronic format. Having examined the contents of the draft report, it appears to be largely a factual statement of events that occurred in relation to the Ballybeg waste licence issue:

> "The Department says that the matter being investigated related to the issue of a Waste Permit by the Council and goes on to make what, in circumstances where it is not in dispute that the LSAS carried out an investigation, is a somewhat bizarre claim that 'The Local Government Audit has no role in examining environmental matters'."

Commenting that she should not have to remind the Department of the Environment of the definition of "environmental information" set out in the Directive and in the Regulations she went on to do just that quoting art.3(1) of the AIE Regs and its definition of "environmental information", any information in written, visual, aural, electronic or any other material form. There was no doubt but that matters relating to the issue of a waste licence come within art.3(c), measures (including administrative measures) ... designed to protect those elements [of the environment], and probably also fall within other elements of the definition including art.3(f), the state of human health and safety ... conditions of human life, cultural sites and built structures ... affected by the state of the elements of the environment ... or through those elements, by any of the matters referred to in paras (b) [factors, ... affecting or likely to affect the elements of the environment] and (c).

In any case, she considered that the matters, including investigation of allegations about non-compliance with licensing measures, are sufficiently connected to factors and measures which affect the environment to be classed as environmental information:

> "Whether the LGAS has any role in examining environmental matters or not, the fact is that it purported to conduct an investigation into matters concerning measures to protect the environment, (namely the regulation of waste disposal in a specific case) so that the records thus created comprise environmental information for the purposes of the Regulations and the Directive."

The LGAS had claimed on behalf of the Department that its report was exempt from release under arts 8(a)(iv) and 9(2)(c) of the AIE Regs. It contended, under art.8(a)(iv), that the reference to the FOI Acts 1997 to 2003 invokes s.21(1)(a) of that Act which provides that a request may be refused if access to the record concerned could, in the opinion of the head, reasonably be expected to "(a) prejudice the effectiveness of tests, examinations, investigations, inquiries or audits conducted by or on behalf of a public body or the procedures or methods employed for the conduct thereof":

> "According to the LGAS, this provision has been 'successfully' invoked in the past in protecting the independence of the Service. I am not sure as to what tests of success the Department is referring in this regard and I have been unable to locate any record of a finding of my Office affirming a decision of a public body to withhold the records of the LGAS under the FOI Acts. In any case, a 'blanket exemption' without particular reference to the content of the records and the harm or prejudice which would flow from release would not be acceptable under the FOI Acts nor under the Regulations and Directive in this case."

The CEI then referred to *Sheedy v Information Commissioner* [2005] IESC 35 as authority that with regard to s.21(1) of the FOI Act the onus to show prejudice was on the Department, in this instance LGAS. In her evaluation of LGAS's argument it is clear that that onus was not discharged:

> "In arguing that article 8(a)(iv) protects the draft report from release, the LGAS refers me to provisions of the Local Government Act 2001 in relation to the independence of the audit function. Clearly, such independence is vital to the proper functioning of the audit service. However, it does not follow that release of a draft report of the type at issue here which, in my opinion, discloses nothing about the independence of the audit service or about its methodology in carrying out value for money audits or other of its investigative functions would prejudice or interfere in any tangible way with the fundamental principle of 'auditor independence'. Similarly, the Department has not convinced me that the principle of the auditor having his or her own discretion in relation to how an audit is carried out would be undermined in any way by allowing access to the information in this particular draft report. In my view, the Department has failed to adduce any substantial arguments which would lead me to conclude that the serious adverse affect on the confidentiality of the proceedings of public authorities necessary to apply the exception would result from release of the draft report."

Department claim unfounded The Department had also claimed that the draft LGAS report is exempt from release under art.9(2)(c) as it is still in the course of completion or is an unfinished document:

> "Given that the draft report was prepared in 2005 and a letter was sent

to the Minister dated 21 December 2005 setting out the opinion of the LGAS in the matter, I cannot see how this draft report can be considered to be in the course of completion, more than three years later. There is no suggestion of any further activity on the part of the LGAS in this matter since 2005."

Public interest concerns Whilst it was not strictly necessary the CEI made some general comments on the public interest:

> "There is a strong public interest in the public being aware of how allegations about waste management, the administration and regulation of permits and the overall issue of pollution resulting from unauthorised dumping of waste are handled. I can find little in the Department's submissions which would support or outweigh this public interest in release. In the case of this draft report, I would add that it seems to me that the fact that the main LGAS file has, apparently disappeared without explanation, strengthens the public interest in as much information as possible about this environmental controversy being released so that the public is aware of measures taken to investigate the allegations made."

Refusal of access to complaint files *Geoghegan and the Environmental Protection Agency (EPA)* Case CEI/09/0004, October 28, 2009, considered the following articles of the AIE Regs: art.4(1) information that is otherwise required to be made available to the public; art.7(3) form or manner in which information is to be provided; art.7(5) information which is not held. The CEI found that the EPA was justified in its part refusal of the request but varied the basis for the decision to reflect the correct provisions of the AIE Regs.

The relevant sections of the articles considered are quoted below:

> 4.(1) These Regulations apply to environmental information other than, subject to sub-article (2), information that, under any statutory provision apart from these Regulations, is required to be made available to the public, whether for inspection or otherwise.
>
> 7.(3)(a) Where a request has been made to a public authority for access to environmental information in a particular form or manner, access shall be given in that form or manner unless—
>
> (i) the information is already available to the public in another form or manner that is easily accessible, or
>
> (ii) access in another form or manner would be reasonable.
>
> (b) Where a public authority decides to make available

environmental information other than in the form or manner specified in the request, the reason therefor shall be given by the public authority in writing.

7.(5) Where a request is made to a public authority and the information requested is not held by or for the authority concerned, that authority shall inform the applicant as soon as possible that the information is not held by or for it.

The appellant had requested access to the report carried out by an EPA inspector on his land and to other information relating to the appellant's complaints to the EPA about air emissions from Aughinish Alumina.

EPA misapplied EPA Licensing Regulations The CEI noted that in its original decision, the EPA had refused access to the information sought on the basis of art.4(1). The CEI's investigator had asked the EPA to identify the particular statutory provision under which it was required to make the information sought available to the public and had been advised that it was obliged to provide access to its licensing files under art.23 of the Environmental Protection Agency (Licensing) Regulations 1994 (S.I. No. 85 of 1994), as amended by the Environmental Protection Agency (Licensing) Regulations 1995 (S.I. No. 76 of 1995) (EPA Regulations). Following examination of these Regulations, the investigator "was not satisfied that the information sought in this request was in fact required to be made available under these EPA Regulations which appear to specify material relating to licence applications only." Following further communications with the EPA, it accepted this to be the case and advised that the information identified as being on the public file is there as an administrative arrangement rather than on foot of any statutory requirement.

EPA confusion on complaints file It was clear from the schedule of records provided by the EPA that no records were held in relation to some of parts of the request:

> "This had not been made clear by the EPA in either its original or internal review decision although I must point out that both decisions referred to 'information that the EPA has in its possession in relation to activities for which it has granted an IPPC (Integrated Pollution Prevention Control) licence ... is made available for public inspection'. The EPA did not at any stage give the impression that all of the information sought was actually held by it."

The CEI continued:

> "There appears to be some confusion as to what information is placed

on the public file in regard to complaints made about the operation of a facility by a licensee. The EPA's publication 'Procedure for Public Viewing of Files' says that public access is available to information on enforcement of licences including all correspondence from the licensee, the EPA and third parties. The procedures further say that 'complaints relating to the facility' are included. However, the description of the 21 records released to the Appellant—which were apparently not on the public file—includes correspondence from the EPA to the licensee as well as internal memoranda and information relating to a complaint. I do not consider that this is evidence of any intent to conceal information; nonetheless it may point to a need to clarify for the public the circumstances whereby, for whatever reason, not all records relating to complaints are on files available to it."

Information "not held" Referring to the authority of "The Aarhus Convention: an Implementation Guide" (ECE/CEP/72; see *Annual Review of Irish Law 2008*, p.372) the CEI noted that if the public authority does not hold the information requested, it is under no obligation to secure it. However, she noted further that the Aarhus Convention goes on to suggest that failure to possess environmental information relevant to a public authority's responsibilities might be a violation of art.5, para.1(a) of the Convention which relates to the requirement that public authorities collect, possess and disseminate environmental information. She pointed out that a similar though not identical provision in relation to records "not held" exists in s.10(1)(a) of the FOI Acts and explained that she was guided in her approach as CEI by the Office of the Information Commissioner's experience over the past 11 years, an approach upheld in *Ryan v Information Commissioner*, unreported, High Court, May 20, 2003 (*Annual Review of Irish Law 2006*, p.414):

> "In cases where the public authority claims not to hold the environmental information requested, I consider that my role is to decide whether the decision maker has had regard to all the relevant evidence and to assess the adequacy of the searches conducted by the public authority in looking for relevant records. The evidence in 'search' cases generally consists of the steps actually taken to search for the information along with miscellaneous other information about the records management practices of the public body insofar as those practices relate to the information in question. On the basis of the information provided, I form a view as to whether the decision maker was justified in coming to the decision that the information is not held for or by the public authority. It is not normally the my function to search for records."

In summary, the CEI considered it reasonable for the EPA to take the view that as the information requested is available on publicly available files, it should not be required to make the information available in another form and, rejecting art.4(1) as the basis for the decision, found that art.7(3) applies to the information sought which is held by the EPA and that art.7(5) applies to that information which is not held.

Common courtesy, common sense? A is obliged by statute to investigate complaints and to make its findings available to the public on request. B makes a complaint to A about C. A investigates B's complaint but refuses to give B his own copy of its findings because they have been published by A for public access. In the normal course of events might we have expected A, as a matter of courtesy, as a matter of sound management and administrative principles, to give B a copy of the findings as soon as they become available? What is missing from our analysis so that when we reconsider the problem where A is the Environmental Protection Agency and B is the appellant Geoghegan, the answer is that A is neither expected nor required to make the information sought available to B? It seems to us, admittedly in the possible absence of all the information, that if common courtesy and common sense applied there would have been no necessity for a formal request from Mr Geoghegan to the EPA in the first instance.

REPORT TO EUROPEAN COMMISSION

The CEI notes that during 2009 the Department of the Environment, Heritage and Local Government made Ireland's first report to the European Commission on the operation of the Directive, which is mandatory on Member States under art.9 of the Directive. *Review of Implementation of EU Directive 2003/4/EC on Public Access to the Information on the Environment. Report by Ireland. Monitoring period: 1 May 2007–31 December 2008* (Directive Review) is available on the Department's website *www.environ.ie*. The review was conducted by questionnaire to relevant public bodies.

CEI's opinion ignored In her annual report the CEI references discussions her office had with the appropriate officials in relation to the Directive Review. She records that among the issues discussed was "the fact that the appeal fee is seen as a deterrent to applicants particularly in cases where responses to requests are so inadequate as to constitute 'non-reply' or a deemed refusal under the Regulations where no decision is issued within the statutory timeframes."

The Directive Review notes the relatively low level of requests. Thus:

> "[I]t is not considered possible to conclusively demonstrate a linkage between the introduction of the Directive and increased or decreased

> involvement of civil society/stakeholders in environmental matters, decision making process etc" (Directive Review, p.3).

It notes further:

> "One area of concern that has been highlighted is that the AIE Regulations could be used as a means to circumvent the fees which apply under Ireland's Freedom of Information legislation" (Directive Review, pp.3–4).

No reference whatsoever was made to the CEI's view that the appeal fee is viewed as a deterrent. The concern is that the members of the public, on whose behalf all public bodies should be acting, might be asking for environmental information under the European Directive as a means of avoiding charges under Freedom of Information. There is no thought here to the possibility that the appropriate request mechanism might in fact be under the Directive. There is no reflection whatsoever on the legislative imperative of both the Directive and of Ireland's Freedom of Information legislation which is to release requested records in as non-restrictive a manner as possible.

OMBUDSMAN

The Ombudsman is governed by the Ombudsman Act 1980. In addition to hard copy, documents referred to may be found at the Ombudsman's website *http://www.ombudsman.ie*. The following is based on the Office of the Ombudsman Annual Report 2008. Mr Michael Mills was appointed first Ombudsman in 1984. He was succeeded by Mr Kevin Murphy in 1994, who was succeeded by the present incumbent, Ms Emily O'Reilly, in mid-2003; hence references to publications may refer to "he" or "she" depending on the date of publication.

Information Commissioner and Ombudsman compared Whereas both the Information Commissioner and the Ombudsman deal with matters of administrative accountability, as has been noted previously, there are significant differences in the statutory role and responsibility of each Office (*Annual Review of Irish Law 2000*, p.276 et seq.; *Annual Review of Irish Law 2001*, p.409 et seq.; *Annual Review of Irish Law 2002*, p.310 et seq.; *Annual Review of Irish Law 2003*, p.395 et seq.; *Annual Review of Irish Law 2004*, p.330 et seq.; *Annual Review of Irish Law 2005*, p.470 et seq.; *Annual Review of Irish Law 2006*, p.422 et seq.; *Annual Review of Irish Law 2007*, p.359 et seq.; *Annual Review of Irish Law 2008*, p.386 et seq.)

OMBUDSMAN'S SPECIAL REPORT TO BOTH HOUSES OF THE OIREACHTAS

Section 6(5) of the Ombudsman Act 1980 states:

> Where it appears to the Ombudsman that the measures taken or proposed to be taken in response to a recommendation [as a result of an investigation] are not satisfactory, he may, if he so thinks fit, cause a special report on the case to be included in a report under subsection (7) of this section.

Lost At Sea Scheme In December 2009, the Ombudsman issued a special report to both Houses of the Oireachtas in accordance with s.6(5) as well as s.6(7) of the Act. Issuing a special report is an extreme action and it is more usual for Government departments to come to an agreement with the Ombudsman. So serious is such an action, and so inadequate was the response of the Oireachtas, that the Ombudsman introduced her Annual Report for 2009 by focussing on this issue which reverberated into 2010 and is unresolved as at September 2010. The Ombudsman noted that the decision and recommendation in her report on the Lost at Sea Scheme was rejected by the Department of Agriculture, Fisheries and Food. She continued as follows:

> "While the Department is free in law to reject my recommendations, this is only the second time in the twenty-five year history of the Office that this has happened. The previous episode – relating to a series of complaints against the Revenue Commissioners – was successfully resolved with the assistance and support of the Oireachtas.
>
> Subsequent media coverage and commentary on the special report highlighted issues around the credibility and integrity of the institution of the Ombudsman and the relationship with the Houses of the Oireachtas." *Annual Report of the Ombudsman 2009*, p.10.

Background In 1990, a new regulatory system was introduced which effectively limited the overall fleet capacity of the Irish sea-fishing fleet. The Lost at Sea Scheme was designed to address the needs of those boat owners who had lost their boats at sea between 1980 to 1989 and who would otherwise have had a boat on which replacement capacity would have been assessed under the new regulatory system at the time of its introduction. If successful under the Scheme an applicant would have been granted capacity in their own right which would have enabled them to carry on a tradition of fishing.

The Ombudsman received six complaints from persons asserting that they were unfairly denied benefit under the Scheme. Only one was upheld by the Ombudsman, that of the Byrne family. Their boat, the MFV Skifjord had tragically sunk off North West Donegal in October 1981. The owner and skipper, Francis Byrne, lost his life along with his 16-year-old son Jimmy, and three other crew members. His widow had been left with a young family of five boys and three girls. The family did not become aware of the existence of the scheme until after the closing date for applications and when they did apply the then Department of Communications, Marine and Natural Resources had rejected their application. The Byrne family then sought the assistance of the Ombudsman. The Ombudsman concluded that whereas the Byrne family failed to comply with all of the eligibility conditions of the Lost at Sea Scheme, the design of the Scheme and the manner in which it was advertised were contrary to fair and sound administration and that these shortcomings were factors in the Byrne family not qualifying for assistance under the Scheme.

The Ombudsman held that:

> "1 The Byrne family application did not meet at least two of the conditions of the Lost at Sea Scheme, as published. The family was adversely affected by the decision to refuse Ms Winifred Byrne's application under the Scheme.
>
> 2 The way the Lost at Sea Scheme was designed was contrary to fair and sound administration. The specific weaknesses in the design process included, lack of adequate research, lack of thorough documented analysis of the pros and cons of the various criteria and a failure to include provision for discretion in the vetting of applications.
>
> 3 Given that this was a finite, once-off Scheme, aimed at a specific class of individuals the Scheme was not advertised adequately. The advertising process should have been more thorough, comprehensive and targeted. In addition some prospective applicants were put in a more advantageous position than others as they were written to directly by the Department and the Minister to inform them about the Scheme when it was launched. Overall, the manner in which the Scheme was advertised was contrary to fair and sound administration.
>
> 4 There is clear evidence of poor record-keeping practices leading up to the sign-off of the Scheme, including a paucity of records, lack of written records of meetings and deliberations, a lack of written analysis of the various drafts of the Lost at Sea Scheme and limited records of the interactions/directions between the Minister and his officials." *Lost At Sea Scheme Report*, p.81.

She recommended that financial compensation be paid to the Byrne family. The Department of Agriculture, Fisheries and Food, which has taken on responsibility for these matters, refused to accept the recommendation. It was consequent on this rejection that the Ombudsman issued her Report to the Oireachtas. This lengthy and comprehensive Report which includes the responses to the Ombudsman's findings of the Department and the then

Minister, Frank Fahey TD, may be found at *www.ombudsman.gov.ie/en/Reports/InvestigationReports/14December2009-LostatSeaScheme*.

Failure of Oireachtas The matter is still unresolved at the time of writing, i.e. no final recommendation has issued from the Houses of the Oireachtas. Dividing on party political lines the Dáil initially voted not to refer the Ombudsman's Report to the Joint Committee on Agriculture, Fisheries and Food for further deliberation. A subsequent attempt at a meeting of the Committee to have the report considered also failed. It was only following a media controversy that eventually the Joint Committee on Agriculture, Fisheries and Food did request both the Ombudsman and the Department to address it. Readers are referred to the Ombudsman's Speeches webpage *www.ombudsman.gov.ie/en/SpeechesandArticles/Ombudsmansspeeches*, most particularly her Statement to Joint Oireachtas Committee on Agriculture, Fisheries and Food, April 21, 2010 and her earlier public addresses, "In the Public Interest: Lessons from the Ombudsman's Experience" address at Institute of Public Administration & Chartered Institute of Public Finance and Accounting – Conference on Good Governance, March 9, 2010 and "Challenge and Change in the Irish Public Service in 2010" address at the Public Affairs Ireland Conference, March 24, 2010.

Ombudsman's Findings In the meantime, the Ombudsman's findings which encompass the substantive issues and points of disagreement are quoted below. Those elements not essential to the narrative have been excluded.

> "In this case, I have had to consider, not just the Department's decision to refuse the Byrne family's application under the Lost at Sea Scheme, but also questions pertaining to the purpose, design and publication of the Scheme. The latter questions are relevant in this particular case because of the nature of the Scheme. It was a non-statutory, once-off scheme, designed to benefit a specific class of persons and, most importantly, was time-bound. Applicants had a once-only opportunity of qualifying for, and benefiting from the terms of the Scheme. In essence, my approach to this case was to consider first whether the Byrne family actually met the eligibility conditions of the Scheme - and it is clear from this report that they did not meet at least two of the stated conditions - and second, given the circumstances of the family's tragic loss and the stated purpose of the Scheme, to consider whether from the outset, it was properly designed and later, adequately published. In other words, my investigation considered not just the question of whether the Byrne family met the conditions of the Scheme, but also whether the design of the Scheme and the publication arrangements were factors in their not qualifying under the Scheme in the first place.

The case is also unusual in that it embraces the actions both of a Minister and those of his officials. Most of the complaints I examine, relate solely to the actions of officials. This is hardly surprising. One only has to think of the myriad decisions made by civil and public servants as they go about the daily business of delivering services to the public. In terms of the overall number of transactions, the actual number involving Ministers, and, in turn, the potential number of complaints relating to their actions, will always be relatively low. Of course, in law, insofar as civil servants are concerned, all acts of a Department and of its officials are the acts of the Minister by virtue of the legal status of a Minister as a corporation sole. This remains the position despite the changes to the accountability of Secretaries general and senior civil servants provided for in the Public Service Management Act, 1997 ...

... In contrast to most cases that I examine, the present case demonstrates clear evidence of the active participation of both the Minister and his officials throughout the Scheme formulation process. He and his officials were deeply involved in defining the objectives of the Lost at Sea Scheme, in designing it, (for example, the Minister amended certain elements of the Scheme criteria which restricted its overall scope and protected it from being abused (see 5.16 [p.46 of Report]), developing the eligibility criteria and bringing the Scheme to the attention of some prospective applicants.

It is also clear that the Minister and his officials held opposing views about the desirability of introducing such a scheme in the first place. While the Minister was clearly determined to introduce a scheme and saw it as desirable, based on his first-hand knowledge of a number of hardship cases which had come to his attention. By contrast, the officials were concerned that it would be difficult to limit the Scheme to the genuinely deserving cases, that this would open the floodgates to other claims and, in turn, erode the Department's policy on regulation and the allocation of tonnage and licences.

There is nothing intrinsically wrong with this approach to designing a scheme. In essence, the approach encapsulates how government works. Considerations ranging from political imperatives, known hardship cases, a desire to address an injustice, protection of the regulatory process in relation to the allocation of tonnage and licences and the public interest, all coalesce and the task of balancing these competing interests results in compromise. Nonetheless any compromise cannot lose sight of the principle of equity in relation to everyone potentially affected by that compromise.

As I have outlined in this report, there is very clear documentary evidence from the Department's files in relation to the Minister's determination to proceed with a scheme. There is also clear evidence, again outlined in my report, of the reasons why the officials were opposed to the introduction of a scheme. However, the Department's files contain little or no evidence as to how the Minister and his officials reconciled these opposing views and arrived at a compromise and the specific criteria which became the basis for the published scheme. What is clear is that the actions of both the Minister and his officials resulted in a scheme which was too focused on known cases and which wrongly excluded some deserving cases. Its overall design was faulty, it left no scope for the exercise of discretion in the event of further deserving cases coming to light following the receipt of applications and paid insufficient attention to the basic Principles of Good Administration and the Ombudsman's Guide to Standards of Best Practice for Public Servants ...

... In this particular case, it seems to me that the officials set about designing a scheme which was fair and equitable and which potentially would allow for other cases to qualify above and beyond those cases which had already come to their attention. The Minister, too, seemed to be of similar intent; he is on record as stating that he was anxious to ring-fence genuine cases and if this meant that 50 cases ended up being eligible then he would not be concerned as long as they were genuine. However, my fundamental point is that the Scheme as implemented did not, in fact, properly reflect its purpose and intent. More thorough research on lost at sea cases should have been carried out, throughout the Department, for the reasons I have set out at 7.5(b) [p.65 ff. of Report] and 7.6 [p.72 ff. of Report]. As a result, the criteria did not capture every deserving case and there was no room to exercise discretion in relation to those small number of cases with unforeseen circumstances which did not meet the criteria but which, nevertheless, fell into the category of cases that the Scheme was intended to cover. I believe it would have been possible to administer the Scheme on this basis while at the same time confining it to those cases that it was intended to cover." *Lost At Sea Scheme Report*, pp.76–80

Local authority charges for photocopying planning documents July 2009 Earlier in 2009 the Ombudsman had laid another section 6(7) Report before the Oireachtas. This may also be accessed in full on the website. The rationale for this Report was stated in the Introduction.

"Public participation in the planning process is an important and valuable element of the planning system. To facilitate the involvement of third parties, planning legislation gives the public the right to inspect and obtain copies of certain types of planning documents. However, the imposition of excessive charges for photocopying such documents can deter members of the public from participating fully. This may not only

> be unfair to the individuals concerned but it can also undermine public confidence in the openness and transparency of the planning system.
>
> Over the past number of years I have received complaints from members of the public about the level of fees being charged by local authorities/planning authorities for photocopies of extracts from planning files. It has been apparent that there has been inconsistency across local authorities in the amounts being charged for photocopies and I have been concerned that the level of fees being charged by some local authorities appeared to be excessive. Where the procedures for making and processing planning applications is standard throughout the country, it seems to me that charges for copies of planning documents should be relatively uniform across all planning authorities. I highlighted the issue in my first Annual Report in 2003 and have referred to it in most of my subsequent annual reports. As I have continued to receive complaints about excessive charges, I have decided to carry out another review across local authorities and report on my findings."

As a consequence of the interaction between the Ombudsman and the Department of Environment, Heritage and Local Government, the Department issued guidelines to all planning authorities in August 2005, Circular Letter PD 4/05. The investigation indicated that this Circular Letter has had little or no impact on the level of charges for photocopying planning documents across the local authorities surveyed. The Ombudsman called on those local authorities who are overcharging to now review their charges, by reference to that Circular and to revise their charges. Should this not happen she stated that she may have no option but to investigate the matter further.

MISUSE OF OMBUDSMAN TITLE

It has been a consistent and justifiable concern of the Ombudsman that the proliferation of appointments using that title diminishes the authority of the Office. We wrote in *Annual Review of Irish Law 2002* under the heading "Imperfect Understanding of Role of Ombudsman" that acceding to interest group requests to appoint an ombudsman:

> "… without due consideration for the exacting requirements of independence for such an office could tend to undermine the principles on which his Office is based. Indeed, the misapplication of the title 'Ombudsman' might conceivably result in bringing elements of the function into disrepute".

Having analysed the flawed Office of the Ombudsman for Children as created by statute we concluded as follows:

> "**Independence of Ombudsman a requirement** In establishing any new positions that might bear the title 'Ombudsman' it could be of value to consider the following comments of Mr. Kevin Murphy, the second appointee to the post, in his introduction to a statement of strategy for his Office for the period 1997 to 1999:
>
> > 'I am required by law to be independent in the exercise of my functions and this independence is the foundation stone of the Office of the Ombudsman. I must be able to operate without being influenced by Government action. Not alone must my Office be independent in fact, it must also be seen as such by those who use the service I provide. The Constitution Review Group recommended that a new Article be inserted in the Constitution confirming the establishment of the Office of Ombudsman and providing for the independent exercise of such investigative and other functions of the Office as may be determined by law. I welcome this recommendation and agree with the Group that such a constitutional guarantee of independence would reinforce freedom from conflict of interest, from deference to the executive, from influence by special interest groups, and that it would support the freedom to assemble facts and reach independent and impartial conclusions'" (*Annual Review of Irish Law 2002*, p.310 et seq.).

Legal Services Ombudsman The statute establishing the Legal Services Ombudsman (Legal Services Ombudsman Act 2009 (No. 8 of 2009)) might be used as a textbook example that the Ombudsman's worst fears as cited above have been realised. One may be forgiven for having thought that a Legal Services Ombudsman (LSO) was being appointed to investigate complaints taken by members of the public against members of the legal professions related to the performance of their function. Indeed s.9 applies:

> (1) The functions of the Legal Services Ombudsman are—
> (a) to receive and investigate complaints,
> (b) to review under section 32 the procedures of the Bar Council and the Law Society for dealing with complaints made to those bodies,
> (c) to assess the adequacy of the admission policies of the Law Society to the solicitors' profession and of the Bar Council to the barristers' profession,
> (d) to promote awareness among members of the public of matters concerning the procedures of the Bar Council and the Law Society for dealing with complaints made to those bodies, and
> (e) to carry out any other duties and exercise any other powers assigned to the Ombudsman by this Act.

> (2) The Legal Services Ombudsman has all powers that are necessary for the performance of the functions of the office.

Section 9(c) requires the LSO to assess the adequacy of the admission policies. How does this duty have any relationship to the investigation of complaints regarding services to the public? Surely any problems relating to admissions are more in the realm of education or competition policy and ought not be a part of the role of complaints regulator? Our comments on the founding statute of the Ombudsman for Children are equally valid here:

> "Such a role compromises the independence and objectivity of an Ombudsman as an impartial investigator seeking redress where appropriate. While the statutory establishment of an office-holder performing these functions may well be necessary, and while it may be considered that such an office-holder is the appropriate person to investigate [complaints re admission to the legal professions], ascribing such a person the title 'Ombudsman' demonstrates a lack of comprehension of the Ombudsman function" (*Annual Review of Irish Law 2002*, p.311).

Based on this statute it is difficult to see how anybody could consider this Office satisfying the "independence" requirement of an Ombudsman. Under s.11 the office-holder may not even appoint a secretary or, assuming funds allowed, a cleaner, without the consent of two Ministers, the Bar Council and the Law Society:

> (1) Subject to subsection (2), the Legal Services Ombudsman may, from time to time, appoint persons to be members of the Ombudsman's staff.
>
> (2) The Legal Services Ombudsman may appoint a person under subsection (1) only with the consent of the Minister and the Minister for Finance having, prior to seeking that consent, consulted with the Bar Council and the Law Society in respect of any appointment under that subsection.
>
> (3) Persons appointed under subsection (1) are to be employed on such terms and conditions relating to remuneration (including allowances for expenses and superannuation) or other matters as, after consulting with the Bar Council and the Law Society, the Legal Services Ombudsman determines with the consent of the Minister and the Minister for Finance.

Whilst one might surmise that such a restrictive practice was not the intention of the legislators and that this provision was meant to apply to the LSO's more senior staff, i.e. the investigators, the statute allows for no exceptions.

Furthermore, at the time of writing the Minister for Justice, Equality and Law Reform, the responsible Minister, is a solicitor and the Minister for Finance is a barrister. Indeed, the Minister for Justice, Equality and Law Reform has traditionally been a member of the legal profession. Add to that mix the gag provision referred to at the beginning of this chapter:

> 16(2) The Legal Services Ombudsman when giving evidence under this section shall not question or express an opinion on the merits of any policy of the Government or on the merits of the objectives of such policy.

It is not that "independent" is an unlikely word to characterise the office of Legal Services Ombudsman. Independence does not appear to feature.

OMBUDSMAN (AMENDMENT) BILL

We anticipated in last year's *Annual Review*, p.386, that the long-awaited Ombudsman (Amendment) Bill would be passed into law before the end of 2009. Unfortunately, at the time of writing this has not yet happened. In her Annual Report 2009, p.14, the Ombudsman comments that subject to its enactment, the Bill will bring some 95 additional public bodies under her Office's remit. This will pose considerable challenges in terms of preparing her staff to deal with a wide range of new public bodies and schemes, briefing the new public bodies on the role, functions and procedures of her Office, putting appropriate liaison arrangements in place and dealing with a greatly increased volume of complaints from members of the public. However, as we noted last year a number of organisations appear to have been exempted from the ambit of the Ombudsman in the proposed amended Second Schedule to the original Act. We again ask the question, by what logic is a public body excluded from an oversight regime the purpose of which is to ensure good administration?

STATUTORY NOTICES OF NON-COMPLIANCE WITH OMBUDSMAN REQUESTS

Section 7 A section 7 notice is a statutory demand for the provision of information required by the Office of the Ombudsman Office in examining a complaint and is normally only issued as a last resort when there has been an unacceptable delay on the part of the public body in providing the requested information (*Annual Review of Irish Law 2002*, p.314; *Annual Review of Irish Law 2003*, p.396; *Annual Review of Irish Law 2004*, p.330; *Annual Review of*

Irish Law 2005, p.470; *Annual Review of Irish Law 2006*, p.424; *Annual Review of Irish Law 2007*, p.360; *Annual Review of Irish Law 2008*, p.387).

Eight section 7 notices were issued in 2009 and once again the Ombudsman has recorded the timelines involved for each notice. Details include the date of request for the required report, dates of issue of the first and final reminder notices, and dates pertinent to any extensions requested with the date of acknowledgment and receipt of communication by the public body if any.

Three of the section 7 notices were issued against Waterford (HSE South). A single s.7 was issued against each of Dublin South City (HSE Dublin Mid-Leinster); Donegal (HSE West); HSE (Health Repayment Scheme); Meath (HSE Dublin North East); Cork County Council (*Annual Report of the Ombudsman 2008*, pp.23–24).

SECTORAL OMBUDSMEN

Financial Services Ombudsman We noted in the *Annual Review of Irish Law 2006*, p.426 that a Supreme Court appeal, not yet decided, had been taken against Finnegan P.'s judgment in *Ulster Bank Investment Funds v Financial Services Ombudsman (FSO)* [2006] IEHC 323. The issue in that case was to determine the scope of the appeal taken under s.57CL of the Central Bank Act 1942, as amended by s.16 of the Central Bank and Financial Services Authority of Ireland Act 2004. In *Square Capital v Financial Services Ombudsman* [2009] IEHC 407 McMahon J., acknowledging that there was an appeal to the Supreme Court, was, nevertheless, happy to adopt the test recommended by Finnegan P. in the absence of any authority from the Supreme Court to the contrary. *Ulster Bank* held that to succeed on an appeal against a decision of the Financial Services Ombudsman, the plaintiff must establish as a matter of probability that, taking the adjudicative process as a whole, the decision reached was vitiated by a serious and significant error or a series of such errors. Applying that test he dismissed the appeal.

Transparency required in financial advice The case concerned an investor who had been recommended to purchase property, an investment with which she was disappointed. After some probing by the Financial Services Ombudsman (FSO) "the Ombudsman extracted, with some difficulty, an admission from the appellant that it in fact owned the apartments" it had sold to the investor. The Deputy FSO, whose finding was subsequently upheld by the FSO, had concluded that:

> "the respondent failed in its overall duty of care to the complainant. Best practice dictates that the respondent should have been utterly transparent about the precise nature of its interest in the apartments.

> Clear records should have been kept to demonstrate that same was expressly communicated to the complainant prior to her investment. The respondent should not have left itself open to the charge subsequently made by the complainant – either expressly or impliedly – that the apartments were recommended on some improper basis and/or that the respondent could not advise on, and/or facilitate, her purchase of same in a disinterested manner."

Jurisdictional issue McMahon J. upheld the FSO's right to determine what came within his jurisdiction for adjudication. He noted that s.2 of the Central Bank and Financial Services Authority of Ireland Act 2004, further amended s.2 of the Central Bank Act 1942 so as to provide that "'financial service provider' means a person who carries on a business of providing one or more financial services". It also provides that a regulated financial service provider means, inter alia, a financial service provider whose business is subject to regulation by the Bank or the Regulatory Authority. Section 57BX(2) of the 2004 Act provides:

> Except in the case of a complaint that may be within the jurisdiction of the Pensions Ombudsman, the Financial Services Ombudsman has sole responsibility for deciding whether or not a complaint is within that Ombudsman's jurisdiction.

Section 57BY(1) of the Act provides: "The Financial Services Ombudsman shall investigate a complaint if satisfied that the complaint is within the jurisdiction of the Financial Services Ombudsman."

Arising from these definitions McMahon J. found that the decision as to whether or not a complaint falls within his jurisdiction is one that falls to the Ombudsman to determine.

> "This is not to suggest that the court never has a role to play in interpreting the Act, but it should intervene only in clear cut cases and then, only if such a case contains a serious and significant error. It is significant to note that the appellant has not brought judicial review proceedings to quash the decision for want of jurisdiction."

Compensation Section 57CI(4)(b) provides that if the complaint is found to be wholly or partly substantiated, the FSO may, inter alia, order the respondent "(d) to pay an amount of compensation to the complainant for any loss, expense or inconvenience sustained by the complainant as a result of the conduct complained of". McMahon J. recorded that the Office of the Ombudsman is different from an ordinary court of law and that the provisions of the legislation mean that he has greater flexibility and choice in fashioning an appropriate remedy in the cases that come before him. Observing that the relevant provision enables him, for example, to mitigate or change the conduct complained of or a practice relating to that conduct McMahon J. was of the opinion that it was important, therefore, that appropriate latitude should be given to the Ombudsman in determining what the appropriate remedy is in the circumstances of each individual case.

Garda Síochána Ombudsman Commission (GSOC) The relevant website is *www.Gardaombudsman.ie*. Mr Dermot Gallagher was appointed Chairman of the GSOC in April 2009.

STATUTES AND STATUTORY INSTRUMENTS

Legal Services Ombudsman Act 2009 (No. 8 of 2009) The Act is considered above under Ombudsman.

Central Bank Act 1942 (Financial Services Ombudsman Council) Levies and Fees Regulations 2009 (S.I. No. 500 of 2009) made by the Financial Services Ombudsman Council in accordance with ss.57BE and 57BF of the Central Bank Act 1942 (as amended) amend the Central Bank Act 1942 (Financial Services Ombudsman Council) Levies and Fees Regulations 2006 (S.I. No. 556 of 2006) and provide for a scheme of levies on regulated entities to fund the operation of the Financial Services Ombudsman's Bureau for the year ended December 31, 2010.

Freedom of Information Act 1997 (Section 17(6)) Regulations 2009 (S.I. No. 385 of 2009) prescribe certain classes of individuals who may apply under s.17 of the Freedom of Information Act 1997 (No. 13 of 1997) for amendment of records containing certain incorrect, incomplete or misleading information having regard to relevant circumstances and to guidelines published by the Minister for Finance.

Freedom of Information Act 1997 (Section 18(5A)) Regulations 2009 (S.I. No. 386 of 2009) prescribe certain classes of individuals who may apply under s.18 of the Freedom of Information Act 1997 (No. 13 of 1997) for information regarding acts of public bodies having regard to relevant circumstances and to guidelines published by the Minister for Finance.

Freedom of Information Act 1997 (Section 28(6)) Regulations 2009 (S.I. No. 387 of 2009) prescribe the classes of individual whose records will be made available to parents and guardians, and the classes of requester to whom the records of deceased persons will be made available, having regard to relevant circumstances and to guidelines published by the Minister for Finance.

These Regulations and Guidance Notes are discussed above.

Local Elections (Disclosure of Donations and Expenditure) Act 1999 (Period for Reckoning Election Expenses) Order 2009 determines the period for the reckoning of election expenses incurred by or on behalf of a candidate, designated person, national agent of a political party, or third party at the local elections to be held on June 5, 2009, in accordance with s.12B of the Local Elections (Disclosure of Donations and Expenditure) Act 1999, as amended.

Section 12A of the said Act, as amended, specifies limits on electoral expenditure which may be incurred by a candidate, designated person and national agent during the period specified in the order.

Land Law, Landlord and Tenant Law and Conveyancing

DR FIONA DE LONDRAS, School of Law, University College Dublin

ADVERSE POSSESSION

In *lster Investment Bank Ltd v Rockrohan Estate Ltd* [2009] IEHC 4 it was claimed that court orders for the enforcement of a debt are not subject to a limitation period under the Statute of Limitations 1957. While an action for enforcement of debt must be taken within the limitation period, once an order has been granted under such an action, its exercise or a claim for ancillary relief arising thereunder need not take place within six years. The decision appears, however, to be based to a large extent on the nature of the arrangement between the parties. Irvine J. noted that:

> "The argument of Rockrohan contending for adverse possession based on the provisions of the above section appears to be based on a misunderstanding as to the nature of the present well charging order proceedings. The proceeding (sic) have as their foundation stone a covenant by Rockrohan to discharge certain liabilities. That covenant created an equitable charge but conveyed no legal or equitable estate in those lands to UIB as is clear from the decision in *Ezekiel*. Time could never run against UIB as it has never had any title or right to occupation of the lands."

However, moving beyond that analysis, Irvine J. also held that even if the application for possession were governed by Ord.42 rr.23 and 2, there were sufficient grounds for the court to exercise its discretion to grant the necessary leave to issue execution at this point.

LANDLORD AND TENANT LAW

The Residential Tenancies (Amendment) Act 2009 confirmed the validity of all appointments to the Dispute Resolution Committee of the Private Residential Tenancies Board made since the coming into effect of the Residential Tenancies Act 2004 (s.2(1)). In addition, it provides that all Tenancy Tribunals constituted under the 2004 Act are valid (s.2(1)) and that all decisions of a

Dispute Resolution Committee or a Tenancy Tribunal, which would have been in contravention of s.159 of the 2004 Act (providing for appointment and composition of the Dispute Resolution Committee) were it not for this 2009 Act, "shall be, and be deemed always to have been, valid and effectual for all purposes" (s.2(2)). This is subject to the provision that if s.2(1) and (2) should be found to be in contravention of the constitutional rights of any person, "the operation of that subsection shall be subject to such limitation as is necessary to secure that it does not so conflict but shall otherwise be of full force and effect" (s.2(3)).

The question of service charges and the equitable right of set-off and deductions from rent and service charges arose for consideration before Dunne J. in the High Court in the case of *Irish Life Assurance Plc v Quinn* [2009] IEHC 153. The plaintiff in this case claimed that the defendant tenant was in arrears of rent and had, furthermore, failed to pay the service charges that were properly owed under the conditions of the commercial lease between the parties. While there was no dispute as to the arrears of rent, the defendant claimed that the service charges could not be demanded as a result of the lack of auditor's certificates in relation to them and, furthermore, that the landlord had failed to ensure good estate management resulting in a loss to the defendant's business that it was entitled to deduct from any sums owed on the basis of the right of set-off. As to the first argument, the court considered the terms of the lease between the parties which permitted the landlord to seek from the defendant an amount in service charges ascertained and certified on an annual basis. Clause 3.2(vii) of the lease, however, also provided that on each gale day advance payment of the service charge could be demanded at the landlord's discretion, with the amount charged to be fair and reasonable and subject to certification as to it being so fair and reasonable in all of the circumstances by the landlord or his agent. There was, therefore, no dispute as to the landlord's entitlement to seek a service charge payment. The defendant argued, however, that the landlord was not entitled to enforce the service charge in the absence of the certificates. In this respect the court noted that according to the lease, the landlord did not have any right to re-enter on the basis of the advance service charges but that there was nothing in the lease that disabled the plaintiff landlord from maintaining an action in respect of those charges even before the certificate had been issued. This was subject to the proof by the landlord that the advance payment of the service charge demanded but unpaid was fair and reasonable. Thus, even though on the terms of the lease itself the landlord could not re-enter the premises, the issuance of proceedings was not precluded.

The court then proceeded to consider the claim in respect of set-off. The defendant argued that the landlord had failed in the duty of good estate management because of the failure to replace a previous anchor tenant within the shopping centre with another tenant of similar quality, and because of the fact that one-third of the remaining units were unfilled within the general premises. The result of this, it was contended, was that the defendant's business suffered, causing an unquantifiable loss that could be off-set against the monies owed. The lease itself provided that payments were to be made "without any deductions" and this, combined with s.48 of the Landlord and Tenant Amendment Ireland Act 1860 ("Deasy's Act") formed the basis of the landlord's argument that deductions of the proposed nature were not permissible in this case. Section 48 provides that:

> All claims and demands by any landlord against his tenant in respect of rent shall be subject to deduction or set off in respect of all just debts due by the landlord to the tenant.

The judgment of Maguire P. in *MacCausland and Kimmitt v Carroll and Dooley* (1938) 72 I.L.T.R. 158, interpreting that section as limiting statutory set-off to liquidated sums by the landlord only, was applied by Dunne J. in this case. However, the question of the equitable right of set-off remained and in this respect Dunne J. held that a leasehold provision referring to the payment of rent and service fees "without any deductions" did not preclude reliance on equitable set-off. She therefore considered the claim on that basis and, based on her application of *Prendergast v Biddle*, unreported, Supreme Court, July 21, 1957 and *Moohan and Anor v S & R Motors (Donegal) Ltd,* unreported, High Court, Clarke J., December 14, 2007 concluded that no set-off was permitted here. The defendant had not made any effort whatsoever to quantify the alleged losses and, in addition, no question as to set-off or complaint as to good estate management had been raised in correspondence prior to the issue of proceedings in this case.

Foley & Anor v Mangan [2009] IEHC 404 concerned a complex conveyancing arrangement between the parties, focused on an attempt to secure relief from forfeiture. The defendant was the owner of a large amount of farmyard in North County Dublin and, as he was in some financial difficulty, agreed to sell the plaintiff a large amount of land but subject to the land being leased back to him for a period of four years and nine months *and* to an option to purchase the land within the currency of that lease. The transaction took place by means of three agreements—a contract for the sale of land made conditional upon both the lease and an option agreement, the lease, and an option agreement. The arrangement contained a number of clauses relevant to these proceedings including a clause in which the defendant undertook to provide the plaintiffs with 205 acres of alternative land for croppage per annum (found to be in satisfaction of part of the financial rental requirements) (Special Condition 12); a clause relating to waste, annoyance and nuisance (Clause 7); and a clause relating to insurance (Clause 9). It was claimed that the defendant was in breach of all three and, therefore, that the plaintiff was entitled to effect a forfeiture for non-payment of rent as well as forfeiture for breach of conditions (in which case the forfeiture would be a statutory one under s.14 of the Conveyancing Act 1881). On the basis of the evidence before her, Laffoy J. concluded that there was no basis for forfeiture for non-payment of rent *or* for breach of Clause 9; the balance of the judgment was therefore focused on forfeiture for breach of Clause 7 and a claim for relief from forfeiture.

As a result of the failure to properly manage the release of slurry and effluent from cattle sheds and the ensuing pollution of the land, the court found that the defendant was in breach of Clause 7. This gave rise to a statutory right of forfeiture, but that itself required compliance with s.14 of the Conveyancing Act 1881, including the service of a notice of forfeiture. Section 14 requires that a forfeiture notice would include a statement of an alleged breach and, if that breach were not remedied within a reasonable period of time, re-entry proceedings could then be progressed. In this case it was claimed that the notice did not sufficiently state the alleged breach, however, Laffoy J. found that outlining the breach in general terms was adequate: there was no need to go into specifics provided it indicated what steps were required to remedy the breach, as was the case here. Secondly, it was claimed that there was no reasonable period for remedy pursuant to the notice. The court found that where a specific period of time is mentioned on the section 14 notice and is considered to be too short, the tenant can always approach the landlord and ask for an extension, the refusal of which request is likely to go to the reasonableness of the time period. In this case there was no specified time period, therefore, the period of time is from issue of the notice (March 2, 2006) to the issue of proceedings to enforce the notice (July 28, 2006). It was clear that because the defendant denied the breach he had no intention of remedying it and, furthermore, that a five-month period was quite adequate for the remedy of the breach of Clause 7. Thirdly, the court clarified that acceptance of service of the notice by the defendant's solicitor was effective in the same way as acceptance of service by the defendant himself would have been. Therefore, s.14 had been complied with in respect of the issue of the notice of forfeiture.

The court then considered whether there was a defence against forfeiture in this case. First, it was found that there had been no waiver—although the plaintiff had been in contact in respect of the land after the proceedings commenced, it was settled law that correspondence subsequent to the service was not a waiver (*McIlvenny v McKeever* [1931] N.I. 161). Furthermore, Laffoy J. held that issuing proceedings are a final and unequivocal determination that the landlord will rely on forfeiture and deprive himself of other contractual remedies (*Moffat v Frisby* [2007] 4 I.R. 512). Thus, there had been no waiver here. Section 14 of the Conveyancing Act 1881 also allows for statutory relief to be granted. In this respect, the court held that this is part of the court's discretionary jurisdiction "to be exercised largely on the same principles as the general equitable jurisdiction to afford relief which may be invoked in cases of forfeiture for non-payment of rent". The court must, therefore, look at the totality of the circumstances in the case in assessing whether to grant relief. In this case the lease was part of a broader conveyancing arrangement including the option agreement and forfeiture of the lease would impact upon that option agreement and the defendant's capacity to exercise it. Taking this into account, together with the bona fides of the plaintiff and the conduct of the parties, Laffoy J. granted relief from forfeiture on the basis of s.14(2), but subject to three conditions: (1) timely completion of a sale under the option agreement; (2) a personal undertaking from the defendant to comply fully with all waste and pollution requirements and statutes; and (3) that the defendant would be liable for the costs of the plaintiff.

In the important decision of *Anthony Kidney & Ronan McNamee v Julian Charlton & Edward Charlton* [2009] M.R. 1, the Master of the High Court considered the meaning of upwards only rent reviews in commercial leases. The lease in question related to premises on Dawson St in Dublin and included a standard clause allowing for the appointment of an arbitrator for the purposes of rent review every five years. The Master considered whether such a clause meant that, pursuant to a rent review, the rental payment can never be reduced. In this respect he noted that an upwards only rent review clause can be either threshold (i.e. requiring that rent never go beneath the rent payable at the commencement of the lease) or ratchet (i.e. requiring that the rent would not go beneath the rent payable immediately preceding the rent review). Having considered the nature of contractual interpretation including the role of the parties' intention, public policy and the founding principle that parties are presumed to be acting reasonably, the Master noted that rent review clauses ought to be read closely and carefully considered. All the surrounding circumstances—including the public policy implications of allowing for a windfall in times of recession and the preoccupation in Irish policy with fair rents—ought to be taken into account. Having found that parties are assumed to know the difference between a threshold and a ratchet upwards only rent review clause, he concluded that such a clause could be interpreted as being of either kind. He then proceeded to explain the interpretive method thus (pp.8–9):

> "The thought process sequence is as follows: firstly, because it's a long term or relational contract, the parties must have intended to co-operate towards that end and to be fair in their ongoing dealings with each other. And, secondly, because they intended to be fair in all respects, all uncertain clauses, including an ambiguous rent review clause, are to be interpreted in that light.
>
> There is clear mutual security in a clause which both protects the lessor's stream of income from falling below that which was the basis of his funding for his asset at the outset, and the provision which shares the risk and protects the lessee from any subsequent downturn in trading environment which would otherwise imbalance the relationship and generate a windfall for the lessor.
>
> Likewise, in regard to the actual arbitration, same must be carried out transparently, and demonstrably fairly. A system in which rent

> reviews are apparently adjudicated by estate agents whose day job is the marketing of like property usually by reference to selling points such as 'strong rental growth potential' is *prima facie* a system which gives rise to significant and legitimate misgivings."

Bearing all of this in mind, and noting that arbitrators ought to take close account of the clarification of the law offered within the decision, the Master concluded that an upwards only rent review does not necessarily preclude a reduction in rent. Rather, as his decision shows at some length, it will be a matter of interpretation in each case.

SOLICITORS' UNDERTAKINGS

Bank of Ireland Mortgage Bank v Coleman [2009] IESC 38 (May 5, 2009) concerned the remedies available where a solicitor is found in breach of an undertaking. In this case the solicitor's undertaking included a promise not to release the amount of €250,500 advanced by the bank to the solicitor until such time as the solicitor had received a duly executed mortgage from the borrower to the Bank of Ireland. The solicitor, however, advanced those monies before the receipt of this mortgage and the Bank of Ireland sought compensation for breach and the repayment of the entire amount of the undertaking to be ordered by the court exercising its inherent disciplinary jurisdiction over its officers, including solicitors. The Supreme Court confirmed the position as outlined in *IPLG Limited v Stuart* [1992] IEHC 372 that courts retain this jurisdiction notwithstanding the Solicitors Act 1960. This jurisdiction was said to be both compensatory and punitive and, where its exercise is in question, there were two important analytical steps: (1) do the circumstances in question warrant the exercise of the jurisdiction at all, and (2) if so, what form should that exercise take. The court noted the importance of considering the undertaking as a whole and of seeing the individual clause in question within its context. This did not, the court held, mean that an isolated obligation can *never* be enforced, but rather that a contextual consideration is required. In addition, the court held that the exercise of this discretion ought not to be oppressive to the solicitor in question—rather any compensation ordered ought to be just in the circumstances and this will not necessarily mean that the compensation ordered is to be equal to the amount of monies advanced on the basis of the undertaking. Applying these principles to the case in question, the court concluded that there was a basis for exercising discretion but that, taking all of the circumstances into account (including the generality of the practice complained of), it would be oppressive to order repayment of the entire sum advanced. In addition, the court found that the bank had carelessly acted on an overvaluation of the property in question, and, in fact, compensation should be calculated based on the *real* value of the security being acquired through the mortgage. Importantly, Geoghegan J. noted that where a bank is fraudulently misled by conduct to which a solicitor is party this will have an impact on the way in which the court exercises its discretion:

> "... the special supervisory jurisdiction of the court invoked by summary proceedings is discretionary in nature. In this particular case where the bank appears to have carelessly acted on an overvaluation of the property it was, therefore, going to be at any rate left with a much lesser security than it anticipated. In those circumstances it would not be appropriate to measure the compensation that might be ordered to be paid by the solicitor as the actual amount of the loan, unless, of course, the bank had been misled as a consequence of fraudulent conduct to which the solicitor had been party".

In *AIB Plc v Maguire & Ors practicing as Seamus Maguire & Co Solicitors* [2009] IEHC 374, the High Court had the opportunity to refine and apply the principles laid down by the Supreme Court in *Coleman*. This case once again concerned the failure to comply with a solicitor's undertaking to a lending bank. The plaintiff bank in this case sanctioned a loan in the amount of €3,000,000 for the purchase of property in Co. Wexford known as Moongate. Pursuant to a solicitor's undertaking to deal with the conveyance in a manner that protected the bank's interest as mortgagee, and following a decision by the bank to neither engage their own solicitor nor seek an independent valuation of the property, the monies were drawn down into the defendant firm's client account. Very shortly afterwards those funds were used in the process of purchasing a property in Dalkey for which the bank had previously refused to provide financing and the solicitor's undertaking was never complied with. All of the funds were used in the purchase of this property and the previous mortgage that existed on the Moongate property was never redeemed. None of the parties to the case disputed that the undertaking was not complied with, that the loan had been called in by the bank, and that the borrowers were now in no position to pay that loan. Neither was it disputed that the failure to comply with the undertaking was that of an individual solicitor in the defendant firm and that once it came to the partners' attention the firm had acted in an entirely appropriate and professional manner. The central question in this case was whether the court ought to allow the undertaking to now be complied with (which would cost the defendant firm in the region of €1,500,000), notwithstanding the delay, rather than order the repayment of the entire loan amount. Referring to the Supreme Court's decision in *Coleman* as reflecting a somewhat "benign" approach, the High Court in this case spent a considerable amount of time assessing whether it fell into the *Coleman* exception, i.e. cases where "the bank had been misled as a consequence of fraudulent conduct to which the solicitor had been party".

Peart J., thus, outlined the principles of *Coleman*:

"1. The Court has an inherent jurisdiction in matters concerning the conduct of solicitors, being officers of the court, including but not confined to compliance with their undertakings.
2. It is both a punitive and compensatory jurisdiction.
3. It is discretionary and unfettered in nature requiring each case to be considered on its own facts and circumstances.
4. In its exercise, the Court is concerned to uphold the integrity of the system, and the highest standards of honourable behaviour by its officers – a standard higher than that required by law generally.
5. The order made by the Court can take whatever form best serves the interests of justice between the parties.
6. In the matter of undertakings, the Court must consider the entire undertaking in order to reach a conclusion as to its real ultimate purpose.
7. The Court may order compliance with the undertaking, though late, where there remains a reasonable possibility of so doing.
8. Even where the undertaking may still be complied with, the Court may nevertheless order the solicitor to make good any loss actually occasioned by the breach of undertaking, which may or may not be the entire of the sum which was the subject of the undertaking.
9. Where compliance is not possible to achieve by the time the Court is deciding what order to make, if any, it may order the solicitor to make good any loss actually occasioned by the breach of undertaking.
10. Carelessness or other form of negligence on the part of the person affected by the undertaking, and in relation to the matter the subject thereof, may be a factor which the Court will have regard to when determining what order may be fair and just.
11. Any order the Court may make ought not be oppressive on the solicitor. Nevertheless, gross carelessness or other conduct considered sufficiently egregious by the Court, though falling short of criminal behaviour or even professional misconduct, will entitle the Court, should it consider it just to do so, to order payment of the entire sum which was the subject of the undertaking, and not simply a lesser sum in respect of loss actually occasioned by the breach of undertaking."

Peart J. then proceeded to add another principle, which he linked to No. 11 above:

> "It seems to me that the special supervisory jurisdiction being exercised by the Court in these matters is not unlike an equitable jurisdiction, given the wide discretionary nature thereof, and its objective of ensuring

> that justice is done between the parties in a broad sense. In my view, therefore, it seems to me that it is not inappropriate or otherwise wrong for this Court to have regard to the overall behaviour of the solicitor, somewhat akin to seeing whether a person who is claiming an equitable relief has come to court with clean hands, even where the undertaking may be still reasonably capable of being completed, and even where the loss actually occasioned and sustained by the claimant may be less than the entire sum which was the subject of the undertaking."

This was said to be integral to the rationale for the court's jurisdiction in this area, i.e. the upholding of professional standards and conduct by solicitors:

> "In cases of deliberate, conscious or reckless breach of an undertaking by a solicitor, and not one resulting from mere mistake, oversight, inadvertence or other human frailty, a situation cannot be allowed to exist whereby the Court is seen to tolerate less than honourable and professional behaviour, by permitting a solicitor who has acted thus, egregiously, and in a way that is deliberate and utterly reprehensible, to simply walk away from that with permission to comply late with his undertaking, and pay whatever sum has resulted directly from the breach, and perhaps leave the other party with a substantial loss to bear. To my mind, such an order may be appropriate where the breach has been accidental or otherwise not deliberate, or through inadvertence or other human frailty, but that an egregious, deliberate and fundamental breach must be treated differently in order to take account of and mark its distinct character, and the court's absolute disapproval and condemnation thereof."

The court here was satisfied that the case fell within the exception to *Coleman* and, therefore, that a non-benign approach was appropriate and permissible. It also rejected the claim that ordering a full repayment would be oppressive because the plaintiffs had been contributorily negligent as a result of their failure to appoint a solicitor and get an individual valuation for the property (which was now valued at around €620,000). Having heard expert testimony on the matter, Peart J. held that the bank had followed standard practice in relation to the conveyance. The court, thus, found that the appropriate exercise of discretion in this case was to order for the full repayment of the loan amount together with interest due to date.

MORTGAGES

Anglo Irish Bank Plc v Fanning [2009] IEHC 141 concerned a large mortgage of over €8,000,000 taken out by Fanning, using his home as security. A portion of these monies was for the refinancing of the residential property but the vast majority was intended for the financing of a large share purchase in Smart Telecom (of which Fanning was the CEO). The defendant claimed that the monies advanced for the purposes of acquiring the shares were advanced not on the basis of the security but rather on the basis of assurances from Mr Murtagh. At this point, the mortgagee bank was attempting to take possession of the property and the defence related primarily to the debt relating to the share purchase, rather than the debt relating to the refinancing of the home which was treated by the parties as an essentially separate debt. On that basis, Dunne J. in the High Court found that there was a default on the loan relating to the refinancing and, therefore, that Anglo Irish Bank was entitled to take possession. In addition, the defendant had argued that the court ought to adjourn proceedings to a plenary hearing in order to litigate the issues raised by the defendant in respect of that part of the loan used to purchase Smart Telecom Shares. Dunne J. endorsed the view of Finlay C.J. in *National Irish Bank Limited v Graham* [1995] 2 I.R. 244 that such a plenary hearing is for the purpose of resolving a factual dispute, the resolution of which is necessary to reach decision in a case. On the basis of the facts before the court there was no basis for such an adjournment: although the arrangement was atypical in many ways there was no basis to challenge the amount said to be owed, no deficiency relating to the execution of the indenture of mortgage, and no basis upon which it might be said that any collateral agreement with Mr Murtagh could effect the mortgagee's capacity to enforce the loan.

In *ACC Bank Plc v Fairlee Properties Ltd & Ors* [2009] IEHC 45, the High Court considered questions relating to the failure to produce title documents when requested in respect of mortgaged property. It was not disputed that the mortgagee bank had an obligation to produce same upon request or that it had breached what was described as "the standard of care and/or professional service which it would wish to give to its clients" (para.27). The plaintiff, however, attempted to rely on *Gilligan & Nugent v National Bank* [1901] 2 I.R. 513 in order to exclude liability. *Gilligan* related to water damage to title documents and, for the purposes of this case, the relevant principle arising from the case was that there was no action in damages for a mortgagor against a mortgagee relating to negligence in the safekeeping of the documents *prior* to redemption. Finlay Geoghegan J., however, distinguished *Gilligan* on a number of bases. Firstly, normal banking and conveyancing practice had changed since the time of *Gilligan*; while in that case the references were to actual redemption, in contemporary practice it is standard for documents to be produced on accountable receipt and, therefore, in advance of actual redemption, especially where a property is being refinanced. Secondly, *Gilligan* could be distinguished because it related to the condition of documents and not to the statutory obligation to produce same (Conveyancing Act 1881, s.16). Finally, *Gilligan* predated the important decision of *Donohue v Stephenson* [1932] A.C. 562 and the development within that case of the so-called "neighbour principle" in tort. While *Gilligan* was based primarily on considerations of an implied term within the mortgage, the neighbour principle is also relevant and can be a sufficient basis for the imposition of a duty of care (para.39):

> "It must have been reasonably foreseeable to the plaintiff that if it was careless in the storing of the title-deeds such that they could not produce them on request, that such carelessness would be likely to injure the defendants. As is clear from the subsequent decisions, that, of itself, is not now sufficient to find in law the existence of a duty of care. The Court must consider the reasonableness in the imposition of such a duty of care and public policy may play a role in that finding. I am satisfied on the facts of this case that it is reasonable to impose a duty of care on the plaintiff as mortgagee or chargee who received the title documents to development properties over which it has been given security, to take reasonable care in the storage of those title documents such that it could, at all material times, and in particular in connection with a proposed redemption from an agreed refinancing either produce them for inspection pursuant to s. 16 of the Act of 1881, or, if they are agreeable to do so, make them available to the mortgagor's solicitor on accountable [sic] receipt, when requested."

The duty of care is then measured by standard tort mechanisms.

CONVEYANCING

Hannon & Ors v BQ Investments [2009] IEHC 191 concerned trustees of the Thomand Football Club who sought an injunction compelling the defendant to construct and make available a right of way pursuant to a contract for the sale of land from August 25, 2005. Condition 10 of that contract provided that, "a right of way over the roadway having a width of six metres with a footpath on both sides and appropriate public lighting" would be provided to the plaintiffs in order to ensure access to football pitches and a clubhouse that were to be developed. Following the completion of the conveyance, however, neither the sports pavilion (pitches and clubhouse) nor the right of way referred to within Condition 10 had in fact been constructed. The defendants argued that the obligation in respect of the right of way did not arise until the pitches and clubhouse had been built; on the contrary, the plaintiffs argued that the obligation within Condition 10 was not subject to any such condition precedent. In the High Court, Laffoy J. rejected the defendants' argument, holding that there were no words within Condition 10 to evidence an intention to make the obligation subject to a condition precedent. Rather than being for that purpose, the reference to "the football pitches and the clubhouse" within Condition 10 was intended to set the limitations of the right of way and to interpret them as making the obligation contingent upon construction of the pitches and clubhouses would be to imply additional words into the contract. As a result, the defendant was found to be in breach of the contractual obligation contained within Condition 10. Because of a number of surrounding circumstances including a compulsory purchase order pursuant to the Limerick Regeneration Project, it was unlikely that the pitches and clubhouse would in fact be constructed and damages for breach of the condition were awarded.

JUDGMENT MORTGAGES

Although the chronology of facts in the case of *Barnes & Anor v The Land Registry* [2009] IEHC 371 was somewhat complicated, the decision of the High Court in that case was concerned with situations in which the respondent might be obliged to remove judgment mortgages from the Folio. The case originated in a dispute as to hedge cutting on or near a boundary line between the applicants' land and that of their neighbours. This dispute had been resolved in favour of the respondent and resulted in costs being awarded against the applicants. As a result of the failure to pay these costs, judgment mortgages for taxed costs were placed on the applicants' land, in relation to which well charging orders were issued in 2004. The applicants did not make an appearance at those equity proceedings, following which one acre of land was subjected to public auction and a bid of €170,000 was made and accepted, although—as a result of the present proceedings—the sale had not yet been completed. The applicants had applied to the respondent for removal of the judgment mortgage burdens on May 6, 2004 but this application was refused. They now claimed that the judgment mortgages ought to have been removed by the respondent as they were alleged to have been based on orders of Barr J. of December 7, 2001 which no longer stood. This contention was, however, found to be incorrect in fact by the court, which instead found that these orders were not set aside. The applicants' claim in this respect had been based, inter alia, on clear misunderstandings as to jurisdiction and the proceedings that had taken place relating to those orders. Furthermore, the applicants had failed to make an appearance at the equity proceedings for enforcement of the judgment mortgage or to raise these concerns then. O'Neill J., thus, found that in the absence of any challenge to those orders at the time at which the equity proceedings were taking place *and* on the basis of clear compliance with s.6 of the Judgment Mortgages Act 1850, on the face of the affidavits, the respondent had had no grounds upon which to remove the judgment mortgages as burdens from the Folio.

In the important and carefully considered case of *AIB Plc v Dormer & Roe* [2009] IEHC 586, the High Court considered whether an order for sale on foot of a judgment mortgage enured for the benefit of all those with incumbrances over the land in question, thereby bringing them within the scope of Ord.33 r.8 of the Rules of the Superior Courts and ensuring that the Statute of Limitations

1957 ceased to run against those incumbrancers at that time. Order 33 r.8 provides:

> Any incumbrancer subsequent in order of priority to the demand of the plaintiff, in case any lands or property the subject of such suit shall remain unsold, after provision for the plaintiff's demands and those of prior incumbrancers, shall be at liberty to apply to the Court for an order directing a sale of such unsold lands or property, or a competent part thereof, for payment of the demands subsequent to that of the plaintiff, which may have been proved as aforesaid; and the Court may accordingly direct such sale, if of opinion that such incumbrancers, or any of them, would be entitled to have their demands raised by a sale of such lands or property; or may direct a receiver to be appointed or continued over such unsold land or property, for the benefit of such subsequent incumbrancers and distribute the funds to be received by such receiver accordingly.

Roe—the notice party in this case—had obtained judgment in the sum of IR£26,139 against the defendant on October 14, 1993, which judgment was then registered as a judgment mortgage against the defendant's interest in the lands in Folio 14365, County Laois on December 17, 1993. The plaintiff in this case had secured a well charging order in respect of the same lands on July 17, 1995. In her wide-ranging judgment, Finlay Geoghegan J. considered that although *Harpur v Buchanan*, on which the notice party placed heavy reliance, was understood to mean that an order for sale would enure of all incumbrancers (thereby stopping the limitation period against them at the point of commencement of proceedings), it seemed to have been decided without the cases of *Re Nixon's Estate* (1874) 9 Ir. R. Eq. 7 and *Re Colclough* (1858) 8 Ir. Ch. R. 330 being opened to the court (para.25). In those cases it appeared that the order for sale might enure for all incumbrancers inasmuch as they would seek a share of the proceeds of sale. This was not the relief sought in the case at bar, where the notice party sought an order for sale and as between *Harpur* and *In Re Nixon's Estate* in particular, she appeared to prefer the latter, describing its reasoning as "persuasive" (para.28). However, she went on to note the limited utility of this conclusion in the present case as:

> "The above and other authorities to which I was referred do not expressly consider the impact of an order for sale on the application of a Statute of Limitations (and obviously not the Act of 1957) to an incumbrancer who has not yet made a claim or proved in the proceedings and who, as a puisne incumbrancer, applies for or to take over an order for sale where the plaintiff's debt has been discharged and the plaintiff does not want to proceed with the sale." (para.29)

In respect of such cases she found it necessary to ascertain the meaning of the following portion of O'Connor M.R.'s judgment in *Harpur* (at 3 of *Harpur* and para.29 of *Dormer*):

> "A mortgagee suit is also a suit on behalf of all the incumbrancers in the sense that all incumbrancers must be ascertained and paid out of the proceeds of sale so far as they go."

While she agreed with the interpretation of this dictum from *Royal Bank of Ireland v Sproule* [1940] Ir. Jur. Rep. 33 (that "when both a sale takes place and incumbrancers claim or prove then the proceedings and/or order for sale enures for the benefit of such proving incumbrancers" (*Dormer*, para.30)), Finlay Geoghegan J. turned her attention primarily to cases—such as the one at bar—where neither of these scenarios had occurred.

In her analysis, Finlay Geoghegan J. helpfully considers the matter in each of the three relevant time periods which she, thus, classifies (at para.31):

> "(i) From the date of commencement of the proceedings to the date upon which the order for sale comes into effect, and
> (ii) From the date upon which the order for sale comes into effect until an advertisement for incumbrancers is published, and
> (iii) Subsequent to the advertisement for incumbrancers."

She concluded that in the first period a plaintiff owes no obligation to any other incumbrancer; neither does any other incumbrancer acquire any right by reason of the existence of the proceedings (para.32). The extent of the obligations in the second period appears to be somewhat dependent on the nature of the order that arises from the proceedings. As noted in para.34 of the judgment, Ord.15 r.31 of the Rules of the Superior Courts gives the court jurisdiction to order that proceedings be served on other parties. In this case no such order had been made and neither had any other parties joined the proceedings. In this case the matter was settled between the parties after the order had been made and in those circumstances the court held:

> "[T]here is nothing in any of the judgments referred to which suggests an obligation on a plaintiff, even after an order for sale becomes absolute, to proceed with the sale if it wishes to vacate the order for sale and discontinue". (para.34)

That then raised the question of whether, in circumstances such as these, an incumbrancer had acquired any actual rights (rather than potential rights) on the basis of the order for sale, subsequently vacated.

In this relation, Finlay Geoghegan J. found that an incumbrancer accrued no such rights from the order for sale because, on what was described as "a careful reading" of the authorities, she held that:

> "[T]he benefit identified appears to have been that those incumbrancers who came in and proved in the proceedings were entitled to be paid in accordance with their respective priorities out of the proceeds of sale (if any)". (para.35)

This is notwithstanding the fact that a practice had developed in the examiner's office to direct a plaintiff who, after the notice to proceed has been served and before the advertisement for incumbrances, wishes to apply for an order vacating the order for sale to give notice to all incumbrancers appearing on searches. That practice was not, however, based on any judgment, nor did it affect the court's finding in the case (para.37). Indeed, at the conclusion of the judgment, the court opined "subject to any appeal that might be taken against the judgment" that, "it may not be appropriate to continue [this] existing general practice in the Examiner's office" (para.52).

The third phase (i.e. subsequent to the advertisement for incumbrancers), involves somewhat different considerations provided "one or more incumbrancers have come in and proved in the proceedings within the time specified" (para.38). Should the plaintiff proceed with the sale at that point the proved incumbrancers would be entitled to payment from the proceeds in accordance with priority. However, those incumbrancers would not, it was held, be in a position to compel sale—the plaintiff may still opt to vacate the order for sale in which case the incumbrancers could apply for an order for sale under Ord.33 r.8. In paras 40–41, Finlay Geoghegan J. considered the effect of that Rule thus:

> "40. I am satisfied that … O. 33, r. 8, in its terms, only applies to an incumbrancer who has already proved in the proceeding prior to the date upon which the application is brought. As appears from the wording of the rule, the application envisaged by rule 8 is an application by an incumbrancer for an order directing a sale of unsold lands 'for payment of the demands subsequent to that of the plaintiff which may have been proved as aforesaid' (emphasis added). The reference to 'which may have been proved as aforesaid' is a reference to proof under the preceding rule 7. The later part of the rule provides that the Court may make such an order if it is of opinion that the applicant incumbrancer and any of the incumbrancers 'would be entitled to have their demands raised by a sale of such lands …' As the notice party herein is not an incumbrancer who has proved, I will leave over the issue as to the date upon which this requires the Court to form the view that the applicant incumbrancer who has proved would have been entitled to an order for

> sale. Such dates potentially include the date of the order for sale, the date upon which it came into effect, the date upon which the incumbrancers claimed in the proceedings or the date of application.
>
> 41. Order 33, rule 8 is consistent with the absence of any obligation on a plaintiff to proceed with an order for sale even where incumbrancers have proved in the proceeding. It provides, in the alternative, a procedure by which as is sometimes said the incumbrancers who has proved may take over carriage of the order for sale. The underlying fairness and purpose of this rule would seem obvious. If a plaintiff whose debt has been discharged is not obliged to proceed with the sale for the benefit of other incumbrancers who have proved in the proceeding, then such incumbrancers as persons who have already participated by making a claim in the proceeding, should be entitled in the existing proceeding to proceed with the sale provided, of course, they are at the relevant date entitled to have their debt realised out of the sale. An incumbrancer who had proved in the proceeding might well have decided not to commence separate proceeding and if he were not permitted to do so might have permitted his claim to become statute-barred. He may also have incurred costs in proving his claim."

The court did note, however, that there may be some circumstances where an incrumbrancer who had not proved might be capable of coming within the Rule. In this relation, Finlay Geoghegan J. referred to "an incumbrancer who was already joined as a party to the proceedings or participated in some way, [but] has not formally proved" (para.43). The court did not elaborate on that point but, as considered below, it arose for consideration in the subsequent case of *Bank of Ireland v Moffitt* [2009] IEHC 545.

Finally, the court considered the boundaries of any inherent jurisdiction to consider an application from an incumbrancer (who was not already a party to the proceedings or who had not yet proved in the proceedings for an order for sale of the lands), to take over the proceedings in the name of the plaintiff. This was so even though no such contention was made in the proceedings at hand. An incumbrancer who had not proved or is not a party to the proceedings is, the court held,

> "[a]t most ... a person who may potentially have benefited either from the proceeding or the order for sale if the plaintiff had advertised for incumbrances and if he had made a claim within the time specified in any advertisement" (para.46).

Finlay Geoghegan J. concluded that such jurisdiction can be exercised only if the notice party had established an entitlement to have his judgment debt raised by a sale of the land at the time of his application. Furthermore, in this case, no steps had been taken by the notice party to seek to enforce the judgment debt since he secured a judgment on October 14, 1993. Indeed, the notice party was now acting as a result of the decision of the plaintiff to take action relating to the debt owed to it, which the plaintiff bank was now happy had been discharged. "In those circumstances", the court held, "it would be unjust to direct a sale for the purpose of enabling the notice party realise a debt which is otherwise not now recoverable" (para.50).

Dormer was subsequently considered in *Bank of Ireland v Moffitt* [2009] IEHC 545. It was contended that Finlay Geoghegan J. had been mistaken as to the law in her finding that well charging orders enured only for incumbrancers who had proved. Secondly, it was argued that, even if the decision in *Dormer* was correct, the applicant/notice party (ACC Bank) in this had participated and engaged with the examiner to the extent to fall within the additional classification briefly considered in *Dormer*. Finally, the applicant/notice party claimed that, unlike in *Dormer*, there had been no unwarranted delay in this case. McMahon J. in the High Court considered the decision as to proved incumbrancers in *Dormer* and concluded that the decision was correct as to the law and there was no reason to depart from the reasoning therein (para.18). In respect of the second claim—that the applicant/notice party had sufficiently engaged or participated with the examiner to counteract the lack of proof—the court found that they had not. At para.29, McMahon J. held:

> "Bearing in mind that the ACC was not a party, had been given notice of the need to prove its debt and chose not to do so and that the level of participation in the proceedings by the ACC was of a particularly low level, I do not believe this was the kind of case Finlay Geoghegan J. had in mind when she made those comments. I do not believe that the facts before me, in this court, are such as to prompt me to accommodate the ACC within the exceptional circumstances that the learned judge was contemplating."

While this is not an in-depth consideration of the question of participation/ engagement it might be inferred from the low level of engagement and the reference to "exceptional circumstances" that a relatively high level of engagement would be required to bring an unproved incumbrancer within an order. Finally, the court was satisfied that its inherent jurisdiction could not be exercised as a result of delay. This case differed slightly from *Dormer* inasmuch as the applicant/notice party did not seek a new order for sale; rather it sought to be substituted in an existing order for sale. It was argued that, as a result, Ord.33 r.8 was not relevant and, consequently, *Dormer* was of limited relevance. McMahon J. was not swayed by this argument and concluded that:

> "… to point out, as the ACC does, that insofar as it is a prior as opposed to a puisne incumbrancer (as mentioned in O. 33, r. 8) and that the rule only applies to where some of the property is sold, does not to my mind

affect the basic proposition of law that, to benefit from an order for sale, the incumbrancer must have proved its debt" (para.37).

COMPULSORY ACQUISITION

In *McNicholas & Anor v Mayo County Council & Anor* [2009] IEHC 379, McGovern J. was asked to consider the suitability of an access route provided to the plaintiffs following the construction of a bypass that cut across their former access. The plaintiffs are the owners of a residence and adjoining lands in Co. Mayo. In order for the construction of a bypass, some of those lands were subject to a compulsory purchase order and duly purchased. Section 49(4) of the Roads Act 1993 provides for the provision of "suitable alternative access" where, on the basis of such acquisition, one is "is permanently deprived of reasonable access to or from his property or from one part of his property to another". The access in this case was provided by means of a flyover and access road which, it was claimed, was particularly steep, sub-standard, roughly surfaced and surrounded by an unsightly wall. The plaintiffs sought injunctive relief relating to this access on two bases: first, that the first-named plaintiff suffered from vertigo and the access as constructed was unsuitable given his condition; and secondly, that they had withdrawn an objection to planning permission on the understanding that access would be constructed along an alternative route and, in the end, this was not done.

As to the claim of vertigo, the court held that the access road—which it found to not be unusually steep—was a perfectly normal flyover and access road and, if the first-named plaintiff suffered from vertigo while driving on it, that had "nothing to do with the suitability of the access road" (para.12), although it might call into question whether he ought to be driving. As to the second basis, the court found as a matter of fact that an alternative was offered to the plaintiffs with a deadline attached and that they chose that alternative only *after* that deadline had passed and, for practical reasons, the alternative was no longer available to them. The court found that suitable access could have been constructed had the plaintiffs acted more reasonably and that they ought to take some responsibility in that relation. At the same time, it was found (and conceded by the defendant County Council) that the access road was paradoxically legal (because it had planning permission) and sub-standard (because it was constructed on lands insufficient for purpose). The defendant County Council ought, the court found, to have built the access on other lands which they could have acquired and had failed to explain adequately why that was not done. The court did not, however, grant the injunctive relief sought. Neither did it grant damages as there was an arbitration on the Compulsory Purchase Order forthcoming at which, it was found, the questions relating to damages for unsuitability of the access could be adequately considered.

LAND AND CONVEYANCING LAW REFORM ACT 2009

2009 saw the passage and enactment of the most wide-ranging piece of property legislation since the foundation of the State. Following a protracted and multi-party law reform process, the Land and Conveyancing Law Reform Act 2009 was introduced with implications in areas of property law as diverse as estates, freehold covenants, judgment mortgages, mortgages, party structures, contracts and conveyances, and co-ownership. In essence, the Act comprises a wholescale reform or, in some cases, codification of property law within the State. A full survey of the provisions is available in Maddox, *The Land and Conveyancing Law Reform Act 2009: A Commentary* (Dublin: Round Hall, 2009) and Wylie, *The Land and Conveyancing Law Reform Act 2009: Annotations and Commentary* (Dublin: Bloomsbury Publishing Plc, 2009).

Law Reform

In 2009 the Law Reform Commission maintained its highly impressive output, publishing three reports and seven consultation papers on subjects ranging from family law to debt enforcement, evidence, criminal law, the civil liability of Good Samaritans and advance care directives.

ADVANCE CARE DIRECTIVES

In the *Annual Review of Irish Law 2008*, pp.430–431, we discussed the Law Reform Commission's Consultation Paper, *Bioethics: Advance Care Directives* (LRC CP 51–2008). The Commission has since published its *Report on Bioethics: Advance Care Directives* (LRC 94–2009), containing its final recommendations on the subject. It emphasises that these recommendations "do not alter or affect" the current criminal law on euthanasia and assisted suicide, which "constitute forms of homicide".

The Commission recommends that an appropriate legislative framework should be enacted for advance care directives, as part of the reform of law on mental capacity in the Government's Scheme of a Mental Capacity Bill 2008.

The proposed legislative framework should apply to advance care directives that involve refusal of treatment, subject to certain conditions to be specified in the legislation. An advance care directive should be defined as the expression of instructions or wishes by a person of 18 years with capacity to do so that, if (a) at a later time and in such circumstances as he or she may specify, a specified treatment is proposed to be carried out or continued by a person providing healthcare for him or her, and (b) at that time he or she lacks capacity to consent to the carrying out or continuation of the treatment, the specified treatment is not to be carried out or continued. As mental health care raises distinctive issues in relation to consent, the Commission prefers that its recommendations regarding the proposed legislative framework should not apply in that context.

The Commission recommends that the principles of autonomy, dignity and privacy of the individual should form part of the legislative framework for advance care directives. The legislation should make it clear that a person is entitled to refuse medical treatment for reasons that appear not to be rational or based on sound medical principles and to refuse medical treatment for religious reasons. The Commission maintains its opposition, however, to the exercise of autonomy by a patient who wishes to *continue*, as opposed to refuse treatment against the doctors' judgment. We criticised this inconsistency with the principle of respect for autonomy in the *Annual Review of Irish Law 2008*, pp.430–431.

The Commission is perhaps at its weakest when it seeks to engage in philosophical debate. Witness the following passage, designed to act as a refutation of John Keown's argument ("The Legal Revolution: From 'Sanctity of Life' to 'Quality of Life' and Autonomy" (1998) 14 *Journal of Contemporary Health Law and Policy* 253 at 253) that the emergence of the concept of autonomy has eroded the principle of the sanctity of life:

> "While the State has an interest in preserving life, this interest must be balanced against the right of a person to decide how they live their life. Indeed, the Commission agrees with the view that the sanctity of life is not necessarily consistent with keeping a person alive at all costs. Treatment which is excessively burdensome, which is of no medical benefit, or treatment which is against the clearly stated wishes of the patient, but which does keep a patient alive, is not consistent with the principle of the sanctity of life. As Hamilton CJ noted [in] *In re a Ward of Court (No 2)* [1996] 2 IR 79, the right to life 'includes the right to have nature take its course and to die a natural death'. A person can choose to decline treatment which has no curative effect and which is intended merely to prolong life" [para.1.95 of the report].

The passage provokes a couple of observations. The implication that the choice is between ending a life and keeping a person alive "at all costs" is a false one: such an approach has never received the support of law or medicine, both disciplines acknowledging that doctors are not obliged to "strive officiously to keep alive" by imposing extraordinary treatment on an unwilling patient. Those who argue for effective protection of the right to life seek no more than that life be protected from neglect (as where, for example, a necessary treatment, of an ordinary rather than extraordinary kind, is denied to a patient) or from direct intentional termination, by euthanasia, suicide or abortion. Doctors are free to provide pain relief even where this shortens the life of the patient; patients are free to decline burdensome or futile medical treatments and let nature take its course. But that is very far from the proposition that "treatment which is against the clearly stated wishes of the patient, but which does keep a patient alive, is not consistent with the principle of the sanctity of life". If a person with no serious medical condition but with suicidal intent refuses treatment in circumstances where the treatment is minimally invasive and the person is in good physical condition as long as he or she continues to take the treatment—a tablet a day, for example—one can scarcely deny that the law's acquiescence in that refusal raises an issue of consistency with the principle of the sanctity of life, however strongly one may support that acquiescence from the perspective of the right to autonomy. Cf. Wilnott, "Advance Directives Refusing Treatment as and Expression of Autonomy: Do the Courts Practice what they Preach?" (2009) 38 *Common Law World Review* 295.

The Commission goes on to recommend that the existence of any advance care directive, including an advance care directive involving the appointment of a health care proxy, be brought to the attention of the court when (as envisaged in the Scheme of a Mental Capacity Bill 2008) it considers the appointment of a personal guardian.

The Commission considers that the Government's Scheme should be extended to provide that a person may appoint an attorney under an enduring power of attorney (EPA) to make decisions regarding life-sustaining treatment, organ donation and non-therapeutic sterilisation, provided that these are expressly provided for in the EPA. In general, in the event of a conflict between the terms of an EPA executed under the Powers of Attorney Act 1996 and an advance care directive, the EPA should take priority. The Commission also proposes that a health care proxy may be appointed under an advance care directive.

The Commission reaffirms the proposal made in the Consultation Paper that, for reasons of public policy, a direction in an advance care directive involving the refusal of basic care should not be enforceable. What are involved here are such aspects as warmth, shelter, oral nutrition and hydration and hygiene measures. It recommends that palliative care should be regarded as part of basic care. Whilst in agreement with the English Law Commission that people should be entitled to refuse pain relief because they might prefer to remain alert, the Commission notes that palliative care encompasses more than just pain relief. The importance of ensuring that a person die "with dignity and in the least amount of pain possible" led the Commission to the conclusion that palliative care should come within the scope of basic care, which a person should not be entitled to exclude by an advance care directive.

The Commission recommends that an advance care directive may include a refusal of artificial life-sustaining treatment, intended to sustain or prolong life and supplanting or maintaining the operation of vital bodily functions that are incapable of independent operation. The Commission is of the opinion that "to require a person to be suffering from a terminal condition before they can refuse artificial life-sustaining treatment would be unduly limiting on a person's autonomy".

Turning to the question whether advance care directives should include an instruction not to provide, or to withdraw, artificial nutrition and hydration, such as through a nasogastric tube or by PEG feeding, the Commission notes the debate, nationally and internationally. In *In re a Ward of Court (No. 2)* [1996] 2 I.R. 79, the Supreme Court characterised this process as medical treatment: see our critical observations in the *Annual Review of Irish Law 1995*, pp.166–168. The Commission quotes the relevant passage from the Irish Medical Council's *Guide to Ethical Conduct and Behaviour*, 6th edn (2004), para.22.1, which, in striking contrast to the approach taken by the judges in that decision, states:

> "Access to nutrition and hydration remain one of the basic needs of human beings, and all reasonable and practical efforts should be made to maintain both."

(The seventh edition, published after the Commission's Report, contains a somewhat more nuanced provision, para.19.1, as follows:

> "Nutrition and hydration are basic needs of human beings. All patients are entitled to be provided with nutrition and hydration in a way that meets their needs. If a patient is unable to take sufficient nutrition and hydration orally, you should assess what alternative forms are possible and appropriate in the circumstances. You should bear in mind the burden or risks to the patient, the patient's wishes if known, and the overall benefit to be achieved. Where possible, you should make the patient and/or their primary carer aware of these conclusions.")

The Commission seeks to find a *via media*. Since the issue is an important one, it is worthwhile giving the full flavour of the Commission's analysis:

> "In the context of advance care directives, the Commission considers that the focus should be on the specific circumstances of the person. Thus whether artificial nutrition and hydration is classified as basic care or life-sustaining treatment will depend upon the circumstances of the case. For example, for a stroke victim who has temporarily lost the ability to swallow ANH must be considered as basic care. This type of care is necessary to keep a person comfortable and is vital to support the body's defences against disease. Food and water should not become medical treatment merely due to the process in which it is administered. After all, 'food and water do not perform the same function in the body that medical treatments do': 'Bopp —Nutrition and Hydration for Patients: The Constitutional Aspects' (1988–1989) 4 *Issues Law and Medicine* 3 at 43.
>
> Where there is no possibility of recovery or where the administration of ANH would be considered invasive and providing no real improvement to the patient, ANH would be considered artificial life-sustaining treatment. In such a case, ANH is not about improving a person's condition, but merely sustaining their life artificially."

The Commission in this context quotes Sheperd, "In Respect of People Living in a Permanent Vegetative State and Allowing Them to Die" (2006) 16 *Health Matrix* 631 at 681:

> "For people in a permanent vegetative state, tube feeding is less like these acts of common decency and more like a ventilator because the provision of nutrition and hydration through a PEG tube is not about respecting the body's integrity or its appearance but solely about sustaining life."

The Commission goes on to say that it considers that determination of whether ANH is artificial life-sustaining treatment or basic care "cannot be made without the input of a medical professional". It recommends that the proposed Code of Practice on Advance Care Directives should include guidance for medical professionals and authors of advance care directives for situations in which ANH will be considered life-sustaining treatment or, as the case may be, basic care. It adds, however, that it considers that, in the case of an advance care directive that includes a refusal of ANH, it would not be appropriate for a health care professional to decline to implement the directive merely where he or she is of the opinion that this would be contrary to the best interests of the patient or has a conscientious objection to the withholding of ANH: "In deciding whether ANH is basic care or artificial life-sustaining treatment, the decision should be based on the health care professional's medical and professional judgment only". This proposal to deny the entitlement of conscientious objection is a source of concern. we return to the issue later in our analysis of the Report.

The Commission recommends that a Code of Practice on Advance Care Directives should be prepared under the proposed statutory framework by the proposed Office of Public Guardian, based on the recommendations of a multi-disciplinary working group established for this purpose by the Office of Public Guardian, with input sought from organisations and groups such as the Health Service Executive, the Medical Council, An Bord Altranais, patients' groups, the Irish Hospice Foundation and Health Information and Quality Authority (HIQA).

In the Consultation Paper, the Commission invited submissions on the status of "Do Not Resuscitate" (DNR) orders. Submissions received made it clear that ambiguity surrounding DNR orders had created "real difficulties in health care practice". Irish studies had shown that decisions on DNR orders were taken at too junior a level, that the patient was not included in the decision-making process and that there was low quality of DNR documentation. DNR decisions were often taken by a doctor without consulting the patient concerned.

The Commission recommends that the Code of Practice on Advance Care Directives should contain guidelines on the process of putting in place a DNR order. The guidelines would provide that, before a DNR order is made, there is to be a consultative process, that this be documented on the patient's chart and that it be made by the most senior available member of the healthcare team.

The Commission considers that, for the time being, the legislative framework for advance care directives should apply only to adults. (In its *Consultation Paper on Children and the Law: Medical Treatment* (LRC CP

59–2009), the Commission returns to the topic: see below p.589.) There would be a rebuttable presumption of mental capacity. Those making such directives should be encouraged to consult with a healthcare professional. In cases where refusal of life-sustaining medical treatment was involved, the decision would have to be an informed one. A competent person would be entitled verbally to revoke an advance care directive even where it was in written form. While the Code of Practice on Advance Care Directives should recommend that they be reviewed regularly, this should not be compulsory, though a healthcare professional might "take into consideration the lapse of time between the creation of the advance care directive and its activation". (The Commission does not elaborate on the permitted consequences of such consideration.)

A register of directives should be established. The Commission goes into some detail about the entitlement of a person who has made an advance care directive to appoint a healthcare proxy—who is "likely to be a close friend or relative"—to make decisions on his or her behalf. The idea is that such a person will be able to fill in the gaps that will inevitably arise through unforeseen circumstances and provide supplementary information about the maker's wishes in the event of his or her incapacity. The line between information provision and decision-making may not, however, always be easy to draw. This does not particularly alarm the Commission, which recommends that, while a proxy can be given a general power to refuse healthcare decisions, it should not extend to artificial life-sustaining treatment, which would require explicit authorisation by the maker of the directive.

The Commission proposes that a healthcare professional should not be liable if he or she followed an advance care directive which the professional believed to be valid and applicable. The absence of a due care requirement is curious. One would have imagined that the test set out by the Supreme Court in *Dunne v National Maternity Hospital* [1989] I.R. 91 would apply. It is hard to identify policy reasons for a more indulgent standard in this context. In the reverse situation, where a professional has acted contrary to the advanced care directive, the Commission is conscious of the practical difficulties facing the professional in emergency circumstances and of the interesting philosophical question as to whether the continuation of life, contrary to the terms of a directive, can properly be characterised as harm. (Kelly J.'s decision in *Byrne v Ryan* [2007] IEHC 207 throws some light on the issue.) The Commission recommends that a good faith defence apply to persons who acted in good faith, contrary to an advance care directive of whose existence they could not reasonably have been aware.

But what of a situation where a health service professional wishes not to comply with an advance care directive on conscientious grounds? The Medical Council, quoted by the Commission, requires doctors with a conscientious objection to a course of action to explain this and to make the names of other doctors available to the patient (6th edn, para.2.6; 7th edn, para.10.2). The Commission takes a contrary view. It states that it:

> "... recognises the conflict which can occur between (*sic*) a health care professional who has a conscientious objection to an advance care directive. Nevertheless, due to the importance of ensuring that the proposed legislative framework can give real meaning to the autonomy, dignity and privacy of a person, the Commission has concluded that a health care professional cannot have a legal right to refuse to follow an advance care directive if they have a conscientious objection".

This approach is unfortunate. The ethical dimension to medicine has been at its core for millennia. Forcing doctors and nurses by legal sanction to act contrary to their ethics, apart from failing to respect that tradition, is not in the interests of society.

CHILDREN AND MEDICAL TREATMENT

In its *Consultation Paper on Children and the Law: Medical Treatment* (LRC CP 59–2009), the Law Reform Commission addresses the question of when children should have legal capacity to consent to medical treatment. This is a complex crossroads where changing norms and practices relating to parenting, children's autonomy and sexual behaviour present challenges to traditional approaches. The subject is complicated further by the constitutional uncertainties. The Constitution in Arts 41 and 42 articulates a coherent philosophy on how to harmonise parental autonomy and societal intervention for the welfare of the child. The Supreme Court in *North Western Health Board v HW and CW* [2001] 3 I.R. 622 interpreted this as affording considerably greater deference to parental autonomy than the language of these Articles, or their underlying philosophy, would appear to warrant: see our analysis in the *Annual Review of Irish Law 2001*, pp.316–338.

The real area of uncertainty is in regard to cases where children's autonomy may come into potential conflict with the "right and duty" of their parents to exercise their guardianship functions in regard to their children. We simply have no useful case law on this issue. (The Supreme Court mysteriously avoided the issue in *McK v Information Commissioner* [2006] I.R. 210.) It would be quite mistaken to infer from the absence of that case law that children's autonomy has no protection under the Irish Constitution. Clearly it has. The problem is to assess where the line should, or will, be drawn in any particular factual circumstances.

One of the areas of greater sensitivity is teenage sexual behaviour and the associated matter of contraception. Today more teenagers than in the past, at younger ages than formerly, engage in sexual behaviour. They have access to some contraceptives but not all kinds, notably the pill. If a 15-year-old consults a doctor, what is the legal position?

The answer is far from certain. The whole question of minors' capacity to consent to medical treatment was traditionally obscure and there was no definitive case law, in Ireland or elsewhere. Gradually, the concept of a "mature minor" gained some support. On this concept, courts built the idea that, whereas minors generally lacked capacity to consent, minors with sufficient maturity should be recognised as having capacity. In Britain in 1969 and in Ireland in 1997, statute intervened. The relevant provision was poorly drafted. Section 23 of the Non-Fatal Offences Against the Person Act 1997 provides:

> (1) The consent of a minor who has attained the age of 16 years to any surgical, medical or dental treatment which, in the absence of consent, would constitute a trespass to his or her person, shall be as effective as it would be if he or she were of full age; and where a minor has by virtue of this section given an effective consent to any treatment it shall not be necessary to obtain any consent for it from his or her parent or guardian.
>
> (2) In this section "surgical, medical or dental treatment" includes any procedure undertaken for the purposes of diagnosis, and this section applies to any procedure (including, in particular, the administration of an anaesthetic) which is ancillary to any treatment as it applies to that treatment.
>
> (3) Nothing in this section shall be construed as making ineffective any consent which would have been effective if this section had not been enacted.

A few points about this section may be noted. First, it says nothing expressly about the position relating to the consent of a minor under the age of 16. If subs.(1) were viewed in isolation, the *inclusio unius est exclusio alterius* rule of construction might possibly indicate a legislative intent that 16 should be the minimum age for a lawful consent by a minor. When one takes account of subs.(3), however, it seems that the Oireachtas has decided to leave open the question whether a minor under 16 has the capacity in any circumstances to consent, without reference to the minor's parents or guardians. Section 23, therefore, only partially clarifies the law.

The second point concerns the nature of consent by a minor who has obtained the age of 16. The section throws no light on what is necessary to constitute such consent. The reference in subs.(1) to "an effective consent" does not refer to the quality of the consent; it merely relates back to the earlier part of the sentence where legal effectiveness is conferred on the consent by reason of the fact of its being provided by the minor. The courts may be disposed to treat the question of the minor's consent as "one of fact", dependent on the circumstances of the case, including the particular minor's age and maturity (or lack of it) as well as the nature of the medical treatment.

This leads to the third point, which concerns the implications of the section for parents or guardians. As has been mentioned, it is plain that Arts 41 and

42 recognise the trusteeship role of parents in the upbringing and protection of their children. Legislation cannot subtract from this constitutional remit though it can attempt to clarify it in specific contexts.

Even if s.23 had never been enacted, it is generally accepted that part of the trusteeship role of parents in relation to the details of the lives of their children is to recognise and respect the burgeoning capacities of their teenage offspring to make autonomous decisions regarding their values, beliefs and choices as to life plans, associations, friendships and loves. While fully acknowledging the difficult task of parenting, it seems certain that a court would not hold to be unlawful the decision of a 16-year-old to undergo a small medical intervention—such as an operation on his or her broken finger—without the consent of the minor's parents. But if the case involves a serious medical intervention with significant risks, and if there is a strong argument that the intervention is not truly for the minor's welfare, the legal position becomes less clear. Presumably the parents could take wardship proceedings, in which the welfare of the minor would be the paramount consideration. In the absence of wardship proceedings, a doctor, before the enactment of s.23, might have apprehended that to go ahead with the intervention without the consent of the parents could expose the doctor to the risk of litigation, either by means of a claim for damages or an injunction.

The enactment of s.23 must have eased these anxieties, though it cannot have removed them completely. The provision that a minor's consent is legally effective and that "it shall not be necessary to obtain any consent for [the treatment] from his or her parent or guardian" could be interpreted in one of two ways. On one view, it means that the parents or guardians are thereby disentitled in any case to take any legal steps in respect of the treatment, whether before or after it takes place, so far as it impacts on the welfare of the minor. On the other view, what s.23 does is to render the consent lawful to the extent that it can not be regarded as being in breach of the civil or criminal law by reason merely of the failure to obtain the consent of the parents or guardians. On this latter view, the trusteeship function is not disturbed and parents or guardians remain entitled (to the uncertain extent that they have such an entitlement) to take proceedings with respect to the treatment in the same way as they can with respect to any other activity, not in breach of the civil or criminal law, in which their minor child engages.

In the famous decision of the House of Lords in *Gillick v West Norfolk & Wisbech Area Health Authority* [1986] 1 A.C. 12, the majority held that minors under the age of 16 have capacity to receive contraceptive treatment from doctors without parental consent if they have sufficient maturity to make the decision. Lord Fraser set out guidelines, which have received widespread endorsement:

> "[A] doctor could proceed to give advice and treatment provided he is satisfied in the following criteria:

1) that the girl (although under the age of 16 years of age) will understand his advice;
2) that he cannot persuade her to inform her parents or to allow him to inform the parents that she is seeking contraceptive advice;
3) that she is very likely to continue having sexual intercourse with or without contraceptive treatment;
4) that unless she receives contraceptive advice or treatment her physical or mental health or both are likely to suffer;
5) that her best interests require him to give her contraceptive advice, treatment or both without the parental consent."

The Commission is impressed by this approach. It provisionally recommends that legislation should be provided in legislation that a person who is 16 years of age is presumed to have capacity to consent to health care and medical treatment. It goes on to propose that a person between 14 and 16 years of age could, subject to certain requirements, be regarded as capable of giving consent to healthcare and medical treatment, provided he or she has the capacity to understand the nature and consequences of the treatment being provided. These requirements would include imposing on the medical practitioner the need to be of opinion that the patient understands the nature and consequences of the proposed treatment, that he or she encourage the patient to inform his or her parents or guardians, consider the best interests of the patient and have due regard to any public health concerns. These recommendations would not legalise any healthcare treatments that are prohibited or shall be prohibited in any other statutory form.

The Commission goes on to recommend that it should be lawful for a healthcare professional to provide healthcare and medical treatment to a person between 12 and 14 years of age, provided that the health care professional has complied with certain requirements, including that the medical practitioner:

> notify the parents or guardians of the child and take account of their views;
> take account of the views of the child in question;
> consider the best interests of the patient;
> and have due regard to any public health concerns.

Again, these recommendations would not legalise any healthcare treatments that are prohibited or shall be prohibited in any other statutory form.

The Commission recommends that it should be provided in legislation that a person who is 16 years of age is presumed to have capacity to consent and refuse health care and medical treatment. In the context of refusal of life-sustaining treatment a person who is 16 years of age may make an application to the High Court to have his or her purported refusal appraised. A person aged between 14 and 16 could (subject to the same requirements that apply to those aged 16 and over) be regarded as capable of giving consent and refusal to healthcare and medical treatment, provided he or she has the capacity to understand the nature and consequences of the treatment in question. Children aged under 14 years of age would not be regarded as being capable of refusing medical treatment.

The Commission provisionally recommends that it should be provided in legislation that a person who is 16 years of age is presumed to have capacity to make an advance care directive. It considers that the Mental Health Act 2001 (the "2001 Act") be amended, with a separate section for people under the age of 18 and invites submissions on the form and content of guiding principles. All children and adolescents admitted and treated under the 2001 Act would have access to an independent advocate. There is perhaps a certain anomoly in authorising a child to make a decision designed to bring about his or her death while not authorising a child to marry or engage in a wide range of other activities. For a broad analysis, see Barry Lyons, "Dying to Be Responsible: Adolescence, Autonomy and Responsibility", (2010) 30 *Legal Studies* 257.

The Commission proposes the introduction of a third category of informal admission for children and adolescents who are admitted under the 2001 Act by parental consent. It "does not seek to differentiate between issues of capacity and consent in relation to physical and mental health" and concludes that "therefore" the recommendation it makes in relation to minors and medical treatment generally, with its differential standards based on the age of the minor, should apply in the context of mental health.

The Commission provisionally recommends that a mental heath tribunal (with an age-appropriate focus) rather than the District Court should review the admission and treatment of children and young people as involuntary patients for the purposes of the 2001 Act. It invites submissions on the administration of treatment to children and adolescents admitted as involuntary patients under the 2001 Act.

CIVIL LIABILITY OF GOOD SAMARITANS

In the Torts chapter, below, p.726, we discuss the Law Reform Commission's *Report on the Civil Liability of Good Samaritans and Volunteers* (LRC 93–2009).

CRIMINAL LAW

In the Criminal Law Chapter, above, pp.385, 391 and 408, we discuss the Commission's *Report on Defences in Criminal Law* (LRC 95–2009).

FAMILY RELATIONSHIPS

In its *Consultation Paper on Legal Aspects of Family Relationships* (LRC CP 55–2009), the Law Reform Commission addresses a range of issues relating to the rights and responsibilities of parents, grandparents and others in relation to children.

The Commission first addresses the question of terminology. Some of the traditional expressions, notably "custody" and "access", reflect an emphasis on the rights of adults rather than of children. There has been a move internationally to replace these terms by "day-to-day care" and "contact", for example, and a tendency to replace "guardianship" by "parental responsibility". The Commission provisionally recommends that a broad statutory definition of parental responsibility be introduced. Perhaps one should be a little slower to abandon the concept of guardianship. After all, it reflects the notion of responsibilities for the child's welfare as well as rights. Our present constitutional dispensation is founded on a normative basis in which the relationship between parents and their children involves an inexorable interconnection between right and duty. In Art.42.1, the State "guarantees to respect the inalienable right and duty of parents to provide, according to their means, for the religious and moral, intellectual, physical and social education of their children".

Turning to the registration of births, the Commission identifies two misunderstandings which have discouraged the registration of a child born outside marriage in the names of both parents: many people believe that this gives the father guardianship rights and that it may negatively affect the mother's entitlement to social welfare payments. The Commission considers that the child's right to know his or her identity is a reason for seeking to encourage parents to include both names on the birth certificate. It is of opinion that, for the time being at least, it is appropriate to retain the distinction between birth registration and the ascription of guardianship (or "parental responsibility", as it prefers to describe it).

The Commission invites submissions on whether it would be appropriate to impose a statutory duty on a registrar to make enquiries of a mother who comes in alone to register the birth of a child as to whether she wishes to include the father's details on the birth certificate. It also invites submissions on whether there should be a statutory duty on a registrar to inform the mother of the option of re-registering the birth at a later stage to include the father's details.

The Commission invites submissions on whether it would be appropriate to introduce compulsory joint registration of the birth of a child or, less radically, on whether a non-marital father should be able to provide his details independently to the registrar, to be registered once it is confirmed that he is the father. There are proposals for compulsory joint birth registration in England, subject to very limited exceptions. It is to be hoped that the Commission does not make such a recommendation in its final Report. Important issues relating to the right to privacy are involved.

In it *Report on Illegitimacy* (LRC 4–1982), nearly three decades ago, the Commission recommended that the parents of children born outside marriage should, as a general principle, have the same guardianship rights as parents of children born within marriage. It considered that the principle of equality which underlay its proposal to abolish the status of illegitimacy of children could not tolerate discrimination between guardianship of fathers based on marital status. It contained special proposals designed to deal with particular cases, such as where a child is conceived by rape and there is a prospect that the rapist father may seek to assert guardianship rights.

The Status of Children Act 1987 did not implement the Commission's proposal. In the present Consultation Paper, the Commission invites submissions on the proposal, without evincing great enthusiasm for it. In favour of taking this step, it may be argued that it most effectively respects the principle of equal rights for children. As long as unmarried fathers are excluded from guardianship rights as extensive as those of fathers of children born within marriage, there is no prospect of that equality of rights. Moreover, the entire thrust of the Consultation Paper, reflecting the normative and cultural trends of recent decades, is to place greater emphasis on the rights and welfare of children and to regard guardianship as not simply a parental right but a right of the child involving clear parental responsibilities. Viewed from that perspective, to retain distinctions in guardianship based on the marital status of parents is to preserve an ancient discrimination against children. The special cases of rapist fathers and of sperm donors in assisted human reproduction can be dealt with by way of specific exception from the general principle.

The Commission provisionally recommends that a central register should be established to keep account of the existence of statutory declarations agreeing parental responsibility/guardianship of children. The Commission invites submissions on whether the proposed register should be managed by the General Register Office and on whether it should be publicly available to search. In *ER O'B v Minister for Justice, Equality and Law Reform* [2009] IEHC 423, O'Neill J. rejected the argument that the absence of such a register was unconstitutional. (We discuss the decision in the chapter on Family Law, above, pp.487–488.) Nothing said in O'Neill J.'s judgment should, however, be regarded as amounting to opposition to the Commission's proposal.

The Commission provisionally recommends the removal of the leave stage provided for by s.11B(2) of the Guardianship of Infants Act 1964, as inserted by s.9 of the Children Act 1997. The Commission also invites submissions as to whether the categories of persons who can apply for access/contact should be expanded to include persons with a bona fide interest, as is currently provided for by s.37 of the Child Care Act 1991.

The Commission invites submissions on the possibility of extending the right to apply for access/contact to include the child and on whether there should be a specific requirement in Irish law that the wishes of the child be considered in making a decision on an application for contact by a member of the child's extended family.

The Commission provisionally recommends extending the right to apply for custody/day-to-day care to persons other than parents or guardians of the child where the parents are unwilling or unable to exercise their responsibilities. Such rights would be extended to the same category of persons who can currently apply for leave to apply for access/contact. It also invites submissions on whether it would be appropriate to develop a procedure to extend guardianship/parental responsibility to a step-parent.

LEGAL ASPECTS OF CARERS

In its *Consultation Paper on Legal Aspects of Carers* (LRC CP 53–2009) the Law Reform Commission puts forward provisional recommendations on how the law should be reformed to ensure that appropriate standards are in place for professional carers, in particular those engaged in the provision of care to vulnerable people in their homes. The Health Act 2007 (the "2007 Act") specifies that the Health Information and Quality Authority (HIQA) is the regulatory and standard-setting body for residential nursing homes but it does not empower the HIQA to set comparable standards for the provision of healthcare in the home setting.

The Commission provisionally recommends that s.8(1)(b) of the 2007 Act be amended to extend the authority of the HIQA to include the regulating and monitoring of professional domiciliary care providers. HIQA should publish standards which should be specifically tailored for the domiciliary care setting, building on existing HIQA standards for the residential care setting. The proposed standards should ensure that domiciliary care is provided in a manner that promotes the wellbeing and independence of service users in their own homes.

The Commission provisionally recommends that the terms and conditions of the provision of care be agreed and recorded in a care contract, in order to offer the maximum protection for the service recipient. The care contract would contain clear policies and procedures in relation to the handling by the carer of money and personal property of the service recipient. The care contract would also set out specific policies and procedures in relation to the management of a service recipient's medication.

The Commission endorses the proposal in Head 27 of the Government's Scheme of Mental Capacity Bill 2008 to create an offence of ill treatment or wilful neglect as involving an important protective element in the context of domiciliary care.

The Commission invites submissions as to whether the form of protection for people who report concerns about incidents of possible abuse contained in the Protection of Persons Reporting Child Abuse Act 1998 should be extended to apply in the context of professional domiciliary care. It also proposes that Pt 9A of the Health Act 2004, which deals with disclosure of abuse, be amended, to ensure that employees of domiciliary care providers will be covered by the protected disclosure safeguards.

LIMITATION OF ACTIONS

In the Chapter on Limitation of Actions, below, pp.624–627, we analyse the Law Reform Commission's *Consultation Paper on Limitation of Actions* (LRC CP 54–2009).

PERSONAL DEBT AND DEBT ENFORCEMENT

The Law Reform Commission in September 2009 published a *Consultation Paper on Personal Debt and Debt Enforcement* (LRC CP 56–2009) and in May 2010 published an *Interim Report on Personal Debt Management and Debt Management* (LRC 96–2010). The Interim Report deals with actions that can be put in place in the short term, against the background of the present economic crisis, pending long-term solutions that could realistically take some time to implement. The Interim Report follows the advice of a Working Group on Personal Debt Management and Debt Enforcement, composed of people from Government departments, statutory bodies and representative bodies.

The Interim Report is distinctive in recording specific actions on debt management and enforcement that have already been put in place or are in train as a result of the deliberations of the Working Group.

The Consultation Paper focuses on personal insolvency law and legal debt enforcement proceedings. It proceeds on the assumption of the validity of the normative distinction based on whether a debtor cannot, or merely will not, pay his or her debts. It acknowledges that this distinction does not in truth signify two categories of persons but rather indicates two ends of a spectrum.

The Commission provisionally recommends that a licensing system should be introduced for the debt collection industry. Subject to specified exceptions, all debt collectors and debt collection agencies should be obliged to hold a licence before operating a debt collection business.

The Commission proposes that the Bankruptcy Act 1988 be replaced because it does not provide an adequate and effective system of personal insolvency law. It recommends that a thorough review of the 1998 Act should be undertaken with a view to introducing a new Bankruptcy Act. The creation of a consumer insolvency system should involve both non-judicial debt settlement and judicial insolvency procedures. The Commission invites submissions as to whether a debt settlement scheme should be limited to consumer debtors, or whether small business debtors should also be included.

The Commission provisionally recommends that debt settlement and bankruptcy procedures should not be denied to debtors merely because such debtors cannot afford to make any repayment to creditors. "Zero-payment" plans should be available in the case of a debtor who has no available income above that required for maintaining a reasonable standard of living. The duration of the repayment period under the debt settlement scheme should be three to five years.

The Commission proposes that, subject to appropriate exceptions, enforcement through an instalment order must first be attempted, or at least considered, before other enforcement mechanisms may be used. An instalment order should not be made in the absence of accurate information about the debtor's means and ability to pay. Creditors should be entitled to apply for a garnishee order without first attempting enforcement through execution against goods. Garnishee orders should not deprive debtors of the funds necessary to maintain a minimum standard of living for themselves and their dependents. The term "garnishee order" should be replaced with a term which more clearly describes the process involved, such as "attachment of debt order" or "third party debt order".

The Commission invites submissions as to the desirability of introducing an attachment of earnings mechanism for the enforcement of all judgment debts against individuals receiving regular income and as to whether social welfare payments should be subject to attachment under attachment of earnings orders. An attachment of earnings order should be available only where less restrictive enforcement mechanisms are unavailable or are ineffective; and an attachment of earnings order should be used only where the debtor has been provided with an opportunity to repay the judgment debt (by instalment order) and has defaulted.

As part of the policy of promoting appropriate and proportionate enforcement, the Commission provisionally recommends that the current position of over-reliance on enforcement by execution against goods should be removed and that this mechanism should be available only where it is necessary, proportionate and not overly restrictive. It invites submissions as to the possible introduction of a two-tier system of execution against goods, involving a distinction between domestic and commercial premises. The Commission proposes the introduction of a code of practice to regulate the procedure of execution against goods in civil debt cases and it invites submissions as to whether legislation should provide for "walking possession" arrangements (under which the sheriff and debtor agree that the debtor's goods have been seized but that they should remain in the custody of the debtor and not be sold until the debt has been paid).

The Commission provisionally recommends that the current rules on the seizure of goods owned by third parties should be codified. The primary rule should be that only the goods of the debtor should be capable of being seized. The Commission, however, provisionally recommends that jointly owned property should be capable of being seized subject to the protection of the interests of joint owners.

The Commission proposes that the procedures for the imprisonment of debtors under the Debtors (Ireland) Act 1872 and the Enforcement of Court Orders Acts 1926 to 2009 should be repealed in the context of a reformed system of court-based enforcement. If imprisonment is to be retained as a remedy of last resort against "won't pay" debtors, a single new procedure should be enacted; orders for imprisonment must continue to be made by a court and not by the proposed enforcement office.

Legal Profession

GENERAL: LEGAL SERVICES OMBUDSMAN

The Legal Services Ombudsman Act 2009 (the "2009 Act") provides for the establishment and functions of a legal services ombudsman to oversee complaints concerning both solicitors and barristers. The 2009 Act contains the first statutory regulation of complaints concerning barristers, solicitors having already been subject to independent review by the solicitors' adjudicator. The 2009 Act also provides, significantly, that the legal services ombudsman has statutory authority to assess the adequacy of the admission policies of the Law Society of Ireland and the Bar Council of Ireland. At the time of writing, it is expected that the first appointment will be made by the end of 2010 (see speech by the Minister for Justice and Law Reform, Law Society of Ireland, May 21, 2010, available at *www.justice.ie*).

OECD 2001 report and Competition Authority 2005 and 2006 reports The origins of the 2009 Act can be traced to the Organisation for Economic Co-operation and Development's (OECD) wide-ranging 2001 *Report on Regulatory Reform in Ireland.* The 2001 OECD report had recommended that a number of professions, including the legal profession, be investigated from the point of view of whether they complied with OECD guidelines on competitiveness. The 2001 report also argued that the control of education and entry into the profession should be removed from the Law Society of Ireland and the Honourable Society of King's Inns, though it also accepted that close ties should be maintained with and to them in order to ensure quality of entrants and the content of education and training. Following the 2001 OECD report, the Government requested the Competition Authority to complete an examination of the regulation of the legal profession. This led to the Competition Authority's preliminary report, *Study of Competition in Legal Services* (2005) and its final report, *Competition in Professional Services: Solicitors and Barristers* (2006).

One of the Competition Authority's key recommendations was that the current self-regulation of both branches of the legal profession, solicitors and barristers by, respectively, the Law Society of Ireland and the Bar Council of Ireland should be replaced by external regulation. In effect, under this proposal, the regulatory role of the Law Society and the Bar Council would be transferred to an independent Legal Services Commission, leaving the Law Society and the Bar Council with a representative role only. For other aspects of the Competition Authority's reports, and subsequent developments by the Law Society and the Bar Council, see *Byrne and McCutcheon on the Irish Legal System*, 5th edn (Dublin: Bloomsbury Professional, 2009), Ch.3.

The position in England and Wales, and in Northern Ireland The Competition Authority's proposal reflected developments that had been proposed for England and Wales by the 2004 Clementi Report, *Review of the Regulation System for Legal Services in England and Wales: Final Report*. The Clementi Report was implemented by the (UK) Legal Services Act 2007, which established the Legal Services Board, and which became fully operational on January 1, 2010. The Legal Services Board is the external regulator under the 2007 Act for the "approved regulators", the Solicitors Regulatory Authority and the Bar Standards Board, which now exercise independent regulatory functions for the two branches of the profession in England and Wales. Thus, the Law Society for England and Wales and the Bar Council for England and Wales now exercise representative roles only.

It is notable that, by contrast, the 2006 Bain Report, *Legal Services in Northern Ireland: Complaints, Regulation, Competition* had taken a different approach to external regulation for Northern Ireland. The Bain Report concluded that regulation of the professions should continue to be discharged by the Law Society for Northern Ireland and the Bar Council in Northern Ireland, subject to a supervisory role by a proposed Legal Services Oversight Commissioner assisted by the Lord Chief Justice for Northern Ireland. At the time of writing (June 2010), this has not yet been implemented. Thus, a Lay Observer for Solicitors, which was established in 1976, continues to oversee complaints against solicitors made to the Law Society for Northern Ireland, while the Professional Conduct Committee (PCC) of the Bar Council in Northern Ireland continues to deal with complaints concerning barristers. It is possible that, in the wake of the devolution of justice powers to the Northern Ireland Assembly in 2010, and the appointment of a Northern Ireland Minister for Justice, a new review of legal services may occur.

Response to Competition Authority reports The Government's response to the 2006 Competition Authority report was that a legal services commission would not be established. Instead, the Government concluded that a legal services ombudsman be established to oversee complaints concerning both solicitors and barristers. This Government response was ultimately enacted by the Oireachtas in the 2009 Act. In effect, it can be said that this represented a preference for the model of external regulation proposed in the Northern Ireland 2006 Bain Report rather than that proposed for England and Wales in the 2004 Clementi Report. It is worth noting in this respect that this analysis was ultimately acceptable to both the Law Society and the Bar Council. This can be seen reflected in the unusual fact that, while some small amendments to the Legal Services Ombudsman Bill 2008—which became the 2009 Act—were made at committee stage in the debate in Dáil Éireann, not one amendment was tabled for the committee stage debate in Seanad Éireann. While, as stated during the Seanad debate, this can be seen as a tribute to the high standard of legislative drafting involved, it may also be seen as reflecting a consensus within the profession as to the reforms ultimately enacted in the 2009 Act. This consensus does not, of course, reflect the analysis in the Competition Authority's 2006 final report. Nonetheless, it is worth reiterating that the result of the 2009 Act is that the external regulation of the legal profession in this State has much in common with that in Northern Ireland, and that both jurisdictions differ in that respect from the arrangements in place in England and Wales.

Main functions of Legal Services Ombudsman The main functions of the Legal Services Ombudsman in the 2009 Act are: to investigate complaints; to review the procedures of the Law Society and Bar Council for dealing with complaints made to those bodies; to assess the adequacy of the admission policies of the Law Society to the solicitors' profession and of the Bar Council to the barristers' profession; and to promote awareness among members of the public of matters concerning the procedures of the Law Society and the Bar Council for dealing with complaints made to those bodies.

Overview of complaints procedures During the Oireachtas debate on the 2009 Act, the main elements of the current complaints procedures for solicitors and barristers were outlined.

It was pointed out that the Solicitors Acts 1954 to 2008 (the "1954 to 2008 Acts") regulate the solicitors' profession. In particular, Pt 3 of the 1994 Act makes detailed provision for the investigation of complaints against solicitors. Complaints to the Law Society generally fall into two broad categories, complaints of misconduct and complaints of inadequate service or excessive fees. The Law Society's complaints and client relations committee, which includes lay members, determines complaints lodged directly to it by members of the public. Complaints of misconduct against solicitors may be made by clients to the Society or the Solicitors Disciplinary Tribunal. Where a complaint of misconduct has been made to the society in the first instance, it may be referred by the society to the tribunal and such complaints would then be liable to attract the heavier end of the scale of sanctions. The Solicitors Disciplinary Tribunal is an independent statutory tribunal appointed by the President of the High Court to investigate complaints of misconduct against solicitors under the 1994 Act. Members of the tribunal are appointed by the President of the High Court and include lay persons.

The Law Society may refer complaints to the tribunal and every client of a solicitor has a right to make a direct application to the tribunal. The tribunal has limited judicial powers and its primary function is to establish by evidence and documents the facts of a complaint and to decide whether misconduct is proven. Where there is a finding of misconduct, the tribunal can impose a sanction on the solicitor ranging from admonishment to a direction to pay restitution of a sum not exceeding €15,000 to any aggrieved party. In more serious cases the tribunal may refer its finding and recommendation to the President of the High Court, who ultimately will decide on the nature of the sanction to be imposed on the solicitor. The powers of sanction available to the High Court range up to striking the solicitor off the roll. If either party is unhappy with a decision of the tribunal, this may be appealed to the High Court.

As to barristers, it was pointed out during the Oireachtas debate on the 2009 Act that they must comply with the Bar Council's code of conduct which was updated in 2006 in response to the Competition Authority's 2006 final report, discussed above. Complaints against barristers by members of the public are dealt with under the Bar Council's disciplinary code. A client may make a complaint about a barrister who has failed to maintain proper professional standards, has committed professional misconduct or has brought the profession into disrepute. Complaints against barristers are made to the Bar Council's professional conduct tribunal comprising barristers and lay persons. The complaints are handled in private and may be dealt with by way of an oral hearing. If a complaint goes to an oral hearing, both parties are invited to attend and both may be legally represented. The tribunal's decision may be appealed by either party to a three-member appeal board, chaired by a High Court judge with the two other members nominated by the Bar Council and the Attorney General. Where there is a finding of misconduct against a barrister, the disciplinary code prescribes penalties ranging from an admonishment to a fine to disbarment.

It was stated in the Oireachtas during the debate on the 2009 Act that approximately 1,700 complaints against solicitors and 20 against barristers have been made per annum in recent years. This was in the context of there being over 8,000 practising solicitors and more than 2,100 practising barristers as of 2009.

We can now turn to discuss in detail the main provisions of the 2009 Act.

Detailed provisions of 2009 Act Sections 4 and 5 of the 2009 Act provide for the establishment of the Legal Services Ombudsman and his or her appointment by the Government on the nomination of the Minister for Justice and Law Reform. Specified persons not eligible for appointment include practising barristers or solicitors, members of the Law Society, members of the Bar Council or benchers of the Society of King's Inns.

Section 6 of the 2009 Act provides that the period of office of an Ombudsman will not exceed six years, but the person appointed may be reappointed for a second or subsequent term. It also provides for the manner in which the Ombudsman may resign from office, the circumstances in which the

Government may remove the Ombudsman from office and the circumstances in which a person ceases to hold the office of Legal Services Ombudsman.

Section 9 of the 2009 Act sets out the general functions and powers of the Ombudsman: to receive and investigate complaints, review the procedures of the Law Society and the Bar Council for dealing with complaints made to them by clients of barristers and solicitors, assess the adequacy of the admission policies of the two professional bodies and improve public awareness of their complaints procedures.

Section 11 provides for the appointment of staff to the Office of the Ombudsman and for the engagement of professional and other advisers and the delegation to a member of the staff of certain functions assigned to the Ombudsman.

Part 3 of the 2009 Act provides that the Office of the Legal Services Ombudsman will be funded entirely by means of a levy on the two professional bodies. Section 12 provides for advance funding from the Government at the set-up stage, which will be recouped from the two professional bodies. Section 13 provides for financial accounting and audit matters by the Ombudsman, including audit by the Comptroller and Auditor General and the presentation of the audited accounts to the Minister for Justice and Law Reform and the Houses of the Oireachtas.

Section 14 requires the Ombudsman to make various periodic reports to the Minister, including an annual report on the performance of the functions of the office and a report on its effectiveness and the adequacy of its functions within two years of its establishment. The Ombudsman may also make a special report to the Minister on a matter of particular gravity or in other exceptional circumstances. The Ombudsman is required to make a special report on any other matter if so requested by the Minister. All reports must be laid before the Oireachtas and published.

Under s.15 of the 2009 Act, the Ombudsman is also required to produce an annual report on the adequacy of the admission policies of the legal professions. The report must specify the numbers admitted annually to legal practice for the year in question and an assessment as to whether the numbers admitted are consistent with the public interest in ensuring the availability of legal services at a reasonable cost. This report must also be laid before the Oireachtas and published.

Sections 16 and 17 provide for the appearance of the Ombudsman before the Committee of Public Accounts and other committees of the Houses of the Oireachtas. Section 18 provides for various publications to be privileged for the purposes of the law of defamation, namely, any matter in a report of the Ombudsman laid before either House of the Oireachtas and publications by the Ombudsman directed to particular persons or bodies. The general reform of the law by the Defamation Act 2009 is discussed in the Torts chapter, below.

Section 19 provides for the payment each year of a levy to the Minister by the Law Society and the Bar Council to meet the approved expenses of the Ombudsman. These expenses equate to the full operating costs and administrative expenses of the Ombudsman in the preceding year and comprise salaries, superannuation, office accommodation and related costs and legal costs incurred in issuing or defending legal proceedings. The Law Society and the Bar Council will each be liable to pay 10 per cent of the approved expenses and the remaining 80 per cent will be paid pro rata by the two bodies according to the relative numbers of complaints made to the Ombudsman in regard to solicitors and barristers. Section 19 also provides for other matters concerning the levy, including late payment. Section 20 empowers the Minister for Justice and Law Reform to make regulations to provide for various matters related to the levy.

Section 21 deals with the Ombudsman's functions concerning complaints, investigations and reviews. A complaint may be made by a client of a solicitor or barrister to the Ombudsman concerning the handling by the Law Society or the Bar Council of a related complaint against a solicitor or barrister. A complaint may also be made by a client of a solicitor to the Ombudsman about a decision of the Law Society to make or refuse a grant from its compensation fund established under the 1954 to 2008 Acts. Section 22 provides for the types of complaints which may be made to the Ombudsman, including complaints of inadequate investigation and failure to commence or complete an investigation of a related complaint within a reasonable time.

The Legal Services Ombudsman may seek the resolution of complaints in such a manner as he or she considers appropriate and reasonable, and the Ombudsman may establish and publish procedures to be followed in regard to the receipt and investigation of complaints. The Ombudsman must conduct investigations in private. To ensure full cooperation with the investigation of a complaint, the Ombudsman has the power to require the provision of information or attendance of any person before him or her as appropriate. In the event that a person fails to comply with a request for information or attendance, the Ombudsman may apply to the High Court for an order requiring compliance. Section 27 creates the offence of obstruction of the Ombudsman in the performance of his or her functions, which is punishable by a fine not exceeding €2,000 on summary conviction.

The Ombudsman has power to issue directions and make recommendations to the Law Society and Bar Council. In particular, following investigation the Ombudsman may, if not satisfied that the related complaint was adequately investigated, direct the Bar Council to reinvestigate it under the Bar Council's disciplinary code or direct the Law Society either to conduct a second investigation or refer the complaint to the Solicitors Disciplinary Tribunal for an inquiry on the grounds of alleged misconduct. The Ombudsman may make other directions and recommendations to either body, including that the Law Society must make, or increase, a grant out of its compensation fund.

The Ombudsman may request the professional body to respond within a specified period to a direction given or recommendation made. In the event of an unsatisfactory response, the Ombudsman may make a special report to the Minister, which must be published. The High Court is empowered to enforce directions made by the Ombudsman and provision is also made for referral of any question of law by the Ombudsman to the High Court for determination.

A key function of the Ombudsman is to keep under review the procedures of the Bar Council and Law Society for receiving and investigating complaints about barristers and solicitors. Section 32 provides that the Ombudsman may examine the complaints procedures of the two bodies, the cooperation of barristers and solicitors with these procedures, the effectiveness of the procedures and the time taken to complete investigations. In addition, the Ombudsman may examine random samples of complaints made to the Bar Council and Law Society, complaints relating to specific matters and statistical information, including information on multiple complaints against individual barristers or solicitors. Arising from his or her review, the Ombudsman may make written recommendations to the Bar Council and Law Society to improve their complaints investigation procedures and requesting the cooperation of barristers and solicitors with these procedures. If not satisfied with their response to the recommendation, the Ombudsman may direct that the recommendation or an amended recommendation be implemented. Where the Ombudsman considers it appropriate, in regard to a particular class or classes of complaint, the relevant professional body may be directed to put in place specific procedures to address such complaints.

Full and complete records must be kept by both professional bodies of all investigations and proceedings relating to complaints and must be made available to the Ombudsman on request. Legal proceedings may only be commenced against the Ombudsman with the leave of the High Court on notice to the Ombudsman. Confidentiality of information in the possession of the office of the Ombudsman is ensured by s.35 of the 2009 Act, which provides that the Ombudsman or a member of his or her staff may not, except in accordance with law, disclose any information obtained other than in specified circumstances.

As noted in the Oireachtas debate, the 2009 Act represents an important part of a series of measures to support the better regulation of the legal professions. The other measures included the enactment of provisions in Pt 3 of the Civil Law (Miscellaneous Provisions) Act 2008 which strengthened and clarified the law on regulatory matters in regard to solicitors (see *Annual Review of Irish Law 2008*, pp.40–44) and of the Legal Practitioners (Irish Language) Act 2008 which modernised Irish language training requirements for solicitors and barristers (see *Annual Review of Irish Law 2008*, p.432).

At the time of writing, it is expected that the first Legal Services Ombudsman will be appointed by the end of 2010. In indicating this, the Minister for Justice and Law Reform emphasised that he intended to request the Legal Services

Ombudsman to prepare a report under the 2009 Act concerning admissions to the two branches of the legal profession, with particular emphasis on the representative nature of the mix of persons being admitted to the profession (rather than the totality of the numbers). It is notable that this focus on admission to the profession reflects a matter that was specifically raised in the 2001 OECD *Report on Regulatory Reform in Ireland* (discussed above), from which the 2009 Act may ultimately be said to derive. It also indicates that, while the external regulatory model in the 2009 Act does not go as far as the model used in England and Wales in the (UK) Legal Services Act 2007, the remit of the Legal Services Ombudsman is not confined to oversight of complaints-handling by the two professional bodies within the legal profession.

SOLICITORS

Undertaking for loans The Solicitors (Professional Practice, Conduct and Discipline—Secured Loan Transactions) Regulations 2009 (S.I. No. 211 of 2009) provide that a solicitor shall not, in general, give an undertaking to, or for the benefit of, a bank, credit union or other financial institution or person in relation to a secured loan transaction in which the solicitor or a connected person has a beneficial interest. This general prohibition is subject to a notice requirement, namely, that the solicitor has given specified notice and the bank, credit union or other financial institution or person has both acknowledged receipt of such notice and consented to the solicitor providing the undertaking. The 2009 Regulations arose in response to major difficulties in recent years concerning undertakings given by solicitors, in particular in connection with secured loans (including mortgages) on land.

Legislation

BRIAN HUNT, Solicitor

TABLE OF ACTS ENACTED DURING 2009

Number	Short Title	Date of Passing *Denotes commencement upon passing
1	Anglo Irish Bank Corporation Act 2009	January 21, 2009*
2	Residential Tenancies (Amendment) Act 2009	January 28, 2009*
3	Gas (Amendment) Act 2009	February 17, 2009*
4	Electoral (Amendment) Act 2009	February 24, 2009*
5	Financial Emergency Measures in the Public Interest Act 2009	February 27, 2009*
6	Charities Act 2009	February 28, 2009
7	Investment of the National Pension Reserve Fund and Miscellaneous Provisions Act 2009	March 05, 2009
8	Legal Services Ombudsman Act 2009	March 10, 2009
9	Electoral (Amendment) (No. 2) Act 2009	March 25, 2009*
10	Social Welfare and Pensions Act 2009	April 29, 2009*
11	Industrial Development Act 2009	May 19, 2009*
12	Finance Act 2009	June 03, 2009
13	Financial Services (Deposit Guarantee Scheme) Act 2009	June 18, 2009
14	Financial Measures (Miscellaneous Provisions) Act 2009	June 26, 2009*
15	Nursing Homes Support Scheme Act 2009	July 01, 2009
16	Aviation (Preclearance) Act 2009	July 08, 2009
17	European Parliament (Irish Constituency Members) Act 2009	July 08, 2009
18	Broadcasting Act 2009	July 12, 2009*
19	Criminal Justice (Surveillance) Act 2009	July 12, 2009*
20	Companies (Amendment) Act 2009	July 12, 2009*
21	Enforcement of Court Orders (Amendment) Act 2009	July 14, 2009*
22	Housing (Miscellaneous Provisions) Act 2009	July 15, 2009

Number	Short Title	Date of Passing *Denotes commencement upon passing
23	Public Health (Tobacco) (Amendment) Act 2009	July 16, 2009*
24	Health Insurance (Miscellaneous Provisions) Act 2009	July 19, 2009*
25	Health (Miscellaneous Provisions) Act 2009	July 21, 2009
26	Harbours (Amendment) Act 2009	July 21, 2009*
27	Land and Conveyancing Law Reform Act 2009	July 21, 2009
28	Criminal Justice (Miscellaneous Provisions) Act 2009	July 21, 2009
29	Oireachtas (Allowances to Members) and Ministerial and Parliamentary Offices Act 2009	July 21, 2009*
30	Local Government (Charges) Act 2009	July 21, 2009
31	Defamation Act 2009	July 23, 2009
32	Criminal Justice (Amendment) Act 2009	July 23, 2009*
33	European Union Act 2009	October 27, 2009
34	National Asset Management Agency Act 2009	November 22, 2009
35	Defence (Miscellaneous Provisions) Act 2009	November 24, 2009*
36	Courts and Court Officers Act 2009	November 24, 2009
37	Public Transport Regulation Act 2009	November 27, 2009*
38	Labour Services (Amendment) Act 2009	November 9, 2009
39	Foreshore and Dumping at Sea (Amendment) Act 2009	December 15, 2009
40	Forestry (Amendment) Act 2009	December 20, 2009
41	Financial Emergency Measures in the Public Interest (No. 2) Act 2009	December 20, 2009
42	Appropriation Act 2009	December 20, 2009*
43	Social Welfare and Pensions (No. 2) Act 2009	December 21, 2009
44	Houses of the Oireachtas Commission (Amendment) Act 2009	December 21, 2009
45	Companies (Miscellaneous Provisions) Act 2009	December 23, 2009
46	Statute Law Revision Act 2009	December 23, 2009

ACTS AND STATUTORY INSTRUMENTS

Volume of legislation During the year, 46 Acts were enacted. This is a very significant increase on the 25 Acts enacted in 2008. As ever, the subject-matter of the Acts enacted is reflective of the policy priorities of the Government in

2009—approximately seven of the Acts arise directly from the onset of the financial and banking crisis.

Unplanned legislation The year saw the enactment of a number of pieces of emergency or unplanned legislation much of which was enacted as a direct result of the financial and banking crisis. For example, the passing of the Anglo Irish Bank Corporation Act 2009 necessitated the recall of the Houses from their Christmas break. The Bill was published on January 20, was passed by the Dáil that same afternoon and was passed by the Seanad later that evening.

A further piece of emergency legislation which arose as a result of the financial crisis was the Financial Emergency Measures in the Public Interest Act 2009 which was passed by the Dáil within three days of its publication and was passed through all stages in the Seanad in two further days.

Other examples of the emergency/unplanned legislation include: Investment of the National Pensions Reserve Fund and Miscellaneous Provisions Act 2009; Residential Tenancies (Amendment) Act 2009; and the Enforcement of Court Orders (Amendment) Act 2009, which was introduced as a consequence of issues raised by the High Court decision in *McCann v Judge of Monaghan District Court* [2009] IEHC 276.

The introduction of emergency/unplanned legislation can have a number of consequences: first, such legislation often undergoes a curtailed legislative process through both Houses; and secondly, such legislation consumes drafting time and parliamentary time which should otherwise have been consumed by legislation which was planned in advance. Therefore such legislation can cause the Government's Legislative Programme to run off-course.

Availability of legislation Difficulties continued to be experienced in 2009 in relation to the availability of legislation in electronic form. One example of this relates to the Housing (Miscellaneous Provisions) Act 2009 which although promulgated on July 15, 2009, did not become available on the website of the Houses of the Oireachtas until November 13, 2009. This delay seems to have arisen because a practice appears to have been adopted within the offices of Houses of the Oireachtas to delay the publication of Acts in electronic form until such time as an Irish language translation of that Act becomes available. This approach may have been adopted as a result of the Supreme Court decision in *Ó Beoláin v Fahy* [2001] 2 I.R. 279.

Format of legislation In July 2009, the Clerk of the Dáil circulated a proposal for the adoption of a revised format in respect of primary legislation. The purpose of the format changes is to make legislation easier to read. The proposed changes include: a reduction in the margins used on each side of the page so that the text runs wider across the page; the discontinuance of placing marginal notes beside sections in favour of the adoption of headings to accompany each section; and, the printing of the long title of each Bill in lower case. However, as of mid-2010 the proposed revised format has not yet been adopted.

Legislation Directory Formerly known as the Chronological Tables of the Statutes, the Legislation Directory has not been updated for several years. However, the updating of the Legislation Directory is now the responsibility of the Law Reform Commission. An enhanced and updated version of the Directory was made available in the second half of 2010.

Statute law restatements A number of Statute Law Restatements were completed by the Law Reform Commission during 2009 and will be finalised and presented to the Attorney General during 2010. In 2010, the Commission is expected to publish its *Second Programme of Statute Law Restatements* identifying the sets of Acts which will be restated during 2010 and 2011.

Translation unit The expansion of the translation unit of the Houses of the Oireachtas was announced in 2009, the completion of which sees the establishment of two separate units, one dealing with primary legislation and the other dealing solely with secondary legislation. See "Government to Run Second Translation Unit", *Irish Times,* May 18, 2009.

CONSOLIDATION ACTS

Land law Though not strictly a consolidation measure, 2009 saw the enactment of the Land and Conveyancing Law Reform Act 2009. The Act is based on a draft Bill which had been prepared by the Law Reform Commission and was contained in its *Report on the Reform and Modernisation of Land Law and Conveyancing Law* (LRC 74–2005). The Act reforms many aspects of land law and it also effected the repeal of over 130 pre-1922 Acts including the De Donis Conditionalibus1285; Quia Emptores 1290; Statute of Uses 1634; Renewable Leaseholds Conversion (Ireland) Act 1868; and a number of Settled Land Acts.

Companies Acts The long-awaited Bill to consolidate the Companies Acts is tentatively expected to be published in Autumn 2011 at the earliest, with enactment to follow some time after.

Criminal law In 2009, the Minister for Justice published the second Annual Report of the Criminal Law Codification Advisory Committee (2008). The

Annual Report indicates that the Committee considered a first draft code of provisions on non-fatal offences against the person.

Courts Acts It is understood that the Law Reform Commission, in conjunction with the Department of Justice, are continuing to work towards the publication of a consolidation Bill to consolidate the 60 or so Courts Acts.

LEGISLATIVE PENALTIES

Fines Bill 2009 In April 2009, the Government published the Fines Bill 2009. The stated purpose of the Bill is to provide for the updating of fines contained in legislation by way of classification. It does so by providing that in future fines shall be classified as a "class A fine", "class B fine", etc. up to a "class E fine", with each class having a maximum value. The updating of penalties in pre-existing legislation is provided for by the provision of a table which attributes a classification to such pre-existing level of fine. The Bill also requires a court to take into account a person's financial circumstances prior to imposing a fine and also allows for the payment of fines by instalment.

The Fines Bill 2004, published as a Private Members' Bill by Fine Gael, similarly proposed a mechanism for the indexation of fines by reference to the Consumer Price Index.

PARLIAMENTARY AFFAIRS

Parliamentary guillotine Five sitting days prior to the summer recess, controversy arose in the Dáil regarding the use of the guillotine to curtail parliamentary debates. Deputy Eamon Gilmore outlined the extent to which various pieces of legislation were being rushed through the House:

> "Yesterday we had one and three quarter hours allocated for the debate on the Health Insurance (Miscellaneous Provisions) Bill 2008 to which there were 84 amendments on Report Stage. Three and a half hours were allocated for the debate on the Land and Conveyancing Law Reform Bill 2006, to which there were 41 amendments on Report Stage. Today, it is proposed to allocate two to two and a half hours for the debate on the Criminal Justice (Miscellaneous Provisions) Bill 2009, to which there are 18 amendments on Report Stage. It is then proposed to allocate one and a half hours for the debate on Report and Final Stages of the Companies (Amendment) Bill 2009 to which there is one amendment. Finally, it is proposed to allocate four and three quarters hours to deal with all Stages of the European Parliament (Irish Constituency

> Members) Bill 2009, relating to the method of payment to Members of the European Parliament, to which, I understand, no amendments have been tabled." (687 *Dáil Debates* (July 2, 2009)).

Deputy Gilmore also highlighted the extent to which the guillotine would be applied to the following week's business:

> "I also draw attention to the arrangements for next week. By my count, there are 12 proposals involving a guillotine. Four of the items of legislation the House is being asked to deal with next week are entirely new and have not appeared before the House thus far. Two of the Bills have yet to be published …" (687 *Dáil Debates* (July 2, 2009)).

As stated by Hogan & Whyte (*JM Kelly: The Irish Constitution*, 4th edn (Dublin: Butterworths, 2003) at para.4.5.05), a question arises as to "whether an attempt by a majority in either House to stifle or curtail debate on a particular Bill might be justiciable by the courts on the ground that the imposition of such a guillotine on parliamentary debate infringed Article 20". They go on to say that this is something which they feel is unlikely and in support of that view they cite the dictum of O'Flaherty J. in *O'Malley v An Ceann Comhairle* ([1997] 1 I.R. 427 at 431) where he said that as regards matters concerning the internal workings of the Dáil, "it would seem inappropriate for the court to intervene except in some very extreme circumstances ...". However, Hogan & Whyte subsequently seem to leave open the possibility of such an intervention, conceding that the jurisdiction of the courts to consider a question such as this "has not yet been fully explored" (*JM Kelly: The Irish Constitution* at para.4.5.09).

Legislative Programme A departure from the Government's Legislative Programme is often a cause of annoyance for members of the opposition. Such concerns caused one member of the Houses to suggest:

> "There should be a programme of legislation for the year and not simply a list of Bills issued by the Chief Whip, which sometimes ends up being essentially an aspirational document that bears no resemblance to reality in respect of the introduction of legislation. Members should know when they are going to deal with blocs of legislation in this House. Deputies should have plenty of time to prepare for debating on such legislation." (Deputy Joanna Tuffy—690 *Dáil Debates* (September 24, 2009)).

Role of legislators The view of one member of the Dáil on the role of her fellow members was articulated as follows:

> "People continually cite the need for Deputies and Senators to act as legislators, which of course is a highly valuable part of their work. Members should be doing more in this regard and should spend more of their time in the House as legislators. … I have always considered that the most valuable contributions I have made in this House have been when dealing with legislation." (As stated by Deputy Joanna Tuffy during the Second Stage debate on the Statute Law Revision Bill 2009—690 *Dáil Debates* (Second Stage, September 24, 2009)).

During a subsequent debate on that legislation, a Senator remarked that, "as politicians, we have various duties, sometimes very far removed from the legislative side of the equation. However, our primary duty, as legislators, is to reflect on, amend, if necessary, and propose legislation." (As stated by Senator Paul Bradford during the Second Stage debate on the Statute Law Revision Bill 2009—199 *Seanad Debates* (Second and Subsequent Stages, December 10, 2009)).

Titles of legislation The formal and often technical nature of titles which are attributed to legislation was, in recent times, raised by a member of the Seanad who observed that legislation in the United States is often given a user-friendly name, such as the No Child Left Behind Bill which was concerned with access to, and delivery of, education. Senator Paul Bradford suggested that if a similar matter were being addressed by the Irish legislature, the associated legislature would be entitled "Education (No.7) (Amendment) (Guarantee of Rights to Education) Bill 2011". He expressed the view that. "[b]y using such language we remove the law from the public. If we were to use more user-friendly titles for legislation, it might help the public to understand what we are about and the legislation we were passing." (199 *Seanad Debates* (Second and Subsequent Stages, December 10, 2009)).

STATUTE LAW REVISION

Statute Law Revision Act 2009 The enactment of the Statute Law Revision Act 2009 marks the third major piece of legislation dedicated solely to the task of statute law revision. The stated purpose of the Act is to repeal two categories of Acts: first, private Acts pre-dating 1751; and secondly, local and personal Acts pre-dating 1851, on the basis that they have either ceased to have effect of have become unnecessary. Sch.1 of the Act identifies 138 Acts which are expressly retained, and Sch.2 identifies the 1351 Acts which are repealed.

Previous Statute Law Revision Acts In the history of the Irish Statute Book a number of statute law revision Acts have been enacted. Prior to independence we have had the Statute Law Revision (Ireland) Act 1878 and also the Statute Law Revision (Ireland) Act 1879. Post independence, seven Statute Law Revision Acts have been enacted in Ireland, they are: Fisheries (Statute Law Revision) Act 1949; Fisheries (Statute Law Revision) Act 1956; Statute Law Revision (Pre-Union Irish Statutes) Act 1962; Statute Law Revision Act 1983; Statute Law Revision (Pre-1922) Act 2005; Statute Law Revision Act 2007; and, the present Act—Statute Law Revision Act 2009.

In addition to pure statute law revision Acts, the repeal of a substantial number Acts has also been effected by other pieces of legislation. For example, the Land and Conveyancing Law Reform Act 2009 has effected the repeal of over 130 pre-1922 statutes.

The Statute Law Revision Act of 2005 Act repealed 207 Acts; the 2007 Act effected the repeal of 3,226 Acts; and this current Act repealed 1,351 Acts. Minister of State Carey pointed out that this Act, "when combined with previous Statute Law Revision Acts will represent one of the largest statute law revision programmes undertaken anywhere in the world".

The process In preparation for this current Act, over 3,000 private Acts and over 7,500 local and personal Acts were examined. During the process 138 Acts were identified as being suitable for retention and 1,351 Acts were identified as being suitable for repeal.

This assessment involved ascertaining the extent to which non-Irish Acts applied to Ireland and also involved a determination as to whether the Acts in question had already been repealed and, if not, whether their repeal should be effected. As explained by Minister of State Carey, in all of these matters a cautious approach was taken.

Consultations formed an important part of the process of assessing the continued relevance of each Act. In the period from September 2007 to February 2009, Government Departments, semi-State bodies, local authorities, particular individuals and the wider public (in total numbering 246 contacts) were all consulted as part of the preparation for this Act. Public notices were placed in national newspapers and further details regarding the proposed were set out on the website of the Office of the Attorney General.

Subject-matter of Acts The Acts which are retained date from 1537 up to 1850 and cover a diverse range of topics, including the settlement of estates of individuals; the provision of water services in certain districts; the development of harbours at certain locations; and the development of railways.

The Acts which are repealed span the period 1534 to 1850 and their subject-matter are equally diverse and include the confirmation of the marriage of certain individuals; the vesting of lands; the facilitation of the sale of lands in order to enable the payment of debts; and, the provision of relief in respect of forfeited estates. Acts providing for the naturalisation of certain individuals are also a significant feature. As Minister of State Carey explained, "[u]ntil 1844 a resident born outside of the United Kingdom could only become a British citizen by means of an Act of Parliament". (199 *Seanad Debates* (Second and Subsequent Stages, December 10, 2009)).

During Second Stage in the Dáil, Minister of State Carey drew Members' attention to one particular Act which was assessed in the preparation of the Bill, which indicates that Sir Arthur Guinness was responsible for causing the re-opening, in 1877, of St Stephen's Green in Dublin to members of the public. He also referred to an Act which provided for the naturalisation of George Friedrich Handel so as to make him a subject of the kingdom of Great Britain. His naturalisation was said to coincide with him being commissioned to compose a piece for the coronation of George III. The Minister of State also made reference to an Act whose purpose was to provide for the removal of the surplus population of Ireland "to a healthy and thinly-populated country". An Act from 1714 enabled the Prince of Wales to qualify himself for the office of Chancellor of the University of Dublin (Trinity College). The Minister of State also made reference to an Act which provided the necessary approvals for the construction of the Anna Livia Bridge and for the provision of lighting on Parnell Square.

Deputy John Deasy pointed out that the legislation "takes in the reign of James I and Charles I and we get a sense from these Acts the kind of turmoil which existed in Ireland during the 17th century in particular". (690 *Dáil Debates* (September 24, 2009)). He also observed that:

> "[o]ne also obtains from the Bill an impression of how divided Irish society was in the past. It contains numerous references to Protestant issue – namely, protestant children. We must remember that in 1641 Catholics owned approximately 60% of the land of Ireland. By 1776, Catholic land ownership stood at 5%".

Deputy Deasy also drew the House's attention to a piece of legislation whose purpose was to enable John Viscount Molesworth and Richard Molesworth to make leases in respect of lands near St Stephen's Green and Dawson Street. In Deputy Deasy's view, the land in question was in all likelihood, the land upon which Dáil Éireann currently stands.

Deputy Ó Caoláin was of the view that:

> "The Bill is chiefly of interest to legal historians and family historians, given the nature of some of the Acts dealing with the naturalisation of individuals and the disposal of private estate. … A large number of them deal with land ownership and inheritance. There is also much to do with seizure, reminding us of the long history of upheaval, plantation and confiscation, particularly in my province of Ulster."

Future statute law revision initiatives Exchanges in the Houses during the course of the debates on the previous Statute Law Revision Bills indicated that the ultimate objective of the project was to result in the publication of a code of laws which would only contain Acts which had been enacted post-independence.

The next phase of the project was expected to involve an examination of Charters and Letters Patent and also Statutory Rules and Orders. That would then be followed by an examination of post-independence legislation with a view to repealing unnecessary and obsolete Acts.

The Taoiseach informed the Dáil that "further elements of the [statute law revision] project will be postponed pending the availability of the necessary funding". (673 *Dáil Debates* (February 3, 2009)). Later in the year, in response to a question regarding the future of the statute law revision project, Minister of State Carey stated: "[w]e are committed to [continuing the project] but, like everything else, it must be done within the available resources. We will see how it can be done." (199 *Seanad Debates* (December 10, 2009)).

When looked at in isolation, the efficacy of statute law revision as an end in itself may of course seem questionable. Statute law revision ought to be regarded as being but one step in broader process of tidying up the statute book and making it more accessible in a real sense; it is a process which should ultimately result in the publication of a statutes in-force database.

IRISH STATUTE BOOK

Irish Statute Book website During 2009, the Office of the Attorney General published the Report detailing the results of its value for money review of the Irish Statute Book website entitled *Maintenance of the Electronic Irish Statute* (February, 2009).

The Report also reveals the results of a survey which was conducted amongst users of the ISB website. The Report states that the website receives, on average, 9,400 visits per day (at p.28). It found that 90 per cent of users surveyed reported that the ISB website was "very useful" or "essential" (at p.12). The Report found that amongst users, there is "a high demand for a more frequently updated eISB than is currently provided ... In terms of the overall timeliness of production, there is a clear message that user expectations are not met by the current production arrangements" (at pp.20 & 21). The Report indicates that 73 per cent of those surveyed believed that constant updating of the website is necessary (at p.26). The Report estimated that the cost of supporting the ISB website during the period 2001–2006 was €1.76 million (at p.7).

Significantly, the Report reveals that there are no permanent staff assigned to the maintenance of the Irish Statute Book (ISB) website. The Report also concedes that the ISB website is updated "at irregular intervals".

The Report acknowledges the existence of an obligation to make legislation accessible which is imposed upon the State by virtue of the fact that "the legal system imputes knowledge of all laws to those within its jurisdiction" (at p.11). It quotes from a letter which the then Attorney General sent to the then Taoiseach (letter dated April 2, 1996), which stated:

> "The position is much worse now than in the middle of the last century. The State makes a lot of law and operates on the basis that ignorance on the part of a citizen is no defence. It does virtually nothing however to make the laws known."

One of the principal conclusions of the Report is that, "the production of the eISB is essentially a legislation publishing exercise beyond the core competency of the Office" (at p.2). The Report makes a number of assertions which are intended to support this stance. For example, at p.15, it states: "The production of the eISB has become a legal publishing exercise for which the AGO is not the most appropriate strategic owner."

At p.26 it states:

> "The AGO is fully engaged with its core functions and does not have sufficient resources to improve the functionality of the eISB to the degree required by its users ...".

At several points in the Report, the authors are forthcoming as regards the Office of the Attorney General's future commitment towards the maintenance of the Irish Statute Book website, stating:

> "The AGO is not in a position to prioritise the function of producing and improving the eISB as a primary goal or strategy … There is no spare capacity for the AGO to take on the job of producing the enhanced eISB that is now desired." (at p.14)

In what may spell bad news for the future of the Irish Statute Book website, the authors of the Report felt unable to identify any one State entity that ought to have responsibility for the production of the ISB website:

> "There is a lack of consensus in relation to which appropriate body should assume authority for the eISB and it is clear that its future production will be an inter-departmental collaborative project." (at p.14)

The Report tentatively alludes to possible suitors for the ISB website:

> "A more suitable organisation for producing the eISB is a body with electronic publishing expertise operating within the ambit of the Better

> Regulation agenda with the supportive collaboration of the other suppliers of eISB content." (at p.32)

The Report goes on to confirm that, in the interim, the AGO's continued role in updating the website is "subject to the availability of resources" (at p.14) and pledges that it will continue to fulfil its current role vis-à-vis the Irish Statute Book website "until such time as the most appropriate strategic owner … is identified and takes up the role" (at p.15).

The Report touches upon the issues of the authenticity of print-outs from the ISB website for use in court. The Report states that before the electronic version of an Act could be considered as an official version "it would be essential to proofread the entire database" (at p.21). The incidence of known errors regarding the accuracy and reliability of the current text present particular difficulties for the reliability of the current database.

The need to upload newly enacted legislation to the ISB website within a short time following its enactment or making is all the more pressing now given the preference which many people have for electronic legislation rather than the paper form. The need for greater functionality is equally important, functionality which allows the user to view legislation in its "in-force" state, incorporating all amendments which have been made. The comments of the Attorney General in his letter to the Taoiseach (quoted above) mean that the justification of the need for such accessibility is not in contention.

With the development of the EU N-Lex Project, which will serve as a common access portal for sources of national law of EU Member States, the ISB website has a wider import beyond our shores. The fact that the ISB website has been formally submitted to the EU Publications Office as being the source database for legislation in Ireland means that it will have a wider audience, an audience who will have an expectation that like the legislative databases of many other countries, the ISB website is up to date and provides full functionality.

EU LEGISLATION

Scrutiny of EU Legislation The scrutiny of EU legislation is carried out by the Joint Committee on European Scrutiny. Established in October 2007, the Committee has a membership of 11 members of the Dáil and four members of the Seanad. The Joint Committee was a successor to the Sub-Committee on European Scrutiny.

Under the European Union (Scrutiny) Act 2002, the Government is obliged to lay copies of all EU legislative measures before the Houses within four weeks of its initial publication, along with an explanatory statement which has been prepared by the Minister with responsibility for the relevant portfolio. The explanatory statement summarises the aim of the proposal, highlights any implications for the State, indicates the anticipated negotiation period, and also indicates the expected implementation date.

The Orders of Reference of the Joint Committee indicate that its primary function of the Joint Committee is to scrutinise proposals for legislation which are being developed by the EU institutions and to report on those matters to the Houses of the Oireachtas.

In practice, the Joint Committee subjects every legislative proposal emerging from the EU to some degree of scrutiny. In a sense its serves as a filtering mechanism—sorting out the relevant measures from the less important ones.

According to its Annual Report published in 2009—*Sixth Annual Report on the Operation of the European Union (Scrutiny) Act 2002* (2009)—the Joint Committee met 27 times over a 14-month period. During that time, it considered 833 documents, 746 of which were legislative proposals. Of the 833 documents considered by the Joint Committee, a surprising 77 per cent of the proposals considered by the Joint Committee were identified as not warranting any further scrutiny. A mere 8 per cent (63) of the documents were deemed to be of such significance that they warranted further scrutiny.

As is demonstrated by its Sixth Annual Report, the Joint Committee clearly has a very demanding workload. In the 14-month period examined by its Annual Report, the number of documents considered at meetings of the Joint Committee seems to have ranged from a high of 166 proposals to four or even zero proposals.

REGULATORY IMPACT ANALYSIS

Revised RIA Guidelines In June 2009, the Taoiseach published the Revised RIA Guidelines. The Revised Guidelines, which replace the original Guidelines dating from 2005, implement a number of recommendations which arose from a review of RIA which was published by the Taoiseach in 2008. Significantly, the Revised Guidelines remove the distinction between a screening RIA and a full RIA. The Revised Guidelines are also more prescriptive as regards the assessment of implementation costs.

Publication of RIAs The publication of RIAs and the apparent difficulty in accessing the reports of completed RIAs was the subject of discussion in the Dáil. Deputy Denis Naughten criticised the failure of most Departments to establish a dedicated webpage for RIAs, and cited the Department of Social and Family Affairs as being the only Department with such a webpage in place. By way of response, the Taoiseach stated: "... the overriding co-ordination role of my Department means we must try to ensure there is better uniformity of presentation". And the Taoiseach undertook to take the matter up with the various Departments. (673 *Dáil Debates* (February 3, 2009)).

Limitation of Actions

BANKRUPTCY

In *Minister for Communications v W* [2009] IEHC 413, the applicants sought an order dismissing a bankruptcy summons. The Minister and another party had claimed that the applicants were indebted to them for nearly €6 million inclusive of interest on foot of a certificate of taxed costs accrued in 1998 pursuant to a High Court order. The bankruptcy summons was served in 2009. The applicant claimed that, since s.11(6)(b) of the Statute of Limitations 1957 provided that "no arrears of interest in respect of any judgment debt shall be recovered after the expiration of six years from the date on which interest became due", the claim for interest made in the case was not correct and that the amount of the debt claimed was overstated and inaccurate. The respondents argued that the Statute of Limitations only barred the remedy of recovery of all the interest but did not extinguish the entitlement of the creditors to claim interest for a period in excess of six years. They also relied on Ord.76 r.12(4) which provides that "[n]o objection shall be allowed to the particulars unless the court considers that the debtor has been misled by them."

McGovern J. dismissed the summons. Although it seemed to him that the applicants could hardly have been misled by the manner in which the interest had been stated as the rates of interest and the periods for which they were claimed were fully set out in the particulars of demand, there did, on the other hand, seem to be an issue as to whether interest beyond the period of six years could be claimed and, if not, whether a correct liquidated sum had been claimed. In McGovern J.'s view, this was a real and substantial issue and one which was "at least, arguable" and which had some prospect of success.

ESTOPPEL

In the *Annual Review of Irish Law 2006*, p.451, we noted *Murphy v Grealish* [2006] IEHC 22, in which MacMenamin J. evinced little hesitation in applying the estoppel principle to overcome the limitation defence where there had been several "clear and unambiguous" assurances that liability would not be in issue. The Supreme Court affirmed the decision: [2009] IESC 9. Geoghegan J. (Kearns and Macken JJ. concurring) sought to reconcile Keane C.J.'s remarks in *Ryan v Connolly* [2001] 2 I.L.R.M. 174 with the diversity of approaches favoured by Henchy, Griffin and Kenny JJ. respectively in *Doran v Thomas*

Thompson and Sons Ltd [1978] I.R. 223. In *Ryan v Connolly*, Keane C.J. had observed that:

> "[t]he fact that a defendant had expressly and unambiguously conceded the issue of liability in a case will not necessarily of itself make it reasonable for the plaintiff to assume that he can defer the institution of proceedings beyond the limitation period."

Geoghegan J. considered it "perfectly clear" that Keane C.J. had been intending to follow the principles laid down in *Doran*. When the judgments in *Doran* and *Ryan* were carefully studied, two important factors emerged:

> "The first is that an admission of liability is all important in considering an issue of estoppel preventing reliance on the Statute of Limitations. Indeed on one reading of the judgment of Henchy J., in particular, one might almost believe that it was a determining factor. I do not believe, however, that he or either of the two other judges in that court would have intended to convey that. In that particular case, there was in fact no admission of liability.
>
> The second factor which emerges from the two cases is the useful correction in this regard made by Keane C.J. ... It clearly could not be the law that merely because there was an admission of liability a plaintiff could ignore the Statute of Limitations with impunity. It is in that context that Keane C.J. uses the word 'necessarily' in the passage cited."

Keane C.J.'s "clearly correct cautionary note" had to be balanced against what Henchy J. said in *Doran*:

> "Where in a claim for damages such as this a defendant has engaged in words or conduct from which it was reasonable to infer, and from which it was in fact inferred, that liability would be admitted, and on foot of that representation the plaintiff has refrained from instituting proceedings within the period prescribed by the statute, the defendant will be held estopped from escaping liability by pleading the statute. The reason is that it would be dishonest and unconscionable for the defendant, having misled the plaintiff into a feeling of security on the issue of liability and, thereby, into a justifiable belief that the statute would not be used to defeat his claim, to escape liability by pleading the statute. The representation necessary to support this kind of estoppel need not be clear and unambiguous in the sense of being susceptible of only one interpretation. It is sufficient if, despite possible ambiguity or lack of certainty, on its true construction it bears the meaning that was drawn from it. Nor is it necessary to give evidence of an express intention to deceive the plaintiff. An intention to that effect will be

read into the representation if the defendant has so conducted himself that, in the opinion of the court, he ought not to be heard to say that an admission of liability was not intended."

In *O'Reilly v Granville* [1971] I.R. 90, both Ó Dálaigh C.J. and Walsh J. had also invoked the concept of unconscionability in this context, as indeed MacMenamin J. had done in the instant case. Interestingly, Geoghegan J. observed:

> "I would leave open the question till it arises in some appropriate case as to whether a plea of statute bar can be defeated in some situations by unconscionable conduct but which could not be said to give rise to an estoppel. Quite apart from the judgments of Ó Dálaigh C.J. and Walsh J., the High Court judgments of Costello J. and Kelly J., though reversed on the particular facts, might give some credence to a wider principle of unconscionability rather than the much narrower concept of estoppel with its stricter rules."

FATAL INJURIES

In *Farrell v Coffey* [2009] IEHC 537, Dunne J. refused to permit an amendment to a personal injuries claim which would have had the effect of converting it into one for fatal injuries after the decease of the original plaintiff. She had no difficulty in distinguishing the facts of the case from those in *Krops v Irish Forestry Board Ltd* [1995] 2 I.R. 113, which we analysed in the *Annual Review of Irish Law 1995*, pp.365–366. She stated:

> "A fatal injuries claim is different to a personal injuries claim. This is so even if the claims arose out of the same facts. The nature of the claim and the damages that flow from the set of facts giving rise to the cause of action are different. The parties are different. The situation in this case seems to me to be quite different to the situation in the *Krops* case … The amendment in that case was limited to the addition of a cause of action in nuisance where the plaintiff relied on the same facts and circumstances to ground that cause of action. The facts pleaded in that case could have given rise to a claim arising both in negligence and nuisance. All of the elements necessary to ground the claim in nuisance had been pleaded. In the circumstances the amendment of the pleadings in that case meant that the statute could not be pleaded in respect of the cause of action in nuisance but as was pointed out there was no new allegation of facts and, in those circumstances, it was held that no injustice was done by allowing the amendment …
>
> By contrast, in these proceedings, it seems to me that the plaintiff is

> attempting by means of the proposed amendment to set up an entirely new case, i.e. a fatal injuries case, using the vehicle of the personal injuries case. In effect, the plaintiff is seeking, by amendment of the original proceedings, to bring a new claim on his own behalf and on behalf of the statutory dependants. If permitted to do so, the defendant would be deprived of his right to rely on the statute. The amendments sought to be made in this case would bring about a change of significance in the nature of the proceedings. Accordingly, in my view, allowing the amendments in the circumstances of this case would prejudice the defendant."

In the instant case, the plaintiff had offered "no explanation of any kind" as to why he sought to reconstitute the proceedings instead of issuing new proceedings to bring a fatal injuries claim pursuant to statute within an appropriate time.

FRAUD

In *O'Sullivan v Rogan, practising as Rogan and Morgan Solicitors* [2009] IEHC 456, the plaintiff, a retired farmer, aged 90 and residing in a nursing home, claimed damages from his solicitors for negligence, misrepresentation, breach of contract, breach of duty and breach of statutory duty, arising from a transaction involving the sale of lands in 1999. The claim was that the defendants had failed to advise the plaintiff properly in transferring his property at a substantial undervalue which amounted to divesting himself of his entire property. A plenary summons was issued in 2008. The defendants invoked the Statute of Limitations 1957. The plaintiff in reply sought to rely on s.71 of that Act, which provides:

> (1) Where, in the case of an action for which a period of limitation is fixed by this Act, either –
> (a) the action is based on the fraud of the defendant or his agent or of any person through whom he claims or his agent, or
> (b) the right of action is concealed by the fraud of any such person,
>
> the period of limitation shall not begin to run until the plaintiff has discovered the fraud or could with reasonable diligence have discovered it.

The defendants by motion sought the striking-out of the proceedings as being statute-barred, by way of a preliminary issue.

The plaintiff emphasised that he was not making a case for damages for fraud but alleged that the failure of the defendants to advise the plaintiff in

March 1999 that he had a cause of action against them due to their failure to advise him properly on the transaction involved amounted to a fraudulent concealment. The defendants, he claimed, "knew well" that they were not properly advising him.

Hedigan J. declined to dismiss the proceedings and ordered a plenary hearing. He observed:

> "In the most unusual facts of this case it is not clear, nor can it be at this preliminary stage, just what the precise actions were surrounding the events which gave rise to these proceedings."

He quoted passages from three English decisions, the latter of which had been approved in Ireland in *McDonald v Bain* [1991] I.L.R.M. 764. In *Kitchen v Royal Air Force Association* [1958] 1 W.L.R. 569, Lord Evershed, speaking of an equivalent English provision, had observed that:

> "It is now clear … that the word 'fraud'… is by no means limited to common law fraud or deceit. Equally, it is clear that no degree of moral turpitude is necessary to establish fraud within the section. What is covered by equitable fraud is a matter which Lord Hardwicke did not attempt to define 200 years ago and I certainly shall not attempt to do so now, but it is, I think, clear that the phrase covers conduct which, having regard to some special relationship between the two parties concerned, is an unconscionable thing for the one to do towards the other."

In *Applegate v Moss* [1971] 1 Q.B. 406, Lord Denning M.R. had said that the provision applied whenever the defendant's conduct had been such:

> "... as to hide from the plaintiff the existence of his right of action, in such circumstances that it would be inequitable to allow the defendant to rely on the lapse of time as a bar to the claim".

In *Keane v Victor Parsons & Co* [1973] 1 W.L.R. 29 Lord Denning M.R. had observed:

> "In order to show that he concealed the right of action by fraud, it is not necessary to show that he took active steps to conceal his wrongdoing or breach of contract. It is sufficient that he knowingly committed and did not tell the owner anything about it. He did the wrong or committed the wrong secretly. By saying nothing he kept it secret. He conceals the right of action. He conceals it by fraud as those words have been interpreted in the cases. To this word 'knowingly' there must be added 'recklessly'."

The Master of the Rolls had gone on to say:

> "If however the defendant was quite unaware that he was committing a wrong or a breach of contract it would be different. So if by an honest blunder he unwittingly commits a wrong ..., or a breach of contract ... then he could avail himself of the Statute of Limitations."

Hedigan J. commented:

> "What exactly was the conduct of the defendants in this case at the time? It is not clear and I believe cannot become clear until the full facts of the case are teased out. If it turns out that what occurred amounts to the kind of conduct referred to in *Kitchen, Applegate* and *Keane*, then it may well be that s.71 will apply and save the plaintiff from the statute. If, on the other hand, it is found to be conduct which whilst negligent was unattended by fraudulent or deceitful behaviour then, as pointed out by Denning M.R. in *Victor Parsons*, the defendant may avail himself of the statute."

Owing to the centrality of the defendants' conduct in relation to the event at the time and owing to the inevitable conflicts in relation to it which could be resolved only by plenary hearing, Hedigan J. remitted the issue to plenary hearing.

In *Task Construction Ltd v Devine practising as BCM Hanby Wallace & Company* [2009] IEHC 74, where the plaintiffs' action for negligence in relation to a transfer of property in 1986 involved an allegation that too little stamp duty had been paid, Dunne J. rejected the plaintiffs' contention that s.71 had any application. She stated:

> "In these proceedings, the alleged fraud could only be a fraud on the Revenue, if indeed there is any fraud. It is impossible to see how such an alleged fraud could have occasioned any loss to the plaintiffs or either of them. In any event, even if there was a fraud on the Revenue, and I am far from convinced that there was ... such a fraud is a matter for the Revenue to pursue—not the plaintiffs herein."

GUARANTEE DEBENTURE

In *Ulster Investment Bank Ltd v Rockrohan Estate Ltd* [2009] IEHC 4, Irvine J. held that an application for possession made many years after the making of an order declaring a sum well charged on foot of a guarantee debenture was not defeated by the Statute of Limitations as it was not capable of being characterised as a fresh "action". In coming to his conclusion, Irvine J. drew inspiration from English authorities and *Yorkshire Bank Finance Ltd v Mulhall* [2008] EWCA Civ 1156. Irvine J. also considered that there were practical reasons why s.11(6)(b) of the Statute of Limitations should be so interpreted:

> "The relief granted by the court in proceedings brought on foot of an equitable mortgage or charge provides the plaintiff with the right to recover monies outstanding by seeking a sale of the defendant's lands. That sale is under the control of the court and is for the benefit of all who may have a charge or encumbrance burdening the land. The plaintiff's ability to realise a defendant's assets is not entirely within its control …
>
> Any number of complications may arise, unrelated to any default on the part of a plaintiff, which could result in the lands charged not being sold within six years of obtaining a well charging order. On the basis of [the defendant]'s arguments, a plaintiff might find itself unable, because of matters outside its control, including obstruction tactics on the part of a defendant, to recover the sums due for principal and interest which a defendant had contracted to pay at the time the charge was created. All of these factors would suggest that it is unlikely that the legislature intended to impose any time limit on firstly, the right of a plaintiff to enforce a well charging order, secondly, its rights to take such steps as might prove necessary to enforce that order or thirdly, its right to recover interest on the monies outstanding on foot of such order."

The defendant argued that it had acquired adverse possession, but Irvine J. considered that this was based on a misunderstanding as to the nature of the well charging order proceedings:

> "The proceedings have as their foundation stone a covenant by Rockrohan to discharge certain liabilities. That covenant created an equitable charge but conveyed no legal or equitable estate in those lands to UIB as is clear from the decision in *Ezekiel* [*v Orakpo* [1997] 1 W.L.R. 340]. Time could never run against UIB as it has never had any title or right to occupation of the lands."

For the avoidance of doubt, if the court was wrong in its conclusion as to the nature of the application for possession and if the application was governed by Ord.42 rr.23 and 24, Irvine J. was "entirely satisfied" that UIB had established good reason for the exercise by the court of its discretion to grant the necessary leave to issue execution. In *Smith and Genport Ltd v Tunney* [2004] IESC 24, the Supreme Court had concluded that it was not necessary for a plaintiff applying for relief under Ord.42 rr.23 and 24 to show the existence of unusual, exceptional or very special reasons for a successful application to issue execution more than six years after the date of an order or judgment once there was something to which the judge could attach the court's discretion.

JUDGMENT MORTGAGE

In *AIB PLC v Dormer* [2009] IEHC 586, Finlay Geoghegan J. held that a judgment mortgagee's entitlements had been extinguished by s.38 of the Statute of Limitations 1957. The relevant period prescribed by s.32(2)(a) for actions claiming the sale of land subject to a mortgage is 12 years from accrual of the right of action. Section 38 provides that, at the expiration of the prescribed period, the right of the mortgagee to the principal sum and interest secured by the mortgage is to be extinguished. Counsel of the judgment mortgagee had argued that s.38 should not be taken literally since to do so could lead to the extinction of the right of a judgment mortgagee's right to principal and interest where proceedings were commenced, but not concluded, a short period before the expiry of the 12 years. Finlay Geoghegan J. rejected this argument since she considered that a court would "normally" determine a plaintiff's claim in accordance with the position between the parties at the date of commencement of the proceedings.

In the *Dormer* case, the applicant incumbrancer had sought an order for sale, pursuant to Ord.33 r.8 of the Rules of the Superior Courts, of lands over which the plaintiff had obtained an order for sale. The plaintiff no longer wished to proceed with the sale and the applicant, a puisne incumbrancer, sought to be substituted as plaintiff in the proceedings.

It was argued on behalf of the applicant that old case law established that an order for sale made by a court enured for the benefit of all incumbrancers, including the applicant, who were entitled to take over carriage of the proceedings and enforce the order for sale, after the plaintiff's demands had been satisfied. Finlay Geoghegan J. concluded, however, that, where the court extended the benefit of its order to other incumbrancers, although broad language had sometimes been used, in no case had an order been made when the incumbrancer had not proven its debt.

In *AIB PLC v Vickers* [2009] IEHC 587, Finlay Geoghegan J. applied the reasoning she had favoured in *Dormer*. In *Bank of Ireland v Moffitt* [2009] IEHC 545, McMahon J. expressed complete agreement with Finlay Geoghegan J.'s approach in relation to facts not dissimilar to those in *Dormer*.

LAW REFORM

The Law Reform Commission, in its *Consultation Paper on Limitation of Actions* (LRC CP54–2009), provisionally recommends radical changes in the law, on the basis that the present statutory code is in need of fundamental reform and simplification.

The Commission proposes the introduction of new "core regime" legislation governing limitation of actions, based on a set of limitation periods applying to the majority of civil actions, with limited exceptions which would provide for special limitation periods. There would be a uniform basic limitation period of general application, which would apply to a wide range of civil actions, subject to a limited number of exceptions. The Commission proposes the introduction of either:

(a) one basic limitation period of general application, running for a period of two years; or
(b) three basic limitation periods of specific application, running for periods of one, two and six years respectively.

Subject to rules concerning the date from which the basic limitation period is to run, the introduction of a two-year limitation period would be sufficient for the majority of actions. The basic limitation period should run from the date of knowledge of the plaintiff. There would also be an ultimate limitation period, of general application, of 12 years' duration, running from the date of the act or omission giving rise to the cause of action. It would apply to personal injuries actions. The Commission defends its extension of the "long stop" rule to personal injuries actions as follows:

> "The Commission considers that special considerations arise in respect of the application of an ultimate limitation period to personal injuries actions. History demonstrates that many forms of personal injuries lay dormant for years if not decades. The imposition of a strict ultimate limitation period to such actions may have harsh results for persons who do not become aware of their injuries until after the expiry of the limitation period. That notwithstanding, there is an underlying danger in allowing the prosecution of civil actions long years after the act or omission giving rise to the cause of action, especially in terms of a risk of unfairness to the defendant. It is recalled that the Courts retain an inherent jurisdiction to strike out claims for want of prosecution even where a statutory limitation period has not yet expired, and it is considered that this jurisdiction plays a role in ensuring that trials do not proceed simply because they are not statute-barred, where there is a risk of unfairness to the defendant."

One may pause to reflect on whether this argument is sufficiently strong to warrant the denial of any recompense to the victim of tortiously inflicted insidious injuries, no less real because of their latent character. The phenomenon of latent physical injury is well established. It can arise in long-term relationships such as employment, where the employer usually has the means of preventing the occurrence of insidious injury and greater resources for discovering its occurrence than the employee. To use an inflexible "long stop" rule to deny the injured employee a right of action in these circumstances seems unjust.

Under the Commission's proposals, the courts would continue to exercise their inherent jurisdiction to dismiss a claim for prejudicial delay or want of prosecution. The Commission provisionally recommends that the term "disability" should not form part of a revised, modern limitations regime.

The Commission considers that, in light of the proposal in the Government's Scheme of a Mental Capacity Bill 2008 to establish a new guardianship system for adults whose mental capacity is limited or who lack mental capacity, the proposed limitations regime should not allow for any exception to the running of either the basic or the ultimate limitation period in the event that the plaintiff is an adult whose mental capacity is limited or who lacks mental capacity. The Commission comments:

> "Fairness to plaintiffs must, of course, not be sacrificed to that end but the Commission is satisfied that sufficient protection will be available to plaintiffs provided that recent developments in the areas of guardianship and capacity … are brought to fruition. These developments envisage a co-ordinated system whereby persons who are incapable of managing their own affairs would be protected by a guardian. Indeed, in that respect, the Commission notes that there are good reasons for supporting the approach that plaintiffs may benefit from bringing proceedings as early as possible, subject to suitable safeguards."

There would be no exception to the running of either the basic or the ultimate limitation period in the event that the plaintiff is under the age of 18 and is in the custody of a competent parent or guardian who is conscious of his or her responsibilities and is capable of commencing proceedings on behalf of the plaintiff. The courts would have a residual discretion, exercisable in exceptional cases and subject to the interests of justice, to allow proceedings to be commenced by a plaintiff who had not reached the age of 18 before the expiry of the ultimate limitation period. There is, of course, a constitutional dimension which needs to be considered. In *O'Brien v Keogh* [1972] I.R. 144, the Supreme Court was concerned about cases where the minor was in the custody of a parent who was the potential defendant in an action in which the minor would be plaintiff. One possible solution would be to craft an exception specifically dealing with this category of case. The Commission does not favour this approach, emphasising that its proposed limitations regime is intended to be streamlined, simplified and of universal application and that it should have as few exceptional rules as possible.

The new limitations regime would not contain any provision for postponement where the plaintiff is a convicted prisoner. An acknowledgment or part payment would have no impact on the running of either the basic or ultimate limitation period.

The Commission provisionally recommends that the concept of postponement in circumstances where the action is based on the fraud of the defendant or the defendant has fraudulently concealed the cause of action from the plaintiff should not be incorporated into a new limitations regime which includes a discoverability test of general application. Similarly, the Commission proposes that the defence of mistake should not be incorporated into a core limitations regime which includes a discoverability test of general application.

MARITIME CLAIM

In *McGuinness v Marine Institute* [2009] IEHC 177, Dunne J. satisfactorily resolved an important question of interpretation relating to s.46(2) of the Civil Liability Act 1961. Section 46(1) deals with cases where damage is caused to one or more vessels by the fault of two or more of them. Subsection (2) provides as follows:

> Where, by the sole or concurrent fault of a vessel damage is caused to that or another vessel or to the cargo or any property on board either vessel, or loss of life or personal injury is suffered, by any person on board either vessel, then, subject to subsection (3) of this section, no action shall be maintainable to enforce a claim for damages or lien in respect of such damage, loss of life or injury unless proceedings are commenced within two years from the date when such damage, loss of life or injury was caused; and an action shall not be maintainable to enforce any claim for contribution in respect of an overpaid proportion of any damages for loss of life or personal injuries unless proceedings are commenced within one year from the date of payment.

Subsection (3) provides that any court having jurisdiction to deal with an action to which subs.(2) relates may extend the limitation period "to such extent and subject to such conditions as it thinks fit".

In the instant case the plaintiff, while on a vessel, had been injured at sea when struck by a number of boxes of ray on board the vessel. He sued his employer and the owner of the vessel. Clearly only one vessel was involved. The claim wended its way to PIAB; while PIAB was considering it, the limitation period ran out, the defendants claimed. The plaintiff's riposte was that s.50 of the Personal Injuries Assessment Board Act 2003 stopped the clock while the claim was before PIAB. The defendants replied that claims under s.46(2) had not been included in those covered by s.50. This was undoubtedly true; the issue thus resolved itself into whether a claim such as the plaintiff's, which did not involve a collision between two or more vessels, actually fell within the terms of s.46(2).

The truth of the matter is that s.46(2) was poorly drafted. It sought to replicate s.8 of the Maritime Convention Act 1911 but used language capable, on one strained interpretation, of extending to claims involving events occurring on only one vessel. The legislative history makes it plain that this was not the intent. Dunne J., applying a textual analysis, concluded that the subsection could only have application to personal injury actions suffered by an individual on board one of two or more vessels. This conclusion was strengthened, in her view, when regard was also had to subs.(1).

> "Section 46 as a whole seems to me to lay out the statutory scheme applicable to collisions between vessels. Looking at the scheme as a whole as contained in s.46 it seems to me that it is clearly the intention of the Oireachtas that the provisions of s.46 are only intended to apply to circumstances involving collisions arising from the fault of two or more vessels. On that basis I am satisfied that the arguments of the plaintiff herein are correct insofar as they relate to the interpretation of s.46(2)."

Dunne J. went on to hold that, if she were mistaken in that view and the plaintiff's claim was statute-barred, she would have no hesitation in exercising her discretion under subs.(3) in the plaintiff's favour. The fact that his claim was still being considered by PIAB when the statutory period ran out, rendering it legally impermissible for the plaintiff to issue proceedings, was a circumstance outside his control.

NEGLIGENCE CLAIM FOR PURE ECONOMIC LOSS

Is is well established that, in negligence actions for pure economic loss as opposed to personal injury (which are dealt with by the Statute of Limitations (Amendment) Act 1991), the limitation clock begins to tick from the time the injury is sustained, regardless of a plaintiff's reasonable failure to become aware of the fact of the commission of the tort or of the damage caused. In *Task Construction Ltd v Devine practising as BCM Hanby Wallace and Company* [2009] IEHC 74, Dunne J. reiterated the traditional rule. The plaintiffs' claim was for alleged negligence in regard to the execution of a deed in September 1986. The second-named plaintiff alleged that he had not seen the deed until 2006. Dunne J. observed:

> "Assuming for the sake of argument that there was negligence on the part of the defendant, the tort was complete in September 1986. That is when the cause of action accrued to any party who suffered a loss as a result of the alleged negligence. The second named plaintiff seems to be attempting to introduce a test of 'discoverability'. This is a concept that has been rejected by the courts in a number of cases, eg. *Morgan v. Park Developments Limited* [1983] I.L.R.M. 156, *Hegarty v. O'Loughran* [1990] 1 I.R. 14, *Doyle v. C. and D. Providers (Wexford) Limited* [1994] 3 I.R. 57 and *Tuohy v. Courtney* [1994] 3 I.R. 1. It is clear from those authorities that, in a case such as this, the test of discoverability does not apply."

By way of contrast, Irvine J.'s decision in *Darby v Shanley (practising as Olwen Shanley and Company Solicitors)* [2009] IEHC 459, whilst adhering to the same principles as to discoverability, had a happier outcome from the plaintiffs' standpoint. The defendant solicitor had been involved in the making of a will of an elderly lady in 1997 and the preparation of a deed of transfer of land by her in 1998, to the plaintiffs' benefit. After the death of the testatrix in 1999, her husband initially asserted his claim to a legal right in his late wife's estate under the Succession Act 1965 and some time later took probate proceedings seeking to overturn these transactions. The proceedings were compromised, with the plaintiffs' benefit being reduced. The plaintiffs initiated proceedings against the defendant, in 2004 and 2007 respectively.

It was argued on behalf of the defendant with respect to the claim for alleged negligence in relation to the will, that the six-year limitation period had elapsed on the basis that it had commenced, at the latest, on December 8, 1999, the date when the widower had claimed his legal right to his late wife's estate. On behalf of the plaintiffs, it was contended that time could not run against them without their knowledge.

Irvine J. accepted the principle that, unless the plaintiffs' claims had been instituted "within six years from the date upon which their respective causes of actions accrued", the claims must fail. She held that the claims were not statute-barred. The cause of action for negligence in relation to the preparation of the will was complete only upon the date on which the probate proceedings were settled, "that being the date upon which it could be stated both plaintiffs had sustained a loss arising from the negligence alleged against the defendants." That loss was ascertainable from the terms of the settlement.

PRACTICE AND PROCEDURE

Addition of parties In *Leisure Management Corporation Ltd v AIG Europe (Ireland) Ltd* [2009] IEHC 365, Peart J. permitted the addition of certain parties as plaintiff, under Ord.15 r.13 of the Rules of the Superior Courts, in an action by an insured against an insurer which had repudiated liability to indemnify the insured for an award of damages in a tort action. The defendant argued that the claims of the proposed additional parties were statute-barred and that, on that account, the court should not permit their addition. Peart J. demurred, observing that:

> "Whether or not the claims of any of the plaintiffs are statute-barred is a matter to be raised by way of defence to the claim, and will require evidence and legal submissions before the matter can be finally determined. This is not a case where it is already beyond any possible doubt that the claims are statute-barred. The defendant can plead these matters so that they can be determined."

Renewal of plenary summons In *Baulk v Irish National Insurance Co Ltd* [1969] I.R. 66, the Supreme Court acknowledged that:

> "[t]he fact that the Statute of Limitations would defeat any new proceedings, which might be necessitated by the failure to grant the renewal [of the plenary summons] sought, could itself be a good cause to move the Court to grant the renewal."

In *Jachman v Getinge AB* [2009] IEHC 612, McMahon J. cited these observations when he stated:

> "It is true that this is a factor which the courts have taken into account in deciding to renew summonses in the past… But it is not the only factor. Further, the court's duty is [to] both parties in the litigation and as O'Flaherty J. stated in *Roche v. Clayton* [1998] 1 IR 596 at p. 600: 'The Statute of Limitations must be available on a reciprocal basis to both sides of any litigation.'"

McMahon J. noted that, in *O'Brien v Fahy*, Supreme Court, March 21, 1997, Barrington J. had engaged in this balancing exercise, in setting aside the renewal of the summons. After acknowledging the serious consequences for the plaintiff of refusing a renewal order, Barrington J. had gone on to state:

> "On the other hand the defendant did not know nor was she given any warning that a claim would be made against her and her solicitor has sworn an affidavit saying that, as a result, were a claim to be now made the plaintiff would be greatly prejudiced in the defence of the case as it is now nearly four and a half years since the alleged accident and he says at this stage it is extremely difficult, if not impossible, to investigate all the circumstances surrounding the accident. It appears to me that the lapse of such a time without knowing that claim was going to be

> made is something which itself implies prejudice and the defendant and her solicitor are prepared to swear affidavits that in fact it is not a theoretical prejudice but an actual prejudice which the defendant would suffer; one must set that against the loss to the plaintiff, if as a result of a refusal to renew the summons which is out of time, her claim became statute-barred."

In the instant case, the defendants would not be seriously prejudiced by a renewal of the summons. The injuries sustained by the plaintiff were sufficiently serious to have made it reasonable for the first-named defendant to apprehend litigation once it had become aware of the accident. The facts that some employees had left the company and that the first-named defendant had relocated its office were "hardly serious prejudices". Moreover, the period of time between the date of the accident and the date on which the first-named defendant first became aware of an intention to involve it in the litigation was three and a half years.

In *O'Keeffe v G & T Crompton Ltd* [2009] IEHC 366, Peart J. set aside an order to renew a plenary summons issued in 2001 in a tort action by an employee against his employer. A delay of several years had occurred on account of pressure of work in the plainfiff's solicitor's office. Peart J. pointed out that Ord.8 r.1 of the Rules of the Superior Courts permitted renewal where reasonable efforts had been made to serve the defendant or where there was "other good reason". In the instant case the reason for the delay was not a good one. The defendants would be prejudiced by the delay. As regards the prejudice to the plaintiff, Peart J. commented:

> "Clearly every plaintiff whose claim is barred in this way will always be prejudiced where any new summons issued thereafter will be fatally vulnerable to a plea by a defendant under the 'Statute of Limitations'. Yet, that fact has been found not, of itself, to justify renewal … On the evidence before me the plaintiff personally is blameless … That personal blamelessness is the best foot that he can put forward on this application. Everything else is against him. While there can be no doubt that a litigant is vicariously liable for the actions of or inaction by his/her solicitor, the question of his/her own personal blameworthiness is a relevant factor when considering the balance of justice between the parties, but it cannot on all occasions trump clear prejudice facing the other party in defending the claim …
>
> The defendants are entitled to a hearing within a reasonable time. They cannot get that, and to force them to defend this claim after such a long time is tantamount to expecting them to do the impossible and leave them unfairly disadvantaged to the extent that the plaintiff might well have a clear and unimpeded run to the finishing line."

Amendment of statement of claim In *Smyth v Tunney* [2009] IESC 5, Finnegan J. quoted extensively from Keane J's judgment in *Krops v Irish Forestry Board Ltd* [1995] 2 I.R. 113. He summarised the present law on amendment as follows:

> "[A]n amendment will be allowed if it is necessary for the purpose of determining the real issues in controversy between the parties. The addition of a new cause of action by amendment will be permitted notwithstanding that by the date of amendment the Statute of Limitations had run if the facts pleaded are sufficient to support the new cause of action. Facts may be added by amendment if they serve only to clarify the original claim but not if they are new facts. Simple errors such as an error in date or an error as to location which do not prejudice the defendant and enable the real questions in controversy between the parties to be determined will be permitted."

In the instant case, the amendment sought by way of the addition of causes of action did not satisfy these requirements. In order to sustain the new causes of action additional facts were required to be pleaded. The Statute of Limitations "m[ight] well have run".

In *Webb v Minister for Finance* [2009] IEHC 534, the plaintiff, a member of the defence forces, took proceedings against the army arising from a collision between two armoured personnel carriers in 2002. The claim related exclusively to the manner in which the driver of one of the vehicles had driven it. In 2008 the plaintiff sought to amend the pleadings to include allegations that the army authorities had "failed to provide a full and comprehensive medical service" to him, had failed to monitor his condition and had delayed an MRI scan for years following his accident, as well as leaving him to perform duties inappropriate to his medical condition.

The defendant argued that the plaintiff was in fact seeking to pursue a new cause of action, for medical negligence against the Army Medical Corps, which would be statute-barred. The plaintiff argued that he could not reasonably have been aware of the alleged neglect of his condition until he had access to medical records in 2006.

Herbert J. held that the amendment sought by the plaintiff should be granted. He stated:

> "In the instant case I find that the plaintiff, though seeking to introduce into the existing action a claim which was not originally made, is not attempting to add a new and distinct cause of action. It is reasonably arguable—the determination of the issue must await the hearing of the action—that it was a direct, foreseeable and proximate consequence of the already pleaded negligence that the plaintiff might require medical treatment and, a failure to provide proper treatment might cause him

further damage, even if the nature and gravity of that damage was not reasonably foreseeable. Even though the proposed amendment must inevitably result in new facts being added to the case already pleaded, in my judgment, the new claim is germaine to, connected with and, arising out of the original cause of action and is not a new cause of action."

The outcome was surely correct but one may suggest respectfully that it could more convincingly have been achieved by severing the claims. There do seem to have been two separate issues, although of course there was a common ongoing employment relationship between the parties. The alleged breach of the duty of the army authorities to monitor the physical condition of their soldiers is, as it were, a violation of a free-standing obligation, unaffected by the separate question of whether the physical condition of any particular soldier causes concern as a result of some completely separate act of negligence by the army to the soldier. If a limitation issue arose in respect of the claim for the alleged neglect by the army medical authorities, it could have been addressed under the provisions of the Statute of Limitations (Amendment) Act 1991.

PROCEEDS OF CRIME

Under legislation dealing with the proceeds of crime, an application may be made by the Director of Public Prosecutions (the "DPP") for forfeiture of property seized and detained on suspicion that it represents the proceeds of criminal activity. The application must be made within two years from the making of the first detention order. In *R v DPP* [2009] IEHC 461, the applicant argued that an application is "made" only when the DPP or his representative actually stands up in court and makes the request. Clark J. rejected his argument. She stated:

> "It would be quite extraordinary in the context of that time limit to introduce a procedure whose lawfulness and compliance could only be assessed when the court is actually addressed by the applicant. Such an interpretation would introduce uncertainty or vagueness in the assessment of those stated limits which would be neither desirable nor necessary and serve no useful purpose. Such an assessment of a time limit would be imprecise and subject to the vicissitudes and vagaries of Court calendars and work loads and cannot have been intended by s.39(1).
>
> If the applicant's arguments were accepted, it would mean that the DPP could be put into a position where he could apply for forfeiture several months before a Circuit Court hearing but would still have to apply to the District Court to extend the period of detention of the money to ensure that the application for forfeiture was made during

> the period while the case was being detained pursuant to s.38 which would be unworkable."

SEXUAL ABUSE

Section 48A(1) of the Statute of Limitations 1957, as inserted by s.2 of the Statute of Limitations (Amendment) Act 2000 (the "2000 Act"), provides as follows:

> A person shall, for the purpose of bringing an action –
> (a) founded on tort in respect of an act of sexual abuse committed against him or her at a time when he or she had not yet reached full age, or,
> (b) against a person (other than the person who committed that act), claiming damages for negligence or breach of duty where the damages claimed consist of or include damages in respect or personal injuries caused by such act,
>
> be under disability while he or she is suffering from any psychological injury that –
> (i) is caused, in whole or in part, by that act, or any other act, of the person who committed the first mentioned act, and
> (ii) is of such significance that his or her will, or his or her ability to make a reasoned decision, to bring such action is substantially impaired.

In *O'D v Minister of Education and Science* [2009] IEHC 227, the plaintiff, born in 1956, claimed that he had been the victim of ongoing sexual abuse while at school. An affidavit sworn on his behalf quoted from a report by a clinical psychologist in whose care the plaintiff was, expressing the opinion that the plaintiff had lacked the capacity to make a complaint until he had sought help through the national counselling service in 2001. Counsel for the fourth-named defendant argued that this evidence was not admissible, invoking Lardner J.'s decision in *RT v VP* [1990] 1 I.R. 545 and the Supreme Court decision of *JF v DPP* [2005] 2 I.R. 174.

Dunne J. rejected the argument. *RT v VP* was not of great assistance as it had involved an application for nullity of marriage where a consultant psychiatrist had given evidence about the respondent without having met the respondent. In the instant case, the consultant psychologist had interviewed the plaintiff on five separate occasions. In *JF v DPP*, the applicant for judicial review had sought to have the complainant in criminal proceedings assessed by an expert nominated by him, and the request was refused. The applicant brought an application to strike out the relevant paragraphs of the statement of opposition and the supporting affidavits of a psychologist and the relevant parts of the complainant's affidavit. This was refused by the High Court but the Supreme Court reversed that decision. Hardiman J. made broad statements in regard to the entitlement of access to the complainant of the applicant's expert. Dunne J. could not agree with the submission that the fourth-named defendant in the instant case was in the same position as the applicant in *JF v DPP*. The lack of fair procedures that existed in *JF v DPP* did not exist in the instant case.

Dunne J. found it somewhat surprising that there had been no reference to the fact that the plaintiff had, in fact, been examined by a consultant psychiatrist on behalf of the defendants. There had been nothing to stop the fourth-named defendant from exhibiting a report of that expert, had it seen fit to do so. The evidence before the court in the form of the plaintiff's solicitor's affidavits, and the exhibits, had not been controverted in any way by the fourth-named defendant. In those circumstances, it would be inappropriate to disregard it.

In *FW v JW* [2009] IEHC 542, the plaintiff, aged 24, took civil proceedings against her 91-year-old grandfather for sexual abuse when she was a young child. The plenary summons was issued in 2008. Since the claim was apparently one for trespass to the person (assault), the relevant limitation period was six years from the time the plaintiff attained majority. Thus no issue arose under the Statute of Limitations. The defendant sought, successfully in the outcome, to have the proceedings dismissed on the ground of delay. Charleton J. quoted s.48A(1), introduced by the Statute of Limitations (Amendment) Act 2000. He commented:

> "The law as to delay was not changed, however, by the Act. An action for sexual abuse even commenced within the limit of the statute or as extended by s.48A of the Act of 2000 must still be dismissed by the court for unfairness if that ground is proved."

He quoted s.3 of the 2000 Act which states:

> Nothing in s.48A of the Statutes of Limitations, 1957, (inserted by s.2 of this Act), shall be construed as affecting any power of a court to dismiss an action on the ground of there being such delay between the accrual of the cause of action and the bringing of the action as, in the interests of justice, would warrant dismissal.

Charleton J. commented:

> "There may be circumstances where it can be said that the delay in commencing proceedings was caused by the action of the defendant. In some instances that can be a dangerous conclusion to reach. To so conclude in this case would be to accept, without ever having heard the plaintiff, that the cause of her troubles was what she alleges against

> her grandfather, the defendant, in this case. Circumstances may be different where as a result of an accident … a person is left disabled. Even there the conclusion that the defendant is responsible should be approached with caution since it may be apparent that a car accident or an incident at birth led to a disability but the issue as to whether there was negligence may be the central point in the case."

The plaintiff had made a formal complaint about the alleged sexual abuse to the Gardaí in Mayo in 2003 when she was aged 18. Charleton J. noted that, "[d]isgracefully, the matter [was] not followed up when the file [was] transferred to the appropriate station in Dublin". When the plaintiff made a complaint about this failure to the Garda Ombudsman Commission in 2008, the adjudication was that the matter had been negligently handled and the relevant Garda officer was fined what Charleton J. described as "the very small sum" of €150.

In dismissing the claim, Charleton J. emphasised the prejudice caused by the death of the plaintiff's grandmother, who could have given important relevant evidence, and the fact that several years had passed from the time of the reporting of the alleged abuse to the notification by the plaintiff's solicitors to her grandfather of an intent to sue:

> "Any person wronged … is entitled to seek damages. Even allowing for the fact that the plaintiff was put through the horrible experience of imagining that the Gardaí might deal with her claim efficiently, and to be disappointed over some years in that regard, I cannot look at a delay of five years before the warning letter as being excusable. There was no conduct akin to acquiescence on the part of the defendant and it seems improbable to find as a fact that the plaintiff was unable to approach a solicitor's firm."

Charleton J.'s analysis provokes a few reflections. First, the idea that an 18-year-old victim who had informed the police of the commission of serious crimes should be regarded as worthy of a negative assessment in failing to initiate civil proceedings quickly thereafter in the face of gradually unfolding gross neglect by the police seems a little stern. Should one really be required to engage in such proactivity, against the background of dereliction of duty by the State, as a condition of sacrificing one's constitutionally protected right of action?

Secondly, the relevance of the legislation of 2000 to litigation taken by victims of sexual abuse who reach adulthood and who initiate litigation within the limitation period thereafter needs further consideration. As a result of decades of legislative inanition following *O'Brien v Keogh* [1972] I.R. 144, a long delay can occur (as in the instant case) between the time of the alleged commission of the tort and the attainment by the plaintiff of majority. When assessing an application to have a claim dismissed on the basis of delay before the litigation has commenced, a court is not entitled to dismiss the claim simply by virtue of the passage of this long time but is entitled to require of newly adult plaintiffs in such circumstances not to dally. The 2000 Act seeks to deal with cases where adult plaintiffs are under a disability resulting from psychological injury caused by the sexual abuse which substantially impairs the plaintiff's ability to initiate the litigation. Should not a court examine the question whether, during part or all of the period of minority, following the abuse, the child was thus affected? Of course, the obvious reason for not doing so may seem to be that the Statute of Limitations is not in any event operating against the child during this period and that, since the rationale of minority is sufficient to preserve the child's right of action, it would be otiose to have regard also to the type of consideration that the 2000 Act contemplates for adults. As against this, when examining the delicate issue of delay, the fact that a plaintiff, even during minority, was so affected by the abuse as to render him or her incapable of initiating (or encouraging the initiation of) litigation, is surely of relevance in understanding the full picture. Incidentally, the possible relevance of the 2000 Act in the instant case does not fully emerge from the judgment.

SURVIVAL OF ACTIONS

In *Prendergast v McLaughlin* [2009] IEHC 250, O'Keeffe J. was called on to resolve a difference of judicial opinion as to how to identify the commencement of a cause of action involving a promise to bequeath property. If the promisor dies without having fulfilled that promise, has the cause of action already vested at the time of his or her death or does the death without having fulfilled the promise generate the vesting of the cause of action? The point is of real practical importance because s.9 of the Civil Liability Act 1961 prescribes a strict two-year limitation period after the death of the defendant for causes to action that have survived against the estate of the deceased. Section 8(1) provides that, on the death of a person, "all causes of action (other than excepted causes of action) subsisting against him shall survive against his estate."

The facts alleged in *Prendergast v McLaughlin* were familiar enough in Irish rural life: an elderly farmer promising to confer a testamentary benefit on a neighbour who had helped him with the farm work for many years. The net point at issue was whether the action based on that alleged promise, initiated more than two years after the death of the alleged promisor, was defeated by s.9 of the 1961 Act.

In *Corrigan v Martin*, High Court, March 13, 2006 (Circuit Appeal), Fennelly J. had come to the clear conclusion that a claim such as this foundered after two years. He had stated:

> "Firstly, I am satisfied that the correct interpretation of the plaintiff's cause of action's in the light of ... section [8] is that the obligation of the deceased was to perform the contract during his lifetime and not at the moment of his death. Hence, the cause of action was complete immediately before his death. It is unnecessary to decide how long before the death. The cause of action, therefore, subsisted at the moment of death and survived against his estate by virtue of section 8(1). Secondly, I am satisfied that the Oireachtas intended by the strong and clear language of section 9(2) to apply a maximum two year limitation period to all claims against the estates of deceased persons. Section 8(1) applies to 'all causes of action (other than excepted causes of action) subsisting against him' (none of the excepted cases is relevant). The Oireachtas intended that provision to apply to all causes of action coming into existence right up to the point of death itself. It is unreal and almost metaphysical to distinguish between causes of action existing immediately prior to the death and those which matured on the death itself. I do not believe that the Oireachtas can have intended to make such fine distinction. It would serve no useful purpose which has been identified in this case."

By way of contrast, in *Reidy v McGreevy*, High Court, March 19, 1993, where the son of the deceased claimed to be remunerated for staying at home and working his father's land as the result of promises by his father that he would exercise a special power of appointment in favour of the plaintiff, Barron J. had concluded that:

> "[t]he claim could not be maintained until the death of the testator because it could not have been ascertained until then, that he had failed to honour his promise. Of course if he had repudiated his promise in his life time, this would have given rise to a cause of action at that stage."

O'Keeffe J. favoured Fennelly J.'s approach. The cause of action was founded in "contract or quasi-contract". The breach of the deceased's promise to bequeath the lands "could only have occurred during the life time of the deceased and the cause of action therefore accrued before the death of the deceased." The plaintiff's claim could alternatively be based on promissory estoppel or equity. As such it was not a claim arising after the death of the deceased but one subsisting at death, "namely, the failure of the deceased to execute a will bequeathing the lands to the plaintiff during his lifetime".

Local Government and Housing

BUILDING CONTROL

Disability access and fire certificate The Building Control Act 2007 (Commencement) Order 2009 (S.I. No. 352 of 2009) brought ss.5 and 6 of the Building Control Act 2007 (*Annual Review of Irish Law 2007*, pp.424–425), which amended ss.6 and 7 of the Building Control Act 1990 concerning disability access and fire certificates, into operation on September 30, 2009. The Building Control (Amendment) Regulations 2009 (S.I. No. 351 of 2009) amended the Building Control Regulations 1997 (*Annual Review of Irish Law 1997*, p.447) and set out revised requirements concerning the notice of commencement of certain building works; the statutory declaration for such notice; the need to obtain a regularisation certificate (with statutory declaration), a revised fire safety certificate or a disability access certificate/revised disability access certificate in respect of certain works and the fees for such applications. The 2009 Regulations came into force on October 1, 2009.

LOCAL GOVERNMENT CHARGES

Residential property charge The Local Government (Charges) Act 2009 (the "2009 Act") provided for the imposition on the owners of certain residential properties, not being a person's primary residence (or mobile home, an exclusion added at a late stage of the Oireachtas debate on the 2009 Act) of the payment of an annual charge in respect of each such property concerned to the local authority in whose area the residential property is situated. The Local Government (Charges) Act 2009 (Commencement) Order 2009 (S.I. No. 279 of 2009) brought the 2009 Act into operation on July 24, 2009. The Local Government (Charges) Regulations 2009 (S.I. No. 278 of 2009) set out certain procedural and related matters for the purposes of levying the €200 charge applicable under the Local Government (Charges) Act 2009.

HOUSING

The Housing (Miscellaneous Provisions) Act 2009 (the "2009 Act") gave legislative effect to the programme of social housing reform measures outlined in the 2007 document *Delivering Homes, Sustaining Communities* which had been published by the Department of the Environment, Heritage and Local Government. The 2009 Act provides for a strategic approach to delivery and management through the use of housing services plans; a more objective basis for assessing need and making allocations; and a more developed statutory basis for the rental accommodation scheme. It also contains the legislative framework for the incremental purchase scheme and for the adoption by housing authorities of strategies to address anti-social behaviour. The 2009 Act deals with five major matters: functions of housing authorities; incremental purchase arrangements; tenant purchase of apartments; affordable dwelling purchase arrangements; and claw-back arrangements.

Functions of housing authorities Part 2 of the 2009 Act (ss.10 to 42) outlines, for the first time, the range of functions of housing authorities. The 2009 Act did not alter the basic distribution of functions across the different levels of local government but it provides for better planning and integration of services by providing for housing services plans, which take a broader strategic perspective at county and city level. The 2009 Act provides that the key function of housing authorities is to provide a housing service. Section 10 provides that this service comprises a range of different housing supports including social and affordable housing, management, maintenance and regeneration. Sections 12 and 13 deal with funding issues. Section 12 replaces s.15 of the Housing Act 1988 (the "1988 Act"), listing the various types of support for which grants or subsidies may be provided by the Exchequer. Section 13 deals with resources available to local authorities from sales or claw-backs and provides that these should be placed in a single fund to be used for housing purposes with the prior approval of the Minister. Sections 14 to 18 refer to the core of strategic planning and operational delivery of housing services, as defined in s.10. They deal with the making, by local authority members, of housing services plans and with the preparation, by managers, of housing action programmes to implement these plans.

The housing services plans provide a strategic focus for the planning of housing services, including delivery and ongoing management. It was explained during the Oireachtas debate on the 2009 Act that the plans build on the multi-annual housing action plans introduced on an administrative basis in 2004. Placing them on a statutory footing provided the necessary framework for engagement with the elected members and a link to work undertaken in preparing housing strategies in the context of development plans. Under s.14 elected members are obliged to make a housing services plan not later than six months after the current development plan is made, and s.15 sets out the matters to be taken into account including the development plan, the demand for social and affordable housing and the need to deliver housing in a way that supports sustainable communities. Section 17 provides for a variation of the plan to be initiated by the manager or the Minister.

Section 18 provides for the making of housing action programmes. The programmes will be, in effect, the delivery mechanism for the plans and will be prepared by the manager. It was stated during the Oireachtas debate that the housing services plans would contain high level goals and objectives, while precise annual targets for programmes would be set out in the housing actions programmes, which would probably be of a three-year duration.

Sections 19 to 22 of the 2009 Act deal with providing social housing support, providing the necessary legislative underpinning *Delivering Homes, Sustaining Communities*; that housing support should be tailored to individual needs as they evolve over their life cycle; and that the delivery of such support must take account of the broader sustainable communities agenda. Section 19 updates and replaces s.56(1) of the Housing Act 1966 and gives powers to housing authorities to purchase, build, lease, etc. dwellings or sites and enter public private partnerships for the purpose of providing social housing support through a variety of methods. In providing such accommodation, s.19(4) obliges local authorities to have regard to their housing services plans as well as ensuring that they provide a mixture of house types to meet the needs of a range of different household types and to counteract undue social segregation.

Section 20 is the basis for the assessment of need and provides extensive ministerial regulation-making powers to set eligibility criteria, classify need and determine the form of this assessment. Section 21 allows for the individual assessments to be summarised in a prescribed form for a variety of purposes, including the making of a housing services plan under s.16. This replaced the previous triennial assessment of need provided for in the Housing Act 1988 and provide for a more timely and clearer picture of the scale and nature of housing need in each local authority area and across the country. Section 22 replaces s.11 of the 1988 Act and provides housing authorities with a new approach to allocating dwellings. Each authority must adopt a new allocation scheme which will allow for local discretion within the national framework.

Sections 23 to 27 of the 2009 Act deal with the rental accommodation scheme, commonly known as RAS. RAS was introduced in 2005 and is aimed at providing a new housing option for people in receipt of social welfare rent supplement who have a long-term housing need. Sections 23 to 27 provide a comprehensive statutory framework for RAS so that it forms part of an integrated suite of social housing options. Section 24 contains the power for a housing authority to enter into a rental accommodation availability agreement. Under this agreement, the provider makes the accommodation available for a period either for a sitting tenant or for any tenants allocated to the property by the housing authority. There are certain requirements to be met by the provider before entering into an agreement under s.24(2) and the terms and conditions associated with that agreement are set out in s.24(4). Section 25 deals with the tenancy agreement, a "chapter 4 tenancy agreement", between the person making the dwelling available and the tenant. It outlines what should be in the agreement and s.25(5) sets out additional obligations to those under the

Residential Tenancies Act 2004 (the "2004 Act"). These include payment of the rent contribution to the housing authority and provisions in regard to tenancy termination under the 2004 Act. Any breaches of these obligations can give rise to terminations. The 2009 Act therefore provides a more developed statutory base for RAS to ensure it can continue to evolve and play an important role in broadening the range and choice of social housing options.

Sections 28 to 35 also form part of the social housing governance regime dealing with local authority responsibilities regarding housing stock, including tenancy agreements, rent schemes and a new requirement to adopt antisocial behaviour strategies. Section 31 provides for an authority to make a rent scheme setting out the manner in which it will determine rents taking account of national parameters set out in regulations.

Section 35 requires each housing authority, by reserved function, to adopt an antisocial behaviour strategy for the prevention and reduction of antisocial behaviour in its housing stock. It was accepted in the debate on the 2009 Act that local authorities, as landlords of some 120,000 dwellings, have a duty to secure and protect the interests of their tenants by abating and preventing such behaviour in their estates. Section 35 therefore specifies the principal objectives of a strategy, notably the promotion of co-operation with other agencies, including the Gardaí. It also provides the matters that may be dealt with in a strategy and sets out the bodies that must be consulted in drawing up a strategy. The 2009 Act (Sch.2, Pt 5) also amended the definition of antisocial behaviour in the Housing (Miscellaneous Provisions) Act 1997 to extend it to include damage to property and graffiti and significant impairment of the use or enjoyment of a person's home.

Sections 36 to 42 of the 2009 Act require housing authorities to develop homelessness action plans. These sections place on a statutory footing, the relevant elements of the 2008 policy document *The Way Home: A Strategy to Address Adult Homelessness in Ireland.* Section 37 of the 2009 Act provides that a homelessness action plan must specify the measures proposed to be undertaken to address homelessness in the administrative area or administrative areas concerned by the housing authority or housing authorities, as the case may be, the Health Service Executive, specified bodies, or approved bodies or other bodies providing services to address homelessness or the performance of whose functions may affect or relate to the provision of such services. It must include measures to achieve the following objectives: (a) the prevention of homelessness, (b) the reduction of homelessness in its extent or duration, (c) the provision of services, including accommodation, to address the needs of homeless households, (d) the provision of assistance under s.10(b)(i) of the 2009 Act, as necessary, to persons who were formerly homeless, and (e) the promotion of effective co-ordination of activities proposed to be undertaken by the bodies referred to in this subsection for the purposes of addressing homelessness in the administrative area or areas concerned.

Incremental purchase scheme Part 3 of the 2009 Act (ss.43 to 49) provides for an incremental purchase scheme. This involves transferring full title of the new house to the householder on the payment to the housing authority or approved body, as appropriate, of a proportion of the purchase price. The housing authority or approved body places a charge on the property in its favour for the portion of equity not paid for, declining over time until the charge is eliminated. In return, the buyer pays the mortgage and accepts full responsibility for the maintenance of the home. Eligible households, as defined in s.43, include those assessed as eligible for social housing support by reference to s.20 and, subject to some conditions, existing tenants who wish to transfer to homes made available under the scheme. Section 44 provides that incremental purchase may apply to newly-built houses by housing authorities or approved housing bodies and to new houses that are vacant or come onto the market in the coming into force of the Act. Section 45 provides the power to sell a dwelling under the arrangement by means of a transfer order and sets out the terms and conditions that should apply. Section 46 sets out, in detail, how the incremental features of the scheme will operate. It requires the housing authority or approved body to put a charge, by way of a charging order, on a house that it has sold under the scheme. The charging order creates a charged share in favour of the housing authority or body, equivalent to the discount granted off the purchase price. The charged share is reduced in equal proportions over the period of the charge. The reduction in the charged share for the first five years of occupancy is not applied until that period has expired and the section also provides for the authority or body to clear the charge when it expires.

Section 48 deals with the control on resale of incremental purchase dwellings. If the incremental purchaser wishes to resell the house during the charge period, the housing authority or the approved body concerned has the first option of buying it at the proportion of the market value equivalent to the prevailing share of the equity that is not charged. The resale of an incremental purchase house in the market is subject to the consent of the housing authority or body, which may refuse consent for specified reasons, including antisocial behaviour by the prospective purchaser or in the interest of good estate management. Where an incremental purchaser resells his or her home in the market he or she must make a payment to the authority or body calculated as the proportion of the market value of the house equivalent to the prevailing charged share.

It was pointed out in the Oireachtas debate on the 2009 Act that the incremental purchase scheme offers a number of key benefits. For families, the scheme offers the earliest possible start on the path to home ownership for those willing and able to undertake a house purchase. In addition, giving the buyer responsibility for repair and maintenance of the home helps build up the householder's stake in the property. The scheme is also structured to make it attractive for people to put down long-term roots in the community and to commit to an area, thereby contributing to more stable and integrated communities. For the State, the scheme will provide an opportunity to extract additional value for money from capital expenditure through our social housing investment programme. It will allow for capital funding to be recycled quickly which can be then used to provide additional social housing without the need for additional Exchequer finance. The full details of how the scheme will operate will be spelled out in ministerial regulations to be made under the 2009 Act.

Tenant purchase of apartments Part 4 of the 2009 Act (ss.50 to 77) facilitates the introduction for the first time of a scheme of tenant purchase for local authority apartments. It was stated in the Oireachtas debate on the 2009 Act that the scheme is based on a long-standing arrangement in the private sector for the ownership and management of multi-unit residential developments. Under the statutory scheme in the 2009 Act, housing authorities must conduct a tenant plebiscite in individual apartment complexes proposed for designation by the housing authority for tenant purchase. Where the plebiscite shows that a minimum number of tenants are in favour of designation and that a minimum number of tenants are willing to serve as directors of a management company if they proceed to buy their apartments, the housing authority may designate the complex. The housing authority will transfer ownership of each designated complex to a new management company established for the purpose, which will immediately lease all apartments back to the authority while retaining ownership of the common areas and services. The housing authority will continue to let the apartments to the existing tenants who, subject to meeting the prescribed minimum tenancy requirement, will have the option of buying them from the authority under the incremental purchase arrangements. Sales will proceed provided that the first sale takes place within a specified period after designation and that a minimum proportion of all the apartments in the complex are to be sold.

The housing authority will continue to be the landlord to tenants in the apartments that remain unsold in the complex. The tenants of local authority apartments will be able to purchase their homes for a proportion of the market value with a charge being placed on the property in favour of the authority or the body concerned for the portion of the equity not paid for, declining over time until the charge is eliminated. The charge share will reduce in equal annual equities releases over 20 to 30 years of occupancy of the property unless the housing authority invokes provisions allowing for the suspension of the releases in cases where the purchaser breaches the terms of the lease. This means that the equity stake not purchased at the outset, in effect the discount, will be given free of charge to the purchaser provided the terms of the scheme are complied with fully. If the tenant purchaser wishes to resell the apartment during the charge period, the authority has first refusal in buying it back. If the authority declines to buy back the apartment, the tenant purchaser may sell it on the market in which case he or she must pay the authority the value of any outstanding charge on the property.

Affordable dwelling purchase arrangements Part 5 of the 2009 Act (ss.78 to 96) deals with affordable dwelling purchase arrangements and provide for the introduction of significant changes in the way affordable housing is made available for sale under various affordable housing schemes. They provide for a shift to an equity sharing arrangement and away from the previous procedures which involved a time-limited claw-back in return for a discounted house. Part 5 provide the legislative powers necessary for this equity sharing arrangement, together with enabling powers for an open market component to replace the previous shared ownership scheme in due course. Under the arrangements set out in the 2009 Act, the purchase transaction will be largely unchanged from the purchaser's perspective. However, instead of the units being sold at a discounted price as they previously were, with the value of the discount being subject to a claw-back that reduced over time, the housing authority will, under the 2009 Act, take a stake in the affordable unit sold. The purchaser will have the option of either buying out the outstanding stake in steps or, alternatively, at the end of a fixed period of 35 years. The various affordable housing schemes will continue to operate unchanged as the means of supplying affordable units but third purchasers will have the single affordable housing purchase mechanism available to them. The stake held by the housing authority will be equivalent to the percentage below the market value at which the property is sold to the affordable purchaser. Generally, affordable housing units are sold at 20 per cent to 25 per cent below the market value.

Claw-back arrangements Part 6 of the 2009 Act (ss.97 to 99) deals with the application of claw-back arrangements to the provision of sites for private housing and grants paid for extensions under the adaptation grants for older people and people with a disability. In the latter case, the claw-back applies in the event of the extended dwelling being sold within five years of the grant payment while, in the case of what is known as the low cost sites scheme, the claw-back mirrors the arrangements already in place under affordable housing schemes.

Planning and Development Law

GARRETT SIMONS, SC

QUARRIES

Introduction The use of planning legislation to regulate quarries has presented a number of practical difficulties over the years. Quarrying activities differ from most other types of development in that the works are carried on over a period of years, even decades. This is to be contrasted with the erection of a structure, for example, where the works phase takes place over a relatively short period of time. The extension of quarrying activities to previously unworked lands also presents conceptual difficulties. In particular, the courts have struggled for some time now as to which pigeon hole, i.e. development works or material change of use, quarrying activities best fits into. See generally, G. Simons, "Enforcement against Quarries: a New Approach Required" (2008) 15 I.P.E.L.J. 148.

Matters are further complicated by the fact that quarries which had commenced excavation prior to October 1964, i.e. the date upon which planning control came into force in its modern form, were regarded as having established use rights. The Supreme Court had interpreted this in *Kildare County Council v Goode* [1999] 2 I.R. 495 as permitting a quarry operator to complete such quarrying activities as could reasonably have been contemplated as of October 1964, without the necessity of obtaining planning permission. This is so, seemingly, even where the quarrying activities involved an extension into previously unworked lands. The special treatment afforded to so-called pre-1964 quarries does not sit comfortably with the requirements of the EIA Directive and, in particular, the obligation to obtain "development consent" in respect of any significant extension of the surface area of the site.

An attempt was made under s.261 of the Planning and Development Act 2000 to enhance the level of control exercised over quarries under the planning legislation. Section 261 imposed an obligation on the owners and operators of quarries to register those quarries with the relevant planning authority. Thereafter, the planning authority had powers to impose conditions on the continued operation of the quarries or, where certain criteria were fulfilled, to require the carrying out of an assessment of the environmental impact of quarrying (EIA) in the context of an application for planning permission.

It has to be said that s.261 is somewhat unhappily worded, and the precise meaning and effect of same is not always entirely clear. A number of judgments of the High Court during the course of 2009 have, however, clarified certain aspects of s.261, as follows.

Nature of registration process The nature of the registration process was considered in *Pearce v Westmeath County Council*, unreported, High Court, Hanna J., December 19, 2008. A local resident sought to challenge the planning authority's actions in (i) registering a particular quarry, and (ii) imposing a requirement to make a planning application accompanied by an EIS. Hanna J., while expressing some puzzlement as to what disadvantage the imposition of requirements intended to regulate quarrying activities could cause to local residents, accepted that the decision to admit a quarry to the s.261 system was, in principle, amenable to judicial review. The planning authority's decision was not, in the view of the court, a mere administrative one triggered by the merest evidence as to the longevity of the quarry, but one which involved a process of public consultation and necessitated "some degree of measured consideration". Hanna J. went on to rule that the court in reviewing the decision of the planning authority must apply the *O'Keeffe v An Bord Pleanála* [1993] 1 I.R. 39 principles and found on the facts of the case that the planning authority did have before it sufficient evidence to support the decision to bring the quarry within the rubric of s.261. The application for judicial review was therefore dismissed.

The legal effect of registration and the subsequent imposition of conditions under s.261(6) was considered in detail in *Pierson v Keegan Quarries Ltd* [2009] IEHC 550. The quarry operator argued that it was implicit in a decision to impose conditions on the continued operation of a quarry under s.261(6) that the relevant planning authority had decided that the quarry was not an unauthorised development, by reason of its use as a quarry prior to October 1, 1964. This decision of the planning authority was—according to the quarry operator—subject to the statutory judicial review procedure applicable under s.50 of the Planning and Development Act 2000 (as amended in 2006). The argument continued to the effect that any challenge to the validity of the decision that the quarry was authorised development could only be brought by way of an application for judicial review: it was not permissible to bring enforcement proceedings under s.160 of the Planning and Development Act 2000, as such proceedings would involve a collateral attack on the planning authority's decision. The High Court rejected these arguments:

> "Neither the reasoning stated to underlie the introduction of s.261 or the departmental guidelines, lend any support to the respondent's arguments as to the effect of the section at the conclusion of the registration process, either as to the status of an otherwise unauthorised quarry or the right of an interested party to invoke the provisions of s.160 of the 2000 Act.

> Further, in my view, the plain reading of the section itself makes the respondents arguments untenable.
>
> This lengthy and detailed section does not state and neither can it be inferred from its wording, that the planning authority has the power when operating the s.261 process to make a binding determination that a quarry in respect of which registration is sought, if registered subject to conditions, is thereafter exempt from the need to apply for planning permission, if at the time it applied for registration it was an unauthorised development. If that had been the intention of the legislature, it would have been so stated in the section. Neither does s.261 provide that any decision made to register a quarry subject to conditions renders that quarry immune from a challenge to its status as an allegedly unauthorised development under s.160 of the 2000 Act. If the decision of a planning authority to impose conditions was intended to have such fundamental and significant legal implications, I believe that the same would have been clearly set out in the section."

The High Court drew attention to the fact that there was only limited provision for public participation under s.261, with no right of appeal to An Bord Pleanála afforded to members of the public, and to the fact that judicial review of the decision to impose conditions on a quarry would not provide a suitable forum within which to resolve a factual dispute as to whether a particular quarry has an established pre-1964 user.

Statutory time limits Section 261 prescribed time limits within which a planning authority was required to give notice of its intention either to impose conditions on the continued operation of a quarry, or to require the submission of a fresh planning application (accompanied by an EIS). The time limits were two years and one year respectively. Unfortunately, a number of planning authorities failed to take action within the prescribed time limits. A question then arose as to whether or not the time limits were mandatory, in the sense that a failure to act within time was fatal. One of the principal objectives of s.261 is to allow for renewed control to be exerted over established quarries in the interests of proper planning and sustainable development. The section is also intended to ensure compliance with the requirements of the EIA Directive. There is a strong public interest in the achievement of each of these objectives, and it would be unfortunate if same were to be frustrated merely because of delay on the part of a planning authority. Indeed, in so far as development subject to the EIA Directive is concerned, it is arguable that a planning authority, as an emanation of the State, is obliged to set aside or discard any provision of national law which prevents EU law from having full force and effect: the time limits under s.261 cannot be regarded as mere procedural rules within the competence of the State—subject only to the requirements of effectiveness and equivalence—because they affect the very substance of the obligation to carry out the assessment.

The question as to whether the time limits should be regarded as mandatory or directory was considered by the High Court in *Browne v Kerry County Council* [2009] IEHC 552. The High Court held that the time limits were mandatory, and that even a short delay in complying with same would be fatal. Hedigan J. placed emphasis on the fact that the legislation did not provide any power to extend time, nor was there any provision to indicate what is to happen if time is exceeded. The judge also emphasised the fact that s.261 had the effect of conferring an important jurisdiction on a planning authority to interfere with the constitutional rights of citizens:

> "Turning first to the issue of whether the time period in section 261(6)(a) of the 2000 Act is mandatory as opposed to directory, it is important that the Court should remain cognisant at all times of the constitutional right, which the applicant holds under Article 43 of Bunreacht na hÉireann, to the quiet enjoyment of his property. With this in mind, it is necessary to analyse the wording of the provision with a view to discerning its plain and literal meaning."

With respect, the correctness of the finding that the time limits are mandatory is open to question. Section 261 imposes an obligation on a planning authority to take certain action in the public interest. Further, the section requires that that action be taken within a specified period. Significantly, the time period for taking action required to meet the objectives of the EIA Directive is much shorter (one year) than the general time limit under s.261(6) (two years), suggesting that there is a particular urgency in meeting the requirements of the Directive.

The logic of the High Court judgment is that the obligation of a planning authority to act simply evaporates as soon as the one- or two-year period expires. This finding is based on an unjustified assumption that the time limits were intended to protect the quarry operator. It is at least arguable, however, that the purpose of the time limits was to protect the public interest, by ensuring that planning authorities take the necessary measures to regulate the environmental impact of quarries urgently. The fact that a planning authority fails to act within time should not be taken as absolving the planning authority thereafter from taking the necessary measures. Rather the duty remains, and a member of the public would be entitled to take proceedings before the courts seeking an order of mandamus directing the planning authority to act. The time limits under s.261(6) and (7) are unlike most of the other time limits under the planning legislation, which require certain steps to be taken within a particular period as part of an *overall* sequence of events. Thus, for example, a submission on a planning application must be made within a five-week period. Any delay in this regard cannot be overlooked, as it would have a knock-on effect on the obligation of the planning authority to make a decision within an overall period of eight weeks. There is no such knock-on effect in the context of s.261(6) and (7).

The judgment is also open to the criticism that no proper weight was given to the fact that where the legislature intended a time limit to be absolute under the planning legislation, it says so in terms and prescribes what is to happen. Thus, for example, it is expressly provided that a failure to make a submission on a planning application within the time limits results in that submission having to be disregarded. Elsewhere, it is expressly provided that a failure to make a decision on an application for planning permission within the time limit results in a default decision at the planning authority stage. Section 261(6) and (7) are silent on the consequences of a failure to meet the time limits, and it seems odd to read into the legislation an intention to allow significant environmental impacts to go unaddressed merely because of a delay on the part of a planning authority.

The judgment in *Browne* has since been followed in *Kells Quarry Products Ltd v Kerry County Council* [2010] IEHC 69. On the facts of that case, the planning authority had delayed in notifying the quarry operator of its intention to impose conditions on the continued operation of the quarry. The effect of this delay was that the quarry operator was not afforded the statutory six weeks within which to respond. The planning authority conceded that the quarry operator was entitled to have the notice set aside, and sought to have the matter remitted to it. The High Court refused to remit the matter, saying that it would serve no useful purpose to do so in circumstances where the two-year time limit on imposing conditions had elapsed, citing *Browne*:

> "That case is a clear authority for the proposition that the time limit fixed in s.261(6)(a) is mandatory. That being so, I cannot see any point in remitting this matter to the respondent for the purpose of going through the exercise of allowing the applicant to furnish submissions on the conditions to be imposed, given that the time for the imposition of conditions has now passed and that there is no provision in the legislative scheme of the Act for the extension of the two-year period. In other words, no purpose would be served by the remittal of the matter to the respondent."

The judgment in *Browne v Kerry County Council* also examined the separate question as to whether, in calculating the one- or two-year period, any allowance had to be made for the Christmas holiday period. Section 251 of the Planning and Development Act 2000 provides that, in calculating any time limit referred to in the Act, the period between December 24 and January 1 (both days inclusive) shall be disregarded. Hedigan J. ruled as follows at para.[20]:

> "The question for the Court therefore is whether section 251 of the 2000 Act may be applied in such a fashion as to effectively extend the two year time period by 9 days in respect of each year, giving rise to a total extension of 18 days. The provisions of section 251 are plain and unambiguous. It is expressly provided that the period between the 24th of December and the 1st of January each year, both days inclusive, shall be disregarded in the calculation of time limits. The applicant has contended that to apply this provision to time limits of more than one year would result in patent absurdity; for example, a time limit which was nominally 12 years on the face of the statute would in fact be calculated at the considerably lengthier period of 12 years and 108 days. He thus argues that the provision can only logically be applied to time limits of less than one year. However, I am unable to agree with this submission. There is no basis within the wording of the 2000 Act or otherwise for the imposition of such a specific limitation on the effect of section 251 by this Court. The provision is undoubtedly capable of effecting a quite serious extension of more lengthy time limits, and such extension will no doubt be of significance in many cases such as the present one. This effect could be described as curious, and its merit might well be open to debate, but it cannot in my view be construed as 'absurd' within the meaning of the 2005 Act."

Nature of conditions under s.261(6) Section 261(6) allows for the imposition of conditions on the continued operation of a quarry. Section 261(7), conversely, allows for the imposition of a requirement to apply for planning permission subject to EIA.

The High Court ruled on the nature and extent of conditions which can be imposed under subs.(6) in three "test" cases in *MF Quirke v An Bord Pleanála* [2009] IEHC 426. In brief, the quarry operators had argued that the power under s.261(6) was confined to the imposition of conditions on the continued operation of a quarry. Any condition which required the *cessation* of quarrying activities—whether by imposing a physical limit (horizontal or vertical) on the area of quarrying activities, or by requiring that planning permission be obtained—was said to be the antitheses of this. The quarry operators drew attention to a number of differences between the powers under subss.(6) and (7), and sought to argue that, in the absence of any provision for compensation, subs.(6) could not be relied upon to achieve a similar result to that provided for under subs.(7). Great play was made of the reverence which has traditionally been shown to established use rights, i.e. development commenced prior to October 1964.

The High Court held that the legislature had, through s.261, introduced a "fresh regulatory scheme" for quarries, and that any argument to the effect that because a quarry was being operated in a certain way over 40 years ago, i.e. pre-October 1964, it should continue in the same manner must be untenable:

> "It could never be said that there was an unrestricted right to use property for any activity, including quarrying, regardless of the effects that activity had on the enjoyment of other persons of their lives, health and properties. Many activities are regulated and restricted in a variety of statutory codes in the interest of the common good. I see no difference in principle or in substance between these statutory regulatory regimes and the type of regulation provided for in s.261(6). In all cases the activity restricted by statute would have been unregulated or unrestricted before the enactment of that type of legislation."

Mr Justice O'Neill held that the power to impose conditions under s.261(6) was a wide one:

> "In the absence of a description of the types of conditions to be imposed in s.261(6) and in light of the wide criteria under which conditions may be imposed (i.e. '*in the interests of proper planning and sustainable development*') I am satisfied that the conditions that can be imposed on the operations of quarries can encompass the wide spectrum of the various normal planning concerns as these are or are likely to be affected by the works carried on at a given quarry in its particular location. To suggest that a condition which required the obtaining of planning permission at some stage in the future was *per se ultra vires* s.261(6) is, in my judgement, to impermissibly restrict the scope of s.261(6), in effect, adding to the language of the subsection words of restriction which are clearly not there, and, therefore, not intended to be there by the Oireachtas. In my view, whether one adopts a literal approach or a purposive approach to the interpretation of s.261(6), the result will be the same."

Conditions may be imposed pursuant to s.261(6) controlling blasting even where some blasting had been carried out historically. The High Court ruled that blasting is merely a method of extraction, and thus cannot be considered to be synonymous with, or an integral part of, an existing right to quarry. It would be nonsensical to attempt to regulate current quarrying activity on the basis of an historical position 40 years earlier, i.e. as of October 1964. Even if a quarry operator could demonstrate an existing blasting use as of the statutory registration date, i.e. April 2004, the imposition of a condition prohibiting blasting would nevertheless be permissible if An Bord Pleanála found that it was in the interests of proper planning and sustainable development. The legislature has provided for controls to be imposed on registered quarries regardless of existing use rights.

It follows from the judgment that conditions of the following type are allowed under s.261(6):

- conditions regulating blasting activities;
- conditions restricting the area, whether horizontal or vertical, within which quarrying activities can be carried out; and
- conditions requiring that quarrying activities cease within a specified period unless planning permission has been obtained in the interim.

Use of explosives The interaction between the planning legislation and the legislation governing the use of explosives (in particular under Directive 93/15 on the harmonisation of the provisions relating to the placing on the market and supervision of explosives for civil uses) was considered by the High Court in *MF Quirke & Sons v Maher* [2008] IEHC 428. The respondent Garda superintendent had refused to authorise the transfer and use of explosives at the applicant's quarry on the basis that the planning authority had informed him that the planning permission for the quarry did not permit the use of blasting. The High Court held that it was reasonably and rationally open to the respondent to form a prima facie view, on being apprised by the planning authority that the planning permission did not authorise the use of blasting, that to approve the transfer of explosives could well be to authorise an unlawful activity. It was not necessary for the planning authority to have gone as far as issuing an enforcement notice, still less was it necessary for there to have been a judicial determination, in the context of enforcement proceedings, that the permission did not authorise the use of blasting.

The judgment is also of note in that it confirms that a planning permission falls to be interpreted in light of the content of the EIS submitted with the planning application. The decision to grant planning permission had, as is common, made express reference to the "plans and particulars" lodged. Herbert J. stated that the EIS was clearly a "vitally important part of these plans and particulars". Herbert J. placed great emphasis on the fact that no reasonable lay reader looking at the EIS would understand same as authorising the applicant to carry out blasting at the quarry.

PLANNING CONDITIONS

Points of detail Planning conditions often leave over points of detail to be agreed subsequently between the developer and the planning authority. The legality of this practice under the previous planning legislation was upheld by the Supreme Court in *Boland v An Bord Pleanála* [1996] 3 I.R. 435; express provision has since been made for such conditions under s.34(5) of the Planning and Development Act 2000 (as amended by the Planning and Development (Strategic Infrastructure) Act 2006).

The decision of the planning authority to "agree" a compliance submission made pursuant to such planning conditions is amenable to judicial review. The planning authority enjoys a very limited discretion in this regard, and is required to faithfully implement that which has already been decided in essence. See *Gregory v Dun Laoghaire Rathdown County Council*, unreported, Supreme Court, July 28, 1997 and *O'Connor v Dublin Corporation (No. 2)*, unreported, High Court, O'Neill J., October 3, 2000.

The nature of the planning authority's role in this regard was considered in detail by the Supreme Court in *Kenny v Dublin Corporation* [2009] IESC 19. Fennelly J. emphasised that a planning permission is to be interpreted according to objective criteria, and that the subjective beliefs either of the applicant or the planning authority are not relevant or admissible as aids to interpretation. The judge went on, however, to state that an objective interpretation is not the same as a literal interpretation, and to explain that where a condition is unclear, ambiguous or contradictory it may be necessary to look to the purpose underlying the condition. This principle is illustrated by the approach which the Supreme Court took to two of the planning conditions in issue in *Kenny*. The first of these required that the height of one of the proposed buildings be reduced by the omission of the "first floor". The stated reason for the imposition of the condition was "the interest of visual amenity". The developer proposed to omit a floor *other than* the first floor: this was because the first floor had a design feature intended to avoid flat façade monotony, involving a "step out" or protrusion from the other storeys. The planning authority agreed to this departure from the literal wording of the condition. The Supreme Court held that to insist on a literal interpretation of the condition, and to require the omission of the first floor, would be unrealistic and pointless. The true objective of the condition was the reduction in the height of the building, and this objective had been achieved. There was no evidence that An Bord Pleanála chose the elimination of the first floor, rather than any other floor, in order to secure the desired reduction in height, or that it wished to alter the composite elevation in any way.

The second example, then, involved a condition which required that no services be laid within 10 metres of the bole of any of the trees to be retained on-site. The evidence before the court indicated that the 10-metre condition had been breached to a lesser or greater degree in the case of 16 out of 275 trees. The judgment characterised this as a case of non-compliance with the literal terms of a condition, though to a minor if not trifling degree, and refused to grant judicial review by reference to such an "inconsequential discrepancy".

Conditions regulating use of land The High Court in *Quinlan v An Bord Pleanála* [2009] IEHC 228 rejected an argument that it was unlawful to impose a planning condition regulating *use* on the occasion of an application in respect of limited *development works*. On the facts, the applicant had made two separate planning applications, one for the alteration and refurbishment of an existing structure; the second for an extension. An Bord Pleanála, on appeal, upheld a planning condition restricting the use of the structure to use as an embassy, and excluding use as a general office. The High Court rejected the contention that because the applications for planning permission were for development by way of "works" only, without any change in use, a condition as to use could not be imposed. An Bord Pleanála was entitled to clarify the use to which the premises could be put by the imposition of a planning condition which reflected the established use, and ensured that there could be no misunderstanding as to the permitted use of the property. The High Court ruled that, given the planning history of the lands, the planning condition was reasonable and was related to the permitted development.

JUDICIAL REVIEW: PROCEDURAL

Promptness Prior to the amendments introduced to s.50 of the Planning and Development Act 2000 by the Planning and Development (Strategic Infrastructure) Act 2006, certain decisions of planning authorities were subject to conventional judicial review. The eight-week statutory time limit thus did not apply, and instead an applicant was required to move promptly and, in any event, within certain outer time limits (six months in the case of certiorari). The general view is that an application made within the outer time limits will not normally be defeated by delay, notwithstanding the overriding obligation to move promptly. The judgment in *Kenny v Dublin Corporation* [2009] IESC 19, however, emphasises that the question of delay must be assessed in the context of the particular circumstances of each case. On the facts of *Kenny*, the application for leave to apply for judicial review was not moved until the second last day of the six-month period, and concerned a challenge to a large scale ongoing development. The Supreme Court stated that this was a particularly clear case of failure to apply promptly for judicial review. The applicant had been aware of the facts giving rise to the potential challenge from an early stage, and indeed had threatened judicial review proceedings, but failed to follow through until the "eleventh hour".

The relationship between the statutory eight-week time limit under s.50 of the Planning and Development Act 2000 (as amended in 2006) and the requirement to move "promptly" under Ord.84 of the Rules of the Superior Court 1986 is not entirely clear. The judgment in *O'Connell v Environmental Protection Agency* [2001] 4 I.R. 494; [2002] 1 I.L.R.M. 1 suggests that proceedings issued within eight weeks might nevertheless be dismissed if, on the facts of the case, this was not prompt enough. A recent judgment of the European Court in the context of public procurement, however, suggests that the absence of a clearly defined time limit might be contrary to legal certainty: Case C–456/08 *Commission v Ireland.*

The difficulties which can arise where related decisions are subject to different time limits are illustrated by the facts of *Talbotgrange Grange Homes*

Ltd v Laois County Council [2009] IEHC 535. The case concerned a challenge to a statutory direction issued by the Minister for the Environment, Heritage and Local Government pursuant to s.31 of the Planning and Development Act 2000. The ministerial direction required the relevant planning authority to vary its development plan. The planning authority had no discretion in this regard, but was required to comply with the direction. The development plan was duly varied and public notices of the variation published.

The applicant in the judicial review proceedings sought to challenge both the ministerial direction itself, and the subsequent variation of the plan by the planning authority. The first decision was subject to the general time limits under Ord.84 of the Rules of the Superior Courts 1986; the planning authority's variation was subject to the eight-week time limit prescribed under s.50 of the Planning and Development Act 2000 (as amended in 2006).

The High Court considered that the principal decision being challenged was that of the Minister and that an applicant who had arguable grounds for challenging such a decision should not be shut out merely because he or she might be outside the eight-week time limit applicable to the planning authority's subsequent variation of the plan. The variation was merely an administrative step—the source of the alleged wrong was the ministerial direction. The crucial time limit therefore was that applicable to the ministerial direction. The High Court held on the facts that the applicant was on constructive notice of the making of the ministerial direction once it had been laid before the Houses of the Oireachtas. In the alternative, even if time were only to run from the date of *actual* notice, the applicant had failed to explain adequately a delay in excess of two months in issuing judicial review proceedings. The applicant was not entitled to hold off issuing proceedings pending a response from the Minister to a request for further information. In the judgment of the court, it would be a "counsel of perfection" for a party to obtain all relevant information from, say, a Government department before proceeding with an application to quash a ministerial order. If reasons or new information subsequently emerged during the course of proceedings which undermined a plea that inadequate reasons were given or that a decision was irrational, this could be addressed in terms of costs. The application for judicial review was therefore dismissed on grounds of delay.

"Other act done by" As a result of amendments introduced under the Planning and Development (Strategic Infrastructure) Act 2006, the statutory eight-week time limit now applies not only to decisions made by a planning authority or An Bord Pleanála, but also applies to any "other act done by" the relevant body. One possible consequence of this is that if a person becomes aware that an error has been made during the course of the planning process, it may be necessary to move for judicial review then: if the person instead awaits the final decision, judicial review proceedings might be time-barred.

This question was considered briefly in *Treacy v Cork County Council* [2009] IEHC 36. The applicant for judicial review complained that the local authority had erred in rejecting as invalid a submission which he had sought to make in respect of a planning application. It was argued against him that any application for judicial review should have been brought once his submission was rejected. Hedigan J. held that in the absence of any prejudice to the other parties arising from the alleged delay, it would not be appropriate to refuse leave on this basis.

Time limits and default planning permission There is some controversy as to whether the eight-week time limit under s.50 of the Planning and Development Act 2000 (as amended in 2006) extends to proceedings claiming a default planning permission. A default decision to grant planning permission arises by operation of law, and thus there may be no *positive* act on the part of the planning authority to challenge. (The obvious exception is where the planning authority makes a decision to refuse permission which the applicant claims is out of time. The decision to refuse is clearly caught by the statutory judicial review procedure.) This question was considered in *Ryan v Clare County Council* [2009] IEHC 115. Hedigan J., having noted that a claim that a default permission has arisen does not rest comfortably within any of the categories listed within the statutory judicial review, held on the particular facts of the case that the operative date from which time began to run was the date on which the planning authority rejected the applicant's assertion that a default permission had arisen.

"Review procedure" under the EIA Directive Article 10a of the EIA Directive (as inserted by Directive 2003/35) requires Member States to provide a "review procedure" whereby the substantive or procedural legality of decisions, acts or omissions subject to the public participation provisions of the EIA Directive may be challenged. The "review procedure" must fulfil certain requirements: in particular, it must be fair, equitable, timely and not prohibitively expensive. Ireland has chosen to provide this "review procedure" in the form of statutory judicial review before the High Court.

The existence of two levels of decision-making under the planning legislation, namely the first-instance decision of the planning authority and an appeal thereafter to An Bord Pleanála, had led some to believe that the appeal to the board also constituted a "review procedure". This misconception has now been dispelled by the High Court in *Cairde Chill an Disirt Teoranta v An Bord Pleanála* [2009] IEHC 76; [2009] 2 I.L.R.M. 89. Cooke J. emphasised that what art.10a required was a review of the "development consent", which is defined as the "decision of the competent authority or authorities which entitles the developer to proceed with the project". In the case of an appeal to An Bord Pleanála, it is the board's decision which will constitute the "development consent".

> "Where, as in the present case, the objector has initiated the administrative appeal, it is the decision of the Board which will constitute the 'development consent' for the purpose of the Directive and that decision, when it is made, is clearly amenable to judicial review before the High Court if the necessary grounds are shown to exist. The judicial review by the High Court is precisely the procedure envisaged by Article 10a in that the High Court has jurisdiction to quash the decision of the Board if it is shown to be vitiated by any material irregularity in the Board's procedures leading to its adoption or by any material error or failure on the Board's part in applying correctly the substantive criteria and conditions of proper planning and sustainable development governing the assessment of the proposed development."

The High Court went on to state that art.10a does not require a Member State to ensure access to a procedure for review of the procedural legality of an *initial* decision on a planning application in advance or in lieu of a possible review of such a decision before an administrative authority whose own decision is then amenable to review before a court of law as regards its substantive and procedural legality.

Infringement proceedings before European Court In Case C–427/07 *Commission v Ireland*, the European Commission took infringement proceedings against Ireland, alleging that the State had failed to adopt the laws, regulations and administrative provisions necessary to implement art.10a, or to notify the Commission of such measures. Judgment was delivered by the European Court on July 16, 2009. It is important to note that these proceedings were very much in the form of a preliminary application, in that they were concerned with the narrow question of whether Ireland had put in place implementing measures, rather than with the quality or effectiveness of such implementing measures. See para.[49] of the judgment:

> "The second complaint, considered in its various parts, as pleaded in essence by the Commission, thus relates exclusively—as the Commission, moreover, confirmed at the hearing—to the failure to transpose certain provisions of Directive 2003/35, without any criticism of the quality of transposition, and, consequently, no such criticism may properly be raised by the Commission in the context of this case."

Thus it remains open to the Commission to bring a second round of infringement proceedings, challenging the quality of transposition.

One of the findings which the European Court did make was as to the costs of judicial review proceedings. Article 10a requires that the "review procedure" not be prohibitively expensive. The European Court accepted Ireland's argument that this requirement did not preclude the making of a costs order against an unsuccessful applicant, provided that the costs were not prohibitively expensive. The court, however, criticised the fact that there was no legislative provision under national law which required a court to ensure that the procedure will not be prohibitively expensive. It is a well established principle of EU law that the provisions of a Directive must be implemented with unquestionable binding force and with the specificity, precision and clarity required in order to satisfy the need for legal certainty: the existence of a general *discretion* on the part of the Irish courts in respect of costs did not fulfil this requirement for legal certainty.

The European Court declined to make any finding on the separate question as to whether the locus standi requirement under s.50 of the Planning and Development Act 2000, namely the "substantial interest" requirement, is consistent with art.10a, on the basis that the quality of transposition was a matter for another day. Interestingly, the more recent judgment of the European Court in Case C–263/08 *Djurgården-Lilla Värtans Miljöskyddsförening* (Swedish underground power cables) suggests, on one reading, that a requirement for "prior participation" in the administrative stage of decision-making is inconsistent with the provisions of art.10a:

> "[…] members of the public concerned, within the meaning of Article 1(2) and 10a of Directive 85/337, must be able to have access to a review procedure to challenge the decision by which a body attached to a court of law of a Member State has given a ruling on a request for development consent, regardless of the role they might have played in the examination of that request by taking part in the procedure before that body and by expressing their views".

Issue-specific locus standi An applicant for judicial review is required under s.50A of the Planning and Development Act 2000 (as inserted in 2006) to demonstrate a "substantial interest" in the matter which is the subject of the application. A gloss has been added to this rule by the courts whereby an applicant may be precluded from pursuing a particular argument before the High Court if that ground had not been previously raised in the course of the planning process. This has been described as "issue-specific" locus standi. A recent example of this is provided by the judgment in *Quinlan v An Bord Pleanála* [2009] IEHC 228: the applicant was not entitled to rely on an argument based on a particular provision of the development plan in circumstances where the point had not been raised before the board.

"Substantial interest" The nature of the interest required in order to qualify as a "substantial interest" was considered by the High Court in *Treacy v An Bord Pleanála* [2009] IEHC 136. One of the complaints made by the applicant for judicial review was that the effect of the local authority's rejection of his submission on a planning application was that he was shut out from making an appeal to An Bord Pleanála. The High Court held that the loss of this procedural right could not per se give rise to a "substantial interest". Rather, the applicant would have to demonstrate that an interest peculiar or personal to him was affected by the proposed development:

> "The interest to which it refers must be in the application for planning permission itself. An insubstantial interest in such a planning permission cannot be converted into a substantial interest because of the loss of the right to appeal to An Bord Pleanála in respect of the decision made therein. To hold otherwise would be to elevate form above substance. Other than this claim to a lost right of appeal, the applicant makes no real claim to any substantial interest in his pleadings herein. The high point of his claimed interest is that his holiday home is located nearby. During the hearing it was, in fact, difficult to determine where exactly his property was located in relation to the notice parties' property. It became clear that it was below and out of sight of that property, a large part of which itself had no sight of the applicant's property. The two properties were adjoining, although the proposed housing development would be at some distance from the applicant's property."

The High Court ruled on the facts that the applicant had failed to discharge the onus of proof on him in this regard.

JUDICIAL REVIEW: SUBSTANTIVE

O'Keeffe principles The judgment of the Supreme Court in *O'Keeffe v An Bord Pleanála* [1993] 1 I.R. 39 continues to act as a brake on the evolution of judicial review of planning decisions. The Supreme Court in *O'Keeffe* ruled that the courts would only ever engage in a merits-based review of planning decisions in exceptional circumstances. This judgment has given rise to a critical distinction between questions of fact and degree, in respect of which the courts will defer to An Bord Pleanála, and questions of law, in respect of which no such deference is required. A recent example of an error being characterised as involving a question of law is provided by *Usk and District Residents Association Ltd v An Bord Pleanála* [2009] IEHC 346. One of the issues raised in the case concerned the manner in which An Bord Pleanála had assessed the environmental impacts of the proposed development, a waste landfill facility. Earlier cases, such as that of *Klohn v An Bord Pleanála (No.*

2) [2008] IEHC 111; [2009] 1 I.R. 59; [2008] 2 I.L.R.M. 435 had held that the carrying out of an environmental impact assessment (EIA) involves the exercise of expert planning judgment, and thus is normally subject to review by the *O'Keeffe* principles. Thus had the only issue in *Usk* involved a challenge to the reasonableness of the board's assessment of the environmental impact, the applicant would have had to demonstrate that the board's decision flew in the teeth of fundamental reason and commonsense. In fact, the challenge in *Usk* was more nuanced, and raised an issue as to the correct division of function between An Bord Pleanála, on the one hand, and the Environmental Protection Agency (EPA) on the other. In brief, prior to the enactment of the Planning and Development Act 2000, there was a rigid demarcation between the respective competences of the two bodies: An Bord Pleanála, in determining a planning application, was precluded from considering the risk of "environmental pollution" arising from the waste disposal activity. The issue in *Usk* was as to whether the assessment of the environmental impact of the *construction* of the landfill liner was a matter for An Bord Pleanála or for the EPA. MacMenamin J. held that it was a matter for An Bord Pleanála, and that the board had erred in law in deciding that it was a matter for the EPA. This error of law went to jurisdiction. The board had, in the judgment of the court, drawn its own jurisdictional line in the wrong place and it should have dealt with environmental pollution caused by the construction works.

An example of a case falling on the other side of the line is provided by *O'Connor v Cork County Council* [2009] IEHC 560. The case concerned the circumstances in which a local authority is entitled to "take in charge" roads and open spaces in a residential development. The relevant statutory provision, s.180 of the Planning and Development Act 2000, provides for the taking in charge of infrastructure such as road, sewers, etc. in circumstances where the development has "been completed to the satisfaction of the planning authority" in accordance with the planning permission and conditions. The question before the High Court was as to the standard of review to be applied to the decision of a local authority that the development had been completed to its satisfaction. O'Neill J. emphasised that the statutory requirement that the development be satisfactorily completed was for the benefit of the local authority, in that it was undertaking an onerous obligation in taking an estate in charge. The appropriate standard of review was, therefore, that under the *O'Keeffe* principles.

In a number of judgments in 2009, the High Court has characterised decisions as to whether particular acts were "exempted development" as being within the expertise of An Bord Pleanála, and thus subject to the protection of the *O'Keeffe* principles. In *Quinlan v An Bord Pleanála* [2009] IEHC 228, Dunne J. held that the question of whether use as an embassy constituted use as an office within the meaning of the "use classes" under the Planning and Development Regulations 2001 was a matter of planning expertise:

> "The issue as to whether a use comes within a specific use class is a matter which is appropriate for determination by the Planning Authority/the Board. I would have thought that it is precisely the sort of question that should be left to planners who have the appropriate knowledge and expertise to evaluate the different use classes and what may or may not fall within a particular class."

A similar conclusion was reached in *Satke v An Bord Pleanála* [2009] IEHC 230. Hanna J. held that An Bord Pleanála's decision that certain works would interfere with the character of the landscape—and thus would be excluded from the benefit of exempted development—could only be successfully challenged if it could be demonstrated that there was simply no evidence to support the decision. Hanna J. did, however, draw a distinction between the board's finding in respect of the character of the landscape and a separate finding in respect of a right of way. The court held that a right of way was a "distinct legal concept", and there was no evidence to support the board's finding in this regard.

It is the writer's view that the question of whether a particular act is or is not exempted development involves the application of a legal concept to a particular set of facts. It is submitted therefore that it is more properly characterised as a question of law and should not attract the *O'Keeffe* principles. The issue in *Quinlan v An Bord Pleanála*, for example, involved a question of statutory interpretation, namely whether an office use within the meaning of the "use classes" extended to use as an embassy. It is difficult to understand why the courts should defer to An Bord Pleanála on such an issue. This is especially so in circumstances where the High Court, in the exercise of its jurisdiction to grant a planning injunction under s.160 of the Planning and Development Act 2000, regularly has to adjudicate on whether acts which are alleged to involve unauthorised development are, in truth, exempted development. In this regard, it is respectfully submitted that the approach of Ryan J. in *Michael Cronin (Readymix) Ltd v An Bord Pleanála* [2009] IEHC 553 is to be preferred. That case involved judicial review of a determination of An Bord Pleanála on a section 5 reference. Ryan J. stated that it is very much the province of the court to see that the board and its inspector have properly applied the law, have properly construed the relevant legislative provisions and have as a result asked the right questions.

Article 10a of the EIA Directive As noted above, as a result of amendments introduced to the EIA Directive by Directive 2003/35, Member States are required to provide a "review procedure" in respect of certain planning decisions. More specifically, the "review procedure" applies to challenges to "the substantive or procedural legality of decisions, acts or omissions subject to the public participation provisions of" the EIA Directive. The High Court has, on a number of occasions in 2009, rejected the argument that the reference to challenges to the "substantive" legality of decisions gives rise to an entitlement to merits-based review of planning decisions. In *Cairde Chill an Disirt Teoranta v An Bord Pleanála* [2009] IEHC 76; [2009] 2 I.L.R.M. 89, Cooke J. held that art.10a does not require the Member States to ensure access to a procedure for review of the merits of a development project for which a development consent has been granted. This approach has been subsequently approved of in *Usk and District Residents Association Ltd v An Bord Pleanála* [2009] IEHC 346 and in *Hands Across the Corrib Ltd v An Bord Pleanála* [2009] IEHC 600.

Duty to give reasons Under s.34(10) of the Planning and Development Act 2000, a planning authority (and An Bord Pleanála on appeal) is required to state the "main reasons and considerations" for its decision on an application for a planning permission. The statutory wording in this regard was introduced in order to give effect to the requirements of the EIA Directive; the wording under the Local Government (Planning & Development) Acts had simply imposed an obligation to state reasons. The case law of the European Court on reasons is therefore relevant in this regard: see, for example, Case C–75/08 *Mellor*. That case concerned the nature of the obligation to give reasons for a "screening" decision, i.e. a decision as to whether sub-threshold development is likely to have a significant effect on the environment, rather than a decision to grant or refuse development consent. There is no *express* duty under the EIA Directive to give reasons for a "screening" decision; nevertheless the European Court emphasised that for the "effective protection" of a right conferred by European law, it was necessary that interested parties have full knowledge of the relevant facts in order to allow them to decide whether there is any point in applying to the courts. It is submitted that this link between the duty to give reasons and effective judicial review should always be borne in mind in assessing the adequacy of reasons: legal errors on the part of a decision-maker can all too readily be shielded from challenge by an uninformative statement of reasons.

The Irish courts have traditionally shown considerable indulgence to planning authorities and An Bord Pleanála, and have treated the statutory requirement as imposing an almost minimal obligation to give reasons. This trend continued in 2009, as illustrated by the following cases. In *Sweetman v An Bord Pleanála* [2009] IEHC 599, the High Court reasserted the traditional view that, in assessing the adequacy of reasons it is legitimate to have regard to the report of the inspector appointed by An Bord Pleanála. This is to be contrasted with the earlier judgment in *Deerland Construction Ltd v Aquaculture Appeals Board* [2008] IEHC 289; [2009] 1 I.R. 673, where the High Court, in the context of a similarly worded legislative provision, had emphasised that the statutory duty required the reasons to be stated in the decision itself, not in some other document. With respect, it is submitted that the approach in *Deerland Construction Ltd* is to be preferred, and is more consistent with the statutory language. On the facts of *Sweetman*, the High Court ruled that, even without reference to the inspector's report, the reasons stated in the decision would have been adequate. This finding would appear to impose a facile obligation on a decision-maker: one of the central issues in the planning appeal before An Bord Pleanála had been whether the proposed road scheme would "adversely affect the integrity of" a European site within the meaning of art.6(3) of the Habitats Directive. The relevant part of the board's decision simply stated that:

> "... while having a localized severe impact on the Lough Corrib candidate Special Area of Conservation, [the road project] would not adversely affect the integrity of this candidate Special Area of Conservation".

With respect, this constitutes little more than the statement of a *conclusion*; the reasons upon which that conclusion is based are not disclosed. The inspector's report, by way of contrast, had contained a discussion as to the environmental impact of the road project in terms of the direct loss and fragmentation of a priority habitat type. Given the importance of the habitats issue in the planning appeal, one would have thought that the board in its decision would be required to state the reasons for its conclusion on this issue.

O'Neill v An Bord Pleanála [2009] IEHC 202 concerned the statutory requirement on a decision-maker to state the "main reasons" where the decision to grant or refuse permission differs from the recommendation in the planning inspector's report. The High Court emphasised that there was no obligation to provide detailed reasoning equivalent to that contained in the report: only the "main reasons" were required. Further, the board's decision had to be read in conjunction with the attached planning conditions. The High Court attached significance to the fact that certain conditions imposed by the board addressed planning concerns—especially in respect of visual amenity—which the inspector had raised in her report. The court concluded that whilst the board's conclusions on the issues of size and visual amenity differed from those of the inspector, it was nonetheless clear that these considerations were to the forefront of the board's deliberations.

A rare example of a planning decision being set aside for inadequate reasons is provided by *Usk and District Residents Association Ltd v An Bord Pleanála* [2009] IEHC 346. Planning permission had been sought for a waste landfill facility on the site of a former quarry. Part of the application site was subject to an earlier High Court order in enforcement proceedings directing the restoration of the lands to a condition suitable for an agricultural after-use. The carrying out of such restoration works might have affected the environmental baseline of the application site in terms of, for example, the import or export of soil and materials. The board's inspector had taken the view that the planning application was premature in circumstances where there was no certainty as to whether the baseline conditions of the site as set out in the EIS, and upon which the proposed development of the landfill facility was predicated, could be guaranteed. An Bord Pleanála, in its decision to grant permission, stated that the board "considered that this is a legal matter". The High Court held that this represented a failure on the part of the board to address itself to the necessity to give adequate reasons. The issue was not a legal matter, rather it was "essentially a purely planning matter which arose from a legal decision of the High Court" in the earlier enforcement proceedings. The High Court judgment in the judicial review proceedings suggested that reasons were particularly required in light of the planning effect of any compliance with the restoration order, which had been made some five-and-a-half years previously.

Finally, the judgment of *Satke v An Bord Pleanála* [2009] IEHC 230 considered the situation where there is no *express* statutory duty to give reasons. The case concerned a decision of An Bord Pleanála on a reference under s.5 of the Planning and Development Act 2000. The High Court noted that there was no statutory duty to state the main reasons for not following the recommendation in the report.

DEFAULT PLANNING PERMISSION

Material contravention of development plan It is well established that a default planning permission cannot arise in circumstances where the proposed development would involve a material contravention of the development plan. This is because a planning authority can only ever grant permission for such development by going through the special voting procedure under s.34(6) of the Planning and Development Act 2000. These important procedural safeguards would be set at naught were default permission to be available in the case of development in material contravention of the development plan. The failure—whether accidental or deliberate—of the planning authority to make a decision within the time limit cannot produce a result, i.e. the grant of planning permission, which it would not otherwise have been entitled to bring about.

There was some dispute, however, as to whether in order to qualify for a default permission the proposed development had to be of a type which would normally be permitted under the development plan. In particular, a distinction had been drawn in some of the case law between development of a type which would normally be permissible under the relevant plan, and other development which was merely open for consideration. This issue has now been resolved by the Supreme Court in *Abbeydrive Developments Ltd v Kildare County Council* [2009] IESC 56; [2010] 1 I.L.R.M. 187. The Supreme Court indicated that the only relevant test was whether the proposed development would involve a material contravention of the development plan. If it would, then a default permission could not arise. If the proposed development would not involve a material contravention, the fact that development of that type might only be "open for consideration" under the plan—and thus would require the planning authority to exercise its discretion favourably in order to grant permission—does not preclude a default permission arising.

Local area plan There is no restriction under the Planning and Development Act 2000 on the circumstances in which a planning authority may grant planning permission which would involve a material contravention of a local area plan (LAP). Thus an LAP enjoys a lesser status than a development plan. (It is proposed to correct this anomaly under the Planning and Development (Amendment) Bill 2009.) Notwithstanding this difference in treatment between the two types of plans, the High Court in *Ryan v Clare County Council* [2009] IEHC 115 rejected a claim for a default permission on the basis that the proposed development would contravene the LAP. See in particular paras [49] and [50] of the judgment as follows:

> "The integrity of the planning process is a vital national interest. Bad planning decisions sentence generations to live with the consequences thereof. The courts, in interpreting the legislation should, in my view, never lose sight of this overarching national interest. Not only must a development be in accordance with the County Development Plan, regard must also be had to the Local Area Plan. The court cannot itself act as a planning authority and therefore, unless it is incontrovertibly shown that a default permission would be fully in accordance with the Local Area Plan it cannot be allowed. In this case, as I have already noted, there is good reason to suspect that the proposal would contravene the housing policies set down in that Plan.
>
> In light of the foregoing, I am satisfied that default planning permission should not issue in this case. Even a bare default decision must avoid contravening the County Development Plan while also remaining in keeping with the Local Area Plan. The importance of the rights of neighbouring residents whose properties may be adversely affected by a particular development cannot be ignored. In those circumstances, I refuse the applications for both declaratory relief and for an order of *mandamus*."

With respect, the correctness of this finding must now be in doubt, especially given the subsequent judgment of the Supreme Court in *Abbeydrive Developments Ltd v Kildare County Council* [2009] IESC 56; [2010] 1 I.L.R.M. 187 (discussed above at p.665). Any requirement that the proposed development be "fully in accordance with" either plan appears to involve precisely the type of subjective assessment which the Supreme Court eschewed in *Abbeydrive Developments Ltd.* The only relevant test is whether the proposed development would materially contravene the plan. Moreover, as already noted, there is no limitation under the (unamended) Planning and Development Act 2000 on the circumstances in which a planning authority may grant planning permission which would involve a material contravention of a LAP, as opposed to a development plan.

"DEVELOPMENT" AND "EXEMPTED DEVELOPMENT"

Unauthorised development The question of whether An Bord Pleanála has jurisdiction to grant planning permission where it is alleged that there is related unauthorised on-site development was considered in *Murphy v An Bord Pleanála* [2009] IEHC 38. Planning permission had been sought, inter alia, for a first floor extension to be built over an existing single storey structure. The applicant for judicial review alleged that the existing single storey structure constituted unauthorised development. The High Court found, on the facts, that the existing single storey structure was not included as part of the development in respect of which planning permission was being sought. Accordingly, in deciding to grant permission An Bord Pleanála was not purporting to approve the existing single storey structure:

> "In this case the planning permission did no more than assure the applicant that as regards the planning legislation, the particular development sought would be lawful. That development was in respect of a first floor extension and did not extend to the ground floor. If an earlier development by the developer was unauthorised and/or unlawful, the planning permission granted did not, either by law or by implication, authorise or permit such earlier development. It cannot be said on the basis of the law as identified by Keane J. that the decision of An Bord Pleanála implicitly approved the earlier development as the development which was approved did not deal with the earlier development."

The High Court went on to hold that, on the facts, there was no obligation on An Bord Pleanála to make a determination as to whether the ground floor structure was an unauthorised development or an exempted development.

Extension of structures Under s.4(1)(h) of the Planning and Development Act 2000, works for the "maintenance, improvement or other alteration" of any structure are "exempted development" provided that the works do not materially affect the external appearance of the structure. In *Michael Cronin (Readymix) Ltd v An Bord Pleanála* [2009] IEHC 553, the High Court had to consider whether an extension to a structure (on the facts, an extension to a concrete yard) constituted exempted development. The resolution of this issue turned on whether the words "maintenance, improvement or other alteration" qualified the *type of works* which came within the exemption, or whether the words merely qualified the *purpose* for which the works were carried out. On the latter interpretation, any type of works would come within the exemption provided that the works were for the purpose of maintaining, improving or altering the relevant structure. To put the matter another way, the general definition of "works" under s.2 of the Planning and Development Act 2000 expressly includes "extension"; the question is whether the exemption under s.4(1)(h) is confined to a subset of works, i.e. works involving maintenance, improvements or other alteration. The High Court held that an extension can be an improvement or an alteration, and that An Bord Pleanála had erred in confusing the purpose for which works were carried out with the kind of activities which might be carried out. This aspect of the case has been certified for leave to appeal to the Supreme Court.

Material change in use The High Court in *Michael Cronin (Readymix) Ltd v An Bord Pleanála* [2009] IEHC 553 had to consider the approach that An Bord Pleanála should take in determining whether there has been a material change in the use of land. On the facts, a surfaced concrete area had been extended and was being used for the purpose of drying and storing concrete blocks. The High Court had earlier found that the works involved in extending the concreted area had constituted "exempted development". The High Court held that, given this fact, An Bord Pleanála's inspector, in assessing whether there had been a material change in use, had erred in having regard to the environmental impact which the construction and extension of the concreted area might have.

> "[I]t seems to me that the Inspector should have looked at the concreted area and asked the question whether the use of that area of land for storing or resting or drying blocks in connection with block making operations constituted a material change of use in all the circumstances. She did not do that. She addressed herself to the question whether the concreted surface itself amounted to a material change of use and that is where, in my view, she fell into error and did indeed conflate works and use, as submitted by the applicant."

DEVELOPMENT PLAN AND LAP

Executive and reserved functions The making of a development plan is a reserved function, i.e. a function of the elected members of the local authority rather than a function of the executive. By way of contrast, the making of a local area plan (LAP) is normally a function of the manager, i.e. an executive function. The default position is that the manager "makes" the LAP. There is provision made, however, for the elected members to intervene in the process by way of resolution.

The division of function between the executive and the elected members was considered in detail by the High Court in *Farrell v Limerick County Council* [2009] IEHC 274; [2010] 1 I.L.R.M. 99. A majority of the elected members had attempted to re-zone an area outside the village of Adare. The attempted re-zoning was contrary to the advice of the professional planning staff. The manager, having taken legal advice, decided that the purported resolution of the elected members was not effective to amend the draft plan. The LAP was subsequently "made" without the attempted re-zoning. The owners of some of the affected lands sought to challenge the manager's actions in the High Court. The challenge failed. The first issue the High Court had to address was whether the manager had jurisdiction to treat the purported resolution as ineffective. McGovern J. held that there is a line of authority to the effect that a local authority manager is only required to give effect to a *lawful* resolution of elected members, citing *Child v Wicklow County Council* [1995] 2 I.R. 447 and *Wicklow County Council v Wicklow County Manager*, unreported, High Court, Ó Caoimh J., February 26, 2003.

On the facts, the High Court held that the resolution was invalid in a number of respects. In particular, the resolution failed to recite the reasons for the attempted re-zoning, and the elected members had failed to address the environmental, cultural, architectural and heritage issues arising from the proposed re-zoning.

STATUTORY DEVELOPMENT AGREEMENT

Section 47 agreements Section 47 of the Planning and Development Act 2000 provides for statutory development agreements. Such agreements may be made between the local authority and a person interested in land in its area. The distinguishing feature of such an agreement is that it runs with the land in that it binds subsequent owners of the land as if it were a restrictive covenant.

The agreement must be for the purpose of "restricting" or "regulating" the development or use of the land. The Supreme Court in *McHugh v Kildare County Council* [2009] IESC 16; [2009] 2 I.R. 407 held, in the context of the similarly worded provision of the previous legislation, that an agreement to transfer the ownership of land to a local authority did not come within the section. The court held that "restricting" or "regulating" the development or use of lands is something of a quite different nature to transferring their ownership.

Practice and Procedure

MARTIN CANNY, BL

ABUSE OF PROCESS

Successive proceedings and the rule in *Henderson v Henderson* The *Bula v Tara Mines* saga finally reached its conclusion in 2009 with the judgment of the Supreme Court in *Bula Ltd v Crowley* [2009] IESC 35; unreported, Supreme Court, April 3, 2009. The court held that proceedings that sought to impugn the propriety of the sale of the plaintiff's zinc mine at Nevinstown, Co. Meath were an abuse of process as all grounds of challenge to the contract for sale of the mine should have been raised in the receivership motion for directions (reported sub nom *Bula Ltd v Crowley (No. 4)* [2003] 4 I.R. 430). Denham J. held that the rule in *Henderson v Henderson* (1843) 3 Hare 100 applied and that it was an abuse of process to pursue those reliefs in new proceedings. In *McHugh v AIB Plc* [2009] IEHC 340; unreported, High Court, Dunne J., July 7, 2009, Dunne J. struck out the plaintiff's action in circumstances where it sought the same reliefs as extant proceedings which were still before the courts. She also indicated that if a notice of discontinuance had been properly served in the earlier proceedings, the latter proceedings would still be an abuse of process if the reason why they had been instituted was to sue a party whom the plaintiff had been refused liberty to join as a co-defendant in the earlier set of proceedings.

Attempts to relitigate matters by setting aside final orders The plaintiff in *Talbot v McCann Fitzgerald Solicitors* [2009] IESC 25; unreported, Supreme Court, March 26, 2009 also found the Supreme Court to be unreceptive to his attempt to relitigate earlier proceedings. Although the plaintiff's application to review an earlier final order of the Supreme Court was firmly refused, the judgment of Denham J. is of interest as it contains a useful review of the principles involved, as set out, inter alia, in *Belville Holdings Ltd v Revenue Commissioners* [1994] 1 I.L.R.M. 29 and *Bula Ltd v Tara Mines Ltd (No. 6)* [2000] 4 I.R. 412.

Test to be applied when proceedings alleged to have no chance of success While cases such as *Barry v Buckley* [1981] I.R. 306 establish that the courts have jurisdiction to dismiss proceedings which have no prospect of success by means of a preliminary application (on grounds that the further prosecution of those proceedings is an abuse of process), Clarke J. in *Salthill Properties Ltd v Royal Bank of Scotland Plc* [2009] IEHC 207; unreported, High Court, Clarke J., April 30, 2009 emphasised the exceptional nature of such an application. The judgment is of interest as Clarke J. held that, on the affidavit evidence put before the court for the purpose of the strike-out application, the plaintiffs had not established a prima facie case. However, as it could not be assumed that probative evidence would not be revealed at the discovery stage, Clarke J. held that it was inappropriate and premature for the court to dismiss the proceedings, although he signalled that the application could be renewed at the close of opening submissions at the trial of the action if no further evidence was revealed in the discovery process.

SECURITY FOR COSTS

Applications for security for costs against a corporate plaintiff In both *Connaughton Road Construction Ltd v Laing O'Rourke Ireland Ltd* [2009] IEHC 7; unreported, High Court, Clarke J., January 16, 2009 and *Ferrotec Ltd v Myles Bramwell Executive Slimming Services Ltd* [2009] IEHC 46; unreported, High Court, Dunne J., February 5, 2009 the defendant sought security for costs from a corporate plaintiff pursuant to s.390 of the Companies Act 1963. The main issue in both applications was whether the plaintiff had established that its impecuniosity was due to the wrongdoing alleged in the proceedings. In *Connaughton Road Construction*, Clarke J. criticised the lack of detail provided in the affidavits filed by the plaintiff as to the likely division of anticipated profits between the corporate plaintiff and the landowner on whose land a development was to have been built. Due to this failing, and the absence of detailed accounts from the plaintiff, Clarke J. ordered that security should be lodged. In *Ferrotec Ltd*, Dunne J. noted that although the plaintiff would have been profit-making if the entire contract sum claimed had in fact been paid to it, as it had been loss-making prior to entering into this contract, and as its accounts were out of date, she also ordered that security be lodged. A subsidiary issue of delay was found not to be fatal to the claim. An issue of considerable practical importance also touched upon in *Connaughton Road Construction Ltd v Laing O'Rourke Ireland Ltd* was that Clarke J. indicated that he would measure the quantum of security to be lodged rather than sending it for assessment by the Master of the High Court, once the plaintiff had been afforded an opportunity to respond to the defendant's estimate of the likely costs of the action.

JURISDICTION – REGULATION 44/2001 AND THE LUGANO CONVENTION

Jurisdiction to stay Irish proceedings in favour of earlier commenced US proceedings In *Goshawk Dedicated Ltd v Irish Life Receivables Ireland Ltd* [2009] IESC 7; unreported, Supreme Court, January 30, 2009, the Supreme Court (on appeal from [2008] IEHC 90; [2008] 2 I.L.R.M. 460) referred a question to the European Court of Justice on the correct interpretation to be given to Regulation 44/2001. The question is as follows: whether, when a defendant is sued in its country of domicile, it is inconsistent with Regulation 44/2001 for the courts of a Member State to decline jurisdiction or to stay proceedings on the basis that proceedings between the same parties and involving the same cause of action are already pending in the courts of a non-Member State and therefore first in time. This important question had been raised in *Owusu v Jackson* (Case C281/02 [2005] E.C.R. I–138) but had not been answered by the European Court of Justice in its decision in that case.

Jurisdiction under the Lugano Convention In *Ryanair Ltd v Bravofly Ltd* [2009] IEHC 386; unreported, High Court, Kelly J., July 30, 2009, Kelly J. refused the plaintiff liberty to join a co-defendant in circumstances where that party had already issued proceedings against it before the courts of Switzerland. As arts 21 and 22 of the Lugano Convention gave jurisdiction to the court first seised of the dispute, he held that no purpose would be served by allowing the joinder of the additional party.

Exclusive jurisdiction clause: incorporation into contractual dealings In *O'Connor v Masterwood (UK) Ltd* [2009] IESC 49; unreported, Supreme Court, July 1, 2009, the Supreme Court confirmed that ordinary principles of contractual interpretation apply in cases where a party wishes to rely on a clause conferring exclusive jurisdiction on a foreign court pursuant to art.23 of Council Regulation 44/2001. As the clause was contained in the written standard terms of the defendant, which the plaintiff had signed, the court held that it was operative and that the courts of Rimini, Italy had exclusive jurisdiction to hear the dispute. In *Ryanair Ltd v Bravofly* [2009] IEHC 41; unreported, High Court, Clarke J., January 29, 2009, Clarke J. held that a defendant who denied that a binding contract governed its relationship with a plaintiff could still argue that if the contract was enforceable, it was entitled to rely on an exclusive jurisdiction clause. Based on this conclusion he held that the plaintiff's standard terms applied to the claim against that defendant and that the Irish courts had no jurisdiction to hear the proceedings.

INJUNCTIONS

Variation of *Mareva* injunction In *Daly v Killally* [2009] IEHC 172; unreported, High Court, Kelly J., March 27, 2009, the plaintiff obtained a *Mareva* injunction freezing the assets of the defendant. The defendant applied to vary the terms of the order so as to allow him to pay his living expenses, legal fees and mortgage payments on his properties. Kelly J. followed English case law such as *A v C* [1981] 2 All E.R. 126 and held that the court did have jurisdiction to vary a *Mareva* injunction so as to allow for the payment of the types of expenses outlined by the defendant, although he reduced the figure for living expenses which would be paid out of the frozen monies to a sum which was more agreeable to the court.

Right of bank to exercise its security over property subject to a *Mareva* injunction *Dowley v O'Brien* [2009] IEHC 566; unreported, High Court, Clarke J., December 21, 2009 involved an application by Anglo Irish Bank Plc to vary a *Mareva* injunction which had frozen the assets of fraudster Breifne O'Brien. The order sought liberty to realise certain assets subject to the order over which the bank had security and to exercise rights of set-off between monies subject to the injunction and debts which Mr O'Brien owed to the bank. Clarke J. held that a typical *Mareva* injunction places no barrier in the way of a financial institution making a bona fide exercise of any power of set-off or security realisation. The only exception is where a *Mareva* injunction is granted in support of a claim for proprietary relief (i.e. in support of a claim that the plaintiff owns the property in question) in which case this would not be allowable. Thus, Clarke J. refused to vary the order on grounds that Anglo Irish Bank plc did not need liberty from the court to exercise its security rights.

PLEADINGS AND PARTICULARS

Scandalous, irrelevant and unparticularised pleadings While the courts are reluctant to supervise the manner in which a party pleads its case, Ord.19 r.27 of the Rules of the Superior Courts 1986 confers a broad discretion on a court to strike out any part of a pleading which is unnecessary, scandalous or prejudicial. In *Ryanair Ltd v Bravofly* [2009] IEHC 41; unreported, High Court, Clarke J., January 29, 2009, Clarke J. held that the defendant had pleaded allegations of abuse by the plaintiff of its market position and aggressive behaviour which were not relevant to the causes of action relied on its counterclaim. Those allegations were struck out of the pleading. However, the plaintiff's application to strike out an unparticularised plea of anti-competitive activity was refused (although the defendant was ordered to provide further particulars). Clarke J. followed *National Education Board v Ryan* [2007] IEHC 428 and held that as wrongdoing of this nature was usually concealed, the defendant would be entitled to seek discovery prior to being forced to provide full particulars of the allegations it intended to make at trial.

Further and better particulars in a libel action In *Quinn Insurance Ltd v Tribune Newspapers Ltd* [2009] IEHC 229; unreported, High Court, Dunne J., May 13, 2009, the defendant published an article which alleged that the plaintiff, inter alia, recruited serving Gardaí to investigate claims and settle them as quickly as possible on its behalf and that it offered "sweeteners" to solicitors to settle cases. The plaintiff brought libel proceedings and later sought particulars of the identities of the Gardaí and claims managers against whom the claims were alleged. Dunne J. considered the case law on what particulars must be provided in a libel action, in particular *McDonagh v Sunday Newspapers t/a the Sunday World* [2005] 4 I.R. 528, and held that the case was adequately pleaded and that the plaintiff was not entitled to be told the identities of the parties in question.

DELAY AND DISMISSAL OF ACTIONS

Refinement of the legal principles: relevance of the European Convention on Human Rights A large volume of reserved judgments were delivered in 2009 on applications to dismiss proceedings on grounds of delay or want of prosecution. *Annual Review of Irish Law 2008* (Dublin: Round Hall, 2009), pp.494–496 and Delany, "Dismissal for want of prosecution—Has the test changed?" (2010) 28(1) I.L.T. (n.s.) 11 both gave some consideration to the apparent conflict between the judgments of the Supreme Court in *Stephens v Paul Flynn Ltd* [2008] IESC 4; [2008] 4 I.R. 31 and *Desmond v MGN Ltd* [2008] IESC 56; [2009] 1 I.R. 737. The judgment of Kearns J. in *Stephens v Paul Flynn Ltd* enthusiastically endorsed the relevance of the European Convention on Human Rights ("ECHR") whereas the judgments of Geoghegan and Macken JJ. in *Desmond v MGN Ltd* deprecated the relevance of the ECHR and stated that the principles set out in *Primor Plc v Stokes Kennedy Crowley* [1996] 2 I.R. 459 remain unaltered. While Dunne J. in *Rooney v Ryan* [2009] IEHC 154; unreported, High Court, Dunne J., March 31, 2009 followed the majority approach set out in *Desmond v MGN Ltd* [2008] IESC 56; [2009] 1 I.R. 737, the case law of the European Court continued to be referred to in a number of cases, including *Mannion v Bergin* [2009] IEHC 165; unreported, High Court, Hedigan J., March 13, 2009 and *Re Hocroft Developments Ltd; Dowall v Cullen* [2009] IEHC 580; unreported, High Court, McKechnie J., December 5, 2009. As the language used in formulating the test in any of the cases is imprecise, the differences of emphasis revealed by these judgments should not be overstated as a judge hearing an application to dismiss proceedings for want of prosecution has an almost unfettered discretion once an initial period of "inordinate" delay is established.

Lapse of time and prejudice: sexual abuse cases The Supreme Court in *JR v Minister for Justice, Equality and Law Reform* [2007] IESC 7; [2007] 2 I.R. 748 held that civil actions alleging sexual abuse raise particular issues in relation to defendant culpability for delays in instituting suit. If the actions of a defendant caused the delay in bringing the proceedings the delay may be excusable and the plaintiff's right to carry on his delayed claim may outweigh the defendant's rights. This approach was followed in *MO'S v WO'S* [2009] IEHC 161; unreported, High Court, Dunne J., April 2, 2009 where Dunne J. allowed the plaintiff to continue her proceedings which involved allegations of sexual abuse that allegedly occurred between 1960 and 1996. The same result was arrived at in *JS v A McD* [2009] IEHC 95; unreported, High Court, Dunne J., February 20, 2009. By contrast, in a number of decisions it has been held that either the degree of prejudice caused by the delay in instituting proceedings or the lack of an adequate explanation for the plaintiff not bringing proceedings at an earlier date led to the court dismissing the proceedings: see, for example, *J O'D v Minister for Education and Science* [2009] IEHC 227; unreported, High Court, Dunne J., May 13, 2009; *JD v DO'K* [2009] IEHC 422; unreported, High Court, Hedigan J., October 6, 2009; *D O'F v Minister for Justice* [2009] IEHC 496; unreported, High Court, Hedigan J., November 11, 2009 and *FW v JW* [2009] IEHC 542; unreported, High Court, Charleton J., December 18, 2009.

Want of prosecution The judgments of the High Court delivered in 2009 on applications to dismiss proceedings for want of prosecution do not ease the task of the legal profession in advising clients on whether or not proceedings will be dismissed for want of prosecution. On the question of what prejudice must be established, while the judgments of Hedigan J. in *Mannion v Bergin* [2009] IEHC 165; unreported, High Court, Hedigan J., March 13, 2009 and *Re Walsh Western Computer Services Ltd* [2009] IEHC 505; unreported, High Court, Hedigan J., November 19, 2009 might suggest that a lengthy period of delay is of itself prejudicial, this approach has not been widely followed and lengthy periods of delay were found not to be prejudicial in other cases, such as *Rooney v Ryan* [2009] IEHC 154; unreported, High Court, Dunne J., March 31, 2009. Similarly, in *Killeen v Padraig Thornton Waste Disposal Ltd* [2009] IEHC 131; unreported, High Court, McKechnie J., March 18, 2009, McKechnie J. held that the fact that delay in instituting proceedings had prejudiced the defendant by reason of the death of its main witness during that period of delay was not of itself sufficient to warrant the proceedings being dismissed. A large number of other judgments were delivered in 2009 on applications to dismiss for want of prosecution which all apply the principles as set out in

Primor Plc v Stokes Kennedy Crowley [1996] 2 I.R. 459. These judgments indicate that the attitude of the courts to litigant delay is still quite forgiving, although perhaps less so than previously: see *Fortune v Revenue Commissioners* [2009] IEHC 28; unreported, High Court, O'Neill J., January 23, 2009; *Razaq v Allied Irish Banks plc* [2009] IEHC 176; unreported, High Court, Herbert J., March 6, 2009; *Corcoran v McArdle* [2009] IEHC 265; unreported, High Court, Laffoy J., March 3, 2009; *Desmond v Times Newspapers Ltd* [2009] IEHC 271; unreported, High Court, Dunne J., June 12, 2009; *O'Keeffe v G & T Crampton Ltd* [2009] IEHC 366; unreported, High Court, Peart J., July 17, 2009; *C (a person of unsound mind) v McG* [2009] IEHC 438; unreported, High Court, McCarthy J., September 18, 2009.

THIRD PARTY PROCEEDINGS

Applications to set aside third party notice Section 27(1)(b) of the Civil Liability Act 1961 imposes an obligation on a defendant who wishes to join a third party to proceedings to do so "as soon as is reasonably possible". The fundamental question of "how long is too long" in relation to the issuing of a third party notice is not a matter which has been given a definitive answer in the decided cases to date, as the circumstances which may excuse a period of delay (in whole or in part) can vary dramatically. However, in *Robins v Coleman* [2009] IEHC 486; unreported, High Court, McMahon J., November 6, 2009 it was noted in para.2.13 of the judgment that delays (properly calculated) of 15, 16 and 18 months have been found to be acceptable in previous cases but that longer periods have been found to be excessive. Although the question of whether the delay has prejudiced the third party has been held not to be a relevant factor in most cases (see *Murnaghan v Markland Holdings Ltd* [2007] IEHC 255; unreported, High Court, Laffoy J., August 10, 2007; *contra Ward v O'Callaghan*, unreported, High Court, Morris P., February 2, 1998), in *Robins v Coleman*, McMahon J. held that prejudice is a factor which is of relevance in assessing whether the third party notice had been served as soon as was reasonably possible. On the facts of the case, McMahon J. held that most of the delays prior to applying to issue and serve a third party notice had been explained and excused and in the circumstances the third parties' applications were refused.

The effect of delays in bringing an application to set aside a third party notice In *S Doyle & Sons Roscommon Ltd v Flemco Supermarket Ltd* [2009] IEHC 581; unreported, High Court, Laffoy J., December 2, 2009, Laffoy J. confirmed the well established rule (see e.g. *Boland v Dublin City Council* [2002] 4 I.R. 409) that a third party who wishes to set aside the third party notice must not delay in bringing that application. In *S Doyle & Sons Roscommon Ltd* *v Flemco Supermarket Ltd* a delay of six months coupled with the delivery of a notice for particulars and a consent order in a motion for judgment in default of defence was held to preclude the third party from then applying to set aside the third party notice.

DISCOVERY

Application to restrict disclosure of discovered documents to expert witnesses In *Kroger Inc v O'Donnell* [2009] IEHC 385; unreported, High Court, Kelly J., July 31, 2009, the defendant was ordered to make discovery to the plaintiff in a copyright infringement case. It sought to limit the parties who would have access to the discovered documents to the expert witnesses who were retained by the plaintiff, on grounds that any wider disclosure would cause unnecessary damage to their legitimate interests in the material remaining confidential. Kelly J. accepted that the court had the jurisdiction to make the order sought by the defendants. However, he refused to impose the restrictions sought, although he directed that only one employee of the plaintiff would be allowed to access the documents and that this employee would have to give an undertaking that he would not make use of the information other than for the purpose of prosecuting the proceedings.

Attachment and sequestration of assets for failure to make discovery In *Ulster Bank Ireland Ltd v Whittaker* [2009] IEHC 16; unreported, High Court, January 21, 2009, Clarke J. noted that although they are seldom pursued, the remedies of attachment and sequestration of assets are, in principle, available if there is a breach of a discovery order. However, as the order served on the defaulting party lacked the "penal endorsement" required by Ord.41 r.8 of the Rules of the Superior Courts 1986, Clarke J. refused the application to attach that party.

Relevance and necessity Several reserved judgments on discovery applications were delivered in 2009. In *Linfen Ltd v Rocca* [2009] IEHC 292; unreported, High Court, MacMenamin J., March 13, 2009, MacMenamin J. applied the well established principles governing discovery applications to a case where the plaintiff was alleging professional negligence and breach of fiduciary duty against a firm of solicitors who had acted for both sides of a transaction. The decision is also of interest for the brief consideration of the circumstances in which the file of a professional adviser will not be within the power or procurement of the client who retained that adviser. In *CB Richard Ellis v Dunne* [2009] IEHC 251; unreported, High Court, Kelly J., May 22, 2009, Kelly J. refused most of the discovery sought by the defendant counterclaimant in circumstances where his allegation that the plaintiff was a disloyal fiduciary which took a secret profit on a transaction was not supported by a factual basis set out on affidavit. Instead it was held to be a fishing expedition; in addition the court stated that much of the discovery sought was excessively broad. In *Croke v Waterford Crystal Ltd* [2009] IEHC 158; unreported, High Court, Birmingham J., March 31, 2009, the plaintiff sought discovery of internal communications in support of its allegation that the plaintiff's cause of action had been fraudulently concealed. MacMenamin J. ordered that discovery should be made of internal communications, except for communications with the defendants' lawyers as these would all be privileged and no purpose would be served by discovering them. In *Hansfield Developments Ltd v Irish Asphalt Ltd* [2009] IESC 4; unreported, Supreme Court, January 23, 2009, the defendant sought non-party discovery from the insurer HomeBond in proceedings where the plaintiff developer alleged that the defendants had supplied quarry materials containing an excessive amount of pyrites. Non-party discovery was sought from HomeBond of documents relating to its involvement with remediation of defects at a housing estate (unrelated to either the plaintiff or defendants) where similar problems had occurred, and documents in its possession relating to changes in the relevant national standards. The discovery was refused on grounds that it was not relevant or necessary to the proceedings: documents within the first category as these were not probative to the proceedings and those in the latter category as this was a matter more suitable to expert evidence.

PRIVILEGE

Litigation privilege: dominant purpose test In *Hansfield Developments Ltd v Irish Asphalt Ltd* [2009] IEHC 90; unreported, High Court, McGovern J., February 17, 2009, the defendants sought an order pursuant to Ord.31 r.18 of the Rules of the Superior Courts 1986 allowing them to inspect documents over which privilege had been claimed. The facts of the case are set out in the previous paragraph; the documents in question were communications between the plaintiff and the insurer HomeBond. McGovern J. followed the judgment of O'Hanlon J. in *Silver Hill Duckling Ltd v Steele* [1987] I.R. 298, which held that for litigation privilege to arise the dominant purpose for the document coming into existence should have been the purpose of preparing for litigation then apprehended or threatened. McGovern J. held that the dominant purpose for the documents being created was to remedy the problems which had been encountered and not for the purpose of litigation. A second argument raised by the plaintiff was that any documents exchanged with HomeBond did not lose the privilege attaching because the parties shared a common interest in the litigation. McGovern J. followed *Moorview Developments Ltd v First Active Plc* [2008] IEHC 274; [2009] 1 I.R. 274 and held that no common interest existed between the parties.

Waiver of privilege: disclosure to third parties and deployment in litigation In *Redfern Ltd v O'Mahony* [2009] IESC 18; unreported, Supreme Court, March 4, 2009, the Supreme Court delivered its judgment on cross-motions seeking inspection of allegedly privileged documents on grounds that privilege had been waived. The disclosure by the plaintiff had been to a joint venture partner in the course of contract negotiations and was stated to remain confidential. The court applied its recent judgment in *Fyffes plc v DCC Plc* [2005] 1 I.R. 59 and held that privilege had not been waived as there had only been a limited disclosure to a party with a common interest. The alleged waiver by the defendants arose by virtue of the fact that their pleaded defence put in issue their intention and state of mind as a result of the receipt of privileged legal advice. The court held that as the content of the legal advice was not relied upon, but only the fact that legal advice had been received, no waiver of privilege had occurred.

A further ruling on the question of privilege in the "pyrites litigation" was delivered by McKechnie J. in *Hansfield Developments Ltd v Irish Asphalt Ltd* [2009] IEHC 420; unreported, High Court, McKechnie J., September 21, 2009. The legal issues ruled on by the court in this judgment overlap with an earlier judgment in the same proceedings (see [2009] IEHC 90) and with *Redfern Ltd v O'Mahony* [2009] IESC 18, which are both referred to above, namely the scope of litigation privilege and loss of that privilege through disclosure. The issue of common interest privilege was discussed in somewhat greater length in this judgment, with McKechnie J. giving a reasonably broad interpretation to the doctrine.

For similar reasons to those relied on by the Supreme Court in *Redfern Ltd v O'Mahony* [2009] IESC 18, Cooke J. in *Ryanair Ltd v Murrays Europcar Ltd* [2009] IEHC 366; unreported, High Court, Cooke J., May 18, 2009 refused to make an order allowing the defendant to inspect a privileged expert report which had been obtained by the plaintiff. The report had been referred to in an affidavit, but Cooke J. held that this did not amount to "deployment" of the document in the litigation in the manner required by the case law, such as the judgment of Clarke J. in *Byrne v Shannon Foynes Port Company* [2007] IEHC 315; [2008] 1 I.R. 814.

TRIAL OF A PRELIMINARY ISSUE

Facts relating to preliminary issue must not be in dispute In *Murray v Fitzgerald* [2009] IEHC 101; unreported, High Court, MacMenamin J., February 27, 2009, MacMenamin J. followed the guidance set out in *Nyembo v Refugee Appeals Tribunal* [2007] IESC 25; [2008] 1 I.L.R.M. 289 and held that the court should only direct the trial of a preliminary issue (pursuant to Ord.25 or Ord.34 of the Rules of the Superior Courts 1986) if there was agreement on the facts for the purposes of the trial of the preliminary issue. As the facts were fully disputed, and as the trial of the preliminary issue which was sought would involve duplication of matters which would arise in any event at the full hearing, the court refused the application for the trial of a preliminary issue.

O'Sullivan v Rogan [2009] IEHC 456, unreported, High Court, Hedigan J., October 16, 2009 is an example of the problems which can arise where a preliminary issue is tried when the facts are in dispute. The defendants in this case alleged that the proceedings brought against them were statute-barred. However, the plaintiff raised an allegation of fraudulent concealment (within the meaning of s.71 of the Statute of Limitations 1957) which was denied by the defendants and which depended on certain disputed factual allegations advanced by the plaintiff. The court held that it was not possible to resolve the issue without the case progressing to trial on oral evidence.

SUMMARY JUDGMENT

Application of the test for summary judgment A large number of judgments on applications for liberty to enter final judgment were delivered in 2009 as the country's economic fortunes receded. The test as set out in cases such as *Aer Rianta CPT v Ryanair Ltd* [2001] 4 I.R. 607 and *Harrisrange Ltd v Duncan* [2003] 4 I.R. 1, namely whether a defendant can establish a "fair or reasonable probability of having a real or bona fide defence" was applied by the courts in the applications for summary judgment which it had to determine. For examples of the application of these principles in 2009 see: *Consular Gestion SGHC SA v Optimal Multiadvisors Ireland Plc* [2009] IEHC 173; unreported, High Court, Kelly J., March 27, 2009; *Bank of Ireland Plc v Walsh* [2009] IEHC 220; unreported, High Court, Finlay Geoghegan J., May 8, 2009; *Danske Bank A/S trading as National Irish Bank v Durkan New Homes* [2009] IEHC 278; unreported, High Court, Charleton J., June 26, 2009; *GE Capital Woodchester Ltd v Aktiv Kapital* [2009] IEHC 512; unreported, High Court, Clarke J., November 19, 2009 and *Ringsend Property Ltd v Donatex Ltd* [2009] IEHC 568; unreported, High Court, Kelly J., December 18, 2009.

Relevance of a cross-claim in an application for summary judgment The recent decision of Clarke J. in *Moohan v S & R Motors (Donegal) Ltd* [2007] IEHC 435; [2008] 3 I.R. 650 on the relevance of a disputed cross-claim to an application for summary judgment was followed in two judgments delivered in 2009. In *Killerk Ltd v Houlihan* [2009] IEHC 358; unreported, High Court, Kelly J., July 16, 2009, Kelly J. entered judgment for the full amount of a claim but placed a stay on the proportion which had been bona fide claimed as special damages (but not a further element which was not properly explained on affidavit) in a cross-claim which was being pursued at arbitration, until the determination of the arbitration. In *Irish Life Assurance Plc v Quinn* [2009]

IEHC 153; unreported, High Court, Dunne J., March 31, 2009, the defendant tenant attempted to set up a counterclaim seeking unliquidated damages for breach of covenant in answer to the plaintiff landlord's claim for arrears of rent. Dunne J. held that the court would not allow a "last ditch effort" to avoid judgment which had been raised at the last moment. She entered judgment for the rent arrears and left the defendant to pursue its claim for damages for breach of covenant in separate proceedings.

Application for summary judgment on the reliefs claimed in a special summons In *Anglo Irish Bank Corporation Plc v Fanning* [2009] IEHC 141; unreported, High Court, Dunne J., January 29, 2009, Dunne J. set out clear guidance for the procedure to be followed where a defendant advances a defence on affidavit in proceedings brought by way of special summons where a plaintiff seeks an order for possession of mortgaged property. She held that the court should apply the test for summary judgment set out in cases such as *Aer Rianta CPT v Ryanair Ltd* [2001] 4 I.R. 607 and *Harrisrange Ltd v Duncan* [2003] 4 I.R. 1 and should ask itself whether the defendant had satisfied the court that there was a fair or reasonable probability that he had a real or bona fide defence.

TRIAL OF PROCEEDINGS

Application to stay proceedings until related actions are determined In *Kalix Fund Ltd v HSBC Institutional Trust Services (Ireland) Ltd* [2009] IEHC 457; unreported, High Court, Clarke J., October 16, 2009, Clarke J. gave guidance as to when it would be appropriate to stay (or defer) proceedings until the court gave its judgment in a related action. The proceedings before the court were among the 47 actions which were issued arising out of the collapse of Bernard L Madoff Investment Securities LLC. The defendants in one of the main actions sought an order directing that the majority of the actions should await the determination of the lead case. Clarke J. refused that application as it would have unnecessarily delayed most of the actions. Instead, he directed that the actions be case-managed by a single judge and that common issues tried and resolved in a speedy fashion. In the somewhat more straightforward case of *Kelly v Lennon* [2009] IEHC 320; unreported, High Court, Clarke J., July 2, 2009, Clarke J. stayed further prosecution of High Court proceedings prior to the determination of an arbitration which would have a significant bearing on the reliefs sought in the High Court proceedings.

Disjoinder of issues to be tried In *O'Flynn v Buckley* [2009] IESC 3; unreported, Supreme Court, January 22, 2009, the Supreme Court refused the Motor Insurers' Bureau of Ireland's ("MIBI") application to strike out proceedings which had been brought in breach of an obligation to sue the MIBI separately where it is alleged to have been a concurrent wrongdoer with a traced motorist who had a subsisting policy of insurance. Giving the judgment of the Supreme Court, Kearns J. held that it would have been more appropriate for the MIBI to have applied for a disjoinder of the issues to be determined at trial pursuant to Ord.18 r.1 of the Rules of the Superior Courts 1986 and that the approach pursued by it was unduly technical.

Application for a trial by jury In *Bradley v Maher* [2009] IEHC 389; unreported, High Court, Clarke J., July 31, 2009, the defendant applied for an order that the plaintiff's libel claim against him be tried by a judge and jury. The plaintiff objected on grounds that other aspects of its claim together with the defendant's entire counterclaim would have to be tried by a judge sitting without a jury, and that unnecessary duplication would arise. Clarke J. applied the decision of the Supreme Court in *Sheridan v Kelly* [2006] 1 I.R. 314 and held that although the court had a discretion to direct a hybrid trial which would involve the trial of certain issues before a jury and some without a jury (pursuant to Ord.36 r.7 of the Rules of the Superior Courts 1986), the balance of justice lay in favour of all issues being tried once before a judge sitting alone.

Application for the taking of an account Order 2 r.1(3) and Ord.37 r.13 of the Rules of the Superior Courts 1986 provide for the taking of an account. This relief is mainly sought in cases where an incumbrancer seeks an order for sale and in cases involving a partnership dispute, but in *Aforge Finance SAS v HSBC Institutional Trust Services (Ireland) Ltd* [2009] IEHC 565; unreported, High Court, Clarke J., December 21, 2009 it was argued that an investor in a fund related to Bernard L Madoff Investment Securities LLC was entitled to an order directing that an account be taken. Clarke J. directed that a preliminary issue be tried as to whether a fiduciary or trustee relationship existed such that the taking of an account would be appropriate. The judgment also sets out the procedure to be followed if the taking of an account is ordered.

AMENDMENT OF PLEADINGS

Adding a cause of action which would be statute-barred if pursued in separate proceedings In *Smyth v Tunney* [2009] IESC 5; unreported, Supreme Court, January 23, 2009 the plaintiff sought liberty to add allegations of the publication of a libel to further parties to its pleaded case, in circumstances where the amendments would have been statute-barred if pursued in separate proceedings. Finnegan J. followed the judgment of Keane J. in *Krops v Irish Forestry Board Ltd* [1995] 2 I.R. 113 and refused the plaintiff liberty to amend, stating that, "[f]acts may be added by amendment if they serve only to clarify the original claim but not if they are new facts". For similar reasons to the foregoing, Dunne J. in *Farrell v Coffey* [2009] IEHC 537; unreported, High Court, Dunne J., December 4, 2009 refused the plaintiff leave to amend the proceedings so as to convert a personal injuries action into a wrongful death action, in circumstances where new proceedings claiming damages for wrongful death would have been statute-barred.

Amendment of title of party to correct a clerical error Order 63 r.1(15) of the Rules of the Superior Courts 1986 allows for the making of an application to amend the title of a party to proceedings to correct a clerical error. If an order is granted under this rule that party is deemed to have been a party to the proceedings from the outset, and no limitation consequences arise by reason of the amendment. In *Sandy Lane Hotel Ltd v Times Newspapers Ltd* [2009] IESC 75; unreported, Supreme Court, November 14, 2009 the plaintiff instituted proceedings claiming damages for libel in June 1998. In 2005 the plaintiff brought an application in which it sought an order amending the title of the plaintiff to "Sandy Lane Hotel Co Limited". The company in whose name the proceedings had been brought was in fact the holding company of the correct plaintiff, following the renaming of a number of related companies in 1997. The Supreme Court refused the application, with Hardiman J. giving a narrow interpretation to Ord.63 r.1(15) in holding that a "clerical error" must involve "a mistake made in the course of a mechanical process such as writing or copying" as distinct from a mistake arising from "lack of knowledge, or wrong information, in the intellectual process of drafting language to express intentions". He held that the error in this case was not a clerical error but instead was due to a mistaken belief and a failure to ascribe any significance to the change of name in 1997.

NOTICE OF DISCONTINUANCE

Withdrawal of notice of discontinuance In *Smyth v Tunney* [2009] IESC 5; unreported, Supreme Court, January 23, 2009, the plaintiff in 1998 served a notice of discontinuance on a defendant to a libel case whom he had alleged was vicariously liable for the alleged libel. Following a finding of liability against that party in related proceedings in 2002 the plaintiff sought liberty to withdraw the notice of discontinuance. The Supreme Court held that the plaintiff was not entitled to withdraw the notice as it had been served as a result of a conscious and deliberate decision, although it did not go so far as to say that a notice of discontinuance could never be set aside.

Probate and Succession Law

DR ALBERT KEATING, BCL, LLB, LLM, DLitt, BL
Senior Lecturer WIT

INTRODUCTION

Section 8(1) of the Civil Liability Act 1961 provides that on the death of a person on or after the date of the passing of the Act all causes of action subsisting against him shall survive against his estate. Section 9(2) of the 1961 Act goes on to provide that no proceedings:

> … shall be maintainable in respect of any cause of action whatsoever which has survived against the estate of a deceased person unless either – (a) proceedings against him in respect of that cause of action were commenced within the relevant period and were pending at the date of death, or (b) proceedings are commenced in respect of that action within the relevant period or within the period of two years after his death, whichever period first expires.

The relevant period mentioned in s.9(2) means the period of limitation prescribed by the Statute of Limitations 1957. Until the judgment of O'Keeffe J. in *Prendergast v McLaughlin* [2009] IEHC 250 there were two differing views as to whether ss.8 and 9 of the 1961 Act applied to causes of action based in equity for which no period of limitation is prescribed in the Statute of Limitations 1957, and also, on the point in time at which such causes of action were maintainable and became subject to the period of limitation provided by s.9(2)(b). In *Corrigan v Martin*, unreported, March 13, 2006, Fennelly J. stated that s.8(1) of the 1961 Act governed all causes of action coming into existence right up to the point of death itself, and when referring to s.9(2)(a) and (b), that an action cannot be maintained unless the plaintiff can bring himself within one of the two sub-paragraphs. This is not affected by the fact that there is no "relevant period" for the purposes of the Statute of Limitations. He went on to say that he was satisfied that:

> "[T]he correct interpretation of the plaintiff's cause of action in the light of the section is that the obligation of the deceased was to perform the contract during his lifetime and not at the moment of his death. Hence, the cause of action was complete immediately before his death. It is unnecessary to decide how long before his death."

Barron J. in *Reidy v McGreevy*, unreported, High Court, December 3, 1986, held the view that whether a cause of action based on a constructive trust is one available against the deceased, and so capable of being barred after the lapse of two years from the date of his death, is dependent upon the facts of the case. But whatever the facts, "the claim could not be maintained until the death of the testator because it could not have been ascertained until then" that he had failed to honour his promise. But he added that if the testator had repudiated his promise in his lifetime this would have given rise to a cause of action at that stage. O'Keeffe J. in *Prendergast v McLaughlin* had the option of choosing either the analytical approach adopted by Fennelly J. in *Corrigan v Martin* or the equitable approach of Barron J. in *Reidy v McGreevy*. Apparently, he preferred the reasoning of Fennelly J.

Fennelly J.'s analysis In *Corrigan v Martin*, unreported, March 13, 2006, Fennelly J., when referring to s.8(1), stated that the Oireachtas intended that provision to apply to "all causes of action" coming into existence right up to the point of death itself, and when referring to s.9(2)(a) and (b), that an action cannot be maintained unless the plaintiff can bring himself within one of the two subparagraphs, in this case subpara.(b). He stated that:

> "This is not affected by the fact that there is no 'relevant period' for the purposes of the Statute of Limitations. The applicable period is the one that which 'first expires'. That may or may not be the two-year period. If the 'relevant period' expired within two years of death, the claim is barred. If there is no such period, it is barred after two years. I believe this interpretation is in accordance with common sense and the clear intention of the legislature."

In that case the plaintiff, a nephew of the deceased, was injured while working on the deceased's farm. The deceased was not insured and the deceased in consideration of the plaintiff forbearing to issue proceedings for the injury sustained agreed to transfer or devise his lands to the plaintiff. The plaintiff sought specific performance of the agreement outside of the limitation period prescribed by s.9(2)(b) of the 1961 Act. There is no "relevant period" in the Statute of Limitations 1957 limiting the time within which a specific performance suit must be instituted. Nevertheless, Fennelly J. categorised the plaintiff's cause of action as one falling within s.8 of the 1961 Act. He was satisfied that:

> "[T]he correct interpretation of the plaintiff's cause of action in the light of the section is that the obligation of the deceased was to perform the contract during his lifetime and not at the moment of his death. Hence, the cause of action was complete immediately before his death. It is unnecessary to decide how long before his death."

He was further satisfied that "the Oireachtas intended by the strong and clear language of section 9(2) to apply a maximum two year limitation period to all claims against the estates of deceased persons". He went on to say that it:

> "… is unreal and almost metaphysical to distinguish between causes of action existing immediately prior to the death and those which matured on the death itself. I do not believe that the Oireachtas can have intended to make such fine distinction. It would serve no useful purpose which has been identified in this case".

The courts favour the early vesting of estates, and he stated that:

> "[T]hose charged as executors or administrators of estates of deceased persons are entitled and, indeed, bound to carry out their tasks with reasonable expedition and that creditors of the estate and, ultimately, the beneficiaries are entitled to have the estate administered within a reasonable time. I believe the Oireachtas deliberately chose to impose a short but fair time limit on claims so that these desirable objectives would be achieved."

Barron J.'s resort to equity In *Reidy v McGreevy*, unreported, High Court, Barron J., December 3, 1986, the plaintiff, a son of the deceased, claimed remuneration for staying at home and working the deceased's land as a result of promises made by the deceased that if he worked the land the deceased would exercise a special power of appointment in his favour. No such power was exercised in the plaintiff's favour. The plaintiff based his claim on the existence of a constructive trust and one that was not defeated by the two-year time limit in s.9(2)(b) of the 1961 Act. Barron J., recognising that the plaintiff's claim was based upon the existence of a constructive trust as identified in *Re JR, A Ward of Court*, unreported, High Court, October 2, 1992 by Costello J., held that where "it would be unconscionable to disregard a promise such as that alleged here, the court will declare the existence of a constructive trust". He then addressed the question "whether such a claim is one available against the promisor and so capable of being barred after the lapse of two years from the date of death". He thought that the nature and extent of the claim was dependent upon the facts, but whatever the facts, "the claim could not be maintained until the death of the testator because it could not have been ascertained until then, that he had failed to honour his promise". However, he went on to say that, "if he had repudiated his promise in his lifetime, this would have given rise to a cause of action at that stage".

***Prendergast v McLaughlin* [2009] IEHC 250** In *Prendergast v McLaughlin* the plaintiff sought a declaration that he was entitled on the death of the deceased to the entire beneficial interest of the lands comprised in the estate of the deceased pursuant to promises made to him by the deceased during his lifetime that the interests in the lands would devolve to the plaintiff after his death and further pursuant to consideration given him by the plaintiff. The court, however, had first to determine as a preliminary issue whether the plaintiff's claim was statute-barred pursuant to the provisions of ss.8 and 9 of the Civil Liability Act 1961.

The following facts were agreed between the plaintiff and defendant for the purpose of determining the preliminary issue:

(i) The deceased and John Dempsey, a late brother of the deceased, were bachelors and even though the deceased owned another farm they lived together in a farmhouse and lands situate at Ballinamona, Clara, Co. Kilkenny.
(ii) The plaintiff assisted both the deceased and his late brother in working and maintaining the farmlands at Ballinamona for a period in excess of 25 years prior to the date of the death of the deceased. During this time the deceased and his brother repeatedly told him that the farmlands at Ballinamona would be left to him after they both had died. He relied upon these repeated promises and assurances and continued to provide assistance in the management and running of the farm at Ballinamona.
(iii) On or about the month of July 1998, a meeting took place between the deceased, his late brother John Dempsey, and another late brother William Dempsey, and the plaintiff. At that meeting, John Dempsey, the owner of the lands, stated he was leaving the lands in Ballinamona to the plaintiff. The deceased, John Dempsey and William Dempsey agreed to this arrangement and with this assurance the plaintiff continued to provide assistance in the working of the farm at Ballinamona. John Dempsey made a will on April 7, 1997 leaving the lands at Ballinamona to the deceased. He died on July 11, 2000.
(iv) Six or seven weeks before the death of the deceased he asked the plaintiff to visit him. The deceased informed the plaintiff during the course of this visit that he had given instructions to a solicitor to make a will leaving the farmlands at Ballinamona to the plaintiff. Thereafter, the plaintiff continued to assist the deceased with the management and maintenance of the farmlands at Ballinamona until his unexpected death on August 28, 2003. On or about July 2003, the deceased instructed his solicitor to make a draft will which was not executed by the deceased.
(v) The deceased died intestate on August 28, 2003, and the

defendant, a nephew of the deceased, extracted a grant of letters of administration intestate to his estate on February 27, 2006.

(vi) The proceedings did not issue until July 25, 2006.

It was submitted on behalf of the defendant that the plaintiff's cause of action was "a subsisting cause of action" within the meaning of s.8 of the Civil Liability Act 1961. It survived against the estate of the deceased as a claim based on the sole ground that the deceased failed to fulfil the alleged promise that he had made in his lifetime to leave certain farmlands to the plaintiff in consideration of the plaintiff continuing to assist him and his predeceased brother in their farming work. It was, therefore, a claim based on an alleged breach of contract and had been so pleaded. The deceased died on August 23, 2003 and as there was no proceedings in being at the time of his death, in order to come within the relevant limitation period provided by s.9 of the 1961 Act these proceedings ought to have been commenced within two years of that event, that is on or before August 22, 2005. Proceedings were not commenced until July 25, 2006. Hence, it was submitted that the plaintiff's claim was statute-barred under the provisions of s.9(2)(b) of the 1961 Act. Section 9 provides that no proceedings shall be maintained in respect of "any cause of action whatsoever which has survived against the estate of a deceased person" unless those proceedings come within paras (a) or (b). Reference was made to the words "any cause of action whatsoever" in s.9(2). It was submitted that the meaning of this phrase was clear and unambiguous and that the words should be given their natural and ordinary meaning in accordance with the norms of statutory interpretation. Reference was made to *DB v Minister for Health and Children* [2003] 3 I.R. 12, where the Supreme Court reiterated with approval the dicta of the Supreme Court in *Howard v Commissioners of Public Works* [1994] 1 I.R. 101, including the following passage from Denham J.:

> "Statutes should be construed according to the intention expressed in the legislation. The words used in the statute best declare the intent of the Act. Where the language of the statute is clear we must give effect to it, applying the basic meaning of the words."

It was further submitted that there was no necessity to look beyond the literal interpretation of the words in s.9(2) as they are clear and unambiguous. The phrase "any cause of action whatsoever" must include all actions that can be maintained by one person against another or howsoever arising including proceedings including equitable relief. The use of the word "whatsoever" brings all actions into account. The legislature intended to introduce an absolute time period outside of which the estate of the deceased person could not be troubled by litigation, notwithstanding the possible harshness that might occur. The plaintiff's cause of action in the proceedings, whether grounded in contract, quasi-contract or equity, fell within the statutory definition of "any cause of action whatsoever". The plaintiff's cause of action was founded in contract or quasi-contract. He was suing the defendant in his capacity as personal representative of the deceased for breach of the deceased's promise to bequeath the lands to him. That breach could only have occurred during the lifetime of the deceased, and the cause of action therefore accrued before the death of the deceased. Even in the event of the plaintiff basing his claim on promissory estoppel it would be a claim not arising after the death of the deceased, but a claim subsisting, because the claim can only be founded on some unconscionable conduct of the deceased during his lifetime.

The defendant relied on the decision of Fennelly J. in *Corrigan v Martin*, unreported, March 13, 2006 where the court held that a cause of action on foot of a promise to leave lands to a plaintiff was a cause of action subsisting at the date of death and consequently the provisions of s.9(2) applied. Fennelly J. categorised the plaintiff's cause of action as one falling within s.8(1) as follows:

> "Firstly, I am satisfied that the correct interpretation of the plaintiff's cause of action in the light of the section is that the obligation of the deceased was to perform the contract during his lifetime and not at the moment of death. Hence, the cause of action was complete immediately before his death. It is unnecessary to decide how long before the death. The cause of action, therefore, subsisted at the moment of death and survived against his estate by virtue of section 8(1). Secondly, I am satisfied that the Oireachtas intended by the strong and clear language of section 9(2) to apply a maximum two year period to all claims against the estates of deceased persons. Section 8(1) applies to 'all causes of action (other than excepted causes of action) subsisting against him' (none of the excepted cases is relevant). The Oireachtas intended that provision to apply to all causes of action coming into existence right up to the point of death itself. It is unreal and almost metaphysical to distinguish between causes of action existing immediately prior to the death and those which matured on the death itself. I do not believe that the Oireachtas can have intended to make such fine distinction. It would serve no useful purpose which has been identified in this case."

Fennelly J. dismissed the plaintiff's submission that as the Statute of Limitations 1957 did not impose a statutory limitation period for claims seeking specific performance, then s.9(2) did not apply to such claims as there is no relevant period within the meaning of s.9(1). The court held that s.9(2) was clear in that no action was maintainable unless it was instituted within the earlier of the time periods set out in s.9(2)(a) or (b).

Accordingly, it was submitted that the plaintiff's cause of action comes within s.9(2), and was not maintainable against the estate of the deceased since it fell outside of the relevant periods allowed under either paras (a) or (b) of s.9(2). The Act of 1961 allowed no exceptions based on equity.

The plaintiff submitted that his claim was to enforce the fulfilment of a promise upon which, for many years, he placed reliance by acting to his material detriment. The claim was based in equity as an equitable/proprietary/promissory estoppel giving rise to a constructive trust. The plaintiff referred to *McCarron v McCarron,* unreported, Supreme Court, February 13, 1997; *Basham v Basham* [1987] 1 All E.R. 405; *Bank of Ireland v O'Keeffe*, unreported, High Court, Barron J., December 3, 1986 but relied primarily on the decision of Barron J. in *Reidy v McGreevy*, reported, High Court, Barron J., December 3, 1986, dealing with a claim based upon the existence of a constructive trust in relation to a limitation period, especially the passage:

> "The claim based upon the existence of the constructive trust is covered by the decision of Costello J., in *J.R. a Ward of Court*, delivered on 2nd October, 1992. Where it would be unconscionable to disregard a promise such as that alleged here, the court will declare the existence of a constructive trust. The question that arises here is whether such a claim is one available against the promisor and so capable of being barred after the lapse of two years from the date of his death.
>
> The nature and extent of the claim is dependent upon the facts. What may be unconscionable upon one set of facts, may not be upon another set. So, depending upon the facts, the plaintiff may be entitled to an estate in property; to a charge over it; or to nothing. But whatever the facts, the claim could not be maintained until the death of the testator because it could not have been ascertained until then, that he had failed to honour his promise. Of course if he had repudiated his promise in his lifetime this would have given rise to a cause of action at that stage."

It was further submitted that a will speaks from death and that the failure of a will to satisfy a promise cannot speak any earlier. Any concept about wrong in law or equity involved both obligation and breach. The defendant's concept of limitation confused the two elements. Until the contingency in a promise is breached, no wrong has been done. The operation of s.9 of the 1961 Act was based on the survival of a subsisting cause of action against a deceased. Until the deceased died no cause of action arose. This was the fundamental logic that underlined the judgment of Barron J. in *Reidy v McGreevy.* No special principle of interpretation of s.9 was required. Its meaning was plain: where a person can be sued whilst alive, the claim must be issued within two years of his death at the latest. This was not changed merely because s.9 referred to "any cause of action whatsoever".

The plaintiff further submitted that the promise of inheritance created an interest equivalent to that of a beneficiary who has six years' right of action after death. There was no discordance in the availability of this period with any policy of finality. A personal representative can be sued on his contract for the same length of time, and if he distributes without regard to liabilities, he may likewise be sued. If the defendant argues that a period of two years manifested a policy for early closure of claims, the argument showed no awareness of the context of administration.

O'Keeffe J., however, found that the plaintiff's cause of action was primarily one based in contract or quasi-contract for breach of the deceased's promise to devise the lands to him. The breach could only have occurred during the lifetime of the deceased and the cause of action therefore accrued before the death of the deceased:

> "I also conclude, based on the agreed facts that the plaintiff's claim can alternatively be based on promissory estoppel or equity. As such it is not a claim arising after the death of the deceased but a claim subsisting at death, namely, the failure of the deceased to execute a will bequeathing the lands to the plaintiff during his lifetime. I do accept that the evidence relating to such cause of action emerged after death, the plaintiff's cause of action in contract, quasi-contract or in equity subsisted during the lifetime of the deceased. I reject the plaintiff's submission to the contrary."

He preferred the reasoning of Fennelly J. in *Corrigan v Martin* to that of Barron J. in *Reidy v McGreevy*. In *Corrigan v Martin*, Fennelly J. analysed in detail the interplay between ss.8 and 9 of the Act. There was no such analysis or examination of the two sections in *Reidy v McGreevy*. Referring to s.8(1), which applies to all causes of action, Fennelly J. stated that:

> "The Oireachtas intended that provision to apply to all causes of action coming into existence right up to the point of death itself. It is unreal and almost metaphysical to distinguish between causes of action existing immediately prior to the death and those which matured on the death itself."

When a cause of action had survived the estate of the deceased s.9(2) provided two alternative periods in paras (a) and (b), and (a) did not apply as no action was pending on the date of death of the deceased. The period provided under s.9(b) is the earlier of the relevant periods, being the expiry of the limitation period under the provisions contained in 1957 Act, or alternatively the period of two years from the date of death of the deceased. As the deceased died on August 28, 2003 proceedings ought to have been issued by August 27, 2005, the period of two years after the death of the deceased. The proceedings did not issue until July 25, 2006 and, accordingly, O'Keeffe J. held that the plaintiff's claim, whether it arose in contract, quasi-contract or in equity, was statute-barred.

Safety and Health

AIR AND WATER POLLUTION

Air pollution: burning of waste The Waste Management (Prohibition of Waste Disposal by Burning) Regulations 2009 (S.I. No. 286 of 2009) (the "2009 Regulations") prohibited the practice of burning of waste, by making it an offence to do so under waste legislation. The 2009 Regulations were expressed to be made under "sections 7, 18 and 39 of the Waste Management Acts 1996 to 2008", but this should, correctly, have been a reference to the relevant sections of the 1996 Act, as amended, since the use of the collective citation "Waste Management Acts 1996 to 2008" is meaningless in this context. The 2009 Regulations were also made under s.53 of the Air Pollution Act 1987.

Regulation 4(1) states: "Except as provided for in Regulation 5, a holder of waste shall not dispose of it by burning." Regulation 5 contains an exemption from the 2009 Regulations which enables farmers, as a last resort, to dispose of wastes generated by agricultural practices. Thus, reg.5 provides that the prohibition in reg.4:

> shall not apply when the following conditions are fulfilled—
>
> (a) the burning of waste relates solely to material consisting of uncontaminated (free of dangerous substances, preservatives or other artificial impregnation or coating) wood, trees, tree trimmings, leaves, brush, or other similar waste generated by agricultural practices, but excluding garden and park wastes and cemetery wastes and wastes arising from infrastructural development works, provided that such burning is done as a final measure following the application of the following waste hierarchy—
>
> (i) waste arisings are reduced in accordance with best agricultural practice,
>
> (ii) waste is reused where practicable,
>
> (iii) is recycled through shredding and use as compost or wood chippings, where practicable, and
>
> (iv) is salvaged for use as fuel where practicable.

The 2009 Regulations came into force on July 27, 2009.

Air pollution: heavy metals The Arsenic, Cadmium, Mercury, Nickel And Polycyclic Aromatic Hydrocarbons in Ambient Air Regulations 2009 (S.I. No. 58 of 2009), made under s.52 of the Air Pollution Act 1987, implemented Directive 2004/107 relating to arsenic, cadmium, mercury, nickel and polycyclic aromatic hydrocarbons in ambient air. The 2009 Regulations specify target values to be attained, from December 31, 2012, for concentrations of arsenic, cadmium, nickel and benzo(a)pyrene (a measurable indicator of the level of polycyclic aromatic hydrocarbons) and also specify monitoring requirements for mercury and other polycyclic aromatic hydrocarbons. The 2009 Regulations also require the Environmental Protection Agency (EPA) to assess the concentrations in the ambient air and deposition rates of the pollutants concerned and to undertake the monitoring necessary for this purpose. The EPA must also take the necessary measures, in consultation with local authorities and other bodies concerned, to address breaches of the target values but such measures should not involve disproportionate costs. The EPA must also ensure that other areas are maintained below the target values and endeavour to preserve the best ambient air quality compatible with sustainable development. The EPA must also send an annual report to the Minister for the Environment, Heritage and Local Government and to the European Commission. The 2009 Regulations also provide for the dissemination of public information, including information on any breaches of the target values, the reasons for the breaches, the area(s) in which they occurred and appropriate information regarding effects on health and impact on the environment.

Marine pollution The European Communities (Marine Equipment) Regulations 2009 (S.I. No. 259 of 2009) revoked and replaced the European Communities (Marine Equipment) Regulations 2003. They implemented Directive 96/98 on Marine Equipment, as amended by Directive 98/85, Directive 2001/53, Directive 2002/75, art.5 of Directive 2002/84 and Directive 2008/67. The European Communities Environmental Objectives (Surface Waters) Regulations 2009 (S.I. No. 272 of 2009) implemented Directive 2008/105 on environmental quality standards in the field of water policy, Directive 2000/60 on establishing a framework for Community action in the field of water policy (the Water Framework Directive) and Directive 2006/11 on pollution caused by certain dangerous substances discharged into the aquatic environment of the Community. The 2009 Regulations apply to all surface waters and provide for: the establishment of legally binding quality objectives for all surface waters and environmental quality standards for pollutants; the examination, and where appropriate, review of existing discharge authorisations by public authorities to ensure that the emission limits laid down in authorisations support compliance with the new water quality objectives/standards; the classification of surface water bodies by the EPA for the purposes of the 2000 Water Framework Directive; the establishment of inventories of priority substances by the EPA; and the drawing up of pollution reduction plans by coordinating local authorities (in consultation with the EPA) to reduce pollution by priority substances and to cease and/or phase out discharges, emissions or losses of priority hazardous substances. The 2009 Regulations also revoke and replace the Local Government (Water Pollution) Act 1977 (Water Quality Standards for Phosphorus) Regulations 1998 and the Water Quality (Dangerous Substances) Regulations 2001.

Water pollution: fertilisers/nitrates The European Communities (Good Agricultural Practice for Protection of Waters) Regulations 2009 (S.I. No. 101 of 2009) revoke and replace with amendments the European Communities (Good Agricultural Practice for Protection of Waters) Regulations 2006 and 2007, with effect from March 31, 2009. The 2009 Regulations implement Directive 91/676 concerning the content and monitoring of action programmes to combat nitrate pollution (the Nitrates Directive), as amended by Directive 2000/60 on establishing a framework for Community action in the field of water policy (the Water Framework Directive). The 2009 Regulations provide a statutory framework for good agricultural practice to protect waters against pollution from agricultural sources. They include measures such as: periods when land application of fertilisers is prohibited, limits on the land application of fertilisers, storage requirements for livestock manure, and monitoring of the effectiveness of the measures in terms of agricultural practice and impact on water quality.

CHEMICALS

Agricultural chemicals The European Communities (Authorization, Placing on the Market, Use and Control of Biocidal Products) (Amendment) Regulations 2009 (S.I. No. 84 of 2009) amended the European Communities (Authorization, Placing on the Market, Use and Control of Biocidal Products) Regulations 2001 in order to implement Directive 2008/75, Directive 2008/77, Directive 2008/78, Directive 2008/79, Directive 2008/80, Directive 2008/81, Directive 2008/85 and Directive 2008/86. These Directives added a number of chemicals used in the agriculture context which are regulated by Directive 98/8, which was implemented by the 2001 Regulations. The chemicals in question are: carbon dioxide, thiamethoxam, propiconazole, IPBC, cyclohexylhydroxydiazene 1-oxide, potassium salt (K-HDO), difenacoum, thiabendazole and tebuconazole. The 2009 Regulations came into force on March 11, 2009.

EXPLOSIVES

Cluster munitions and anti-personnel mines The Cluster Munitions and Anti-Personnel Mines Act 2008 (the "2008 Act") allowed for the ratification of the 2008 Convention on Cluster Munitions (which had been signed in Dublin on May 30, 2008 at the conclusion of an international conference on the subject). The 2008 Act also gave further effect to the 1997 Convention on the Prohibition of the Use, Stockpiling, Production and Transfer of Anti-Personnel Mines and on their Destruction. The 1997 Convention had already been implemented under the Explosives (Land Mines) Order 1996 (*Annual Review of Irish Law 1996*, p.530), made under the Explosives Act 1875.

It was explained during the Oireachtas debate on the 2008 Act that it should be seen against the general background of international humanitarian law, the branch of the law concerned with the conduct of armed conflict. Once an armed conflict begins, international humanitarian law applies to limit its effects, in particular by limiting the right of the parties to an armed conflict in their choice of methods and means of warfare. It also requires them to spare those who do not, or can no longer, take a direct part in hostilities, thereby protecting civilians in addition to captured and incapacitated combatants, from the effects of conflict. The basic rule of international humanitarian law in the protection of the civilian population in times of armed conflict is that the parties to the conflict must at all times distinguish between civilians and combatants and between civilian objects and military objectives. The rule permits them to direct their operations against combatants and military targets only. Indiscriminate attacks are prohibited. In that respect, where a weapon is incapable of distinguishing between civilian and combatant or where it is prone to use in such a manner that the effect is similar, it will tend to violate this general basic rule. It has been found, however, that just as with anti-personnel mines, the general rule has not been sufficient in itself to prevent the atrocious humanitarian consequences arising from the use of cluster munitions. A number of states continued to insist that it was possible to observe the basic rule and still use cluster munitions. This was the background to the development of the "Oslo process" in which a number of states, including Ireland, joined together to prepare a new instrument of international humanitarian law dealing specifically with cluster munitions, culminating in the 2008 Convention on Cluster Munitions.

It was pointed out in the debate on the 2008 Act that, historically, cluster bombs have had significant humanitarian consequences in every conflict in which they have been used, and they have repeatedly caused excessive harm to civilians. Among the first uses of cluster munitions was an attack on Grimsby during the Second World War, where many civilians were killed and injured by munitions that had not exploded upon impact. The weapons subsequently formed part of NATO arsenals during the Cold War. They were used on an enormous scale during the Vietnam War, with Laos, which was not even a declared participant in that war, becoming the most affected country in the world. In excess of 260 million sub-munitions were dropped during that conflict and at its end it was estimated that 80 million of them were left unexploded. They continue to cause civilian casualties, restrict access to land and impede social and economic development in that country. Cluster munitions were also used extensively during the conflict in the 1990s in Kosovo. Almost 235,000 sub-munitions were dropped across the region against a range of mobile and static targets during the NATO campaign in 1999. Human Rights Watch has documented 75 civilian deaths and injuries as a direct result of cluster munitions during the bombing campaign. They continued to affect civilians there even after hostilities had ceased. By 2008, at least 152 post-conflict casualties are estimated to have been caused by unexploded bomblets.

The primary purpose of the 2008 Act is to create offences in respect of the use, development, production, acquisition, stockpiling, retention or transfer of cluster munitions and explosive bomblets as required under the convention. Similar provision is made for anti-personnel mines which, as already mentioned, gives further effect to the 1997 Convention on the Prohibition of the Use, Stockpiling, Production and Transfer of Anti-Personnel Mines and on their Destruction.

Section 2 of the 2008 Act defines the key terms in the Act, notably, a cluster munition, an explosive bomblet and an anti-personnel mine. These are identical to the definitions in the 1997 and 2008 Conventions. Section 5 empowers the Minister for Foreign Affairs to declare by order which states are parties to the 2008 Convention on Cluster Munitions. This is necessary for the purposes of co-operation with those states under s.7 of the 2008 Act. A similar provision enabling the Minister to declare by order the states parties to the 1997 anti-personnel mine ban convention is made in s.8.

Section 6 makes it a criminal offence, with certain exceptions set out in s.7, to use, develop, produce, acquire, possess, retain or transfer a cluster munition or an explosive bomblet. It is also an offence to assist, encourage or induce the commission of such an offence. Any such act committed outside the State on board an Irish ship or aircraft or by a member of the defence forces is also an offence. Section 6 gives effect to the requirement under art.9 of the 2008 Convention to take all appropriate measures to implement the convention, including the imposition of penal sanctions to prevent and suppress any prohibited activity.

In accordance with the 2008 Convention, s.7 permits certain acts that might otherwise be offences under s.6, namely, retention or acquisition of a limited number of cluster munitions or explosive bomblets for development of and training in detection, clearance and destruction of these munitions, or for the development of counter-measures. This is in accordance with art.3 of the convention. It also provides for their possession in the context of criminal investigations or proceedings and their transfer to the defence forces or another state party for the purposes of their destruction.

Provision is also made to enable the defence forces to participate in United

Nations mandated peacekeeping forces with a state or states that may not be party to the 2008 Convention on Cluster Munitions, in accordance with art.21 of the 2008 Convention. This is the so-called "interoperability" provision of the Convention which, it was noted during the Oireachtas debate on the 2008 Act, had been "the most difficult issue to resolve in the negotiations" in the final 2008 conference in Dublin leading up to the signing of the Convention. Section 7(4) of the 2008 Act ensures that future participation by the defence forces in UN-mandated peacekeeping operations will be consistent with the Convention. Its purpose is to ensure that no member of the defence forces, while serving abroad with military personnel of states that are not party to the Convention, such as in a UN peacekeeping mission, may find himself or herself criminally liable for an inadvertent, unintended or unavoidable act that might otherwise be an offence. The 2008 Act makes clear that under no circumstances may he or she expressly request the use of cluster munitions. It was stated during the Oireachtas debate that "it is very unlikely that section 7(4) of the [Act] will ever be invoked."

Section 9 makes the use, development, production, acquisition, possession, retention or transfer of an anti-personnel mine an offence, in accordance with art.9 of the 1997 Anti-Personnel Mine Ban Convention. Certain exceptions are permitted, in accordance with the Convention, and these are provided for in s.10.

Sections 11 to 15 of the 2008 Act (which was added to the Act during its passage through the Oireachtas) provides that any statutory investment mandate is qualified by a requirement to exclude investments in the manufacturers of cluster munitions and anti-personnel mines. They set down the requirement to avoid initial investments of public monies directly or indirectly in manufacturers of prohibited munitions. They also set out clear requirements and guidelines for dealing with circumstances where such investments occur despite best efforts to avoid them.

Section 17 provides for penalties to be imposed upon summary conviction and conviction on indictment of an offence under s.6 (relating to cluster munitions) and s.9 (relating to anti-personnel mines). The maximum penalty for conviction on indictment is 10 years' imprisonment and/or a fine of €1,000,000. Section 18 is a standard provision to ensure that corporate bodies do not avoid responsibility for conduct prohibited to individuals. Section 19 allows for the forfeiture of items to the State and is necessary to ensure that a cluster munition, explosive bomblet or anti-personnel mine seized during the investigation of a suspected offence is not returned to a claimant under the Police (Property) Act 1897 but is sent for destruction. Section 19(2) allows the court to recover from the offender the cost of destroying cluster munitions or anti-personnel mines following a successful prosecution.

Identification and traceability of explosives for civil uses The European Communities (System for the Identification and Traceability of Explosives for Civil Uses) Regulations 2009 (S.I. No. 133 of 2009) implemented Directive 2008/43 setting up, pursuant to Directive 93/15, a system for the identification and traceability of explosives for civil uses. The 2009 Regulations also amended the European Communities (Placing on the Market and Supervision of Explosives for Civil Uses) Regulations 1995 (*Annual Review of Irish Law 1995*, p.438). The 1995 Regulations had implemented the 1993 Directive, which as the title of the 1995 Regulations makes clear, deals with the regulation of placing on the market and supervision of explosives for civil uses. The aim of the 2008 Directive is to strengthen the control of explosives for civil uses, which in turn is connected with helping to combat terrorism. The 2009 Regulations require the unique labelling of explosives in accordance with the requirements in the Schedule to the Regulations. Manufacturers, traders and users of explosives are also required to tighten record keeping and stock management. This should allow the identification and traceability of an explosive from its production site and its first placing on the market until its final user and use, thereby assisting in the prevention of theft and ensuring that any thefts or losses are quickly detected. Penal sanctions for those who contravene the 1995 and 2009 Regulations are prescribed (and in the case of the 1995 Regulations were increased by the 2009 Regulations): on summary conviction, a fine not exceeding €5,000 and/or 12 months' imprisonment; on conviction on indictment, a fine not exceeding €20,000 and/or three years' imprisonment. In accordance with the timeframe laid down in the 2008 Directive, the 2009 Regulations come into force on April 5, 2012.

MANUFACTURING STANDARDS

Cosmetics The European Communities (Cosmetic Products) (Amendment) Regulations 2009 (S.I. No. 191 of 2009) further amended the European Communities (Cosmetic Products) Regulations 2004 in order to implement Directive 2008/88, Directive 2008/123 and Directive 2009/6 with a view to improving the safety of cosmetic products. The 2009 Regulations came into force on May 21, 2009.

Medical equipment The European Communities (Active Implantable Medical Devices) (Amendment) Regulations 2009 (S.I. No. 109 of 2009) amended the European Communities (Active Implantable Medical Devices) Regulations 1994 in order to give effect to Directive 2007/47. Similarly, the European Communities (Medical Devices) (Amendment) Regulations 2009 (S.I. No. 110 of 2009) amended the European Communities (Medical Devices) Regulations 1994 in order to give effect to Directive 2007/47.

SAFETY, HEALTH AND WELFARE AT WORK

Prosecutorial delay In *J Harris Assemblers v Director of Public Prosecutions* [2009] IEHC 344, Hedigan J. refused to prohibit, on grounds of delay, the trial on indictment of the applicant (an unlimited company) under the Safety, Health and Welfare at Work Act 1989 (since replaced by the Safety, Health and Welfare at Work Act 2005: *Annual Review of Irish Law 2005*, pp.604–618). The case arose against the following chronological background. In January 2000, the applicant company sold a Hino Grab/Crane Lorry (the lorry) to South Midland Construction Co Ltd (the SMC Group). In November 2002, while in the ownership of the SMC Group, the lorry was involved in a fatal accident. As a result of this, the lorry was inspected by a Health and Safety Authority (HSA) inspector on the same date. In November 2003, the Director of Public Prosecutions directed the HSA to initiate a prosecution under the 2005 Act against the SMC Group. In April and June 2004, the lorry underwent further inspection by the HSA inspector. Also in June 2004, the HSA inspector met representative employees of the applicant company. Both employees furnished statements to the HSA inspector, prior to which no caution was administered. Later in June 2004, the HSA inspector carried out another inspection of the lorry, during which he observed that the top proximity sensors of the crane feature on the lorry were absent from their proper location. In September 2004, a further meeting was held between the HSA inspector and the same representative employees of the applicant company. Again no caution was administered. In early October 2004 the HSA inspector's investigation file in respect of the applicant was passed to the HSA's prosecution committee for review. It was then forwarded to the HSA's legal department in late October 2004.

In May 2005, in *People (DPP) v South Midland Construction Co Ltd*, the SMC Group pleaded guilty in the Circuit Criminal Court to charges of breaching ss.6(1) and 6(2) of the Safety, Health and Welfare at Work Act 1989 (general duties of employers: see now s.8 of the Safety, Health and Welfare at Work Act 2005), and was fined €100,000. In December 2005 the review of the HSA inspector's investigation file by the HSA's legal department was completed and it was transmitted to the office of the Chief Prosecution Solicitor, which is part of the Office of the Director of Public Prosecutions (DPP). In February 2006, the Chief Prosecution Solicitor's office requested further information on behalf of the DPP and, as a result, a series of additional statements were taken during March and April 2006. In May 2006, the HSA replied to the office of the Chief Prosecution Solicitor with the information that had been requested. In June 2006 a further request for information on behalf of the DPP was made and, in November 2006, the HSA supplied the information.

In January 2007, the DPP issued directions to proceed with the prosecution of the applicant. The DPP also directed that additional evidence should be gathered and this was duly compiled and forwarded to the DPP in April 2007. Later in April 2007, summonses relating to the sale of the lorry were issued by the District Court and were served on the applicant company in June 2007. They contained the following charges:

(a) That the applicant, being a supplier within the meaning of the 1989 Act, and a person to whom section 10(1) thereof applies, did, on or around the 4th of September, 2003, fail to take such steps as were necessary to secure that persons supplied by the applicant with the lorry were provided with adequate information about the use for which it had been designed or had been tested and about any conditions relating to the lorry so as to ensure that when in use, dismantled or disposed of it would be safe and without risk to health, contrary to section 10(1)(b) and section 48(1)(a) of the 1989 Act; and

(b) That the applicant, being a supplier within the meaning of the 1989 Act, and a person to whom section 10(1) thereof applies, did, on or around the 4th of September, 2003, supply the lorry and did fail to ensure that it was designed, constructed, tested and examined so as to be safe and without risk to health when used by a person in a place of work, contrary to section 10(1)(b) and section 48(1)(a) of the 1989 Act.

In December 2007, a book of evidence was served on the applicant and the case was sent forward to the Circuit Criminal Court for trial on indictment. The applicant sought disclosure of certain documents from the DPP and, following a lengthy period of correspondence, this request was ultimately acceded to in July 2008. In October 2008, the applicant was given leave to apply for an order of prohibition in respect of that pending trial.

The applicant argued that the DPP had acted in breach of its right to natural and constitutional justice in failing to initiate the prosecution within a reasonable time. The applicant company argued that this was inexcusable and unwarranted in the circumstances and had resulted in prejudice to the applicant in the preparation of its defence to the charges. As already indicated, Hedigan J. rejected this argument. He referred with approval to the decision of the Supreme Court in *Devoy v Director of Public Prosecutions* [2008] IESC 13, in which Kearns J. had set out the following applicable principles:

"(a) Inordinate, blameworthy or unexplained prosecutorial delay may breach an applicant's constitutional entitlement to a trial with reasonable expedition.

(b) Prosecutorial delay of this nature may be of such a degree that a court will presume prejudice and uphold the right to an expeditious trial by directing prohibition.

(c) Where there is a period of significant blameworthy prosecutorial delay less than that envisaged at (b), and no actual prejudice is demonstrated, the court will engage in a balancing exercise between the community's entitlement to see crimes prosecuted and the applicant's right to an expeditious trial, but will not direct prohibition unless one or more of the elements referred to in *P.M. v Malone* [2002] 2 I.R. 560 and *P.M. v Director of Public Prosecutions* [2006] 3 I.R. 172 are demonstrated.

(d) Actual prejudice caused by delay which is such as to preclude a fair trial will always entitle an applicant to prohibition."

Applying these principles, Hedigan J. stated that, first, the prosecutorial delay in question was not so severe as to merit, by itself, an order of prohibition. The delay between September 2003, when the alleged offences were said to have occurred, and April 2007, when the summonses were ultimately served, was "undoubtedly a lapse of time deserving of the court's attention but does not seem to be so egregiously lengthy as to entitle the applicant to the relief sought without any further consideration of the circumstances." Hedigan J. therefore considered whether any specific prejudice had arisen as against the applicant which had affected, or would affect in the future, its ability to defend the criminal charges in question. In this regard, Hedigan J. noted that there were no problems relating to the unavailability of witnesses or of documentary evidence. Indeed, he noted that two of the applicant's employees were capable of providing quite detailed recollections, on affidavit, of the events surrounding the sale of the lorry, for the purposes of the present proceedings.

He then went on to apply the balancing test set out by the Supreme Court in the *Devoy* case. Hedigan J. commented:

> "In doing so, the court must weigh the community's entitlement to see that criminal offences do not go unpunished against the applicant's right to an expeditious trial in due course of law. This exercise must, of course, be performed in view of the circumstances of the case as a whole."

Hedigan J. accepted that the delay in the present case was a significant one, and one which had not been contributed to by any fault on the part of the applicant. However, in Hedigan J.'s view, a considerable portion of the period which elapsed prior to the service of the summonses has been adequately explained in the affidavit of the HSA inspector involved in the case. He accepted that diligent investigations were taking place between April and October 2004, and that almost the entire calendar year of 2006 was spent obtaining further evidence and directions in respect of the then possible prosecution of the applicant. The period of 14 months from October 2004 until December 2005, however, was explained only by virtue of a backlog of work within the HSA's legal department. In Hedigan J.'s view, this was not a satisfactory justification and amounted to a prima facie violation of the applicant's right to an expeditious trial.

The question then in the present case was whether this inexcusable delay was sufficient to overpower the community interest in seeing a prosecution occur. Hedigan J. stated that the offence with which the applicant was charged was undoubtedly a serious one, and that the prosecution of corporations and individuals who culpably engage in the supply of such hazardous devices is a matter of the utmost public importance. On this basis, he could not accept that the period of blameworthy delay which did occur in the present case was of sufficient gravity to warrant the prohibition of the applicant's trial. He added that "the importance of safety in the workplace is a consideration of the utmost importance in contemporary society". On these grounds, as already indicated, Hedigan J. refused to make the order of prohibition.

Road works and enforcement notices In *Cork County Council v Health and Safety Authority* [2008] IEHC 304, Hedigan J. held that the Health and Safety Authority (HSA) was empowered under s.66 of the Safety, Health and Welfare at Work Act 2005 (the "2005 Act") (*Annual Review of Irish Law 2005*, pp.604–618) to serve enforcement orders connected with roadworks at a time where roadworks were actually being carried out or were imminent, but not otherwise. The HSA had, under s.66 of the 2005 Act, served an improvement notice on Cork County Council requiring it to put in place improved procedures and control measures concerning the use of dense bitumen macadam (DBM) road surface on roads and other incomplete surface dressings outside 60 km speed limit zones. The improvement notice in this case came against the background of concerns that a number of road fatalities had occurred in the State arising from the use of DBM by various local authorities (acting as road authorities as defined in the Roads Act 1993) as a road surface dressing. The HSA's approach was based on its concern that, first, a DBM surface was unsafe for road users, and secondly, that workers "on site" would be, or could be, endangered when the final road surface was applied if correct traffic control measures were not in place. Cork County Council appealed the making of the improvement notice to the District Court under s.66 of the 2005 Act and the judge then stated a case to the High Court setting out a number of questions of law. It was acknowledged that this was, in effect, a test case that would determine a series of similar improvement notices that had been served by the HSA on other local authorities in respect of DBM.

In approaching the case, Hedigan J. pointed out that the 2005 Act is a penal statute because it imposes a criminal sanction for non-compliance. This being so, under the relevant rules of statutory interpretation, it must be strictly interpreted, that is, it must be interpreted as having no more scope than the relevant words—in this case in s.6 of the 2005 Act—appear to mean. Furthermore, Hedigan J. also held that any improvement notice issued under the 2005 Act must be so clearly drafted as to leave the recipient in no reasonable doubt as to what actions are required for compliance. He referred to the comments of O'Neill J. in *Dundalk Town Council v Lawlor* [2005] 2 I.L.R.M. 106 at 112, where he had considered the validity of a planning enforcement notice:

> "[I]t [is] imperative that the precise steps required by the council be set out with precision and clarity because in the absence of that being done it becomes difficult to the point of impossible for a person served with the notice to know how far they must go in order to ensure compliance with an enforcement notice and hence the avoidance of criminal liability. If the steps required are not set out with precision and clarity the person served with the notice may find themselves having to guess or speculate as to what they must do to achieve compliance."

One of the complaints made by the Council in this case was that the HSA was not entitled to serve the improvement notice in this case because it was focused primarily on the safety of road users, rather than of workers. The Council therefore argued that the use of s.6 of the 2005 Act in this case was outside the "dominant purpose" of the 2005 Act, the Long Title to which the Council pointed out had also referred to its purpose being to implement Directive 89/391, the 1989 EU "Framework" Directive on safety and health at work. Hedigan J. agreed that this argument by the Council "must be correct". He added (at para.24):

> "It is clear that the dominant purpose for which the [HSA has] issued the improvement notice is the protection of road users from a DBM surface which it considers to be unsafe, because it does not have sufficient skid resistance. The concentration on traffic control and monitoring on the site of possible future works whilst indeed a laudable concern is, it seems to me, essentially governed by the purpose of ensuring a certain final road dressing is laid. This dominant purpose has nothing to do with the safety and welfare of workers at work and is not in my judgment, a purpose within the scope of the [2005] Act."

On one reading of the final sentence of this passage, it is arguable that Hedigan J. appears to indicate that the safety of road users is not contemplated by the 2005 Act, or of the 1989 Directive on safety and health at work which, as indicated, it implements. If so, this would be an incorrect view of the scope of the 2005 Act (a point discussed in more detail below). A better view of this sentence is that it merely states that, in the particular circumstances of this case, the focus on road users was impermissible. This appears to be the approach Hedigan J. took in an earlier passage where he stated (at para.22):

> "[The HSA] addressed [itself] to safety issues arising while DBM surfaces were in use between phases of work, that is, after the site of roadworks that had existed had been demobilised and the road opened to traffic but before a final surface was laid. During that period of time no road workers would be on site. In fact no site would exist."

This appears to make clear that the problem in the present case was that no work was being carried on at the time. To some extent, however, Hedigan J. reverts later in his judgment to his view that the HSA can never contemplate risks to road users and must limit its concern to "workers". In this respect, having quoted the definition of "place of work" in s.2 of the 2005 Act as including "any place… land or other location at, in, upon or near which, work is carried on whether occasionally or otherwise" he comments (at para.25):

> "The [2005] Act at such time and place is therefore, in my view, applicable and the HSA may give such directions as are within the scope of the Act and for a purpose prevailed therein, that is, the health and safety of workers at work."

In this passage Hedigan J. appears to conflate the concept of "place of work" with "place where workers are at work". This is simply not what the 2005 Act states, and as already indicated the scope of the 2005 Act, extends well beyond the protection of employees. This is made clear in a number of provisions in the 2005 Act. Thus, s.11 of the 2005 Act (which implemented art.8 of the 1989 EU Directive 89/391 already referred to) requires employers to ensure contact with the emergency services. Even more clearly, s.12 of the 2005 Act imposes a specific duty on employers to ensure the safety, health and welfare of "individuals at the place of work (*not being his or her employees*)". Section 15 imposes duties on those in control of places of work to "persons other than employees". In the specific context of the *Cork County Council* case, which concerned a construction project, s.17 of the 2005 Act imposes specific duties on those involved in commissioning a construction project to ensure that, among other matters, it "can be maintained safely and without risk during subsequent use". Section 17(4) provides that a construction project "means any development which includes *or is intended to include* construction work". Section 17(4) thus expressly contemplates the concept that intended future work, not merely current work, comes within the scope of the 2005 Act. Sections 19 and 20 of the 2005 Act, which concern risk assessment and the preparation of a safety statement (in effect, a safety and health management plan) also require employers to include persons other than employees within the ambit of their analysis. These provisions of the 2005 Act make clear that its scope extends beyond the protection of employees and has a wider remit. To that extent Hedigan J. appears to have misread the scope of the 2005 Act.

Nonetheless, it may be that, in the specific manner and circumstances that arose in the *Cork County Council* case, the HSA may be said to have been acting at the edge of the scope of its powers, bearing in mind that at the time it served the notice it is arguable that no roadworks were in place. As already indicated, Hedigan J. held that the HSA was empowered under s.66 of the Safety, Health and Welfare at Work Act 2005 to serve a notice but not necessarily in the circumstances that arose.

The *Cork County Council* case involved 16 separate points of law and Hedigan J. addressed each in turn towards the end of his judgment. The numbering used in the case is followed in the summary that follows.

Q1. Whether s.66 of the Safety, Health and Welfare at Work Act 2005 applies to a local authority. Hedigan J. stated that it was agreed that this question should be amended by the addition of the words "in respect of roadworks carried on by it or on its behalf". He held that the answer to this question was yes but only where there are roadworks in being or imminent and only in respect of the safety of workers on site and road users present or likely to be present at the locus in quo.

Q2. Whether the Health and Safety Authority (HSA) has the power to direct a roads authority as to the manner in which it performs its duties under that Act, whether in circumstances where the National Roads Authority has overall responsibility for the planning and supervision of works for the construction and maintenance of national roads, or at all. Q7. Does the HSA have power under the 2005 Act to issue an improvement notice to roads authorities in respect of the exercise of their statutory functions with respect to the performance of roadworks? Hedigan J. dealt with Q2 and Q7 together. He held that whilst it is the case that s.17 of the Roads Act 1993 grants overall responsibility to the National Roads Authority (NRA) for the planning and supervision of works for the construction and maintenance of national roads, nonetheless, s.13(1) of the 1993 Act expressly provides that, subject to Pt 3, the construction and maintenance of all national and regional roads shall be a function of the council of that county. Thus, whilst planning and supervision of works are a duty assigned to the NRA, maintenance and construction of roads remain a function of the county council. Thus, the answer is yes but subject to the same conditions as set out in answer 1.

Q3. Whether the improvement notice issued by the HSA and served on Cork County Council complied with the provisions of the Safety, Health and Welfare at Work Act 2005, and in particular s.66 thereof, whether on the basis that the improvement notice is sufficiently precise, or otherwise. Q4. May the HSA serve an improvement notice on the basis that the contents of a revised improvement plan are inadequate? Hedigan J. dealt with Q3 and Q4 together and held that, as reasoned above the answer to both was no.

Q5. Does the HSA have power under the 2005 Act to issue an improvement notice in respect of works not in being at the date of issue of the improvement notice? Q6. Does the HSA have power under the 2005 Act to issue an improvement notice in respect of works to come into being after the date of issue of improvement notice? Hedigan J. dealt with Q5 and Q6 together. He held that, it being a necessary pre-condition that an activity (in this case roadworks) is occurring or likely to occur, there must be some clear prospect of activity about to commence. The mere possibility of such activity is not enough. The answer, therefore, was yes but on condition the activity the subject matter of the notice is clearly in prospect and is not merely a possibility.

Q8. Does the HSA have power under the 2005 Act to issue an improvement notice applicable to a type of activity generally as opposed to an actual instance(s) of that activity? Hedigan J. held that because an improvement notice carries a penal sanction for non-compliance, it needs to specify clearly what action is required to be taken in order to avoid incurring criminal liability. A notice addressing itself to a type of activity generally as opposed to a specific activity does not seem capable of doing so. The answer therefore was no. This approach is consistent with the view taken by Murphy J., in the context of fire safety notices served under the Fire Services Act 1981, in *Transactus Investments Ltd v Dublin Corporation* [1985] I.R. 501, discussed in Byrne, *Safety, Health and Welfare at Work Law in Ireland*, 2nd edn (Nifast, 2008), p.540.

Q9. Is a road on which works have ceased for a significant period between phases of surfacing works and opened to traffic during that period, "a place of work" within the meaning of the 2005 Act? Q11. Is a road on which works have ceased for a significant period between phases of surfacing works and opened to traffic during that period a place at which work is "being carried on" within the meaning of the 2005 Act? Hedigan J. dealt with Q9 and Q11 together and held that for the reasons set out above the answer to both questions was no.

Q10. Does the HSA have power under the 2005 Act to issue an improvement notice in respect of a locus which is not a "place of work" within the meaning of the 2005 Act? Hedigan J. noted that it was agreed by the parties that the answer to this question was no.

Q12. Does the HSA have power under the 2005 Act to issue an improvement notice in respect of a locus at which works are not in the course of being carried on? Hedigan J. held that, as noted above, where an activity (such as roadworks) is occurring or is clearly in prospect, then the HSA does have power to issue an improvement notice. As further noted above it is not enough that such activity is a mere possibility, it must be clearly in prospect. The answer therefore was yes, subject to a condition of clear imminence.

Q13. Does the HSA have power under the 2005 Act to issue an improvement notice in respect of risks to persons where such risks arise other than in the course of work being carried on? Hedigan J. held that in light of the above other answers and the reasons given, the HSA may issue an improvement notice in respect of risks to persons which are likely to arise from a course of work which is likely to be carried on. As further noted above, this means work that is clearly in prospect as opposed to work which is a mere possibility.

Q14. Does the HSA have power under the 2005 Act to issue an improvement notice in respect of risks to members of the public where such persons' presence at the locus is not connected to the performance of works thereat? In answering this question, Hedigan J. referred to s.12 of the 2005 Act which requires employers to manage their undertaking in such a way as to avoid risk to individuals at the place of work who are not his or her employees. He also referred to s.65(1) of the 2005 Act, which provides for the power of a HAS inspector to require an improvement plan where of the opinion there is a risk to the safety, health and welfare "*of persons*". In both instances, Hedigan J. concluded that it seems clear that:

> "[W]hether it is the individual contemplated by section 12 or the person provided for by section 65(1), no requirement exists that their presence be connected to the performance of works at the locus in quo. The power of the HSA to issue an improvement notice arises simply from their presence at the locus in quo under section 12 and their existence simpliciter under section 65."

The answer to the question posed was, therefore, yes.

Q15. Does the HSA have power under the 2005 Act to issue an improvement notice to a roads authority in respect of works by an independent contractor to such roads authority? Hedigan J. held that, in respect of the power to issue an improvement notice under s.66(1) of the 2005 Act, the person upon whom the notice may be served is the person who has control over the activity concerned. Where roadworks are being carried out by independent contractors, the local authority in question is not "a person … who has control over the activity concerned" and there is consequently no power to issue an improvement notice under s.66(1) in those circumstances.

Q16. Does s.66(1) of the 2005 Act confer on the HSA an entitlement to serve an improvement notice on a person who is not the addressee of s.12 of the 2005 Act? In answer to this final question in the case stated, Hedigan J. stated that the addressee of s.12 of the 2005 Act is every employer who is managing and conducting his or her undertaking. He held that the purpose of s.12 is to extend the duties imposed on employers by the 2005 Act to persons who, although present at the place of work, are not employees. He concluded that the clear reference in s.12 is to those employers who are exercising such level of control as enables them to meet the obligations imposed by those duties. He also concluded that there would seem little point in serving an improvement notice on a person who is not in a position to comply therewith and the 2005 Act should not be interpreted thus. The answer therefore to this question was no.

In conclusion, the decision of Hedigan J. in the *Cork County Council* case involved important clarifications of the scope of the HSA's enforcement powers under the 2005 Act. It clarified that the HSA retains, under the 2005 Act, important regulatory powers in this area which are very different to those of the NRA under the Roads Act 1993. It also confirms that road works are often to be regarded as a "place of work" under the 2005 Act, as the wide definition of "place of work" in s.2 of the 2005 Act had already made clear. Indeed, road works also fall clearly within the definition of "construction project" in s.17 of the 2005 Act, discussed above, and the Safety, Health and Welfare at Work (Construction) Regulations 2006 (*Annual Review of Irish Law 2006*, pp.516–521). Moreover, reg.97 of the 2006 Regulations, which contains detailed requirements concerning road signage and related matters, has been amended in important respects since the improvement notices in the *Cork County Council* case were served: see the Safety Health and Welfare at Work (Construction) (Amendment) (No. 2) Regulation 2008 (*Annual Review of Irish Law 2008*, p.569). In that respect, it is important to note that the *Cork County Council* case has provided important guidance on the limits of the HSA's regulatory powers under s.66 of the 2005 Act. Equally, however, Hedigan J.'s judgment reiterates the very wide scope of the duties imposed by the 2005 Act on employers and others having control over places of work, including road works, and that these duties apply not just to employees but also to members of the public, including road users.

RADIOLOGICAL SAFETY

Radioactive waste shipments The European Communities (Supervision and

Control of Certain Shipments of Radioactive Waste and Spent Fuel) Order 2009 (S.I. No. 86 of 2009) was, unusually, made under the powers conferred both by s.3 of the European Communities Act 1972, as amended by s.2 of the European Communities Act 2007, and by ss.9(1) and 30 of the Radiological Protection Act 1991. The 2009 Order implemented Directive 2006/117/Euratom, and it also revoked and replaced the European Communities (Supervision and Control of Certain Shipments of Radioactive Waste) Regulations 1994 (*Annual Review of Irish Law 1994*, p.407). The 1994 Regulations had implemented Directive 92/3/Euratom, which was repealed and replaced by Directive 2006/117/Euratom. The 2006 Directive and the 2009 Order impose conditions for the supervision and control of shipments of radioactive waste and spent fuel between Member States and into and out of the Community whenever quantities and concentrations of such waste exceed certain levels. The 2009 Order designates the Radiological Protection Institute of Ireland (RPII) as the competent authority for the purpose of the 2006 Directive, including for the purpose of all authorisations required under the 2009 Order.

The 2009 Order also greatly increased the penalties for offences under its terms by comparison with the 1994 Regulations: on summary conviction, a fine not exceeding €5,000 and/or three months' imprisonment; on conviction on indictment, a fine not exceeding €500,000 and/or three years' imprisonment. This increase in penalties explains the invocation of the European Communities Act 1972, as amended by the European Communities Act 2007, in the preamble to the 2009 Order. The 1972 Act, as amended by the 2007 Act, expressly enabled Regulations made under its terms to create indictable offences, with the associated greater penalties permissible in that context (see *Annual Review of Irish Law 2007*, p.404). It is notable that the preamble to the 2009 Order states that the Minister for the Environment, Heritage and Local Government invoked this power:

> "... to make provision for offences under the [2009 Order] to be prosecuted on indictment ... for the purpose of ensuring that penalties in respect of an offence prosecuted in that manner under the [2009 Order] are effective, proportionate and have a deterrent effect, having regard to the acts or omissions of which the offence consists".

In terms of the terminology used, rather oddly the preamble to the 2009 Order and the text of the 2009 Order refers to the statutory instrument as "these Orders" when it is clear that the term "this Order" should be used. The 2009 Order came into force on March 19, 2009.

TOBACCO CONTROL

The Public Health (Tobacco) (Amendment) Act 2009 (the "2009 Act") amended the Public Health (Tobacco) Act 2002 (the "2002 Act"), as amended (*Annual Review of Irish Law 2002*, p.433 and *Annual Review of Irish Law 2004*, pp.443–447), notably in connection with the advertising and sale of tobacco products, in particular cigarettes. The Public Health (Tobacco) Act 2002 (Commencement) Order 2009 (S.I. No. 242 of 2009) brought the changes made by the 2009 Act into force on July 1, 2009. During 2009 a series of regulations on the advertising and sale of tobacco products were also made, a number connected with the changes to the 2002 Act made by the 2009 Act.

The Public Health (Tobacco) (Registration) Regulations 2009 (S.I. No. 41 of 2009) requires all persons who carry on, in whole or in part, the business of selling tobacco products by retail to register with the Office of Tobacco Control. They also allow the Office of Tobacco Control to collect the information necessary for the establishment and maintenance of the register. The Public Health (Tobacco) (Self Service Vending Machines) Regulations 2009 (S.I. No. 42 of 2009) deal with the retail sale of tobacco products by means of a self-service vending machine on licensed premises or the premises of a registered club. The Public Health (Tobacco) (Retail Sign) Regulations 2009 (S.I. No. 57 of 2009) require that a sign as prescribed in the Regulations be displayed at a premises where tobacco products are sold by retail. The Public Health (Tobacco) (Product Information) Regulations 2009 (S.I. No. 123 of 2009) set out the manner in which a retailer may make information available with a view to assisting customers over 18 who enquire about what tobacco products a retailer has available for purchase. The Tobacco Products (Control of Advertising, Sponsorship and Sales Promotion) (Amendment) Regulations 2009 (S.I. No. 243 of 2009) deleted reg.8(2)(b) of the Tobacco Products (Control of Advertising, Sponsorship and Sales Promotion) Regulations 1991 (S.I. No. 326 of 1991). The effect of this deletion was to ban all advertising of tobacco products internally in premises which are points of retail sale. All these regulations made in 2009 came into force on July 1, 2009. One of the most notable effects was the "blanking out" of any cigarette branding on cigarette dispensing machines in retail shops, as required by the Tobacco Products (Control of Advertising, Sponsorship and Sales Promotion) (Amendment) Regulations 2009.

TRANSPORT

Tachograph: roadside checks The European Communities (Road Transport) (Working Conditions and Road Safety) (Amendment) Regulations 2009 (S.I. No. 51 of 2009) amended the European Communities (Road Transport) (Working Conditions and Road Safety) Regulations 2008 (*Annual Review of Irish Law 2008*, p.638). They provide for the Irish and English language version of the roadside check form to be used for the purposes of the 2008 Regulations.

Social Welfare Law

GERARD WHYTE, Lecturer in Law, Trinity College Dublin

PRIMARY LEGISLATION

As usual, two Acts dealing with, inter alia, social welfare matters were enacted during the year, the Social Welfare and Pensions Act 2009 and the Social Welfare and Pensions (No. 2) Act 2009. In the description of the legislation that follows, I have drawn heavily on the explanatory memoranda accompanying both pieces of legislation.

The Social Welfare and Pensions Act 2009 provides for certain amendments to the welfare code as announced in the 2009 budget. Sections 3 and 4 increase the earnings ceiling for PRSI contributions from employed and optional contributors respectively. Section 5 amends the conditions for receipt of jobseeker's benefit by additionally requiring claimants to participate, if requested by an officer of the Minister, in any appropriate course of education, training or development. It also provides that any day of unemployment in a week in which the claimant receives payment under the Short Term Enterprise Allowance Scheme shall be treated as a day in respect of which jobseeker's benefit was paid. Section 6 similarly amends the conditions for receipt of jobseeker's allowance to require claimants to participate in appropriate courses of education, training and development and also provides for a reduced rate of jobseeker's allowance for claimants under the age of 20 (later raised to 22 by the Social Welfare and Pensions (No. 2) Act 2009) who do not have child dependants. Certain categories of claimant under the age of 20 are exempted from this reduction, including claimants who were in state care in a year before his or her 18th birthday. Section 7 makes similar provision for claimants of supplementary welfare allowance who are under the age of 20 (later increased to 22 by the Social Welfare and Pensions (No. 2) Act 2009). It also stipulates certain conditions that have to be satisfied before rent supplement under the supplementary welfare allowance scheme is payable and also prescribes how rent supplement is to be calculated. A reduction in the amount of early childcare supplement is effected by s.8 while s.9 empowers the Minister to prescribe by regulation the type of information to be provided by claimants when making a claim. Section 10 provides for the payment of up to six months' arrears of domiciliary care allowance where there was good cause for the failure to claim the allowance in time. Finally, Pts 3, 4 and 5 of the 2009 Act provide for amendments to the Health Contribution Acts, the Financial Emergency Measures in the Public Interest Act and the Pensions Acts respectively.

The Social Welfare and Pensions (No. 2) Act 2009 implements certain measures announced in the budget for 2010 and due to come into effect in late December 2009 or early January 2010. It also effects miscellaneous changes to the social welfare code. Sections 3 and 4 provide for various reductions in the rates of welfare payable in respect of claimants and their adult dependants, though it also provides for an increase in the amount payable in respect of child dependants, while s.5 effectively provides for a reduction in family income supplement. Section 6 reduces the rates of jobseeker's allowance payable to claimants under the age of 25, subject to certain exceptions, and also reduces the amount of welfare payable in respect of such a claimant's adult dependant where the claimant has no child dependants. Section 7 provides for reductions in the rate of child benefit while s.8 imposes a four-year time limit for claiming refunds of PRSI contributions. Sections 9 and 10 provide that state (contributory) pension and widow's or widower's (contributory) pension shall only be payable to self-employed contributors once they have paid all contributions due from them while s.11 limits the treatment benefit scheme to the free examination elements of dental and optical benefits and the medical and surgical appliances scheme. Section 12 provides that in determining entitlement to the mortgage interest supplement under the supplementary welfare allowance scheme, mortgage interest will not include the amount of mortgage relief received by a person, any allowance or subsidy payable by a local authority under a shared purchase scheme or any interest payable in respect of a default or delay in making mortgage repayments. The section also defines "institution" for the purposes of s.14 as covering hospitals, convalescent homes or homes for persons with physical or mental disabilities, any premises providing residence, maintenance or care for people therein, prisons or places of detention or any other prescribed institution. Section 13 reduces the rates of supplementary welfare allowance payable to claimants under the age of 25, subject to certain exceptions, and also reduces the amount of welfare payable in respect of such a claimant's adult dependant where the claimant has no child dependants. Section 14 provides that in order to qualify for rent supplement, a claimant must show either that s/he has been assessed by a local authority as having a housing need, or that s/he has resided in rented accommodation for a prescribed period in circumstances where, at the outset of the tenancy, s/he could reasonably have expected to be able to pay the rent but where due to a change of circumstances beyond his/her control, this is no longer possible, or that s/he has resided for a prescribed period in accommodation for homeless people or in an institution as defined in s.12. In order to qualify for various specific welfare payments, a claimant must prove that s/he is habitually resident in the State. Section 15 now provides, inter alia, that a person who does not have a right to reside in the State shall not be regarded as habitually resident therein, thereby disqualifying asylum seekers for receipt of the relevant payments. The section also details the various categories of person deemed to have a right to reside in the State and also lists six categories of person who are not regarded as habitually resident in the State for the purpose of the welfare code. Section 16 extends existing provisions allowing a social welfare inspector accompanied by a Garda to stop and question occupants of a vehicle to cover situations where the inspector is accompanied by an officer of the Customs and Excise instead of a Garda. Pursuant to s.17, an officer of the Minister may require a financial institution to produce records that contain or, in the officer's reasonable opinion, may contain information relevant to a possible contravention of the social welfare code. Section 18 provides for the transfer of information relating to claimants of social welfare payments to the competent authority of another Member State of the European Communities or to an international organisation or other country with which a reciprocal agreement has been made. Section 19 provides that payments made under the Special Civil Service Incentive Career Break Scheme are fully assessable as means for the purpose of social assistance schemes. Finally, s.20 provides for the inclusion of the Health and Social Care Professionals Council and the Road Safety Authority in the list of bodies authorised by legislation to use the Personal Public Service Number as a public service identifier.

SECONDARY LEGISLATION

Twenty-one statutory instruments relating to social welfare matters were promulgated during 2009. In the description of these regulations, I have drawn heavily on the explanatory note accompanying each statutory instrument.

Social Welfare (Consolidated Claims, Payments and Control) (Amendment) (Jobseeker's Benefit) Regulations 2009 (S.I. No. 24 of 2009) These Regulations provide that a person claiming jobseeker's benefit who fails to satisfy the requirement of having 13 qualifying insurance contributions in the governing contribution year will qualify if s/he has 13 paid contributions in either of the two contribution years preceding the governing contribution year or in a subsequent contribution year.

Social Welfare (Consolidated Claims, Payments and Control) (Amendment) (No. 2) (Early Childcare Supplement) Regulations 2009 (S.I. No. 54 of 2009) These Regulations set out the dates on which early childcare supplement will be payable for 2009 and subsequent years.

Social Welfare (Miscellaneous Provisions) Act 2008 (Section 8) (Commencement) Order 2009 (S.I. No. 112 of 2009) This Order provides for the commencement on January 1, 2010 of s.8 of the Social Welfare (Miscellaneous Provisions) Act 2008 which provides that income from dividends arising from stallion fees, stud greyhound fees and profits from the occupation of certain woodlands will be taken into account in estimating reckonable income for PRSI purposes.

Social Welfare and Pensions Act 2008 (Sections 15 and 16) (Commencement) Order (S.I. No. 143 of 2009) This Order provides for the commencement of ss.15 and 16, other than para.(c), of the Social Welfare and Pensions Act 2008 which set out the conditions for eligibility for receipt of domiciliary care allowance, the rates of payment and consequential amendments to allow for the transfer of the administration of the scheme, in respect of new applications made on or after April 1, 2009, from the HSE to the Department of Social and Family Affairs.

Social Welfare (Consolidated Claims, Payments and Control) (Domiciliary Care Allowance) (Amendment) (No. 3) (Early Childcare Supplement) Regulations 2009 (S.I. No. 162 of 2009) These Regulations set out the conditions for receipt of domiciliary care allowance including the various medical procedures to be used certifying the extent of the qualified child's disability and the likely duration. They also include standard provisions in relation to the time limit for making a claim and the payment procedures and also provide for the method to be used for deciding the normal residence of the qualified child and for the payment of a reduced rate of domiciliary care allowance in respect of a qualified child who is resident on a part-time basis in an institution. The Regulations further provide for a medical review procedure that may require the submission of additional medical evidence or require that the child attend a medical examination.

Social Welfare (Miscellaneous Provisions) Act 2008 (Section 22) (Commencement) Order 2009 (S.I. No. 164 of 2009) This Order provides that s.22 of the Social Welfare (Miscellaneous Provisions) Act 2008, providing for the deduction of the income levy from any family income for the purpose of determining entitlement to family income supplement, comes into effect on May 6, 2009.

Social Welfare (Reduction of Payments to Health Professionals) Regulations 2009 (S.I. No. 198 of 2009) These Regulations set out the revised fees payable by the Department to those health professionals in respect of services as indicated in the tables.

Social Welfare (Consolidated Supplementary Welfare Allowance) (Amendment) (Rent Supplement) Regulations 2009 (S.I. No. 202 of

2009) These Regulations provide for an increase to €24 in the minimum weekly contribution payable by a recipient of rent supplement. They also provide for a reduction of the levels of maximum rent until May 31, 2010 in respect of which rent supplement is paid.

Social Welfare (Consolidated Claims, Payments and Control) (Amendment) (No. 4) (Island Allowance) Regulations 2009 (S.I. No. 230 of 2009) These Regulations provide for the addition of Dernish Island in Co. Sligo to the list of prescribed islands for the purposes of the island allowance payable to certain social welfare claimants normally resident on those islands.

Social Welfare (Consolidated Claims, Payments and Control) (Amendment) (No. 5) (Prescribed Time) Regulations (S.I. No. 240 of 2009) These Regulations provide that the prescribed time for making a claim for family income supplement shall be the period of three months from the day on which the person becomes entitled to the payment.

Social Welfare (Miscellaneous Provisions) Act 2008 (Part 5) (Commencement) Order 2009 (S.I. No. 241 of 2009) This Order provides for the commencement of Pt 5 of the Social Welfare (Miscellaneous Provisions) Act 2008 which provides for the dissolution of the Combat Poverty Agency and the transfer of its operations to the Department of Social and Family Affairs.

Social Welfare (Miscellaneous Provisions) Act 2008 (Part 4) (Commencement) Order 2009 (S.I. No. 244 of 2009) This Order provides for the commencement of Pt 4 of the Social Welfare (Miscellaneous Provisions) Act 2008 which amends the Citizens Information Acts 2000 and 2007 to extend the functions of the Citizens Information Board to include the provision of the Money Advice and Budgeting Service and related responsibilities.

Social Welfare (Consolidated Supplementary Welfare Allowance) (Amendment) (No. 2) (Rent Supplement) Regulations 2009 (S.I. No. 265 of 2009) These Regulations provide that to qualify for payment of rent supplement a person must have been residing in rented accommodation or accommodation for homeless persons (or any combination of these) for a period of 183 days within the preceding 12-month period. This provision will not apply to persons who have been assessed by a local authority as having a housing need under s.9 of the Housing Act 1988 (as amended). These Regulations also provide that where a person refuses two offers of accommodation provided by a housing authority within any continuous 12-month period, a supplement shall not be payable for a period of 12 months from the date of the second refusal.

Social Welfare and Pensions Act 2008 (Section 17) (Commencement) Order 2009 (S.I. No. 347 of 2009 This Order provides for the commencement of s.17 (other than subs.(5)) of the Social Welfare and Pensions Act 2008. Section 17 sets out the transitional provisions to allow for the transfer of the administration of the payment of an allowance for the domiciliary care of children from the Department of Health and Children to the Department of Social and Family Affairs.

Social Welfare (Consolidated Claims, Payments and Control) (Amendment) (No. 6) (Nominated Persons) Regulations 2009 (S.I. No. 378 of 2009) These Regulations provide for the payment of social welfare benefits and pensions to a person other than the claimant or beneficiary where that person is nominated by either the claimant or beneficiary to act as agent and receive the payment on his or her behalf or is appointed by the Minister to act as agent on behalf of a claimant who is under 16 years of age and unable to manage his/her own financial affairs. These Regulations specify the circumstances in which such appointments may be made and also set out the duties and responsibilities of the appointed person.

Social Welfare (Consolidated Contributions and Insurability) (Amendment) (Refunds) Regulations 2009 (S.I. No. 563 of 2009) These Regulations provide for the return of health contributions paid by employees in respect of tax-allowable pension contributions where the employees' reckonable earnings exceed the PRSI threshold.

Social Welfare (Consolidated Claims, Payments and Control) (Amendment) (No. 8) (Prescribed Time) Regulations 2009 (S.I. No. 564 of 2009) These Regulations provide for the extension of the time limit within which an application to become a homemaker for the purposes of the state pension (contributory) may be made.

Social Welfare (Occupational Injuries) (Amendment) Regulations 2009 (S.I. No. 565 of 2009) These Regulations provide for changes in the reduced rates of certain occupational injuries benefits arising from the budget.

Social Welfare (Consolidated Claims, Payments and Control) (Amendment) (No. 9) (Treatment Benefit) Regulations 2009 (S.I. No. 578 of 2009) These Regulations amend the definitions of dental benefit and treatment benefit in the light of a reduction in the range of treatments covered under the treatment benefit scheme announced in the budget.

Social Welfare (Consolidated Claims, Payments and Control) (Amendment) (No. 7) (Change in Rates) Regulations 2009 (S.I. No. 584 of 2009) These Regulations provide for changes, arising out of the budget, in the reduced rates of illness benefit; jobseeker's benefit; health and safety benefit; widow's and widower's (contributory) pension; and deserted wife's benefit, and also provide for changes in the rates of tapered increases in respect of qualified adults. The Regulations also provide for changes in the minimum and maximum weekly rates of maternity benefit and adoptive benefit, with effect from January 4, 2010.

Social Welfare (Consolidated Contributions and Insurability) (Amendment) (No. 2) (Contributions) Regulations 2009 (S.I. No. 585 of 2009) These Regulations provide that collection functions relating to certain self-employed contributors shall be carried out by the Revenue Commissioners.

CASE LAW

There would appear to have been only one case concerning social welfare law before the superior courts in 2009. In *Ayavoro v Health Service Executive* [2009] IEHC 66; unreported, High Court, February 6, 2009, O'Neill J. dismissed two judicial review applications brought by the applicant challenging decisions of the welfare authorities in respect of claims for supplementary welfare allowance and jobseeker's allowance. While several of the applicant's arguments were dismissed on the facts, two aspects of this case are worthy of note.

As part of his claim, the applicant alleged that the authorities had treated him in an inhuman and degrading manner contrary to art.3 of the European Convention on Human Rights. This appeared to be based on an implicit contention that the manner in which the authorities processed his various applications pushed him into a form of destitution that was inhuman and degrading, and in support of this argument the applicant relied on the House of Lords' decision in *R. (Limbuela) v Secretary of State for the Home Department* [2005] 3 W.L.R. 1014. In this case, the applicant was an asylum seeker who had been denied social welfare support by virtue of s.55(1) of the UK Nationality, Immigration and Asylum Act 2002. Because he was also forbidden to work, this meant that state action was pushing him into penury. According to Lord Bingham at 1018, an infringement of art.3 occurred if an asylum seeker, "with no means and no alternative means to support himself is, by the deliberate action of the state, denied shelter, food or the most basic necessities of life".

In the instant case, O'Neill J. distinguished *Limbuela* on two grounds. First, unlike the statutory regime in *Limbuela* which provided for a total prohibition on benefit being provided to asylum seekers, the social welfare code pursuant to which Mr Ayavoro was applying for social assistance provided both for an appeal against decisions of deciding and appeals officers, and also for revision of such decisions in light of new information. Secondly, there was no evidence that decisions of the welfare authorities had, in fact, rendered the applicant destitute. By implication, however, O'Neill J. appears to accept that the State may not deliberately deny a person access to the basic necessities of life and in an interesting obiter dictum made in the context of a different aspect of the applicant's case, he stated that the welfare authorities were not entitled:

> "... to make onerous demands [for information] which kept an impecunious person out of benefit for an unconscionable period of time which, in the case of impecuniosity, would ... be a very short time indeed".

While *Limbuela* was concerned with art.3 of the European Convention on Human Rights, a duty on the State not to drive people deliberately into destitution also exists at common law. Thus in *R. v Inhabitants of Eastbourne* (1803) 4 East 103, Lord Ellenborough C.J. said at 107:

> "As to there being no obligation for maintaining poor foreigners before the statutes ascertaining the different methods of acquiring settlements, the law of humanity, which is anterior to all positive laws, obliges us to afford them relief, to save them from starving;..."

This was subsequently cited with approval in *R. v Secretary of State for Social Security ex p. Joint Council for the Welfare of Immigrants* [1997] 1 W.L.R. 275 where the majority of the Court of Appeal held that regulations depriving asylum seekers of the rights to support conferred by the Immigration and Asylum Act 1993 were ultra vires.

While the Irish courts have yet to recognise a constitutional duty on the State to refrain from taking deliberate action that has the effect of pushing people into poverty, other constitutional rights might be successfully relied on by litigants confronted by legislation or state policy having that effect. Thus, in *Dillon v DPP* [2008] 1 I.R. 383, the applicant had been charged with the offence of begging in a public street contrary to s.3 of the Vagrancy (Ireland) Act 1847 and de Valera J. held, inter alia, that this offence infringed the applicant's constitutional freedom of expression. In an earlier case, *Fajujonu v Minister for Justice* [1990] 2 I.R. 151, Walsh J. indicated, obiter, that the State would infringe Art.41 guaranteeing the integrity of the family if it sought to deport the alien parents of Irish citizens on the ground that the parents were unable to support their children in circumstances in which the State had refused the father a work permit.

Returning to *Ayavoro*, one further ruling of O'Neill J. in this case is worth noting briefly. The applicant had argued that, in relation to issues that might disqualify him for receipt of payment such as his habitual residence or whether a regular payment into his bank account was for himself or his mother, the onus of proof rested on the authorities to establish their concerns. This argument was dismissed by O'Neill J. who said that the information given by the applicant to the authorities gave rise to reasonable queries on these points and at all times the onus was on the applicant to provide the necessary documents and information relating to such queries.

Torts

DUTY OF CARE

Pure economic loss *ACC Bank Plc v Fairlee Properties Ltd* [2009] IEHC 45, offers an interesting and novel synthesis of the conceptually distinct issues of the duty of care and remoteness of damage. The plaintiff bank, which had granted commercial facilities to the first defendant, a property development company, which the second defendant had guaranteed, lost the title deeds of the property that had been used as security for the loan. This resulted in restrictions on the second defendant's capacity to carry out development of his property with consequent damage to profits.

Finlay Geoghegan J., in the counterclaim by the second defendant, held that the bank had been under a duty of care in relation to the safekeeping of the title deeds, had breached that duty and was liable to compensate the plaintiff for his economic loss. She distinguished an old Irish precedent, *Gilligan v National Bank Ltd* [1901] 2 I.R. 513, which had held that a bank with which a property owner had deposited his title deeds had not been under a duty of care to prevent them from being damaged by water, rendering them partly illegible. The Queen's Bench Division had overturned a verdict in favour of the property owner, on the basis that no action lay by a mortgagor against a mortgagee prior to redemption. Barton J. had observed:

> "In my opinion, an action for damages for negligence in storing title-deeds does not, at all events before repayment, lie at the suit of a mortgagor against an equitable mortgagee by deposit of title-deeds, because the mortgagee is not a pawnee or bailee of the documents, but the absolute owner of them in the eye of the law; and the mortgagor's remedy, if any, is not by an action for damages but by an application for equitable relief."

Finlay Geoghegan J. considered that *Gilligan* was distinguishable on its facts, since the bank in the instant case had been under an obligation to produce to the defendants the title deeds on redemption; at all times prior to redemption, it was under a statutory obligation, pursuant to s.16 of the Conveyancing and Law of Property Act 1881, to have the title deeds available for inspection. Moreover, *Gilligan* long predated the "seminal decision" in *Donoghue v Stevenson* [1932] A.C. 562 and the development of the "neighbour principle" in the law of torts.

As regards the loss of profits sustained by the second defendant by reason of the delay in carrying out the development of his property, Finlay Geoghegan J. observed:

> "A person in the position of the [bank] must be aware that a developer requires his title documents as security to raise development finance. Further, that he requires development finance to carry out the development. It also appears to me to be reasonably foreseeable to a person in the position of the plaintiff that if a development is delayed this may result in a reduction in the profits achievable by the developer. This may be for a multiplicity of reasons, including additional time carrying the finance on the site purchase costs, potential increases in construction costs and potential variation in the market prices for the development being constructed, in this case, apartments. It is well established that what must be foreseeable is damage of the type suffered, but not necessarily of the exact nature or extent. See, for example, *Burke v. John Paul & Co. Ltd.* [1967] I.R. 277, at p. 285. The nature of the damage claimed is reduction in profits on a delayed development. This was foreseeable. It was also foreseeable that profits might be affected by variations (up and down) in market prices. It is not relevant that the extent of the variation or extent of the loss was not foreseeable."

This principle had to be considered in the context of subsequent developments and, in particular, the decision of the Supreme Court in *Glencar Exploration Plc v Mayo County Council* [2002] 1 I.R. 84, which required the court to address whether it was just and reasonable to impose a duty of care of the scope contended for, in addition to reasonable foreseeability, proximity of relationship and the absence of countervailing policy considerations. In the instant case, it was not disputed that the bank had such close and direct relations with the first and second named defendants as the owners, at least of the equity of redemption in the properties to which the deposited title deeds related, that it must have been reasonably foreseeable to the bank that, if it was careless in the storing of the title deeds such that it could not produce them on request, such carelessness would be likely to injure the defendants.

Finlay Geoghegan J. was also satisfied on the facts of the case that it was reasonable to impose a duty of care on the bank as mortgagee or chargee who received the title documents to development properties over which it had been given security, to take reasonable care in the storage of those title documents. She observed, in relation to the development of the second defendant's property, which was delayed by the loss of the title deeds, that she was satisfied that the reduction in probable profits was damage of a type which came within the scope of the duty of care of the plaintiff on the facts of the application. It was reasonably foreseeable by a person in the position of the plaintiff at the relevant time and it was fair and just to impose the liability on the plaintiff.

This is the first decision in which the separate issues of duty of care and remoteness of damage have been intermingled so as to raise the questions of proximity, countervailing policy considerations and the justness and reasonableness of imposing liability in respect of a remoteness issue. Since the decision of the Privy Council in *Overseas Tankship (UK) Ltd v Morts Docking & Engineering Co (The Wagon Mound No. 1)* [1961] A.C. 388, which treated the question of reasonable foreseeability as a single one, attaching to both the standard of care and remoteness of damage, courts have been puzzled when they encounter fact situations which cry out for a severance between the two questions. Compounding the difficulty is the fact that one of the constituent elements of the duty of care is also reasonable foreseeability. In our analysis of *Gaffey v Dundalk Town Council* [2006] IEHC 436 in the *Annual Review of Irish Law 2006*, pp.549–550, we discussed the unnecessary complexities which follow from a duplication of judicial effort in assessing reasonable foreseeability twice, in the context of duty of care and standard of care, in cases where the facts present an issue of reasonable foreseeability that can be most effectively addressed under the rubric of standard of care. It is novel for a court to require a plaintiff to jump the hurdles of proximity, absence of public policy objections and of reasonableness and justice where the issue is essentially one of remoteness of damage.

The truth of the matter is that the instant case essentially raised a question relating to the duty of care rather than remoteness (though the details of the second defendant's loss undoubtedly could be regarded as involving a remoteness issue). Finlay Geoghegan J. was faced with a quintessential conundrum as to the extent to which compensation should be permitted for negligently-caused pure economic loss. The Supreme Court in *Glencar* was hostile to such claims, though it did not exclude them completely. Undoubtedly the degree of proximity of relationship between the parties was very close and the extent of undertaking and reliance relating to the safekeeping of the title deeds very strong.

Immunity from suit In *Doherty v Minister for Justice, Equality and Law Reform* [2009] IEHC 246, where the plaintiff had initiated litigation against more than 40 defendants, including judges, the Bar Council, the Law Society and Ministers, McGovern J. ordered that the statement of claim be struck out as disclosing no reasonable course of action and as being scandalous, vexatious and an abuse of process. He noted that members of the judiciary and other statutory bodies acting within their jurisdiction enjoyed an immunity from action in negligence. McGovern J. observed:

> "While I appreciate the plaintiff … suggests that in certain instances the judges or other officials may not have been acting *bona fide* in the exercise of their duties, many of the complaints are anecdotal in nature

> and are, in my view, an abuse of process because they are brought for an improper or ulterior purpose, which is to cause embarrassment and vexation to the defendants and they do not fit within the rubric of *inter partes* disputes which are justiciable. In many cases, the plaintiff was not personally affected by the actions of which he complains. The remedy of judicial review is there for persons who have genuine complaints about the manner in which public officials exercise their powers. For example, if they act *ultra vires* or in breach of natural or constitutional justice or fail to carry out their duties towards the plaintiff, such actions are amenable to judicial review and the reliefs of certiorari, mandamus and prohibition are available. But the courts do not exist for the purpose of facilitating individuals to vent their displeasure, and even their anger, at the manner in which public officials carry out their duties."

Later in this chapter (below, pp.750–751) we discuss McMahon J.'s decision in *Kemmy v Ireland* [2009] IEHC 148, in relation to the question of the liability of the State in the context of judicial immunity.

Duty to protect prisoners In the *Annual Review of Irish Law 2008*, pp.593–594, we analysed *Breen v Governor of Wheatfield Prison* [2008] IEHC 123, where a prisoner injured in an attack by another inmate failed in his actions for negligence against the prison authorities. We noted that this decision was one of many over the years in which prisoners had failed in such claims, see Binchy, "Prison Authorities, Attacks on Prisoners and the Duty of Care", (2009) 3 *Quarterly Review of Tort Law* 28. In 2009, two further claims came before the Irish courts; one was partially successful; the other joined the long list of failures.

In *Creighton v Ireland* [2009] IEHC 257, the plaintiff, an inmate of Wheatfield Prison, was very seriously injured when attacked with "a blade of some sorts" by another prisoner in the medical centre whilst awaiting his medication. The three central units of the medical centre were interconnected by separating gates. The separating gate to the dispensary unit was locked and prisoners were admitted to it individually. Two prison officers were present, one to admit prisoners to the unit and return them to the corridor, the other to verify their entitlement to medication. The lower half of the central unit, as it faced onto the corridor, was described by White J. as "solid" and the upper half was barred, "thereby permitting of staff having a limited view of the central units from the corridor".

There had been 12 assaults at the prison from July 18, 2001 to January 18, 2003 (the day before the incident); two of these had occurred in the medical centre. No evidence was given of any risk evaluations having been carried out following the assaults at the medical centre or of any steps having been taken to minimise the potential exposure of inmates to assaults there.

White J. imposed liability on the prison authorities, not for *all* the injuries sustained by the plaintiff but for those of them that could be attributed to the delay in rescuing him caused by the manner in which security was provided in the area of the medical centre. He stated:

> "I am satisfied that it would be unreasonable to expect, or require, the prison authorities to search each and every prisoner every time he exited his cell. Further, I am satisfied that the prison authorities could not have been reasonably expected to have been in a position to prevent an attack on the plaintiff. Equally, however, given the fact that two attacks, involving the use of weapons, had occurred in the Medical Centre within the previous six months, I consider that the failure to place a prison officer or prison officers within the three central units of the Medical Centre and among the prisoners was a failure in the defendants' duty of care to the plaintiff, but only to the extent that such a presence would have resulted in an earlier intervention in, and break up of, the assault. The absence of such a presence inevitably resulted in some time delay in officers going to the assistance of the plaintiff. Speed of intervention would have, in my view, lessened the extent of the injuries sustained by the plaintiff. I do not consider that such a presence could have prevented the head and facial injuries, but I consider, in all probability, it would have been likely to prevent the injuries which the plaintiff sustained to his flank and to his abdomen."

In *Casey v Governor of Midlands Prison* [2009] IEHC 466, the plaintiff, a prisoner at the Midlands Prison, Portlaoise, was injured in an attack by another prisoner using a delft cup when they were in the recreation yard. The two had been involved in a dispute earlier that day relating to the use of a pool table. The cup was a standard type issued to all prisoners. The evidence disclosed that the practice of the prison authorities was to search prisoners when moving beyond their own wing but not when they moved within it. Visiting the recreation yard did not involve moving beyond their wing. An expert witness called on behalf of the plaintiff (who had not been afforded an opportunity of inspecting the Midlands Prison—a matter, surely, of some concern) considered that there should have been "pat[ting] down" searches when prisoners went into a recreation yard, even in their own wing, since scores between prisoners were more likely to be settled outside than in an indoor recreation area, where prison officers would be in closer proximity and there would be no opportunity to hide a potential weapon in outdoor clothing.

Irvine J. dismissed the claim. She was impressed by the fact that it was "the accepted norm of Irish prisons" to permit prisoners to move within their wing to the exercise without being searched. Only three incidents had occurred in the recreation yard in the 12 months before the attack, none of which had involved the use of a weapon. In the same period, 12 assaults had taken place in the indoor recreation area. The assailant in the instant case, though "a nuisance and somewhat of a thorn in the side of the prison service", having assaulted fellow prisoners on two previous occasions (in what the Assistant Governor described as "regular type fighting between inmates"), had not used weapons and had no proven "propensity to carry out vicious assaults on fellow inmates". The system for searches advocated by the plaintiff's expert witness would not have protected prisoners from the use of small and dangerous items.

Irvine J. stated:

> "Of equal importance ... is the fact that the systematic searches proposed by the plaintiff would substantially impinge upon the constitutional rights enjoyed by prisoners as citizens and the requirement that where possible their dignity as human beings should be respected. These searches, which would be visited upon all prisoners potentially as often as three times per day throughout their confinement, would I believe amount to a disproportionate interference with those rights, when weighed against the risk of foreseeable or potential injury absent such system. The plaintiff's submission, if accepted, would force the defendants to abandon much of their efforts to promote a humane model of confinement to protect against a remote risk of injury in the prison yard. To my mind, the defendants' efforts to preserve dignity, generate the notion of citizenship even within the confines of prison life and avoid the unneccessary dehumanisation of prisoners by subjecting them to ongoing body searches, justifies them accepting the remote risk that occasionally some type of injury which would otherwise be avoided if prisoners were always searched on entry to the recreation yard, may occur."

This emphasis on prisoners' dignity is to be welcomed, yet courts should not lose sight of the particularly dangerous environment of prisons where, as the High Court of Australia acknowledged in *New South Wales v Bujdoso* (2005) CLRI 227, "[v]iolence is, to a lesser or a greater degree, often on the cards". It seems likely that the further development of jurisprudence on arts 2 and 3 of the European Court of Human Rights will have an impact in this context.

Duty to prevent injury from youthful excesses In *Harkin v Bundoran Adventure Park Ltd t/a Harrisons Amusements*, High Court, July 16, 2009, reported in *The Irish Times*, July 17, 2009, a young woman aged 17 was injured when the dodgem car she was driving was struck head on by another dodgem being driven by two youths who were "messing" and who had deliberately gone in the opposite direction from other cars, deliberately targeting her. Imposing liability on the proprietors, Herbert J. did not accept that the incident had happened so quickly that it could not have been stopped. He observed:

"This is what teenage boys will do and this is why there are people there to look out for them."

"Good Samaritan" proposals In its Report, *Civil Liability of Good Samaritans and Volunteers* (LRC 93–2009) the Law Reform Commission proposes the introduction of a "Good Samaritan" law, applying to those who provide assistance, advice or care to others injured in an accident, emergency or other circumstance of serious and imminent danger. Liability would be restricted to cases where the "Good Samaritan" is guilty of gross negligence. Individual volunteers who, without any expectation of payment or other financial reward, agree to provide assistance, advice or care to another or for a purpose that is of benefit to the community would also only have to comply with a gross negligence standard. Volunteer undertakings would, however, have to comply with a reasonable care standard.

The Commission is opposed to the imposition of a duty to rescue in any new circumstance. One reason is that the Commission believes that:

> "[w]ere moral wrongdoings to be a cause of action, there could well be numerous types of damage which might be difficult or even impossible to qualify. Certainly, what one person considers immoral or wrong, another person might not. In this regard, enforcing moral obligations could lead to much uncertainty in the law. In particular, it has been argued that the recognition of moral obligations as valid claims would destabilise written law by replacing it with the varied morals of those sitting on the bench."

It has to be said that this is a particularly unconvincing argument. The Commission's aversion to the enforcement of morality revives a debate of half a century ago between Hart and Devlin. But today we are addressing, not the question of personal moral decisions that have no harmful effects on others but precisely the opposite—decisions that will result in others suffering death or injury.

It is curious that the Commission should so strongly favour individualist norms at a time when globally the trend is towards greater recognition of communal solidarity, reflected in enhanced obligations resting on states under global and regional human rights instruments to be proactive in the protection of rights to life and bodily integrity, the trend towards horizontal application of rights and the associated increase in responsibilities resting on non-state actions, personal and corporate.

EMPLOYERS' LIABILITY

Safe place of work and safe systems In *Behan v AIB Plc* [2009] IEHC 554, Murphy J. dismissed a claim by an employee who had injured her knee when the castor of the chair in which she was sitting came in contact with a money bag. She was the senior official in the office where money bags were counted. The money bags were placed in a basket in the centre of the floor. A porter was available to remove the baskets when full.

The essence of the plaintiff's case was that the employer had not taken reasonable care to provide a safe place or system of work since it had permitted the work area to become congested, cluttered and unsafe and had failed to warn her and others of the danger. Murphy J., rejecting the claim, emphasised that the plaintiff had been in charge. Although the system of placing bags in a basket in the centre of the floor pre-dated her coming there to work at this task, she had never complained about it.

Protection from sexual abuse In *Reilly v Devereux* [2009] IESC 22, a soldier, born in 1966, was subjected to sexual abuse by a Sergeant Major from 1989 to 1995. His claim for negligence against the Minister for Defence failed before Johnson J. and the Supreme Court affirmed. The plaintiff had not availed himself of the procedure to bring such concerns to the attention of the superior officers. Johnson J. considered that they had not sufficient information to become aware of the abuse. He observed:

> "It is necessary to look at the incidents and at the evidence in light of the times as they then were. These events took place in the 1980's and early 1990's, at a time when the antennae of the ordinary reasonable person were far less acute to the potentials for sexual abuse or sexual assault than they are today. We must remember that, for the last ten years, the country has been subject to continual reports of sexual exploitation, sexual abuse and sexual assaults, all of which have tended to make the population a great deal more sensitive to matters which twenty years ago would not have drawn any attention whatsoever."

On appeal, this statement was subjected to criticism by the appellant's counsel on the basis that the public awareness of predatory sexual activities already existed at the time of the abuse, but the Supreme Court found it perfectly acceptable. Kearns J. (Denham and Finnegan JJ. concurring) observed:

> "The television programme 'States of Fear' was broadcast by RTE only in 1999. That programme provoked a storm of comment in the media at that time and continued to be debated and referred to for many years thereafter. It prompted many complainants who had been

> sexually abused to come forward. The McColgan abuse case was also the topic of huge media interest, but the much publicised civil hearing also postdated the abuse in this case which ended in 1995.
>
> It is a dangerous exercise in hindsight to apply knowledge and standards of today to events which occurred twenty-five years ago. Homosexual activities were strongly discouraged in the Army at the time and homosexual activities were criminalised until 1993. Accordingly, that orientation and preference was often hidden, notably in a predominantly male environment such as the Army. Further, there was no evidence before the Court that a homosexual person was or is more likely than a heterosexual person to commit a sexual assault. Indeed it can perhaps be best described as offensive to suggest that gay men are more likely to assault a victim than heterosexual men."

One may perhaps wonder whether in fact the past two decades can better be understood as involving an opening up to public acknowledgment of a reality that was indeed understood but simply not discussed.

Stress claims In the *Annual Review of Irish Law 2006*, pp.556–558, we analysed *Berber v Dunnes Stores Ltd* [2006] IEHC 327 in which Laffoy J. imposed liability on an employer in negligence for having failed to respond with due care to its employee's condition of stress. The Supreme Court reversed that decision: [2009] IESC 10. For an insightful analysis, see Neville Cox, "Recent Developments in the Rules Relating to Workplace Stress: The Supreme Court Decision in *Berber v Dunnes Stores*" (2009) 3 *Quarterly Review of Tort Law* 17.

The plaintiff, who suffered from Crohn's disease, had been a buyer in the defendants' employment who was transferred from buying back to store management. He regarded this as a demotion. His relationship with his employers deteriorated. A range of incidents occurred to which the plaintiff took exception. A document entitled "Drapery Management Analysis" was widely circulated among staff by his employers, which included his name under the heading "new trainees". The plaintiff considered this humiliating, defamatory and vindictive. (Finnegan J. (Denham and Hardiman JJ. concurring) observed that the document was "in fact no more than a manuscript duty roster for a particular store for a particular week".) On the plaintiff's insistence, a correction to the document was circulated but not in the terms agreed with him.

Finnegan J. accepted that the employers had fallen under a duty of care in relation to the plaintiff's condition of stress which had come to their notice. He applied the principles set out in *McGrath v Trintech Technologies Ltd* [2005] E.L.R. 49, *Quigley v Complex Tooling and Moulding*, High Court, March 9, 2005 and *Hatton v Sunderland* [2002] 2 All E.R. 1. He considered that the employers had at all stages acted reasonably. The misdescription in the roster had been "a mistake and any harm resulting from the same in my view unforeseeable". The wording in the circular correcting the error was "in substance … as agreed". Although its circulation had fallen short of what had been agreed, it had not been "such as to make injury foreseeable". The same applied to the other matters advanced by the employee as evidence of a lack of due care. Cumulatively they also failed the test of foreseeability. Finnegan J. commented:

> "The appellant responded reasonably to each incident as it arose and the alternative available to the appellant was to abdicate from all control of the manner in which the respondent would carry out the duties of his employment."

PROFESSIONAL NEGLIGENCE

Medical care In *Healy v HSE* [2009] IEHC 221, the plaintiff infant was born with a malrotation of his intestine, which manifested itself by yellow-coloured bile-stained vomit. The consultant paediatrician, although notified that the plaintiff had vomited in this way at least twice, decided to continue observation of the plaintiff rather than refer him immediately for investigation, either by way of a barium meal x-ray or by a paediatric surgeon. The hospital staff, in spite of repeated complaints by the plaintiff's mother that he had vomited bile-stained matter on a number of occasions in the two days following birth, did not investigate her concerns with sufficient efficiency or urgency and did not record accurately the plaintiff's condition. The plaintiff was subsequently discharged without the nursing and medical staff having first satisfied themselves that his vomits had not been caused by a malrotation.

Quirke J. held that the medical and nursing staff had been negligent. As regards the nursing staff, he noted that a further aspect of that negligence was the discharge of the plaintiff when he had sustained a weight loss of 9.5 per cent in the first three days after birth, without warning his parents that they should return to the hospital immediately in the event of the plaintiff's suffering from a further bilious vomit. The plaintiff suffered an acute bowel obstruction which nearly resulted in his death. He spent over seven months in Our Lady's Hospital in Crumlin, where he received exemplary medical and nursing attention. There were several surgical interventions, including five laparotromies.

Quirke J. declined to hold that the consultant paediatrician was shielded from liability by the novus actus interveniens principle. He observed:

> "When [the consultant paediatrician] directed that the plaintiff should be observed for feeding difficulties (and in particular, for vomiting) on 16th February, it must have been foreseeable to him that the standard of observation within the post-natal unit of the hospital was such that

> the plaintiff's serious symptoms might well be missed by the nursing staff.
>
> He had been a consultant paediatrician within Tralee General Hospital for some time and was familiar with its practices and procedures. It was therefore foreseeable by him (although it may not necessarily have been probable or likely) that the plaintiff might be discharged (as he was) on 17th February, 2000, without having been adequately observed for symptoms indicating a probable malrotation and a potential volvulus. He made no further enquiries about the plaintiff's condition. He failed to follow up upon his own recommendations for the plaintiff's investigation and possible treatment …
>
> [The consultant paediatrician] was the most senior person responsible for the care of the plaintiff and for his medical treatment immediately after his birth and whilst he was a patient in the hospital. The members of the hospital's nursing and medical staff were entitled to look to [him] for direction and supervision in the care and treatment afforded to the plaintiff after his birth and while he was in the hospital. [He] was negligent and failed in his duty to provide appropriate care and treatment to the plaintiff.
>
> He also failed to provide the direction and supervision which the nursing and medical staff at the hospital were entitled to expect from him.
>
> Although this concurrent negligence by [him] did not discharge the separate and independent obligations and duties which the medical and nursing staff owed to the plaintiff, it did not absolve [him] from his separate and independent liability to the plaintiff either."

It is not precisely clear why the consultant paediatrician ought to have foreseen that the nursing staff "might well" have missed the plaintiff's serious symptoms. Perhaps the decision can best be understood as being based on his continuing responsibility rather than on the foreseeability of conduct that would have been characterised as constituting a novus actus interveniens in the absence of such foreseeability.

In *English v North Eastern Health Board* [2009] IEHC 189, Charleton J. dismissed a claim for negligence where an operation to deal with the plaintiff's condition of Dupuytren's contracture resulted in the amputation of a finger. The operation had been conducted by a general surgeon working at Louth County Hospital. At the time there were four to five specialist hand surgeons practising in the State. Charleton J. considered that the standard of care which the plaintiff was entitled to expect at that hospital was "that which a careful and competent general surgeon, engaging from time to time in hand surgery, could give." After a review of the evidence, Charleton J. concluded that the plaintiff had not met the burden of proving that the surgeon had failed to provide "the ordinary skill and care appropriate to a general surgeon operating in a county hospital". He added that he had not been convinced by the evidence that the plaintiff would have had a better result, given his condition and the length of time over which Dupuytren's contracture had developed, had he been referred to specialist care from a hand surgeon in a dedicated unit.

Charleton J's approach indicates that the professional standard of care in relation to surgeons should be broken down into two categories: specialist hand surgeons and general surgeons who engage in hand surgery from time to time. The reference to the county hospital suggests (though not very firmly) that a further subcategorisation bearing some similarity to what American courts call the "locality rule" may be envisaged.

Solicitors In *Darby, Shanley practising under the Style and Title of Oliver Shanley & Company Solicitors* [2009] IEHC 459, the defendants were sued for negligence in relation to two transactions in which they gave professional services: the making of a will by an elderly married testatrix in which she gave a life interest to her husband with remainder to members of another family with whom "(a) close family relationship existed", and a later transfer to one of that family of a portion of land. After the testatrix's death, her husband took proceedings asserting his legal right and challenging the validity of the transfer. The proceedings were settled, to the partial detriment of the beneficiaries of will and transfer. A number of these beneficiaries sued the defendant for negligence.

As regards the will, Irvine J. applied the principles set out in *Wall v Hegarty* [1980] I.L.R.M. 124 and *White v Jones* [1995] 2 A.C. 20. She declined to impose liability as the husband's claim would probably have occurred irrespective of whether the defendants had been negligent. Moreover, any negligence found against the defendants had not formed any legitimate basis on which the executrix had been entitled to conclude that the proceedings required settlement in the manner agreed by her.

The transfer raised different issues. Irvine J. concluded that the defendants had been negligent in respect of the intended beneficiary's interests. She stated:

> "A prudent solicitor, acting with Patrick Darby's interests in mind, ought to have been live to the possibility that the circumstances and backdrop to the transfer were such that a potential challenge to the validity of the transfer might arise. The facts that should have made a potential claim of undue influence foreseeable to a prudent solicitor in the present case were as follows:
>
> (a) The age of the transferor.
>
> (b) The fact that Mr. Darby had the plans prepared and brought them into the offices of Mr. Shanley.

> (c) The fact that the site was several acres large and much larger than was needed merely for the construction of a family home.
> (d) The fact that Mr. Darby paid for all the legal work.
> (e) The fact that Mr. Darby brought Mrs. Bird in to execute the transfer.
> (f) The fact that Mrs. Bird and her husband were wholly dependent upon the Darby family, almost to the point that without them, they could not have lived independently.
> (g) The fact that Mrs. Bird came in alone to the office without her husband and in circumstances where they could not have known whether or not she had been taken advantage of by Mr. Darby to the point that she may not even have been able to discuss the transfer with her husband.
> (h) They had no knowledge of Mr. Bird's attitude to the intended transfer.
>
> A potential claim of undue influence being foreseeable, the defendants owed Patrick Darby an obligation to advise him regarding the potential for such a claim and how he could protect himself from such a challenge. The defendants were mandated to advise Patrick Darby to attend an independent solicitor and to warn him that if he did not do so, that he would be exposing the transfer to a potential challenge on the grounds of undue influence. The defendants were mandated to explain to Patrick Darby that if they continued to act on his behalf, and a challenge was made to the validity of the transfer, that he would not be in a position to prove that the advice given to Bridie Bird at the time she executed the transfer was independent of his influence."

In relation to the testatrix, Irvine J. held that the defendants had owed a duty to her to consider the possibility that she was transferring the lands whilst under the undue influence of the Darby family. They had been obliged to make reasonable inquiries of Bridie Bird as to the reasons behind her decision to transfer this property to Patrick Darby and to enquire whether her husband was in agreement with the proposed transfer, given that any challenge to the transfer was likely to emanate from him. In the absence of knowledge of Mr Bird's agreement to the proposed transfer, they had been mandated to advise Bridie Bird of the risk of a claim of undue influence being made at a later date, in which case, if Patrick Darby was not separately represented, it would be difficult to establish that she had acted independently of his influence. If such a challenge were made, then her wishes would be thwarted, with the property she intended to be given to Patrick Darby ending up in the hands of a third party.

HORSES ON THE HIGHWAY

In *O'Brien v Derwin* [2009] IEHC 2, where the plaintiff motorist was severely injured by a wandering horse on the N6 roadway at nighttime, the crucial issue relating to liability was the ownership of the horse. After a detailed examination of the circumstantial evidence, Charleton J. concluded that the defendants owned it. The fencing to their property was broken down because of horses "leaning over it and eating the luxuriant grass verge while putting their weight against it". The horses had been encouraged to eat that way because they had often been fed hay over the fence from the roadway from a vehicle parked there.

RES IPSA LOQUITUR

Unexplained injuries In *Rogers v MIBI* [2009] IESC 30, the Supreme Court reversed Herbert J.'s holding ([2003] IEHC 142) in favour of a man found by a roadside early in the morning having been drinking the previous night in a public house some distance away. The evidence led Herbert J. to conclude that the man had been hit by an unknown vehicle being negligently driven. The Supreme Court made other inferences. Finnegan J. (Geoghegan and Clarke JJ. concurring) observed:

> "My conclusion is that on the evidence adduced at the trial the injuries sustained by the respondent may have been sustained as a result of impact with a motor vehicle and, if so, more likely by a fall resulting from a motor vehicle brushing against him rather than direct impact. Equally, however, they may have been caused by a fall, however precipitated, without any involvement of a motor car. The bruise to the hip and the laceration to the hand do not point to one cause of the other. The mud does not lead to a probability of impact with a car rather than to a fall. There is an unexplained time gap between 3 a.m. and 5 a.m. Where did the respondent sustain his injury? How did he sustain his injury? When did he sustain his injury? These questions are all unanswered by the evidence. It is not permissible to resort to conjuncture to answer these questions. Resort to *res ipsa loquitur* does not provide any answer. Consequently, the applicant has failed to establish causation as a matter of probability. His claim must fail."

Trespass to land In *Presho v Doohan* [2009] IEHC 619, Murphy J. adopted the novel strategy of invoking the res ipsa loquitur principle in a claim for trespass to land. The plaintiff's somewhat dilapidated house on Tory Island gradually disappeared over a period of several months. The cause of the disappearance was by no means clear. The plaintiff was not living there at the relevant time. The plaintiff sued the sole owner of a JCB on the island and a hotel situated beside his vanished house.

Murphy J. noted that the defendants had "benefitted to some extent from the demolition of Mr Presho's house. There was no evidence of lack of motive on their part to show the relative unlikelihood of their interest." The removal of part of the house had required mechanical means. The first defendant, "as the owner of the only JCB on the island", had the capacity and opportunity to remove the stakes identified by Mr Presho on the foreshore.

Murphy J. considered that the doctrine of res ipsa loquitur, "while not entirely dispositive", had some application to the case. Henchy J. in *Hanrahan v Merck Sharp and Dohme* [1988] I.L.R.M. 629, had stated in regard to the doctrine:

> "The ordinary rule is that a person who alleges a particular tort must, in order to succeed, prove (save there are admissions) all the necessary ingredients of the tort and it is not for the defendant to disprove anything. Such exceptions as has been allowed to that general rule seem to be confined to cases where a particular element of the tort lies, or is deemed to lie, *pre-eminently within the defendant's knowledge, in which case the onus of proof as to that matter passes to the defendant*. Thus, in the tort of negligence, where damage has been caused to the plaintiff in circumstances in which such damage would not usually be caused without negligence on the part of the defendant, the rule of *res ipsa loquitur* will allow the act relied on to be evidence of negligence in the absence of proof by the defendant that it occurred without want of due care on his part. The rationale behind the shifting of the onus of proof to the defendant in such cases would appear to lie in the fact that it would be *palpably unfair to require a plaintiff to prove* something which is beyond his reach and which is peculiarly within the range of the defendant's capacity of proof" (emphasis added by Murphy J.).

Murphy J. noted that, while McMahon and Binchy in *Irish Law of Torts*, 2nd edn (Dublin: Butterworths, 1990) were "somewhat critical" of this reasoning of Henchy J., the doctrine was applicable to the circumstances where motivation, capacity and opportunity of the defendants were considered. McMahon and Binchy had pointed out:

> "It is not the case that *res ipsa loquitur* may be invoked only where the evidence is more accessible to the defendant. Of course, proof of the elements of a case based on *res ipsa loquitur* frequently shows superior or exclusive knowledge on the part of the defendant as to how the accident occurred: of the nature of things, those in control of the instrumentality causing the injury are generally more likely to have such knowledge than their victims. But the *res ipsa loquitur* doctrine

> is neither reducible to, nor dependent on, this element … *The whole point of the doctrine is to permit the making of an inferential conclusion that the defendant's negligent conduct caused the plaintiff's injury from the fact that (a) the thing causing the injury was under the defendant's control and (b) accidents such as the one befalling the plaintiff do not ordinarily happen if those in control exercise due care*" (2nd edn, 1989, p.143) (emphasis added by Murphy J.)

Murphy J. noted that the court was entitled to infer, and was satisfied, that it was probable that the first-named defendant's JCB, "whether driven by that defendant or not, was the only 'thing causing the injury'". On the basis of his analysis of the circumstantial evidence and the doctrine of res ipsa loquitur, Murphy J. was satisfied that the plaintiff was entitled to the damages "for trespass and interference".

Undoubtedly the circumstantial evidence in the case required the court to make inferences and come to conclusions on the basis, in large part, of these inferences. The res ipsa loquitur doctrine has been interpreted by some courts and scholars as no more than a graphic instance of circumstantial evidence justifying, though not requiring, the conclusion that the defendant's negligence caused the plaintiff's injury. In the instant case, negligence was not a feature of the claim. The case involved a mystery, just as the facts in *Hanrahan v Merck Sharp and Dohne* did: what had caused the plaintiff's injury? Henchy J.'s analysis has been criticised on account of his failure to make this clear. The first requirement for the application of res ipsa loquitur, that the thing which caused the injury was under the control of the defendant, was the very matter that was in issue in that case. The doctrine had no relevance until that requirement was fulfilled evidentially, yet the doctrine was invoked by Henchy J. precisely to fill that evidential lacuna.

CONTRIBUTORY NEGLIGENCE

Passengers journeying with intoxicated drivers In the *Annual Review of Irish Law 2005*, pp.707–711, we analysed in detail the law relating to claims made by injured passengers who allowed themselves to be driven by drivers who, they knew or ought to have known, were intoxicated. We discussed the decision of *Hussey v Twomey* [2005] IEHC 17, where Peart J. reduced the plaintiff's compensation by 40 per cent. The plaintiff took an unsuccessful appeal to the Supreme Court: [2009] IESC 55. For a clear analysis of the decision, see Ray Ryan and Des Ryan, "Contributory Negligence: Drink Driving and Inexperience Cases Examined" (2009) 3 *Quarterly Review of Tort Law* 6, 6–8.

Kearns J. (Geoghegan and Finnegan JJ. concurring) considered it an "inescapable" conclusion from the evidence that the plaintiff had been well aware of the driver's inebriated condition, having spent an hour in his immediate company in a public house and having had "plenty of opportunities" of seeing him during that time. On her own evidence, the plaintiff had made no effort to ascertain whether he was fit to drive; she "must have been aware" that his driving was likely to be impaired and the circumstances had been "clearly such as to put her on inquiry".

Kearns J. thought it :

> "... fair to say that the society's understanding of the role of alcohol in driving cases has undergone radical change in the space of the last forty years…There has been undoubtedly an enormous sea change in society's attitude to drink driving influenced no doubt by the extent of carnage on our roads and the effectiveness of multiple campaigns which inform the public of the hazards of driving, whilst under the influence of even small quantities of alcohol. It is thus now commonplace, if not yet a universal practice, for groups of people on a night out to appoint one of the group as a designated driver who will drink no alcohol or alternatively to make arrangements whereby no member of the party will be driving under any circumstances. Thus, I think it can fairly be said that any measure of tolerance towards intoxicated drivers and their passengers, if indeed it formerly existed to any appreciable degree, is very much a thing of the past".

Seen in this light, most of the decisions opened to the court in the course of the appeal had to be seen as "carrying a 'health warning'" to the extent that they reflected attitudes from a different time as to the role and responsibilities of an intended passenger in a car about to be driven by a driver who has consumed alcohol.

Kearns J. went on to observe:

> "I can see the attraction of an argument that a passenger who elects to travel with a driver whom he knows to be unfit through alcohol from driving safely should in consequence be seen as thereby surrendering his autonomy and accepting whatever risks ensue thereafter. This fits well with the doctrine of *volenti non fit injuria* because in a sense it can be said that a passenger who elects to travel with a drunken driver is in much the same position as a person who elects to walk blindfold across an eight lane highway. However, the approach of the courts in common law jurisdictions, at least in the latter part of the last century, was to regard such an outcome whereby a claimant failed *in toto* as being unduly harsh … Section 34(1)(b) of the Civil Liability Act 1961 expressly abolishes the defence of *volenti* (save to the limited extent provided by the subsection) and provides that such issues be resolved by references to standards of contributory negligence only. I am satisfied

that the mechanism provided by s.34(1) of the Civil Liability Act, 1961 is sufficiently flexible to allow Irish courts calibrate an apportionment for contributory negligence in a manner which does justice in cases of this nature."

Both sides to the appeal accepted that the following principles applied:

"1. The court may, where a passenger voluntarily elects to travel in a motor vehicle in circumstances where he knows, or should reasonably be aware, that the driver has consumed alcohol, be penalised in contributory negligence.
2. In determining the issue of contributory negligence, the court must approach the issue on an objective basis, though the test cannot itself be absolutely objective in that the personal characteristics of any given plaintiff and the circumstances in which that plaintiff elects to travel as a passenger must be taken into account. A passenger in a given case may be under a disability by reason of age or infirmity, or may be relieved of any responsibility to make enquiry in the particular circumstances, such as in the case of a passenger travelling in a taxi.
3. An intending passenger who has consumed alcohol can not rely on self-intoxication for the purpose of avoiding a finding of contributory negligence and in particular can not rely on self-intoxication in an effort to avoid the consequences of facts which would otherwise have been reasonably discernible to him."

Kearns J. considered that the extent of the apportionment had also to be seen "against the backdrop of changed societal perceptions". In this respect the apportionment of contributory negligence in respect of travelling with an intoxicated motorist was quite different from the type of contributory negligence which arose from the failure to wear a seatbelt:

"In the latter instance the causative effect of the omission may be evident from the fact that a particular passenger may have suffered severe facial injuries from windscreen glass as a result of failing to secure his seatbelt. In the context of a passenger travelling with an intoxicated driver the fault lies in the decision to travel with such a driver in the first instance. The more the passenger should have realised, or did realise, the risk being undertaken, the greater the degree of contributory negligence. There is such scope for a much higher finding of contributory negligence in this context than in the case of a failure to wear a seatbelt."

In *Moran v Fogarty* [2009] IESC 55, decided six months after *Hussey v*

Twomey [2009] IESC 1, the Supreme Court raised from 15 per cent to 35 per cent the deduction for contributory negligence on the part of a passenger in permitting himself to be driven by a driver he knew, or ought to have known, to be intoxicated. The Supreme Court proceeded on the basis that, when asked to interfere with an apportionment of liability, it should do so only where there had been an error of law or a significant disproportion. Finnegan J. (Murray C.J. and Denham JJ. concurring) accepted that the normal reduction should be less than 50 per cent:

> "In general it can be said that the blameworthiness of the driver will be greater than that of a passenger permitting himself to be driven. The decision to drive is that of the driver and it is he that poses the risk to his passengers and to other road users. Accordingly an apportionment to such a passenger will normally be less than that to the driver. However there may be other elements of fault, for example failure to avail of a seat belt. In such circumstances the correct approach for the court is to take an overall view of the blameworthiness of the passenger and arrive at an apportionment which is just and equitable. Should there be two or three elements of fault it is not necessary that the court should ascribe a percentage to each but rather on an assessment of the blameworthiness as a whole an apportionment should be made."

Finnegan J. identified a number of factual circumstances that were relevant to the apportionment of liability. The evening had been "in the nature of a joint venture" in that the plaintiff and defendant had travelled together by car to the bar, with the intention of making the return journey having consumed alcohol. They had spent at least four and a half hours there in each other's company. The plaintiff had consumed between five and seven pints of cider and one short; the defendant had consumed at least six pints. The plaintiff knew, "or certainly ought to have known", that the defendant's ability to drive had been impaired by drink and that he quite clearly ought not to have driven. This was so regardless of whether the defendant's appearance indicated the extent of his impairment as the parties had been in each other's company throughout the evening and the plaintiff had actual knowledge of the defendant's consumption of alcohol.

The greater blameworthiness was that of the defendant:

> "It was his decision to drive to the bar and to drive home notwithstanding his consumption of alcohol. It is he who had control of the car and its driving and it was he who represented a danger not just to the [plaintiff] but to road users and the public in general."

It is worth reflecting on the broader position in relation to passengers travelling with drivers whom they ought to know to be intoxicated. Courts in these islands have long been hesitant to characterise the passenger as *volens* (see, e.g. *Dann v Hamilton* [1939] K.B. 509) though courts in Canada and Australia used to evince less reluctance. Today, as Kearns J. noted in *Hussey v Twomey*, the position in Ireland is governed by s.34(1)(b) of the Civil Liability Act 1961 which, as construed by the Supreme Court in *O'Hanlon v Electricity Supply Board* [1969] I.R. 75, requires proof of some actual communication between the parties from which waiver of the plaintiff's right of action is to be inferred. Such is unlikely where at least one of the parties is intoxicated: cf. *Joe v Paradis* 2008 BCCA 57 (Can LII); *Shariatmadari v Ahmadi* 2009 BCSC 1571 (Can LII). Alternative strategies to defeat the passenger's claim include *ex turpi causa* (cf. *Morris v Murray* [1991] 2 Q.B. 6) or the absence of a discernible duty of care (*Anderson v Cooke* [2005] 2 I.R. 607, analysed in the *Annual Review of Irish Law 2005*, pp.711–712). In *Anderson v Cooke*, the parties had been engaging in the foolhardy escapade of driving exceptionally fast and photographing the speedometer at its highest speed. The driver was sober. The plaintiff's claim was dismissed. Is the foolhardiness of travelling with a drunken driver so very different in principle? Certainly the tenor of Kearns J.'s observations suggests that successful invocation by a drunken driver of any of the full defences is unlikely.

Seat belts In *Moran v Fogarty* [2009] IEHC 55, Finegan J. (Murray C.J. and Denham J. concurring) was satisfied that there had been credible evidence supporting the trial judge's finding, notwithstanding the existence of "some indications to the contrary", that the plaintiff had been wearing a seat belt. The witness who had given evidence to that effect had admitted to having consumed at least five alcoholic drinks, but her recollection of what had occurred prior to the accident had not been tested in cross-examination.

NUISANCE

In *Ambrose v Shevlin* [2009] IEHC 548, construction work had taken place on a roadway on the defendant's property in 1993. Exceptionally heavy rain occurred in February 1994, which resulted in the silting up of a culvert, which in turn led to a stream on the defendant's property overflowing onto the plaintiff's property, causing damage to his home. The plaintiff sued in nuisance and negligence. It appears that Dunne J.'s analysis focussed on nuisance, though the outcome would almost certainly have been the same had it been on negligence. She quoted from Costello J.'s judgment in *Fitzpatrick v O'Connor,* High Court, March 11, 1988, which set out the principles applicable in nuisance claims where water has moved from one premises to another.

Dunne J. considered that the events of the stormy night were so exceptional as not to have been reasonably foreseeable by the defendant. The position in relation to the next two days was different, however. The defendant filled in a breach in the roadway on his land without taking any steps to put in suitable drain pipes to allow any flood water that might accumulate to escape:

> "He should have taken reasonable steps to ensure that there would be no further problem. The result was inevitable. Further flooding took place. This was entirely foreseeable."

Accordingly Dunne J. imposed liability.

DEFAMATION

The Defamation Act 2009 The Defamation Act 2009 introduces some important changes, largely likely to assist media defendants, in the law of defamation. It is substantially based on recommendations made by the Legal Advisory Group on Defamation, established by the Minister for Justice, Equality and Law Reform, in its Report published in 2003, which we analysed in the *Annual Review of Irish Law 2003*, pp.590–602. The legislation has been generally welcomed, though criticisms include its failure to address issues raised by the ubiquity of internet publications.

For analysis of the Act, see Andrew O'Rorke, "Defamation Act Will Facilitate More Sensible, Efficient Justice", *The Irish Times*, January 2, 2010. A "defamatory statement" is defined in s.2 as meaning one that tends to injure a person's reputation in the eyes of reasonable members of society. The Act abolishes the old distinction between libel and slander. Cases of defamation in future will be actionable without proof of special damage: s.6(5). Only one cause of action in respect of multiple publication is permitted save in cases where the court considers that the interests of justice requires bringing more than one action: s.11.

Part 3 of the Act sets out a list of nine defences: truth (in place of "justification" at common law), absolute privilege, qualified privilege, honest opinion (replacing "fair comment"), an offer to make amends, apology, consent to publication, fair and reasonable publication on a matter of public interest and innocent publication.

The onus of proof of the truth of the assertion remains on the defendant but the Act contains a requirement, backed by stern criminal sanctions, that parties, in respect of any pleadings containing assertions or allegations or fact, swear verifying affidavits: s.8. As regards qualified privilege, ss.18(2)(a) and 19(2) effectively reverse the effect of the Supreme Court decision in *Hynes-O'Sullivan v O'Driscoll* [1988] I.R. 436, which we analysed in the *Annual Review of Irish Law 1988*, pp.439–445, by affording a defence where the defendant believed upon reasonable grounds that the person to whom the statement was published had a duty to receive, or interest in receiving, the information contained in it, including cases where the publisher mistook a person for an interested person.

The new defence of apology (s.24) enables an apology to be made without its being construed as an admission of liability.

Section 26 sets out a defence of fair and reasonable publication on a matter of public interest. This, broadly speaking, gives statutory expression to the type of defence that courts around the common law world have constructed over the past couple of decades, the Irish instance being Ó Caoimh J.'s judgment in *Hunter v Gerald Duckworth & Co Ltd* [2003] IEHC 81. Subsection (2) sets out a non-exhaustive list of factors of which the court is to take account in determining whether it was reasonable to have published the statement concerned, somewhat similar to Lord Nicholls's famous list in *Reynolds v Times Newspapers Ltd* [2001] 2 A.C. 127.

Part 4 of the Act sets out the remedies. Significant changes to the former law are prescribed. Under s.28, a person may apply to the Circuit Court for a declaratory order in relation to an allegedly defamatory statement. No damages may be sought or awarded under this section. The court must make the required order if satisfied that the statement is defamatory of the applicant and that the respondent has no defence. The court may also make a correction order and an order prohibiting publication of the statement. Section 29 permits lodgment in court by the defendant without admission of liability. Section 30 enables the court, on the plaintiff's application, to make a correction order directing the defendant to publish a correction of the defamatory statement.

Among the important changes in relation to damages, s.31 permits the parties to make submissions to the court "in relation to the matter of damages" (s.31(1)). Subsection (4) sets out a non-exhaustive list of eleven factors to which the court is to have regard in making an award of general damages. None of these factors is such as would have been unlikely to have otherwise occurred to the jury (or judge, in the Circuit Court). The defendant is permitted to give evidence in mitigation of damages that the plaintiff has already been awarded for substantially the same allegations in other proceedings: s.31(7).

Section 32(1) permits the court to award aggravated damages where the defendant has conducted his or her defence in a manner that aggravated the injury caused by the plaintiff's reputation. Punitive damages may be awarded where the defendant published the statement intentionally to another person, knowing that it would be understood to refer to the plaintiff and knowing or being reckless as to its untruth: s.32(2).

The Supreme Court, on appeal from a High Court decision, may substitute such amount of damages as it considers appropriate: s.13(1).

The court may make an order prohibiting publication or further publication of a statement if in its opinion it is defamatory and the defendant has no defence to the action that is reasonably likely to succeed: s.33(1).

Section 43 provides that where a person has been convicted or, as the case may be, acquitted of an offence in the State, the fact of that conviction or acquittal and any findings of fact made during the course of the proceedings for the offence concerned are admissible in evidence in the defamation action.

Section 38 provides a one-year limitation period for defamation proceedings, significantly reducing that period from six years. An extension of up to two years is permitted, only where the court is satisfied that the interests of justice so require and that the prejudice the plaintiff would otherwise suffer would significantly outweigh the prejudice the defendant would suffer if the extension were given. Section 35 abolishes the common law offence of defamatory libel.

The Act, in s.44, enables the Minister for Justice, Law Reform and Equality by order to recognise a newly established body, the Press Council if satisfied that it complies with the minimum requirements set out in Sch.2 of the Act.

The Act came into force on January 1, 2010: Defamation Act 2009 (Commencement) Order 2009 (S.I. No. 517 of 2009).

Trial by judge or jury? In *Bradley, practising as Malcomson Law Solicitors v Maher* [2009] IEHC 389, Clarke J. considered it "clear that any entitlement to trial by jury in defamation proceedings is purely statutory, and does not derive from the Constitution". He pointed out that defamation proceedings in the Circuit Court do not involve a jury. It had, he observed, never been suggested that there was any constitutional infirmity in that arrangement.

In the instant case, a firm of solicitors took proceedings for defamation and unlawful picketing against a person with a grievance in relation to how they had administered the estate of a relative of that person, who had picketed their premises with allegedly defamatory placards. Clarke J. gave a comprehensive analysis as to the respective merits and drawbacks of the options of a single unitary trial, two fully separate trials and a hybrid trial where the jury would decide only certain issues. He concluded that a single trial, without involving a jury, would be the only fair and just way of resolving all of the issues. He mentioned that he did not consider that the joinder by the plaintiff of the two separate claims for defamation and unlawful picketing was a device to deprive the defendant of an entitlement to a jury trial; rather, it was "obvious" that both aspects of the claim were "real, connected and proper to be decided in one set of proceedings".

In *Kerwick v Sunday Newspapers Ltd t/a Sunday World,* High Court, July 10, 2009, reported in *The Irish Times*, July 11, 2009 and decided 11 days before Clarke J. handed down his judgment, the plaintiff brought proceedings for defamation, a breach of the right to privacy, and negligent infliction of emotional distress arising from the publication of an article in the *Sunday World*. Dunne J. held that, notwithstanding the fact that, in the ordinary way, the defamation claim would have been tried by a jury, the interests of justice required that there be a single trial of all issues and that such a trial could not be before a jury. Dunne J. is quoted in Clarke J.'s judgment as having outlined the difficulties of separating the claims into separate proceedings as follows:

> "Imagine that this case was set down for trial without a jury and that the plaintiff made an application to have the trial of two of the causes of action heard at the same time and the trial of the third cause of action held at a later time. Imagine that there would be two separate assessments made in respect of damages. There would be a duplication of evidence, the case would take longer, the costs would be greater and it is arguable that there could be an overlap in respect of the damages that might be awarded. It is difficult to see how such an approach could be permissible in any circumstances."

(The litigation was settled on July 21, 2009. The *Sunday World* apologised unreservedly for distress caused by the article. *The Irish Times* (July 22, 2009) reported that it was understood that Ms Kerwick would receive substantial High Court damages.)

The defence of justification In *Quinn Insurance Ltd v Tribune Newspapers Plc* [2009] IEHC 229, the defendants published an article alleging that the plaintiffs' insurance company "offered claimants' solicitors a sweetener to settle quickly in an innovative cost-cutting measure" and also had recruited serving Gardaí to investigate claims and settle them as quickly as possible on the company's behalf, according to a confidential internal company memorandum. The plaintiffs sued for defamation. The defendants pleaded justification, stating in their particulars: "The memorandum is authentic, and the defendants are entitled as against the plaintiffs to assume the accuracy of its contents." The plaintiff's sought further particulars of the plea of justification. The defendants' response was that "this is a matter for evidence".

The plaintiffs sought, unsuccessfully, an order from the court requiring further particulars, identifying the claims managers and serving members of An Garda Síochána. Dunne J., after a comprehensive review of the case law, derived the following principles from the earlier decisions:

> "It goes without saying that a party is entitled to know the case being made against them. If necessary, particulars may be ordered to clarify the issues or to prevent the party from being taken by surprise at the trial of the action. However, a party is only entitled to know the broad outline of the case that he/she will have to meet. A party is not entitled to know the evidence that will be given against them in advance of the hearing. Further, it is not usual to order the names and addresses of witnesses to be furnished in advance of the hearing of an action.
>
> The absence of particulars in relation to a plea of justification may result in an order to furnish such particulars, although the level

> of specificity is not as great in this jurisdiction as is required in the jurisdiction of England and Wales. The Rules in England and Wales do require a party pleading justification to set out the particulars of justification in their defence. The Rules of the Superior Courts do not impose a similar requirement on the party pleading justification in this jurisdiction, although it has been noted in a number of decisions that a party pleading justification should not do so lightly or without consideration of the evidence available to support such a plea.
>
> Finally, the names and addresses of potential witnesses may be ordered in circumstances where not to do so would be to the litigious disadvantage to the party pleading justification and to the considerable advantage of a plaintiff in a manner that would be unfair. The overriding principle in deciding whether to order replies to particulars which would have the effect of disclosing the names and addresses of potential witnesses, should be the need to ensure a fair trial for both parties to the litigation."

Applying these principles to the instant case, Dunne J. noted that, given the plea of justification, there was a strong possibility that the defendants would be required to give evidence first. The memorandum would be at the heart of the case being made by them. The plaintiffs had put in issue the genuineness of that document. The defendants relied on it as part of their plea of justification. If that document were found not to be genuine, it was difficult to see how the defendants' plea of justification would be sustained. It was clear that the allegations in relation to the use of serving members of the Gardaí and the allegations in relation to unlawful and unethical practices were derived from the contents of the memorandum. Dunne J. had "little doubt" that the defendants would find it extremely difficult to identify the names and addresses of the serving members of the Gardaí alleged to have been employed by the first named plaintiff or to identify particular claims managers of the first named plaintiff involved in such activities. On the other hand, it would be a relatively straightforward matter for the first-named plaintiff to establish if it had, in fact, employed serving members of the Gardaí for the purposes outlined and to ascertain from its own enquiries within its own business whether it had made use of information improperly obtained on its behalf.

Dismissal for want of prosecution In the *Annual Review of Irish Law 2008*, pp.495–496, Martin Canny discussed *Desmond v MGN Ltd* [2008] IESC 56, in which the Supreme Court, by a majority, declined to dismiss defamation proceedings which he had been "parked" by the plaintiff between 1999 and the issuing of the defendants' motion to dismiss in May 2005, on the grounds that he was awaiting the results of the Moriarty Tribunal. In *Desmond v Times Newspapers Ltd* [2009] IEHC 271, Dunne J. acceded to a similar motion. Whilst not expressing dissatisfaction with the majority's approach, Dunne J. evinced a strong view that a plea of justification should not necessarily constitute a barrier to dismiss. She observed:

> "There is no doubt that a plea of justification is an important factor to be borne in mind in considering and assessing where the balance of justice lies. The fact that a plea of justification has been made in defamation proceedings is not, however, a licence to a plaintiff to allow proceedings to languish indefinitely without any activity. Reference has been made to a number of decisions in which the importance of proceeding with expedition in defamation proceedings has been emphasised. The essence of defamation proceedings is the vindication of an individual's good name. A person's reputation is at the heart of such proceedings. That is why it is necessary for a plaintiff to act quickly in the prosecution of defamation proceedings for the longer a defamatory statement remains unchallenged, the greater the potential damage to a person's reputation. The taint of wrong doing implicit in a plea of justification and the fact that that will be allowed to remain on the record is a significant matter in considering where the balance of justice lies.
>
> Nonetheless, it cannot be the case that a plaintiff's case cannot be dismissed for want of prosecution, only by reason of the fact that there is a plea of justification. One has to ask the question at what point could the defendants be entitled to apply to have these proceedings dismissed for want of prosecution. In my view the defendants in these cases became entitled to apply to have the proceedings dismissed when the plaintiff failed to reactivate these proceedings in 2005 or within a reasonable period thereafter, having reached the decision that it was no longer appropriate to await the outcome of the Moriarty Tribunal. At that point, even on the plaintiff's case, there was no reason not to proceed. The plaintiff attempted to do so in [earlier] proceedings and the MGN proceedings. It was only thereafter that the defendant sought to have those proceedings dismissed for want of prosecution. In these cases, the plaintiff could have reactivated the proceedings, but chose not to do so and has not provided any reason, good, bad or indifferent for that decision. I do not think that the fact that justification has been pleaded in these cases on its own is a sufficient reason to swing the balance of justice in favour of the plaintiff. One has to consider other factors that arise in these cases."

MALICIOUS FALSEHOOD

The Defamation Act 2009 has introduced an important change in relation to the action for slander of title, slander of goods or malicious falsehood, which used to be widely known as the tort of injurious falsehood. Under s.20 of the Defamation Act 1961, headed "Slander of title, etc.", subs.(1) provided that it should not be necessary to allege or prove special damage in either of two circumstances. The first was where the words on which the action was founded were "calculated to cause pecuniary damage" and published in writing or other permanent form (extended to broadcasting by subs.(2)). The second was where the words were "calculated to cause pecuniary damage to the plaintiff in respect of any office, profession, calling, trade or business held or carried on by him at the time of publication." The parallels with the differences between the actions for libel and slander were obvious.

The Defamation Act 2009 abolishes the distinction between these two actions and does not require the plaintiff in a claim for defamation to prove special damage. This has a consequential effect on what was characterised as "Slander of title, etc" in s.20 of the 1961 Act. Section 42, headed "Malicious falsehood", first prescribes the ingredients of the tort. Subsection (1) states that, in an action for slander of title, slander of goods or other malicious falsehood, the plaintiff is required to prove that the statement on which the action is founded (a) was untrue, (b) was published maliciously, and (c) referred to the plaintiff, his or her property or his or her office, profession, calling, trade or business. Subsection (2) provides that, in such an action, the plaintiff is required to prove either (a) special damage, or (b) that the publication of the statement "was calculated to cause and was likely to cause financial loss to the plaintiff in respect of his or her property or his or her office, profession, calling, trade or business."

One difference between the former and current law is that, in the absence of special damage, a plaintiff may now sue successfully in cases where the words are not published in permanent form but are "calculated to cause and likely to cause" financial loss in respect of the plaintiff's property. As against this, formerly, again in the absence of special damage, where the words were published in permanent form, the plaintiff could succeed if they were "calculated to cause" him or her pecuniary damage. Today, whether publication is in permanent form or otherwise, the plaintiff, in the absence of special damage, must do more. He or she must show that the publication was "calculated to cause and was likely to cause" a particular result. The use here of the word "calculated" can scarcely be surplusage. It formerly connoted likelihood rather than intention. Now it must have a separate meaning: "intended" is the obvious candidate. So now the plaintiff must cumulatively prove both intention and likelihood. It is hard to see the merit in this change. A second difference, to the disadvantage of the plaintiff, is that he or she must prove "calculation" plus likelihood of causing him or her financial loss in respect of his or her property. Formerly, where the words were published in permanent form, likelihood ("calculat[ion]") of causing pecuniary damage sufficed.

VICARIOUS LIABILITY

Sexual abuse of employee In *Reilly v Devereux* [2009] IESC 22, where a young member of the Defence Forces had been subjected to sexual abuse by a Sergeant Major from 1989 to 1995, the Supreme Court, affirming Johnson J., held that the military authorities were not vicariously liable. Kearns J. (Denham and Finnegan JJ. concurring) was guided by the decisions of the Supreme Court of Canada in *Bazley v Curry* 174 DLR (4th) 45 (1999) and *Jacobi v Griffiths* 174 DLR (4th) 71 (1999) but distinguished them on the basis that they related to the care of children, whereas the plaintiff in the instant case had been born in 1966. While undoubtedly the Sergeant Major had exercised a supervisory and disciplinary role in relation to the plaintiff, he had not been in the same position as a school teacher or boarding house warden in relation to a child. Kearns J. observed:

> "Nor was the nature of the employment one which would have encouraged close personal contact where some inherent risks might be said to exist as, for example, might arise if the [Sergeant Major] had been a swimming instructor in close physical contact with young recruits. There was no intimacy implicit in the relationship between the plaintiff and the [Sergeant Major] nor was there any quasi-parental role or responsibility for personal nurturing, which was found to exist in the cases where vicarious liability was established. To hold otherwise would be to extend to the Defence Forces a virtual new species of liability where the defendants would be liable for virtually every act or omission of an employee."

Kearns J. noted that such an approach had been firmly ruled out by the Supreme Court in *O'Keeffe v Hickey* [2008] IESC 72. Hardiman J. had there stated:

> "In my view, both justice and the basic requirements of an ordered society require that the imposition of strict liability on a no fault basis be done (if at all) only on the clearest and most readily understandable basis. I do not regard the Canadian cases cited as providing such a basis: quite the opposite, as the two conflicting decisions cited demonstrate, in my view. I do not believe that the expanded basis of vicarious liability represents the law in this jurisdiction, or can be made to do so except by legislation. The consequences of doing this, social as well economic, would be immense".

Hardiman J. had gone on to note the "chilling effect" of any extension of the doctrine of vicarious liability whereby the State would become liable for criminal activities of those in their employment in circumstances where there was no fault attaching to the State. To do so would be not only to make the taxpayer liable for the criminal acts of employees of state bodies, but it would also affect that body's actions in ways which would require it to be considered as a matter of policy before such an extension of the law could be allowed. Kearns J. observed:

> "While the *O'Keeffe* case involved a vulnerable child who was sexually abused by a teacher at school, it need hardly be stressed that the facts of the relationship between the parties in the instant case could hardly be more different. The plaintiff in this case was at all material times an adult. He elected to accept the rigours, the discipline and the camaraderie associated with the life of a professional soldier. It must be accepted that the Defence Forces require an atmosphere of discipline in order to function. A wide extension of liability would undermine the whole operational basis of any army."

Health care *Reilly v Moir* [2009] IEHC 164 serves as a useful reminder that the provision of private healthcare does not always carry with it access to the "deep pocket" of a large institution or its insurers. The plaintiff underwent breast enlargement surgery resulting in unsightly scars, which constituted a permanent disfigurement of a particularly distressing and embarrassing kind. Mr Moir, a London-based surgeon who carried out the operation, at Clane Hospital, frankly admitted his negligence for which he apologised. The way the operation had been arranged was that a company called Precision Lasercare Limited (PLL) advertised the provision of cosmetic surgery. The plaintiff, following an initial telephone call to the company, attended an appointment at Clane Hospital where she had a consultation with Mr Moir. She was happy to go ahead with the surgery. She expected that it would be another London-based surgeon, Mr Carver who would do the operation though this was not a matter of concern to her.

The plaintiff paid the requested fee (£4,050) to PLL. She had no involvement in how the fee was divided between relevant parties thereafter. The relationship between these parties was somewhat complex. PLL, in essence, generated patients through advertising and arranged for them to speak to a suitably qualified surgeon in the hope that the patient would decide to undergo surgery. It would contact a British company Private Patient Services Ltd (PPS), in which Mr Carver had a 50 per cent share, and make arrangements for a qualitied surgeon such as Mr Moir or Mr Carver to come over to Dublin. Mr Moir was not party to any of the arrangements entered into between PLL and PPS. He was simply asked by PPS to travel to Clane Hospital on this particular day in order to perform the plaintiff's surgery. He was never quite sure as to who exactly was in charge of these arrangements, though he knew that there was some arrangement between PLL and PPS. Mr Moir stated in evidence that he and Mr Carver were independent surgeons for whom PPS simply performed some administrative functions, such as controlling their diaries, organising tax returns, and collecting fees. Neither of them was employed by PPS. He stated that, in so far as Mr Carver would on occasion be at Clane Hospital in an adjoining operating theatre, he was available to him for advice or consultation should that need arise, but he rejected any notion that he was working under the direction as such of Mr Carver.

Evidence was given that, before any surgeon could have theatre rights in Clane Hospital, his or her qualifications would have to be checked by the hospital, and that had been done.

Peart J. concluded that, when performing surgery in Ireland, Mr Moir had been acting as an independent contractor:

> "He was not an employee as such of PPS. That company's involvement is confined to the provision of essentially secretarial and administrative services as described. They were the contact point for PLL when arranging for a surgeon to see clients and where necessary to perform the surgery. Their duty obviously involved ensuring that any surgeon so provided was a suitably qualified surgeon, but that is not the same as saying that PPS would be liable for any surgery which was performed negligently, as in this case. Any such negligence is a matter between the patient and that surgeon, and possibly between the patient and PLL with whom the contract for surgery was made. There has been no evidence to even suggest that part of these arrangements involved the giving of an indemnity to PLL in respect of any negligence being found against the surgeon. Those surgeons provided through PPS were not employees of PPS and there is no question of any vicarious liability arising."

The fact that Mr Carver was a 50 per cent shareholder in PPS did not alter his position. He had not been in any way negligent in this case. As it happens, Mr Carver was present at Clane Hospital on the day on which the plaintiff underwent her surgery with Mr Moir. He was operating on other patients in an adjoining theatre at the hospital. While he was available to be consulted by Mr Moir if that need arose, it could not be said that Mr Carver was in any supervisory role in relation to the plaintiff's surgery in the sense that he shared the responsibility to ensure that her surgery was properly performed:

> "Mr Moir was the surgeon. He was fully qualified to perform that surgery, and the responsibility for the unsatisfactory outcome is the responsibility of Mr Moir."

While Clane General Hospital had owed a duty of care to the plaintiff arising from its relationship with her, there was no evidence that it had breached its duty of care to her. It had had no direct involvement in the surgery either directly or on the basis of any vicarious liability, since Mr Moir was not its employee, and the surgeon provided by PLL, through PSS, was appropriately qualified to carry out this operation on the plaintiff.

Thus, the only defendant liable to the plaintiff was Mr Moir who, it appeared, had no insurance cover for his work in Ireland.

Judicial immunity In *Kemmy v Ireland* [2009] IEHC 148, McMahon J. provided a stimulating analysis of the issue of the vicarious liability of the State in the context of judicial immunity. The plaintiff had been convicted of rape and sexual assault and sentenced to imprisonment. The Court of Criminal Appeal had overturned the conviction on the basis that the act of the trial judge, in reading only his note of the complainant's evidence (in response to a request by the jury for the transcript of her evidence) had been "unfair" and had render[ed] the trial "unfair". The plaintiff sought damages from the State for its infringement, through its judicial organ, for the plaintiff's constitutional rights to a fair criminal trial.

McMahon J. examined in detail the principle of judicial immunity. As regards vicarious liability, he observed that "whichever text one favours, the relationship between the State and the judiciary stubbornly refuses to be comfortably accommodated." When one had regard to the constitutional principles of the separation of powers and the independence of the judiciary, it was:

> "... clear that the administration of justice can only be exercised by the judiciary, and its administration is free from any interference by any other person, including the legislature or the executive. It is also clear that this is very different from the duty which a servant (employee) has towards the master (employer) and who must carry out his master's orders at all times. Importantly, under the Constitution, the judge does not receive his power or authority from the State but from the people, is independent in the exercise of his functions and is free from interference from the State, particularly from the other organs of government. The only limit or control on the judge is to be found in the Constitution itself or in the law. For these reasons too, it would be difficult to consider the judge to be part of the State 'enterprise', since his only function is to administer justice as mandated by the people.
>
> For the above reasons it is wholly inappropriate to attempt to describe the relationship between the State and a member of the judiciary in the Master/Servant terminology developed for the purposes of imposing vicarious liability for tortious acts or omissions. Accordingly, in my view, the State cannot be vicariously liable for the errors which a judge may commit in the administration of justice. This conclusion holds in respect of errors which may be described as errors within jurisdiction, and of *a fortiori* to errors which are outside the judge's jurisdiction,

> including those committed, *mala fides*, for which of course, in extreme cases, the judge may lose his personal immunity."

Nor did McMahon J. consider that the State should be directly liable under the Constitution for judicial error. He reasoned as follows:

> "[W]hen the judge is exercising judicial authority he is acting in an independent manner and not only is he not a servant of the State in these circumstances, he is not even acting on behalf of the State. He is not doing the State's business. He is acting at the behest of the people and his mission is to administer justice. In most cases he is merely exercising his discretion and his actions cannot amount to 'torts' at all. For the most part he is immune from civil liability. From this perspective, the State is not directly involved with his activities, does not write his mission and cannot intervene with the judge's exercise of his functions. While in one sense, it may be appropriate to describe the judiciary as an organ of government in the broad constitutional representation of the State, in another sense, when exercising its jurisdiction, the judiciary is truly decoupled from the State. In a sense, there are two principals involved at a constitutional level in the administration of justice, and if the judiciary is immune from suit it seems logical that the State when facilitating the exercise of judicial power through the judiciary should also be entitled to State immunity in that regard.
>
> In a constitutional sense, the State merely provides the scaffording for judicial activity. The State is no longer involved once the judge begins his work. The State may be liable for failing to erect the appropriate scaffolding, but once this is up, and the judge goes about his business, the only liability that arises is that of the judge. To speak of the State's liability for judicial acts in that context is somehow to re-introduce in disguise the concept of vicarious liability, something that I have already rejected."

In *McFarlane v Ireland*, (Application No. 31333/06), on September 10, 2010, the European Court of Human Rights, in the majority judgment, indicated disagreement with what had been stated in *Kenny*. The dissenting judgment, of judges Gyulumyan, Zieriele, Bianku and Power, reveals a far clearer understanding of the subtleties of McMahon J.'s analysis.

DAMAGES

Duty to mitigate damages In *Yun v MIBI and Tao* [2009] IEHC 3, Quirke J. held that the plaintiff, who had been very seriously injured, was not required to subject herself to further surgery which had a 1 per cent to 5 per cent risk of resulting in paraplegia. Some of the doctors were keen on her undergoing the surgery. Matters were complicated by the fact that the plaintiff's psychological condition inhibited her decision-making capacity. Quirke J. considered that the defendants had not discharged the onus of proving that the plaintiff's refusal to undergo the surgery was unreasonable. He noted that the plaintiff's terror of paraplegia had been magnified by the stigma which would attach to that condition in her home region in China. Quirke J. considered that this terror was "not necessarily irrational. It has been shared by others in this jurisdiction and elsewhere".

Dismissal of claims by plaintiffs giving false or misleading evidence Section 26(1) of the Civil Liability and Courts Act 2004 requires the court to dismiss a personal injuries action where the plaintiff gives or addresses evidence that (a) is false or misleading in any material respect, and (b) he or she knows to be false or misleading, unless, for reasons the court must state in its decision, the dismissal of the action would result in injustice being done. The courts have generally been reluctant to dismiss a claim by reason of s.26. On rare occasions, however, they have dismissed claims on this ground.

Gamell v Doyle trading as Lee's House [2009] IEHC 416 is a curious case. The plaintiff was struck and injured by the second-named defendant when they were in the first-named defendant's premises. The plaintiff claimed that the punch came out of the blue; the second-named defendant said that he had been provoked by the plaintiff's lewd references to the second-named defendant's wife. Hanna J. concluded on the evidence that the plaintiff had said "venomous, crude and provocative things" and had engaged in a "tirade of appalling abuse and lewd sexual references", as well as poking the second-named defendant while speaking to him. The second-named defendant, in Hanna J.'s view, had been "subjected to the most outlandish provocation".

On the question of liability, Hanna J. considered that a reduction of 50 per cent of compensation to take account of the plaintiff's contributory negligence was appropriate (rather than an award of contemptuous damages, which he thought more appropriate for defamation cases). The injuries sustained by the plaintiff would have warranted €40,000 if he had been entitled to a full award. Hanna J. went on, however, to completely deny the plaintiff *any* compensation by reason of s.26. The plaintiff's account of what had occurred had been "both fanciful and self-serving and deliberately so".

In the particular circumstances of the case, the dismissal of the claim would not amount to injustice. The second-named defendant had been prosecuted for assault, pleaded guilty and received a suspended sentence of two and a half years imprisonment. The case was thus not one where a plaintiff who had received a significant injury and yet told untruths to a material extent would have to watch an undoubted tortfeasor walk away. The law had taken its course and the second-named defendant had the imposition of a significant, albeit suspended, sentence.

One puzzling aspect of the case is that "personal injuries action" is defined by s.2(1) of the 2004 Act as not including "an action where the damages claimed include damages for … trespass to the person". Section 26 applies only to personal injuries actions. If a punch on the nose is not a trespass to the person, it is hard to envisage what is. The plaintiff's unsuccessful action against the first-named defendant was of course for negligence rather than trespass to the person. Hanna J.'s judgment does not address the nature of the claim against the second-named defendant.

In *Behan v AIB Plc* [2009] IEHC 554, Murphy J. held that s.26 should not be applied against a plaintiff, whose affidavit was, in one reply, "incomplete and, to that extent, … misleading" as he was not satisfied that the plaintiff had known that this reply was false and misleading. Murphy J. noted that subs.(2) did "not provide that she ought to have known".

In *Walsh v South Dublin County Council* [2009] IEHC 518, where Lavan P. dismissed a claim by a plaintiff who alleged that she had been caused to trip over a damaged sluice marker post on a public footpath, he noted that the plaintiff had been "in difficulties from the beginning of her cross-examination". She could not validate her affidavit of verification. He observed:

> "The Oireachtas being concerned with bogus claims has move[d] to ensure that claims are verified. Where an affidavit of verification is sworn and subsequently proven to be wrong then the defending party must pay the price for this."

Lavan J. did not, however, invoke s.26 of the 2004 Act. He simply rejected the evidence of the plaintiff and her witnesses, dismissing the claim on the basis that the plaintiff had "failed, on the balance of probability, to establish a case in negligence" against the County Council.

In *Donovan v Farrell* [2009] IEHC 617, Peart J. declined to conclude that the plaintiff had attempted to exaggerate her injuries by not mentioning previous back difficulties during her pregnancies or by saying to a medical examiner that she could do no gardening when video evidence contradicted this to some extent. Peart J. was "not inclined to penalise her in relation to stating [this] so categorically", even though she ought to have given "a more comprehensive answer to his questions in that regard". In *Singleton v Doyle* [2009] IEHC 382, Peart J. came to a similar conclusion where the plaintiff, seriously injured in an accident in 1999, had failed to inform some of her medical professionals of precisely what injuries she had suffered in an accident nine years previously.

The risks involved in the defendant's unsuccessfully accusing a plaintiff of making a fraudulent claim were made plain in *Hennessy v Cusack t/a Adare Manor Equestrian Centre*, High Court, May 12, 2009, reported in *The Irish*

Times, May 13, 2009. The plaintiff, an inexperienced horse rider attending the defendant equestrian centre, fell from a horse that was not appropriate for his level of expertise. The defence as initially presented to the court was that the plaintiff had not undertaken a riding lesson on the day in question and had not been injured at the centre. In cross-examination, it was put to him that his claim was fraudulent but the claim of fraud was later withdrawn during the trial. Quirke J. noted that the decision to make the claim of fraud had apparently been made by the indemnifiers of the defendant ("understood to be a UK group".) Awarding the plaintiff €75,000, which included €30,000 aggravated damages, Quirke J. noted that the case had been dominated by a most serious allegation of fraud, maintained over two full days of evidence, made with disregard for the consequences on the plaintiff's reputation.

Care costs Clearly, if a plaintiff has been so badly injured that he or she needs care to be provided in terms of nursing assistance or more informal support such as help with dressing and day-to-day living, compensation must be made for this. Professional care of this kind, extending over many years, can come to a substantial sum.

In many cases the care will be provided by a spouse, partner, parent or child of the plaintiff. The courts in these circumstances are willing to compensate the plaintiff though at a rate less than the commercial rate.

In *Yun v MIBI and Tao* [2009] IEHC 318, Quirke J. addressed this matter. The plaintiff had received "continuous and comprehensive" care from her boyfriend over the seven years since the accident, in May 2002, provided by him "in an exemplary manner". Quirke J. stated:

> "The plaintiff is entitled to recover damages to enable her to repay Mr. Cao Zhi for the invaluable, continuous care which she has received from him.
>
> The cost of professional care for four hours every day from the 9th May, 2002, to the 12th December, 2008, has been calculated at €174,916. Mr. Cao Zhi provided far more than four hours care each day to the plaintiff during the past seven years.
>
> When awarding damages for past care provided by parents and family members it has been the practice of the courts to apply remuneration rates significantly less than those which apply to the provisions of professional care. It has never been entirely clear to me why that should be the case. Usually the care provided by parents and family members is commensurate with professional care standards. Often it exceeds those standards.
>
> However, adopting that practice, I am awarding the plaintiff the sum of €85,000, which is somewhat less than 50 per cent of the cost of the

> very least amount of professional care which the plaintiff has required during the past eight years."

In *O'Brien v Derwin* [2009] IEHC 2, Charleton J. declined to award the wife of the plaintiff any compensation for the home care she provided him. The plaintiff had sustained significant brain damage. Charleton J. observed that he was:

> "... not satisfied that on the authorities I am entitled to make such an allowance. My sympathy goes very much in favour of the plaintiff's wife and the tremendous work that she has done. It was apparent even as they were sitting in court that the plaintiff depends upon her and their mutual affection is obvious. It was argued that the alternative to making such an award was to make an allowance in respect of home care. I simply feel that there is no legal warrant for me to do so since the precedents opened to me concern the use of nursing skills to a badly injured plaintiff."

This seems a somewhat harsh holding. The plaintiff's particular needs fell within a zone where compensation has been provided in the other cases over the years.

The cap on damages In *Sinnott v Quinnsworth Ltd* [1984] I.L.R.M. 523, the Supreme Court introduced a rough tariff in relation to damages for pain and suffering. The plaintiff was a young man who, as a result of a motor accident, became "quadriplegic, with paralysis and sensory loss and loss of control of bladder and bowel and totally dependent on others". The Supreme Court reduced a jury award of £800,000 to £150,000. O'Higgins C.J., in a passage with which the other members of the court agreed, expressed the view that:

> "[u]nless there are particular circumstances which suggest otherwise, general damages, in a case of this nature, should not exceed a sum the region of contemporary standards and money values and I am conscious that there may be changes and alternations in the future, as there have been in past."

O'Higgins C.J. arrived at the figure of £150,000, by a slow and somewhat controversial route. He stressed the danger that, in "assaying the impossible" in attempting to provide compensation for very serious injuries, juries were in danger of losing "all sense of reality". Two policy factors made it important that this should not happen. First, the defendant or his indemnifiers could legitimately complain if the sum awarded was "so high as to constitute a punishment for the infliction of the injury". Secondly, it mattered to contemporary society "if, by reason of the amount decided upon and the example which it sets for other determinations of damages by juries, the operation of public policy would thereby endangered". This is an important reminder that awards of compensation are not made in a social vacuum: there is a social price, and there comes a point where the price is simply too high.

The Chief Justice expressed the view that "a limit must exist, and should be sought and recognised, having regard to the facts of each case and the social conditions which obtain in our society". He stressed that "every single penny" of monetary loss or expense to which the plaintiff had been, and would be, put had been provided for under other heads of damages. In assessing general damages, the objective had to be to determine a figure that was fair and reasonable, and to this end it seemed to O'Higgins C.J. that:

> "... some regard should be had to the ordinary living standards in the country, to the general level of incomes, and to the things upon which the plaintiff might reasonably be expected to spend money".

In *Yun v MIBI and Tao* [2009] IEHC 318, the plaintiff, a young woman, sustained very serious back injuries in a car crash, which left her with a most serious psychological condition. Quirke J. described her injury as being "of the utmost gravity", involving "the near total destruction of her life and lifestyle" during the eight years following the accident.

Quirke J. set out in detail the jurisprudence on the cap on general damages. He considered that the following general principles applied to the assessment of general damages where catastrophic injuries have been suffered:

> "1. Where the claimant has been awarded compensatory special damages to make provision for all necessary past and future care, medical treatment and loss of earnings, there will be a limit or 'cap' placed upon the level of general damages to be awarded.
>
> When applying or reviewing the 'cap' on general damages the court should take into account the factors and principles identified by the Supreme Court in *Sinnott v Quinnsworth,* and in *M.N. v S.M.* [[2005] IESC 17] including 'contemporary standards and money values'.
>
> 2. Where the award is solely or largely an award of general damages for the consequences of catastrophic injuries there will be no 'cap' placed upon the general damages awarded.
>
> Each such case will depend upon its own facts so that: (a) an award for general damages could, if the evidence so warranted, make provision for factors such as future loss of employment opportunity or future expenses which cannot be precisely calculated or proved at the time of trial, (b) life expectancy may be a factor to be taken into account and, (c) a modest or no award for general damages may be made where general damages will have little or no compensatory consequence for the injured person.

> 3. There must be proportionality between: (a) court awards of general damages made, (i) by judges sitting alone and, (ii) in civil jury trials and, (b) by statutory bodies established by the State to assess general damages for particular categories of personal injuries."

Quirke J. considered it appropriate to receive expert evidence on Ireland's economic and social history since 1984, when *Sinnott v Quinnsworth* was decided, as well as "future social and economic outlooks", when seeking to review the cap at the time of judgment.

As regards inflation, the expert evidence showed that the equivalent value of the sum of €150,000 (€190,000) in 2007 was €391,400 (applying the Gross Domestic Product Deflator) and €388,740 (applying the Consumer Price Index). In 2008, the CPI yielded a figure of €405,460.

In attempting to identify the "ordinary living standards in the country ... the general level of incomes and ... the things upon which the plaintiff might reasonably be expected to spend money", to which O'Higgins C.J. had referred in *Sinnott,* Quirke J. received expert evidence on the Gross National Product, consumption and average industrial earnings. The statistics regarding the difference between 1984 values and contemporary values are considerably more striking than those relating to inflation. As regards Gross National Product, they suggested a per head increase from £5,900 in 1984 to €39,200 in 2007. Applying this to the sum of £150,000, 1984 values, that sum would have increased to €1,311,000. Household consumption had increased by a multiple of 5.2, yielding €988,000 as the equivalent of €150,000. Average industrial earnings had increased by a multiple of 3.1, yielding an equivalent of €589,000. Further expert evidence relating to earnings in the manufacturing and private sectors, gross national income per head and disposable income per head, showed increases by factors varying between 2.15 and 6.07, giving sums in 2008 values between €409,491 and €1,156,777.

Quirke J. then had to confront the nature and likely future outcome of the recent collapse in the economy. Expert evidence had been given that the consensus view was that GNP per head would fall by at least 4 per cent and possibly as much as 8 per cent in 2009. A further contraction of between 1 per cent and 3 per cent was probable for 2010 and a recovery within the economy was unlikely before the end of 2011 although it could be delayed for a further year. It was unlikely that GNP per head would return to 2008 levels before 2014 or 2015. Quirke J. noted that one of the expert witnesses, Moore McDowell, had:

> "... explained that, whilst the effect of a prolonged recession should have an impact upon the calculation of the 'cap' in catastrophic cases, the adjustment to be made should not be large by comparison with an

> adjustment to take into account social and economic change over a 25 year period".

He had not, however, measured the adjustment to be made.

The pith of Quirke J.'s analysis of the relevance of these data to determining the contemporary of the cap on damages is contained in the following passage of his judgment:

> "The 'cap' on general damages in 2008 should be calculated against the background of living standards and money values applicable within the community in 2008. On the evidence living standards in 2007 were more than five times better than they had been in 1984. Income levels had increased at a rate approximately 50 per cent greater than inflation during the same period. A downturn commenced in late 2007 or early 2008.
>
> No expert evidence has been adduced which would accommodate a scientifically accurate calculation of an adjustment of the 'cap' which, having allowed for inflation, would reflect the significant increases in earning levels and the improvements in living standards which have occurred between 1984 and 2008. Accordingly, I am seeking to achieve that objective on a commonsense basis by making a 25% upward adjustment of the 'cap'.
>
> That upward adjustment increases the equivalent value in 2008 of the 1984 'cap' of IR£150,000 (€190,000) from €400,000 to €500,000.
>
> However, a downward adjustment must then be made to reflect the present and forthcoming reduction in wealth and living standards which commenced in early 2008 and is expected to continue for a further period in excess of five years.
>
> The downward adjustment should not be large for the reasons outlined by Mr. McDowell and also because, on the evidence, it is likely that living standards, after a sharp decline in 2009, will gradually improve before returning to their 2008 levels by 2014 or 2015. I would measure the downwards adjustment at 10%.
>
> That further adjustment reduces the present equivalent value of the 1984 'cap' of IR£150,000 (€190,000) to €450,000."

Quirke J. went on to state that there should be proportionality between court awards of general damages made by judges sitting alone, by juries and by statutory and other bodies established by the State to award general damages. This approach was indicated, though not expressly prescribed, by Denham J. in *MN v SM* [2005] IESC 17, a case dealing with compensation for sexual abuse and exploitation. The idea that cases of that kind or cases of defamation, for example, have any necessary connection with personal injury claims relating to road traffic accidents is a controversial one. It is noteworthy that Canadian jurisprudence does not accept that the same scale of compensation must apply in all contexts.

The *Reddy v Bates* reduction In *Reddy v Bates* [1984] I.L.R.M. 197, the Supreme Court stressed that the high rate of unemployment and redundancies that was then a feature of the economy "must inevitably lead to the conclusion that there is no longer any safe, much less guaranteed, employment". Juries would be required to take that factor into account in assessing future loss of earnings in any given case. In *Cook v Walsh* [1984] I.L.R.M. 208, Griffin J. reiterated this injunction more emphatically. In the decade or more following *Reddy v Bates,* courts faithfully made a reduction in assessing future loss of earnings, generally in the region of 10 per cent to 15 per cent, though reductions smaller and larger than those did occur rarely.

Through the years of the economic boom, the *Reddy v Bates* reduction lived on, though cited relatively infrequently. No judge held that it was wrong to make a reduction of this kind as there was full employment which seemed likely to last indefinitely.

Now that the bad times have returned, courts are willing to spell out the *Reddy v Bates* reduction in stark terms. In *Yun v MIBI and Tao* [2009] IEHC 318, Quirke J. concluded from the evidence that the capital value of the plaintiff's loss of employment, if she had remained in continuous employment as an accountant until she reached the age of 65, was €522,950. He went on to say:

> "That capital sum must be discounted to take account of the factors identified by the Supreme Court in *Reddy v Bates* (and subsequent authorities). The discount must be substantial because of the present and predicted domestic and global economic recession and because of the plaintiff's personal circumstances and aspirations prior to her injury. The discount must also take into account the plaintiff's professed hope to marry and raise a family, which, if realised, would probably have slightly reduced the extent and duration of her earning capacity."

This reduction of more than 30 per cent calls for comment. The fact that Quirke J. refers to both economic and non-economic factors without attempting to allocate their respective weights makes it difficult to assess the degree of reduction which he considered appropriately "substantial" to reflect the "present and predicted" recession. He gives no indication of how long he considers the recession likely to last—a difficult question, of course, but one to which a court must have regard if it is not to project into future decades the present bad state of the economy simply because of the difficulty of the task. As to making even a modest reduction to take account of the plaintiff's professed hope to marry and raise a family, troubling issues arise. A defendant who has injured a plaintiff—male or female—is surely not entitled to obtain a reduction in the amount of compensation paid to the plaintiff for loss of earning capacity simply because the plaintiff discloses a hope that his or her personal life in the future may unfold in a way which would result in his or her failing to utilise that earning capacity fully. A court should be very careful not to proceed on any prescriptive gender-based premises when awarding damages. See Berryman, "Accommodating Ethnic and Cultural Factors in Damages for Personal Injury" (2007) 40 U.B.C.L. Rev. 1, 15–19; Cassels, "(In)equality and the Law of Tort: Gender, Race and the Assessment of Damages" (1995) 17 Advoc. Q. 158, 170–174; Adjin-Tettey, "Replicating and Perpetuating Inequalities in Personal Injury Claims Through Female-Specific Contingencies" (2004) 49 McGill L.J. 309, 326–330.

It is worth noting that in *Moran v Fogarty* [2009] IESC 55, the Supreme Court appeared content to apply the *Reddy v Bates* reduction. Here, Finnegan J. (Murray C.J. and Denham J. concurring) noted that the award made by the trial judge for future loss of earnings had been within the parameters of the evidence adduced. In these circumstances he would not interfere with it. Finnegan J. added, without further elaboration, that the trial judge had "expressly had regard to *Reddy v Bates*". This surely constitutes implicit endorsement of the continuing vitality of the *Reddy v Bates* reduction. At High Court level, Charleton J. in *O'Brien v Derwin* [2009] IEHC 2 reduced the compensation for future earnings by 10 per cent to take account of "ordinary risks such as under-employment and redundancy". He specifically referred to *Reddy v Bates* in this context.

In *Vernon v Colgan* [2009] IEHC 86, Laffoy J. applied *Reddy v Bates* when awarding a 55-year-old plaintiff €120,000 for future loss of earnings. She accepted evidence that his net annual earnings would have remained at €29,000 "continuously into the future until, say, retirement at age 65". This reduction from €290,000 seems notably steep, representing a elimination of over 58 per cent.

In *Quinn v Dunne* [2009] IEHC 144, where the plaintiff's injuries were so serious as to require him to abandon his career as a printer and become a taxi driver, Peart J. made no reduction to take account of *Reddy v Bates* but added:

> "[N]either am I taking account of evidence which has been given to the effect that during 2009 taxi fares are due to be increased. In my view a reasonable and fair balance is struck in this way."

The Book of Quantum Section 22(1) of the Personal Injuries Assessment Board Act 2003 requires the court, in assessing damages in a personal injuries action, to "have regard to" the Book of Quantum published by the Personal

Injuries Assessment Board. Subsection (2) of s.22 provides that subs.(1) is not to operate to prohibit a court from having regard to matters other than the book of Quantum when assessing the damages. For earlier analysis of the Book of Quantum, see Binchy, "The Impact of the New Act on Tort Law" in C. Craven & W. Binchy (eds), *Civil Liability and Courts Act 2004: Implications for Personal Injuries Litigation* (Firstlaw, 2005), pp.68–74.

Judges have generally responded compliantly to this legislative nudge. See *Meagher v Shamrock Public Houses Ltd t/a The Ambassador Hotel* [2005] IEHC 35; *Vega v Cullen* [2005] IEHC 362; *Kerr v Molloy and Sherry (Lough Eglish) Ltd* [2006] IEHC 364; *Davis v Jordan* [2008] IEHC 200. In *Power v Governor of Cork Prison* [2005] IEHC 253, where the plaintiff suffered a head injury with severe headaches, as well as a scar, Herbert J. noted that he had had regard to the Book of Quantum but had "found there was no indicated parameters of compensation for this type of injury". One flash of judicial independence occurred in *McFadden v West* [2005] IEHC 473, where Budd J. observed:

> "The Book of Quantum states that it contains a guideline of injuries and related values. It lists injuries and the levels of compensation ... I have considerable reservations about the usefulness of the P.I.A.B. Book of Quantum as so much depends on one's assessment of the personality of the individual plaintiff and how devastating the effect of the particular injuries have been on such a person with the relevant particular circumstances and character."

In *O'Brien v Derwin* [2009] IEHC 2, we get an insight into current judicial thinking in relation to the Book of Quantum. The plaintiff received permanent brain damage in an accident. He lost his employment. He had difficulty concentrating on reading more than a paragraph in the newspaper. Sometimes even his ability to talk went "a bit haywire". He became obsessive and unable to do more than one task at a time or think about more than one issue at a time. He suffered from anxiety and "negative thought", with random headaches and back pain.

Charleton J. observed that, while counsel had expressed some scepticism in relation to the exercise of having regard to the Book of Quantum, he wished to record that he was grateful for the work done by the Personal Injuries Assessment Board on the issue of general damages. It provided a touchstone against which the cases could be assessed and it was "a useful expert view which can help the court in coming to a conclusion on this difficult issue".

Charleton J. went on to note that, in addition to the plaintiff's main brain injury, he had sustained other smaller bone injuries, a small degree of scarring and "what would normally be highly significant in terms of an injury", the loss of his sense of taste and smell, "which would otherwise attract an award of serious compensation". Charlton J. quoted the following passage from p.4 of the Book of Quantum which seemed to him to be correct:

> "If, in addition to the most significant injury as outlined above, there are other injuries, it is not appropriate to add up values for all the different injuries to determine the amount of compensation. Where additional injuries arise there is likely to be minor adjustment within the value range."

Charleton J. commented:

> "It is clear that the plaintiff has a serious and permanent condition. The Book of Quantum classifies skull fractures and brain injuries under three headings. The first, attracting the least significant amount of damages involves a skull fracture with no loss of consciousness. The second, leading to more significant damage, involves a skull fracture with a brain injury but with no loss of consciousness. Finally, the most serious category involves a skull fracture with intracranial injury and loss of consciousness. For a serious and permanent condition, the maximum amount set is €129,000. An argument was presented that this Book of Quantum was formulated in 2004. That does not mean that the values are out of date, especially at a time when property values are slipping rapidly and when the economy is in serious challenge. It could be that the deflation since that time makes the sums questionable in the other direction, but they seem to me to be a good guide. I think it is correct to award the plaintiff the sum of €120,000 under that heading, and it could be divided as pain and suffering to date in the sum of €80,000 and pain and suffering into the future in the sum of €40,000. As to his fractures, and as his scarring, I propose to add on the sum of €20,000, divided as €10,000 to date and €10,000 into the future. For his loss of his sense and taste and smell I will add the same figure."

It should be noted that the Book of Quantum does not refer to loss of taste or loss of smell. It appears that Charleton J. received no expert evidence on money values. His comments about the rapid decrease in property values do not take account of the escalation of property values in the period before 2004, which resulted in a significant gap between the property-buying power of the *Sinnott v Quinnsworth* "cap" of 1984 and the "cap" in 2004 (reflected in the Book of Quantum). Even though property values have fallen back very considerably from their height, the present "cap" will buy less real estate today than it did in 1984, when €150,000 would have purchased an impressive home.

Pain and suffering In *Vernon v Colgan* [2009] IEHC 86, the plaintiff, born in 1954, was involved in a traffic accident in 2003 in which he received relatively minor physical injuries but very serious psychiatric and psychological injuries. He had a range of symptoms, including panic attacks, suicidal intention for a period, depression, insomnia and nightmares. His relationship of 20 years with his partner ended. Laffoy J. attributed this to his injury; she considered it, "on the basis of the 'eggshell skull' principle" to be "wholly compensatable by the defendant". Laffoy J. awarded €100,000 for pain and suffering to the time of judgment and a further €75,000 for future pain and suffering.

In *Colburn v Sligo County Council* [2009] IEHC 536, O'Neill J. awarded €60,000 general damages to a 71-year-old plaintiff who, three years previously, had tripped on an uneven footpath, resulting in injuries to her elbow and knee and, more seriously, to her neck and lower back. There had been a "very significant degenerative charge" to her back, involving a diffuse protrusion of disc at the L4/5 level. The plaintiff was on a daily regime of anti-inflammatory and analgeric medication. Her mobility had been "hugely hampered". Her condition was likely to continue for the foreseeable future.

In *Quinn v Dunne* [2009] IEHC 144, Peart J. awarded €100,000 general damages for past pain and suffering and €50,000 for future pain and suffering to a man, aged 25 at the time of the accident in 2003, who had sustained injuries to the head, hip, humerus and elbow, as well as other parts of his body. He had a scar on his head ("not of any serious cosmetic significance") and had restricted function of his right shoulder and right arm with activities such as dressing and shaving. He also had some post-traumatic difficulties. It was probable that he would have two hip replacements at some later date.

In *McCahey v MIBI* [2009] IEHC 349, Birmingham J. awarded general damages of €30,000 for past pain and suffering and €37,500 for future pain and suffering to a 65-year-old plaintiff who was knocked from his bicycle in 2006, suffering a fracture to the right tibia as well as fractures to the third, fourth and fifth metatarsals. His ability to cycle was uncompromised but his ability to walk "any distance" had been affected. He had a slight limp.

In *Donovan v Farrell* [2009] IEHC 617, Peart J. awarded €75,000 for past pain and suffering and €20,000 for future pain and suffering to a 59-year-old woman who had received a whiplash-type injury to her neck and a fractured sternum, as well as suffering depression, post-traumatic stress disorder, an inability or unwillingness to drive a car and soft tissue injury to her back which made her pre-existing degenerative changes symptomatic earlier than they would otherwise have been.

In *Singleton v Doyle* [2009] IEHC 382, where the plaintiff suffered serious injuries in an accident in 1999, and had also suffered significant injuries in another accident nine years previously, Peart J. had the difficult task of assessing the extent of damages caused by the more recent accident. The injuries included injuries to her neck and shoulder, damage to her voice (following fusion surgery), having to undergo a cervical rhysotany and ongoing back pain. Peart J. awarded €120,000 for past pain and suffering and €35,000 for future pain and suffering.

In *Moran v Fogarty* [2009] IESC 55, the Supreme Court upheld an award by Johnson J. of €80,000 for past pain and suffering and €140,000 to a young man who had received a moderate brain injury in a traffic accident, which impacted on his pre-morbid cognitive ability. The court was satisfied that Johnson J.'s findings in support of his award were supported by "ample credible evidence".

Transport

AIR TRANSPORT

Aircraft: ramp inspections The European Communities (Safety of Third-Country Aircraft Using Community Airports) (Amendment) Regulations 2009 (S.I. No. 60 of 2009) amended the European Communities (Safety of Third-Country Aircraft Using Community Airports) Regulations 2007 (S.I. No. 754 of 2007) in order to implement Directive 2008/49. The 2008 Directive inserted an amended Annex II into Directive 2004/36 on the safety of third-country aircraft using Community airports, which deals with the criteria for the conduct of ramp inspections on aircraft using Community airports. The 2009 Regulations came into force on February 19, 2009.

Greenhouse gas emissions trading The European Communities (Greenhouse Gas Emissions Trading) (Aviation) Regulations 2009 (S.I. No. 274 of 2009) (the "2009 Regulations") provide for the partial implementation of Directive 2008/101 which extends to aviation activities the EU Emissions Trading Scheme (ETS) in Directive 2003/87 (the "2008 Directive"). The 2008 Directive provides that all flights arriving at and departing from EU airports will be included in the ETS from 2012 onwards; there are some exemptions and these are identified in Sch.1 to the 2009 Regulations. The Regulations provide for the submission of monitoring plans to the Environmental Protection Agency, which has been designated as the competent authority for the purposes of the 2008 Directive. The European Commission's Monitoring and Reporting Guidelines for emissions and tonne-kilometre data from aviation activities, adopted pursuant to art.14(1) of the 2003 ETS Directive, requires aircraft operators to submit their monitoring plans to the competent authority for approval at least four months prior to the start of the first reporting period. The first reporting year is 2010 in accordance with art.1(12)(b) of the 2008 Directive. As such, aircraft operators are required to submit their monitoring plans to the Environmental Protection Agency before the end of August 2009.

Preclearance The Aviation (Preclearance) Act 2009 (the "2009 Act") implemented an Agreement entered into between the Government of Ireland and the Government of the United States of America relating to the provision of preclearance operations at airports in the State for persons travelling by air to the USA. It also empowered the Minister for Transport to make regulations, including regulations designating areas at airports within which preclearance operations may be carried out. The 2009 Act also conferred certain limited functions on preclearance officers within those areas and provided for the seizure and forfeiture of goods not duly declared. The 2009 Act also repealed and replaced the Air Navigation and Transport (Preinspection) Act 1986. The Aviation (Preclearance) Act 2009 (Commencement) Order 2009 (S.I. No. 315 of 2009) provides for the commencement of the 2009 Act, apart from s.19, on August 5, 2009. The Preclearance Area (Shannon Airport) Regulations 2009 (S.I. No. 317 of 2009) designate preclearance areas at Shannon Airport under the 2009 Act, and also came into force on August 5, 2009.

Statistical information The European Communities (Statistics in Respect of Carriage of Passengers, Freight and Mail by Air) Regulations 2008 (S.I. No. 56 of 2009) were, despite the year "2008" in their title, made in 2009 (as their S.I. No. indicates) and came into force on the date they were signed, January 29, 2009. The 2008/2009 Regulations provide for the administrative arrangements to enforce the collection of statistical information on the scale and development of the carriage of passengers, freight and mail by air within the European Union or to and from the European Union, as required by Regulation 437/2003, as implemented and amended by Regulation 1358/2003. The purpose is to ensure comparable, consistent, synchronised and regular data at European Union level. The 2009 Regulations also revoked and replaced the European Communities (Statistics in respect of Carriage of Passengers, Freight and Mail by Air) Regulations 2003 (S.I. No. 715 of 2003).

MERCHANT SHIPPING

Light dues The Merchant Shipping (Light Dues) Order 2009 (S.I. No. 297 of 2009), made under the Merchant Shipping (Light Dues) Act 1983, revoked and replaced the Merchant Shipping (Light Dues) Order 2006 (S.I. No. 138 of 2006). The 2009 Order increased the level of light dues levied on merchant shipping collected from vessels calling to ports within the State from 52 to 57 cents per ton from August 1, 2009. In addition, from August 1, 2009 the 2009 Order increased the maximum number of voyages for which dues may be levied from seven to nine voyages in any one year.

RAIL TRANSPORT

Working conditions: cross-border services The European Communities

(Working Conditions of Mobile Workers Engaged in Interoperable Cross-Border Services in the Railway Sector) Regulations 2009 (S.I. No. 377 of 2009) implemented Directive 2005/47, which gave effect to an agreement between the Community of the European Railways (CER) and the European Transport Worker's Federation (ETF) on certain aspects of the working conditions of mobile workers engaged in interoperable cross border rail services. The 2009 Regulations came into force on September 7, 2009.

ROAD TRANSPORT

Heavy goods vehicles: tolls The European Communities (Charging of Heavy Goods Vehicles for the Use of Certain Infrastructures) Regulations 2009 (S.I. No. 87 of 2009) implemented Directive 1999/62 and Directive 2006/38. Collectively the Directives are known as the Eurovignette Directive and they provide a harmonised EU framework for the charging of tolls and user charges on heavy goods vehicles on certain European motorways. Eurovignette does not require Member States to levy tolls or charges on HGVs, but where they decide to do so they must respect the rules of the Directive. Tolls and charges are to be transparent and non-discriminatory. Tolls for existing schemes must be related to infrastructure costs and tolls for new schemes must be calculated in line with detailed rules set out in the directive. The 2009 Regulations came into force on March 19, 2009.

Licensing of driving instructors The Road Traffic (Driving Instructor Licensing) (No.2) Regulations 2009 (S.I. No. 203 of 2009) (the "2009 Regulations"), made under s.18 of the Road Traffic Act 1968, provide for the first time for the licensing of driving instructors by the Road Safety Authority (RSA). The 2009 Regulations came into force on May 1, 2009 and provide that it is an offence for a professional instructor to teach another person to drive a road traffic vehicle unless the instructor is on the RSA's Register of Approved Driving Instructors (ADIs). On conviction of providing lessons for reward, instructors who are not registered with the RSA as ADIs may be fined up to €2,000 and/or be sentenced to six months' imprisonment, or both. The 2009 Regulations also prohibit a person, until he or she receives an ADI full permit, from advertising themselves as a driving instructor. The 2009 Regulations also set out standards as to the quality and skills of instructors in the State. The regulatory system under the 2009 Regulations has three elements: a three-part ADI exam consisting of driver theory, driving practice and an "ability-to-instruct" test; tax clearance (tax clearance certificate must be produced as proof of tax compliance); and Garda vetting.

Professional drivers: certificates of professional competence The European

Communities (Vehicle Drivers Certificate of Professional Competence) (Amendment) Regulations 2009 (S.I. No. 348 of 2009) amended the European Communities (Vehicle Drivers Certificate of Professional Competence (No. 2) Regulations 2008 (S.I. No. 359 of 2008) to: (a) allow bus drivers holding a certificate of professional competence until December 31, 2009 to complete the first seven hours of training required; and (b) bring the lower age limit for obtaining a driver certificate of professional competence into line with the lower limit for obtaining a driving licence for bus and truck drivers. The 2009 Regulations came into force on September 2, 2009.

Road haulage licences: disqualification criteria The European Communities (Road Haulage and Road Passenger Transport Operator's Licences) Regulations 2009 (S.I. No. 318 of 2009) further implemented Directive 96/26 and Directive 98/76 on admission to the occupation of road haulage operator and road passenger transport operator, by providing for the disqualification of persons with serious convictions from those occupations. The 2009 Regulations came into force on September 10, 2009.

Whistleblower Protection

ESTELLE FELDMAN, Research Associate, Trinity College Dublin

CHILD ABUSE

The question as to whether allegations of child abuse made against the appellant were malicious is a central feature of *P v Information Commissioner* [2009] IEHC 574. The key object of the Protections for Persons Reporting Child Abuse Act 1998 is to protect from civil liability, persons who report child abuse reasonably and in good faith. The Act does not appear to have been applied in any action to date. However, as noted in the judgment in *P v Information Commissioner*, it is possible that a judgment is pending as the appellant is recorded as contemplating the commencement of proceedings pursuant to s.5 of the Act. The Act was analysed in *Annual Review 1998,* pp.653–654 and in Feldman, "Whistleblower Protection: Comparative Legal Developments" (1999) 17 I.L.T. 264. Section 5 states:

> 1) A person who states to an appropriate person that
>   (a) a child has been or is being assaulted, ill–treated, neglected or sexually abused, or
>   (b) a child's health, development or welfare has been or is being avoidably impaired or neglected,
>
> knowing that statement to be false shall be guilty of an offence.
>
> 2) A person guilty of an offence under this section shall be liable
>   (a) on summary conviction, to a fine not exceeding £1,500 or to imprisonment for a term not exceeding 12 months or to both,
>   (b) on conviction on indictment, to a fine not exceeding £15,000 or to imprisonment for a term not exceeding 3 years or to both.
>
> 3) Notwithstanding section 10(4) of the Petty Sessions (Ireland) Act, 1851, summary proceedings for an offence under this Act may be instituted within 2 years from the date on which the offence was committed or, if later, 2 years from the date on which evidence that, in the opinion of the person by whom the proceedings are brought, is sufficient to justify the bringing of the proceedings comes to that person's knowledge.
>
> 4) For the purposes of subsection (3) of this section, a certificate signed by or on behalf of the person bringing the proceedings as

> to the date on which the evidence referred to in that subsection relating to the offence concerned came to his or her knowledge shall be prima facie evidence thereof and in any legal proceedings a document purporting to be a certificate issued for the purpose of this subsection and to be so signed shall be deemed to be so signed and shall be admitted as evidence without proof of the signature of the person purporting to sign the certificate.

P v Information Commissioner is analysed in this *Annual Review* in the chapters on Constitutional Law and on Information Law and the Ombudsman.

GARDA SÍOCHÁNA

Confidential reporting scheme In last year's *Annual Review* (p.641) we noted a report of the crime correspondent of the *Sunday Tribune*, confirmed by the Department of Justice, that there had been a total of three reports of corruption and malpractice referred to the Garda Commissioner, one of which alleged serious malpractice in Cavan. The same correspondent reports that consequent on this disclosure an investigation was launched and the:

> "… Garda commissioner is due to be presented with an extensive file into alleged criminal malpractice and indiscipline by Gardaí in the Cavan/Monaghan district that highlights several potentially criminal acts by Gardaí. An Garda Síochána and the Minister for Justice are also facing a number of High Court legal actions claiming malicious prosecution, sexual harassment and bullying by Gardaí in the Bailieborough district" (Bracken, "Garda commissioner to get report on criminal malpractice", *Sunday Tribune*, January 3, 2010).

At the time of writing no information is available regarding any further use of the confidential reporting scheme.

Confidential Reporting Charter We have previously noted that the legislative purpose of the Garda Síochána (Confidential Reporting of Corruption or Malpractice) Regulations 2007 is for the establishment of a Charter (s.4), *Annual Review 2007*, p.598. We noted in *Annual Review 2008*, p. 642–643, that despite the commencement of the scheme no such charter has been published. Our research for the current *Annual Review* also failed to reveal any charter. Having contacted Garda Headquarters we received an email from the Garda Press Office which is reproduced below.

> "The charter has been established but not placed in the public domain.

> The Garda Commissioner reports to the Minister each year as per SI NO 168 of 2007 see below.

An Garda Síochána do not wish to comment further.

STATUTORY INSTRUMENTS.

S.I. No. 168 of 2007

GARDA SÍOCHÁNA (CONFIDENTIAL REPORTING OF CORRUPTION OR MALPRACTICE) REGULATIONS 2007

Annual report

> 15. (1) Not later than 4 months after the end of each year the Commissioner shall report in writing to the Minister in relation to any confidential reports made during that year and the action taken in relation to them."

Whistleblowing or leaking In July 2009 the Circuit Criminal Court imposed a 12 month suspended jail sentence and a €5,000 fine on Garda Detective Sergeant Robert McNulty who had pleaded guilty to passing on the report on the Dean Lyons inquiry before its official publication contrary to s.37 of the Commissions of Investigation Act 2004. This provision states:

> 37.—(1) A person who receives a draft of a report or part of a draft report from a commission under section 34 shall not disclose its contents or divulge in any way that the draft or part of the draft has been sent to that person, except—
> (a) with the prior written consent of the commission, or
> (b) to the extent necessary for the purposes of an application to the Court.
>
> (2) A person who contravenes subsection (1) is guilty of an offence.

In 1997, Dean Lyons, a homeless drug addict, had falsely confessed to a double murder. According to Garda McNulty's defence counsel his client had been "obsessed" with vindicating his own reputation as highlighted in this matter. Both the draft and final reports had vindicated him. According to the *Irish Times* report of the case (McGreevy, "Suspended Term, €5,000 fine for ex-Garda", *Irish Times*, July 30, 2009), Judge Hogan said that McNulty was under a lot of pressure because of "innuendo and suspicion" and had decided to "jump the gun" by leaking the draft report to the press. "Had he waited for a period of time, he would not be in the trouble he is in today", the judge added. "It is a loss he must bear as a result of his activities." Apparently Garda McNulty had confined the passages leaked to those parts which pertained only to himself and did not affect others named.

Strict liability disclosure provisions There would appear to be strong public policy grounds for s.37 of the Commissions of Investigation Act 2004, and without insider knowledge of the circumstances, it is impossible to conclude whether there was any justification whatsoever for this unlawful disclosure. Nevertheless, it may be noted that when one suffers over years with a burning sense of personal grievance as appears to have been the case with Garda McNulty, it may well become impossible to maintain patient silence whilst waiting for officialdom to act. Whistleblowers might sometimes "jump the gun" not through any bad intention but because they have lost belief that the gun will ever sound. An action that might be described as a leak when taken by somebody high up in an organisation is seldom viewed in any positive light when taken by those down the ranks. In relation to whistleblower protection, alternatives to strict liability offences require consideration. This issue will be revisited in future *Annual Reviews*.

HEALTH SECTOR

Confused accountability The so-called whistleblower provisions for the health sector came into effect on March 1, 2009. According to the *Irish Medical Times* website, Mr Larry Walsh, previously National Director of the joint management/trade union Health Services Partnership Forum, has been appointed by Professor Brendan Drumm, CEO of the Health Service Executive (HSE), as the authorised person to whom protected disclosures should be made under these Health provisions. In an interview with Dara Gantly, Mr Walsh told the *Irish Medical Times* that he will be providing information on cases under general headings to the Department of Health and Children (DoHC) on a monthly basis, and intends to prepare a report for the HSE at the end of his first 12 months in the post. Since it is recorded that Mr Walsh was appointed by the CEO of the HSE this raises many questions not the least of which is, to whom Mr Walsh is responsible and to whom accountable. These are serious issues for those who wish to place their trust in the "authorised person" scheme. Further, although this appointment appears to have been made in or about April 2010, despite extensive internet searches we could find no other reference to this appointment and drew a complete blank in this regard on both the HSE, *www.hse.ie* and DoHC, *www.dohc.ie* websites. In this interview Mr. Walsh explained:

> "that a concerted campaign has been initiated within the HSE to promote the new measures, through the use of posters, material on the Executive's

> intranet, and leaflets to employees containing his contact details. 'But one thing that we have all learned in the health services is that you can never over-communicate,' stated Walsh, who acknowledged not only the challenge in getting this information across to people, but also of gaining their confidence in the process". (Baxter, *Whistleblowers Protected, www.imt.ie/opinion/guests/2009/08/whistleblowers-protected.html* (Last Accessed August 07, 2010)

No confidentiality, no confidence As we have noted in previous *Annual Reviews* there is a real necessity for the identity of a whistleblower to remain confidential, as once the identity is known it becomes possible for retaliatory action to be taken against the whistleblower. However, the Health procedures require the putative whistleblower to reveal their contact details to the authorised person without clearly revealing his contact details. A leaflet entitled "Protected Disclosure of Information Explanatory Leaflet for Health Service Employees" is available on *www.hse.ie/eng/staff/HR/Policies,_Procedures_and_Guidelines/Protected_disclosures_of_information.pdf.*

The following is quoted from the leaflet:

> "The HSE has appointed an 'Authorised Person' to whom protected disclosures may be made. Employees are required to set out the details of the subject matter of the disclosure in writing on the Protected Disclosures of Information Form (attached) and submit it to the Authorised Person at the following address: HSE Authorised Person PO Box 11571 Dublin 2."

A handy form in the leaflet requires the employee to provide contact details any of which would identify the employee. By contrast the authorised person is not in any way identifiable either by name or by the postal box address which means that the communications, far from being confidential, could be accessible to many unidentified persons.

In a separate report the *Irish Medical Times* records that Mr Walsh is actively looking at 10 cases. (Baxter, *HSE has 10 'whistleblowers'*, *www.imt.ie/news/latest-news/2009/08/hse-has-10-whistleblowers.html* (Last Accessed August 07, 2010)) Mr Walsh is quoted as saying that one of the cases involves somebody who has suggested "'that they were expressing a concern under all of the headings laid out in the legislation, and that is in relation to how an entire service was being delivered". The HSE employs 100,000 people, of whom more than 65,000 staff are in direct employment, and a further 35,000 are employed by voluntary hospitals and bodies funded by the HSE (source: HSE Staff Figures and Information webpage sourced on August 13, 2010). Even were the protected disclosures scheme in line with good practice to protect whistleblowers, if that is the nature of the protected disclosures made so far, it is not unreasonable to wonder if the "authorised person" scheme would ever be adequately resourced sufficient to inspire confidence in potential whistleblowers.

In view of the foregoing it is timely to quote the comments on those provisions from the *Annual Review of Irish Law 2007*, pp.596–598.

Criminalising whistleblowers in the health sector *Part 14 of the Health Act 2007 (Protection of Disclosures of Information)* In an appalling development the words "reasonably ought to know to be false" (seemingly taken directly from Protections for Persons Reporting Child Abuse Act 1998) are included in a provision of the health service protected disclosures legislation which states as follows in the Health Act 2007 Pt 14, amending the Health Act 2004:

> 55S.—(1) A person who makes a disclosure which the person knows or **reasonably ought to know to be false** is guilty of an offence.
>
> (2) A person guilty of an offence under this section is liable—
>
> (a) on summary conviction, to a fine not exceeding €5,000 or to imprisonment for a term not exceeding 12 months or to both,
>
> (b) on conviction on indictment, to a fine not exceeding €50,000 or to imprisonment for a term not exceeding 3 years or to both.
>
> (3) Notwithstanding section 10(4) of the Petty Sessions (Ireland) Act 1851, summary proceedings for an offence under this Act may be instituted within 2 years from the date on which the offence was committed or, if later, 2 years from the date on which evidence that, in the opinion of a member of the Garda Síochána, is sufficient to justify the bringing of the proceedings.
>
> (4) For the purposes of subsection (3) of this section, a certificate signed by a Superintendent of the Garda Síochána as to the date on which the evidence referred to in that subsection relating to the offence concerned came to his or her knowledge is prima facie evidence thereof and in any legal proceedings a document purporting to be a certificate issued for the purpose of this subsection and to be so signed is deemed to be so signed and shall be admitted as evidence without proof of the signature of the Superintendent purporting to sign the certificate. (emphasis added)

Who could have any confidence in a system that without any clarity as to who will decide that a person "reasonably ought to know" imposes such draconian punishment for not knowing? So much for acknowledging international expertise, e.g. the Bristol Babies inquiry, that the imperative in the health service in order to encourage more openness is to move away from a culture of blame.

Provisions a mere tag on There are undoubtedly some very positive aspects to the provisions regarding protected disclosures for those providing healthcare. Unfortunately, the manner in which the Oireachtas has passed this most important legislation shows almost utter indifference to the basic premise of providing whistleblower protection, namely, promotion of openness and accountability. The provisions have clearly been tagged onto a Health Act that was about something else entirely. This is illustrated by the Long Title:

> An Act to establish a body to be known as an tÚdarás um Fhaisnéis agus Cáilíocht Sláinte or, in the English language, as the Health Information and Quality Authority and Oifig an Phríomh-chigire Seirbhísí Sóisialacha or, in the English language, the Office of the Chief Inspector of Social Services and to provide for the dissolution of certain bodies; to provide for the transfer of the functions of the dissolved bodies and their employees to the Health Information and Quality Authority; to provide for a scheme of registration and inspection of residential services for older people, persons with disabilities and children in need of care and protection; to provide for the repeal and amendment of certain other acts; and to provide for related matters.

The rush to ensure that good faith whistleblowers in the health services should be encouraged and protected primarily arose out of a whistleblower exposing the tragic circumstances of numerous unnecessary major gynaecological procedures performed by Dr Michael Neary, subsequently struck off the medical register, and subsequently from the revelations regarding abuse of the elderly in residential nursing homes, specifically a covert RTE reporter in Leas Cross Nursing Home, which was subsequently closed down. Hence, an obvious question is to ask who is responsible for downgrading the extraordinary importance of these statutory provisions to a "related matter": was it someone in the Department of Health and Children, was it the Health Service Executive, was it just the inability of the members of the Oireachtas to understand that whistleblower protection should preferably be a stand-alone statute in plain English and failing that a clearly signposted set of provisions. These provisions were included as an amendment to the Health Act 2004 which established the Health Service Executive.

No reassurance for whistleblower Moreover, a member of the health professions considering making a disclosure could obtain no comfort whatsoever from the indigestible appearance, confusing language and slipshod fashion in which these important provisions have been placed on the statute book. The provisions to amend the Health Act 2004 commence at s.103 of the 2007 Act, and continue for approximately 14 pages referencing ss.55A to 55T, 20 sections, of the Health Act 2004, as amended. In that space there are

86 cross references either to sections or subsections of the Health Act 2007 or to sections of 14 other Acts. One of these latter is to s.45 of the Medical Practitioners Act 1978 which was repealed in its entirety by the Medical Practitioners Act 2007 which came into law less than three weeks after the Health Act 2007. Not only would a health professional have difficulty making sense of this, it would require a legal professional of extraordinary stamina as well as ability.

Subject Index